FOREWORD

This is an idiosyncratic book, or so I am told; meaning that it fits into no known category. It is certainly subjective, and it is very personal in the sense that the descriptions reflect my reactions to the appearance, smell and taste of a wine. The words I use will not always be exact, and my conclusions can be challenged. But the extraordinary way in which the first edition was received and the gentle but insistent pressure of both readers and publisher has had two conflicting effects: great encouragement to update, and diffidence verging on reluctance to foist my opinions on an increasingly knowledgeable public.

Eleven vintages have elapsed since the publication of *The Great Vintage Wine Book*, a period that embraces one of the most successful decades in the history of winemaking. Since then, I have travelled even more widely and have been exposed to a far greater wealth of fine and rare wines. Over the past 10 years I have met a surprising number of people, professional and amateur, who have used the book both as a work of reference and as bedside reading. I have been flattered by their appreciative comments. Nevertheless, over this period other tasters and writers, some highly competent, have expanded into the field of critical note-making. The emphasis here is on 'critical', for I often sense a lack of excitement, of simple pleasure, and perhaps an approach betraying more knowledge than understanding.

What I hope I offer is a feel for the style and quality of a vintage, and to a certain extent for the individual wines which are part and parcel of the vintage. The purpose of this book is the same as that of the first edition: to assess a given vintage, and through my tasting notes to trace the wine's development from its original to its present condition, and to make an informed guess at its future.

In this second volume, wines from other districts and countries have been included – in homage and by way of appreciation, but certainly not comprehensively. I shall probably, rightly, be accused of self-indulgence. So be it.

Michael Broadbent
Christie's, London. Summer 1991

Edited and designed by
Mitchell Beazley Publishers
part of Reed International Books
Michelin House
81 Fulham Road
London SW3 6RB

A CIP catalogue record for this book is available from the British Library.

ISBN 0 85533 909 8 (Casebound edition)
ISBN 1 85732 926 0 (Limpbound edition)

Editors:
Diane Pengelly
Elizabeth Bellord
Kirsty Seymour-Ure
Associate Editor:
Susan Keevil
Art Editor:
Rozelle Bentheim
Associate Art Editor:
Paul Drayson
Production: Ted Timberlake
Index: Lyn Greenwood

Managing Editor: Anne Ryland
Executive Art Editor: Tim Foster

Jacket Illustration: Philip Thompson

Typeset in Imprint by
Servis Filmsetting Ltd
Manchester, England
Printed and bound in Great Britain by
Butler & Tanner
Frome, England

CONTENTS

INTRODUCTION

Wines are like people, infinitely variable, endlessly fascinating: commonplace and forgettable, great and memorable. If, on balance, the content of this book tends towards the latter it is because the great and the good are not only more complex and interesting but reflect more clearly than the nondescript their style, quality, condition and drinkability.

This book does not claim to be comprehensive: the notes are not exhaustive, it is definitely not 'definitive' — a term that I have always found presumptuous. It is not a buyers' guide in the good-value-for-immediate-drinking sense. Nor does it seek to rate individual wines with mathematical precision. Its purpose is rather to assess vintages: what they were like, what they *are* like, how the wines of these vintages have fared, their present condition and future promise.

The individual notes have several tasks to fulfil: they should convey the wine's style and drinkability, and as far as possible describe its colour, smell and taste, and taken together they should illustrate the general state and nuances of a given vintage.

A further purpose of this second volume is to draw attention to some 'New World' greats, some lesser-known classics and the *nouvelle vague*. These, compared to the red Bordeaux section, are necessarily sketchy, partly because of space considerations and partly because, though I taste a lot, I cannot presume to be an authority on all wines. I appreciate quality and character and I notice trends: this is what I hope is communicated through my notes.

Source material

All the tasting notes in this book are first hand, 'hand' being the operative word. I have always hand-written my notes, either during or immediately after tasting, into a daybook, in effect an indexed wine diary, in whatever circumstances I find myself. I use it at dinner parties, my own and others', at trade tastings, and at the many extremely valuable horizontal and vertical tastings I attend. Some notes are necessarily skimpy, some, particularly those made at highly structured tastings, are more detailed.

The essential material for this volume has been culled from over 50,000 notes extracted from 90 tasting books. All but minor and non-vintage wines are photocopied, then cut and pasted up alphabetically according to type of wine and vintage. This, in part, accounts for the length of time I have taken to update *The Great Vintage Wine Book* (it is a very time-consuming fetish to note, as I have for the past 39 years, every wine I taste) but at least the notes you read here are the actual descriptions I wrote at the time of tasting.

As head of Christie's Wine Department, I cannot of course spend all day and every day tasting and writing. This is not my business. Nor can I take advantage of all the tastings to which I am invited. I fit in what I can when I can. On the other hand, particularly since the last edition, I have been lucky enough to taste an extraordinarily wide range of fine and rare wines and have conducted, or 'moderated', many outstanding tastings over the past 10 years, most of which are referred to in the text.

Since the last edition, tasters, tasting panels, professional wine writers and critics have proliferated. Methods of tasting, note-taking and assessment have become increasingly sophisticated. I am flattered that so many of my own methods have been adopted.

The level of tasting commentaries in well-established wine journals is high though, as a one-time wine merchant, I believe that the relatively new role of the 'wine critic' emasculates the established trade, pre-empting the roles of the broker, the *négociant*, the importer, the wholesaler (though he was ordinarily an 'order taker') and the retailer. But I respect Robert Parker and much prefer his observations to those of wine writers who happen to have a column in which to air the impressions of their unhoned taste buds. On the plus side, the more respected critics have certainly shaken some poor and idle winemakers out of their ignorant complacency; and good but relatively unknown wines have, happily, been raised from undeserved obscurity.

Rating

At comparative tastings I frequently award points out of 20, usually three for appearance, seven for nose, 10 for taste and overall assessment, to supplement my tasting note, particularly if the latter is brief. A numerical rating reminds me which wine, at that particular moment, I judged to be better than another. But, as all experienced tasters must concede, a wine that is rated highly at one tasting may not rate so highly at another. There are many reasons. It may be because of the context, the sort of tasting, or a consequence of being in a different place at a different time – even atmospheric pressure can affect the taste; then the verdict may depend on whether the taster is on form or, for example, getting over a cold. The permutations are endless. This is why I very rarely publish a numerical rating but stick to a far broader, more flexible star system:

***** Outstanding (vintage or wine)
**** Very good
*** Good
** Moderately good
* Not very good, but not bad
No stars Poor

To give the reader an indication of the present drinkability, and a prediction of ultimate quality of a young vintage, I use brackets:

for example

*(***) means one star for drinking: immature, unready; but an additional three stars show that its potential at full maturity is 'very good'.

A wine rated ***(**) can be drunk with pleasure now but, after further bottle-age, should be 'outstanding'.

Having said this, nothing is finite, nothing is for sure. One of the most difficult tasks of the taster is to assess the potential of very young wine. It is a gift, not a science. Harry Waugh had an unerring and completely natural, unforced feeling for wine tasted in cask. Few tasters have this ability and without it, predicting the future of wines tasted in the spring after the vintage, or even after a year in cask, is a chancy business. Assessing older wines is easier, but even then, nothing is certain – a lot depends on provenance, how and where the wine has been stored, the state of the cork and so forth.

On tasting

One's approach should vary according to the type and age of the wine to be tasted. This is insufficiently understood. Red burgundy and Bordeaux have totally different characteristics: they look, smell and taste different. The taster should not have a good Pauillac in mind when tasting a Côte de Nuits; and someone accustomed to California

Cabernets must shift his sights when faced with red Bordeaux. Still more so with white burgundy and Rhine wines. The German winemaker, even without making the obvious allowances for grape variety, soil and climate, has a totally different approach and goal from his counterpart in Meursault. Just as importantly, it is not sensible to use the same criteria when tasting very young or very old wines. For these reasons I have explained my approach to various types of wine in the introductions to individual sections.

Tasting terms

Many of the tasting terms I use are self-explanatory, many are analogous, some — I freely admit — are less easy to comprehend. Assessing quality and condition is relatively straightforward, but to put precise smells and tastes into words is difficult, often well-nigh impossible. What I hope to convey is an impression of the wine.

For space considerations the glossary that follows has been kept short. My book *Winetasting*, which has been in print since 1968, deals thoroughly with this subject, and the latest Mitchell Beazley pocket edition (1991) lists over 250 words and expressions used in tasting, and includes sections on French, German and Italian terms.

Some readers may find certain expressions far-fetched. Cynics scorn the use of descriptions such as 'old straw', 'linoleum', cheese rind' yet these are not fanciful: the physical and chemical compounds that produce the smell of linoleum, for example, can be present in wine. A petrol or kerosene smell (classic Riesling) is due to various terpenes, rubber to mercaptan, sweatiness to butyric acid, burnt match to free sulphur, grass (Sauvignon) to hexanedienol, banana to amyl or isoamyl acetate.

However, not being a trained oenologist, I tend to describe a smell in lay terms, often the cause of much hilarity amongst my more technically inclined Australian winemaking friends. Nevertheless, though not proud to be ignorant, I write as a lover of wine, not professionally for the professionally equipped. Besides, I feel that to write 'cherry-like' is much more meaningful than cyanohydrin benzaldehyde, the actual element that produces the smell! Similarly, 'peach-like' is more evocative, more recognisable than piperonal, 'pineapple' preferable to ethyl caprylate, and so on.

Making notes

At a tasting I try to follow the same procedure in the same sequence. As soon as possible after the wine has been poured, I swirl it in the glass so that the sides of the glass are rinsed, maximising the surface area of wine and rousing it, then I note the first impression, and the precise time. Leaving the glass where it is I look at it against a white background noting its depth of colour and then, picking it up by the stem, I tilt and manoeuvre it into a position where I can examine its actual hue, from the centre of the bowl to its rim, to judge (in the case of red wine) its maturity. After noting this I then smell the wine again, taking several steady, fairly deep sniffs to extract as much information as possible. I do not, incidentally, swirl the wine in the glass a second time. I note the time again, for it can take 10 to 40 minutes for the nose of a top-class wine, particularly if relatively immature, to gather its forces and develop fully. I often note initial smell, then the scent which evolves in the glass and again, after an hour or so, note its further development. It is amazing what glorious contortions a fine wine can get up to in the glass.

This tasting procedure is then reflected in the notes, which deal with the wine in the following order: appearance (depth, hue); nose (aroma, bouquet, 'off' smells); and taste (dryness, body, fruit, tannins, acidity, as appropriate), the somewhat idiosyncratic semi-colon dividing the three main elements.

The credo

I believe in wine. I believe in its health-giving properties. It is the most supreme beverage. A good wine appeals to more than just the palate. It can be beautiful, it fills one with eager anticipation; its smell can be fragrant and evocative and it does a job by preparing the mouth, setting the vital gastric juices in motion. And then there's the taste. All wine should taste good; it should have a pleasing flavour, should intrigue, should delight, but it also has a job to do. Red Bordeaux, for example, when sipped, cleans the palate for the next mouthful. And it is a most effective aid to digestion.

The impression given by this book might be that I am a cerebral taster. In fact, I drink wine every day, with every meal except breakfast (and salad lunches in the office canteen). But my friends also know that I am a very moderate, cautious drinker. A glass of dry sherry or champagne as an aperitif, a couple of glasses with a meal, enough to accompany an individual dish. No more. Moderation is an unoriginal but not an idle recommendation.

GLOSSARY*

acid, acidity Sound healthy grapes contain natural acidity, which gives the wine its crisp, refreshing quality. Too much acidity will make the tongue curl; a flabby finish results from too little. *See also* volatile acidity.
aftertaste The taste that remains after a particularly fine wine has been swallowed; a fragrant internal bouquet.
alcohol One of the essential components of wine, giving it body and backbone. No smell or taste as such, but 'peppery' on the nose of a young wine, a feeling of weight in the mouth, slight sweetness and warmth as it is swallowed. Alcohol content of 'light' wines varies from around 11 to 14 per cent by volume depending on the sugar content of the grape, which in turn depends mainly on the ripening sun. *See also* chaptalised wine.
aroma The element of smell that derives from the grape.
astringent A bitter, mouth-puckering effect due to excess tannin and acidity.
austere Mainly in relation to taste: hard, somewhat severe. Not a fault, possibly undeveloped and certainly indicating a lack of obvious flesh and charm.
balance The combination and vital relationship of component parts.
beads at the rim The string of little telltale bubbles clinging to the meniscus which, in my experience, is often a warning that an old wine is cracking up. Not to be confused with *spritzig* (qv).
beefy An evocative description: a full-bodied wine with high extract (qv), a sort of chewable quality and texture.
beery The beery, yeasty endtaste of a faulty wine.
beetroot Or boiled beetroot: an analogous description of the root-like, mature Pinot aroma.
bite An acid grip in the endtaste, more than a zestful tang and tolerable only in a rich, full-bodied wine.
bitter Either a fault or due to too much tannin. Normally no fine mature wine should be bitter on the palate, though bitterness is considered a normal and desirable feature of some Italian reds.
bitter almonds An almond kernel, acetate smell usually due to bad fining. A fault.
blackcurrants An evocative smell and taste generally associated with Cabernet Sauvignon and Sauvignon Blanc.
body A physical component: weight of wine, alcohol, extract. Varies according to wine type and vintage. *See* full-bodied.
bottle-age Hard to describe but easily recognisable once you know what to look for: the ameliorating, softening effect of a wine aged in bottle, detected on the nose; a mellow sweetness; on white wines a honey smell.
Botrytis Short for *Botrytis cinerea*, known also as noble rot, *pourriture noble* and *Edelfäule*. The rot which is encouraged to grow on the skins of grapes in Sauternes and the top German vineyards during the delayed harvest. It shrivels the grapes, reduces the water content and concentrates the sugar. The effect on nose and palate is akin to honey.

* *For a full glossary, see* Michael Broadbent's Pocket Guide to Wine Tasting *(Mitchell Beazley/Simon & Shuster)*.

bouquet The element of smell that is a result of the winemaking process and subsequent development in cask and bottle. Loosely synonymous with the nose or general smell of a wine.
burnt Descriptive, like singed (qv). Red wines, dessert wines and hot-vintage wines can have a burnt character on the nose.
capsule 'Cap' for short. Usually lead, sometimes a wax seal over the cork.
caramel Sweet, toffee-like smell. Sometimes indicates an acceptable degree of maderisation as in old Sauternes.
cedar A cedarwood, cigar-box smell characteristic of many fine clarets.
chaptalised A French term for adding sugar to the grape must in years when the natural grape sugar is deficient. Without it these wines would be lacking in alcohol and unstable. Chaptalised wines tend not to keep well, though they can be attractive when young.
cheesy Or cheese rind: a descriptive term, not usually derogatory, applied to some clarets.
chocolaty Also descriptive, applying to the nose. I associate the term mainly with some of the sweeter, heavier, usually blended but not unattractive burgundies. Usually weighty and chunky on the palate.
chunky A term I often use to describe a hefty, somewhat coarse-textured red wine.
clean Fresh and free from faults.
coulure The failure of the buds to develop as a result of bad weather conditions.
cracking-up A disintegrating wine, over-mature, oxidised.
crisp Descriptive. Indicates good level of acidity, particularly in dry whites.
depth Depends on the context: a wine can have depth, ie richness of colour; depth of nose — the opposite to superficial, one has to sniff long and hard to detect its latent fruit and character; depth of flavour, richness, complexity.
developed Usually qualified, eg undeveloped, still immature but implying potential. *See also* well developed.
dumb Usually used in the context of an immature fine red wine with an undeveloped bouquet. Sometimes the dormant bouquet can be aroused by patiently warming the glass in cupped hands.
earthy Evocative and descriptive, nose or taste. Not derogatory in normal contexts. Red Graves can have an earthy taste, so, in different ways, can some Australian and California wines.
esters Smells are conveyed by volatile esters and aldehydes to the receptors in the nose, a chemical process.
estery Peardrops, a faulty, chemical smell.
extract Richness of minerals, trace elements — everything in wine except sugar, water or alcohol.
fading Can apply to colour loss and general decline of bouquet and flavour; the result of age.
fat Usually referring to a combination of sweetness, alcohol, high extract, possibly glycerine, and implies a slight lack of counterbalancing acidity.

finish The endtaste. A good positive finish is essential in a fine well-balanced wine. A poor finish indicates lack of quality, follow-through and acidity.
firm Sound constitution, positive. A desirable quality on the palate.
flabby Soft, feeble, lacking acidity on the palate.
flat The next stage after flabby. Total lack of vigour on nose and on palate; lack of acidity; oxidation.
flowery Evocative. Can refer to nose: fragrant, fresh aroma; developed bouquet; or taste.
fruity Rarely grapey. More a positive, fleshy quality of nose and flavour derived from sound, ripe grapes.
full-bodied A big wine, high alcoholic content and extract; a mouthfilling table wine or a robust young port.
grapey Aroma and taste usually associated with very ripe Rieslings and muscadelle-type grapes.
green Unripe, raw, youthful on nose or palate. Strictly speaking, resulting from unripe grapes, but also loosely used to describe an immature, acidic wine.
hard On the palate, severe, probably still tannic. Not a fault in a young wine.
heavy Over-endowed with alcohol, more than full-bodied; clumsy, lacking finesse.
high-toned The nose of a particularly marked but light volatile character, often associated with considerable fragrance but can verge on, and is probably associated with, highish volatile acidity (qv).
hollow A wine that has a first taste, something of a finish but no middle palate.
honeyed Some young, natural dessert wines, if good, have a distinct smell of honey that deepens with age. Even dry wines, if of good vintages, can develop a mellow, honeyed bouquet as they mature.
iron A character derived from the soil, noticeable more on palate than nose. Lafite often has it, so has Cheval-Blanc. And in a swingeingly metallic, harsh tannic-acid way I have noted it in one or two young Australian and California wines.
kernel, kernelly Smell and taste of peach or almond kernels. An occasional element of white wines, which I, personally, dislike.
lean Self-descriptive. On the palate, sinewy, firm; often the sign of a 'long-distance runner'.
legs The viscous droplets that form and ease down the sides of the glass when the wine is swirled.
long Refers to length of flavour. A sign of quality.
macération carbonique A modern 'whole fruit' method of vinification that at best produces appealingly fresh and fruity wines, at worst superficial, flimsy, tinny ones.
maderised Heavy, flat, 'brown' smell and taste of an overmature oxidised wine.
maître de chai A Bordelais term for a cellar master, responsible for the vinification and ageing of the wine. The maître de chai will also travel to other cellars re-corking the wines of old vintages from his particular château.
meaty Rich 'chunky' nose, almost chewable flavour.
medium-sweet Self-explanatory. Usually too sweet to accompany a main course. A light dessert wine.
mercaptan An unpleasant rubbery smell of old sulphur, mainly on very old white wines.
milky A milk-like smell. Lactic acid. Not a good sign but not necessarily bad or undrinkable.
millerandage The imperfect fertilisation of the grapes, resulting in uneven development and a small crop; caused by the flowering taking place in bad weather.
murky More than deep-coloured: not bright, turbid. Mainly a red wine fault.
must Grape juice in the cask or vat before it is converted into wine.
nutty The smell of cobnuts (tawny port), and a particular and pleasant quality I associate with oak and the Chardonnay grape and with some old amontillado sherries.
oak A smell deriving from maturation in small French oak casks. Adds a certain character and style but can be overdone.
oily Can apply to a particularly unctuous smell or a texture. A highly viscous white wine can also have an oily appearance.
old In a wine context an old nose or old taste implies signs of decay beyond normal maturity.
open knit Can apply to nose or taste texture of a fairly fully developed wine. Forthcoming, loose-knit, loose-textured.
overblown The somewhat unpleasant smell of an overmature or faulty wine.
oxidised 'Brown', old straw smell; flat stale taste of a wine destroyed by the action of air in cask or in bottle through a faulty or shrunken cork.
peacock's tail The way the flavour of certain great burgundies can open up and fan out in the mouth.
peardrops An acetone, spirit-glue smell. A fault, usually in white wines.
peppery The effect of a high alcoholic content in a young wine, noticeably vintage port. Almost a physical, peppery assault on the nose, accompanied by a hot, peppery texture.
piquant A high-toned, overfragrant fruity nose verging on sharp, usually confirmed by an overacidic endtaste. Can still be a refreshing, flavoury drink, but not one to keep.
plummy Can apply to both colour and taste. A thick red-purple appearance; fruit, some coarseness on palate, often indicating an in-between state of maturity, or a particular style.
pricked Distinctly sharper than piquant. Acetic smell, tart. An irremediable fault.
pungent Powerful, assertive smell, linked to a high level of volatile acidity, eg certain old Madeiras.
ripe Smell and taste exhibiting the softness and sweetness resulting from ripe grapes.
round On the palate, a feature of a complete, well-balanced, mature wine. No hard edges.
sharp Acidity on the nose and palate somewhere between piquant and pricked (qv). Usually indicating a fault.
sélection grains nobles **(SGN)** Individually selected overripe *Botrytis*-affected grapes, roughly the equivalent of the German Beerenauslese.
silky Refers only to texture, the feel of a ripe Pomerol, for example.
sinewy Lean, muscular on the palate. Usually a wine of some potential.
singed The smell of some red wines of hot vintages.
smoky Both evocative and descriptive: the smell of burnt oak chips, of wood smoke. For me a pleasant type of smell that I associate with the bouquet of good burgundy and certain other wines.
Spanish root A smell that reminds me of this root, a sort of liquorice. Certain ports have it.
spritzig Or **spritz** for short. A German term. First detectable visually as tiny specks of air in the wine and then as a crisp prickle of youthful acidity and carbon

dioxide in the mouth.
stalky Nose and taste. Not necessarily a fault, but undesirable; common, not an attribute of fine wines. Probably due to unripe grapes or prolonged contact with stalks during fermentation.
stewed An unimpressive, fudged-up, compounded sort of aroma lacking clear-cut fruit. Often from blended, sugared wines. Quality generally lacking.
stringy A texture: on the thin and scrawny side, lacking equability.
sulphury The prickle on the nose, rather like a whiff of a burnt match or coke oven, announcing the presence of sulphur dioxide, a common white wine preservative. Not a fault. Often wears off in the glass but should not be too intrusive.
supple Texture, balance: pleasant combination of vigour and harmony. Highly desirable in a properly developing red wine.
tang, tangy Rich, high-toned, zestful bouquet and endtaste, particularly in old Madeira, Tokay and some other old fortified wines.
tannin An essential preservative extracted from the skins of red grapes during fermentation. It dries the mouth.
tart Occasionally used as a synonym for the natural acidity in wine, but in my book it has an unattractive, even faulty connotation.
tête de cuvée No hard and fast definition, varies according to district, but definitely implies 'the pick of the bunch', from the best cask in a grower's cellar.
thin Deficient, watery, lacking body. Usually used in a derogatory sense. Not a synonym for light.
tinny Metallic, acidic at the back of the palate. A fault, but often tolerable.
toffee-nosed A literal description: sweet toffee, caramel-like smell. Possibly the first evidence of approaching maderisation, but attractive.
unripe A condition of wine arising from the use of unripe grapes containing malic acid, which gives the wine a smell of cooking apples and a raw, somewhat tart, endtaste. A word sometimes loosely used as a synonym for immature.
vanilla Generally associated with certain cask-aged wines.
varietal A distinctive aroma and taste deriving from a specific grape variety.
velvety A textural description: silky, smooth, a certain opulence on the palate.
vinous Having a pleasant enough, positive winey smell and taste but lacking a recognisable varietal (qv) character.
volatile acidity A normal component of wine but undesirable in excess, the danger signs being a vinegary smell and bitter/acid endtaste. Excess volatile acidity cannot be remedied.
weight A measure of the body, *see* alcohol.
well developed Component parts blended together, a desirable state of full maturity.
woody In relation to a wine nose or taste, a pejorative term, as opposed to oak (qv), which is desirable. The result of wine having been kept too long in cask, particularly old casks with rotten staves.
yeasty Undesirable smell, usually accompanied by an unclean, beery endtaste.

RED
BORDEAUX

Ch Lafite

I make no excuses for the dominance of the red Bordeaux section in this, as in the first, edition. It is one of the oldest surviving classic wine districts, certainly the largest in terms of vineyard area and production, and the most important as a market, producing a wide range of wine up to a virtually unassailable quality level. Its standards are emulated by other parts of the Old World as well as what, for want of a better blanket term, we describe as the New World: California, Australia and New Zealand.

Red Bordeaux has been shipped to England since Norman times. Bordeaux was under the English crown for three centuries, when the wine trade almost dominated our economy. And claret, as the English have called it for centuries, still dominates the fine wine market. "Fine Claret" was, as I have always noted with satisfaction, the first wine to appear in a Christie's auction catalogue, "The Property of a Nobleman deceas'd" in December 1766.

What is *so* special about Bordeaux? Not, I submit, the winemaker, not just the *cépages*, but the soil and maritime climate. It is the latter that is almost entirely responsible for vintage variations, the subject of this book. I look upon the soil and vine as mother and father, the winemaker as midwife. As we all know, siblings, despite the same parents, all turn out differently. My view is that the climatic variations take the part of genes, producing the vintage variations which largely dictate the different style, quality and longevity.

Much has been written about Bordeaux and I particularly recommend Edmund Penning-Rowsell's regularly updated tome *The Wines of Bordeaux*, and David Peppercorn's *Bordeaux*. And, to remind yourself of the precise location of each château, Hugh Johnson's *World Atlas of Wine*.

My aim is to summarise the particular character of each vintage, giving brief climatic reasons, but above all to illustrate the character, quality, weight and condition of the wine with up-to-date tasting notes.

Once again, I must remind readers that despite the number of vintages and châteaux recorded, this book does not and cannot claim to be definitive. It is a guide.

1771***

One of the earliest recorded good vintages. The first red Bordeaux vintage to appear in a Christie's catalogue: "Excellent fine flavoured Claret of the year 1771", in March 1776.

Ch Margaux Contemporary bottle, good top-shoulder level. Long black-with-age cork. Incredibly deep-coloured in decanter, paler in glass: still some red with a rich amber rim, not quite bright. Very little on nose at first but no obvious faults. After 30 minutes, developed a slightly quince-like scent and remained sound after 80 minutes in the glass. On the palate distinctly sweet, medium full-bodied, with positive flavour and remarkably good acidity.

*The oldest wine at Desai's Margaux tasting, Los Angeles, May 1987***

1784*****

The greatest vintage of the period.

Ch Lafitte (*sic*) Ullaged. Intensely dark colour, like an old-style brown sherry; an astounding smell, pure balsamic vinegar; yet still sweet, intense, with high extract. But, alas, not drinkable!

At Flatt's Lafite tasting, Oct 1988.

Ch Margaux Level just below top-shoulder. Surprisingly long, very black cork. A glorious, healthy-looking red brown wine with orange rim; the faintest whiff of a bouquet yet rich and meaty; slightly oxidised but rich, holding on to life precariously, and still drinkable. It must have been magnificent.

From a half-bottle tasted immediately prior to recorking, at the château, Aug 1987.

1785***

Latour of this vintage sold at Christie's in 1792.

1787****

No vintage report.

Ch Margaux Level: 1½in (4cm) below wizened black cork. Good depth of colour in the decanter and surprisingly deep in the glass. It had no 'nose' when first poured, but was sound. It took only five minutes of air to bring out the bouquet, sweet and biscuity, with great richness and depth. After 15 minutes it had evolved fully, cheesy, stably. The empty glass remained filled with perfume even after an hour. Distinctly sweet on palate, with a very lively rich flavour, perfect weight, length and finish. The sediment was thick, gritty and puce-coloured.

*Sept 1987******

Ch Branne-Mouton In the decanter the wine was a deep, rich amber. In the glass it looked relatively pale. The nose was closed but sound—not a vestige of oxidation or acetic acid. After 10 minutes it had blossomed, becoming richer, like dunked ginger biscuits, with a touch of coffee and caramel. On the palate, as the air got to it, it was slightly sweet, very richly flavoured with a good thick consistency. Complete. Good acidity. Delicious. An hour later the empty glass still retained a perfect bouquet, noted as "wholesome and wholemeal".

*At the château, June 3 1986******

1791****

Mr Christie, in his wine sale catalogue of May 23 1797, offered six hogsheads of first-growth claret of 1791, opining that the vintage was "considered the best that France has produced for many years".

Ch Margaux Contemporary bottle with striated neck. A later label "Claret Margaux". Rather pale, very little red, touch of orange; light but delicious bouquet that developed a fragrance that reminded me of a mixture of sealing wax and brandy snaps. Strange and ethereal. On the palate, slightly sweet, with perfect flavour, and excellent acidity.

*At Desai's Margaux tasting, May 1987******

1799***

Fairly big crop picked from Oct 5.

Ch Lafite From the château, recorked in 1953. Very much alive, fragrant, faded but fascinating.

*Marvin Overton's Lafite tasting, May 1979******

1803***

Picking began Sept 25. Good wines.

Ch Lafite Warm amber colour; sound, fragrant bouquet; dry, lean but firm.

*Marvin Overton tasting, May 1979****

1806

Ch Lafite A slender, elegantly shaped bottle of the period, one of several old vintages of Lafite, all recorked at the château and released to selected prestigious restaurants in France in the mid-1950s. This particular bottle sold by Le Coq Hardi restaurant, Bougival, and bought by Lloyd Flatt at Christie's in June 1980. Palish warm amber with orange highlights; lovely, sweet, rich, stably bouquet with touch of varnish, which for nearly

three hours surged out of the glass; dry, fairly light, good crisp acidity, firm enough, fragrant finish.
*One of the most beautiful wines at Flatt's outstanding Lafite tasting, New Orleans, Oct 1988******

1814

Picking began Sept 20. Small crop, good quality.
Ch Lafite Ex-château. Recorked mid-1950s. Faded orange amber; dry, light, firm, little fruit. Seemed better after two hours. One of the lessons of the Overton tasting of Lafite was that old claret, notably old Lafite, actually improves with a lot of air.
*At Overton tasting, May 1979***

1825****

Early harvest, Sept 11. Very good, long-lasting wines.
Ch Lafite Recorked at château. Lovely colour; ravishing bouquet and flavour to match.
*At Overton tasting, May 1979******

1832***

Hot dry growing season. Hard wines.
Ch Lafite Tasted twice, the first recorked at the château by Maitre Revelle in June 1987 and opened three months later at Rodenstock's annual tasting: good colour; nose a bit woody at first, rich, opened up attractively; very sweet, stylish, flavoury – a very good drink. The following autumn, a bottle bought at Christie's in 1979: lovely colour, warm peach; very sound, slightly vanilla, gentle fruity bouquet; medium sweetness, medium-full body, good, long, positive and powerful, with the singed-grape flavour following a very hot summer. Perfect tannin and acidity.
*Last noted at Flatt's Lafite tasting, Oct 1988******

1844****

Picking commenced Oct 8. Reckoned at the time to be the best vintage since 1815. Small crop. High prices.
Ch Lafite Recorked at the château, Oct 1953. Rich-looking, beautiful colour; equally full rich bouquet, fragrant, ripe – almost overripe – henhouse scent; on the sweet side, fair body, very positive and lovely flavour, great length, good tannin and acidity.
*At Flatt's Lafite tasting, Oct 1988******

c 1844–1848

Two wines I should like to mention though the precise vintage is not known. The first appears from time to time at auction.
Ch Bel-Air-Marquis d'Aligre Tasted three times in the mid-1980s. Each bottle had a good level, two had a fairly deep rich colour. One brownish amber. The first two had very good old bouquet, a bit vegetal and varnishy but fragrant. The third smelled of mushroom soup and was a bit dried out. The best two were dry, light, faded but elegant.
*Last tasted Sept 1987. At best****
Royal Mail Steam Packet Company's first claret Shipped by Nathl Johnston & Sons, Bordeaux. Three bottles from a Scottish cellar. The ship depicted on the label was launched in 1832, plied between Plymouth and the West Indies and went out of service in 1848. I bought all three bottles at Christie's really for the labels. But the wine was delicious. The first, opened casually at Christie's with Colonel Norman Johnstone, a collateral of the Bordeaux Johnstons, was, to our amazement, well-nigh perfect. The second and third, equally good.
*Last noted June 1984*****

1846*****

Hot summer. Big wines. The finest holding well.
Ch Lafite The first, with a "Harvey's Selection" slip label, at Flatt's Lafite tasting in 1988: good level, fabulous colour; delicate, fragrant bouquet; slightly sweet, medium weight, soft, velvety, marvellous tannin and acidity. A lovely drink and one of the best wines in the entire tasting. More recently: deep colour for age; very good old 'ivy leaf' nose that held well in glass. Still quite tough though not a big wine. Good length. Excellent.
*Last noted during lunch at Lafite, June 1989******

1847****

Abundance of light, flavoury wines, too delicate – at that time – for the English trade though this is hardly borne out by the two top growths tasted. Practically all the 1847s were shipped to Germany, Holland and the US.
Ch Margaux "Cruse Fils Frères, Bordeaux" label. A magnum, level top-shoulder: incredibly deep, intense; gloriously sweet, fruity, almost jammy bouquet; sweet, full-bodied, powerful and rich. Almost too good to be true, and certainly not as predicted.
*At Desai's Margaux tasting, May 1987******
Ch Rauzan Good colour for age, but tell-tale warning 'beads' at rim; extraordinarily sweet, delicate, completely harmonious old bouquet that blossomed in the glass; dryish, medium-light. A delicate, charming wine, soft, scented, with good length.
*From the private cellars at Lafite and tasted there, March 1983*****

1848*****

Ch Lafite First, recently recorked at château, at the Overton Lafite tasting in 1979: still deeply coloured, rich, tannic, extraordinary. A less good bottle at the 1986 Rodenstock tasting: dried out, somewhat decayed but with an attenuated flavour. Most recently at Flatt's Lafite marathon, with an "R Galos Gérant" label, recorked by the Maître de Chai in 1986. Very deep, rich tile-red centre, fine mature rim; a chunky, almost chewy, sweet bouquet which opened up in the glass, rather like warm, rich tea, an overtone of sweaty tannin but virtually faultless; slightly sweet, fairly full-bodied, rich, meaty, still tannic, good length, a touch of bitterness (due to slight cloudiness; it had not settled enough to be decanted bright). Very high marks.
*Last tasted in New Orleans, Oct 1988******
Ch Margaux Picking commenced Sept 4. Production 12,000 cases. Original bottle. Medium colour, very lively, lovely graduation; amazing fragrance, 'ivy leaf' and sealing wax, which gained richness and spiciness in the glass; surprising body for its age, deliciously flavoury, excellent acidity. A lovely drink. This bottle was from the private cellars at Ch Lafite where, at some time, it had been recorked.
*At Desai's Margaux tasting, May 1987*****

1849**

Moderately good year.
Ch Ausone From the château, recorked. A lovely autumnal colour, very lively, almost too good to be true; gentle, slightly smoky and raisiny, opened up, high-toned; dry, medium-light, slightly singed flavour, complete though faded and reduced.
*Sept 1987****

1858*****

An excellent vintage. Healthy harvest towards end of Sept following hot summer. A good crop.

Ch Lafite Seven notes. First, crisp but fragrant, from Lord Rosebery's cellar in 1967. A very good bottle from the Lafite cellars at Overton's tasting in 1979. More recently with original label, warm orange amber; low-keyed but very good, delicate, slightly biscuity bouquet; medium dry, on the light side, flavoury but with slight prickle of acidity. The other bottle with a Loewenthal label, level top-shoulder, probably not recorked. Similar depth of colour, fragrance, and weight. A more beautiful colour, lively and bright; fine, delicate, pure cedary Lafite smell and taste. Bouquet perfection after 10 minutes in the glass, then faded a little. A bit lean but clean, with good tannin and acidity.
*Last tasted at Flatt's Lafite tasting, Oct 1988*****

Ch Mouton-Rothschild Tasted three times, all labelled "Mouton, Bn de Rothschild, Proprietor 1858 R Galos, Gerant, Bordeaux". Original corks. All with good levels. The first tasted at the château: impressively deep in decanter, old brick red in glass, with rich amber rim; completely sound, touch of vanilla, harmonious bouquet; slightly sweet, full, rich, mouthfilling flavour, glorious acidity. The second similar but with teeth-gripping tannins. (I thought it was a 1937 Latour!) The last, at a Rodenstock tasting, had an incredibly awful creosote, tarry smell. Not tasted.
*Last tasted Sept 1987. At best*****

Ch Rauzan From the private cellars at Lafite. Recorked – short plain cork, excellent level. Pale, rather unhealthy amber colour, weak, slight spritz at rim; extraordinary high-toned madeira-like scent, refined linoleum and barley sugar; sweetish entry, dry finish. Light, faded.
At Lafite, June 1986 just.*

1861****

Crop devastated by early May frost, but remaining vines produced very good wine.

Ch Latour With "Café Voisin" label. A wormy old cork, level high shoulder. Fairly deep and brown; delicate, surprisingly sound bouquet with good gentle fruit, ginger and wholemeal biscuits; distinctly dry, on the light side, clean, fresh, sound. Remarkable.
*At Kerry Payne's Fête du Château Latour tasting, June 1981*****

1863**

Small crop, reported at the time to be of mediocre quality.

1864*****

A magnificent vintage picked in great heat. The most beautifully balanced of all the great pre-phylloxera vintages. Lafite said to be the most perfect, not only of the vintage but of all time.

Ch Lafite Five notes, British bottled, château bottled, in bottles and in jeroboam. More recently: in Sept 1987 a bottle recorked at château earlier that year: deep, healthy colour; slightly woody but a rich, substantial and basically sound bouquet; on the sweet side, fairly full-bodied, lovely flavour, perfect balance. Another, recorked by the Maître de Chai in 1986: deep, intense; rich, plummy, malty nose, speedily revealing sweetness, vanilla, then, after 15 minutes, a warm, raisiny bouquet. On the palate a similar sweetness and weight to the previous bottle, slightly chocolaty, with high extract, tannin and acidity.
*Last noted at Flatt's Lafite tasting, Oct 1988******

Ch Margaux Tasted twice. Both bottled by Cruse. The first, at the Desai tasting: fairly deep; slightly yeasty nose, reminding me of Malaga and brandy snaps. Medium sweetness and body, flavoury but slightly acetic. Yet after two hours, a glorious blackcurrant flavour. The second bottle, with original cork and very good level, deep-coloured but acetic.
Last noted at Rodenstock's tasting, Sept 1987.

Ch Latour Level top-shoulder. Beautiful colour but a little on the pale side; overpowering almost sickly sweet, pungent, 'ivy' bouquet; dry, flavoury but . . . .
At Kerry Payne's Latour tasting, June 1981.

1865*****

Another great vintage. Unusually early harvest. Magnificently sturdy wines, more consistently reliable – if well-cellared – than any other pre-phylloxera vintage.

Ch Lafite Tasted on six occasions. The first four, perfectly preserved, from Sir George Meyrick. The fifth, recorked at the château in 1987, had correct depth but very mature colour; low-keyed but very good bouquet, sweet, fruity, meaty. Powerful, excellent flavour, length, firm tannin and acidity in Sept 1987. The most recent, recorked by Whitwhams in 1974: palish, ruddy centre, amber rim; high-toned, slightly varnishy; sweetish, on the light side, flavoury but with touch of acidity.
*Last noted at Flatt's Lafite tasting, Oct 1981. At best******

Ch Margaux Cruse labels. The first bottle ullaged mid-low-shoulder. Slightly cloudy. Switchback bouquet; caramel, strawberry, then after 15 minutes very rich development, next mushroom soup, finally, after nearly two hours, glorious. Palate: sweet, fairly full, rich, remarkable flavour, good tannin and acidity. The second bottle: vinegar.
*At Desai's tasting, May; and Rodenstock's tasting, Sept 1987. At best****

Ch Latour Three notes. The first two enormously impressive but spoiled by too high volatile acidity. Most recently, from the château, recorked. Opaque; rich, harmonious, incredible vinosity; dryish, full-bodied, fabulous flavour, richness and balance, still retaining tannin and acidity. Years of life left.
*At Payne's Latour tasting, June 1981******

Ch Giscours From the private cellars at Lafite, recorked some time ago. High level, broken cork. Palish but warm-hued; an extraordinary scent, warm, fragrant though touch of decay. Held well. A light dryish charmer with acceptably acidic finish.
*At Christie's pre-sale tasting, June 1986****

Ch Laroze Cork like charcoal. Amazingly good colour for its age; high-toned old bouquet, eucalyptus; equally spicy mouthfilling flavour, cloves.
*Sept 1987*****

Ch Rausan-Ségla Level mid-shoulder. Fabulous deep colour; a curiously medicinal scent, TCP and bandages, but held well for over an hour; distinctly sweet, nice weight, very flavoury but equally curious medicinal, iodine-like, aftertaste.
*At Lafite, March 1983****

1867**

Small yield, prices too high for the quality.

Ch Mouton-Rothschild From the private cellars of Lafite, sold at Christie's. Recorked at Lafite. Pale amber, colour tailing off; initial strawberry amyl acetate scent, 20 minutes later very high-toned and malty, after an hour

like linoleum, sickly; very dry, lean, pricked – yet clean.
At Flatt's Mouton tasting, New Orleans, April 1986.

Ch Ducru-Beaucaillou Last recorked at Lafite in 1980. Lively colour, red tinge, perfect gradation; glorious, ripe, rich – topped up with Lafite?! Drying out but clean.
*Bought at Christie's and presented at the Rodenstock tasting, Sept 1987*****

1868***

Curious conditions: heat, then heavy rain in Aug but very hot again either side of an unusually early vintage. Very high prices.

Ch Lafite Perfect capsule, level and original cork. Rich, warm, rosehip colour; medicinal at first but soon blossoming, rich and powerful. After 15 minutes sweaty and medicinal again but then steadied and held well; dry, medium weight, light style, very clean, flavoury.
*At Flatt's Lafite tasting, Oct 1988*****

Ch Margaux Picking started Sept 7. Production: 14,000 cases. Fairly deep; not as harmonious as the 1870 but very clean and forthcoming. After 45 minutes very rich, slightly cheesy, and after 90 minutes faded, slightly chocolaty but sound. Fullish, richly flavoured, excellent tannin and acidity. Dry finish. At Lafite, March 1983. Four years later two bottles, both with new château capsules. Slight bottle variation. Both deepish and lively; one smelling like a venerable *chai*, stably, old Cabernet Sauvignon, the other slightly sour and dusty but powerful. Both fairly sweet and flavoury, one slightly piquant the other very complete, tannic.
*The latter two at Desai's Margaux tasting, May 1987. At best*****

Ch Latour Ex-château, recorked. Good colour, broad, brown rim; high-toned, varnishy nose, combination of mustard and manure, touch of volatile acidity; dry, spicy, citrus-touch, unknit. Not bad.
*At Kerry Payne's Latour tasting, June 1981**

1869****

An extremely good sturdy vintage, following perfect growing season. One of the most dependable of all the pre-phylloxera wines – if well kept.

Ch Lafite A magnificent magnum. When its original greasy black cork was drawn an incredible fragrance was released. Rich, soft, languorous at a century old. Then in 1978, a bottle recorked at the château: rich warm colour; extraordinary bouquet, reminded me fleetingly of Castrol XL motor oil! After 15 minutes rich, ripe, not to say overripe; sweet, fullish, very flavoury, fragrant and spicy.
*Last noted at Flatt's Lafite tasting, Oct 1988*****

Ch Margaux A bottle of the 1869 bought at Christie's had been sent to the château for recorking. Coincidentally, I was there (to recork the 1784). Level mid-shoulder. Despite its ullage, it was in remarkably good condition. On pale side but with a healthy glow; delicately fruity bouquet of great charm; slightly sweet, lightish and fading a little but fragrant, with a lovely aftertaste. It was topped up with a little 1970, a new branded cork inserted and given a new château capsule. Hey presto!
*At Margaux, Aug 1977****

Ch Mouton-Rothschild Three bottles, all from the private cellars at Lafite, and recorked there in 1980. The first pair tasted in 1983, intriguing but tricky. One incredibly rich, malty, overripe, with an acetone smell; rich yet decayed on palate. The other, ullaged, a pretty orange-pekoe tea colour; varnishy smell and taste. Dry. Light. Decadent. The third bottle: very high level, on the pale side but lively; faded and faint but complete. After 25 minutes the bouquet was sweet, reminiscent of pineapple husks and peaches, and held well for a further hour; on the palate fragrant, good length, with an endtaste like apples matured in a loft.
*Last noted at Flatt's Mouton tasting, April 1986*****

Carruades de Ch Lafite Two bottles: the first palish, very mature-looking; deliciously forthcoming rich, fragrant, rose-scented bouquet; distinctly sweet but a faded old lady. The second redder, bouquet of burnt coffee; dry, somewhat over acidic, with spicy finish. Both gamey, light and lacking the length of the *grand vin*.
*Both tasted at Lafite, June 1988****

Ch Marquis-de-Terme Good long cork, excellent level. Palish but very healthy ruddy hue; lovely, very fragrant, 'old ivy' bouquet; fairly full-bodied, rich, excellent flavour, good acidity.
*At Lafite, June 1986*****

1870*****

One of the greatest pre-phylloxera vintages and still magnificent if well kept. Crop reduced by spring frosts, a bakingly hot summer and early harvest – Sept 10 – in good conditions. The result: opaque, massive, concentrated and long-lasting wines.

Ch Lafite Anyone thinking Lafite produces only comparatively pale, light, delicate and feminine wines has never heard of, let alone tasted, the Lafite blockbuster of all time. I have 13 notes. The most spectacularly good was one of the (40) magnums from Glamis Castle. Bottled by Coningham, it had been bought by the 13th Earl of Strathmore, who found it tannic and tough, like red ink. Indeed it took 50 years to come round, according to André Simon who drank it in 1920. This extraordinary stock had remained untouched until the great Glamis Castle sale at Christie's in 1971. One was opened at a dinner at Christie's attended by a dozen or so of Britain's best-known claret experts. It proved to be faultless. Another, bottled by Cruse and tasted in 1980, had just survived a poor, low-shoulder level. More recently, a single bottle, recorked, was similarly perfect at Flatt's Lafite tasting: its appearance still deep, fine and rich; nose rather cheesy and sweaty when first poured, but the bouquet rapidly unfurled and improved for well over an hour in the glass. Still a touch of sweetness, still full-bodied, rich, chewy and still tannic. Top marks.
*Last tasted Oct 1988******

Ch Margaux Three notes, two from the Desai Margaux tasting in 1987. One with wax capsule embossed "Monkhouse & Andersons 1st growth claret" had a fine deep colour, sound and fragrant bouquet; sweetish, rich – magnificent power. The other, presumably recorked at the château was rather lower-keyed and, though flavoury, revealed a touch of decay and edgy acidity. An 1870, with a Sèze Fils Frères label and original cork had been brought back to Margaux with the 1869 previously referred to. This bottle, from another source, had not survived its mid-shoulder ullage. Though rich, it was oxidised. The Maître de Chai refilled it with some of the 1970 Margaux opened to top up the 1869. A plain cork was inserted. It was not re-capsuled. (This is normal practice at the top châteaux. So if you see an uncapsuled bottle with unbranded cork but good level, expect a topped-up 'oxidised' wine).
*Last tasted Aug 1987. At best******

Ch Latour Two excellent notes, including a faultless Scottish bottling: high level; wonderfully deep, intense colour; a most glorious, harmonious bouquet; distinctly sweet, fairly full-bodied yet soft, with perfect balance and

flavour. An aftertaste like warm toast.
*The best wine at Payne's Latour tasting, June 1981******

Ch Mouton-Rothschild From the cellars at Lafite. Rich, deep, intense appearance; a rich, singed tarry nose that blossomed gloriously in the glass and probably at its most sublime after 40 minutes, after which it appeared to fade a little, but retrieved a sort of 'second breath', sustaining for two hours an incredibly rich and pungent bouquet. On the palate: dry yet rich with a similar tarry flavour. Spicy — cinnamon — powerful, retaining good tannin and acidity. Lovely finish.
*At Flatt's Mouton tasting, April 1986******

Ch Cos d'Estournel Marvellous colour, tawny red with intense orange amber rim; rich, complete, harmonious bouquet, with touch of citrus and old oak, magnificent after even an hour in the glass. Incredibly sweet, rich, massive style and in otherwise perfect condition, though fading. Still fairly tannic.
*At Lafite, March 1983******

Ch Gruaud-Larose Also from the Lafite cellars. High level (clearly recorked). Warm amber red; heavenly bouquet, old ivy, ginger and arrowroot, which held for over two hours in the glass; flavour to match. Sweetish, long, slightly spicy, very complete, very fragrant. A beautiful wine.
*At Christie's pre-sale tasting, Oct 1985******

Ch Montrose Tasted twice. Both bottles virtually faultless. Most recently, one from the private cellars at Lafite, recorked at some stage: lovely autumnal colour but not very bright, probably shaken; very sweet, rich, sound bouquet and flavour. Old, oaky, Cabernet character. Dry finish.
*Last tasted June 1986******

Cuvée Marquise de la Tourette Bottled by Greenham & Co, Shanklin, Isle of Wight. Vintage neck label, short cork, top-shoulder level. Medium-pale, no red left; sweet, caramelly nose; good extract, chunky, fruity, soft and rich.
*Sept 1987***

1871**

Smallish, uneven crop following coldest winter since 1829/30. Regarded as inferior by the trade, and low-priced.

Ch Léoville-Barton Original capsule and cork. Top-shoulder level. Very deep colour; very sound, cedary bouquet; dry, medium weight, clean, crisp, excellent tannin and acidity. Drying out, lean but good.
*At Rodenstock's annual wine event, Sept 1987****

1872*

Rain in the middle of the vintage spoiled an otherwise respectable growing season. Few remain. Curiosities only.

Ch Lafite From four different cellars. All fully mature, palish but with a nice glow; the least good delicate but slightly decayed, a bit varnishy, with the smell of rice pudding skin and taste of old tea leaves. The best fragrant, gingery and flavoury. All very dry. Varying degrees of acidity. Summing up: "sear and yellow".
Last tasted at Flatt's, Oct 1988 * *to* **

1873

Literally nipped in the bud by a disastrous frost on April 28. Quarter the average crop. Ordinary quality. None tasted.

1874****

An enormous crop of high quality wine, but now the most variable of the major pre-phylloxera vintages.

Ch Lafite Tasted on 13 occasions since 1967. I have found it at its best from "pristine", original cold English cellars, and then only when the level has been high. In these circumstances it can be a very exciting wine. Colour ranges from fairly pale to fairly deep. Bouquet, at best, is rich, ripe — overripe really, reminding me of the smell of a hen coop. It seems to benefit from plenty of air. All slightly sweet, some very faded, slightly decayed but fragrant, some firm and substantial in balance. On the whole, living dangerously.
*Last tasted at Flatt's, Oct 1988. At best*****

Ch Latour A perfect bottle from Lord Rosebery's cellar in 1967 and a sickly, tart bottle, despite its quite good upper-shoulder level, at Kerry Payne's big Latour tasting.
*Last noted June 1981. At best******

Ch Mouton-Rothschild Four notes. One, at Lafite, had an extraordinary deep colour; rich, chocolaty but partially oxidised nose; drying out, good middle flavour but tailing off. Most recently, recorked at Lafite, medium depth, rosy hue, bright and lively-looking; rich ripe bouquet that blossomed beautifully, sweet, strawberry-like, held well, gentle, fragrant, tobacco-scented; dry, lean but flavoury. Stuffing taken out of it. A bit edgy.
*Last tasted at Flatt's Lafite marathon, April 1986*** *to* ***

Ch Gruaud-Larose Original capsule and cork. Balaresque label. Level mid-shoulder. Deep, too brown, yet, despite some oxidation, an extraordinarily rich bouquet. Once a big wine.
*Provenance, Mme Teysonneau, Sept 1987**

Ch Léoville-Barton Original cap and cork. Level upper-shoulder. Deep, intense, ruby glow; malty, meaty nose yet rich and raisiny. Sweet, fullish, good length, acidity high but tolerable.
*Sept 1987**

Ch Léoville-Poyferré A low-shoulder magnum. Oxidised.
Sept 1987.

Ch Pichon-Baron Original capsule and cork. Excellent level. Very deep, ruby shaded; nose low-keyed but sound; fairly sweet and full, perfect flavour, extract and balance.
*Sept 1987*****

1875*****

The most delicately delicious of all the pre-phylloxera vintages. More reliable than the 1874 and, at its best, still a most beautiful drink. It was an even more copious vintage than the '74, in fact the biggest production in the Gironde from the start of records until 1960. Considered at the time to be too light and evanescent — which just proves that (like 1929 or 1953) claret can be charming from cradle to grave.

Ch Lafite Five notes, and only one, an ullaged, maderised bottle, less than delectable. The most recent, from three magnums all recorked at the château in 1953. A lovely warm, rich, tile-red; very sweet, spicy, cedary bouquet, with an almost confectionery-like scent. Held well. All were sweet, medium weight but full-flavoured, glorious fruit, fragrant. Sheer perfection. (The unrecorked bottle from the Meyrick cellar was just as, if not more, beautiful.)
*Last tasted at Flatt's, Oct 1988******

Ch Margaux Double-magnum, ullaged mid-shoulder.

Deep, intense, ruby; extraordinary nose like crystallised violets and clean bandages! Fairly sweet, full-bodied and powerful, excellent flavour, still gripped by tannin.
*Sept 1988******

Ch Latour Two magnums, recorked at the château in 1980. Fairly brown; extraordinary bouquet like medicated shampoo. Curious taste of raspberries. Very dry. Most odd.
*At an otherwise excellent tasting of 1875 first growths, Sept 1988***?

Ch Mouton-Rothschild Three ullaged and murky bottles at Heublein pre-sale tastings in 1979, 1980 and 1981. And two magnums, recorked at the château in 1982, at the Rodenstock tasting of 1875s. Medium depth, fine, mature-looking; both had a perfect, sweet, gentle and harmonious bouquet with a whiff of cinnamon and pears. Lovely wine. Sweet, nice weight, perfect flavour and balance. Started to crack up after 35 minutes in glass.
*Last tasted Sept 1988******

Ch Haut-Brion Two magnums, both ullaged mid-shoulder. Fine, medium-deep, good mature rim; one distinctly corky, the other sweet. Old red Graves 'warm tile' bouquet; slightly sweet, delicate, soft, with characteristically earthy and almost chocolaty flavour. Acidity about to overtake it.
*At Rodenstock's 1875 magnum tasting, Sept 1988****

Ch Desmirail Provenance, Fernand Woltner, Paris. Château-bottled and recorked some time ago. Very good level despite loose crumbly cork. Very lively and pretty colour, palish ruby; sweet gentle bouquet, no decay. After 10 minutes a heavenly, ethereal, slightly smoky, and charred raspberry-like scent. Touch of sweetness and fat, very flavoury, piquant. Absolutely delicious despite touch of acidity.
*March 1984******

Ch Léoville Bordeaux bottled. Original capsule and cork. Level mid-shoulder. Brown and tart.
Sept 1987.

1876*

Poor weather conditions. Small crop of uneven quality wines.

Ch Lafite The year the phylloxera appeared at Lafite. Two bottles, one with cork pushed in. The other, recorked at the château and with a very high neck level, had a palish, warm but very mature colour, a bit cloudy; an immediately forthcoming fragrant bouquet, the initial whiff of banana being quickly overtaken by gardenia, then roses — a very floral, attractive scent and taste. Sweet, on the light side, with fine dry finish.
*At Flatt's Lafite tasting, Oct 1988****

1877****

Phylloxera rapidly progressing through Bordeaux. Above average crop of light but charming wines. Can still be delicious.

Ch Lafite A beautiful magnum from the château in 1967. Most recently, a bottle recorked at the château: pale, bright, appealing; lovely fragrant nose, slightly smoky, touch of tangerine, which opened up gloriously; a lovely sweet old wine, still with tannin and acidity, and very good length.
*At Flatt's Lafite tasting, Oct 1988*****

Ch Latour Similar colour to Lafite; most intriguing, intense and flavoury bouquet; sweetish, on the light side and delicate for Latour. Touch of decay and overripe, but lovely.
*At Payne's Latour tasting, June 1981*****

Ch Ausone First tasted in 1983, recorked: palish, beautiful, delicate, perfect weight, texture balance and finish. More recently, similar, with a heavenly Lafite-like delicacy and in perfect condition.
*Last noted at Flatt's Ausone tasting, Oct 1987******

Ch La Mission-Haut-Brion Good colour; slightly singed mocha bouquet; sweet, fairly full-bodied, good flavour, fruit, extract and balance.
*The oldest vintage at Karl-Heinz Wolf's La Mission tasting, June 1990*****

1878****

Commonly and incorrectly referred to as the last pre-phylloxera vintage. The pest was beavering away from the early 1870s to beyond 1900 and indeed is endemic. Nevertheless, 1878 certainly rounded off a magnificent era for Bordeaux.

Ch Lafite de Luze label. Level mid-shoulder. Fine, rich mahogany colour; nutty, oaky nose, very rich but showing age; sweetish, malty, partially oxidised, flavoury but with unclean finish.
At Flatt's Lafite tasting, Oct 1988.

Ch Latour Original capsule embossed with vintage year. Level mid-shoulder; deep, rich ruby; nose and flavour to match. Bouquet of ripe mulberries, attractive flavour, good extract, lovely aftertaste.
*At Rodenstock's tasting, Sept 1987*****

Ch Mouton-Rothschild Several bottles surviving low-shoulder levels in 1978 and 1979. Most recently: a low-shoulder magnum with a predictably maderised nose, slightly raisiny. Touch of sweetness, good length and with surprisingly clean, dry finish.
Last noted at Flatt's Mouton tasting, April 1986.

Ch Cos d'Estournel Attractive appearance but nose creaking, mushroomy, complex and medicinal. A faded old lady. Despite tartness, fragrant and clean.
*At Maurice Renaud's Cercle de Vingt lunch, May 1988**

Ch Gruaud-Larose Good provenance. Making an effort, despite an abysmally low level, and its tartness. Another, bottled by de Luze, original cap and cork, and splendid top-shoulder level: deep rim, high-toned, full-bodied, a bit over acidic and *rancio*.
Last noted at Rodenstock's tasting, Sept 1987.

Ch Larose Brandenburg Frères label. Poor level. Dry, delicate, clinging to life. Clean.
*At Christie's pre-sale tasting, Chicago, Feb 1987***

Ch La Mission-Haut-Brion Recorked 1978. Thick-looking, yet with delicate, fragrant nose and flavour. Sweet, lightish, good length and aftertaste.
*At Desai's La Mission tasting, Los Angeles, Feb 1985****

Ch Pontet-Canet Fully labelled, "Grand Vin", good level for age. Very pale, no red left but lively; a gloriously decadent overripe bouquet; delicate and delicious.
*At Christie's, Chicago, Feb 1987****

Ch Rausan-Ségla Rich, fragrant Café Voisin bottle in 1977. A deep brown oxidised bottle at a Rodenstock tasting.
Last noted Sept 1986.

1879**

Despite dismal weather reports and a small crop, those that have survived are delicately appealing.

Ch Lafite Recorked at château. Fairly pale but lovely bright rosehip colour; sweet, delicate, 'old ivy' bouquet which evolved beautifully in the glass; dry, light, gentle, flavoury, reasonable length and fragrant aftertaste.
*At Flatt's Lafite tasting, Oct 1988****

Ch Ausone Palish amber, bright; delicate, soon developed interesting bouquet, rich, mushroom soup, raisins,

whiff of ginger. Light yet rich, soft, delightful.
*At Flatt's Ausone tasting, Oct 1987****

1880*

As in 1879, poor spring, uneven flowering leading to small crop of not unattractive wines.
Ch Lafite Recorked. Similar appearance to the 1879; a very forthcoming oaky, smoky bouquet and flavour. Slightly sweeter and in some respects better than the 1879, though a bit screwed up at the end.
*At Flatt's tasting, Oct 1988****
Ch Mouton-Rothschild Labelled "Alfred Morton & Co, Bordeaux". Several notes, all from the Ten Broeck mansion cellar. All fairly low-shouldered. Murky though still alive; remarkable nose for age and ullage; soft yet highish acidity. Not at all bad.
*Last at Heublein's, Chicago, May 1980. At best***

1881**

Difficult climatic conditions. Summer hot, early harvest. Small crop of rather tannic wines.
Ch Lafite Old capsule, probably recorked. Top-shoulder. Lovely rich, warm, autumnal red; overripe, gamey, chocolaty nose; fairly sweet, lightish, some fruit and grip, dried raisin finish.
*At Flatt's Lafite tasting, Oct 1988***
Ch Latour Several deep-coloured, sound but severe bottles from the Meyrick cellar in 1970. More recently, a bottle ex-château, impressively deep; sweet, faultless old bouquet; a big, dry wine with excellent flavour, though still tannic.
*At Payne's Latour tasting, June 1981****
Ch Mouton-Rothschild Re-corked by Whitwham's in Feb 1974. Lovely colour, rich, ruddy, intense; gentle whiff of coal-tar soap, rising richly, with touch of cinnamon, fading after 1½ hours; dry, medium weight, excellent flavour, unexpected quality and length. Mildly tannic finish.
*At Flatt's Mouton tasting, April 1986*****
Ch Cantenac-Brown Recorked; healthy 'old heather' nose; dried out.
*At Rodenstock's tasting, Sept 1987**

1882*

The phylloxera gaining hold, also mildew. Light wines. Only one — a poor bottle — tasted.
Ch Lafite Balaresque slip label. Old cork, mid-low-shoulder. Warm amber colour but whiff of banana skins and grubby endtaste due to state of cork and level.
At Flatt's tasting, Oct 1988.

1883

Uneven weather, average crop, light wines.
Ch Lafite Recorked at château. Pale, no red left; curiously beautiful bouquet like crystallised pineapple; dry, very light, washed out and very short.
At Flatt's Lafite tasting, Oct 1988.

1884*

Continuing the run of poor vintages. Despite a good summer, vines affected by mildew, though the phylloxera "wearing itself out".

1885

Half crop of ordinary wines due to mildew and the phylloxera. None tasted.

1886***

Spring frosts and mildew reduced crop. Good late-vintage weather.
Ch Lafite Original short capsule and crumbly cork. Good top-shoulder level. Deep, healthy, rosy colour; fabulously sweet spicy vanilla bouquet; medium sweetness and body, good flavour and balance, dry finish. A surprisingly lovely drink.
*At Flatt's tasting, Oct 1988*****
Ch Mouton-Rothschild Fully embossed capsule, original cork. Level mid-shoulder. Palish tired amber; strange dusty nose; off-taste.
At Flatt's Mouton tasting, April 1986.

1887***

The best vintage between 1878 and 1893, following a warm summer and good harvest conditions. Though mildew under control, only a half-size crop.
Ch Lafite Three notes: in 1976 and 1985, similar: palish, very mature-looking; glorious 'old ivy' and coal-tar nose; slightly sweet, light soft and delicate with an upturned dry finish. But a mid-shoulder oxidised bottle at Flatt's Lafite tasting: too brown, tart and grubby.
*Last tasted Oct 1988. At best****
Ch Margaux Two fragrant bottles from Glamis Castle in 1971 and two others, recorked. The first oxidised and sour, the second with a better, more ruby, colour; sound but low-keyed nose; touch of sweetness, very flavoury, dry finish.
*The last two at Desai's Margaux tasting, May 1987. At best****
Ch Latour Fine, deep, intense; very sound, complete, touch of vanilla, cedar and tangerine peel; sweet entry, dry tannic finish. Good weight and texture. Well-balanced.
*Dinner at Ch Lafite, March 1983*****
Ch Chasse-Spleen Pierre Chabanneau, Bordeaux. Half-bottle. Short cork. Level upper mid-shoulder. Pale, no red left, but healthy glow and bright; dusty old nose, fragrant but highly volatile; warm, pleasing, caramelly flavour. Surprisingly high alcohol. Light, dry, acid finish.
*June 1988**

1888***

Depressing summer saved by a brilliant Sept. Late picking. Large crop of good, elegant, wines.
Ch Lafite Three notes: a charming half-bottle from a Scottish cellar in 1970 and a slightly oxidised bottle 10 years later. The third, recorked at the château, pale, bright, no red left; a charred heather fragrance; dry, light, faded — as though skinned alive or charcoal filtered.
Last noted at Flatt's tasting, Oct 1988.
Ch Latour Very pale, but healthy glow; fragrant, perfumed, 'ivy leaf', mildew affected bouquet; charming, light and lovely.
*At Ch Lafite, March 1983****
Ch Mouton-Rothschild Recorked by Whitwhams in 1980: deep but murky; overblown, very spicy nose and taste.
*At Flatt's tasting, Sept 1988**
Ch Haut-Brion La Mission (*sic*) From the Woltner cellars. Good colour; rich, maderised, coffee-like nose that settled down reasonably well; slightly sweet, lightish, good flavour, assertive yet good end acidity.
*At Wolf's La Mission tasting, June 1990****

1889**

Late vintage due to late flowering. Good harvest. Elegant wines.

Ch Lafite Frail but lovely in 1975. Next, original short capsule and very high level: a rosy glow; fragrant bouquet and flavour, extraordinarily scented, medium weight, some grip, dry finish.
*Last tasted at Lloyd Flatt's, Oct 1988****

1890**

Cold spring, late flowering, late harvest; lovely Sept.

Ch Lafite Provenance, a Rothschild cellar in Paris. Two notes. Both lovely rosehip colour; fragrant; medium sweetness and body, attractive, soft, chewy, good tannin and acidity. Dry finish.
*Last tasted Oct 1988****

Ch Latour Two notes. Both medium-deep, plummy, mature; low-keyed old nose, rather vegetal, 'old ivy' and mace, held well, reminding me of cream cheese; medium sweetness and weight, for Latour. Dusty, pasty, teeth-drying on the palate yet a good drink.
*Last tasted Nov 1990***

1891*

Very late harvest in good conditions following an unsatisfactory spring and summer. Yield severely reduced by *cochylis*.

Ch Lafite Tasted twice. Same provenance, a Rothschild Paris cellar. Recorked in 1957. Both with a broad, open, attractive colour and appealing bouquet; one noted as cedar and tea, the second as fruity, strawberry then honeyed. One dry and light, the other sweeter and fuller, but both silky, sound and pleasing.
*Last tasted at Flatt's Lafite tasting, Oct 1988****

Ch Latour Noted twice, first in 1974. Both bottles poor, one oxidised, the other acetic.
Last sniffed June 1981.

1892* *to* ***

Two severe frosts reduced crop. The rest scorched in mid-Aug by a 110°F sirocco. Then hailstorms. Results irregular.

Ch Lafite The first, from a Rothschild cellar, recorked in 1957, light elegant and attractive in 1976. The second, possibly Bordeaux-bottled, with good upper-shoulder level, fairly pale but bright; light, old but very fragrant bouquet and taste. Slightly sweet, very feminine, long refreshing acid finish.
*The last at Flatt's Lafite tasting, Oct 1988***

Ch Margaux Tasted twice. First, with original cork: extraordinary scented nose but a bit varnishy. Second, with new château capsule, presumably recorked, with bright, attractive appearance; bouquet old and dusty yet with strawberry-plant fruitiness; both bottles on the sweet side, lightish, the latter faded yet complete.
*The last at Desai's tasting, May 1987***

Ch Latour From the château: incredibly rich colour, bouquet and flavour. Sweet nose and taste.
*At Payne's Latour tasting, June 1981*****

1893****

A vintage of success and excess. Warm spring, early flowering. A bakingly hot summer and the earliest harvest on record, Aug 15, resulting in some opulently rich wines. But because of the great heat and abundance, some difficulties and failures.

Ch Lafite Eight notes over the last 20 years, ranging from oxidised (two with bad corks and levels) to luscious. Three in the 1980s, the first fairly deep; harmonious though gamey bouquet; medium-sweet, rich yet delicate (in 1981). A fabulous *impériale* with original label and cork: a lovely colour; faultless, harmonious bouquet, rich yet crisp, perfect weight and balance, refreshingly dry finish in 1987, and, most recently, a bottle recorked by Whitwhams in 1974, palish but warm colour; very rich, cheesy bouquet but with whiff of volatile acidity; medium-sweet, medium-full body, rich, fruity, high extract — but acidity too apparent.
*Last tasted at Flatt's, Oct 1988. On average***. At best******

Ch Margaux Nine notes since 1971. All, save one, very good. The best from Sir John Thompson's cellar sold at Christie's in 1976: gloriously rich colour, bouquet and flavour. Crystalised violets, soft, creamy. The next two at Desai's Margaux: one of the bottles had a protruding cork, a deep deathly colour and appalling smell. The other, from the cellars at Lafite, and recorked, was also deep, but richly coloured; a whiff of decay which dispersed; slightly sweet, full and rich, with positive flavour, though a bit too acidic. Most recently (from the Thompson's sale) excellent level, lively ruby; fragrant, perfect bouquet; slightly sweet, losing weight but lovely flavour and perfect balance. Faultless.
*Last noted at David d'Ambrumenil's dinner, Nov 1989******

Ch Latour Three notes, one ex-château, at the Latour tasting in 1981. All three surprisingly pale, the first with pink cheeks, the other two orange-shaded tawny. The most orange-tinged had a mushroomy nose. The first and last delicate, high-toned, gamey, sweet; yet dried out on the palate, light, faded but fragrant and very drinkable.
*Last tasted at the château, Oct 1981****

Ch Mouton-Rothschild Two opulent and excellent in 1971 and 1972, the third surviving a low-shoulder level and still drinkable.
*Last tasted May 1981, at best******

Ch Cheval-Blanc Double-magnum. Incredibly deep, almost opaque; extraordinary nose, *framboise*, wet cardboard. After one hour, a glorious vanilla scent. Medium-sweet, full-bodied, rich, wild cherry flavour.
With Jacques Hébrard at the Eigensatz tasting of 1893s and 1929s, in Wiesbaden, June 1987. Hors classé.

Ch Pétrus Double-magnum. Short lead capsule. Medium depth, rich; coffee-like, then more like gravy; fairly sweet, full, chunky, high extract, spicy tannic finish. Provenance unknown but impressive.
At Eigensatz's, June 1987.

Ch Brane-Cantenac Palish, lovely; very subdued at first but developed well. Sweet, relatively lightweight, delicious, dry finish.
*At Christie's pre-sale tasting, Oct 1985*****

Ch Cos d'Estournel Two magnums, recorked. One slightly 'corky'. The other of lively appearance; very sweet, a cross between a Rioja and a mildewy 1888; the sweetness of a hot vintage, gamey, tasting as if topped up with something like Lafite 1912 before recorking. A lovely drink.
*At Rodenstock's tasting, Sept 1987*****

Ch Ducru-Beaucaillou Provenance, Rothschild cellars. Good level. Palish but lovely colour with intense amber rim; unknit but rich bouquet; slightly sweet, lively, long, piquant.
*At Christie's pre-sale tasting, Oct 1985****

Ch Montrose Original cork. Medium-deep, a bit shaken; faultless, fragrant, strawberry-like nose; not all sweetness and light but some pleasing, soft fruitiness and

a bit of astringency.
At the Cercle de Vingt, May 1988★★

Ch Pichon-Lalande A pair from an English cellar, one with charcoal-black cork and oxidised, the other with excellent level and sound, original branded cork: rich mahogany colour; soft, warm, fragrant with touch of decay; medium sweetness, soft, lovely texture, dry finish.
Both tasted Aug 1981. At best★★★

1894★

1893 turned inside-out. The previous summer's heat inhibited the vines. There was *coulure* then rain, followed by a small, late harvest.

Ch Lafite Recorked at the château. Fairly pale and weak; delicate, fragrant, lacy old bouquet, singed, toasted; dryish, lightish, frail, faded, watery yet with fragrant endtaste.
At Lloyd Flatt's, Oct 1988★★

Ch Ausone Ullaged and unclean in 1977. More recently: pale, bright, tawny rose; very forthcoming, spicy, slightly varnishy bouquet and palate. Raspberry-like flavour.
Last at Flatt's Ausone tasting, Oct 1987★★

Ch Brown-Cantenac (*sic*). Calvet capsule. Alas, with poor greasy cork and ullaged. Maderised, faded, yeasty.
Nov 1983.

Ch Kirwan Double-magnum purchased at Christie's in Chicago. Deepish, ruby centred; chocolaty, meaty, oak and vanilla; dry, full, chewy but very tannic and with edgy acidity.
At Rodenstock's tasting, Sept 1988★

1895 *at best* ★★★★

Difficult growing conditions. Wet until end July, too dry in Aug and Sept, dangerous heat during vintage.

Ch Lafite Two excellent bottles, one in 1975, the other, recorked by Lafite's Maître de Chai in 1987: a lovely deep colour; sweet, lively yet solidly rich nose; slightly sweet, medium-full, rich, good fruit and good length.
Last tasted at Flatt's, Oct 1988★★★★

Ch Baret An unclassified Graves. Two bottles, both from the Baret sale at Christie's. The first amber-coloured; old, varnishy nose; dry, faded. The next upper mid-shoulder, good colour for age, a bit woody yet some fruit and fragrance.
Last tasted Nov 1984★

Ch La Mission-Haut-Brion A bottle tasted at the château in 1978, recorked 1950, fragrant and delightful. More recently, also from the Woltner cellars: broad, slightly weak rim; extraordinarily forthcoming bouquet, very scented, almost artificial fruit; sweet, lightish, stylish, very flavoury — though touch of linoleum — very drinkable.
Last noted at Wolf's La Mission tasting, June 1990★★★

1896★★★★

An abundant crop of delicate and distinguished wines, but only those in perfect condition have survived.

Ch Lafite Two bottles. The first with Rothschild provenance: attractive, piquant in 1976. The second: recorked by the Maître de Chai: very deep, rich but edge too brown; malty nose; medium, chewy, still tannic, slightly over acidic.
Last noted at Flatt's Lafite tasting, Oct 1988.

Ch Margaux Recorked. Dusty old nose; unpleasant, varnishy.
At Desai's, May 1987.

Ch Latour Two notes. One bottle delicate but dried out in 1971. The other, mid-shoulder, too brown and drab though a surprisingly good old nose and flavour. Dry. Rather acidic.
Last at Payne's Latour tasting, June 1981.

Ch Ausone Bad cork. Tawny, cloudy, oxidised, tart.
At Flatt's, Oct 1987.

Ch Brane-Cantenac Bouquet struggling to the surface, intriguing, developing coffee/chocolate fragrance; dry, one dimensional but very flavoury and clinging to life thanks to residual tannin.
At Lafite, March 1983★★

Ch Giscours Bordeaux bottled, cork branded de Luze. Excellent level. Bright, lively, pretty colour; delicate but well-knit and delectable bouquet; dry, lightish, somewhat faded but sound.
Oct 1981★★★

1897★

Strong on-shore salt winds scorched the vines, resulting in the smallest crop between 1863 and 1910. Just saved by good harvest weather.

Ch Lafite Failed corks leading to ullages spoiled some bottles, but one, recorked at the château in 1957, was light and elegant in 1976. Another, more recently: 'arsenic and old lace', palish, faded, slightly watery but sound.
Last tasted at Flatt's, Oct 1988★★

Ch Latour Two bottles, one Belgian-bottled and quite out of character: not Latour, not even claret-like on the nose. Tart. The other, from the château and recorked: a lovely colour, palish but healthy; slightly sweaty, pear-like but strangely attractive nose; dry, light, delicate.
Both at Kerry Payne's Latour tasting, June 1981★

1898★★ *to* ★★★★

Variable and half-size crop of hard, tannic wines, some of which have survived.

Ch Lafite Two bottles, both recorked, the first in 1976. Identical colour: ruddy tawny; bouquet light, tarry but lovely; on the light side though with a little tannic grip and good flavour. Short.
Last at Flatt's Lafite tasting, Oct 1988★★★

Ch Margaux New château capsule, so probably recorked. Pale, tawny-hued; rich, stably nose; dry, raw, still tannic.
At Desai's tasting, May 1987★

Ch Latour Lovely: good depth; on the verge of decay but perfumed, cinnamon; fairly sweet, lightish, soft and spicy, with delightful fragrance.
Dining at Lafite, July 1985★★★★

Ch Brane-Cantenac Autumnal colour; rich, toasted, fragrant nose, which reminded me of a box hedge, held marvellously. Light, softening yet piquant, fading yet flavoury.
At Lafite, March 1983★★★★

1899★★★★★

The first of the famous twins. A well-nigh perfect vintage to match buoyant times: abundant, high quality.

Ch Lafite Tasted eight times. Has not the body and stamina of the 1900, but at its best it can be superb. An incredibly beautiful bouquet and flavour at the Overton tasting in 1979: one *mise d'AG and E de Rothschild*, ullaged, cloudy and *passé* in 1981, and another, bottled by Eschenauer, very varnishy at Flatt's Lafite tasting in 1988. Most recently a superb, recorked, double-magnum: feminine, fragrant bouquet with a whiff of tangerine and taste to match. Perfect weight, gentle, beautifully balanced.
Last noted at the Eigensatz tasting, May 1989★★★★★

Ch Margaux Five notes, two fragrant, fascinating but fading at the château in 1972, another two at Desai's Margaux tasting in May 1987, one with a Pillet-Will label and new château capsule, presumed to be recorked at Margaux, pale, with an unhealthy orange tinge, soupy, varnishy nose, the other with plain capsule and overprinted label, probably from the cellars at Lafite: a lively colour; beautiful bouquet, delicately fruity; medium sweetness, lightish body, feminine, fragrant, lovely. Margaux at its best. Lastly an *impériale*, with original cork, richly coloured though with an orange amber rim, anticipating a trace of decay, yet with 'legs' like Romanesque arches. A sweet, fragrant, biscuity bouquet which was over-the-top within 30 minutes. On the palate sweetish, medium weight, holding its tannin and acidity. A lovely rich drink even though on the verge of collapse.
*The last at Walter Eigensatz's big bottle tasting, May 1989. At best******

Ch Latour Four notes. At best rich and soft. A bottle from the château showing very well in 1981: good colour; high-toned fragrant bouquet; slightly sweet, delicate, lovely. And a strange bottle from a cellar in Stockholm, bottled by F H Brown, Bordeaux. Poor cork, rich vinegar.
*Last tasted March 1987. At best******

Ch Mouton-Rothschild Four notes, two silky, faded but agreeable pre-1980. A well-nigh perfect bottle, recorked by Whitwhams in 1974, at Flatt's Mouton tasting in 1986: lovely, lively, ruddy colour; gentle fragrant bouquet, coffee, caramel, touch of mint, slightly lactic; perfect weight, a certain milkiness, the style reminding me of a cross between the '53 and '75. Firm dry finish. And a double-magnum, original cork, with an opulent, biscuity, fudge and chocolate bouquet; dry, crisp, lively, good length, highish end acidity.
*The last at Eigensatz's, May 1989. At best*****

Ch Ausone Very rich, raisiny slightly maderised bouquet and flavour. A touch of sweetness, chewy.
*At Flatt's Ausone tasting, Oct 1987***

Ch La Mission-Haut-Brion Two notes. Both bottles from the Woltner cellars. Recorked. The first at Desai's La Mission tasting in 1985: pale but lively; gentle, scented bouquet; dry, light, delicate, piquant. The second, a richer colour but slightly oxidised and sour. Over-the-top.
*The last noted at Wolf's La Mission tasting, June 1990. At best****

Ch Léoville-Barton First tasted in 1976: gentle and attractive. Next, dining at Lafite in Sept 1982: soft, beautiful balance, flavour and weight; I awarded it *six* stars. The following year also at Lafite: fairly deep and intense, beautiful, limpid; very forthcoming bouquet, rich, with an almost powder-puff sweetness. After 30 minutes a bit edgy, then got its second breath. Drying out but with '99 delicacy and gentleness.
*Last tasted March 1983******

At the same tasting at Lafite of wines from the 'exchange of stock' cellars, three other growths:

Ch Brane-Cantenac Lovely in 1971. Next, at Lafite, similar colour to the Poyferré: gentle graduation; harder, less charm, than the Poyferré, different character, depth of fruit; fuller, firmer, nice weight and texture, perfect balance, complete***

Ch Cantenac-Brown Palish, lively; delicate, chocolaty bouquet which opened up beautifully; sweet, delicious, good acidity, perfect****

Ch Léoville-Poyferré Paler and pinker than the Barton; Lafite-like scent and delicacy, blossoming in the glass, meeting the nose half-way, fully evolved after an hour in the glass; touch of sweetness, flavoury, leathery, dry slightly acidic finish***

Ch Rausan-Ségla From Mme Lawton's cellar: excellent level, palish, lively; 'old ivy' bouquet, a bit strained at first but attractive and, the great test, it developed well over two hours; faded but in balance, great length, acidity just in check.
*At pre-sale tasting, Oct 1981*****

1900*****

Perfect weather conditions. A superabundant crop of excellent wines.

Ch Lafite Five notes: opulent, delicious, magnificent at the Overton tasting in 1979. A memorable *Réserve du château* bottle at an equally memorable dinner at the Dolder Grand Hotel in Zurich to celebrate the publication of the German edition of *The Great Vintage Wine Book*: lovely colour, mahogany edge; overripe *gibier* bouquet, like an old cedar cigarbox, or singed hair. Touch of sweetness, fullish weight and style though fading, still with residual tannin. Well over-the-hill but exciting. It cracked up after an hour. Next, an ullaged and oxidised bottle in 1984 and a disappointing bottle at Flatt's Lafite tasting: meat extract and mushroom soup. Unclean finish.
*Last tasted Oct 1988. At best******

Ch Margaux Six notes: perfection. Two bottles at Desai's Margaux tasting, one with original capsule and "Pillet-Will" label, the other with an overprinted label (probably from the cellars at Lafite). Both sound, sweet, soft, rounded. Perfect. Most recently, deep; gentle, restrained; mouthfilling fragrance.
*Last tasted at Rodenstock's Weekend Closing Dinner at the Aalberg Hospiz, Sept 1987******

Ch Latour Three notes, two prior to 1980: magnificent colour, ripe, flavoury, somewhat austere. The biggest disappointment at Kerry Payne's Latour tasting, oxidised, woody.
*Last tasted June 1981. At best****

Ch Mouton-Rothschild Five notes, one acetic. In 1983, from the private cellars at Lafite, very sweet, fairly full-bodied, twist of acidity. A bottle recorked in 1980 at Flatt's Mouton tasting in 1986, with oyster-shell bouquet and flavour. The nose developed beautifully, rich and biscuity, but the overall impression was of a faded mouthful. Two months later, an incredibly rich, thick-looking wine, somewhat cheesy, distinctly sweet, full, fat and chewy.
*Last tasted June 1986. At best******

Ch Ausone Dry, rich yet lean. Lacking excitement.
*At Flatt's Ausone tasting, Oct 1987***

Ch Pétrus Bottled in Scotland. Worn wax seal impressed "1900 Pomerol . . . rtley, Leith": palish, no red left; bouquet fragrant despite decay and pungency; acidic but clean, with amazingly spicy aftertaste.
*At Hans-Peter Frerick's Pétrus tasting, Munich, April 1986***

Ch Brane-Cantenac Lovely autumnal colour; chocolaty, beautifully evolving bouquet; sweet, soft, delicate.
*At pre-sale tasting, Oct 1985******

Ch Figeac An extraordinary burgundy-shaped half-bottle from an English country mansion, with hand written slip label. Hard, protruding cork. Warm glow, red-tinged; old, fragrant, like pomegranate; very sweet, soft, faded but lovely. Faded rose petals.
*June 1988*****

Ch Gruaud-Larose Richly coloured; dry, fullish, peppery, lively.
*Oct 1984******

Ch La Mission-Haut-Brion Ex-Woltner cellar. Level upper mid-shoulder. Healthy blush of red – a bit too red, signalling 'pricked' nose and end-taste. But flavoury.
*At Desai tasting, Feb 1985***

Ch Mouton d'Armailhacq Limpid orange rose; touch of mercaptan – old rubber tyres – which cleared, just.
Oct 1985.

Ch Pichon Lalande Deep, rich; extraordinary scent, touch of volatile acidity; fairly sweet and full, rich, lovely but a hot, edgy finish.
*Sept 1987****

Ch Rausan-Ségla Perfection in 1976. Then two bottles from Mme Lawton's cellar. The cork of one had fallen in *en route* from Bordeaux. Acetic. The other, recorked by Lalande in 1953, fine, deep; similar nose to the 1899 but more robust and substantial. Acidity on the high side but perfectly tolerable.
*Last tasted on the day of the sale, Oct 1981****

Ch Tertre-Daugay Double-magnum: deep and plummy; soft, mellow; delicate, flavoury.
*Sept 1987****

1901*

Uneven vintage due to perverse weather conditions.

Ch Latour Palish orange tawny; intense bouquet, coffee beans and ivy; dry, light for Latour, positive flavour. Faded yet balanced.
*At Kerry Payne's Latour tasting, June 1981***

1902*

Like 1901, difficult growing season. A fairly large crop of ordinary wine.

Ch Lafite Two notes. The first bottle with a short cork at the Overton Lafite tasting in 1979: exquisite but faded and fleeting. At Lloyd Flatt's, pale but ruddy; very fragrant, spicy bouquet, but dry, light and thin.
*Last tasted Oct 1988***

Carruades de Ch Lafite Recorked. Four notes. All creaking somewhat. At best with delicate, herbaceous, spicy bouquet. Mainly dry, all light, tart but drinkable.
*In 1981, 1982, 1984 and at the Flatt's tasting, Oct 1988. At best***

1903

A third dismal vintage. April freezing. Crop reduced. Sunless summer.

Ch Lafite Glass lozenge embossed. Alas, tawny and oxidised.
At Flatt's Lafite tasting, Oct 1988.

Ch Latour Pale, decayed and tart in 1977.

1904****

Excellent growing season. Abundant crop. Rather a Cinderella vintage now but, if kept well, can give much pleasure.

Ch Lafite Four notes, two ullaged and 'off', one, in 1970, faded but fragrant. A good bottle at Flatt's Lafite tasting: palish but warm; very rich, meaty bouquet; dry, light, delicate but with good length. Fragrant.
*Last tasted Oct 1988. At best****

Ch Latour Even better than its reputation. Good level, incredibly deep and youthful appearance; sound cedary nose; fairly sweet, fullish, smooth yet tannic.
*At Bordeaux Club dinner at Harry Waugh's, April 1987*****

Ch Baret Recorked. Subdued tobacco-like Graves character; dry, mouthfilling, though lacking fruit. Good for its age and class.
*From the château. Tasted April 1986***

Ch Brane-Cantenac Palish, amber rim; pungent coffee and chocolate nose developing recognisable Brane-Cantenac *fermier* character and strange whiff of pear skin; a wine of some substance, open, soft, with dry finish. Better than it sounds, but it faded in glass.
*At Lafite, March 1983***

Ch d'Issan From the *caveau privé* of Fernand Woltner. Level upper-mid; firm unbranded cork; very deep colour; old, dusty and dried out.
Nov 1986.

Ch Malescot-St-Exupéry Deep, plummy-coloured; curious bouquet, spice, banana-like, showing its age, vanilla, cheesy; fairly sweet and fullish body, soft, a bit short.
*At Rodenstock's Malescot tasting, Sept 1990**

Ch La Mission-Haut-Brion First noted at Desai's tasting in 1985: despite ullage, healthy glow; gentle, vanilla, creaking and crumbly yet sweet and flavoury. Most recently, palish, attractive; fragrant, tea-like, developed charming biscuity scent; very dry, fairly light, crisp, very flavoury, sound despite end acidity.
*Last noted at Wolf's La Mission tasting, June 1990****

Moulin-Riche The second wine of Léoville-Poyferré. Purchased at the Lawton sale. Recorked by Lalande c1953. Pale but lively; shrugged off its old age and bouquet developed beautifully. Good, surprisingly rich, despite being delicate and faded.
*At home, March 1982****

1905***

An abundant crop of light wines.

Ch Lafite Two notes. The first, in 1976, recorked, with a stem-ginger bouquet and delicate flavour; the second, probably from the same Rothschild family cellar, rich, singed, biscuity, very attractive; a fragrant, 'old cedar' taste and light dry finish.
*Last noted at Flatt's tasting, Oct 1988*****

Ch Margaux Beautiful, silky, lingering in 1969 and a more delicately poised, light, acidic but flavoury bottle.
*Last noted at Flatt's tasting Oct 1988. At best*****

Ch Latour First a strange bottle in 1981 labelled "PR Vours, Le Bouscaut". The air above its low-shoulder level must have been benign for the nose was remarkably sound, though light and faded. Next, a recorked bottle from a New York State mansion, very similar: old oak, nice fruit, once full-bodied, now fading yet still tannic.
*Last tasted March 1985***

Ch Mouton-Rothschild Two notes, both bottles ullaged mid-shoulder. One, in 1977, had survived, sound, delicate. The other had a fabulously rich colour, threw off its wet dog smell, developed a lovely bouquet but was dry, lean and a bit tart on the palate.
The last at Flatt's Mouton tasting, April 1986.

Ch Haut-Brion A half-bottle, just surviving its low level. Though a bit maderised, rich and clean on the palate. Good finish.
*April 1984***

Ch Brane-Cantenac A continuation of the tastings of stock from the private 'exchange' cellars at Lafite. Palish but evenly graduated; very ripe farmyard, medicinal bouquet much liked by some; dry, lightish, crisp, flavoury, nicely balanced.
*March 1983*****

Ch Cos d'Estournel, From the château. Recorked 1983: badly shaken, cloudy, no red left, faded and creaking.
In Miami, Jan 1990.

Ch Figeac A controversial magnum: marvellous colour; at first showing age, whiff of chocolate, then opened up, malty, caramel. After two hours it smelled like a Pineau

des Charentes. An extraordinarily scented flavour, vanilla and raspberries.
At Desai's Figeac tasting at Le Taillevant, Dec 1989. Hard to classify.
Ch Gruaud-Larose One a bit tart, the next, pale but interesting, with marvellously fragrant bouquet and flavour. Dry, light. Refreshing acidity.
*At Heublein's pre-sale tastings in 1980 and 1981. At best***

1906***

A good vintage. Great heat and drought reduced crop. Robust wines, now faded but, if in good condition, still delicious.
Ch Lafite Three favourable notes. Still an attractive wine. Most recently: palish, ruddy amber; fairly sweet nose and palate, soft, flavoury. Exotic but must be drunk soon after pouring.
*Last tasted at Flatt's, Oct 1988****
Ch Margaux 10 notes, six since 1980 including, alas, three poor mid- to low-shoulder bottles. Demonstrating the effect of levels, three bottles from Prunier's cellars in Paris varied, one opaque, flat-tasting low-shoulder bottle, one, upper mid-shoulder, had an oxidised bottle-stink that cleared and was not bad on the palate, and a top-shoulder bottle, the least deep though richly coloured, with a sweet old perfumed bouquet and rich, soft, harmonious flavour.
*Last tasted June 1985. At best****
Ch Latour Fine, deep, classic colour; delicate yet meaty bouquet that held well. Dry and much less impressive on palate. Acetic acid poised to take over.
*At Kerry Payne's Latour tasting, June 1981**
Ch Mouton-Rothschild Recorked 1965. A very lively red; strange, medicinal, but attractive bouquet; lightish, with lovely flavour and delicacy, clean dry finish.
*Best of the 1905 to 1909 flight at Lloyd Flatt's tasting April 1986****
Ch Haut-Brion At best, excellent.
*Last tasted Nov 1979****
Ch Ausone Despite mid-shoulder level, attractive, fragrant and flavoury, with good length.
*At Flatt's Ausone tasting, Oct 1982****
Ch Baret Very good level, nose and taste with earthy Graves character, faded but fragrant.
*At pre-sale tasting Sept 1983****
Ch Brane-Cantenac Three notes, all remarkably good despite two low and one mid-shoulder level. Moral: better an ullaged bottle after a lifetime in a cool cellar than a peripatetic high-level bottle of the same age.
*All from the Prunier cellar, Paris, Oct, Nov, Dec 1982. At best***
Ch Figeac Magnum: palish, rosehip; gentle, fragrant at first then opened up richly, like a thoroughbred stable, but fragile and faded in under two hours; dry, slightly tart finish, but flavoury.
*At Desai's Figeac tasting, Dec 1989***
Ch Marquis-de-Terme Ex-Fernand Woltner cellar. Good level, palish but healthy colour and with a very heavy muddy sediment; lovely old 'singed ivy' bouquet on decanting, afterwards creaking and stalky, finally brightened up. Slightly sweet, rich but faded old lady.
*March 1985***
Ch La Mission-Haut-Brion A very ullaged bottle from the Woltner cellars. Oxidised, yet a decayed fragrance; tart but flavoury.
At La Mission tasting, Feb 1985.

1907**

An abundance of light wines, appealing at the time but lacking staying power.
Ch Lafite Rose-tinged tawny; a touch of sourness failed to conceal delicacy and fragrance, but dry and short.
*At Flatt's Lafite tasting, Oct 1988**
Ch Margaux A flowery Viennese bottling in 1975 and one château-bottled and recorked, pale and pretty-looking, but dusty, acetic taste.
The last at Desai's tasting, May 1987.
Ch Mouton-Rothschild Both bottles from Lafite's private cellars, both similar: pale, open, healthy; initial whiffs of pear-skins, varnish and mushroom stalks cleared, softened and sweetened; despite touch of decay, a good drink, though lean and mild for Mouton.
*Tasted in March 1983 and at Flatt's, April 1986***
Ch Haut-Brion Tawny, weak-rimmed; thick, singed, earthy, and characteristic tobacco leaf nose which developed amazing chocolaty richness and smells of cold tea and pea soup. Dry, light, short. Perfect acidity. Oddly enough it was appealing, when one got used to it.
*At Lafite, March 1983**

1908**

An average year. Some tannin and depth of colour remains but now variable and risky.
Ch Lafite One, recorked in 1957, good but short in 1976, one amber, maderised, tart and grubby.
*Last noted at the Flatt Lafite tasting, Oct 1988. At best****
Ch Margaux Two bottles at the Desai Margaux tasting, both with original château capsules, one with Pillet-Will label, sweetish and attractive, the other, possibly from a Rothschild cellar, very deep and rich-looking but unknit with curious overtones and edgy finish.
*May 1987. At best****
Ch Latour Three good notes. The first, from the de Beaumont cellars in 1974, the next two recorked, lovely in 1976 and showing well at Payne's Latour tasting: remarkably deep, rich and sound, firm, flavoury and tannic.
*Last tasted June 1981****
Ch Mouton-Rothschild Two bottles, with original Bn de Miollis labels, recorked 1980. Lovely autumnal colour; touch of old age cleared, revealing fleeting touch of richness, then faded. Both crisp and flavoury but with acidity lurking at the end.
*At pre-sale tasting in 1985 and at Flatt's Mouton tasting, Oct 1988*** just.*
Ch Haut-Brion An earthy, malty *impériale*.
Dec 1969.
Ch Cheval-Blanc In magnums. Fairly deep, rich; one old, earthy, fragrant, the second with a smell of dried mushroom stalks. Some sweetness, medium weight, a very positive long, singed flavour and wonderful acidity.
*At the château, Sept 1986. The best*****
Ch Pétrus Palish but lively, red-tinged; extraordinary, fragrant, farmyard, medicinal bouquet; sweet, an over-ripe decadently opulent flavour.
*At Frerick's Pétrus tasting, April 1986*****

1909*

Stormy Aug with hail badly damaging healthy crop. Hot sun at end Sept pulled it round. Average crop of light wines. Long past their best.
Ch Lafite Four notes. Faded and thin.
Tasted from 1955 to 1969.
Ch Margaux Recorked. Amber; smell of ox blood. Decayed.
At Desai's tasting, May 1987.
Ch Latour Dry, light, fruity in 1974. More recently, ex-château, recorked: a good rich colour; old but delicate and

mellow; lightish yet sturdy. Dry stringy finish.
*Last noted at Kerry Payne's Latour tasting, June 1981**

Ch Mouton-Rothschild Both from Lafite, recorked 1980. Both palish, rusty-looking; the first—at pre-sale tasting in 1985—a bit dusty on the nose but a very pleasant, sweet old flavour. The second cracking up. Malty, singed nose becoming very smelly, like a Limbourg cheese; raw, short and tart.
Last tasted at Flatt's, April 1986.

Ch Haut-Brion Deepish tawny but pretty; faint at first, then became rich and biscuity (it reminded Eric de Rothschild of a harness room), then the distinct Haut-Brion tobacco 'trademark'; sweet, rich, cracking up but an enjoyable drink.
*Lunch at Lafite, March 1983***

1910

Poor weather. Late improvement for a mid-Oct harvest. Tiny crop of feeble wines.

Ch Lafite Probably recorked. Palish; overripe, gamey; sweet, singed; lightish, lean faded but flavoury. Piquant dry finish.
*At Lloyd Flatt's, Oct 1988***

Ch Haut-Brion Gentle, faded; clinging to life.
*1971***

1911***

Despite storms, mildew and pests, summer heat and drought, a good, small vintage. Some still quite nice, though acidity taking over.

Ch Lafite Recorked by *Maître de Chai* in 1987. A lovely glow; deliciously sweet bouquet, fruit, touch of vanilla; dry, chewy, taste of singed leaves, nice weight, fair length, soft tannin and acidity. Attractive.
*At Lloyd Flatt's, Oct 1988****

Ch Margaux Four notes. All attractive, despite over-maturity. Feminine, fragrant, piquant.
*Last tasted pre-sale, Oct 1985****

Ch Latour Four notes. Variable. Two, one bottled by Berry Bros, oxidised and tart. One, with original cork, lively looking; high-toned, fragrant; distinctly dry, light, short, flavoury—acetic edge.
*The last at Payne's Fête du Ch Latour, June 1981. At best**

Ch Mouton-Rothschild Four notes. Two wines undrinkable. Another pale, orange-tinged; high-toned; tempting but tart. At best, light, faded, tolerable.
Last tasted Sept 1987 Risky.*

Ch Ausone Difficult to decipher label: 1921 or 1911. As it happens the two vintages had something in common and the notes were not dissimilar. Medium-deep; sweet, 'old ivy', spicy, nice fruit, persistance; nicely evolved, lean and long.
*At Flatt's Ausone tasting, Oct 1987****

Ch Cheval-Blanc Four notes. First, mid-1970s in bottles: curiously meaty nose, rich texture, both with original corks; and two magnums, with Cruse capsules, rich, singed, sweet and fleshy.
*Last tasted Sept 1987****

Ch Figeac Pleasant colour; old biscuity nose which evolved into a rich, spicy, scented, beetroot-like bouquet; lightish, mild, gentle, silky texture, acidity creeping up.
*Brought by the Manoncourts to Desai's Figeac tasting, in Paris, Dec 1979****

Ch Gruaud-Larose Open, orange-hued; fully evolved but faint, with gentle fruit and fragrance. Faded and a touch of decay but attractive.

Ch Léoville-Poyferré Deeper, ruddier; sweet, fragrant; dryish, light, mild, pleasant enough but a bit lacking.
*Both tasted at Lafite†, March 1983***

Ch La Mission-Haut-Brion Two bottles: one corked, mushroomy. The other cleaner, improved in glass; medium weight, some elegance, crisp finish.
*Both at Rodenstock's tasting, Sept 1987. At best****

Ch Rausan-Ségla First tasted in 1977: fragrant. Most recently, recorked: autumnal colour, fabulous bouquet and glorious flavour. Sweetish, excellent length. Most drinkable.
*Last noted at Christie's pre-sale tasting, Oct 1985*****

1912**

Rollercoaster conditions: May hot, June unsettled, July satisfactory, Aug cold and wet, Sept fine and warm. An abundance of light wines. Can still be delightful.

Ch Lafite Six notes since 1969. All recorked at the château. All good. Warm, amber rim; fragrant, floral, 'ivy leaf'. Light, crisp, flavoury, with a pleasantly dry, acid finish. A charmer.
*Last tasted at Lloyd Flatt's, Oct 1988****

Ch Latour Original cork. Upper mid-shoulder. Palish; high-toned, cheesy but with a fragrance like the Lafite '12. Slightly sweet, lightish, a faded old lady but flavoury.
*At Payne's Latour tasting, June 1981****

Ch Mouton-Rothschild Original cork. Upper-shoulder. Pale, faded; resiny, acetic. A poor bottle.
At Flatt's Mouton tasting, April 1986.

Ch Ausone Upper-mid-shoulder. Amber, no red, but with healthy glow; distinctly honeyed 'calf's-foot jelly' scent; attractive but well past best.
*At Flatt's Ausone tasting, Oct 1987**

1913

Cold summer. Pests and diseases. Weather improved too late. Abundant, poor. Curiosity value only.

Ch Lafite Calvet slip label. Original cork. Lowish level. Spoiled. Mushroom soup flavour. Dry. Raw.
Poor bottle at Flatt's tasting, Oct 1988.

Ch Latour Two similar notes, both ex-château, recorked. Fragrant in 1977. Light, gentle, touch of sweetness and slightly tart finish.
*Last tasted June 1981***

Ch Ausone Top-shoulder, good colour; scent of freshly picked mushrooms; sweetish but losing fruit, lean but flavoury.
*At Flatt's Ausone tasting, Oct 1989**

1914**

Delayed flowering, reduced crop. Hot Aug. Good harvest. Some excellent wines have survived, just.

Ch Lafite Two recorked. Fragrant, attractive though lacking length in 1976 and 1977. A half-bottle, good level. Amber, maderised. Short.
*Last tasted at Lloyd Flatt's, Oct 1988. At best***

Ch Latour Original cork. Upper mid-shoulder. Too brown, falling apart.
Payne's Latour tasting; June 1981.

Ch Mouton-Rothschild Upper-shoulder. Lovely colour; decayed but fragrant nose and flavour. Gentle but

† *It was customary for leading châteaux to exchange wines. Mouton at this time was a second growth and exchanged with other second growth châteaux. The most highly regarded were Rausan-Ségla, Brane-Cantenac, Léoville-Barton and Gruaud. Those at Lafite were regularly recorked.*

dried out.
At Flatt's Mouton tasting, April 1986.
Ch Ausone Upper-shoulder. Palish; very fragrant bouquet and taste. Lightish, crisp fruit, charming.
*At Ausone tasting, Oct 1987***
Ch Gruaud-Larose Bottled by Reid Bros & Kerr, Pall Mall. Top-shoulder. Lovely brick-red; gentle, sound nose and flavour. Soft fruit. Touch of end acidity.
*From a country house cellar, at pre-sale tasting, July 1980****
Ch La Mission-Haut-Brion First noted at Desai's tasting in 1985: pale; sweet; attractive. Most recently: palish, slightly orange tinge; sweet, creamy, fragrant bouquet; sweet on palate, lightish, singed Graves flavour, pleasing finish.
*Last noted at Wolf's La Mission tasting, June 1990****
Ch Pontet-Canet UK bottled. Drab. Sweet and sour.
Pre-sale, July 1989.

1915

War and pestilence. Wet summer, mildew, pests, labour shortage. Aug and Sept fine but some vineyards abandoned. None tasted.
Ch Latour Declassified. For domestic consumption only.

1916**

Average crop of good though tough wines. The hard tannins, which doubtless made them austere when young, have preserved them.
Ch Lafite From the *cave privée* of Fernand Woltner. Original capsule, top-shoulder. Rich colour, nose and taste. Overripe nose. Good fruit. Bitter, tannic finish.
*At Flatt's tasting, Oct 1988**
Ch Latour Five notes from 1974. A pretty tough wine. Mostly original corks, some wizened. All fairly deep-coloured; showing age; fading, flat though chewy. Still tannic.
*Last tasted April 1987**
Ch Mouton-Rothschild Mid-shoulder; over-mature; decayed, scrawny, dried out.
At Flatt's Mouton tasting, April 1986.
Ch Ausone Upper-shoulder. Fairly deep, rich; sound, sweet, scent of ripe peaches and stem-ginger. Chewy, chocolaty, excellent flavour.
*At Flatt's Ausone tasting, Oct 1987****
Ch Cantemerle Mme Binaud told me that she had helped pick her father's grapes – she was just 16. Two bottles from her cellar. Original crumbly corks, upper-shoulder. Mature but lively; spicy, gingery, complex. Faded, lovely texture, delicate.
*Tasted in May and at the pre-sale tasting in June, 1983****
Ch Léoville-Poyferré Two notes. Good but astringent in 1970. Rich, meaty, alcoholic, rich, delicious.
*Last tasted Oct 1981. At best*****
Ch Le Marque Shipped and bottled by Reid Bros & Kerr Ltd, Albemarle Street. A fortuitously happy purchase from a Northumberland cellar. Several notes. Overripe; an intriguing smell of black treacle, cold tar, grapefruit and mace; dried out, still tannic and acidic – yet delicious.
*Last tasted Dec 1989***.
Ch La Mission-Haut-Brion Three notes: powerful, complete in 1978. At Desai's in 1985: a pretty colour but corked nose. Very dry, leathery. Most recently: richly coloured; fragrant, tobacco-like nose, evolving richly in the glass; fairly sweet but medium-light, rich, cedar and tobacco flavour. A bit edgy.
*Last noted at Wolf's La Mission tasting, June 1990. At best****
'Le Pavillon – Château Margaux' Now known as Pavillon Rouge. Fairly intense and impressive looking, but dry, dusty and raw.
At Desai's Château Margaux tasting, May 1987.
Ch Rauzan-Gassies Upper-shoulder. Very deep, too deep, showing its age. Fig-like nose.
Dec 1985.

1917**

Good flowering, hot June though cooler July and Aug. Early vintage but shortage of labour. Average crop of soft and charming wines.
Ch Lafite Attractive wine from a Paris cellar in 1976. A low-shoulder bottle at Flatt's tasting: nose like a sweet madeira and taste like smoky dry sherry. Not good.
*Last tasted Oct 1988. At best****
Ch Margaux Two similar bottles at Desai's Margaux tasting. Attractive, high-toned, nice weight, style and fruit.
*May 1987****
Ch Latour Seven notes. Variable, from corked to deep rich, fruity and powerful, including a soft Berry Bros bottling in 1981.
*Last tasted March 1983. At best****
Ch Pétrus Deep but murky; pungent, overripe, opulent; flavoury but too sharp.
At Hans Peter Frerick's Pétrus tasting, April 1986.

1918***

Fine spring, warm summer, beneficial rain resulting in good end-of-war harvest early Oct. Healthy but rough. Can still be attractive.
Ch Lafite Several notes reflecting variations of provenance and condition. A recorked bottle at Lloyd Flatt's: lovely colour; fragrant, gentle fruit, whiff of motor oil, fragrant. Sweet, lightish, soft, pleasant but with touch of acidity.
*Last tasted Oct 1988. At best****
Ch Margaux *Grand vin.* Fine, deep; restrained but sound; rich, medium full-bodied, chewy, attractive.
*At Desai's tasting May 1987****
Ch Margaux '*2ème vin*', with Pillet-Will label, tasted twice: fragrant, crisp in 1973 and more mature-looking than the *grand vin*; touch of liquorice; dry, lightish, lean, with touch of pine on flavour.
*Last at Desai's tasting, May 1987***
Ch Latour Several notes. Variable. Best in 1976, soft, perfect balance. Rather too red and high-toned at Fête du Ch Latour: austere raw and edgy.
*Last tasted June 1981. At best****
Ch Mouton-Rothschild Two bottles, both recorked, the first with a Carlu-designed label: beautiful, lively, rosy-hued; gentle, rich almost sickly sweet bouquet; palate drying out but quite nice. The other RC (*Réserve du château*) with old style label "Hers. du Bon de Rothschild/Bn de Miolis, Gérant" drabber looking; old raisiny, chocolate nose; dry, hollow, edgy acidity.
*Both at Flatt's Mouton tasting, April 1986. At best***
Ch Ausone Magnum from Nicolas cellar. Recently recorked. Rich; gloriously evolving bouquet; lightish, flavoury, excellent despite teeth-gripping tannin and acidity. Fragrant aftertaste.
*At Flatt's Ausone tasting, Oct 1987*****
Ch Calon-Ségur Recorked. Mahogany; aged; dry, delicate, faded.
*At Christie's, pre-sale, June 1987**
Ch Léoville-Poyferré Two good notes, first in 1970.

Orange-tinged mahogany; sound, rich, medicinal Médoc nose; very flavoury, good length.
*Last tasted Oct 1981*****

Ch La Mission-Haut-Brion Three notes. Dry, thinning at château in 1978, similar, flavoury but short at Desai's in 1985. Latterly, despite its attractive colour, a corky, acidic bottle.
Last noted at Wolf's tasting, June 1990.

Ch Pontet-Canet Barton & Guestier label. Bright, colourful; fruit sandwiched between initial dustiness and faint whiff of mushrooms. Not bad for age but acidic.
With D Zivko, Chicago, Oct 1982.

1919***

After a good start, damp July encouraged diseases. Then drought and scorched grapes. Variable crop but good quality. Clinging precariously to life.

Ch Lafite Two notes. Light, flavoury in 1976. The second, cork probably original though level well into neck: very good colour; fragrant, rich, gingery bouquet; dryish, medium-light weight and style. A little faded but fragrant, with crisp end acidity.
*Last tasted at Flatt's, Oct 1988****

Ch Margaux Mid-low-shoulder. Palish, lively; decaying but fragrant; the sweetness of well-hung game, light, fading yet still a good drink.
*Dec 1980***

Ch Latour Several notes, some decomposed, some a foretaste of the '20. Pale, pretty; light Cabernet fruit; sweetish, light yet rich.
*Last tasted at the Fête du Ch Latour, June 1981***

Ch Haut-Brion Beautiful colour; smell of old *chai*; delicious, full of flavour and fruit. Good extract masking acidity.
*At Christie's pre-sale tasting, May 1980*****

Ch La Mission-Haut-Brion Four notes. One ullaged and oxidised, another nice if you like high pheasant and runny brie. At Desai's in 1985, a high level bottle: palish, dull with dusty vanilla nose. Dry, light, tight, little flavour and acidic. Most recently, in magnum, deep-coloured; smoky, citrus, old nose; very sweet, very flavoury but slightly bitter and distinctly acidic.
*Last noted at Wolf's La Mission tasting, June 1990**

1920*****

A top-class vintage, heralding one of the best decades in the history of Bordeaux. Perfect flowering, but crop severely reduced by exceptionally cold July and Aug, inducing rot. Saved by a sunny Sept. Smallish production, high quality. The best-kept have survived.

Ch Lafite Two notes: sweet bouquet and lovely gentle fragrance overall. Claret at its most refined – at the Overton tasting, 1979. The second, recorked, not quite right though trying hard to push its attractive fragrance through a mushroomy overtone; elegant, stylish, good length – but an old appley finish.
*At Flatt's Lafite tasting, Oct 1988. At best******

Ch Margaux Two notes: rich yet austere in 1971. A magnum, recorked, with a very complete yet delicate and mildly opulent bouquet; medium full-bodied, good length, austere, dry finish.
*The last at Desai's Margaux tasting, May 1987. On average**** *Could be better.*

Ch Latour Five consistently good notes, justifying its reputation as the best of all the first-growth '20s. Rich, cedary, magnificent at the Overton tasting, 1969. Impressively deep, rich colour pressing against the glass in 1971. A decade later: excellent bouquet, Pauillac cedar and oyster shells, with more to yield; seemed remarkably sweet, rich, wonderful depth, balance, length and aftertaste.
*At the Fête du Château Latour, June 1981******

Ch Mouton-Rothschild Two notes. In 1972: glorious. Colour of rich, faded brick; immediately forthcoming nose, fragrant old oak, yet which opened up further, ginger, gushing, opulent. After 90 minutes, like scented tea. Flavour to match. Full, rich, soft, oaky, perfect length, tannin and acidity.
*Last tasted at Flatt's Mouton vertical, April 1986******

Ch Haut-Brion From a French cellar. Original cork, branded "Heretiers Larrieu". Deepish, orange-tinged; old vanilla; fullish, supple, slightly malty.
*At Christie's pre-sale tasting, April 1987***

Ch Cheval-Blanc Three notes. One oxidised yet drinkable in 1978; the next at Rodenstock's in 1984: very sweet, nice texture but with whiff of volatile acidity. Most recently, a magnum, pale but with a fabulous 'singed ivy', gloriously evolved bouquet and flavour. Very sweet, fairly full-bodied, very fragrant.
*The last at a tasting at the château, Sept 1986******

Ch Brane-Cantenac Two notes, the first in 1976. Both excellent levels; attractive ruddy colour; sweet, very fruity nose and taste. Good acidity.
*The last at a pre-sale tasting, Oct 1985****

Ch Gruaud-Larose Two notes, ex-château, and at Lafite. Rich but mature-looking; rich cheesy cedar nose, spicy; flavoury but starting to crack up.
*Last tasted March 1983***

Ch La Mission-Haut-Brion Roasted and rich, ex-château, in 1978. Two of different provenance at Desai's tasting in 1985: the first, top-shoulder, palish yet ruby; fresh apply nose; lightish, refreshing, a charmer. The other deeper and browner; an extraordinarily fragrant old bouquet, richer. Most recently, a double-magnum at Wolf's tasting: open, mature; lovely, delicate bouquet, gamey (like old hen droppings!); sweetish, nice weight, lovely citrus-touched flavour, creaking and crumbly but lovely.
*At the La Mission dinner in Wiesbaden, June 1990*****

Ch Olivier Labels depicting the turreted château where the Black Prince was born. Several notes, all from Aalholm Castle, bottled by Joh Fr Schalburg: two with levels into neck, a fine, deep rich colour; bouquet of old oak and vanilla, evolving fragrantly in the glass; faded old ladies, sweet in the middle, but with wrinkles. Two others, top-shoulder, were fragrant and charming, seemed softer but acidity catching up. One slightly corky, mushroomy, but sweet and flavoury. Three good, flavoury but all noticeably tart after an hour.
*Last tasted June 1990. At best****

Ch Palmer Deep, rich, full and fine in 1973; similar appearance but overripe nose, very sweet, full and burgundy-like at Rodenstock's.
*Last tasted Oct 1984****

Ch Pichon-Lalande Tasted three times over eight months. All with good levels and corks. Lightish but beautiful colour, soft garnet red; lovely rich delicate old cedar bouquet and flavour. Pleasant weight, refreshing, acidity held at bay.
*All noted in 1980*****

1921****

Exceptionally hot, like 1893, 1895 and 1982. After an excellent flowering, hot summer and early harvest. Baked grapes, high sugar, alcohol and tannin. Some châteaux had difficulty controlling vinification, but many made outstanding wines.

Ch Lafite Recorked. Medium, lively glow; low-keyed, citrus, singed; medium-full, fairly sweet and assertive flavour. Sound. Silky, leathery tannin.

*At Flatt's Lafite tasting, Oct 1988***

Ch Margaux Three notes. The first, in 1970, rich but cracking up. The next two both fairly deep, lively yet mature-looking. One, in 1984, with an almost Pétrus-like thickness of fruit and richness. Most recently a magnum, with Eschenauer slip label but original capsule and cork, top-shoulder, had a hot, singed '21 character, sweet, rich and excellent bouquet. Fullish, harmonious, with great length, finesse and aftertaste.

*Last noted at Desai's Margaux tasting, May 1987******

Ch Latour Extremely good at the Fête du Ch Latour in 1981: deep, fragrant, flavoury, with very dry finish, but a lovely drink. Then a shaken bottle, level mid-shoulder, poor cork. Creaking. Softer and more pleasing after filtering.

*Last drunk at a Bordeaux Club dinner, May 1986. At best*****

Ch Mouton-Rothschild Several notes. All impressive, if variable. Deep, alcoholic, rich in the early 1970s. A bottle and two halves at Flatt's Mouton tasting. The bottle, level upper mid-shoulder, was the best: good depth of colour with lively, ruby glow; high-toned nose, peppery, taut, fading after an hour; surprisingly delicate despite its tannin. Good length, clean and sound. The half-bottles were fragrant, dry, lean and more fragile.

*Last tasted April 1986. At best*****

Ch Ausone Two bottles. One had a rubbed label, hard to tell whether 1921 or 1911. The second was clearly labelled, with high level, presumably recorked. Fairly rich appearance; curious hot, alcoholic nose, reminding me of seaweed and an athlete's sweat (quite attractive really), crisp, appley. A lovely full-bodied, rich, beefy wine, excellent length, dry finish.

*Both at Flatt's Ausone tasting, Oct 1987*****

Ch Cheval-Blanc The star of the vintage, the '47 of the '20s. Five superb bottles on five occasions. First, dining at John Avery's; next at the 'men's lunch', celebrating George Reece's 70th birthday in Los Angeles, then at Rodenstock's tastings in 1984, 1985 and 1986. Five totally consistent notes: none very deep, fully mature, with a 'rosy glow'; all had a marvellously rich yet delicate bouquet, a perfect old lady, ripe; all very sweet, not as full-bodied as one might expect of a '21. Rich, very flavoury, lovely texture, great length. No intrusive end acidity. Perfection.

*Last tasted Sept 1986******

Ch Pétrus Two notes, the first, at Frericks' Pétrus tasting: top-shoulder, medium-deep, healthy; gloriously fruity bouquet, perfection; very sweet, fairly concentrated, beautiful flavour and length. The second, at Rodenstock's, was more subdued, overripe, also very sweet but with higher acidity. Tasted blind, I thought it might have been Cheval-Blanc.

*Last tasted Sept 1986******

Ch La Mission-Haut-Brion Three very good notes: the first in 1978, the second, a magnum, at Desai's La Mission tasting. Another recent magnum; richly coloured; fragrant, singed leaves, tea, tangy; sweet, very flavoury, good length tannin and acidity.

*At Wolf's, June 1990*****

Ch Vincent Palish, orange-tinged; singed, old oak, evolved richly; soft, faded, some Margaux charm and residual tannin.

*Aug 1989***

1922*

Good spring, early summer but spoiled by cold, wet Sept favouring late pickers. Huge variable crop. Now one of the drier vintages of an excellent decade. Drinkable and interesting if well kept and with good levels.

Ch Lafite Two notes, the first in May 1984: palish but rich, with a healthy glow; a faded old lady on the nose and a bit mushroomy; a decayed sweetness and raw acidic edge. At Flatt's tasting: mid-low level, murky and oxidised.

*Last tasted Oct 1988. At best** but risky.*

Ch Latour Doubtless late-picked. Displaying its reputation for producing a decent wine in a poor year. Three notes, in 1975 and 1977 and at the Fête du Ch Latour. All consistent: lovely colour; old but fragrant bouquet; light, flavoury, residual tannin.

*Last tasted June 1981***

Ch Ausone Too brown; beefy 'oxo'dised; grubby.

At Lloyd Flatt's, Oct 1987.

Ch Pétrus Two magnums with Kressman capsules. Impressive colour; one with extraordinary milk chocolate nose, the other more vanilla; one fairly sweet, lactic, curious, the other like strawberry jelly with volatile acidity.

At Rodenstock's annual tasting, Sept 1987.

Ch Beychevelle Three half-bottles from a shipper's cellar in Bordeaux: the first with level below low-shoulder and predictably dead, one mid-shoulder, poor cork, mushroomy nose, rich but cracking up. The third had a better cork but, paradoxically, a lower level. Colour palish, amber-rimmed; light, faded, fruit but tart. Lesson: do not expect too much from half-bottles of old and less-good vintages.

Last tasted Jan 1989.

1923**

Cold wet spring, warm summer, late vintage. Average quality, some charm. Now fragile, though – at best – fragrant.

Ch Lafite Tasted only once, from a curious bottle with strange capsule, bin-soiled label and unbranded cork. Level upper-shoulder, the wine a pleasant surprise. Lovely warm, rich colour; bouquet of toasted coconut, then singed, fragrant; sweet on palate, middleweight, sound, reasonable length, tannin and acidity.

At Flatt's, Oct 1988.

Ch Margaux Two notes in 1960 and 1970: aromatic, velvety. More recently, with new château capsule, high level, so presumably recorked, a surprisingly lively colour, sound on nose and palate. Light, 'medicinal', fragrant but fading; dry, lightish, short.

*Last tasted at Desai's Margaux vertical, May 1987****

Ch Latour Three consistent notes from 1960, 1970 and 1981: an astonishingly deep colour, opaque, huge; showing age on nose, mushrooms rather than fruit, chocolaty, prune-like; rich, chunky, lacking length, dry finish.

*Last tasted at the Fête du Ch Latour, June 1981***

Ch Haut-Brion Noted in 1969, 1976 and twice in 1981. Like the Latour, better on palate than nose. Good corks, excellent levels. Rich but not deep; very sweet, gamey old bouquet. On the palate sweet, lightish, delicate, flavoury, but a bit tart.

*The last two at Will Dickens' Haut-Brion tasting in Florida, May 1981***

Ch Ausone One poor, low-shoulder, bottle, tart and beery.
At Flatt's Ausone tasting, Oct 1987.
Ch Cheval-Blanc Magnum: palish, cloudy; old but fragrant, little depth but no decay; sweetish, light, surprisingly firm and sound.
*At the château, Sept 1986*******
Ch Pétrus Labelled "1er grand cru . . . . F Laporte fils succsr, Négociant". Palish but lively; elegant, fragrant, beetroot-like, overripe. Very dry finish. Slightly tinny edge to nose and palate.
*At Frericks' Pétrus tasting, April 1986******
Other notes:
Carruades de Ch Lafite Two half-bottles, both mid-low-shoulder: muffled, mushroomy noses; lightish reasonably sound, short.
Oct 1988.
Ch Desmirail Overmature, little fruit, clean but acidic.
May 1982.
Ch Lagrange St-Julien. Good colour; calm, sound old cedar bouquet; dried out, lean and a bit tart.
Nov 1983.
Ch Larose (*sic*). Bottled at Aalholm Castle, good level, lovely and lively looking; singed old cedar; sweet, lightish, soft, very pleasant.
*At pre-sale tasting, Nov 1989******

1924***

Conditions like 1978: poor spring, wet summer saved by a wonderful Sept. Abundant. Now living precariously, divinely decadent: advancing age but opulent charms.
Ch Lafite Seven notes dating from 1971, variable but always appealing, at best delectable. In 1986, despite crumbly cork and slight ullage, fragrant and delicious. A faded but gently fruity magnum in spring 1988, and the same autumn a high-level bottle, with original capsule: attractive colour, very fragrant bouquet; sweet, the perfect Lafite weight, citrus-edged fruit, slightly astringent — but delicious.
*Last noted at Lloyd Flatt's, Oct 1988*** to******
Ch Margaux Four bottles and, except for one oxidised, a consistent charmer. Fully evolved, attractive looking; gentle, glorious warm biscuity bouquet; clean, fragrant, touch of acidity.
*Last noted at Desai's Margaux tasting, May 1987. At best*****
Ch Latour Four reasonably consistent good notes between 1976 and 1981. Good rich colour; polished oak nose; lovely flavour, full, crisp, dry finish, good aftertaste.
*Last tasted at the Fête du Ch Latour, May 1981. At best******
Ch Mouton-Rothschild Two superlative notes, first from a jeroboam at the Rodenstock annual in 1985: deep, perfect bouquet, sweetness, weight and flavour. In 1986: lovely colour, glorious sheen; bouquet delicate, harmonious but low-keyed at first though it blossomed in the glass and held well for a couple of hours; slightly sweet, medium weight, luxuriant flavour, length and finish. Lovely.
*Last noted at Flatt's Mouton tasting, March 1986******
Ch Haut-Brion Four notes. Two poor. One a shrunken-corked double-magnum with a whiff of chlorine and taste of stale tobacco at Rodenstock's tasting; two ripe wines from the Dillon cellar. Not a patch on the '26.
*Last tasted Sept 1986. At best*** possibly*****
Ch Ausone Double-magnum recorked at château in 1980: perfect colour; gently rich spicy bouquet with whiff of seaweed — not unlike some medicinal Médocs; slightly sweet, fullish, lovely rich flavour, excellent length, tannin and acidity.
*At Flatt's Ausone marathon, Oct 1987*****
Ch Beychevelle 12 notes from 1976. All half-bottles and varying according to level of wine. Overall, faded, overripe but some charm.
*Last tasted March 1981, at best****
Ch Dauzac A double-magnum served at a Rodenstock dinner. Palish; showing age on the nose. Trace of onion peel. Bouquet held well. A fragrant but faded old lady. Charming. Good length.
*Sept 1990****
Ch Figeac Deepish; extraordinarily rich, scented bouquet, cherry and beetroot; sweetish, lightish, gentle, fragrant. Lovely despite showing its age.
*At Desai's Figeac tasting at Le Taillevant, Dec 1989*****
Clos Fourtet Four slightly variable bottles from Peter Wallenberg's cellar: fairly pale but with a nice glow; light, *gibier*, ripe, chocolaty bouquet; dry, light, good length. Acidity mollified by food.
*Dining at Drottningholm, Sweden, March 1987***
Ch Gruaud-Larose A jeroboam. Medium-deep; fragrant bouquet, overripe, developing an exotic, slightly varnishy scent; sweet, a bit overdone, curious scented flavour with raspberry aftertaste. The cork broke, so if it had been refreshed it must have been some time ago.
*Sept 1990****
Ch Lagrange St-Julien. Masses of half-bottles from the same Bordeaux cellar as the Beychevelle, varying from deep brown and dead to flavoury and attractive.
*Last tasted Sept 1987. At best***
Ch Larose Like the '23, bottled and stored in the cellars at Aalholm Castle, Denmark. First drunk at lunch with Baron Raben-Levetzau, in Aug 1987, next at the pre-sale tasting, and many times since. All had good levels despite short, crumbly corks. Despite age and acidity trying to overtake it, can be delicious. Good colour; ripe old nose; rich — with extract and fruit.
*Last tasted April 1991***
Ch Léoville-Las-Cases Magnum recorked by Whitwham's. Marvellous colour: autumnal tawny red, good legs; beautiful cedary bouquet. Refreshing lightness and deftness of touch. Lovely.
*At a Heublein pre-sale tasting, May 1980*****
Ch La Mission-Haut-Brion A beautiful bottle from the Woltner cellars in 1978. At Desai's tasting in 1985 a deep, somewhat too brown, rich but overripe hen-droppings bouquet; a bit screwed up and cheesy. A dumb and dusty magnum: black treacle nose and endtaste like sour cream. A more impressive double-magnum: deep, lively colour like a '62; sweet old nose and flavour, good fruit, a bit woody.
*The last two served by Karl-Heinz Wolf at his remarkable La Mission tasting and dinner, June 1990. At best****
Ch Nenin Variable, from oxidised to silky and firm.
May 1989.
Ch Talbot From a French cellar. Fairly good level, very attractive colour, slightly orange-tinged; curious high-toned but gentle bouquet; dry, very flavoury, good length.
*At a Christie's pre-sale tasting, June 1980****
Ch Tertre-Daugay Two bottles. Good looking. Bouquet developed richly, then faded. Dry, lightish, cool and a bit tart.
*Both at Lafite, March 1983***

1925

Late and abundant vintage of watery wines. Ignored at the time and fairly dismal now.

Ch Lafite Four notes. One acetic, the next light but quite flavoury. The third, recorked (with figures inadvertantly reversed: branded 1952): initially smoky, sooty nose, then like old army bandages; dry, screwed up and tart. Most recently a rasping, oxidised mid-shoulder bottle.
Last noted at Flatt's Lafite tasting, Oct 1988. Not my most favourite vintage of Lafite.
Ch Latour Attractive colour; low-keyed, rich but sound; dry, clean a bit stalky but quite attractive.
*At the Fête du Ch Latour, June 1981***
Ch Mouton-Rothschild Tasted twice. Palish, drab, unconvincing colour. Un-Mouton-like nose: dusty, though some richness and fragrance developed. Better on palate. Dry, rich but stringy and piquant.
Last tasted — or rather not tasted, it was hopelessly oxidised — at Flatt's Mouton vertical, April 1986.
Ch Ausone A magnum from a cellar in Copenhagen. Better nose and taste than expected. Chewy, chunky, good length.
*At Flatt's Ausone tasting, Oct 1987***

1926*****

Cold spring, poor flowering and long, hot summer. Small crop, high quality, high prices. Incredibly rich wines.
Ch Lafite Three notes in the mid- to late-1970s: rich colour, nose and taste. Cedary bouquet and flavour. Acidity catching up. More recently a poor bottle: pale, amber coloured; slightly oxidised yet fragrant. Not too bad on palate. Lean and clean.
*Last tasted at Lloyd Flatt's, Oct 1988. At best****
Ch Margaux Three notes, all good. The last two bottles, one recorked, the other with original capsule and cork, at Desai's Margaux tasting. A rich, lively, fully evolved colour; bouquet sound, fragrant, opening up beautifully and still glorious after two hours. Sweet, medium weight, heavenly flavour, good length, rich yet delicate.
*Last tasted May 1987******
Ch Latour Tasted five times: always good. Impressively deep, rich colour; crisp, fragrant bouquet of great depth. Cabernet Sauvignon aroma and a slightly medicinal Pauillac scent. Fairly sweet, fullish, chunky. Lots of fruit, high extract. Still tannic and the noticeable acidity merely uplifting the flavour.
*Last tasted dining at the château, April 1990******
Ch Mouton-Rothschild Invasion of *cochylis* reduced the crop by 75%. Three consistent notes, in bottle in 1983, jeroboam in 1985 and most recently in magnum. Very deep, opaque centred; rich, ripe, medicinal — iodine, developing ripe fragrance. The bottle was recorded as fairly sweet, soft, fading but lovely. All three were very flavoury and still fairly tannic. A good, rich wine.
*Last tasted, in magnum, at Flatt's Mouton tasting, April 1986******
Ch Haut-Brion Many notes. In jeroboam, magnum and several bottles, all pretty good, richly coloured, with distinctive Haut-Brion bouquet: coffee ice-cream, brandy-snaps, singed fern, with a touch of maltiness anticipating the more idiosyncratic '28 and '29. Graves, tobacco-like, scent and taste. High extract, very sound, complete, refreshing.
*Last tasted June 1987. At best******
Ch Ausone Two bottles. One mid-upper, the other upper-shoulder. Both fairly deep, rich, with very mature rim; sound, one old and oaky which nevertheless developed a lovely bouquet, the other higher toned, emitting a gloriously spicy, scented, violet bouquet. Both fairly sweet and medium full-bodied, soft, fleshy for Ausone, perfectly evolved.
*Both at Flatt's Ausone tasting, Oct 1987*****
Ch Cheval-Blanc A memorable wine. Six consistent notes over the past 25 years: not very deep but richly coloured; glorious, oaky, singed leaves, rich, ripe bouquet. All but one remarkably sweet, with marvellously mouthfilling flavour. The last, in magnum, from a French private cellar, drier and lighter. Delicate and fading but with finesse and great length.
*Last tasted May 1987. A perfect claret******
Ch Pétrus Glorious. Tasted in April 1986, and in 1987 from a double-magnum. Both fabulously deep, rich and intense; both opulent on the nose, ripe mulberry, figs, concentrated musk; both sweet, full-bodied, with spicy tea-like taste, hefty, great length, still tannic.
*Last noted June 1987******
Ch Calon-Ségur Two magnums, both with loose corks but good levels. Opaque; surprisingly good old-cedar bouquet; full-bodied, chunky, still with good tannin and acidity and no decay. Sweetened in the glass.
*Both tasted in May 1981*****
Ch Cantemerle A recorked half-bottle, tawny, high-toned, about to fall apart.
June 1983.
Ch Cos d'Estournel Fading but nice in 1970. Most recently, with crumbly cork but good level, sound refreshing nose; distinct sweetness, a '26 characteristic, perfect flavour, balance and finish. Excellent.
*Last tasted March 1982******
Ch Dauzac Double-magnum: attractive velvety purple colour; showing age on nose at first. Then a whiff of Médoc sea-breeze, later *gibier*; sweet then dry tannic finish. A bit short, but fragrant.
*Served at Rodenstock's closing dinner, Sept 1990****
Ch Duhart-Milon Deep, rich colour, nose and flavour. Touch of vanilla and leather, very sound, dry, massive extract.
*At Christie's pre-sale tasting, Nov 1983*****
Ch Figeac Deepish, lovely colour; showing age but fragrant, warm, biscuity, with fruit. Drying out, a certain piquancy, tannic finish. Better on nose than palate.
*At Desai's Figeac, tasting Dec 1989***
Ch Léoville-Poyferré An *impériale*: palish, open, fully mature colour; sound, gentle, slightly singed bouquet; lovely weight, elegant, good flavour and balance. Dried out after 40 minutes.
*Sept 1990*****
Ch Lescalles A rarely seen Médoc, bottled in and sold from the Aalholm cellars. Tasted three times, once in the cellar, twice prior to sale. Very attractive, sound, fragrant, delicious.
April to Sept 1989.
Ch La Mission-Haut-Brion Four notes. All with deep rich, thick appearance. In 1973 and 1978 beautiful bouquet and taste. At Desai's in 1985, lacking La Mission's dominant character. Most recently, a magnum from the Woltner cellar: impressively deep; fragrant, no faults. Gentle bouquet that held well developing rich, ripe, stably character; sweet, medium weight, good flavour. But the palate deteriorated, turning sour and edgy.
*Last noted at Wolf's La Mission tasting, June 1990. At best*****
Ch Olivier Danish bottled, lovely colour; good fruit, firm, tannic yet sweet. In remarkable condition.
*From Aalholm Castle cellar, July 1989****.

1927*

Good start, hot July: then cold, wet and windy through to

the late Sept harvest. Few seen.

Ch Latour Three notes, two surprisingly good — bottles from the de Beaumont family (previous owners) and the château cellars, and a pale, varnishy, dry and skinny bottle at the Fête du Ch Latour.

*Last tasted June 1981. At best***

Carruades de Mouton-Rothschild Bought for several reasons: my birthyear, uniqueness, the art nouveau label and sheer curiosity. The Carruades plateau is shared by Mouton and Lafite, though associated with the latter. Bn Philippe declassified the Mouton '27 and a little was marketed as Carruades for the first and last time. (In 1930, 1931 and 1932, the declassified wine was labelled Mouton Cadet.) I had purchased two magnums from an earlier Eschenauer sale, one broke *en route*. The other was ullaged low-shoulder so I never opened it. One day Bn Philippe spotted it in my office display case, so, regrettably, I gave it him. Some years later, some half-bottles appeared at Christie's. I have opened two. Both were ullaged mid-shoulder and surprisingly agreeable. The most recent I opened on my 63rd birthday: good colour; fragile, cedary but nice old nose, slightly sweet, lightish, soft, no obvious decay or over acidity. Delicious to drink, which just goes to show . . . .

*Last tasted May 1990****

Ch Ducru-Beaucaillou Magnum. No capsule, unlabelled, plain cork. Sole identification the records of a Swiss private cellar. Excellent level. Medium-deep, lovely colour; slightly smoky, quite fruity nose when first decanted. Medium weight, lean, citrus-like acidity, flavoury. Lacking length and acidic finish.

*At a Christie's luncheon, Sept 1990**

Ch La Mission-Haut-Brion Surprisingly deep and healthy; a high-toned bracken-like Graves nose; dryish, on the light side, flavoury, short. A touch of acidity, otherwise unexpectedly good.

*At Desai's tasting, Feb 1985***

1928*****

A glorious vintage: good flowering, perfect summer though excessive heat thickened skins. Good harvesting conditions. Intensely deep, high in alcohol and immensely tannic wines. In St-Emilion and Pomerol, there were some soft and luscious wines, the Médocs were uncompromisingly hard. As a result, many have lasted well.

Ch Lafite Not up to '28 standard. Several notes, all remarking on its lovely colour. I preferred the crumbling fragrance of those with original corks to the slightly singed, varnishy scent of those recorked at the château. Dry, fullish body, loads of tannin and acidity.

*Last noted, a recorked bottle showing well at Flatt's Lafite tasting, Oct 1988. At best****

Ch Margaux Six notes, with slight variations but all good, the last three from a magnum and two good-level bottles at Desai's. All had a good deep colour; cedary, singed, fragrant bouquet, a rich development in glass, coffee and chocolate. On the palate, sweet, tanned and tannic. It was for this wine that I first used the phrase 'iron fist in velvet glove'. Lean but chewy.

*Last tasted May 1987*****

Ch Latour Undoubtedly *the* great '28. Undrinkably tannic for 50 years. Approaching its best in the mid-1980s. Many notes. Some variations but no bad bottles. Intensely deep appearance. Needs decanting time and air to bring out its spicy, cinnamon, cedary bouquet. Both dry and surprisingly sweet for a '28, depending on context, and whether the ripe, alcoholic entry or the mouth-scouring tannin uppermost. But a massive, masculine wine, full of tannin yet velvety, with great concentration and length. Another half-century of life.

*Last tasted June 1990******

Ch Mouton-Rothschild Four notes. Red brown and quite attractive though acidic in 1967, 1972 and 1977. A poor, orange-coloured and acetic bottle at Lloyd Flatt's.

Last noted April 1986.

Ch Haut-Brion Between 1926 and the Dillon family purchase in 1935 some peculiar wines were made. The return to classic wines really started in 1945. The '28 tasted on many occasions, has varied from rasping, oxidised, corked and woody to curiously impressive, thick and opulent. Opaque; fig-like, dried leaves nose and taste. Some people like it. Not I.

*Last tasted Oct 1987. At best****

Ch Ausone First tasted at the Peppercorns' in 1983. Next one bottle and two halves at Lloyd Flatt's. The wine has lost colour; rich but crumbling on the nose, some oxidation, a malty touch, fungi; all were somewhat sweet, positive, yet something missing. Dry tannic finish. Not my favourite wine.

*Last tasted Oct 1987. At best***

Ch Cheval-Blanc Four consistent notes. Virtually no tannin in 1955. 30 years on: still deep; gnarled oak nose; sweet entry, unusual softness for a '28 and nice flesh. Dry finish. Not a patch on the '29.

*Last tasted June 1985*** just.*

Ch Pétrus Extraordinarily rich, high-toned bouquet; sweet, jammy, reminiscent of a late-harvest Zinfandel. Good length.

At Rodenstock's tasting, Oct 1984.

Ch Beychevelle Three good notes: deep; pungent; nicely constructed. Rich, ripe, attractive.

*Last tasted May 1986****

Ch Bouscaut Two good notes. Mahogany, almost opaque; massive, masculine; very rich, earthy, still tannic.

*The last from a Paris cellar, at a Christie's pre-sale tasting, Feb 1984****

Ch Calon-Ségur 10 notes from 1954. Deep, rich purple-brown centre, crisp amber mature rim; sweet, concentrated, characterful nose; rich, good length, mouth-puckering tannin.

*Last tasted June 1987*****

Dom de Chevalier Opaque; an old, singed '28, but sound; slightly sweet, massive yet perfectly balanced. Dry finish.

*Dining with Claude Ricard, March 1981*****

Ch Cos d'Estournel Four good notes. The last two Belgian bottled. Sound, fruity, candied-peel bouquet; sweet, full, delicious.

*Last tasted Jan 1990*****

Ch Lascombes Magnum, upper mid-shoulder. Deep plummy brown; old cedar and cheese rind nose; dry, austere, tannic.

*From a good Paris cellar, May 1981***

Ch Léoville-Las-Cases Almost luscious for a '28 when first tasted in 1955. Many notes until 1959, then a gap of over 20 years. Two bottles at the same tasting, the first with sweet waxy bouquet; medium body, elegant, suave, lovely flavour and exquisite aftertaste, the second noticeably deeper but not quite as fragrant, with more bite and grip.

*Last tasted Sept 1981. At best******

Ch Marquis-de-Terme Chr Stausholm, the best wine merchant and bottler in Copenhagen. Very deep, rich; marvellous scent, cedar and old prunes; very dry and tannic, fullish, austere, lean but sound.

*A tough mouthful from the Aalholm Castle cellar, May 1988****

Ch La Mission-Haut-Brion Eight variable notes. The best recorked at the château. Two at Desai's in 1985, one mid-shoulder, sour and oxidised bottle, the second a livelier colour; gentle sound nose; sweet, fullish, rich with tannin, and acidity under control. Most recently: medium-deep; rich, stably nose that developed well, lovely old oak; sweet, fairly full-bodied, good flavour and grip. No faults.
*Last noted at Wolf's tasting, June 1988. At best******

Ch Montrose Rich, mature; iodine and old oak; dry, lighter than expected, lean, austere, plenty of tannin and acidity. Creaking.
*Sept 1990***

Ch Palmer Rich but acidic in 1973. More recently, recorked: deep; baked, singed nose; hard dry finish. None of the charm that Penning-Rowsell noted in the mid-1950s.
*Last tasted March 1981***

Ch La Tour-Haut-Brion Assertive nose, strange, cheesy, later violets; medium sweetness and weight, tea-like fragrance, silky tannins, citrus-like acidity. Attractive in its way.
*At Wolf's, June 1990****

Ch Trotanoy Magnificent. Not very deep, but bright, open, pretty colour; fruity, rich, glorious development in glass; delicious, supple, fruity, good tannin.
*Tasted blind and thought to be a '21 or a '29, Sept 1986******

Some other notes:

Ch Cantemerle Sweet nose (even improved better the next day) flavoury, slight astringency.
June 1983.

Ch Chasse-Spleen Rich, high-toned, sweet, a bit tart.
June 1988.

Ch Duhart-Milon Firm, austere, sound.
Nov 1983.

"Margaux" Amazingly good for an old generic wine. Rich bouquet and flavour, chunky, tannic.
Aug 1989.

Ch Paveil-de-Luze Stausholm bottling, lovely colour; soured old cedar; sweet, soft, good fruit, flavour and length.
July 1989.

Ch Segonzac Also Danish-bottled, fragrant, flavoury, refreshing.
July 1989.

1929*****

The epitome of elegance. Blossomed much earlier than the tannic '28s but, if well kept, can still be superlative. July, Aug and Sept were hot, some beneficial rain mid-Sept prior to picking. This toned down the tannins, alcohol and acidity but left the charm.

Ch Lafite Four poor bottles in the 1970s, six better ones in the 1980s, ranging from distinctly ripe to blatantly overripe. The most interesting notes made at a marvellous tasting of *all* the first growths of the '29, '45, '61 and '70 vintages given by Arthur Hallé in Memphis in 1987. To allow for bottle variation, two bottles of each were tasted. The first bottle of '29 Lafite, despite its crumbly cork, was surprisingly deep and intense; sweet, rich, fragrant — like clean cardboard and blancmange; on the palate also sweet and fragrant. The second was a touch more piquant, not quite as sweet, and shorter. The best noted was an Alexis Lichine selection at Flatt's Lafite tasting in 1988: an attractively forthcoming bouquet; sweet, very appealing, citrus-like acidity. Most recently a jeroboam with a sweet but malty nose, opulent, living dangerously. Not quite right. Rich but cracking up.
*Last noted at Eigensatz's tasting, May 1989. At best***** *but risky.*

Ch Margaux Eight variable notes starting in the early 1970s. Bottle variation due to cork and storage. The pair, at Hallé's tasting referred to above, differed considerably. One bottle, recorked Jan 1984, had a very deep colour, with touch of brown, and not quite bright; odd, medicinal, slightly woody, smelling of apples and pears; a punchy, chewy, flavour but a bit acidic. A second, less deep, more lively looking; gentle, fragrant bouquet, with characteristic Margaux 'violets', still lovely after two hours. On the palate fairly sweet, lively, attractive, with dry finish. Then, in May 1987, three bottles at Desai's Margaux tasting. The first two, with original short capsules, upper mid-shoulder, looked palish and fully evolved; each were fragrant. Delicate, faded, 'arsenic and old lace'. Both had a curious, almost mildewy, taste. The third bottle, recorked, was slightly oxidised. Exactly two years later, an upper mid-shoulder jeroboam at the Eigensatz big-bottle tasting: very deep; spicy and fragrant but volatile acidity taking over. Dry — all the other '29 Margaux were fairly sweet — and bitter on the finish.
*Last tasted May 1989. At best******

Ch Latour Lafite and Haut-Brion were not at their best in 1928 and 1929. Latour made superlative wine in both vintages; but whereas the great tannic '28 was not really mature enough to drink until the late 1970s, the '29, softer and more amenable, developed much more quickly. With only two exceptions, one low-shoulder, one sour, the 15 times I have tasted it since 1955 have elicited glowing comments. Top marks for a recorked bottle at the Fête du Ch Latour in 1981; and an Eigensatz jeroboam — perfection, with time in hand. To sum up: impressively deep, even for Latour, opaque centre, lovely and lively; a truly exciting, richly scented nose, spicy, cloves, eucalyptus, sage. On the palate: immensely sweet and rich for a Médoc, for Latour. Well-endowed with alcohol, extract and fruit. Velvety. A wonderfully full, elongated, shape in the mouth, with marvellous length and glorious aftertaste. .
*Last tasted May 1989****** *(One is tempted to add a sixth star.)*

Ch Mouton-Rothschild Like a great diva, world-renowned but not unsullied. Never tasted in its prime. First noted in 1968, 18 times since: overripe, decadent but an unceasing challenge to nose and palate. At his great Mouton tasting in 1986 Lloyd Flatt served a bottle (excellent), a magnum (slightly oxidised) and a jeroboam (perfection). At best: intensly deep yet luminous, with a fine gradation of colour; ripe, fleshy, corrupt yet with inimitably Mouton Cabernet Sauvignon fragrance, but much else: it evolved, revolved, in the glass. Distinctly sweet, concentrated, spicy, lovely fruit, persistence of flavour. Opulent. Sublime. But gather ye (faded) rose buds while ye may!
*Last tasted May 1989. At best********!*

Ch Haut-Brion 11 notes. Despite not liking it, I am intrigued by its excesses. It looks hefty and concentrated, with a black cherry centre. Nose ranging from treacly, peppery, oaky, and singed heather to coffee, chocolate, caramel and molasses. Very sweet, very full-bodied, packed with fruit, chewy, a taste of black treacle, yet a very dry tannic finish. Not a food wine. More like port, California 'port'.
*Last noted May 1989. At best***** *depending on one's inclination.*

Ch Ausone Tasted only twice. Oxidised at Flatt's tasting in 1987 and, more recently, a curiously scented, *impériale* with a whiff of banana and slightly unclean finish.
Last noted at Eigensatz's tasting, May 1989.

Ch Cheval Blanc One of the great '29s. A charmer, first tasted in 1971. A superb bottle, original cork, decanted 2½ hours before serving at Arthur Hallé's tasting in 1987, and a perfect Eigensatz *impériale* two years later. Neither deep in colour but a rich rosy-hued, tile-red with long legs. Sweet on nose and palate. Bouquet of great depth, fragrant, cedary, the wine from both bottle and *impériale* blossoming in the glass. A gentle, soft, glorious wine with nice weight, good length and excellent acidity. Perfection.
*Last tasted May 1989******

Ch Pétrus My only note is of an *impériale* served at the Eigensatz's: fairly deep with a fully mature amber brown rim; nose slightly singed and chocolaty but improved in the glass, spicy, then bitter truffles. Fairly sweet, fairly full-bodied, rich, with a quite powerful tangy flavour and raw, tannic finish. "Like a farmer with mud on his boots" someone observed. Certainly blunt and unsophisticated compared to the subtler, multi-dimensional Médocs.
*Tasted May 1989***

Ch Brane-Cantenac At peak of perfection in 1954. Creaking when last tasted.
April 1985.

Dom de Chevalier Highly reputed. A superb magnum in 1968 and an equally lovely bottle from a Danish cellar. Beautiful colour; delicate, fragrant; perfect balance, length and aftertaste.
*Last tasted Oct 1981******

Ch Figeac Four consistent notes from 1969. Very deep, thick appearance. In 1975 a rich meaty nose. Most recently like roast beef and rich gravy – but glorious! Fullish, rich, tangy and tannic. Despite lurking acidity, time in hand.
*Last noted at Desai's tasting, Dec 1989*****

Clos Fourtet One of the best-ever Fourtets. Lovely in 1954. 29 years later: very good level; palish, fully mature; gentle old nose and flavour. Slightly sweet, medium-light, positive, delicious.
*Last tasted Oct 1983*****

Ch Gruaud-Larose Rich, sweet-and-sour in 1969. Next, despite loose cork and upper mid-shoulder level, a gloriously rich mahogany colour. Sweet and sour: sweet entry, dry acidic edge and finish. Very ripe, soft, flavoury. Remnants of original '29 plumpness.
*Last tasted Nov 1986.** (Another bottle, labelled "Gruaud-Larose-Sarget", similar level, from an American cellar, with more vinosity, otherwise much the same in Nov 1986***)*

Ch Haut-Bailly Some strange similarities to Haut-Brion: too deep, too brown; rich, malty, almost caramelised Sauternes-like nose; very sweet, fairly full, rich and thick. Astonishing.
*Tasted June 1988****

Ch Larrivet-Haut-Brion Another strange red Graves. Good level but smelly cork. Deep, oxidised appearance; virol/malty nose but some fruit; better flavour than nose. Good weight and acidity. Went well with brie!
*Tasted May 1983***?

Ch Léoville-Las-Cases Deep; its dusty vanilla nose like the smell of fly spray; very sweet, full and rich, fleshy yet tannic. (I thought it was Latour '47!)
*Tasted Oct 1984***

Ch Léoville-Poyferré Regarded as one of the very best '29s, and certainly the finest Poyferré, since the late 19th century. Never tasted at its peak. An upper mid-shoulder bottle in 1984 was a bit too thick and brown; initially a gamey high-toned nose that settled down and held well; lovely weight, flavoury but ancient and edgy. The next bottle was oxidised.
*Last tasted July 1989** If well-kept, at best******

Ch Marquis-de-Terme A good bottle bought from the Fernand Woltner cellar: remarkably deep and lively; very sound nose, developing richly; distinctly sweet, fullish, still fruity. A very good drink. Another, from a Bordeaux négociant's cellar, later, soft, delicious and more than just tolerable, despite its mid-low level.
*Last noted at a pre-sale tasting, July 1988. At best*****

Ch La Mission-Haut-Brion One of the great '29s and the richest of all La Missions. Eight notes. At the Hallé tasting a crumbly-cork bottle had an extraordinary nose, sweet, caramelised – like Yquem '37. Two hours later like soft brown sugar. Flavoury but acetic. The best were all from the Woltner family cellars. Two bottles, in a different state of preservation at the Desai La Mission tasting in 1985. One brown, sweet, malty, full, very dry – clearly oxidised. The other sheer perfection: immense depth of colour; gloriously calm fragrant bouquet, rich, great depth; fairly sweet, full but not too full-bodied, marvellous fruit, vinosity, length and aftertaste. One could almost chew it. Most recently, a magnum at Wolf's: opaque; dumb at first, concentrated, malty, harmonious; immensely sweet, full, very rich and rounded, velvety, mouthfilling, silky tannins. Magnificent.
*Last tasted June 1990******

Ch Pontet-Canet Also renowned. My first experience was a magnificent bottle in 1956. Most recently, two slightly tart bottles, shipped by de Gernon Desbaratz and bottled in Sweden. Despite excellent levels, old, cedary, dried out. Not bad . . . .
*Last tasted March 1987. At best******

Ch Rauzan-Gassies Three variable bottles: the first oxidised, the second a bit dusty, better on palate, though a varnishy smell took over. The third fading a little, yet refreshing and delightful.
*All tasted in Oct 1980. At best****

Two excellent wines shipped, respectively, by A Lalande and J Calvet, and both bottled in Copenhagen by Kjaer and Sommerfeldt: both from the perfect Aalholm Castle cellar:

Ch Duplessis Very deep; sweet, soft, lovely fruit, still tannic rather like a '28.
*Last tasted July 1989*****

Ch L'Enclos Beautiful rosehip red; also soft, and very rich, fleshy, high extract and prune/fig-like fruit.
*Last tasted July 1989*****

1930

The first of three atrocious vintages, a complete crop failure, thanks to inclement weather. Very rarely seen. Even those born in 1930 should give it a miss.

Ch Latour The only '30 tasted. A surprisingly good colour for vintage and age but with tailing-off watery rim; slightly spicy, medicinal nose; dry, fairly light and thin but crisp and very flavoury. Varnishy acidic finish in 1983. More recently, dining at Latour, I noted some intensity and a ruby colour; a rather peppery, egg-and-cress nose that gained a sort of meatiness and, after an hour in the glass, turned sour. Rather chewier and more chunky than the earlier bottle.
*Last tasted Nov 1990**

1931

A reasonable crop. Still not good but much better than 1930. Rarely seen.

Ch Lafite Almost certainly recorked: level into neck. Fairly pale, dull, though warm, appearance; curious soft fluffy nose that developed surprisingly nicely revealing a touch of liquorice, Cabernet and stem-ginger; slightly sweet, light, lean but flavoury. Raw end acidity.

*At Flatt's Lafite tasting, Oct 1988**

Ch Latour Three uninspiring notes: ullaged and sour at Overton's in 1976. A fairly pale, brown, varnishy, skinny, recorked-at-château bottle, and, later, a strangely deep, dusty, old, unharmonious bottle at Rodenstock's, both in 1981. Even Latour couldn't do much in a year like 1931.

Last tasted Sept 1981.

Ch Haut-Brion Five consistently curious notes. Four half-bottles drunk at intervals starting in 1976, and a bottle in Japan. All remarkably deep in colour, impressive for such a poor year, but on the brown side; very rich, malty, molasses nose. Dry, a bracken and black treacle flavour, though surprisingly drinkable, if one ignores the rather varnishy and acidic finish.

*Last noted at Mutsuo Okabayashi's dinner at the Imperial Hotel, Tokyo, June 1989**

Ch La Mission-Haut-Brion A Graves year. Like the Haut-Brion, surprisingly deep and thick-looking. Strangely attractive at Desai's tasting in 1985. Reasonably sound bouquet and taste. Most recently: still very deep and impressive to look at; a low-keyed, singed bouquet reminiscent of plain chocolate; sweetish entry leading to a very dry, edgy finish. But in between, full, rich, tobacco flavour and with grip.

*Last noted at Karl-Heinz Wolf's tasting, June 1980**

Ch La Tour-Figeac Bordeaux-bottled by Eschenauer. Mid-shoulder, deep Bovril colour, oxidised, tart yet a flicker of life.

Pre-sale, Feb 1984.

1932

The third of three ugly sisters. Tiny crop picked without enthusiasm between Oct 10 and Dec 1.

Ch Latour First tasted in 1977. More recently: surprisingly deep but tailing off to a watery rim; high-toned nose, slightly sour and varnishy, like curled autumn leaves; dried out, fairly light, some fruit but tart.

At the château, Nov 1990.

1933***

Small crop due to strong winds during flowering. Ripe harvest. Nice wines. Can still be charming, though surviving precariously.

Ch Lafite Three notes, all delicate, flavoury, with some charm. The third, recorked: a warm, lively, open, mature colour; after a whiff of bottle-stink quickly cleared, the bouquet blossomed deliciously; rich but not remotely fat, medium-light weight, very flavoury, fragrant aftertaste.

*The last at Flatt's Lafite tasting, Oct 1988. At best****

Ch Margaux *Perfection in 1957 and 1966*****

Ch Latour Six notes. Consistent. Full-flavoured, fully ripe. Lovely garnet red with mature mahogany edge; rich, very spicy, high-toned nose; sweetish, nice weight and texture. Opulent yet lean. An exciting wine on the verge of corruption.

*Last tasted at the Fête du Ch Latour, San Francisco, June 1981****

Ch Mouton-Rothschild A pair of half-bottles at Flatt's tasting in New Orleans. The first: a lovely glowing colour; warm, rich, soft, biscuity and gamey bouquet; sweet, edgy, overripe but attractive flavour. The second overripe to the point of decay.

*April 1986*** *Larger bottles doubtless better.*

Ch La Mission-Haut-Brion Four notes. Once a very rich wine. Now losing colour. Brown; overripe, piquant, cocoa-like old nose. In 1978 two flavoury but crumbling bottles. At Desai's in 1985 dry, light, screwed-up and short. Most recently a bottle from the Woltner cellars, rather weak, over-developed appearance; open, attractive, milk and fruit bouquet; sweetish, fairly light, very flavoury, some elegance and deftness but a bit edgy.

*Last noted at Wolf's tasting, June 1990. At best***

1934****

Best of the decade. Good, abundant early harvest. Decidedly over-developed and risky now, though if well-cellared can be delicious. If '33s are like a well-hung pheasant, '34s are like gamey grouse.

Ch Lafite Six notes. Variable. One like seawater and old glue, a tart but striving double-magnum. Then three lively and attractive bottles, and one sweaty and raw. Finally an excellent magnum, probably with original cork, upper mid-shoulder, at Flatt's Lafite tasting: deep, rich, ruddy cherry colour; slightly scented but very rich, with sweaty tannins, some fruit but over-mature. Very sweet and fairly full-bodied. Excellent flavour and condition.

*Last tasted Oct 1988. At its exotic best*****

Ch Margaux Over a dozen notes, ranging from a good bottle in 1954, some creakingly acidic bottles in the 1960s to mid-1980s, and others fragrant, elegant and flavoury. Two fairly recent bottles from a French private cellar, one mid-upper the other top-shoulder. Fairly deep, rich, fully mature looking – as one can expect. Both had a 'cheesy' nose, the first developed richly, the second, though not over-mature, failed to evolve in the glass. Somewhat dried out, reasonable body, positive though superannuated flavour, losing fruit, and with acidity catching up. Another from the same cellar orange-tinged but with a lovely, soft, ripe old bouquet and flavour. Acidity lurking but tolerable.

*Last tasted Sept 1989. At best****

Ch Latour Perfect in the mid-1950s, fine and still tannic in the 1960s, old and strained in the 1970s. By the 1980s, drying out yet still opulent. Lovely rich mahogany colour; bouquet described variously as like celery and boiled fennel, meaty, singed; the sweetness of approaching putrifaction, fairly full-bodied and concentrated but with edgy acidity. Living dangerously, dying reluctantly.

*Last tasted June 1981. At best****

Ch Mouton-Rothschild Approaching its zenith when first tasted in 1955. Starting to show age in the late-1960s. In the 1970s, variable bottles, four tart and over acidic, one fragrant and flavoury, one lovely. At Flatt's Mouton tasting in 1986 more than a whiff of volatile acidity, though flavoury. Most recently from a jeroboam, *Réserve du Baron*, recorked in 1953, at a Rodenstock tasting: lively intense colour; restrained but harmonious nose; sweet, fullish, complete, lovely fruit. Acidity in check.

*Last tasted Sept 1987. Average rating a risky *** at best******

Ch Haut-Brion Six notes. Magnificent in 1955, attractive in 1972, and a deep, malty, bottle from the Dillon New York cellar in 1979. Then a pair in the early 1980s: deep, intense; with a concentrated singed-raisins nose like the black treacle style of Haut-Brion '28/'29. Both were dry and full-bodied with a leathery texture, in excellent condition but idiosyncratic. The second, upper-shoulder, with taste of syrup of figs. The château was ready for the takeover and a change of direction.

*Last tasted May 1981. At best, in its own way****

Ch Ausone Never seen at its peak. First tasted in 1983: beautiful colour, extraordinary scent but drying out and edgy. Next two bottles at Flatt's Ausone tasting, both richly coloured, with overripe bouquet reminiscent of dry bracken and sour cheese. On the palate revealing the

sweetness of decay and a pasty, acidic, dry finish.
*Last tasted Oct 1987. At best**
Ch Cheval-Blanc One of the best '34s. First tasted in 1978: Danish bottled, exquisite. Next, in 1984: lovely glowing worn-tile red; delicate, exquisitely revealing, fragrant, ripe peaches bouquet; 'old ivy', firm shape reminding me of the '71, good length. Then a magnum with similarly glowing colour; ripe, tea-leaf, singed bouquet, faded but not cracking up; a touch of sweetness and nice weight, firm, well-constructed, with beautifully behaved tannin and acidity.
*Last tasted Sept 1986*****
Ch Pétrus Two notes. First in 1986: very deep, rich, 'thick' appearance smell and taste, as if the must had been concentrated. Sweet, full-bodied, rich, but with acidity taking over. Next, an *impériale*, similar but better balanced, a perfect bouquet lasting over an hour, rich on palate, with good grip.
*Last noted at Rodenstock's tasting, Sept 1990*****
Ch L'Angélus An excellent Kjaer and Sommerfeldt Danish bottling. Good level. Good crisp fruit. Attractive, lingering, tannic.
*From Aalholm Castle, July 1989*****
Ch Beychevelle First tasted in Stockholm in 1984 then in 1989, two bottles from the Aalholm cellar shipped by de Luze and bottled in Denmark by Stausholm. All three had lovely translucent colour; excellent bouquet, delicate, held well; soft, yet on the lean side, acidity in check, lovely fragrance. A delicious drink.
*Last tasted Sept 1989*****
Carruades de Ch Lafite Rich colour; well-developed, ripe, chocolaty bouquet; drier, leaner, more austere on palate.
*Oct 1988***
Dom de Chevalier Another lovely '34. Glorious blossoming of bouquet in 1981. Later, dining with Claude Ricard: palish but lovely; showing age, ripe, cheesy, fragrant; slightly sweet, reminding me of a '47. Nice weight, lovely old flavour. A slightly flat profile but a perfect drink.
*Last tasted June 1984*****
Ch Cos d'Estournel Still hard in the mid-1950s. Lovely, ripe, yet somehow still 'green' (reminded me of the '37s) in the mid-1960s, and two rather austere notes in the 1970s. Most recently: deep rich colour, nose and flavour, though a bit woody/corky and drying out.
*Last noted at dinner with Bruno Prats at Ch Marbuzet, May 1986***
Ch Figeac A bottle bought at auction in Lille and drunk at the château in 1986: deep coloured, intense; very rich on nose and palate. Slightly decayed malty bouquet. Huge, fleshy, a hot acetic finish masked by good fruit and high extract. A fairly similar bottle, but a bit sickly on the nose, over the hill and too tart at Desai's Figeac vertical in Paris.
*Last tasted Dec 1989. At best**
Ch Gruaud-Larose A surprisingly harsh bottle in 1964, then one long-stored in Adet Seward's Bordeaux cellars: little red left; smell of old oak and vanilla; tired.
Last tasted July 1987 Should be better than this. See below.*
Ch Gruaud-Larose-Faure Shipped by de Luze, bottled well by Chr Stausholm and immaculately cellared at Aalholm. Impressively deep, ripe, mature colour; low-keyed but sound nose; medium sweetness and body, lovely rich flavour, extract and tannin.
*July 1989****
Ch Marquis de Terme Imported by Hans Andersen, Copenhagen: very deep colour; bouquet of tea and malt; dry, tannic, lean.
From Aalholm, July 1989.
Ch La Mission-Haut-Brion A lovely bottle at the Woltner pre-sale tasting in 1978 and showing well at Desai's tasting in 1985: deep, richly coloured; glorious fruit, blackcurrant-and-glycerine, less full-bodied than expected, but rich, with some charm. And a Woltner magnum at Wolf's tasting in Wiesbaden: opaque, intense, impressive; lovely rich cedar, ripe fragrance; fairly sweet, medium weight yet powerful, complete, lovely flavour and finish.
*Last tasted June 1990******
Ch Palmer Tasted once. Palish and pink-tinged; hard at first but some fruit; dry, fading yet propped up by tannin and acidity.
*Oct 1984***
Ch Rausan-Ségla Jeroboam: very deep, still plummy; showing age on nose, like singed brown paper, but good fruit; sweet, fairly full-bodied, rich, fragrant, excellent flavour, good grip, refreshing acidity.
*At Rodenstock's closing dinner, Sept 1990*****
Ch Talbot Château-bottled, cellared at Aalholm, so about as good as it could be. Good colour; typically high-toned, very fragrant, slightly medicinal bouquet; nice rich entry, weight and flavour. Slightly acidic finish.
*Pre-sale, May 1988****

1935*

Hot dry summer, wet Sept. Abundant, irregular. Few '35s were imported so rarely seen. Of the five tasted only three worth mentioning.
Ch Latour A good, flavoury if slightly acidic bottle from the Comtesse de Beaumont's house in Brittany, at the pre-sale tasting in 1974, and a lively-looking, piquant, loose-knit, very dry bottle at the Fête du Ch Latour.
*Last tasted June 1981**
Dom de Chevalier A rather deathly amber; neutral, then malty; dry, light, faded, edgy but interesting.
*Pre-sale, July 1987**
Ch La Mission-Haut-Brion From the Woltner cellar in 1978, drab and austere. A better bottle at Desai's tasting in 1985: healthy vanillin, blancmange nose; pleasant, light yet chunky. Another Woltner bottle, medium, well-developed appearance; rather feeble apple skin scent; sweet, flowery though lactic.
*Last noted at Wolf's tasting, June 1990. At best****

1936*

Wet summer, fine Sept, late picking. Like the '35s ignored by wine merchants. Not often seen, but some quite flavoury '36s still exist.
Ch Latour A reasonably good bottle from the de Beaumont cellar in 1974, and an even better one at the Fête du Ch Latour: good lively colour; fragrant, charming Cabernet Sauvignon nose; lightish but flavoury and delightful.
*Last tasted June 1981. At best****
Ch Mouton-Rothschild A rather dried out bottle in 1981 but a fairly attractive and flavoury one at Flatt's Mouton tasting. Quite good length. Fragrant but faded, showing acidity.
*Last tasted April 1986. At best***
Ch Ausone "Harvey Selection" slip label. Level upper mid-shoulder. Nice surprise: attractive appearance, bouquet and flavour. No depth of colour, nose or taste, but warm, open, delicate, lightish, charming. Lacking a little length.
*At Flatt's Ausone tasting, Oct 1987****

Ch Cheval-Blanc Deeper but drabber than the '34. A fully evolved, fragrant, high-toned chocolaty bouquet which developed a curious smell like an *entrecôte* grilled on vine leaves. Flavoury but lacking flesh, with acidity leaving it high and dry.
In magnum, Sept 1986.

Ch La Fleur-Pétrus Good deep mature colour; showing age but retaining fruit; soft, some flesh, surprisingly flavoury. Held well.
*At a La Fleur-Pétrus tasting at Corney and Barrow, Dec 1980****

Ch La Mission-Haut-Brion Four notes, two in 1978. Slightly uneven but quite nice. At Desai's La Mission tasting in 1985, looking healthy; ripe cheddar and Cabernet nose; lightish, soft, short but charming. Most recently, deepish, well-developed; swingeing *chèvre* nose; brackish and unattractive.
*Last noted at Wolf's tasting, June 1990. At best***

1937**

A strange year. No rain, but cool from May to mid-Sept, then useful downpours. Harvesting in good conditions. Bottled mainly after the outbreak of war: they were far too tannic to drink. Though highly regarded by the post-war trade, I have never liked them.

At Hardy Rodenstock's wine marathon in Sept 1988, one day was devoted to '37s. His Festival des Jahrgangs 1937 opened with a tasting of 60 red Bordeaux, including all the top growths, in eight 'blocks' or flights, arranged by district. For me, it was akin to visiting a reptile house: combined fascination and repugnance. Allowing for the fact that so much depends on provenance, state of cork and level, my unfavourable assessment of '37 clarets was confirmed. But also confirmed was the superior quality of '37 red Burgundy and white Bordeaux served at a dinner the same evening.

Ch Lafite First noted – a string of tired magnums – at Heublein pre-sale tastings in 1974 and 1975. Two recorked magnums in 1987 and 1988 differed, one, definitely recorked at the château, was delicious: an attractive cigar box bouquet, lovely long flavour, 'ivy and old lace', somewhat attenuated. Three recent bottles, one stringy and ungracious, one ullaged mid-shoulder predictably mushroomy and raw, and a well-nigh perfect bottle, top-shoulder, pale but warm colour; sweet, ripe, cedary bouquet; fairly sweet on palate, but with Lafite delicacy. Delicious.
*The last two at a Christie's lunch, Oct 1988. At best****

Ch Margaux Pretty and charming, but with '37 acidity, in 1970. Three sound bottles in the mid- to late 1970s, two, in slightly different states at Desai's tasting in 1987. Most recently, a rich, tannic magnum. At best, a fairly deep nicely graduated colour; gentle, gnarled oak and cedar bouquet, touch of vanilla and spice; slight sweetness, fuller-bodied than Lafite, chewy, fruit, 'grip', tannin and acidity.
*Last tasted Sept 1988. A good '37****

Ch Latour "Not so hot" but "had bite" in 1955, tired yet tannic a decade later, and a "good but astringent" note in 1966. Of 11 tasted, only two have been brown and oxidised, but I have never liked the wine. The occasional richness of fruit never compensates for its tartness and astringency.
*Last tasted Sept 1988. At best**

Ch Mouton-Rothschild Four notes: a swingeingly acidic bottle in 1972, an oxidised bottle at Flatt's Mouton tasting in 1986, a sweet, pretty good magnum in 1988, and a jeroboam, ullaged mid-shoulder, with a slightly sickly medicinal nose, "iron and oyster shells", full of fruit but with a bitter finish. The best feature is its colour.
Last tasted Sept 1988.

Ch Haut-Brion A fairly good '37, generally deep in colour, a bottle in 1975 and a magnum in 1988, each having a curious bouquet, one tea-like, the other high-toned, citrus, fig-like, rather exotic. Both astringent but the latter made a delicious drink. Two bottles in the late 1970s from the Dillon cellar differed, one concentrated in appearance, nose and flavour, with a malty character reminiscent of the '34, the other lower-keyed. Both flavoury with good fruit.
*Last tasted Sept 1988. At best****

Ch Ausone Ignoring an oxidised bottle in 1975, three fairly consistent notes spanning the next 12 years: lovely rich colour; a strange bouquet of scented old straw which opened up beautifully in the glass, spicy and high-toned; an extraordinary Graves-like tobacco and 'dried bracken' flavour and aftertaste, though it tailed off. With '37 acidity of course.
*A good magnum in Sept 1988. At best****

Ch Cheval-Blanc In 1960: pleasant with a soft middle palate flanked by excessive dryness. In 1977 it seemed leathery, and in 1988, in magnum, quite attractive. Always richly coloured, with a scent of blancmange and old stables. Lots of grip. A good '37.
*Last tasted Sept 1988****

Ch Pétrus A woody, *bouchonnée*, full-bodied yet tart jeroboam. But a better magnum: fairly deep, plummy coloured; bouquet cool and salty like a sea breeze; fairly sweet, medium-full-bodied, flavoury but lean for Pétrus.
*Both at Rodenstock's tasting, Sept 1988. At best****

Ch Batailley Attractive, fragrant in 1978, lightish, fully mature, fragrant and gamey.
*Last tasted May 1981** verging on****

Ch Beychevelle Charming but leathery in 1971. A fairly good upper-shoulder magnum at Rodenstock's. Rich, fragrant though drying out and fading on palate. Nevertheless, attractive.
*Last tasted Sept 1988****

Ch Calon-Ségur In 1961: dry with no middle. Then an austere, acidic magnum in 1978. Fragrant, flavoury, not bad for '37 in 1979. Nine years later at the Rodenstock tasting of '37s, still deep-coloured; a gnarled old oak bouquet that faded in the glass. Dryish, fullish, a similar old oak character on palate, good flavour, grip, tannin and acidity. Not enormously pleasurable but not bad.
*Last tasted Sept 1988***

Carruades de Ch Lafite An attractive magnum, recorked at the château in 1981: fragrant, delicate fruit and cedar, with a second deep, slightly murky, dried-out but tolerable bottle.
*Both at Flatt's Lafite tasting, Oct 1988. At its very best****

Ch Cos d'Estournel Soft, faded in 1970, rich, leathery but not unattractive in 1974, and five recent notes: good but tannic, a magnum flavoury but falling apart, a good Danish bottling with honeyed bottle-age nose, drying out but decent and firm. And a couple, one leathery and astringent, the other better but tasting of old dry leaves. Trying hard, but best avoided.
*Last tasted Jan 1990. At best***

Ch Figeac Toasted and tart amongst Rodenstock's '37s in 1988. Better at Desai's Figeac tasting: fruit, tea, pepper and spice; dry, fullish, rich but raw.
*Last noted Dec 1989**

Ch La Fleur-Pétrus Palish, very mature; sweet, ripe bouquet that held well; dry, lightish, very flavoury, slightly pasty acidity, good aftertaste.
*At La Fleur-Pétrus tasting, Dec 1980****

Ch Gruaud-Larose Two notes in 1976. Both showing age. One astringent, the other rich, short, acidic. Then a top-shoulder magnum at Rodenstock's, lactic and acetic.
Last tasted Sept 1988.
Ch Léoville-Barton A charming and delicate Corney & Barrow bottling.
*1979***
Ch Léoville-Las-Cases A tolerable bottle recorked by Whitwhams in 1988, clean, flavoury; a grubby magnum at Rodenstock's.
*Last noted Sept 1988. At best***
Ch Marquis-de-Terme Four notes in 1976, from rasping, swingeing acidity to "not bad". More recently showing well (from a good French cellar) at a pre-sale tasting: lovely colour, fully mature; powerful meaty 'old oak' bouquet which developed richly; medium weight and style, good, crisp, warm and flavoury, with '37 acidity. A month later an ullaged brown and oxidised bottle.
*Last tasted July 1988. At best***
Ch La Mission-Haut-Brion Four notes. An impressive wine. Médoc-like, good, a bit short in 1973. An opaque, intense-looking magnum with fruity, harmonious, bouquet, and massively full and fruity on the palate at Desai's tasting in 1985. A similar-looking magnum, with original cork and excellent level two years later, smelling of soft old leather, slightly malty, "massive"; another magnum at Rodenstock's tasting of '37s in 1988, full of fruit, complete, tannin and acidity dominant, and with the characteristic tobacco endtaste. Most recently another magnum at Wolf's La Mission tasting: incredibly deep appearance; light but fragrant 'singed leaves' bouquet; very sweet, otherwise like Rodenstock's.
*Last tasted June 1990*****
Ch Montrose Big, black, overloaded with tannin in 1955. Its nose the best feature. 20 years later, loss of colour, mature-looking; fragrant, medicinal bouquet; a good '37. Raw finish. And a magnum: rich, gnarled, acidic old nose; good fruit, substantial, still with loads of tannin and acidity.
*Last noted at Rodenstock's, Sept 1988***
Ch Mouton d'Armailhacq In 1969: fine, deep-coloured; good strong leathery nose; soft yet tough and tannic, attractive in its way. And an oxidised magnum, despite its good level, at a Rodenstock tasting.
*Last noted Sept 1988. At best***
Ch Palmer Two half-bottles tasted in 1976 were deep, rich and flavoury. Most recently a magnum with top-shoulder level: still fairly deep, developing a rusty orange rim; very rich, tangy; nose and palate sweet but decayed. A bit sickly and tart. One of the least astringent of the '37s at the Rodenstock marathon.
*Last tasted Sept 1988***
Ch Rausan-Ségla A tolerably good Corney & Barrow bottling in 1979, softening, with old, charred, firm flavour, and, more recently, two upper mid-shoulder bottles with high-toned 'oyster shell' nose, dry, lean, a bit tart but not bad.
*The last at the Rodenstock tasting, Sept 1988**
TASTED ONLY AT RODENSTOCK'S FESTIVAL DES JAHRGANGS 1937 IN SEPT 1988:
Notes arranged by level of the bottle or magnum:
Top-shoulder
Ch Cantenac-Brown Magnum, lean, flavoury, spoilt by volatile acidity.
Ch Canon Magnum, spicy, uplifting, bouquet, violets; sweet, crisp, fruity, elegant, silky tannins. An excellent '37.
Ch Canon La Gaffelière Three bottles, all oxidised.
Dom de Chevalier Magnum, fragrant; attractive.
Ch Cap de Mourlin A bit acidic.
Ch Carbonnieux Oxidised.
Ch Dauzac Magnum, rich, not bad.
Ch Ducru-Beaucaillou Magnum, delicious.
Ch La Gaffelière Magnum, fruity but tart.
Ch d'Issan Magnum, oxidised.
Ch Lanessan Two bottles, quite pleasant though tart finish.
Ch Larcis-Ducasse Magnum, lean, short, acidic.
Ch Léoville-Barton Magnum, lean, tannic.
Ch Petit Faurie de Soutard Three bottles: quite good.
Ch Pichon-Lalande Magnum, recorked, very flavoury but edgy acidity.
Ch Pontac-Monplaisir Magnum, not bad.
Ch Smith Haut-Lafitte Two bottles, one maderised, the other fruity but a bit tart.
Ch Talbot Magnum, tart.
Ch Trotanoy Magnum, low-keyed, delicious fruit, but harsh finish.
Vieux Ch Certan Magnum, slightly volatile but good flavour.
Upper-shoulder
Ch Branaire-Ducru Cedary, lean, slightly tart.
Ch Pichon Baron Magnum, excellent bouquet, good fruit, very tannic.
Ch Pontet-Canet Magnum, classy bouquet; attractive, with '37 acidity.
Ch Pontet-Clauzure Four bottles, cardboardy, rich, tart.
Mid-shoulder:
Ch Chapelle Madelaine Orange colour, banana smell.
Ch Grand-Puy-Lacoste Magnum, over the hill.
Ch Maucaillou Woody.
Ch Pape-Clément Magnum, lovely colour; fragrant, but well over-the-hill.
Ch Pavie Magnum, deep, plummy coloured; rich, figgy, chocolaty nose; sweet, fullish, some fruit but touch of decay. Finish a bit astringent.
Ch Pavie-Macquin Three bottles, fresh, fruity, hen coop bouquet; raw and tart (a better bottle in 1987).
Oxidised mid-shoulder:
Ch L'Angélus, Ch Brane-Cantenac Magnum,
Ch Camensac, Clos Fourtet, Ch La Garde,
Ch Grand La Lagune, Ch Haut-Bailly,
Ch Léoville-Poyferré, Ch Pavie-Decesse,
Ch Haut-Simard.

1938*

Late harvest due to lack of sun. Below average quantity and quality. Mainly consumed by the end of the war.
Ch Lafite Tasted once. A pale green wartime bottle. Good top-shoulder level. Palish but healthy; sweet, vanilla bouquet, pure crystallised ginger; dry, reasonable weight, lean, firm, clean and sound.
*At Flatt's Lafite tasting, Oct 1988****
Ch Latour Five notes: a poor bottle in 1966, three fairly good in 1977 and 1978, nicely coloured, rich, though a bit over acid. At the Fête du Ch Latour tasting, in a clear glass wartime bottle, upper-mid-shoulder: nose showing age, fungi but fragrant; dryish, lightish for Latour, pleasant but fading. Dry finish.
*Last tasted June 1981***
Ch Mouton-Rothschild Good upper-shoulder. Surprisingly good depth of colour; mild, a bit lactic and creaking; overripe, very dry, edgy-acidic.
*At Flatt's Mouton tasting, April 1986**

Ch La Mission-Haut-Brion Same weight as the '36. High acidity in 1978. A much better bottle at Desai's tasting in 1985: lively, attractive colour; very fruity, distinct Cabernet, delicate. It closed up a bit, but was spicy; dryish, chewy, medium weight, masculine, like a minor '48. More recently, a similar description. Surprisingly pleasant and easy.
*Last noted at Wolf's La Mission tasting, June 1990****

1939*

Late summer, cold, wet. Very late harvest. Abundance of light but fragrant wines. Rarely seen. Avoid, unless provenance and condition impeccable.

Ch Lafite Tasted only once. Wartime bottle, plain capsule. High-shoulder. Palish, fully developed colour, brown-rimmed; pleasant rich mint bouquet that developed well, spicy, gingery; dryish, lightish, lean, very flavoury.
*At Flatt's Lafite tasting, Oct 1988****

Ch Latour Four notes: old, tired, smelly, feeble but holding on, rotten grapes but some elegance. The last, in clear glass bottle, mid-shoulder, dead brown, oxidised.
*Last tasted at Fête du Ch Latour, June 1981. At best**

Ch Mouton-Rothschild An acceptable if acidic bottle in 1978. A decade later, in wartime bottle, upper-shoulder level, palish but healthy; an odd malty-meaty, cheesy, overripe nose; dry, over mature, sour.
Last noted at Flatt's Mouton tasting, April 1988.

Ch Baret Crumbly cork showing signs of weevil, level still top-shoulder. Sweet, sweaty-saddle nose; fragrant but faded. A bit varnishy.
*Ex-château at pre-sale tasting, Sept 1983**

Ch Felloneau An interesting, attractive but decaying and rarely seen wine from Macau.
*Last tasted Sept 1987**

Ch Figeac Two notes, the first in a green wartime bottle with short capsule, good level: fairly deep; mushroomy though sweet, good fruit on the nose but developed a whiff of brown banana and started cracking up. Very sweet, soft, with twist-of-lemon acidity leaving the mouth dry. Later the same year: very sweet, chocolaty nose, a bit caramelised; overall dry, light, just a bit of edgy acidity.
*Last noted at Desai's Figeac tasting, Dec 1989**

Ch La Mission-Haut-Brion At Desai's in 1985: fully developed; gentle, spicy bouquet; medium dry, medium-light weight, spicy Cabernet flavour, short, sound but fading. A similar bottle at Wolf's La Mission tasting to which I would add vanilla, touch of iodine, then chocolaty bouquet; delicate, fragrant, touch of end acidity.
*Last tasted June 1990***

1940**

A reasonably good vintage, richly coloured and attractive. If well-cellared can still be quite nice.

Ch Lafite Tasted once. High-shoulder. Deep rich red brown; better than expected, low-keyed but harmonious, medium weight, flavoury, very dry finish.
*At Flatt's tasting, Oct 1988***

Ch Margaux An odd half-bottle from a Bordeaux cellar, level upper mid-shoulder. Medium; curious at first but developed fragrance. Lightish. Acidity catching up. *Pre-sale tasting, June 1988**

Ch Latour Eight notes between 1967 and 1975 and two since. In every instance intensely deep-coloured. Apart from one oxidised bottle, rich bouquet noted; lively, fruity but not mellow. Strong classic flavour, fairly full-bodied, quite a bite. The word "chunky" crops up several times. Like a '62. Most recently, at a Christie's pre-sale tasting in Chicago: very deep; dry, stern, full of fruit and tannin.
*Last tasted Sept 1990***

Ch Mouton-Rothschild Three wartime bottles opened at Flatt's Mouton tasting, one mid- and two top-shoulder. Each of the latter had a healthy, rich, beautiful colour with very mature amber rim; a gloriously forthcoming bouquet, the characteristic Mouton Cabernet Sauvignon aroma developed spicily, holding well. Sweet, full, soft, lovely, ending with a crisp, very dry finish.
*All tasted April 1986. At best*** perhaps**** allowing for age and vintage.*

Ch Cheval-Blanc Magnum. Fairly deep, still some ruby, fine mature rim, long legs; fragrant, sweet, slightly cheesy, good depth. After an hour the bouquet was light, gentle, very sound. Slightly sweet palate, medium-full body, with excellent, rather assertive, singed tobacco leaf flavour. Good length, tannin and acidity. An attractive wine.
*At the château, Sept 1986*****

Ch Fleur-Pétrus Palish, mature-looking; high-toned, fragrant, delicate, touch of rot; dry, lightish, nice flavour, vinosity and condition.
*At Corney & Barrow's, Dec 1980****

Ch La Mission-Haut-Brion Fragrant and flavoury at the Woltner pre-sale tasting in 1978. At Desai's in 1985: palish, nice colour though fairly brown; a thick, dusty, slightly corky yet rich bouquet that developed well; slightly sweet, medium weight, surprisingly pleasant rich flavour. Very complete. Another very good bottle from the Woltner cellar, bought at Christie's and noted at Wolf's recent La Mission tasting. Excellent bouquet. Good firm wine in well-nigh perfect condition.
*Last tasted June 1990*****

Ch Pontet-Canet Bordeaux bottled by Sichel. Intense, opaque centre; a rather 'cold' oaky, leathery nose and flavoury. Dry tannic finish. Just sound enough.
*Pre-sale tasting, Chicago, April 1984**

Ch La Tour-Haut-Brion Medium-deep; good, forthcoming, chocolaty nose; very sweet though lightish, fragrant, flavoury, a bit short.
*At Wolf's tasting, June 1990****

1941**

Good summer, difficult late vintage. Better than its reputation. Rarely seen but more than merely interesting.

Ch Lafite Top-shoulder. Medium, broad, fully evolved colour; an amazingly good bouquet, spicy, touch of 'old ivy', marvellously evolving fragrance; dry, medium weight, clean, crisp, fat.
*At Flatt's Lafite tasting, Oct 1988*****

Ch Latour In good condition, but severe in 1969. Rich nose but very austere in 1978; a deeply coloured bottle and a smell like freshly peeled mushrooms and wooden boxes in damp cellars; the sweetness of decay, lightish, flavoury, some charm. A surprisingly fragrant aftertaste.
*The last at the Fête du Ch Latour, June 1981. At best***

Ch La Mission-Haut-Brion A flavoury bottle at the Woltner pre-sale tasting in 1978. In 1985, at Desai's tasting, a rich damson colour, brown-tinged; very sound nose; dryish, lightish, healthy and flavoury despite a touch of end acidity. Another Woltner bottle at Wolf's tasting fairly similar, though a coffee-like bouquet noted that evolved richly: stables and brown sugar! Rather lean.
*Last tasted June 1990***

1942**

Good spring and summer, poor Sept. Some pleasant wines, mainly consumed by the mid-1950s. Some have more than survived.

Ch Lafite Four notes. Showing age but not bad in 1974, 1975 and 1976. A good high-shoulder bottle at Flatt's Lafite tasting: a warm, healthy colour; attractive bouquet of ginger and vanilla, a bit peppery, evolved nicely; medium sweetness and weight, chewy and fruity.
*Last tasted Oct 1988. At best*****

Ch Latour Opaque, loaded in 1964, dry and powerful in 1976. At the Fête du Ch Latour: very deep, with cedar rim; nose like milk chocolate, showing age, but it held well in glass; on the palate, dry, short, uncharming.
*Last tasted June 1981**

Ch Mouton-Rothschild Surprisingly deep and intense, but with unhealthy bead at rim; low-keyed but harmonious when first poured, after two hours developing a rich vanilla/caramel, farmyard scent; dryish, fairly full-bodied, rich, very good flavour and texture but a bit short.
*Lunch at Lafite (boiled eggs and toast!) March 1983****

Ch Ausone Excellent level. Very attractive, rich, mature colour; beautiful, slightly meaty, forthcoming, harmonious bouquet; dry, medium weight, fragrant, refreshing, with a very satisfactory finish.
*At Flatt's Ausone tasting, Oct 1987*****

Ch Cheval-Blanc Pale green bottle, short cork, good upper-shoulder level. Pleasantly warm colour; nose pricked: whiff of banana but some fruit; basically good flavour spoiled by acidic finish.
Opened by Douglas Logan-Kuhs, Dec 1987.

Ch Figeac Medium-deep; nose not quite right: stalky, stably though with crisp fruit and spice. Slightly sweet, medium, quite nice though faded flavour. Fragrant finish.
*At Desai's Figeac tasting, Dec 1989***

Ch La Fleur-Pétrus Medium pale; high-toned cress-like bouquet, old but good; overall lean and dry but very flavoury.
*At Corney & Barrow's, Dec 1980****

Ch Lascombes Recorked 1971. Very good colour, star-bright; showing age and touch of decay on the nose, though some softness and fruit; the sweetness of maturity, lightish, body sagging, crumbling acidity. Not a bad drink.
*A vertical tasting at the château, in Feb 1985***

Ch Léoville-Poyferré Mid-shoulder. Deep, slightly too brown but with quite good old cedary nose. Medium weight, a bit tart but not bad.
Aug 1989.

Ch La Mission-Haut-Brion First noted at Desai's tasting in 1985: palish but pretty with a rosy glow; a light, gentle fragrance, not much support, some decay; dry, light, raw, acidic. A bottle of similar appearance and nose at Wolf's tasting, but in better condition. A sweeter, very pleasant, easy wine.
*Last noted June 1990. At best****

Ch Palmer Plain label, unbranded cork. Rich mahogany; singed; dry, lightish, tart but drinkable.
*Ex-chateau, pre-sale, May 1991***

Ch Petit-Village Opaque centre, healthy maturity; sound, harmonious bouquet, Cabernet Franc, cedar and tobacco; medium entry, dry finish. Good sturdy wine. Excellent, if old, oaky flavour. Tannic.
*Dinner at Ch Marbuzet, May 1986****

1943*** *to* ****

Good flowering, a hot dry summer. The best of the wartime vintages. Some wines almost as impressive as the 1945s, but the common denominator being a rather short blunt finish. Still worth looking out for.

Ch Lafite One note: top-shoulder. Very healthy colour; light but sound nose quickly evolving into a beautiful, delicate bouquet; dry, medium weight, a bit screwed up but very flavoury with good finish.
*At Flatt's Lafite tasting, Oct 1988****

Ch Margaux 10 fairly consistent notes since 1975. Fairly deep, rich mature colour; bouquet generally good, variously described as broad, vanilla, lovely 'old brick' perfume, subdued, touch of decay, rich. However, consistently dry on palate, fairly full-flavoured though 'fern-like' and 'old leaves' noted. Blunt-ended, lean, its edgy acidity tamed by food. A pretty good, always interesting drink.
*Last tasted Feb 1988. At best****

Ch Latour Eight notes, first in 1954 when it was still full and hard. Rich and powerful in the mid-1960s and continuing to improve. Fine, deep autumnal colour; consistently good nose: lovely, delicate yet concentrated, cedar, peppery, fragrant. Overall dry, medium full-bodied, crisp, flavoury. More acidity than tannin. Rich but lacking length.
*Last tasted July 1981. At best*****

Ch Mouton-Rothschild Bottled Aug 1946. Three notes. A good bottle (at Lafite), decanted at 10am, and served at 1.30pm. Fabulously deep colour; whiff of old age when poured, but by 2pm developing spiciness, and at 3.30pm gently faded. Nice weight. Very flavoury. Dry finish. And at Flatt's Mouton tasting a lovely ruddy colour; pronounced *cassis* bouquet which opened up fragrantly and, after an hour, sheer perfection. Slightly sweet, medium-full, marvellous fruit, flavour, balance and aftertaste.
*Last tasted April 1986. At best*****

Ch Ausone Top-shoulder. Rich, lively, attractive appearance; most unusual sweet rich and appealing bouquet; fullish, good, rich and rounded. Dry finish. A bit short.
*At Flatt's Ausone tasting, Oct 1987****

Ch Cos d'Estournel An interesting but unexciting bottle in 1974; a good recorked bottle in 1985. Rich, good-looking; initially a touch of kerosene on nose but developed nicely; crisp, faded. Most recently, a top-shoulder bottle, less healthy looking but with better nose than expected, cedary, very attractive. Rich, a bit edgy and with the usual '43 bluntness.
*Last tasted June 1988. At best****

Ch Figeac The first vintage vinified by Thierry Manoncourt. Attractive rich vanilla nose which developed an almost sickly sweetness, creamy, strawberry-like. Sweetish, medium weight, good fruit, flavour and balance.
*Brought by Manoncourt to Desai's Ausone tasting, Dec 1989****

Ch La Fleur-Pétrus Open-knit, overripe *gibier* yet attractive cress-like bouquet; full, flavoury but very dry and with teeth-gripping acidity.
*At Corney & Barrow's, Dec 1980**

Ch La Mission-Haut-Brion At Desai's in 1985: a beautifully soft, rich colour; warm, glowing, slightly toasted bouquet; medium sweetness and body, good crisp fruit, excellent mid-palate, reasonable length, and complete. An equally, good magnum at Wolf's La Mission tasting: incredibly deep colour; bouquet of 'hot

bricks' and ripe mulberries; full, sweet, ripe, rich.
*Last noted June 1990*****

1944**

Variable weather conditions, mainly favourable though hot, thundery summer. Rain towards the end of harvest. A fairly big crop of lightish wines of irregular quality. At best a charmer.

Ch Lafite One of the charmers, particularly in the mid-1950s. Dry, lightish, refined, soft and silky, with dry finish in 1968, and, despite excellent level, a disappointing bottle at Flatt's Lafite tasting. It had a forthcoming but slightly soapy, scented bouquet which nevertheless developed, fig-like and richly. A slightly malty flavour. Dry finish.
*Last tasted Oct 1988. At best****

Ch Latour Four notes in the 1950s, 1960s and 1970s. All a bit unbalanced but with good mature fruit and flavour and marked acidity, the best being recorked in 1976. And two in the early 1980s, one mid-shoulder: tawny, 'oxo'dised (like meat extract, not completely gone) and tart. A distinctly lighter style of Latour, piquant and flavoury.
*Last tasted June 1983. At best***

Ch Mouton-Rothshild Bottled in 1947. Top-shoulder. Deeper appearance than expected. Its bouquet could only be Mouton: rich, high-toned, berry-like, developing fine elegant spiciness in glass. On the palate sweet, medium weight, very flavoury though a touch of hardness and rawness. Very dry spicy finish.
*At Flatt's Mouton tasting April 1986****

Ch Haut-Brion Two delicate, healthy half-bottles in 1979. Two bottles 1981, both in palish green wartime bottles. The first, high level: not much red left but alive and bright; fragrant freshly-peeled mushroom nose; slightly sweet, light, delicate, an attractive drink. The other, with level just below top of shoulder, looked like an old tawny port yet seemed crisper and fresher and developed well.
*Last tasted May 1981, at best****

Ch La Mission-Haut-Brion Interesting but with some reservations in the 1970s. A delicately appealing bottle, doubtless from the Woltner family cellars, at the Wolf tasting: palish; attractive bouquet but with questionable overtones; sweetish, on the light side, showing age, short but a pretty drink.
*Last tasted June 1990**

Ch Pontet-Canet Shipped by Cruse and bottled by Rutherford Osborne and Perkin, their London agents. A deliciously ripe bottle in 1979. In 1989: level into neck, original short, slightly loose, but firm well-stained cork; beautiful ruby and tile-red colour; sweet, lightish, glorious flavour, decent length, light, silky and leathery tannin and acidity. A charmer.
*At a dinner party, May 1989*****

1945*****

A truly great year, measuring up to the pre-phylloxera 1865 and 1870. Big, highly concentrated wines, extremely tannic, long-lasting. After an agreeable early spring, bad frosts in May nipped the vines in the bud. Then came hail and diseases followed by a summer of drought and exceptional heat which thickened the skins and increased the sugar. The small harvest of very ripe and concentrated grapes began early, on Sept 13.

As there had been little replanting during the war and pre-war depression years, the vines were all mature, so although mistakes occurred, those wines made traditionally by experienced maîtres de chai were superb.

Many '45s will take 50 years for the excessive drying tannins to ameliorate. The best have survived and will continue to improve. Those less well made, less fleshy, are drying or have already dried out.

Ch Lafite 25 notes since 1967, in bottles, magnums and double-magnum. Surprisingly little bottle variation, remarkably consistent character and style. Not deep-coloured, but lovely, lively, intense, rich, with fine mature rim. Initially a low-keyed nose but it blossoms in the glass, churning out a fabulous, biscuity, spicy, slightly citrus-like penetrating fragrance. A distinct touch of sweetness on the palate, by no means a heavyweight, more of a middle-weight, elegant and stylish, svelt yet with some concentration, great length and dry finish. At its best, simply lovely.
*Last noted in Chicago at Christie's pre-sale tasting of Lloyd Flatt's cellar, Sept 1990***** Drink now to beyond the year 2000.*

Ch Margaux 18 notes since 1971. Except for three maderised bottles, consistently good. Deeper-looking than Lafite, lovely, rich, and still with a vigorous blackberry hue. The bouquet unfolds in the glass, revealing rich, ripe mulberry-like fruit, a cigar box scent, immense and intense fragrance. On the palate a touch of ripe grape and high alcohol sweetness, rich, velvety, yet still tannic, fairly full-bodied, a beautiful wine with years of life in hand.
*Last tasted at the Penning-Rowsell's '45 first-growth dinner, June 1990***** Drink now to beyond 2000.*

Ch Latour Magnificent. One of the best ever. Still extremely vigorous and youthful in 1965: "a good strapping drink", and "10 years' life left" – an understatement. It had mellowed, less deep, less dense but still lively and rich, with a fine mature rim in the mid-1960s, its bouquet crammed with fruit. Now more forthcoming, fully evolved, fragrant, spicy Cabernet Sauvignon, cinnamon and eucalyptus, worth giving it time in the glass. Still full-bodied, crammed with fruit, extract, flesh. Great length. Tannins ameliorating but still gripping it firmly. Over the last 25 years, 22 bottles, and only one poor one.
*Last tasted at Penning-Rowsell's '45 dinner, June 1990***** Drink now to well into the next century.*

Ch Mouton-Rothschild The greatest ever Mouton. Astonishing still; still a "Churchill of a wine". Tasted well over two dozen times since 1954: "loaded with all good things"; "full of vigour". It has lost scarcely any of its brilliant concentration of colour, opaque-centred, intense, as if it were trying to exert pressure on the sides of the glass. Now showing maturity at the rim. Incredible bouquet: immediately forthcoming, with a vigorous fragrance, a sort of essence of Cabernet Sauvignon, spicy, cinnamon, eucalyptus. Like the Latour it appears to have become sweeter but is still full-bodied, very rich, very concentrated, mouthfilling, spicy, still borne aloft by its alcohol, acidity and tannins, though the latter are softening – a little. What a wine. I have often given it 21 out of 20, and *six* stars!
*Last tasted at the Penning-Rowsells', June 1990***** Drink now to well into the next century.*

Ch Haut-Brion Another great wine. Consistently fine. One of Haut-Brion's best-ever vintages. 21 excellent notes, just one poor bottle. It seems to have regained depth of colour with age, again almost opaque but with mature amber rim. On nose and palate, it is different from its Médoc peers. More earthy, but not in a clodhopping way, and with a tobacco-like element to its taste. The bouquet variously described as gentle and fragrant, sweet, vanilla and chocolate, warm, spicy, complete — and always remarkably good. Pretty full-bodied, yet velvety, with loads of sweetening and enriching alcohol, its tannin masked by richness and extract. Great length, wonderful aftertaste.

*Last noted June 1990***** Drink now to well into the 21st century.*

Ch Ausone Huge and unready in the mid-1950s; astringent in 1974; a dried leaf character in 1975 and at Desai's tasting in 1986, though it had a deep, intense, beautiful colour and powerful flavour. Despite its length it lacked fruit and was dried out. The magnum at Flatt's Ausone tasting was too brown, poor.

*Last tasted Oct 1987. At best***

Ch Cheval-Blanc Tasted over a 10-year period since 1977. Totally different from the mammoth '47 and not as good as the '48. Possibly some vinification problems: a whiff of over-high volatile acidity on three occasions and touch of decay on another. At best, one of a pair at Arthur Hallé's first-growth tasting, with perfect original cork, decanted 2½ hours before serving: medium, rosy-hued, touch of orange maturity; a beautiful bouquet, fragrant, with great depth and which evolved gloriously in the glass: another 3 hours later fully opened, with wonderful cedary vinosity. Distinctly sweet but gently faded, elegant and with lovely flavour and good length.

*Last tasted April 1987. At best**** Drink now.*

Ch Pétrus I have noted this pretty rare and almost priceless wine on eight occasions. No doubt about it: a very great wine. At the beginning of the 1980s opaque, retaining fairly convincing depth and intensity, and very lively-looking; soft, milky, vanilla noticed on the nose, yet perfectly evolved, very fragrant, full of fruit. On the palate fairly sweet, now less massive, but a rich, soft, chewy charmer. Perfect weight, rich, good length, with some acidity peeping through.

*Last noted at Johan Bjürklund's Pétrus tasting, April 1990***** Drink now.*

Many of the following notes were made at Desai's mammoth tasting of '45s in Feb 1986:

Ch Batailley Good wine: full and fruity in 1957, rich, with some depth in 1972 and two good cork, good-level bottles at Desai's tasting: magnificent colour; sound, fleshy, glorious nose; fullish, lovely mid-palate fruit, nice dry finish.

*Last noted Feb 1986*****

Ch Beychevelle Dry and severe in 1957, four good notes in the 1960s and four in the 1970s, three lovely, but one, bottled by Justerini and Brooks, acetic. Two bottles at the Desai horizontal, both with good levels, one with blackened cork and corky, the other ruby, rich, flavoury, with some elegance but a bit raw.

*Last tasted Feb 1986. Averaging****

Ch Calon-Ségur First noted in Nov 1952 as "well rounded. Pleasing in every way" but "too young". Since then I have tasted and drunk it a dozen times. The initial tannin gave the impression of dryness and austerity right through the 1970s. Its former depth of colour has mellowed but is still gloriously rich ('45s, like '61s, have a distinctive concentration of colour). Almost identical notes over a recent three year period: two château-bottled, a magnum at Desai's tasting of '45s, and the last shipped by Calvet and bottled by Carl Permins Vinhandel, Copenhagen. All had a lively, ripe, fragrant, distinctly cedary bouquet; all much sweeter with age despite a fair amount of residual tannin giving the wines a dry finish. Rich, concentrated, firm. Good.

*Last tasted July 1989****

Ch Cantemerle A pair of '45s, from different sources, both with excellent levels, noted at Desai's tasting: opaque, intense-looking yet with a gentle, fragrant, attractive bouquet that blossomed, strawberry-like, in the glass. Nice weight, shapely, still fairly loaded with tannin and acidity.

*Last tasted Feb 1986*****

Ch La Conseillante First tasted in 1977: an intense yet rapier-like flavour. Two, bottled by Harveys, had a beautiful depth of colour, rich, ripe smell and lovely mellow-brick flavour, though drying out on the finish. Most recently a superb bottle from the Aalholm Cellars bottled by Joh Fr Schalburg. Level still well into neck. Fully mature but warm and alive; lightly honeyed bouquet; sweet, losing weight yet still plump, soft, delicate and lively.

*Last tasted July 1989*****

Ch Cos d'Estournel First tasted in 1959: fruit and balance, needs time. Still a bit raw in 1968 but developing richly, probably at peak in 1972. A pair at Desai's tasting: fabulous colour, low-keyed slightly scented bouquet, touch of sweetness, perfect flavour, texture, balance.

*Last tasted Feb 1986*****

Ch La Croix de Gay Three notes. All bottled by Harvey's. Two in 1965: good, mahogany-coloured, still full of fruit and tannin, and, nearly 20 years later, its bouquet now suave and gentle, developing tea-like fragrance; stylish but losing weight and a bit edgy on the finish.

*Last tasted Feb 1986. Now, just reaching****

Ch Croizet-Bages Four notes in the 1960s summed up as "a great minor wine". Most recently: very mature, rich; lovely old cedary bouquet; sweet entry, very dry slightly acidic finish, nice weight, good flavour.

*Last tasted April 1991****

Ch Ducru-Beaucaillou The first '45 I tasted, the month I came into the trade, Sept 1952. "Slightly earthy" nose; "rather too dry and rough". In 1972, a double-magnum was still opaque, with a peppery, snuff-like nose, fine but searingly dry; and just over 10 years later, at Desai's tasting, a mid-shoulder magnum, *too* deep, a bit sour. And an excellent top-shoulder bottle: fragrant, classic biscuity bouquet; lean, flavoury but still retaining a bit of raw tannin and acidity. Most recently: dried out but rich. Good length.

*Last tasted Dec 1990. At best****

Ch La Dominique Very fine wine. Eight notes. Totally undrinkable in 1954; enormous, unready in 1961, but softening in the late 1970s. More recently: deep, redder than the '49; a rich and exciting wine, its high extract, meatiness and richness just managing to mask volatile acidity.

*Similar notes in 1979, 1983 and, last, in July 1988**** but living dangerously.*

Clos L'Eglise A highly volatile Justerini & Brooks bottling in 1977 and, at the Desai tasting, a Bordeaux-bottled magnum, with excellent level: almost opaque; a hard, taut, Cabernet Franc nose, distinctly sweaty; strange, flat, leafy flavour. Rich but raw.

*Last tasted Feb 1986. Risky. At best***

Ch L'Enclos The lightest and driest of the Pomerols shipped by Cruse, bottled by Rutherford's, tasted in 1974. Next, with silky texture, rich though dry, and one woody, unclean, Bordeaux-bottled.

*The last two at Desai's tasting of '45s, Feb 1986. At best****

Ch Figeac Just one note. Deep, intense, ruby centre; an extraordinary bouquet, sweet, crystallised violets almost Mouton-like; sweet, full, brackish, tobacco-like flavour, overloaded with tannin.

At Desai's Figeac tasting, Dec 1989.

Ch La Fleur-Gazin Mahogany colour, cold nose but lovely flavour and excellent condition in 1972, but a single bottle with poor level at the Desai tasting smelled of roast beef, its fragrance and silky Pomerol texture striving ineffectually to surface.
*Last tasted Feb 1986, at best****
Clos Fourtet Two hard and stalky bottles in the early 1970s and a variable pair, both with excellent levels, and good fruit hemmed in by rawness and high tannin content. Unattractive.
Last tasted Feb 1986.
Ch Le Gay Two soft, velvety, upper-mid-shoulder bottles in 1978, a bit edgily dry at the end; and in 1984: a beautiful upper-shoulder bottle with deep, lively colour; bouquet rich and ripe after decanting, sagged a little an hour later but then gained its second breath and settled down nicely. Fabulously rich flavour, great concentration, a warm alcoholic glow, leathery tannic finish reined in by superb aftertaste. Another, more recently, just surviving a mid-low-shoulder level. Still magnificent despite whiff of oxidation.
*Last tasted July 1990. At best******
Ch Grand Puy-Lacoste A consistently well-run property making top class, uncompromising wine in a traditional way. Unassuming, little tasted, consequently undervalued. A magnum in 1986 marred by the cork, but a superlative bottle in 1988: very deep, opaque centre, intense; crisp, classic Pauillac nose; a touch of initial sweetness, full-bodied, concentrated. In marvellous state of preservation — needs another 20 years.
*Last tasted June 1988****(*)*
Ch Gruaud-Larose 10 notes, from a beautiful big fruity and just drinkable wine in 1954, in variable states of drinkability in the 1960s, coming into its own in the mid-1970s and nicely poised on its maturity plateau in the second half of the 1980s. A perfect Army & Navy stores bottle at the Desai tasting, and, most recently, a magnum: still deep and richly coloured; sweaty and tannic at first, taking time to develop a ripe gingery fruit bouquet; distinctly sweet, fleshy, full of fruit and tannin.
*Last noted Nov 1989****(*)*
Ch Langoa-Barton Three notes. All Bordeaux bottled by Barton & Guestier. An attractive bottle in 1974, another rich and intense in 1981, and a superb magnum despite its mid-shoulder level at the Desai tasting: deep, perfect, richly coloured; sound, fragrant, medicinal Médoc bouquet that developed beautifully; good fruit. Very dry crisp tannin and acidity.
*Last tasted Feb 1986*****
Ch Léoville-Barton 10 notes. In 1954 raw, tannic, nowhere near ready; in 1957 hard. "Flavour like a good cigar". Softening in the 1960s, an elegant Berry Bros bottling in 1971, and superb château-bottled in 1972. Exciting but rather astringent in 1985, and three different bottlings at Desai's tasting: Corney & Barrow's a real beauty, an unknown bottler less good, and Cockburn & Campbell's a bit tart. Most recently a lovely, fragrant, cedary, soft château bottling.
*Last tasted April 1991. At best*****
Ch Léoville-Las-Cases Nine variable notes, one "soft" and another "too thin", bottler unknown, in 1954. Fine-flavoured and elegant in 1971, deep but thinning, (a bottle from a cellar in Bordeaux) at a Heublein pre-sale tasting in 1972, then five mainly excellent notes in the 1980s: fabulous colour; sound, rich nose opening up most beautifully; still very tannic. The most recent a lovely rich wine from Aalholm Castle, shipped by Cruse and bottled by Kjaer & Sommerfeldt.
*Last tasted July 1989. At best****(*). If well-cellared should continue to improve.*
Ch Léoville-Poyferré Contradictory comments in 1954, and a Saccone & Speed bottling noted simply as a "big wine" in 1955. A bottle and a magnum "austere despite beautiful bouquet" in the mid-1960s, and similar remarks about a Cockburn & Campbell bottling 10 years later. Most recently a pair at Desai's tasting confirmed its depth, fragrance but very austere tannic finish.
*Last tasted Feb 1986. Appearance and nose***** Palate, a grudging*****
Ch Lynch-Bages Four rather unflattering notes in the mid-1950s and early 1960s: a rather exaggerated Cabernet Sauvignon character being its best attribute. A pair, both with short original corks and good top-shoulder levels, at Desai's tasting, one with very deep colour, a glorious, fully developed spicy Cabernet Sauvignon cassis nose, full of body and flavour. The other smelled of mushrooms.
*Last tasted Feb 1986. For appearance and bouquet*** For palate*****
Ch Malescot St Exupéry A surprisingly soft but characterful half-bottle in 1955. Next, 11 years later, a pair, levels upper- and top-shoulder, both excellent: the usual '45 depth; bouquet highly scented, violets, cassis, spicy, gingery; lovely crisp fruit, dry tannic finish.
*Last tasted Feb 1986. Nose***** Palate*****
Ch La Mission-Haut-Brion With the '29, one of the greatest La Mission vintages. 11 uniformly excellent bottles from the mid-1970s. A powerhouse of colour, ruby encircling a virtually black core; ripe, spicy, herbaceous bouquet of great depth; a heavily loaded palate, masculine, vigorous, very tannic, with characteristic tobacco endtaste.
*Last noted June 1990***** Drink now and well into the next century.*
Ch Montrose Impressive but tough and tannic in 1985. A pair at Desai's tasting the following year, one dried out and tart, the other, with a very high level: great luminosity; rich, spicy; attaining some softness, very sound, but lean, leathery, tannic.
*Last tasted Feb 1986. Optimistically ***(*) but might dry out completely before it mellows.*
Ch Mouton d'Armailhacq Six notes: flavoury but lacking charm in the late 1960s, some fragrance and a degree of delicacy in 1977, and a pair with different provenance at Desai's tasting. Both good, the first rather spicy finish, Lynch-Bages like, and, like so many of the originally very dry '45s, sweetening with age. Piquant, stylish, very flavoury. The other: fragrant and delicious.
*Last tasted Feb 1986. At best*****
Mouton-Cadet Without wishing to sound superior, I would not normally think of including a branded table wine. But this bottle from a cellar in Los Angeles was fully mature, sweet, rich and attractive.
*At Christie's pre-sale tasting, Chicago, June 1985****
Ch Palmer Five notes. Full, tough, classic in 1971. A poor London bottling and magnificent château bottling in 1973. At Desai's tasting, two bottles with excellent levels; fabulous colour; a cool bouquet that took off, stalky then gingery; lovely crisp fruit but lacking the opulence of the '61. Tannic.
*Last tasted Feb 1986*****
Ch Pichon-Longueville, Baron Seemed a bit too brown and old on the nose but marvellous on the palate in the mid-1970s. Rich and penetrating in 1985, but a rather dried out, raw bottle at Desai's tasting. Still fairly deep but, unlike many '45s, the bouquet not its best feature: strange, singed, dried bracken.
*Last tasted Feb 1986. At best****

Ch Pontet-Canet Over a dozen notes. First, Bordeaux-bottled (it used never to be bottled at the château), a boiled beetroot aroma, lovely, full, raw and hard in 1954, still 'black strap' in 1961 and noted as hard and austere in 1971. It started to mellow in the late 1970s and by the mid-1980s a rich, sweet, lovely wine. However the bottlings vary: the best being an original Cruse bottling noted in 1986 though three bottles at the same tasting were oxidised, pricked, tart. Others very good. Variations in colour too. Best bouquets perfect, classic, slightly medicinal, ozone, biscuity. More recently, a perfect half-bottle.
*Last tasted June 1990. At best*****

Ch Rausan-Ségla 10 notes. In magnums, the odd half-bottle and various English bottlings, so hard to sum up. First tasted in 1965: youthful, lacking middle. "Volatile acidity" crops up in the late 1960s and 1970s. The best were three château-bottled magnums in 1975, 1977 and 1979. All opaque; rich, complex bouquet, hovering on the brink; all very dry, velvety yet hard and austere. And, most recently, two Berry Bros bottlings, one excellent—with rather a '28 character, the other, around mid-shoulder, gnarled, tannic, with end acidity.
*Last tasted July 1988. At best*** Will not improve.*

Ch Rauzan-Gassies Five notes. Flavoury but 'green' in mid-1950s and spoiled by raw acidity in the early 1960s. At the Desai tasting one bottle oxidised, the other too deep, with beads at the rim proclaiming that all was not well. Overblown, sweet, spicy, acidic.
*Last tasted Feb 1986. At best***

Clos René Shipped *en barrique* by Cruse and bottled in London by their UK agents. Perfection in 1974, and a couple of bottles at Desai's tasting, both soft and lovely. But—the weakness of most Pomerols—the nose, sweet and rich, is unsubtle and does not blossom like the best Médocs. Handsome rosy-cheeked peasant.
*Last tasted Feb 1986. At best*****

Ch Talbot Dry, rich but austere in 1976. Two excellent-level bottles at Desai's. Black cherry; marvellous fruit and spicy bouquet (cinnamon) which opened up in the glass; now sweet, concentrated, with lots of everything. A very good '45.
*Last tasted Feb 1986******

Ch La Tour-Haut-Brion Pretty good but acidic in 1978. At Desai's in 1985 a strange weedy fish-skin bouquet; lean, austere, a bit tart. Not a patch on its big brother, La Mission. A raw, coarse bottle at the Wolf tasting.
*Last noted June 1990**

Ch Trotanoy Incredibly rich, oily nose in mid-1970s but cracked up quickly, though powerful and silky on palate. At Desai's, two bottles, both château-bottled, from the Nicolas cellars in Paris: good levels; one curiously scented, soft and chewy, the other fully evolved, very fragrant but with an odd cough-mixture smell. Sweetish, full-bodied, rich, chunky.
*Last tasted Feb 1986. At best*** but cracking up?*

Vieux Ch Certan A mammoth. Fantastically concentrated and impressive in the mid-1970s. A decade later still quite opaque; an incredibly sweet, toffee-chocolate nose; vast molasses-like flavour. Crude and tannic. But clearly oxidation wielding a heavy stick.
Last tasted Feb 1986?

The following tasted only at Bipin Desai's '45 vintage marathon in Feb 1986:

Ch Brane-Cantenac Two bottles, both with excellent levels, yet one slightly sour. The other good: deep, rich; fine cedar fragrance; good fruit but very tannic.
***** Drink soon before it dries out.*

Ch Branaire-Duluc-Ducru Château bottled, from a Danish cellar. Good level, a bit drab, old, tired and tart.

Ch Cantenac-Brown Another pair, upper-shoulder levels, one a bit tart, the other sweeter.
*At best***

Dom de Chevalier Another pair, one with level into neck, opaque centre, pretty intense; sweet, harmonious, chocolate, cedar and olive bouquet; medium sweetness and body, marvellous silky texture, dry tannic finish. The other, top-shoulder, good but seemed less fruity.
*At best****

Ch La Fleur Two London bottled with excellent top-shoulder levels, both black as Egypt's night, smell of sweaty feet and glue, yet developing a pleasanter rich farmyard scent. Both rich, one a bit raw, the other more elegant.
*At best****

Ch La Fleur-Pétrus Magnum, excellent level. Very deep, glorious colour; strangely attractive linseed oil and mint smell and taste. The bouquet developed in the glass, perfectly lovely after an hour. A dry, powerful chewy wine. Very good in its way ***

Ch La Gaffelière Beautiful: rich, ruby centre; glorious fruit, almost literally blossomed in glass; medium-sweet, medium-full body, ripe fruit, lovely dry finish and aftertaste. Perfection *****

Ch Grand La Lagune One, bottled by Cockburn & Campbell, rich, chewy but inelegant, the other with strange fragrance.
*At best***

Ch Haut-Bailly Magnum, very high level. Fabulous colour; ripe, scented, earthy Graves nose and tobacco flavour. Lacking concentration but with great style and good aftertaste ****

Ch Kirwan Both Bordeaux bottled by Schröder & Schÿler. Rich; fragrant cedar and Cabernet; good, crisp, fairly long dry finish ****

Ch Lafon-Rochet Two bottles, different sources. Both with upper mid-shoulder level. One teak-coloured; singed, vinous nose which later smelled like an old ashtray. Dry, rich but decayed. The other drying out but more delicate.
*At best***

Ch Nenin Two bottles. One with overripe pigsty smell (butyric acid) and raw, the other slightly better.
*At best**

Ch La Pointe Fabulous colour; initial whiff of bananas cleared to reveal marvellous fruit, rich yet delicate. Great vinosity, lovely texture, good length
***** and will develop further.*

Ch Pichon-Longueville, Lalande A pair, one Selection Nicolas', top-shoulder, fabulously deep colour; rich fully-developed mocca bouquet; fullish, singed coffee bean flavour, lots of tannin. And an upper-shoulder Raymond Baudouin Selection, rich, slightly deeper but with a whiff of volatile acidity.
*At best****

Ch La Tour-Carnet Two bottles, the first with a curiously attractive, fragrant, raw blackcurrant scent; slightly sweet, fullish, fruity, crisp and flavoury. The other similar, with an appealing raspberry-like aroma ***

Ch La Tour-de-Mons Magnum, high level. Glorious cedar and ruby colour; fabulous bouquet; full, rich, plump, complete, good length *****

1946

Previously described as more of an "odd" than "off"

vintage. Late flowering, summer hot enough but very wet the first half of Sept. Late picking in hot Oct sun.

Ch Lafite Tasted once, at Flatt's Lafite tasting. Top-shoulder. Deep, rich, fine mature colour; sweet, fully evolved vanilla fudge bouquet, soft fruit, then caramelly; slightly sweet, fuller body than expected, chewy, tannic, lacking elegance and length but otherwise surprisingly good.
*Oct 1988*****

Ch Latour Several notes. Opaque, astringent, 'black strap', impressive in 1964; good bottles in late 1960 to mid-1976 though twist of raw acidity noted. A very good recorked bottle ex-château at the Fête du Ch Latour tasting in 1981: very sound, finished dry and a bit short. Most recently an oxidised bottle.
*Last tasted March 1989. At best****

Ch Mouton-Rothschild Certainly not an off-vintage taste. Deeper and more drinkable than the '45 in 1971, lively and lean in 1976, an excellent if trifle austere *Réserve du Château* bottle at Flatt's Mouton tasting in 1986 and, coincidentally, earning almost identical marks at the Latour/Mouton tasting in Wiesbaden. Deep, attractive, still some red. At both recent tastings, initial spiciness blurred by what I thought might be mercaptan, but both cleared and opened up. Touch of sweetness leading to dry yet spicy finish. Rich. Chewy. Pretty good fruit.
*Last tasted March 1989*****

Ch Lascombes Richly coloured; fascinating, rich nose, with cedar and fruit; sweet, soft, rather gravelly old flavour, some acidity but good.
*At the Rouët cellar pre-sale tasting March 1985****

Ch La Mission-Haut-Brion Four, first in 1978, all from the Woltner family cellars. Lovely colour, ruby centre; dusty vanillin nose; dry, lean, flavoury but tannic and acidic. Most recently too brown, dry, rich but oxidised.
*Last tasted June 1990. At best****

1947*****

One of the famous post-war trio. Totally different in style from the concentrated '45s and superbly elegant '49s. Renowned for ripeness richness and softness, but acidity always knocking at the door as a result of the very hot vintage conditions. Harvesting from Sept 19 in almost tropical conditions. Exceptionally high sugar content and almost overripe grapes making opulent, heady wines.

Delicious in the mid-1950s and, if stored well, still providing an exciting mouthful. Some have coped better with the innate risky, though exciting and enlivening, acidity.

Ch Lafite 14 notes, fairly consistent. A beautiful, well-balanced wine in the late 1950s. Not deep, always fairly maturing-looking. By the mid-1980s further evolution of bouquet which, in turn, developed in the glass. Touches of iodine, iron, vanilla, 'medicinal' Pauillac but always fragrant. Sweetish, a full-flavoured wine with elegance and power, and excellent acidity. The best probably the magnum at a Marin County Wine & Food Society dinner in 1986.
*Last tasted Oct 1988**** to***** Fully mature.*

Ch Margaux Seven variable notes. Beautifully drinkable by the late 1950s, but a couple in the mid-1960s: "lacking Margaux femininity and charm", then "surprisingly big and coarse". Always a deep, richly coloured, combining power and delicacy in 1970s. One with slightly singed bouquet belching out heat, but a bit malty, and another, perfect, at the Desai Margaux tasting. In 1988, two bottled by Hankey Bannister, one oxidised, the other showing age though mellow and attractive. Most recently, Belgian-bottled, van der Meulen: tawny; extraordinary honeyed fruit; very sweet, a bit souped up but in excellent condition.
*Last tasted Sept 1990. At best*****

Ch Latour 12 notes: a brief "very big wine" in 1954, three, variable in the 1960s, one over-volatile; three variable in the 1970s, with noticeable acidity again in two of them. Better notes in the 1980s: consistently deep and rich-looking, more red than the '45; a bricky, gnarled oak, cheese-rind bouquet. Fairly full-bodied, still powerful, excellent flavour retaining tannin and considerable acidity.
*Last two notes at the Frericks/Wodarz vertical of Latour and Mouton in March 1989**** A rich roller coaster, needs drinking.*

Ch Mouton-Rothschild First tasted in 1961, then still youthful. Since then, nine mainly admiring notes, save for one corky and strained. At its peak between 1969 and 1979. A fairly deep, attractive translucency. Its best feature a fabulously fragrant Mouton bouquet. Touch of sweetness on palate, losing weight, lightly fruity, lacking great length but with very good aftertaste.
*Also last noted at the Mouton/Latour tasting in March 1989**** Still attractive.*

Ch Haut-Brion Few notes. "far too strong" in 1957. Maturing considerably, stylish though hard in 1971.
Doubtless fully mature: drink now.

Ch Ausone A lovely magnum in 1976 and a very attractive bottle at Flatt's Ausone tasting. Never very deep, now palish, broad, open, orange-tinged; strange bouquet that speedily opened out fragrantly, holding well thereafter. Refreshing acidity. A lot to it.
*Last tasted Oct 1987**** Drink up.*

Ch Cheval-Blanc I have tasted this monumental wine nearly two dozen times. Whilst admiring it, wonderously, I like it less and less as a drink. In the late 1950s: sheer perfection, very rich, knocking the first-growth Médocs into a cocked hat by the mid-1960s. Four very good Harvey's bottlings straddled across three decades and two rather acidic Belgian bottlings by J van der Meulen in 1977, several excellent château-bottled magnums and a curious marie-jeanne. Still virtually opaque; a proportionately vast nose, ripe mulberries, liquorice and lint bandages, figs and, occasionally, mushrooms. A sweet, full, rich, loaded yet soft, wine. High alcohol, extract, tannin and acidity. I now find it too port-like.
*Last tasted Sept 1989. At best***** Drink up, or keep for the next generation.*

Ch Pétrus First drunk in 1971: rich, rounded, fabulous wine. A drier, leaner Belgian-bottled wine in 1977. Full marks in magnum at Frericks' in 1986 and again, in bottle, at the recent 'Stockholm' vertical. Very deep, with very mature rim; rich, ripe, stolid, slightly malty nose; very sweet, very full-bodied, almost burning with alcohol, chunky, laden with tannin and acidity. Magnificent.
*Last tasted April 1990***** Perfection. Will keep.*

Ch Baret An unclassified Graves. Two bottles from the château, one with cork weevil and touch of sourness, the other deep, mature, with coffee-like nose; soft, pleasing.
*Last tasted Nov 1983****

Ch Batailley Perfectly balanced, a "wine of great character" in 1955, and, 35 years later, still deep, slightly chocolaty, with rich extract and high alcohol.
*Last tasted June 1989****

Ch Calon-Ségur Six notes. A "lovely big wine" in 1954, deep, sweet and complete by the mid-1970s, one slightly ullaged and overblown in 1980. Recently two excellent bottles, shipped by Dourthe and bottled by Kjaer and Sommerfeldt, from the Aalholm cellars. Deep and rich in appearance, nose and taste. Excellent, toasted, bouquet; sweetish, still tannic.

*Last tasted Sept 1989*****

Ch Cantenac-Brown A lively, chocolaty, sweet, cheesy double-magnum at a Rodenstock tasting. On the edge.

*Tasted Sept 1986** Risky.*

Ch Canon Consistently well made wine. Deepish, warm, fully developed powdery chocolaty bouquet; sweet, soft, perfect.

*June 1989******

Ch Ducru-Beaucaillou Four notes. Seemed best in the 1960s. By 1973 a touch of overripeness and acidity. Most recently, a magnum, still opaque; a whiff of old age but with attractive citrus bouquet; marvellous sweetness and flavour, 1959 weight but noticeable acidity.

*Last drunk at the château, Sept 1982*** but well past its best. Drink up.*

Ch Figeac Soft and lovely in 1986 and a good magnum from the château at the recent Desai Figeac tasting. Rich, meaty, glorious, almost overwhelming bouquet. Sweetish, fairly full-bodied, good tannin and acidity. Beautiful.

*Last tasted Dec 1989******

Ch La Fleur First admired in 1955. A rich but slightly crumbling Harvey bottling in 1974, then a fully mature and charming bottling by Cruse's London agents. A drier but well-balanced Belgian bottling in 1977, and a superlative Danish wine – shipped by Cruse, bottled by Schalburg – from the Aalholm cellar: rich to eye, to nose, to palate. Sweetish, enormous body, high extract, still tannic. Perfection. Not surprisingly, Baron Raben's favourite wine.

*Last tasted Aug 1987***** Will keep.*

Ch La Fleur-Pétrus 'Premier grand 1er cru, Haut Pomerol'. Two notes. Deep, fine, rich, mature in appearance, on nose and taste. Thoroughly ripe and fleshy – yet firm.

*Last tasted Dec 1980*****

Ch Haut-Bailly Three bottles at dinner, all top-shoulder, consistent. Hardly any red left; restrained bouquet which developed the old stable and biscuity smell I associate with good old claret. An end-burst of almost Mouton-like fruit. Delicate, overall sweet, good length, nice acidity.

*At Peter Wallenberg's in Sweden, March 1987*****

Ch La Mission-Haut-Brion Six notes since 1973 and all, I suspect, from the Woltners' private cellars. An almost opaque magnum at Desai's tasting; rich, ripe, very scented bouquet; sweet, lively, crammed with flavour. Drank well long after opening. Most recently: deep; intriguing cedar and tobacco; fleshy with length.

*Last noted at Wolf's tasting, June 1990******

Ch Montrose Still fairly deep; attractive, mature, fragrant sea breeze and leather bouquet; full-bodied, plump, firm core but velvet cladding. Lovely.

*Last tasted Aug 1984*****

Ch Palmer Four notes between 1955 and 1966. Three, bottled by Harveys, were soft and fruity but on the verge of cracking up. More recently, I presume château bottled: a beautiful colour, still sporting a shade of cherry red; heavenly bouquet, rich, mealy, high-toned, living dangerously; sweet, fragrant, glorious, the touch of '47 acidity giving it a fillip.

*Last noted at a Castle Hotel, Taunton, Wine Weekend, Nov 1985**** Drink up.*

Ch Pichon-Baron Rather tart in 1955 and two astringent notes in the 1970s. Most recently a good bottle from Aalholm Castle. Level into neck. Fine deep rich appearance, nose and taste. Slightly chocolaty. Good length. Deft touch of tannin and acidity.

*Last tasted July 1989, at best****

Ch Pontet-Canet Never château bottled. Always either bottled by Cruse, the proprietors, in Bordeaux or shipped in cask. Lovely Pauillac nose but still rather 'green' in 1956. A beautiful, well-preserved Cruse-bottled jeroboam in 1973. Overripeness and fragrance noted in 1978. Lively-looking, 'singed', rich but slightly tart in the early 1980s, and a fairly intense-looking, rich, ripe-smelling double-magnum spoiled by slight woodiness. Even baked brie could not tame its raw acidity.

*Last noted May 1986. Now** and cracking up.*

Ch Rausan-Ségla Two elegant, flavoury bottles, late 1970s. Most recently: opaque, intense; stalky, volatile; dry, raw.

*Last tasted Jan 1991. At best*****

Ch Talbot Seven notes, first – very attractive – in 1968. Two, shipped by Cruse and London bottled by their London agents were also very attractive despite whiff of volatile acidity. Three quite recently: a superb château bottling at a Christie's pre-sale tasting in Chicago – fully evolved but sheer perfection, and a couple from Aalholm, shipped by Cordier, bottled by Carl Permins, excellent levels, very mature-looking, typical Talbot ripe hen-house nose; soft, delicious *à point* but one a bit sharp-ended.

*Last tasted Sept 1989, at best*****

Other post-1980 notes:

Ch Beauséjour-Bécot Very deep; magnificent, huge, fleshy in 1982 ****

Ch Haut-Sarpe Five variable notes all in the early 1980s. A deep rich-vintage colour, bouquet at best creamy, rich but tending to crack up. Mainly sweet and spicy, sometimes creaking and *passé*.

*Last tasted July 1983. At best****

Ch Smith-Haut-Lafitte Shipped by Eschenauer, the proprietor, bottled by Schalberg. High level, perfect colour; sweet, honeyed, lingering bouquet and flavour. Bit of an acidic bite at the end.

July 1989.

Ch La Tour du Pin-Figeac Deep, fruity, stylish, attractive.

*Sept 1983****

Ch Trottevieille Vanilla and liquorice bouquet, spicy but a bit lean and past its best.

*June 1989***

1948***

A strange, never popular vintage. Perverse due to baking heat in May then a miserable June, causing *coulure*. July opened cold but warmed up. Aug cold and wet. Rot set in. Sept was fine, warm and dry.

Ch Lafite 10 notes, from 1954 "lovely wine", mellow but a bit short in late 1950s, flavoury in the 1960s, exciting and stylish but showing age in the late 1970s, a superb marie-jeanne dining at Lafite in 1985, and high marks at Flatt's tasting. Surprisingly satisfactory. Still well coloured, fully mature; beautiful bouquet, variously described as delicate, fragrant, tangerine and oyster, developing marvellously with air; crisp, still tannic, overall dry. Flavour like red Graves, dry leaf, bracken-like – yet very attractive.

*Last noted at a Bordeaux Club dinner at Christ's College, Cambridge, Nov 1989*****

Ch Margaux First tasted in 1975, rich but high acidity.

Five years later: very deep, with a red tinge, mature-looking; delicate, perfectly harmonious bouquet; dry, certainly not a beefy '48, notably fragrant, tannic.
*Last tasted Feb 1980*****
Ch Latour Big, dark and 'green' in 1956 then not tasted again until 1971. Variable: spicy, pronounced Cabernet aroma, strong, austere, zestful but astringent. Judging from nine well spread notes, a powerful, assertive wine displaying the raw, tannic side of the '48s.
*Last tasted March 1989. At best*****
Ch Mouton-Rothschild Four notes. Fabulously rich bouquet, surprisingly green and unready in 1969. A magnum showing well at Flatt's Mouton tasting in 1986, particularly its beautifully developed nose. Almost identical marks at the Mouton/Latour tasting in Wiesbaden: still deep, attractive; lovely Mouton aroma, rich, scented, roses; medium weight, assertive, fruity yet 'dried leaves' like Lafite '48, still tannic.
*Last tasted March 1989*****
Ch Cheval-Blanc 12 notes. Black strap, unready and, though good, not very appealing in the early 1960s. By the mid-1980s well-nigh perfect: fabulously deep colour, citrus-like fragrance, surprisingly sweet, full-bodied, with perfect flavour, richness and balance. A rather sour-cream, black treacly nosed, pungent magnum in 1986, an eccentric Avery-bottling a year later: opaque; smell of singed raisins — reminded me of an Australian liqueur muscat, thick, tannin masked by high extract. More like port. The last four, Danish-bottled by K Dorf Petersen from the cellars at Aalholm Castle. Baron Raben had three bins full, 182 bottles, their labels and levels all perfect. Deep, richly coloured; soft gentle nose which opened up with a strawberry-like fragrance; sweet, rich, soft, lovely flavour, tannin and acidity.
*Last noted at pre-sale tasting, Sept 1989*****
Ch Pétrus First noted at Frerick's tasting in Munich in 1986. Black plum colour; singed; sweaty, almost sickly sweet nose; huge, tough, tannic. Impressive but. . . .
Next and last tasted at the 'Stockholm' vertical May 1990.
Ch Baret Despite cork weevil and a slightly reduced level, a good rich colour, earthy Graves character, sweeter and milder than expected.
Sept 1983.
Ch Ducru-Beaucaillou Only tasted once: rich, mature colour; fragrant, overripe, classic bouquet; dry, lean, very flavoury but raw. I thought it was Lafite '34.
*Oct 1984****
Ch La Mission-Haut-Brion One of the top '48s, though I have had one oxidised and one austere brackish bottle. Perfect in the early 1960s, fabulous in 1978. Incredibly deep-coloured; very fine, rich, gingery bouquet; typically earthy Graves flavour, dry, fragrant aftertaste. Latterly assertive but austere.
*Last tasted June 1990*****

1949*****

A thoroughly exciting great classic vintage, the third of the magnificent post-war trio. Due in part to mature vines and traditional winemaking by experienced Maîtres. Jan and Feb the driest on record; cold and rain during flowering caused disastrous *coulure* though late June was fine. July the hottest and driest ever; Aug too dry. Sept stormy. Fine for harvest late Sept. Fine, supple, well-balanced wines produced. The best still superb.
Ch Lafite Light, lacking fruit and disappointing when first tasted, with three similar notes in 1955. Then a jump to 1970: a bottle recorked at Ch Latour in 1968. Again, disappointing, astringent. Since then, nearly 20 notes, most sizes of bottle and some variation. A little too often piquant, somewhat over-acidic, not always showing at its best. But six of the last seven notes, all in the 1980s, have been good: medium-deep, lovely, mature appearance; delicate, fragrant essences, sometimes an almost burgundian vegetal scent (Los Angeles, 1983), apricots; on the palate generally noted as sweet, ripe, delicate, smooth texture, rich yet touch of leanness. Certainly very high marks at Flatt's Lafite tasting in 1988. An exciting, excitable '49.
*Last tasted Aug 1989. At best******
Ch Margaux 10 notes. Soft and rounded in the mid-1950s. A creaking Chalié Richards bottling in 1970, a very good, elegant Block Grey and Block bottling from a nobleman's cellar in 1986. Since then I have noted its pretty colour, fully evolved fragrant bouquet, distinct sweetness on palate, perfect weight and flavour, great length and dry finish.
*Last tasted Sept 1989, at its best, and as it should be******
Ch Latour Over two dozen mainly admiring notes. A dark, big, raw wine in 1954. It started to bloom, silky textured, fruity yet still loaded in the late 1960s, then several magnificent magnums towards the end of the next decade. One or two raw and acidic (badly kept?); one fragrant on nose but hard and woody. Four mid-1980s notes all good: still fairly deep, ruby-tinged — youthful for age; exciting, often exquisite, rich Cabernet bouquet; full-bodied yet fully developed, lots of fruit, sweet entry, dry fragrant finish. A recent bottle, at the Latour/Mouton tasting was a bit maderised and austere.
*Last tasted March 1989, at best***** mainly **** Not as great as the '45 but will continue to develop.*
Ch Mouton-Rothschild A supremely beautiful wine from start to finish. 17 rave-review notes — just one woody bottle in 1985. Its hallmark, from the mid-1950s to the 1980s, has been its fragrance and delicacy; at its best, seemingly from the early 1970s to the present and doubtless beyond. Recent notes: very deep, rich, intense colour with good mature rim; an archetypal Mouton nose, immediately forthcoming, sweet, spicy, exquisite, developing a richly unusual scent of tea and rose leaves. Touch of sweetness, by no means a heavyweight, combining softness, delicacy, charm and a certain femininity.
*Last tasted March 1989******
Ch Haut-Brion Over a dozen rather variable notes. Distinctly green and unready in the mid-1950s, pleasing, refreshing in 1960s, its bouquet becoming sweeter in the 1970s when I noted a very rich, complex, earthy, though still slightly astringent palate. Happily showing well at the sale at Christie's in 1985 to mark the 50th anniversary of Haut-Brion's purchase by the Dillon family. More recent notes: still deep, almost '45-like intensity and '28 Haut-Brion density; very fragrant earthy, tobacco-leaf and clover honey bouquet; fairly sweet, chewy, concentrated, the characteristic Graves bracken and tobacco taste, with an unsuspected acidity lurking beneath.
*Last tasted Oct 1947, at best**** Needs drinking.*
Ch Ausone One bottle soft yet tannic and classic, and another full-flavoured but acidic in the mid-1950s. Strange, singed, characterful and a very attractive drink in the early 1970s, and showing well at Flatt's Ausone tasting. Never my style of wine, the most idiosyncratic of all the first growths, it seems to look old and brown from the start, though often impressively deep. Strange old nose, open, cheesy, rich — develops spiciness. On the last occasion sweetish, nice weight, flavour perfect in its way,

soft, fleshy with good length and finish.
*Last noted Oct 1987*** to**** Almost a matter of taste.*
Ch Cheval-Blanc Nearly 30 notes. It is superb. In 1954, when first tasted, I noted it "more rounded and advanced than (the good) '50. Very pricy". Noted as a "sapling" and disappointing in Jan 1959 and "beautifully balanced one of the best '49s", only 10 months later. Must have been me rather than bottle variation. One or two English bottled: a tart Harvey's half-bottle, a fabulous rich Justerini & Brooks in 1978 and two excellent Corney & Barrows. The wine gained in stature as it aged, seeming to reach its apogee in the mid-1980s, give or take one or two oxidised (château) bottles. Recent notes, summarised: very richly coloured, a glorious *tuillé* or Provençal tile red, beautifully graduated; sweet, scented cedar and warm brick bouquet, truffles noted (at Overton's 50th birthday dinner, a jeroboam). Taste to match. Distinctly sweet, soft, harmonious, *à point*. A great '49.
*Last tasted Sept 1990. At best******
Ch Pétrus The first of my four notes was made at Frerick's tasting in 1986. The '49 got my top marks. This really is a very great wine. Deep, impressive, mulberry-coloured; ripe mulberry-like bouquet too. Sweet, full, soft, velvety yet with life-sustaining grip. Perfect.
*Last tasted May 1990******
Ch Beychevelle At its elegant best. It even looks elegant, never deep, even aged 10, despite full flavour and youthful bite. Very drinkable in 1965, a superb magnum in 1974 but a somewhat unbalanced bottle the following year. Most recently a marvellous Berry Bros bottling: fine mature colour; lovely bouquet and flavour, Lafite weight, gentle dry finish. Elegant, elegant, elegant.
*Last tasted March 1983. At best***** and worth looking out for.*
Ch Bouscaut Three notes. Curiously attractive. Most recently, at the château, very deep with brick red rim; interesting bouquet, whiff of raspberry then of black treacle; dry, gravelly, pebbly Graves character, a bit dried out but sound.
*Last tasted Sept 1986***
Ch Cantemerle In 1966, 1977 and 1983, its first notable feature a marvellous colour, deepish, garnet tinge; next its exquisite, perfumed, flowery bouquet; elegant, flavoury, thinning a little but, for me, what claret is all about.
*Last tasted May 1983*****
Ch Certan Certainly a Pomerol year. Soft and velvety in 1974. Most recently, shipped by Cruse and bottled by Rutherford's, their London agents: top-shoulder; medium, rich, fully mature; showing age initially, but rich, sweet, beetroot-like, developing beautifully; on the palate sweet, lightish, rounded, fragrant. A charmer.
*Last tasted Jan 1989*****
Ch La Conseillante Two notes. First, as it should be, a stunningly beautiful wine. More recently a curious semi-oxidised bottle, too brown, nose like beef extract, sweetish, massive, drinkable—just.
*Last tasted April 1982. At best*****
Ch Cos d'Estournel Showing promise in 1954. Three attractive but slightly acidic Justerini & Brooks bottlings in 1969/1970. Most recently: medium, mature; ripe, 'ivy leaves' like a rare old Beychevelle, even Lafite; delicate, good length, still supported by tannin and acidity though the latter is taking over. I rated it highly as a drink.
*Last tasted March 1984*****
Ch Figeac Very exciting. Noted twice in mid-1950s: a big black but smooth wine, and thrice in the 1980s. Still fabulously deep with a lively, almost youthful, ruby tinge; one however (in 1986) was woody and smelled like an abandoned ashtray. More recently, crisp fruity bouquet, flavour. Lastly arguably the top wine at Desai's Figeac tasting in Paris. Opaque, intense; lovely, fragrant, spicy Cabernet Sauvignon fruit; medium sweetness and weight, raspberries and cream flavour, perfect balance, gorgeous aftertaste.
*Last tasted Dec 1989***** and time in hand.*
Ch Grand-Puy-Lacoste Like Cantemerle, a superbly run estate at this time. Deep, ruby, lively; superb fruit; dry.
*Feb 1988*****
Ch Gruaud-Larose 10 notes. Soft and pleasing even in 1952, a hint of Burgundy in 1953, delicious, fruity in 1974. 10 years later a magnum, more complex, very flavoury. Then variously noted as "elegant", "soft", "velvet", "perfect balance" and, in the 1980s, still not a poor bottle. Château bottled, mulberry ripe, fleshy, still elegant. Two superb Block Grey and Block bottlings: still deep, plummy, intense; waxy, cedary, no faults; sweet, mouthfilling, soft, lovely fruit. Perfection.
*Last tasted May 1987***** Will last.*
Ch Lynch-Bages Several notes over the past 25 years. Magnificent but still a bit 'green' in 1961. Described for the first time as the 'poor man's Mouton' in the mid-1970s. Two variable bottles recently: one deep, lively; a citrus fruit bouquet; and sweet warm, spicy—a lovely wine, the other paler, showing more maturity and caramelised.
*Last tasted April 1987. At best*****
Ch La Mission-Haut-Brion A great '49 and, in the opinion of the Woltners, the best ever La Mission. Equalling their '29. Eight notes, first in 1971, all, I think, from the Woltner family cellars. All superb. A magnificent magnum at Desai's tasting in 1985: sweet, full, fleshy. An almost exaggerated fine red Graves flavour reminiscent of toasted bracken, dried leaves, tobacco.
*Last tasted June 1990******
Ch Montrose For me, the high period of this *2ème cru* St-Estèphe. Huge, magnificent, rather austere in 1972. Still very deep, intense; the smell of a fine mature claret. Bottle-age but no faults. Sweet, gentle nose; sweet, smooth and ripe on the palate. Silky leathery tannins, wonderful length, spicy. A joy to drink.
*Last tasted April 1985*****
Ch Palmer Advanced enough to enjoy in the early 1950s. "Lovely, sweetish" noted at the château on our first visit to Bordeaux in 1955. Most recently in magnums, both with very good levels. Fairly deep; rich colour, nose and flavour. Fully evolved, waxy, cedar cigar box and old leather bouquet which then soured. Wonderful ripeness though a hint of decay.
*Last tasted Nov 1980*****
Ch Rausan-Ségla First briefly noted in 1954. Several bottles at a big dinner in 1980. On my table it was excellent: very deep, magnificent colour; scents of cedar, tobacco, smoky, stably, touch of cheese rind (if these smells do not sound very appetising, in combination they make up a glorious mature Margaux bouquet); soft, at peak. Dry leathery-tannic finish. Others had poorer bottles. Another pair three years later, one corked, the other still intensely coloured, a bouquet that opened up, but though a good flavour, dried out and disappointing. Most recently: very deep, ripe, powerhouse of fragrance, sweetish, rich, lovely, elegant but tannic.
*Last tasted Jan 1991. At best*****
Ch Talbot In 1962 mature-looking, high-toned, silky. A certain austerity and astringency noted then and in the mid-1970s. Two excellent, impressively deep, rather

severe and masculine bottles from the Cordier cellars in 1981 and, more recently, showing some age and rawness though with a classic Cabernet nose.
*Last tasted Oct 1984, at best****
Also tasted in the 1980s:
Ch Baret Graves. Opaque, rich, very flavoury, with tannic acid finish.
Ch Duhart-Milon Fragrant, silky texture, nice weight and balance, creaking a bit but good.
Ch Larcis-Ducasse Thick, tawny, sweet but over-the-hill.
Ch La Tour-de-Grenet Lussac St-Emilion. Another Danish-bottled wine from Aalholm. Despite excellent level, a bit odd. Nose developed well, but somewhat overblown. A minor wine doubtless at its best in the 1950s.

1950**

In the hungry-for-stock post-war years of rationing and restrictions, the British trade took aboard the abundant 1950s. Useful wines. Many notes in that decade, fewer since.
Ch Lafite Lovely nose, lightish, attractive, supple and a good drink in 1959, two similar in 1962 but piquant acidity noted in 1965. Bouquet of 'cold tea', light, flavoury in 1975. Most recently, a magnum: medium, mature; light, showing age, then fragrant and biscuity, fully evolved bouquet within the hour; attractive, very Lafite weight and flavour. Dry, slightly acidic finish. A good refreshing drink but not a great '50.
*Last noted during lunch at Lafite, June 1988****
Ch Margaux Justifiably reputed to be one of the best '50s. 12 notes, first in 1956: lightish, good. A quick developer, its colour maturing and already fragrant, soft and attractive by the early 1960s but continuing delightfully through the 1970s, ripening nicely. I thought it was at its peak in 1973 but a magnum at Desaï's Margaux tasting was delectable. Never deep in colour it smelled at first like wet cardboard, a bit edgy but after minutes in the glass revived, generating the inimitable gentle Margaux fragrance. A wine of elegance and charm. Lovely flavour. Exquisite aftertaste.
*Last noted May 1987**** Drink soon.*
Ch Latour First tasted in 1960 when though fairly full-bodied was, surprisingly for Latour, nice to drink at that age. Its strength noted through the 1960s, fine but peppery. Completely satisfactory in the early 1970s, lovely silkiness and perfect balance. Later more cedary, more earthy, some colour loss. By La Fête du Château Latour in 1981 it had a pretty colour, complex, fragrant Cabernet nose, some sweetness, flavoury but no great length. At the Frericks/Wodarz Latour and Mouton tasting it was rich but not deep; quite good Pauillac cedar bouquet but little development; flavoury, with a lightly peppery acidic finish. On the decline.
*Last tasted March 1989. Now***
Ch Mouton-Rothschild First tasted in 1956: a cassis nose "rather like Malescot". A "wine to drink" (not to lay down). Consistently lovely nose in the 1970s but noted as drying out, thin, austere on the palate. In the mid-1980s, still a lovely, lively ruby colour; strange piquant Cabernet nose, open, attractive, appealing, but faded within 30 minutes. The palate sound, a bit austere, lean, tannic and lacking length. Otherwise a good drink.
*Last noted at Flatt's Mouton tasting, April 1986****
Ch Haut-Brion No recent notes. Rich and attractive in 1975.
Probably still quite nice.
Ch Ausone Tasted only twice, with a 30-year gap. Fragrant, a good drink in 1957, and a lively, though very mature-looking bottle from Aalholm at Flatt's Ausone tasting. Curious unharmonious bouquet and odd, shortish flavour, though both nose and palate improved in the glass.
*Last tasted Oct 1987**
Ch Cheval-Blanc 20 notes. A poor start with a woody Saccone & Speed bottling in 1954 but pleasing the following year despite little bouquet. Seemed to go through a long, under-developed period, noted variously as "green" and "raw" right through the 1960s, despite looking mature. Variable notes in the 1970s, two volatile, disappointing, château-bottled, and another two agreeable Bordeaux-bottled. It did however keep its colour, "red for age", "good ruby", "surprisingly deep" noted in the 1980s, whereas, though fragrant, the bouquet showed its age. Storage conditions apart, some of the inconsistencies due to poor late bottlings. A volatile, varnishy J Lyons', a slightly raw, lean Harvey's bottling; both tasted in 1983. The best was a Corney & Barrow half-bottle in 1982, with a deep colour and sheen; fragrant, elegant, lovely flavour but drying out. Lastly a rich château-bottled magnum, very forthcoming though a bit overripe, soft, easy and a bit lactic.
*Last tasted Sept 1986. Average** Chancy.*
Ch Pétrus A good reputation from the start. Only tasted once: a fine, deep, plummy, still youthful appearance (tasted blind, I thought it was the '48); bouquet of tea and mint, a bit peppery on nose and palate. A very powerful, spicy wine.
*At the 'Stockholm' tasting, April 1990*****
Ch Beychevelle Tasted twice: light, fruity, pleasant and good value in 1954 and, 35 years later, palish, over-mature orange amber rim; fragrant medicinal Médoc bouquet; light, easy, lean-skinned, its initial flesh lost — but good length.
*Last tasted April 1989****
Ch Figeac Opaque, packed with fruit, still tannic after 15 years. Dark; spicy, Latour-like Cabernet Sauvignon nose; rich, malty but tannic in the mid-1980s. Most recently, from the château: still surprisingly deep, cherry red, fairly intense; peppery, Cabernet nose, developing crisp blackberry-like fragrance; full-bodied but rather raw and tannic.
*Last noted at Desaï's tasting Dec 1989. At best*** Drying out.*
Ch La Fleur-Pétrus Surprisingly deep; unknit bouquet showing age and decay, though a slightly sweet, soft and very pleasant flavour. Touch of bitterness.
*Dec 1980***
Ch Le Gay First tasted, château-bottled, in 1972: firm, delicate, touch of volatile acidity but lovely flavour. Most recently, Avery-bottled: palish, fully mature; an initial whiff of volatile acidity which blew away revealing lovely 'warm brick' fragrance; medium sweetness and weight, sound, attractive, nice silky texture.
*With Tony Mitchell at Dyrham Park, April 1984*****
Ch La Mission-Haut-Brion One of the richest and best of all the '50s. Tasted 10 times including two good Harvey's bottlings in the 1960s. A consistently deep coloured, rich, earthy wine noted as of "1st growth calibre" in the early 1970s but showing some age on the nose later that decade. An intensely deep magnum with sweet bouquet and flavour, rich, marvellous fruit but ending with a question mark at Desaï's tasting in 1985. Most recently, a bottle from the Woltner cellars, still very deeply coloured; low-keyed but sound, peppery Cabernet nose; sweet and surprisingly plump, fleshy and

rounded. Much better than Haut-Brion.
*Last tasted in Wiesbaden, June 1990*****
Ch Palmer Seven variable notes. Slightly piquant, tannic, Harvey's bottlings in 1955 and 1956, a so-so château bottling in 1970 and four in the 1980s, all shipped by Sichel & Co, but bottlers unknown. All past best, drying out but flavoury.
*Last tasted Sept 1987**

1951

Terrible, the worst post-war vintage and one of the most disastrous ever. Inclement weather: cold, wet spring, foul June, July hot but thundery, Aug very cold, Sept some hot days, cold nights resulting in unripe grapes. Thin, meagre, acid wines.
Ch Lafite Just two notes from the 1980s. Fairly pale, bright, ruddy tinged; light medicinal 'dried leaves' bouquet, but fragrant and flavoury despite a thin mouth-curling acidity.
Last at Flatt's tasting, Oct 1988.
Ch Latour Eight less than complimentary notes, raw in 1955, dull in the 1960s, two austere but not bad in the 1970s. Three totally oxidised, one with grape rot on the nose. Frankly awful.
*Last sniffed, but not tasted, March 1989 minus **
Ch Mouton-Rothschild Three notes: green and raw in 1963 and a passable upper-shoulder level bottle with surprisingly good colour; low-keyed, sound, fragrant, gingery nose; some sweetness, light, good flavour though lean, lacking length and marked tannin and acidity.
Last noted at Flatt's Mouton tasting, April 1986.
Ch La Mission-Haut-Brion Palish, weak-rimmed; light, delicate, vanilla nose; dry, light and acidic. Even Henri Woltner had his hands tied by the appalling weather.
At Desai's, Feb 1985.
Ch Baret An unclassified red Graves showing better than expected. Despite short cork and signs of weevil, a better colour than the '52, little fruit but some fragrance, albeit like damp cardboard. Dry, light, lean, surprisingly flavoury.
*Three notes in 1983**

1952** *to* ****

Opening promisingly, the over-tannic Médocs have retained their hardness, despite good fruit, whilst some superb St-Emilions and Pomerols were made, and have survived. A warm, promising spring, with exceptionally good flowering conditions and a hot summer. Sept, however, was cold and the mid-month harvest took place in unfavourable conditions. This was a vintage of considerable variation in quality, style and condition. Apart from La Mission and the better right bank wines, not a vintage to get excited about.
Ch Lafite A disappointing wine, though my mid-1960s notes were quite favourable: nice quality, fruit and balance, very flowery, though "astringent" and "earthy tang" creep in later that decade. Variable notes in the 1970s. A rich, ripe-nosed magnum in 1980, austere at Lloyd Flatt's and, more recently, at pre-sale tastings in Chicago: a curious medicinal nose reminding me of bad breath; dry and faded.
*Last tasted Feb 1989, at best*** Drink up.*
Ch Margaux Also lacking the charm of the '53. Eight mainly critical notes. Severe and unforthcoming in the late 1960s, "clenched, holding back" in the early to late 1970s. A richly coloured magnum at Desai's Margaux tasting, with an instantly rich, biscuity scent that faded, lots of grip and tannin. Finally, a surprisingly nice bottle, despite its peripatetic background: imported *Mis en bouteille* by Lorentz Petersen, sold to a Danish customer, exported by Whitwhams to Maison Portier in New York, finally consumed with a renowned Japanese connoisseur at the Imperial Hotel, Tokyo. But it was showing its age.
*Last tasted June 1989** Drink up.*
Ch Latour 18 notes. A bit raw and unready when first tasted in 1962, "surprisingly drinkable" despite its tannin in the mid- to late 1960s, austerity and asperity creeping in to the notes in the mid-1970s. Two poor bottles at the Fête du Château Latour in 1981, one oxidised, the other acidic, doubtless due to poor storage. Of the four most recent, two were soft, rich, spicy, one being overtaken by acidity. Appearance still very deep, rich, mature; nose at first a bit dusty with highish volatile acidity but which developed fragrance; a bit stalky, nice weight, slightly raw on finish.
*Last noted dining at the château, April 1990, now** to*** Drink up.*
Ch Mouton-Rothschild Six notes, all interesting. Packed with fruit but hard in the mid-1960s, silky, leathery-textured, deep and flavoury in the 1970s. In 1986, at Flatt's Mouton tasting: magnificent colour, deep, intense ruby; intriguing bouquet, milky, gingery Cabernet Sauvignon on take-off, holding back a bit after 10 minutes, then fragrant and scented. A fine, firm, masculine wine, still tannic.
*Last tasted April 1986**** Time in hand.*
Ch Haut-Brion Just six notes. A lovely, pronounced and characteristic earthiness in the mid-1960s but, 10 years later, signs of cracking up, very dry and tannic. Characterful but not a patch on La Mission '52.
*Last tasted Feb 1987** Drink up.*
Ch Ausone That 1952 was infinitely more successful in St-Emilion than the Médoc is clearly demonstrated by even that odd-man-out, Ausone. Considered to be light and pleasing, an early developer in 1953, confirmed when I first tasted it in May 1960. Despite its strange colour, pale, almost brown, the result of overripe grapes lacking vivid skin colour, it was in fact very agreeable in the early 1960s. Two excellent Belgian bottlings in 1977, one, bottled by Decannière, firm, well balanced, but with Ausone's idiosyncratic nose, "more root than fruit" I noted, the other a sound van der Meulen bottling. By the early 1980s it was beginning to creak. A good, flavoury but edgy Harvey half bottle, an autumnal looking Avery magnum with varnishy old fruit, overmature, soft but with a sandy texture. Most recently at Flatt's Ausone tasting an oxidised van der Meulen bottling and one, top-shoulder, from the château: rich, healthy appearance despite fully mature brown rim; nose a bit brackish at first but developing a rich, warm old bouquet. Dry, quite a bite, fuller bodied than expected. A survivor.
*Last tasted Oct 1987. At best***
Ch Cheval-Blanc One of the best '52s. Over a dozen notes: a slow starter in 1954, a remarkably fine and drinkable Gloag's (Perth) bottling and silky texture also noted on Harvey's bottlings, all in the early 1960s. Reached its plâteau of perfection in the late 1960s and cruised firmly through the 1970s with time in hand. A perfect bottle, in 1987, very deep, sweetish, lively and again silky. One, oxidised smelling of brown sugar and virol, stewed and port-like on palate. Most recently, an excellent top-shoulder bottle with good long cork. Rich, plummy, red core, fully mature rim; lovely bouquet that held well; still fairly sweet and full, chewy extract. A very

good drink.
*Last noted at a Christie's Boardroom lunch, April 1990**** Though unlikely to improve, it will keep.*
Ch Pétrus Six notes: finely textured, soft but powerful in the mid-1970s, a beautiful bottle at Harry Waugh's Bordeaux Club dinner in April 1987, a fine, deep cherry red; harmonious, fragrant; fairly sweet, high alcohol content but soft and fleshy. Most recently a rather too thick and murky bottle at the Stockholm group Pétrus tasting, oxidised and cracking up.
*Last tasted April 1990. At best******
Ch L'Angélus A most agreeable wine shipped in cask by Calvet, bottled by Kjaer & Sommerfeldt and perfectly cellared at Aalholm Castle. Mature, sweetish, equally perfect weight and balance, demonstrating again how good the '52 St-Emilions can be, how reliable the Copenhagen merchants' bottlings, and the benefit of excellent storage conditions.
*Pre-sale tasting, July 1989*****
Ch Beychevelle A peak period for this château. A deeply coloured; low-keyed but harmonious old bouquet, better when first poured; sweetish, full-bodied, rich yet with dry finish.
*Delicious drink in May 1986*****
Ch Cantemerle One of my favourite châteaux of this period but only two notes: a bit austere in 1971, much later a good bottle, excellent level, palish, gentle, mature appearance; sweet, ripe, slightly cheesy but firm bouquet, getting lighter and softer. Came round nicely in the glass.
*At home, Sept 1984****
Dom de Chevalier A good '52: earthy, lots of grip. Looked like a '61, with some '62-like acidity, fairly full, chunky and peppery.
*Last noted dining at the château, March 1981*** Possibly**** now. Alas, small production, but if found should be very good.*
Ch Figeac Though appearing to mature quickly, with a well-developed nose, it was fairly tannic in the early 1960s. Yet, at Desai's, a bottle from the château still exhibited a fullish, youthful colour; a gentle, harmonious, broad, citrus bouquet though a little dull after the '53 and '55. Very dry, fullish, slightly malty, singed flavour and lots of grip.
*Last tasted Dec 1989*** Will keep.*
Ch Langoa-Barton Nice wine. Tannic when young. A lovely, cedary Justerini & Brooks' bottling in 1974. Most recently, a magnum, bottled by Barton & Guestier: good colour, tannic and masculine.
*Last tasted Nov 1989*** Will keep.*
Ch Léoville-Las-Cases Strangely, rather meagre and light from the start. Still dumb in 1958. Notes in the mid-1960s to mid-1970s depended somewhat on the bottling: some still tough; a British Transport Hotels bottle with curious bouquet and slightly bitter finish; a very attractive, albeit astringent, Avery bottling. The last noted was bottled by K Dorph-Petersen, from Aalholm Castle: high level, medium depth of colour, lovely gradation; warm, deep, classic, cedary bouquet; surprisingly soft and fleshy, nice weight, good but not too intrusive tannin.
*Last tasted July 1989. At best*****
Ch Léoville-Poyferré Eight restrained notes. Even the Maître de Chai preferred his '50. But there had been much replanting, and young vines do not produce wines of quality and depth. I thought it well-balanced in 1956; a wishy-washy, poor (English-bottled?) specimen in the mid-1960s it was made up for by a deep, cedary, tough-yet-rich Avery bottling in 1973 and one or two good château-bottlings. From the mid-1970s it was beginning to creak a bit. A decade later: deep, brown-rimmed; bouquet of dried leaves; dry, still fullish body, but raw and tannic. Neither fruit nor charm.
*Last noted Oct 1985**
Ch La Mission-Haut-Brion One of the best '52s, though I first tasted it when it was over 30 years old. Four notes, two slightly variable bottles at Desai's tasting in 1985: one with hard, tannic, strong, earthy character, the other softer and silkier. In 1988, dry with pronounced tobacco-leaf flavour. Most recently: very deep appearance; sweet, slightly chocolaty nose, with good fruit, developing very rich-extract figgy bouquet, opening up gloriously. I found it sweet, fairly full-bodied, flavour endorsing the bouquet, well balanced. The latter two both ex-Woltner family cellars.
*Last noted at Wolf's La Mission tasting, June 1990. At best***** Drink now to 2000.*
Ch Montrose A consistently big, impressive wine. Deep but vigorous and not browning by the mid-1970s, equally deep and fresh on the nose, and surprising elegance and harmony noted. More recently: still very deep in colour; bouquet opened up in glass; surprisingly sweet for Montrose and for a '52, ripe, its tannin being assimilated though still teeth-gripping.
*Last noted at a Saintsbury Club dinner, Oct 1986**** Drink now to 2000+.*
Ch Pichon-Longueville, Baron Just two notes: a rather severe, tannin laden Chalié Richards' bottling in 1968 and a still tannic but attractive Justerini bottling: top-shoulder level; lovely rich cedar red and mature colour; very good, rich, slightly cheesy bottle-age bouquet; now on the lighter side of medium but soft, fleshy, nice, gentle despite dry tannic finish.
*Pre-sale, May 1987*** Drink now to 2000.*
Other 1952s tasted in 1980s:
Ch Baret Variable, from tough, tannic and malty to quite good.
1989.
Ch Batailley Deep, pleasing.
1980.
Ch Croizet-Bages Old-oak appearance and bouquet though sound, full, rich and surprisingly sweet on palate in May 1986.

1953*****

Undoubtedly my favourite claret vintage. Wines of charm, style, elegance; beautiful for drinking even without food. Happily, a major vintage of my early wine trade career, which is one of the reasons I have over 500 tasting notes. Many wines are still unbelievably beautiful. An early spring dogged by two months of nightly frosts. Flowering started well but cold and rain caused some *coulure*. However the end was hot, thundery weather. Aug was one of the finest in living memory. However, rain delayed the harvest in mid-Sept. It paid to wait. Picking commenced on Oct 2 in perfect weather.
Ch Lafite A wine of infinite delicacy and charm, never robust but a sweet survivor. My first note in 1960. A last minute order in a restaurant, and not decanted, it was dumb, rather green and *just* drinkable. I had not learned in those days about the need for good claret, particularly Lafite, to breathe. Lovely from the mid-1960s, immensely fragrant through the 1970s and 1980s. Bottles, magnums, jeroboams tasted and consumed in England, France and the US. 34 notes, only one being less than admirable. Throughout the 1980s surprisingly deep (for

vintage and for age) with a lively appearance. Consistently lovely bouquet that opens up fragrantly, fully evolved after 30 minutes in glass but holding well thereafter: cedar, sometimes very slightly chocolaty, delicate. Gentle sweetness on the palate also constantly noted: ideal weight and balance, lovely flavour, charm, length. Simply perfect.

*Last tasted Aug 1989***** Despite its delicacy, will survive, like the 1875.*

Ch Margaux Another splendid '53. Condensed and unready in the early 1960s, it developed fairly quickly and by the early 1970s was "rich, deep and velvety". The 13 notes since 1979, five from magnums, have been, with the exception of an odd half-bottle, uniformly ecstatic: sublime, blossomy, very feminine, great length, superb aftertaste. Also, several times recently noted as deeper than expected, though showing considerable maturity. Touch of iodine or oyster shell on the nose evolving into a pure rose scent; fairly sweet, rich, yet delicate and lacy.

*Last tasted in April 1988******

Ch Latour For some reason or other the odd-man-out in 1953, the '52 and, particularly, the '55 being superior. First tasted in 1955, unready. Deep and big in heart towards the end of the 1960s, mouthfillingly delicious and opulent in the early 1970s. Thereafter the notes become more critical: "agreeable but . . .", "four-square", "inelegant". In the 1980s still deep and intense with a lively red tinge; aroma of highly polished eucalyptus, oysters, even clams — certainly a medicinal Pauillac fragrance. Unlike Lafite and Margaux, consistently dry, fullish, a sort of raw fruit, occasionally scrawny, flavoury yet unexciting.

*Last tasted March 1989. Now, at best****

Ch Mouton-Rothschild A luscious wine, almost a caricature of itself. 16 notes. Lovely yet leathery in the early 1960s. Glorious in the 1970s with spicy, gingery Cabernet Sauvignon aroma. Sweet, blackcurrant scented; fleshy exciting, heart on sleeve: the Tchaikovsky of claret. Some acidity beginning to peep through in the mid-1980s but still glowing, glorious, a most exciting drink.

*Last noted at pre-sale, in Chicago, Feb 1989***** Will continue to thrill.*

Ch Haut-Brion First tasted in cask, on my first visit to Bordeaux, summer 1985. Excellent but distinctly different in character and flavour to the first growth Médocs. By the mid-1960s silky, great vinosity, earthy flavour. Seven notes through the 1970s: reaching its plateau of perfection. In the 1980s, medium-deep, lively centre yet almost amber rim; strange coffee, chocolate, earthy, hot-pebbles fragrance, uniquely Haut-Brion; distinctly sweet with singed, earthy, bracken tobacco-like flavour, lovely texture, elegance and length. Most recently: beautiful nose but appears to be drying out.

*Last tasted Nov 1989******

Ch Ausone Good, particularly in its youth. Quite a bite in the early 1970s, and an overblown magnum. Can be attractive: soft rich brown molasses nose noted; crisp and flavoury. Last tasted at Flatt's Ausone tasting: good colour and bouquet but swingeingly dry.

*Oct 1987****

Ch Cheval-Blanc Several samples from different shippers tasted in 1956. All had good potential. Well-developed fragrance and silky texture noted in the early 1960s and many magnificent château-bottled specimens through the 1970s. In the 1980s, three rather souped-up Harvey's bottlings: caramel on nose, sweet palate, almost port-like. Château-bottled halves also a bit overripe, sweet, stably, with beautiful texture but a flavour like brussel sprouts. However, most recently, a Harvey's bottling, one I considered absolute perfection: soft, fleshy, ripe, in excellent condition.

*Last tasted June 1987. Variable. At best*****

Ch Pétrus 18 notes, first in 1956. Not the usual deep-velvet sort of Pétrus, comparitively light but very attractive then, and either side of 1960. Fractional acid instability in 1970 though it was fragrant, soft and rich. Just over half my notes have been made since 1980, mainly château-bottled, nearly half of which have been less than admiring including a poor Harvey's bottling with a nose like beef *consommé* and calf's-foot jelly. At its best, the bouquet has been noted as cedar, fennel, coffee and chocolate and, to mix a district and a grape analogy, more Médoc than Merlot. However, a fabulously mouth-filling magnum in 1986 at Frericks', Munich and at the recent 'Stockholm' tasting: pretty colour, mature; very pleasant fragrant bouquet, slightly medicinal (as in Munich), spicy but with a curious overtone like wet dog; fairly sweet, as always, firm, charming, but a bit tart on the finish.

*Last tasted March 1990. At best**** Drink soon.*

Ch Batailley Quite a few notes from 1960 when it seemed at its best. A pronounced Cabernet character, flavoury, refreshing, delicious but acidity catching up.

*Last tasted June 1989*** Drink up.*

Ch Branaire Five, bottled by Nicolas. Plain and rather shaky corks, hence slightly variable levels, all tasted in 1984: mellow brick colour; with the now fleeting charms and fleshy delights of a good '53 Médoc. And similar château-bottled.

*Last tasted in May 1985*** Drink up.*

Ch Calon-Ségur Very popular in this era. Several notes from 1955–1960, mainly English-bottled: '53 softness and fruit masking its usual firm tannins. A good château-bottled magnum in 1980 followed, exactly two years later, by another: very deep for a '53, opaque centre, mahogany rim; marvellous old cedary bouquet, classic Médoc; fullish, soft, velvety, rounded, complete, harmonious despite its dimensions.

*Last noted at a Saintsbury Club dinner, Oct 1983***** Drink soon.*

Ch Cantemerle One of my favourite '53s. Over 20 notes. Lovely from the start. Most drinkable in 1959, perfect in mid-1960s, seemed at its peak a decade later, two of the best noted being a Wine Society bottling and two excellent Dutch bottlings. Two château-bottled magnums, each "still a charmer", in 1981. By the mid-1980s beginning to show its age: loss of colour, palish but healthy tile-red; smell redolent of warm tiles, delicate, fragrant, though it faded; an overripe sweetness, lightish. Still a charmer.

*Last tasted at Dr Mauliner's, Feb 1983**** Drink up.*

Ch Certan du May Another lovely '53. Like many Pomerols better on palate than nose. First tasted in 1956, drinking beautifully by 1959. Most recently a Harveys of Bristol bottling, with good long cork: lovely mature colour; very delicate, fragrant bouquet that blossomed in the glass, though a touch too much volatile acidity. Sweetish, medium weight, very flavoury, fragrant and refined though lacking a little flesh and length.

*Last noted at a Bordeaux Club dinner at Christ's College, Cambridge, June 1987**** Drink up.*

Ch La Conseillante Two notes: sweet and lovely, château-bottled, in 1969, and an Avery half-bottle: lively, flavoury.

*Last noted at a pre-sale tasting, Sept 1983*** Drink now.*

Ch Cos d'Estournel Making less *charpenté*, less longer-lasting wines than Montrose at this period. Fully developed by the mid-1970s but showing age. Variable a decade later.

*Last tasted Feb 1985. At best*** Depends on condition.*

Ch Ducru-Beaucaillou First tasted in 1967 from a hogshead imported and bottled by an old friend, John Snell. By the mid-1970s, château bottled, deep, bouquet like a cedar cigar box; elegant and holding well, and, a decade later, a very similar description. All the components there but a bit short.

*Last tasted Feb 1989**** Should still be good.*

Ch Figeac Three notes. It was sweetish, fat and lovely in 1962, perfection in 1986. Most recently: still fairly deep, fully mature; an immediately soft, warm, earthy fragrance that blossomed beautifully. The residue still lovely after nearly two hours in the glass. Dryish, medium weight, crisp yet with some softness, excellent firm flavour, tannin and acidity.

*Last noted, a bottle ex-château, at the Desai tasting, Dec 1989**** Perfect now.*

Ch La Fleur-Pétrus Deep, lovely; a full-bosomed beauty completely ready, with dry finish.

*Two notes Dec 1980**** Drink soon.*

Ch Giscours Two notes: perfect in 1975. Fairly deep; stylish bouquet that developed beautifully and, after half an hour or so exposed to air, had that lovely classic mature Médoc smell of warm wholemeal ginger biscuits; sweetish, fullish, ripe yet firm and dry. Good length.

*Last tasted March 1981**** Doubtless still good.*

Ch Grand-Puy-Lacoste Not tasted until the early 1970s, but a string of "perfect" notes through to the mid-1980s: lovely colour, rich, mature; sweet, cedar and vanilla nose, minty, great depth; also rich yet dry on the palate. Delicate, fragrant, perfect style, good acidity.

*Last tasted Feb 1985***** Now to 2000+*

Ch Gruaud-Larose First tasted in 1958, and a soft, charming ready-to-drink magnum in 1961. Several subsequent consistently good notes. Beautiful appearance, lovely *tuillé* colour, nice gradation and glow; glorious bouquet of warm tiles and cedar, spice, ginger; sweetish, rich, rounded, perfect weight and balance.

*Last tasted Sept 1987***** Drink now to 2000.*

Ch Langoa-Barton First tasted in 1956: light but with tannic dryness. Flavoury, well balanced through to mid-1960s. All bottled by Harvey's, including three top-shoulder, upper-mid- and mid-shoulder. All had survived and were very drinkable. Now on the sweet side, with good cedary nose and flavour but fading.

*Last tasted Dec 1983*** Drink soon.*

Ch Léoville-Barton First tasted (bottled by Harvey's), with the Langoa, in 1956. A good, lovely, attractive wine. Léoville-Barton was only bottled at the château in small quantities and I have tasted only one in 1962. It was showing some age. Then in the mid-1970s came a batch of excellent Berry Bros bottlings and, most recently, another Harvey's bottling: excellent level, into the neck, short, but perfect cork. Palish but gloriously glowing rosehip colour; soft, fragrant bouquet which churned out of the glass for an hour. On the palate the sweet entry of a perfectly mature old wine, lightish, lovely flavour, now overmature but delicate and delicious.

*Last tasted July 1988**** Drink up.*

Ch Léoville-Las-Cases First noted Feb 1955. Good potential. By 1964 it had developed nicely though with time in hand. One or two good enough London bottlings, then, in the early 1970s two perfect château bottlings: soft, velvety, at peak and positively luscious for Las-Cases. Still a fabulous rich, cedary, spicy bouquet; soft, velvety, multi-dimensional — the more one sniffs and sips, the more it has to offer.

*Last tasted July 1988******

Ch La Mission-Haut-Brion Noted it briefly "fullish, well made" in 1955. 17 consistently good notes since then. Flavour better than nose, particularly if one is partial to the idiosyncratic 'smoky twigs' peat or tobacco taste of La Mission. Seemed perfect from the mid-1970s. A fabulous, tarry-scented magnum at Desai's tasting though at the recent line-up in Wiesbaden a bottle from the Woltner cellar was comparitively low-keyed on the nose but very elegant, with, again, that peat and tobacco-like taste.

*Last tasted June 1990**** Will go on.*

Ch Palmer Tasted in 1955 twice, from cask: unusual, flowery style. Through the 1960s I noted its fullness, fragrance and fairly pronounced Cabernet character, both in Harvey's and château-bottlings. Very rich, fruity, flavoury in the mid-1970s and, a decade later, a fragrant, attractive but tiring and slightly short double magnum.

*Last noted at the Rodenstock tasting at Yquem, Sept 1986. Not one of the best Palmers*** Drink up.*

Ch Pichon-Longueville, Lalande An excellent '53. First tasted in 1972: classic, elegant, stylish. Silky textured in a marie-jeanne in 1978. "A perfect dinner wine" in 1980. Two Nicolas bottlings: one lovely, the other, with a crumbly cork, drier and more acidic; and most recently another delicious marie-jeanne: lovely warm tile-red; "old cedar", medicinal Pauillac bouquet that opened up gloriously; medium sweetness and weight, silky, now lean but well clad. Dry but fragrant finish.

*Last tasted at Yquem, Sept 1986**** Drink now, or, if well stored, beyond 2000.*

Ch Rausan-Ségla Three notes, none château bottled. A very rich, fat, David Sandeman bottling, full of vinosity, in 1968, a totally different unknown London bottling in 1975, extraordinarily dry, 'green' and hard and, most recently, an Avery's bottling that seems to split the difference: high level, into neck; surprisingly deep, rich, thick even; lovely biscuity nose that held well for 2½ hours. Dry, lighter in body than its appearance suggested, piquant citrus-like flavour, good length.

*Last tasted Oct 1988. At best*** Drink soon.*

Ch Rauzan-Gassies Although the '53 had quite a good reputation, only noted once: fairly deep, fully mature amber rim; sweet, harmonious though with a whiff of *fungi*.

*Pre-sale, Sept 1989** Drink soon.*

Ch Talbot Attractive, lively, but lacking '53 charm. Too strong and meaty early in 1956; softening but still green in the early 1960s; deep rich and tangy, including a most attractive Avery's bottling, in the 1970s. A perfect *impériale* in 1983 and, most recently, a beautiful double-magnum: lovely, lively colour; well-developed, bricky, cedary bouquet and flavour; overall dry, excellent length, fragrant aftertaste.

*Last noted at lunch at one of Rodenstock's remarkable wine weekends, Sept 1987**** Drink now to 2000+*

Also tasted 1980:

Ch Baret A lean, elegant, flavoury unclassified Graves.

Nov 1983.

Ch Carbonnieux Like a much older wine, raw, no charm.

April 1991.

Ch Prieuré-Lichine Mature-looking; sweet, soft, fragrant and harmonious bouquet; fairly sweet, medium

weight, rich, flavoury, long and lovely.
Oct 1988.
Vieux Ch Certan Medium-deep colour, slight bead of carbon dioxide at rim; harmonious bouquet, touch of vanilla, honey and later toasted coconut; dryish, silky, charming and still perfect.
April 1984.

1954*

A poor year and, wedged between the 1953 and 1955 vintages, not sought after by the trade. But it is a wonder that any drinkable wine was made. One of the coldest summers ever. Those who managed to hold out started picking on Oct 11 in perfect weather which saved what was left of the crop from complete disaster. Not surprisingly the wine was heavily (and officially) chaptalised. Some winemakers coped better than others. Of little interest now.
Ch Lafite First tasted in cask, July 1955: better than Mouton, more guts but too acidic. Several notes a decade later: distinct Cabernet aroma, turning into a light, attractive drink. Good level, fairly pale, very mature looking; a rather nice, sweet gingery, bouquet—but failed to note its taste.
*Last noted at Flatt's Lafite tasting, Oct 1988**
Ch Margaux Not very good. Three notes: unimpressive in cask, chaptalised, dry, dull.
Not tasted since 1976.
Ch Latour 10 notes: in cask, fairly forthcoming and plausible in the 1960s and five in the 1970s when it was probably at its best. Still quite deep, intense and red; a peppery nose and finish. Caramel fudge-like nose, fruity, chunky, blunt.
*Last noted at the Mouton/Latour tasting in Wiesbaden, March 1989**
Ch Mouton-Rothschild Skinny in cask. In 1983, a fragrant flavoury bottle from the château. Soft, chewy, drinkable at Flatt's tasting: surprisingly good colour, rich, mature; medicinal old-straw nose; fairly light, flavoury, dried out and short. Most recently, at the Mouton/Latour tasting, oxidised.
*Last tasted March 1989. At best**
Ch Haut-Brion Not good. Poor in cask. 20 years later fully mature, austere, little fruit.
Not tasted since 1963.
Ch Ausone Tasted only once: good level; very healthy colour; bouquet medicinal, coffee and chocolate; on the light side, flavoury, chewy, reasonable length, dry finish.
*Showing well at Flatt's Ausone tasting, Oct 1987***
Ch Cheval-Blanc "Interesting", in March 1956. Two notes in the mid-1970s. Quite a good very mature colour; fully ripe, cheesy nose and taste, plus earthiness and iron tang.
Still interesting when last tasted in 1976 Though 'drink up' was recommended.*
Dom de Chevalier Sweet, bland, nice bouquet; very flavoury, attractive and holding well in 1969. Recently a low-shoulder, scummy brown, dead bottle. Both shipped by Cruse, the first bottled by Grierson's, the second bottled in Copenhagen. The bottler let down by the cork.
*Last tasted March 1990. At best***
Ch L'Evangile Fairly sound old nose; lightish, no fruit, tart finish.
Tasted chez Malcolm Forbes, New York, Feb 1986.
Ch La Mission-Haut-Brion One note. Thanks to Woltner's skill, a charming wine, attractive looking, bouquet of sea-shells, liquorice and caramel. Slightly sweet, easy, slightly bitter finish.
*At Desai's La Mission tasting, Feb 1985***

1955****

An important year in its day. Coming after the sturdy '52s and lovely '53s, both absorbed at reasonable prices by the trade, the '55s were welcomed, despite slightly higher cost prices. Not regarded as long-lasters they were mainly consumed in the 1960s. I have hundreds of notes, the vast majority made prior to 1970 and only a few dozen châteaux noted in the 1980s.

Late spring-like Feb, March cold and frosty, flowering in fine weather followed by rain then heat. Aug hot and dry. Welcome Sept rain swelled the grapes for fine harvesting conditions.

An above average but largely forgotten vintage. The best, and best-kept, are still lovely.
Ch Lafite In my early days in the trade I was not despatched to Bordeaux on the firm's business, and our summer busman's holidays were spent each year in a different European wine district. Tasting first growths in cask was not my business, which is why my first notes on the '55 Lafite were made in 1961. Although fairly deep-coloured it was already showing some maturity: "browning". Its bouquet was developing and it had a lovely flavour, though at the time I thought it had only moderate life expectancy. Nearly 30 years later—how inaccurate my inexperienced prognostications—it was showing well, lovely, stylish. A touch of astringency throughout the 1970s, its bouquet becoming more fragrant, a lovely aftertaste developing. Of the two dozen notes, half made since 1980, not one poor bottle, half-bottle, magnum, or *impériale*. The most detailed note was made at a Bordeaux Club dinner I gave in 1986. Despite its peripatetic existence: imported by Berent-Vandervoort & Co, San Francisco, sold to a gentleman in Los Angeles from whom I obtained it, hand carrying it back to London. It was delicious, and its delicate, slightly medicinal Pauillac bouquet developed gloriously over two hours, half in decanter then in glass. Although losing some colour it can still be surprisingly deep, rich, intense even. Bouquet still very forthcoming and fragrant; dryish, perfect weight, crisp, slightly citrus flavour, good length. A beauty.
*Last tasted Aug 1989***** Drink now to 2000.*
Ch Margaux Also first tasted in 1961. Similar, then, in many ways to Lafite, though I noted it as full, silky and more tannic. It paled sooner and tasted fully mature by the mid-1960s. "Fragrant" crops up repeatedly, so does "elegance", and "perfect weight". End acidity noticeable but not sufficient to detract from all its other virtues.
*Last tasted April 1989. On average**** Drink now to 2000.*
Ch Latour Totally different from Margaux in weight and style when first tasted in 1961. A longer life predicted: deep purple, huge, dumb, compressed nose, and palate packed with fruit, tannin and acidity. Many notes, all good. It remained deep, richly coloured and powerful throughout the 1960s and 1970s, though its bouquet continued to evolve in bottle. Still fairly deep with lovely gradation of colour to mature rim; cedary bouquet which needs coaxing out of the glass, originally dry, it now appears sweeter as the tannins have ameliorated. It remains full-bodied, fleshy, spicy, with a firm backbone. A top Latour vintage, better than the '52 and '53.
*Spectacularly lovely when last tasted at a Christie's Wine Course Master Class, Dec 1990***** Beautiful now but will continue to mature well into the 21st century.*
Ch Mouton-Rothschild The great attraction of Mouton is the immediacy of its high-toned Cabernet Sauvig-

non aroma. In 1961 like the Latour '55: a youthfully deep appearance, full, fruity and loaded. In 1968, initially underestimating its life span, I gave it up to 20 years. 12 notes from early to mid-1970s, deep though maturing; fabulously rich, blackcurrant, biscuity bouquet; firm, later delicate and most attractive flavour. Three notes in the 1980s: still a magnificent colour, deep, translucent; opulent *cassis* nose and amazing flavour. Touch of leanness and good, firm tannins and acidity.
*Last noted at a Christie's pre-sale tasting, Chicago, Oct 1987******

Ch Haut-Brion 10 notes from 1961–1979, two half-bottles since. Never very deep, yet rich, ruby-centred. The nose is consistently earthy, with lovely, ripe, soft and gentle progressions. Haut-Brion is always the odd-man-out, quite different in taste from the first-growth Médocs: earthy, tobacco, sometimes charred, bracken-like or tarry, but — since the last war — consistently well made and elegant. A fine wine but a bit more austere than its peers.
*Not tasted since Oct 1983***(*)? Hard to judge its peak. Probably continuing to evolve.*

Ch Cheval-Blanc I confess to being partial to Cheval-Blanc. From the beginning of this century, it has performed remarkably evenly, and, at times, as in 1921, 1929 and 1947, has scaled incredible heights. However, up until 1962 not all was château-bottled. Of the 20 '55 Cheval Blancs tasted, over half a dozen have been English-bottled. Moreover, as sizes have ranged from half-bottles to double-magnums, my notes have been understandably varied, from gnarled, twisted, flat, brown and weak to soft and lovely. Cheval-Blanc often has a pronounced iron character, derived I believe from the soil. The last few notes, four bottled at the château, have been full of praise: still deep with a lovely mature mahogany rim; very open, fragrant bouquet; all sweet, completely rounded, with lovely balance and texture, *à point*. The most recent have been Berry Bros' bottlings. There were variations but the best had lovely, sweet, vinous, harmonious bouquet; equally lovely flavour and balance.
*Last tasted May 1986. At best***** Drink now.*

Ch Pétrus A magnum, loaded with tannin in 1967. 10 notes follow its progression through the 1970s, always dry (tannic), huge yet velvety. I must have used the phrase "iron fist in velvet glove" about this time. Typically deep, magnificent, suede textured in 1975. Five notes since then: "magnificent but not Médoc", lacking zest, in 1983; then a lean and tannic half-bottle; an equally lean yet ripe, fragrant and refreshing magnum at Frerick's tasting in Munich. A disappointing bottle: opaque, meaty, malty, sweet, soft, rich but cracking up.
*Last noted at the 'Stockholm' tasting, April 1990. At best*****

Ch Beauséjour A Calvet sample, light and delicate in 1956 and a soft, fully mature bottle at a pre-sale tasting, with a very sweet, very fruity, port-like nose. Delicious.
*Last tasted July 1983*****

Ch Bel-Air-Marquis-d'Aligre A lightish "good lunch wine" noted in 1967, stylish, elegant, very Margaux, nicely developed by 1979. Two years later, an attractive mature brick/garnet-red; harmonious bouquet; drying out a bit, light, pleasant.
*Not tasted since Jan 1981. Then****

Ch Beychevelle Pleasing, lightish, nice in 1959, a delicate but dubious London bottling in 1968 and an extremely attractive bottle, deep, soft and flavoury.
*Last tasted May 1986. At best*****

Ch Calon-Ségur A good '55, full, fruity and, surprisingly, not over tannic in the late 1950s; probably at its best in the mid-1960s–early 1970s but "cedary, very flavoury though a touch of piquancy" noted in 1978. Most recently a poor, acidic, English bottling.
*Last tasted in July 1985. At best****

Dom de Chevalier Two notes, soft, delicate, good in 1961 and, 20 years later, still a fine colour; an open, welcoming nose; touch of sweetness, nice weight, supple and easy, lovely flavour, length and aftertaste.
*Last tasted March 1981**** Doubtless still attractive.*

Ch Cos d'Estournel Three notes: one lovely, one woody in 1972. More recently a very attractive-looking bottle, beautifully developed, dry finish. Needed drinking.
*Last tasted March 1981*** Drink up.*

Ch Figeac Lovely, even as a cask sample in 1956. Light, silky, pronounced Cabernet Sauvignon flavour, scented and most attractive in the 1960s. 20 years later: an excellent magnum from the château, deepish but very mature-looking; rich, opaque, delicate, fragrant — violets — bouquet. Dryish, nice weight, flavour and texture.
*Last noted at Desai's Figeac tasting, Dec 1989*****

Ch Gruaud-Larose Consistently good. Despite its fairly deep appearance and body, sweetish and very drinkable in the early 1960s. A lovely Harvey's bottling in 1964 and an equally attractive Dolamore's bottling nearly a decade later. Now some colour loss, fully mature; very positive, very fragrant, classic, cedary, blossomed beautifully; medium weight, fleshy, even velvety, "perfect claret" in 1981 but fading a little now.
*Last tasted April 1986. At best*****

Ch Lagrange St-Julien. Severe, touch of bitterness in the 1960s, dry but attractive in 1973 and two J Lyons bottlings, one pleasing in 1967, the other, nearly a decade later, creaking.
Last tasted July 1986 Avoid.*

Ch Langoa-Barton Several notes, various bottlings, mainly Barton & Guestier, Bordeaux. Noted as full, fairly "green", short and expensive, a couple of nice Harvey's bottlings in the mid-1960s. Most recently, B & G: perfect colour; fragrant nose; very flavoury.
*Last noted, pre-sale, Chicago, March 1985****

Ch Lascombes Seven consistently good notes from 1958. It seemed fully mature in the mid-1970s but was still a delight, perfectly balanced in 1982 though poised for a decline. Now fully developed, sweet, soft, lightish, tannin receded and fruit fading — yet elegant.
*Last tasted Feb 1985. At best**** now** or*** depending on condition.*

Ch Léoville-Barton Bottled in Birmingham and at the château, both lacking charm in the mid-1960s, then a sound London bottling and a good magnum. Most recently, from the château: surprisingly deep; sweet, rich, slightly chocolaty, vanilla, bottle-age bouquet; fairly sweet and full. Agreeable chunky wine.
*Last tasted at the Barton dinner at Brooks's, Nov 1989. At best****

Ch La Mission-Haut-Brion Nine notes. Showing great vinosity and potential yet with a tannic bitterness that ran through to the mid-1970s. Earthy, full of iodine and iron, its bouquet had reached perfection in 1978. Amazing depth and intensity at the Desai tasting in 1985; magnificent, with idiosyncratic tobacco taste, in 1986 and very high marks at Wolf's La Mission tasting: a lovely, lively, fully opened-up wine in all respects. Tannins now softened. Sweet and ripe.
*Last tasted June 1990***** Will continue.*

Ch Mouton d'Armailhacq Agreeable but a bit of a bite in the 1960s. 18 years on, and labelled "Baron Philippe", deep-coloured for a '55; scented, overripe; very flavoury.
*Last tasted Feb 1986** Needs drinking.*

Ch Nenin Sweet and rich in cask and, bottled by

Harvey's in 1957, very scented. Several other notes including a silky but bitter-ended Justerini & Brooks' bottling in 1968. Quite a nice château-bottling: deepish, mature, sweet, sound, lovely Pomerol texture.
*Last tasted in June 1984***
Ch Les Ormes-de-Pez Sweet but tannic in 1958, full of fruit tannin and acidity in the early 1960s. After another quarter century still very deep but fully mature; bouquet and palate high-toned, crisp, fruity, overmature, touch of acidity.
Last tasted May 1986. Drink up.
Ch Palmer Not a great Palmer. Beginning to show age, though quite rich on nose and palate, in the early 1960s. Two critical notes in the mid-1970s and, a decade later: delicate, scented, vegetal nose; lightish, some elegance, dry finish.
*Last tasted Nov 1985** Declining.*
Ch de Pez Nicely made, at best (in magnum) in 1980 and, most recently, a good if unexciting bottle.
*Last tasted July 1988** Dependable.*
Ch Pichon-Baron Two fairly good notes in 1974 and three favourable in the mid-1980s. Still a fine deep colour; rich, lean, chewy, a bit '62-like.
*Last tasted April 1985****
Ch Rausan-Ségla Fragrant though unready in the early 1960s, a tart Dutch bottling in 1978. Most recently, with branded cork, curiously overripe bouquet; dry, fairly light, soft, quite nice fruity, tannic.
*Last tasted Jan 1989***
Ch Trotanoy A somewhat contradictory but fragrant and refreshing wine: fine colour; harmonious, fragrant; dry, lean, elegant.
*Last tasted in M Jacques Rouët's cellar in Paris, July 1984****
Vieux Ch Certan A perfect magnum.
*Feb 1989*****
Tasted in the 1980s:
Ch Baret This minor, unclassified Graves showing consistently well despite signs of cork weevil: lovely colour, fragrant, flavoury. ***
Ch Gontier Côtes de Blaye. Bottled by Justerini & Brooks: remarkably soft and nice in 1964; showing pleasing survivability 25 years after the vintage. **
Ch Ripeau Drying out, lacking style.

1956

An appallingly severe winter, unprecedentedly bad spring damaged vines, cold Aug, excessively wet Sept, brief respite for picking from mid-Oct. My few notes of this vintage, repeat "surprisingly" (nice) surprisingly often! But, meagre and thin; only of the faintest interest now.
Ch Latour Typifying Latour's ability to produce a fairly good wine in a poor year. Distinctly impressive in colour, nose and flavour though short in 1970. Becoming a bit tart though flavoury in the mid- to late 1970s. Although richer and redder than the '63 at the big Latour tasting in 1981, a bit raw. Most recently at the Latour/Mouton tasting in Wiesbaden: medium, still red and with some intensity; subdued but quite good nose, its original Cabernet fruit now cedary. Drying out, lightish though some body, acidic finish.
*Last tasted March 1989**
Ch Mouton-Rothschild Also deep for an off-year, medicinal, very flavoury, piquant in 1973. Similar appearance at Flatt's Mouton tasting in 1986: strawberry-scented, sweetish, lean, flavoury, but tailed off. And at Wolf's tasting, surprisingly good colour, bouquet, taste. Light, fragrant, spicy Cabernet nose. Lightish, soft, very flavoury, with dry acidic finish.
*Last noted March 1989**
Ch Ausone Surprisingly deep in 1976, cheesy, sound, dry, a bit austere. And at Flatt's Ausone tasting some colour-loss but attractive-looking; unexpectedly good nose that developed richly; on the light side, short, dry finish.
*Last tasted Oct 1987***
Ch Lynch-Bages Deeper than anticipated but very brown; sweet, medicinal Pauillac nose; dry, light, very mature, not bad finish.
*March 1985**
Ch La Mission-Haut-Brion Frankly two rather different assessments. At Desai's tasting in 1985 I noted it as very mature-looking; light, open, cheesy nose; dry, lightish, lean and short. At Wolf's recent tasting: a surprisingly deep, impressive appearance; a most unusual nose, like the smell of a linen shop, sweaty, chaptalised. Some sweetness and more body, surprisingly rich and chewy. (The bottle came from the Woltner cellars via Christie's.)
*Last noted June 1990. At best, a good '56, almost*** Drink up.*
Ch Respide Schröder & Schÿler. Sweet, light, managing to be both flabby and acidic.
March 1991.

1957*

One of my least-favourite vintages, though it was never considered a poor year. Even in their heyday, the mid-1960s, the wines were over-acidic.

A strange growing season: very mild Feb, incredibly hot March; frosts in April, severe in May, poor flowering, Aug coldest on record. Small, unripe crop picked from Oct 1 in record heat.
Ch Lafite Nine notes, better on nose than palate. Attractive, *cassis* in cask. Ripeness and elegance on nose but a certain rawness and acidity noted thrice in the mid-1970s. Seemed to have settled down by the early to mid-1980s: tangerine, creaking with overmaturity, drying out, a bit meagre. Sunday lunch at Lafite, accompanying oysters and sausages, in 1984. Short, tolerable if piquant acidity.
*Last tasted March 1990**
Ch Margaux Tasted in cask and from cask sample, restrained but not unattractive. Tried hard to be fragrant in the mid-1970s, though always a bit tart and 'screwed up'. On the whole dry, raw, not very well-balanced, though a decent magnum at Desai's Margaux tasting: very high level; touch of cherry-ruby; quite attractive, refreshing nose; nice weight, refreshing though acidic finish.
*Last tasted May 1987***
Ch Latour Not too bad a start: a big, black wine in cask, fruity, with loads of tannin. Seemed best in the mid-1960s, thereafter one of my least-liked vintages of Latour, not helped by two fairly recent bottles, one raw and tart, the other, at the Wolf tasting, oxidised.
Last noted March 1989.
Ch Mouton-Rothschild First tasted, a deep, lovely, fruity, Cabernet-flavoured wine in 1961, and six times since. Still quite deep and red; forthcoming, wet dog and typically spicy Mouton medicinal Cabernet Sauvignon aroma. Very flavoury, some charm, despite its raw '57 acidity.
*Last noted March 1989***
Ch Haut-Brion First noted in cask. Quite flavoury, nicely balanced. In the early to mid-1960s: good though restrained nose and a lovely, deep, earthy flavour. Acidity

noticeable, but silky. By the mid-1970s showing a great deal of maturity, loose-knit, unimpressive; and, a decade later, fully developed, ripe bouquet; spicy, flavoury but raw.
*Last tasted May 1985**
Ch Ausone Tasted in cask and from a cask sample in 1958: soft, chocolaty, curious, already browning. By the 1960s not as advanced as the colour indicated. Piquant, flavoury in 1971. Most recently, a bottle from the château at Flatt's tasting: fairly deep, thick and somewhat shaken; nose muffled at first but then tried to please; dry, flavoury, reasonable length, touch of '57 acidity.
*Last tasted Oct 1987**
Ch Beychevelle Two Army & Navy Stores' bottlings, both having scented, fragrant, high-toned Cabernet noses with whiff of volatile acidity; dry, elegant, flavoury, lovely acidity.
*Oct 1987****
Ch Gruaud-Larose First tasted in cask, Sept 1958. Deep, rich, full of fruit, tannin and acidity. Two tart bottlings, David Sandeman's and British Transport Hotels', in the early 1970s and an impressively deep, château-bottled magnum in 1983, still fruity, rich, chunky but showing its age, with noticeable acidity and touch of bitterness.
*Last tasted May 1983***
Ch Léoville-Barton Two quite attractive English bottlings in the mid-1960s, and one note since: quite rich-looking though not deep; old cedar nose, creaking a bit; dry, better flavour than smell, '57 acidity, lacking charm but not a bad drink.
*Last tasted Dec 1982**
Ch Léoville-Las-Cases A dozen notes, ranging from an attractive cask sample through different bottlings to a deep, dusty, dry, raw but very flavoury château bottling. Noticeable but tolerable acidity. Though never wholly satisfactory a relatively good '57.
*Last tasted Oct 1985. At best***
Ch Lynch-Bages From cask, many notes, many bottlings. Quite an attractive wine. At best in the mid-1960s, a Harvey's and a château bottling showing well: a good mouthful, though the typical Lynch-Bages Cabernet spiciness at best in the early 1970s. Most recently: medium, rich, orange-tinged; pronounced *cassis* nose, touch of sweetness, nice weight, soft, 'warm', flavour enhanced not destroyed by volatile acidity.
*Last tasted Sept 1987. At best*** but risky.*
Ch La Mission-Haut-Brion One of the very best '57s. Tasted three times in 1978, all bottles from the Woltner cellars. Consistent notes: deep, almost '61 opacity; attractive bouquet — calm sea, hot pebbles, sacking and iodine. Reads oddly, but the same on palate. Showing well at the Desai tasting in 1985 and a deep, fairly intense magnum at the recent Wolf tasting (also Woltner stock); tough, peppery, rich old oak bouquet; touch of sweetness, fairly full-bodied, rich fruit, silky leathery tannins.
*Last tasted June 1990**** Will keep.*
Ch Pichon-Baron 'Green' but flavoury in cask, quite nice though austere 11 years on. Now fully mature; ripe, cheesy, surprisingly attractive bouquet; lean, flavoury, dry, refreshing but not over-acidic.
*Last tasted Nov 1983. At best****
Also tasted in the 1980s:
Ch Beauséjour St-Emilion. Richly coloured, flavoury, sweetness masking acidity. **
Ch Belair St-Emilion. Tasted in cask at Ausone, and unimpressed. Pasty and acidic in 1989.
Ch Croizet-Bages Piquant.
Ch Pique-Caillou Mérignac, Graves. Rich, cheesy, slightly sweet, soft, warm and agreeable. Slightish touch of volatile acidity at end. **
A poor 1957:
Ch Marquis d'Alesme-Becker Acidic and spoiled by mercaptan.

1958**

A soft, easy, attractive vintage sandwiched between the much-bought '57s and heavily invested-in '59s. These underrated wines were, however, much liked by some of the top English connoisseurs who found them charming, and inexpensive, when at their best in the mid- to late 1960s. Basically no faults but short and lacking stamina. Feb mild, March cold and snowy, April mainly cold and wet. Good flowering in June. Warm, dry summer but late harvest.
Ch Lafite Four notes, the first quite good, flavoury and clean but bitter on finish. A gentle, femininely ripe and attractive bottle in 1975, and in 1985 very mature-looking; bouquet ripe though thin and medicinal; light but stylish on palate. Lastly an impressive *impériale* produced by Lloyd Flatt for lunch between Lafite tasting 'flights': fairly deep, rich, mature; full, fruity bouquet that became very fragrant; rather sweet, lovely rich fruit, but sandy texture mingled with some tannin and acidity. Certainly very drinkable.
*Last noted Oct 1988. At best*** Drink up.*
Ch Margaux A touch of bitterness in the mid-1960s. Not worthy of *grand vin* status. An agreeable but not outstanding bottle in 1971 and, a decade later, despite its good, fully mature colour, drying out and a bit stringy.
*Last tasted May 1981. At best***
Ch Latour Many notes: dull, stodgy, indifferent, austere when young. But lovely and spicy, though short, in 1986. At the recent Frericks/Wodarz Latour/Mouton tasting it had lost its original depth of colour; its nose harsh though fragrant, a bit varnishy, not bad fruit though acidity noticeable. Not very interesting.
*Last tasted March 1989***
Ch Mouton-Rothschild Deep, rich, exciting in the late 1970s. An attractive, fragrant but verging on smelly, rich but short bottle at Flatt's Lafite tasting in 1986; and, at Wolf's: fully mature appearance; soft, sound, tea-like bouquet that faded a little; hollow, short, dry finish yet lacking acidity.
Last tasted March 1989 On its way out.*
Ch Haut-Brion Touch of bitterness, woolly nosed, complete but dull — an adjective appearing four times in the mid-1960s. Developing in the 1970s: soft, agreeable, earthy flavour, but not classically balanced. Most recently: earthy, ripe, high-toned; dry, lightish, somewhat raw.
*Last tasted May 1985** Declining.*
Ch Ausone So-so cask sample. Three notes in 1970s: loose knit, little to it. Yet coming into its own at Flatt's Ausone tasting: though fully mature, with touch of carbon dioxide, a very forthcoming, heavenly, rich bouquet; on the dry and lightish side, lean but flavoury.
*Last tasted Oct 1987. At its best****
Ch Cheval-Blanc Rather dull initially but pleasant enough through the 1970s to the early 1980s. Latterly a remarkably attractive magnum, still ruby, with rich 'legs'; good, scented, cedary bouquet; fairly sweet.
*Last tasted at the château, Sept 1986. At best****
Ch Pétrus Tasted twice. In 1973: fairly deep, velvety; little nose; rich, soft, fluffy, 'stunned', mute, unexciting, holding back. Most recently, at the 'Stockholm' group

tasting: medium depth, mature, not very bright; showing age, slightly medicinal, then biscuity; very sweet, medium full-bodied, fruity but edgy.
*Last tasted April 1990*** Will not improve.*
Ch L'Arrosée The first vintage tasted of a St-Emilion château that has only recently come into prominence. However, not a very impressive start: three notes made in the early to mid-1980s: plummy coloured yet fully mature; indefinable nose.
*Last noted March 1984. At best***
Ch Cos d'Estournel Two notes, soft, flavoury in the mid-1970s but an ullaged, faded and nondescript bottle a decade later.
*Last tasted June 1983. At its best probably***
Ch Gruaud-Larose Five notes, from 1969. A sound, easy, cedary wine, fragrant, soft, short, and now on its way out.
*Last tasted June 1984. At best**** Drink up.*
Ch La Mission-Haut-Brion Remarkably good. Three consistent notes, mid- to late 1970s: very deep, rich, mature-looking; fabulous, almost jammily rich, earthy, Graves bouquet; huge yet soft, iron tang, dry. An easy charmer, though short at the Desai tasting in 1985. Most recently at Wolf's: still surprisingly deep for a '58; a curious, meaty mocha-like nose; pleasant citrusy acidity, lacking length.
*Last tasted June 1990****
Ch Montrose Aged 10 showing an almost too-good-to-be-true maturity and bouquet; well made and a bit hard, as always, fruity, short. Aged 23, palish, very mature; sweet, harmonious, vanilla bouquet; nice weight, delicious flavour.
*Last tasted Dec 1981****
Also tasted in the 1980s:
Ch Baret Graves. Rich, mature; ripe earthy nose; agreeable, flavoury, short.
Ch Beauséjour St-Emilion. Orange tangy, old, thin and edgy.
Ch Malescot-St-Exupéry Characteristically exaggerated Cabernet Sauvignon scent and taste; dry; flavoury.
Ch Pavie Surprisingly deep but with touch of woodiness.

1959★★★★★

A magnificent, full-throated vintage. It also marked the end of an era of good and poor but rarely dramatic vintages. 1959 was the first (not the last) to be hailed as the "vintage of the century". Then, a bit of back-tracking, (as with the '82): '59s, it was said, lacked acidity. Great wines were produced but, as with '82 and '47, hot weather provided some winemakers with problems. Although this *was* a great vintage, most minor wines were probably at their best after 10 years.

Unusually fine, sunny weather in Feb and March, April variable, improvement in May, June fine, July almost too hot, Aug fine and warm, Sept hot though very wet from the 13th. Good harvesting conditions from the 23rd. Average quantity, high quality. The best are still marvellous.

Ch LAFITE *24 notes since 1975. Undoubtedly a great wine. Very rich, fragrant, elegant, though hefty for Lafite. Plenty of life. Good notes from the mid-1970s to the 1980s, with the exception of a rather 'hot' slightly acidic bottle at Flatt's marathon in 1988. Most recently Walter Eigensatz presented us with bottles, magnums, a double-magnum, a jeroboam and an* impériale *which were tasted blind in random order. The* impériale *I noted as "firm", with "great length" and "needs more time". The jeroboam was perfect and just surged out of the glass. The double-magnum seemed the most supple and ready; the magnums excellent; the bottles slightly variable.*

Overall, Lafite '59 has a deep, lively appearance, ruby centre grading off to a fine, mature rim; marvellously fragrant bouquet, touch of vanilla, cedar, citrus fruit, spice — it keeps evolving in the glass. Distinctly on the sweet side — ripe grapes, alcohol, extract, all the appropriate component parts. Fairly full-bodied, crisp, firm, yet fleshy, lovely flavour and great length. Last tasted Sept 1990★★★★★ *Will keep.*

Ch MARGAUX *Another excellent and relatively sturdy '59. Lovely even aged five. Still almost opaque and with a beautiful, classic bouquet and flavour in the early 1970s. "Sweet, charming, soft and velvety" in the mid-1970s, though two austere bottles at Heublein pre-sale tastings. Out of nearly 30 notes made over the past quarter-century, six have been disappointing, probably due to varying storage/provenance. And although velvety, often noted, never elegant. Summing up: now medium-deep, fully mature-looking; lovely, crisp, minty, old oak and cedar bouquet at its zenith; touch of sweetness — though some drying out a little — fairly full-bodied, glorious flavour; rich, soft, well balanced, great length, still tannic.* Last tasted at Lay & Wheeler's Margaux event in Colchester, Nov 1990★★★★★ Drink soon.

Ch LATOUR *Nearly three dozen notes. Apart from one woody bottle at the Frericks/Wodarz tasting in 1989, all in marvellous condition. Indeed the wine is virtually indestructible. In 1963: black; packed with fruit; loaded with tannin. Retaining its depth of colour through the 1960s and 1970s. Like Jane Russell, mean, moody and magnificent. A huge mouthful, packed, austere. Massive and masculine throughout the 1980s. Still very deep, opaque centre, maturing edge; a misleadingly gentle, cedary nose with the mulberry character of intense, ripe Cabernet Sauvignon. Full-bodied, rich yet still very tannic.* April 1990★★★★(★) *Will continue to develop well into the next century.*

Ch MOUTON-ROTHSCHILD *Magnificence piled upon magnificence. With the exception of a rather malty, oxidised bottle at Flatt's Mouton tasting in 1986, consistently superb. An embarrassingly large number of notes dating from March 1963. Always very deep but with not quite the opacity of Latour, its most striking feature throughout has been the fabulously fragrant, exotically rich and spicy Cabernet Sauvignon nose. Harmonious, with layers of cedar, cinnamon, eucalyptus. A touch of sweetness on the palate, open, fleshy, still packed with fruit, great length, beautiful aftertaste.* Last tasted March 1989★★★★★ *Will continue beyond 2000.*

Ch HAUT-BRION *Yet another great wine. In well over 30 notes only one rather disappointing bottle, a second bottle at the same tasting being good. Initially not as deep or intense as the aforementioned first growths, it displayed a mature browning of the rim way back in 1963 and, on the palate, seemed surprisingly soft and forward. Yet on the nose it remained relatively dumb and undeveloped through to the mid-1970s. More surprisingly still, it has not only gained in stature over the years but also in depth and intensity of appearance, with a lovely, fragrant bouquet exhibiting the Haut-Brion hallmark: tobacco. Reached its plateau of maturity in the mid-1980s. Still perfection. Now medium-deep; top-class, well-developed, harmonious bouquet and flavour. Touch of sweetness, medium-full body, suave, elegant.* Last tasted June 1990★★★★★

Ch AUSONE *Tasted twice, first in 1971. Certainly good in its way. And fairly recently: fine, rich colour, nose and palate. Lovely yet not very forthcoming bouquet. Substantial, chewy, good grip but lacking the fat of the great '59s.* Last noted at Flatt's Ausone tasting, Oct 1987★★★

Ch CHEVAL-BLANC *Sweet, rich and rounded in the early 1970s. Perfect: slightly sweet, soft and velvety in the late 1970s, since when not tasted.* ★★★★ Doubtless delicious.

Ch PETRUS *A full, sweet, fleshy wine first tasted in 1972 and since in magnum and jeroboam. Consistent notes: fine, lively colour; gloriously ripe, fragrant bouquet, liquorice and mint; full of fruit, flavour, extract, tannin. Yet rather an obvious wine, lacking the subtle nuances of the great Médocs.* Last noted at the 'Stockholm' Group tasting, April 1990★★★★★ *Years of life ahead.*

Ch BARET *I always think minor red Graves are delicious to drink, and always good value, when young. The '59 Baret was starting to mature nicely two and three years after bottling. Identical notes: on nose "sweet, pure honey"; both attractive on palate, the first still a bit 'green', a year later crisp and agreeable. Three notes in the* *mid-1980s: a homely, soft, earthy wine with dry finish.* Last tasted, pre-sale, March 1985*** Drink up.

Ch BATAILLEY *First noted, a Harvey's bottling in 1961: "attractive, not great". Seemed at its best (château bottling) in the late 1960s, typically plummy. Not bad in the mid-1970s and, a decade later: palish, very mature; nose still fruity and attractive; lacking length but pleasing.* Last tasted June 1983** Drink soon.

Ch BEYCHEVELLE *An exciting wine, deep, full and soft in 1963. Then two excellent English bottlings, J Lyons and British Transport Hotels, both well-nigh perfect in the mid-1960s. In 1983 an extraordinary Army & Navy bottling, marvellously deep, intense; hefty, meaty but harmonious bouquet; massive, velvety mouthful, and, later that year, a fully evolved, fragrant, somewhat overripe château bottling with flavour and charm — but needed drinking.* Last tasted Nov 1983*** Drink up.

Ch CALON-SEGUR *Four different British bottlings in the late 1960s, all hefty, all good. 14 years later a very sweet, chunky, somewhat overblown château bottling.* Last tasted Nov 1983** Drink up.

Ch CANON *Consistently rich. First in 1967, a J Lyons bottling with a nose like fried bacon. Two château bottlings in the 1980s. Now fully mature, lovely colour; sweet, glorious bouquet; drying out a little, fine, no great length but good aftertaste. The most dependable of châteaux.* Last tasted Oct 1985**** Drink up.

CARRUADES DE CH LAFITE *I confess I have always liked the light, feminine style of Carruades. Seven notes, all good: elegant, silky and a perfect drink in the late 1960s. Consistently fragrant and attractive through the 1970s. More recently, still a good colour; stylish, cedary four-star bouquet; a lovely wine, good fruit, flavour, dry finish, holding well.* Last tasted Nov 1983***

Dom de CHEVALIER *Deep, spicy, dry, fullish, crisp fruit; stylish, un-Graves-like, and with time in hand.* Last tasted Jan 1983****

Ch CISSAC *Despite devastation by frost in 1956, after which they replanted 75% Cabernet Sauvignon, a small amount of excellent wine was made in 1959. A magnum, bottled by Dr Snell in Cheshire, was still green but attractive in 1967. A château bottling nearly 25 years after the vintage was superb: magnificent appearance; deep, rich, classic bouquet; full-bodied yet soft, lovely, fruity and perfect, retaining tannins for longer life.* Last tasted April 1983 ****

Ch COS D'ESTOURNEL *An excellent '59. First noted in 1965 as beautifully made and balanced but needing more time. "Loads of tannin, years of life" noted through to the early 1970s, then a leap of 12 years. Several more notes. Showing particularly well, with charm but quite a bite, at Desai's tasting of '59s. Most recently: no longer deep but a lovely tile-red; fully developed, rather pheasanty, overripe bouquet; sweet entry, still quite a mouthful, masking ever-present Cos tannin.* Last tasted Jan 1990**** Past its peak but good.

Ch DUCRU-BEAUCAILLOU *"Classic" crops up in six of my seven notes. For such a well-liked château I cannot think why I did not taste the wine until it was nine years old: an excellent Berry Bros bottling, equally well balanced in the early 1970s. The rest château-bottled, fine and "classic" from the late 1960s through the 1970s. Still surprisingly deep — two notes in the early 1980s — very fragrant though peppery; the fullness and sweetness only achieved in a hot, ripe-grape vintage. Most recently, an excellent Berry Bros bottling: medium-deep, fine mature appearance; very sound nose, rich, harmonious but low-keyed. Flavour to match. Lots of extract, tannin and acidity giving it a dry finish.* Last tasted Sept 1990**** Still drinking well if properly cellared.

Ch GRAND-PUY-LACOSTE *An uncompromising, masculine Pauillac, packed with fruit and tannins, verging on the astringent. Attractive but pretty tough from the late 1960s to the mid-1970s. Crisp and peppery at Desai's '59 tasting in 1983. Most recently, from an* impériale*: very deep, intense yet lively, with long legs; rich, ripe, very fruity bouquet, perfection after 20 minutes, glorious, gingery an hour later. Full-bodied, very good quality and length. Very tannic, rather peppery finish.* Last tasted Sept 1987**** Time in hand.

Ch GRUAUD-LAROSE *Many notes, over half English bottled: by J Lyons, Dolamore, Saccone & Speed, British Transport Hotels, Godfrey & Duchene and the always dependable Army & Navy Stores.* All *good, which demonstrates that we knew how to bottle in those days. From the mid-1960s, a fruity, attractive wine. Two oxidised and one laden with mercaptan, all château bottled, in the early 1980s. The most perfect, an Army & Navy Stores bottling noted in 1983: still very deep, bouquet slow to develop but worth waiting for; very rich, fruity. A most attractive drink. Most recently, from an* impériale*: minty, opulent, multi-dimensional nose; full, fleshy, alcoholic, extract masking tannin.* Last tasted Sept 1987**** Still a lovely mouthful.

Ch d'ISSAN *Opaque and raw in 1962 and still unready though well balanced in the late 1970s. An excellent Harvey's bottling in 1986: sweet, fragrant bouquet; shapely. Most recently, château-bottled magnums: deep, velvety; scented; sweet, fullish, soft, rounded. Needs drinking.* Last tasted April 1991***(*)

Ch LAGRANGE *St-Julien. Quite nice when young but variable notes. Through the 1960s depending on the bottling. Rich appearance but 'so-so' 20 years on. Most recently a rather edgy Justerini & Brooks bottling.* Last tasted Nov 1983* Avoid.

Ch La LAGUNE *Tasted only once: lovely colour; vinous, elegant, mulberry-rich nose; sweet, lovely texture fruit and weight. "Perfect now".* At Desai's tasting of '59s, Nov 1983****

Ch LANGOA-BARTON *A good '59. Excellent mouthful in 1970, an attractive, fragrant bottle at the Desai tasting and, later the same month, a fully mature but equally fragrant Justerini & Brooks bottling.* Last tasted Nov 1983***

Ch LASCOMBES *Quite attractive in the mid-1960s, but, more recently, too plausible (could a '59 have been chaptalised?), overmature, lactic, vanilla nose and somewhat rasping finish.* Last tasted Nov 1983. At best*** Probably better to avoid.

Ch LEOVILLE-BARTON *A lovely wine from the start. Well made, well balanced, almost ready yet long-lasting capability even in 1963. With the exception of a Tylers bottling cracking up in the early 1970s, exceptionally good notes, improving as the years go by. A good colour; sweet, cedary, fragrant, classic bouquet; very sweet on the palate, medium full-bodied, nice texture, glorious richness and depth. Sweet to the end. A charmer.* Last noted at the Barton dinner at Brooks's, Nov 1989*****

Ch LEOVILLE-LAS-CASES *Although most of my dozen or so notes relate to château bottling, some are English, one Belgian bottled, all good. A classic, velvety yet tannic 'welterweight', showing particularly well in the 1970s. Still fairly deep, with a lovely, rich, old cedar nose. Noted as "claret at its best" in the mid-1980s.* Last tasted June 1984**** Will continue.

Ch LEOVILLE-POYFERRE *The first six notes made between 1967 and 1970 were mainly of various English merchants' bottlings and a bit lacking in admiration, except once, bottler unknown, a "classic with 10–20 years of life ahead". Notes made in the 1970s and 1980s, all of château bottlings, are very complimentary. Attractively rich; lovely, sweet, harmonious bouquet; fairly sweet, reasonably mouthfilling, soft, rounded — a "stunning '59".* Last tasted Nov 1986****

Ch LYNCH-BAGES *Unready for nearly 10 years, it seemed to turn the corner either side of 1970 with lovely Berry Bros and perfect IECWS bottlings noted, and, less good, by J E Jameson and Marshall Taplow. Very recently a dried out and scraggy double-magnum. Now medium-deep; spicy, vanilla blancmange bouquet; good fruit, rich, but piquant acidity noted on several occasions. Past its peak.* Last tasted Sept 1987. At best****

Ch La MISSION-HAUT-BRION *Bringing to a close a magnificent decade for the Woltners. Distinctly dry, full-bodied, velvety yet loaded with tannin in the early to mid-1970s. By the mid-1980s sweetening up. An impressively hefty wine at Desai's in 1985 and, most recently, at Wolf's comprehensive vertical, a magnum, still very deep, thick, rich-looking; a very sweet, fairly evolved, lovely, rich nose with fig-like fruit; sweetish, full-bodied, rich and rounded, still plenty of tannin, acidity and good length.* Last tasted June 1990***** Years of life ahead.

Ch MONTROSE *Very much a Montrose vintage. Very deep, hefty, made to last. Quite a few English bottlings noted in the 1970s, Justerini's being particularly good. The phrase "iron fist in velvet glove" used yet again: a splendid château bottling tasted in 1979, also referred to as "broad shouldered", and in 1983 as "rock of ages"! Still a huge, chunky, but beautiful balanced wine.* Last tasted Nov 1983****(*) Can take further bottle-age.

Ch MOUTON-BARON PHILIPPE *Very deep and rich in the early 1970s, a Green's and one S H Day bottling. Another Green's bottling showing well at Desai's horizontal. By the mid-1980s, very mature-looking; a crisp, acidic yet very attractive bouquet, and flavour to match. But lean and a bit too piquant.* Last tasted Nov 1983** Past its best.

Ch PALMER *The first few notes from 1969–1975 all of English bottlings, and all very rich. Two magnums, deep, impressive in 1979 and 1980, and six subsequent notes. Consistently a big vintage appearance, ruby-centred, though rim now maturing; ripe mulberry, spicy, cedary, scented bouquet; sweet entry, a huge, chunky, fleshy wine, with masculine muscle but velvety texture. Beautiful endtaste.* Last tasted; a magnum at dinner, Nov 1985*****

Ch PAPE-CLEMENT *Two elegant and refined British Transport Hotels bottlings in the late 1960s, supple and ready. Charming, château bottled, in 1972. Never deep in colour, a palish brick red at Desai's tasting of '59s in 1983, bouquet teasingly fragrant, cigarettes and cedar, but with a whiff of volatile acidity; soft, medium weight, moderate length and a very dry finish. Then a stalky, woody bottle.* Last tasted Dec 1984. At best*** Fading.

Ch PHELAN-SEGUR *From 1965 to 1973, three variable but overall unimpressive bottles, astringent yet not bad. At Desai's tasting of '59s good flavour but rough and raw.* Last tasted Nov 1983. Avoid.

Ch PICHON-BARON *Impressively deep-coloured from the start. Still opaque in 1983. Magnificent, though somewhat piquant Cabernet Sauvignon nose and flavour in the early 1970s. Great class, huge, massive, like Montrose with knobs on, rather '45-like, and awarded very high marks at Desai's tasting. Still intense though browning; ripe, rich bouquet but showing signs of cracking up. Thick, tannic, chewy but drying out.* Last tasted Feb 1985. At best****

Ch PICHON-LALANDE *After a good start, restrained in 1966, three bad Charles Kinloch bottlings in 1969 and various others, all adequate but unready, in the 1970s. Never quite as deep as the Baron; rich, fragrant bouquet; touch of sweetness and reasonable weight, fleshy, soft and attractive though showing its age.* Last tasted June 1987***

Ch PONTET-CANET *10 notes, almost all English bottled, including three surprisingly disappointing by the usually dependable Army & Navy Stores. Berry's and Rutherford's good in the 1970s and an unknown rich, rounded bottling in 1984.* Last tasted Feb 1987. At best**** but variable.

Ch RAUSAN-SEGLA *'Green' and dumb in the mid-1960s, a couple of good notes in the early 1970s. Most recent: still deep-coloured, very rich, singed, slightly malty and distinctly tannic.* Last tasted Nov 1983**

Ch RAUZAN-GASSIES *Many notes, all qualified, ranging from "lacking balance and character" in 1963, to traces of volatile acidity through the late 1960s and 1970s. Mature, orange-tinged; a fragrant but distressed nose, slightly better flavour. Short.* Last tasted Nov 1983* Avoid.

Ch TALBOT *Over a dozen notes, including consistently good English bottlings and, because of storage conditions, slightly variable château bottlings. Probably at its best, certainly impressively rich, in the late 1970s, early 1980s. By and large a fine '59 but drying out a little.* Last tasted Sept 1987. At best*** Worth seeking.

Ch La TOUR-HAUT-BRION *Four notes since 1978,*

all Woltner stock. Consistently deep, hefty, tannic, positive. Last noted at Karl-Heinz Wolf's tasting: deep but less definition than La Mission; fragrant, scented, singed Graves nose; medium dryness, fairly full-bodied, nice fruit, tannin and acidity. Last tasted June 1990*** Will keep.

VIEUX CH CERTAN *Six notes, from a good but unready Berry Bros bottling in 1967. Cedary nose and velvety texture in the mid-1970s though over-acidity occasionally noted. Not tasted since the early 1980s when it was still deep-coloured, with a rich, outstandingly good nose and taste, fullish, soft, well-balanced.* Last tasted Jan 1982****

TASTED IN THE 1980s:

Ch L'ANGELUS *Sweet, well developed, touch of bitterness.*

Ch BEAU SEJOUR BECOT *Dry, a bit lean, showing age.*

Ch BLISSA *An instantly attractive, still tannic Côtes de Bourg.*

Ch La CLOTTE *Very mature, elegant in the late 1960s, but two recent notes, one sound but dull, one woody.*

Ch FRANC-MAILLET *Pomerol. Justerini & Brooks, dry, hard, ungracious.*

Ch GISCOURS *Palish and mature for a '59, and a poor bottle recently.*

Ch GUADET-ST-JULIEN *Amber rim, chunky, sound but dull.*

Ch LAUJAC *A fine, deep, sound, but drying out Army & Navy stores bottling.*

Ch NEXON-LEMOYNE *Ludon. A fine, very deep, rich Corney & Barrow bottling.*

1960★

Roughly as important though not as attractive as 1958. At best, light luncheon wines: flavoury, refreshing. Almost all but the best should have been drunk in the late 1960s to early 1970s. Bought by the trade as stopgaps between the '59 and '61 vintages. Despite frosts in April and May, perfect flowering. June warm and dry but July and Aug cool and wet. Sept variable, late harvest mid-Oct.

Ch LAFITE *15 notes. Stalky, little to it even in the mid-1960s. A pleasant enough luncheon wine in the mid- to late 1970s. 10 years on, age conferring more fragrance and flavour – but: pale, almost more orange than red; sweet, slightly caramelly; soft, light, quite pleasant but certainly not of* grand vin *quality or with any future.* Last tasted in an impériale, Sept 1990*

Ch MARGAUX *Obscure and astringent from 1964 to 1971, then, as with Lafite, more interesting with bottle-age. By the mid-1980s gentle, scented, sugared nose and flavour. Fairly light. Dry finish.* Last tasted July 1984**

Ch LATOUR *Fragrant, piquant Cabernet aroma and taste, short and unready up to the late 1960s/early 1970s. A decade later still fairly deep-coloured for vintage and age; cedary nose; a bit sharp, crisp, overall dry.* Last tasted March 1989** In decline.

Ch MOUTON-ROTHSCHILD *Good notes throughout the 1970s. Very pronounced piquant Cabernet Sauvignon aroma; quite a dishy mouthful. Four good notes in the 1980s: good colour; open, intriguing, attractive, singed-ginger bouquet; touch of sweetness, light, flavoury, short, with end acidity.* Last tasted March 1989** Drink up.

Ch HAUT-BRION *Soft, light, forward in 1964, bland yet tinny and ageing fast by the early 1970s, then not tasted for 14 years. Light but sound, attractive, flavoury, dry finish.* Last tasted May 1985**

Ch CHEVAL-BLANC *Pale and fully mature-looking yet uncertain nose and taste by late 1960s. A dry old-tasting bottle in 1976 but an amber-rimmed, autumnal-nosed, yet lean and flavoury bottle a decade later.* Last tasted Sept 1986*

Ch DUCRU-BEAUCAILLOU *Soft, ready though short and with touch of bitterness in the mid- to late 1960s, piquancy and edginess slightly marring an otherwise light, quite stylish drink in the 1970s and early 1980s.* Last tasted Feb 1980* Just.

Ch FIGEAC *Strawberry-like, flavoury, in 1965, but a poor bottle in 1975 and a deep, brown, oxidised bottle more recently.* Last tasted March 1985. Decidedly risky.

Ch LAFON-ROCHET *Palish, light but delicious in 1978. Sound, touch of sweetness, little character, short when last tasted* July 1985*

Ch La LAGUNE *Most extraordinary: mild but very nice in 1974. More recently a singularly sweet, full, fleshy and well-balanced bottle.* Last tasted May 1985***

Ch LYNCH-BAGES *Several notes. A rather contrived, twisted caricature of the Lynch-Bages Cabernet* cassis *style. Surprisingly good healthy colour though with a fading, crumbling nose; very positive, flavoury but acidic.* Last tasted Sept 1982*

Ch MALESCOT-ST-EXUPERY *A piquant, flavoury note in 1967 and a surprising bottle from the château very recently. I thought it was a '59: impressively deep, mature brown rim; sweet on nose and palate, full-flavoured, showing age but lovely.* Last tasted Sept 1990***

Ch La MISSION-HAUT-BRION *A good 1960. Roasted, earthy nose and flavour. Approaching its best in 1970. At Desai's La Mission tasting in 1985, sweet, chaptalised, strange flavour, short, but showing well at Wolf's tasting: sweet, chocolaty nose; distinctly sweet on palate, fairly light but lovely, easy, charming.* Last tasted June 1990***

OTHERS TASTED IN THE 1980s:

Ch BARET *Dry, lean, pleasant enough.*

Ch CISSAC *Surprisingly deep, sound, quite nice, a bit raw.*

Ch La CONSEILLANTE *Tinge of orange; unknit but interesting, very flavoury.*

1961★★★★★

A magnificent vintage, vying with 1945 as the greatest since World War Two. What produced the conditions which enabled such intensely rich wines to be made? First the potential crop was severely reduced by poor flowering conditions. Rain at the end of July was too early to flesh out the remaining grapes and was followed by drought in Aug. All the soil nutrients were concentrated on fewer and smaller grapes. Finally a sunny Sept brought the grapes to full maturity, thickening the skins to provide colour and tannin. The high concentration of sugar converted into a proportionately high alcoholic content, and thick, sunburnt skins added colour and tannin. I have over 900 notes on '61s, covering just short of 200 châteaux. Overall, those wines with abundant flesh and fruit as well as high alcohol and tannins took time, sometimes 20 years, to reach pleasing drinkability; but those lacking concentration and on the lean side when younger have dried out, becoming acerbic, and will not recover. The best are supreme examples of the finest reds in the world.

Ch LAFITE *I was well into my Christie's career when I first tasted '61 Lafite: dry, refined, long and elegant in 1975. Then a couple of rather woody, scraggy bottles, immediately replaced by a lovely magnum at Dr Taams's epoch-making horizontal of '61s in 1978. Since when, over two dozen notes: fragrance is the operative word, but Lafite often takes time to open up, which is why detractors compare it unfavourably with the more immediately dramatic Mouton, the deeply impressive Latour, the obvious fleshy delights of Pétrus and the instantly forthcoming great Napa Cabernet Sauvignons.*

I confess that I decant old and fine wines timidly, tending to do so late, preferring to allow the wine to develop with air in the glass. But for once, as host at a Bordeaux Club dinner in April 1984, after standing the bottle for several days I decanted it at 6.50pm into an open-topped carafe. The nose at this stage had a rich, slightly earthy medicinal fragrance. It was served at 8.30 and by 9 o'clock the bouquet had blossomed fabulously. By 9.50 it was fully opened out, spicy, biscuity, retaining incredible intensity in the glass for another hour. On the palate it was dry, medium full-bodied, rich, very flavoury, with good acidity, length and aftertaste. Like the nose, the flavour seemed sweeter and 'warmer', sheer perfection after time in glass. Last tasted Oct 1989***** Drink now to well after the turn of the century.

Ch MARGAUX *Forget the am/pm nonsense (ante and post-Mentzelopoulos). The '61 Margaux is a great wine. First tasted in 1964, when it had a lovely flavour despite its unreadiness. Very rich, well-constituted, refined, great length noted in 1967. 27 notes, not one poor bottle. Fragrance is its hallmark, scented even: violets, ripe mulberries, cedar. Originally fairly deep but by no means opaque, it now has a lovely soft, autumnal colour, mellow brick red with a warm amber rim; also, like Lafite, it needs time in decanter and glass to open up. Its nose can be a bit dusty at first. On the last occasion, a delicious half-bottle, it had almost* fraise des bois *fruitiness of bouquet, blossoming gloriously, sweet, incredibly rich. Its initial youthful, tannic dryness had sweetened and softened, yet it kept a perfect grip on itself.* Last tasted July 1988***** Lovely now. Decades of life ahead.

Ch LATOUR *Not surprisingly, immensely deep, opaque-centred when young but, though still retaining considerable depth of colour, now less intense, with a lovely mature rim. Its nose dumb, rather severe in the late 1960s, has of course developed, but even after two decades appeared to be closed up and low-keyed, though it develops a gingery, cedary, fig-like fragrance with air. A huge, packed, fleshy, austere but magnificent wine, due to its high alcohol and tannins. Almost chewable. I have tasted more Latour than any other '61, some 30 or so notes, and believe that, like the '28, it will need a full half-century to come round.* Last tasted Sept 1990***(**) Unready. Drink 2000+

Ch MOUTON-ROTHSCHILD *First tasted in 1963: deep, dumb, and peppery but packed with fruit. Its opacity and intensity of appearance has never faltered but the crisp, rich Cabernet Sauvignon nose has loosened. In the early 1980s, sometimes spiky and with a whiff of asparagus but, given even a short time in glass, displaying the classic Mouton style. Originally dry, tannic, now with a distinct incoming sweetness, still full-bodied, yet soft and opulent. A glorious wine.* Last tasted March 1989***** Drink now and well into the 21st century.

Ch HAUT-BRION *Stalky and austere around the time of bottling, yet after only a year in bottle seemed relatively soft and forward. Many notes. As always, a totally different style, different taste, from its Médoc peers. But like them, an unmistakable depth of colour, just as the '45s had. A singed, tobacco and tea-leaves scent, harmonious — no harsh edges — confident, elegant and superb in its own slightly idiosyncratic way. An elegant, silky texture, as opposed to the more rustic, vigorous La Mission. Never very dry, it now has a pleasing sweetness, perfectly assimilated tannins and acidity, balance and length. Beautiful.* Last tasted Sept 1990***** Drink now and for many years to come.

Ch AUSONE *Five notes. In 1971: "not as great as most '61 Médocs though a more stylish, lighter and elegant version of Ausone '59". Unconvincing, slightly woody and austere in 1983, far more impressive in 1984 and a commanding* impériale *at Walter Eigensatz's in Wiesbaden in 1987. A massive, chunky wine, though still with a touch of tannic bitterness. Later that autumn: deep, very rich-looking; with mature rim; lovely, sweet, harmonious bouquet; dry, medium-full body, distinctive Ausone dried-leaf taste. Showing well but not my style of wine.* Last noted at Flatt's Ausone tasting, Oct 1987. Difficult to place. Perhaps***(*)

Ch CHEVAL-BLANC *Consistently producing wine of the quality to warrant its* 1er grand cru classé *(A) status. Many notes to endorse this. Deep, rich, velvety but with a touch of astringency when young, the wine has evolved beautifully. Opaque, intense and with unplumbable depth in 1983. The nose reminded me of a Fonseca port, liquorice, then prunes and raisins. But a whiff of volatile acidity* *was confirmed on the end palate. A very sweet, fairly full-bodied, soft, easy, agreeable wine, fully mature. Still incredibly deep, its rippling bouquet variously noted as flowery, medicinal (often a touch of iron in Cheval-Blanc), rich, and so forth. Consistently sweet, perfect weight, lovely flavour but sometimes a light, citrus touch. Anyway I like it.* Last tasted Oct 1987***** Drink now.

Ch PETRUS *Leaving aside the fact that this is one of the most excessively priced stars of the international saleroom, a pretty good mouthful of wine. "Rich" in well over a dozen notes since 1967; "black as Egypt's night", even after 18 years in bottle: magnificently opulent on nose and palate. From then on: appearance consistently deep and velvety though now showing signs of maturity; a bouquet that defies description, "rich ripe mulberry Merlot" noted regularly, also, after time in the glass, scented, spicy, vegetal, wholemeal, and then a sort of tarry cinnamon. Very sweet, immensely full-bodied, firm yet fleshy, velvety, with high extract masking tannin, lovely texture, slightly chocolaty, crammed with fruit. Worth every penny. . . .* Last noted at the 'Stockholm' Group tasting, April 1990*****
Magnificent now, and no end in sight.

Ch BATAILLEY *I wonder if, by 1963, English wine merchants still knew how to bottle wine of a vintage like '61? Hawkers of Plymouth unbalanced and acidic; Saccone & Speed not very interesting; Justerini & Brooks, fairly recently tasted, more like a '62, high-toned, lacking flesh. Some I described as hollow, some, mainly I presume château bottled, much better. Most recently deep, ripe, crisp, rich, still tannic.* Last tasted June 1989. At best***

Ch BEYCHEVELLE *First tasted in July 1963: attractive but, despite tannin and acidity, possibly an early developer. Evolving well 10 years later, and simply lovely aged 15: deep, soft, firm, velvety. More concentrated, judging from two notes in 1978, including one (19 out of 20) at Dr Taams's tasting of '61s, and, in 1981, superbly rich, ripe, almost burgundian and packed with fruit though not obtrusively so, at which stage it had reached its peak. More recently a degree of colour-loss, now fully mature-looking; fragrant but occasionally showing its age. Sweet, fullish, rounder and rich. The last three noted all bottled by Berry Bros: cedary, delicious, soft and attractive, yet lean. Perfect with food.* Last tasted April 1990**** Drink up.

Ch BRANAIRE-DUCRU *Variable, the best noted in 1979, château bottled, in New York with the Aarons. Spicy, singed, delicious but not great.* Last tasted Feb 1986. At best***

Ch BRANE-CANTENAC *Six mainly unsatisfactory notes. Probably the weakest of all the* 2ème cru classé *'61s. Fully mature by the early 1980s. Then a magnum, very mature-looking, with cardboardy nose and bitter finish.* Last tasted Feb 1986. At best**

Ch CALON-SEGUR *20 notes spread evenly over 21 years from 1967, half of them in the 1980s. Despite the expected tannins it developed quite quickly and, like a successful marriage, improved with age. An excellent bottling by Gloag's of Perth, in 1985, and a particularly attractive château bottling in 1986: deep; marvellous, harmonious, tea-like fragrance; some sweetness, full-bodied, sleek and sinewy. Tannic finish.* Last tasted Feb 1988. At best **** Will keep.

Ch CANTEMERLE *Three good notes: fragrant, with delicacy and great charm (1981 and 1986) but, more recently, a poor bottle.* Last tasted Jan 1988. Should be rated****

Ch CHASSE-SPLEEN *Some early notes. Three, English bottled, were variable but two, château bottled, both from a country house cellar in Northumberland, tasted in the 1980s, were impressively deep with equally deep bouquet, crisp, fruit and old oak (majestic English trees, not old barrels). Full yet soft, rich yet tannic. A massive, chewy wine.* Last tasted July 1986***(*)

Dom de CHEVALIER *Four notes since 1981. All deep-coloured, lively and appealing; gentle, harmonious bouquet that expanded in the glass, rich, great complexity, honey, tobacco and spice. Overall dry, perfectly packed.* Last tasted Oct 1986****

Ch COS D'ESTOURNEL *Magnificent, very tannic. A long life predicted, even in the mid- and late 1970s. Its original depth of colour translated into a luminous ruby, and its bouquet beautifully developed by the mid-1980s. Rather a singed, hot year, roasted character and flavour, but perfect fragrance, concentration, texture and aftertaste. Still tannic.* Last tasted Jan 1990****(*)

Ch CROIZET-BAGES *Rich, curious, "try again" noted in 1968. By the early 1980s fairly well developed. Never very deep, now a mature, nicely graduated garnet; Pauillac spice and fruit; touch of sweetness, nice lift-off of flavour, lightly tannic.* Last tasted Oct 1987**** Drink soon.

Ch DUCRU-BEAUCAILLOU *Over 30 notes well spread over 22 years and never less than excellent. Extremely high (19½ out of 20) marks at Dr Taams's '61 tasting in 1978 and only half a point below Palmer and Pichon-Lalande at Dr Skinner's '61 classed-growth tasting in 1986. A lovely, stylish drink throughout the 1970s, but in the 1980s showing some colour-loss and maturity, yet with a fully developed classic, cedary bouquet. The overall impression was of a dry wine, but age is appearing to sweeten it as the tannins soften. Lovely wine, lovely texture.* Last tasted Nov 1989***** but no longer upwardly mobile.

Ch L'EVANGILE *Four notes. Beautiful wine: still opaque, intense; herbaceous, spicy; sweet, packed with fruit, lovely texture. A rich mouthful.* Last noted at L'Evangile tasting at Spenier, May 1991****

Ch FIGEAC *Figeac's unusually high Cabernet Sauvignon content, very apparent in the late 1960s, has developed, alongside a forthcoming burgundy-like opulence in the early 1980s, to a deep, rich, stewed blackberry and vanilla. Still an impressively deep, intense and surprisingly youthful appearance, and now very sweet on the palate: soft, elegant, fruity, its richness masking life-supporting tannin. Food not needed to accompany this wine.* Last noted, a bottle from the château, at Desai's Figeac tasting, Dec 1989***** Probably perfection into the early decades of the next century.

Clos FOURTET *A rather untypical St-Emilion and a poor '61. Deep but lacking charm in 1975. Bottles in 1981, 1986 and latterly all spoiled by high acidity.* Last tasted June 1989. A little tart: avoid.

Ch LA GAFFELIERE *The acidity here merely brings out the flavour. Rounded and ready by the early 1970s, now, despite verging on the overripe, a glorious colour (acidity again); a very high-toned, fragrant bouquet; sweet, fruity, flavoury.* Last tasted June 1989*** Living precariously.

Ch LE GAY *Uneven and uncertain, high acidity and severity noted in its earlier years, but a superb bottle at a Bordeaux Club dinner. Rich, cherry red yet mature; very sweet nose, yet delicate, harmonious, opening up in the glass and retaining its fragrance for two hours; silky, smooth, leathery. Few overtones but lovely.* Last noted April 1984. At best****

Ch GAZIN *Many notes, several bottlings, from 1964 to 1986. With the exception of one deep, massive, unready bottle in 1981, variously described as lightweight for a '61, easy, flavoury but also dull, to which (at Dr Skinner's tasting) I added "open ended, rather feeble".* Last tasted Feb 1986* Avoid.

Ch GISCOURS *Seemed best when young. Slight rawness and acidity noted since 1981. Strangely, a bottle with a loose cork which fell in turned out to be quite a rich, flavoury drink, despite a car journey and with only one hour to settle before decanting.* Last tasted June 1989. Now only** Not highly recommended.

Ch GLORIA *Five glorious notes. Deep, fragrant, well-balanced.* Though not tasted since Feb 1981, I will bank on at least***

Ch GRAND-PUY-LACOSTE *Various bottlings in the early years, all good. Five excellent notes, four château bottled and one by Berry Bros, since 1980. Still fairly deep-coloured, ruby centre leading to fine, mature rim; delicious bouquet, still with firm, taut Cabernet Sauvignon aroma; full, fruity, crisp, with quite a lot of tannin and acidity.* High marks at Dr Skinner's classed-growth tasting of '61s, Feb 1986***(*)

Ch GRUAUD-LAROSE *Still fairly deep-coloured; glorious fruit; a fairly sweet mouthful despite its dry finish. Fullish, soft, rich, ripe and fleshy.* Last tasted Jan 1989***** A lovely drink now. Will keep.

Ch HAUT-BATAILLEY *Some below-standard English bottlings noted in the late 1960s, but in recent notes, all château bottled, challengingly attractive. Intense, almost exaggerated* cassis *fragrance. Crisp, silky, with good aftertaste.* Fairly high marks at Dr Skinner's tasting, Feb 1986*** Drink now.

*Ch d'*ISSAN *Refined, good texture but unready in the late 1960s, then a jump to a trio of deep, marvellously rich, classic Margaux bottles in 1981, 1982 and 1983. Good balance and length.* Last tasted Sept 1983****

Ch KIRWAN *One bottled by Schröder & Schÿler, the proprietors, and one by their London agent. The latter, in 1969: exciting and showing promise; the former rich, chunky, flavoury but with some sharpness on the finish.* Last tasted Sept 1982**

Ch LAFON-ROCHET *Two pleasant English and two rich château bottlings in the 1970s. More recently: deep, firm and flavoury, a distinctly singed coffee bean, bracken-like nose on two occasions, with teeth-gripping tannic finish.* Last tasted, without enthusiasm, Feb 1986*

Ch LAGRANGE *St-Julien. Relatively good notes from 1968 to 1977 but unimpressive in the 1980s. A bit raw and short. Later fragrant but slightly stalky, dry, lean. And a corky bottle.* Last tasted Feb 1986*

Ch LANGOA-BARTON *Six notes since 1981, alas three rather poor, the others quite nice. The last, a magnum, with a lively pink tinge; sweet, cigar box nose; flavoury, lightish, crisp citrus-like fruit and acidity.* Last tasted Feb 1986**

Ch LASCOMBES *First tasted and in fine form in the early 1970s: a "marvellous mouthful". A rich, chunky bottle in 1978 and 1979, but other bottles at the same time showing a bit of acidity which became more and more noticeable in the early 1980s. At best, very flavoury and refreshing, but a distinctly acetic Justerini bottling in 1984.* Last tasted Dec 1984. Well past best.

Ch LATOUR A POMEROL *One superb note. Pomerol at its best: deep ruby; glorious uplifting fruit; sweet, fleshy. A fabulous mouthful.* Feb 1986*****

Ch LEOVILLE-BARTON *11 good notes, three in mid- to late 1970s. Elegant, nice texture. But though firm and correct, of seven notes in the 1980s, two were poor bottles and the emphasis was on "lean". Nice weight. Most recently deep; soft, sweet cedar; fullish, chewy, extract, citrus touch.* Last tasted June 1991. At best****

Ch LEOVILLE-LAS-CASES *Mostly noted admiringly from 1967 to 1978, and even more so from 1980. Still a fine, deep, intense appearance though maturing; bouquet closed at first, sometimes dumb and dusty, but invariably and speedily developing a lovely classic, cedary fragrance. Positive, well-filled, shapely, still substantially loaded with tannin and acidity.* Last tasted Feb 1986****(*)

Ch LEOVILLE-POYFERRE *Various bottlings, nice wine. All château bottled, all seven notes made since 1980 uniformly good. Appeared to me at its most fragrant and glorious, a '61 with finesse, from 1983 to 1985, though tannin and, particularly, end acidity, becoming more noticeable.* Last tasted Feb 1986*** Attractive but possibly drying out.

Ch LYNCH-BAGES *Various and varying bottlings. At best a typically Mouton-like* cassis *nose, gingery, allspice. Six château bottlings in the 1980s, all good; a vinegary IECWS bottling and, most recently, an excellent Berry Bros bottling. Very rich, very flavoury.* Last tasted April 1990****

Ch MAGDELAINE *Soft, charming and lovely in the 1970s. A couple of poor bottles in 1981. Most recently: fine deep, luminous ruby; beautifully developed and harmonious bouquet; sweet, full, rich, chewy. Should be better known. Certainly in the Canon class.* Last tasted Feb 1986****

Ch MALESCOT-ST-EXUPERY *Tasted over 30 times. Piquant, flavoury. Deep, concentrated, Cabernet Sauvignon. Attractive but less blackcurranty than usual, very flavoury but specious. Four notes in 1986: fleshy, spicy, acidity creeping up. Two, recently, one in a marie-jeanne: still fairly deep; toasted, spicy, four-square nose; good flavour but lean and with quite a tannic bite.* Last tasted Sept 1990**

Ch La MISSION-HAUT-BRION *First tasted almost 20 years after it was made. 12 notes since 1981 at which stage it was opaque, with a bouquet of vast dimensions, sweet, complete, and distinctive tobacco flavour. Enormously impressive in a hectoring sort of way, with a touch of rawness. Otherwise consistently good notes. A magnum: still incredibly deep; restrained yet harmonious, coffee-like bouquet; still very sweet on palate, full-bodied, fleshy, with fabulous flavour. Masculine. Just one point below the ripe, suave Haut-Brion.* Last noted at Wolf's tasting, June 1990***** Will keep.

Ch MONTROSE *An archetypal tough Montrose, dry, raw and severe when young and* still *unready, though very impressive, 20 years after the vintage. Coming into its own in the mid-1980s, still with a deep '61 appearance, and marvellous fruit and fragrance when coaxed out of the glass. Soft, fleshy, yet a touch of sinewy leanness, still peppery with alcohol, and a long, somewhat mouth-puckering dry tannic finish.* Last tasted Feb 1986**** Still developing.

Ch MOUTON-BARON PHILIPPE *Usually crisp, often delicate, very flavoury, and, despite initial depth of colour, a lighter style of '61. By the mid-1980s very pretty though fully mature-looking; gentle, fragrant, Cabernet aroma, strawberry and gardenia scented; light style, lean, flavoury, lacking length. A pleasing, refreshing drink.* Last tasted in magnum Feb 1986*** Unlikely to gain much with age.

Ch PALMER *One of the least disputed greats of '61. First encountered as a rather restrained Berry Bros bottling in 1972 and evolving remorselessly with burgundian richness in the late 1970s. 15 unequivocably admirable bottles plus a magnificent magnum in the 1980s, and several bottles and a magnum in 1990. Still a deep, velvety appearance though now mature. Bouquet of great depth, fleshy, fragrant, ripe mulberry, and further qualified by totally inadequate expressions, the least of which is "glorious". Sweet, mouthfilling fruit and flavour, voluptuous, multi-dimensional. Just superb.* Last tasted, at a dinner given by Michel Klatt, Nov 1990***** A great future.

Ch PAPE-CLEMENT *Six notes since 1978. Very deep, mahogany, four fairly recently. Characteristic tobacco-like red Graves smell and taste. Firm; fragrant, elegant, quite sweet, lovely texture, still tannic despite its maturity.* Last tasted Nov 1990****

Ch PAVIE *Rather unimpressive when bottled and some variable performances since, including two acidic Grants' bottlings in the early 1970s and straightforward but rather dull château bottlings in 1978 and 1981, followed by two malty oxidised bottles, one dumb, dry, singed. More recently a bit austere and lacking length though the most recent really quite nice. But not a great Pavie nor a particularly good '61.* Last tasted June 1989. On average**

Ch PHELAN-SEGUR *Seven notes, all English bottled and quite good, between 1968 and 1975. Three, château bottled, in the 1980s, deep, cedary, with medicinal Médoc noses. Loose-knit, not bad.* Last tasted Feb 1986**

Ch PICHON-LONGUEVILLE, BARON *Three passable English bottlings between 1968 and 1976, and four poor château-bottled specimens, all with high volatile acidity spoiling an otherwise flavoury wine.* Last tasted Feb 1986. Avoid.

Ch PICHON-LONGUEVILLE, LALANDE *Infinitely better than the Baron. Again, my earlier notes all of English bottlings, which tend to be sold more speedily than château bottled. Five of the latter since 1981. All delicious. Vanilla on nose, plus fruit. Soft, rich, fragrant, good length and finish.* High marks at Dr Skinner's '61 tasting in Feb 1986**** Now completely mature.

Ch PONTET-CANET *The first 10 notes, 1967 to 1975, all English bottled, J Lyons the worst, too long in wood; the Army & Navy Stores the best. Five bottled by Cruse, the proprietors, in Bordeaux (Pontet-Canet was never bottled at the château at this period), tasted between 1979 and 1986, consistently excellent: very rich, almost Latour-like in its concentration. Impressive but lacking charm.* Last tasted Feb 1989. Could even achieve*****

Ch RAUSAN-SEGLA *Quite promising when young. The best, château bottled, from a perfect Northumberland cellar in 1981, sporting the rich '61 robe, that oh-so-beautiful scent as it was being decanted, and soft, ripe, Margaux character. More recently, a penetrating bouquet, cedar, vanilla, spicy; high alcoholic content, rich, long, 'cheesy', tannic.* Last tasted Sept 1986**** And life ahead.

Ch RAUZAN-GASSIES *Toasted, lean, raw, lacking length.* Last tasted March 1983.

Ch TALBOT *Quicker developing than expected. Now very ripe, appealing, fragrant — touch of fennel — and a whiff of decay. Nice though.* Last tasted April 1987****

Ch La TOUR-HAUT-BRION *Strange but attractive. Sweet, chunky, chewy.* June 1990***

Ch La TOUR-DE-MONS *A copybook example of a well-made* bourgeois *claret; lovely after a decade but lacking the* cru classé *pedigree, which boils down to what the French call* terroir, *to develop and age gracefully. Half a dozen notes since 1986. All ripe, good up to a point but coming apart at the seams.* Last tasted, April 1990. Now**

Ch TROTANOY *Six notes, three in the 1980s. A magnificently deep-coloured wine; developing a multi-faceted bouquet, exciting, rich, black treacle; rich yet tannic, lean, elegant, chewy. Marvellous texture.* Last tasted Jan 1986***** Will keep.

ALSO TASTED IN THE 1980s:

Ch L'ANGELUS *Nice texture but drying out.*

Ch BARET *Graves. Seven notes, all deep, rich, good for its class.*

Ch BEAU SEJOUR BECOT *Very deep, plummy, fleshy and firm.*

Ch BEAUSEJOUR-FAGUET *Soft, velvety, spicy.*

Ch BELAIR *St-Emilion. Beautiful colour, fragrant, charming, needs drinking.*

Ch BOYD-CANTENAC *Fragrant, a rather specious charmer.*

Ch LA CABANNE *Not bad but raw, showing age.*

Ch CANON *Superb.*

CARRUADES DE CH LAFITE *Fruity, flavoury, nice weight. Drink up.*

Ch CISSAC *Packed with fruit though drying out.*
Ch CITRAN *Pale for a '61, well past best.*
Clos L'EGLISE *Deep, forthcoming and fragrant, impressive yet fleshy, still tannic.*
Ch FERRIERE *Fragrant and flavoury.*
Ch La GRACE-DIEU *Rich, chewy, gentle.*
Ch GRAND-PUY-DUCASSE *Raw and unimpressive.*
Ch LYNCH-MOUSSAS *(Berry Bros) Fabulous colour and nose, lean, very dry but fruity.*
Ch de MIRAIL *Graves. A minor minty charmer.*
Ch MONBOUSQUET *Several notes: rich, chunky, needs drinking.*
Ch MOULINET *On its way out.*
Ch PETIT-VILLAGE *Soft, straightforward. Not a heavyweight. Needs drinking.*
Ch ST-PIERRE-BONTEMPS-ET-SEVAISTRE *Not bad but a bit raw.*
Ch La TOUR-DU-PIN *Lovely colour, crisp, fruity, lots to it.*
Ch VILLEMAURINE *Lovely flavour and texture.*
VIEUX CH CERTAN *Disappointing.*

1962★★★★

A very good vintage but undeservedly overlooked. Upstaged by the great, concentrated '61s, the '62s can still be exciting, flavoury and racy. Though generally lean they are elegant and stylish. A distinct redness gives advance notice of fairly high fixed acidity, their only weakness, but even this, at best, merely adds to their zest. Delicious with food. The top wines well worth looking out for. Cold, wet weather to end May. Good flowering mid-June, very hot summer and autumn with welcome showers. Late harvest from Oct 9 in good conditions. Of the 190 châteaux recently tasted, the following entries are the most representative.

Ch LAFITE *22 notes. From the early 1970s a stylish, refined, elegant wine. Depth of colour has changed little. It retains its lively red core leading to a lovely broad mature edge; sweet, gingery, fragrant bouquet; lightish but firm style, lean, very flavoury, spicy, crisp dry finish. Last noted, pre-sale, in Chicago, Sept 1990★★★★*

Ch MARGAUX *First tasted in cask. Like the Lafite, very crisp and stylish, though its rawness — the '62 acidity — noticeable for almost 20 years. Still fairly deep and plum-coloured; attractive bouquet, violets, leaving marvellous fragrance in the emptied glass; nice weight, fruit, lean, elegant, lacking the length of a great vintage. Very dry finish. Acidity just in check. Last tasted Sept 1987★★★★ but only just.*

Ch LATOUR *First tasted in 1965: deep purple, packed tight with fruit, a raw edge leading to a hard tannic-acid finish. Otherwise very impressive. More recently, at the Latour/Mouton tasting in 1989: deep, intense red; fine cedar and fruit; full, firm, crisp. Last tasted Sept 1990★★★★*

Ch MOUTON-ROTHSCHILD *First tasted in 1965 and its fresh Cabernet Sauvignon aroma has persisted, past a peppery stage in the mid-1970s to a soft, broad richness. Depth and intensity seem almost unchanged, still with its youthfully red tinge. Fairly full-bodied with a lovely flavour, tannic yet delicate, lean, good acidity. Last noted at Frericks' tasting March 1989★★★★ Hard to predict but no signs of weakness.*

Ch HAUT-BRION *Naturally astringent in cask, but between five and 10 years old, very soft, rich and attractive. A velvety texture first noted in 1971. Still very deep, a fine ruby; fragrant but initially restrained bouquet, developing in the glass; fairly sweet, fairly full-bodied, lovely fruit and with Haut-Brion elegance and distinctive Graves taste. Last tasted June 1990★★★★ and should continue 10–20 years.*

Ch AUSONE *In the early to mid-1970s rather pale and mature-looking though with a pleasant nose. Four good notes in the 1980s. Most recently, at Flatt's Ausone tasting, a lively, attractive though not deep appearance; light, delicate, fragrant, slightly singed bouquet; dryish, lightish, easy yet crisp, fully mature, good length and finish. One of the most attractive Ausones I have ever tasted. Last noted Oct 1987. A generous★★★★★ Drink now.*

Ch CHEVAL-BLANC *Many notes from mid-1960s. Medium depth, less aggressively red than the Médocs. Now a mellow brick red; at best a lovely, slightly tobacco-like bouquet; soft, gentle yet lively. The last eight notes show bottle variation, including a woody bottle, some better developed than others, some harder, some with more acidity. Last tasted Sept 1987. At best★★★*

Ch PETRUS *10 very consistent notes spread evenly from 1967. A deep sweet rich wine from the start. Now medium-deep and mature-looking; very fragrant bouquet, mint, violets, ripe mulberries; a very sweet, opulent mouthful, good fruit, extract, length, perfect tannin and acidity. Last tasted Sept 1990★★★★★ This will see us all out.*

Ch BATAILLEY *Harvey's bottling fruity but a bit coarse aged four. Berry Bros acidic in 1974, and a fairly deep, cedary, chunky, rich and fruity château bottling at Rodenstock's tasting of '62s. Last noted Sept 1987. At best★★★*

Ch BELAIR *St-Emilion. Fully mature, orange-tinged; idiosyncratic, dried-leaves character opening up fragrantly. Nice weight, elegant and easy. Sept 1987★★★*

Ch BEYCHEVELLE *Lightish and fairly forward when young but seems to have come into its own in the early to mid-1980s. Deep-coloured; rich, spicy nose and flavour, marvellous aftertaste. Great style. Almost '61 quality. Most recently a good Berry Bros bottling, deep, mature, soft, very pleasant. Last tasted Dec 1985. At best★★★★*

Ch BRANE-CANTENAC *Typically ripe meaty nose, a bit dull though advanced in 1969. Then at Rodenstock's '62 marathon: palish, slightly orange-tinged; bouquet curiously rich but very attractive in its way; dry, lean, with some class. Last tasted Sept 1987★★ Drink up.*

Ch CALON-SEGUR *Over a dozen notes. A youthfully astringent Harvey's bottling; two very flavoury Justerini & Brooks bottlings in the mid-1970s, a touch of acidity showing, with fruity château bottlings interspersed. In the 1980s an attractive, well-developed Hedges & Butler bottling; a well-evolved, lean, fruity, château bottling and a very good* impériale: *deep, still youthful, fruity, lovely bouquet, medium dryness and fullness, showing well.* Last noted at Rodenstock's '62s tasting, Sept 1987**** Will continue to develop.

Ch CANON *Two copybook notes in 1967. A firm, rich, flavoury mouthfiller. Lively, deep, cherry-centred, fully evolved.* The last, a jeroboam, in Sept 1987**** Lovely now. Will keep.

CARRUADES DE CH LAFITE *Six notes from 1969. A lightish, delightful, early developer, peaking in the late 1970s but continuing in a fragrant citrus-like way. Showing well in half-bottles at Flatt's. Very sweet, rich, fully evolved bouquet and flavour.* Last tasted Oct 1988***

Ch La CONSEILLANTE *One early but encouraging note in 1966 and two recent tastings confirm its high quality. A beautiful magnum, at peak at Rodenstock's '62s tasting and, a year later, a lovely soft garnet red with touch of cherry; equally warm, soft, leafy-arboured bouquet; soft, very flavoury.* Last tasted July 1988**** Perfect now but will keep.

Ch COS D'ESTOURNEL *Seven notes in the 1980s: all, except two brown and oxidised magnums at Rodenstock's, very good including a deep, lovely, extraordinarily fragrant, soft and fleshy Justerini & Brooks bottling.* Last noted Sept 1987. At best***

Ch DUCRU-BEAUCAILLOU *15 mainly good notes, varying bottlers, Berry Bros being as good in 1988 as in 1971. At the same tasting a lovely château bottling: pleasant weight, colour and body; a beautiful upturned spicy bouquet; touch of sweetness, crisp, lively flavour and acidity.* Last noted June 1988. At best**** but now on a bit of a knife-edge.

Ch FIGEAC *Several notes including good English bottlings tasted prior to 1978. A rich, cedar, menthol and vanilla-nosed double-magnum at Rodenstock's '62s tasting, elegant, lean, flavoury, and an almost identically noted bottle at Desai's Figeac tasting: medium depth, open, mature; vanilla again, beautiful development of bouquet; distinctly sweet, soft, chewy, fruity. Dry finish.* Last tasted Dec 1989**** Ready.

Ch La FLEUR-PETRUS *Attractive in 1974, fully developed by 1980. Most recently: richly coloured, orange-tinged maturity; rather idiosyncratic, ripe mulberry nose; sweet, fruity, soft yet tannic.* Last noted, Rodenstock's '62s tasting, Sept 1987***

Ch La GAFFELIERE-NAUDES *(the same as La Gaffelière, the Naudes being dropped nowadays). Various good bottlings prior to 1980, thereafter it had nothing to offer. Attractive, flavoury but hot and acid-etched.* Last noted, in magnum, at Rodenstock's, Sept 1987** Drink up.

Ch GAZIN *10 notes, mainly château bottled, mainly good. As agreeable to drink in 1980 as in 1971. More recently, at Rodenstock's: open, fragrant, touch of mushroom soup, very flavoury, slightly tinny finish.* Last tasted Sept 1987*** but declining.

Ch GISCOURS *Six good notes between 1962 and 1979 when acidity was beginning to push through. Tasted once in the 1980s: rich colour, fully mature; low-keyed, rather static but classic 'cheesy' bouquet; dry, high-toned flavour, more positive than nose. Refreshing.* Last noted at Rodenstock's tasting, Sept 1987** Drink up.

Ch GRAND-PUY-LACOSTE *Varying bottlings prior to 1980, all château bottled since. Crisp, high-toned, flavoury in the early 1980s. Magnum at Rodenstock's rich, plummy, pink-tinged; very fragrant; dry, medium-full, lean, classic, good fruit.* Last tasted Sept 1987***

Ch GRUAUD-LAROSE *Many notes since 1966. All good. Several recent notes. Still deep and lively; gloriously evolved, rich, tarry bouquet; fullish, now a bit lean, but with good length and dry finish. Still a fine drink.* Last tasted Feb 1989****

Ch HAUT-BATAILLEY *Two good notes. Cedary, complex in 1973. Now fully mature, slightly orange-tinged; very fragrant spicy nose; touch of sweetness, fullish, flavoury, some flesh but overall lean. Good length.* Last tasted Sept 1987****

Ch KIRWAN *Several rather raw, stalky bottlings in the 1960s. Then a jump of 18 years when it was served, ingeniously, with caviar, langoustines and black truffles.* At a grand cru dinner, Ch Haut-Brion, June 1987*** After that it can survive anything.

Clos des JACOBINS *Pleasant, flavoury in 1975. Maturing nicely, spicy, fragrant, soft, delightful and original. Lovely texture.* Last tasted Oct 1983*** Doubtless surviving.

Ch LANGOA-BARTON *A charming and agreeable Barton & Guestier bottling in 1969, an excellent but still unready Berry Bros magnum the next year. Most recently: in magnums from the château: deep, red-tinged; very fragrant, distinct Cabernet nose; touch of sweetness, nice weight, crisp and flavoury.* Last noted at Brooks's Barton dinner, Nov 1989***

Ch LASCOMBES *Fruity, chunky and tannic in 1970. Three consistent notes in the 1980s: cherry red; fragrant, shapely, no harsh edges; surprisingly sweet but with refreshing '62 acidity — nice fruit. Complete.* Last tasted Sept 1987*** and more to come.

Ch LEOVILLE-BARTON *Good, slightly austere, château and Berry Bros bottlings between 1969 and 1975. Showing well at Rodenstock's '62s tasting: rich colour and nose; classic, fragrant, cedar and tea leaves. Lean, elegant, nice weight, slightly lacking length, overall dry.* Last noted Sept 1987*** Will survive.

Ch LEOVILLE-LAS-CASES *Many notes, all good except two corked bottles in 1986, the third being superb, "perfect claret". Recently: deep, rich, velvety appearance; subtle, harmonious, rich cedary, meaty nose of great profundity; substantial, fleshy, good fruit, length and aftertaste.* Last tasted Sept 1987***** Will continue.

Ch LEOVILLE-POYFERRE *Not in the same class as Las-Cases and with less drive than Léoville-Barton. Nevertheless, in magnum, a similar depth and weight to the Barton, less red, more mature-looking; bouquet, though not very well-knit, developed nicely; dry, light style, easy charm.* Last tasted Sept 1987. Just about*** but lacking conviction.

Ch LYNCH-BAGES *A vintage tailor-made for Lynch-Bages, bringing out its typically exuberant Cabernet scent and taste. Many notes, various bottlings, all favourable up to the late 1970s when* *the acidity seemed to be catching up. Seemed at its peak, certainly a magnificently flavoury bottle, in 1980, a rich spicy Corney & Barrow bottling in 1983 but, at Rodenstock's, disappointing, with more than a whiff of volatile acidity and cheesy, lactic taste. Last tasted Sept 1987. Now a risky** or, at best****

Ch MAGDELAINE *I have always had a soft spot for this too little known wine. Good notes. Rich, velvety in the 1970s. Then a string of half-bottles, still with good fruit, silky tannins, nice weight. Last tasted May 1991****

Ch MALESCOT-MARGAUX *(same as St-Exupéry). Should really be called St Exuberant: flavoury, sometimes outrageously so, like Lynch-Bages but somehow a little coarser and lacking the latter's dazzling style. Savoury but over-acidic in 1987. Most recently, in a marie-jeanne, rather lacking character though still tannic. Last tasted Sept 1990***

Ch MEYNEY *Four notes, only one recent: lively red; peppery, clean; lightish, lean, flavoury, dry finish. Last tasted in double-magnum, Sept 1987***

Ch La MISSION-HAUT-BRION *12 notes. Impressive yet somehow not wholly satisfactory. Several recent notes, virtually all ex-Woltner cellars, some in magnums. Still quite deep, crisp and lively-looking; very forthcoming, very fragrant but strange old dried-leaves character; fairly sweet and full-bodied, a rich and powerful wine, well-endowed with alcohol but perhaps over-endowed with acidity. Last noted at Wolf's tasting, June 1990*** For those who like living dangerously.*

Ch MONTROSE *Several notes, including two good Justerini & Brooks bottlings, from 1968 to 1975. Austere but attractive. Then, 12 years on, showing well at Rodenstock's '62s tasting: lovely, flavoury, lean, with dry finish. Last tasted Sept 1987**(*) The old Montrose style. Needs plenty of bottle-age.*

Ch MOUTON-BARON PHILIPPE *Lively, fragrant, a pleasant easy fruitiness, just enough flesh, good length. Last noted Sept 1987****

Ch PALMER *Good notes from 1965. Perhaps the most impressive, an* impériale *at a Saintsbury Club 'meeting' in 1984 when it almost achieved the depth and fleshy ripeness of the '61. Similarly rich and fruity in magnums at Rodenstock's and, most recently, some loss of colour, but lovely; a warm-brick, harmonious, mulberry nose that opened up delectably; slightly sweet, medium-full body, fleshy, with an attenuated, slightly acidic finish, otherwise a perfect drink. Last tasted June 1988*****

Ch PAPE-CLEMENT *Many notes, but tasted only once since 1977. One of my favourite '62s. Now fully mature, rich, but with a touch of orange; extraordinary, open, Lafite-like fragrance; touch of sweetness, light Médoc-like style, flavoury and charming. Last noted at Rodenstock's, Sept 1987*****

Ch PAVIE *After a rough start, seemed to have reached a satisfactory level in the 1980s. Rich, ripe, farmyard bouquet and taste. Soft, nice texture, lean but flavoury, crisp acidity. Last tasted Sept 1987****

Ch PICHON-BARON *Six rather half-hearted notes made between 1969 and 1975. Then one quite nice bottle: deep, rich, yet with a piquant dry finish. Last tasted May 1981. To be on the safe side***

Ch PICHON-LALANDE *Also a slow starter, but attractive by the mid-1970s. A rich, thick-looking,* impériale *at Rodenstock's tasting, flavour better than nose though the latter was opulent and quite sweet. Last tasted Sept 1987***

Ch La POINTE *Three typically silky Pomerol English bottlings in the 1960s, another good bottle in 1973, and showing well at Rodenstock's. Beautiful luminosity; warm, rich, hefty nose; fairly sweet and full, some rich fruit and extract. One of the best La Pointes I can recall. Last tasted Sept 1987**** Lovely now.*

Ch PONTET-CANET *Masses of notes, Bordeaux and English bottled, and variable. Tasted only once since the 1970s, in the Rodenstock line-up of '62s. High-toned but attractive nose. Sweet, fullish, spicy, flavour enhanced but the acidic tail wagging the dog. Last tasted from a double-magnum, Sept 1987***

Ch RAUSAN-SEGLA *Many notes between 1964 and 1975, 'green' appearing quite frequently. Age has softened it a little. Fully evolved bouquet of some delicacy. Quite stylish. Nice acidity. Last noted Sept 1987***

Ch RAUZAN-GASSIES *Just three notes. Quite nice in 1968. A double-magnum at Rodenstock's in 1987: good colour, jammy, heavily chaptalised nose; fullish, thick, fruity, lacking length. More recently, very mature-looking; touch of marzipan on the nose; a bit raw. Last tasted Sept 1990**

Clos RENE *Several worthy Harvey's bottlings noted up until the early 1970s including a superbly silky château bottling in 1968. Still fairly deep; sweet, high-toned, blancmange-like nose; rich, meaty, earthy. Citrus-like end acidity. Last tasted Sept 1987*** Clearly a Pomerol year, though all but the top wines now past their best.*

Ch de SALES *Three nice, silky and forward Harvey's bottlings in the 1960s, and several bottles with varying levels, the best being lovely, as was a double-magnum later that year: medium, mature; low-keyed but nice fruit and some depth; "sweet, easy" again, attractive, light style. Last tasted Sept 1987****

Ch TALBOT *Many notes, various bottlings, all good. The last two bottled in Copenhagen by Kjaer & Sommerfeldt: warm, rich, vinous, delicious. Last noted at the Aalholm Castle cellar pre-sale tasting, Sept 1989**** Very much alive and kicking.*

VIEUX CH CERTAN *Two notes: fullish, soft, velvety, good grip in 1973. Curiously alcoholic nose, almost like cognac, fullish but lean dry finish. Last tasted Sept 1987***

OTHER '62s LAST TASTED IN THE 1980s:

Ch L'ARROSEE *Lively, attractive, but a bit thin and sharp.*

Ch BARET *Surprisingly good classic Graves character, flavoury but drying out.*

Ch BEAUREGARD *Pomerol. Fragrant, agreeable, lean yet fleshy.*

Ch BEAU SEJOUR BECOT *Firm, fruity.*

Ch BELGRAVE *A fruity but rather soft, mushy jeroboam.*

Ch BOUSCAUT *Curious magnum, boiled sweets, very flavoury, faded away.*

Ch CHASSE-SPLEEN *Dry, raw and tannic.*

Ch CISSAC *Twice: hard-nosed yet very flavoury, rich, chewy.*
Ch COUFRAN *In magnum, fully developed, delicious, though a bit dried out.*
Ch CROIZET-BAGES *Delicious.*
Ch L'EVANGILE *Fragrant, flavoury, with citrus touch on nose and palate. Fully evolved.*
Ch FOMBRAUGE *Chunky, fruity but coarse, lean, uninspiring.*
Ch GLORIA *A minor classic.*
Ch LATOUR A POMEROL *Nice weight, medicinal, ripe.*
Ch MARQUIS-DE-TERME *Rich, fruity, fragrant, with strange smell of tripe; a bit hollow, though flavoury.*
Ch Les ORMES-DE-PEZ *Rich, also very flavoury but crumbling.*
Ch PRIEURE-LICHINE *Plummy; cedar and fruit; pleasant punchy style, lean, dry finish.*
Ch SMITH-HAUT-LAFITTE *Deep, intense, fragrant, lovely vinosity and texture, mouthfilling and elegant.*
Ch SOUTARD *Fully mature; scent like the skin of roast chicken; soft, flavoury, easy. Needs drinking.*
Ch du TAILLAN *Meaty, holding well.*
Ch TAILLEFER *Tart.*
Ch TERTRE-DAUGAY *Citrus, tinny, sweet but sharp.*
Ch TROTTEVIEILLE *Fruity, no finesse.*

1963

A poor, dismissable vintage. Wedged uncomfortably between the much-bought '62s and the generally well-liked '64s, the trade could afford to by-pass the '63s, which is why relatively few have been tasted.

An instance of 'don't shoot the pianist'. Even the most gifted winemaker could not do much after a growing year which was inhibited by poor flowering conditions, and a cold, wet summer, causing rot. Sun came too late to salvage the small crop. Mainly light and acidic; though some just passable, flavoury and piquant wines were made.

Ch LAFITE *Thin in 1967. Five recent notes all at pre-sale tastings. Rosehip pink, pale, and watery rimmed; surprisingly fragrant though frail bouquet; dry, thin, short but flavoury. Despite heavy chaptalisation and few* cuves *being selected, it was short-sighted to market this as the* grand vin. *Last tasted Oct 1988**
Ch MOUTON-ROTHSCHILD *Not unattractive in cask. Two fairly recent notes, both made at major vertical tastings: pale and orange-tinged; delicate but decayed with chocolaty chaptalised character; surprisingly sweet, light, a bit skinny and tinny, otherwise inoffensive; and a fragrant but faded, lightly acidic old-tasting double-magnum. Last noted Sept 1990**

Ch La MISSION-HAUT-BRION *Four notes, two recent: an unexpectedly good colour; very sweet, stewed, chocolaty, medicinal (oyster shell) nose that improved in the glass; fairly dry, piquant, chaptalised, tobacco-plus-fruit flavour. Slightly bitter finish. Last noted at Wolf's tasting, June 1980** *Just.*
Ch MONTROSE *Four notes. The most recent: colour lively, not too bad; light, slightly malic but quite attractive nose; fairly light, flavoury, acidic, but could be worse. Last tasted Sept 1987**

LAST TASTED MAINLY IN THE MID-1970s–80s:

Ch MARGAUX *Five notes. Quite nice but not Margaux.*
Ch LATOUR *Surprisingly deep-coloured and nice nose for a '63; dry, short, not bad.*
Ch HAUT-BRION *Doubtless now thin and faded.*
Ch BEYCHEVELLE *Browning, stewed nose, some richness but raw and short.*
Ch CALON-SEGUR *Prematurely aged.*
Ch COS D'ESTOURNEL *Consistently one of the best '63s.*
Ch DUCRU-BEAUCAILLOU *Relatively rich, but raw.*
Ch PONTET-CANET *Pale, pretty, piquant, quite flavoury.*

1964★★ to ★★★★

Deservedly popular in its early days, now, like the '62, largely forgotten. Yet not only were many attractive wines made but some are still beautiful to drink and, moreover, singularly good value at auction (which is about the only place to buy them). Those 'in the know' dwell on the heavy rains which descended on parts of the Médoc, separating the AR from the PR (ante rain, post rain), as if, somehow, the fate of the entire vintage depended on this.

The growing season was favourable save for heavy rain part-way through the Médoc harvest. Mild wet winter, pleasantly warm spring, excellent flowering conditions. Summer hot and dry ensuring, by mid-Sept, a sound, ripe harvest. The story is that continuous torrential rainfall cut the harvest in two. To a certain extent this is true. Most started picking towards the end of Sept, and the rain started on Oct 8. However, the early-ripening Merlot had been picked, favouring, in particular, Pomerol and St-Emilion. Also much of the Cabernet Sauvignon had been brought in. Those who delayed picking the Cabernet in order to gain extra ripeness *were* caught. Médoc picking dates are shown where known. The Graves were less affected, and Pomerol and St-Emilion hardly at all.

Ch LAFITE *Picking from Sept 26 to Oct 16. Rain came halfway through, and it shows. Eight notes since 1980 variously describe the wine as flavoury but short and scraggy though, at Flatt's mammoth Lafite tasting in New Orleans in 1988, a bottle and a jeroboam were not bad. The former had a rich, attractive colour, crisp strawberry-scented fragrance, flavoury, chewy even, but with a slightly bitter finish. Out of jeroboam, at lunch, it looked surprisingly deep and relatively full-bodied and tannic. Had a special cask been put aside for the* grands formats, *or had it been refreshed at the château before recorking? Most recently, even more complimentary: medium, still youthful though mahogany-rimmed colour; sweet, ripe bouquet that settled down harmoniously; touch of sweetness, lightish weight, nice flavour, dry finish. As if the wine had taken a second breath.* Last tasted July 1990** No great future but no signs of collapsing.

Ch MARGAUX *Picked from Sept 19 to Oct 15. Attractive in cask and in its earlier years. Certainly better than the '64 Lafite. Three notes in the 1980s. The more recent, a magnum at Desai's in 1987: medium-deep; fragrant yet peppery, open-knit, fully evolved nose; slightly hard and assertive mid-palate. Touch of end acidity giving it a dry and not very classy finish. Most recently, a deep-coloured jeroboam with fragrant though stalky nose, good fruit, stern and tannic, needing time.* Last tasted Sept 1990**

Ch LATOUR *Picking started Sept 25 and finished the day before the rains came. Consequently a vastly superior wine, the finest of the '64 Médocs. Many notes, 12 since 1980. Still virtually opaque; lovely scent, spicy, violets, crisp yet ripe; sweet, fairly full-bodied, rich, velvety, well laden with fruit, nicely balanced.* Last noted, dining at the château, Nov 1990***** Will keep.

Ch MOUTON-ROTHSCHILD *Late-picked, Oct 1–16, and though not unattractive, a shadow of its normal self. Five notes in the 1980s all noting lack of length. The colour, though palish, quite lively and attractive; soft, gentle, strawberry-gingery nose, quite different from the usual blast of Cabernet Sauvignon. Light, flavoury but unconvincing.* Last noted, Frericks/Wodarz Latour and Mouton tasting, March 1989. At best**

Ch HAUT-BRION *Clearly fewer problems in the Graves. Several notes in the early to mid-1980s. Fairly deep, lively; intriguing, smoky, pitch pine and vanilla bouquet; perfect flavour, albeit with that characteristic tobacco taste, well balanced. Sleek, some tannin but nicely matured. Perfect now but will keep well.* Last tasted March 1991****

Ch AUSONE *Five recent notes. Idiosyncratic as always, but a good wine. At Flatt's Ausone tasting in 1987, an attractive mature colour; rich, roasted, broad, fully opened-out bouquet; taste of dry leaves and tobacco (charred wood in an earlier note). Overall dry. And most recently, caramel sweetness noted on the nose, surprisingly nice, some charm.* The last at a 1er grand cru St-Emilion dinner at Cheval-Blanc, June 1989***

Ch CHEVAL-BLANC *A lovely wine, one of my favourite — certainly one of the best — '64s. Many notes: attractive in cask and fairly quick-maturing. Consistently delicious since the late 1960s, and for years to come. A wine with lovely legs, a gloriously rich bouquet, fairly sweet, fairly full-bodied, ripe fruit, soft, rich, refreshing.* Last tasted June 1989. Perhaps an over-generous*****

Ch PETRUS *The year when Mouiex purchased a half-share. My original rave notices based on six tastings between 1976 and 1978 have certainly since been qualified. In 1986, at Frericks' vertical, all in magnums; a lovely deep cherry red; curious, intriguing, tea-like, but at first less-than-harmonious bouquet, though it settled down; fullish, round, chunky, very fruity and flavoury, quite a punch, but nowhere near the top of the post-war range of vintages. A pleasant, soft, fleshy bottle in 1987. Next, at the 'Stockholm' tasting: deep, rich, lively, not unlike the '61 but a bit too red, hinting at the acidity to come; again, tea-like, slightly peppery, fragrant but with distinctly high volatile acidity which, for me, spoiled its finish. Yet, most recently, a deep, sweet, rich and rounded bottle with good finish. Whether bottles are now variable or some are tiring I do not know.* Last tasted Nov 1990. At best****

Ch BATAILLEY *Picked Sept 22 to Oct 12. Slightly sweet, lean and spicy.* Tasted June 1987***

Ch BEYCHEVELLE *A rich but slightly acidic* impériale *in 1982. Two notes mid-1980s, chunky rather than elegant. Most recently: good colour; low-keyed but pleasant scent; remarkably sweet, soft, supple, persistent, dry finish.* Last tasted dining at the château, April 1991. At best****

Ch CANON *Lovely wine. Two notes in 1981; recently, one in bottle, one in magnum. Rich, ruby, mature; very harmonious bouquet, soft yet crisp. Perfect maturity and depth; sweet, fullish, rich, fleshy, still tannic.* Last tasted April 1989**** Will continue.

CARRUADES DE CH LAFITE *Deeper than the* grand vin. *A good note in 1984, fragrant and charming, but more critical at Flatt's Lafite tasting: rather stewed nose, coarse and a bit chocolaty.* Last tasted Oct 1988*

Dom de CHEVALIER *Very nice wine. Six notes. At lunch at the Domaine in 1986, the best note: very deep but fully mature-looking. Decanted at 12.30pm it was first poured a minute before 3pm: sweet mushrooms, harmonious bouquet that, after 20 minutes, seemed to have been overcome by fatigue and the lateness of the hour, yet, another 20 minutes later, had recovered its equilibrium, gentle, spicy, biscuity. On the palate, perfectly shaped, sweet, soft, fleshy. Lovely texture. A perfect drink. At a big dinner party there, a year later, slight bottle variation, one a bit edgy, one rich and earthy, the third perfect: smooth, excellent balance and weight.* Last noted June 1987. At best****

Ch CROIZET-BAGES *Picked Sept 28 to Oct 13. Rich, ripe, lovely.* At peak when last tasted, March 1986***

Ch FIGEAC *Like Concorde: bumpy take-off, steep climb, then supersonic, reaching cruising altitude in the mid-1970s. My last three notes from an* impériale, *a double-magnum and a magnum. The first at Gravetye Manor in 1980; decanted into eight decanters four hours before serving: opaque, four-square, touch of iron, solid and complete. In 1981 an equally opaque double-magnum, iron again (from the soil), a gentle giant. More recently, a magnum at Desai's Figeac vertical: still intense and youthful-looking for its age; bouquet full of fruit, held back a little then opened up; slightly sweet, full-bodied, very rich, fig-like flavour, rounded, fine.* Last tasted Dec 1989**** Plenty of life ahead.

Ch GAZIN *Several notes, all good, but tasted only once since 1976. Now showing considerable maturity; a bouquet reminding me of rich, old, polished* *mahogany; chewy, flavoury, touch of volatile acidity. Last tasted Dec 1985*** But needs drinking.*

Ch GRUAUD-LAROSE *Picked Sept 24 to Oct 17. Of the 20 noted, half have been UK bottled. Even allowing for bottle variation, not entirely satisfactory. Seemingly at its best, indeed demanding to be drunk, from 1976 to 1983. A lovely, rich, fruity château bottling and an unknown English bottling in excellent condition in 1983. Then another splendid UK bottling in 1988, and two the following year, flavoury but tart. Last tasted Feb 1989. A bit of a lottery. At its best****

Ch LANGOA-BARTON *Several notes. Rather an ungracious wine, austere, cracking up. Last tasted Dec 1985**

Ch LEOVILLE-LAS-CASES *Picked Sept 24 to Oct 9. A good '64 in its early days but variable, from the mid-1970s. Six notes in the 1980s. At its best a classic, cedary bouquet; soft, fleshy. Recently two, both English bottled, quite nice, the last, Berry Bros, deep but maturing, nose rather subdued, full-bodied, good fruit, a bit leathery. Last tasted April 1989. At best****

Ch LEOVILLE-POYFERRE *A dozen variable notes prior to 1980, only one since: good colour, correct nose, medium sweetness and body. Soft, ready and waiting. Last tasted Feb 1986***

Ch MALESCOT-ST-EXUPERY *A strangely exuberant wine. Tasted only twice since 1976. Still quite deep; nose rather hard, spicy and medicinal, then brambly blackcurrant; unusual flavour, a bit hollow and short, lean, almost skinny but a sweet fruity, berry-like finish. Very drinkable. Last tasted from a marie-jeanne, Sept 1990***

Ch La MISSION-HAUT-BRION *Tasted seven times in the 1980s, latterly all from the Woltner cellars. A deep, chocolaty, chewy wine, full of fruit, a slow, still tannic developer yet a whiff of volatility, adding to its crisp, tangy finish a slight acidic edginess. If anything, this, for the time being, seems merely to enhance its flavour. Last noted at Wolf's tasting, June 1990**** A pretty ripe, rumbustious character.*

Ch MONTROSE *Picked Sept 21 to Oct 2. Tasted many times, from cask, through to the mid- to late 1980s. Effects of early picking noticeable. A big wine: Montrose at its sturdiest best. Two excellent Berry Bros bottlings in 1985. The most recent, château bottled: incredibly deep and youthful-looking; lovely, classic, harmonious bouquet, but with leathery tannic character; overall dry, fairly full-bodied, chunky, crisp, loads of life, very tannic. Last tasted April 1987*** (**) A great future if you like stern, uncompromising wine. I predict perfection around 2010.*

Ch PALMER *Picked Sept 21 to Oct 8. Although all the grapes harvested by the time rain swept the Médoc, a disappointing Palmer. Tasted in cask and found a little lacking, confirmed by my rather variable notes since. At best a good chunky mouthful, but showing age. Last tasted 1981***

Ch PAPE-CLEMENT *Variable bottlings prior to 1980. Most recently, château bottled: deepish; slightly malty nose; very sweet, distinct Graves taste of tobacco and old ferns. A bit coarse. Not a patch on the '62. Last tasted Oct 1989**

Ch PAVIE *Many notes from 1963, including two raw, volatile, Grants bottlings. But on the whole, quick-developing and pleasing, completely ready, sweet, soft, gently rounded and delightful. Last tasted 1981. Then*** and doubtless, if well cellared, still attractive.*

Ch PICHON-LALANDE *Picked Sept 23 to Oct 12. Good wine, though only tasted once since 1978. Now medium weight, fully evolved colour, nose and taste. Full, sweet, opulent bouquet and palate. Last tasted May 1986*** Will continue to please.*

Ch ROUGET *Several notes over a 10-year period. By the mid-1980s still quite deep and richly coloured; a broad, harmonious bouquet; touch of sweetness, medium-full body, soft, rich, rounded and fully evolved. Last tasted July 1984*** Quite possibly a pleasing mouthful now.*

Ch de SALES *A woody sample in 1965. Good Harvey's bottling in 1979. More recently: fairly deep and youthful for age; very good, open-knit fruit; lovely flavour and aftertaste but short, tannic. Last noted at Vinton's, ex-Skinner cellar, Jan 1983****

Ch TALBOT *Picked Sept 24 to Oct 17. Several notes, various bottlings, prior to 1980, and three since. Usually less rich, more masculine than Gruaud, still medium-deep, lively, noticeably red-tinged; crisp, tight-knit, cherry-like fruit, fragrant, scented. Dry, crisp, fruity. Nice wine. Last tasted April 1989****

Ch La TOUR-HAUT-BRION *Still fairly deep, peppery, sweetish, chunky, flavoury, but with whiff of volatile acidity. Last tasted June 1990***

Ch TROTANOY *Interesting, yet curious in 1972 and 1977. Still deep, red-tinged but overmature-looking; fruity but with peppery alcohol and a whiff of volatile acidity on nose and palate. Full, chunky, raw tannin, iron and a slightly tinny finish. I expected more of Trotanoy and '64. Last tasted Sept 1987**

OTHER '64s TASTED IN THE 1980s:

Ch BEAU SEJOUR BECOT *Chunky but faded. Dry yet with a chaptalised character and almost '69-like acidity.*

Ch BEAUSEJOUR-FAGUET *Fine, rich, mature, good length.*

Ch BOYD-CANTENAC *Mature, chunky, inelegant but nice.*

Ch CANTEMERLE *Rich, plummy, some sweetness, chunky, lacking Cantemerle's customary charm and elegance.*

Ch CAPBERN-GASQUETON *Soft, fruity.*

Ch CARBONNIEUX *Curious mixture of richness and light, dry, Carbonnieux style.*

Ch CISSAC *Very attractive.*

Ch COUFRAN *Soft, broad, delicious, well balanced.*

Ch La FLEUR-PETRUS *Not tasted since 1980: a good mature colour; cream-cheese nose; sweet, flavoury, some flesh but short acidic finish.*

Ch GRAND-PUY-LACOSTE *Usual deep, rather hard, uncompromising style, but good and will keep.*

Ch d'ISSAN *Several notes. Seemed at best in the mid-1980s. Slightly lacking character and acidity now becoming noticeable.*

Ch LAFON-ROCHET *Surprisingly good. Several notes. A good ripe vintage, rich, with some charm.*

Ch LANESSAN *Light, stylish, lean, crisp.*

Ch LASCOMBES *Fully developed in the early 1980s. Quite a good chunky '64.*

Ch LEOVILLE-BARTON *Uneven; just one satisfactory Henekey bottling in 1982: amazingly deep colour, nice nose, rich, ripe, slightly edgy.*

Ch du TERTRE *Fairly deep, fragrant, delicious in 1985.*

Ch La TOUR-CARNET *Forthcoming, smoky, spicy, overripe but exciting bouquet; sweet, slightly tart but attractive.*

Ch La TOUR-DE-MONS *Completely mature, ripe, rich, appealing.*

VIEUX CH CERTAN *Surprisingly deep, good, rather bland, broad, meaty Pomerol nose; soft, chunky, very complete and well balanced.*

1965

Vying with 1963 for the poorest vintage of the decade. Rightly dismissed by the trade, which had a surfeit of '64s, with '66s in the offing. The weather did not give even the most gifted winemaker much of a chance. Flowering uneven and protracted, heavy rains throughout summer; Sept both wet and humid, causing rot, but improving later. Small crop of variable ripeness. Wines mostly thin and acidic, some flavoury but weedy.

Ch LAFITE *Hardly a* grand vin *and noted in the mid-1970s as passable light luncheon wine. Six recent notes, all from the same English Rothschild cellar as the '63. Pale rosehip tawny; delicate, medicinal but quite fragrant; light, a fraction of fruit, a bit acidic. Slightly more to it than the '63. Last noted at a pre-sale tasting, July 1988* just.*

Ch MOUTON-ROTHSCHILD *Pale but pretty at Flatt's tasting; muffled nose; dry, light, little to it but holding up. Most recently, not dissimilar. Nose a bit smelly despite a mild spiciness — trying terribly hard to be Mouton. Crisp, a bit sour and, of course, short. Last noted, at the Frericks/Wodarz Latour and Mouton tasting, March 1989. Being generous**

Ch HAUT-BRION *Surprisingly good colour, deeper than the '64; a fully developed though small, cheesy, nose; dry, light, not disagreeable, passable acidity. Two bottles, last noted May 1985**

Ch La MISSION-HAUT-BRION *Surprising depth of colour noted both at Desaï's in 1985 and at Wolf's more recently. A curious piquant, fragrant but superficial, fishy oyster-shell nose; both noted as sweet, with a rich chaptalised taste, a bit metallic, tails off. At the most recent Rodenstock wine weekend: surprisingly fragrant and fruity nose; flavour attractive. Last tasted Sept 1990***

THREE OF THE BETTER '65s LAST TASTED IN THE MID- TO LATE 1970s:

Ch Latour Ch Beychevelle** Ch Montrose**

1966★★★★

A very important and still somewhat underestimated vintage, mainly because of its willowy leanness and the time it has taken to come round, in many cases a full 20 years. It has always been a favourite vintage of mine, one I regard as in the classic claret style.

Mild winter, early spring and the crucial flowering in fine weather. Summer cooler and drier than average, though July fairly wet. A sunless Aug made up for by very hot sun during the crucial ripening period in Sept. Somewhat unsettled towards the end, but sound grapes harvested in perfect weather from Oct 6.

The vintage is more uniformly successful on the right bank, the best being superb and beautiful to drink now. In the Médoc there are some weak links, particularly in what I call the hinterland, like Listrac and Moulis, though the best are glorious and will continue to develop.

Ch LAFITE *Many notes. I shall just concentrate on two, a bottle decanted at 6.45pm and first poured at 8.30pm by which time the bouquet had had time to develop. It was already very forthcoming, fragrant, complex, with hints of iron and sage, eventually soft, 'warm' and biscuity. A touch of sweetness as it crossed the lips, a pleasant weight, neither too heavy nor too light, a delicious flavour, cedary, firm, with dry finish — the sort of level of tannin and acidity that leaves the mouth clean and dry, anticipating the next sip. Then at Flatt's '200 years of Lafite' tasting in New Orleans, autumn of 1988: appearance medium-deep, a fine gradation of colour stretching to a pleasantly mature rim; at 10.26am when the glasses were put before the seated tasters, having been decanted earlier and poured just before service, the bouquet was already forthcoming, rich, stylish. At 10.32 it already had developed a fine, classic cedar nose, depth, more to come. It was at this stage that I first tasted the wine. At 10.46 the bouquet had developed, and an hour later was exquisite. On the palate it was a good, crisp flavour, touch of iron, lean and refreshing, excellent aftertaste — and more time in hand. Last tasted Sept 1990****(*) Will develop further with bottle-age.*

Ch MARGAUX *Seven recent notes. Margaux, often the same weight as Lafite, but with different characteristics, also benefits from thoughtful decanting and time in glass. Also, like Lafite, elegant; sometimes, as with this '66, a bit more fleshy and velvety. At Desaï's extensive Margaux vertical in Los Angeles, 1987, a magnum: fairly deep in colour; oyster shell-like fragrance, developing sweetness. Ripe and elegant. Medium sweetness, fairly full-bodied, lovely shape and texture, good flesh and great length. And, most recently, at a Miami Wine & Food Society dinner: a lively cherry red, almost opaque at the centre; crisp, berry-like fruit developing great fragrance over one hour in the glass, high-toned, minty; still fairly lean and tannic yet with an* *innate delicacy.* Last tasted Jan 1990****(*) Could take another 20 years' bottle-age, and needs plenty of decanting time.

Ch LATOUR *About the least ready, slowest maturing of all the '66s. 18 notes since 1980: consistent, unyielding. Original opacity toned down a little, plummy, starting to show some maturity; nose hard at first but opens up richly, fine, firm fruit, spicy, cedary; touch of ripe sweetness soon overtaken by dry, leathery tannins. Huge; beefy; sinewy; full of fruit. Great length; unready.* Last tasted Dec 1990**(***) Needs at least 10 years and will surely last another 50.

Ch MOUTON-ROTHSCHILD *Several recent notes, three at major tastings: Flatt's vertical in 1986, at a monumental horizontal of '66s organised by the Commanderie de Bordeaux in San Diego also in 1986, and, most recently, at the Frericks/Wodarz comparative tasting of Mouton and Latour. To summarise: fairly deep, moderately intense; fine crisp Cabernet Sauvignon nose, developing further fragrance, spicy, holding well; fairly dry, medium-full body, crisp yet fleshy, good fruit, long and lean.* Last tasted March 1989****(*) Will continue well into the 21st century.

Ch HAUT-BRION *First tasted, a cask sample, in 1967 and 18 notes since. An excellent '66. Showing marvellously well at Wolf's line-up of La Mission and La Tour-Haut-Brion. Still very deep, most impressive, almost opaque but with maturing rim; sweet, almost chocolaty bouquet, rich, alcoholic, evolving gloriously in the glass; fairly sweet, fairly full-bodied (but not as sweet or full as La Mission), perfect balance and fruit. Power combined with elegance.* Last tasted June 1990***** Magnificent now. Many more years of life.

Ch AUSONE *In its own quaint way, a very good Ausone. Lovely, well-developed, flavoury by the mid-1970s, it now seems to have dried out. Three recent notes, showing best at Flatt's Ausone tasting: medium-deep, richly coloured, mature; delicate medicinal nose evolving richly and fragrantly; dry, medium weight, with the curious lean, dried leaves, almost Graves-like taste. But flavoury, with good vinosity and length.* Last tasted Oct 1987****

Ch CHEVAL-BLANC *The epitome of elegance. I much prefer this to the renowned '47. Seven recent notes, in magnum at the château, and elsewhere: marvellous depth and luminosity; "glorious" bouquet noted several times, forthcoming, scented—milk chocolate and the smell of a sawmill—toasted, cinnamon . . . in short, fragrant. Distinct touch of sweetness on palate, medium-full body, perfect weight, balance, shape and length. Silky and elegant yet with good tannin and acidity.* Last tasted April 1987***** Will continue for another quarter-century if well kept.

Ch PETRUS *A hefty cask sample in 1967, then a jump to 1984, 'iron fist in velvet glove' followed by three fascinating tastings: Frericks' vertical in magnums in 1986 and the extensive '66 horizontal in San Diego and, most recently, at Johann Bjürklund's in London. Summary: very deep, thick appearance, yet mature; rich, fruit just oozing out, almost coffee-like and malty but in every instance it developed fabulous fragrance; sweet, full-bodied, chunky yet soft, high extract, loaded with fruit, good length, ripe yet still tannic.* Last tasted April 1990****(*) Lovely now, will keep for ages.

OF THE MANY OTHER '66s LAST TASTED IN THE 1980s:

Ch L'ANGELUS *At peak in the mid-1970s. Nevertheless still forthcoming, with raspberry-like fragrance and flavour. A touch of sweetness, nice weight, fully mature.* Last tasted Nov 1986** Needs drinking.

Ch BATAILLEY *Always reliable, the '66 is perhaps more elegant and refined than usual. Nice weight, losing tannin, good flavour.* Last tasted June 1989*** Ready.

Ch BEYCHEVELLE *Impressive in cask, and, since then, 12 well-spread notes, all good. From the start, and still, a very deep, intense and rich appearance. Seemed to me at its soft, velvety best after only eight or nine years, but has become even more sweet, fleshy—for a '66, and attractive.* Last tasted Aug 1987****

Ch BOYD-CANTENAC *Sweet, nice weight, pleasant, easy, slightly short.* Nov 1986***

Ch BRANAIRE-DUCRU *Medium, mature; most appealing, cedary, scented, spicy bouquet; sweetish, very fruity, with refreshing acidity.* Last tasted Nov 1986. Perhaps an over-generous**** Lovely now.

Ch BRANE-CANTENAC *Puzzling. Several easy and attractive bottles up to 1980. Five overmature-to-oxidised bottles in the mid-1980s. Most recently, two lean and over-evolved bottles.* Last tasted Nov 1986.

Ch CALON-SEGUR *Many notes. Initially rather coarse and tannic, therefore slow developing. Reached an agreeable staging-post in 1975 and has continued to evolve. Elegant, complete and surprisingly sweet, though still sporting a dry, tannic finish.* Last tasted June 1987***(*) Will continue to improve.

Ch CANON *I am a great admirer of Canon. Its customary flesh and fruit provides a perfect foil for the '66 tendency to leanness. Sweet and agreeable in 1975, even more so a decade later. A very forthcoming, fragrant, fully evolved, bramble, blackberry-like fruit, nose and taste. Chunky but elegant. Great length.* Last tasted Nov 1986***** Superb. Will keep.

Ch CANON-LA-GAFFELIERE *A quick-maturing, easy wine, at best in 1970 and, more recently, though slight bottle variation.* Last tasted Nov 1986** Drink up.

Ch CANTEMERLE *Although an IECWS bottling was showing well in 1975 almost every note since ends "not ready", "needs time", "almost ready", though the nose is invariably fragrant. A fine, crisp, dry, flavoury wine.* Last tasted Nov 1986***(*) A claret man's claret. Worth waiting for.

Ch CANTENAC-BROWN *A string of notes from 1971. With the exception of a recent oxidised bottle, all fulsomely flavoury.* Last tasted Nov 1986*** Drink up.

CARRUADES DE CH LAFITE *Noted more for its slender charm than longevity, very agreeable in*

1978 but by the mid-1980s fully evolved, over-the-top really, and drying out. Last tasted Nov 1986** Drink up.

Dom de CHEVALIER *A firm Berry Bros bottling, with good texture and balance, and a couple, château bottled in 1986. Still deep, fragrant, classic, full-flavoured and still tannic.* Last tasted Oct 1989***(*)

Ch La CONSEILLANTE *Fine wine, now very ripe, with rich, raspberry-like fruit; stylish, silky tannins, notable aftertaste.* Last tasted May 1991**** Drink now.

Ch COS D'ESTOURNEL *First tasted in cask, and 14 well-spread notes, excluding one oxidised bottle, confirm its initial promise. Has mellowed in colour and sweetened on palate. Lovely classic, cedary nose; lovely weight and feel, lean but fleshy, a touch of liquorice.* Last tasted Jan 1990**** Will keep.

Ch CROIZET-BAGES *Various bottlings since 1969. A well-constituted wine, thoroughly ripe and ready now: warm, crusty Cabernet nose; chunky, fruity.* Last tasted Nov 1986*** Drink soon.

Ch DAUZAC *Several notes. Firm, spicy. Best aged 10, trace of acidity at 20, but still very flavoury.* Last tasted Nov 1986*** Drink up.

Ch DUCRU-BEAUCAILLOU *A mass of notes. Quite a bite when young. Still stern and unyielding even after 15 years. Never very deep in colour but consistently dry. Vinous, cedary, silky yet lean.* Last tasted Feb 1989***(*)

Ch DUHART-MILON *A bit raw in the late 1970s, then a sudden burst of maturity. Now fairly sweet, soft, ripe, agreeable.* Last tasted Nov 1989*** Drink soon.

Ch L'EVANGILE *Deep, fruity in 1975, in 1986 still opaque, intense; beautiful fruit; and full, loaded, good texture, austere.* Last tasted at Spencer House, May 1991***(*)

Ch FIGEAC *Sweet, soft and attractive even in cask, and through the 1970s. Now fully evolved colour, bouquet and taste. A cedary thoroughbred, the unusually high percentage of Cabernet Sauvignon very apparent. Fairly sweet, shapely, beautiful.* Last noted at Desai's tasting, Dec 1989*****

Les FORTS DE LATOUR *A very agreeable mouthful in the early 1970s. It has developed a lovely, deep, fruity nose; lean but tasty, just a trace of coarseness betraying young vines.* Last tasted Nov 1986*** Drink soon.

Ch FOURCAS-HOSTEN *Just to demonstrate that not all '66s are good, a hinterland Médoc: six fairly dismal notes from 1975. Austere, stalky, edgy acidity.* Last tasted July 1988.

Clos FOURTET *Not at all bad though unexciting: lovely colour, rich chocolaty nose; decent flavour, lean, very dry finish.* Last tasted Nov 1986**

Ch La GAFFELIERE *This name triggers a characteristic flavour enhanced, or at least propped up, by fairly high acidity. Tasted in cask and nearly a dozen times since, and varying from oxidised, 'old socks', and stalky to citrus-like fruit. Often attractive but usually qualified. Its nose unravels interestingly, and it is now soft, rich and complete.* Last tasted Nov 1986. At best*** but risky.

Ch GAZIN *Nice nose but a bit lean in cask. Good flavour and texture in 1976. 10 years later, a beautiful bouquet, good depth and length. Most recently tasted from a double-magnum: a cherry-like colour and bouquet, the latter quickly opening up. Good depth and length. Still with tannin and acidity.* Last noted Nov 1986***(*)

Ch GISCOURS *The sort of '66 that might never completely come out of its shell. Fine; but five recent notes repeat "lean", a bit unyielding, and a medicinal Médoc nose. Packed with fruit but a touch of greenness.* Last tasted Nov 1986**(*)?

Ch GLORIA *Nice fruit and balance. Lacking length.* Last tasted Nov 1986***

Ch GRAND-PUY-LACOSTE *Many notes. A good but uncompromising classed-growth Pauillac in an uncompromisingly good vintage. Given air, a beautiful bouquet. Dry, firm, lean, sinewy, long, classic.* Last tasted Jan 1987***(*) Possibly ***** in the next century.

Ch GRUAUD-LAROSE *20 notes including two English bottled: all good. Full and fruity, an appealing wine yet lacking grace and finesse. In 1990 in double-magnums, the first from Dr Robert Charpie's cellar: still deep; laden with fruit, some spice; a very satisfactory mouthful. The second at the château. But time in hand.* Last tasted June 1991***(*) Will continue to develop.

Ch HAUT-BAILLY *A charmer, soft, earthy, velvety through the 1970s. Very sweet, fragrant.* Last tasted Nov 1986****

Ch HAUT-BATAILLEY *Fruity, cedary, cheesy, fragrant. Elegant, good length.* Last tasted Nov 1986***(*)

Ch d'ISSAN *First noted in 1983 over lunch at the château: it was deep, rich, soft, fleshy and suave. In 1984, a case from Christie's: delicious; lovely colour, excellent consistency, good length. An unknown Bordeaux bottling creaking a bit. Most recently two Berry Bros bottlings, one scented but tart, the other flavoury.* Last tasted April 1991. At best**** Ripe.

Ch LAFON-ROCHET *Plummy, smoky, spicy, quite good.* Last tasted Nov 1986**

Ch LAGRANGE *St-Emilion. Earlier notes not very favourable. The two most recent quite attractive, though acidity high.* Last tasted April 1987. At best** Avoid.

Ch La LAGUNE *A most un-Médoc-like Médoc. Five notes, four since 1985. A curious yet mouthfilling, flavoury wine. Most recently: distinctly sweet nose, fruity, very fragrant, oaky flavour and aftertaste.* Last tasted Feb 1989. At best*** Try it.

Ch LANESSAN *Many notes, varying from blackberry to bland. Quite nice flesh.* Last tasted Nov 1986** Drink now.

Ch LANGOA-BARTON *Slight bottle variation. Lean, refreshing, good length.* Last tasted Nov 1986. At best***

Ch LASCOMBES *Six notes in the 1980s. Impressively deep and vibrant colour; nose like a dairy: vanilla, cheesy, slightly sour. Better on palate, but rather a mish-mash, though a very nice bottle in 1985.* Last tasted Nov 1986**

Ch LEOVILLE-BARTON *A copybook '66. My original lean long-distance runner. Classic, fragrant, elegant.* Last tasted Nov 1989****

Ch LEOVILLE-LAS-CASES *First tasted in cask, and*

*many times since. With the exception of two strangely acidic Army & Navy Stores bottlings in the late 1970s, some pretty good notes. By no means a heavyweight, svelte, good fruit and balance. Dry finish. Last tasted Feb 1987***(*)? Future a little uncertain, despite its pedigree.*

Ch LEOVILLE-POYFERRE *Attractive, mature; nose a bit hard and stalky beneath its classic fragrance. Flavoury, good length, dry finish. Last tasted Nov 1986. At best****

Ch La LOUVIERE *Full of bounce in 1975, and delicious now: lovely colour, bouquet and flavour. Surprisingly sweet, nice weight, elegant. Last tasted March 1987*****

Ch LYNCH-BAGES *Uneven notes in the 1970s. Over the past three years, three: one in magnum, delightfully spicy, very fragrant, positively exotic, drinking well. Last tasted May 1989. At best*****

Ch MAGDELAINE *A rich, long-haul wine. Two excellent recent notes: lively, luminous; glorious bouquet; slightly sweet, perfect weight, flavour and grip. Harmonious. Elegant. Years of life. Last tasted June 1989**** More to come.*

Ch MALESCOT-ST-EXUPERY *Superficial, speciously attractive. Lacking length. Nov 1986***

Ch MARQUIS-DE-TERME *Initially piquant and attractive, three horribly overblown bottles in 1980 and 1986. Yet a deep, rich, sweet and chunky bottle in 1987. Last tasted Jan 1987. At best***

Ch La MISSION-HAUT-BRION *Woltner's 'no-problem' wine. (They used their* vin de presse *'66 to boost the '65!) Many notes, 10 since 1984. Overall: impressively deep, intense appearance; extraordinary nose, vigorous, high-toned but not completely knit and with a distinctive whiff of volatile acidity, not unlike the '70 La Mission. An exciting mouthful. Very sweet, full-bodied with flesh and fruit. A slightly metallic finish. After the Karl-Heinz Wolf tasting in 1986, an* impériale *was consumed at dinner: perfection. Last noted May 1991. At best***** Living life to the hilt.*

Ch MONTROSE *A premature cask sample in Feb 1967. Developed well through the 1970s, with loads of fruit and tannin. Still deep, still tannic but worth hanging on to. Last tasted Feb 1988**(**)*

Ch MOUTON-BARON PHILIPPE *Pleasing in the mid-1970s and a charmer a decade later. Pretty colour; brandy-snaps bouquet; light style. Last tasted Nov 1986****

Ch NENIN *At its best, elegant, stylish, and now fully developed. Last tasted Nov 1986**** Drink up.*

Ch PALMER *Many consistently good notes: medium-deep; lovely mulberry-ripe fruit, rich, fleshy; a sweet, beautifully balanced, mouthfilling wine. Last noted June 1991**** Will develop further.*

Ch PAPE-CLEMENT *Still deep-coloured; crisp fruit; touch of Graves, earthy, tobacco flavour, lean, and beginning to creak at the joints. Last tasted in magnum, Nov 1986** Drink up.*

Ch PAVIE *Early maturing, completely developed, lightweight but attractive. Last tasted Feb 1987***

Ch PICHON-BARON *Deep, intense; concentrated nose; a huge alcoholic mouthful. Last tasted Nov 1986***(*) Impressive. I hope it will develop further.*

Ch PICHON-LALANDE *Lively; 'warm', cedary scent; soft, lovely fruit, balance, aftertaste. Last tasted Nov 1986**** Lovely now; will keep.*

Ch PONTET-CANET *A wine of delicacy and finesse. Most recently an impressive Berry Bros bottling with an immediate yet prolonged fragrance, showing age but very attractive. Last tasted April 1990*** Unlikely to improve.*

Ch RAUSAN-SEGLA *From cask to maturity, a satisfactory, well-balanced wine. Now mature, a perfect weight, elegant, clean-cut. Delicious. Last tasted Nov 1986**** Will keep.*

Ch RAUZAN-GASSIES *Dry, lean, austere, with teeth-gripping tannin. Last tasted Nov 1986**

Ch TALBOT *Lean, austere in the 1970s. Softening mid-1980s. Deepish; lovely; sweet, rich and ready. Last tasted Dec 1990*****

Ch La TOUR-HAUT-BRION *First tasted in 1978, ripe, spicy. A decade later, sweet, chunky, rich. Latterly deep, attractive; far less full-bodied than La Mission or Haut-Brion but sweet and soft, with an odd iodine and oyster-shell nose and taste, very appealing in its way. Last tasted June 1990*** Drink now to 2000.*

Ch TROTANOY *The last three notes in the mid-1980s: deep, rich; lovely bouquet, elegant, spicy, rich, hefty, expanded in glass; fairly full-bodied, complete, fairly dry, tannic finish but fragrant aftertaste. Most recently noted at Rodenstock's annual tasting, Sept 1987**** Drink now – will keep.*

CHATEAUX TASTED ONLY ONCE SINCE 1980 AND STILL SHOWING WELL:

Ch Balestard-La-Tonnelle; Ch Baret; Ch Beauregard; Ch Beau Séjour Bécot; Ch Beauséjour Duffau-Lagarosse; Ch Belgrave St-Laurent; Ch Bouscaut; Ch de Camensac; Ch Carbonnieux; Ch Chasse-Spleen; Ch Cissac; Ch La Croix-de-Gay; Ch La Fleur; Ch La Fleur-Pétrus; Ch La Garde; Ch Le Gay (Berry Bros); Ch Haut-Bages-Averous; Ch Lagrange Pomerol; Ch Latour à Pomerol; Ch Les Ormes-de-Pez; Ch Petit-Village; Ch Prieuré-Lichine; Ch de Sales; Ch La Serre; Ch du Tertre; Ch La Tour-Figeac; Ch La Tour-de-Mons; Ch Trottevieille; Vieux Ch Certan; Ch La Violette.

VARIABLE OR MEDIOCRE IN THE 1980s:

Ch Belair St-Emilion; Ch Durfort-Vivens; Ch Ferrière; Ch Grand-Pontet; Ch Haut-Bages-Monpelou; Ch Livran; Ch Lynch-Moussas; Ch Marquis d'Alesme-Becker; Ch Monbousquet; Ch Phélan-Ségur; Ch La Pointe; Ch Siran; Ch La Tour-Carnet; Ch La Tour-Martillac; Ch Villegeorge; Ch Yon-Figeac.

RECENT POOR BOTTLES:

Ch Cos Labory; Ch Curé-Bon-La Madeleine; Ch Grand-Puy-Ducasse; Ch Lestage; Ch Pédesclaux.

1967*

By and large, the '67s peaked in the mid-1970s and most were cracking up in the 1980s. Flowering was late, the summer hot and dry; the vital ripening period was cold and wet, the last week of Sept hot. Early Oct cool and damp, then better weather interrupted by heavy rain. An uneven crop of relatively unripe grapes. The wines, particularly in the Médoc, were heavily chaptalised, giving them an early but spurious attraction which did not help them develop or keep. The earlier-picked Merlots in Pomerol seemed to have fared better.

Ch LAFITE *Raw in cask, some fragrance and charm by the mid-1970s. A decade later fairly pale, very mature-looking, watery rimmed; showing age on nose, dried leaves; one bottle sour and woody, one unknit and volatile. However, at Flatt's tasting, lightish and lean, quite flavoury but with surprising length. Last tasted Oct 1988** Drink up.*

Ch MARGAUX *Eight notes. Also quite nice in the mid-1970s but in decline since then. Not a bad colour; a scented but low-keyed nose that faded in the glass; some fruit but raw, acidic, no finish. Last tasted May 1987* Not bad with food. Drink up.*

Ch LATOUR *Several notes from 1969 and, despite its depth of colour (still opaque in the mid-1970s), it was surprisingly soft and generous. Raw and lacking refinement in the early 1980s. Now medium-deep and plum-coloured; a light touch of scent and fragrance, of fruit and ginger; medium body, soft fruit, chunky, short. Last noted at the Frericks/Wodarz tasting in March 1989** One of the best '67s, but drink up.*

Ch MOUTON-ROTHSCHILD *A similar pattern of pleasant, unexceptional notes from 1974 but lack of finish, even tartness and bitterness noticed towards the end of the decade. Similarities noted at Flatt's Mouton tasting in 1986 and the Mouton-Latour tasting in Germany: palish but attractive, open, mature appearance; sweet and equally attractive nose, piquant Cabernet, though no depth; lightish, plausible, overall dry and lacking balance. Last tasted in Wiesbaden, March 1989***

Ch HAUT-BRION *Four notes, none recent: earthy, quite nice. At a III Form Club dinner, Jan 1979** Doubtless it has deteriorated.*

Ch AUSONE *Two notes: bland and drinkable in 1971 and, at Flatt's tasting: pale, the most mature-looking of the flight; chocolaty, chaptalised nose; dry, light, lacking middle but a surprisingly pleasant if lactic flavour. Last tasted Oct 1987* Drink up.*

Ch CHEVAL-BLANC *Many notes in the 1970s. An occasional "disappointing" but mainly "agreeable", though no future. A fairly substantial colour still; rather sweaty nose; soft, drinkable, but lying on a doormat of tannic acid. Last tasted Feb 1986** Not for keeping.*

Ch PETRUS *Velvety, rich but shapeless in 1978. Lacking cohesion but a good '67 at Frericks' tasting in 1986. Most recently: medium-deep, rich colour; restrained but nice fruit, touch of volatile acidity; initial sweetness, some body but short and edgy. Last noted at the 'Stockholm' tasting, April 1990***

Ch BRANE-CANTENAC *Loose-knit, soft but rather acidic in the 1970s. Three recent notes show palish, mature colour; sweaty nose; sweetish, on the light side, quite agreeable flavour but short and with '67 acidity. Last tasted May 1987** Not bad. Drink up.*

Ch CALON-SEGUR *Dry, lean, crisp, short. Last tasted June 1987**

Ch DUCRU-BEAUCAILLOU *A pretty good '67, luminous, dry, crisp, quite flavoury. Last tasted Sept 1987***

Les FORTS DE LATOUR *More impressive than the '66 when launched in 1972. Later, austere, charmless. Probably at its best either side of 1980. Green, lean, short. But not a bad '67. Last tasted Nov 1981** Drink up.*

Ch MALESCOT-ST-EXUPERY *Two notes in 1977, flavoury but green and hard. Most recently, an* impériale, *quite attractive in its way. Lean, crisp, pleasant to drink but needs drinking. Last tasted Sept 1990***

Ch La MISSION-HAUT-BRION *One of the best '67s. Deep, chunky, fruity, earthy and a good mouthful in the mid- to late 1970s. A decade later, a bit sour-ended at Desai's tasting, and, three notes later: medium depth but with an open, attractive colour; well-developed, sweet, tobacco-like Graves nose; touch of sweetness, medium weight, good flavour, its edgy acidity probably unnoticeable with food. Last noted at Wolf's tasting, June 1990***

Ch MONTROSE *Many notes. Pleasant but unknit in the mid-1970s. Raw and ungracious in 1981. A good Berry Bros magnum though "no future" in 1985. A jeroboam in 1986, raw again, with a Chinon or Bourgueil-like piquancy of fruit and acidity. Most recently a deep, leathery-textured jeroboam, full, fruity. Last noted at Rodenstock's, Sept 1990. At best***

Ch PALMER *Flavoury, fragrant when young. Three tart English bottlings in the 1970s. In 1990, a very impressive and enjoyable bottle at the château: deep but very mature; soft, scented nose; very sweet, fullish, velvety, well-balanced. Last tasted pre-sale, June 1991*** At best a very attractive '67.*

Ch PRIEURE-LICHINE *Quite good colour; crisp, tannic Cabernet nose; surprisingly sweet and flavoury. Perfectly tolerable acidity. A good '67. Last tasted Oct 1988***

Ch RAUSAN-SEGLA *High-toned, some charm but little to it in the 1970s. Now pale, fully mature; faded nose; though sweet on palate, piquant, quite flavoury. A wine with the stuffing taken out of it. Last tasted April 1989**

OF THE MANY '67s TASTED IN THE 1980s, THE FOLLOWING WERE REASONABLY GOOD, ALTHOUGH ALMOST WITHOUT EXCEPTION THEY HAVE THE EDGE OF ACIDITY:

Ch Baret; Ch Boyd-Cantenac; Ch Branaire-Ducru; Ch Canon; Ch Cantemerle; Carruades de Ch Lafite; Clos L'Eglise; Ch La Fleur-Pétrus; Ch Haut-Bailly; Ch d'Issan; Ch de Lamarque; Ch Lascombes; Ch Léoville-Barton; Ch Léoville-Poyferré; Ch Malartic-Lagravière; Ch Magdelaine; Ch Pape-Clément; Ch Pavie; Ch Rauzan-Gassies; Ch Talbot; Ch La Tour-Haut-Brion.

LESS GOOD, SKINNY, ACIDIC IN THE 1980s:

Ch Belair St-Emilion; Ch Belgrave St-Laurent; Ch de Camensac; Ch Canon-La-Gaffelière; Ch Cissac; Ch Courant; Ch Croizet-Bages; Ch Larrivet Haut-Brion; Ch Pichon-Baron; Ch Pichon-Lalande; Ch Siran; Ch La Tour-Carnet.

1968

An atrocious vintage. Cold spring, uneven flowering, sunless summer save for July, Aug the coldest and wettest for years. Timorous sun in Sept failed to ripen the fairly large crop picked early to mid-Oct. Avoid.

Ch LAFITE *Not* grand vin, *even a* petit vin. *Very pale, almost rosé from the start. Now a faintly glowing amber; shallow, vanilla, gingery nose; dry, light, flavoury but short. Last noted at Flatt's Lafite tasting Oct 1988★ Skeletal but drinkable.*

Ch LATOUR *Thin, short and bitter in cask. At the Frericks/Wodarz tasting in 1989: a better colour than Mouton, but with unknit, indistinct nose; some fruit, quite attractive flavour though short and raw. More recently, a magnum: seemed quite fragrant and classic; dry, with crisp, fruity taste. Lean, leaving tannins bare. Last tasted Sept 1990★★*

Ch MOUTON-ROTHSCHILD *Thin, tart but flavoury in the mid-1970s. Similar, hardly a glimmer of life to the eye, at Flatt's tasting in 1986. At the Frericks/Wodarz Latour and Mouton tasting: a chocolaty, caramelly, chaptalised but not unattractive nose, though weak, medicinal and short on palate. Last noted, March 1989★*

Ch HAUT-BRION *Not bad in 1974 and noted in 1984 as having a surprisingly deep and lively colour; a strange, hard and closed-up nose; dry, stalky but not bad for a '68. Last tasted May 1985★*

Ch CHEVAL-BLANC *Declassified.*

Ch PETRUS *Four notes since 1979. Most recently: some richness but with orange-brown mature rim; nose stewed tea and old leaves, distinctly vegetal but opened up, like a wet labrador! On the palate surprisingly sweet, heavily but well chaptalised, nice weight, Pomerol texture, liquorice taste. Just shows what well-timed picking and careful selection of Merlot can do. Last noted at the 'Stockholm' tasting, April 1990★★*

Ch CANTEMERLE *Stewed, raw. June 1982.*

Ch DUCRU-BEAUCAILLOU *Not bad but rasping in the early to mid-1970s. Weak tea colour; sweet, passable, chaptalised nose; good for a '68 though short. Last tasted in June 1982, then a generous★★ Doubtless faded.*

Ch GRUAUD-LAROSE *Three notes since 1976. Some colour; nose not bad, at least it develops; raw, yet soft and flavoury. Last tasted in Oct 1983★★*

Ch La LAGUNE *Three notes. Sweet, caramelly,* macération carbonique *sort of fruit. Chaptalised, light and thin. Last tasted March 1985.*

Ch La MISSION-HAUT-BRION *Pale, open-knit; feebly fragrant: raisiny sherry, vanilla then chocolate on nose; sweet, light, strange pasty flavour, short. Last noted at Wolf's tasting, June 1990★*

Ch La TOUR-HAUT-BRION *Deep and quite rich for a '68; light, easy, quite nice. Nov 1986★★*

1969★

1967, 1968 and 1969 remind me of the proverbial British Rail sandwich: dry and curling on each side, a scraping in the middle. Lean and acidic from the start, yet not unattractive when young, the '69s evolved too quickly and rapidly faded. Despite its shaky start, the '69s were snapped up, fuelled by inflationary demand and a small crop.

A poor flowering in bad weather and a cold June were followed by a reasonable July and Aug. Rain in Sept hampered ripening but fine weather followed to the early Oct harvest.

Frankly, a vintage to be avoided, though the occasional good bottle can still make a refreshing luncheon wine.

Ch LAFITE *Some piquant charm in the mid-1970s, intriguing, some complexity but a bit thin at Edmund Penning-Rowsell's 10-year first-growth tasting. Nine years on and three notes, the last at Flatt's Lafite tasting: medium depth, completely mature rim; somewhat medicinal and chocolaty but quite pleasing bouquet; dry, nice weight, surprisingly attractive flavour, the '69 acidity quite refreshing. Last tasted Oct 1988★★ Certainly better than the '67 but no future.*

Ch MARGAUX *Astringent and charmless from the early 1970s. Not noted since Penning-Rowsell's 10-year tasting: medium depth; little bouquet, "cold" but with some delicacy; dry, lightish, piquant and short. Somehow manages to be flat and acidic at the same time. Last tasted March 1979★ Skinny, and unlikely to have improved.*

Ch LATOUR *Huge and raw in 1970. Sharp, peppery, austere, twist of bitter lemon throughout that decade. The deepest and crispest-looking of the first growths in 1979 but, though a big mouthful, dull. Two years later, at the* Fête du Ch Latour *tasting, unknit and raw. Finally at the Frericks/Wodarz Latour and Mouton tasting: appearance almost as deep as the '70. On the nose raw, peppery and piquant though it developed a more interesting cedar and brick-dust scent, then, after nearly 20 minutes, some semblance of fragrance. Medium weight for Latour, a strange, sweaty, stalky taste, tannic texture and raw acidity. Last tasted March 1989. Unattractive, unlikely to improve.*

Ch MOUTON-ROTHSCHILD *Fruity and forward in 1970, lacking the characteristic Cabernet Sauvignon spiciness. At Penning-Rowsell's tasting a milky, un-Mouton-like nose, with green, swingeing finish. Seven years later, at Flatt's Mouton tasting, more mature-looking, less lively than the '67; a quite attractive, light, fragrant bouquet, though something lacking; palate light and soft yet with short sharp end. Two later notes: most recently at the Frericks/Wodarz tasting:*

palish, fully evolved; a forthcoming but superficially scented aroma; very dry, fairly light, lean, medicinal taste, acidic. Last tasted March 1989★ Refreshing, but no future.

Ch HAUT-BRION *Astringent in cask. Later dry and peppery. At Penning-Rowsell's in 1979: some depth of colour, a touch of iron earthiness and sweetness on the nose, and a soupçon of fat and softness to counter its austerity. Tasted once since. A closed bouquet; dry, quite flavoury, tolerable '69 acidity, fairly short.* At pre-sale tasting, May 1985★ Not bad but no future.

Ch AUSONE *Only three notes: flavoury, piquant in the mid-1970s, and at Flatt's tasting a surprisingly pleasant colour though insipid rim; quite fragrant and nicely evolved; dry, fairly light, rather lean but flavoury.* Last noted Oct 1987★

Ch PETRUS *Six notes. Bouquet slow to evolve, but speciously flavoury in the mid-1970s, the most complete and rounded of the first growths in 1979; fleshy but one-dimensional in 1984. Then, in magnum, at Frericks' tasting in Munich: medium, mature, weak rim; a cold, powdery Spanish-root nose; surprisingly sweet and agreeable on the palate though touch of bitter acidity on the finish. Attractive but weak.* Last tasted April 1986★★ Will probably keep but is unlikely to improve.

Ch GRUAUD-LAROSE *Started off with a bang, extraordinarily rich in cask, and is still banging on. Some fruit, flavoury but a bit hard-edged in the mid-1970s. Still quite deep and rich-looking, with amber brown mature rim; fruity, vanilla, piquant nose; surprisingly sweet, fair body and flavour despite '69 acidity.* Last tasted Nov 1989★★

Ch LEOVILLE-LAS-CASES *Also started off well, quite impressive in cask but despite one good note, "dry", "hard", "uninteresting" even "scraggy" as the decade progressed. Then 10 years later: medium depth with a rather weak, mature rim; soft, vanilla nose; and on the palate not unlike the Gruaud-Larose. Acidity in check.* Last tasted Nov 1989★★

Ch MAGDELAINE *Several notes: two in the mid-1980s. Good colour, still a bit of cherry red; light but fragrant bouquet; well constituted, overall dry, flavoury, tolerable acidity.* Last tasted March 1985★★ Probably still drinkable.

Ch La MISSION-HAUT-BRION *Three well-spaced notes over the past 12 years. Not much development: all medium, mature-looking; bouquet the best feature, some fragrance; all with sharply acidic finish. Most recently, the wine had a quite attractive, refreshing sea-breeze whiff. Dry, fairly lightweight, not bad flavour but lean, mean and acidic.* Last noted at Wolf's La Mission tasting, June 1990. Not up to standard and will not improve.

Ch MOUTON-BARON PHILIPPE *Two notes: maturing, unknit, chaptalised but, in 1977, really more attractive than its elder brother, Mouton-Rothschild. In 1984 rather pale and feeble; bouquet fully stretched — but like thin elastic, about to break; not unappetising, but little to it.* Last noted, pre-sale, Chicago, Sept 1985★ Drink up.

SHOWING REASONABLY WELL IN THE 1980s:

Ch Baret; Ch Batailley; Ch Beau Séjour Bécot; Ch Branaire-Ducru; Ch Cissac; Ch Dauzac; Ch Gaffelière-Naudes; Ch La Tour-Haut-Brion; Ch Lascombes; Ch Montrose; Ch Pichon-Lalande; Ch Rauzan-Gassies.

NOT SHOWING WELL IN THE 1980s:

Ch Beychevelle; Ch de Camensac; Ch Cantenac-Brown; Ch Cos d'Estournel; Les Forts de Latour; Ch La Lagune; Ch Malartic-Lagravière; Ch Nenin; Ch Pavie; Ch du Tertre.

1970★★★★

A turning point. After the ups and downs of the 1960s, 1970 presented a big, bold front, as if heralding a renaissance, ready to meet the challenges of a fully aroused international market. It was in fact a doubly satisfactory vintage, combining the twin commercial virtues of large quantity and high quality. It was one of those rare years in which the main grape varieties, Cabernet Sauvignon, Cabernet Franc, Merlot and Petit Verdot reached full maturity concurrently. The growing season started with a late spring, followed by blossoming in good weather — important for crop size. Great heat and drought in July; Aug forbiddingly cold and stormy. Hot sunshine throughout the harvest, which began early Oct.

Despite some disappointments, this is by and large still an impressive vintage. The best St-Emilions are lovely now, Pomerol a bit mixed. The red Graves fairly even, and good. The best Médocs are magnificent but need more bottle-age; some lesser classed growths drinking well, some scrawny and unappealing. A hundred or so châteaux noted, a selection from those tasted recently.

Ch LAFITE *Fine, deep and elegant in cask, characteristic length noted, and an incredible aftertaste, through the 1970s. 15 notes during the 1980s. Originally considerable depth of colour, now medium-deep. Nose, though well developed, opens up in the glass, fragrant, touch of vanilla. The first sip has the sweetness of maturity and bottle-age, fairly full-bodied, silky, delicate yet mouthfilling, great length, beautiful aftertaste, with tannin and acidity to prolong its life.* Last tasted April 1989★★★★(★) Drink now or leave for one's children.

Ch MARGAUX *A deep and chunky Margaux, more of a '59 than a '53 in style. Over a dozen notes from 1974. A wine of richness and complexity. Still fairly thick and intense-looking; nose noted as restrained though giving the impression of great depth of fruit. Rather dry, fairly full-bodied, four-square, rich, substantial, good length. Still tannic.* Last tasted Aug 1987★★★(★) Hopefully★★★★★ in due course.

Ch LATOUR *A blockbuster. Opaque and heavily laden in cask. Paradoxically, I enjoyed it in its adolescence, the late 1970s; of 15 bottles since 1980, four have been either woody, corked or oxidised which, even allowing for storage variation, is unsatisfactory. At its recent best it is still impressively deep; nose marvellously mellow and reassuring, singed, fruit and cedar, then wave after wave of rich chocolate and spice; sweet entry, massive, a gloriously rich monumental wine, with a little bit — rather, a lot — of everything.* Last tasted Dec 1990**(***) *Fully developed by 2010–20.*

Ch MOUTON-ROTHSCHILD *Powerful but austere around the mid-1970s. The most high-toned of the first growths, a touch of leanness and acidity tagging along with the tannin noted in the 1980s. At Flatt's Mouton tasting: flavoury, edgy and lacking charm. Still fairly deep though showing some maturity and less intense than expected; soft, low-keyed fruit, with the fairly characteristic medicinal Pauillac scent and Cabernet Sauvignon aroma. Sweet entry, dry tannic acid finish. Reasonably full-bodied, fruity, flavoury yet lean and lacking charm. Somehow not as impressive as it should be. Time will tell.* Last tasted May 1991**(**)? *Hard to advise.*

Ch HAUT-BRION *Curiously it appears to have deepened in colour, though now, despite its richness and a degree of intensity, it is showing some maturity. Haut-Brion has a smell and taste unlike its Médoc peers; indeed, all it has in common with the other first growths is, happily, great quality, style and finesse. Bouquet variously described as gravelly, hot pepper and iodine, tobacco, also as both coffee and tea! The palate more consistent: touch of ripe sweetness leading eventually to a dry, still tannic finish. Medium full-bodied, touch of leanness, lovely silky texture, elegant and complete.* Last tasted June 1990****(*) *Drink now if you like a characterful mouthfiller, or wait 10–20 years.*

Ch AUSONE *As usual, far fewer notes. Tasted twice in 1976, twice in 1986, and in 1987 at Flatt's Ausone tasting: medium-deep, an attractive rosy-hued mature-looking wine; fragrant bouquet, touch of coffee, a lovely rich gingery fruit, vanilla and strawberry; fairly dry, medium weight, a soft, chewy wine with a slightly singed flavour, rounded, complete, though slightly lacking in length. A very good wine, though Ausone is not everyone's cup of tea.* Last tasted Oct 1987**** *Drink now to 2010, or beyond.*

Ch CHEVAL-BLANC *Good in cask, promising a long life. Slowly developing though rich and elegant. Eight consistently admiring notes from the 1980s. My top wine in a blind tasting of '70s, in Bordeaux, Sept 1986. It was rich-looking, had a glorious bouquet, complex, cedar and ripe fruit, and was sweet, full, rich, soft and fleshy. In short, perfection. It still is.* Last tasted Feb 1989***** *Lovely now, will keep.*

Ch PETRUS *A lovely, very rich mouthful in cask. In 1976, though somewhat closed on the nose, eminently drinkable. Several notes over past 10 years. I seemed to like it best in the early to mid-1980s: deep, rich, fleshy, with an astonishing flavour of ripe mulberries. Fabulous magnum at Frericks' in 1986, but, more recently, almost too sickly sweet. Maturing well at the 'Stockholm' tasting, nose restrained and a bit woody at first but developed a light but lovely fragrance; very sweet, on the lightweight and lean side for Pétrus, slightly lacking fruit, dry, faintly tart finish.* Last noted, blind, April 1990**** *Perhaps overcritical. Time will tell.*

Ch L'ANGELUS *Pink-tinged, feminine and gentle in 1975. A decade later, a medium-pale, mahogany, mature colour; sweet, fruity and agreeable on the nose; medium dryness and weight, good flavour and nicely balanced, with unobtrusive tannin and acidity.* Last noted, pre-sale, Oct 1985*** *Should be lovely now.*

Ch d'ANGLUDET *Tasted twice in 1976 — a nice wine. A decade later: good colour; sweet on nose and palate. Rich. Chunky.* Last noted, pre-sale, March 1986*** *Should be nice now; will keep.*

Ch BATAILLEY *A number of notes from 1975 to 1987 including English bottlings, a good Berry Bros anda recent lean, woody bottling by Davies & Son. Also a château-bottled magnum showing its age. Acidity noted in the four tasted since 1983. Flavoury though.* Last tasted Oct 1987. At best*** *Not worth keeping.*

Ch BEAU SEJOUR BECOT *Three notes. Completely ready in 1982. Nice fruit, decent length.* Last tasted Jan 1988*** *Drink soon.*

Ch BEL-AIR-MARQUIS-D'ALIGRE *Deep, impressive; fragrant, ripe; a lovely soft, fleshy mouthful.* Tasted twice, autumn 1985*** *Drink soon.*

Ch BELGRAVE *Rather undistinguished* 5ème cru classé *Médoc. Unknit and stalky in the mid- to late 1970s and not much better now, its most notable feature being a deep, rich colour, though even this has a slightly rusty orange, mature tinge, and a hefty, port-like flavour. Very tannic.* Last tasted Oct 1988** *Not yet ready but I wouldn't wait.*

Ch BEYCHEVELLE *Deep, fruity, stylish in cask. Drinking nicely in 1978. A decade later, still remarkably deep in colour; rather dusty, cheesy nose, sweet, full, but not heavy, attractive but twinge of overmaturity. A chunky rather than elegant Beychevelle. Still tannic.* Last tasted Dec 1988***(*) *Drink now or, say, within 10 years.*

Ch BOYD-CANTENAC *Before and after 1980 deep, fairly full-bodied, a bit raw and unready. Now maturing; a reasonable well-developed 'medicinal Médoc' bouquet; flavoury and attractive.* Last noted, pre-sale, Oct 1987** *Might just benefit from more bottle-age.*

Ch BRANAIRE-DUCRU *Soft and chocolaty in cask. Three recent notes: lovely colour; sweet, slightly lactic but fragrant; a mildly fleshy charmer with touch of acidity.* Last tasted Jan 1990* *No great future.*

Ch BRANE-CANTENAC *Many notes, from a plummy cask sample. It seemed to show best either side of 1980. Notes since then dwell on its very distinctive, overripe, farmyard nose: manure, pigsty, hen droppings, which some people find attractive. I don't. Nevertheless a very flavoury wine with good soft fruits, decent length though a trifle piquant.* Last tasted Dec 1990**

Ch CALON-SEGUR *Fragrant in cask, evolved*

plausibly. Chewy, meaty, more Pomerol than St-Estèphe in its texture and vinosity. An attractive, well-developed bouquet. Last tasted Sept 1988*** *Though still tannic, probably best to drink soon.*

Ch CANON *Consistently reliable. Good notes on the '70 over 15 years. Still fairly deep, lively; a rich, harmonious bouquet, prune-like fruit and a whiff like a spent firework; touch of sweetness, nice weight, excellent flavour and balance, chunky but not coarse.* Last tasted Jan 1988**** *Lovely now. Will keep.*

Ch CANON-LA-GAFFELIERE *A bit sugary. Needs drinking.* Last tasted May 1986**

Ch CANTEMERLE *A vintage like 1970 does not suit the Cantemerle style. Dumb but mouthfilling in 1973, touch of austerity but some elegance in the early 1980s. Most recent: a nice healthy colour; sweet, tannic, nose; medium weight, quite nice fruit, bit tinny, dry tannic finish.* Last tasted Feb 1991**(*) *No great improvement.*

Ch CANTENAC-BROWN *First tasted in cask alongside the '71. Fatter, more complete. Five good notes in the mid- to late 1970s. A decade later: medium-deep, mature-looking; nice, rich, typically chocolaty nose; dry, fullish, complete, still tannic.* Last tasted July 1990**(*)

Ch CARBONNIEUX *Austere in early 1970s, dry, lean, chunky in early 1980s. Most recently: soft, harmonious, fullish, fleshy, very tannic, slightly woody.* Last noted dining at the château, April 1991*** *Just.*

Dom de CHEVALIER *Tasted over a 10-year period. Wonderfully fragrant bouquet, raspberries, typical Graves 'warm brick', cedar-box scent, developing even more deliciously after an hour in the glass. Ripe sweetness, fairly full body, spicy, elegant. Lovely.* Last tasted Sept 1986**** *Probably peaking now.*

Ch CISSAC *First tasted in 1977 and a dozen times since. Variable. Despite suspicions of high volatility most were good. An amazingly sweet nose; chewy, chunky, still tannic.* Last tasted, a bottle from the château, Oct 1990. *At best**(*)*

Ch COS D'ESTOURNEL *Bruno Prats' first vintage. The wine has an uncompromising masculinity and is loaded with St-Estèphe tannin. An old-fashioned Cos. Most recently: a lively ruby colour; dry fruit and spice, opening up in the glass beautifully; good, crisp, fruity, mouthfilling, tremendously tannic.* Last tasted July 1990**(**) *Like a '28. Probably needs another 20 years. It could achieve******

Ch CROIZET-BAGES *Crisp and fruity.* Last tasted March 1986**(*)

Ch DUCRU-BEAUCAILLOU *Many usefully spaced notes, starting with a concentrated, gutsy cask sample in spring of 1972, and a dozen good notes since 1983. Like Cos, a deep-coloured, mouthfilling, masculine wine. Rich garnet with ruby highlights; the bouquet over the past five years softening, coming out of its shell, mulberry, ripe, cedary, harmonious; big but agreeable weight. Rich and satisfying — up to a point, for it is still very tannic — plus the fruit, extract and balance to guarantee a long life. Most recently: glorious colour, classic nose, rich and powerful.* Last tasted Nov 1990***(**) *Patience will be rewarded.*

Ch DURFORT-VIVENS *Rather overripe and acid-etched.* Last tasted April 1988**

Ch L'EVANGILE *Seven variable notes from 1976. Consistently tannic. Most recently: deep; lovely, scented, touch of tangerine; rich, chewy, chunky. Lacks Pomerol charm.* Last tasted May 1991**(*)

Ch de FIEUZAL *I was not bowled over when I first tasted this in 1973, but shortly after, I discovered its attractiveness. Still deep, fragrant, crisp fruit, nice weight.* Last tasted Oct 1989***(*)

Ch FIGEAC *A glorious '70, challenging its great rival Cheval-Blanc for sheer drinkability, though noticeably different in style. Over 12 notes, all but two (one tart, one corky) singing its praises. Most recently at Desai's Figeac tasting: lovely, lively, still relatively youthful-looking; an exalted fragrance spiced with strawberry-like fruit; distinctly sweet and ripe, fairly full-bodied, vigorous, crisp acidity, most attractive.* Last noted Dec 1989**** *Exciting now but lacking the rotundity and staying power of Cheval-Blanc.*

Ch La FLEUR-PETRUS Cépages: *50:50 Merlot and Cabernet Franc. Not wholly up to its very high reputation. Notes in 1983 and 1986 all qualified in some way: unknit, touch too high volatile acidity, curious; perhaps I was nit-picking for otherwise it is fragrant, very attractive, stylish, with a distinctive silky Pomerol texture.* Last tasted Sept 1986. *Might warrant**** A wine for rich men who like a challenge.*

Les FORTS DE LATOUR *Purple, stalky and raw when tasted in cask in Jan 1971. "Interesting to see development" noted. Still an intense ruby colour; bouquet, with air, vanilla and cedar pencils, fragrant. It has gradually sweetened up and now has a delicious spicy, almost eucalyptus flavour. A pretty good mouthful, tannin noticeable but not too intrusive.* Last tasted Nov 1990**(*) *More drinkable now than the* grand vin, *but will not improve to the same extent.*

Ch GAZIN *Not big but quite rich, rather jammy.* Last tasted July 1976**

Ch GISCOURS *Impressive in cask, its opaque, rich, intense appearance has scarcely changed; bouquet harmonious and packed with fruit, plummy, fig-like. Sweetness, high alcoholic content, extract, fruit and flesh manages thinly to disguise the heavily laden tannin. More like port! 13 consistent notes since 1982.* Last tasted Nov 1990*(****) *Well worth keeping.*

Ch GLORIA *It was around this time that the late Henri Martin first established the reputation of Gloria. Many notes. At peak either side of 1980. Spicy, almost gooseberry-like fruit. Still sweet, fleshy and attractive.* Last tasted Nov 1990*** *Drink soon.*

Ch GRAND-PUY-LACOSTE *A concentrated, impressive cask sample in 1972, then a string of notes in 1979, fragrant and firm; six in the 1980s. A classic, slow-maturing Lacoste, still very deep-coloured and vigorous; characteristically crisp, berry-like nose and taste, with spicy Cabernet fruit, good length, still tannic.* Last noted at the closing dinner of the International Wine & Food Society Convention at the Regent Hotel, Kowloon. Slight bottle variation but I rate this***(**) *Will be incomparable in 20 years.*

Ch GRUAUD-LAROSE *The sort of '70 that makes one wonder whether the Médocs of this vintage will ever come round. After 20 notes spanning 12 years I still have reservations. Ignoring one corky and four oxidised bottles, there is a tartness allied to its body and tannin that makes me wonder. At best a deep, attractive, luminous red; lively fruitiness on nose and palate. Last tasted Sept 1988**(*)? I won't bother to wait.*

Ch HAUT-BAILLY *Has the advantage of long-tried* terroir, *though it was at Loudenne with the late Martin Bamford that the '70 alerted me to Haut-Bailly. The initial cask sample had a typical, straightforward, earthy Graves character which it has retained. A 'thick', sturdy, rich wine. Beautifully developed when last tasted in the mid-1980s. Doubtless even lovelier now*****

Ch HAUT-BATAILLEY *Almost always leaner and more elegant than the contiguous and similarly classified Batailley. The '70 a slow developer. Now medium-deep, rich, fairly mature-looking; equally rich bouquet, toasted, good depth, more to come; and, with bottle-age, distinctly sweet, softening, with nice weight and flavour. Last tasted Sept 1989*** Enjoy now.*

Ch LAFON-ROCHET *Despite its promixity to Cos and almost backing onto Lafite, just across the* jalle, *somehow it often lacks class and certainly lacks charm, though the '70 reasonably fragrant, with pretty good fruit and length. Still tannic. Last tasted Jan 1991**(*)*

Ch LAGRANGE *St-Julien. 12 notes. Quite nice and fruity, taxiing in the mid-1970s, but has never achieved lift-off. Dull, austere, a bit edgy. Last tasted Sept 1988(*)*

Ch La LAGUNE *Unusually, for this most 'burgundian' of all Médoc classed growths, a rather slow starter in this vintage. Quite a few notes from a nice-textured cask sample, but for over 10 years deep, dumb, full and unready. Suddenly, two mulberry rich, agreeable notes in 1983 and subsequently, including a lovely soft fruity Grants of St James's bottling. Rich, plummy and attractive. Needs decanting time. Last tasted July 1991***(*) Nice now, will open up even more.*

Ch LANGOA-BARTON *Nice wine. Recently, a magnum from the château: very deep by candlelight; classic 'medicinal' Médoc nose, touch of spearmint; refreshing but not really ready. Seemed more advanced in bottle, with a lovely, slightly scented cedary bouquet, nice weight, deft touch, lightly tannic finish. Last noted at Brooks's Barton dinner, March 1990***(*)*

Ch LASCOMBES *Just four good, consistent notes, straddling nearly 10 years. Deep, classic claret nose; touch of sweetness, fairly full-bodied, rich, fleshy, all the components in place. Last tasted Nov 1986. Now probably***(*) A satisfactory drink but more to come.*

Ch LATOUR A POMEROL *One note only. Deep, rich; good nose; drier and more tannic than expected. April 1987***(*)*

Ch LEOVILLE-BARTON *Several notes. Austere in the late 1970s. Four noted as stalky, old wood in early to mid-1980s. Most recently: lovely colour; classic, biscuity; dry, lean, flavoury yet bottle variation. Last tasted Jan 1991. At best*** Drink up.*

Ch LEOVILLE-LAS-CASES *Austere in cask, but by 1976 had developed a lovely nose, dry, fine and elegant. 12 notes in the 1980s. An excellent wine, still fairly deep, rich but showing some maturity. A soft, harmonious, slow-to-emerge but cedary, fragrant smoky bouquet; full, rich, fleshy yet still tannic. Last tasted Dec 1989**(***) Should turn out well.*

Ch LYNCH-BAGES *A marvellous wine. Opaque and concentrated in cask, with the unmistakable Lynch-Bages crisp blackcurrant (70% Cabernet Sauvignon) aroma. By far the deepest and most intense in a vertical tasting in 1984 of vintages ranging from '71 to '83. Crisp, full, fleshy, full of flavour and zest. Last tasted Feb 1986***(*) But clearly more excitement ahead.*

Ch MALESCOT-ST-EXUPERY *Just two notes. A good Dutch bottling in 1977 and, recently, an* impériale *at Rodenstock's Malescot tasting: impressively deep; broad, open, fruit, touch of tangerine; sweetish, full-bodied, rich, extract and fruit, nice texture, very tannic and fairly high acidity making it undrinkable without food. Last noted Sept 1990. With food****

Ch La MISSION-HAUT-BRION *Absolutely magnificent and extraordinarily concentrated in cask. A wine of vast dimensions, huge, tannic, through the 1970s, but volatile acidity noticeable since the early 1980s. Although this to some extent enhances the bouquet, it produces a raw acidic finish. Rich, chunky, flavoury but aggressive. Immensely impressive but flawed. Last noted, at the Karl-Heinz Wolf tasting, June 1990*** It will never throw off its acidity, but don't be put off.*

Ch MONTROSE *Apart from one terrible British Transport Hotels bottling in 1976, magnificent. An archetypal, massive, long-lasting, old-fashioned Montrose. Opaque, intense; amazingly rich, singed, leathery tannin, highly alcoholic nose. Ripe entry. Latour-like body, strength and length. A lovely, rich mouthfiller. Last tasted Nov 1990***(**)*

Ch MOUTON-BARON PHILIPPE *Although bigger than usual, as always a charmer. 12 notes over 12 years. Pretty well developed, rich, flavoury. Just a touch of acidity. Last tasted March 1986. Ready then** Drink soon.*

Ch PALMER *Not tasted in its early years but quite a few notes over a 10-year span. Still incredibly deep and intense; a bouquet that seems to lie in wait, hard but then pungent, biscuity, liquorice, rich fruit and spice; the flavour explodes in the mouth. A rich consistency, chewy, fleshy, impressive. Last tasted Nov 1989****(*) A lovely mouthful now, and will continue well into the next century.*

Ch de PEZ *At harvest time in 1970 the proprietor, encouraged by Martin Bamford, vinified his four* cépages *separately. Tasted in cask, then in bottle, the individual varietals were interesting but not as satisfactory as the final — traditional — blend. Good fruit, nice balance, still tannic. Last tasted Jan 1987. Now likely to be***(*) Will never be more than very good for its class.*

Ch PHELAN-SEGUR *Same classification, same district but nowhere near as good as the Pez. Last tasted March 1985* Best forgotten.*

Ch PICHON-BARON *Disappointing. Touch of coarseness.* Last tasted Nov 1981* Retaste.

Ch PICHON-LALANDE *Infinitely superior to its neighbour across the road. Forthcoming even in cask, and a peppery Cabernet Sauvignon aroma well into the mid-1970s, and, though impressive, still a bit austere a decade later. Now mature, well-developed, rich, crisp, cedary bouquet; lovely weight and style, fruity.* Last tasted Dec 1989**** Delicious now but should continue unabated for 10 years or so.

Ch RAUSAN-SEGLA *A wonderful colour; rich though not overwhelming bouquet; plump, fleshy, lots of tannin, good acidity.* Last tasted Sept 1986***(*) Should be a pretty good mouthful now, and more to come.

Ch ST-PIERRE (BONTEMPS ET SEVAISTRE) *A decade of notes. Despite impressive depth of colour, an early developer. Lovely bouquet; soft, ripe, fleshy, velvety.* Last tasted May 1985*** Perfectly well evolved then and probably delightful now.

Ch de SALES *Delicious in cask and through the 1970s. Soft, pleasing, completely ready by 1982. Now medium-pale, very mature-looking; soft, gentle bouquet; sweet, on the light side for a '70.* Last tasted March 1991** Drink up.

Ch TALBOT *Seven notes, from 1974. Straightforward. Leaner, as usual, than Gruaud. A couple of "dumb" and "dusty" notes in the early 1980s. Still plummy; ripening — sweet, rich nose; seems to be sweeter on palate, fairly full-bodied, good tannin and acidity.* Last tasted July 1990***(*)

Ch La TOUR-CARNET *One of the less-than-impressive classed growths. A bit four-square, lean, medicinal.* Last tasted June 1988*

Ch La TOUR-HAUT-BRION *Following its progress in parallel with La Mission, more stalky and raw in cask but a gradual opening up. Rich, fruity and attractive by the mid-1980s. Finally, at Wolf's tasting, alongside La Mission and Haut-Brion itself, it had a very odd bouquet, like the singed top of a rice pudding. Dry, fruity, flavoury but a trifle acidic.* Last noted June 1990**(*)

SOME OTHER '70s TASTED IN THE 1980s AND SHOWING WELL:

Ch Beauregard Pomerol; Ch Carbonnieux; Ch La Clusière; Ch Coufran; Ch La Dominique; Ch Duhart-Milon; Ch Fombrauge; Ch Fourcas-Hosten; Clos des Jacobins; Ch La Louvière; Ch Loudenne; Clos du Marquis; Ch Nenin; Ch Pibran; Ch Pomies-Agassac; Ch Prieuré-Lichine; Ch La Tour-de-Mons; Ch Tronquoy-Lalande; Ch Yon-Figeac.

TASTED IN THE 1980s, MEDIOCRE OR VARIABLE:

Ch Baret; Ch La Gaffelière; Ch Haut-Beychevelle-Gloria; Ch de Lamarque; Ch Meyney; Ch Pape-Clément.

TASTED IN THE 1980s AND POOR:

Ch Croque-Michotte; Clos Fourtet; Ch La Grave Trigant de Boisset; Ch Pavie-Decesse; Ch Pouget Margaux.

1971****

Overpriced at the time, and undervalued since. A thoroughly enjoyable vintage still giving a good deal of satisfaction and particularly successful in Pomerol, St-Emilion and Graves. I have in fact upgraded 1971 since the last edition on the basis of my notes made since 1980. Though it does not have the really long-term potential of the finest '70s, the best of the '71s give great pleasure.

The growing season: a cold wet spring and May and June similar. Summer warm and pleasant, with light rains to swell the grapes. A respectable ripening month followed by a small harvest in good weather, early Oct. Production of about half that of 1970, and an overheated market, resulted in high prices. Then came 1972 and the slump.

Many notes, the following being a representative selection, some of the most recent being made at a tasting of '71s organised by Farr Vintners.

Ch LAFITE *Nine notes. From early on it had a rather weak as opposed to intense rim, always a tell-tale sign, was a fairly light, easy wine after about eight years and fully developed for the past eight. Showing well at Lloyd Flatt's in Oct 1988. Most recently: medium-pale, open, very little red; a very forthcoming, almost exotically fragrant nose, strawberries, violets; slightly sweet, lightweight and style. Easy, fragrant. Dry finish. Speciously attractive.* Last noted, Farr Vintners, Nov 1990*** Drink up.

Ch MARGAUX *Picking started Sept 28. Production 16,000 cases. Surprisingly deep and still quite youthful-looking after eight years, but fully evolved with a delicately rich and fragrant bouquet; a crisp, fruity, charmer at Desai's in 1987. Most recently, palish, pretty, mature; sweet, fragrant, fruity but unknit; dry, crisp, fruity flavour. A little on the raw side. A good drink but drying out.* Last tasted Nov 1990*** Drink soon.

Ch LATOUR *14 well-spread notes from cask onwards. From the start, deep, rich, almost with a '70 denseness, now mellowing though still quite intense. Good nose. Rich, meaty yet some hardness concealing further potential. Four-square, full of chunky fruit and vinosity, far less charm and fragrance than Lafite, Margaux or Mouton but better balanced than all three.* Last noted, Farr Vintners, Nov 1990***(*) Worth keeping.

Ch MOUTON-ROTHSCHILD *More notes on this than any other '71. Fairly deep, more of a cherry red and still with a crisp youthful plumminess of colour. Trying hard to be fragrant with deceptively raw fruit when first decanted, needing an hour or so to open up, eventually delicious, spicy; surprisingly sweet, lean, flavoury, good length. Touch of bitterness on the finish.* Last tasted Nov 1990***(*) Needs time and air.

Ch HAUT-BRION *Several notes. As deep as the '70 but more piquant. A sweet, fragrant, rather caramelly coffee-like nose and an assertive pebbly-*

tobacco flavour. Slightly sweet entry, fleshy, elegant, medium weight, silky, fruity, slightly raw, very dry finish. Most recently a lovely, elegant, double-magnum. Last noted at Haut-Brion dinner, Brooks's, March 1991****

Ch AUSONE *Just four notes, first in cask, then after three years in bottle, next 11 years later — both the latter noted as much deeper in colour than the '70. Most recently: quite good bouquet, slightly vegetal, forthcoming touch of liquorice; dryish, medium weight, assertive, idiosyncratic flavour, nice texture — silky drying tannins. Tails off a bit.* Last noted, Farr Vintners, Nov 1990*** Strange character. Will keep.

Ch CHEVAL-BLANC *Very deep, spicy in cask. "Well-balanced" noted over half a dozen times. Deep, attractive, lovely gradation of colour; a glorious bouquet, harmonious, swelling, still spicy — eucalyptus; slightly sweet, perfect weight, an elegant, smooth, well-timed wine with more flesh than the Médocs. Most recently, showing considerable maturity; sweet, fragrant bouquet; silky texture. A lovely wine.* Last tasted Nov 1990**** Drink now to 2000.

Ch PETRUS *Opaque in cask, a lovely Pomerol texture noted, plump yet tannic. Evolving well, marvellously fleshy and fragrant by the mid-1980s. Also tasted in cask and over six times since. Now losing colour and mature though still lively; a sweet, sweaty with tannin, jammy fruit, whiff of sage bouquet; fairly sweet and full-bodied, chunky, rich, rather malty, lovely texture, almost '75-like tannin.* Last noted, Farr Vintners, Nov 1990****(*) Long life ahead.

Ch BATAILLEY *Quite a few notes including an agreeable Berry Bros bottling in 1985. Plumminess of the early 1980s now much paler and fully mature; sweet but unexceptional nose; pleasing, with enough richness and fruit. Very drinkable though lacking finesse.* Last tasted July 1989** Drink soon.

Ch BEYCHEVELLE *Tasted several times from 1976 to 1983; only once since. Consistently good notes: appearance now fully mature, orange-tinged; vinous, cedary bouquet; nice weight, elegant, well-rounded, soft yet slightly more acidity than expected though this would not be noticeable with food.* Last tasted Nov 1990*** Now to 1998.

Ch BRANAIRE-DUCRU *Medium, mature, orange-tinged; fully mature, rather unusual, very distinctive bouquet, violets, liquorice; full-flavoured, rich, chewy, tannin well-masked. Good shape.* Last tasted Nov 1990*** Now to 1996.

Ch BRANE-CANTENAC *Some find this rather medicinal-Médoc, ripe barnyard-smelling wine attractive, which it is in its way. To my surprise I found it very appealing, a lovely scent; silky, gentle, fragrant, ready.* Last tasted Nov 1990*** Now to 1995.

Ch CALON-SEGUR *Strangely, only three notes. An attractive wine, a good '71 and a good Calon. Nice weight, flavour and length.* Last tasted Jan 1986*** Drink now. Will keep.

Ch CANON *Excellent aged 10 and still very attractive. Now on the pale side of medium, open, mature but richly coloured; open-knit, fragrant bouquet that evolved sweetly in the glass; very fragrant with sinewy, dancing acidity, lean for Canon. Dry finish.* Last tasted Nov 1990**** Now to 1998.

Ch CANON-LA-GAFFELIERE *Eight notes spanning the 1980s. Never very deep, now fairly pale and with an orange-tinged maturity. But despite this and a plausible sweetness of nose, an agreeable drink, soft, light, flavoury.* Last tasted July 1979** Drink up.

Ch CANTEMERLE *A return to elegance, even in cask. Fragrant and flavoury in 1982. Most recently: deep, lovely mature appearance; an extraordinarily forthcoming bouquet, a gusher, mixture of underarm and violets! Multi-faceted and exotic. Medium sweetness, medium-full body, very rich, lovely flavour and finish. Well clad and time in hand.* Last tasted Nov 1990**** Now to 2000.

Ch CERTAN-GUIRAUD *Palish, very mature appearance; fragrant, singed, coffee-like, attractive but unknit bouquet; very sweet, a rich mouthful. Lovely wine.* Last tasted Nov 1990**** Now to 1998.

Ch CERTAN-DE-MAY *Very confusing, all these Certans and to add to the confusion, this was made at L'Evangile. Deep, rich; rather over-rich, Virol (malty) nose; sweetish, full-bodied, lots of fruit, flesh, length and good dry finish.* Last tasted Nov 1990**** Now to 2000.

Dom de CHEVALIER *Fully mature by 1980. Most recently, open-knit, tinge of orange; soft, fully-evolved bouquet, tea, chocolate, fading violets; consistently dry, medium-light weight and style, very flavoury but lean. Tannin and acidity to sustain it.* Last tasted Nov 1990*** Now to 2000.

Ch CISSAC *Many notes since an early cask sample. A good example of a reliable and always reasonably priced* cru bourgeois. *Now mature. Quite elegant and shapely.* Last tasted Nov 1990** Drink soon.

Ch La CONSEILLANTE *An early developer. Fine and fleshy by the mid-1980s. Recently medium-deep, mature; a sweet, very attractive bouquet of considerable depth; dry, fullish, perfect balance.* Last tasted Nov 1990**** Now to beyond 2000.

Ch COS D'ESTOURNEL *Distinctly leaner than the '70. Mature but not very distinguished by 1980. A decade later: attractive, open-knit bouquet; very dry from start to finish. Lacking flesh.* Last tasted Nov 1990** Unexciting. Unlikely to gain much with further bottle-age.

Ch La DOMINIQUE *Just one note: deepish, lovely colour; fragrant, very rich, considerable depth, but touch of silkiness; dry, full-bodied, good length, very tannic.* Nov 1990***(*) Now to beyond 2000.

Ch DUCRU-BEAUCAILLOU *Good notes in the 1970s. Still fairly deep, red, flavoury but dry and a bit insubstantial in 1980s. Most recently, at Farr Vintners, I ran contrary to most of the other blind-tasters, finding the nose overripe and sweaty, dry, fullish, a rather herbaceous and* fermier *flavour. I also found the finish a bit raw. Clearly a matter of taste.* Last noted Nov 1990**?

Ch L'ENCLOS *Deep, rich, mature; rich, chocolaty nose that grew in the glass, very sweet, very fragrant; flavour to match. A very assertive wine, tannic and humus rich.* Nov 1990**** Now to 2000.

Ch L'EVANGILE *Fairly deep, mature; strange, sweaty tannic and unknit at first but air enriched it; a rich mouthful too, with piquant fruit and a lot of tannin. Worth risking considerably more bottle-age. Nov 1990**(**) 1992–2000?*

Ch FIGEAC *Eight notes since 1976 on this Jekyll and Hyde wine. Late-picked. One of Thierry Manoncourt's favourite wines. Sometimes showing signs of overmaturity, loss of vigour. At Desai's Figeac tasting in 1989 an opulently rich, forthcoming bouquet, vanilla, leaving a strong jammy scent in the glass. Very sweet, full-flavoured, a warm attractive wine with spicy aftertaste. Positively exotic on nose but more austere on palate at Farr Vintners tasting. Last noted Nov 1990**** Drink soon.*

Ch La FLEUR-PETRUS *Five notes. An attractive, well-constituted wine, fragrant and very appealing by 1980. A decade later: still deep-coloured; fleshy, harmonious bouquet; touch of ripe sweetness, full of body and flavour, good fruit and lots of grip. Last tasted Nov 1990**** Now to beyond 2000.*

Les FORTS DE LATOUR *First tasted in 1979, attractive on nose, a pleasing weight, flavour and balance. A couple of years later I found it bland-nosed; soft, agreeable, a bit empty, needing drinking. Most recently: fairly deep, rich, mature; open, attractive and fragrant on nose and palate. A bit lean. Certainly not a heavyweight. Last tasted Nov 1990*** Now to 1996.*

Ch La GAFFELIERE *A pleasing and quick developer but still soft and delicious well into the mid-1980s. Last tasted Nov 1986*** Drink soon.*

Ch Le GAY *Very deep in colour and with great depth of nose and palate. A lovely full-bodied wine. March 1985**** Will keep.*

Ch GISCOURS *An extraordinary wine. Initially opaque, still unusually deep with intense black cherry centre; vigorous, full of fruit, fragrant; a pretty huge mouthful, rich, fleshy, soft yet tannic. Last tasted July 1989***(*) Impressive now. Will keep.*

Ch GRAND-PUY-LACOSTE *Several notes in the 1970s: rich, stylish, a bit 'green'. Firm and flavoury in 1980. A decade later: medium, mature; crisp fruit, harmonious bouquet; touch of sweetness, medium-full body; good, straightforward flavour, length and finish. Lean but stylish. Last tasted Nov 1990***(*) Now to 2000+*

Ch La GRAVE TRIGANT-DE-BOISSET *Mouiex's purchase of La Grave in 1971 was somewhat ill-timed. The vines had been so badly hit by hail that it affected the taste of the wine. In desperation they left it for three years before bottling it. The wine is now sensationally attractive: a medium-deep, mature colour; immediate fragrance which evolved beautifully in the glass; sweet, full, fleshy, a glorious wine. Rave notices at Farr Vintner. Nov 1990***** Drink now.*

Ch GRUAUD-LAROSE *Many consistent notes: good, fruity, tends not to open up, lacking finesse. Still fairly deep, rich, mature-looking; sweet, rather meaty, 'medicinal' nose and flavour, lean, crisp, dry, slightly metallic tannic finish. Last tasted Nov 1990*** Should keep well but unlikely to change its character.*

Ch HAUT-BAILLY *At this period 34% Cabernet Sauvignon, 16% Cabernet Franc, 26% Merlot. 24% old vines. By the mid-1980s a harmonious, chocolaty Graves bouquet; shapely, pleasant weight and flavour, tannic finish. Most recently: lovely colour, mature; rich, forthcoming, exotic bouquet; smooth, velvety, a touch of red Graves, chocolaty, earthy character, good finish. Last tasted Nov 1990**** Lovely now, will keep.*

Ch HAUT-BATAILLEY *So disarmingly plausible and flavoury in the mid-1970s it was hard to foresee room for improvement. But, well made and beautifully balanced, it has ever since appeared to be 'at peak' and will doubtless continue. Elegant. Lovely. Last tasted Dec 1989*** or, to be more generous****

Ch HAUT-BEYCHEVELLE-GLORIA *Soft, light, attractive. Last tasted Dec 1987** Drink up.*

Ch La LAGUNE *Initially slow to mature. By the mid-1980s, plum-coloured; peppery, spicy, almost spiky non-varietal fruit nose; dry, lean, flavoury but a bit raw. Most recently: still deep-coloured; distinctly meaty, rather strange nose reminding me of calf's-foot jelly, rich; moderately good, touch of coarseness. A middling '71. Last tasted Nov 1990. Just*** Drink up.*

Ch LANGOA-BARTON *Tasted only in the early 1980s, consistent notes: most attractive, mature; warm, ripe, appealing bouquet and flavour. Nice texture. Charming. Last tasted July 1984*** Should still be very good.*

Ch LATOUR A POMEROL *Surprisingly, not deep, mature; crisp fragrant bouquet which developed richly; fuller body than its appearance indicated, good soft mid-palate, attractive. Nov 1990**** Now to 1998.*

Ch LEOVILLE-BARTON *A fragrant early developer which is still a charmer, with silky texture, nice weight and flavour. Dry finish. A wine with class and style. Last tasted Sept 1989**** Drink now, will keep.*

Ch LEOVILLE-LAS-CASES *Rather austere when young, my last six notes show progressive maturity. Still fairly deep; 'classic' and 'cedar' seem to be the key words, latterly the nose very sweet and biscuity; good flavour and texture but a bit stern and lacking the deft Barton touch. Dry finish. Last tasted Nov 1990***(*)*

Ch LYNCH-BAGES *A bit insubstantial and now fully mature; curious high-toned nose, slightly medicinal but rich and flavoury. Appealing in its way. Last tasted Nov 1986***

Ch MAGDELAINE *Palish, mature; low-keyed at first, developing a strange rich meatiness on the nose; distinctly sweet, fuller body than appearance indicated, rich, chocolaty, slightly singed. I liked it. Nov 1990*** Drink now to 1998.*

Ch MALESCOT-ST-EXUPERY *Soft rich colour; open-knit, sweet, attractive bouquet; flavoury, fruity, touch of rawness around the tannic finish. Drinking well in marie-jeanne, a touch of rawness around its tannic finish at a tasting two months later. Last noted Nov 1990. Just*** Drink now to 1998.*

Ch MARQUIS D'ALESME-BECKER *Touch of iron. Pleasant enough. Aug 1986***

Ch La MISSION-HAUT-BRION *Rich and flavoury*

in cask, and since. Consistently favourable notes. Still very deep; immediately fragrant, harmonious, citrus-like fruitiness, plus coffee and iodine; distinctly sweet, fairly full-bodied, complete, tobacco taste, great length. I much prefer this to the '70. Last tasted Nov 1990**** Lovely now, will keep.

Ch MONTROSE *Many notes. Good wine. Except for a woody bottle, displaying marvellous fruit though tannic in the early 1980s. "Clean cut" and "not as hard as expected" in the mid-1980s. Two recent notes: though fairly deep still, very mature-looking; a very Médocain nose, iodine, oyster shell; dry, lean, lacking length and charm, not that charm is a Montrose feature, rather, masculinity. Just a little disappointing. Last tasted Sept and Nov 1990**(*) Worth keeping in case . . .*

Ch PALMER *A slow developer seeming to struggle inwardly through the 1970s and early 1980s. Still fairly deep, rich ruby, but showing some maturity; lovely, sweet, rich, cedary bouquet taking the place of the earlier plummy fruitiness; touch of sweetness and flesh, soft, rich, complete, attractive. Needs air. Last tasted Nov 1989**** On the plateau now, should continue.*

Ch PAPE-CLEMENT *Though not generally highly regarded around this time, I have good notes on the '71, particularly around 1980 when I noted it as stylish, with an excellent earthy Graves flavour, balance and length. Fine, a bit lean in 1986. Most recently: a lovely mature colour; rich, meaty yet relatively low-keyed, classic nose; very distinctive Graves tobacco flavour. Dry finish. Last tasted Nov 1990**** Now to 2000.*

Ch PAVIE *Not tasted prior to 1980, but many notes throughout 1980s. Pleasant, elegant, with nice texture though lacking fat. Clearly a beverage wine — a whiff of "tea" in 1985 and "chocolate and coffee" recently! Last tasted Nov 1990*** Drink soon. I think it is drying out.*

Ch PHELAN-SEGUR *10 notes over 12 years, none very complimentary. A heavily chaptalised, rather smelly wine, raw and somewhat artificial though I have quite enjoyed it at lunch. Last tasted Feb 1988* I only mention it as a warning.*

Ch PICHON-BARON *At five years of age its appearance hinted at a quick-maturing wine though its very dry, somewhat astringent palate gave one pause for thought. Most recently: deep, crisp, fairly intense; strange, vanilla, fairly powerful nose; fullish, piquant fruit, assertive and very tannic. Last tasted Nov 1990**(*)? Hard to know how this will turn out.*

Ch PICHON-LALANDE *First tasted in the mid-1980s when I noted it twice as fully mature; sweet, with a rather sugared nose; a bit lean, flavoury, but pleasant enough. Most recently, similar remarks. Fully evolved, open-knit, chaptalised but attractive. Neither of the '71 Pichons great. Last tasted Nov 1990** Drink soon.*

Ch RAUSAN-SEGLA *Deeper than expected; showing maturity and bottle-age, like brown toast, autumnal, specious; despite an edge of acidity I thought it delicious, silky, completely ready. At the château, Sept 1986** Drink up.*

Ch de SALES *Always an easy-going wine and at its best in a vintage like '71. Early-maturing, very attractive at seven years of age and still soft, rounded and agreeable seven years later. Last tasted Oct 1984** Probably still very pleasant.*

Ch TALBOT *The Cordier reds seem a bit lacking in '71. The usually masculine Talbot is fairly deep and spicy but "raw" noted twice in the mid-1980s. Unyielding, except with a good mouthful of beef. Most recently: a lovely rich colour, now showing signs of maturity; classic cedar nose, fragrant; lean but powerful, still rather tannic. Last tasted Nov 1990**(**) Give it time.*

Ch La TOUR-HAUT-BRION *Rich and flavoury but lacking the length of its elder brother and a bit raw. Most recently: still a deep ruby with an extraordinary nose, iodine at first, then very rich, biscuity, fragrant — its best feature. Dry and lean. Last noted Nov 1990**(*) 1994–2000*

Ch La TOUR-DU-PIN-FIGEAC *On the Pomerol side of St-Emilion and more like a chaptalised version of the former. Very mature. A rather old leathery flavour. Just to demonstrate that the less grand St-Emilions are not much better than the equivalent Médocs even in a vintage like '71. Last tasted Sept 1986**

Ch TROTANOY *Several notes in the mid-1970s and one in the mid-1980s clearly proclaim a remarkable wine. Until then, almost opaque; a rich, plummy Merlot-like Pétrus; full, rich, velvety. Now maturing; high-toned, fragrant bouquet of great depth; still fairly sweet, a rich fleshy mouthful, lovely flavour and texture. Last tasted Nov 1990**** Now to beyond 2000.*

VIEUX CH CERTAN *A soft supple wine, its depth of colour, lovely texture and flavour noted in 1985. Most recently: rich, maturing appearance, bouquet of fruit and walnuts, a bit hard at first but opened up; rich, chocolaty flavour though lightish style. Silky tannic finish. Last tasted Nov 1900***(*) Drink now to 2000.*

THE FOLLOWING WERE SHOWING WELL IN THE EARLY TO MID-1980s:

Ch Beauregard Pomerol; Ch Beau Séjour Bécot; Ch Cantenac-Brown; Ch Carbonnieux; Ch Duhart-Milon; Dom de L'Eglise; Clos Fourtet; Ch Haut-Sarpe; Ch Lascombes; Ch Moulinet; Ch Mouton-Baron Philippe; Ch Petit-Village; Ch Plince; Ch Prieuré-Lichine; Ch Ripeau; Ch La Tour-de-Mons; Ch Troplong-Mondot.

AGREEABLE MINOR WINES IN THE 1980s:

Ch d'Arcins; Ch Baret; Ch Bel-Orme-Tronquoy-de-Lalande; Ch La Clotte; Ch Fombrauge; Ch de Lamarque; Ch Lynch-Moussas; Ch Magnan-La-Gaffelière; Ch Petit-Faurie-de-Souchard; Ch Pontet-Clauzure; Ch Roquetaillade-La-Grange; Ch Trottevieille; Ch Yon-Figeac.

NOT SHOWING WELL IN THE 1980s:

Ch Boyd-Cantenac; Ch Croizet-Bages; Ch Gressier-Grand-Poujeaux; Ch Pomys; Ch Pontet-Canet.

1972

Not so much bad as dreary. Few were remotely good even when young yet, as is well known, a madness overcame Bordeaux and château proprietors, egged on by *négociants*, pushed prices over the top. Folly and cupidity ran hand in hand in an overheated market. It signalled the collapse.

Cold spring, late flowering. Apart from warm July, a miserable summer with cold and heavy rain in Aug. Sept and Oct fine and dry. But because of the late flowering an extremely late vintage. A large, uneven crop of relatively unripe grapes. I tasted a large number of wines in the mid- to late 1970s. At this early stage, some were quite nice but they were almost all pre-mature and had all the signs of petering out; though by dint of careful chaptalisation, some drinkable wines were made. But chaptalisation is like a peroxide blonde who fails to keep up the treatment. Most '72s have been consumed. The few remaining command deservedly low prices on the open market. But at these prices some of the top growths are not bad value.

Ch LAFITE *Not, of course, a* grand vin *in quality, but by no means as poor as the '63, '65 or '68. After a year in bottle it was beginning to show signs of maturing, was fragrant and surprisingly nice. Four very recent notes indicate a tolerably flavoury wine, food ameliorating its raw end acidity. Not a bad colour. Fully mature. Rather indifferent, unknit nose but on each occasion the inimitable Lafite fragrance has surfaced, given time in decanter and glass, even noted as "opulent" at Flatt's Lafite tasting. Cheap enough anyway. Last tasted, a half-bottle decanted at Brooks's, June 1990*** For casual consumption not serious cellaring.*

Ch MARGAUX *Just five notes, the first two the autumn following the bottling, at that time one of the deepest '72s, but bitter. An interesting double-magnum in 1983, deepish; an immediate impression of quality and style on the nose but less interesting on palate. More recently, a bottle, a positive though not strong mature colour; singed, meaty bouquet, some fragrance; dry, lightish, sound. Some pretence of quality. Last tasted Jan 1986***

Ch LATOUR *Quite a few notes, plummy-coloured, hard and stalky when young, still a bit raw and screwed-up in the early 1980s. An indistinct nose that developed oddly, unknit. Dry, short, undistinguished. Last noted, Frericks/Wodarz Latour and Mouton tasting, March 1989**

Ch MOUTON-ROTHSCHILD *A travesty: raw in cask, but some characteristic Cabernet Sauvignon lurking which has, amazingly, taken hold. A pretty but rather weak orange-tinged red; light yet crisp and quite attractive bouquet; dry, unbalanced but with a zestful blackcurrant flavour and acidity. Last noted alongside the Latour, March 1989***

Ch HAUT-BRION *Tasted once. One of the palest '72s; vestiges of fragrance battling with sour, unripe grapes; dry, fairly light, unimpressive, though in its way, flavoury. May 1985**

Ch AUSONE *Also only one note. Curiously, a similar depth of colour to the '70 though rather more orange, palish, bright and lively-looking. Low-keyed vanilla nose and flavour; dryish, on the light side, some fruit, with end acidity. At Flatt's Ausone tasting, Oct 1987**

Ch CHEVAL-BLANC *Noted as one of the best '72s but not tasted since 1975.*

Ch PETRUS *At an extensive tasting of '72s in 1975 Pétrus did not rate highly. A rather thin-for-Pétrus magnum at Frericks' in 1986, chaptalised, with smell of beetroot and dried tea leaves. The following year, palish, fully mature appearance, more fruity nose; not bad but short. Last noted, pre-sale, Chicago, April 1987* Ideal for label buyers lacking taste.*

Ch BEYCHEVELLE *Many notes from the 1980s, at least nine at pre-sale tastings. Most recently a lively-looking rosy-claret hue; sweet, completely chaptalised nose; dry, a bit raw—just a faint vestige of Beychevelle fragrance and charm. Last tasted May 1987**

Ch CALON-SEGUR *Four notes in the mid-1980s. Pale, orange-mature, amber green rim; chaptalised nose: brown sugar, singed brown paper. Not as bad as it looks. Dry, light, piquant flavour. Last tasted May 1986.*

Ch DUCRU-BEAUCAILLOU *Not bad. Some fragrance and flavour when young. Six consistent notes in the 1980s. A passable bouquet, sweet, soft, medicinal; flavoury, not too light or thin but a slightly tinny finish. Last tasted May 1987***

Ch La LAGUNE *Rather jammy fruit in 1975. Most recently: palish but rich and orange-tinged; sweet, quite attractive coffee-plus-chocolate chaptalised nose; sweeter than most on palate, chunky but with teeth-gripping bitter acid finish. Last tasted Sept 1989. Try with sausages.*

Ch MALESCOT-ST-EXUPERY *At three years old palish, advanced, peppery and loose-knit, a jammy sort of Cabernet Sauvignon character emerging in the late 1970s. Most recently, an* impériale *at Rodenstock's Malescot tasting: medium; open, chaptalised nose, whiff of rotten grapes; medium dryness and weight and not at all bad to drink. Some fruit. A bit raw. Last noted Sept 1990***

Ch La MISSION-HAUT-BRION *Stalky and raw in the mid- to late 1970s. Four recent notes. The usual '72 pale orange tinge; also heavily chaptalised, with a fully-developed coffee and chocolate nose and taste of brown sugar wrapped in brown paper. Coarse, short, with bitter finish. Last noted at Wolf's tasting, June 1990.*

Ch MONTROSE *Cheesy, fragrant but unknit nose; dry, lean, a bit raw. Last tasted Oct 1985.*

Ch PALMER *Nine notes since 1975. At its best around 1980. Unknit but not bad. Brown-rimmed; heavily chaptalised, stewed-fruit nose. An odd, chunky wine with a finish like old apples and dried leaves. Last tasted Oct 1984.*

Ch TALBOT *One note. Rather root-like burgundian nose. Dry, light, fruity. Not bad. March 1984**

Ch La TOUR-HAUT-BRION *One note. More*

attractive than La Mission. Surprisingly flavoury. Nov 1986**

NOT BAD IN THE EARLY/MID-1980s:

Ch Baret; Ch Beau Séjour Bécot; Ch Bernard-Raymond; Ch Branaire-Ducru; Ch Brane-Cantenac; Ch Canon-La-Gaffelière; Ch Citran; Ch Gazin; Ch Gloria; Ch Haut-Batailley; Ch Lascombes; Ch Latour à Pomerol; Ch Lynch-Bages; Ch Les Ormes-de-Pez; Ch Rausan-Ségla; Ch Smith-Haut-Lafitte; Ch La Tour-de-Mons; Ch Trotanoy; Ch Verdignan.

MEDIOCRE EVEN BY '72 STANDARDS IN THE EARLY 1980s:

Ch Batailley; Ch Boyd-Cantenac; Ch de Camensac; Ch Cissac; Ch Fourcas-Hosten; Les Forts de Latour; Ch Léoville-Poyferré; Ch Marquis d'Alesme-Becker; Ch Mouton-Baron Philippe; Ch Trottevieille.

POOR IN THE EARLY 1980s:

Ch Cissac; Ch Fourcas-Dupré; Ch Pavie; Ch Phélan-Ségur.

1973**

It was as if the vines had been allowed to run riot, unpruned, untrained. Nevertheless it was a vintage with at least some charm compared to the grim '72s and graceless '74s. Some of the more conscientious proprietors appear to have been highly selective, both of grapes (see Pétrus) and of vats. Many made pleasant easy and early drinking. Some can still be surprisingly nice and they have the virtue of being unwanted, therefore inexpensive.

Growing conditions: warm spring to June, rainy July, hot Aug, some rain again in Oct. A large, healthy but much diluted crop.

Ch LAFITE *Several notes. Lovely in 1977. At 10 fragrant but a bit rough-textured. In 1988 a flavoury well-nigh perfect post-theatre supper wine. Never very deep in colour, now palish and fully mature-looking. It certainly has Lafite's fragrance and characteristic blossoming in the glass. Medium-sweet, medium-light, lacking the length and depth of a really good vintage but flavoury.* A bottle from the château. Last noted Sept 1989** Enjoy now, but will keep a further 10 years or so.

Ch MARGAUX *Two notes. An early-matured charming wine in 1978. Next, deeper than expected; fragrant though a touch of stalkiness and volatility. Light weight and style. Nice texture. Insubstantial, overall dry. Bouquet its best feature.* Last noted, at Edmund Penning-Rowsell's, a bottle cellared since the mid-1970s, March 1984** Enjoyable but unlikely to have improved.

Ch LATOUR *Unusual for Latour to exude charm when young. The '73 certainly did in 1977, but a certain lack of balance noted in 1979. Ten notes in the 1980s. Still with some of its customary richness of colour and some intensity, now mature. Bouquet of old cedar and mint. First sip distinctly sweet but a rather raw tannic acid end. Lacking fruit but light and easy for Latour.* Last tasted Dec 1990** Unlikely to improve.

Ch MOUTON-ROTHSCHILD *Some refinement and a good flavour but tinny acidity noted in 1977 and 1984. A pretty colour though weak-rimmed; a fully evolved, fragrant though not very Moutonish aroma, probably muted owing to chaptalisation, but a sweetish, light, short but pleasantly easy wine.* Last noted, Frericks/Wodarz tasting, March 1989** Enjoy now.

Ch HAUT-BRION *Two notes. I placed it second at Penning-Rowsell's 1973 first growth tasting in 1984. Lively-looking, and with the totally different Haut-Brion smell and taste. A whiff of coffee beans and 'Smarties', vinous, developed well. Medium dry, fuller-bodied than expected, soft yet powerful, iron-tobacco flavour, good texture and aftertaste.* Last tasted July 1987*** Some room for improvement.

Ch AUSONE *Palish, a bit brown and dull; a smoky fruity bouquet, fairly fragrant, opening up a little: ginger and strawberry. On the light side, soft mid-palate, overall dry and bit acidic.* At Flatt's Ausone tasting, Oct 1987*

Ch CHEVAL-BLANC *Two notes in the mid-1980s. A good open-knit colour; an initial whiff of fresh-picked mushrooms, mild, fragrant — my wife noted "lavender". Some sweetness, nice weight, soft gentle texture, good flavour and finish.* Last tasted, in magnum, dining at the château, Sept 1986*** Lovely now. Will keep.

Ch PETRUS *Made from highly selected grapes to ensure richness. A purple, full-bodied but fluffy, loose-knit and bitter cask sample in 1974. A decade later colour still intense, with matching depth of nose. But a bit four-square and unexciting. Most recently, still colourful, long-legged and ruby; bouquet a bit woody and restrained, hard to pin down. It did not open up like a Médoc. Sweet, medium weight, some power, pleasant enough but no great length.* Last noted, 'Stockholm' tasting, April 1990**

Ch L'ARROSEE *Pale, mature, stewed fruit, sound but insubstantial.* July 1985*

Ch BATAILLEY *Usually dependable, rather obviously chaptalised and 'showing her hems' (acidity).* July 1987*

Ch BEL-ORME-TRONQUOY-DE-LALANDE *Longer title than palate. A decade of notes from 1976 ("little to it"). Not even as pleasing as some minor '72s and '74s.* Last tasted March 1986*

Ch BEYCHEVELLE *10 variable notes over 12 years, starting with a stalky cask sample. Next, hollow, old socks; one distinctly oxidised bottle, another quite nice, and "as good as it will ever be" noted in 1983. Nondescript.* Last tasted July 1986. At best*

Ch BRANAIRE-DUCRU *Opposite Beychevelle's elegant front drive, the more homely Branaire made a better job of the '73. A good cherry red; a pleasant lightish flavoury wine.* Last tasted May 1984, but probably perfectly drinkable**

Ch BRANE-CANTENAC *If Branaire is 'homely', Brane is distinctly more rustic. At the big Gault-*

Millau tasting in Paris in 1976 the '73 seemed prematurely aged, developing a rather oily old nose. "Mature" and "manure" noted in 1980. Now orange-tinged with a cheesy, chaptalised, light, medicinal nose; yet quite flavoury though with a touch of over-acidity. Last tasted, in magnum, March 1990. At best★

Ch CALON-SEGUR *Quite pleasing, fragrant and with nice texture a year after bottling and showing well around five years after the vintage. Then six notes, starting with a soft, rounded magnum in 1980, but mainly steady deterioration after that. Several bottles in the 1980s. Overmature, orange-rimmed; a somewhat overblown bouquet; lightish, quite attractive but creaking.* Last tasted June 1987. Not worth pursuing now.

Ch CANON-LA-GAFFELIERE *Two recent notes: pale, no red left; sweet, scented, high-toned; light, easy, not disagreeable.* Last noted, pre-sale, July 1979★

Ch COS D'ESTOURNEL *Light and easy though with a touch of astringency in the later 1970s, now palish, fully mature-looking; a rather attractive 'ivy leaf', gentle, spicy almost Graves-like nose; some sweetness, a light easy pleasant drink despite a tingle of end acidity.* Last noted, Hollywood Wine Society, Jan 1990★★

Ch CROIZET-BAGES *Colour and nose showing signs of fatigue. Better on palate. Fairly stylish but tails off.* Last tasted March 1986★

Ch DUCRU-BEAUCAILLOU *Slow starter. Uneven. Probably at best in early 1980s. Bouquet trying hard, with whiffs of cedar, cinnamon, wholemeal biscuits; quite attractive but lacking stuffing.* Last tasted Nov 1984. At best★★

Ch GRUAUD-LAROSE *Fairly deep, vigorous and tannic in 1975, it came 7th in the Gault-Millau tasting of '73s and was probably at its best in the early 1980s. Many notes. Still very deeply coloured for a '73, some fruit, fleshy but a bit dull.* Last tasted Jan 1990★★

Ch d'ISSAN *Light but with adequate fruit in cask. Very straightforward. An easy, attractive lunch wine.* Last tasted June 1985★★

Ch La LAGUNE *A sweet, soft and fruity cask sample in 1974 and six good notes since. At its best, either side of 1980, an almost burgundian richness, flavoury, plausible. Most recently: palish, no red left; a very sweet, chocolaty, chaptalised nose, flowery. Not bad.* Last tasted Jan 1987★★ Needs drinking.

Ch LASCOMBES *Fairly deep and relatively concentrated when young but within five years had taken on a very brown tinge and was distinctly unknit on nose and palate. Colour developing a warning prickle; odd, though almost opulent, nose; very sweet, interesting texture, fulsome and flavoury but living dangerously.* Last tasted April 1988★ Drink up.

Ch LEOVILLE-LAS-CASES *Tasted five times in the early to mid-1980s. Deep for a '73; superficial, chaptalised bouquet; slightly bitter finish.* Last noted Dec 1984.

Ch LEOVILLE-POYFERRE *Neither bad nor very good in its youth. Showing age, dry, light, crisp, unexciting.* Last tasted Jan 1984★

Ch LYNCH-BAGES *Deep, but unyielding and rather dull when young. Four recent notes: still quite a good colour for a '73; sweet bouquet, some charm, with that rather medicinal Pauillac nose and flavour. Piquant. Not bad at all.* Last tasted April 1987★★

Ch MALESCOT-ST-EXUPERY *By 1980, palish, mature-looking with a bland, sugared nose. Dry. Light. Agreeable. A decade later, an* impériale *palish and pretty; a gentle, meaty malty nose, open, vinous, quite attractive; sweet, lightish, well chaptalised and a very pleasant drink.* Last noted at the Rodenstock/Malescot dinner, Sept 1990★★★

Ch La MISSION-HAUT-BRION *"Flavoury" the most consistent adjective from its gravelly early days. "Fragrant" applied to the bouquet from the mid-1980s: sweet, surprisingly spicy, tobacco leaf. Now medium-pale, mature; a bouquet with a touch of honeycomb and TCP; medium-sweet, on the light side for La Mission, a pleasant, easy flavour. Short.* Last noted at Karl-Heinz Wolf's, June 1990★★ Drink now.

Ch MONTROSE *Touch of orange at rim, chocolaty, chaptalised, with curious light metallic tin foil smell and taste.* Not *the usual long-haul wine. Mediocre.* April 1988★

Ch PALMER *Apart from the odd woody bottle and one dried up, an attractive, flavoury wine from the late 1970s to its peak in the early 1980s. By the mid-1980s rather pale and insubstantial; innocuous nose, a delicate touch of fruit; slightly sweet, light, some charm. Most recently, a pleasant bottle from the château.* Pre-sale, May 1991★★ Drink up.

Ch PHELAN-SEGUR *I thought nothing of this when it was young but it rallied. Still a surprisingly sweet-nosed wine, jammy yet bland. Easy. Quite a pleasant drink.* Last tasted July 1979★★

Ch PIBRAN *Orange-tinged; vanilla; lean, scraggy, taste of seaweed, acidic. Once a nonentity, always a nonentity.* May 1989.

Ch PICHON-BARON *Pretty colour; delicate yet fully developed and pleasing bouquet; quite flavoury and attractive.* Last tasted April 1988★★ Nice now, fading but not fast.

Ch PRIEURE-LICHINE *A plausible charmer. Fragrant, attractive, piquant blackcurrant scent; slightly sweet, light, flavoury, with refreshing acidity.* Last tasted Oct 1988★★

Ch RAUSAN-SEGLA *Cask sample signalled an early but pleasing developer. Satisfactory in the late 1970s and quite nice eight years later. Palish, fully mature; some fruit; dry, a bit raw but flavoury.* Last tasted May 1986★★

Ch SMITH-HAUT-LAFITTE *Fragrance, fruit and style despite its raw youth. One more recent note. Beetroot-tinged, weak rim; beetroot nose too, vegetal, chaptalised; a silky charmer.* Last tasted Oct 1987. Almost★★★

Ch TAILLEFER *Harmless, charmless, fruitless and hard.* July 1985.

Ch TALBOT *Plummy-coloured, a bit skinny shortly after bottling. Began to show class soon after. At its best in the early 1980s. Paler and much more mature-looking than his elder sister, Gruaud; sweet, fragrant; open, easy and curious flavour. Piquant.* Last tasted June 1991★★ Drink up.

Ch La TOUR-HAUT-BRION *Two fairly recent notes: from Woltner stock in Nov 1986, rich-looking for a '73, fragrant, flavoury and with some length. The following spring, an old brown tinge noted, and an odd cedary Graves nose that nevertheless developed beautifully in the glass. Fairly assertive, earthy, tobacco flavour, fair body, very dry finish — went well with Camembert! Last tasted April 1987*** Should still be drinking quite nicely.*

PLEASANT DRINKING IN THE EARLY 1980s:

Ch Beau Séjour Bécot; Ch Canon; Ch Cantemerle; Ch Cantenac-Brown; Ch Cissac; Ch Cos Labory; Ch Coufran; Dom de L'Eglise; Ch La Fleur-Pétrus; Les Forts de Latour; Clos Fourtet; Ch Gazin; Ch Grand-Puy-Lacoste; Ch Pape-Clément; Ch Pavie; Ch Pavie-Decesse; Ch Simard; Ch La Tour-Bicheau.

MEDIOCRE IN THE EARLY 1980s:

Ch du Glana; Ch Haut-Bages-Libéral; Ch Lagrange St-Julien; Ch Langoa-Barton; Ch Léoville-Barton; Ch Marquis-de-Terme; Ch Mouton-Baron Philippe; Ch Puy-Blanquet; Ch Rauzan-Gassies; Ch La Rose-Trintaudan; Ch La Tour-St-Bonnet.

1974

Unbalanced wines, raw, totally lacking charm and grace. Little potential when young and the few that remain not very appealing now. To make matters worse, the volume of wine was prodigious — there were serious worries that the wine lake of unwanted '72s, '73s and '74s would never be absorbed by the market.

The prime blame can be laid on the weather, for despite an encouraging start, good flowering (which dictates the potential quantity of the harvest) and a fine, warm, dry summer, the ripening period was hindered by grape-swelling rain in Sept; and it continued cold and wet throughout the Oct harvest.

Many '74s were tasted in the mid- to late 1970s and have been omitted from these notes. Those not good in the early to mid-1980s will certainly be no good now.

Ch LAFITE *18 notes dating from 1985. One of the things I like about Lafite is the ability of its bouquet to evolve fragrantly. On the first occasion, after 90 minutes in the glass, all I noted was "chlorine", and added "opulent but depraved". At Lloyd Flatt's three years later, a fishy metallic nose and taste — I gave it very low marks. It is now pale, fully mature-looking, and I still note a tinny overripe character and lack of length. It is hollow yet flavoury in an odd sort of way. Last tasted Oct 1988. Don't let me put you off. It is drinkable.*

Ch MARGAUX *Two notes. Low-keyed at first, it developed a gentle Margaux fragrance. Dry, medium-full, positive, with short, clean, crisp, tannic finish. Some charm, and quite flavoury. Last tasted at Penning-Rowsell's tasting, March 1985***

Ch LATOUR *Many notes from 1976. Deep plummy purple, a bit stewed and short. Scrawny, raw, slightly twisted in the early 1980s. In 1985, alongside the other first growths, not at all bad, a comparatively good flavour, if undemonstrative, and with the best future. More recently, still fairly deep, red-tinged; some vinosity, more solidity and depth than Mouton. Medium dryness and body, passable flavour. Tannic. Short. Last noted at the Frericks/Wodarz Latour and Mouton tasting, March 1989**

Ch MOUTON-ROTHSCHILD *Attractive though raw in the late 1970s. Similar marks to Latour at Penning Rowsell's, but a very critical note at Flatt's Mouton tasting the following year: a sort of metallic, fishy smell and taste. Consistently good colour though. A crumbling Cabernet Sauvignon aroma, lacking depth; dry, on the light side and with the tinny medicinal taste previously noted. Last noted at the Latour/Mouton tasting, March 1989**

Ch HAUT-BRION *Not a bad start in 1976. Surprisingly deep at Penning-Rowsell's in 1985: warm brick and liquorice, Graves nose, resembling later a chocolate liqueur. Dry, hard, unmistakable Haut-Brion tobacco tang. Not quite as good as the Margaux. Three notes later: showing some maturity; nose reminded me exactly of a choc ice. Medium sweetness and weight. Silky tannin. Easy. A very pleasant drink. Last tasted June 1990****

Ch AUSONE *Quite a good note in 1978 though advanced state of maturity clearly apparent, then orange and latterly a touch of brown. On the nose, fruit subsided, rather singed character, smoky, dusty; drying out on palate though some weight. Overall impression: dried leaves, ferns. Last noted, Flatt's Ausone tasting, Oct 1987. Distinct lack of appeal.*

Ch CHEVAL-BLANC *Just one note, at Penning-Rowsell's: medium-deep; nose curious at first but developed an interesting lily-of-the-valley fragrance, plus a touch of rot. Slightly sweet, nice firm flavour but a bit hollow. Dry tannic finish. Some charm. Preferred to Haut-Brion and the first-growth Médocs. March 1985***

Ch PETRUS *Two notes. First at Penning-Rowsell's in 1985: very deep; quite good herbaceous nose, vanilla, leathery tannic; fairly sweet and full, richer than all the other first growths, cheesy, lovely fruit, dry finish. Then, in magnum, a decidedly different character, less deep in colour, very light, slightly mushroomy nose that improved in the glass, fragrant, tea-like. On the palate lighter, leaner, tannic. This was at a vertical tasting, wedged between '73 and '75. Last noted, Frericks' Pétrus evening, April 1986**

Ch BEYCHEVELLE *On the light side, but not bad: mature, vanilla nose, dryish, nice texture. Pre-sale, Amsterdam, Oct 1985***

Ch BRANE-CANTENAC *Orange-tinged; mercaptan nose; poor. Pre-sale, Amsterdam, Oct 1985.*

Ch CALON-SEGUR *Several notes. Quite an attractive colour; sweet, oaky but refreshing bouquet; dry, quite pleasant but somehow combining softness with rawness. Short. Last tasted June 1987**

Ch CANTEMERLE *On Concorde in 1981 — before I joined the British Airways tasting panel. It had a cheesy, old socks nose, dry, short, dull. Confirmed by several notes after that, "cheese" repeated, though some fragrance, some fruit. But raw.* Last tasted Nov 1984.

Ch La CONSEILLANTE *Palish, orange-tinged. Positive flavour, some length.* Pre-sale, Amsterdam, Oct 1985★★

Ch COUFRAN *Rather raw and dull.* Last tasted July 1986.

Ch DUCRU-BEAUCAILLOU *Tasted in 1976, 1979 and at pre-sale tastings in Amsterdam. Fairly light, chunky, tannic, uninspiring.* Last noted Oct 1985★

Ch DUHART-MILON *Now fairly pale, very mature-looking, orange-rimmed; curious fudge-like nose; very sweet, very odd flavour — like burnt paper. Dry, a bit tart.* Last tasted Oct 1989.

Ch FIGEAC *Two notes but, at last, not unattractive '74. Lively piquant fruit on the nose. Slightly sweet, not very well knit but an agreeable drink.* Last noted, Amsterdam, Oct 1985★★

Les FORTS DE LATOUR *Several notes. Fairly deep, not much nose, reasonable body, some fruit and flesh. Still a bit raw.* Last tasted April 1987★

Ch GAZIN *Not very impressive in its youth, but some fruit though lean and tannic.* Last tasted in Amsterdam, Oct 1985★

Ch La GRAVE-TRIGANT-DE-BOISSET *Rich and ruby; straightforward nose and flavour, marron and spices, some flesh. A good '74.* Nov 1985★★★

Ch GRUAUD-LAROSE *A firm fruity cask sample. Showing quite well in 1983 and subsequently. Bouquet a bit muffled but an agreeable flavour. Touch of tartness but a tolerable '74.* Last noted, pre-sale, Oct 1988★★

Ch LEOVILLE-LAS-CASES *Earlier notes harped on lack of balance, loose-knit, rawness; but at least a lively colour and a vestige of fruit on the nose. Dry, fairly light and lean.* Last noted Oct 1985★

Ch LEOVILLE-POYFERRE *First tasted in 1980 on a cruise in the Mediterranean. The wine was kept in a hot storeroom; hardly surprising that it smelled stewed and cardboardy. But even when well cellared, not much better, though at the Amsterdam tastings it was tolerably flavoury.* Last noted Oct 1985★ Just.

Ch LYNCH-BAGES *A string of notes from 1978, each stressing its even more than usually medicinal Pauillac nose: it smelled of lint, bandages and iodine. Poor flavour and horrid endtaste. Having read Peynaud I concluded that this was due to grey rot.* Last expectorated Nov 1985 — ugh!

Ch MALESCOT-ST-EXUPERY *Fairly deep appearance but with woody nose, very unknit and unmellow on palate. This solitary dismal note in 1980 endorsed a decade later: a marie-jeanne, by now fairly pale, nose pure iodine, very dry, raw — frankly awful.* Last tasted Sept 1990. Avoid.

Ch La MISSION-HAUT-BRION *12-year span of consistent, fairly good notes. A load of fruit when young, though with a strange chlorine-like whiff plus tangerines. Showing quite well, chewy, fleshy at Desai's in 1985. Most recently: still very deep, intense and relatively immature-looking; crisp; tight, low-keyed bouquet; medium sweetness and fullish weight. Fruit. That strange ozone and oyster-shell taste. Coarse but very drinkable.* Last noted at Wolf's tasting, June 1990★★

Ch MONTROSE *Plummy-coloured; a bouquet like sour cream, some fruit but tart; very dry, stern and somewhat forbidding.* Last tasted, Amsterdam, Oct 1985★ Might have softened a little by now.

Ch SMITH-HAUT-LAFITTE *Fragrant, gamey fruit; extraordinarily flavoury and spicy for a '74, as if made by the* macération carbonique *method and matured in new oak casks.* Last tasted in Oct and Nov 1986★★

Ch TALBOT *Quite attractive in cask. It eventually became a good old British Airways standby. Still fairly deep, medium weight, some fruit.* Last tasted (incorrectly listed as '76) supersonic at 57,000 feet, Jan 1986★★

Ch La TOUR-HAUT-BRION *Fairly deep; good, sweet if a little crude; distinct medicinal smell and taste, inharmonious yet fruity and a jolly good drink.* Last tasted Nov 1986★★

PERFECTLY DRINKABLE IN THE EARLY 1980s:

Ch Beau Séjour Bécot; Ch Citran; Ch La Fleur-Pétrus; Ch La Lagune; Ch Langoa-Barton; Ch Lascombes; Ch Latour à Pomerol; Ch Léoville-Barton; Ch Meyney; Ch Pichon-Lalande; Ch Sociando-Mallet; Ch Soutard; Ch du Tertre; Ch Trotanoy.

UNKNIT, RAW, FLAVOURY, DRINKABLE IN THE EARLY 1980s:

Ch L'Angélus; Ch Canon; Ch Chasse-Spleen; Ch Cissac; Ch Fourcas-Dupré; Ch Grand-Puy-Lacoste; Ch Haut-Bages-Monpelou; Ch Mouton-Baron Philippe; Ch Patache d'Aux; Ch Pavie; Ch Rausan-Ségla; Ch St-Pierre-Bontemps-et-Sevaistre; Ch La Tour-Carnet; Ch Verdignan.

POOR IN THE EARLY 1980s:

Ch Bellefont-Belcier; Ch St-Bonnet; Ch Hanteillan; Ch Puy-Blanquet.

1975★ to ★★★★

An enigma. Pronounced a *vin de garde* by the Bordelaise and, after the dreariness of the previous three vintages, a distinct turn for the better. It also coincided with the end of the Bordeaux slump. Pre-1980 I noted depth, richness and intensity of colour, thickened by the high extract all too noticeable on the palate. Full of fruit too. But the *tannin*. Swingeingly tannic. Apart from a few exceptionally well-structured wines, I think the majority are going rusty, almost literally, for the tannin is turning the colour of the wine sear and yellow, prematurely orange-tinged, instead of a fine gradation to a soft, mature red-brown rim. The better wines saved by extract and fruit.

Mild, wet winter; warm start to spring with cold spell and frost; favourable flowering promising a reasonable size of crop, but hot, dry weather from May to mid-Sept prevented fleshing, despite some gentle rain before the harvest, which began around Sept 26. Hot sun thickened the skins and was responsible for the deep colour, hefty tannins, and high levels of alcohol. Time will tell.

Ch LAFITE *A lovely spicy wine in cask and showing well at three major tastings in 1979, despite a tendency to leanness and tannin. The tannic dryness much in evidence subsequently, though at present shielded by good fruit. Still fairly deep in colour; sweet, rich, very fragrant nose, though at Penning-Rowsell's '75 first growth tasting, after just over an hour I noted that it smelled like furniture polish (a good make!). Fairly sweet on the palate initially, nice weight — quite full-bodied for Lafite, open-knit, with good texture, fruit and extract. But . . . ? Last noted at the Flatt tasting, Oct 1988***(?) Drink now, or keep in the hope that it will open up and soften towards the end of the century.*

Ch MARGAUX *Four notes. Holding its initial depth of colour though maturing. Consistently noted a sweaty, tannic nose, though with good fruit; touch of sweetness on the palate leading to a very dry, tannic finish. Richly packed, touch of iron, flavoury, pretty good length. Last tasted April 1989**(**) Drink 2000+*

Ch LATOUR *19 notes. Predictably opaque and massive in cask. Although impressive, retained a notable astringency. "Touch of old boots" at Sotheby's tasting of '75s in 1984. Showing well against the other first growths at the Penning-Rowsells' in 1986: a gloriously deep colour; classic, the best balanced, the tannin being well clad. In bottle, magnum and jeroboam at the Frericks/Wodarz tasting, the last being far less developed than the bottle. The magnum, from the château, had a very agreeable scented bouquet yet despite its silky texture was extremely tannic. Complete, fruit and flesh. Last tasted June 1991***(*)*

Ch MOUTON-ROTHSCHILD *Mean, moody and magnificent. Great depth of colour, packed with fruit, bouquet most striking. But tannic. 12 notes plus one woody bottle since the mid-1980s. Noted in bottle and jeroboam at the Frericks/Wodarz tasting in 1989: still deep, with a black cherry centre, maturing rim; crisp Cabernet nose, initially shy but developing an attractive, almost Graves-like tobacco, fern-like fragrance, deep, singed; fairly sweet, full of alcohol, extract, fruit, flavour. Despite its silkiness, teeth-gripping tannin. Most recently: very rich, medicinal nose; dry, fruity. Swingeing metallic tannin. Last noted June 1991**(*)? 1995–2000?*

Ch HAUT-BRION *Well-spread notes spanning 14 years. Never quite as deep as the first-growth Médocs, but rich, velvety, with a broader, more mature rim; nose restrained, tight and light. Warm, earthy, hot, peppery, almond oil, then developing a fig-like Cabernet fragrance. The typical Haut-Brion tobacco-like flavour, firm yet soft, fruity, yet dry-as-a-brick tannin. About equal to Lafite at Penning-Rowsell's 75th first growth tasting. Impressive alongside La Mission but touch of coarseness. Notable intensity and length. Now bricky orange mature rim; gloriously rich, earthy bouquet; sweet, assertive, verging on pungent. Last noted June 1991***(*) Now to 2000.*

Ch AUSONE *As usual, infrequently tasted; and one of the few major vintages missing at Flatt's Ausone event. Good sweet nose but severe overall at 3½ years. At the Sotheby tasting in 1984: fairly deep, lively, cherry-tinged; bouquet developing beautiful richness, fig-like; with body, strength, backbone and a singed flavour. Overall both rich and raw. Not noted since May 1984**(**)?*

Ch CHEVAL-BLANC *Six notes. Still impressively deep but browner than the first-growth Médocs; slightly medicinal, iron, earthy but warm fragrance; distinctly sweet, fairly full-bodied, fleshy, lively, fruit, suave, elegant for a '75, good length. Tannic, but not as obtrusive as its peers. Last tasted June 1988***(*) Drink now, but should be mellower just beyond 2000.*

Ch PETRUS *Seven notes, five since the mid-1980s. By and large a most impressive mouthful. Soft, fleshy, fragrant, and despite strange, bitter tannins, showing well, particularly on the palate at Penning-Rowsell's. Still deep, rich, intense and slightly immature-looking; restrained, rather peppery nose, touch of old wood, depth of fruit — but its bouquet, as often with Pétrus, not its most interesting feature. On the palate, very sweet, full, fleshy. Loads of fruit, extract and tannin, like leather in silken sheets. Last noted at the 'Stockholm' tasting, April***(**) Long life.*

Ch BATAILLEY *Deep; rich, sweet, fruity; a fairly full-bodied, fleshy, chunky wine. Tannin not too obtrusive and showing well though it palled a little. Last tasted in May 1990*** Drink now to 2000+*

Ch BEYCHEVELLE *Six notes in the 1980s. Rich, thick-looking; sweet, leathery, tannic nose, cedary, stylish; fuller bodied and 'broader' than usual style and lacking Beychevelle charm. Fleshy, fruity, overall dry. Finishes a bit abruptly. Last tasted Sept 1986**(*) I do not see enough improvement ahead to warrant long cellaring.*

Ch BRANAIRE-DUCRU *Richly coloured though now less deep, and developing an orange tinge; very ripe, fragrant bouquet; rich palate, quite attractive, yet with tannic rawness. Last tasted Feb 1990** Drink up.*

Ch BRANE-CANTENAC *From the start almost a caricature. Strong, smelly, cask sample, inelegantly but appositely described by a fellow MW as "dry shit", and consistently odd on the nose: oily, unknit, sweet, as if over-chaptalised, possibly mercaptan. Flavoury but raw. Last tasted Jan 1989**

Ch CANON *Fairly good colour, with even gradation to a fairly mature rim; rather raw and unknit at first but there was a rich swelling of bouquet; very positive entry, good middle flavour, fullish body, fairly rounded, tannic. Last tasted, Nov 1989*** Probably best before 2000.*

Ch CANTEMERLE *Original. Deep, but slightly toned down purple; fruity, crisp, still immature, high-toned bouquet and flavour. Stylish. Last tasted June 1987**(**) Should turn out quite well.*

Ch CANTENAC-BROWN *Many notes through the 1980s. Appearance not deep to begin with, rather weak-rimmed; characteristic chocolaty nose, somewhat unknit but quite rich, cheesy, gingery; medium dryness and weight and easy, plausible. A somewhat tart finish.* Last tasted Oct 1989** Drink up.

Dom de CHEVALIER *Seven consistent notes: raw, tannic, tart, lean. Yet some richness, and with a quite attractive flavour.* Last tasted Oct 1989** Disappointing; will not improve.

Ch CISSAC *Half the crop lost to hail in 1975. 10 notes since 1983. Still fairly deep; leathery, vinous nose; full-bodied, some flesh, flavoury but very tannic.* 1987*(*)

Ch COS D'ESTOURNEL Cépages: *65% Cabernet Sauvignon, 35% Merlot, the latter crop being reduced by* coulure; *40% new oak used. Impressive, though severely tannic in cask. Now medium-deep, a good crisp colour but developing an orange rim; attractive bouquet, sweet, fragrant, singed, piquant, fruity; fairly sweet, very flavoury, touch of liquorice, good length, swingeingly tannic. A good '75 but I question its balance.* Last noted at Michèle Prat's tasting, Jan 1990*** Drink now to, say, 2000.

Ch COS LABORY *From a nondescript cask sample, consistently unimpressive. Orange-tinged; smell of sweaty feet; dry, flavour enhanced by volatile acidity.* Last tasted Jan 1988.

Ch DUCRU-BEAUCAILLOU *Over a dozen notes since quite impressive cask samples in 1976 and 1977. Still fairly deep, browning; consistently restrained nose, with some fruit and vinosity and a touch of spiciness longing to be dragged out. Dry, some substance, flesh and fruit, but a bit one-dimensional, astringent and with mouth-drying tannins.* Last tasted Feb 1990*(*). I do not see this outliving its tannic grip.

Ch DUHART-MILON *Most extraordinary: the Pétrus of Pauillac in 1975! Richly coloured, slightly orange rim; lovely fruit, strawberries, raspberries, exotic ripe mulberries — too good to be true; very sweet, full, fleshy, soft, forward. Clearly immensely ripe grapes. Aftertaste like La Tâche.* 1984****

Ch L'EVANGILE *Opaque, full of fruit, extract, alcohol. Loaded with tannin. Impressive but a bit raw.* At Spencer House tasting, May 1991**(*)?

Ch FIGEAC *A late harvest starting Sept 25 after a little rain. Small crop, high extract. Frankly, an odd-ball, fragrant and flavoury at the Gault-Millau tasting in 1979 and an equally delicious bottle in 1989. 36 distinctly woody bottles supplied by the château for a convention dinner in Frankfurt in 1988, yet a sweet, full, though tannic bottle only two months later. Lastly, from the château, at Desai's Figeac tasting: strange, stalky nose; dry, flavour of iodine and old seashells: horrid.* Last tasted Dec 1989. Judgement suspended.

Les FORTS DE LATOUR *Deep, impressive, mature orange rim; quite good, slowly developing nose; touch of sweetness, chunky, lacking middle, very tannic but very drinkable.* Last tasted May 1990**(*) Will keep but will not improve.

Ch GISCOURS *Many notes since 1979. Still very deep though brown-rimmed; medicinal, tea-like, stewed, fruit, somewhat lacking in zest; better on the palate: sweet, full of alcohol, extract, fruit. Fleshy, flavoury but too tannic.* Last tasted Dec 1989*(**) Quite a mouthful. Could well soften and improve. Say 2000–20.

Ch GRAND-PUY-LACOSTE *An impressively fruity wine when young. Still richly coloured though developing that '75 rusty orange mature rim; quite spicy, fragrant, Pauillac Cabernet fruit and cedar; nice weight, good, fruit, rich, very tannic but satisfactory. Slight bottle variation, one being slightly milder, lighter and shorter.* Last tasted Feb 1987**(**) Drink 1995–2015.

Ch GRUAUD-LAROSE *Opaque, tight-knit, concentrated in cask. A decade later still deep; relatively undemonstrative bouquet, fruit there but a hard core; a big, taut, tannic wine.* Last tasted April 1986*(***) Unready but worth keeping an eye on. Drink, say, 1995–2015.

Ch KIRWAN *Several notes, none bad, none enthusiastic. Straightforward, quite nicely made, lean, very tannic.* Last tasted Jan 1991** Probably a little development in hand.

Ch LAGRANGE *St-Julien. Low-keyed but quite harmonious; medium-full, rounded, extract. An easy flavoury style.* Last tasted July 1989** Drink soon.

Ch LANGOA-BARTON *Now mellow, very mature-looking; original hardness ameliorated, quite a pleasant, crisp, rich bouquet but with a distinct, somewhat overripe, sweaty-saddle flavour. Reasonable length, lean, interesting.* Last tasted Sept 1986** Drink now.

Ch LASCOMBES *Nowhere near ready in the early 1980s, a touch too much acidity noted at the Sotheby tasting in 1984, and with distinctly high volatile acidity on the last two occasions. Still richly coloured; citrus, bay leaves nose; lots of fruit but inelegant. Mouth-puckering.* Last tasted April 1987. No great urge to taste again.

Ch LATOUR A POMEROL *Two fairly recent notes. Sweet, vanilla, harmonious bouquet that faded rather than developed, a not untypical Pomerol characteristic; first sip intriguing, full-bodied, citrus-like fruit and acidity, silky but very tannic.* June 1988**(*) I look forward to seeing how this progresses.

Ch LEOVILLE-BARTON *11 notes, the first two admiring, but those since 1982 critical in one way or another. Quite deep, attractively coloured, somehow combining youthfulness with a mature orange tinge; ripe, sweaty, leathery nose; dry, piquant fruit and acidity. Some grip, certainly tannic.* Last tasted June 1989*(*) Hard to know how this will develop; certainly not gracefully.

Ch LEOVILLE-LAS-CASES *Very attractive towards the end of the 1970s. 12 notes since confirm its quality. Still a fine deep ruby; sweet, slightly vanilla, immensely rich bouquet of great depth; slightly sweet, full of alcohol, extract, fruit. Magnificent middle palate but still very tannic.* Last tasted June 1988**(**) Worth keeping and trying again after 2000.

Ch LEOVILLE-POYFERRE *A curious cask sample in 1976 but fragrant and quite attractive in the early 1980s. Opening wine at Sotheby's tasting of '75s in 1984: mediocre Médoc. More recently, showing quite a bit of maturity in colour and on nose. Rich, fruity, fairly mouthfilling but very tannic.* Last tasted April 1987**(*) Peaking modestly around 1995.

Ch LYNCH-BAGES *A strange wine. Unimpressive in the late 1970s: stalky, common nose though flavoury. Later notes more complimentary: maintaining its deep, intense appearance; a powerful bouquet, brambles, cherry stones, vanilla and oak, cedar, with characteristic medicinal Cabernet Sauvignon aroma; a distinct touch of sweetness, almost burgundy-like, with loads of fruit. Crisp, alcoholic, and lots of tannin and acidity. Unready. Last tasted June 1988*(**) Might develop extraordinarily over the next 10 years to say*****

Ch MALESCOT-ST-EXUPERY *Spicy but lacking flesh in 1979. Six notes from 1984 more or less confirm this. A most untypical Malescot nose, with none of the usual strident Cabernet aroma but rather an open, caramelised, as if heavily chaptalised, smell, latterly of vanilla, tea, and leaf mould. Somewhat artificial flavour, lacking fruit and on the light side. Soft yet tannic. Last tasted Feb 1990* Unimpressive.*

Ch La MISSION-HAUT-BRION *First tasted at the château in 1978. Immensely impressive, deeper and plumper than Haut-Brion, but felt like cold pebbles in the mouth. "Screwed up" noted at the Vintners Club tasting in California in 1980. Variously noted at Sotheby's in 1984, at Desai's La Mission tasting in 1985 and at the Woltner pre-sale tasting 1986. Last tasted alongside Haut-Brion and La Tour-Haut-Brion at Wolf's extensive tasting. Still very deep, thick, intense; extraordinary medicinal bouquet, TCP and bandages, which happily simmered down. "Pickled peach" noted earlier, also iodine. A full, fleshy wine. Good length but highish acidity and bitter tannins. Mahler with a touch of Bartok. Never Mozart! Last tasted June 1990*(***) For those with exotic tastes and a sound constitution. Probably excellent with wild boar.*

Ch MONTROSE *A dry, hard, severe cask sample, and very slow development. By 1984 beginning to show its paces. Never quite as deeply coloured as expected and beginning to show maturity; undemonstrative nose, classic, cool as a sea breeze, considerable depth and latent fruit. Loaded with all the major component parts. Solid, delicious, but needs many years of bottle-age. Last tasted/noted Feb 1985*(***) Drink 2000–2030 or thereabouts.*

Ch MOUTON-BARONNE PHILIPPE *A comparatively early, easy, elegant charmer, but with tannin overcoming the fruit. Medium depth of colour; fragrant, crisp, fruity nose but a very dry, rather raw palate. Stylish but with a touch of bitterness. Anorexic. Last tasted Oct 1986.*

Ch PALMER *Lots of fruit but oppressed by tannin. Cinnamon noted earlier; spicy, peppery in the mid-1980s, when I wrote "beginning to confirm my worries about the '75s". Now palish, fully mature, orange, old oak and iodine; dry, raw, tannic, tart. Last tasted at the château June 1991* Avoid.*

Ch PAPE-CLEMENT *"The most Médoc-like Graves" noted in 1978, 1984. Another mid-1980s note: velvety, perfect balance. Most recently: still very deep; tannic; dry, fullish, austere. Last noted May 1991*** On decline?*

Ch PAVIE *An impressive, deep, crisp, rich cask sample, and steady evolution. It started to shed some of its colour and was weakening at the rim by the mid-1980s and displayed a touch of '75 orange maturity recently. An open, well-developed bouquet, vanilla and crisp fruit. Slightly sweet, pleasant, medium weight, easy to drink despite hefty tannins. Possibly a little more to come but the tannin will outlast the fruit. Last tasted Sept 1988**(*)*

Ch PAVIE-DECESSE *At best early 1980s. Now fully evolved; rustic; thick, chewy. Last tasted Nov 1990** Drink up.*

Ch PICHON-BARON *An easy, quick-maturing wine judging by its appearance in the early 1980s, but a bit unknit and rather rough textured. Some fragrance, but not very good; overall dry, chewy, a bit raw, touch of bitterness. Last tasted Feb 1987* Not to be pursued.*

Ch PICHON-LALANDE *Far superior to the Baron from its early years. Many notes. Still fairly deep; classic Pauillac nose; very dry, full-bodied, fairly concentrated, a fair amount of fruit and very tannic. Lunch at Lord Paget's in 1984 and sample from his excellent cellar. Last tasted pre-sale, Feb 1988**(**) Still a bit hard. Say 1995–2010.*

Ch PONTET-CANET *Took a full 10 years to achieve a semblance of maturity. Still quite rich and deep, a shade of orange; rather stern, classic nose; iron, leathery tannin; touch of sweetness and softness. Some fruit, a touch of class and a pleasant enough drink despite the tannin. Last tasted March 1987**(*) Could do with more bottle-age, say 1995 or soon thereafter.*

Ch PRIEURE-LICHINE *Two notes. Speciously fragrant, very sweet, flavoury but lacking conviction in 1984. More recently, orange-tinged; low-keyed, medicinal nose, still sweet, quite attractive. A rather tinny, tannic finish. Last tasted Oct 1988** Drink up.*

Ch RAUSAN-SEGLA *Very agreeable either side of 1980, with a particularly attractive aftertaste. A souped up, stewed, oxidised bottle at Sotheby's in 1984, and one subsequent note: fully mature, orange-amber rim; interesting nose, no harsh edges. Whiff of paraffin. Quite well clad, rich, fair extract, chunky fruit, tannic. Enigmatic. Last tasted Sept 1986** A great future unlikely.*

Clos RENE *Three notes. Richly coloured but now too orange; smooth, sweet, rather meaty nose; distinctly sweet, fairly mouthfilling, silky Pomerol texture, very tannic. Last tasted June 1988**(*) Probably at its best now. Might develop further.*

Ch de SALES *Many notes spanning 11 years. Now showing a tinge of orange maturity; consistently pleasing if not great nose, sweet, chunky; equally sweet and chunky on palate. Soft, fruity, most drinkable. Last tasted Feb 1990*** Drink now.*

Ch ST-PIERRE-BONTEMPS-ET-SEVAISTRE *Three good notes. Deep, very intense; rich, complex, appealing fruit; very positive, plummy, fleshy, flavoury, complete. 1984**(*)*

Ch SMITH-HAUT-LAFITTE *Light, stylish, elegant. It quickly developed a very sweet, fresh cream, Belgian chocolate sort of scent. But though fragrant, not for long keeping. 1984***

Ch du TERTRE *Rich, very flavoury. 1981**(*)*

Ch TERTRE-DAUGAY *Odd nose; broad, chocolaty flavour. Very dry, tannic finish. 1984*(*)*

Ch TALBOT *Less opaque, more piquant fruit than Gruaud in cask. Firm, severe yet elegant towards the late 1970s. My best notes in 1984. Still deep, intense; typically ripe Talbot nose; dry, stylish, attractive but lean. Notable tannin and acidity.* Last tasted Feb 1987**(*) Try again in 1997, though it is unlikely to relax completely.

Ch La TOUR-HAUT-BRION *From 1978 to 1986 noted for its marvellous fruit. Surprisingly—for a '75, and La Tour—soft, easy, almost elegant. Appearance much more evolved than La Mission. Sweet, somewhat chocolaty nose, later, in glass, like fudge; slightly caramelly flavour and soft tannins.* Last tasted June 1990*** Nice now but will keep.

Ch TROTANOY *Extraordinary 15–16 days* macération. *Showing well late 1970s. Highly developed nose, bananas, raisins; thick, chunky in 1984. Now deep, plummy, mature; figgy, almost malty; rich, chewy, tannic.* Last tasted Nov 1990**** in its way. Future?

GOOD THOUGH TANNIC IN EARLY TO MID-1980s:

Ch Beau Séjour Bécot; Ch Bel-Orme-Tronquoy-de-Lalande; Ch Calon-Ségur; Ch La Conseillante; Ch La Dominique; Ch l'Eglise; Ch La Fleur-Pétrus; Ch La Gaffelière; Ch du Glana; Ch Haut-Bailly; Ch Haut-Sarpe; Ch d'Issan; Clos des Jacobins; Ch La Lagune; Ch Lanessan; Ch Larcis-Ducasse; Ch La Louvière; Ch Magdelaine; Ch Malartic-Lagravière; Ch Marquis d'Alesme-Becker; Clos du Marquis; Ch Meyney; Ch Les Ormes-de-Pez; Ch Patache d'Aux; Ch de Pez; Vieux Ch Certan.

MODERATELY GOOD, PERHAPS LACKING BALANCE IN THE MID-1980s:

Ch Boyd-Cantenac; Ch de Camensac; Ch Cormey-Figeac; Ch Croizet-Bages; Ch Durfort-Vivens; Ch Fourcas-Dupré; Clos Fourtet; Ch Gazin; Ch Haut-Bages-Libéral; Ch Haut-Batailley; Ch Lafon-Rochet; Ch Lynch-Moussas; Ch Rauzan-Gassies; Ch Trottevieille.

POOR IN THE EARLY TO MID-1980s:

Ch Belgrave St-Laurent; Ch Canon-La-Gaffelière; Ch Chasse-Spleen; Ch Gloria; Ch Grand-Puy-Ducasse; Ch Livran; Ch Loudenne.

1976★★ to ★★★★

A charming, easy, attractive vintage but, like a pretty girl, without the bone structure to turn her into a beautiful woman. A complete contrast to the 1975, the '76 could be drunk while the *vin de garde* '75 was being guarded.

The year of exceptional heat and drought in northern Europe. The weather broke in Sept, interrupting the picking which began on Sept 15. A large number of wines tasted, many up to the early 1980s and quite a few of them never since then. But the minor wines were quickly and rightly sold and consumed. Most of these have been omitted. Most should be drunk soon.

Ch LAFITE *Absolutely delightful the first autumn after bottling and has continued more sturdily than I anticipated over the past 10 years. Showing particularly well in the mid-1980s and voted second unanimously, at Penning-Rowsell's 1976 first growth tasting (which included Pétrus, Ausone and Cheval-Blanc). Elsewhere noted as good but by no means great, and not all that obviously 'Lafite'. Many notes. Recently a most attractive magnum, bright and appealing; nose subdued at first but evolved in the glass, very fragrant, minty; dry, a certain delicacy, refreshing. Two months later, in bottles, at a very grand dinner party, it appeared quite deep in colour and fairly full-bodied. Served blind, I jumped straight to the 1976 vintage but not to Lafite as I noted a somewhat chunky coarseness. Reasonably well balanced, it will continue.* Last tasted Aug 1990***(*) Now to 2010.

Ch MARGAUX *Four notes. Seventh out of the eight at Penning-Rowsell's first growth tasting, March 1987. Although easy to drink, it lacked vigour, unable to take off. A magnum at Desai's tasting had a similar weakness of rim; initially restrained nose though it opened up a little, whiff of paraffin in 1984, obvious chaptalised character. It still managed to be a charmer, though with a somewhat short, rough finish.* Last noted at Desai's Margaux tasting, May 1987** Drink up.

Ch LATOUR *15 notes: opaque and raw in cask but, for Latour, a relatively quick development. Surprisingly pleasant to drink in the early 1980s. Nevertheless, alongside its peers at Penning-Rowsell's in 1987 it was unanimously voted sixth. A bit dull. Most recently: now a pleasant, open, mature, medium depth of colour; rich bouquet, nice fruit, touch of ginger, harmonious, good vinosity, opened out fully; seemed distinctly sweet, fullish, though with an easy, soft, slightly caramelly flavour.* Last noted at the Frericks/Wodarz Latour and Mouton tasting, March 1989***(*) Drink now. Will continue, softening further.

Ch MOUTON-ROTHSCHILD *Its nose the best feature, a crisply fragrant, slightly spicy Cabernet Sauvignon. A touch of sweetness on the palate and very flavoury throughout the 1980s, but a touch of astringency, lack of length and attenuated finish marking it down from very good to merely quite good. Most recently, deepish, translucent; fruit and extract but flavoury.* Last tasted Sept 1990*** Drink soon.

Ch HAUT-BRION *12 notes. Cask sample: good fruit and flavour. Pleasantly developed by the mid-1980s: marvellous in magnums, and a pair of bottles with warm-brick, Graves character, nicely evolved, marvellous aftertaste. I voted it third at Penning Rowsell's '76 vintage dinner. Still deep, fine, firm, mature; a most forthcoming, fragrant, biscuity bouquet; medium sweetness and weight, well developed, harmonious. Very dry finish.* Last noted at Karl-Heinz Wolf's tasting, June 1990**** Lovely now, will keep.

Ch AUSONE *After a period in the dumps, a renaissance: Pascal Delbeck's first vintage as winemaker. An impressive, though very austere ex-cellar sample in 1978. Not tasted again until the mid-1980s, the most recent at Flatt's Ausone tasting: medium-deep, rich, attractive appearance; immediately forthcoming bouquet, fairly sweet, spicy — sage, and rich evolution in glass; medium weight, lively, taut yet chewy and chunky.* Not tasted since Oct 1985***(*) *Probably at best now but should keep and develop further.*

Ch CHEVAL-BLANC *First tasted April 1978. Iron, earthy character. Showing very well in the early 1980s and voted first, by all at Penning-Rowsell's in 1984 (Ausone was the only first growth not represented). Deep and youthful then, now medium-deep and showing some maturity; a gentle, smoky, cedary and berry-like fragrancy; always a distinct sweetness, with lovely texture noted more than once. Easy to drink, most attractive.* Last tasted Dec 1988**** *Lovely now. Will keep.*

Ch PETRUS *First tasted in 1980, a deep, rich mulberry Merlot, and six times since.* Not *all that impressive in 1983, a rather charmless, disappointing magnum at Frericks' tasting in 1986 and in 1987 noted as good, thick, well made but came fifth out of seven first growths. Most recently: now medium-deep, fully evolved; a rather cool, dumb, slightly peppery nose, touch of spice emerging; medium-sweet, medium-full body. Characteristic silky Pomerol texture, light leathery tannic finish.* Last noted at the 'Stockholm' tasting, June 1990**(*) *A good drink but not really worth the current prices being paid.*

Ch BRANAIRE-DUCRU *Well over a dozen consistent notes, starting with a pleasant, chunky cask sample in 1977. Throughout, a good colour, fruity, high-toned, well-chaptalised nose; always slightly sweet, pleasing weight, soft, fleshy. Completely ready.* Last tasted Jan 1989*** *Drink now.*

Ch CALON-SEGUR *Two notes in the same month. Mature; rather high-toned, but with agreeable fruit and flavour. Though lightweight, a bit faded and short. Not a patch on the '75.* Last tasted June 1987** *Drink up.*

Ch de CAMENSAC *A bit green at the edges in the late 1970s, it seemed to be at its relatively modest best in the early 1980s, flavoury, easy. Now palish, fully mature. A recent bottle a bit woody and feeble.* Last tasted July 1979* *Drink up.*

Ch CANTEMERLE *Showing best, soft, delicate, harmonious, at the MW tasting of '76s in 1980. Later noted, apart from one woody and one corky bottle, as agreeable to drink. Most recently: still an attractive colour, rich ruby core, mature edge; low-keyed nose; very sweet on the palate, a nice weight, drinking pleasantly but touch of acidity noticeable.* Last tasted April 1990** *Drink up.*

Ch CHASSE-SPLEEN *Many notes from 1980. (Our everyday claret at home for some time.) Probably at best in the early 1980s when it showed great class and style, "delectable, delicious". Rather strangely, a vastly deep, alcoholic, iron-clad, tannic jeroboam, clearly made to last, tasted in 1984. Now fully developed; ripe, cheesy, fragrant bouquet; slightly sweet, nice weight, very attractive but a touch of tartness noticeable.* Last tasted April 1990. *Now** Drink up.*

Ch CISSAC *At its best in the mid-1980s. Elegant, easy. Fairly undemonstrative though harmonious nose; dry, lean, pleasant enough.* Last tasted Sept 1988** *Drink up.*

Ch La CLOTTE *Almost tempted to buy this. Such a marvellous name. An oddly sweet, sugared, slightly chocolaty un-claret-like wine.* May 1988* *Drink this and most relatively minor '76 St-Emilions now.*

Ch COS D'ESTOURNEL *A good '76. Showing some elegance even in cask, clearly destined to develop more quickly than the '75, but, in the event, holding back until the early 1980s. Now mature-looking, its nose difficult to get to grips with, but an agreeable weight and flavour.* Last tasted June 1988*** *Drink soon.*

Ch COS LABORY *Raw and short at a trade tasting in 1978. Lean but not too bad in 1980. Now fairly pale with an old, cheesy nose. Under palate I just wrote "terrible".* Last tasted July 1987. *Not recommended.*

Ch La DAUPHINE *Fronsac wines are bluff and honest and keep well. Though not too impressed when first tasted in 1982 I went ahead and consumed many a perilously mature bottle. At its best an easy, attractive drink, nice weight, soft. But really past its best. Flavoury but fading.* Last tasted May 1990*

Ch DUCRU-BEAUCAILLOU *Conflicting notes, even from cask samples within a month of each other in the spring of 1977. Mind you, samples drawn from the cask and brought by a London importer, via a* négociant *in Bordeaux, for presentation at a trade tasting can go out of condition fairly quickly. I would not buy on the pre-view show of one cask sample, but would merely use it as an indicator. Tasted in cask in April 1978 I thought it stylish and fruity. A charming early developer in 1979. Then raw and hard, harsh even, in 1980, firm in 1985, and palish, mature, easy and pleasant in 1987. Then a contradictory note: "surprisingly deep, plummy, fairly intense, almost '75-like; peppery, rich, nice 'biscuity' development; fairly full-bodied, mouthfilling, fruity, somewhat coarse texture, surprisingly tannic".* The last noted at a Wine and Food Society dinner in Puerto Rico, Feb 1988. *Probably*** Ready to drink.*

Ch DUHART-MILON-ROTHSCHILD *Six consistent notes. Pretty colour; fragrant, cress-like; dry, light, refreshingly piquant.* Last tasted Nov 1986*** *Not for keeping.*

Ch FIGEAC *First tasted the year it was bottled, and eight times since. In its early days I found it rather severe, with an impressive intense colour like a ruby port. But it started to mature nicely in the early to mid-1980s. Indeed my best notes were made in 1984 and 1985: marvellous fruit, fragrant, spicy, silky texture, with flavour opening up in the mouth like a rich burgundy, yet with a clean, dry finish. Later, dining at Figeac, it seemed tough for a '76; but it had to compete with delicious fresh-picked asparagus. Most recently: medium-deep, a sweet, wide open, attractive bouquet and flavour. Dry, medium weight, a bit plausible.* Last noted at Desai's tasting, Dec 1989**** *Drink soon.*

Les FORTS DE LATOUR *Six notes. A bit low-keyed, nice texture but short in 1981. Then softened up after the mid-1980s. Quite a good, classic flavour when tasted in 1988, for British Airways, but I found it austere, lacking elegance and style at 52,000 feet. But the other passengers liked it. Still deep and lively, fruity, but a bit raw.* Last tasted March 1989** A lusty claret. Age will not confer other qualities.

Ch GISCOURS *Speaking of lusty claret, here is one of the deepest coloured, chunkiest, most tannic '76s. Initially very hard, still firm. A lot of fruit and flesh. Drinking best in 1982.* Last tasted March 1988. At best*** Will probably keep.

Ch La GRACE-DIEU *A relatively minor but very pleasing St-Emilion with a ripe, vegetal, almost burgundy-like nose. Sweet, soft, earthy.* At a Jurade de St-Emilion lunch at the Black Swan Hotel, Helmsley, Nov 1988***

Ch GRAND-PUY-DUCASSE *A mature orange-brown edge, like some '75s. Sweet, ripe, a bit on the edge, but an attractive drink.* Noted twice at pre-sale tastings, in July 1989**

Ch GRAND-PUY-LACOSTE *Many notes, from 1978. A firm, uncompromising Pauillac even in a vintage like 1976. A bit hard at first. A lively, youthful, cherry red; touch of vanilla, cedar, blackcurrant; crisp, fruity, stylish, tannin and acidity.* Last tasted April 1991***(*)

Ch GRUAUD-LAROSE *Many notes over 12 years. A crisp, flavoury wine. Yet the words "woody" and "stalky" crop up between 1978 and 1990, not to mention two corked bottles. Drinking well in the mid-1980s. A fair amount of fruit but a bit lean for Gruaud.* Last tasted May 1990. Hard to place*** just. Probably best to drink soon.

Ch LABEGORCE *A reliable Dourthe Monopole wine. Mature. Nice nose, soft, touch of iron, very slight woodiness but overall attractive.* June 1986**

Ch La LAGUNE *"Chunky, fruity" noted in cask, after bottling and 12 times in the 1980s. Despite some tannin, high ratings at comparative tastings of '76s in 1982 and 1984. Still a lovely deep colour; rich, plummy nose, rather port-like; touch of ripe sweetness, fairly full-bodied; fleshy, fruity, soft, very agreeable.* Last tasted July 1988***(*) Lovely now, will continue.

Ch de LAMARQUE *A minor, easy to drink wine. Chaptalised nose; sweetish, on the light side.* Last tasted Dec 1989** Drink up.

Ch LANGOA-BARTON *16 notes since 1980. A chunkier wine than Léoville, developing a particularly ripe, rich, honeyed, cedary bouquet. Perfectly mature in 1986, I noted "needs drinking" in 1987. Now looking very mature, with an orange tinge; scented, fragrant, almost overripe; sweetening up with a rich middle palate, slightly lacking in length and with a twist of end acidity.* Last tasted Aug 1988*** Drink up.

Ch LASCOMBES *Piquant, mouthwatering bouquet; soft, ripe, sweet, fruity. More acidity than tannin. Twist of tangerine on nose, bay leaf on palate. Refreshing and flavoury with food.* Last tasted Feb 1985** Drink up.

Ch LEOVILLE-POYFERRE *Rather overripe nose; quite flavoury but drier and less attractive than Langoa and lacking the length of Las-Cases.* Last tasted Nov 1986**

Ch LYNCH-BAGES *Although its characteristic Cabernet Sauvignon aroma was very noticeable in cask, not noted subsequently. A slightly raw, crisp, fruity fragrance. Distinctly sweet, with silky texture. Lightish, nice weight and style. At best a charmer though its end acidity a bit marked.* Last tasted July 1989**

Ch MAGDELAINE *I noted a latent softness in a cask sample in the spring of 1978 which has been the prevailing note since. Beautiful colour, rich, lively; gloriously open, sweet, mulberry-like nose; distinctly sweet on the palate, mouthfilling body and taste. Zesty orange-peel finish. Some bottles from a slightly too warm, dry cellar were more developed, browner, flat tasting, with touch of aniseed.* Last tasted July 1987. At best**** Drink now, but will keep.

Ch MEYNEY *Fairly deep but mature; liquorice, spice, quite nice, fruit, dry, medium full-bodied, firm, tannic.* Last tasted Jan 1989** Not very exciting and not worth waiting for the tannin to soften.

Ch La MISSION-HAUT-BRION *Most impressive at the MW tasting of '76s in 1980. Six eulogising notes since; displaying fragrance and charm at Desai's tasting in 1985. Most recently: still deep, with mature brown rim; nose low-keyed at first, developing attractive Cabernet fruit and tobacco bouquet; medium sweetness and weight. Very pleasant flavour, lacking a little length, with a curious bitter-tea finish yet fragrant aftertaste.* Last noted at Wolf's tasting in June 1990***(*) A good mouthful, perhaps a little more to come.

Ch MONTROSE *Firm in cask. Well made. Good grip. Good deep ruby colour. Nose a bit cheesy, good fruit. Nice weight, crisp, chunky, dry, silk-clad tannic finish.* Last tasted July 1985**(*) Doubtless softening and will probably keep quite well.

Ch PALMER *Never very deep though richly coloured. Most original nose at four years: intriguing combination of fruit and the smell of the* chai. *Crisp and spicy. Blossoms in the glass and improves on palate too. Distinctly sweet overall, not very full-bodied, soft, some acidity but not much tannin. Delicious.* Last tasted Oct 1986. Bouquet**** Palate*** Drink soon.

Ch PAPE-CLEMENT *Ripe mulberry, soft, attractive in its youth. Seemed to age fast, for by the mid-1980s it was palish and very mature-looking. Showing age on the nose too, and a lack of vigour; dryish, on the light side, with hot Graves flavour, quite nice balance, soft yet edgy. No great future.* Last tasted Oct 1986** Drink up.

Ch PETIT-VILLAGE *Severe and tannic in cask in spring 1977. Opening up quite quickly with a sweet, delicious fragrance and taste in the early 1980s. Still quite deep but mature in the mid-1980s, nose a bit sweaty at first but opened up richly; soft entry, fleshy, even a bit of fat, good weight but dry, with slightly bitter tannic finish.* Last tasted Oct 1986*** Could well have lost that bitterness and, just possibly, warrant****

Ch PICHON-LALANDE *Quite a few notes. Surprising how quickly it developed. From 1980 onwards a delight to drink: harmonious, stylish. In 1985 "claret at its most beguiling". Seemed to have become sweeter. Mouthfilling but not heavy, with mouthwatering acidity, nice weight, well balanced.* Last tasted June 1986**** Probably at its best then but *doubtless still a charmer.*

Ch de SALES *Fully mature, touched with orange; soft, meaty; on the light side, easy, a bit chocolaty, ready.* Last tasted Jan 1991** Drink now.

Ch TALBOT *Six good notes. Sweet, spicy bouquet, a bit like Léoville-Barton. Slightly preferred to Gruaud at the same tasting. Maturing nicely, ripe-nosed, nice weight, style and softness. Dry finish.* Last tasted Feb 1986***(*) Good to drink now, probably a little more in hand.

Ch La TOUR-HAUT-BRION *Just one note. Fully mature. Loose-knit, chaptalised, but nice flavour. Short.* Nov 1986** Drink soon.

Ch TROPLONG-MONDOT *A typical run-of-the-mill St-Emilion: always reliable but rarely reaching the heights. Fairly deep colour. Soft, chewy, very pleasant.* March 1985*** Drink soon.

Ch TROTANOY *An impressive ex-cellar sample, with more flesh and a better finish than La Fleur. Still deep, thick, rich. Sulphide noted in one of the bottles. Had a chaptalised feel about it, but probably due more to natural richness and extract.* Last tasted Sept 1985*** Probably at peak now.

A BRIEF SUMMARY OF OTHER WINES TASTED IN THE EARLY TO MID-1980s:

Ch L'ANGELUS *Deep colour for a '76. Nicely developed; chunky; rounded.* 1986***

Ch BATAILLEY *Quite rich and flavoury. Fruit. Nice weight.* 1985***

Ch BEAU SEJOUR BECOT *Soft, complete, delightful style. For early drinking.* 1984***

Ch BELAIR *St-Emilion. Crisp, attractive.* 1983***

Ch BEYCHEVELLE *10 notes. Fairly deep colour. Not the charmer expected. Quite good fruit, some flesh but the overall impression lean and tannic for the year. Might be worth risking more bottle-age.* 1984**(*)

Ch BRANE-CANTENAC *Not very deep. Maturing. Relatively lightweight but pleasing. Good length and aftertaste.* 1984***

Ch CANON-LA-GAFFELIERE *Most attractive colour; very sweet nose; lightish, fruity, very agreeable.* 1982***

Ch CANTENAC-BROWN *Stalky and acidic cask sample. Two variable bottles in 1980, one oxidised, the other dry and acidic. The last, woody. Avoid.* 1982

Ch CARBONNIEUX *Palish and pink; a rather light, superficial style, scented, crisp. Best when young.* 1982**

Dom de CHEVALIER *Palish. Mature. No harsh edges, nice fruit. Dry, light weight and style. Elegant. Refreshing.* 1985***

Ch CROIZET-BAGES *Rich, spicy nose; flavoury, stylish but a touch of wood.* 1986**

Ch L'EVANGILE *Fairly deep but surprisingly brown; rich yet unknit and lacking fruit. Dry, slightly raw finish.* 1982*

Ch La FLEUR-PETRUS *Fragrant; very easy and attractive. Refreshing dry finish.* 1980**(**)

Clos FOURTET *Rather jammy nose; chewy, flavoury, fleshier than usual but slightly bitter finish. Pleasant fruit, but in a rather hard stalky casing.* 1983*(*)

Ch GAZIN *Very hard at first but softened quite quickly. Lovely fruit, very fragrant and forthcoming for a young Pomerol. Medium dryness and weight. Rich, ripe, good finish. Probably at best.* 1983***

Ch HAUT-BAILLY *Tasted once in its youth but impressed by its typical Graves tobacco nose and an earthy quality like rich humus. Rich on the palate too, very attractive, some finesse and a good aftertaste.* 1980***

Ch HAUT-BATAILLEY *Quite good depth of colour; good nose, flavour and balance.* 1982***

*Ch d'*ISSAN *Deep mahogany; nose seemed to display all the Bordeaux* cépages, *and developed well; soft, caramelly, touch of lemon and sugar; lightish in style and weight. Noticeable tannin and acidity drying off an otherwise good opening flavour.* 1983***

Ch KIRWAN *Two not very interesting bottles.* 1980

Ch LAFON-ROCHET *Quite nice nose; firm, fleshy, easy style but not much charm. Hard dry finish.* 1985**

Ch LAGRANGE *St-Julien. Rather weak though quite agreeable. Little character.* 1985**

Ch LEOVILLE-BARTON *Fairly deep; dry, mingling some richness with delicacy and charm. Classic weight. Good aftertaste.* 1984***

Ch LEOVILLE-LAS-CASES *Beautiful colour, consistently good notes: good nose, very convincing flavour from beginning to end. Lovely texture and shape.* 1984**(**)

Ch MALESCOT-ST-EXUPERY *Pretty colour; fragrant and appealing nose; light style, easy. Malescot at its most charming and feminine but not made to last.* 1982**

Ch MOUTON-BARONNE PHILIPPE *Palish, light, easy, though with a bit of a bite. Little to it. Not for keeping.* 1982**

Ch PAVIE *A bit of an ugly duckling. By the early 1980s some fragrance, high-toned; on the light and dry side. A bit lacking but pleasant to drink. Not for long keeping.* 1982**

Ch PICHON-BARON *One note: delicious.* 1980***

Ch La POINTE *Good vinosity, touch of iron on nose and palate, sweet entry, tannic finish with nice earthy middle flavour and Pomerol texture.* 1984***

Ch PONTET-CANET *A firm fruity wine, with Pauillac crispness. Several notes, last in 1980 when it was showing well, with notably persistent flavour. Probably still attractive.* 1980***

Ch RAUSAN-SEGLA *No recent notes. It was fairly advanced with a plausibly sweet, high-toned nose and flavour. Then a delicious drink but not a long laster.* 1980**

Ch RAUZAN-GASSIES *Ruby-tinged; medicinal, chocolaty; dry, a bit skinny and raw.* 1984*

MINOR WINE TASTING WELL IN THE EARLY TO MID-1980s:

Ch Grand-Barrail-Lamarzelle-Figeac; Ch Bel-Orme-Tronquoy-de-Lalande; Ch Cap-de-Mourlin; Ch La Cardonne; Clos du Clocher; Ch Coufran; Ch Fonroque; Ch Haut-Bages-Averous; Ch Moulinet.

PLEASANT THOUGH LACKING IN THE EARLY TO MID-1980s:

Ch Citran; Ch Closerie; Ch Fourcas-Hosten; Ch Larrivet-Haut-Brion; Ch Marquis d'Alesme-

Becker; Ch du Tertre; Ch La Tour-Martillac; Ch La Tour-de-Mons.

POOR IN THE EARLY TO MID-1980s:

Ch Larose-Trintaudon; Ch Smith-Haut-Lafitte.

1977

A disastrous growing year. Severe spring frosts decimating some vineyards, affecting many; late flowering; cold, wet June, extremely wet July, first half of Aug hot and dry, then cool and damp. The driest Sept since 1851, a fairly late, sunny harvest starting early Oct in the Médoc and, unusually, later in St-Emilion. The autumn sun saved the day, but in most instances the damage had been done. The wines were not too bad for early drinking – indeed I have few later notes – but, having bought heavily the impressive '75s and the attractive '76s, the trade gave the '77s a miss.

Ch LAFITE *First tasted 10 years after the vintage at one of Penning-Rowsell's annual first growth tastings. In 1988 at Flatt's Lafite tasting, quite pleasant, and in 1989, a magnum from the château. Very consistent notes: surprisingly deep, ruby yet mature – far richer and livelier than Latour or Margaux. Crisp, low-keyed bouquet which developed some fragrance. Dry, light, lean, quite flavoury but a bit tart.* Last tasted Sept 1989* Drink up.

Ch MARGAUX *Also not tasted in its youth. Flavour noted in 1983 as "rather like La Tâche 1975", and at Desai's Margaux tasting in 1987 as "like a Domaine de la Romanée-Conti – a sort of root-like, earthy flavour". Fragrant, some delicacy and grip at Penning-Rowsell's in 1987. Two notes two years later. Now fairly pale, fully mature with orange tinge; a sweet, chaptalised nose which opened up and held spicily for two hours. Medium dry, lightish, flavoury but with a slightly acidic finish.* Last tasted Sept 1989* Drink up.

Ch LATOUR *Six notes since 1981. Initially fairly deep, now medium-pale, more red than Mouton. It seemed to churn out fruit and, with a reasonably rounded, cedary flavour, came first out of seven top growths of Bordeaux at Penning-Rowsell's tasting in 1987. Curious nose, touch of sweetness – a well-chaptalised wine. Medium-light for Latour, a bit austere though quite pleasant.* Last tasted Sept 1989* Drink up.

Ch MOUTON-ROTHSCHILD *Six notes. A bottle in 1983 had a sweaty-saddle nose, was light and flavoury. Quite attractive in colour, smell and taste, though lacking length and with a touch of bitterness at Flatt's Mouton tasting in 1986. The fleshiest and richest, it came third out of the first growths in 1987. Now fairly pale with a very mature rim; a light, sweaty, superficial, watered-fruit nose which nevertheless opened up. Medium dry, light, easy, short.* Last noted at the Frericks/Wodarz Latour and Mouton tasting, March 1989* Drink up.

Ch HAUT-BRION *Tasted only once. Surprisingly deep and intense in colour, thick, ruby, touch of carbon dioxide; sweet, forthcoming, cheesy nose; fairly sweet on the palate, some flesh yet lean on the finish. Smoky, cigarette-like flavour – tobacco, autumn leaves. Short, slightly bitter finish – better with cheese.* Last noted at Penning-Rowsell's first growth dinner, Dec 1987* Drink up.

Ch AUSONE *Surprisingly deep though mature, with touch of orange at rim. A curiously warm, fluffy nose, slightly chocolaty, medicinal; medium dry, medium-light, soft, easy, short, with powdery finish.* Flatt's Ausone tasting Oct 1987* Drink up.

Ch CHEVAL-BLANC *Rated second of the first growths at Penning-Rowsell's in 1987. A pleasant, open appearance; sweet, beetroot-like chaptalised nose, citrus fragrance; slightly sweet, medium body, somewhat chocolaty, quite flavoury. Most recently, dining at the château: good, flavoury but drying out.* Last tasted April 1991** Drink up.

Ch PETRUS *First tasted in magnum at Frericks' in 1986: surprisingly deep; rich nose but dry and lean on palate. A corky, woody bottle at Penning-Rowsell's in 1987. Most recently, still deep and attractive to look at; very rich prune-like nose, almost too sweet; yet again dry on the palate, fairly full-bodied for a '77, gritty, very tannic finish.* Last noted, Rodenstock's annual tasting, Sept 1988* Might keep but will not improve.

Ch DUCRU-BEAUCAILLOU *First tasted in cask: surprisingly deep; some fruit on nose and palate. Light. Short. A de Luze cask sample in May 1978. Chunky. Dry finish. Most recently: very mature, orange-tinged; somewhat vegetal, unknit but some fruit; quite good flavour. Not bad.* Sept 1990* Drink up.

Ch GLORIA *Palish, orange maturity; first whiff off-putting, hydrogen sulphide, hen droppings, iodine, but recovered, crisp, trying hard to be fragrant; dry, light, lean, flavoury.* Sept 1990*

Ch GRUAUD-LAROSE *Medium depth, mature, weak-rimmed; quite a good, meaty nose; medium dryness and body, quite nice flavour and texture. Short.* Jan 1988** No point in keeping.

Ch LEOVILLE-POYFERRE *A good long stained cork – better quality than the vintage warranted. Fairly pale, mature-looking; light but fragrant, medicinal Cabernet Sauvignon nose; light, flavoury, dry finish, acidity tolerable.* Two notes in 1986**

Ch MEYNEY *Palish, orange-tinged; chocolaty, chaptalised, unknit but not bad; sweet, light, soft, short. Little to it.* Sept 1990.

Ch La MISSION-HAUT-BRION *Six notes, all bottles from the Woltner cellars. Fairly deep in 1981 with a light, jammy, sugared nose, soft middle palate, hard bitter finish. Fairly scented, piquant, lean and flavoury at Desai's tasting in 1985. Noted again in 1986 and 1988. Most recently: a fully evolved colour; scented, citrus, Cabernet bouquet, like soft brown sugar; lightish for La Mission, a short, quite nice 'ivy leaf' flavour. Quite nice now – probably the best '77 for current drinking.* Last noted, Karl-Heinz Wolf's La Mission tasting, June 1990***

Ch PICHON-LONGUEVILLE, BARON *Four notes over four consecutive years; the first two observed to be palish and brown-rimmed, nose a bit screwed-up, rotten grapes, chaptalised — yet a light easy luncheon wine. The last two: a "surprisingly deep" appearance; nose rather raw, crisp, hard; spicy, tannic, hollow, passable acidity. Last tasted April 1987★*

Ch La TOUR-HAUT-BRION *First tasted in cask in Sept 1978 at La Mission. Fruity, piquant, slightly bitter. In 1981 it showed considerable colour change, fairly pale, weak-rimmed; raw on nose and palate, thin but flavoury. In 1986, similar appearance; some fragrance; dry, light, flavoury, short. Last tasted Nov 1986★★*

PASSABLES. LAST NOTED IN THE EARLY TO MID-1980s:

Ch BEAU SEJOUR BECOT *Palish; indeterminate; lightish, soft yet with raw finish. 1982*

Ch BEYCHEVELLE *Surprisingly deep for a '77, mature-looking; positive but unknit nose; touch of sweetness, fairly lightweight, nice flavour, bitter finish. 1982*

Ch BRANE-CANTENAC *Palish, weak-rimmed; open and blown in 1982, cheesy, chaptalised. Smelly. Dry. 1985*

Ch CANTEMERLE *Attractive colour; piquant, light, better flavour than nose, but raw. 1982★*

Ch FIGEAC *Well-developed colour, distinct brown rim; one-dimensional nose, sweaty, not much fruit; light, tongue-cutting acidity. 1984★*

Les FORTS DE LATOUR *Surprisingly good colour, cherry red; strong whiff of Cabernet Sauvignon, vanilla; remarkably attractive, crisp, fruit, dry, somewhat raw bitter finish. 1983*

Clos FOURTET *High-toned, peppery; good flavour and texture. Nicely put together. 1982★★*

Ch LANGOA-BARTON *Picked in good weather, no rot; fairly deep and firm-looking; sweet, pleasant, chaptalised nose, some fruit, touch of liquorice; soft middle, light, quite nice. 1982★*

Ch LASCOMBES *Fairly weak; stalky little nose; light, raw, short. 1982*

Ch LEOVILLE-BARTON *Surprisingly deep and youthful-looking; little nose; dry, lean, raw, not bad. 1984★*

Ch LEOVILLE-LAS-CASES *A deep, very flavoury, tannic cask sample in 1978 and some ripeness and fruit in 1979. Surprisingly deeper in colour than the '76, at the château in 1982, with soft, Merlot nose yet more Cabernet on palate. A year later, still good-looking but muffled, almost sickly, on the nose; distinctly sweet, yet raw and then skinny and shallow. 1983*

Ch LYNCH-BAGES *Surprisingly deep though quick-maturing; pronounced Cabernet Sauvignon aroma — 95% in the final blend as the Merlot was spoiled; flavoury but raw. 1982*

Ch MOUTON-BARONNE PHILIPPE *Well chaptalised; dry, soft, easy. 1982*

Ch PICHON-LONGUEVILLE, LALANDE *Fruity and agreeable cask sample, spring 1978. Not a bad colour; sweet, fruity, attractive nose; dry, piquant Cabernet flavour. A bit thin. 1985*

1978★★★

An important but by no means great vintage. A dreadful spring, poor flowering, and worse summer: so bad that by the middle of Aug growers were in despair. The weather improved and Sept was warm and sunny, fully ripening those grapes that had survived. Reviewing my notes, Pomerols seem to fare best; whilst some Médocs are scraggy, others are hearteningly attractive. A vintage in demand now for trading and current drinking, but not easy to generalise about, hence fairly extensive coverage of individual wines.

In addition to the notable first growth verticals, two horizontal tastings, one at Sotheby's in 1985, and, three years later, to celebrate its decade, a particularly useful range presented by Robert Paul, a leading Miami lawyer. The latter tasting opened with a flight of the six top St-Estèphes, then 16 St-Juliens, seven red Graves, 11 St-Emilions and nine Pomerols. The following day 11 Margaux, 12 Pauillacs. Though this sounds exhausting it was a well-paced tasting and certainly put the major wines of Harry Waugh's oft-quoted "year of the miracle!" into perspective a decade after the vintage. On balance, most are passing their peaks, few will reward long keeping.

Ch LAFITE *Seven notes. Key words throughout "soft", "fragrant", though it took about five years to loosen up. Identical notes and score at a tasting in 1985 and, at Penning-Rowsell's first growth dinner in 1988, positive, even assertive with good length and aftertaste. Though rich and scented at Flatt's Lafite spectacular later the same year, lower marks, probably due to context. Most recently: appearance now medium-deep, fairly mature; immediately forthcoming, sweet, touch of malt, then biscuity. Consistently noted as slightly sweet, medium weight, soft, flavoury, elegant, with lean dry finish. Ready. Last tasted June 1991★★★ Now to 2000.*

Ch MARGAUX *Many notes, probably due to its important pivotal position: the first vintage of the new Mentzelopoulos ownership and management. A Merlot ensemble tasted in cask in April 1979, very deep yet soft and supple despite its youth; next, at Harvey's* en primeur *tasting in Jan 1980. Then, showing well, with lovely flavour and length at an MW tasting of '78s in 1982. A crisp sage-and-onion spiciness and silky leathery tannins at Desai's Margaux tasting in 1987. Still deep, intense, crispness on nose and palate noted again at Penning-Rowsell's 10th year first growth dinner. Most recently: crisp, intense, still youthful; soft, fragrant, though static, berry-like nose; sweetish, velvety texture, attractive fruit, very dry. Last tasted June 1991★★(★) 1994–2000? Hard to say how this will progress.*

Ch LATOUR *First tasted Jan 1980: opaque, dumb, peppery, intense, concentrated and tannic. In short, Latour. Nine usefully spaced notes. Same rating as Lafite though totally different in style and development at the 1985 tasting, a fraction higher at the Penning-Rowsells' in 1988. Still impressively deep; crisp fruity bouquet. At two Christie's Wine Course Master Classes in 1990: much as just described but though fairly deep, not intense. The nose, though rich, cedary, lacks the true ripe sweetness and evolution in the glass of a great vintage. An impressive fleshy mouthful, but in a line-up, wedged between the '82 and the '75, lacking conviction. Most recently tarry, dusty nose, distinctly tannic.* Last tasted June 1991***(*) 1994 to beyond. A longer life than most '78s.

Ch MOUTON-ROTHSCHILD *Many notes, starting in the spring of 1982. A much plummier and less decisive colour than its peers, and quicker maturing. Moderate rating at Flatt's Mouton vertical in 1986 and a rather muffled double-magnum at Rodenstock's later that autumn. Nose a bit disappointing; chunky, cheesy, nice fruit but lacking excitement at Penning-Rowsell's in 1988. Most recently, though deep, fully mature and a bit weak at the rim; low-keyed, crumbly, brambly fruit; on the sweet side, medium weight, soft, easy, pleasant but no great future.* Last noted at the Frericks/Wodarz Latour and Mouton tasting, March 1989** Good as a drink, but not great.

Ch HAUT-BRION *At Harvey's* en primeur *tasting Jan 1980, pleasing and forthcoming on the nose, immediately agreeable on palate, "an early developer", and more expensive than the Margaux. The strong, idiosyncratic Haut-Brion Graves tobacco flavour noted in 1982, a silkiness of texture and rich bouquet developing by the mid-1980s: prunes, ripe mulberries, cloves. Nine notes later, at Penning-Rowsell's in 1988, showing quite a bit of maturity. Its sweet fudge-like nose somehow reminded me of Bassett's Liquorice Allsorts, which is not very helpful to American readers. Gentle on the palate, citrus touch, with the strange, inimitable earthy Graves tobacco-leaf endtaste. Slightly sweet, nice weight and flavour. Two consistent recent notes. Drinking well at the bi-annual dinner of the Institute of Masters of Wine in March 1990 and, three months later, harmonious, fragrant, elegant and attractive.* Last tasted June 1990*** Agreeable now. Good not great.

Ch AUSONE *This was a renaissance period for Ausone. First tasted in 1982, still notably tannic in 1985, cherry red, quite rich on the nose, not a heavyweight, good flavour but lean at Flatt's Ausone tasting in 1987 and swingeingly tannic, with an almost Graves-like taste of old leaves at Robert Paul's mammoth tasting of '78 red Bordeaux, Feb 1988. Three months later at the Penning-Rowsells': fairly deep, lively, attractive colour; nose at first like beef-tea, soon opened, elegant, suave, then biscuity — a soft confection. Medium-dry entry, crisp fruit, lively, quite a bit of grip, combining some roundness with fair length. Elliptical is the word.* Last noted May 1988*** Nice now, will develop further.

Ch CHEVAL-BLANC *First noted at the MW tasting in 1982 and a month later at a pre-sale tasting. A rich, chunky, fruity wine. By the mid-1980s, an earthy, iron nose, ferns, violets — high marks for its appeal. Sweet, loaded with fruit, fleshiness and spice. Two notes Feb 1988, showing well at Bob Paul's, sweet, soft, rich, and three months later at Penning-Rowsell's. Still deep but showing some maturity; a forthcoming bouquet, touch of vanilla, slightly herbaceous, fully evolved; lovely texture, also with an elliptical shape in the mouth: it enters, swells, closes firmly. High marks.* Last noted April 1991**** Lovely now, will continue to please.

Ch PETRUS *Five notes. Developing nicely by the mid-1980s. A rather curious magnum at Frericks' vertical in 1986: raspberry, mushroom soup bouquet, soft, flavoury. Not great. Rather malty-nosed, chunky, and with an unconvincing finish at Bob Paul's tasting in 1988. Certainly not top. Three months later at Penning-Rowsell's, a luscious mulberry-fruit bouquet plus that strange roast beefiness; fairly sweet, fleshy, a bit severe. Most recently, medium-deep, open, fairly mature; very forthcoming nose, fragrant, beautiful in its way though with rich coffee and toffee towards the end. By now distinctly sweet, mouthfilling but not a heavyweight. Soft. Fragrant finish. Pretty good, but not a great Pétrus.* Last noted at the 'Stockholm' Pétrus tasting, April 1990*** Should continue into the 21st century.

Ch L'ANGELUS *Two consistent notes, the first in 1985. Not very deep-coloured but rich, thick, even and maturing. Long legs. Nose rather unknit initially but had distinct strawberry-like fruit. Medium sweetness and weight. Good flavour and lovely silky texture. Stylish.* Last noted, controversially, at Bob Paul's, Feb 1988*** Drink soon.

Ch d'ANGLUDET *First tasted at Harvey's, Jan 1980. Pleasant enough though it lacked finish. In 1981 I noted "south Rhône" on the nose, meaning a curious, spicy character — doubtless from the soil. Angludet has a character all of its own. A bit stalky and raw in the early 1980s, some later development. At Bob Paul's tasting, in magnum, deep, intense, still youthful-looking; an equally immature, leathery (tannic) nose which soon exuded an extraordinary spiciness that faded a little, leaving it crisp and fragrant. A distinctly dry wine. Still immature, uncompromising, tannic yet fragrant.* Last tasted Feb 1988**(*) Hard to say when and if this will soften before it dries out.

Ch BATAILLEY *Many notes as I have it in my cellars. Always reliable if rarely achieving great heights, it showed well at Bob Paul's tasting, fully evolved, elegant, on the lean side. Now with a Talbot-like, ripe, stably nose; fairly dry, nice weight, pleasant balance, dry finish.* A decent Sunday lunch wine, last noted Nov 1990*** Drink now before it dries out.

Ch BEYCHEVELLE *Uneven notes in the mid- to late 1980s. Showing slightly better in 1985, well developed, 'cheesy' and easy, then distinctly odd on the nose, very hard and metallic on palate, tasted twice in 1987. A pair at Bob Paul's tasting. One was piquant, loose-knit, coarse, the other more fragrant, easier yet tannic.* Last tasted July 1988** Variable, not for keeping.

Ch BOYD-CANTENAC *Surprisingly deep, still ruby; richly fragrant, multi-faceted nose; medium depth and weight, delicious flavour and fruit, good* *length, tannin and acidity.* Last tasted Jan 1987*** Not great but pleasing. Drink now to 2000.

Ch BRANAIRE-DUCRU *Its initial deep ruby started to mature from 1983–85. A rather superficial but attractive bouquet which blossomed spicily in the glass. A lightish, very pleasant drink.* Several notes. Last tasted Feb 1989*** Now to 1995.

Ch BRANE-CANTENAC *I liked the nose and flavour but thought it had rather an attenuated, slightly sharp finish at Harvey's, Jan 1980. Its characteristic, rather high-toned, hen-coop scent was noted in 1985, but I also found it very sweet, fleshy, velvety yet lean. At Bob Paul's the nose a bit smelly though it developed a gentle, toasted bouquet. And on the palate, once again, fairly sweet, soft, chewy, ripe, with tannic iron finish but with lots of character and life. Now starting to show an orange-tinged maturity.* Last tasted March 1990*** Good in its way. Lush. Drink now.

Ch CALON-SEGUR *A bit lacklustre. In the mid-1980s: possibly over-chaptalised, lean, lacking substance and more like a tannic '77. Nice fruit on the nose but a bit hollow. Then at Bob Paul's tasting: colour well developed; nose closed and tannic at first, then slightly caramelly, opening up, sweet, strawberry-like; rich but with a touch of rot, of chaptalisation. Very dry finish.* Last tasted Feb 1988* Not to be pursued.

Ch de CAMENSAC *Two notes. Still deep, immature in 1988. Low-keyed, some fragrance; full-bodied, flavoury but with masculine sweetness, tannic, iron.* Last noted at Bob Paul's, Feb 1988* Doubt if it is worth waiting for the hardness to wear off.

Ch CANON *First tasted at Harvey's in Jan 1980. A lovely wine, even then. Showing very well when last tasted in the mid-1980s: fairly deep, thick (extract), rich, maturing; a cool, gentle, fragrant bouquet; slightly sweet, mouthfilling, rich, long in the mouth, tannin for keeping, acidity for life enhancement. Well made, as always.* Last tasted May 1985. Then***(*) Doubtless lovely now and more to come.

Ch CANON-LA-GAFFELIERE *Never deep, early maturing; consistently sweet nose, rich, complete; sweet on the palate too, with a rich, earthy flavour. Pleasant, with style and shape.* Last tasted July 1989*** Now to 1995.

Ch CANTEMERLE *Some good notes from 1982–85: delicious, classy. But a stalky, lean bottle and one oxidised, both from the same stock in 1986. Perhaps not well kept. I was a tremendous admirer of the style of Cantemerle in the 1950s but things have slipped. However, I am giving the '78 the benefit of the doubt.* Last tasted June 1986. Taste again.

Ch CERTAN-DE-MAY *Rather curiously uneven bottles at tastings in 1985 and 1988. Of the first pair, one was cardboardy and odd, the other marvellously rich, chewy and very good though still tannic. At Bob Paul's one was corky and unclean, the second sweet, 'warm', biscuity. A lovely wine.* Last tasted Feb 1988. At best****

Dom de CHEVALIER *Still cerise and immature, peppery, a bit raw in 1985. Developing well in the late 1980s. Now showing some maturity; distinguished, rich, scented bouquet; nice weight and style, lean touch of Graves earthiness, fragrant aftertaste.* Last tasted April 1991*** Now to 1998.

Ch CISSAC *Consistently well-run property and reasonably priced wines. Several notes, all good. A particularly good nose; pleasant flavour, weight and finish.* Last tasted Oct 1988*** Now to 1998.

Ch CLERC-MILON-MONDON *Good colour and fruit but raw in the early 1980s. More recently surprisingly sweet, fleshy and chewy but with a bitter, tannic finish.* Last tasted Sept 1989** Unlikely to benefit from further bottle-ageing.

Ch La CONSEILLANTE *Seemed at its best in 1985, deep, impressive; rich, lovely fruit, since when it seems to have dried out. Even at Bob Paul's 1988 tasting there seemed to be a touch too much volatile acidity, piquant and lean despite its richness. Mature-looking in 1989, fruity but with a very dry finish. Six notes.* Last tasted Feb 1990. Now a disappointing**

Ch COS D'ESTOURNEL *Another '78 on Harvey's shopping list. In Jan 1980, deeper, more intensely purple than Montrose; crisp, almost raspberry-like nose; very attractive. Still lively and youthful, rich and harmonious, fragrant and very drinkable at Bob Paul's in 1988. Most recently, presented by Michèle Prats at a Cos tasting for the Hollywood (Florida) Wine Society: much more mature-looking, a rather woody bottle, lacking a little grace. The* cépages *mix in 1978 was 60% Cabernet Sauvignon, 40% Merlot. 30% new oak.* Last tasted Jan 1990. Allowing for a below-par bottle*** Now to 2000.

Ch COS LABORY *Palish, pretty, chaptalised, dry, lean. A woody bottle in 1983. Minor, hardly of classed-growth quality.* Last tasted May 1987*

Ch COUFRAN *Several notes. In June 1988 I had the very great honour to be the Président of the annual Fête de la Fleur of the Commanderie du Médoc et des Graves held at Coufran and hosted by the owner, Jean Miailhe. One of the wines served and showing well was his '78. Two recent notes. One woody, stalky, the other fully mature; sweet, 'old oak'; nice weight, spicy, tannic.* Last tasted June 1991. At best*** Will keep but might not improve.

Ch CROIZET-BAGES *Usually a very fruity wine, almost an exaggerated Cabernet Sauvignon character though little finesse. Flavoury, rounded, rather short, tannic.* Last tasted Feb 1988**

Ch CURE-BON-LA-MADELEINE *Two notes. Palish, mature, somewhat weak-rimmed; rather vegetal burgundy-like nose which developed a very pleasant scent. Medium sweetness and weight. Crisp fruit. Quite attractive.* Last noted at Bob Paul's, Feb 1988** Drink up.

Ch DAUZAC *Best, bright, delicious, rounded, in 1984; two woody/corky bottles at a tasting in 1985. Fully evolved, fragrant but faded, needing drinking.* Last noted at Bob Paul's, Feb 1988* Drink up.

Ch DUCRU-BEAUCAILLOU *13 notes, starting with a rich and classy ex-Kressman cellars sample in June 1979. My most detailed note was made at the Banker's Club in San Juan in 1986 at a tasting I conducted for the Confraria Puertorriqueña del Vino. It was good. Later, fragrant and stylish, at Bob Paul's. Still a good rich colour, brick red and cherry; very harmonious bouquet, no harsh edges,* *sweet, fruity — also on the palate. Delicious, lacking the length of a great vintage, and with end acidity. Two recent notes, Feb 1989*** Drink soon.*

Ch DUHART-MILON-ROTHSCHILD *Two notes. Quite nice Pauillac character, chunky, chewy, rather raw tannins. Less than spectacular. Last tasted Feb 1988** Now to 1995.*

Ch DURFORT-VIVENS *Pure blackcurrants on nose and very flavoury in the early 1980s. Fully evolved appearance; amazingly forthcoming aroma, sweet, spicy, liquorice. Full-flavoured, lovely shape and texture, extraordinary fruit and spice. Tannic. Last tasted Sept 1986 but cannot wait to taste it again. Almost too good to be true.*

Ch L'EVANGILE *I used to mix up L'Evangile, and L'Angélus. Both sound divine. A very nice wine. Fragrant and lovely — two notes in 1982, stylish in the mid-1980s, and showing well at Bob Paul's. Very deep, rich; intriguing, scented bouquet; sweet, fleshy, lively, slightly piquant. Last tasted May 1991**** Lovely now. Drink soon.*

Ch FIGEAC *Tasted from the cask, eight days after* soutirage, *it was like a Beaujolais Nouveau. Developing well in the mid-1980s with characteristically explosive Figeac bouquet, fragrant, strawberry-like. Fairly sweet, fruity, giving a citrus touch to the dry finish. Showing well at Bob Paul's. Also at Desai's Figeac tasting, Dec 1989*** Attractive now, and will gush ahead for a further 10 or so exciting years.*

Ch La FLEUR-GAZIN *Palish, slight, light, easy, short. May 1989**

Les FORTS DE LATOUR *A thick-stemmed sort of wine. In the early 1980s with the same plummy look as the* grand vin. *Showing quite well at Sotheby's tasting of '78s in 1985 though lacking charm. A poor, woody bottle en route. Now easing, with nice fruit. Last tasted Jan 1988***

Clos FOURTET *Remarkably soft and ripe in 1981. One attractive and one corked at a tasting in 1985. Now plummy-coloured; rich, gingery nose; chunky yet lean, fruity, flavoury, with citrus-like acidity enlivening and uplifting the bouquet and flavour. Last noted at Bob Paul's, Feb 1988** just, to be generous, possibly*** Drink soon.*

Ch Le GAY *Deep, rich; sweet, luscious fruit; very attractive. April 1988*****

Ch GAZIN *Good notes. Deep, rich, mature-looking; equally deep rich bouquet, spicy, blackcurrant fruitiness; sweet, medium weight, fleshy, taste of violets, velvety tannins. Last noted at Bob Paul's, Feb 1988**** Now to 2000.*

Ch GISCOURS *Many notes. An odd-man-out. Extraordinarily deep colour, thick, opaque-centred; absolutely stuffed with fruit and extract, with surging development of bouquet; rich, full, fleshy. Virtually chewable. Almost Latour-like in its massiveness. Impressive but not exactly loaded with charm or finesse. Last tasted April 1988***(*) if you like block-busters.*

Ch GLORIA *Initially lean and stringy, it seems to have filled out a little. Reasonably soft and easy. Last tasted Feb 1988** Drink now.*

Ch GRAND-PUY-DUCASSE *Three notes since 1985. Crisp, lean, unimpressive. Last tasted July 1989**

Ch GRAND-PUY-LACOSTE *Many notes. Lively, classic, elegant, pleasant even at four years of age with a meal. Yet it is fairly loaded with tannin. Still deep, intense, black-cherry red; nose harmonious but subdued at first sniff, then a lovely Cabernet fragrance emerges. Smooth texture, elegant, lovely fruit, crisp, still a bit on the hard side. Last tasted Feb 1989***(*) Drink now or keep.*

Ch GRUAUD-LAROSE *16 notes from the early 1980s. Three opaque, medicinal. Still fairly deep, mature-rimmed, with quite a heavy sediment when last decanted. A typically ripe, high-toned, Cordier-style nose; dry, a fairly good mouthful, with good fruit but a bit lean and raw — four recent and similar notes. Last tasted March 1991*** Drink whilst still fruity and flavoury.*

Ch HAUT-BAILLY *Like many middle-class Graves, it tends to develop early: the '78 was very pleasant after only two years in bottle. A good rich colour; sweet, attractive nose; medium sweetness and body, an equally good, rich, consistency, decent length and finish. Last tasted at dinner in Paris, March 1988*** Very pleasant now and should be so for 10 or more years.*

Ch HAUT-BATAILLEY *As always, totally different in style from the adjacent and similarly classified Batailley. A pleasing ex-cellars sample in June 1979 and the following Jan a nice, too-easy sample on Harvey's* en primeur *list. Leaner than Batailley, it gathered pace with some good "agreeable", "fruity" comments in the mid-1980s. Seemed a bit hesitant, flavoury but a bit lacking at Bob Paul's but, a few days later, the best bottles from the château showed well at a presentation by Xavier Borie, at a Ducru, Haut-Batailley and Grand-Puy-Lacoste tasting in Hollywood, Florida. Star-bright; flavoury; sweet through and through, soft and lovely. Last tasted Feb 1989*** Drink now.*

*Ch d'*ISSAN *Fleshy, not too tannic in cask, the spring of 1980. Vinous, sinewy, full-flavoured and exciting in the mid-1980s. More recently: plummy, long legs; sweet, crisp, Cabernet nose, very stylish; medium sweetness and weight. Soft, fleshy, elegant. Last noted at Bob Paul's, Feb 1988*** Nice now. Probably best before 2000.*

Clos des JACOBINS *Two fairly recent notes: deep youthful cherry ruby; good nose, crisp, good fruit and vinosity; fairly full-bodied, good earthy flavour, nicely clad but rather severe. Very dry tannic finish. Last tasted at Bob Paul's Feb 1988**(*) Allow a further five years.*

Ch KIRWAN *Plummy, unconvincing; stewed fruit and vanilla; some softness and flesh. Last tasted Dec 1990***

Ch LAFON-ROCHET *Medium, still youthful; peppery fruit, burst of fragrance; light crisp fruity style. Lean. Very dry tannic acid finish. Last tasted Feb 1988*(*) Will probably dry out.*

Ch LAGRANGE *St-Julien. Six notes. Sweet, good fruit in the early 1980s but has gained little. Probably best in the mid-1980s. Most recently, pink-tinged; quite agreeable citrus-like fruitiness; flavoury but lean. Very dry tannic acid finish. Last tasted Nov 1989**

Ch La LAGUNE *Sweet chunky cask sample in June 1979 and 10 evenly spread subsequent notes. The opening description still applies. Still richly* *coloured, if less deep; bouquet opens up in glass; less fleshy, more crisp and lean. Agreeable.* Last tasted Feb 1989*** Drink now to 2000.

Ch LANGOA-BARTON *A number of notes since 1981, all confirming its attractiveness. Nose still retains its youthful aroma of Cabernet Sauvignon, strawberry, vanilla, opening up in a spicy, herbaceous, almost flowery way after two hours in the glass. Touch of sweetness, good body, pleasant easy style.* Last noted at Bob Paul's, Feb 1988*** Ready but will keep another 10 years or so.

Ch LASCOMBES *Seven notes. Aged four moving from a stage of evolution to reduction. Three years later, a reassuringly harmonious, if low-keyed nose. Tannic but with deft touch and charm. Noted then as a "middle distance runner. Good in 5 years". An accurate prediction for it has developed quite well, a chunky wine with chocolaty nose and flavour, still holding its tannin.* Last tasted Jan 1988** Drink now to 2000.

Ch LEOVILLE-BARTON *Many notes. First tasted in July 1981: well-knit. A lovely flavour in the early 1980s but a certain austerity, even tartness. This rather citrus-like acidity has persisted but serves to give the wine a crisp uplift to nose and flavour. Bouquet classic, cedary, 'medicinal-Médoc' opening up most fragrantly. Tasted on two occasions, including Bob Paul's, in Feb 1988. A perfect medium-weight claret, very much to the English taste. But more recently have noted a rather hard tannic edge so it might dry out. Give it plenty of air.* Last tasted June 1989*** Drink now.

Ch LEOVILLE-LAS-CASES *11 notes. Impressive in cask in June 1979 and in Jan 1980, noting its depth of colour, pronounced nose, intensity and aftertaste, superior to Ducru at the Harvey's* en primeur *tasting. Steady development. At Bob Paul's: still deep, rich, fairly youthful; sublime nose—rich, deep, Cabernet Sauvignon, great character; slightly sweet, reasonably full-bodied, extract, softness. Extra dimensions, dry finish. A polished performance.* Most recently, attractive; a lovely mouthful. Last tasted Feb 1991****

Ch LEOVILLE-POYFERRE *Two notes. Mature appearance; forthcoming, fragrant; medium sweetness and weight. Soft, quite stylish. Citrus-like fruity zest.* Last noted at Bob Paul's, Feb 1988** Drink soon.

Ch LYNCH-BAGES *Softer and chunkier than neighbouring Haut-Batailley in 1982. A hard, stalky woodiness noted on three different occasions. Flavoury and quite fruity but not a typical or particularly good Lynch-Bages. Tannic.* Last tasted Feb 1988**

Ch LYNCH-MOUSSAS *Surprisingly fruity and attractive.* Oct 1988**

Ch MAGDELAINE *One of my favourite St-Emilions. A good '78. Still deep, lively; lovely bouquet that evolves beautifully in decanter and glass; distinctly sweet, full-bodied, rich fruit, tannin for keeping, marvellous aftertaste.* Last tasted Feb 1988**** Excellent mouthful now. Will keep.

Ch MALARTIC-LAGRAVIERE *A second-rank but consistent Graves. Maturing ruby; pleasant bricky bouquet; nice weight, quite flavoury.* July 1989**

Ch MALESCOT-ST-EXUPERY *Packed with fruit and tannin in cask. Attractive, lean but still tannic in 1985. Most recently, an* impériale *from the château: deep ruby; fully evolved fruit, later spicy; dry, medium weight, lean, surprisingly aggressive.* Last noted at Rodenstock's tasting, Sept 1990*(*) Will probably dry out before it matures.

Ch MEYNEY *Fairly deep, rich; 'cheesy' fruit; some flesh, fruit and tannin.* Last tasted May 1991***

Ch La MISSION-HAUT-BRION *Seven notes since 1984, latterly all from Woltner cellars. Seemed to be at its silky best in 1985/6 for at the two most recent tastings I have reservations about its finish. Still a deep, comparatively youthful ruby; a sweet, fragrant bouquet its best feature; slightly sweet on palate, powerful, attractive but a hard, slightly bitter finish. Alongside Haut-Brion '78, La Mission is rather raw and coarse.* Last noted Nov 1990. For me*** For those who like its gruff style**** Drink now to 2000.

Ch MONTROSE *10 notes since early 1980s. Medium, maturing; nose closed at first but fruit emerged from the depths. Fairly full-bodied, nice flesh, texture. Class. Long dry tannic finish.* Last tasted March 1991***(*) Risky putting an extra potential star on a '78 but Montrose has always been a slow developer and usually worth the wait.

Ch MOUTON-BARONNE-PHILIPPE *Always a light easy style of wine. It was so in 1982, and still is. Appealing, with a lean and deft touch.* The last out of magnum, Oct 1989*** An attractive drink.

Ch PALMER *I noted it as beautifully rounded, well put together, with expansive mulberry-like aroma in 1980. I also noted, in 1985, that though very agreeable I did not think it would live to a great old age. Indeed it was probably at its very best aged 10: glorious scent, piquant fruit, vanilla, opening up marvellously into an almost overwhelming compôte of raspberry, blackberry and violets. Distinct sweetness, full-flavoured, soft, fleshy, still with decent tannin and acidity. Showing equally well at Bob Paul's tasting in 1988, and recently, tasted blind at the château.* Last noted June 1991**** Lovely now.

Ch PATACHE D'AUX *From the sublime to the immodest. First noted at a Christie's pre-sale tasting in 1982: pink, bright, spicy, easy and attractive. Still rather weak in colour, its chaptalisation now noticeable, but pleasing enough.* Last tasted May 1989* Drink up.

Ch PAVIE *A very attractive '78. Two very good notes, first in 1985. Now deep, lively, maturing; crisp fruit opening up most fragrantly, rose cachou and a hint of tobacco leaf. Distinctly sweet entry, fairly full-bodied, packed with fruit and gingery spice. Delicious.* Last noted at Bob Paul's, Feb 1988**** Drink now to 2000.

Ch PAVIE-DECESSE *Intriguing. Fragrance; original flavour, sweetish, good flesh, soft, attractive.* Last tasted Nov 1990*** Drink now.

Ch PEDESCLAUX *Pedestrian. A smelly, sweaty, coffee-cum-chocolate chaptalised nose. Too sweet. Rather short.* Feb 1988.

Ch de PEZ *The opening wine at Bob Paul's comprehensive celebration of the first decade of the '78s at the Biltmore Hotel, Coral Gables. It was* *still as tannic as I had found it when first tasted in 1980. A short burst of fragrance. Quite nice — best with food, as noted in 1986. Last tasted Feb 1988***

Ch PICHON-LONGUEVILLE, BARON *Only tasted twice but high marks at Sotheby's tasting of '78s in 1985 and at a smaller tasting of '78s organised by a Danish journal at Ch Langoa in 1986. In each case a notably deep, intense appearance; a gloriously exciting five-star bouquet; medium-sweet, full-bodied. A powerful, spicy wine with good flesh and fruit. Marvellous components but perhaps a trifle coarse. Last tasted Sept 1986. Then***(*) I hope to taste it again.*

Ch PICHON-LONGUEVILLE, COMTESSE DE LALANDE *To give it its full title following Mme de Lencquesaing taking over the reins from her brother Alain Miailhe. Almost as deeply coloured as Giscours and performing very well in 1982 and 1984, though I thought it was 'showing its hem' — chaptalisation — mid-1980s. Latterly good, and happily so at Bob Paul's tasting of '78s, as the indomitable May de Lencquesaing was in the front row: still very deep and plummy; a rich, fruity and fleshy nose which evolved opulently. Fairly sweet and full-bodied, blackberry-like fruit and spiciness derived from new oak barrels — cinnamon and cloves. Good length and aftertaste. A top '78. Last tasted Feb 1991**** Lovely now. Will keep.*

Ch PONTET-CANET *Four notes from the mid-1980s onwards and none impressive. A bit stalky and raw. Seemed to smell more of old wood than new oak. Last tasted Jan 1989* Avoid.*

Ch PRIEURE-LICHINE *Rich ripe nose and taste. Attractive. Good length and finish. Last tasted Oct 1988*** Drink soon.*

Ch RAUSAN-SEGLA *Four notes from 1985. Medium weight, fully evolved colour; sweet Cabernet fruit and vanilla nose that developed attractively; fairly dry, lightish weight and style. Lean, flavoury, tannic. Last noted at Bob Paul's, Feb 1988*(*) Drink now. Likely to dry out.*

Ch RAUZAN-GASSIES *Four notes ranging from indifferent to dreary. In essence, poorly made. Whiffs of volatile acidity, old socks, stalkiness. Confusing tastes. Some fruit, grubby finish. Last tasted April 1989. Avoid.*

Clos RENE *Two bottles at Bob Paul's, one unclean, sweet-tasting but stalky, the other in excellent condition, clean, nice fruit, delicious. Feb 1988. At best**** Drink now to 2000.*

Ch de SALES *First encountered in 1982 at the restaurant Jean Ramet in Bordeaux. It coped admirably with liver in raspberry vinegar. Noted as rather plausible — de Sales often is — with a nice tarry taste in 1985, and showing quite well at Bob Paul's. It always seems to mature quickly and now certainly looks very mature; nice enough nose; sweet, lightish, earthy. Touch of acidity. A peasant but pleasant. Last tasted Feb 1988** Drink up.*

Ch SMITH-HAUT-LAFITTE *Nine notes. Quite nice though unexciting in the early to mid-1980s. Soft, easy, with typical Graves earthiness. Nice balance. Last tasted Jan 1989*** Drink now.*

Ch TALBOT *Copious notes from 1983. Still fairly deep. The usual and somewhat idiosyncratic ripe, almost overripe, pigsty nose harnessed to considerable fruit, blackberry-like. Very attractive in its way. Probably best in the mid- to late 1980s. A popular taste but it appeals less to me, usually reminding me of farmyards and rusty nails. Last tasted Feb 1990. For me** For some**** Not for the next century.*

Ch La TOUR-CARNET *Not for the first time, failing to live up to its classed growth status. But not bad. Last tasted June 1988***

Ch La TOUR-HAUT-BRION *Agreeable. Nice texture and flavour in 1982. Seemed to gain in richness. Deep, rich, good. Last tasted, Oct 1986*** Now to 2000.*

Ch La TOUR-MARTILLAC *Rather unimpressive in cask. Four notes and 10 years later, though pale and light, quite nice to drink. Last tasted Oct 1989** Drink up.*

Ch TROTANOY *A marvellous '78. Displaying enormous charm in 1985 and, at Bob Paul's, deep, rich, mature-looking; exciting fruit on the nose, rich, milky — like a strawberry/blackberry milkshake. Silky. Sweet, mouthfilling extract. Rich, rounded, delicious. Last tasted May 1991***** Perfect now. Will doubtless last beyond 2020.*

Ch VERDIGNAN *An agreeable, easy wine in 1984. Seems to have sweetened up a little. Very pleasant and good value, though fails to sustain interest. Last tasted Sept 1990***

VIEUX CH CERTAN *Another good '78 Pomerol. Very deep, plummy, retaining youthful appearance; bouquet needs sorting out, but fragrant. Sweet, fairly full-bodied, good texture, rounded, decent length, good acidity. Last tasted Feb 1988*** Drink now to 2000+*

GOOD, DRINKING WELL IN THE MID-1980s:

Ch Beau Séjour Bécot; Ch Le Bon-Pasteur; Ch La Cardonne; Ch Chasse-Spleen; Ch Couvent-des-Jacobins; Clos L'Eglise; Ch Haut-Bages-Averous; Ch Petit-Village; Ch St-Pierre-Sevaistre; Ch La Tour-de-Mons; Ch La Tour-du-Pin-Figeac.

GOOD ENOUGH, DRINKING WELL IN THE MID-1980s:

Ch Carbonnieux; Ch Chambert-Marbuzet; Ch Citran; Ch La Fleur-Pétrus; Ch La Gaffelière; Ch Lagrange Pomerol; Ch La Louvière; Ch Monbousquet; Ch Moulinet; Ch Nenin; Ch Les-Ormes-de-Pez; Ch Plince; Ch Tertre-Daugay; Ch La Tour-Figeac; Ch Troplong-Mondot; Ch Villemaurine.

MINOR, QUITE GOOD IN THE MID-1980s:

Ch Caronne-Ste-Gemme; Ch Fombrauge; Ch La Garde; Ch Les Grandes-Murailles; Ch Haut-Sarpe; Ch Labégorce-Zédé; Ch Lalande-Borie; Ch Lanessan; Ch Larcis-Ducasse; Ch Marquis d'Alesme-Becker; Ch Maucaillou; Ch Phélan-Ségur; Ch Verdignan.

INDIFFERENT OR UNBALANCED IN THE MID-1980s:

Ch Belair St-Emilion; Ch Bel-Orme-Tronquoy-de-Lalande; Ch Bouscaut; Ch Cap-de-Mourlin; Ch Larose-Trintaudon; Clos l'Oratoire; Ch Pibran; Ch du Tertre.

1979★★

The '79 vintage came onto a London market sated with '75s, '76s and, in particular, '78s. At the first trade tasting, several times referred to below, the wines were impressively deep-coloured and uncompromisingly tannic. These '79s remained 'on the shelf', in an old maid sense, until the mid-1980s, after which they began to be mopped up, having achieved some maturity whilst remaining good value.

Long wet winter, damp spring, good flowering in St-Emilion but, meanwhile, storm damage had reduced some crops in the Médoc. July dry but not hot, Aug dry and unusually cold. Sept was little better. The overall result, a huge harvest – the biggest in Bordeaux since 1934 – of small, healthy grapes that lacked flesh and ripeness. The consequences are illustrated in my notes. Clearly, many of the wines of the Graves and from the right bank, particularly Pomerol, have turned out well. Only the best, those with flesh, will keep and improve further. For many further ageing will just leave a lean, barren, tannic shell of a wine.

Ch LAFITE *First tasted prior to the Lafite-Rothschild dinner at Boulestin, Sept 1980. Not surprisingly, an immature purple, impressive but very tannic. Next at a Lafite tasting led by Eric de Rothschild at the 'California Wine Experience', autumn 1983. By that time, a lively ruby; low-keyed, rather hard nose that took an hour to unfold; dry, raw, loaded with tannin, crisp, good length. Next, long but lean at the MW tasting of '79s in 1984. Still very deep with a strange uncharacteristic bouquet, rich vinosity and almost Pétrus-like flesh. Dry, full, four-square, tannic at Flatt's Lafite tasting in 1988. The following Feb, at Penning-Rowsell's first growth first decade dinner, both nose and flavour beginning to emerge: high-toned, fragrant, evolved, elegant, with a citrus touch. On the palate rather medicinal, very flavoury, dry with noticeable acidity. Most recently, served in double-magnums, opaque, massive, tannic, unready. It slaughtered the lamb for a second time. Last noted at the Justerini & Brooks Queen's Award luncheon at the Banqueting House, Whitehall, Nov 1989★★(★) Will it ever come round?*

Ch MARGAUX *10 notes. First tasted Oct 1981: opaque, fragrant, full of fruit. Consistently intense; a fabulous colour but with a low-keyed nose that needed much exposure to air to develop. Rich, well clad, good texture and fragrance. Tannic. At Desai's Margaux tasting in 1987 one bottle was corked, the other dumb, dry, tannic and lacking the length expected of a first growth. In 1988, in Puerto Rico, served impossibly cold which made it seem even more raw and tannic. Most recently, with seven other '79 first growths (including Pétrus): still very deep, intense and retaining youthful looks; light, fragrant at first but opened up with good rounded fruit for a limited period. Dry, firm, crisp, lovely flavour. Lacking flesh and length. Last tasted Feb 1989★★(★) The best to be expected is a fragrant but lean wine.*

Ch LATOUR *First noted in June 1981. Deep, full, very impressive but raw. Subsequent notes rather off-putting: old socks, distinctly smelly, raw and slightly bitter at the MW tasting of '79s in 1984, extraordinarily overripe nose, cheesy, sweaty feet. In 1987, very tannic. Not showing very well at Penning-Rowsell's: opaque; smelling of animal fat, pork and boot polish; chunky but lacking flavour. Most recently, still very deep and youthful, dark cherry red; very unattractive and most extraordinary bouquet: very cheesy, bandages, dung. Happily a better flavour than nose. Sweetening up a bit though still tannic, chunky, with farmyard aftertaste. Last noted at the Frericks/Wodarz Latour and Mouton tasting, March 1989 ? Leave some until 2030 or give it a miss.*

Ch MOUTON-ROTHSCHILD *First tasted in 1983. Though still youthful it had good vinosity and style. Tasted 11 times since. Attractive, lean but with good flesh and fair fruit. Lovely nose and very high marks at Penning-Rowsell's '79 first growth dinner. Most recently, still fairly deep but developing; a rather hot, spicy, spirity nose, rich, though more chocolate than fruit; fairly full-bodied. A bit raw, and very tannic. Last tasted Oct 1990★★(★) Will the tannin take over? Suggest mid-term drinking, say around 1995–2000.*

Ch HAUT-BRION *Well over a dozen notes dating from the first London trade tasting of '79s given by French Wine Farmers in April 1980. Not very deep. Dry. Tannic. In 1984 I noted a spicy nose, showing quality but obscured by tannin. Yet an impressive mixture of softness and tannin and fragrance. At Penning-Rowsell's in 1989, still a fine deep ruby colour; initial scent of tar, opening up gloriously; very dry, fairly full-bodied, characteristic brick-dust and tobacco taste, a bit lean. Most recently, lovely colour, lower-keyed, more harmonious than La Mission, good fruit, soft silky tannins. Last noted March 1991★★★(★) 1995–2010.*

Ch AUSONE *Three very consistent notes. A total contrast to the other first growths: relatively pale, pink-tinged; an immediately attractive nose, sweet, rich, hints of strawberry and chocolate; medium dryness and body, crisp fruit, silky tannic texture. Last noted at Penning-Rowsell's, Feb 1989★★★(★) Drink now to 2000.*

Ch CHEVAL-BLANC *Outstandingly the most attractive wine at the extensive MW tasting of '79s in 1984. Most recently, fairly deep in colour, rich legs; a beautifully evolved bouquet, cloves, cinnamon and honey; on the sweet side, elegant, svelte. An original flavour. Last noted at Penning-Rowsell's, Feb 1989★★★★ Drink now to beyond 2000.*

Ch PETRUS *Eight notes. Very impressive when young: opaque, intense; sweet, loads of grip. Tannin very noticeable at the MW tasting in 1984. Next, at Frericks' vertical tasting in magnums, 1986: a bit hard, peppery, and stalky on the nose; sweet, rather rough-textured, acidity noted again. Most recently, losing depth of colour and now beginning to show maturity; fragrant though still peppery nose, tea-like scent; drying out, medium weight, still tannic and with a consistent thread of acidity.*

*Last noted at the 'Stockholm' tasting, April 1990*** Not a top Pétrus vintage and more likely to decline than improve. Drink now to 2000.*

Ch BATAILLEY *Good deep ruby colour; straightforward; fairly dry, medium-full, tannic, fruity, no finesse, no great length, but an agreeable drink. Last tasted June 1986** Now to 2000.*

Ch BEYCHEVELLE *Flavoury in cask, evolving through 1980s. Still deep; rich, cedary; sweetish, full-bodied, flesh, tannin and iron. Last tasted April 1991***(*) Now to 1998?*

Ch BRANAIRE-DUCRU *Fairly deep ruby; fragrant; crisp, fruity, pleasantly dry tannins. Attractive. Last noted in Oct 1989*** Drink now to 2000.*

Ch BRANE-CANTENAC *Still very deep though beginning to show some maturity; very pronounced and characteristic ripe, rancid, bucolic fragrance and taste. Soft and rich for a '79 and not over-tannic. Last tasted Jan 1988*** Drink now to 1995.*

Ch CALON-SEGUR *Intensely deep and purple when first tasted in spring 1980, fairly full of fruit, alcohol and tannin. Still plummily deep, consistently sweet fruity nose. Enters sweet, finishes dry and somewhat astringent. Fairly full-bodied, nice texture but seemed a bit lean and lacking middle. Last tasted Feb 1990**(*) Drink now, though might mature further.*

Ch CANON *Still very deep, intense; nose peppery and complex when in cask, now all fruit and spice. Good texture when young, now sweet, fullish, fleshy, as '79s go, with cloves and cinnamon from the use of new oak. Very good. Last tasted Nov 1988**** Drink now to beyond 2000.*

Ch CANON-LA-GAFFELIERE *Medium, mature-looking; sweet, agreeable nose, touches of vanilla and strawberry; dry, medium weight, sinewy, silky. Last tasted July 1989*** Drink now to 1995.*

Ch CANTEMERLE *An acidic note in 1985 but a better one in 1987: deep, still youthful; a rather thick-fruit nose; soft, fleshy, quite nice but not the charming Cantemerle of the mid-1950s. Last tasted March 1987** Probably as ready as it ever will be.*

Ch CHASSE-SPLEEN *Three good notes from the mid-1980s. Deep cherry red; very good nose, crisp, fruity; certainly dry and tannic but also with flesh and fruit. Demands food, is softened by cheese. Last tasted Feb 1989**(*) A little more to come, but no point in keeping even the top wines of this class over 15 years.*

Dom de CHEVALIER *All notes from the mid-1980s. Deep, intense; nose takes time to develop. Described by my son as smelling like an ashtray, not an obvious Graves character. More positive on palate. Good texture, rich but a bit raw. Last tasted April 1985. Now probably**(*) Drink now to 2000.*

Ch CLARKE *Lavish Rothschild investment in a* bourgeois *Médoc. First tasted in 1985 with the keen young members of the Sommelier Society of Palm Beach. Quite nice, but pale and not very '79-ish. Most recently an open, fairly forthcoming, biscuity bouquet but, though still relatively pale and starting to mature, the rather severe '79 tannins noticeable. Last tasted July 1989** Drink up.*

Ch COS D'ESTOURNEL *Big storm during flowering meant a small crop at Cos.* Cépages: *55% Cabernet Sauvignon, 45% Merlot. First tasted April 1980: it was even deeper and tougher than Montrose. Subsequently noted a change in colour from plummy purple to lively cherry-cum-ruby, slow to mature. Nose consistently restrained, needs coaxing out of the glass, but most recently noted the scents of tea and liquorice. Though still tannic, seems to have sweetened up. Crisp fruit. Nice weight. Last noted at the Hollywood Wine Society Cos tasting, Jan 1990*** Can be drunk now, will keep.*

Ch DASSAULT *Another lavishly endowed property, this time in St-Emilion. Two notes: very deep, still youthful-looking; pronounced vanilla, blancmange, new oak character; very sweet, full, rich, fruity, tannic. Certainly more successful than Ch Clarke, but '79s on the right bank are less severe than those in the Médoc. Last tasted Nov 1988*** Drink soon.*

Ch DUCRU-BEAUCAILLOU *A dumb, dry, austere but straightforward cask sample. Agreeable fruit, good texture, but mouth-drying tannins and severity in the mid-1980s. The last three notes all indicate deep but maturing appearance and, consistently, a stalkiness, almost wood, on the nose, very dry and austere on palate. Last tasted Feb 1989*(*)? Unlikely to soften due to lack of flesh and fruit.*

Ch FIGEAC *A huge crop. Still 'working', green, stalky and tough cask sample in April 1980, yet remarkably well evolved at the MW tasting of '79s in 1984. Delicious, mouthwatering and worth keeping. Good notes: "glorious but unknit" bouquet, sweet, piquant, flavoury in 1987 and 1988, but a rather cool note at Desai's Figeac tasting. Colour still fairly deep. Plausible. Last tasted Dec 1989*** Drink now to 2000.*

Les FORTS DE LATOUR *First tasted Dec 1981 at the Ch Latour headquarters in Millbank Towers, London. Opaque and raw but laden with young fruit. Many notes since. Despite its uncompromising tannin I have found it surprisingly nice, with a lovely, deep, ruby colour, very sweet, fragrant nose, full-flavoured, with some flesh and silkiness of texture. Infinitely more attractive than the* grand vin. *Last tasted May 1989**(*) 1993–2000+*

Ch FOURCAS-HOSTEN *Surprisingly pleasant in the mid-1980s and, more recently, still very deeply coloured, full-bodied but with good flesh ameliorating to some extent the high tannin content. Last tasted June 1988**(*) Drink now to 1995.*

Ch La GAFFELIERE *Pleasant colour but already mature, slightly orange-tinged; dry, lightish, with an easy, somewhat chaptalised, style. Jan 1988** Drink soon.*

Ch Le GAY *Pomerol running more or less to form, being more inclined to Médoc severity than St-Emilion rusticity. Fine deep colour, maturing; light, berry-like aroma; sweet entry, very dry, 'hot', tannic, teeth-gripping finish. Good fruit sandwiched in between. July 1988*(**) Say 1995–2010.*

Ch GISCOURS *All notes on Giscours from the mid-1980s. An interesting wine, packing a punch, rich, chewy, elegant despite its assertiveness. Needs coaxing in the glass and more time in bottle. Last tasted Jan 1985**(**) 1993 to well beyond 2000.*

Ch GLORIA *Rather nice. From 1982 onwards, showing well, lots of fruit, good flavour and balance. Still deep; a rather extraordinary nose, ripe fruity,* *spice, a powdery fragrance; touch of sweetness, fairly full-bodied, flavoury.* Last tasted Jan 1988**(*) Drink now to 2000.

Ch GRAND-PUY-DUCASSE *Weak-rimmed; sweet, chaptalised nose; dry, rather flat, weak and watery for a '79.* Last tasted July 1989*

Ch GRAND-PUY-LACOSTE *Extraordinarily minty nose, unusual taste and good aftertaste — cask sample, spring 1980. Showing well, silky tannins, fruit and length at the MW tasting in 1984. More recently still a deep immature ruby; attractive, spicy, blackcurrant, soft fruit aroma; dry, fairly full-bodied, good length, a bit austere. A top-class wine needing decanting time, air and coaxing now, preferably more bottle-age.* Last tasted June 1988*(***) Should keep and develop beyond 2010.

Ch GRUAUD-LAROSE *Many notes. A big chunky, fruity wine. Still very deep and plummy; nose cool, with Médoc oyster shell, iodine nose soon opening out into a rich, ripe-smelling wine; dry and tannic yet with loads of mouthfilling fruit giving it a certain softness.* Last tasted March 1989***(*) Drink now to well beyond 2000.

Ch HAUT-BAILLY *Consistent notes: rich vinosity, touch of liquorice and vanilla; a slightly sweet, soft, fleshy, fragrant and attractive wine.* Last noted June 1987. Probably*** Ready for drinking.

Clos des JACOBINS *Interesting mix: 8% Cabernet Sauvignon, 47% Merlot; 45% Cabernet Franc. Fragrant, whisper of raspberry; dry, fullish, crisp, flavoury.* Last tasted July 1987*** Drink soon.

Ch LAGRANGE *St-Julien. Fairly deep; attractive, crisp, fruity nose; quite nice flavour, with sort of slithery leathery tannins. A bit pinched.* July 1988*(*) Not really worth pursuing. Say 1992–1998.

Ch LANGOA-BARTON *Spicy, clove-like, attractive when young. Several notes in the mid-1980s. "True Bordeaux nose" (me), "mothballs and lavender" (my wife). Certainly well bred but a bit hard. More recently opening up a bit, lovely nose, lean yet rich and shapely.* Last tasted June 1988**(*) Probably best 1993–2010.

Ch LASCOMBES *Several rather variable notes from 1982. Impressively deep rich colour; nose somewhat low-keyed; some ripeness and sweetness, positive, fair fruit, teeth-gripping tannin and upturned edge.* Last tasted April 1988*(*) On balance, so-so: 1992–1998?

Ch LEOVILLE-BARTON *Not a deep-coloured or hefty '79. Ruby; a certain delicacy and fragrance after time in glass; fairly dry, lean yet with some fleshiness. Lacking fruit, and with refreshing citrus-like acidity.* Jan 1990*** Now to 2000.

Ch LEOVILLE-LAS-CASES *17 notes. Showing well at the French Wine Farmers' tasting in April 1980 and subsequently. Fascinating tasting of individual* cépages *from casks in June 1982, and the final blend (63% Cabernet Sauvignon, 12% Cabernet Franc, 20% Merlot, 5% Petit Verdot) noted at a Christie's Wine Course tasting two years later: intense pink purple; fairly ripe aroma; overall dry but impressive. Most recently: still deep though showing some maturity; an earthy, tannic, cedary nose, far less appealing since 1988 than in the early to mid-1980s. Medium-full body, quite nice fruit, tannins softening but a bit lean and stringy. Flavoury.* Last tasted April 1990*** "Ready to fly" at a British Airways Wine Committee tasting and might as well be flown. Drink now to 1995.

Ch LEOVILLE-POYFERRE *The usual '79 depth of colour. Showing quite well at a Christie's Wine Course in 1986.* Cépages: *65% Cabernet Sauvignon, 5% Cabernet Franc, 30% Merlot. Rather chocolaty nose, positive, on the soft and silky side, not too tannic, pleasant.* Last tasted March 1989*** Drink now to 1996.

Ch La LOUVIERE *Many notes, mainly from mid-1980s and representing red Graves at several Christie's Wine Course sessions.* Cépages: *80% Cabernet Sauvignon, 20% Merlot, the Cabernet coming out very noticeably on the nose, blackcurrant and strawberry, and, after some time in the glass, honeyed, complete, black treacle and ginger. Mouthwatering acidity and touch of tannin bitterness. Lean. Nice texture. Unready, but will it improve greatly?* Last tasted June 1987**(*)? Drink 1992–1998.

Ch LYNCH-BAGES *Many notes, from a cask sample, spring 1980. Initially low-keyed on the nose though by the mid-1980s a more recognisable, crisp, Cabernet Sauvignon aroma. Original depth and intensity ameliorating. A bit raw, lean and severe though fairly full-bodied and with crisp fruit. Not tasted recently but not a top Lynch-Bages.* Last noted July 1987*(**) Drink whilst still crisp and lively.

Ch La MISSION-HAUT-BRION *11 notes, from 1984, mainly Woltner stock, at pre-sale tastings and at two major verticals, the first Desai's in Los Angeles in 1985 and, most recently, Wolf's in Wiesbaden. Very consistent notes: appearance deep, nose restrained at first, then a burst of characteristic Graves tar and tobacco, finally, with more air, rich, crisp, biscuity. On the palate medium dryness and weight, fairly beefy, nice fruit, impressive though not as massive as one might expect. A touch of bitterness in tannic finish.* Last tasted June 1990**(*) 1992–2010.

Ch MONTROSE *Nine notes, from a dumb, tight-knit tannic cask sample, through a period of fruit and charm, despite its tannin, in the mid-1980s. Latterly its nose a bit uninteresting, wet cardboard plus Médoc iodine, but an underlay of fruit coming to the surface with air; a misleading touch of sweetness, nice weight and balance, reasonable length, touch of bitterness yet surprisingly drinkable for a tannic '79 St-Estèphe.* Last noted April 1988***(*) Now to 2000+

Ch PALMER *Five notes, from mid-1980s. Very individualistic wine: glorious colour; a fleshy, mulberry-like fruitiness on the nose; fully developed and surprisingly — for a '79 — sweet and fleshy on the palate. Chewy richness, flavoury, masked tannin and acidity.* Last tasted at the château, June 1991***(*) Some more development but not for long keeping.

Ch PAVIE-DECESSE *Deep, good fruit, lean, leathery, spicy.* Last tasted Nov 1989*(**) 1992–1998.

PAVILLON ROUGE DE CH MARGAUX *Many notes in the mid-1980s. Particularly interesting as the second Mentzelopoulos vintage. Noted as 75%*

Cabernet Sauvignon, 20% Merlot, 5% Petit Verdot. Youthful ruby; nose fragrant but hard; nowhere near ready, raw, with marked tangerine-like acidity, yet attractive, vigorous, though teeth-gripping. Then trying to mature, spicy, fragrant, lean but attractive. An overpriced adolescent. Last noted Nov 1990** Drink soon.

Ch PICHON-LONGUEVILLE, BARON *Seven notes. Predictably opaque in the early 1980s, firm, not very interesting. Still fairly deep, nose low-keyed, hard, tannic; crisp fruit, quite attractive, good length but severe.* Last tasted Oct 1988*(*) *Difficult to imagine that this will develop sufficiently in bottle to warrant long cellaring.*

Ch PICHON-LONGUEVILLE, LALANDE *10 notes. Cask sample in April 1980, crisp fresh fruit and good aftertaste; similar characteristics noted at the MW tasting of '79s in 1984, plus a lovely texture. Brilliant with pheasant and roast veal sausage stuffed with shitake and basil in Boston, 1987. Most recently, still a gloriously deep ruby colour; pepper, cedar, fruit opening up beautifully, fragrantly, in the glass; fairly full-bodied, soft silky leathery texture, dry finish.* Last tasted Nov 1990***(*) Now to 2010.

Ch de SALES *Forthcoming, soft and easy even after only one year in bottle, partly due to the 66% Merlot, but also its* terroir. *The initial somewhat ingenuous fruit on the nose developed into an intriguing mish-mash. Better on palate, like fruit salad.* Last tasted Oct 1986** Drink up.

Ch TALBOT *Deep; ripe, sweaty tannins with quite pronounced Cabernet fruit on nose and palate. Dry. Fairly impressive.* Last tasted Feb 1989**(*) *Drink now, probably more to come and will keep.*

Ch La TOUR-CARNET *From a normal '79 depth of colour in the mid-1980s, a steep dive into orange-tinged maturity. Not much bouquet; nice weight, leathery tannic texture, moderate length and quality.* Last tasted April 1988*

Ch La TOUR-HAUT-BRION *Several notes. Very deep, intense, cherry red in the mid-1980s, still deep; a complex, rather strange nose, medicinal, touch of caramel and orange peel, but evolving quickly and attractively in the glass. Overall dry, its original hardness and austerity now showing as a crisp fruitiness.* Last noted at Wolf's tasting, June 1990**(*) 1992–2000+

Ch TROTANOY *Six notes. A cask sample of considerable potential, a deep purple richly textured bottle in 1982, showing elegance, though lean, at the MW tasting in 1984. Most recently, still deep, retaining fairly youthful good looks; a rich, distinctly sweet, forthcoming bouquet; touch of sweetness and richness on entry but a very tannic finish.* Last noted May 1990**(**) *Worth hanging on to.*

Ch YON-FIGEAC *Several recent notes. Quite a good, rich, fruity mouthful.* Last tasted March 1979** Drink now.

'79s TASTED SINCE 1985:

Ch BEL-ORME-TRONQUOY-DE-LALANDE *Very deep, tough, tannic.*

Ch de CAMENSAC *Deep yet mature, fairly sweet, good fruit, tolerable tannin.*

Ch CROIZET-BAGES *Deep nose developed nicely; very attractive fruity flavour, reasonable length, dry finish.*

Ch La FLEUR-GAZIN *Well-graduated colour, cherry red to maturing rim; touch of caramel at first, evolving harmoniously in the glass; lovely Pomerol texture, soft despite slightly bitter tannic finish. Very agreeable.*

Ch LANESSAN *Opaque, mature edge; classic cheese rind nose; dry, fairly substantial, mouthdrying tannin.*

Ch La LOUVIERE *Many notes. Impressively deep; good, peppery, Cabernet aroma; silky texture, some extract partially masking tannin, mouthwatering acidity.*

Ch MARBUZET *50% Cabernet Sauvignon, 10% Cabernet Franc, 40% Merlot. Still purple-tinged; crisp fruit,* fraise des bois; *interesting flavour, teeth-gripping tannin, lean.*

Ch MARQUIS-DE-TERME *Dry, raw, tannic.* April 1986

Ch MOUTON-BARONNE-PHILIPPE *First tasted in 1982. Not very deep then, it matured quickly; a very lightly fragrant bouquet; lean, easy-going. A decent lunch wine.*

Ch La POINTE *Highly polished appearance and taste. Soft, harmonious nose developing honey, ginger and cinnamon; silky texture, adequate flesh, tannin and acidity. Very attractive.*

Ch POTENSAC *Wholesome but unready.*

MINOR, QUITE GOOD WINES TASTED IN THE MID-1980s:

Ch du Calvaire; Ch Canon-Fronsac; Ch Caronne-Ste-Gemme; Ch Cissac; Ch Couvent-des-Jacobins; Ch Potensac; Ch Pouget; Ch La Rose-Trintaudon.

RAW TANNIC MINOR WINES TASTED IN THE MID-1980s:

Ch Caillou.

SHOWING WELL EARLY TO MID-1980s:

Ch d'Angludet; Ch Beau Séjour Bécot; Ch Belair St-Emilion; Ch Bouscaut; Ch Cap-de-Mourlin; Ch Croque-Michotte; Ch La Dominique; Ch L'Enclos; Ch Faurie-de-Souchard; Ch La Fleur-Pétrus; Ch La Grave Trigant; Ch Haut-Bages-Averous; Ch Haut-Batailley; Ch Haut-Marbuzet; Ch Haut-Pontet; Ch Haut-Sarpe; Ch Latour à Pomerol; Ch Magdelaine; Ch Malartic-Lagravière; Ch Malescasse; Ch Maucaillou; Ch Moulinet; Ch Nenin; Ch Les Ormes-de-Pez; Ch Petit-Village; Ch St-Pierre-Sevaistre; Ch La Tour-Martillac.

QUITE GOOD IN THE EARLY TO MID-1980s:

Ch L'Angélus; Ch Balestard-La-Tonnelle; Ch Brame-les-Tours; Ch Cadet-Piola; Ch Canon-de-Brem; Ch Carbonnieux; Ch Clerc-Milon-Mourlin; Ch La Clusière; Ch Coufran; Ch Duhart-Milon-Rothschild; Ch d'Issan; Ch Larmande; Ch Millet; Ch Olivier, Clos de l'Oratoire; Ch Pavie; Ch Petit-Faurie-de-Soutard; Ch Pique-Caillou; Ch Prieuré-Lichine; Ch Rauzan-Gassies; Ch Rouet; Ch Smith-Haut-Lafitte, Clos St-Martin; Ch Troplong-Mondot.

NOT GOOD ENOUGH IN THE EARLY TO MID-1980s:

Ch Barreyres; Ch Beaumont Cussac; Ch Cantenac-Brown; Ch Kirwan; Ch Lafon-Rochet; Moulin des Carruades; Ch Pape-Clément.

TOO TANNIC, UNBALANCED IN THE EARLY TO MID-1980s:

Ch Les Grandes-Murailles.

1980

The splendid decade of the '80s got off to a rather limp start, rather like that of the '60s. Indeed, red Bordeaux of the 1980 vintage has something in common with that of the 1960. Both a bit thin and acidic, though, at their best, are very pleasant light luncheon wines; both were best in the pink of youth; neither had the possibility of enhanced flavour or profitability that might ordinarily come of prudent cellaring. Spring was cool, flowering prolonged and uneven; summer cold and wet but Aug hot. Sept was warm but sunless which slowed the ripening process. Early Oct was very wet but improved for a very late and small harvest.

Ch LAFITE *For some reason or other, I did not taste the '80 in its formative years. The first note was made at a Christie's pre-sale tasting in June 1988, the next four months later, at Flatt's marathon Lafite tasting in New Orleans; then, exactly a year later a bottle from the château at a boardroom lunch, and latterly at Penning-Rowsell's annual first growth dinner. At Flatt's the colour seemed, in a 1980–85 flight, surprisingly deep. Consistent notes on nose: crisp, fruity, fragrant, attractive with a whiff of oysters or iodine. Fairly dry, on the light side, lean but nice fruit, lacking the length of a top vintage and with some astringency on the finish. Last tasted March 1990**(*) Really a light luncheon wine with just fractional room for improvement. Drink now to 1995.*

Ch MARGAUX *First tasted in cask, Oct 1981: deeper than expected, some fragrance. Next at Schaefer's: stewed fruit nose, slightly bitter, acid finish. Then at the château, Sept 1984, with Emile Peynaud, who informed us that the grapes were picked from Oct 17, the latest harvest of this century. It seemed already to have started to mature, showing some softness, some spice. Showing quite well at Desai's tasting in 1987. Forthcoming, fragrant; an attractive bilberry-like flavour; easy, for drinking. And most recently at Penning-Rowsell's 10th year dinner: deep, fairly intense ruby; closed and peppery at first but evolved well, sweet spicy scent like brandy-snaps; medium dryness and body, flavoury, silky tannins, crisp, short. Last noted Nov 1990**(*) A very pleasant short-term light luncheon or late dinner wine. Drink now to 1995.*

Ch LATOUR *Two notes: the first at the Frericks/Wodarz twin vertical tasting of Latour and Mouton in March 1989, the second at the Penning-Rowsells' mentioned above. Fairly deep, a good colour. Nose curious, dumb at first though with underlying fruit. In each instance, after 10 minutes in the glass the bouquet developed richly, a whiff of beetroot and the 'sweat' of tannin; medium dryness and weight, quite a good fruity mouthful. A bit astringent on the finish, tannin, iron. Last tasted March 1990**(*?) Not an attractive drink. It might ameliorate a little with, say, five more years' bottle-age.*

Ch MOUTON-ROTHSCHILD *Many notes, starting in March 1983 with a bottle from the château to make a note for their label exhibition catalogue. I found it plausible and ready for drinking after less than a year in bottle. (It was bottled during the month of June 1982.) At Flatt's extensive tasting in 1986 it looked a relatively pale quick-developer, nose pleasing, touch of sweetness, lacking length but an attractive drink. Virtually identical notes at the Frericks/Wodarz Latour and Mouton tasting in 1989 and, in 1990, at the Penning-Rowsells': holding its colour though a bit weak and watery at the rim, the sign of a lesser vintage. Nose restrained at first but evolved, meaty, fruity, gingery. Pleasant to sip, quite nice fruit, a bit raw, with sandy-textured tannins. Last tasted March 1990** Plausible. Drink it whilst it still has fruit.*

Ch HAUT-BRION *First tasted in May 1987 with the Duc de Mouchy and Jean Delmas at the château. In a short range, 1978–82, it did not show too well, though the colour was better than expected. Straightforward, lightish, short "a luncheon wine" in May 1985; then, aged 10, at the Penning-Rowsells': medium, ruby tinted, lively looking. Decanted at 7pm and poured at 8.15, the nose had had time to evolve, very forthcoming and fragrant, a sweet, attractive Graves character. On the light side with the characteristic bricky, tobacco-like, flavour. Finished a bit short with an endtaste like burnt brown paper. Always* much *more agreeable to drink than describe. Last tasted March 1990**(*) Drink now to 1995.*

Ch AUSONE *Two somewhat contradictory notes. At Flatt's vertical in 1987 I noted it as pale, fully evolved in colour; thin, minty, tinny and unknit on nose and palate — and short. At the Penning-Rowsells' comparison of first growths the bouquet, initially dusty and waxy, developed quite pleasantly, tea-like; sweeter and less skinny than at Flatt's. Loosely constructed but no bitterness. Last tasted March 1990* Drink up.*

Ch CHEVAL-BLANC *First tasted from the cask, Sept 1982, noting a surprisingly good colour. Nearly eight years later, at the Penning-Rowsells': colour still good; curious nose: sour cabbage at first, then evolved fragrantly with noticeable 'iron' character I associate with Cheval-Blanc, from the soil I believe, later, distinctly vegetal. But on palate most attractive. Sweet, a nice weight, silky texture, very flavoury, elegant, dry finish. Voted best of the first-growth '80s that evening. Last tasted March 1990*** Drink soon before the charm wears thin.*

Ch PETRUS *First two notes made at Hans-Peter Frericks' Pétrus tasting in Munich: in magnum, a pretty cherry red; reluctant bouquet opening up* *slowly. After an hour in the glass it was sweet, strawberry-like with a snuff-like spiciness. On the palate a plausible chaptalised sweetness. An attractive drink. And drink it we did, from an* impériale, *with caviar served like porridge. Christian Mouiex agreed that the beluga was delicious but did nothing for the Pétrus! More recently at the Penning-Rowsells': a fishy, herbaceous nose, not strawberry this time but ripe mulberry, slightly malty. A specious wine. Last tasted June 1991*** Drink now to 2000.*

Ch BRANE-CANTENAC *Quite a good, rich nose, light and flavoury in its butyric acid, hen-droppings way. Last tasted Oct 1986. Disinclined to taste again.*

Ch CALON-SEGUR *First tasted in cask, Oct 1981. Very flavoury, not bad at all. More recently, now on the pale side; sweet, high-toned, lightly medicinal, quite attractive bouquet; lightish, soft, easy. Last tasted June 1987** Drink now.*

Ch CERTAN-DE-MAY *Labelled "Ch Certan, De May de Certan". Surprisingly deep and youthful-looking; good, crisp Cabernet Franc nose; dry, medium weight, good fruit, tannic. A bit of '79 in the blend? Pre-sale April 1988** Drink now to 1996.*

Dom de CHEVALIER *Tasted once. Very evolved, mature, orange-tinged rim; chocolaty, earthy Graves nose, sweet, vanilla; quite nice. Chaptalised, pebbly, earthy, dry tannate/iron finish. At the château May 1986** Drink now to 1995.*

Ch CROIZET-BAGES *Palish, mature; sweet, chaptalised nose and taste. Rather raw edge. Oct 1987**

Ch DUHART-MILON-ROTHSCHILD *Palish, mature; sweet, meaty; quite nice flavour, short, dry, slightly acidic finish. Ex-château, Oct 1989**

Ch La FLEUR *Good colour, mature; sweet, liquorice-like, chaptalised Pomerol nose; dry, lighter than it looks. Not bad. April 1987*(*) Drink soon.*

Les FORTS DE LATOUR *Several notes. Quite a good colour, though on the last occasion I thought it was showing some premature ageing on nose and palate. Stewed fruit. Touch of bitterness. Last tasted Aug 1987. Not too keen on this.*

Ch GRAND-PUY-LACOSTE *Deep, dry, flavoury but lean, raw, with hard tannins. Nov 1986**

Ch LAGRANGE *St-Julien. Medium, translucent, distinct orange tinge of prematurity; low-keyed nose, hard to pin down; touch of sweetness, on the light side. A nice, easy, soft, chaptalised wine. Short. At a* Decanter *tasting, July 1988** Drink soon.*

Ch LANGOA-BARTON *First tasted in Sept 1982: a rather superficial, light, easy wine. Four years later, mature; lightly fruity nose. An attractive, flavoury luncheon wine. Last tasted April 1986** Drink soon.*

Ch LEOVILLE-LAS-CASES *Several notes. Soft, supple and easy when first tasted at the château, Sept 1982. One of the best '80s, as it was one of the best '60s: in fact quite a similarity. Richly coloured when last seen and, though not unattractive, more appealing in its first flush of youth. Last tasted Nov 1986** Drink up.*

Ch LEOVILLE-POYFERRE *A couple of notes. Maturing; hard, peppery little nose; dry, lacking character, short. Last tasted Oct 1986. Drink up.*

Ch LYNCH-BAGES *At the château, Sept 1982: raw. Fleeting flavour, more acid than tannin but drinkable in 1984. More recently, still rather deep for an '80, lively cherry red; an attractive, lightly fruity lunch wine. Last tasted Jan 1987** Drink soon.*

Ch La MISSION-HAUT-BRION *First noted at Desai's in Feb 1985: surprisingly deep, as deep as the '81; low-keyed; dry, rather raw and tannic. Nose seemed more evolved in 1986 but distinctly tannic. Most recently at Wolf's extensive tasting of Woltner wines, losing some colour, mature; fruit, pepper, tea on the nose, no development. Dry, light, austere, cheesy. Not bad but not very appealing. Last tasted June 1990* Not worth holding on to.*

Ch MONTROSE *Palish, weak-rimmed; sweet, earthy, slightly pungent fruit; light, soft despite some iron-like tannin. Not bad. Pre-sale, July 1986* Drink soon.*

Ch MOUTON-BARONNE-PHILIPPE *Many notes from the mid-1980s. Now pale, fully mature, little red; light, rather medicinal stewed-fruit nose; dry, light, thin, short, yet a certain delicacy and not without flavour. Last tasted April 1988* Drink up.*

Ch PALMER *Like Léoville-Las-Cases, Palmer made notably good '60s and '80s. A sweet fleshy nose that developed strawberry-like scent; distinctly sweet on palate too, nice chunky flavour. Juicy. Texture a bit coarse. Last tasted Aug 1987*** Drink now to 1995.*

PAVILLON ROUGE DE CH MARGAUX *Fragrant and flavoury in 1985. But in 1987 I thought it a bit green and stalky, raw and short. Most recently, seemed sweeter, lightish, ready. Last tasted Nov 1990* Drink up.*

Ch PICHON-LONGUEVILLE, LALANDE *Distinctly raw in cask, July 1981. After a year in bottle quite pleasing, dry, light, almost a charmer. When last tasted still holding a good, deep colour; sweet, medicinal Pauillac nose; flavoury, piquant. Last noted Sept 1986** Drink up.*

Ch PONTET-CANET *Medium-pale, maturing; sweet, jammy nose; light, dry, tart finish. Scarcely even a lunchtime wine. Jan 1989. Drink up.*

Ch La TOUR-DU-PIN-FIGEAC *Only included to demonstrate that a wine of this calibre and vintage is best drunk young. Deep, intense, with some youthful appeal, quite nice fruit and flavour in 1983. Showing premature ageing on nose, short and a bit drab in 1989. Last tasted March 1989. Drink up.*

VIEUX CH CERTAN *Palish, mature; sweet, chaptalised nose. Bottle variation, one seeming to show a bit of rot on the palate, the other drier, fresher and fruitier. Feb 1989**?*

SHOWING QUITE WELL, PROBABLY STILL DRINKABLE:

Ch Cantemerle; Ch La Cardonne; Ch Clos St-Martin; Ch Croque-Michotte; Ch Dauzac; Ch La Dominique; Ch Grand-Puy-Ducasse; Ch Guadet-St-Julien; Ch Meyney; Ch Les Ormes-de-Pez; Ch Le Pin; Ch Prieuré-Lichine; Ch La Serre; Ch Siran; Ch Troplong-Mondot.

1981★★ to ★★★★

Underrated, certainly undervalued on the open market. The wines tend to be lean, making this vintage less immediately appealing than, say, the '76 and far less obvious than the multi-dimensional '82s by which it was completely upstaged. This was a vintage of elegance. However, they *do* vary. Those wines which were skinny as opposed to agreeably lean and elegant are not worth pursuing. There are, however, plenty of nicely constituted wines, many delicious now, some needing more time in bottle.

Spring neither early nor brilliant but perfect conditions for flowering. Then cold and wet. Until a sunny Aug through to the harvest around the end of Sept, soon after which heavy rain stopped the picking for several days. Some dilution, but generally no harm done.

Ch LAFITE *Five fairly recent notes. Showing quite well at Flatt's Lafite tasting in 1988, crisp, fruity, lean. Still rather youthful; bouquet hard and spicy though with some depth and fragrance; touch of sweetness, fair length, tannic, lacking flesh and extract but quite nice in 1989. Most recently, developing nicely; soft, gently fragrant; good fruit, flavour, texture.* Last noted at Penning-Rowsell's '81 first growth tasting, June 1991 ★★(★) 1997–2007

Ch MARGAUX *First tasted in cask, in Sept 1982: opaque, good fruit, tannin and guts, then again the following May, in* barriques. *Almost overwhelming the smell of new wine was the pungent smell of cement in the new second-year cellar. Much drier and leaner than the '82. Next tasted in Sept 1984, a year in bottle. Still, intense; nose well-knit though understated. As tannic as the '82 but more sinewy. Reminded me of the '66. A rather green, lean and slightly woody bottle at Desai's Margaux tasting in 1987. More recently: still deep, youthful; good crisp fruit, opening up well; dry, fullish, lean, raw but flavoury.* Last noted at the Penning-Rowsells', June 1991 ★★(★) 1996–2010

Ch LATOUR *Not as big and black as expected. Fragrant but unknit though with crisp fruit in the mid-1980s. Bottle variation at the Frericks/Wodarz Latour and Mouton tasting in March 1989, one rather woody and stalky, the other more evolved. Fairly full-bodied, rich, more extract than Mouton. Most recently: deep; biscuity, fragrant, cedar, Cabernet Sauvignon; dry, lovely flavour, crisp fruit, lacking the length of a great vintage, swingeingly tannic finish.* Last tasted June 1991 ★(★★)? Say 1996–2015

Ch MOUTON-ROTHSCHILD *Six notes. Showing well at Flatt's Mouton tasting in 1986: convincing, good classic nose and taste. Despite its '81 leanness, surprising softness and flesh. At the Frericks/Wodarz tasting: its appearance was only fairly deep, seemingly quite evolved; youthful brambly fruit, vanilla scented; flavoury but a bit austere. Most recently, lovely crisp colour; dumb when first decanted but opened up beautifully, flowery, delicious, sweet and spicy; dry, crisp fruity flavour, some flesh, touch of tannic bitterness. A cross between the '71 and '66.* Last noted at the Penning-Rowsells', June 1991 ★★★(★) 1993–2010

Ch HAUT-BRION *Eight notes. First tasted May 1983: little nose, firm, elegant. The following spring, at a tasting of '81 red Graves: good depth of colour, a totally different nose to La Mission, more cedary, more harmonious, less dramatic; lovely mid-palate and elegance. Reticence noted in the mid-1980s, some maturity showing by 1988 and, a year later, a touch of maltiness on nose and palate. Most recently medium-deep, rich, fairly mature appearance; marvellous vinosity, cool, high-toned, opening up well; touch of sweetness, medium body, lean but with good structure. Very idiosyncratic brick-dust and tobacco taste.* Last tasted at the Penning-Rowsells', June 1991★★(★) Now to 2015.

Ch AUSONE *Just two notes, the first at Flatt's exhaustive vertical: medium-deep ruby; two-part nose, slightly sweet, vegetal; medium dryness and weight; lean but fruity. At the Penning-Rowsells', nice colour, still youthful; malty at first, tobacco, ferns and fruit; rather earthy Graves-like flavour, unusual. It grew on me.* Last noted June 1991★★(★) 1993–2005

Ch CHEVAL-BLANC *Six notes. First tasted in Sept 1982: very deep; rich, very good nose; quite a bite. More acidity than the Pomerols. Sweetness noted consistently through the mid to late 1980s. Most recently: deep, very attractive, fragrant well-developed nose; powerful, attractive.* Last noted June 1991★★★(★) Now to 2010.

Ch PETRUS *Five notes. Black; dumbness, concealing depth of fruit; full, fleshy, rich, complete — sort of puppy fat a year after the vintage. Next, in magnum, at Frericks' Pétrus tasting in 1986: medium-deep, plummy, spicy bouquet developing, meaty, calf's-foot jelly. At the 'Stockholm' Group blind vertical tasting in 1990, one of the few vintages I got right. Maturing; a bit hard at first but opened up, crisp fruit; rather leathery texture, acidity noticeable. Most recently decanted in the office, tasted, then taken to the Penning-Rowsells'. Four hours later, opulent, mulberry-like fruit; seemed sweeter, full of fruit flavour though blunt.* Last noted June 1991★★★(★) Drink now to 2005.

Ch L'ANGELUS *Three recent notes. Fairly deep, now starting to mature; an attractive, rich, very sweet nose; sweet on palate too, medium weight though alcoholic, unusual soft blackberry-like fruit. Soft and fleshy for an '81. Nice tannin and acidity.* Last tasted July 1990★★★ Now to 2000+

Ch BEAUREGARD *Pomerol. Indeterminate colour; one bottle stalky, woody, rather raw and short. Another, two months later, from the same stock, mature, not very impressive appearance; light, hard nose which developed slightly then faded; dryish, medium-light, lean, short.* Last tasted Sept 1990★ Drink soon.

Ch BEYCHEVELLE *First tasted, a cask sample, at a de Luze trade tasting in London, April 1982: deep, very fragrant, spicy new oak. In Jan 1988: fairly deep though murky, maturing; almost artificial scent and flavour. Dry; hollow. Most recently, fully mature; singed, a spicy immediacy; not bad flavour though strange bitterness on finish.* Last noted March 1991** Drink up.

Ch BOUSCAUT *Five notes, "dull" in March 1984, "boring" in 1985, "dull" again and "tails off". "Mean and lean with a flat dry end" at a recent tasting of '81s. Though not wholly without merit, certainly not my favourite '81 red Graves.* Last tasted July 1989*

Ch BRANAIRE-DUCRU Cépages *75% Cabernet Sauvignon, 20% Merlot, 5% Petit Verdot. A mass of notes, starting in April 1984. Although a bright healthy cherry red, not very deep; whiff of tangerine peel; a light, refreshing charming young wine. In 1987: lovely fragrance, raspberry, cedar, mouthwatering; a gentle, silky touch with crisp dry finish. Now fairly mature, a bit weak at the rim; quite a ripe little nose; nice crisp fruit. Light easy style. More acidity than tannin.* Last tasted June 1991** Drink now to 1996.

Ch BRANE-CANTENAC *Five recent notes. Though some richness, not deeply coloured, indeed overall a bit feeble, orange-tinged; an extraordinary bouquet; better on palate than appearance and nose indicated. Fruit, extract, grip. Not my style of wine, but interesting.* Last tasted Sept 1990*** in its way. Drink now to 1996.

Ch CALON-SEGUR *At the de Luze cask sample tasting in the spring of 1982, flavoury but a bit lacking, a phrase also used in 1987, and latterly. An attractive, medium, very mature colour; moderate nose; lean, not enough girth, very dry tannic finish.* Last tasted Sept 1990* I do not foresee a great future.

Ch CANON *Good wine, colour development still restrained; fragrant, distinctive nose and flavour. Some sweetness, light tannins, refreshing acidity.* July 1989*** Now to 2000.

Ch CANON-FRONSAC *A relatively minor wine now Moueix owned. No relation to the Canons from St-Emilion. Fronsac is the village name and commune. To add to the confusion, Canon-Fronsac is the name of a local classification higher than Fronsac, as well as that of a château. Lighter and less dense than '81 Pomerols. Light fruit. Agreeable.* June 1988** For current drinking.

Ch CANON-LA-GAFFELIERE *Five recent notes. Medium, maturing; light but forthcoming, quite pleasant bouquet; touch of sweetness and liquorice, medium-light, lean, flavoury.* Last tasted Jan 1991** Drink soon.

Ch CANTEMERLE *Five notes. Never deep in colour though retaining a youthful cherry red blush. Bouquet, or should I say smell, of tripe and onions; lacking fruit and a touch of end bitterness noted in 1985. Lean, crisp, a bit insubstantial.* Last tasted Sept 1988*(*) No great future.

Ch CANTENAC-BROWN *Plummy; low-keyed yet fragrant; broad style but unfinished cask sample in April 1982. In 1986, similar appearance, little nose, lightish, soft, pleasant enough. More recently, still looking a bit immature; sweet, jammy fruit on nose, and relatively chunky for an '81.* Last tasted Jan 1988** Say 1992–96.

Ch CARBONNIEUX *First tasted in March 1984. Youthful ruby; charming, some fruit; nice, refreshing, easy style predicted despite bitter tannins. By 1988, cherry red; nose seemed to have closed up; uncompromisingly lean though good length. Three recent notes: now paler, more advanced in colour; nose now fully developed, sweet, jammy, chocolaty; on the light side, light refreshing fruit, more acidity than tannin.* Last tasted Jan 1991** Drink soon.

Ch La CARDONNE *First noted in May 1984 at a tasting I conducted in Bremen, and three more times that year. Soft fruit nose, very pleasant, easy, no great length. Spiciness noted on the nose, chewy — less skinny than some '81s.* Last tasted Jan 1985** For drinking now.

Ch CHASSE-SPLEEN *Several notes in the mid- to late 1980s. Initially deep and intense, now medium, rich, maturing. Pleasant enough nose and flavour. Medium weight though with crisp light style. Attractive.* Last tasted April 1990*** Drink now to 1996.

Dom de CHEVALIER *I found this spicy, scented and delightful in the spring of 1984. A year later noted as unaggressively Graves, a middle-distance wine, just a little meagre. Latterly, three notes: still deep and youthful-looking; curiously sweet, high-toned nose, vinous, scent of black treacle; medium dryness and weight, lovely rich flavour, fruit and texture. Slightly bitter tannic finish.* Last tasted Sept 1990***(*) Drink now to 2000+

Ch CISSAC *I have always had a soft spot for this rather hard wine. Dependably made, never overpriced. So: 14 notes at regular intervals from a rather dry, severe, unready bottle in Sept 1984. Still deep though maturing at the edges; good, straightforward, leather-tannic-Médoc nose; overall dry, fair body, good length for its class and year. A good 'food wine'.* Last tasted May 1989** Drink soon.

Ch COS D'ESTOURNEL *70% Cabernet Sauvignon, 30% Merlot; and 30% new oak used in 1981. A fragrant cask sample with lovely flavour at the de Luze tasting, April 1982. Evolving pleasingly through the mid-1980s. Michèle Prats reported a violent rainstorm during the harvest which caused some lack of concentration and charm, but otherwise an agreeable wine, maturing, gentle bouquet, cedary, some depth. Dryish, lightish, soft for an '81. An attractive drink.* Last noted Jan 1990*** Drink now to 2000.

Ch COUFRAN *Another favourite* bourgeois claret, *though the '81 not wholly satisfactory. Not as lean as some '81s, not as fleshy as the '82 or even the '79. Now fully mature; a curiously fudge-like, singed nose; fairly dry, reasonable body and texture. Unexciting.* Last tasted July 1988** Drink soon.

Ch CROIZET-BAGES *Two recent notes. Lively, maturing; crisp, fruity, piquant nose and flavour. Bouquet evolves well in glass.* Last tasted July 1990*** Drink now to 1996.

Ch La CROIX-TOULIFAUT *A* nouvelle vague *Pomerol. Many recent notes. Fairly deep; fragrant, high-tuned, like apple sauce; sweetish lovely texture, chewy fruit, touch of tarry tannin and rawness on finish. Attractive.* Last tasted June

*1991**(*) Drink now to 1998.*

Ch La DAUPHINE *A wine almost always as elegant as the château itself; a Fronsac trying hard to be a Pomerol. 65% Merlot, 35% Cabernet Franc. Six detailed notes in the mid- to late 1980s. Even in an unobvious vintage like '81 "good" appears in every note of colour, nose, palate. The Fronsac traits all in evidence: beautiful cherry red colour, wholesome fruit, firmness and good value. Fragrant, edge of honeycomb nose; dry, fullish, firm, fruity, good balance and length. Touch of bitter tannin on finish. Last tasted May 1988**(*) Probably ready now to 1998.*

Ch DUCRU-BEAUCAILLOU *Very austere cask sample, April 1982. Tasted ex-cask at the château that autumn: firm, good grip, tannic but not overladen. Several notes in 1987: soft, black cherry red; wholesome, harmonious nose that opened up with air; lean, by no means a heavyweight, refreshing fruit and acidity. An Englishman's claret, restrained. Last noted at a Wine & Food Society tasting of Ducru, Las-Cases and Gruaud-Larose, conducted in Boston, Oct 1987. Then*(**) Now probably**(*) Drink 1992–2000+*

Ch DUHART-MILON *Two recent notes: fairly deep, plummy; good bouquet; cedar, tea, honey; overall dry but with some flesh. Well made. Flavoury. Last tasted Sept 1990**(*) Drink now to 2000+*

Ch L'EVANGILE *Fairly deep but with mature rim; sweet nose, quite good fruit, forthcoming, stylish, though faded after an hour; distinct touch of sweetness on the palate, very distinctive rounded Pomerol style, with extract. Oaky aftertaste. Last tasted Sept 1989*** Now to 2000.*

Ch FIGEAC *Six notes since the mid-1980s. The first, stalky and hard, two with poor noses, one stalky and woody though very flavoury, the other corky — at the same tasting. Three better bottles: almost an '82 richness of colour developing a 'rusty' mature rim; fully evolved, forthcoming bouquet, rich, peppery, liquorice, tobacco; slightly sweet entry, very flavoury, dry, leathery, lightly tannic finish. Last tasted Sept 1990. At its best*** Drink soon.*

Les FORTS DE LATOUR *Deep, immature; full of fruit but unyielding. Massive, raw, with tannic acid finish. I don't see this coming round. For masochists. Last tasted Jan 1988(**)*

Clos FOURTET *Medium, mature; deep, slightly stewed, rather smelly, cheesy, nose; distinctly sweet on palate, soft, chocolaty fruit, a bit flat and tannic. Last tasted Sept 1990* Now to 1995.*

Ch La GAFFELIERE *Several recent notes: medium-deep, rich, mature appearance; warm, soft, fruity bouquet; touch of sweetness, nice weight, flavour and length. Crisp, fragrant, dry finish. Last tasted June 1991*** Now to 2000.*

Ch GAZIN *One of several cask samples presented by de Luze in April 1982. I thought it was delicious: a delicate, extraordinary, crystallised violets nose and sweet on palate. I had been beguiled by its youthful charm for by 1986, though good, it clearly needed time. Interestingly, I noted "violet scented" again in 1989 and good texture, fruit and grip in 1990. However, a magnum after seven years in a cool, damp English bond was developing slowly. Medium-deep, rich, misleadingly mature-looking; soft, cedar and iron nose; soft, fruity and fleshy on the palate too but with a dry tannic and iron finish. Not quite ready. Last tasted Oct 1990**(*) Possibly**** 1993–2000+*

Ch GRAND-PUY-LACOSTE *First tasted from the cask with the Bories, April 1982. Low-keyed, classic Pauillac, Cabernet Sauvignon aroma; dry, taut, austere. In 1988, though still quite youthful-looking, the nose had opened up, harmoniously; slowly coming out of its shell, flavoury but lean and still dry on the finish. Worth keeping and coaxing. Last tasted July 1988*(***) 1995–2010*

Ch La GRAVE TRIGANT DE BOISSET *First tasted with Jean-Pierre Mouiex in a very impressive line-up of '79 and '81 Pomerols in Sept 1982. Plummy and plump-looking in the mid-1980s, chewy and rich despite tannin. Later, lovely bouquet, slightly singed fruit; fairly sweet, good body, a curious, dry blackberry flavour. Softened as it warmed up. Paradoxically, I thought it tasted more like a Graves than a Pomerol. Last noted June 1988***(*) Now to 2000+*

Ch GRUAUD-LAROSE *Many notes from the mid- to late 1980s. Still fairly deep, intense, masses of fruit, rich, blackberry-like; surprisingly sweet, full-bodied, rich, chewy, chunky, soft and fleshy for an '81. Pronounced rusty and rustic aftertaste. Extremely good in its way. Last noted Feb 1991***(*) Now to 2010.*

Ch HAUT-BAILLY *Scented and spicy, in March 1984, still virtually opaque, spicy on the nose, with a crisp, very refreshing, flavour. Last tasted Oct 1989*** Now to 2000.*

*Ch d'*ISSAN *First noted in Dec 1982 at a* Vente aux Enchères de Vins de Bordeaux en Primeur *pre-sale tasting: a desultory wine event conducted in Paris with telephone links to Christie's. Its good fruit had by 1988 developed many facets: elegant, scented, Médoc-medicinal; surprisingly sweet, classy, with a lovely, firm, ascending flavour and good, soft tannin finish. Endorsed by two later notes. Still very deep in colour, fleshy for an '81. Very agreeable. Last tasted April 1989***(*) Now to 2000+*

Clos des JACOBINS *First tasted in 1986. Unexpectedly deep yet starting to mature. Next noted as a bit weak and plummy; unsettled nose, dumb, peppery, tight, whiffs of mint and fish; raw edge, tannin like rusty nails. A rather more generous note in 1987. Most recently, maturing, light fruit, lightish weight and style. A minor wine. Last tasted Dec 1988** Drink up.*

Ch KIRWAN *Noted at a Schröder & Schÿler tasting in London in May 1984: a bit hard; not bad. In 1989 still pink-tinged; low-keyed; straightforward but unexciting. Most recently, medium-pale, starting to show maturity; light fruity nose; surprisingly sweet entry, fairly lightweight, a bit pinched and lean. Not enough fruit or extract to balance the tannins. Last tasted Jan 1991** Drink up.*

Ch LAFON-ROCHET *Dry and lean at the best of times. The '81 very much so. Noted at a Christie's pre-sale tasting, Nov 1989**

Ch LAGRANGE *St-Julien. Four recent notes. Not very deep but pretty; slightly lactic and honeyed; distinctly sweet, lightish and easy on the palate.*

Refreshing acidity. Quite attractive. Last tasted Sept 1990** Drink now.

Ch La LAGUNE *Deep; whiff of camphor though fragrant; curious flavour, chunky and rough-textured cask sample, April 1982. Three recent notes. Still fairly deep, plummy red, mature; crisp, high-toned fruit on nose and palate. Volatile acidity, indicated by particular redness of colour, on nose and finish. But a plausibly attractive drink.* Last tasted July 1990** Drink up.

Ch LANESSAN *Deep chestnut red, lovely gradation; good straightforward claret smell, touch of iodine. Pleasant sweetness, weight, fruit, tannin and acidity.* Jan 1989**(*) Now to 2000.

Ch LASCOMBES *First tasted in cask, Aug 1982: impressively purple, very fragrant, good fruit. Then two notes in 1985: its pristine purple now a lively ruby; nose low-keyed, a bit hard, quite nice young jammy fruit; surprisingly sweet and gentle entry, lots of fruit, dry tannic finish. Slight but well formed. Most recently a stalky, horrid half.* Last tasted Nov 1990. At best*** Drink soon.

Ch LEOVILLE-BARTON *Deep, hard, firm but flavoury, in cask June and Sept 1982. Tasted again in March 1983 with Anthony Barton. Not the final blend. Marvellous depth and opacity; almost malty richness on nose and with a soft ripeness that reminded me, despite its tannin, of a '53 or '59. Perhaps it was its beguiling youthfulness, or the context, for in 1989 I found it low-keyed and austere. Most recently lean and unyielding.* Last tasted March 1991. Probably needs coaxing, and a little more time.

Ch LEOVILLE-LAS-CASES *First tasted, ex-cask, with M Delon, Sept 1982: intense purple, distinct St-Julien cedar on nose; medium weight, surprisingly delicate flavour. By 1985 the colour a beautiful ruby cherry, still intense, with youthful, crimson edge; a low-keyed, gentlemanly nose, calm and classic; good fruit, acidity, considerable charm but lacking punch. Restrained but pleasing, elegant but a dry, slightly 'green', finish in 1986, a couple of notes in 1987, one very detailed: classic cedar-pencil nose, complete, no harsh edges; nice quality, flavoury, refreshing, fleshier than Ducru, with a burst of fruit towards the back of the palate. Most recently still impressively deep; a bit of bottle-stink which cleared, good fruit on nose and palate, quite powerful. A good '81.* Last tasted July 1989**(**) Now to 2000+

Ch LEOVILLE-POYFERRE *Not very deep; spicy, Cabernet Sauvignon aroma; austere, citrus-like acidic finish at the de Luze cask sample tasting in April 1982. Opening up on the nose but lean, skinny and tinny in the mid-1980s though quite good crisp fruit noted later on. More recently, still immature but a bit weak; firm fruit on nose, evolving quite nicely. Seems to have sweetened up, though still with teeth-gripping tannin and acidity.* Last tasted July 1989*(*) I doubt if it will much improve.

Ch La LOUVIERE *Three detailed notes during the latter half of the 1980s. A soft red, maturing; consistently pleasing nose, sweet, soft fruit, harmonious; overall dry, agreeable fruit, rounded though short, with a rather austere tannic finish which should have simmered down a little by now.* Last tasted May 1988**(*) Say 1992–98.

Ch LYNCH-BAGES *A plethora of notes from very fragrant and flavoury cask samples, April 1982, and from the cask at the château that autumn. Qualified notes in the mid-1980s: not as impressive as its beautiful colour though some elegance and crisp fruit. Touch of bitterness. Lacking length. Seemed to pull out, soft fruit on the nose complementing the loss of colour and impending maturity. From the start, a sweet entry noted, medium-full body, very flavoury. Tannins now less abrasive.* Last tasted Oct 1988**(*) Should continue to develop and could, just, earn another star. Say 1992–2000.

Ch MAUCAILLOU *Many notes. Starting to mature in 1985, nice fruit, touch of tannic bitterness. Recently, attractive colour; curious fruit, strawberry, mint and iron, opening up, gentle, honeyed; nice weight. Dry, pleasant drink.* Last tasted June 1991**(*) Now to 1998.

Ch La MISSION-HAUT-BRION *First noted, March 1984 at a big tasting of '81 Graves prior to a charity wine auction at the Savoy Hotel: glorious fruit, Cabernet and eucalyptus; aggressive on palate. Lean, dry, sinewy at Desai's in 1985, identical notes in 1986 and 1988, though good fruit again observed. An austere, woody bottle in 1989 and, most recently, at Wolf's tasting: still fairly deep; sweet, rich mulberry-ripe fruit nose. (Jean Delmas noted "truffles"). Nice weight, good crisp flavour, citrus-like acidity and touch of tannic bitterness.* Last tasted June 1990**(*) Now to 2000+

Ch MONTROSE *Not tasted recently but a lovely smelling cask sample in April 1982. The other two notes made in April 1985. The first at a tasting conducted for Len Evans in Bulletin Place, Sydney, the other at the 'VIEW AUSTRALIA '85 Commemorative International Judging'. Pink-rimmed, for Montrose, and looking like an uncharacteristically early developer; nose low-keyed but harmonious; also, for Montrose, a light style, mild and easy-going.* Last tasted, wearing a clinically white jacket, in Melbourne, May 1985. Should be drinkable by now.

Ch MOUTON-BARONNE-PHILIPPE *As this is by no means a plump wine even in plump vintages, the '81 is understandably lean. Yet it has some flesh. Six notes in the mid-1980s. Quite deep in colour; fruit on the nose, but also sweaty tannins; overall dry, crisp, fruity.* Last tasted Aug 1987. Then totally unready but doubtless a little more evolved by now. Optimistically*(**) 1992–98

Ch NENIN *Translucent, silky, fragrant, a lightweight charmer with swingeingly tannic finish in 1985. Almost sickly sweet nose and taste, odd, short in 1989 — but it had a very dry cork. Most recently: fully evolved, sweet, slightly chocolaty nose; still fairly sweet on palate, flavoury, a bit edgy.* Last tasted Sept 1990** Drink soon.

Ch Les ORMES-DE-PEZ *Spicy, quite nice in cask. Evolving well. Very flavoury. Most recently: medium-deep, rich colour; medium dryness and weight. Soft yet with some grip.* Last tasted July 1988**(*) Now to 1998.

Ch PALMER *Fragrant and spicy, a quick developer, in Jan 1983. In 1985: ripe mulberry fruit — the*

Palmer hallmark. Sweet and fleshy on palate but not a big wine. Very agreeable. A nice swell of fruit in the mouth, reasonable length and a certain charm noted in 1986, attractive, fleshy, in 1987. Most recently: now maturing; forthcoming, sweet, almost jammy nose; attractive, flavoury, lightish, delicious now. Last tasted June 1991**** Now to 1998.

Ch PAPE-CLEMENT *Better flavour than nose: wood noted in 1984, slightly chalky cedar in 1989, a bit cardboardy recently. Touch of sweetness, easy, quite good flavour and length. Lean. Rather more acid than tannin.* Last tasted Dec 1990*(*) Drink soon.

Ch PAVIE *Fragrant cask sample in April 1982, and "fragrant" noted in two of the three most recent notes. Nice wine, lovely flavour, slightly sweet, silky, good fruit, length and aftertaste.* Last tasted Sept 1990*** Now to 1998.

Ch PHELAN-SEGUR *Some fruit, dry, lean, crisp, raw.* Last tasted Jan 1991**

Ch PICHON-LONGUEVILLE, BARON *Also noted at the de Luze cask sample tasting in London in April 1984: quite different from the Comtesse, more open, jammy on the nose, softer and shorter. Bouquet well developed; elegant. A year later rather 'green', raspberry-like fruit on nose, fairly high acidity; attractive; steady evolution. 10 consistent notes, all rating it attractive but lacking a bit of length. Acidity noticeable but it serves to bring out the flavour. Touch of sweetness on nose and palate.* Last tasted July 1990*** Now to 1998.

Ch PICHON-LONGUEVILLE, COMTESSE (previously LALANDE) *Deeper colour, more fragrant Cabernet Sauvignon on the nose than the Baron, with taut, spicy eucalyptus flavour and excellent aftertaste, April 1982. Six notes since. Ruby colour, like port, in the mid-1980s; high-toned, spicy nose; stylish but tannic. More recently: beginning to show some maturity; sweet, nicely evolved bouquet; lovely flavour and fruit, velvety tannin and acidity. A top '81.* Last tasted Sept 1990***(*) Now to 2000+

Ch PONTET-CANET *Two fairly recent notes. Deep; quite good, honeyed, spicy nose; soft, rich, fullish, nice fruit, good acidity.* Last tasted July 1989*** Now to 2000.

Ch PRIEURE-LICHINE *First tasted at the château in Sept 1983: more pink than purple, tight-knit and lean. By 1988 it had loosened up. A light, easy style of wine. Most recently: not very deep, now mature-looking; nose forthcoming, vanilla, a bit stalky at first but a jammy sort of fruit developed. A plausibly attractive flavour. Chaptalised fruit. Pleasant enough.* Last tasted July 1989** Drink soon.

Clos RENE *Two recent notes. Good colour and good fruit on nose and palate. Fullish; firm; tannic.* Last tasted Sept 1990*** Now to 2000.

Ch SIRAN *Surprisingly deep; dry, a bit medicinal but a good drink.* April 1990** Now to 1996.

Ch TALBOT *10 notes from 1985. Consistently deep colour. Also the consistently ripe farmyard smell typical of Talbot. Palate a contradictory mixture: soft, yet very tannic; rich; yet lean, flavoury. Earthy, iron, dry finish. I like this style of wine less and less; almost the antithesis of an understated gentlemanly St-Julien. It is, however, very popular.* Last tasted Feb 1989*(**) 1994–2000

Ch La TOUR-DE-MONS *Three fairly recent notes. An interesting funnel of scent, tea-like, very sweet, sweaty tannins; nice fruit; dry, a bit acidic.* Last tasted Jan 1991** Drink soon.

Ch La TOUR-DU-PIN-FIGEAC *Four recent notes. Fairly deep though mature; so-so nose, chaptalised. One bottle woody. Light easy style. Short.* Last tasted Jan 1991* Drink up.

OTHER '81s LAST TASTED IN THE MID-1980s, PLUS ONE-OFF NOTES OF MINOR WINES:

*L'*AMIRAL DE BEYCHEVELLE *2ème vin. Nice flesh. Very attractive.* 1987

Ch BEAUMONT *Good for its class and the vintage. Ready.* 1985

Ch BEAU SEJOUR BECOT *Several notes. Good in cask. Good nose; fullish, fleshy, attractive.* 1985

Ch BELGRAVE *Quite nice fruit.* 1986

Ch BEL-ORME *Nicely put together, lean, stylish.* 1986

Ch CITRAN *Spicy, fleshy, firm, tannic.* 1984

Ch CLARKE *Gloriously deep colour; good fruit; nice flesh, very tannic, attractive.* 1987

Ch COS LABORY *Using new oak, for this vintage. Quite nice fruit; taut; flavoury. Fragrant aftertaste.* 1984

Ch COUVENT-DES-JACOBINS *Honeyed, vinous nose; silky yet lean. Touch of liquorice. Long, rather hard finish.* 1986

Ch DAUZAC *Not very deep; crisp fruit; stylish, nice texture, easy.* 1986

Ch L'EGLISE-CLINET *Deep; big wine, good fruit. Delightful.* 1985

Ch de FIEUZAL *Sweet, chocolate and spice; dry, good fruit, tannic.* 1984

Ch La FLEUR-PETRUS *Although only tasted in cask, an important wine, sweet, attractive, an early developer.* 1982

Ch FOURCAS-DUPRE *Attractively sweet and fruity on the nose but dry, lean and a bit stingy on the palate.* 1988

Ch GISCOURS *Intense Cabernet aroma; very sweet, full, rich, chunky.* 1986

Ch GRAND-BARRAIL-LAMARZELLE-FIGEAC *Not as grand as its name. Nondescript colour, tailing off; jammy nose and endtaste. Bitter, like aspirin.* 1980

Ch GRAND-PONTET *Sweet, nice fruit, easy style.* 1985

Ch GRESSIER-GRAND-POUJEAUX *Sweaty saddle nose; dry, tannic, fullish, raw.* 1987

Ch HAUT-BAGES-AVEROUS *Stalky in cask, but turned out delightfully.* 1985

Ch HAUT-BATAILLEY *"Charm and fruit" plus remarkable aftertaste noted in cask in the autumn of 1982 and New Year 1983. Hope to try it again.* 1983

Ch de LAMARQUE *Good depth; blackcurrant aroma; pleasing if a little severe.* 1985

Ch LAROSE-TRINTAUDON *Medicinal, hen-coop nose and aftertaste but soft on the palate, nice fruit, dry finish.* 1989

Ch LATOUR-POMEROL *Immensely impressive.* 1982

Ch MALARTIC-LAGRAVIERE *Very attractive.* 1984

Ch MALESCOT ST-EXUPERY *Palish, piquant, flavoury, tannic.* 1986

Ch de MARBUZET *High percentage of Merlot (56%) for*

St-Estèphe. Quite nice fruit. Citrus-like acidity. A bit austere. 1987

Ch MARQUIS D'ALESME-BECKER *Opaque, still immature-looking; dumb, still peppery; an uncompromising dry, big, mouthfilling wine. 1988*

Ch MEYNEY *Cordier-style fruit, raw, tannic, but not bad. 1988*

Ch PALMIER *Not to be confused with Palmer. Fleshy, fullish, agreeable. 1987*

PAVILLON ROUGE DE CH MARGAUX *Good depth of colour; fishy Cabernet aroma, fragrant; nice flesh, crisp fruit, preferred to the* grand vin. *1987*

Ch PETIT-VILLAGE *Sweet, ripe, rustic nose; chewy, chunky, touch of iron on finish. 1986*

Ch de PEZ *Beautiful colour; fragrant, mouthwatering nose; assertive, peppery, good though raw fruit. Rather coarse textured. 1988*

Ch PIBRAN *Low-keyed, dry, lean, touch of tangerine-like acidity. 1989*

Ch Le PIN *Opaque; medicinal nose, developed nicely, lovely flavour though bitter tannins which should now have ameliorated. 1984*

Ch La POINTE *Good fleshy Pomerol nose; full of fruit and tannin. 1985*

Ch POTENSAC *Flattering notes in New York, Feb 1986. Three months later, tasted at the château: deeper than the '83; peppery and closed at first but opened up a little in the glass. Dry; a bit raw; very tannic. 1986*

Ch RAUSAN-SEGLA *Small fruity nose; mouthdrying tannins, low-keyed, shallow, even, but flavoury enough and should make a decent restaurant wine. 1986*

Ch La RIVIERE *Very deep colour; muffled mulberry nose; dry, fullish, but neutral. 1989*

Ch ST-PIERRE-SEVAISTRE *Impressively deep; sweaty, leathery smell like a '79. Plummy, chewy, masculine, no finesse or elegance but agreeable enough. 1985*

Ch La TOUR-CARNET *Richly coloured; curious fruit on the nose; dry, firm, quite nice flavour and texture. 1986*

Ch La TOUR-HAUT-BRION *Ruby; good though tannic nose; medium dryness and weight; flavoury. 1986*

Ch TROTANOY *Impressive. Long life predicted. 1982*

Ch VERDIGNAN *Dry, lightweight luncheon wine; raw tannins, fruity but hollow. 1987*

VIEUX CH CERTAN *Rich, maturing; high-toned and a bit stalky on nose and palate. Fullish, nice flesh but, somehow, hollow. 1987*

Ch La VIOLETTE *Palish, very mature; rather overblown, chocolaty, chaptalised. Light and easy. 1988*

1982★★★★★

A vintage of great proportions and equally great importance. It has been described, with some accuracy, as more like a California Cabernet Sauvignon than claret. It was first met with overpraise, then worries about whether wines so sweet, so full of fruit and thus so drinkable have a long future; worries that the very high tannin content which makes that future possible will dominate as the fruit fades, leaving it high and dry.

The harvest was very big, the grapes unusually ripe. After a mild, frostless, dry spring, flowering took place early and in excellent conditions, at which stage an early harvest and a large crop could be predicted. July was hot. Towards the end of that month there was some light rain which continued intermittently through a cooler but fine Aug followed by a particularly hot, dry Sept, which accelerated the ripening and resulted in one of the earliest harvests in recent years. It is, however, a mistake to think that the exceedingly hot dry weather continued throughout the Bordeaux harvest. The Merlot was, as usual, the first to be picked, in Pomerol and St-Emilion from around Sept 9 in conditions of great heat outside and in the *cuves*. The Cabernet Sauvignon was picked, in the bigger Médoc vineyards at any rate, over the second two weeks of Sept in very pleasant but by no means subtropical heat.

A particularly useful tasting of right bank '82s was given by Robert Paul, a distinguished Miami lawyer with an extensive private cellar, in Feb 1989. 35 guests including the proprietors of Châteaux Ausone, Canon, Figeac, Gazin and Pavie, attended an all-weekend event, tasting 48 Pomerols in four sessions on the Saturday and 47 St-Emilions on the Sunday. Interestingly there was little evidence of problems arising out of the hot vintage conditions. Most recently at a tasting of '82 (against '83) Margaux organised by *Wine* magazine. These occasions are invaluable for putting quality, condition and development into perspective.

Ch LAFITE *First tasted in 1985. It was a good cherry red but not as deep as Margaux or Latour; a nose of great depth and immediately forthcoming on the palate. Mouthfilling flavour, a long, hard, tannic finish and notably good aftertaste. Looking over eight notes since then, intensity of colour is a feature, the rim changing from its pristine purple to a softer, starting-to-mature red after about five years in bottle. At the same time its bouquet has been gathering momentum. On the last two occasions, at tastings conducted in Tokyo six months apart, the nose has been surprisingly forthcoming, sweet, with lovely strawberry-like fruit, then spice (cinnamon), harmonious, fragrant, lingering. On the palate a soft, rich entry (a feature of all wines made from very ripe grapes, and high in alcohol, a combination associated more with the top California Cabernets). Fairly full-bodied yet with a feminine style. Lovely middle palate, good length, tannin high but well masked by fruit and extract. A fine wine.* Last tasted Nov 1989**(***) *Should reach its plateau of maturity shortly after the turn of the century. A long life predicted.*

Ch MARGAUX *11 notes. The* grand vin *first tasted in cask, May 1983: quite opaque with vivid, purple rim; very sweet, fleshy nose, but on the palate that flesh overwhelmed by the tannins. Tasted again in* *cask in Sept 1984, two months before it was due to be bottled: a ripe, mulberry richness of fruit, fabulously mouthfilling. Showing magnificently in Chicago in 1985. Although dumb and dusty on the nose at first, it developed richly at Bipin Desai's Margaux tasting in 1987 and had a beguiling softness on the palate despite its tannin content. At the Shibata tasting in Tokyo in 1989, it was the least mature-looking of the first growths and certainly immature on palate. But the nose was minty, peppery with high alcohol, leathery with tannin, yet with the scent of Cabernet Sauvignon which opened up in the glass and continued to churn out endlessly. A crisp Cabernet flavour, lovely structure and balance but quite unready. Recently, tasted blind amongst a range of '82 and '83 Margaux district wines, I rated the '82 Ch Margaux outstandingly the best; better even than the usually higher-rated '83. Bouquet of coffee, allspice. Sweet, velvety, great depth. Last tasted Aug 1990*(****) Keep. It would seem premature to start drinking it before 2000. I foresee it at its best between 2010 and 2030.*

Ch LATOUR *Many notes. First tasted at the château at the time of bottling in Sept 1984: predictably opaque, nose dumb, massively tannic. Showing well at the Schaefer/Christie's tasting in 1985: glorious nose, marvellous vinosity yet peppery and tannic. A huge, fleshy wine, sweet, fruit, great length. By spring 1989, at the Frericks/Wodarz Mouton and Latour tasting, though deep, the colour was more evolved than the Mouton. High-toned, cedary nose, good fruit, opened up well. A big chunky wine, touch of iron on its austere finish. Most recently, still very deep and intense, with black cherry colour but starting to mature at the rim; well knit. Loaded with fruit, like a harvest festival; sweet, mouthfilling but somehow lacking charm and finesse. Tannic. Last tasted Dec 1990(*****) 2010–2040*

Ch MOUTON-ROTHSCHILD *Nine notes from 1985. A magnificent wine. Full marks at Flatt's Mouton tasting in April 1986: wonderful intensity of colour, glorious depth of nose; sweet, full, rich, plump — ripe flesh, Rubensian — mulberry-like Cabernet Sauvignon taste. But a slightly metallic, very tannic element holding it in check. Still very deep, with '82 thickness of colour, bramble-like nose, spice, alcohol; a huge mouthful, dry, fragrant aftertaste. Needs time in bottle, decanter and glass. Last noted at the Frericks/Wodarz tasting, March 1989(*****) 2010–2030, or thereabouts.*

Ch HAUT-BRION *Totally different* cépages *from first-growth Médocs: more or less 50:50 Cabernet and Merlot. Ten notes. First tasted in cask, rather hastily, with the Duc de Mouchy and Jean Delmas in May 1983. Impressively deep. Fleshy. Again in Sept when I was informed that the highest-ever tannin content at Haut-Brion had been recorded. Cigar-box nose, very tannic/iron on palate. It was bottled in Nov 1984. Though still intensely purple, the wine had developed well after only two years in bottle: glorious mulberry-ripe fruit and new oak spice; rich, powerful. The characteristic warm tile, tobacco flavour, noted in 1986. By the summer of 1989 the colour was changing: softer, more plummy. Distinctly sweet nose, coffee, chocolate, cedar and iodine, opening up, rich biscuity. Very distinctive Haut-Brion red Graves flavour reminiscent of autumn leaves. Still deep; harmonious; sweet entry, full, alcoholic, ripe, velvety yet very tannic. Last tasted March 1991**(***) 1997–2025*

Ch AUSONE *(50% Cabernet Franc, 50% Merlot). A totally different ballgame in St-Emilion in 1982. Great heat, grapes enormously high in sugar, low in acidity. It was reported in* The Wine Spectator *that Pascal Delbeck, the winemaker who had done so much to achieve the renaissance at Ausone, had added a "tiny" amount of tartaric acid after the acid in the wine had "collapsed". I first tasted it in cask in May 1983. It seemed firm, with good flavour, length and finish. In the autumn of 1986 I thought it had a rather spongy, earthy, character. Next, in 1987, at Flatt's Ausone tasting, it was medium-deep, a lively ruby cherry colour; rather low-keyed at first but quite nice fruit opening up on the nose. A big, flavoury wine but not as thick, as high in extract, as I expected. Most recently, plummy-coloured, still somewhat immature-looking; the bouquet herbaceous, scented, spicy; on the palate, a very idiosyncratic character and taste conjuring up dry bracken and tobacco. Frankly not my type of wine. Last noted at Robert Paul's extensive tasting of 1982 St-Emilions, Feb 1989(***) For fans of Ausone drink 1995 — ?*

Ch CHEVAL-BLANC *(60% Cabernet Franc; 34% Merlot; 1% Cabernet Sauvignon; 5% Malbec). First tasted in cask, with Jacques Hébrard, in May 1983. A broad, spicy, toasted nose and taste, good length and aftertaste. Next, at the Schaefer/Christie's tasting in May 1985. A sweet, slightly caramelly, gingery nose. A charmer, fragrant, spicy, cloves and cinnamon, not remotely a heavyweight, lovely aftertaste. Later that autumn a gloriously aromatic magnum, fabulous flavour, tannic of course. Full marks at Robert Paul's tasting of '82s in Feb 1989: very sweet, well rounded. In Tokyo it was slightly deeper than Haut-Brion but a similar colour, with lovely gradation and long romanesque-arch legs; a soft, fragrant, harmonious bouquet; sweet, soft; very pleasant weight, too good to spit out. Lovely wine. Last tasted June 1989****(*) Drink now to 2020.*

Ch PETRUS *First tasted blind, at the Simi Winery in Sonoma in June 1985 alongside their 'regular' Cabernet Sauvignon. I rated Pétrus half a point higher than the Simi but well below Mouton '82. The following spring, in magnum, at Frericks' vertical. Deep. Long legs. Citrus-like nose that developed gloriously. Fleshy, great depth of fruit, complete but hard. The last of my half-dozen notes made at the 'Stockholm' Group tasting: deep, rich, intense, maturing; nose a bit dusty, minty; also a bit woody, lacking the 95% Merlot flesh of previous bottles. Silky leathery texture, very tannic. An impressive mouthful but lacking the elegance of Cheval-Blanc and the, frankly, more interesting first-growth Médocs. Needs plenty of time. Last tasted April 1990(****)? 2000+*

Ch BATAILLEY *Plummy-coloured; slightly sweet, medium-full body, rich, chunky, delicious. An* *early developer. Sept 1987**(*) Now to 2000.*

Ch BEYCHEVELLE *First tasted in cask, May 1983: opaque, fragrant, lovely texture. In June 1987 at the annual Fête de la Fleur, presided over by HRH The Duke and Duchess of York. Now beginning to show some maturity; developing extraordinary fruitiness on nose and palate, yet dry, crisp, a bit medicinal, fleshy, tannic. In an in-between state like some other Médocs. Last tasted March 1991**(*)? Hard to say when this will be at its best. Beyond 2000.*

Ch BOYD-CANTENAC *Chunky, raw in cask. Still fairly deep; very attractive rich roasted coffee bouquet; fairly full, chunky, fruity, good tannic finish. Last tasted Aug 1990**(*) Now to 2010.*

Ch BRANAIRE-DUCRU *Soft, stylish and appealing even after one year in cask. Still deep and rich in appearance; lovely bouquet; sweet, charming though tannic. Last tasted Nov 1988**(*) Now to 2000.*

Ch BRANE-CANTENAC *Lively-looking, the usual farmyard whiff, some softness and flesh — it seemed a bit too open and soft after a year in cask. Also seemed an early developer, despite tannin, in 1986. Five notes since: taking on a mature orange-tinged rim, a dusty roasted coffee nose, rich in its way. Quite a full, fleshy, flavoury mouthful though still tannic. Frankly, I can never make up my mind about Brane-Cantenac. Last tasted June 1991**(*) Now to 2000. Very much a personal choice.*

Ch CALON-SEGUR *First tasted in cask, May 1983: surprisingly forthcoming nose though sweaty and cheesy with tannin; chunky, rich. Six months later, a honeyed quality. A good Calon. Fairly concentrated fruit, rich, chewy after three years in bottle. More recently still almost opaque, with black cherry centre and attractive, translucent gradation; vinous, cedar and vanilla nose, yet still a bit hard and unyielding. Good fruit and silky leathery tannins. Very dry finish. Last noted at a tasting conducted for a new branch of the Wine & Food Society, Santa Domingo, Feb 1989*(***) 1995–2020*

Ch de CAMENSAC *Unknit and raw after a year in cask. A rather common Rhône-like nose, but quite good fruit noted in the late 1980s. Most recently, deep but maturing, a rather 'cool' nose; touch of sweetness, medium weight, nice and easy, some tannin. Not really up to classed-growth standard. Last tasted May 1990** Now to 1995.*

Ch CANON *Six notes. First tasted in cask, May 1983: opaque, intense; a dumb, tight-knit nose, yet a full, soft, lovely flavour — ripe mulberries and spice. Starting to evolve in the mid-1980s, a low-keyed but self-assured wine, not spectacular at first sniff but full of fruit and flesh. Tannic. Still deep, very rich-looking, starting to mature; an unusual, very original, rich, pear-like fragrance of great depth; slightly sweet, full in the mouth, rich, rounded. Last tasted Feb 1989**(**) I am tempted to add another star. 1995–2030*

Ch CANTEMERLE *Tasted from the cask with the Maître de Chai in Sept 1983. The wine had marvellous intensity and fruit, sweaty with tannin, prune-like. Notable richness and length. A couple of months later, similar, then not seen for another five years. Sweet, meaty, vanilla, harmonious nose, no harsh edges; rich and chewy. Good wine. Last tasted July 1988**(**) Now to 2010.*

Ch CANTENAC-BROWN *First noted at a de Luze tasting in May 1983. It was the palest and least impressive of 20 '82s, seemed empty and had a beery finish. Now palish, mature; a forthcoming, sweet, quite appealing bouquet with the chocolaty character noted in the original sample, which is a characteristic of the château. By no means a hefty '82, with slightly tinny, rather severe tannic finish. Last tasted Aug 1990*(*) Not a top '82. Drink now to 1996.*

Ch CAPBERN-GASQUETON *Formerly known just as Capbern. Three notes in the mid-1980s. Deep, youthful; nice fruit on nose and palate. Last tasted June 1987*(**) Say 1995–2010.*

Ch CERTAN-DE-MAY *Showing well at the Paul tasting. More recently, deep, velvety; good fruit, fleshy, full-bodied. Slightly bitter tannins ameliorated by mouthfuls of boeuf Wellington. At a Bordeaux Club dinner, Aug 1990**(**) 1995–2015*

Ch CHASSE-SPLEEN *Consistently one of the best-made* bourgeois *Médocs. Several notes, all good. Excellent component parts, well assembled. Beef and flesh and fruit. Though tannic, a good drink. Give it air. Last tasted Aug 1988***(*) Now to 2000.*

Dom de CHEVALIER *Extraordinarily fleshy and fruity on nose, developing sweet, cinnamon spiciness; flavour to match. Full, almost fat for Chevalier. Very dry finish. Last tasted June 1988*(***) 1995–2020*

Ch CISSAC *Another reliable and always reasonably priced* cru bourgeois exceptionnel. *First tasted in cask: intense, oaky, lovely style. Still deep, harmonious though tannic nose; slightly sweet, full, fleshy. Last tasted Jan 1988**(*) Now to 2010.*

CONNETABLE TALBOT *The second wine of Cordier's* cru classé *of that name. One of the reassuring aspects of the 1980s is the number of second wines, evidence of greater selection; the best* cuves *being kept for the* grand vin, *in this case Ch Talbot. The wines made from younger vine stocks, relegated to the second division, are usually good and always good value. Brick red, sweet, biscuity, almost jammy nose; very tannic, fruit and extract, a bit austere. Needs food. Jan 1988(**) 1993–98*

Ch La CONSEILLANTE *Has been making magnificent wines for years, long before the Mouiex family started to make their name synonymous with Pomerol. Extremely high marks at Bob Paul's tasting in 1989, notably for its fine fragrance and wonderful flavour, length and aftertaste. Now maturing nicely, a sweet, soft, lovely wine. Last tasted Sept 1990***(**) Now to 2010.*

Ch COS D'ESTOURNEL *First noted at the de Luze tasting in May 1983: totally different from Montrose and Calon on the nose, and almost alarmingly easy to taste despite its youth. Similar notes vis à vis Montrose six months later. However, once in bottle it tightened up, but still had a distinctive bouquet. Described as firm, lean and taut in 1985; a classic, cedary nose, developing through 1986; fragrance in 1988. Most recently at a Cos tasting conducted by Michèle Prats: still fairly deep with characteristic '82 thickness, extract, tarry nose; sweet, full-bodied, rich, rather bitter tannins, better with food. Last* *noted Jan 1990**(**) 1995–2010*

Ch COUFRAN *Mialhe family. Untypically, for a* bourgeois *St-Estèphe, almost 90% Merlot. Most recently, noting an unusual light, crystalline, crusty sediment, rich ruby yet maturing in colour. Fullish body, chewy, chunky. Last tasted June 1991**(*) 1992–2010*

Ch CROIZET-BAGES *First noted, in cask, Nov 1983. Impressed by its fruit and flavour in 1986. Most recently a rich deep colour; sweet, mulberry-ripe Cabernet Sauvignon nose; fairly sweet on the palate, full-bodied, spicy tannin, new oak — cloves and cinnamon. Packed with fruit, drinking well. Last tasted June 1989***(*) Now to beyond 2000.*

Ch La DAUPHINE *Particularly good in this vintage. Fleshy, harmonious, mouthfilling, high alcohol, still tannic. Oct 1985***(*) Probably drinking well now to 2000.*

Ch DAUZAC *Two very good notes in 1986: soft, fleshy, well clad. Now maturing, losing its puppy fat. Nice wine. Last tasted blind (at* Wine *magazine), Aug 1990**(*) Drink now to 2000.*

Ch DESMIRAIL *An infrequently seen third growth, first tasted in cask, Nov 1983: not very deep; raw and stalky, though soft and flavoury on palate. Most recently, tasted blind, now palish and fully mature-looking, nose sweetened up, quite fragrant. Dryish, lean, citrus-like acidity. Quite attractive. Last tasted Aug 1990** Drink soon.*

Ch DUCRU-BEAUCAILLOU *Visited the château on Sept 21, six days after picking had started. The Merlot had a tremendously high must weight, according to Jean-Eugène Borie as high as the '47. First tasted as a cask sample in May 1983. Deep, intense, good length and uplift. Next, showing well at the Christie's/Schaefer tasting of '82s in 1985. It had a beautiful cedar vanillin nose, tannin clothed with flesh, great potential. Several good notes since, the last made at Xavier Borie's presentation at a Hollywood Wine Seminar: although losing its pristine depth, still immature-looking; very harmonious, vanilla bouquet; sweet and fairly full-bodied for Ducru, rich chunky fruit, mouthdrying tannins. Last tasted Feb 1989**(**) 1995–2020*

Ch DUHART-MILON *Sweet, cheesy, chunky, tannic. Jan 1989**(*) Now to 2000.*

Ch DURFORT-VIVENS *One of the less distinguished second growths. First tasted, in cask, Nov 1983: not very deep, jammy, loose-knit. Quite a pretty colour, silky textured but weak ending in 1985. A better note at a British Airways tasting in May 1990, attractive but something lacking. Most recently, at* Wine *magazine's blind tasting of '82 and '83 Margaux. Palish, open, a bit weak-kneed. Last noted Aug 1990** Drink soon.*

Ch L'EVANGILE *Showing extremely well at Bob Paul's tasting of '82s, Feb 1989. Still opaque, intense; dense but fragrant, scented, opened up beautifully; rich, massive, silky tannins, good length, dry finish. Last noted at Spencer House tasting, May 1991***(**) 1992–2010*

Ch FERRIERE *Palish, fully mature, weak-rimmed; well-developed bouquet, fragrant; lean, firm, quite good length, tannic. Tasted Aug 1990*(*) Drink soon before the fruit fades leaving the tannin high and dry.*

Ch FIGEAC *One of the best of all the de Luze cask samples presented in May 1983. The unusually high proportion, for St-Emilion, of Cabernet Sauvignon noted then and since. Very distinctive style. Glorious nose and almost exaggerated flavour noted in 1988, and two similar notes in Feb 1989. Extremely high marks at Bob Paul's tasting, and at Desai's tasting that Dec. Most recently: limpid red; intense berry-like aroma, very fragrant, appealing, plausible, touch of caramel and liquorice; new oak spiciness almost too obtrusive, sweet, rich, rounded, yet lots of grip. Silky, crisp tannic finish. An exciting wine. Last noted Feb 1991***(*) Possibly**** Drink now to 2010.*

Ch La FLEUR *St-Emilion. An easy, quite attractive wine. Three notes in 1987** Drink soon.*

Ch La FLEUR-PETRUS *Always top class. Impressively deep; sweet, rich, fragrant, chocolate and violets. Evolved perfectly in the glass; an unusual Spanish-root flavour that swelled in the mouth, silky, dry tannic finish. Just a little stalky and severe. At Robert Paul's, Feb 1989**(**) 1992–2000+*

Ch FOMBRAUGE *Relatively minor, reliably made, reasonably priced St-Emilion. Several notes. Nice weight, fleshy, tannic. Last noted pre-sale, Nov 1989*(*) Drink soon.*

Ch GISCOURS *Though not very deep, intensely fragrant and spicy in cask. Now sweet on nose and palate. Good rich ripe fruit, tannin and acidity. Very attractive. Last tasted June 1991***(*) Now to 2010.*

Ch GLORIA *Two notes in the mid-1980s. Good fruit, very flavoury, tannic. Last tasted Sept 1987**(*) Now to 2000.*

Ch GRAND-PUY-DUCASSE *Also tasted only in the mid-1980s. Very deep; fairly full-bodied, fleshy, soft yet very tannic. Last tasted March 1987*(*) 1995–2000*

Ch GRAND-PUY-LACOSTE *Impressive cask sample in May 1983. Opaque, very fragrant. The clove-like spiciness of new oak noted later that autumn. A slow developer. Two recent notes: intensity the keynote, of appearance, nose and taste. Deep blackcurrant colour and aroma. Marvellously crisp fruit. Complete. Still tannic. Last tasted Feb 1989*(***) 1995–2020*

Ch GRUAUD-LAROSE *In cask in 1983, sweet, packed with fruit and tannin. Still immensely deep in the mid-1980s, flesh and fruit contained and dominated by high alcohol and tannin. Several recent notes, still intense, plummy, immature; gloriously rich, fruit, tarry, medicinal; sweet, full flavoured, chewy, rich, pronounced though silky tannins. Needs time. Last tasted May 1990*(***) 1995–2015*

Ch HAUT-BAILLY *Several recent notes. Medium-deep, maturing; distinctive, rich, earthy; sweet, tobacco, tannic. Last tasted April 1991***(*) Now to 2000.*

Ch HAUT-BATAILLEY *Cask sample in May and tasted in cask, Nov 1983. Not very clear-cut, a bit raw, disappointing. Recently tasted alongside the other Borie châteaux, Ducru and Grand-Puy-Lacoste. Paler and leaner than both, more evolved in colour and on nose, stylish but still a little disappointing. Last noted Feb 1989★★(★) Now to 1996.*

Ch d'ISSAN *Almost completely replanted in 1945 when the Cruse family bought the property. Now 33 ha of vines. 12 new stainless steel tanks installed in the early 1980s and some stylish wines being made. The '82 was first tasted in Sept 1983 just after* soutirage *(it was explained that this was like a man who after taking 'the waters', is leaner but fitter!): a note of prunes and walnuts. Spicy. Stylish. Lovely fruit noted in 1988. Most recently medium colour, mature; rich, very sweet, coffee-like nose; very pleasant crisp citrus flavour, goodish length and tannic. Last tasted June 1991★★(★) Say 1992–98.*

Ch KIRWAN *First tasted in 1985. More fat and flesh than usual. Two more recent notes. Losing colour; very sweet, roasted coffee beans and caramel bouquet and flavour. Thick '82 texture. Curious soft yet dry tannic finish. Last tasted Aug 1990★★(★) Now to 2000+*

Ch LABEGORCE-ZEDE *Good rich colour; rich, nice firm fruit, very tannic. Last tasted Aug 1990★★(★) 1995–2000*

Ch LAFON-ROCHET *Leathery, firm, fruity in cask. Still very deep and immature-looking four years later. Glorious Cabernet Sauvignon, bilberry-like nose; dry, very tannic, lean for an '82. ★(★★) 1995–2010*

Ch LAGRANGE *St-Julien. Two recent notes: intensely deep, just starting to show maturity; low-keyed at first, packed with fruit, developed fragrance; slightly sweet, fairly full-bodied, Spanish-root flavour; silky tannins. Last tasted May 1990★★(★) 1992–2000+*

Ch La LAGUNE *Masses of notes, from cask sample, May 1983 and twice in cask that Sept. At that stage the wine was fairly predictably opaque; spicy from the new oak; full of fruit. An exciting wine at a tasting in June 1985 of '82 classed growths: gorgeous nose, fruity and spicy. One recent resinous bottle. Now plummily deep; a fabulous rich vegetal bouquet; very sweet for a Médoc, flavoury. Still spicy, good fruit. Last tasted June 1991★★★(★) Now to 2000.*

Ch LANESSAN *Three good notes. Deep, good fruit, delicious. Last tasted March 1989★★★ Now to 2000.*

Ch LANGOA-BARTON *First tasted with Anthony Barton in Sept 1983. Opaque, dumb, more flesh than usual. Still deep, rich; rich, fragrant, tannic nose; on the dry side, nice weight, chunky fruit. Last tasted June 1991★★(★) 1993–2010*

Ch LASCOMBES *First tasted at the château in 1985. I was enormously impressed. Full of mulberry-ripe fruit, fleshy yet loaded with tannin, extract, alcohol. Most recently: medium, fully mature; whiff of coffee, with fruit on the nose; still a touch of sweetness, pleasing weight, nice citrus-like fruit, flavour and finish. Good tannin and acidity. Last tasted June 1991★★★(★) Now to 2010.*

Ch LEOVILLE-BARTON *Three notes from autumn 1983, first tasted alongside the '82 Langoa, at the château. More peppery, quite different. Lovely flesh, flavour and length, though a lean touch and very tannic. Similar notes through the mid-1980s. Still a fine deep colour, a jewel-like ruby; classic cedar nose, very pleasing, no harsh edges though a bit unyielding. Dry. A bit straight-laced but nice fruit and texture. Leaves fragrance in the mouth. Last tasted Sept 1990★★(★★) 1995–2015*

Ch LEOVILLE-LAS-CASES *A sample from Vat 8, at eight days old, was vividly purple, smelling of fruit, alcohol, bananas and acetone — very high acidity. A year later, still opaque, intense. Extra dimensions on nose. Classic. Tannic. Three detailed notes in the mid-1980s. Most recently: deep but just starting to mature; nose rather unyielding, all the component parts still waiting to combine. High alcohol content, tannic, but with a lovely burst of fruit mid-palate. Long life ahead. Last tasted Oct 1987★★(★★) Possibly★★★★★ in due course: say 1995–2020.*

Ch LEOVILLE-POYFERRE *First noted at the de Luze cask sample tasting in May 1983. Quite nice fruit but lacking depth. That Sept I thought it quite good but lacking, though subsequent notes have been fairly complimentary. Still intensely deep; rather medicinal, tannic and slightly stalky nose; fairly dry, fullish, quite a lot of fruit. Last tasted May 1991★(★★) 1995–2005*

Ch La LOUVIERE *Graves. Noted at a vertical tasting at the château in 1987. Sweet nose, like new leather. Chunky. Fruity. Tannic. Very good. More recently, deep but maturing, rather a 'woolly' nose; Pomerol-like, silky, tannic texture. Last tasted April 1989★★(★) Now to 2000.*

Ch LYNCH-BAGES *10 notes, from an attractive, fruity cask sample in May 1983. Remarkable for its very distinctive bouquet: medicinal, oyster shells, peppery, much fruit, touch of vanilla, all combining to blossom in the glass. Soft and fleshy from the start despite the '82 tannins. Loads of fruit, extract. Chunky, touch of iodine. A very good mouthful. Last tasted Sept 1990★★(★★) Now to 2010.*

Ch MALESCOT-ST-EXUPERY *First tasted Nov 1983. Nice fruity wine. Most recently from an* impériale *at Rodenstock's Malescot tasting: deep, plummy; peppery at first. Opened up after 10 minutes, and after 20 minutes rich, almost pungent fruit. 10 minutes later a complete change. A mouthfilling, spicy, tannic wine with good extract, drinking well. Last noted Sept 1990★★(★★) 1992–2010*

Clos du MARQUIS *The second wine of Léoville-Las-Cases and, not surprisingly, better than many a classed-growth* grand vin: *very deep, attractive bramble-like fruit. Full-flavoured, chewy, tannic. Last tasted May 1988★★(★) Now to 2000.*

Ch MARQUIS D'ALESME *Very sweet, rich, tannic nose; full-bodied, good fruit, citrus touch, fair length. Aug 1990★★(★) 1993–2000*

Ch MARQUIS-DE-TERME *Hard, almost stalky but fragrant. Dry, lean, crisp fruit and tannic. Aug 1990★(★) 1993–2000*

Ch La MISSION-HAUT-BRION *Eight notes. First tasted Sept 1984, two months after bottling. Meaty, mouthfilling. Showing well at Desai's tasting the following year: chewy, fleshy, marvellous tannin and acidity. Subsequent notes remark on its lovely texture, flesh, length. At a tasting in 1987, preferred it to Haut-Brion. A lovely colour, still fairly deep, rich, maturing; sweet nose, low-keyed at first. After an hour* *reminded me of fresh walnuts. Medium dry, fairly full-bodied, good extract, fruit, loads of tannin. Fine wine with good future.* Last noted at Wolf's tasting, June 1990***(**) 1992–2020

Ch MONTROSE *Showing well, predictably tannic, at the de Luze tasting in May 1983, also in Sept, at Tastet & Lawton's in Bordeaux, a good, rich, fleshy, freshly drawn cask sample. Bouquet developing well in the mid-1980s, with lots of flavour, fruit, grip. Most recently, still deep but maturing; attractive harmonious bouquet and flavour. Unusually 'sweet' for Montrose, nice texture, slightly astringent finish.* Last tasted May 1990*(****) 1995 or, if you can wait, to 2030.

Ch Les ORMES-DE-PEZ *Deep, rich; rather exuberant henhouse scent, good fruit beneath; slightly sweet, medium full-bodied, soft, fruity yet slightly bitter stalky tannic finish.* Last tasted July 1988**(*) 1993–2005

Ch PALMER *First tasted May 19 1983, ex-cask, with Franck Mähler-Besse who informed me that the assemblage had been made early April. Samples were taken from wine in new and old casks, the former being crisper and more astringent, the latter sweeter and softer. Lovely ripe mulberry-like fruit, fleshy but not as impressive as expected. Two more cask samples in Nov 1983, when I noted "for once, in its class, 3ème", that is to say not a super-second, let alone of first-class quality like the inimitable '61. In 1985 I noted the nose as fleshy but elusive and a bit watery and lacking. Better notes in 1986, one being at a particularly interesting tasting of top '82s from Bordeaux and California organised by* The Wine Spectator. *Wedged between Ch Margaux and Inglenook Cask Reserve, it had developed a lovely fragrance, was warm, soft, fruity but a bit short. For drinking soon! Most recently, palish, fully mature; sweet, rich, gingery bouquet; chewy, good flavour, tannic.* Assez bien, *but not a top '82.* Last noted at the Château, June 1991**(*) 1993–2000

Ch PAPE-CLEMENT *Two recent notes. Nose a bit hard. Firm, lean yet good chunky flavour.* Last tasted Feb 1988(***) 1995–2005

PAVILLON ROUGE DE CH MARGAUX *Bottled in June 1984, was first tasted that Sept. Deep cherry; rather muffled nose; rather raw. In 1987, noted colour denser, but leaner on palate than the* grand vin, *and, a year later, surprising sweetness and silky texture. Next: liquorice, big mouthful. At* Wine *magazine's tasting of '82 and '83 Margaux, medium-deep; very fragrant, spicy nose; lean, fragrant, dry finish.* Last noted Aug 1990**(*) 1992–2000

Ch PICHON-LONGUEVILLE, BARON *Three recent notes. Very deep yet showing maturity; cool, unusually sweet, fleshy, rounded but distinctly tannic.* Last tasted May 1990**(*) 1993–2005

Ch PICHON-LONGUEVILLE, LALANDE *Excellent cask sample at the de Luze tasting in May 1983 and, later that month, tasting from the cask with the Maître de Chai: marvellous fruit, rich, spicy. Equally adulatory note, in cask later that autumn. Good development through the mid-1980s but, curiously, not tasted since then. Needed decanting time and air in glass to reveal its all. Tannic of course.* Last tasted Sept 1986. Doubtless now**(**) 1992–2015

Ch PONTET-CANET *Understandably tannic in cask, a rather appley nose, citrus flavour. Latterly good fruit but hard, firm, still immature.* Last tasted May 1988*(*) Need to retaste.

Ch POUGET *A rather obscure Margaux* 4ème cru classé. *Slightly woody, very tannic in cask. At* Wine *magazine, blind tasting: deep, very impressive colour; very rich but slightly stalky, very sweaty tannic nose; sweet, full, rich yet lean, rather metallic tannic finish.* Last tasted Aug 1990*(*) 1993–2000

Ch PRIEURE-LICHINE *Dined at Prieuré with Alexis Lichine on Thursday Sept 23 1982. The Merlot which started to be picked on the Monday was all in, and the Cabernet Sauvignon was under way. It was tasted in cask exactly a year later, then again in Nov 1983. A nice wine, the usual lean touch despite richness of the '82 grapes. A very poor corky, rubbery bottle in 1986, chunky but unready in 1988. Now losing colour, maturing, coffee and fruit, sweetish, easy, attractive flavour, relatively unobtrusive tannin, refreshing acidity.* Last tasted June 1991*** Now to 1998.

Ch RAUSAN-SEGLA *Dry, very spicy, lean and tannic in cask, Nov 1983. Next noted in Oct 1985: pleasant, unaggressive yet tannic and with hard nose which took time to evolve in the glass. Chewy, chunky, rough, bitter tannin, immature. Still teeth-grippingly unready a year later and a consistent note the following spring: mouthfilling, considerable length, lean, masculine, touch of bitter aloes. Several recent notes: orange-tinged maturity; cedar, vanilla, coffee and fruit, touch of volatile acidity. Drying, consistently lean, crisp, tannic, piquant end acidity.* Last tasted May 1991. Drying out?*(**) Hard to predict.

Ch RAUZAN-GASSIES *Deep, plummy; blackcurrant aroma; straightforward, tannic, rather raw, no great length, noted twice in cask, Nov 1983. Now medium, mature, some '82 richness; forthcoming nose, rich, coffee-like, intriguing fruit; dry, lean but not bad. Very tannic.* Last tasted Aug 1990*(**) 1994–2010

Ch SIRAN *Medium, attractive, mature; sweet, ripe, tannic nose; medium dryness and body. Firm. Very tannic finish.* Aug 1990*(*) 1992–98

Ch SMITH-HAUT-LAFITTE *Not very deep, mature-looking; good fruit, vanilla and strawberry nose; an attractive, easy, stylish wine with nice texture.* Tasted only once, May 1988*** Drink soon.

Ch TALBOT *Opaque, good fruit, spicy, tannic in cask. Several recent notes: still almost opaque; sweet, sweaty, typical Talbot whiff of barnyard and ripe fruit; full, fleshy, soft, rich but tannic. I suspect this will always be tough, yet popular.* Last tasted May 1990*(***) 1993–2010

Ch du TERTRE *For many years one of the more obscure classed growths of the Médoc. Not very deep; curious, raw nose though attractive on palate in cask a year after the vintage. Now fairly pale and fully mature; coffee-like nose; lean, citrus-tinged flavour and acidity. Not a very typical or effective '82.* Last tasted Aug 1990* Drink up.

Ch La TOUR-CARNET *Yet another rather unconvincing classed growth. Just two notes, the first in 1984: dumb; tannic and lacking compensating fat. Somewhat more recently, a warm fruity though not fully evolved nose; quite nice fruit sandwiched between a soft entry and astringent finish. I do not foresee much bottle-age benefit. Last tasted April 1987*(*) Now to 1995.*

Ch La TOUR-HAUT-BRION *First tasted in Sept 1984, two months after bottling. Smelled of chocolate cake. Spicy. Tannic. Two years later: deep, ruby; very sweet nose; a rich, fruity mouthful. Last tasted Nov 1988. Probably**(*) Now to 2000.*

Ch TROTANOY *The extraordinary heat at vintage time endorsed by the* cuve *readings when I visited the* chais *on Sept 22. On Sept 16 the temperature in the vat had been 33°C in the morning, 27°C in the afternoon. On the 17th 21°, 18th 21° and 23°, 19th 23°, 20th 23°, on the 21st it rose to 25° in the morning and to 26° in the afternoon, finally, the day of my visit, it was 29°C. Clearly it had survived this tropical heat for at Robert Paul's tasting it showed well and gained high marks: deep, still youthful, the least mature of the flight which ranged from Gazin to Pétrus. Classic, shapely but indefinable nose; fairly sweet and full-bodied, rich, fleshy, yet with silky tannins. Good length. Feb 1989**(**) Possibly***** Drink now to 2015.*

OTHER '82 POMEROL AND ST-EMILION CHATEAUX TASTED ONLY, OR LAST TASTED, AT ROBERT PAUL'S IN FEB 1989:

*Ch L'*ANGELUS *Already fairly mature-looking, slightly orange-tinged; sweet on nose and palate. Rich, chocolaty bouquet. Chunky, oaky, tannic, touch of liquorice on finish**(*) Drink soon.*

*Ch L'*ARROSEE *Noted at a trade tasting in April 1984: an open easy style, sweet though with tinny tannins. At Bob Paul's: still a youthful tinge; some fragrance and fruit; soft, chewy, quite nice wine*** Drink soon.*

Ch BALESTARD-LA-TONNELLE *Deep, warm, brick red with orange highlights; rich, slightly singed nose; sweet, medium weight, soft, dry finish** Drink now.*

Ch BEAUREGARD *First tasted in 1988. Attractive; lovely fragrant raspberry-like fruit; pleasant; chewy, 'warm' and inviting*** Drink now to 1995.*

Ch BEAU SEJOUR BECOT *Fairly deep but mature; very sweet, rather strange flavour, good length but a bit raw*(**) Drink soon.*

Ch BEAUSEJOUR-DUFFAU-LAGARROSSE *Very deep, intense, cherry red; rich, but undeveloped, peppery, vanilla nose; crisp fruit, a bit stalky, very dry tannic finish*(**) 1995–2005*

Ch BELAIR *Deep, plummy; high-toned, spicy bouquet and taste. No great length. Acidic*(*) Drink soon.*

Ch Le BON-PASTEUR *Distinctly raw and austere in 1985. Still impressively deep, with crisp, elegant, eucalyptus bouquet; fairly sweet, full, richness masking tannin**(**) Now to 2020.*

Ch BOURGNEUF-VAYRON *Rich, soft, velvety despite iron-like tannic finish*(*) Now to 2000.*

Ch CADET-PIOLA *Deep yet maturing; assertive, thick with fruit and tannic nose and palate. Two notes in 1989**(*) Now to 2000.*

Ch CAP-DE-MOURLIN *Jacques. A split estate, each part run by the family of this name. Deep, rich, mature; assertive, whiff of slightly sour cream cheese but gentle fruit. Sweetish, tangy finish*** Drink soon.*

Ch CAP-DE-MOURLIN *Jean. Less definition of colour; very sweet, attractive bouquet, after 20 minutes like chocolate ginger biscuits. Also sweet on palate, rather rough texture, nice fruit*** Drink soon.*

Ch CERTAN-GIRAUD *Small vineyard producing a rich, spicy wine. Sweet finish*** Drink soon.*

Ch CLINET *A bit too brown; slightly oxidised; very sweet, soft yet woody and bitter. Poor bottle?*

Clos du CLOCHER *Tiny 6-ha vineyard. Nicely evolved, crisp, flavoury, short** Drink up.*

Ch La CLUSIERE *Minty, fragrant; medium sweetness and weight, good mid-palate, tails off a bit** Drink up.*

Ch COUVENT-DES-JACOBINS *Soft, fleshy yet good tannins. July 1989*** Drink soon.*

Ch La CROIX *Maturing, touch of rust at rim, sweet fleshy nose and palate. Good fruit and length*** Now to 2000.*

Ch La CROIX DU CASSE *Rather weak-rimmed. Well-named, though volatile acidity rather than any* casse. *Avoid.*

Ch La CROIX DE GAY *Orange-tinged in 1985, distinctly so in 1989, laden with tannate of iron and both times showing signs of oxidation. A winemaking fault, probably overheated must.*

Ch La CROIX ST-GEORGES *Attractive colour, bouquet and flavour. Jan 1988*** Drink soon.*

Ch La CROIX-TOULIFAUT *(100% Merlot) A rather newly fashionable wine first tasted in 1985: easy, forward. But both bottles at the Paul tasting were rusty-edged and slightly woody. Try again.*

Ch CROQUE-MICHOTTE *Rich, ruddy, blackberry colour; nose initially peppery, fruit plus chlorine, but opened up nicely; sweet, soft, fleshy. Lacks finesse*** Drink now.*

Ch CURE-BON-LA-MADELEINE *Chocolaty, hollow; very sweet, curious flavour, some oxidation. Probably due to winemaking.*

Ch DASSAULT *Still immature-looking yet a very assertive, forthcoming though raw fruity aroma; piquant, lean, dry finish. Young vines?*(*) Try a later vintage.*

Ch La DOMINIQUE *Spicy oaky nose and flavour. Sweet, interesting texture**(*) Now to 2000.*

*Clos L'*EGLISE *Fully mature, orange-tinged; pleasant, fragrant, orange blossom bouquet; sweet, slightly caramelly, delicious but future reservations** Drink up.*

*Ch L'*EGLISE-CLINET *Beautiful, glowing colour; rather Médoc-like nose; a rich mouthful, silky, leathery tannins, lovely texture. Needs time in bottle and in glass. Two good notes, both Feb 1989**(**) 1995–2020*

*Ch L'*ENCLOS *Attractive, raspberry-like fruit; sweet, fullish, rich fruit, good length and aftertaste***(*) Now to 2010.*

*Ch L'*ENCLOS HAUT-MAZEYRES *Lovely colour; unusual crisp nose, unforthcoming, liquorice (from Malbec); chunky, chewy, rather coarse textured, very dry tannic finish(**) Cannot predict future.*

Ch FEYTIT-CLINET *Fully evolved in appearance, on*

*nose and palate. Very sweet, jammy fruitiness. Plausibly attractive**** Drink now.

Ch La FLEUR *Fairly deep, attractive, maturing; good rich cheese-rind nose, sweet, fruity; flavour of chocolate and liquorice with silky leathery tannins***(**) Now to 2010.

Ch La FLEUR-GAZIN *Fairly mature; lovely fragrant raspberry-tinged bouquet; appealingly easy wine, with citrus-like acidity. Lacking length***(*) Now to 2000.

Ch La FLEUR-DU-ROY *Fully evolved; crisp fruity; raw, short. Not bad. Minor wine** Drink up.

Ch FONPLEGADE *Smell of fruit and bad teeth but flavoury in 1986. A rather better note later that year, but put off by a smelly, overripe, hen-droppings nose and horrible aftertaste. Taste of dull, flat, wet cardboard at Bob Paul's tasting.*

Ch FONROQUE *Still a youthful cherry red; peppery; raw, acidic, undeveloped.* Give it a miss.

Clos FOURTET *First tasted in cask in May 1983. Even then a very forthcoming nose, nice texture. A great improvement on some earlier vintages. At Bob Paul's, an easy-looking wine; forthcoming, rich, gingery, fruity nose; uncharacteristically sweet for Fourtet, and on the light side. Clearly much new oak used, judging by the cloves and cinnamon flavour**** Drink now to 1995.

Ch La GAFFELIERE *A rather acidic cask sample, and acidity still noticeable at the Paul tasting. Fruity, unknit bouquet; soft, rounded, fruity but not as good as it ought to be*** Drink soon.

Ch Le GAY *Lovely dark cherry colour; low-keyed, hint of violets, touch of liquorice; flavoury but hard, good fruit, very tannic.* Last tasted May 1989(***) possibly**** Say 1995–2015

Ch GAZIN *Rich, mature-looking; light, rather restrained strawberry scent; sweet, fullish, soft, rounded. Tannic iron finish***(**) Now to 2010.

Ch GOMBAUDE-GUILLOT *Not very forthcoming. Hard, very tannic. Not very interesting**

Ch GRAND-BARRAIL-LAMARZELLE-FIGEAC *Open-knit appearance, nose and taste. Very sweet, fairly lightweight*** Drink now.

Ch Les GRANDES-MURAILLES *Deep, richly coloured; quite pleasant fruit and fairly sweet but with pronounced tobacco taste and a rather tinny dry finish. Not bad*** Drink soon.

Ch GRAND-PONTET *Plummy, chewy, chunky. Straightforward**(*) Drink soon.

Ch La GRAVE TRIGANT DE BOISSET *Attractive appearance and taste. Bouquet reminiscent of walnuts, fruit; sweet, good body, richness masking very dry tannic finish***(**) Now to 2010.

Ch HAUT-SARPE *Showing well in 1985 and at the Paul tasting: deep, crisp, maturing; oaky, spicy; good chunky fruit, correct tannins**** Now to 2000.

Clos des JACOBINS *An extremely good note in 1986, black cherry colour; fleshy, harmonious nose; glorious ripe fruit, nice weight. Also showing well at the Paul tasting. Very forthcoming, blossomy nose, roses, strawberries, almost too plausible; chunky fruit, violets, spice**** Now to 2000.

Ch LAGRANGE *Pomerol. Fairly deep but fully developed; strangely fragrant, walnuts, lots of fruit; very sweet, soft, attractive, easy**** Now to 2000.

Ch LARCIS-DUCASSE *Mixed feelings in cask, quick-maturing yet a bit hard. Now, though quite deep, distinctly mature, touch of orange; first whiff like chlorine but developed strawberry-like fruit; despite jammy flavour, rather hard and flat.* Probably better to avoid.

Ch LARMANDE *Rich, plummy; crisp, high-toned, good fruit; fairly sweet, good body, spicy new oak flavour and tannic finish. "The poor man's Figeac," I noted***(*) Now to 2000.

Ch LATOUR A POMEROL *Deep colour and fruit. Fragrant. Dry, powerful, fig-like flavour, very tannic, good length***(**) 1993–2015

Clos La MADELEINE *Attractive, maturing; forthcoming bouquet, vanilla and fruit; interesting flavour, light touch**** Now to 2000.

Ch MAGDELAINE *Rich, mature; nose tight, crisp and peppery at first but developed nicely; sweet, full, rounded, richness masking tannins. Another excellent Mouiex property****(*) Now to 2010.

Ch MATRAS *Mature; curious coffee and chlorine whiff, the latter clearing; open-knit, dry, baked leaf taste**

Ch MOULINET *Sandy soil. Nicely evolved, refreshingly fruity nose and taste. Vinosity. Silky texture. Good length***(**) Now to 2005.

Ch NENIN *Fully mature, pleasing appearance; fragrant nose, vinous, honeyed, harmonious. On the light side, spicy, elegant, good dry finish**** Now to 2000.

*Clos de l'*ORATOIRE *Mature. Hardly any red; corky, woody, slightly oxidised nose and taste. Short. Bad bottle or bad wine?*

Ch PAVIE *Two excellent cask samples in May 1983 and showing well at Bob Paul's tasting in 1989. Heavy sediment noted. High-toned, herbaceous, cress and fruit nose, lovely, crispy, spicy; slightly sweet, just as it was when young, good body, chewy, vanilla pods and fruit, good length****(*) Now to 2010.

Ch PAVIE-DECESSE *Still immature-looking; fragrant, crisp, berry-like aroma; pleasant, dry***(*) Now to 2000.

Ch PAVIE-MACQUIN *Very fragrant, pleasant fruit, strange style on nose; unusual fruit, nice style on palate. Lacking length*** Now to 1995.

Ch PETIT-VILLAGE *Mature-looking; fabulous mocha bouquet developed; distinctly toasted spicy flavour in 1986. At Bob Paul's, rim browning; deep, rich, earthy oaky nose; substantial wine, extract masking tannins, but rather hard dry finish. Some complexity**** Now to 2000.

Ch Le PIN *A half-bottle sample sent to me by Richard Walford in Nov 1983. Very impressive too. Another the following spring: rich ripe Merlot, with spice. Then at Bob Paul's in 1989, still deep, but maturing; glorious bouquet, rich, fruity; fairly sweet, full body, fruit, liquorice, lots of tannin, velvety texture. High marks***(**) Now to 2010.

Ch PLINCE *Not very deep, open, mature; nose developed well in the glass, rich, attractive; sweet, curious, slightly sooty taste, vanilla and tobacco aftertaste*** Drink soon.

Clos RENE *Impressive, unyielding but good in 1987. At Paul's tasting of '82s: still very deep, plummy; bouquet nicely evolved, fruit, vinosity; touch of sweetness, good body and fruit but not exciting. Very tannic**(**) 1993–2000

Ch RIPEAU *Plummy; crisp fruit; flavoury, positive, good finish. Bottle variation. At best just about*** Now to 1996.*

Ch La ROSE-FIGEAC *Fairly deep, appealing; crisp, fruity, spicy; medium sweetness and body. Chewy, chunky, attractive. Minor wine. Weak, slightly watery finish** Drink soon.*

Ch ROUGET *Fully evolved colour; slightly varnishy nose; quite nice, a bit dull, short, leathery tannic finish*(*) Drink soon.*

Ch de SALES *The biggest vineyard in Pomerol. Usually an easy wine and certainly so at the opening de Luze cask sample tasting in May 1983. Pleasing in every respect at the Paul tasting: well-developed colour, nose and taste. Silky Pomerol texture. Moderate length*** Drink soon.*

Ch SOUTARD *Deep, still immature-looking; low-keyed, restrained, mint and cress nose; sweet, quite good weight, broad fruity flavour. Tannic**(*) Now to 1998.*

Ch TAILLEFER *Maturing nicely; crisp, citrus fruit aroma, unknit but appealing; iron-tinged tannins, rather acidic yet watery finish* Drink up.*

Ch TERTRE-ROTEBOEUF *Another recently fashionable château and certainly delicious when tasted in 1987: sweet, soft, touch of tannic bitterness**(*) 1992–98*

Ch La TOUR-FIGEAC *Unforthcoming a year after the vintage, but well developed by 1989. Rich, mature appearance; earthy nose and taste; medium sweetness and body, soft, rounded, good tannin and acidity*** Now to 1998.*

Ch La TOUR-DU-PIN-FIGEAC *(Moueix) Very confusing: two owners, each with part of the same vineyard, Mouiex owning 9 ha, Belivier 10.5 ha. Surprisingly, Moueix's was high-toned, lean, stringy and rather acidic.*

Ch TRIMOULET *Fairly mature. Heavy sediment noted. Sweet, soft, quite nicely fragrant; light style, flavoury, lacking length** Drink up.*

Ch TROPLONG-MONDOT *Dusty, muffled nose then a touch of tangerine. Sweetish, rounded, straightforward** Drink soon.*

Ch TROTTEVIEILLE *First tasted in May 1983: quite good fruit, nice but unexciting. A common touch. At Robert Paul's, one bottle corked, the second impressively deep; good nose; soft, pleasant enough*** Drink soon.*

Ch VIEUX-FERRAND *A tiny 3-ha vineyard. Colour fully evolved; surprisingly interesting nose which developed well; lightish, lean, crisp, flavoury*** Drink now.*

Ch VIEUX-SARPE *Fine deep colour; earthy, low-keyed; medium-sweet, full-bodied, a touch of harshness. Interesting but not appealing*(*) 1993–98?*

Ch VILLEMAURINE *Very deep, immature; attractive nose and plausible flavour. Sweet, soft yet dry, tannic, brackish finish** Drink soon.*

Ch La VIOLETTE *Whether it was pure imagination or not, it actually smelled of violets; attractive, crisp, new oak. Rather sweet, fairly full-bodied, chunky, cheesy, coarse*(*) 1992–98*

Ch YON-FIGEAC *Very deep, beginning to mature; sweet, quite pleasant fruit; dry, lean, straightforward, a bit short*(*) Drink soon.*

BRIEF NOTES ON SOME OTHER '82s WITH YEAR LAST TASTED:

Ch d'AGASSAC *Pleasant, tannin, fruit**(*) 1987*

Ch de BARBE *Soft and ripe for Bourg** 1989*

Ch BEAUMONT *Cheesy; sweet, easy** 1991*

Ch BOUSCAUT *Immature, fairly hefty*(*) 1989*

Ch CARBONNIEUX *Light and lean for an '82. Tannic** 1985*

Ch La CARDONNE *Very deep; cheesy; good fruit*(*) 1988*

Ch FOURCAS-HOSTEN *Straightforward, dry, tannic*(*) 1988*

Ch du GABY *Canon-Fronsac. Smell of seaweed; sweet, soft, quite nice* 1989*

Ch La GURGUE *Metallic, unknit nose; dry, lean, minor. 1990*

Ch HAUT-BAGES-AVEROUS *Opaque; full of fruit and charm**(*) 1986*

Ch HAUT-BAGES-LIBERAL *Deep, rich, spicy; soft yet tannic**(*) 1987*

Ch HAUT-BAILLY *Deep, soft, rich, fleshy. Tannic***(*) 1990*

Ch HAUT-BEYCHEVELLE-GLORIA *Sweaty, tannic, dry, medicinal*(*) 1988*

Ch HAUT-MARBUZET *Opaque; rich, fleshy**(*) 1985*

Ch LAROSE-TRINTAUDON *Rich, sweaty, liquorice; fullish, soft, fruity** 1988*

Ch LARRIVET-HAUT-BRION *Lovely; soft, sweet; very original flavour*** 1991*

Ch LESTAGE *Very tannic but pleasant enough*(**) 1990*

Ch MALARTIC-LAGRAVIERE *Forthcoming, fragrant, citrus; very flavoury, deft style but lean for '82*** 1989*

Ch MALESCASSE *Very deep. Rich, tannic, lacking grace*(*) 1986*

Ch de MARBUZET *Full, rich, chewy, tannic*(**) 1986*

Ch MEYNEY *Very deep; tough; rich, chewy, quite stylish, tannic-iron finish(**) 1988*

Ch MILLET *Graves. Nice texture but stalky and common* 1986*

Ch MONBOUSQUET *Deep, rich, maturing; low-keyed; broad, easy, chocolaty, extract masking tannin*** 1990*

Ch PATACHE-D'AUX *Intense, black cherry; flavoury, excellent value** 1988*

Ch PAVEIL-DE-LUZE *Comes into its own in a vintage like '82. Sweet, brown sugar nose; very sweet on palate, delicious, fruity, soft tannins, for drinking soon. 1987*

Ch PIBRAN *Deep, velvety; sweet, full, rich, fleshy, extract and tannin**(*) 1989*

Ch PIPEAU *Deep; dumb; fullish, rich, good texture and extract*** 1988*

Ch POTENSAC *Opaque; dumb; a big, fleshy, powerful wine, short very dry finish(**) 1986*

Ch La SERRE *Opaque; glorious fruit; dry, full-bodied; packed with fruit, tannic**(*) 1988*

Ch La TOUR-ST-BONNET *Deep, rich; chunky, rustic, quite flavoury** 1989*

Ch VERDIGNAN *Deep ruby; nice weight, delicious flavour, good tannins*(**) 1988*

1983★★★

After the encouraging but uneven start to the decade, 1983 seemed to usher in a period of normality and calm, though it is arguable whether there ever is such a thing as a 'normal' vintage in Bordeaux. Certainly a swing back after the excesses of the '82 vintage to a useful and reasonably priced vintage with some very attractive wines for medium-term drinking. Perhaps not as well constructed or well balanced as the '85s.

A mild winter, cold wet spring, slow start to vegetation. First half of June fine and dry, permitting a good start to flowering, but cooler weather caused some *millerandage*. July and Aug exceptionally hot, interspersed with summer storms, keeping the *vignerons* busy with sprays. The latter half of Aug was drier; then cooler, Sept fine with good harvesting conditions in early Oct.

Apart from two early trade tastings in London, my first major exposure to the vintage was a tasting of 46 châteaux, all leading growths, but not the firsts, at Christie's. It was reported that wines of the "greater Margaux district" (my description) were particularly successful in 1983 and this was borne out at a blind tasting of '82 and '83 vintages organised by *Wine* magazine in Aug 1990; I thought Ch Margaux '82 stood head and shoulders above them all.

Ch LAFITE *Showing extremely well at Flatt's Lafite tasting in Oct 1988. I gave it identical overall marks to the '82 and '85. Fairly deep, fine, light violet rim; very attractive fruit on the nose, chunky, 'thicker' than the '85, violets; touch of sweetness, medium-full body, lovely fruit, fairly tannic finish. Similar notes three months later. Most recently, fragrant cedary bouquet noted but still a swingeingly dry finish. Needs food.* Last tasted Nov 1990★★(★★) 1995–2015

Ch MARGAUX *Picking began Sept 29. First tasted in cask, Sept 1984: opaque; attractive, youthful fruitiness; fairly full-bodied, loads of fruit and tannin, with length and savour. Showing well at Desai's Margaux vertical in May 1987: still opaque; low-keyed at first but opened up in the glass. Very good fruit, balance. Next at the château in the spring of 1988. The bouquet took ages to open up. Quite unready, yet that summer a more developed bottle, deep cherry colour; sweet, fragrant, with marvellous depth of fruit. Richness of bouquet and taste, "almost chocolaty" noted in Aug 1990. Still surprisingly deep and youthful; vanilla on nose, very fragrant; also surprisingly sweet — as red wine goes, very good fruit. Tannic. However, at both recent tastings I was more impressed with the '82.* Last tasted at Lay & Wheeler's Margaux evening, Nov 1990★(★★★) 1995–2015

Ch LATOUR *First tasted in the* chai *in Sept 1984. Deep but not opaque, intense purple; delicious young fruit and vinosity though still raw; dry, fairly full-bodied, lean, nice texture. Most recently at the Fericks/Wodarz Latour and Mouton tasting in Wiesbaden: rich, colour more evolved than the Mouton; cedar, touch of 'linoleum', good chunky fruit — totally different character from the Mouton; medium dryness, not a heavyweight but rich, fleshy, fine. Very attractive.* Last tasted March 1989★★(★★) 1995–2020

Ch MOUTON-ROTHSCHILD *Sample ex-cask with the legendary Maître de Chai, Raoul Blondin, in Sept 1984 (they had just finished bottling the '82). Good lively colour but not very deep. 18 months later, at Flatt's Mouton tasting, lovely colour; lean, very crisp, fruity nose that blossomed beautifully in the glass; fairly full-bodied, more open-knit and less flesh than the dense '82. Good length. Still raw and tannic. High marks but two points beneath the '82. More recently, at the Latour and Mouton tasting in Wiesbaden: appearance still immature; a most appealing, crisp cherry-like fragrance, gloriously evolved, considerable depth of fruit; lovely flavour and weight, well balanced. Dry finish. A certain austerity.* Last tasted March 1989★★(★★) 1995–2020

Ch HAUT-BRION *Tasted only once at the château, alongside La Mission and La Tour-Haut-Brion: very deep; low-keyed, harmonious, with a whiff that reminded me of thoroughbred stables; medium-dry, fairly full-bodied, good mid-palate, lovely texture, good length.* Sept 1984(★★★)

Ch AUSONE *Tasted only once, at Flatt's Ausone tasting: fairly deep, rich-looking but a different sort of appearance from the '82; quite different on the nose too, a sort of elegant, rich, more-of-a-Pomerol style. Medium full-bodied, silky texture, nice length, good potential.* Oct 1987★★★(★) Now to 2000+

Ch CHEVAL-BLANC *Intense, fleshy, tannic in 1985. Most recently: mature; sweet, like soft brown sugar; also sweet on palate, medium weight, silky tannins, pleasant drink by itself.* Last tasted at the château, Nov 1990★★★★

Ch PETRUS *High marks at Frericks' tasting in Munich, April 1986, in magnum: very deep, intense ruby; very sweet, chunky almost jam-like fruit on the nose but still hard on the palate, very full-bodied, crisp, spicy mid-palate, dry finish — touch of iron in the tannin. Exactly four years later, in bottle, now medium-deep and maturing; lovely, rich biscuity bouquet, then muffled, rather chocolaty, yet, after only 15 minutes, sweet, perfect; fairly sweet on the palate too but not as massive as the magnum tasted in 1986. Chewy, chocolaty, maturing.* Last noted at 'Stockholm' Group tasting, April 1990★★★(★★) Now to 2010.

Ch L'ANGELUS *Attractive cask sample at Nathl Johnston's trade tasting of '83s in London in the spring of 1984: very deep; curious, crusty, raspberry aroma; sweet, rich, lovely flavour. Then, in Oct, at a mammoth tasting of* grand cru *'83s at Christie's, dazzled by its fragrance, fruit and spice. Four years later four stars again, at a British Airways tasting, this time for its flavour, lovely fruit, texture. 16 months later, there had been noticeable colour loss, now broad and open, fairly mature-looking. A bit* too *sweet on the nose; easy, ready.* Last tasted May 1990★★★ Drink soon.

Ch d'ANGLUDET *Four recent notes, three at Distillers' Livery dinners, one tasted blind at* Wine *magazine's tasting of '82 and '83 Margaux. Quite a good, rich, well-developed colour. Flavoury, though a touch of raw tannin.* Last noted at the Mansion House, Sept 1990**(*) Now to 1996.

Ch BATAILLEY *Several notes. Plummy, forward; medicinal Pauillac nose; lean for Batailley though with some fruit.* Not *very exciting.* Last tasted July 1989** Drink soon.

Ch BEAU SEJOUR BECOT *Rich ruby in 1985, fully mature-looking only three years later; fleshy Merlot fruit, like an '82; slightly sweet, rich, spicy, fruity, flavoury, good length. More acidity than tannin.* Last tasted Nov 1988*** Drink soon.

Ch BEYCHEVELLE *Deep, fairly full-bodied, spicy, very tannic. Most recently, still deep, surprisingly; curiously artificial, rich, vegetal nose; chewy but lean. Dry. So so.* Last tasted April 1991** Drink soon.

Ch BOYD-CANTENAC *Tasted only once, blind. Fairly deep, maturing; strangely agreeable, scented bouquet; medium dryness and weight, nice texture, lissom, good dry finish.* Aug 1990*** Now to 2000.

Ch BRANAIRE-DUCRU *Sweet, fleshy, very pleasant, quick-maturing. Pale for its age. Attractive but unimpressive.* Last tasted July 1988** Drink soon.

Ch BRANE-CANTENAC *A somewhat beery, unready, cask sample in April 1984 — one of the risks of bringing cask samples to London too early in the spring. But, at the* grand cru *tasting in Oct, fragrant and delicious. By 1990 fully mature, a rich, coffee-like, plausible bouquet; sweet, fullish, rich, good length. Most recently ripe but with raw finish.* Last tasted April 1991*** Drink soon.

Ch CALON-SEGUR *A dry, lean, unimpressive cask sample in the spring of 1984. More recently, medium, mature-looking; stylish nose; sweet at first sip, flavoury. I liked it but others did not, some finding it too tannic.* Last tasted May 1988. Clearly not wholly satisfactory. Need to retaste.

Ch CARONNE-STE-GEMME *Six notes of a useful Livery Company luncheon wine. Advanced, flavoury, touch of metallic bitterness.* Last tasted May 1990** Drink up.

Ch CHASSE-SPLEEN *Can always be relied upon to make the best of the prevailing vintage conditions. Deep, rich colour and fruit. Good extract for the year. Tannic.* Feb 1988*(**) 1992–98

Dom de CHEVALIER *A pretty, cherry-coloured cask sample, attractive and fragrant in May 1984. Good style, shape and length. Holding its depth of colour and youthfulness; very pleasing fruit; lovely flavour, elegant but tannin consistently noted.* The last four notes from Jan to Dec 1988**(**) 1984–2000+

Ch CISSAC *Good, fairly deep, attractive, maturing; very fragrant; good flesh and balance. A rich little wine.* Last tasted March 1989*** Now to 1996.

Clos du CLOCHER *Lovely colour, maturing; a bit subdued at first but developing fig-like fruit, spicy, agreeable; slightly sweet, medium weight, good fruit, cinnamon and cloves, dry finish.* Last tasted Nov 1989**

CONNETABLE TALBOT *The second wine of Ch Talbot. Several recent notes. Fairly deep, cedary colour; harmonious; pleasant fruit, nice weight, good acidity, mouthdrying tannins.* Last tasted Oct 1990** Now to 1995.

Ch COS D'ESTOURNEL *Frankly I don't know about this: a sort of smelly, overripe, medicinal style of wine, surprisingly sweet despite its tannin, medium full-bodied, good fruit. Better flavour than nose.* Last tasted Nov 1989. In its way*** Now to 1996. Hard to say.

Ch COUFRAN *Attractive soft Merlot nose, its initial raw tannin easing off. Nice fruit. Easy.* Last tasted Feb 1988** Drink soon.

Ch CURE-BON-LA-MADELEINE *Palish, advanced; pleasant, sweet, fairly light, soft and flavoury.* July 1990** Drink soon.

Ch DAUZAC *One of the palest '83s at the extensive* grand cru *tasting in 1984, with a sweet, open, pleasant nose and taste. Moderate quality. Six years later: not much change in colour, nose and taste. Well chaptalised. Attractive in its way.* Last noted at Wine magazine's tasting of '83 Margaux, Aug 1990** Drink soon.

Ch DESMIRAIL *Showing well at the '83 Margaux tasting. Sweet, harmonious bouquet; flavoury, elegant, fair tannin and acidity.* Aug 1990*** Now to 1998.

Ch DUCRU-BEAUCAILLOU *An intensely purple cask sample in April 1984, good fruit, very tannic, and in Oct the clove-like spiciness of new oak and good length noted. Appearance consistently deep and rich, like an '82; classic nose, good fruit and flesh. Good wine.* Last tasted March 1989**(*) Now to 2000.

Ch DUHART-MILON *Two fairly recent notes. Good colour, distinctly more developed than the '85; attractive, fragrant, fruity nose and flavour. Medium weight, light style.* Last tasted Jan 1989*** Now to 1998.

Ch DURFORT-VIVENS *Appearance not very deep but noted as having a very attractive nose "with deep tannic underlay" at Christie's* grand cru *tasting in Oct 1984; "sweet, medium weight, flavoury, of no great length but nice". Words which still applied six years later though it now looks fully mature, and the nose has taken on a rich, chunky, toasted, coffee-like scent. Orange-tinged and still tannic — going rusty.* Last noted at Wine magazine's tasting, Aug 1990*** Drink now to 1995.

Ch L'EVANGILE *Opaque, intense; most unusual deep, hot fruit; sweet yet very tannic. Like port without sugar.* Twice, May 1991**(**)? 1993–2000

Ch FERRIERE *Not often seen but bearing out the success of the '83 vintage in Margaux. Fully mature but rich appearance; sweet, nicely chaptalised nose; medium sweetness and weight, light tannins, deft touch of citrus fruit acidity. Very attractive.* Tasted Aug 1990*** Drink now to 1995.

Ch de FIEUZAL *I have always liked this class of red Graves and find the '83 Fieuzal a charmer. First noted, crisp and fragrant, at a Thorman Hunt tasting in May 1984, and again at Christie's in Oct: figs and blackthorn nose, though, in the context of 46 other '83s, noted as "pleasant enough". Lacking length. More recently, paler in colour, nose sweaty, tannic, opening up with a strawberry-like* *fragrance. Light, charming, "a pretty little thing", with slightly bitter, lingering mouthdrying tannin.* Last tasted June 1990*** Now to 1996.

Ch FIGEAC *Three fairly recent notes: clearly a very fragrant, most attractive wine. Still a lovely deep plummy colour; an exciting, rich, spicy, very forthcoming nose; a very flavoury mouthful, oaky, spicy, with touch of iron, tannic bitterness but glorious aftertaste.* Showing brilliantly at Desai's tasting, Dec 1989**** Now to 1998.

Les FORTS DE LATOUR *Three recent notes. Ripe, fully developed; sweetish, soft, easy, short.* Last tasted at Latour, Nov 1990** Drink now.

Ch FOURCAS-HOSTEN *Surprisingly rich though maturing; lightish, with crisp, pleasant fruit and light dry tannic finish.* July 1990*** Drink now to 1996.

Ch La GAFFELIERE *Poor cask sample shown at Nathl Johnston's trade tasting in April 1984. Perhaps they were rushing samples to London to pre-empt de Luze. Anyway, the out-of-condition bottle should have been spotted and removed. Two recent notes, both of which stress the clove-like spiciness of new oak, an attractive and unusual flavour, but something lacking.* Last tasted Dec 1989** Drink up.

Ch GISCOURS *By no means a block-buster, in fact noticeably* not *deep at the* grand cru *tasting, Oct 1984, though delicious with hint of delicacy and forwardness. Seven recent notes. Now palish, very mature; sweet, chaptalised nose.* Last tasted June 1991*** Drink soon.

Ch du GLANA *Bottled by Berry Bros. Deep, plummy; rich, meaty nose; fairly sweet, medium-full body, chunky, fruity.* Last tasted Nov 1989** Drink soon.

Ch GLORIA *Maturing nicely in colour; sweet, almost '82 chunkiness, tannin, vanilla; an attractive lunch wine with what might be a touch of gallic acid? Bitterness accentuating its dry finish.* Jan 1990** Now to 1995.

Ch GRAND-PUY-LACOSTE *Many notes, including cask samples at four trade tastings in 1984: richly coloured, fruity, spicy, lean — as usual — and classic. Summarising four more recent notes: still fairly deep, slow — also as usual — to shed its youthful sheen; rich, lovely fruit; touch of sweetness, medium-full body, flavoury, with crisp dry finish. Undervalued.* Last tasted Aug 1990**(**) 1992–2000+

Ch GRUAUD-LAROSE *Immediately forthcoming, fragrant, piquant Cabernet Sauvignon fruit, a little unknit but with long dry finish at the* grand cru *tasting, autumn 1984. Several detailed notes since. Showing considerable potential at a vertical tasting of Gruaud at one of Christie's Wine Course sessions in 1985. Gentle, more relaxed and harmonious than the '81, but positively opulent on the palate in 1987. More recently, though still deep, and developing, I have noted a hard edge to the fruit, more medicinal on the nose, but still very flavoury. Tannin and acidity on finish. Like a chubby-cheeked child growing up and looking for guidance.* Last tasted March 1990**(*) Say 1992–98.

*Ch d'*ISSAN *Initially deep in colour, with a curious high-toned, farmyard smell and taste, sweet but raw, Oct 1984. A very detailed but frankly inconclusive note exactly three years later, and unimpressive at the recent blind tasting of Margaux. Medicinal, hen-droppings nose; lean, light tannins and acidity. Rather disappointing.* Last tasted Aug 1990*(*) 1992–98?

Ch KIRWAN *I have frequently found Kirwan rather dull. The '83 is, happily, attractive. Showing quite well at Hall and Bramley's tasting of the Schröder & Schÿler range, 'S & S' being Bordeaux* négociants *as well as the proprietors of Kirwan. Also showing quite well at* Wine *magazine's tasting of '83 Margaux: deep, rich, excellent colour; equally rich, and sweet though tannic nose; sweet on palate, nice fruit, chewy, attractive.* Last tasted Aug 1990*** Now to 1998.

Ch LABEGORCE-ZEDE *An impressive early cask sample, deep-coloured, with rich ripe fruit though very tannic. At the recent Margaux tasting; still deep, still rich, but showing some maturity; lovely fruit and fragrance; dry, medium-full body, a bit lean but very flavoury, good length, dry tannic finish. I gave the nose very high marks. I shall stick my neck out and add an extra star.* Last tasted Aug 1990***(*) Now to 2000.

Ch LAGRANGE *Pomerol. Four notes during the latter half of the 1980s. Lovely, lively, luminous red; sweet, strawberry-like fruit on the nose; smooth and confident. Nice wine.* Last tasted Nov 1987*** Drink now to 1998.

Ch LAGRANGE *St-Julien. Three good, fairly recent, notes. No harsh edges; a sweetish, attractive, easy, fruity wine with adequate tannin and acidity.* Last tasted July 1988*** Now to 1998.

Ch La LAGUNE *Idiosyncratic as usual: thick plummy colour; spicy, a curious open-knit almost Rhône-like fruity character, but still raw and stalky at two cask sample tastings in the spring of 1984. More recently, two notes, each, coincidentally, finishing with a question mark. Now maturing nicely, it has an almost '82 chewy denseness; rich, ripe fruit on nose and palate. Very drinkable.* Last tasted Dec 1990*** Now to 1996.

Ch LANGOA-BARTON *Fully mature; very sweet, scented, touch of mint, liquorice; dryish; fairly light in style and weight, lean, dry, slightly coarse finish.* Nov 1990** Now to 1998.

Ch LASCOMBES *Tasted, still in cask, in Feb 1985. Fine, intense magenta colour; pleasant young crisp Cabernet fruit, vanillin and tannin. More of a conventional claret style than the '82 tasted alongside. Nice weight. Pleasing acidity. I gave it fairly high marks at the tasting of '83 Margaux! Now medium, fairly mature-looking; sweet, rich, coffee/chocolate nose; sweet, fairly full-bodied, very attractive fruit, length and grip.* Last tasted Aug 1990***(*) 1992–2000

Ch LEOVILLE-BARTON *Tight-knit, crisp, lean, spicy and tannic in 1985. Three recent notes: medium-deep, lovely colour; crisp, high-toned, fragrant; dry, lean though good vinosity, a bit raw on finish.* Last tasted March 1991**(*) 1993–2000

Ch LEOVILLE-LAS-CASES *A deep, firm, very tannic and impressive cask sample, then not tasted again until the mid-1980s when it was still, not surprisingly, immature though positive, well clad and with good fruit. More recently, still fairly youthful-looking; good fruit; loads of tannin,* *extract and fruit. A multi-dimensional '83. Last tasted Nov 1989**(**) 1995 to well beyond 2000.*

Ch LYNCH-BAGES *Tasted four times in 1984. At two trade tastings in London, in April and May: very forthcoming, flavoury; an easy-going, attractive, fruity wine. Also at Christie's Advanced Wine Course in July and at the* grand cru *tasting in Oct. Several subsequent notes, the early* cassis-*like aroma changing, though still forthcoming and sweet; sweet on the palate too, with a rich yet easy and charming character and adequate tannins. Last tasted Oct 1990*** Now to 2000.*

Ch MALARTIC-LAGRAVIERE *A delicious, citrus fruit-flavoured cask sample in May 1982. The name Malartic to me conjures up the expectation of highish volatile acidity, and I certainly notice it on the nose and palate of the '83. (A dash of VA raises the tone of the nose and, to a certain extent, brings out the flavour.) Lean, flavoury, with a slightly gravelly texture. Last tasted Oct 1989** Drink soon.*

Ch MALESCOT ST-EXUPERY *Three recent notes. An extraordinarily evolved, almost too blatantly plausible sweet fruitiness on the nose, though undoubtedly fragrant; with some charm, crisp, berry-like fruit on the palate, a touch of acidity and slight bitterness on the finish. Last noted at a Malescot session at Rodenstock's wine weekend. An* impériale *served at dinner, Sept 1990**(*) A bit of a roller-coaster. Now to 1998.*

Ch de MARBUZET *A dependable St-Estèphe from the Prats 'stable'. Rather lean and austere in the mid-1980s, but, more recently, the nose now rounded, almost too agreeable, with lovely, soft yet mouthwatering fruit. Fleshy, nice weight and texture. A touch of astringency on the finish. Very agreeable. Last tasted Nov 1989*** Now to 1998.*

Ch MARQUIS D'ALESME-BECKER *Only one note on this and the following Marquis, both noted at the Margaux tasting. I found this the lesser of the two: medicinal, unknit, dry, lightish, lean. Aug 1990* Modest future.*

Ch MARQUIS-DE-TERME *Deep, maturing; rich, fruity, tannic; medium sweetness, almost '82-like extract. Aug 1990*(**) 1993–2000*

Ch MEYNEY *Deep, impressive, black cherry; low-keyed but sweet and pleasant, with some Cabernet* cassis, *even cream — also a whiff of wet nappies! Lots of fruit, good length, very tannic. June 1990*(**) 1993–98*

Ch La MISSION-HAUT-BRION *First tasted in Sept 1984 at Haut-Brion with Jean Delmas: intensely purple; marvellously spicy nose and taste. Oak. Tannic. Most recently at Wolf's tasting: still deep, ruby-tinged; very appealing, crisp Cabernet Sauvignon nose and taste. Fairly full-bodied. Lacking tannins. Last tasted June 1990*(***) 1994–2000+*

Ch MONTROSE *A slightly sweet, lovely, spicy, very tannic cask sample in April 1984. Three more recent notes: still fairly deep but maturing; curious cheesy nose and flavour. Still slightly sweet, spicy fruit, bitter tannin finish. As usual taking longer than most to develop. I would give it lots more bottle-age. Last tasted Dec 1989*(**)? Possibly**** in due course, 1995–2000+*

Ch PALMER *I first noted this at a vertical tasting of Palmer at the Swedish Wine Festival in Malmö, in March 1986, and that its* encépagement *was 45% Cabernet Sauvignon, 35% Merlot, 5% Cabernet Franc and 15%, unusually high, Petit Verdot. Opaque centre, black cherry, leading the eye to its purple rim, and with legs like Gothic arches. Tannic, hard, stalky, mouthwatering nose which, nonetheless, opened up gloriously over an hour in the glass. Sweet, pleasant fruit, yet raw, teeth-gripping tannins. Not one of my top marks at the* Wine *magazine Margaux tasting though I noted it as richly coloured and nicely developed with good length, tannin and acidity. At a recent vertical at the château I liked it less the more I tasted. Last noted June 1991**(*)??*

PAVILLON ROUGE DE CH MARGAUX *Deep cherry red; sweet, very attractive nose, lovely, fruity, opening up nicely; fairly dry, rich yet lean, slightly stalky, good fruit, tannic. I actually gave it half a mark more than the* grand vin *at the '83 Margaux tasting. Last noted Aug 1990**(**) 1993–98*

Ch PICHON-LONGUEVILLE, BARON *Showing well: lovely fruit, very flavoury, at one of the early cask sample tastings. In May 1988, I also thought it attractive though lacking some length. Equally attractive six months later: medium-deep cherry red; fruit on nose and palate, dry, fullish. Last tasted Nov 1988**(*) Now to 1998.*

Ch PICHON-LONGUEVILLE, LALANDE *First tasted in April 1984, then at the* grand cru *tasting that autumn: deep, almost '82 richness of colour; fragrant, ripe mulberry sort of fruit, though tannic; dry, some of the innate '83 leanness but an interesting shape, crisp, good length and delightful. More recently, distinctly 'thicker' and fleshier than the Baron, rich though still tannic, and with the anticipated extra dimensions. Last tasted Nov 1988**(**) Now to 2000+.*

Ch Le PIN *A sensationally good half-bottle brought to Christie's tasting room in April 1984: deep purple; extraordinarily spicy, cloves, cinnamon, with echoes of Mouton-Rothschild at its exotic best. Flavour to match. Fragrant aftertaste. Another sample, this time from the grower, tasted eight months later, evincing similar reactions though I noted with a weaker rim than another Pomerol, Le Gay. However it had a very rich, ripe mulberry-Merlot nose, was startlingly rich on the palate, with a spicy oakiness and dry finish. Not bad! Last tasted April 1988**** Now to 2000.*

Ch PONTET-CANET *First noted in 1986: flavoury, fragrant. Shaping up nicely. Good length. And again, with strawberry-like scent, flowery, just a little lean. More recently, lively bouquet, not too dry, medium weight, citrus-like refreshing acidity, very flavoury. Last tasted May 1988***(*) A fourth star gratuitously offered though I have made a note to retaste. Say 1992–98.*

Ch PRIEURE-LICHINE *Four notes, all consistently unenthusiastic, from a rather cardboardy cask sample with bitter tannins at the big tasting of* grands crus, *Oct 1984, to three made more recently. Now mature-looking; a rather stewed, sweaty nose; dry, lean — as it often is — certainly lacking flesh, even a bit raw. Disappointing. Last tasted Aug 1990★ Drink up.*

Ch RAUSAN-SEGLA *Though at a marking time stage when first tasted in 1986, I thought it delicious and similar in style to the '85, though more muted on the nose. Charming fruit and great possibilities. Two recent notes: lovely fruit and grip, medium-deep, a glorious nose despite tannins still lurking in the background. Good fruit, full-bodied, firm, very tannic. Needs time. Last tasted Aug 1998★★(★★) 1993–2000+*

Ch RAUZAN-GASSIES *Tasted only once. Rich appearance but woody, possibly earthy nose. The second bottle smelled of BO (body odour). Better on the palate. Some softness and richness. A touch of tannate of iron. Might improve. At the* Wine *magazine tasting of '82 and '83 Margaux, Aug 1990★(★)?*

SARGET DE GRUAUD-LAROSE *Unmistakably from the Cordier stable. Medicinal, rich jammy fruit; ripe and rustic. Dry finish. Tannic bitterness. Extraordinary aftertaste. Two recent notes, last in Jan 1990★(★) or★★(★) depending on the individual. Now to 1996.*

Ch SIRAN *First noted, a cask sample, at the Thorman Hunt tasting, May 1984. Informed that two-thirds new oak used and that the eminent Emile Peynaud had been advising for over 20 years. His description was* vin corsé *and tannic, very meaty* (charpenté), *harder than the '82 but that after the malolactic fermentation it would become something like the '78. The wine had some depth of colour; fruit and elegance on the nose; dry, lovely flavour, blackcurrants and cinnamon. Six years on, at the blind tasting of '83 Margaux, it had matured fully in colour; its bouquet was sweet, plausible, a bit smelly — this would be the tannin. Dry, chewy, chunky, with slightly bitter tannic finish. Quite nice. I must find a bottle of the '78 to compare. Last tasted Aug 1990★★(★) just. We'll see — say 1992–98.*

Ch TALBOT *A fairly powerful fruity cask sample in April 1984, and by Oct the familiar farmyard whiff noted. Very rich. More recently: still surprisingly deep; rustic fruity nose; tannic. Not to my taste. Last noted June 1991★★ Drink soon.*

SHORTER NOTES ON '83s:

Ch BELAIR *St-Emilion. Mature, sweet, earthy. 1990★★★*

Ch BELGRAVE *St-Laurent. Light, crisp, hard, not bad fruit. 1990★★*

Ch BEL-ORME-TRONQUOY-DE-LALANDE *Nice weight, slightly bitter finish. 1989★★*

Ch BOURGNEUF *Mature-looking though tannic, coarse. 1988(★★)*

Ch de CAMENSAC *Plausibly sweet. 1988★★*

Ch CANTEMERLE *Chunky fruit, lacking charm. 1988★★*

Ch La CARDONNE *Pleasant enough. 1988★★*

Ch CLARKE *Attractive. Ready. 1991★★★*

Ch FOMBRAUGE *An easy charmer. 1987★★*

Ch Le GAY *Unusual fruit, rich, soft yet tannic. 1988★★★(★)?*

Ch La GRACE-DIEU *Raw fruit. 1988★★*

Ch La GURGUE *Style as weird as name. Severe. 1990★*

Ch HAUT-BAGES-LIBERAL *Rustic, crisp, fleshy. 1987★★*

Ch HAUT-BAGES-MONPELOU *Sweet nose, light yet leathery. 1989★*

Ch LANESSAN *Stalky fruit, bitter tannins. 1987★*

Ch LATILLE-CAMELON *Taste matches name, sweet, soft, plausible. 1989★★*

Ch La LOUVIERE *Noticeable oak when young. Agreeable fruit, fragrance. 1987★★★*

Ch du LYONNAT *Strawberry jam. Almost spreadable. 1988★★*

Clos du MARQUIS *Good fruit but slightly astringent. 1988★★*

Ch MAYNE-VIEIL *Good fruit. Developed prettily. 1989★★★*

Ch OLIVIER *Good fruit, unsatisfactory finish. 1988★*

Ch PATACHE D'AUX *Farmyard, estery. Preferred in cask. 1988★?*

Ch PAVIE-DECESSE *Lively, sweet, attractive. 1988★★★*

Ch de PEZ *Sweet and easy. 1989★★★*

Ch RESPIDE *Palish, sweet, light, refreshing. 1990★★*

Clos du ROCHER *Attractive, nice fruit, silky tannins. 1989★★★*

Ch ROUET *Dry, light, pleasing. 1989★★★*

Ch du TERTRE *Fully evolved, specious. 1990★★★*

Ch La TOUR-CARNET *Attractive in cask. Fully mature, pleasant enough. 1988★★*

Ch TROPLONG-MONDOT *Dry, full, tannic. 1988★★(★)*

NOT TASTED SINCE 1986. SHOWING WELL THEN:

Ch Couvent-des-Jacobins; Ch Haut-Bages-Averous; Clos de L'Oratoire; Ch Pavie; Ch Petit-Village.

'83s NOT NOTED SINCE EARLY CASK SAMPLE TASTINGS AND SHOWING PROMISE:

Ch Andron-Blanquet; Ch L'Arrosée; Ch Beauregard, Pomerol; Ch Canon; Ch Carbonnieux; Ch L'Enclos; Clos Fourtet; Ch Haut-Bailly; Ch Haut-Batailley; Ch La Tour-Haut-Brion; Ch La Tour-Martillac.

NOT SHOWING PARTICULARLY WELL IN CASK:

Ch Balestard-La-Tonnelle; Ch Cantenac-Brown; Ch Cos Labory; Ch Ferrande; Ch Grand-Puy-Ducasse; Ch Pique-Caillou; Ch La Tour-Haut-Vignoble; Ch Villemaurine.

1984★

An unsatisfactory year in several respects, but all stemming from extreme weather conditions and, most significantly, the failure of Merlot throughout Bordeaux. The worst affected were those districts like St-Emilion and Pomerol, which normally rely on a high percentage of Merlot. Though less serious in the Médoc, the unusually high proportion of Cabernet Sauvignon upset the balance of the wines, resulting in rawness and hardness. In short, a difficult year, the Médocs lacking grace but with the right bank suffering most.

The cause was a warm April which advanced the vegetation. May cool, torrential rains halting the development of the vines. June very hot, so flowering too fast resulting in severe *coulure*, affecting particularly the Merlot. July and Aug dry and warm. The weather in Sept, the crucial ripening period, deteriorated and cyclonic rainfall followed. Picking commenced towards the end of Sept/early Oct. Hurricane 'Hortense' on Oct 5 caused minor damage.

Not many tasted. Some were deep and raw, some others weak and fairly raw. In both instances, mainly unbalanced, unknit, lacking charm and not for keeping. Only the best endowed will benefit from further bottle-ageing. Main virtue: now inexpensive. Drink up.

Ch LAFITE *Deep, surprisingly thick and plummy-coloured at Flatt's Lafite tasting, Oct 1988, with crisp, distinct Cabernet Sauvignon aroma; dry, medium full-bodied, rather raw and very tannic. 12 months later, a magnum from the château: still immature; some fragrance; surprisingly soft silky texture, flavoury, light style, dry as dust. Most recently: the same depth as the '85 but more evolved, and weaker rim; bouquet low-keyed, hard, peppery and then emerged, scented. Better than expected. Last tasted Nov 1990(**) Not for long keeping though it could do with further bottle-age.*

Ch MARGAUX *Picking commenced Oct 1, 90% Cabernet Sauvignon. Tasted only twice, first at Desai's vertical in 1987: deep, fairly intense, immature rim; young raw smell of the* chai*, oak, unknit, even a whiff of volatile acidity. Chunky, fruity but very tannic. Most recently: medium-deep, some signs of development; vanilla, some fruit on nose and palate, but raw. Last tasted Nov 1990(**) Drink soon.*

Ch LATOUR *First tasted in Sept 1986: closed, tannic nose; reasonably fleshy despite raw tannic finish. More recently: deep, more mature-looking but weaker rim than Mouton; curious nose, surprisingly forthcoming, developing nicely in the glass but unknit; fairly full-bodied, more rounded than the Mouton. Crisp Cabernet flavour, slightly bitter tannic finish. Last noted at the Frericks/Wodarz Latour and Mouton tasting, March 1989(**) Probably worth bottle-ageing but will never be great.*

Ch MOUTON-ROTHSCHILD *A cask sample produced for Flatt's Mouton vertical in April 1986: fairly deep though not very intense; quite nice fruit; dry, medium full-bodied, lots of fruit but raw. And, three years later, at the Latour and Mouton tasting: deep, crisp; an immediately attractive, typical Mouton Cabernet Sauvignon nose, but then noted "veal", bramble, and, after 30 minutes, sweaty tannin. Very dry, fullish, crisp, hard, flavoury but ungracious and short. Considering that Mouton is an archetypal Cabernet Sauvignon claret, clearly Cabernet Sauvignon alone is not enough, it needs to have a secure growing season and unhampered ripeness. Last tasted March 1989*(*) Will probably soften a little with bottle-age.*

Ch CHEVAL-BLANC *Fairly deep, attractive ruby; nothing special about the nose, either way. Touch of sweetness, not bad mid-palate but tannic/bitter finish and lacking length. Got worse in the glass. Tasted only once, lunching at the Travellers' Club, Jan 1990.*

Ch PETRUS *I recall walking past the vineyard in the early autumn of 1984: scarcely a grape to be seen. Straggly clusters, the vines looking more like a field of stubble. What little wine was made was all consigned to the US. Not tasted.*

Ch d'ANGLUDET *Maturing; lean, metallic nose and palate. Dry. Rather raw. April 1989*

Ch BEYCHEVELLE *Managed to produce about 8% Merlot. Medium depth, maturing; quite flavoury but not much future. Two notes, last in Aug 1987**

Ch CISSAC *First noted, pure Cabernet, quite flavoury but with a slightly bitter finish in 1987, and each year since. Bravely shown at a recent Cissac tasting: medium, plummy colour; indifferent nose; medium dryness and body, not bad fruit but raw. Last tasted Oct 1990**

Ch DUHART-MILON *Magnum. Fairly deep black cherry colour, starting to mature; curiously fishy, oyster shell, metallic nose; medium dry, fairly full-bodied, firm but blunt, with quite nice chunky fruit and not unreasonably dry finish. Yet curiously raw with food. Last tasted Oct 1988**

Ch L'EGLISE-CLINET *Considering that the make-up normally includes 80% Merlot, a fairly satisfactory wine made. Nose sweet, rather jammy, some sweetness on palate, fairly lightweight, broad chaptalised flavour. Early developer. July 1987** Drink up.*

Ch L'EVANGILE *Palish, mature; soft, sweet, cardboard and strawberry; light, dry, bitty finish. Somewhat tart. May 1991**

Ch FIGEAC *Medium depth, advanced maturity; rather flat, chaptalised, iron-tinged nose; medium weight, not bad fruit, dry finish. Figeac's percentage of Cabernet Sauvignon plantation is unusually high for St-Emilion, Merlot being only 30%. Noted at pre-sale tasting: a well-known wine merchant trying to ease out of '84s, July 1987***

Les FORTS DE LATOUR *Crisp fruit; surprisingly soft. Nov 1990** Drink up.*

Ch du GLANA *Two recent notes. Not at all bad. Some richness. Tannic. Last tasted Sept 1989**

Ch LASCOMBES *Selective late-picking and careful sorting increased costs by 50%, though the small production was of reasonable quality. Certainly impressive in cask: intense ruby; assertive Cabernet Sauvignon aroma and flavour; dry, tannic, clean-cut but raw. Very deep, impressive colour noted after bottling, the nose and taste being very spicy. Dry, full-bodied. Last tasted Nov 1986. Need to retaste.*

Ch LEOVILLE-LAS-CASES *As always, relatively fleshy and well clad. Two notes in the mid-1980s, then very deep, intense, youthful; glorious fruit, the best '84 tasted; certainly finer than most. Last noted July 1987*(**) Need to retaste.*

Ch LYNCH-BAGES *Opaque in cask, dumb but deep, rich and fruity. A year later I thought it rather common and stalky on the nose, dry, fairly full-bodied but raw and short. Two years later, opening up and maturing, but rather smelly and rough-textured. Needs strong cheese. Last tasted Oct 1988(*)*

Ch MALESCOT-ST-EXUPERY *Palish, fully developed; light, fragrant nose but dry, lightish and short. Jan 1989* Drink up.*

Ch MEYNEY *Four fairly recent notes. Deep, impressive, maturing; cherry-like fruit; full-bodied, tannic with tinges of earth and iodine. Perfectly drinkable as an* ordinaire. *Last tasted June 1991*★★

Ch La MISSION-HAUT-BRION *Deep, plummy; quite good nose, scented, touch of lime; fleshier than expected. Some ripe fruit, but lacking length. Noted at Wolf's tasting, June 1990*★★(★) *Now to 1998.*

Ch MONTROSE *The weakest of a small group of '84 Médocs tasted at VinExpo in June 1985. Lacking the usual Montrose depth; curious overtones, peppery, cloves; fluffy, indeterminate, short, rather bitter. Last tasted July 1987*(★)

MOULIN DES CARRUADES *Two fairly recent notes. Quite attractive soft ruby; acceptably fragrant nose and flavour. Very tannic. Rawness rubbed off by, and quite refreshing with, food. Last tasted Oct 1989*★

Ch Les ORMES-DE-PEZ *Very deep; strange, hard, stalky nose; quite nice fruit, very positive but rather ordinary, common even. Last tasted Oct 1986*★

Ch PALMER *Medium, rather dull and plummy; not bad fruit on nose and palate; unthrilling in April 1989. Recently at the château: palish, orange-tinged; pleasant though immature fruit; light, short, rather raw and bitter finish. Not bad. Last tasted June 1991*★

Ch PICHON-LONGUEVILLE, BARON *Palish, maturing; neutral nose; dry, crisp Cabernet Sauvignon flavour. Rather raw. Oct 1988*★(★)

Ch PICHON-LONGUEVILLE, LALANDE *Medium-deep, beginning to show a little maturity; sweaty tannic nose and flavour. Aug 1990*(★★)

Ch PRIEURE-LICHINE *Palish, quick developer; nose a bit stewed; hard fruit, unsurprisingly raw and short. In magnum, Oct 1988*★

Ch RAUSAN-SEGLA *Very deep, plummy, youthful appearance; forthcoming nose, crisp, bramble-like fruit with flavour to match. Tannic. May 1988*★★(★) *Now to 1998.*

Ch La TOUR-CARNET *Medium-pale, faintly plummy, weak-rimmed; odd, rather artificial piquant fruitiness which opened up quite fragrantly; dry, fairly light, easy, flavoury. Short and spiky. Last tasted June 1988*★★

Ch La TOUR-HAUT-BRION *Just one not very recent note. Surprisingly pale; raw fruit on nose; open oyster shell, metallic fruit flavour and rather hollow. July 1988*★

BRIEF, MAINLY OLDER, NOTES ON SOME OTHER '84s:

*L'*AMIRAL DE BEYCHEVELLE *Ruby; strangely scented; loads of new oak, raw, very tannic. 1988*★

Ch CANTENAC-BROWN *Fairly deep, full-bodied, quite rich and chewy. 1986*★★

Dom de CHEVALIER *Over 80% Cabernet Sauvignon. Fairly deep; restrained though some fragrance; not bad, quite a concentration of tannin. 1986*★★

Ch CORBIN *St-Emilion. Fairly deep, touch of sweetness, chunky, fruity. Surprisingly agreeable. 1987*★★

Ch COS D'ESTOURNEL *Piquant, stalky Cabernet fruit, very dry, raw, tannic. 1986*(★)

Ch COS LABORY *Palish, weak-rimmed; sugary fragrance; light, easy flavoury. Needs drinking. 1986*★

Ch GISCOURS *Characteristically deep; a very odd though fruity nose, unknit; full, flavoury, chewy, tannic. 1986*★(★)

Ch GLORIA *Some fruit; dry, chunky, dull. 1987*★

Ch HAUT-BAGES-AVEROUS *Very deep; stalky; dry, fullish, some flesh and fruit but raw. 1986*★

Ch La LAGUNE *Deep, plummy; curiously attractive fruitiness on nose and palate. Very flavoury. 1987*★★

Ch de MARBUZET *Dry, lean, raw fruit, tannic. 1986*(★)

Ch PETIT-VILLAGE *Small crop but managed 50% Merlot. Fragrant, dry, slightly acidic, short but very flavoury. 1986*★★

Ch PIBRAN *Advanced colour, mature, orange-tinged; low-keyed, touch of coffee; dry, rather tinny. 1989*

1985★★★★★

This seems to be a universally good vintage, certainly in Europe: superb Tuscan wines, the best red burgundy and almost certainly the best vintage port of the decade – and beautifully balanced claret. I have a feeling that, for me, this vintage will turn out to be almost as entrancing as '53.

A winter with heavy frost damage in Jan. The spring was wet with severe storms, including locally devastating hail in May and June. However, the weather during the crucial flowering period was good and this was followed by a hot July, with some rain, a cooler, dry and rather dull Aug, and Sept was the driest on record. It was also hot, the temperature exceeding that in 1959, 1964, 1975 and 1982 though not capping 1961. Some picking commenced around Sept 22 but those who held back were rewarded with fine harvesting conditions throughout Oct.

Apart from tasting from the cask, and from cask samples in London, the first really comprehensive surveys were the *grand cru* tasting of 69 '85s, at Christie's in April 1987, and two major *Decanter* magazine blind tastings of top-growth Médocs. Rarely have I made so many consistently good notes on so wide a range of wines. It seems that almost every one, in every district, produced happily balanced wines. Not block-busters. Claret at its ingenuous best.

Ch LAFITE *Five recent notes: fairly deep, lovely cherry red; the nose, as so often, subdued at first but nicely refined and with very good fruit, developed fragrantly in the glass, toasty, elegant, great potential; medium-dry, medium-full body, very good fruit, tannin and acidity. Long, a bit lean. More recently: perfect weight, beautifully balanced. Should make a perfectly understated claret of distinction. Last tasted Dec 1990*★★(★★★) *1995–2015*

Ch MARGAUX *First tasted in cask, June 1987. Though deep, not as intense as the one-year-old '86 but certainly more open, more fragrant and distinctly fleshier. Tasted again two months later when I went to the château to recork Marvin*

Shanken's half-bottle of the 1784. I noted the sweet young fruit and spicy new oak on the nose of the '85, still in cask. A rich, mouthfilling wine with soft fruit despite youthful tannin. Then twice recently. One slightly corky and austere, the other sweet, harmonious, velvety, elegant. Last tasted Dec 1990**(***)

Ch LATOUR *Seven notes. First tasted in the cellars just before fining, Sept 1986. Intensely purple; high-toned, citrus touch; full, fleshy, fascinating, with distinct blackcurrant flavour. Six recent notes: At the Latour/Mouton tasting in Wiesbaden, March 1989: medium-deep, more evolved than the '86; meaty, shapely nose that developed richly in the glass; attractive fruit, length and aftertaste. Very stylish. At two Christie's Wine Course Master Classes: an appealing colour, not as deep as expected; beautiful well-developed bouquet, sweet, chocolate fudge, though with underpinning hardness; wonderful sweetness and fruit on the palate. Full-bodied but rounded. Taste of pistachio nuts. All the component parts. Beguiling. Lovely to drink even now though a good long life ahead.* Last tasted Dec 1990**(***) Soon to 2010 or beyond.

Ch MOUTON-ROTHSCHILD *First tasted in cask in June 1986: marvellously deep, rich colour yet not opaque; glorious fruit though, as with the Latour, a hard foundation; full, fleshy, yet a bit lean. Two notes in 1989: nose reminding me of brambles and violets, classic, fine but a bit severe. And at the Frericks/Wodarz Latour and Mouton tasting: deep though far more advanced than the '86; pleasant youthful spiciness and fruit, also a meatiness — veal — and alcohol. Less spectacular on the nose than the '86. Medium dry, fairly full-bodied; slightly austere despite its flesh and fruit. Tannic. Most recently: glorious nose; elegant, lovely texture and beautiful aftertaste. My highest mark at the most recent* Decanter *blind tasting of '85 Médocs.* Last noted Dec 1990**(***) 1998–2015

Ch AUSONE *Tasted only once, at Flatt's vertical of Ausone: medium-deep, lively, immature; lovely, luscious young fruit, plausible, attractive, tannic yet almost sickly sweet nose; on the palate full, fruity with good length. Attractive.* Oct 1987**(**) Say 1992–2005.

Ch CHEVAL-BLANC *In cask: deep and purple; curious, somewhat taut, low-keyed nose; nice weight, shape and very good fruit. Most recently: rich, maturing; first a whiff of iron, clover, mint, opening richly, almost pungent; sweet, full of fruit, extract, excellent length, balance. Lovely.* Last tasted March 1991***(**) Now to 2010.

Ch PETRUS *Showing well at Johann Bjürklund's Pétrus tasting: medium-deep, very distinctly ruby; the nose was very forthcoming, seemingly fully evolved, rich, sweet and chocolaty when first poured, then held back a bit and after an hour opened up fully and finally, after over two hours in the glass, had a glorious ripe mulberry aroma. On the palate, medium sweetness and medium-full body with lovely fruit, flavour, perfect balance, tannin and acidity.* April 1990***(**) Now to 2020.

Ch L'ANGELUS *First noted sample, at Nathl Johnston's sample presentation, May 1986: rich, stylish. Also showing well at the* grand cru *tasting at Christie's in April 1987. An elegant, shapely wine. Two years later: sweet, agreeable, harmonious nose; sweet on palate too, with very attractive flavour, fruit, tannin and refreshing acidity.* Last tasted April 1989*** Drink now to 1998.

Ch d'ANGLUDET *Five recent notes: good colour, deep, rich, still rather youthful; very distinctive nose, ripe, curiously scented, spicy; remarkably soft, delicious flavour, good dry tannic finish and crisp acidity.* Last tasted July 1990****

Ch BATAILLEY *Eight recent notes: attractive plummy colour; soft, sweet, agreeable nose, lovely fruit, no harsh edges; palate mirrors nose: sweet, uplifting flavour, nice weight, reasonable length dropping to a soft tannic finish. Archetypal Batailley: fruit rather than finesse. A pleasant drink.* Last tasted Feb 1991*** Now to beyond 2000.

Ch BELGRAVE *Two notes: quite nice fruit but nothing special. Sweet, bland. If it cannot make its fifth growth standard in a vintage like '85, it never will.* Last tasted Dec 1990**

Ch BEYCHEVELLE *Three varying and unhelpful cask samples at Nathl Johnston's first trade tasting of '85s. Next noted in Aug 1987, a month after the bottling had finished: though hard-nosed, surprisingly soft and easy on the palate. Showing well in Jan 1989 and in Dec the same year. Almost identical notes 12 months later: deep, plummy colour; attractive, fragrant, blackberry-like citrus nose; fairly sweet, nice weight, flesh, vinosity and texture. Soft tannins. Attractive.* Last tasted Dec 1990***(*) Now to 2000+

Ch BOYD-CANTENAC *An attractive, easy, soft wine at the* grand cru *tasting in April 1987. Next in Jan 1989, not much colour change; interesting, peppery, candle-wax bouquet, with quite good depth; medium dryness and weight, pleasant texture, fair length. A poor, woody bottle at the most recent tasting.* Last tasted Dec 1990. At best**(*) Now to 2000.

Ch BRANAIRE-DUCRU *Rather weak-rimmed; sweetish nose, very nice fruit; dry but lean, peppery and lacking flesh in April 1987. Latterly pink-tinged, still sweet-nosed, vinous, fragrant. Dry, nice weight, quite pleasant. Refreshing acidity. Agreeable enough but not top class.* Last tasted Dec 1990*** Now to 1998.

Ch BRANE-CANTENAC *The usual, overripe, sweaty, farmyard nose; distinctly sweet on palate, full-bodied, certainly full-flavoured, rich, spicy — glorious, in its opulently rustic way.* Last tasted Dec 1990*** Now to 1998.

Ch CALON-SEGUR *A cask sample in May 1986 seemed a bit artificial to me; much better from the cask tasted at the château that Sept: good depth, and good fruit. In April 1987 the wine was distinctly sweet, its tannin masked by body and fruit. By Jan 1989, still deep though forward; straightforward, young, peppery and fruity nose; full-bodied, nice texture, good tannin and acidity. Less impressed most recently, finding the sample bottle rather sickly and sweaty on the nose and a bit short.* Last tasted Dec 1990**(*)?? 1995–2010.

Ch de CAMENSAC *Eight recent notes. Nice wine, for a change approaching its classed-growth* *classification: medium-deep; very attractive crisp Cabernet nose; slightly sweet, soft, easy and appealing.* Last tasted June 1991*** Now to 2000.

Ch CANON-LA-GAFFELIERE *Fruity and agreeable in April 1987. Exactly two years later: fairly deep, still youthful; soft, sweet, fruity nose and flavour. Perfect now.* Last Dec 1990*** Now to 1998.

Ch CANTEMERLE *Three consistent and not altogether enthusiastic notes. In April 1987, hard chewy, tannic. At the two* Decanter *tastings, deep and fairly intense though maturing; low-keyed, slightly malty, a bit smelly though sweet, quite rich and fruity on the palate. But not a top '85 or a notably up-to-standard Cantemerle.* Last tasted Dec 1990** Now to 1996.

Ch CANTENAC-BROWN *Three fairly recent notes: very deep, plummy, still immature; sweet, hefty, vegetal nose that developed vanilla, strawberry and honeycomb fragrance in the glass; sweetish, full-flavoured, nice texture. Attractive, not great.* Last tasted Jan 1989*** Now to 1996.

Ch La CARDONNE *At its most agreeable in a vintage like '85. Nice fruit. A pleasantly balanced, delicious drink.* Last tasted Feb 1991*** Now to 1995.

Ch CHASSE-SPLEEN *An excellent cask sample in May 1986: lovely fruit and spice. A year later: fragrant, cedary nose, noticeable length, good aftertaste. More recently still a fairly thick black-cherry colour; low-keyed at first, tannic but with good fruit support; a pleasant, currant-like richness of fruit, some flesh, slightly bitter tannins and good acidity. Settling down for a good mid-term run.* Last tasted Feb 1988***(*) 1992–98

Dom de CHEVALIER *First tasted at the château in May 1986. Production a modest 4,500 cases. Deep purple, very forthcoming nose, full of fruit, spice, iodine; fullish, lean and fragrant. A year later, a rich, sweaty, tannic nose; very good flavour and balance. More recently, still deep and youthful; a good fruity mouthful. Overall dry.* Last tasted Jan 1988**(**) Say 1993–2005.

Ch CLERC-MILON-MONDON *Slight prickle of carbon dioxide when shown — a cask sample — in April 1987 but nose very beguiling. Almost identical rating at the two* Decanter *tastings: still very deep, but maturing; fragrant, almost opulently ripe nose; nice flavour and weight, tannin and noticeable acidity.* Last tasted Dec 1990*** Now to 1998.

Ch CLINET *Very good wine. Showing well — rich, fleshy, delicious in April 1987. Two years later: deep, youthful; nice fruit; distinctly sweet, good extract and flavour.* Last tasted at lunch at Ch Canon, April 1989***(*) Now to 2000+

Ch COS D'ESTOURNEL *First tasted in cask at the château: elegant, cedary, fruity, spicy. Showing very well in Jan 1989: blackberry, bramble-like fragrance and flavour. Great potential. 12 months later, at the Hollywood Wine Society Cos tasting, still a deep, rich, ruby; lovely, sweet, harmonious, cedary, slightly tarry scent; perfect balance and length. Developing well.* Last tasted Dec 1990***(*) 1992–2010

Ch COS LABORY. *Deep yet relatively forward in appearance. At the Jan 1989 tasting I found the nose surprisingly open and evolved, less so at the most recent tasting though with good depth of fruit. Very pleasant flavour. Silky tannins.* Last tasted Dec 1990**(*) 1992–2000

Ch CROIZET-BAGES *Seems to be developing too quickly; sweet, plausible nose and flavour. Too easy.* Jan 1989** Now to 1995.

Ch DAUZAC *Deep; sweet, forthcoming nose, a bit uneven; medium full-bodied, some concentration yet an easy elegant style, oaky, tannic. Lacking length.* Last tasted Dec 1990*** just. Drink now to 1996.

Ch DESMIRAIL *Initially youthful, intense; a consistently fragrant bouquet, crisp, nicely evolved, violets. Flavour to match. Medium weight. Attractive.* Last tasted Dec 1990*** Now to 2000.

Ch DUCRU-BEAUCAILLOU *Dry, good texture, moderate length in May 1986. A year later dumb, sweaty, tannic nose; rich; fullish, tannic on palate, quite good aftertaste. I thought it a bit stalky and lacking length at the Jan 1989* Decanter *tasting but, the following month, presented by Xavier Borie at a tasting it showed reasonably well: deep, plummy, intense, bright; rather medicinal nose, iron, vanilla but developed a pleasant scent after a time in glass; crisp fruit. Straightforward.* Last tasted Dec 1990**(**) 1995–2010

Ch DUHART-MILON *Four recent notes: deep; minty, rich Cabernet Sauvignon aroma; pleasant sweetness and weight, soft fruit, reasonable extract, very attractive flavour.* Last tasted May 1991*** Now to 1998.

Ch DURFORT-VIVENS *Showing quite well at the* grand cru *and two* Decanter *tastings: deep; classic, some depth; fairly full-bodied, crisp yet ripe fruit, extract, tannin and acidity. Moderating now.* Last tasted Dec 1990**(*) 1992–2000

Dom de L'EGLISE *Pomerol. Medium-deep, velvety, maturing, open, already browning at the edge; lovely fruit and flesh. Rather Graves-like scent. After 15 minutes became almost malty, then honeyed. Distinctly sweet on the palate. Lovely rich fruit. Interesting texture. A beautiful yet contradictory wine.* June 1990**** But drink soon!

Ch L'EVANGILE *Gloriously deep; lovely fruit; beautiful flavour, silky tannins, good length. A charmer.* At Spencer House, May 1991***(*) Now to 2000.

Ch FERRIERE *Medium-deep, crisp, youthful; nicely developed, biscuity, very fragrant; lovely flavour and texture, tannic finish.* Jan 1989*** 1992–2000

Ch de FIEUZAL *Showing well in May 1986 and very attractive at the April 1987* grand cru *tasting; fairly sweet, harmonious, crisp fruit, tannic.* Last tasted April 1991*** Now to 2000.

Ch FIGEAC *First tasted in cask at the château in May 1986. Lovely wine, full of fruit. Showing well at Desai's Figeac tasting: fairly deep, plummy; very fragrant; full-flavoured, soft yet good grip, combination of fruit and oak. Very attractive.* Last tasted Dec 1989**** Now to 2000.

Les FORTS DE LATOUR *Deep, plummy; good fruit, vanilla, depth; fullish, surprisingly soft.* Last tasted at Latour, Nov 1990*** Now to 2000.

Ch GISCOURS *Fragrant but a distinct 'Virol' maltiness, reminding me of '28 Haut-Brion, and, in Jan 1989, strange, very tannic bottles. Now maturing; slightly malty, chaptalised blackberry nose; sweet on the palate, fairly full-bodied, fruit and grip yet bland. Lacking '85 charm. However, looking very mature and tasting sweet and bland at the most recent* Decanter *line-up. Last tasted Dec 1990**? 1992–2000*

Ch GRAND-PUY-DUCASSE *Fragrant, spicy and attractive cask sample at H Sichel's tasting, May 1986. In Jan 1989: still deep, youthful; sweet, fragrant, brambly yet unknit; also fairly sweet on palate. Slightly medicinal, tannic finish. Quite a nice mouthful, elegant yet some reservations. A good Ducasse. Last tasted Dec 1990**(*) 1992–98*

Ch GRAND-PUY-LACOSTE *An excellent, firm, spicy cask sample at Nathl Johnston's tasting, May 1986. An opaque, classic, no tricks bottle in April 1987, going through a rather severe period at the first* Decanter *tasting in Jan 1989 and, the following month, at the Borie tasting in Hollywood (Florida). Still deep, plummy; classic but restrained; excellent future. Last tasted Dec 1990**(***) 1995–2015, the longer the better.*

Ch GRUAUD-LAROSE *Three recent notes: still impressively deep, intense; fragrant, crisp, lively, harmonious nose; touch of sweetness, agreeable weight, flavour, style. Pleasing fruit, flesh and length. Last tasted Dec 1990***(**) Now to 2005.*

Ch HAUT-BAGES-LIBERAL *A yeasty, bitter, unready cask sample in May 1986 — why are wines shown to the trade in this condition? In Jan 1989 nose hefty, hard and alcoholic at first but developed fragrance; good flavour, texture, tannin and acidity. Remarkably high marks at the most recent tasting: impressively deep, maturing; richly evolved, ripe, fruity nose; sweet, full-bodied, soft, fleshy. A lovely wine. Last noted Dec 1990**(**) 1993–2000*

Ch HAUT-BAILLY *Good fleshy cask sample, May 1986. Spicy 1987. Now medium-deep; sweet nose; extraordinarily rich, rustic, assertive. Last tasted April 1991***(*) Now to 2000+*

Ch HAUT-BATAILLEY *Delightful cask sample, May 1986. Elegant, attractive at the* grand cru *tasting the following spring. Two uneven bottles at the first* Decanter *tasting, one slightly stalky, both dry and stringy. Showing some maturity at Xavier Borie's tasting, but slight stalkiness noted again — wet straw, a whiff of Cabernet Sauvignon. Three months later, stalky nose again; sweet, rather strange flavour. At the most recent* Decanter *tasting, opaque though maturing; dumb and dusty at first, then fragrant; nice weight, elegant. Perhaps lacking a little length. Last tasted Dec 1990**(*)? Drinkable now to 1998.*

*Ch d'*ISSAN *Four notes. Fragrant, high-toned, a bit lean but stylish, in April 1987. Then in Jan 1989 medium-deep; scent of violets, good depth of fruit; medium weight, flavour, still rather unknit, tannic finish. Most recently: also tasted blind, sweet, soft, harmonious bouquet and flavour. Lovely wine. Last tasted Dec 1990**** Now to 2000.*

Ch KIRWAN *Also noted at the* grand cru *and the two* Decanter *blind tastings. Gloriously rich fruit on the nose with interesting and unusual citrus-touched fruit on the palate when young. Still deep; sweet, harmonious, forthcoming bouquet, violets again, like the d'Issan; loose-knit but full, fleshy and flavoury. Last tasted Dec 1990*** Now to 2000.*

Ch LAFON-ROCHET *Even in a vintage like '85, a tannic, fairly severe, uncompromising sort of wine. Noted at the* grand cru *and both* Decanter *tastings. Still very deep, just starting to mature; dumb and dusty nose, plummy fruit; medium dryness and weight, well put together but notably tannic. Needs time. Last tasted Dec 1990*(**) 1995–2005*

Ch LAGRANGE *St-Julien. Four recent notes: impressively deep; nose not very clearly defined but vinous, cedary; distinct sweetness, fairly full-bodied with nice, easy plummy fruit and adequate tannin and acidity. High marks at a recent blind tasting: nose like port and coffee; soft, rich, fleshy. Last tasted Dec 1990**** Now to 2000.*

Ch La LAGUNE *Showing well, rich, very spicy, at Nathl Johnston's tasting, May 1986, also at the first* Decanter *tasting: deep; glorious nose combining fruit and spices; fairly sweet, rich, pleasant weight, beguiling oak, good tannins. Very pleasant. Last tasted Jan 1989***(*) Now to 2000+*

Ch de LAMARQUE *Nice colour; curious, high-toned, peppery nose but flavoury and charming at the April 1987 tasting at Christie's. Opening up yet sweaty and a bit disappointing on the nose though with a nice touch of sweetness, medium-light, soft, quite nice. Last tasted Dec 1989** Now to 1996.*

Ch LANGOA-BARTON *At the 1987* grand cru *tasting: richly coloured, good fruit; lean, dry, tannic. In Jan 1989: fruit still a bit raw, but an attractive, easy wine at the first* Decanter *tasting. Most recently, elegant yet a touch of stalkiness. Last noted Dec 1990*** 1992–2000+*

Ch LASCOMBES *In April 1987, fairly harmonious, satisfactory. At the Jan 1989* Decanter *tasting, still deep, intense, youthful-looking; slightly caramelly, well-developed nose; sweet, medium full-bodied, rich, harmonious, nice texture, good tannins. Fairly similar notes at the most recent tastings. Perhaps a touch of weakness on the finish. Last noted Dec 1990**(*) 1993–2005*

Ch LEOVILLE-BARTON *At the H Sichel tasting in May 1986, Anthony Barton thought his own cask sample was not showing well, yet it was spicy and relatively soft. The following spring, very crisp, fruity and tannic. Lovely flavour and texture. My most recent note not good but I must give it the benefit of the doubt. Others marked it more highly. Last tasted Dec 1990***(*) 1992–2000*

Ch LEOVILLE-LAS-CASES *M Delon rarely condescends to produce sample bottles for tastings, though I do not blame him for not risking to ship early cask samples. As it happens, I was able to taste his '85 in cask in May 1986. Though restrained on the nose, it harboured marvellous fruit and vinosity, and was a full, rich classic young wine on palate. Colin Parnell must have used his editorial powers of persuasion for bottles of Las-Cases* were *in both* Decanter *magazine's line-ups of '85s. Still very deep, intense and youthful; fine, classic nose. Firm. Flavoury. A star, waiting in the wings. Last tasted Dec 1990**(***) 1995–2015*

Ch LEOVILLE-POYFERRE *In May 1986, attractive but a lighter style than the next door sample,*

Ducru-Beaucaillou. In Jan 1989: nose sweet, meaty; fairly full-bodied, rich, good fruit. Most recently: deep; brambly fruit; nice wine. Last tasted Dec 1990*** *Now to 2000.*

Ch LYNCH-BAGES *Cask samples showing well at both London trade tastings, May 1986: opaque, intense; lovely crisp fruit, fleshy, spicy, 'medicinal' Médoc fragrance. The following April, similar, some leanness noted but good firm flesh, gingery. By autumn 1988, rich and plummy, lovely fruit, length, tannin and potential. Still a deep youthful appearance in Jan 1989; a very original fragrance, flavour and silky texture. Good weight, nice aftertaste. A good, rich, flavoury wine.* Last tasted Dec 1990***(**) *Now to 2005.*

Ch LYNCH-MOUSSAS *Attractive but a bit superficial at the* grand cru *tasting in 1987. Fragrant, flavoury, easy at the most recent* Decanter *tasting.* Last noted Dec 1900** *Now to 1996.*

Ch MALESCOT-ST-EXUPERY *Four recent notes. The best, from an* impériale *at Rodenstock's Malescot tasting and dinner: rich, fruity, crisp, medium-dry, fairly full-bodied, ripe, spicy. Touch of iron on the tannic finish. A pretty good, very fruity bottle at the recent* Decanter *tasting. Better nose than palate.* Last tasted Dec 1990*** *Now to 2000.*

Ch de MARBUZET *First tasted at Cos in May 1986: opaque; spicy, dusty, fig-like fruit; dry, crisp. Most recently: still fairly deep; a pleasant, high-toned nose with "dusty", I noted again, fruit; full, fleshy, fruity, pleasant.* Last tasted June 1991*** *Now to 2000.*

Ch MARQUIS D'ALESME-BECKER *Two notes, both at* Decanter's *blind tastings. Tannic, rather stalky, appley nose; dry, full-bodied, tannic, severe in Jan 1989. Impressive yet not attractive.* Last tasted Dec 1990(*) *Future uncertain.*

Ch MARQUIS-DE-TERME *These 'aristocrats' from Margaux tend to be a bit confusing. Three recent notes: strange, figgy, port-like nose in Jan 1989 at both* Decanter *tastings, flavoury, unknit yet overall attractive. Showing quite well at a pre-sale tasting in July 1989: deep, still youthful; attractive Cabernet Sauvignon aroma; touch of sweetness, medium-full body, rich, suave, pleasant enough, fairly tannic. Most recently, some elegance and suavity noted.* Last tasted Dec 1990**(*) *1993–2005*

Clos du MARQUIS *This Marquis is of Las-Cases, the second wine of that* 2ème cru. *First tasted (a cask sample) May 1986 and, later the same month, at the château. First a bit raw though with good fruit. Fresh from the cask, the nose a bit young and stalky but softer on palate. More recently, at a Wine & Food Society tasting: still a notably deep plummy purple; nose like stewed blackberries or blackberry and apple pie! Sweaty tannins. Dry, full-bodied, rich, chewy, dry tannic finish. A commendable performance for a second wine.* Last tasted Nov 1989*(**) *1994–2000+*

Ch La MISSION-HAUT-BRION *Just one note: deep, lively; nice ripe mulberry-like fruit which opened up gloriously; medium-dry, lovely fruit, weight, balance, tannin and acidity. Excellent.* Noted at Wolf's La Mission tasting, June 1990***(**) *1995–2020*

Ch MONTROSE *Full-bodied, rich, very assuring bottle in April 1987* grand cru *tasting. In Jan 1989, relatively immature; rather hard, good length, with fruit and other component parts to ensure a long life. Still very deep; rich nose; sweet, suave and elegant for a relatively young Montrose.* Last tasted Dec 1990**(**) *1995–2010*

Ch MOUTON-BARONNE PHILIPPE *Three recent notes: opaque, immature; a curious sweaty, leathery, tannic nose though quite good fruit; fairly full-bodied with extract masking tannins. Rather severe for the combination of Baronne Philippe and '85 and needing more bottle-age. Rather disappointing.* Last tasted Dec 1990*(**). *Try from 1995.*

Ch PALMER *Five fairly recent tastings: opaque, intense; gloriously sweet, crisp, fragrant, fruity nose; ripe, rich, soft mid-palate fruit but tannic finish. Lovely wine. Maturing.* Last tasted June 1991***(**) *1995–2015*

Ch PAPE-CLEMENT *An important vintage. New owners. Consultant Ribereau-Gayon. Now 50% Merlot. Cask sample May 1986: rich fruit, flesh, high extract, new oak. Spring 1987: full, chewy, medicinal. Recently: opaque centre, plummy; lovely, sweet, fruit, tannins; also sweet palate, lovely vinosity, touch of tar and Graves tobacco taste.* Last noted April 1991***(*) *1992–2000+*

Ch PAVIE *Cask sample showing well, May 1986: fairly sweet, lovely fruit though very tannic. For some reason or other I thought it a bit un-Pavie-like. Seemed even sweeter the following spring. More recently, an impressive colour; marvellous harmony of vanillin, strawberry; distinctly sweet on the palate, with soft fruit and excellent flesh, good weight, texture and length.* Last noted at a Jurade de St-Emilion tasting, York, Nov 1988***(*) *Now to 2005.*

Ch PEDESCLAUX *Three recent notes. Penultimately, in Jan 1989: very deep, plummy; rich, slightly malty, marmalade-like nose; slightly sweet, fairly full-bodied, lovely flavour, decent length, soft tannins. However, tasted speedily and blind at the most recent tasting I was less impressed and thought it had a curious endtaste.* Last noted Dec 1990*(*)? *1992–98*

Ch PICHON-LONGUEVILLE, BARON *Six recent notes: deep, intense; rich nose, of brambles, wild cherry, slightly medicinal; medium weight, crisp but chewy, fleshy, spicy tannins.* Last tasted Feb 1991***(*) *1994–2000*

Ch PICHON-LONGUEVILLE, LALANDE *An impressive cask sample, May 1986. However, I thought the nose a bit lean, oaky, varnishy and unforthcoming at the* grand cru *tasting the following spring, attractive on the palate but not tangibly a "super second". At the first* Decanter *tasting, nose more developed, rich, brambly, chocolaty, alcoholic; fairly full-bodied, with a fragrant Cabernet savour. Similar rating at the most recent tasting. Rich. Fleshy. Good but not great.* Last tasted Dec 1990***(*) *1993–2005*

Ch La POINTE *Two recent notes: medium-pale, quick-maturing; sweet smell and taste. Chocolate, fruit and walnuts on the nose. Soft. Easy. Attractive.* Last noted at pre-sale tasting, July 1990*** *Now to 1996.*

Ch PONTET-CANET *Interestingly, half the price of*

Beychevelle and a fraction of the price of Ducru and Pichon Lalande, at Nathl Johnston's '85 cask sample tasting May 1986. Seemed full of fruit. Tannic of course. Then at Christie's in April 1987, I noted a curious, "green", high-toned nose overlaying new oak; rich, full-bodied, very oaky and very tannic on palate. At the two Decanter *tastings, still fairly deep; an immediately forthcoming, high-toned, multi-part nose: meaty, sweaty cheese rind tannin, fruit, and a whiff of bandages (iodine, lint); a cool, crisp, fruity, citrus-like flavour, some elegance, an interesting texture and leathery tannic, slightly unconvincing finish. Will be interesting to see how this turns out. Last tasted Dec 1990**(*) 1993–2000*

Ch PRIEURE-LICHINE *Refreshing but unknit nose, lean, very flavoury in April 1987. Opening up by Oct 1988. Four consistent notes since then: a very pretty, luminous cherry red; an appealing, fragrant, piquant but still not completely harmonious bouquet; fruity, lean, crisply refreshing. Rather superficial, but very flavoury. Nice texture. Good length. Last tasted Jan 1991*** Now to 1998.*

Ch RAUSAN-SEGLA *Six notes. First tasted from half-bottle cask samples in Sept 1986: low-keyed, immature, Cabernet Sauvignon aroma, tight-knit, new oak spiciness. Despite its youthfulness a sweet young thing, cloves, cinnamon, not too tannic. Good fruit though leanness noted the following spring. 12 months later, the bouquet developing well, mulberry, touch of tar; fullish, shapely, silky, good length. Three more recent notes: still fairly deep; rich, fragrant bouquet and flavour. Nice sweetness and weight. Fleshy. Pleasing aftertaste. Last tasted Dec 1990***(*) Now to 2000.*

Ch RAUZAN-GASSIES *Three notes. Less deep, more developed than the Ségla; sweet, slightly malty, caramelly nose. Sweet, nice weight, lacking charm and a bit hollow but quite attractive and a good Gassies. Last tasted Dec 1990*** Now to 2000.*

Ch de SALES *Consistent in style, easy, modest weight, very pleasant crisp fruity nose and flavour. July 1990*** Now to 1998.*

Ch ST-PIERRE-SEVAISTRE *Two consistent notes. First, Jan 1989: deep, fairly intense; vinous, medicinal, with overripe rusticity on nose and palate, particularly noticeable in the aftertaste. But sweet, fruit and flavoury in its rather idiosyncratic way. Virtually identical notes at both* Decanter *blind tastings. Not to my taste. Last noted Dec 1990** Now to 1998.*

Ch TALBOT *Showing well at the* grand cru *tasting, April 1987: crisp, citrus-scented nose; lovely fruit, flesh, spicy new oak and good aftertaste. Tasted blind in Jan 1989: fragrant but sweaty, tannin, vanilla and fruit; nice texture, dry tannate of iron finish at the first* Decanter *tasting. Most recently, deep but starting to mature; developing the idiosyncratic, medicinal, high profile smell and taste which I noted at the time, rudely, as "mad cow disease". Yet sweet, soft and flavoury. But I dislike this character as much as 'peach kernels' in white wine. Last tasted Dec 1990*** in its way. Will be a ripe, flavoursome mouthful for quite a time, and doubtless popular.*

Ch du TERTRE *A bit green on the nose but easy-going on palate in May 1987. More recently, mixed feelings on nose but pleasant on palate: a crisp, delightful, quick developer. Last tasted Jan 1989** Now to 1998.*

Ch La TOUR-CARNET *Smell and taste reminded me, in April 1987, of wet sawdust. A couple of pre-sale tasting notes in 1988: agreeable fruit, pleasant enough. At the first* Decanter *tasting (not shown at the second) it seemed to be rather hefty in appearance, on nose and palate, quite good fruit but unexciting. Last tasted Jan 1989** Now to 1998.*

SOME OTHER '85s TASTED FAIRLY RECENTLY:

Ch CISSAC *Good combination of fruit and tannin. Nice wine. Oct 1990***

Ch de CLAIREFONT *The second wine of Prieuré-Lichine: cherry red; crisp, mouthwatering fruit; very attractive, flavoury, a bit raw, adequate tannin. Nov 1989***

Ch COUFRAN *Very deep, with density of an '82; fairly full-bodied, lovely fruit but very tannic. July 1988**(*)*

Clos L'EGLISE *Opaque; great depth; soft and rich. July 1988*****

Les FIEFS DE LAGRANGE *The second wine of Ch Lagrange: good, fruity, spicy, vinous. July 1988****

Ch FOMBRAUGE *Quite nice fruit, no great length, tannic. June 1990*(*)*

Ch du GLANA *Fruity, nice weight, agreeable. May 1991****

Ch GRAND-PONTET *Pretty; caramel; easy, attractive, lean. Feb 1991****

Ch HANTEILLAN *Sweet, tannic; strange, fleshy yet austere. Sept 1989*(*)*

Ch LABEGORCE *Quick-maturing; open-knit; lean, 'mild and bitter'. April 1988***

Ch LAMOTHE-CISSAC *Agreeable fruit, crisp, dry. Jan 1988***

Ch LAROSE-TRINTAUDON *Rather oily nose; quite nice but a very odd, charred, endtaste. July 1988**

Ch MAUCAILLOU *Very tannic though loaded with fruit. Sept 1988*(**)*

Ch MEYNEY *Deep; hard, tannic, unexciting. Sept 1990***

Ch MILLET *Light. Pleasant enough. July 1988***

Ch OLIVIER *Black cherry; rich, oaky; good flavour, fruit and extract. Tannic. Oct 1989**(*)*

PAVILLON ROUGE DE CH MARGAUX *Good nose; chewy, chunky, crisp, fruity, tannic. Nov 1990****

Ch de PEZ *Unusual vinosity, nice texture. Jan 1989****

Ch PIQUE-CAILLOU *Consistently agreeable. Mar 1991****

Ch POUGET *Margaux. Rich appearance and nose. Dry, good weight and vinosity. Dec 1990****

Ch du ROCHER *Brilliant ruby; rich fruit; lovely flesh and fruit, leathery texture. Nov 1988***(*)*

Ch La SERRE *Deep, youthful; plausible, lively, citrus-edged; nice weight, spicy finish and aftertaste. Nov 1988****

Ch La TOUR-DE-MONS *Ruby; sweet, harmonious; fruity, tannic, unready. Nov 1990**(**)*

Ch TRONQUOY-LALANDE *Ruby; crisp, tannic, agreeable. Jan 1988**(*)*

Ch VERDIGNAN *Curiously perfumed vanillin; light and easy. July 1988***

NOTED ONLY FROM CASK SAMPLES AT CHRISTIE'S, SPRING 1987:

OUTSTANDING, GREAT FUTURE: *Ch Canon; Ch La Conseillante; Ch La Croix-de-Gay; Ch Petit-Village.*

SHOWING WELL, GOOD FUTURE: *Ch L'Arrosée; Ch Balestard-La-Tonnelle; Ch Beaumont; Ch Beauregard, Pomerol; Ch La Cabanne; Ch Haut-Bages-Averous; Ch La Louvière; Ch Les Ormes-de-Pez.*

SHOWING WELL, GOOD MEDIUM-TERM DRINKING: *Ch Cap-de-Mourlin; Ch Carbonnieux; Ch Clarke; Ch Fourcas-Dupré; Clos Fourtet; Ch Labégorce-Zédé; Ch Nenin; Ch Siran; Ch Troplong-Mondot.*

LIGHT, PLEASANT, QUICK MATURING: *Ch Larrivet-Haut-Brion; Ch Malartic-Lagravière; Ch Smith-Haut-Lafitte; Ch La Tour-Martillac.*

MINOR, PLEASING: *Ch Fonplégade; Ch Fourcas-Hosten; Ch de France; Ch Greyssac.*

MINOR, GOOD ENOUGH: *Ch Fonroque; Ch Hortevie; Ch Haut-Bergey.*

LESS GOOD, WEAK: *Chevalier de Védrines; Ch Côte-de-Baleau; Ch Loudenne; Ch Malescasse; Ch Ripeau.*

1986(★★★★)

An important and somewhat controversial vintage, over-hyped at the time, though still highly regarded by some notable authorities. One thing is certain, the '86 red Bordeaux are, on the whole, firm, fruity but severe and tannic wines. At their best they will be lean, long-distance runners — possibly a cross between the steeliness of the '66 Médocs, the crispness and weight of the '62s, and the macho masculinity of the '75 Médocs. Those with insufficient extract and flesh to support their fruit might well go out like the tide, leaving the hard tannins high and dry.

As usual, the growing conditions were not precisely the same in all districts. The winter of 1985/6 was quite severe but without the frost damage suffered early in 1985. The spring was cold and wet, retarding growth. May and June were fine and warm, enabling the vegetation to catch up and for the flowering to take place in ideal conditions, promising another bumper harvest, particularly of Merlot. Hottest and driest weather for 20 years until mid-Sept when there were a couple of days of rain. Less welcome was a violent storm on Sept 23 that dumped 4 in (10 cm) of rain on Bordeaux and its immediate surroundings, the southern Médoc and the Graves. However, the skies cleared and picking began around Sept 29; the Merlot first and the Cabernet Sauvignon being picked in glorious Oct weather. It was the biggest harvest since the war and most promising.

My first comprehensive tasting of '86s was arranged by Peter Vinding for L'Union des Grands Crus and held at Christie's in May 1988, the most recent organised by the Institute of Masters of Wine in London in Nov 1990. These notes have, of course, been augmented by miscellaneous tastings in cask and, subsequently, in bottle.

My present impression is that the best, like Mouton, are magnificent and will be superb — but in many years time. The less than excellent might well be avoided: I cannot foresee great developments. Choose the best, put them in your own cellar — too expensive to keep that long in a trade cellar — and forget them for 15 years or more.

Ch LAFITE *Two recent notes, first at the MW tasting of '86s: fine, deep, immature appearance; minty, cedary fragrance, with some depth of fruit. Fairly full-bodied, good mid-palate fruit, crisp, citrus-like, very flavoury, not overladen but firm tannin and acidity. Long, lean and taut yet full of fruit. A long-haul wine.* Last tasted Nov 1990(★★★) Possibly★★★★ in due course. 2000+

Ch MARGAUX *Tasted three times ex-cask at the château, first in June 1987, next in Aug: lovely colour, rich, deep, intense purple; exciting fruit and flesh, spicy; distinctly lean, taut and masculine, excellent length. Again the following April: very fragrant nose, the cinnamon of new oak, fairly dry, medium-full body, with good flesh on its bones. Very tannic. Two recent notes, the first at the MW tasting: impressively deep, intense, still immature; distinctive nose, violet-like fragrance but hard; fairly full-bodied, lovely flavour, quite sweet fruit leading to a crisp, tannic acid finish and notably good aftertaste.* Last noted at Lay & Wheeler's Ch Margaux evening, Nov 1990(★★★★) 2010–25

Ch LATOUR *First tasted from a cask sample, Sept 1987: lovely fruit; fairly full-bodied, lean though some flesh and a long, long wait until it has matured (in drinkability and in price). Next tasted at the Frericks/Wodarz Latour and Mouton tasting in March 1989. Rather surprisingly less deep and more open-knit than Mouton, immature, rich legs. Sweet, hefty nose. After 20 minutes, good spicy, gingery development, rich, brambly. Fairly dry, full-bodied, good crisp flavour, austere, bitter tannins. At the MW tasting, a more evolved colour than Mouton; nose unknit, but some fruit — a sort of toasted Cabernet Sauvignon. Fairly full-bodied, very flavoury, citrus-like piquancy, good texture. Loaded with tannin. Lean. Crisp fruit. Good length. Reasonable flesh. Considerable potential.* Last noted at the château, Nov 1990(★★★★) 2010–30

Ch MOUTON-ROTHSCHILD *A spectacular wine and certainly a top '86. Outstanding at the Latour/Mouton tasting in March 1989: opaque* *centre, intense immature purple; raw young fruit and spice, a rich, almost thick, blackcurrant aroma tirelessly churning out, sweet, with considerable depth; fabulous flavour, packed tight with fruit, very tannic, fragrant aftertaste. And at the recent MW tasting: the most magnificent depth of colour; totally different style from Lafite and with 'toasted' Cabernet fruit like Latour, only more complete and more intense. Lovely fruit on the palate. Crisp. Very flavoury. Plenty of tannin and acidity. Last noted Nov 1990(*****) A long wait.*

Ch HAUT-BRION *Very deep, marvellous colour; distinctly sweaty tannic nose, touch of chocolate; full-bodied, very chewy, loads of tannin. Astringent. Tasted with Jean Delmas at La Mission, Nov 1990(****) A long-haul wine.*

Ch CHEVAL-BLANC *Medium-deep; sweet, reasonable fruit, some depth; lean for Cheval-Blanc, rather raw dry finish. At MW tasting, Nov 1990(***)? Say 1998–2010?*

Ch PETRUS *Crisp, lively, ruby colour; immediately sweet, rich aroma, slightly gingery nose, beautiful, then biscuity. Well after an hour in the glass, lovely. Very sweet and full-bodied, rich, fleshy with a caramel, fudge-like flavour and aftertaste. Noted at the 'Stockholm' tasting, April 1990(*****) 1996–2016*

Ch L'ANGELUS *First noted at the* grand cru *tasting in May 1988: good colour; rather sweaty tannic nose; medium full-bodied, some softness and extract. A bit hard to get to grips with, a similar comment made the following spring. Most recently: impressively deep; rather cool, withdrawn nose; sweet, fleshy yet astringent. Last tasted May 1990(**) 1996–2006*

Ch d'ANGLUDET *Medium-deep; fragrant, rather idiosyncratic nose; relatively light style, very attractive, nice fruit at the May 1988 tasting. A soft red colour; fragrant, ripe and rustic; fruit and iron. Last noted June 1991(***) 1992–2000*

Ch BATAILLEY *Deep, crisp colour, nose and palate. Good fruit. Spicy. Flavoury. Good length. April 1990*(**) 1992–2000*

Ch BEYCHEVELLE *First tasted in the deep, stone, first-year cellar, Aug 1987: less intense, more open-knit and lacking the length of the Ch Margaux I had tasted the day before. Very tannic. Next, at the* grand cru *tasting in May 1988: very fragrant, medicinal, spicy new oak, lean and sinewy. Exactly two years later, plum-coloured, crisp fruit, a touch of sweetness despite its astringency. At the MW tasting: medium-deep, appreciable colour loss though still rich; a very odd iodine nose, flavoury but with a very dry bitter finish. My lowest mark of the nine classed-growth St-Juliens. Last tasted Nov 1990(**)? Time will tell.*

Ch CANON *Beautiful colour; nose rich, spicy though rather closed; medium-dry, excellent weight, fruit, extract and flavour in May 1988. At the MW tasting: medium-deep, lovely colour, starting to mature; a touch of stalkiness but good depth of fruit on nose and palate. Attractive, spicy flavour but lean for Canon and very tannic. Should make a good bottle, eventually. Last tasted Nov 1990(****) 1993–2000+*

Ch CANTEMERLE *Three notes. Surprisingly sweet and forthcoming in May 1988 but with a 'hot' bitter finish. May 1990: plummy; rather vegetal fruit; open, loose-knit and, six months later, not remotely as deep as most '86 Médocs, starting to mature; sweet, touch of strawberry on nose though a trace of stalkiness; initial sip still sweet but leaving the mouth very dry. Medium weight, lean though with something to chew. Lacking the old Cantemerle charm. Last noted at the MW tasting, Nov 1990(**) Unpredictable.*

Ch CANTENAC-BROWN *Medium, rather unconvincing appearance; quite attractive nose, a flicker of fragrance. Some fruit but frankly uninteresting, raw, tannic. Noted Nov 1990(**) For mid-term drinking.*

CARRUADES DE CH LAFITE *Medium-deep, poised to shed its youthfulness; attractive fruit, spice and fragrance; flavoury but lean, hard and dry. Like an* haute couture *model. Tasted Nov 1990(***)?*

Ch CHASSE-SPLEEN *Once again demonstrating what intelligence and competence can do with a* cru bourgeois. *First noted at the May 1988 tasting: a distinctly light style, almost the colour of a good young Fleurie; an immediately forthcoming nose, vanilla, cedar, nice fruit. Stylish. Elegant. A good long flavour. And at the MW tasting: a hard foundation to its pleasant fruitiness; a touch of sweetness and flesh to balance its tannins. Last tasted Nov 1990(***) 1992–98*

Dom de CHEVALIER *French Wine Farmers are often the first to bring cask samples to London. They showed a range of '86s as early as March 1987, including a rather raw, tannic but stylish Dom de Chevalier. Kressman's tasting followed two months later: deep; restrained, complete; good crisp fruit. By May 1988 losing a little depth of colour; still low-keyed yet very fragrant; lean, elegant, understated. At the MW tasting: ruby; nose opening out, rich, with a scent of new leather, stylish, very masculine and still extremely tannic. Last noted Nov 1990(***) 1994–2000+*

Ch CLERC-MILON *Impressively deep; nose of soft fruit and tannin; relatively sweet, chewy, fruity, attractive and very tannic. Noted at the MW tasting, Nov 1990(***) 1995–2000+*

Ch La CONSEILLANTE *Medium, maturing; very sweaty tannic nose but good fruit; medium sweetness and weight, good texture, stylish. A touch of bitterness on the finish. Nov 1990(***) Should develop well, say 1994–2000.*

Ch COS D'ESTOURNEL *68% Cabernet Sauvignon, 30% Merlot, 2% Cabernet Franc; the first vintage in which Cabernet Franc grapes used; 90% new oak. At Michèle Prats' presentation, Jan 1990: the vanilla of new oak noticeable. A fine substantial wine yet with '66 leanness. Good fruit, good length. Similar notes 10 months later. A fairly deep and intense colour; a crisp cherry-like fragrance and flavour, and acidity. Tannic of course but not overdominant. Last tasted Nov 1990(****) Should make an attractive, firm bottle, say 1996–2010.*

Ch COUFRAN *Three recent notes. Deep, rich, opaque centre; lovely rich fruit and spicy new oak on the nose. Dry, fairly full-bodied, with loads of fruit* *and grip. Very tannic. Opened on the Saturday evening it tasted better at Sunday lunchtime.* Last noted Oct 1990**(*) Now, if you like a lusty wine. Now to 2000.

Ch DAUZAC *A very good note at the* grand cru *tasting, May 1988: notable sweetness and fruit. Two years later, still deep, immature; fragrant, tannic nose opening up nicely in the glass. Medium-full body, nice fruit and flesh despite a lean '86 tendency and mouth-drying tannins.* Last tasted May 1990(***) 1993–2000

Ch La DOMINIQUE *A very good note at Eduard Kressman's cask sample tasting in May 1987: harmonious, sweet, lovely fruit. Still deep but starting to mature; rather burgundian nose; silky, easy style yet tannic.* Last tasted May 1990*(**) An attractive mid-term drink 1992–98.

Ch DUCRU-BEAUCAILLOU *Only one note. Very deep, intense, immature; forthcoming nose, good fruit and depth though with touch of stalkiness; unusually sweet, respectable weight, fruit, flavour, extract, tannin and acidity. Impressive.* Tasted Nov 1990(****) 1995–2010

Ch DUHART-MILON *Showing well at Percy Fox's tasting in Jan 1989: very distinct blackcurrant, Cabernet Sauvignon aroma; surprisingly sweet and full of fruit, though lean and tannic. Still impressively, youthfully, deep; fragrant bramble-like aroma; agreeable sweetness and weight, adequate flesh, appealing fruitiness. Good mid-term drinking.* Last tasted Nov 1990(***) 1993–98

Ch L'EVANGILE *Lovely, brick red; sweet, California-like fruit; dry; lean, leathery tannins.* May 1991(****) 1993–2000+

Ch de FIEUZAL *I have a soft spot for this class of red Graves. They have a useful tendency to drink well when young, yet they last. I have very good notes made in 1987, 1988 and 1989. Initially intensely deep and purple-tinged, now deep ruby; lovely fruit from the start, a rich mulberry-like character noted; sweet, medium weight, more flesh and extra dimensions compared with most of the '86 Graves. Delicious.* Last tasted April 1989*** Drink now to 1996.

Ch FIGEAC *Slight stalkiness haunting its crisp, distinctly Cabernet Sauvignon, oriental aroma in May 1987 and 1988. Sweet, attractive, good length. At Desai's tasting in Dec 1989 it somehow had the look of a quick developer. Nevertheless it was harder and lower-keyed on the nose and leaner and drier on the palate than the '83 or '85, but with crisp Cabernet Sauvignon fruitiness much in evidence. A '66 style of wine. A year later: medium, maturing in appearance; strawberry-like fruit, touch of mint and tannin, not fully knit; fairly sweet and fullish body, good fruit, length, acidity and of course tannin. Will, as so often, make a very flavoury, slightly over-dramatised mouthful.* Last tasted Nov 1990*(***) 1992–2000

Les FORTS DE LATOUR *At the MW tasting: less deep than expected; quite a bit of fruit but rather raw and very tannic. Later the same month: intense; slightly varnishy though crisp fruit on nose and palate.* Last tasted at Latour, Nov 1990(**) 1996–2010

Ch GISCOURS *Opaque in May 1988, with a rich port-like nose, prunes, mulberries; sweet, full-bodied with a curious stewed-fruit flavour. Almost Pétrus-like substance and fruit. In Dec 1989, still rich but not as deep; curious nose, fragrant, rich, stably. Chewy. Tannic. A lookalike note a year later, "mulberry" occurs again, also the sweetness and rich fruit. An extraordinary mouthful, still tannic.* Last tasted Nov 1990(****) For those with a taste for the brawny. Say 1994–2005.

Ch GRAND-PUY-LACOSTE *Opaque; packed with fruit and spice, good extract yet lean, in May 1987. The following year, tasted from the cask, intense, tannic, impressive. Latterly, at the MW tasting: fairly deep, still immature, attractive-looking; a lively citrus-tinged Cabernet Sauvignon aroma, spice, considerable depth of fruit; fairly full-bodied, good fruit, lean, characteristically supple, very tannic. A sinewy long-distance runner.* Last tasted Nov 1990(****) 2000+

Ch GRUAUD-LAROSE *Showing well at the* grand cru *tasting in May 1988: opaque; full of fruit, rich, rounded. Exactly two years later an almost identical note. Most recently, still impressively deep and youthful; nose now much more forthcoming, ripe, more herbaceous; distinctly sweet on palate. A good rich fruity mouthful with extract masking tannins.* Last tasted Nov 1990(****) 1992–2005

Ch HAUT-BAGES-LIBERAL *Identical marks for appearance, nose and palate in May 1988 and at the MW tasting. Now a very appealing colour; open-knit, fruity nose; very flavoury, crisp fruit, easy style.* Last tasted Nov 1990**(*) Now to 1998.

Ch HAUT-BAILLY *Three recent notes. Fairly deep, plummy, on the point of losing its pristine youthfulness; distinctly sweet, very fragrant nose; good fruit. An easy attractive wine with a useful crunch of tannin and acidity.* Last tasted Nov 1990*** Now to 1998.

Ch HAUT-BATAILLEY *Intensely deep; good fruit and taut style, in May 1987. Still fairly deep, very attractive, beautifully graded colour; tannic, stalkiness over its fruit; very assertive flavour.* Last tasted Nov 1990(***) 1995–2005

Ch LAGRANGE *St-Julien. Three notes. A half-bottle distinctly more restrained and raw than a bottle in July 1988 and, more recently, a very forthcoming, soft-fruit nose. Dry, fullish, lean though reasonably well clad, tolerable, nicely integrated tannin.* Last tasted Nov 1990(***) Say 1994–2000.

Ch La LAGUNE *Deep, rich, 'thick' extract; sweet, long, fruity in cask. Very fragrant, fruity and crisp, but one of the hardest, most tannic La Lagunes I can recall.* Last tasted Dec 1989(****) 1994–2000+

Ch LANESSAN *Six notes, from a beery, unready, cask sample in March 1987 to a plum-coloured, caramel-nosed and silky bottle, with "raw", "so-so", "slightly coarse", "screwed up" notes in between.* Last tasted June 1991(*)

Ch LANGOA-BARTON *Very deep, immature; good fruit, very spicy new oak; relatively light style, lean, attractive, lacking a little length. This was at the* grand cru *tasting in May 1988. Now less deep; nose and flavour attractive but not fully integrated. Good fruit. Dry. A lanky somewhat raw-boned youth. Probably still lanky, a trifle* *dour but dependable, in its middle age. Last tasted Nov 1990(***) 1996–2010*

Ch LEOVILLE-BARTON *An intensely deep cask sample in May 1988, with lovely fruit, spicy oak, stylish, well-clad tannins. Now medium-deep; good depth of fruit and tannin on the nose and palate. Firm, masculine, good length, very dry. Last tasted Nov 1990(***) 1996–2010*

Ch LEOVILLE-LAS-CASES *Noted only once, at the MW tasting. Magnificent colour, impressively deep and intense; forthcoming and harmonious nose, good fruit and tannin. Medium dryness, fullish body, more flesh than most, good length, tannin and acidity. Nov 1990(****) 1995–2015*

Ch LEOVILLE-POYFERRE *Noted at annual tastings since May 1987 when, for me, it was showing best. In 1988, a combination of fragrance, sweaty tannins and coarse flavour. In 1989 noted as unknit, though with firm fruit. And, most recently, a fairly deep cherry red; forthcoming and initially attractive fruit on the nose but a stalkiness noted and tannin that resembled smelly feet. Dry, not very full-bodied, quite attractive flavour but very lean with an abundance of both tannin and acidity. Last tasted Nov 1990(**) 1995–2000*

Ch LYNCH-BAGES *Lovely wine. Good, fruity cask sample in May 1987, fragrant nose, palate and aftertaste noted at the* grand cru *tasting in May 1988, and packed with flavour that autumn. At the recent MW tasting a glorious colour; rich harmonious nose; touch of sweetness, fairly full-bodied and positive, very individual flavour. Tannin and crisp acidity. Last tasted Nov 1990(****) 1993–2015*

Ch MALESCOT-ST-EXUPERY *Three recent notes. The first and last (in bottle): not very deep in colour; with very sweet, agreeable, fragrant Cabernet Sauvignon nose, and flavour to match. In between, in an* impériale, *peppery, austere, and undrinkably tannic. Last tasted Nov 1990*(**) 1994–2000+*

Ch La MISSION-HAUT-BRION *Still virtually opaque, its colour seeming to press hard against the sides of the glass; nose sweet and surprisingly open with touch of caramel and pronounced Cabernet Sauvignon aroma. I upgraded it an hour later as it had developed a gloriously rich mulberry-like fruit. On the palate dry, fairly full-bodied, crisp fruit, a lean '66-type touch. Good potential. Tasted Nov 1990(****) 1996–2015*

Ch MONTROSE *Cask samples in March and May 1987, next at the* grand cru *tasting 12 months later. Consistently deep, dumb, oaky and laden with tannin. But good fruit and length. Still fairly deep, rich; pleasantly sweet at first sip, good body. Notable fruit currently suppressed by the tannins. Time will reveal all. A classic Montrose needing plenty of bottle-age. Last tasted Nov 1990(****) 1998–2020*

Ch MOUTON-BARONNE PHILIPPE *Very deep, still immature; hard, lean, low-keyed, crisp fruit nose, and flavour to match. Attractive though, and, once past the tannin, with a fragrant aftertaste. Tasted Nov 1990(***) 1993–2005*

Ch PALMER *First noted at the* grand cru *tasting at Christie's in May 1988: muffled fruit, good length, very tannic. In 1990: still impressively deep, black cherry; forthcoming, mulberry-like fruit; leathery tannins, enough flesh. Most recently: still deep; very fragrant; delicious, shapely, tannic, good future. Needs plenty of time. Last tasted at the château, June 1991(*****) 1995–2010*

Ch PAPE-CLEMENT *New* cuverie. *Stainless steel taking place of cement vats. In May 1988, very deep, rich, intense; quite good fruit on the nose, plus earthy iron Graves character. Surprisingly soft and fleshy despite tannin. Now less deep but still rich-looking; nose a bit hard and stalky; sweet, good weight, quite nice fruit. Lean and tannic. Last tasted Nov 1998(***) 1993–2000*

Ch PAVIE *First tasted and much liked in May 1988. Two similar recent notes. Pristine intensity now less deep and on the point of change; appealing though not fully integrated nose, sweet, slightly strawberry-like; nice flesh, fruit, open character, touch of rawness which should ease off. Last tasted Nov 1990*(***) 1992–98*

Ch de PEZ *Crisp and tannic in May 1988. Not much change. Sulphur on the nose. Light for St-Estèphe and '86, but flavoury. Last tasted Nov 1990(**) 1992–98*

Ch PICHON-LONGUEVILLE, BARON *Six notes, the first an attractive, spicy, oaky cask sample in April 1987, the next, flavoury though lean and tannic in May 1988, and again shortly after bottling. Soft fruits and spice in Dec 1989 reflecting my earliest note, but stalky astringency noted the following May. Most recently, at the MW tasting, less deep but rich and losing its virginity; nose sweet, sweaty and a bit muffled; nice texture, quite good flavour but lacking real quality and style. Last tasted Nov 1990(**) 1995–2000*

Ch PICHON-LONGUEVILLE, LALANDE *Two recent notes. Less deep than expected though still immature; crisp, citrus-like fruit on nose and palate, higher-toned than the Baron; touch of sweetness, medium-full body, good length, lean but flavoury. As always, a wine with extra dimensions. Last tasted Nov 1990(****) 1996–2010*

Ch RAUSAN-SEGLA *Showing well at the* grand cru *tasting in May 1988: opaque; elegant, bilberry-like aroma; lovely fruit flavour and weight. Two recent notes: still intensely, impressively deep and rich; an original nose with distinct Margaux violets, hard though fruity. Going through a raw interim stage with bitter tannins. Lean. Will need much bottle-age. Last tasted Nov 1990. Optimistically(***) 1998–2015*

Ch SIRAN *A very deep, lean though shapely and very tannic cask sample in April 1987. More recently, medium-deep, vividly coloured; crisp, lime blossom fragrance; fullish body, quite good flesh and fruit but unexciting. As much acidity as tannin. Last tasted May 1990(***) 1994–2000*

Ch SMITH-HAUT-LAFITTE *Showing moderately well in May 1988, sweet — rather jammy — fruit on the nose, now a rather strawberry-like scent. Never very deep, now relatively light and forward for an '86, borne out on the palate. Sweet, easy, refreshing. Last tasted Nov 1990**(*) 1992–98*

Ch TALBOT *Consistent notes and not much development since the May 1988 tasting; if anything, closing up. Its pristine purple now beginning to hint, misleadingly, at maturity; its very distinctive tarry, medicinal, farmyard smell effectively masking, just as the raw tannins are overcoming, the fruit. Very flavoury. Reminds me of the '79. Gutsy.* Last tasted Nov 1990(★★★) 1996–2010

Ch La TOUR-DE-BY *My everyday wine for drinking at home for some time. First noted at a Thorman Hunt trade tasting in April 1987. Noting it as "agreeable" I should have bought it then, ex-cellar. It was, and is, an example of a lusty young wine: a beguiling combination of good fruit and spicy new oak. The sort of good-value minor Médoc to watch out for, though one should not expect even a well-made* bourgeois *claret to take on extra dimensions and suavity with age. Nevertheless, I shall keep a few bottles back.* Last tasted June 1990★(★) Now to 1995.

Ch La TOUR-MARTILLAC *Woody, raw in May 1987. Fruit and flesh though still raw in 1988. Deep; dry, fullish, slightly bitter.* Last tasted March 1991(★★)? 1993–96

Ch TROTTEVIEILLE *Though labelled* "1er grand cru classé", *the equivalent in St-Emilion of La Tour-de-By in the Médoc, though softer in appearance on nose and on palate. Ruby colour, sweet nose, curious fluffy texture and new oak apparent.* Last noted, June 1991★★

OTHER '86s TASTED RECENTLY:

Ch La CARDONNE *Sweet nose but unusually severe and tannic.* Last tasted Jan 1989★(★★)

Ch CISSAC *Deep; fragrant; raw, very tannic.* Oct 1990(★★★)

Ch CLARKE *Deep, velvety; attractive fruit and new oak nose and taste.* June 1991(★★★)

Ch CLINET *Spicy, rich, chunky fruit.* Last tasted April 1989★★(★★)?

Ch COUFRAN *Four notes, first in 1988. Still deep, immature; good fruit; rich, tannic.* Last tasted June 1991(★★★)

Ch HANTEILLAN *Hard, chunky, uninteresting.* Last tasted June 1991(★★)

Ch HAUT-BAGES-MONPELOU *Quite attractive.* April 1991★★(★)

Ch LAROSE-TRINTAUDON *Maturing; good fruit; rich, decent length, attractive.* June 1991★★(★)

Ch OLIVIER *Immature; curious, medicinal; odd but flavoury, nice weight.* June 1991(★★)

Ch ROQUETAILLADE-LA-GRANGE *Rich, biscuity; sweet, attractive.* May 1991★★

Ch ROUDIER *Montagne-St-Emilion. Deep, sweet, plausible, inexpensive.* June 1991★★

Ch La TOUR-ST-BONNET *Ripe fruit, raw tannin.* Last tasted Feb 1991★(★)

Ch VERDIGNAN *Opaque; hard, tannic, unappealing.* Last tasted June 1991(★)?

NOT NOTED SINCE THE *GRAND CRU* TASTING, MAY 1988:

SHOWING WELL, CLASSIC, GOOD FUTURE: *Ch Lascombes; Ch Les Ormes-de-Pez; Ch Prieuré-Lichine.*

SHOWING WELL, MID-TERM: *Ch Balestard-La-Tonnelle; Ch Branaire-Ducru; Ch Carbonnieux; Ch d'Issan; Ch Lafon-Rochet; Ch Pavie-Decesse; Ch La Pointe; Ch Pontet-Canet; Ch Poujeaux; Ch du Tertre.*

SHOWING WELL, EARLY DRINKING: *Ch La Cabanne; Ch Cap-de-Mourlin; Ch Canon-La-Gaffelière; Ch de France; Ch Greysac; Ch Larmande; Ch La Louvière; Ch Malartic-Lagravière; Ch Malescasse.*

SHOWING MODERATELY WELL, DRINK SOON: *Ch Belair, St-Emilion; Ch Fourcas-Dupré; Ch Haut-Bergey; Ch Larrivet-Haut-Brion; Ch Monbrison; Ch Olivier; Ch Troplong-Mondot.*

DISAPPOINTING: *Clos Fourtet.*

RATHER COARSE, ORDINARY: *Ch Beaumont; Ch Fonréaud.*

1987★★

Whatever one says about this vintage sounds condescending. If not, strictly speaking, a good vintage, it is certainly not bad. By and large, the wines do not have a lengthy future; they are not for long cellaring and certainly not the quality of claret to invest in. Nevertheless, it is a better, more agreeable, vintage than the '84, useful to consume whilst waiting for the '88s to start coming round.

The weather conditions: a long cold winter and spring (−22°C (18°F) recorded in Jan) followed by dismal, drawn-out flowering during a cold, wet June. July and Aug mixed, mainly cool and lacking sun, then an extremely hot Sept. By early Oct the weather became unsettled and rain set in during the harvest. The first comprehensive tasting of '87s was again organised by Peter Vinding for L'Union des Grands Crus at Christie's, May 1989, providing many of the following notes.

Ch LAFITE *Surprisingly deep but, less surprisingly, more evolved than the '88. First bottle a bit corky, the second with harmonious, low-keyed, vanilla nose that opened up, with a touch of liquorice, fruit, then a warm, toasted scent; nice weight, somewhat hard, slightly woody. Despite its dry tannic finish, an early developer.* Tasted Nov 1990★(★) Say 1993–98.

Ch MARGAUX *Tasted in cask, April 1988: fairly deep; young raw fruit on the nose; dry, lean and raw on palate too. Also from cask, two months later: although lacking middle, noted that it should make a pleasant lesser Margaux. Again in cask in April 1989, medium-deep, plummy-coloured; the sojourn in cask producing a cinnamon and cloves spiciness. Touch of sweetness, lean, flavoury, some charm but still austere. Most recently: medium-deep, open, youthful — a lovely ruby colour; nose low-keyed but floral, touch of lime blossom, good* *vinosity; incredibly sweet on the palate, a pleasant weight, spicy, nice grip though lacking length. Pleasant mid-term drinking.* Last tasted four months after bottling, Nov 1990*(**) 1992–2000

Ch LATOUR *Bottled in May 1989 and first tasted in April 1990: medium depth and developing quickly; sweet yet low-keyed nose, touch of ginger and fudge; dry, medium weight, lean, flavoury. At the château seven months later: similar notes, light fruit on nose and palate, earthy softness, an early developer.* Last tasted Nov 1990*(**) Should make good mid-term drinking, say 1993–2000.

Ch MOUTON-ROTHSCHILD *Deep; sweet, very fragrant, open-knit fruit; very sweet on palate, medium weight, rich, chewy, very forward, lovely flavour. Will make very attractive mid-term drinking.* Tasted Nov 1990*(**) 1992–99

Ch HAUT-BRION *Medium-deep, fairly well evolved; sweet, forthcoming vanilla nose, rather unknit, crusty bread-like fragrance; medium sweetness and weight, broad; open, tobacco-like flavour. Good mid-term.* Tasted Nov 1990*(**) 1991–98

Ch AUSONE *Not tasted.*

Ch CHEVAL-BLANC *Tasted at the château in 1989. Not very deep; very fragrant and agreeable nose; sweetish, fairly light, easy. A pleasant early developer.* May 1989** Now to 1995.

Ch PETRUS *Not tasted.*

Ch BEYCHEVELLE *A very odd bottle in 1989. More recently: plummy; muffled fruit, oil of cloves; chewy, flavoury, spicy.* Last tasted March 1991** Drink now.

Ch BRANAIRE-DUCRU *A very sweet, strawberry-scented, plausible wine. Light grip of tannin and acidity.* Tasted May 1989*(*) Drink soon.

Ch BRANE-CANTENAC *Sweet, positive fruit, and very flavoury. More acidity than tannin. Really very agreeable.* Tasted May 1989**(*) Now to 1996.

Ch CANON *Plummy; fragrant; dry, medium full-bodied, excellent fruit.* Tasted May 1989*** Now to 1996.

Ch CANON-LA-GAFFELIERE *Medium; sweet, attractive nose; firm, well made.* Tasted May 1989*** Now to 1996.

Ch CANTEMERLE *A curiously attractive, light, chaptalised nose, with touch of tar; fairly sweet, on the light side, open, soft fruit, lacking length but agreeable.* Last tasted May 1990** Now to 1996.

Ch CANTENAC-BROWN *Not much depth; an immediacy about the nose and flavour. Lightish, pleasant enough fruit, short.* Tasted May 1989** Drink soon.

Dom de CHEVALIER *Very pleasant mulberry-like fruit on nose and palate. Medium dryness and weight. A good '87.* May 1989*** Drink soon.

Ch CLINET *Very deep; strangely appealing nose, oak, figs, Rhône-like. Sweet and fleshy but with a raw finish. Odd. Certainly not to my taste.* Two notes in April 1989.

Ch La CONSEILLANTE *Sweet, good fruit but stalkiness noted in April 1989. A year later, settling down and opening up: very fragrant, strawberry-like nose; a very sweet, open, easy wine.* Last tasted May 1990*** Drink soon.

Ch COS D'ESTOURNEL *Deep; 'cold', stalky almost woody nose and taste. Some extract, but raw.* Tasted May 1990. Retaste.

Ch La CROIX DE GAY *Fairly deep; rich, fig-like fruit; medium-full body, rich, almost malty, high extract. Presumably the result of selecting the ripest Merlot grapes; so much easier for the owner of a small vineyard in Pomerol than of a large property in the Médoc. Having said this, '87 is '87. The wine is only as good as the growing season permits.* Tasted April 1989** 1991–97

Ch DUHART-MILON *Medium-deep, more evolved than the '88; low-keyed yet meaty, the nose developed nicely in the glass, soft, vanilla; dryish, nice weight, a pleasant, relatively easy, fruity wine with a touch of bitterness on the finish.* Tasted at Lafite, Nov 1990*(*) Drink soon: say 1992–97.

Ch DURFORT-VIVENS *Attractive colour; very pleasant nose, fruit and new oak; sweet, medium-full body, positive flavour, nice grip, touch of citrus-like acidity.* Tasted May 1989**(*) Now to 1997.

Ch de FIEUZAL *Four notes between April and Nov 1989. An interesting red Graves, well worth keeping an eye on. An attractive cherry red; distinctly sweet, agreeable, strawberry-like nose, touch of caramel. At each of the last two tastings, an amazing development after an hour in the glass. Dry, medium-light in weight and style. Pleasant fruity entrée, positive flavour though lacking intensity. Agreeable.* Last tasted Nov 1990** Drink soon.

Ch FIGEAC *Just one note. Medium depth; sweet, chaptalised, unknit but attractive, quick-developing nose; medium-light, very agreeable, easy to drink. Not a long-haul wine.* Dining at the château, April 1989** Drink soon.

Les FORTS DE LATOUR *Medium, youthful but quick developer; open, attractive nose; medium-light weight, straightforward, a bit neutral, easy, short.* Last tasted at Latour, Nov 1990** Now to 1995.

Ch GISCOURS *Paler than usual, immature. A sweet, almost jammy nose, meaty, medicinal, fruit and spice; medium dryness and weight, crisp, fragrant, fruity, good finish combining citrus-like acidity and bitter tannins. Making a serious effort.* Last tasted Dec 1989(**) Worth watching out for. Drink say 1992–98.

Ch GRUAUD-LAROSE *Deep, immature, long legs; low-keyed, slightly stalky at first, but cool classic fragrance developing in the glass; slightly sweet, medium weight, silky texture, loose-knit and easy. Some style.* Tasted May 1990*(**) 1992–98

Ch HAUT-BAILLY *Advanced; light, fruity nose; sweetish, light style, pleasant, easy. Good for early drinking.* Tasted May 1989** Now to 1996.

Ch d'ISSAN *Palish; sweet, easy, pleasing nose and palate. Quick maturing.* Tasted May 1989** Now to 1997.

Ch KIRWAN *Medium; muffled, slightly cheesy nose; chunky, chewy, short.* Tasted May 1989** Now to 1995.

Ch LAFON-ROCHET *Very positive fruit on nose; surprisingly sweet, soft and easy on the palate. Short. Less austere than usual.* Tasted May 1989** Drink soon before its 'puppy fat' wears off.

Ch LAGRANGE *St-Julien. Nine months after the vintage: impressively deep, opaque, purple;*

fragrant though an immature stalkiness and new oak apparent; dry, flavoury, still raw of course. No great length. At the Decanter *tasting, July 1988(**) 1992–97*

Ch La LAGUNE *Medium-pale, cherry red; sweet, spicy, very attractive nose; medium-sweet, medium-light, chewy, chunky, very flavoury, plausible, spicy new oak. Tasted Dec 1989**(*) 1992–96*

Ch LANGOA-BARTON *Medium; surprisingly sweet, soft, harmonious, vanilla nose; sweet on the palate too, chewy, fruity, adequate tannin, very attractive. Tasted May 1989**(*) Now to 1997.*

Ch LARRIVET-HAUT-BRION *Medium-deep; very appealing nose, fruit, oak; a sweet, soft, rich mouthful, nicely rounded. Tasted May 1989*** Drink now.*

Ch LASCOMBES *Plummy; rather smelly nose, broad, fruit, caramel; undistinguished and indistinctive on the palate. Rather raw. Tasted May 1989(*)?*

Ch LEOVILLE-BARTON *Medium, fairly forward; very good nose, sweet, rich; adequate body, positive, stylish, good length for an '87. Tasted May 1989*(**) 1992–2000. Worth looking out for.*

Ch LEOVILLE-LAS-CASES *Encouragingly deep plummy appearance but nose reminded me, at first whiff, of a field of rotting cabbages though, after 15 minutes in the glass, it did develop a much more acceptable fragrance; some body, some flesh, some tannin. Not bad but undistinguished. Tasted May 1990(**)? In view of Delon's reputation, worth trying again to see what a bit of bottle-age can do.*

Ch LEOVILLE-POYFERRE *Medium, ruby; very sweaty, tannic nose; tongue-twisting, mouthdrying acidity and tannin. I cannot see this frog turning into a prince. Last tasted May 1989. Try again?*

Ch LYNCH-BAGES *First noted at Jean-Michel Cazes' tasting in London, Oct 1988: a fine deep youthful appearance; attractive young fruit and spicy new oak; nice weight, chunky, moderate length, tannic. Seven months later, a cask sample at the* grand cru *tasting at Christie's: still very deep; glorious fruit on the nose; dry, positive flavour, tight-knit tannin and acidity. Last tasted May 1989*(**) 1992–2000*

Ch La MISSION-HAUT-BRION *Medium-deep, open-rimmed, somewhat indeterminate appearance; medicinal nose — iodine, ozone, TCP — developing quickly in the glass; fairly light and easy for La Mission. Distinctive aftertaste. An early developer. Tasted June 1990**(*) Now to 1997.*

Ch PALMER *In May 1989: medium-deep; light, fruity. An easy, rather 'green' but attractive '87. Last tasted June 1991(**) Now to 1997.*

Ch PAPE-CLEMENT 50% *new oak. Medium-deep, purple-tinged; curiously rich, fig and port-like nose and taste. Rather strange. Must retaste. From cask sample, May 1989 ?*

Ch PICHON-BARON *Fairly deep; sweet, forthcoming, fruity, attractive nose; flavour to match. Chunky. New oak. An appealing '87. Consistent notes. Last tasted May 1989**(*) 1992–2000*

Ch PONTET-CANET *In May 1989: medium colour and weight. A strange, rather common, slightly malty, stalky nose; dry, passable but unexciting. More recently, tasted blind: still immature; very odd nose, like medicated lint; tarry taste. Last noted June 1991 ?*

Ch PRIEURE-LICHINE *First tasted at Harvey's, Oct 1988: a deepish, appealing, sweet-nosed and fruity wine. A cask sample at the* grand cru *tasting in May 1989 was not showing quite as well, a bit hollow, stalky tannins and lean. More recently, plummy-coloured; distinctly sweet, almost jammy fruit; lightish, some style, touch of bitterness on the finish. Will make a pleasant, refreshing luncheon wine. Last tasted July 1990*(*) 1992–97*

Ch RAUSAN-SEGLA *Interestingly, this was declassified.*

Ch TALBOT *Medium-deep; very fragrant, fruity, with style and depth; dry, a good positive character and flavour. One of the best '87 cask samples at the* grand cru *tasting, May 1989**(**)*

VIEUX CH CERTAN *Deep; low-keyed, slightly malty nose; dry, good weight and flavour, respectable tannin and acidity. Quite impressive. Tasted April 1989*(**) Now to 1997.*

OTHER '87s TASTED RECENTLY:

Ch BATAILLEY *Weak rim; quite nice fruit. June 1991***

Ch BEAUMONT *Plummy, slightly stalky, passable cask sample. Recently, one bottle corked, the other attractive minor Médoc. Last tasted June 1991***

Ch CISSAC *Dry, rather raw and acidic. Oct 1990**

Ch L'EVANGILE *Soft, chaptalised nose; sweet, easy, ready. May 1991***

Ch MAUCAMPS *Deep; sweet, full, fleshy, good fruit. June 1991*** for its class.*

Ch MEYNEY *Maturing; surprisingly good fruit, pleasant, chewy. Last tasted June 1991****

Ch TERTRE-ROTEBOEUF *Meaty nose; soft, light, very drinkable. Aug 1990***

Ch La TOUR-DE-BY *Several notes. Well made. Plummy. Nice weight, agreeable though tannic. Last tasted June 1991*(*)*

'87s TASTED ONLY, OR LAST NOTED, AT THE *GRAND CRU* TASTING, MAY 1989:

SHOWING WELL: *Ch L'Angélus; Ch d'Angludet; Ch Bouscaut; Ch de France; Ch Gazin; Ch La Louvière; Ch Les Ormes-de-Pez; Ch Pavie-Decesse; Ch Villemaurine.*

PLEASANT ENOUGH: *Ch Beauregard, Pomerol; Ch Cap-de-Mourlin (Jacques); Ch Coufran; Ch Dauzac; Ch Fonplégade; Ch Fonréaud; Ch Fourcas-Dupré; Ch Fourcas-Hosten; Ch Greysac; Ch Haut-Bergey; Ch Monbrison; Ch Pique-Caillou; Ch de Lamoureux.*

ORDINARY: *Ch Balestard-La-Tonnelle; Ch Cos Labory; Ch Lanessan; Ch Poujeaux; Ch Troplong-Mondot.*

QUESTIONABLE, TASTE AGAIN? *Clos Fourtet; Ch Malescasse; Ch Siran.*

1988★★★★

Unquestionably, very good. Having tasted a wide, representative range of '88s and '89s, I am impressed by the quality of both vintages and their complementary styles. Same *terroir*, same *cépages*, same vine husbandry, same winemaking methods: yet there are marked differences due entirely to subtle weather variations during the growing season. The '88s are firm, manly, well constituted, destined for a long life; the '89s are also well constituted but more pliable, with more charm, and will develop more quickly. For a time they will run neck and neck. In the 1980s time-scale, the '89 is to the '88 what the '85 is to the '86. The latter pair remind me, though less dramatically, of the '29 and '28. But, as always, time will tell.

The winter and spring of 1988 were more than usually wet. Though spring frosts were avoided, the later flowering conditions were not ideal. July to Sept was drier than usual, the monthly temperatures being about average. Oct not dissimilar to 1985. A significant factor was the uneven maturity of the different grape varieties which made life tricky for growers, particularly of Cabernet Sauvignon in the Médoc, but those in the Graves and, in particular, St-Emilion and Pomerol had fewer problems. Most of the notes, other than the first growths, were made at two tastings. The first, in Bordeaux, April 1989, was of a wide range of Margaux at Ch d'Issan, St-Julien and Pauillac at Ch Langoa, Pomerol and St-Emilion at Ch Canon, and Graves and Sauternes at Ch Carbonnieux. Not all the tasting conditions were ideal, some too cold, some too cramped. Then, happily, an almost identical range was presented to the trade and to wine journalists at a Livery Company Hall in London exactly a year later, which helped firm up one's impressions. Noticeable was the marked change in colour after a further 12 months in cask. Almost invariably the pristine opacity and purple tinge had changed to a less deep, more plummy colour. More importantly: a remarkable consistency of quality. A vintage to buy and to keep.

Ch LAFITE *First tasted in April 1989, in the cold cellars at Lafite and from ice-cold glasses. Not surprisingly the nose was closed, dumb, yet, with a cupped warm hand and a bit of coaxing, there emerged a scent of freshly sharpened pencils, crystallised violets, and the spiciness of new oak. Fairly full-bodied, an extraordinary brambly fruit flavour, good length, very tannic. 12 months later, alongside the '89, medium-deep; a minty, fragrant nose; nice flesh and flavour but I thought it lacked the length of the '89. It was bottled in July 1990 and my next notes were made in the bright new tasting room at the château. Lovely colour; nose closed at first but after 15 minutes in the glass was lovely, firm and spicy. An assertive, quite powerful wine. Good fruit. Still hard.* Last tasted Nov 1990(★★★★) *A good, fairly long-distance runner. Say 2000–2020.*

Ch MARGAUX *Initially tasted at the château in April 1989. We were informed by Paul Pontallier that the vines, from July 1988, were under stress which slowed their maturity. The sample, from the vat, was virtually opaque, certainly intense; its nose was lovely, fragrant, with the spicy, beguiling scent of new oak; a touch of sweetness, medium-full body, crisp, lean, virile, very tannic. It was bottled late Aug–early Sept 1990, and I next tasted it roughly six weeks later: still deep, with a lovely, intense purple rim; a fascinating powdery, toasted marshmallow scent, good fruit, and very fragrant after 10 minutes or so in the glass. Seemed very sweet, with good flesh and length. An aftertaste of violets. New oak spiciness very apparent at this stage but it will simmer down. Lovely wine.* Last tasted at the château, Nov 1990(★★★★) *Great future.*

Ch LATOUR *This was not tasted during the* grands crus *tour in April 1989. I first tasted it at the château the following April though it had only recently been fined. Next tasted in Sept 1990, not long after it had been bottled. Very deep, mulberry-centred, purple-rimmed; nose unsettled though plenty of fruit; very powerful, aggressive even on the palate, very good but astringently dry. Two months later, in a fascinating line-up of recent vintages at Latour, the colour of cherry brandy, certainly more intense than the '89; a good crisp, scented cedar and Cabernet Sauvignon aroma; full-bodied, good fruit and some soft flesh waiting in the wings, or, to change the metaphor, clasped to the bosom. A very tannic wine. But, in years to come, all will be revealed.* Last tasted Dec 1990(★★★★) *An archetypal, old-fashioned Latour that will need a great deal of bottle-age, and patience.*

Ch MOUTON-ROTHSCHILD *Bottled June/July 1990. Tasted only once: fine, deep, intense, plummy-coloured wine that looked younger than the '89. Singed, meaty, brambly fruit on the nose, remaining firmly tucked into the glass. Surprisingly sweet, full-bodied, very firm, very tannic but fleshier than I expected.* Tasted at the château, Nov 1990(★★★★) *Another classic long-haul wine.*

Ch HAUT-BRION *Very deep, intense purple; very fruity, distinct Cabernet aroma, great depth; touch of sweetness, full-bodied, very rich fruit, extract, velvety yet very tannic. Due to be bottled from Nov 26, three days before I tasted it.* With Jean Delmas, Nov 1990(★★★★) *Likely to mature sooner than the first-growth Médocs. Say 1998–2020.*

Ch AUSONE *Very deep. Virtually opaque; despite its youthfulness, very forthcoming, excellent fruit, of distinctly first-growth quality; fairly full-bodied, very rich, packed with fruit, high extract, slight taste of tobacco and new oak, spicy, good length. Should turn out well.* Tasted at the château, April 1989(★★★★) *2000–20.*

Ch L'ANGELUS *Three notes. Twice in April 1989: very deep, good fruit, new oak apparent. Most recently, 12 months later: losing its initial depth of colour, though very rich-looking; a very forthcoming nose, with whiff of chocolate and fudge; distinctly sweet, medium weight, good fruit, adequate tannin and acidity. Surprisingly attractive. Last noted at the* grand cru *tasting at Merchant Taylors Hall, April 1990*(***) For fairly early drinking; say 1994–2000.*

Ch d'ANGLUDET *Deep, fairly intense. Different, distinctive and really rather extraordinary character, particularly on the nose, which often reminds me of the Rhône, in this case a fragrant Hermitage. Good flesh and fruit. Soft tannins. Impressive. Fractionally higher marks a year later. Now plummy purple; again with a very distinctive smell and taste, fruity, crisp, sweet and attractive. Good aftertaste. Last noted April 1990*(***) for its class. 1996 to well beyond 2000.*

Ch BEYCHEVELLE *Initially a very distinctive cedar oak, spiciness on nose and taste. Sweet but tannic. A year later: medium-deep, plummy; nose opened up, green tea, eucalyptus; seemed incredibly sweet on palate, chewy, fruity, pretty good length, tannin and acidity. Last noted April 1990(****) 1996–2000+*

Ch BRANAIRE-DUCRU *Initially opaque; dumb; strange flavour and style and a slightly yeasty taste. 12 months later, less deep, more plummy though still, of course, immature. Fruit and tannin on the nose; very sweet on the palate, with an attractive easy fruitiness despite its tannin and acidity. A further note the following month. In an interim state. Last noted May 1990(***) Good but rarely more than good. Should make an agreeable mid-term drink, say 1997–2010.*

Ch BRANE-CANTENAC *Deep, rich; unknit but crisp fruit; easy, open but yeasty in April 1989. A year later colour advanced; very sweet, spicy nose and taste. A quick developer. Last tasted April 1990(***) 1993–2000*

Ch CALON-SEGUR *A very good Calon though I found it not wholly satisfactory at the '88 line-up at Langoa in April 1989. At the tasting in London: impressively deep, opaque core, intense rim; sweet, well-balanced nose; sweet for Calon-Ségur, fullish, lovely fruit and texture. Last tasted April 1990(****) 1995–2020*

Ch CANON *April 1989: opaque; a strange meaty nose supported by rich* cassis-*like fruit; a hefty wine, very tannic. A year later, less deep but rich appearance; nose a bit closed but with good fruit and depth; sweet, chunky, lovely fruity-acid endtaste. Good life ahead. Last tasted April 1990(****) 1994–2010*

Ch CANON-LA-GAFFELIERE *Opaque, intense; nose undeveloped but sweet, with good fruit; dry, fine texture and flavour. Bitter tannins. Considerable evolution after a further year in cask; very rich; nose combining fruit and oak; sweetening up on the palate, nice weight, delicious flavour. Loads of fruit and sufficient tannin and acidity. A marked change in winemaking; a château to watch. Last noted April 1990*(***) 1992–2000+*

Ch CANTENAC-BROWN *April 1989: very deep, intense; one of the most evolved of the group of Margaux: sweaty, spicy, oaky, plausibly attractive. Almost identical marks a year later. Rich nose; fairly sweet, nice weight, rich, crisp. Dry finish. April 1990*(**) 1993–2000+*

Ch CARBONNIEUX *Very consistent notes, no faults but not very distinctive nose in April 1989, nondescript – and an identical mark a year later. Some sweetness, the customary rather light and lean style, attractive, flavoury, piquant. A refreshing, well-made, unpretentious wine. Last tasted April 1990*(**) Now to 1998.*

CARRUADES DE CH LAFITE *First tasted at Lafite in icy conditions. Vivid purple; cold, dumb, hard, tannic. In London, more evolved: light but lively, spicy nose; nice weight, open-knit, chewy, flavoury. More serious and less charm than Carruades of the 1950s and 1960s, but perhaps this is the nature of the '88 vintage. Last tasted April 1990(***) 1994–2000+*

Ch CHASSE-SPLEEN *Showing well at both the April tastings, in 1989 and 1990. Very flavoury, the distinctive spiciness of new oak. Top of its class, but a wine for good mid-term drinking, not for one's grandson. Last tasted April 1990(***) 1993–98*

Dom de CHEVALIER *Just one early note. Fragrant, lively, oaky; firm, on the lean side but with adequate flesh, lovely fruit, good balance, tannic. Good future. Tasted April 1989(****) 1995–2015*

Ch CLINET *Considerable division of opinion amongst tasters at the '88 session at Ch Canon in April 1989. I was in the minority, finding the Clinet very appley on the nose and with a strange, common, Côtes du Rhône nose. A week later, at a trade tasting in London, without reference to the earlier notes, I described it as having a stewed apple and cloves nose, raw and very tannic, with "strange, stalky, Rhône flavour". 12 months later I* still *found it curious, smelling of cress and spice, though very distinctive, with a rather attractive blackberry flavour. I shall look forward to tasting it when it has a bit of bottle-age. Last tasted April 1990**??*

Ch COS D'ESTOURNEL *A barrel sample, not the final blend, presented by Michèle Prats at a Cos tasting in Florida in Jan 1990: opaque, intense purple rim; youthful, vigorous fruit, very attractive; touch of sweetness crossing the palate to final dry finish. Nicely balanced. Three months later, another cask sample at the* grand cru *tasting in London. Lovely fruit, fairly full-bodied. Chunky but distinctly tannic. Good future. Last noted April 1990(****) 1996–2020*

Ch La CROIX DE GAY *High marks at both April tastings. Medium-deep, richly coloured; lovely fruit, a crisp ensemble of cherries and raspberries spiced up with new oak, and with great depth. Fairly sweet at first sip, pleasing weight, most attractive, almost plausibly so. Crisp, new oak. Tannic. Last tasted April 1990(****) 1993 to beyond 2000.*

Ch DUCRU-BEAUCAILLOU *In April 1989: opaque; dumb, unyielding; dry, fullish, firm, oaky, bitter tannins; but a classic understated Ducru. More recently, still a fine deep purple; a bit stalky and hard. Astringent even. Needs a good deal of bottle-age to bring it into line. Last noted May 1990. Based on form and the vintage(****) We will see – but it will take another 10 years to soften.*

Ch DURFORT-VIVENS *Twin tastings: April 1989,*

very deep, intense; April 1990, medium-deep, rich appearance; crisp spicy fruit — identical description and marks; attractive fruit on palate but rather raw tannin/acid finish. Needs time. Last noted April 1990(★★★) 1998 to beyond 2000.

Ch DUHART-MILON *Good blackberry-like fruit; crisp, chewy at the April 1989 tasting. Most recently, at Lafite: still deep purple; closed and hard and dusty at first. Took 45 minutes to ease and open. A nice weight and good flavour but, as yet, hard and restrained. Needs plenty of bottle-age.* Last noted Nov 1990(★★★) 1998 to well beyond 2000.

Ch L'EVANGILE *Showing considerable potential in April 1989. Most recently: good colour; sweet, forthcoming fragrance; good, positive flavour, length, texture, balance, and tannin for keeping.* Last tasted May 1991★(★★★) Probably 1996–2015.

Ch de FIEUZAL *Tasted twice in April 1989, in Bordeaux and in London: opaque; lovely fragrance, new oak; distinct touch of sweetness, good fruit, spicy, tannic. And, 12 months later, still impressively deep; highish-toned, very crisp, fruity nose; almost too speciously spicy and oaky — trace of cloves. But very attractive. I find this class of red Graves very appealing and deserving to be better known.* Last tasted April 1990★(★★) 1992–2000

Ch FIGEAC *Several notes. A glorious wine. Opaque; dumb but concentrated; a big wine when tasted in April 1989, but it seemed much more perfumed at a London trade tasting later that month; rich, nice texture. At Desai's Figeac tasting that Dec, it was displaying a lovely combination of spicy new oak and Cabernet Sauvignon on nose and palate. The following spring, at the London tasting, its colour was softening and starting to evolve despite a fair amount of tannin. Good length. Attractive.* Last tasted April 1990★(★★★) 1993 to beyond 2000.

Clos FOURTET *Immensely impressive, opaque appearance in April 1989 but with curious nose, like a brown apple core, sweet, slightly caramelly, tannic; sweet on palate, fullish, with good fruit, spicy new oak taste. Simmering down in colour a year later, the nose more open but with sweaty tannins still apparent. Also noted as surprisingly sweet and speciously attractive.* Last noted April 1990(★★★) 1993 to beyond 2000.

Ch La GAFFELIERE *Deep, plummy-coloured; minty nose; curious flavour, tobacco, conjuring up dry bracken, more Graves-like than its usual somewhat swaggeringly fruity self. Astringent too. I must try it again. Needs bottle-age.* Tasted April 1990(★★)?

Ch GAZIN *Consistent notes at the two, year-apart, April tastings. Impressively rich-looking; stylish, good fruit on nose and palate. Slightly sweet, fairly full-bodied, nice texture, with good soft tannins.* Last tasted April 1990★(★★★) 1995–2015 or thereabouts.

Ch GISCOURS *April 1989: its appearance was like snow at Christmas, "deep and crisp and even", though after 12 months longer in cask distinctly less deep. Nose initially subdued though with fleshy fruit, which a year later had opened up sweetly. Full of flavour, extract masking tannins, good length. Very complete and a seemingly 'easy' Giscours in a fairly substantial vintage. Should turn out well.* Last noted April 1990(★★★★) 1998–2020

Ch GRAND-PUY-LACOSTE *As always, a fine but uncompromising wine that makes no concessions to popular, plausibly fruity fashions in taste. For Cambridge dons to cellar, and eventually to linger over in the Senior Common Room. Two virtually identical notes, a year apart. Very deep; dumb but intrinsically very rich, tight-knit blackberry nose, still with the pepperiness of alcohol and immaturity. Medium full-bodied, sturdy rather than massive. Sinewy, tannic.* Last tasted April 1990(★★★★) 2000–20

Ch GRUAUD-LAROSE *Impressively deep though otherwise hard to fathom at the April 1989 tasting. Nose dumb. Tannic. Bitter. A year later it had stretched its legs, the nose reminded me of Beychevelle's 'green tea' but with the typical Cordier-style ripe fruit. Seemed sweeter too, fullish, chunky, fruity, decent length, tannin. Should run to pattern.* Last tasted April 1990(★★★★) 1998–2020

Ch HAUT-BATAILLEY *Deep; crisp fruit, tannic; good length and balance, crisp tannic finish. Firm, well made. Good future.* Tasted April 1989(★★★) at least. Say 1998–2015.

Ch d'ISSAN *Lovely wine. At the earlier tasting, crisp peppery fruit, fragrant — reminded me of a newly opened cigarette packet (Virginia, not Gauloises!). Lovely fruit, flesh, new oak and length. A beauty. Although a year later I noticed a considerable evolution of colour, I gave it even higher marks on the palate. Relatively sweet, nice weight, lovely rich fruit.* Last tasted April 1990(★★★★) 1995 to beyond 2010.

Ch KIRWAN *Rarely the most exciting of wines, an agreeable enough '88. Not very deep. Looking like an early developer. New oak and tannin uppermost when first tasted though it evolved quite sweetly in the glass. Nice weight, relatively — for an '88 — open-knit, soft and agreeable. Light, easy style despite its tannins.* Last tasted April 1990. A hesitant(★★★) Say 1994–2000+ It will be interesting to see how this turns out.

Ch LAFON-ROCHET *For me an austere, unsmiling, tannic wine. Well dressed but with a stiff collar. And so it was when I first tasted the '88. Opaque. Spicy with new oak. A year later, low-keyed, quite good fruit but hard. Touch of sweetness on the way in. Needs time.* Last tasted April 1990. A hopeful(★★★) in due course.

Ch LANESSAN *Hard, muted in April 1989. Most recently: very deep, intense; medicinal, immature; nice weight, texture, attractive fruit.* Last noted June 1991(★★★)

Ch LANGOA-BARTON *Amongst its* grand cru *peers in the new reception-cum-tasting room at Langoa, it developed its customary masculinity, rather raw, distinctly tannic. The following spring, in London, looking thick with chunky fruit and extract, with a touch of iron in its soul and lean like its proprietor. A good mid- to long-term claret.* Last tasted April 1990(★★★) 1998–2020

Ch LASCOMBES *Less deep and more evolved than most at the April 1989 tasting. Quite attractive but seemed to me to lack conviction and length. Distinctly lacking in '88 colour a year later and the nose, though fruity, was hard. I omitted to taste the wine. Oversight or lack of interest?* Last noted, if not in full, April 1990 ?

Ch LEOVILLE-BARTON *Opaque, intense; dumb but firm; touch of sweetness, medium full-bodied, lovely fruit, flavour and fragrance, with oaky aftertaste. Almost identical comments and marks a year later. An understated classic.* Last tasted April 1990(****) 1998–2020 and beyond.

Ch LEOVILLE-POYFERRE *Two notes in April 1989. Very deep; piquant, slightly stalky and raw. A year later medium, plummy-coloured; low-keyed, fruity but unknit; stalkiness and rawness noted again. Loaded with acidity and tannin. It will take time to shake off the latter. Not enthralled.* Last tasted April 1990(**)? Future uncertain. Taste again after some bottle-age.

Ch LYNCH-BAGES *Showing well, April 1989: opaque; very fruity, toasty, spicy nose and flavour. The following April, nose a bit closed and palate tight-knit but very flavoury. A month later, intensely deep; nose low-keyed at first but, given time in glass, mulberry-like fruit emerged. The wine seemed to be sweeter at every stage tasted, fabulous mouthfilling flavour, richness masking astringency. Will make a marvellous drink given bottle-age.* Last tasted May 1990(****) 1996–2020.

Ch LYNCH-MOUSSAS *Surprisingly good wine: deep; forthcoming Cabernet Sauvignon aroma and a sweet, almost pure blackcurrant flavour at the April 1989 tasting. 12 months later, simmered down a little but nose quite advanced, chewy, fruity and attractive.* Last tasted April 1990(***) 1995–2000

Ch MALARTIC-LAGRAVIERE *I always used to associate Malartic with piquant, often high, volatile acidity; yet flavoury. Like so many red Graves of its class, there has been great improvement and the '88 is good. A straightforward, fruity, if unexciting, cask sample tasted in the cold, crowded cellars at Ch Carbonnieux in April 1989. More tasters, but happily more space, at Merchant Taylors Hall. Like many Graves, it was starting to lose its initial depth of colour, which is misleading, for though they reach their plateau of maturity sooner than their equivalents in the Médoc, they last well. This wine was sweet and delicious, with a touch of refreshing acidity as a sort of afterthought.* Last tasted April 1990(***) 1993–2010

Ch La MISSION-HAUT-BRION *Bottled in Sept 1990, the wine was a lovely, fairly intense ruby; low-keyed at first, a bit raw, with touch of liquorice and iron, but after an hour in the glass I noted good fruit and some sweetness on the palate. Full-bodied, chewy, with mouthdrying tannins. Will need time to show its paces.* Tasted at the château, Nov 1990(****) 1998–2020 or so.

Ch MONTROSE *Good wine. Deep. Lovely flesh and fruit sitting atop its tannins. Good length. Endorsed a year later. Needs time, as always.* Last tasted April 1990(****) 1998–2020

Ch PALMER *Although widely regarded as a 'super second' it does not hit the button quite as regularly as La Mission or even Las-Cases. The '88 is good but not great. It was certainly showing well at the April 1989 tasting: rich, toasty nose with good, sweet underlying fruit. Rich, fleshy, with fragrant aftertaste. A trace of stalkiness noted the following April, though very appealing on palate. In Nov 1990: rich open nose; fullish, firm, good crisp flavour. Most recently, at the château, plummy, immature; distinctive; open-knit, less impressive.* June 1991(***)?? 1996–2010

Ch PAPE-CLEMENT *Noted at the two April tastings. In 1989 opaque; fragrant nose, full of fruit, new oak spice. Powerful. Very tannic. A year later, medium-deep, richly coloured; softened and sweetened on nose and palate. Tannins less obtrusive.* Last tasted April 1990(***) 1996–2015 or beyond.

Ch PAVIE *80% new oak. Medium-deep; low-keyed but good crisp fruit. Lean. Tannic. The following April, nose developing well, rich fruit; sweetening up, nice weight, good balance, delicious flavour.* Last tasted April 1990(****) 1996–2015.

Ch PAVIE-DECESSE *(Also owned and made by Jean-Paul Valette). An intensely purple cask sample in April 1989; warm, toasty; fruity nose and flavour. Rich. Soft tannins. High marks at the 1990 tasting. Attractive sweetness, good crisp firm fruit and good length.* Last tasted April 1990(****) 1995–2015

Ch PICHON-LONGUEVILLE, BARON *Immensely deep, vividly purple at the April 1989 tasting at Langoa. Tight-knit fruit on nose. Full, crisp, impressive. In London the following April: opening up on the nose; sweet on palate with spicy, oaky beguiling flavour. Endorsed a month later; sweet, full-bodied, fleshy, full of fruit, well balanced.* Last tasted May 1990(****) 1998–2020+

Ch PICHON-LONGUEVILLE, LALANDE *Opaque; good fruit but closed; fullish, elegant but — for me — something lacking at the opening tasting. The following April I thought it had the sort of overwrought fruit I associate with Brane-Cantenac. At another tasting, two months later, the colour was certainly impressively deep; nose spicy, oaky at first, a sort of pasty vanilla noted later; some softness and flesh. Fairly, but not very, full-bodied. Chunky. Good. But whether it will pull ahead of the Baron across the road, time will tell.* Last tasted May 1990(***?) 1996–2015?

Ch La POINTE *Noted at the two April tastings. Leaner, crisper and more tannic than usual but still managing to advertise its customary early development. Nice wine.* Last tasted April 1990(***) 1993–2005.

Ch PONTET-CANET *I thought this was — to say the least — the most peculiar of all the '88 classed growths at the April 1989 tasting at Langoa. Good appearance: very deep; nose not bad either, fruit, oak, but with a very sweaty, tannic overtone. But most odd on the palate, with a taste of stale tobacco, and excessive tannin. Terrible. Unhappily, the second tasting a year later in London merely confirmed the first assessment. Colour and nose no problem, but it had a taste of creosote. I read recently that Emile Peynaud was advising, so perhaps it will emerge, phoenix-like.* Last tasted April 1990 ?

Ch PRIEURE-LICHINE *Nice fruit, gingery, new oak,*

attractive. Pleasing flesh and fruit. Good aftertaste. Retasted ex-cask two months later. Cedary nose, long tannic finish. Good life ahead and a very good Prieuré. Last tasted June 1989(***) 1996–2010 and beyond.

Ch TALBOT *Very good wine. Identically high ratings at the April 1989 and 1990 tastings. Lovely crisp fruit. Enough flesh. Interesting flavour. Good future.* Last noted April 1990(****) 1998–2020

OTHER '88s TASTED RECENTLY:

Ch BEAUMONT *One bottle corky, stalky, the other very attractive.* June 1991*(**)

Ch La CARDONNE *Plummy, immature; undeveloped, dry. Not the usual easy charm.* June 1991(**)

Ch CISSAC *Lively; good fruit; fullish, well balanced.* Nov 1990*(**)

Ch FOURCAS-HOSTEN *Cedary, flavoury but slightly yeasty sample in April 1988. Now maturing though fruit as yet undeveloped, fairly full and rich. Good enough, unexciting.* Last tasted June 1991(**)

Ch LALANDE-BORIE *Very deep, immature; slightly stalky, tannic.* June 1991(**)

Ch La TOUR-DE-BY *Sturdy, dependable.* April 1991(**)

Ch TROTTEVIEILLE *Soft fruit yet stalky; severely tannic.* Jan 1991(**)

OTHER '88s TASTED APRIL 1989 AND APRIL 1990:

QUITE GOOD THOUGH RAW AND TANNIC: *Ch Balestard-La-Tonnelle(**) Ch Cos Labory(**) Ch La Tour-Martillac(***)*

NEED TO TASTE YET AGAIN: *Ch Cap-de-Mourlin; Ch Villemaurine.*

OTHER '88s NOTED ONLY ONCE, AT APRIL 1989 TASTING:

GOOD FUTURE: *Ch Cantemerle(****) Les Forts-de-Latour(***) Ch Haut-Bailly(****) Ch Larmande(***) Ch Larrivet-Haut-Brion(***) Ch La Louvière(***) Ch Olivier(***) Ch Les Ormes-de-Pez; Ch Rausan-Ségla(****) Ch Siran(***) Ch Smith-Haut-Lafitte.*

QUITE GOOD, TANNIC: *Ch Beaumont(**) Ch de Chantegrive(**) Ch Citran(***) Ch Coufran(***) Ch Dauzac(**) Ch de Lamarque(**) Ch Monbrison(**)*

LIGHTER STYLE, QUICKER MATURING: *Ch Dassault(**) Ch Ferrande, Ch Fombrauge(***) Ch Fonplégade(***) Ch Fourcas-Dupré(**) Ch Méaume(**) Ch Notton(**) Ch Pique-Caillou(**)*

UNIMPRESSIVE: *Ch Bouscaut; Ch de France; Ch Greyssac; Ch Haut-Bergey.*

NEED TO RETASTE (POSSIBLY POOR CASK SAMPLE): *Ch Boyd-Cantenac; Ch Croizet-Bages; Ch Fonréaud; Clos des Jacobins; Ch Lagrange, St-Julien; Ch Larcis-Ducasse; Ch Malescasse; Ch Nenin; Ch Pouget; Ch Poujeaux; Ch du Tertre.*

1989*****

A most attractive vintage, complementing the firmer, somewhat sterner '88s perfectly. By tasting a wide range in Bordeaux over the space of four days, the character and the style of the vintage came over loud and clear: thoroughly appealing wines, with a deft touch, an agreeable balance of fruit, extract without the 'thickness' of the '88s, plus the three vital parts needed to enrich, enliven and sustain: alcohol, tannin and acidity. In some ways like the '85s, and many will provide those wise enough to have invested modestly with pleasurable drinking over a 10 to 20-year period.

A hot year. Well above average temperatures in May advanced the vegetation some three weeks ahead of normal. Flowering began early and took place under excellent conditions, thus ensuring a big crop. June was unbelievably hot, with the heat continuing through July and Aug. The average summer temperature equalled that of 1945. Over the previous half century, only 1949 had been hotter. There were frequent local rainstorms though these merely swelled and refreshed the gasping grapes. The harvest was the earliest since 1893.

If the star ratings appear to rate a very large number of wines fairly equally, this is in itself testimony to the evenness of quality perceived during four days of tasting in Bordeaux in Nov 1990.

Ch LAFITE *Tasted at the château in the spring and autumn of 1990. Initially opaque, as can be expected in a good year, and intense, the vivid purple pressing the sides of the glass; nose taut, a bit unyielding; the sweetness of ripe grapes, full-bodied, firm flesh, like the sort of young girl's bottom that elderly Frenchmen have a predilection for pinching. Good texture, length, tannin and acidity. More recently, the nose low-keyed at first but after 20 minutes developed a beautiful scent of spice and fruit. Some of the inherent '89 charm apparent. Sweet, great length. Will make an archetypal Lafite, combining power and elegance.* Last tasted April 1991(*****) 2005–25, but will be drinkable either side of these dates.

Ch MARGAUX *First tasted in April 1990 with Paul Pontallier who informed me that the make-up of the '89* grand vin *was 77–78% Cabernet Sauvignon, about 15% Merlot, 5% Petit Verdot and 2–3% Cabernet Franc. Alcohol a moderate 12.8%. Good depth, yet not opaque. Very forthcoming, spicy ripe fruit, touch of raspberry, whiff of new oak. Fairly sweet. Soft tannins, I was told, add sweetness, as does lower acidity. Already delicious, lovely, fleshy. In Nov, beguiling scent, more than fruit — perfume; flesh and puppy fat. Latterly, recently fined, one more racking before bottling: ripe, sweet. Similar weight to the '90 but lovely silky texture, flavour. Should turn out beautifully.* Last tasted April 1991(*****) Say 2000–25.

Ch LATOUR *Also tasted with other recent vintages, including Forts de Latour, in the spring and autumn of 1990. The wine's depth and colour at this stage could well be imagined; its nose developing very good fruit and flesh, as did the palate. Full-bodied with 100% new oak providing a very spicy aftertaste. Most recently: fabulous cedar and Cabernet aroma; lovely fruit and components. Rarely the easiest of red Bordeaux to get to grips with at an early stage, it holds great promise. Last tasted Nov 1990(*****) 2005–30*

Ch MOUTON-ROTHSCHILD *In April 1990: intense purple; tight-knit, glorious fruit, spicy, characteristic* cassis *Cabernet Sauvignon aroma; fairly dry, full-bodied, powerful, great length, spicy aftertaste. In Nov, noted its luminosity; nose already harmonious, wonderful flesh and depth of fruit, then a touch of ginger and youthful pepperiness; mouthfilling, slightly bitter tannins, vigorous. By the second spring, deeper than the '90, exotic nose, Mouton at its immensely fragrant best. Sweet, great length. Fabulous. Last tasted April 1991(*****) Beyond 2000.*

Ch HAUT-BRION *First tasted in Nov 1990, with Jean Delmas at La Mission. Opaque but less intensely purple-edged than La Mission. Nose restrained but after 15 minutes, rich and spicy, violets, new oak. On the palate distinctly sweet, full, fleshy, well endowed with ripe fruit. Most recently, first in the* chai *then, comparatively at the La Mission. Superb. Great future. Last noted April 1991(*****) 2000–25*

Ch AUSONE *At the '89 tasting in St-Emilion: very deep with a distinctly oaky nose, revealing good fruit and spice. Taste to match. A touch of '89 softness and a good aftertaste. Should develop well. Tasted Nov 1990(****) 1995–2015*

Ch CHEVAL-BLANC *Tasted on Nov 23, three days before refining. Deep-coloured; low-keyed but fragrant, new oak, great depth — alongside the other* 1er grand cru classé *St-Emilions it had unquestionably an extra dimension. Medium-sweet, medium full-bodied — not remotely the weight of the first-growth Médocs. Soft, fleshy, with distinctive style and elegance, length and new oak aftertaste. A beauty. Noted at the tasting at the* Maison du Vin *in St-Emilion arranged for me by Jean-Paul Valette. Nov 1990(*****) 1998–2020*

Ch PETRUS *In Nov 1990: opaque, intense, purple; firm, hard, unyielding but good fruit; full of alcohol, extract, flavour. More than firm. A stern blackberry taste. Highly impressive. Latour-like substance and weight though with inimitable Pétrus flesh. All this concentration the result of the 'green harvest': a ruthless thinning of bunches to concentrate all nature's efforts into the remaining grapes. Most recently: sweet, full, very tannic, great length. Last tasted from the cask, June 1991(*****) Beyond 2000.*

Ch BATAILLEY *Very deep, fairly intense; lean but with good fruit; slightly sweet, fullish body, nice spicy finish. Usually dependable, Batailley at just about its best. Nov 1990(****) 1996–2015*

Ch BEYCHEVELLE *Opaque; highly oaked, almost speciously spicy; soft, fleshy, fruit and spice again on the palate. Nov tasting(***) 1999–2020*

Ch Le BON-PASTEUR *Medium-deep though rich; distinctly different from the usual run of Pomerols: meaty, figgy; full-bodied, fairly powerful, well endowed with fruit and extract. Good length. Warranting its bijou reputation. Tasted Nov 1990(****) 1997–2015*

Ch BRANAIRE-DUCRU *Very deep; fruit and spice. Loads of new oak. Dry, medium weight, chunky tannins. Not great but should turn out pleasantly enough. Tasted Nov 1990(***) 1996–2006*

Ch CANON *After Cheval-Blanc consistently the best of the* 1er cru classé *St-Emilions. Its quality, vintage after vintage, stands out like a beacon. Very deep, fairly intense; low-keyed fruit and oak quickly developing fragrance, touch of liquorice. Medium sweetness, fullish body, lovely fruit, perfect shape in the mouth: a persuasive entry, an elliptical swelling of flavour, firm finish. Tasted Nov 1990(*****) 1997–2020*

Ch CANON-LA-GAFFELIERE *Now run by the young Count de Neipperg and his wife who live at the château, there has been a marked improvement in the winemaking. The '89 is opaque at the core, with an intense, plummy purple rim; very sweet, fig-like richness of fruit, and oak on the nose; fairly sweet on the palate, good weight, nice texture. Will make an attractive drink. Tasted Nov 1990(****) 1995–2005*

Ch CANTEMERLE *Opaque, intense; fruit, tannin, oak, spice; perfect weight, good texture, tannin and acidity, up to the standard if not the charm and style of the mid-1950s. Tasted Nov 1990(****) 1998–2015*

Ch CANTENAC-BROWN *Deep but open-knit; low-keyed yet fragrant, developing a curious cheesiness; medium dryness and weight, the customary broad, chocolaty character and flavour. Lacking conviction. Tasted Nov 1990(**?) 1996–2006*

CARRUADES DE CH LAFITE *Nov 1990 showing decidedly better in the new tasting room than in the freezing cellar in the spring. Medium-deep, promising an early start; nose open, flowery, then cedary and, after 30 minutes or so, elegant, lovely; nice weight and style. Fragrant. A charmer. Carruades and a vintage like '89 make excellent bed-fellows. Last tasted April 1991(****) 1995–2010*

Dom de CHEVALIER *Olivier Bernard, who arranged the tasting of red and white Graves for me, said that this Merlot produced an exceptionally high degree of tannin. I cannot say that I noted the excess, though it was tannic and clearly destined for long life. The wine had a very deep, fairly intense appearance; low-keyed yet honeyed at first, and quickly evolving, displaying the Domaine's vinosity and style at its best. A chewy, chunky wine. Good fruit — and future. Tasted Nov 1990(****) 1998–2020*

Ch CLERC-MILON *Dumb but fleshy, oaky tannins in April 1990. A year later: deep, velvety; opulent, mulberry and violets; sweet, full of fruit, very tannic. Last tasted April 1991(***) 1995–2005*

Ch La DOMINIQUE *Showing distinctly well in the St-Emilion line-up, probably number three, after Cheval-Blanc and Canon. Opaque; nose restrained, yet with lovely concentrated fruit; some sweetness, fullish body, well endowed and fleshy. Soft-textured. Oaky aftertaste.* Nov 1990(****) 1997–2015

Ch DUCRU-BEAUCAILLOU *Opaque; harmonious nose, cedar, firm, understated but good; dryish, medium-full body, good fruit, soft and rounded yet with its complement of tannin and acidity. A classic Ducru with a good future.* Tasted at Langoa, Nov 1990(****) 1999–2020

Ch DUHART-MILON *First tasted in the cellars at Lafite April 1990. A startlingly bright purple; nose chilled into submission but good fruit and length. Developing nicely after seven more months in cask and, tasted less hurriedly in a well-lit room, its virtues easier to appreciate. By now, very attractive fruit on the nose, beguiling, almost jammy; sweet, good weight and flavour, the leanness of a fit youth. Tannic, delicious.* Last tasted April 1991(***) 1996–2010

Ch L'EVANGILE *Distinctive, sweetish, elegant in Nov 1990, richness and tannin noted April 1991. Less intense than the '90; curious spearmint nose; seemed drier, doubtless the new oak and tannin. Lean. Nice flavour.* Last tasted May 1991. Hopefully(****) 1996–2010

Ch FIGEAC *Very good, very distinctive. And as so often, a fishy nose, rich, fragrant, blackberry/bramble fruitiness, subsiding to a gentle harmonious, almost caramelly sweetness. Distinctly sweet on the palate too. Mouthfilling fruit and flavour. Lively, charming. Spicy dry finish.* At the tasting in St-Emilion, Nov 1990(****) 1995–2015

Ch La FLEUR *This small compact Pomerol district manages to harbour a profusion of similar sounding vineyards. La Fleur, unencumbered, is a Moueix wine. Opaque, intense. Very rich nose with characteristically concentrated, fig-like fruit; fairly sweet, fairly full-bodied, certainly full of fruit, extract and flavour. An amplitude of flesh, but happily more Renoir than Rubens.* Nov 1990(****) 1997–2015

Ch La FLEUR-DE-GAY *A tiny vineyard sited between Vieux Ch Certan and Pétrus, producing — from 100% Merlot — a maximum of 2,000 cases. Good but not exceptional. Yet another cult wine.* Tasted with another fairly wide range of Pomerols at Ch Jonqueyres, Nov 1990(****) 1997–2015

Ch La FLEUR-PETRUS *One of the top Pomerol wines, yet rather low-keyed, distinctly undemonstrative. Dry, medium-full body, rather lean and very tannic.* Nov 1990(****) Needs time, say 1999–2020.

Les FORTS DE LATOUR *Using 40% new wood, the wine, when first tasted in the spring of 1990, seemed even deeper in colour than the* grand vin, *though, despite its power, certainly not as good. At the autumn tasting, still intensely purple; nose exhibiting nice young fruit, its original slight stalkiness now noted as a somewhat varnishy oak. Pretty full-bodied, with good fruit, crisp tannin and acidity. More recently showing well; beautiful fruit, cedar, mulberry; sweet, lovely flavour and texture. Certainly impressive.* Last tasted at the château, April 1991(****) 1995–2000

Clos FOURTET *Very deep, fullish, soft fruit, pleasant at the first showing in April. One of the deepest looking in the Nov line-up: a plummy purple; a forthcoming, slightly stalky but rich fruit and scent of new oak. Soft fruit noted again, adequate tannin and acidity. Spicy finish.* Last tasted Nov 1990(***) 1995–2010

Ch La GAFFELIERE *Very deep purple; distinctive and very fragrant nose; medium dryness and weight, unusual style, loose-limbed, citrus-like acidity, very flavoury, good finish. Whereas Clos Fourtet seems constantly to need that extra touch of inspiration, it comes naturally to La Gaffelière, though it is not always channelled in the right direction. It works in '89.* Tasted Nov 1990(****) 1995–2005

Ch GAZIN *Also fairly inspired in '89. Crisp, rich, brambly fruit. Peppery new oak. Fairly full-bodied. Tannic. Attractive.* Nov 1990(****) 1996–2010

Ch GRAND-PUY-LACOSTE *Another winner, another classic. Opaque, low-keyed crisp fruit opening up in the glass, revealing the rich Pauillac Cabernet character. Full-bodied, packed with good crisp fruit, tannin and acidity. Long life.* Nov 1990(****) 2000–25

Ch La GRAVE TRIGANT-DE-BOISSET *The nose of La Grave points in the direction of the Rhône rather than the left bank of the Gironde. It is certainly harmonious, but I cannot envisage the eventual unravelling of bouquet and flavour, or the finesse of its Médoc counterpart in a good vintage. However, like all the top Pomerols it has an immediacy of appeal, and I can see why they are so popular.* Tasted Nov 1990. A grudging(****) 1996–2010

Ch GRUAUD-LAROSE *Opaque, intense; nose and taste typically packed with fruit. Fairly full-bodied. Very good wine.* Nov 1990(****) 2000–2025

Ch HAUT-BAILLY *Deep, completely straightforward, soft fruit and oak. Could not be a better example of dependable Graves.* Tasted Nov 1990(****) 1997–2015

Ch HAUT-BATAILLEY *An elegant, medium-weight, Pauillac. Fragrant and stylish.* Nov 1990(***) 1996–2015

*Ch d'*ISSAN *Lovely deep texture and colour; good fruit, weight and flavour. Deft touch of new oak. Elegant.* Nov 1990(****) 1997–2015

Ch LANGOA-BARTON *Opaque; fragrant, spicy, cedary nose; dry, medium-full, good, crisp, firm.* Nov 1990(****) 1998–2010 and beyond.

Ch LATOUR A POMEROL *One should be able to detect these Mouiex Pomerols because of their fig-like concentration of fruit. Deep, fleshy, tannic.* Nov 1990(****) 1997–2015

Ch LEOVILLE-BARTON *Excellent, with dimensions added to its understated masculinity. Opaque, intense; immediate cedar and spice, then the soft sweetness on the nose that is simply very good despite being low-keyed. Medium dry, medium full-bodied, crisp fruit, good texture and all it needs to make an Englishman's claret.* Nov 1990(****) 1999 to beyond 2020.

Ch LEOVILLE-POYFERRE *Poyferré back to its pre-1930 form. Opaque, intense; rather well-polished new oak on the nose, but crisp fruit and, after time* *in glass, nice scent; dry, very oaky, good fruit. Tannic. Nov 1990(****) 2000–2020+*

Ch LYNCH-BAGES *Also showing well, indeed at its best. Opaque, intense; marvellous rich Cabernet* cassis *fruit on the nose; full of body, fruit, extract. A rather unusually fleshy character. Good length, tannin and acidity. Nov 1990(****) 1998 to beyond 2020.*

Ch MAGDELAINE *Very deep, rich; low-keyed but prune-like richness of fruit; fairly sweet, full-bodied, fleshy, concentrated, good shape. Two good notes, in Nov 1990**(**) 1993–2005*

Ch La MISSION-HAUT-BRION *Opaque, intense; more open and fruity than the '88, but less so than the '89 Haut-Brion. Scent of tar and chocolate. On the palate, sweet, full-bodied, rich, fruity and very tannic. Tasted at the château, not long after it had been fined. Nov 1990(****) 1998–2025*

Ch MONTROSE *Opaque, intense purple; lovely scent of fruit, cedar, oak. Fairly full-bodied, laden with fruit, flesh, tannin and acidity. An excellent classic wine needing plenty of bottle-age. Nov 1990(****) 2000–2030*

Ch MOUTON-BARONNE PHILIPPE *In April 1990: ruby; pleasant, crisp, oaky nose; dry, medium body, light style. But tight-knit. A year later developing nicely, seemed sweeter, fruity. Both at the château, last in August 1991(***) 1995–2005*

Ch PALMER *First tasted at the line-up of '89s at Langoa, and at Palmer. Very deep, rich; cold and closed in the cellars but warmer and showing more generosity at the tasting: nose of cedar, new oak, developing gloriously in the glass with the mulberry-rich fruit that is Palmer at its best. Surprisingly sweet, medium full-bodied, soft, fleshy, rounded. Most recently, at the château: deep; lovely; silky tannins. Last tasted June 1991(*****) 1998–2020*

Ch PAPE-CLEMENT *The improvement of recent years very noticeable. Deep; a lovely fragrant nose combining fruit and oak; palate to match. Fullish, elegant. Nov 1990(****) 1998–2020*

Ch PAVIE *Very deep; open-knit, fruity nose; citrus-like fruit and acidity, a flavoury, relatively quick-developing wine. Nov 1990(***) 1996–2010*

Ch PAVIE-DECESSE *Very deep, crisp, purple; very pleasant fruit; sweet, medium body, flavoury, attractive. Nov 1990(***) 1995–2005*

Ch PICHON-LONGUEVILLE, BARON *Opaque, intense; straightforward, classic nose, cedar, fruity, oak, depth; medium-full body, good fruit and extract. Very satisfactory. The new régime shows. Nov 1990(****) 1999–2020*

Ch PICHON-LONGUEVILLE, LALANDE *Very deep; rather exaggerated, overripe nose. Very disappointing. Clearly not showing well. Nov 1990 (?) Must taste again.*

Ch PONTET-CANET *As with the '88, I found this very strange and not to my liking. Nose varnishy, cedar, fruit, then liquorice — a curious woody Spanish-root smell. Medium weight. Raw. Nov 1990(?) I must see how this fares in bottle.*

Ch PRIEURE-LICHINE *In Nov 1990: lovely colour; soft, open, fruity nose, touch of stalkiness; on the sweet side, easy-going though adequate tannin and acidity. Last tasted June 1991(***) 1993–2003*

Ch RAUSAN-SEGLA *Very deep, intense; fruity, vinosity, elegance; medium-full body, firm, good fruit, length and aftertaste. Nice wine. Nov 1990(****) 1998–2010*

Ch RAUZAN-GASSIES *Medium, open appearance; sweet and rather advanced on the nose; developing a curious blackberry-like aroma; flavoury, open-knit. Not bad but, as so often, not up to its* 2ème cru *classification. Nov 1990(**) 1994–2000*

Ch SIRAN *Never great but consistent in style, lean and, at its best, elegant. Very deep, velvety appearance; fragrant, cedary nose; dry, leathery tannins but svelte. Tasted in April and Nov 1990(***) 1996–2016*

Ch TALBOT *Opaque, intense; very strange fig-like smell. Not right. Bad sample. Nov 1990(?) Retaste.*

Ch TROTANOY *Deep though advanced colour; nose tight and peppery at first but developed scented fruit; fairly full-bodied yet with a lean elegance and silky texture. Good tannin. A lovely wine. Nov 1990(*****) 1997–2020*

OTHER '89s TASTED ONLY ONCE, NOV 1990. STARS GIVE A ROUGH INDICATION OF ITS PERCEIVED QUALITY AND FUTURE:

*Ch Andron-Blanquet(**) Ch L'Angélus(***) Ch d'Angludet(***) Ch Balestard-La-Tonnelle(***) Ch Beau Séjour Bécot(****) Ch Beauséjour (Duffau-Lagarosse)(****) Ch Beau Site(**) Ch Bourgneuf(***) Ch La Cabanne(***) Ch Canon-de-Brem(***) Ch Cap de Mourlin(**) Ch Carbonnieux(***) Ch de Carles(***) Ch Certan de May(****) Ch Clinet(****) Clos du Clocher(***) Ch Cos Labory(**)? Ch Couvent-des-Jacobins(**) Ch La Croix(****) Ch La Croix du Casse(***) Ch La Croix de Gay(****) Ch La Croix-St-Vincent(***) Ch La Dauphine(***) Ch Dauzac(***) Clos L'Eglise(***) Dom de L'Eglise(****) Ch L'Enclos(***) Ch Feytit-Clinet(***) Ch de Fieuzal(****) Ch Fonroque(***) Ch Fourcas-Dupré(***) Ch Fourcas-Hosten(**) Ch de France(***)? Ch Haut-Bergey(***) Clos des Jacobins(**) Ch Kirwan(**) Ch La Fleur-Gazin(** at least) Ch Lafon-Rochet(***) Ch Lagrange, Pomerol(***) Ch Larrivet-Haut-Brion(**? retaste) Ch La Louvière(**? retaste) Ch Lynch-Moussas(***) Ch Malartic-Lagravière(***) Ch Mazeris(***) Moulin du Cadet (the third wine of Lafite)(**) Moulin de Duhart (the second wine of Duhart-Milon)(**) Ch Moulinet(***) Ch Olivier(***) Ch Les Ormes-de-Pez (retaste); Ch Patâche d'Aux(**) Ch Petit-Village(****) Ch Plince(**) Ch Rahoul(***) Ch Siaurac(**) Ch Smith-Haut-Lafitte(***) Ch Taillefer(**) Ch La Tour-de-By(**) Ch La Tour-Martillac(* retaste) Ch Trottevieille(***) Ch Yon-Figeac(***)*

1990(★★★★)

1989, 1990: once again miraculous vintage twins? Certainly very similar weather conditions: both years abnormally hot (an average 18.7°C in 1990, 18.6°C in 1989) with low rainfall, (80mm against average 136mm).

Judging wine the spring after the vintage is a chancy game. After so little time in wood, sweet young fruit can be beguiling, hardly hinting at the changes to come as it evolves in new or partially new oak. The following notes are therefore presented diffidently. Having said this, it *is* clearly a very good vintage.

Jan to March was unusually warm and sunny, reaching up to 25°C on Feb 24, heralding an early spring. Beneficial rain in April. May very hot, dry and sunny. Flowering finished early June. July was so hot (30 days of temperatures over 30°C; 38.8°C on July 21) that the sap was blocked, impeding maturation. Aug warm and dry. Harvest around mid-Sept. There was some talk of too much tannin and too little acidity; but if a wine has ample fruit, alcohol, extract and tannins, it does not need proportionately high acidity (as for example, the '82s and '59s).

Except for the first growths, the following notes were made in April 1991 at Ch L'Angélus (the St-Emilions and Pomerols), at Ch de Fieuzal (Graves), and at Ch Prieuré-Lichine (Margaux). The tastings were organised by the *Union des Grands Crus*. Unfortunately, I was unable to stay on for the important Pauillac and St-Julien tasting.

Ch LAFITE *Opaque, purple; dumb, cedary, smoky; sweet, medium weight, surprisingly soft and easy. Amenable tannins. Attractive but outshone by the '89.* At the château, April 1991(****)?

Ch MARGAUX *Green pruning, or crop thinning, was first practised at Margaux in 1986. Severe in 1988 and 1989 because of big potential crops, even more so in 1990. 30% of new vine grapes were culled. Very deep, intense purple; low-keyed but fragrant, deft use of new oak; medium-full, lean, stylish, supple, good fruit. Tannins not excessive.* Ex-cask, April 1991. At least(****)

Ch LATOUR *Fabulous depth of colour; nose difficult to assess; severe, tough, chewy, very good flavour but very tannic.* At the château, April 1990, probably(*****)

Ch MOUTON-ROTHSCHILD *Fine, deep; low-keyed, unknit fruit and new oak; sweet, fullish, good fruit, drying tannins. Upstaged by the spectacular '89.* At the château, April 1991. Early days(****)?

Ch HAUT-BRION *In* barriques *since Jan. Opaque; hard, cedary, violets, fruit; dryish, full-bodied, flesh, fruit and elegance, good tannins and acidity.* From the cask, April 1991(****)

Ch AUSONE *Tasted from two casks. Fabulous, brilliant purple; the first with lovely fruit aroma, the other more restrained; on palate both fairly sweet, full-bodied, fleshy, lovely. Firmer and more tannic from Demtos cask. Surely will turn out to be one of the best-ever Ausones.* In the cellar, with Pascal Delbeck, April 1991(*****)

Ch CHEVAL-BLANC *Not very deep; forthcoming, fragrant; sweet, fullish, chewy, attractive flavour, length, balance, and finesse.* At the château, April 1991(*****)

Ch PETRUS *Opaque; fruit and already oaky; fairly sweet, fullish, fleshy, lovely fruit, less tannic than the '89.* From the cask, June 1991(*****)

A SELECTION TASTED FROM CASK SAMPLES:

Ch L'ANGELUS *Black; distinctive, raspberry-like then black treacle; fullish, tarry taste, slightly watery finish.* At the château, April 1991(***)

Ch d'ANGLUDET *Very deep; distinctive, fragrant, violets, a good combination of fruit and new oak; soft, flavoury, citrus-like fruit acidity. Delicious.* April 1991(****)

Ch BOUSCAUT *Opaque, intense; dumb, new oak; full-bodied, high extract, fruit, tannic. Shapely but not long.* April 1991(***)

Ch CANON *First sample bottle totally wrong: rather pale; over-opulent; fragrant but strange. The second deep, rich; fruit and typical Canon flesh; fairly sweet, fullish, fragrant aftertaste.* April 1991(*****)

Ch CANON-LA-GAFFELIERE *Opaque, velvety sheen, rich legs; massive, blackberry, oak — like dust of sawn wood, then rich, mulberry and tar; good fruit, balance, length.* April 1991(****)

Ch CANTEMERLE *Soft fruit; very distinctive, open, an early developer.* April 1991(***)

Ch CANTENAC-BROWN *Vivid purple; forthcoming, sweaty, stably; sweetish, chewy, characteristic chocolaty flavour, tannic.* April 1991(****)

Ch CARBONNIEUX *Deep but not intense; very sweet, forthcoming, lovely fruit; very attractive, easy, early developer.* April 1991(***)

Dom de CHEVALIER *The Cabernet Sauvignon considered better than in 1988 and 1989, the Merlot less good. Alcohol lower than the '89. Opaque; closed yet good fruit; medium-sweet, fullish, rich, chewy, slightly sandy texture, judicious new oak, extra dimensions compared with most other red Graves.* April 1991(****)

Ch CLERC-MILON *Glorious, spicy, mulberry-ripe Cabernet Sauvignon nose and taste. Sweet, nice weight, crisp.* April 1991(****)

Ch CLINET *Intense black; malty, blackberry-like fruit; very rich, plummy.* April 1991(****)

Ch La CONSEILLANTE *Opaque; harmonious fruit; sweet, rich, high alcohol(?), rounded, classy.* April 1991(****)

Ch DAUZAC *Intense purple; good fruit, sweaty tannins; softer and rounder than expected. Good fruit but a bit weak.* April 1991(***)

Ch DUHART-MILON *Dumb, straw-like; sweetish, loose-knit but nicely balanced, soft tannins.* April 1991(***)

Ch L'EVANGILE *Gloriously deep, rich; ripe, mulberry; fairly sweet, luscious fruit, new oak, cloves aftertaste. Loaded — one could almost spread it on bread.* Tasted at Lafite in April and at Spencer House in May 1991(*****)

Ch de FIEUZAL *Intense purple; very distinctive style, smoky, oaky, good fruit, length.* April 1991(****)

Ch FIGEAC *Deep plummy purple; delicious fruit, very dry, tannic, iron finish.* April 1991(*****)

Les FORTS DE LATOUR *Opaque, impressive; low-keyed, nice fruit; very sweet, fairly full-bodied, very good flavour.* April 1991(****)

Clos FOURTET *Very deep; dumb, then classic fruit, evolved well; entirely straightforward.* April 1991(*** possibly ****)

Ch GAZIN *Opaque; stalky at first but good fruit emerged; very tannic.* April 1991(***)?

Ch GISCOURS *Opaque, immense; rich, high alcohol, syrup of figs; sweet, thick, impressive but odd. Soft tannins.* April 1991(***)

Ch HAUT-BAILLY *First a cask sample, then from the cask. Intense, lovely colour; extraordinary scent, good fruit, vanilla; rich, fullish, good fruit, length, taut, tannic.* Last tasted at the château, April 1991(****)

Ch d'ISSAN *Opaque, intense; low-keyed but good, fig-like richness; sweet, lovely flavour, texture and balance, Margaux violets and charm.* April 1991(****)

Ch KIRWAN *Deep; light at first, fruit, tannin; unknit; sweet, soft, quite good fruit, tannic.* April 1991(***)

Ch LASCOMBES *Opaque; violets and sawn wood; sweetish, soft, open-knit.* April 1991(***)

Ch La LOUVIERE *Opaque; open, rich, slightly cheesy, then almost caramelly, sweet, full of fruit. Flavour to match. Sweet, soft tannins, an easy, early developer. Perhaps lacking acidity.* April 1991(**)

Ch MALARTIC-LAGRAVIERE *Open-knit; light fruit, evolved; dry, lightish in weight and style, easy, lacking length. An early developer.* April 1991(**)

Ch MALESCOT-ST-EXUPERY *Opaque; forthcoming, high-toned, unknit but fragrant; sweet, crisp fruit, flavoury but rather hollow. Tannic.* April 1991(** possibly ***?)

Ch La MISSION-HAUT-BRION *Opaque; lovely fruit, depth; dry, medium-full body, crisp, very good length, tannins.* At the château, April 1991(****)

Ch MOUTON-BARONNE PHILIPPE *Black cherry core, ruby rim; low-keyed, violets; sweet, very pleasing fruit, soft tannins, almost too easy, yet good length.* April 1991(***)

Ch PALMER *Showing well in April. Very deep; good crisp, mulberry-like fruit; distinctly sweet, medium-full body, soft fruit, good length, dry tannic finish. Attractive. Good potential.* Last tasted at the château, June 1991(****)

Ch PAPE-CLEMENT *Interesting new developments. Irregular ripening in 1990, great selection needed. Vats bled, removing 12% of juice. 75% new oak. Opaque; soft, vanillin, curiously lean, open-knit, spicy oak, then vegetal; sweet, medium-full body, soft, chewy, the most Médocain in flavour and character, touch of oyster shells, iodine. Spicy new oak aftertaste. Tannic.* April 1991(****)

Ch PAVIE *Opaque; low-keyed, ripe fruit; fullish, well balanced, positive finish.* April 1991(****)

Ch PRIEURE-LICHINE *Crisp purple; crisp fruit, better on palate than nose. Leather and spice.* April 1991(*** perhaps ****)

Ch RAUSAN-SEGLA *Opaque; very rich brambly fruit; sweet, fullish, firm, elegant, good texture.* April 1991(****)

Ch RAUZAN-GASSIES *Deep, though with weak purple rim; open, unknit; very sweet, soft fruit, quite nice and easy.* April 1991(***)

OTHER '90s TASTED APRIL 1991:

Ch BAHANS-HAUT-BRION *Surprisingly sweet yet with tannic bitterness*(**)

Ch BALESTARD-LA-TONNELLE *Nose like cod-liver oil and black treacle; austere, very tannic*(**)

Ch BEAUREGARD *Pomerol. Strange, unknit, stalky, easy*(**)

Ch La CABANNE *Curious; light, attractive*(**)

Ch CAP DE MOURLIN *(Jacques) Opaque; good fruit, high-toned, early developer*(**)

Ch La CARDONNE *Soft, sweet, delicious*(***)

CARRUADES DE CH LAFITE *Intense; meaty, leathery, silky texture: more substance, less charm than I associate with Carruades*(**)

Ch CHASSE-SPLEEN *Opaque; crisp young fruit; fullish, firm tannic*(****)

Ch CITRAN *Opaque; blackberry, rich; fullish, chewy, fruity*(***)

Ch CLARKE *Intense purple; good young fruit, slightly short*(**)

Ch La CROIX DE GAY *Unyielding nose; sweetish, fleshy, good fruit, balance, length*(****)

Ch DASSAULT *Good, fruity, oaky, excessively tannic*(**?)

Ch FONPLEGADE *Deep, dumb, hidden fruit, lean, short*(***)

Ch FONREAUD *Plummy; soft, short*(*)

Ch FOURCAS-DUPRE *Purple; concrete-like, then figgy; soft, not much flavour, short*(*)

Ch FOURCAS-HOSTEN *Opaque; sweet cedar and fruit; soft, fruity, very tannic*(**)

Ch de FRANCE *Opaque, intense, rich legs; sweet, very attractive fruit and new oak. Early developer*(***)

Ch LABEGORCE *Touch of tangerine; soft fruit, some fat and substance but specious*(**?)

Ch LARCIS-DUCASSE *High-toned, varnishy; lightish, not much fruit or flesh*(*)

Ch LARMANDE *Unknit; soft fruit, chewy, very tannic*(**)

Ch LARRIVET-HAUT-BRION *Scented; original flavour, texture, iron finish. Retaste*(**?)

Ch LATOUR-HAUT-BRION *Deep purple; full, fleshy, blackberry, blackcurrant; sweet, fullish, soft tannins, tobacco taste*(***)

Ch MALESCASSE *Intense, velvety; brambly, loose-knit; crisp, dry*(**)

Ch MARTINENS *Plummy; extraordinary aromas and flavour, ginger, blackberry, tangerine. Crisp, tannic*(***)

Ch MAUCAILLOU *Very distinctive mint, raspberry nose, taste. Lacking acidity and length. Early developer*(**)

Ch MONBRISON *Soft fruit and tannins. Shapely. Some charm*(***)

Ch NENIN *Quite nice fruit, balance. Early developer*(**)

Ch OLIVIER *Opaque; dry, full, rich fruit, good extract, tannic*(***)

Ch PAVIE-DECESSE *Tight-knit, blackberry; attractive fruit, good tannin and acidity. Early developer?*(***)

Ch PETIT-VILLAGE *Fragrant, distinctive, fair length*(***)

Ch PIQUE-CAILLOU *Intense, figgy; good fruit, length, almost tarry taste, metallic tannin*(***)

Ch La POINTE *Meaty; crisp, fruity, easy*(**)

Ch SMITH-HAUT-LAFITTE *Deep; earthy; soft fruit, tannic, lacking length(**)*
Ch La TOUR-MARTILLAC *Impressive colour and nose, slightly scented; full-bodied, lots of fruit, very tannic, fragrant new oak aftertaste(***)*
Ch TROPLONG-MONDOT *Opaque, intense, rich; brambly; sweet, soft, chewy, easy, correct tannin and acidity(****)*
Ch VILLEMAURINE *Oaky, varnishy nose, taste. Needs time(**?)*
VIEUX CH CERTAN *Plummy; fragrant; straightforward(***)*

1991?

Is it possible for the run of splendid vintages to continue? If so, it would run contra to previous experience. Fairly severe frosts have reduced the potential harvest, some districts hit harder than others. At Cheval-Blanc and Pétrus I was informed that the crop would be 10% of normal, and the replacement buds indicated a late harvest. We shall see. Meanwhile, make the most of the superlative decade of the 1980s.

DRY WHITE BORDEAUX

In this edition, as they are totally different in character and purpose, I have split the dry white and sweet wines into separate sections.

The post-war history of sweet white Bordeaux has been one of economics and taste. Suffice to say that over the past decade both have moved in Sauternes' favour. But unlike the dry whites, the production of Sauternes is largely dictated by the weather: the fortunate combination of sun to ripen and sweeten the grapes and morning mists to induce *Botrytis*. Cold and rain can be terminal. Happily the market and the weather have worked unusually well together over recent years. The other important difference is that the best sweet whites will not only keep but will improve with bottle-age.

Like most dry white wines, dry white Bordeaux is made to be drunk young and, with a few exceptions, does not benefit from bottle-age. Only the top quality Graves need and repay keeping. Graves is, of course, the best known dry white wine district of Bordeaux. In the old days, indeed well into the 1950s, the white wines from this district were often yellow, sulphury-nosed, four-square and, frankly, drab. The combination of more up-to-date winemaking methods and concentration on the more acidic and zestful Sauvignon Blanc grape variety at the expense of the more sedate Sémillon has changed the scene, largely, but not completely, for the better. However, opinion now is that the present trend towards light, very dry acidic wines has gone too far, for there is no doubt in my mind that the traditional combination of Sémillon and Sauvignon Blanc, when well handled, produced wines of character. If I want to drink a Sancerre-type wine I prefer to drink Sancerre. Moreover I have noted a comparatively recent trend to give Sauvignon Blanc some time in new oak casks which adds a spiciness verging on speciousness. My own feeling is that new oak and Sauvignon Blanc are uneasy bedfellows, if not completely incompatible, unless the wine is reasonably well endowed with fruit and extract.

The two great white Graves, Haut-Brion and Laville-Haut-Brion, followed closely by Dom de Chevalier, are about the only dry white Bordeaux that benefit from bottle-age, and then, principally, in the better vintages. Indeed, Haut-Brion positively needs, but is rarely given, bottle-age, the small production being snapped up and all too speedily consumed. Outside the Graves area the two best known dry white Bordeaux of note are 'Y', Ygrec, made by Lur-Saluces at Yquem, and, in the Médoc, Pavillon Blanc de Ch Margaux. Frankly, I find both extremely variable. Of late there has been a tendency for château proprietors in Sauternes and Barsac to make a dry wine, rather like a bookmaker laying off bets, presumably to build up an acceptable market lest weather conditions prevent their making a sweet wine. It is somewhat ironic that this has occurred during a period particularly favourable for the production of classic Sauternes, with a market to match. Frankly I am unimpressed by most dry Sauternes.

As with most other types of wine, only the best are worth keeping, and few will survive poor storage conditions.

1926****

Very good vintage. For obvious reasons not often seen.

Pavillon Blanc de Ch Margaux Just to remind us that Pavillon Blanc is not just a Mentzelopoulos innovation. Top-shoulder level; orange amber with gold highlights, slightly cloudy; forthcoming waxy bouquet with a whiff of old tom-cats; medium dry, lovely rich crisp flavour, not unlike an old dry Vouvray. Firm dry finish.
*May 1987****

1928*****

Outstanding. The best dry white wine vintage of the decade and arguably the most satisfactory and long-lasting of the century. Firm, full-bodied, well endowed with all the necessary component parts including life-enhancing acidity.

Ch Haut-Brion A great classic wine – at its best. Just two bottles noted, one woody/corked. The second: lovely amber colour; old waxy bouquet, which developed rich, stably, straw and lanolin scents; medium dry, excellent consistency and texture on the palate. Slightly maderised but otherwise clean and sound.
*At a joint Christie's/Chicago Wine Company dinner, April 1982****

Ch Laville-Haut-Brion Fairly deep, richly coloured; powerful bouquet, like old apricots and apples in a loft; dry, fairly full-bodied, austere. Maderised like an old Sauternes but with underlying quality.
*From the Woltner cellars, at Karl-Heinz Wolf's La Mission tasting in Wiesbaden, June 1990***

Ch Bouscaut "Extra dry". Startlingly rich orange-gold colour, bright; whiff of old lanolin, linoleum and mushroom skin, but developed a soft honeyed bouquet; dry, firm, lightly honeyed one-dimensional flavour, good acidity.
*Sept 1986***

Pavillon Blanc de Ch Margaux Pure yellow gold; low-keyed, dough-like nose; dry, fullish, great length, excellent acidity. Barley-sugar bottle-age taste.
*May 1987****

1929****

Good vintage. Ripe, less firm wines than the '28s. If stored in perfect conditions, still more than just interesting.

Ch Laville-Haut-Brion Lively orange gold; no faults: lovely, harmonious bouquet, honeyed bottle-age, ripe apricots; fairly dry, excellent flavour, flesh, balance. Surprisingly good, life sustaining acidity.
*From the Woltner cellars, June 1990******

Pavillon Blanc de Ch Margaux Orange gold, more like an old cognac; a bit mushroomy at first, but opened up, smoky, honeyed bottle-age, good in its way; meaty and somewhat maderised but an agreeable barley-sugar flavour and good acidity.
*At the Rodenstock annual tasting, Sept 1990****

1933***

Ch Laville-Haut-Brion Lovely bright gold; toasted Sémillon, nice fruit; dry, on the light side. Pronounced almond kernel taste, and acidic.
*At the Wolf tasting, June 1990***

Ch La Louvière Upper mid-shoulder level; lovely yellow gold; light, but fragrant, pleasant waxy old Sémillon bouquet; dry, lightish, lean, kernelly taste, good acidity. A nice surprise.
*June 1988***

1934****

Extremely good vintage.

Ch Laville-Haut-Brion Gold sheen; glorious, virtually faultless honeyed bottle-age bouquet; fairly dry, nice weight, firm, fleshier than the '33, good finish.
*June 1990*****

Ch Lafite Labelled "Vin de Château Lafite 1934" with Carruades corks. Dry and attractive but lacking extra dimensions.
*March 1978****

1935***

Ch Laville-Haut-Brion The colour of say, Climens, of this age; lovely bouquet, honey, orange blossom, touch of caramel; dry, fullish, firm, barley-sugar aftertaste. In excellent condition.
*Another Woltner/Wolf wine, June 1990*****

1936**

Ch Laville-Haut-Brion Lemon gold; rather raw but attractive, acidulous lime blossom bouquet; very dry, light, steely; clean but with teeth-gripping acidity.
*Woltner/Wolf tasting, June 1990***

1937*****

An excellent white Bordeaux vintage. The excessive acidity which made the reds too astringent helped enliven the whites. However, acidity now seems to be taking over and the dry whites are not showing as well as the '28s and the immediate post-war vintages. And, for more understandable reasons, are nowhere near as good as the still fabulous Sauternes.

Ch Haut-Brion Lovely yellow gold; sweet, gentle, harmonious nose, touch of lemon, honeyed vanilla; dry, rather raw and distinctly acidic.
*Sept 1988***

Ch Laville-Haut-Brion Excellent level; deepish warm gold; soft, lanolin bouquet that opened up beautifully, crème caramel, honey and milk fudge; drying, fullish, harmonious. No faults: indeed a perfect though unexciting flavour.
*March 1987*****

Ch Bouscaut Amber gold; soft, creamy, honeyed; touch of sweetness, waxy, honeyed vanilla flavour, excellent acidity but a bit short, and with a touch of bitterness.
*Sept 1988***

Ch Carbonnieux Straw gold; powdery, mushroomy; very dry, too tart.
Sept 1988.

La Perle Blanche A Monopole (branded wine) of Mähler-Besse. Deep gold; sweet, honeyed, Barsac-like nose; medium-sweet, rich, honeyed bottle-age flavour, sound though short.
*Served by the Mähler-Besse family at Ch Palmer, Nov 1990****

1938**

Ch Laville-Haut-Brion Colour of old gold or brass buttons in need of a polish; smell of old peach skins, biscuits; dry, masculine, good length, fairly high fixed acidity. Good for age and vintage.
*June 1990***

1939**

Ch Laville-Haut-Brion Its best features colour and bouquet: fairly deep gold colour and fragrant bouquet. On the palate dry, lightish, steely, rather sour.
*June 1990**

1940***

Ch Laville-Haut-Brion Rich amber gold; waxy Chenin Blanc-like nose with touch of *citronelle*; medium dryness and body, firm, excellent condition.
*Woltner/Wolf tasting, June 1990****

1941**

Ch Laville-Haut-Brion Orange gold; raw, acidic but some depth, and with honeyed bottle-age; dry, firm, lean, hard acidic finish. In excellent condition.
*June 1990***

1942***

Ch Laville-Haut-Brion Yellow gold, pale for age; sweet, attractive, pasty vanilla bouquet; medium dryness and weight, well balanced and in excellent condition.
*June 1990****

1943*****

Better for white than for red, but few remain as most were consumed during the immediate post-war period.
Ch Haut-Brion Level upper mid-shoulder, greasy cork. Slight sediment. Very good colour, palish yellow amber; first whiff, old but sweet and caramelly but it shed the stale air from its ullage and opened up in the glass, rich, old peaches and honey. Fabulous after three hours. Sweet, full-bodied, a good old waxy taste, dry finish.
*Purchased in 1986 and served at a Bordeaux Club dinner at Christie's, April 1990****
Ch Laville-Haut-Brion Beautiful limpid appearance; sound but rather unforthcoming nose; dry, fairly full-bodied, firm acidity. A touch of coarseness when tasted after the '45 and '49.
*June 1990***
Ch Carbonnieux Amber gold; barley-sugar, Sauternes-like bouquet; bone dry, waxy Sémillon flavour, firm and sound.
*May 1986****

1945*****

Good vintage. Still holding well if properly cellared. Worth seeking out the best. Rare and expensive.
Ch Laville-Haut-Brion Marvellous wine, first tasted at La Mission in 1978. Most recently, a bottle from the Woltner family cellars sold through Christie's: medium-pale yellow gold; fabulous bouquet reminding me of the orange blossom of Yquem, with bottle-age scent of clover honey; surprisingly dry after the richness of bouquet, lean, firm, steely, good length, excellent acidity.
*Last noted at Karl-Heinz Wolf's tasting, June 1990******
Ch de Valoux Despite good level and good cellar, acetic. Minor and not made to last.
April 1981.

1946*

Ch Laville-Haut-Brion Orange-tinged; sweet, chocolaty, acidic; dry, good body and flavour but a bit coarse, with pasty end acidity.
*June 1990***

1947****

A softer riper year than 1945. Can still be good.
Ch Laville-Haut-Brion Marvellous warm amber gold; fabulous, pure honeycomb bouquet which blossomed in the glass; dry, fairly full-bodied, assertive, lovely rich flavour but with a rather unexciting finish.
*Last tasted June 1990*****

Two minor wines tasted in the early 1980s, both from a private cellar in Paris:
Dom de Jaussans Cérons. Good nose but drying out a bit and short**
Blanc de Susbielle Graves Supérieur. Yellow gold; honeyed bottle-age; on the sweet side and perfectly balanced***

1948***

A good firm dry white vintage.
Ch Laville-Haut-Brion Sweet, fragrant, 'caramac' (soft, fudge-like caramel) nose; dry, lean, touch of peach kernel, highish acidity, good aftertaste.
*June 1990***
Ch Laville-Haut-Brion *Crème de Tête.* Bright amber; lovely, honeyed, harmonious, slightly 'singed' bouquet; medium dryness and fullness, but grubby endtaste.
*Sept 1988**
Pavillon Blanc de Ch Margaux Good level and cork. Buttery gold; old honeyed Sémillon; dry, firm, a nice backbone of acidity, in excellent condition.
*Pre-sale tasting, Nov 1981****

1949****

Post-war vintage dry whites were snapped up by merchants and speedily sold to and consumed by their customers. Worth looking out for the best.
Ch Laville-Haut-Brion Several notes including some variable bottles at a dinner in 1979. Most recently: yellow gold, pale for age; lovely ripe waxy Sémillon nose, lively, with whiff of lime (acidity) and barley-sugar (bottle-age). Dry, lightish, delicate, good length and fragrant aftertaste. Despite rather high acidity, lovely.
*Last noted at the Wolf tasting, June 1990*****
Ch Le Pape Preignac. Palish yellow; lovely honeyed Sémillon; dry, soft, honeyed aftertaste. Very agreeable.
*At pre-sale tasting, Nov 1988****

1950**

Ch Laville-Haut-Brion Touch of old gold; milky, slightly smoky nose that quickly opened up, churning out a pleasing scent. Dry, fullish, assertive, caramelised flavour and aftertaste.
*June 1990***

1951

Terrible year. None tasted.

1952***

A good firm vintage. Haut-Brion was outstanding at five years old and if kept cool and undisturbed it will probably still be good. Only Laville tasted recently.
Ch Laville-Haut-Brion Palish, weak-rimmed; curious, goats cheese, leathery nose; dry, medium weight, masculine, austere.
*June 1990***

1953***

An attractive vintage.
Ch Laville-Haut-Brion Medium, yellow, and, like the '52, with a watery edge; low-keyed but crisp, honeyed nose, walnuts; dry, medium full-bodied, four-square, lacking length, charm and acidity though with a fairly fragrant barley-sugar aftertaste.
*June 1990***
Graves 'Royale' A good example of a Bordeaux merchant's (de Luze) Monopole. Once pale, changing after over 25 years in bottle to buttercup yellow; a mainly

Sémillon waxy, honeyed bouquet reminiscent of old Chenin Blanc; medium dryness and weight, very attractive but lacking length and finesse.
*Two consistent notes. Last tasted Dec 1982****

1954

Despite dismal wet summer, some passable Graves made.
Ch Laville-Haut-Brion Surprisingly lovely and lively in 1970. In 1990, a pleasantly forthcoming bouquet, honey and cold tea; fairly dry, nice weight, good acidity.
*Last tasted June 1990****

1955****

The best vintage of the mid-1950s.
Ch Haut-Brion Poor cork. Amber gold, orange-tinged; smell of rich old straw; dry, fullish, tangy, good extract and acidity, a bit maderised.
*Oct 1988**
Ch Laville-Haut-Brion Five virtually perfect notes between 1977 and 1979. Also showing well in 1982. Most recently: pure yellow gold; a very pronounced and distinctive nose: sheepskin, goats cheese, the rind of Camembert; medium dry, soft, slightly bitter finish. Should be more attractive than this.
*Last tasted June 1990. At best*****
Ch Carbonnieux Good level but colour too amber; sherry-like nose; dry, appley, maderised. Carbonnieux rarely seems to have staying power.
Oct 1981.

1956

Terrible reputation. None tasted.

1957**

Dry, acidic.
Ch Laville-Haut-Brion Rather dull, orange-tinged; fragrant, floral, refreshing nose; dry, nice weight and flavour. Good acidity.
*June 1990***

1958*

Of little interest.
Ch Laville-Haut-Brion Palish lemon gold, weak rim; little nose though a trace of underlying honey. Not giving up. Dryish, soft, with touch of woodiness on the finish.
*June 1990**

1959*****

A great vintage for red, sweet *and* dry white Bordeaux. The exceptionally hot summer produced grapes with a high sugar content, alcohol and extract. But the dry whites perhaps lacked the refreshing counterbalancing tartaric acid and, as in all hot vintages, carried the risk of high volatile acidity.
Ch Laville-Haut-Brion Lovely burnished gold; clearly a touch of *Botrytis*, plus honeyed bottle-age; medium dry, fairly full-bodied, lovely flavour, balance and aftertaste.
*June 1990*****
Vin Blanc de Lafite Drunk on two occasions at the château, first in 1984. Consistent notes: pale for age, possibly due to the highish sulphur dioxide content noticeable on the nose, otherwise mildly honeyed. Dryish, somewhat four-square though with some richness. A bit short, with a trace of volatile acidity on the finish.
*Last tasted June 1988***
Ygrec Rich yellow gold; glorious bouquet, sweet, honeyed, almost like Yquem itself, with highish volatile acidity; verging on the sweet, full, very rich, fabulous flavour, great length.
*The oldest and one of the best of a vertical of Ygrecs tasted at Ch d'Yquem, Sept 1986******

1960*

Not very good.
Ch Laville-Haut-Brion First tasted in 1978 when I found it fragrant but piquant. An identical note made in 1986. Next served at the opening dinner at Rodenstock's ninth Rare Wine tasting. Six bottles, all sound. On our table: a glowing yellow; nose restrained, a touch sharp and peppery; dryish, surprisingly good flavour but teeth-gripping acidity. Most recently, a maderised bottle.
*Last tasted June 1990. At best**
Ygrec Two notes: fairly deep colour; 'green', kernelly, touch of 'kerosene'; dry, lean and with more body than expected. An oily richness yet lean and skinny. Not very appealing.
*Last tasted at Yquem, Sept 1988**

1961****

Very good. Some excellent wines still to be found.
Ch Haut-Brion Surprisingly pale for age; on the palate dry, fairly austere with fairly marked end acidity. But it developed nicely, even sweetened, in the glass.
*Last tasted Feb 1982***
Ch Laville-Haut-Brion Variable. Aged four the wine was glorious. I thought it the finest Graves I had ever tasted. Good notes through the 1970s and a superb bottle given to me at Le Grand Véfour in 1982, a positive yellow yet still, after 21 years, retaining a youthful green tinge; harmonious waxy, honeyed bouquet; dry, some plumpness, lovely flavour, length and acidity. Two recent bottles, both poor. Drab and grubby at Wolf's tasting, unharmonious, old sulphur, raw, aggressive and rubbery.
*Last tasted Sept 1990. At best*****
Dom de Chevalier First tasted at the château in Oct 1981. Despite its Sémillon character, M Claude Ricard said it was 60% Sauvignon Blanc but that the soil dominated. Still fairly pale for age; nose developed surprising spice and pungency; dry, medium weight, very good but a bit bland.
*Last tasted Feb 1986*** Needs drinking.*
Ch Fieuzal Palish gold; good clean, firm, fairly dry wine with slightly honeyed bottle-age, waxy Sémillon flavour and excellent acidity.
*Aug 1984*****
Pavillon Blanc de Ch Margaux Yellow gold; fragrant bouquet, sweet, honeyed, considerable depth; dry, flavour of barley-sugar, excellent acidity.
*Several notes. Last tasted May 1987*****

1962****

A very good vintage. Attractive wines, still showing well.
Ch Haut-Brion Six bottles. Wine mostly straw-coloured, some with a tinge of orange; pronounced Sémillon nose which improved in glass; dryish, full, rich, nutty and showing age. Others distinctly paler with lemon-fresh nose and palate, more fragrant.
*All tasted Sept 1988** to****
Ch Laville-Haut-Brion Six remarkably consistent notes from 1967 to 1982, all stressing its softness and delicacy; mild and easy. But a rather discordant recent note: honeyed but hard, with a trace of my unfavourite almond kernel on nose and palate. Good golden colour

though. Dry, with slightly 'hot' acidic finish.
*Last noted at the Wolf tasting, June 1990. At best*** Either tiring or bottles now becoming variable.*
Ygrec Nose dumb at first then developed vinosity and a glorious spicy fragrance; fairly dry, elegant, shapely, ageing gracefully.
*At Yquem, Sept 1986***(*)*

1963

Abysmal.
Ch Laville-Haut-Brion Pale lemon; a hefty dose of sulphur did nothing for the nose; light, dull. Poor even in 1968. Probably scarcely drinkable now.

1964

Nothing like as good as the red Graves. Dull and dismal.
Ch Haut-Brion Not tasted since 1976***
Ch Laville-Haut-Brion Several unenthusiastic notes between 1968 and 1978. Recently, a curious pair, dull yellow, sharp-nosed and oddly flavoured.
Last tasted, Oct 1980.
Ch Laville-Haut-Brion *Crème de Tête*. Distinctly better though unassertive in the late 1970s, an out of condition bottle in 1988 and, most recently, medium-pale gold; quite attractive floral, honeyed bouquet; medium dryness and body, soft, rich flavour but lacking length.
*Last tasted June 1990. At best***
Dom de Chevalier Palish and fresh on nose for age, but touch of bitterness on finish.
Sept 1984.
Ygrec Having failed to make Sauternes, Yquem just managed a dry white. Low-keyed, vanilla nose, reminded me of a cold fish-slab; dry, lean but flavoury.
*Sept 1986**

1965

As thin and acidic as the reds.
Ch Laville-Haut-Brion Two notes. Dry and raw in 1978. Now a palish yellow gold; surprisingly good nose, lemon and honey; dry, firm, short, rather weak, slightly bitter and acidic.
Last tasted June 1990.
Ygrec Lemon yellow. Some bottle variation, one smelled of the cellar, the other honeyed; dryish, surprisingly assertive, flavoury but high acidity.
At the château, Sept 1986.

1966***

A good vintage, with firm, well-constituted wines. If kept well cellared, still very attractive – if you like your dry whites with bottle-age.
Ch Haut-Brion First tasted in 1971. In 1980, colour a bit too deep; bottle variation: one poor, the other nutty, showing age; both fairly powerful. This should have been much better.
*Last tasted in Mexico City, April 1980***
Ch Laville-Haut-Brion Impressive from first to last. Several good notes dating from 1971. Now a bright yellow; marvellous vinosity; medium dry, good body, soft, honeyed, peach and vanilla flavour, fine balance and aftertaste.
*Last tasted June 1990*****
Dom de Chevalier Several notes since 1984. Now a pronounced yellow; good, soft, creamy, somewhat Sauternes-like nose; dry, medium weight, a waxy rather four-square wine apart from its fairly high fixed (tartaric) acidity. Holding well.
*Last noted at Ch Latour, Nov 1990****
Grand Vin Sec de Ch Doisy-Daëne At this period, the minor châteaux of Sauternes were having a tough time and Doisy-Daëne, a Barsac, introduced a dry white. Rich, toasty old Sémillon nose; dry, pleasing, holding well.
*March 1986****
Ygrec Despite bottle variation: one slightly mushroomy, the other honeyed and flowery, one of the best of a sadly variable range tasted at the château in 1986. Most recently, a bright yellow gold; lovely, fragrant, honeyed nose; fairly dry, barley-sugar flavour, good shape and length.
*Last noted Sept 1990****

1967*

The grapes were so superb at Ch Yquem that none were wasted on making Ygrec. But, though the acidity of this vintage should have served the dry whites well, the net result is unsatisfactory.
Ch Haut-Brion Several notes since 1971: consistently pale; kernelly Graves nose; fairly marked acidity.
*Last tasted Sept 1989**
Ch Laville-Haut-Brion A variable performer, first tasted in 1972 and, on the whole, disappointing. Acidity noticeable from the squeeze-of-lemon nose to the bone-dry finish. All had an almond kernel flavour. Most recently, watery rim; nose like freshly peeled mushrooms and managing to be both fat and flat as well as acidic.
Lasted tasted June 1990.
Ch Couhins-Lurton Fresh spicy fragrant nose, but a bit rasping and coarse in the mouth. Never meant to be kept.
Oct 1989.
Ch La Louvière Pale for age, very bright; touch of lemon, like Hermitage Blanc; dry, excellent, slightly waxy flavour. Remarkably good.
*In magnums at La Fête de La Fleur, at Louvière, June 1991*****

1968

An atrocious year for both red and white Bordeaux: cold, wet, sunless.
Ch Laville-Haut-Brion Tolerable in 1978. Now bright yellow; surprisingly good waxy Sémillon and cherry stones nose; aggressively dry.
*Last tasted June 1990**
Ygrec Ch d'Yquem not marketed, and even Ygrec could not fit the bill. A dry, raw wine.
At Yquem, Sept 1986.

1969*

By and large, rather acidic wines. Lesser châteaux should have been drunk by the early 1970s.
Ch Haut-Brion Intriguing but acidic in 1978. Raw-edged in 1982. In 1985: deepish yellow-gold; gloriously rich, nutty bouquet and flavour. Dry, fullish body, sustained by its acidity.
*Last tasted May 1985. Then*** but probably declining.*
Ch Laville-Haut-Brion Eight notes, the first in 1978. Seemed at best in the mid-1980s. Pale, highly polished, lemon-tinged; smoky honeyed Sémillon and peach kernel nose which developed well in the glass; fairly mild entry but overall dry and steely, like a fine Chablis. Good length. An excellent '69.
*Last tasted June 1990****
Ygrec Lively lemon gold; low-keyed but fragrant 'lino-leum' nose; dry, assertive, with hard column of acidity.
*At Ch d'Yquem, Sept 1986**

1970★★★

A good year. Ripe grapes with a high sugar content producing wines with more generous alcohol than acidity. But the best have kept well.

Ch LAVILLE-HAUT-BRION *A powerful, alcoholic wine first tasted in 1978. Lovely colour; rich, fragrant, intense and complex nose; fairly dry, mouthfilling, with crisp acidity.* Nov 1986★★★(★)

Dom de CHEVALIER *Quite a few notes from 1973. Good colour; harmonious, the sort of nose which reminds me of Chenin Blanc; medium dryness and weight, lovely waxy flavour, texture and balance.* Last tasted July 1988★★★(★)

1971★★★★

A lovely vintage, the best of the decade, combining flesh and firmness, elegance and length. The top wines still excellent and will keep.

Ch LAVILLE-HAUT-BRION *Two identical notes, in 1978 and 1986: incredible colour, rich yellow; Barsac-like bouquet; full-bodied, magnificent. Most recently, a fabulous amber gold; outstanding, rich, full, honey and mint leaf; medium dry, superb length, fragrant aftertaste.* Last noted June 1990★★★★★

Dom de CHEVALIER *Very yellow; nutty, harmonious. After 15 minutes developed fragrance, after 35 minutes sweet perfection, and after an hour a touch of aniseed; dryish, mild, supple. A perfectly balanced wine.* May 1985★★★★

YGREC *Honey-gold colour; equally honeyed and gloriously full rich bouquet; medium dry, fullish, firm, elegant.* Tasted at Ch d'Yquem, Sept 1986★★★★

1972

As dreary as red Bordeaux.

Ch LAVILLE-HAUT-BRION *Three recent and consistent notes: palish yellow; smell of old honey and peaches; dryish, soft, easy, short.* The opening wine of Karl-Heinz Wolf's tasting, June 1990★

YGREC *Straw-tinged; extraordinary, kerosene-like smell. Dry, raw, very peculiar.* At Ch d'Yquem, Sept 1986.

1973★★

Some quite pleasing and inoffensive wines. Drink up.

Ch LAVILLE-HAUT-BRION *Three fairly recent notes. Buttery yellow colour; Sémillon honeycomb nose; bone dry, fresh, acidic, reasonable length.* Last tasted Oct 1988★★

YGREC *Lovely golden colour, orange-tinged; honeyed, soft, peachy; dry, firm, a bit short but pleasing.* Sept 1986★★

1974

Lacking in grace, like the reds.

Ch LAVILLE-HAUT-BRION *Three notes: first tasted, grubby and raw in 1978. In 1988: honeyed bottle-age, piquant nose, acidic Sauvignon Blanc uppermost. Dry, a bit short.* Last tasted Oct 1988.

1975★★★★

A good vintage, arguably better than the over-tannic reds. Nice now but the best will develop further.

Ch HAUT-BRION *Pale; lemon vanilla Chardonnay-like nose; dry, firm. "More time in bottle" noted in 1982–83*★★★(★)? Probably delicious now.

Ch LAVILLE-HAUT-BRION *Three notes, all Woltner stock. Lovely in 1982, glorious in 1986. An attractive palish yellow; soft ripe Sémillon nose and taste; medium dry, with the richness of ripe grapes, power and good length.* Last tasted Oct 1988★★★(★)

Dom de CHEVALIER *Vaseline-like Sémillon nose; medium dryness, full body and rich kernelly flavour. Touch of harshness.* May 1985★★(★)

La PERLE BLANCHE *Monopole. Waxy, creamy, Sémillon; medium dry, nice smoky flavour. Touch of peach kernels (see also 1937).* With the Mähler-Besse family at Ch Palmer, Nov 1990★★

1976★★★★

A very agreeable vintage. Like the Sauternes (and, coincidentally, like 1976 Rhine wines), initially more highly regarded than the 1975. Drink up.

Ch HAUT-BRION *50% Sémillon, 50% Sauvignon Blanc. Complex and assertive in 1979. Glorious honeyed bouquet, marvellous fruit, touch of pineapple; dry, medium body, lovely flavour, soft. Acidity adequate.* Last tasted May 1985★★★★ Probably at peak now.

Ch LAVILLE-HAUT-BRION *Seven consistent notes from 1978 onwards. Pale yellow initially, now lemon gold; nose almost overpowering, glorious, honeycomb; dry, powerful though not full-bodied, stylish and striking yet not long on palate.* Last tasted Oct 1988★★★★ At peak now.

Dom de CHEVALIER *Palish yellow; sweet, pleasant vanilla nose of no great depth. Rather static. Good, straightforward, worthy rather than inspiring. Quite nice acidity.* Last tasted Sept 1990★★

1977

The worst growing conditions of the decade. Winemakers hardly had a chance. Avoid.

Ch LAVILLE-HAUT-BRION *First tasted in cask. Three notes later: palish yellow; fully-developed, very pronounced waxy, kernelly, Sémillon nose; dryish, dull, short but not bad. Last tasted Oct 1988*★

YGREC *Two bottles at the château in 1986, both with a curious juniper-like nose; a rather startling flavour with touches of linoleum, kerosene and almond kernels. Most recently, a rather drab olive green; nose better than expected; fairly dry. Last tasted Sept 1990.*

1978★★★★

A most attractive vintage but, as in the case of most white Bordeaux, only the top châteaux worth keeping or seeking out.

Ch HAUT-BRION *Two notes: a rather woody, but otherwise impressive bottle in 1985. In 1987: perfection. Vanilla, blancmange nose; lovely flavour, length, acidity. Long life ahead. Last tasted June 1987*★★★★(★)

Ch LAVILLE-HAUT-BRION *Two notes. Pale; fragrant; dry, lean, nice acidity. To which I add lovely, buttery, vanilla nose and soft, rich, lovely flavour and aftertaste. Last noted April 1990*★★★(★)

Ch CARBONNIEUX *Pale, immature, sulphury in April 1980. Most recently: good colour for age; gentle waxy bouquet, honeyed bottle-age and lemon; dry, firm, Sémillon dominant but good acidity. Last noted dining at the château, April 1991*★★★

Dom de CHEVALIER *Soft, easy and attractive. At lunch with Jean-Pierre Mouiex, Sept 1982. Will doubtless have developed well*★★★ *or*★★★★*?*

PAVILLON BLANC DE CH MARGAUX *The first Mentzelopoulos dry white. Dry, lightish but firm, crisp and surprisingly attractive in May 1981. It has retained its appeal, its youthful appearance, pale, green-tinged, but with bottle-age has developed extra dimensions. The bouquet reminds me sometimes of Chenin Blanc, of a good Napa Chardonnay, of a fine oaky white burgundy. Dry, medium body, firm, harmonious, excellent acidity. Pavillon Blanc seems to fluctuate wildly in style from vintage to vintage. This, for me, is still the best. Last tasted at a Ch Margaux dinner at Brooks's Club, April 1988*★★★★

'R' RIEUSSEC SEC *Three samples, some with, some without oak and varying from dry to medium dry. Without wood, fully evolved: vanilla and honey scented, the sweetest, fullest and richest, with a pleasant, normal kernelly flavour. With Eric de Rothschild and Professor Peynaud at Ch Rieussec, Sept 1984*★★

YGREC *50% Sémillon, 50% Sauvignon Blanc; 100% new oak. Bottled in March 1981. Six notes. First tasted in 1982 when relatively unknit. By 1987 it developed an impressive colour; rich lanolin and marzipan nose; dryish, assertive flavour, good length. Unattractive, kernelly taste in 1988, in addition I have recently noted "kerosene". Last tasted Sept 1990.*

1979★★★

Good vintage. Firm wines, holding and developing nicely.

Ch HAUT-BRION *Lightly spicy; dry, rather strange peachy, kernelly flavour. But should have developed well by now. Tasted May 1985*★★★

Ch LAVILLE-HAUT-BRION *Five variable notes. Pale; first impression like the crust of unripe Brie, vanilla, peach kernels; distinctly dry, strange, sweaty cheese-rind flavour, powerful, steely. Intriguing. Most recently, smelling of pear skins and a bit woody. Last tasted June 1990. Should be*★★★ *but I have reservations.*

Ch CARBONNIEUX *Three notes, from 1983. Earthy, fruity nose; dry, excellent flavour. The initial teeth-gripping acid edge softened. Last tasted at Casa de Campo in the Dominican Republic, Feb 1989*★★★

Dom de CHEVALIER *In 1985: obstinately hazy; creamy, vanillin oak nose; rounded, mouthfilling. More recently, very pale, lime-coloured, bright; hardly any nose at first, then opened up a little, soapy and spicy; firm, good flavour, reasonable length. Last tasted Sept 1990*★★★ *Drink now.*

PAVILLON BLANC DE CH MARGAUX *Four notes. Star-bright; slightly vegetal, minty, mouthwatering nose; dry, refreshing acidity. Attractive. Last tasted before lunch at the château, June 1987*★★★

YGREC *Unready and too hot and sharp in 1983. A couple of gradually evolving bottles in 1986. Distinctly yellow; rather raw nose, lemon, pineapple husk; dry, crisp, palate-filling, good finish. Last tasted Sept 1987*★★★

1980★

Insubstantial and not worth pursuing:

Ch HAUT-BRION *In 1985: light, fragrant, nutty; dry, rather ordinary and no length. Most recently, nose like linoleum. Unattractive. Last tasted Feb 1989.*

Ch LAVILLE-HAUT-BRION *Green-tinged; hard, not much fruit, dry, light, nutty flavour, short. Oct and Nov 1988*★

Ch CARBONNIEUX *Sauvignon Blanc 75%. Three notes in mid-1980s. Bright, yellow, appealing; mouthwatering redcurrant aroma; dry, twist of lemon acidity. Refreshing. Last tasted March 1985*★★

YGREC *Pale; unknit nose: honey, kernels, violets; strange flavour of violet cachous. At Yquem, Sept 1986*★

1981★★ to ★★★

Assez bien: good enough, probably at best in the mid-1980s but the top wines will have developed with bottle-age.

Ch LAVILLE-HAUT-BRION *Three notes: dry, fullish, nutty. Last tasted Oct 1988★★(★)*

Dom de CHEVALIER *Two good notes. Dry, mild, stylish, elegant. Last tasted May 1985★★★*

PAVILLON BLANC DE CH MARGAUX *Palish, bright; smoky, fruity and fragrant; medium dryness and body, smoky-oaky flavour. Good acidity. Last tasted Nov 1990★★★*

OTHER DRY WHITES:

Ch BOUSCAUT *Pale; scented; dry, quite nice.*
Ch DOISY-DAENE Sec. *Fresh vanilla; dry, soft, gentle.*
Ch LYNCH-BAGES *Pale; a bit sweaty; dryish, pleasant enough.*
Ch MALARTIC-LAGRAVIERE *Adequate.*
Ch OLIVIER *Deepish yellow; waxy, harmonious; fairly dry, nice ripe flavour.*
Ch RAHOUL *Dry, crisp, fruity, refreshing.*
REVERDON *(the dry white of Ch Coutet) Honeyed, good body and flavour but lacked acidity.*
'R' RIEUSSEC Sec. *Dryish, soft, 'kerosene' taste.*

1982★★★

A thoroughly ripe vintage. Nicely constructed wines, the minor to be consumed quickly, the top châteaux improving with bottle-age.

Ch HAUT-BRION *A powerful wine first tasted dining at the château in May 1983. Like an oaky Montrachet, impressive but premature. Still pale, star-bright; nicely evolved bouquet, waxy Sémillon, fruit and vanilla with flavour to match. Last tasted Nov 1990★★★(★) A magnificent mouthful now. Will develop further. Now to, say, 2000.*

Ch LAVILLE-HAUT-BRION *First tasted in spring 1984. Pale; crusty bread-like nose; lively, good length. Now taking on colour; a powerful smoky vanillin nose and flavour. Last tasted June 1990★★★(★) Now to 1997.*

Ch LAVILLE-HAUT-BRION Crème de Tête. *Palish; heavy waxy Sémillon nose; dry, fairly full-bodied, rather austere, hard. Needs more time in bottle. Oct 1988★★(★★?) 1992–2000*

Dom de CHEVALIER *Very small production, only 200 cases. Scent of apricots and pineapple; powerful, full of fruit, good acidity. Excellent, worth seeking out. May 1985★★★(★★)*

Ch CARBONNIEUX *65% Sauvignon Blanc, 35% Sémillon. Seven notes. Unknit and piquant in 1983. Seemed best in 1986, having developed a more yellow colour; ripe grapes and bottle-age on nose, a touch of honeycomb and vanilla; overall dry but hefty for Carbonnieux and not as zestful as in lighter vintages. Last tasted Dec 1987★★★*

PAVILLON BLANC DE CH MARGAUX *100% Sauvignon Blanc; 12% alcohol. Picking commenced Sept 10, in wood until May 1983 and sold after one year in bottle. Minty, fresh, and* nerveux *in 1984. Positive colour; superficially waxy and harmonious nose but with* sauvage *Sauvignon 'tom-cats' lurking beneath; medium dryness and body. A nice fleshy wine. Served as an aperitif, but would have been better with the fish course when last tasted at Ch Margaux dinner at Brooks's, April 1988★★★(★)*

Ch RIEUSSEC Sec. *Much experimentation with the relatively new dry 'Sauternes'. The first, six months in wood: an extraordinary pungent, apricot, kernelly nose; tasted like cheap sherry. The next, three months in wood: touch of oak; straightforward, complete, but slightly rubbery finish. Two samples using no wood at all, one fragrant, dry, with a sort of detached acidity and taste of almond kernels, the other deeper, fuller, fatter and rounder. Rather curious. Then richly coloured; distinctly sweeter, heavier, with a curious wet straw taste. At the château, with Eric de Rothschild and Emile Peynaud, Sept 1984.*

1983★★★★

An extremely good, well-balanced vintage. Good body, fruit and acidity. More zestful than '82. Lovely now.

Ch HAUT-BRION *Three mid-1980s notes. Pale; charred oak nose, strangely spicy, with twist of lemon; dry, very distinctive, firm, lemon vanilla flavour, stylish, with spicy oaky finish. A great future. Last tasted June 1985★★★(★★)?*

Ch LAVILLE-HAUT-BRION *In cask: a waxy shoe-polish nose, vanilla and pineapple; overall dry, good acidity — and future. Tasted six weeks before bottling, Sept 1984. Probably★★★(★)*

Ch CARBONNIEUX *Five notes. Distinctly yellow; minty; dry, positive, well balanced, excellent acidity. Probably the best white Carbonnieux I have ever tasted. Last tasted Oct 1989★★★*

DOISY-DAENE Sec. *Very bright; fresh as a sea breeze; slightly scented, almost Gewürztraminer-like flavour. June 1988★★★*

PAVILLON BLANC DE CH MARGAUX *100% Sauvignon Blanc, fermented and aged in new oak. Four notes. Now a waxy yellow green; unusual, fragrant, fruity, vanilla, mint leaf nose, latterly reminding me of laurel and hay; medium dry, on the light side, soft and ripe, yet with crisp lemon-like acidity. Most attractive but lacking length and not for long keeping. Last tasted Nov 1990★★★ Drink soon.*

Ch RIEUSSEC Sec. *Pale; fresh, 'green'; dry, lightish, nice fruit, piquant acidity. First tasted at the château, then at the inaugural tasting for brokers at Ch Lafite, Sept 1984.*

1984

Lacking in grace and rather acidic.

ALL TASTED IN 1986 AND 1987:

Ch CARBONNIEUX *Highly polished, mouthwatering appearance; refreshingly acidic aroma; overall dry, good length, fairly marked acidity but a nice drink (several notes).*

Dom de CHEVALIER *Oaky, spicy, austere; full-flavoured, like a young Bâtard-Montrachet.*

Ch de FIEUZAL *60% Sauvignon, 40% Sémillon. Piquant. A smell of wet nappies and taste of almond kernels. A fairly substantial wine with good acidity.*

Ch REYNON *Agreeable raw blackcurrant aroma; unsubtle but nicely made.*

Ch de ROCHEMORIN *100% Sauvignon Blanc. Mouthwatering, redcurrants and tom-cats; dry, light, cleansing acidity. Three consistent notes. Not bad.*

1985★★★ *to* ★★★★★

A potentially great year but a dramatic demonstration of the difference between the top and lesser châteaux. The latter to be drunk young, the former benefiting greatly from bottle-age.

Ch HAUT-BRION *First tasted, prematurely in* impériale, *June 1987: lovely, bright, positive colour; unknit, hard, touch of vanilla but rich; fairly dry, full-bodied, most recently: waxy, lemon, opened up in glass; though some softness and fat, needing bottle-age. Considerable potential. Last tasted March 1991★★(★★) 1994–2010*

Ch LAVILLE-HAUT-BRION *Pale but rich; very fragrant, delicate, lovely scent; dry, fullish, firm, vanilla flavour, hard acid backbone. Destined for a long life. Sept 1990★★(★★★) 1992 to beyond 2000.*

Dom de CHEVALIER *First tasted in cask. Like a precocious child, impatient, trying to walk and talk. Aromas of pineapple, apricots and pears, plus the spiciness of new oak. Still very pale; very fragrant bouquet; medium dry, ideal weight, balance and lovely flavour. Last tasted Sept 1990★★★(★) Now to 1998.*

PAVILLON BLANC DE CH MARGAUX *Two recent notes. Very pale, lime-tinged; a most pronounced aroma of tom-cats, spearmint and armpits; fairly dry, light, lean, scented, grapey and acidic. Exciting, to say the least. Last tasted Sept 1990★★ Drink soon.*

YGREC *First tasted in Sept 1986. Lemon-tinged; fresh, unremarkable Sauvignon Blanc aroma; easy on the palate. In 1989, richness and fat nicely 'cut' with acidity, drinking well. Two recent notes: gaining colour, more yellow; light but fragrant clover honey nose; medium dryness and weight, well balanced, good flavour though a touch of what I merely call* "noisette"*. Certainly a good Ygrec. Last tasted Oct 1990★★★ Now to 1995.*

1986★★★★

Variable. Haut-Brion Blanc not marketed: the crop was too abundant, very diluted, so no selection made.

'R' RIEUSSEC BLANC *Now under the aegis of the Domaine Barons de Rothschild. Admittedly only tasted once, a stray half-bottle: very pale; smell of apple skins and kerosene, and a horrible taste. Oct 1990.*

'Y' YGREC *Touch of linoleum on nose; dry, medium weight, pleasantly acidic. June 1989★★(★)*

OTHER '86s TASTED IN 1988 AND 1989:

Ch BARET *Pale, light and dry.*

Ch BONNET *A well-made Lurton wine, star-bright; a fresh grapiness and mouthwatering acidity.*

Ch CARBONNIEUX *Soapy, horrible. To be fair, I should re-taste.*

Ch de CHANTEGRIVE *Vanilla, Sauvignon crispness, light.*

Ch LARRIVET-HAUT-BRION *60% Sauvignon, 40% Sémillon. Very pale, green-tinged; clean, fresh, fragrant, displaying the waxy honeyed Sémillon and mouthwatering acidity of the Sauvignon Blanc. Touch of bitterness on the finish.*

Ch La LOUVIERE *Another Lurton family wine: pale; fresh, crisply fruity and attractive; dry, fragrant.*

Ch MALARTIC-LAGRAVIERE *Positive, indeed fulsome, aroma; nice flavour and acidity.*

Ch OLIVIER *Too pale, rather ordinary.*

Ch RAHOUL *Curious boiled sweets fragrance, quite attractive.*

Ch SMITH-HAUT-LAFITTE *Too fragrant and flavoury, verging on artificial.*

Ch La TOUR-MARTILLAC *Odd, again rather boiled-sweet artificiality but quite flavoury.*

1987★★

Better for white than red. Pleasing enough, refreshingly dry white, mainly for early consumption. The use of new oak very apparent.

Ch HAUT-BRION *Very small crop. Cool, nutty, cress and mint aromas, strangely, after 30 minutes in the glass reminding me of milk chocolate; medium dryness and weight, soft, open flavour. Light end acidity. At La Mission, Nov 1990★★ Not for keeping.*

Ch LAVILLE-HAUT-BRION *Palish; waxy, buttery Sémillon aroma; similar dryness and body to Haut-Brion, but broad, peach kernelly flavour. Soft finish. Also tasted at La Mission, Nov 1990★★ Drink soon.*

Dom de CHEVALIER *Some yellow pigment; low-keyed; dry, medium body, firm, good length. May 1989★★(★)*

Ch COUHINS-LURTON *Two recent notes. Well made. Pleasant colour; fragrant aroma; dry, light. Fruit and oak, neither overstated. Nov 1990★★*

Ch La LOUVIERE *Several notes. Aroma of raw blackcurrants. Dry, light, short and sharp. Refreshing. Last tasted April 1991★★*

Ch PAPE-CLEMENT *Palish; nose almost sickly sweet; medium dry, very assertive, waxy flavour and* *teeth-gripping acidity.* At lunch at the château, Nov 1990*

PLEASANT, IF RATHER OAKY, DRY WHITES:

Ch FIEUZAL
Ch RAHOUL
Ch La TOUR-MARTILLAC *Very pale, fresh, spicy, appealing.*

OTHER 1987s:

Ch BOUSCAUT *Fragrant but short.*
Ch de CHANTEGRIVE *Passable.*
Ch LARRIVET-HAUT-BRION *Pale; soapy; vanilla.*
Ch SMITH-HAUT-LAFITTE *Little nose or flavour. Dry, lean, good acidity.*

1988***

Potentially a very good vintage when, in April 1989, I tasted a wide range of Graves Blanc in the *chai* at Ch Carbonnieux. However, many were 'undignified' and a bit soapy. I also noted a lot of new oak being used and it was there that I first had the feeling that oak and Sauvignon Blanc do not make a wholly compatible marriage. But we shall see. More have since been tasted.

Ch HAUT-BRION *Pale, slightly green tinge; low-keyed, cress-like nose that after 10 minutes in the glass took on a fresh mint-leaf fragrance; fairly dry, fairly full-bodied, lean but fruity. Very crisp acidity. Good wine. Needs bottle-age.* Tasted Nov 1990(****) 1993 to beyond 2000.

Ch LAVILLE-HAUT-BRION *Pale; delicate Sémillon, immature lemon-like acidity, very slight trace of caramel and mint; medium dryness, perfect weight, good crisp flavour, acidity and finish.* Also tasted Nov 1990(****) 1992–2000

VIN SEC DE CH COUTET *Minty, scented, Sauvignon Blanc aroma and flavour. Dry. Trace of almond kernels in the endtaste.* Oct 1990**

Ch DOISY-DAENE *Grand Vin Sec. More* sec *than* grand. *Very pale; unknit, crisp, youthful fruit; dry, lightish, not much character. Good enough acidity.* Oct 1990**

Ch FIEUZAL *In March 1989, high-toned, tom-cats; flavoury, fragrant. Settling down: lemon and melon; medium dry, delicious taste, good acidity and aftertaste.* Last noted April 1991***

AMONGST THOSE DRY WHITE GRAVES SHOWING VERY WELL IN THE SPRING OF 1983 AND WITH CONSIDERABLE POTENTIAL:

Ch CARBONNIEUX *Though not bright, an attractive spearmint nose, good if latent flavour, fragrance and length, with spicy aftertaste.*

Dom de CHEVALIER *Good fruit, fragrance and flavour, a touch of 'soapy' oak but rich and anticipating an attractive future.*

Ch SMITH-HAUT-LAFITTE *An exotic almost Muscat scent, crisp, very flavoury.*

1989*****

An altogether extraordinary year. The intense heat during the summer months resulted in the grapes ripening early, too early and too ripe for dry white wines. In order to avoid over-ripeness the grapes were picked in Aug and early Sept.

M Olivier Bernard very kindly laid on a tasting at Dom de Chevalier of white Graves cask samples in Nov 1990. Unless otherwise stated all my notes were made there. In addition in Oct 1990 *Wine* magazine arranged a blind tasting of dry wines made at certain châteaux in Barsac and Sauternes, almost all of which seem to me to have been an unmitigated disaster.

Ch HAUT-BRION *A small crop and very small* rendement, *picked in Aug. First noted in Nov 1990: distinct yellow tinge, the deepest of the group of recent vintages of Haut-Brion and Laville. Nose 'cool', vanilla and pineapple, opening up fabulously; medium-sweet, full-bodied, assertive, rich, full of fruit. Spicy, cloves, new oak taste and aftertaste. Tasted again just over two months after bottling. Great quality confirmed. Marvellous fruit, persistence of flavour.* Last tasted April 1991(*****) 1995–2010

Ch LAVILLE-HAUT-BRION *First tasted at La Mission, Nov 1990: medium pale yellow; spicy, fruity, oak and pineapple. Its style and character reminded me of a rich Australian Chardonnay! Medium dry, medium full-bodied, with lovely, broad, very spicy flavour. Dry finish. Most recently: glorious in every respect. Wonderful vinosity. Aromatic. The best Laville ever.* Last tasted April 1991(*****) 1994–2010

Dom de CHEVALIER *Lovely fruit and oak on nose; flavour of vanilla and butter. Good length, considerable depth. Dry finish.* At the château, Nov 1990(****)

Ch PAPE-CLEMENT *15% Muscadelle, the rest made up more of less equally of Sémillon and Sauvignon Blanc. Fermented in oak, 10–12 months in* barrique. *Immature, muffled pineapple and gooseberry-like aromas; dry, rather austere and acidic. Refreshing. Should turn out quite well.* At the château, Nov 1990(***)

OTHER '89 GRAVES BLANCS TASTED IN NOV 1990:

Ch BOUSCAUT *70% Sémillon, oaky nose, dry, straightforward. Good length***(*)

Ch CARBONNIEUX *Very light, slightly oaky nose; good flavour, soft, ripe, easy. For early drinking****

Ch CHANTEGRIVE *Mainly Sauvignon. Light, peachy, varnishy, Sauvignon tom-cats aroma; good positive flavour, nice use of oak***

Ch de FIEUZAL *Still on its lees. Not bright. Raw. Unready to taste.*

Ch LARRIVET-HAUT-BRION *An odd, light, varnishy scent; dryish, fullish, soft, broad. For quick consumption**

Ch La LOUVIERE *Very pleasant combination of Sémillon*

*and Sauvignon (85%) aromas. Good flavour**(*)*

Ch MALARTIC-LAGRAVIERE *100% Sauvignon Blanc, and it shows. Strident tom-cats aroma and flavour. Dry, hollow, thin**

Ch OLIVIER *70% Sémillon. Exceedingly pale; immature smell of pears and apple cores; dry, light, austere***

Ch RAHOUL *100% Sémillon. Good, light, immature, pineapple aroma; soft, nice fruit and oak. Still a bit raw*(*)*

Ch SMITH-HAUT-LAFITTE *Attractive vanilla and pineapple nose and flavour. Dry, crisp, fresh**(*)*

Ch La TOUR-MARTILLAC *Light, nutty, immature nose; fairly dry, medium full-bodied, very straightforward flavour, touch of oak**(*)*

1989 DRY WINES MADE AT CHATEAUX IN BARSAC AND SAUTERNES, TASTED BLIND, OCT 1990:

Ch CAILLOU Sec. *Very pale; immature, estery nose; fairly dry, soft, soapy, a bit flat.*

Ch DOISY-DAENE *Good colour; lots of oak and nice fruit; fairly dry, nice weight, soft, soapy, oaky flavour. Lacks acidity***

'G' Ch GUIRAUD Sec. *Yellow; unusual, fragrant; dry enough. Hard to pin down. Acidified? Dry finish.*

CORDIER BRUT DE LAFAURIE *Cordier brute, more appropriate. Appley Tokay-like nose; dry, fairly light, almond kernels, boring. Not bad.*

Ch de MALLE Sec. *Judging from the nose, a high percentage of Sauvignon Blanc. The flavour a pale shadow of the pronounced aroma. Flat.*

LE SEC DE RAYNE-VIGNEAU *Too pale; neither clear nor clean; dryish, 'warm', 'mealy', dull.*

1990

Another hot summer resulting in ripe grapes and an early harvest. The first vineyard to start picking was Château Pape-Clément in Pessac. The white grapes are low in acidity and the Sauvignon Blanc, picked first, will probably lack the definitive Sauvignon aroma and taste. Sémillon and the smaller crop of Muscadelles were harvested from mid-Sept. A range tasted, with the reds, in April 1991. Too early to judge as many were still 'working'. With the exception of the few top growths, most for early drinking.

Ch HAUT-BRION *Lovely colour; youthful pineapple, light honeyed fruit; dry, fullish, firm, acidic. Still raw. At the château, April 1991(****) 1996–2010?*

Ch LAVILLE-HAUT-BRION *Yellow gold; gently scented pineapple and oak; medium-sweet, slightly soapy vanilla flavour, as yet unknit. At La Mission, April 1991(****) 1995–2010*

OTHER '90s TASTED AT CH FIEUZAL, APRIL 1991:

Ch BOUSCAUT *Hazy; dry, nice fruit, good acidity(***)*

Ch CARBONNIEUX *Hazy; attractive fruit; fairly dry and light, easy, fragrant aftertaste(***)*

Ch CHANTEGRIVE *Unready. Light easy style(**)*

Dom de CHEVALIER *Palish, bright; lovely, forthcoming, good fruit; dry, medium weight, good balance(****)*

Ch de FIEUZAL *Very yellow; Sauvignon Blanc uppermost, pineapple, grapefruit; crisp fruit, acidity. Flavoury(***)*

Ch La LOUVIERE *Yellow gold; soft, slight soapiness on nose and taste, but lively fruit(***)?*

Ch OLIVIER *Unready; grapey; dry, lean, short but good acidity(**)?*

Ch RAHOUL *Soft yellow; plausible, quite nice fruit(**)*

Ch SMITH-HAUT-LAFITTE *Cloudy; fragrant enough; distinctive, medium dry(***)?*

Ch La TOUR MARTILLAC *Pale, hazy; slightly minty; dry, soapy(**)?*

SAUTERNES

Château d'Yquem

1747

Ch d'Yquem Mid-18th century dumpy straight-sided amber-green hand-blown bottle. Hand-written label and two slip labels "Château d'Yquem", "circa 1740" and "1747 Sauternes de Sauvage". Original crumbly cork. Wine oxidised: deep amber brown with tawny rim; curious, light, high-toned, banana skin nose; still residual sweetness and body but lean, sharp and with yeasty finish. A curiosity of unknown provenance but contents clearly the same age as the bottle.
At Hardy Rodenstock's Raritäten Weine-Probe, Sept 1987.

1784*****

The first well-documented major Sauternes vintage. Letter from Thomas Jefferson, then American envoy in Paris, to M Diquem (*sic*) in 1787: "I know yours is one of the best crus of Sauternes wine", accompanied by an order "directly from your hand" for 250 bottles of the "first quality, of the year 1784".
Ch d'Yquem* Bottled Jan 1788. Contemporary hand-blown bottle with deep punt and sharp pontil marks, 18th century wheel engraving "Ch d'Yquem Th J 1784". Deep amber gold in decanter but paler amber in glass, bright and lively; scented vanilla, blancmange; still sweet, perfect weight, balance and acidity. Flavour of peaches and cream, dry finish.
*Rodenstock tasting, Wiesbaden Oct 1985******

1811*****

The renowned 'Comet' vintage.
Ch Yquem Hand-blown bottle of burgundy-like shape with striated neck. Cork like blackened polished oak. Labelled "Chateau Yquem, Marquis A M de Lur-Saluces 1811 Grand Vin Sauternes." Lovely colour, warm glowing amber; smell of old cellars, raisins and sweat; still sweet, fullish body, raisiny flavour, pasty acidity.
*At Ch d'Yquem, Sept 1986*** (for its age).*

EARLY TO MID-19TH-CENTURY

Ch Yquem The most beautiful bottle I have ever seen: slender 'club'-shaped, cylindrical, blue glass, most likely Russian, embossed with the arms of the Sauvage family and with applied glass and enamel flower decorations. Original black-edged cork; fairly deep colour, a warm red brown, tea-like, with amber-green rim; nose a combination of singed raisins and old malt whisky, developing in the glass, pungent, prune-like, old stables. Still sweet and surprisingly rich with a positive flavour. This bottle was found by Hardy Rodenstock in Leningrad. The Russian Court and nobility were long-time lovers and buyers of the finest Sauternes.
Opened in the presence of the Comte de Lur-Saluces at Ch d'Yquem, Sept 1986.

1825****

Ch Yquem Bordeaux-bottled by Chabeau, level upper mid-shoulder. Amber tawny with green tinge; beautiful scent, incredible fragrance: after an hour like ethereal fruit salad. On the palate sweet, fullish, concentrated, with fig-like flavour, marvellous acidity and aftertaste.
*The highlight of Bud Moon's Yquem tasting in Chicago, Feb 1988******

* *From 1789–1855 the château was known as Yquem; before and after as d'Yquem.*

1847*****

The most renowned vintage between 1811 and 1921.
Ch Yquem Labelled "Château Yquem, Lur-Saluces, 1847, Sauternes". Deep old amber with apple-green rim; rich, raisiny bouquet, amazing power, vanilla-scented peaches and cream; still sweet, full-bodied, positively thick, very intense, concentrated, great length. One of the greatest wines ever tasted.
*Tasted three times in April and Sept 1986******
And with Cruse label, high shoulder: surprisingly pale for age and vintage; pungent and peppery nose, reminiscent of dead bracken; tart and bitter.
The biggest disappointment of the Moon tasting, Feb 1988.

1848****

Ch Yquem First, at the château in 1987: L Tampier Bordeaux label and capsule. Original cork, excellent level. Medium-deep amber, green rim; very sweet, creamy vanilla bouquet, honeyed, great depth, orange blossom; medium sweetness and body, very assertive flavour but a bit hard, with backbone of acidity.
*At the château, Sept 1987****

Next, château-bottled: level into neck. Surprisingly pale for age, an attractive buttery yellow; gentle, soft, creamy bouquet; still sweet, medium weight, very good acidity.
*Last noted at Bud Moon's tasting, Feb 1988*****

1858****

Ch d'Yquem A half-bottle in 1981 labelled "Ch Yquem Sauternes, Keyl & Co, Bordeaux". K & C capsule. Original cork branded "1858 Yquem". Low-shoulder. Drab amber gold with bright lemon rim; sweet old Sémillon nose, slightly oxidised; fairly dried out, flavour not bad but yeasty aftertaste. Next, from a Scottish cellar, with glass shoulder button embossed "CHATEAU YQUÈM HAUT SAUTERNES, GRAND CRU" and slip label. Cork slightly shrunk. 1½in ullage. Good colour though slightly cloudy, with deep amber edge; nose like old Tokay essence, rich, honeyed, toffee-like bouquet that held and developed well; very sweet, rich, concentrated, excellent acidity, length and aftertaste.
*Last tasted at Yquem, Sept 1986. At best*****

1859***

Ch Rieussec Labelled "P Mayé Prop". Original cap, label and cork. Very good level for age. Colour of brown sherry, opaque centre, amber-green rim; bouquet of amazing power, richness and depth, vanilla and black treacle; very sweet, powerful, very high acidity masked by body and extract.
*Sept 1987******

1861***

Ch d'Yquem Very deep tawny-tinged amber; incredible power and concentration, figs and raisins; intensely sweet, concentrated, fabulous singed crème brûlée.
*Rodenstock tasting, Oct 1985******

1864*****

Ch d'Yquem Cruse et Fils Frères capsule, label and cork. Excellent level, though cork fell in. Very deep colour, graduation from amber brown to pronounced amber rim; relatively low-keyed yet perfect bouquet, honeyed, mint leaf; high acidity controlled by grape sugar and extract, rich, fat.
*At Yquem, Sept 1987****(*)!*

1865*****

Ch d'Yquem Identical label and similar deep colour to the 1864. Excellent level. Bouquet noticeably less assertive, developed well, soft, barley-sugar; sweet, soft, delicate, perfect.
*At Yquem, Sept 1987******

1867**

Ch d'Yquem A three-quarter-full bottle. Deep old amber; maderised yet alive – deep, caramelly yet clean. High sugar content, alcohol and acidity keeping it alive.
*June 1972***

1868*

Ch d'Yquem Dried out.
June 1971.
Ch Coutet Pfungst & Co. Fragrant. Very good.
*Twice in 1977*****

1869*****

Ch d'Yquem Sensationally good magnum with Peter Palumbo at Bougival in 1969, a bottle at Rodenstock's tasting in 1984 and another, with Cruse label with Le Cercle de Vingt at Le Fondation Cartier. All fairly deep warm amber with tinge of orange and a yellow-green rim; very sweet vanilla, apple crumble, peaches, crème brûlée bouquet; the last two bottles sweet, rich, yet with a lean deft touch and powerful blancmange flavour.
*Last tasted May 1988******
Ch La Tour Blanche Incredibly deep colour. By candlelight looked like a red wine; intensely rich vanilla fudge nose; still sweet, fullish, very rich flavour like the caramelised top of crème brûlée, fabulous extract, acidity and aftertaste.
*Dinner at Lafite, Sept 1982******

1871****

Ch d'Yquem Château-bottled. High level top neck. Dark tawny; rich but slightly sharp bouquet, old, deep honey, held well; sweet, assertive, somewhat pasty flavour, backbone of acidity. *Feb 1988***

Next: level upper-shoulder. Bright, medium-deep amber; rich toasted bouquet, singed barley-sugar and apricots; still very sweet, powerful, concentrated, rich yet dry finish.
*At Bud Moon's tasting, Chicago, Feb 1989*****

1872

A poor vintage. Presumably the Lur-Saluces family in need of capital as the "whole of the stock remaining in the cellars of the Marquis de Lur-Saluces" sold for a "lump sum" to M Jules Clavelle. The stock comprised 240 *barriques* of the 1871 Yquem, 440 of the 1870 and 20 of the 1865, 40 *barriques* of Coutet 1868 and 32 (in bottles) of the 1861, and 28 *barriques* (in bottles) of Filhot 1865. (*Reported in Ridley's trade gazette, June 1872.*)

1874****

Ch d'Yquem Variable, depending on level, from syrup of figs to crème brûlée.
Last tasted in 1975.

1875*****

Ch d'Yquem Bottled by Brandenburg Frères. Excellent in May 1978, considering its low level. Tasted twice more recently, both with Cruse labels. The first deep-coloured; perfect bouquet, rich, harmonious, great depth; sweet, full, rich, marvellous structure. The second, upper mid-shoulder; tea-coloured; old, creaking, sour, dried out.
*Last tasted Sept 1988. At best******

1876**

Ch Coutet Lur-Saluces. Original capsule, label, cork. Level mid-shoulder. Pure amber, like an old Sercial, with lime-coloured edge; reminded me on decanting of calf's-foot jelly but it opened up, vanilla, blancmange, barley-sugar; drying out a little and acidity catching up, slightly malty flavour, touch of bitterness. Good for age and level.
*Brought by Bob Paul on New Year's Day 1988***
Ch La Tour Blanche Re-corked Sept 1987. Bright amber; brown sugar and sour honey, caramel beneath; completely dried out and faded, yet clean acidity.
*With Le Cercle de Vingt, May 1988**

1878*****

Ch Filhot Brown, dried, thin, acidic.
May 1976.

1880

Ch Filhot Lur-Saluces. Original capsule, label, cork. Excellent level. Deepish but glorious colour, warm orange amber, green rim; honeyed, rich Sémillon character, barley-sugar; dried out, pasty end acidity.
*Sept 1987**

1881

Ch d'Arche A half-bottle labelled "mis en bouteille special (*sic*) Novembre 1886, Paul Paris . . . Imported by Robert Steel, Philadelphia". Château capsule, wired bottle. Fairly deep old amber; old honey, crème brûlée, drying out, taste of black treacle.
*June 1983**

1884**

Ch d'Yquem Upper mid-shoulder. Orange tinge; most unusual bouquet, lightly caramelly, vanilla, seemed to be cracking up but held amazingly well; most attractive flavour, tangerine.
*Oct 1984****
Ch de Rayne-Vigneau Lovely but a bit short.
May 1976.

1888**

Ch d'Yquem Drying out. Rather austere.
Feb 1977.

1890**

Ch d'Yquem Old notes, variable levels. At best (in 1975) soft and lovely.

1892*

Ch d'Yquem Quite good, dry finish in 1975. Then, at Schloss Johannisberg in 1984, medium, warm amber; good, sound, classic nose; medium sweetness and body, very good crisp positive flavour, dry finish. Most recently, a poor bottle, cloudy; old, murky, sherry-like; flavour not as bad as nose.
*Last tasted Feb 1988. At best****

1893***

Clos Haut-Peyraguey Château capsule, branded cork. Lovely warm amber; old, crème brûlée; still some sweetness, rich, very good flavour, excellent acidity.
*At Bordeaux Club dinner Oct 1981*****

Ch Suduiraut Mid-shoulder. Amber tawny; crème brûlée, twist of lemon and vanilla, developed orange blossom scent; medium-sweet, excellent flavour and condition.
*Sept 1985*****

1895

Ch d'Yquem Level mid-shoulder. Palish amber; high-toned, acetone; dried out, acidic, yeasty finish.
March 1981.

1896****

Ch d'Yquem Deep rich warm amber; excellent, classic but verging on unctuous; sweet, fullish, rich, with firm flavour, balance and acidity.
*Top marks at Schloss Johannisberg, March 1986******
Ch Filhot Fading but interesting.
*April and June 1975**
Ch Sigalas-Rabaud Rich, tangy.
*April 1975****

1899****

Ch d'Yquem Tasted three times. Old but interesting in 1973. At the Schloss Johannisberg tasting, in 1984: palish, warm amber; light, scented ferns, creamy, and after 30 minutes, perfection; medium sweetness, lightish style and weight, gentle but crisp flavour, lots of charm. Most recently, a badly ullaged bottle, caramelised, dried out.
*Last tasted March 1985. At best*****
Ch Suduiraut Two notes. In 1981: deep oloroso amber; excellent condition, caramel cream; still sweet, full, rich. Next, upper-shoulder, perfect colour, orange-tinged gold; glorious orange blossom nose; sweetish, medium weight, soft, slightly lacking length but with warm glowing aftertaste.
*Last tasted at Christie's with D Logan-Kuhs, Sept 1985*****
Ch La Tour Blanche Unbranded cork. Very good level. Light powdery sediment. Decanted: bright warm amber gold; low-keyed waxy Sémillon nose; medium-sweet, some body and fat, good condition.
*From Mme Lawton's cellar, July 1981****

1900****

Ch d'Yquem A beautiful bottle in 1972. In 1984, a low-shoulder bottle, deep; maderised nose; yet still sweet and surviving. A third, Bordeaux-bottled by H Wulffe. High-shoulder. Colour of warm oloroso; bouquet of nutmeg, old honey, very rich; fairly sweet, full-bodied, concentrated but lacking a little length.
*Last tasted at Bud Moon's, Feb 1988****
Ch La Tour Blanc (*sic*) Mid-shoulder, slight sediment otherwise bright buttery gold; pure Sémillon, honeyed lanolin; still fairly sweet and quite powerful, good acidity.
*An oddity from the Aalholm Castle cellar, July 1989****

1904****

An excellent vintage.
Ch Coutet Crumbly cork. Deep-coloured like a '21; lovely, fragrant, crème brûlée bouquet; medium-sweet yet very rich. Perfect condition.
*Dec 1979*****
Ch Filhot Deep amber; very good barley-sugar bouquet developing an orange blossom fragrance, held well; medium-sweet, full-bodied, caramelised but delicious.
*April 1987*****
Ch de Rayne-Vigneau Very good in 1976. Next: recorked. Very high level. Warm gold amber with pale apple-green rim; lovely bouquet, barley-sugar bottle-age, glorious; medium sweetness and weight, yet high extract, rich, with dry finish.
*From the cellars at Lafite, Dec 1986******
Ch La Tour Blanche Healthy tawny amber; soft, creamy, old crème brûlée, touch of tangerine; drying out, powerful, tangy, with very good acidity.
*From Mme Lawton's cellar, Oct 1985****

1905

Haut-Sauternes Barton & Guestier. Upper-shoulder. Rich old gold colour, with nose and taste to match.
*Pre-sale tasting, Chicago, Feb 1987****

1906****

A classic Sauternes vintage.
Ch d'Yquem Fairly deep, amoroso-like colour, with pronounced apple-green rim; intensely rich, high-toned, ethereal, touch of acetone, meaty but ambrosial bouquet of considerable depth; still fairly sweet, full-bodied, rich, silky texture, acidity, great length, dry finish.
*Sept 1985******
Ch d'Arche Opaque, intense; syrup of figs, malty, iodine; sweet, chewy. Oxidised but interesting.
Sept 1985.
Ch Lafaurie-Peyraguey Fabulous bouquet; very rich.
*From the château, May 1976*****

1909****

Ch d'Yquem Deep rich warm amber; hefty and slightly sickly crème brûlée bouquet; medium-sweet, full-bodied and very rich, positive acidity, taste of marron glacée.
*At Schloss Johannisberg, Nov 1984*****
Ch Lafaurie-Peyraguey Beautiful wine.
*Ex-château Sept 1976*****

1911***

Ch Filhot Top-shoulder. Very bright amber gold, pale for age; surprisingly youthful, fragrant bouquet, honeyed bottle-age, trace of almond kernels; drying out and fading though still sound with a long, gentle, caramel flavour.
*Sept 1984****

1912

Ch d'Yquem Very bright medium-pale yellow; touch of vanilla and pear, youthful; dry, raw, with unclean finish.
At Bud Moon's tasting, Feb 1988.
Haut-Sauternes Barton & Guestier. Very good colour, medium gold; heavenly, honeyed, bottle-age bouquet; medium sweetness and weight, sound but short.
*From an old cellar in Ohio, April 1984****
Ch Lafaurie-Peyraguey "Fred. Grédy, Proprietor". Original cork. Top-shoulder. Fairly deep, luminous oloroso colour; caramelised, slightly citrus; sweetish, taste of old barley-sugar, good acidity, dry finish.
*April 1985***

1913**

Ch d'Yquem Level upper-shoulder. Very pale for age, like an old fino, greenish rim; nose not very Sauternes-like at first but after 1½ hours nicely developed, gentle, vanilla; completely dried out, but clean.
*At the Moon tasting, Feb 1988**
Ch Lafaurie-Peyraguey Lovely bouquet; medium-sweet, lightish, zestful. *Ex-château, Sept 1976****

1914***

Ch d'Yquem Drying out a little, but fine, rich.
*Tasted in 1969 and 1973*****

Ch Caillou Barsac. Upper-shoulder. Lovely rich lanolin yellow; low-keyed but sound, old honey and mint; medium-sweet, lightish, soft, clean, dry finish.
*From a Paris cellar, Nov 1988****

Ste Croix-du-Mont Excellent level. Buttercup yellow; old, waxy Sémillon nose; medium-sweet, lightish, excellent flavour, pleasant though pasty acidity. Remarkable for class and age.
*Purchased at Christie's, consumed at an Avery dinner, Bristol, July 1981****

Ch Filhot Deep amber brown; old, singed, full, rich but maderised; yet still sweet and surprisingly rich. Showed well even after a '45 Yquem, though not in the best of condition.
*Oct 1984***

Ch Lafaurie-Peyraguey Topaz; beautiful bouquet; excellent.
*Ex-château, Sept 1976*****

Ch de Rayne-Vigneau Good.
*May 1975****

1915**

Ch Lafaurie-Peyraguey Two half-bottles, one dried out, one nice.
*In 1976. At best***

1917

Ch Lafaurie-Peyraguey Drying out. Short.
*Ex-château, Sept 1976**

1918**

Ch d'Arche At best, pleasant and holding well.
*Several notes in 1974***

Ch Climens Good level, cork and colour for age; light, creamy, slightly cheesy, high-toned nose; sweetish, rich flavour reminiscent of lanolin, vaseline and lemon curd, with dry, crisp, slightly acidic finish.
*Feb 1984***

Ch Lafaurie-Peyraquey Lovely lime-shaded amber; beautiful, rich, barley-sugar bouquet and flavour. Still sweet, soft, good length and fragrant aftertaste.
*Sept 1990*****

1919**

Picking in Sauternes commenced Sept 20.

Ch d'Yquem Good level. Unexpectedly pale lemon yellow, bright but insipid; light, waxy, powdery vanilla; medium sweetness and weight, slight caramel flavour but good acidity.
*At Bud Moon's tasting, Feb 1988**

Ch de Rayne-Vigneau Lovely colour, lively yellow amber; very rich, mature, crème brûlée; medium-sweet, lovely soft lanolin-like flavour with gentle acidity.
*Pre-sale tasting, Nov 1983*****

1920***

A good Sauternes vintage overshadowed by the '21. Picking began Sept 15.

Ch d'Yquem An air of quality, going downhill but drinkable.
*Once noted, 1955**

Ch Doisy-Dubroca Amber; rich, fragrant; sweet, rich, touch of caramel, good fruit and excellent acidity.
*Half-bottles from Prunier's at pre-sale tastings, Oct and Dec 1982****

Ch de Rayne-Vigneau Good bright colour; bouquet lovely and lively, touch of caramel; fairly sweet, medium weight, excellent flavour, zestful acidity.
*Nov 1983*****

1921*****

A quite remarkable white wine vintage throughout the European wine districts. Following a summer of exceptional heat, picking commenced Sept 14.

With good provenance and ideal storage, there is no reason why these '21s should not be in beautiful drinking condition and keep beyond the turn of this century.

Ch d'Yquem Considered the greatest Yquem since 1847, with mammoth component parts, high sugar content and extract in particular, giving the wine unusual depth of colour, weight and power. I have been privileged to drink this wine 15 times over the past 20 years. Tasted twice in 1983, twice in 1984, (one corked and drying out). In 1984, one of the most interesting: bottled in Switzerland (1921 was the last vintage to be shipped in cask by Lur-Saluces), a Swiss green glass bottle, pictorial label and short cork. Fairly deep colour, bright but with tartaric acid crystals; classic crème brûlée bouquet; sweet, full-bodied, very rich, perfect flavour, drying out on the finish. In 1986, from magnums in 1987 and, more recently, at Bud Moon's Yquem tasting in Chicago. Slight variations, depending on provenance, condition: very deep orange amber, rosehip, Bual madeira-like colour; all had glorious bouquets, very rich, honeyed, singed raisins, peach and orange blossom, sometimes like vanilla and orange candied peel, sometimes a bit chocolaty and Bual-like; ranging from medium-sweet to very sweet, always full-bodied, concentrated, assertive, with marvellous intensity, and perfect counter-balancing acidity — a unique combination of power and beauty.
*Last tasted Feb 1988******

Ch Climens In 1977 seemed to lack '21 richness. More recently in jeroboam: fairly deep amber brown; heavy, rich, crusty caramel; still sweet, fairly full-bodied, meaty, caramelised flavour with just enough acidity.
*Last tasted Feb 1985****

Ch Lafaurie-Peyraguey Fairly deep but lively. A healthy orange tinge and lime-coloured rim; singed, Tokay-like, raisiny, rich apricot nose; medium-sweet, full-bodied, rich, tangy, burnt toffee flavour and good, teeth-drying acidity.
*Sept 1990*****

Ch de Ricaud Loupiac. Bouquet developed well in the glass; medium sweetness and weight, very good flavour and balance, dry finish.
*Oct 1982*****

Ch La Tour Blanche First tasted in Feb 1987, upper mid-shoulder, rarely a problematic level with old Sauternes: lovely old gold; glorious bouquet, peaches and barley-sugar; fairly sweet. Perfection. And three other bottles, one corked with murky muffled mushrooms smell, and dried out. The other two very good.
*Last tasted Sept 1987. At best******

1922*

Abundant, light and lacking. Picking began too early, Sept 12.

Ch d'Yquem Drying out. Not bad.
*Last tasted in 1976**

Ch de Myrat Barsac. A half-bottle, mid-low-shoulder. Palish amber, apple-green rim; surprisingly rich, crusty caramel; sweetish, rather light but clean, flavoury, with good acidity. An unexpected pleasure.
*June 1988***

1923***

Not bad. Picking began Sept 27.

Ch d'Yquem Firm flavour, crisp, drying out.
*Last tasted in 1977****

Ch d'Arche Pugneau Two notes. Glorious, lively, old gold; barley-sugar and caramel; still sweet, fullish, rich, caramelised. One with rather high acidity.
*From a Paris cellar, March 1989. At best****

Ch Guiteronde 2ème cru 'Haut Barsac'. Good levels. Lovely colour, orange gold-tinged; low-keyed at first but developed a sweet, powdery, 'Joy'-reminiscent scent! Still sweet, classic flavour, good length, one with a slightly bitter finish.
*A pair of surprisingly attractive half-bottles, from Prunier's cellar, Paris, Oct and Dec 1982*****

1924***

Picking began Sept 16.

Ch d'Yquem Luscious in 1977. A bottle in less than good condition at Schloss Johannisberg in 1984: slightly cloudy, an initial whiff of brewer's yeast which wore off; better flavour than nose and richer than the '26. More recently, level upper-shoulder: lovely old gold colour with slight but noticeable orange tinge (common to all these '24s); beautiful bouquet of barley-sugar and orange blossom; soft, perfect weight, flavour and aftertaste.
*At Christie's pre-sale tasting in Chicago, Nov 1986. At best******

Ch Guiraud Half-bottle, level top-shoulder, reasonable cork. Bright amber, apple-green rim; lovely, sweet, honeyed, caramelised bouquet; medium sweetness and weight, rich, good barley-sugar flavour, reasonable length, acidity marked but in check.
*Last tasted Sept 1988*****

Ch Guiteronde Good capsules, labels, levels. Vintage not on labels but branded on corks. Rich gold; one with an odd, spicy, mint leaf nose, the others sweet, fragrant, waxy vanilla; medium-sweet, lightish, one high-toned and crisply acidic, with better nose.
*Half-bottles from Prunier's, Oct and Dec 1982** to ****

Ch Rabaud-Promis Very good level but cork pushed in. Buttery yellow gold; lovely, sweet, classic nose; medium sweetness and weight, good flavour, quite powerful, excellent acidity and overall condition.
*Also from Prunier's, pre-sale, Nov 1982*****

1925**

Picking began Sept 27. Originally quite good. Now variable.

Ch d'Yquem Appears not infrequently at auction, but based on a dried out, bitter-tasting bottle Feb 1968, I would not pay a high price. But perhaps I was unlucky.

Ch Lafaurie-Peyraguey Full and fat.
*April 1976****

1926****

Picking began Sept 22. Very good, now drying out.

Ch d'Yquem Slight variations. Very good in 1975: deepish warm amber; honeyed, slightly peppery nose; Sémillon-dominated flavour. Rather severe and lacking fragrance at Schloss Johannisberg in 1984. One with noticeably high acidity in Nov 1986, and, more recently a bottle with attractive colour; curious smell reminiscent of an indoor swimming bath, an hour later minty. Drying out though rich, with pasty vanilla caramel flavour and good acidity.
*Last tasted Feb 1988** to ****

Ch Filhot I noted in 1976 a chlorine smell, a description which, coincidentally, matches up with the Yquem above. But another half-bottle more satisfactory: palish, lemon and gold tinged; rich waxy old honeyed Sémillon; dried out, fading, lean but flavoury, clean.
*June 1988***

Ch de Rayne-Vigneau Deep orange gold, crème brûlée; rich but drying out. Caramelised but clean, scented, with very good acidity and aftertaste.
*Nov 1990*****

Ch St-Amand Preignac. Good levels. Bouquet almost sickly sweet; sweet, lemon curd flavour, rich, clean, attractive.
*Last tasted Dec 1982****

1927**

Picking began Sept 20. A wash-out for red Bordeaux but evidently better conditions for a late harvest in Sauternes.

Ch Doisy-Védrines Fairly deep amber with very pronounced green rim; extremely good, rich, sound, crème brûlée; medium sweetness and body. End acidity effectively masked by remarkably rich old flavour.
*At Ch Latour, Oct 1981*****

Ch Filhot Yellow gold; peach kernels; dried out.
Not helped by raspberry vacherin, July 1981.

Ch de Rayne-Vigneau Two recent notes: top-shoulder, excellent level for age; medium-deep, orange amber; bouquet of peaches, apricots, honey and spice; drying out a little but still rich, powerful, good length though abrupt finish. Lovely barley-sugar aftertaste.
*Last noted May 1990*****

Ch La Tour Blanche As it is my birth-year, tasted and drunk six times, consistently good. Most recently: good level despite crumbly cork. Deepish amber, green rim; lovely old crème brûlée nose; still sweet medium-full, rich, slightly caramelised taste, good acidity.
*Feb 1984*****

1928****

Picking began Sept 18. A contrast in style to the more luscious '29s. Firm. Keeping well.

Ch d'Yquem Tasted a dozen times. Colour varies from lemon gold to rich warm amber, at least one with a slight brownish sediment; intense bouquet, toasted, crème brûlée, vanilla and twist of lemon, peach and orange blossom, ethereal yet sometimes a bit hard; medium-sweet (for Yquem), rich, assertive, with crisp acidity giving it a dry finish.
*Last tasted Oct 1985******

Ch Climens Eight notes, all fairly consistent. Reassuringly good in a half-bottle in 1980. More recently: medium amber gold, lime-edged; spicy, orange blossom, lemon curd, continuously evolving bouquet, a wonderful scent; medium-sweet — drying out a little, crisp, fragrant, excellent acidity and length.
*Last tasted May 1988*****

Ch Filhot Several notes. Amber, caramelly nose and flavour. At its best crisp and flavoury.
*Last tasted Sept 1990***

Ch de Rayne-Vigneau Lovely, bright old gold; orange, peach, crème brûlée; drying out but lovely, perfect weight, balance and acidity. Leaves mouth fragrant.
*Dec 1985*****

Ch Suduiraut Two notes, both good: glorious colour, orange-tinged amber gold; bouquet of dried apricots and barley-sugar, intensity and depth; still fairly sweet, fullish, rich, flavour to match nose. Beautiful aftertaste.
*June 1984 and June 1988******

1929*****

Picking started Sept 23. A glorious vintage. A better balanced, sweeter, softer lusciousness than either the '21

or the '37. If kept in good condition, still perfection. However, '29s tend to be deep in colour, Yquem in particular, to the extent that those who are unaware of this tend to assume that the wine is maderised. Not so.
Ch d'Yquem Noted with purring satisfaction on several occasions. Deep, rich amber, some rose-tinted tawny, all beautifully coloured; the top note of its bouquet seems to be "cream", peaches, apricots, peeled sultanas, rich, slightly toasted; always sweet, full of body, extract and flavour, concentrated, with great length and exquisite aftertaste.
*Last tasted Feb 1988***** Another 50 years of life.*
Ch Climens I am a great admirer of Climens and this must be its greatest-ever vintage. A wonderful deepish amber gold colour with green rim; soft, marvellous bouquet, far more crème and far less brûlée than most old dessert wines, touch of mint leaf; consistently sweet, rich and fat but not hefty or unctuous, with acidity performing like a discreet accompanist. Perfect.
*My last note is dated March 1983, but I re-live it endlessly******
Ch Filhot Several consistent notes. Rich, meaty bouquet; medium, neither sweet nor dry but full-bodied, soft and rich. Good length. Dry finish.
*Last tasted Sept 1990****
Ch Guiraud Level mid-shoulder. Fairly deep straw amber; excellent nose, character, quality, condition. Rich crème brûlée; medium sweetness and body, soft, ripe, rich. Surely one of the best-ever Guiraud.
*Feb 1981******
Ch Laville Preignac. (Not to be confused with Ch Laville Haut-Brion.) Plain capsules, Bordeaux bottled by Eschenauer. Level 1½in below cork, which fell in. Fabulous colour, warm old gold, touch of orange; lovely creamy, honeyed bottle-age and *Botrytis* bouquet which held perfectly for over two hours; medium sweetness and body, perfect flavour and balance, lovely acidity, still very fresh.
*Bordeaux Club dinner at Christie's, April 1984******
Ch de Ricaud Loupiac. Three half-bottles, two in 1982. Beautiful colour; perfect herbal fragrance; still very sweet, fairly powerful, perfect save for the lack of length of a wine of its class.
*All from the Prunier cellar, Paris. Last tasted Nov 1986*****

1930

Disastrous year. Yquem not marketed.

1931

Picking began Sept 21. Not a notable year. Depression and depressing. Poor weather and, when it came to bottling and selling, a poor market.
Ch d'Yquem Consumed on five occasions. One poor bottle, low-shoulder, cork fell in. Maderised, appley, high acidity. The others not at all bad, notes consistent. The most recent with fully embossed capsule and cork, body label, Eschenauer slip label and Julius Wile neck label (shipper and American importer, respectively), level upper-shoulder. Deep amber — looked almost like a red wine in the decanter; almost sickly sweet nose, pure caramel, slightly malty; medium sweetness and weight, caramelised taste, still rich, with good dry acidic finish.
*Last tasted New Year's Eve 1989. At best***

1932

No sun; scarcely any grape sugar, virtually no alcohol.

1933*

Picking began Sept 20. Not a notable success.
Ch d'Yquem The cork fell in. Colour old gold, but bright; nose like old blancmange; still fairly sweet, not bad considering the vintage and its condition, good acidity keeping it afloat. Clean finish.
*Dec 1990**
Ch Lafaurie-Peyraguey Variable, even from the château; one oily, one with some richness and a good flavour.
*Last tasted July 1976. At best***

1934****

Picking began Sept 17. The best year for Sauternes between '29 and '37.
Ch d'Yquem Medium-deep, warm-looking; very sound classic nose, slightly caramelly, fragrant, orange blossom, rich and lovely after one hour in glass; fairly sweet and full, good rich flavour, crisp, excellent balance.
*At Bud Moon's tasting, Chicago, Feb 1988*****
Ch Coutet Perfect colour, medium yellow gold; perfect nose, sweet, lovely soft, lanolin-like; medium sweetness and body, very lively, stylish, good flavour, length and acidity.
*Nov 1983******
Ch Filhot Palish yellow, orange-tinged; crisp, fragrant; drying out, barley-sugar flavour. Nice but second rank.
*May 1987****
Ch Lafaurie-Peyraguey Several excellent half-bottles.
*1977 and 1978*****
Ch de Tastes Ste-Croix-du-Mont. Amber; caramelly; medium-sweet, attractive smoky lanolin flavour, highish crisp acidity. Three notes.
*Last tasted Feb 1982***

1935**

Picking began Sept 25. Bottled just before the outbreak of war. Scarce.
Ch d'Yquem Noted several times since 1970. Apart from a curious palish yellow colour, variable. An attractive delicate-nosed wine, peachy, touch of pineapple; medium-sweet, lightish body and style, elegant, low-keyed but firm, delicate but complete in 1986. An odd, unpleasantly sweaty-smelling bottle at the Moon tasting.
*Last tasted Feb 1988. At best****

1936**

Picking began Oct 2. Mediocre year.
Ch d'Yquem Level into neck. Medium, slight orange tinge, very bright; a curious bouquet, slightly peppery, somehow reminded me of salmon, others of wild cherries; medium sweetness and weight, quite flavoury, lean, clean, good acidity.
*At the Moon tasting, Feb 1988**
Ch d'Arche Eight fairly consistent notes: a lovely orange-tinged amber gold; harmonious, honey and vanilla bouquet; medium sweetness and body, attractive lemon Sémillon, barley-sugar flavour. Good for age, vintage and class.
*Last tasted Sept 1985****

1937*****

Picking began Sept 20. Like 1921 a year famed for white wines rather than red. Great in Sauternes, and the best Sauternes, well kept, are still superb.
Ch d'Yquem Tasted on many occasions, at least nine times during the 1980s. Fairly consistent, the slight variations doubtless the result of less good cellaring. The latter included a too deep, brownish amber bottle with tolerable, though maderised, malty nose. Normally, and at best, a deepish glowing amber gold with touch of

orange (never as deep as the '29 or '21); perfect bouquet (how can one put perfection into words?); honeyed, fragrant, orange blossom, gushing forth an endless succession of scents from seemingly immeasurable depths. On the palate sweet, full-bodied, rich, concentrated, ambrosial barley-sugar, wonderful length, acidity, aftertaste. Most recently a magnum: an explosive bouquet and almost exaggerated flavour.
*Last tasted Sept 1988******
Ch Climens Tasted six times. Most recently: medium-deep warm amber; rich but high-toned, minty bouquet; sweet, creamy rich flavour, rather high acidity but lovely.
*Sept 1988*****
Ch Coutet Several notes. Deeper coloured than expected. Old gold, amber-green rim; low-keyed, caramelised nose; drying out but rich crème brûlée flavour, excellent acidity.
*At Lloyd Flatt's in New Orleans, May 1981*****
Ch Gilette *Crème de Tête*. Rich yellow, gothic-arched legs; honey and straw, slightly vanilla and minty bouquet that softened and sweetened in glass; very sweet, full, rich, creamy, crisp, high acidity giving a dry finish.
*Sept 1988*****
Ch Lafaurie-Peyraguey All good notes. Lovely amber gold; rich, honeyed, barley-sugar bouquet; full-flavoured, waxy, honeyed, excellent acidity. Drying out.
*Last tasted Sept 1988*****
Ch de Ricaud Loupiac. Variously recorded as "crème de tête," "vin de tête" and "tête de cuvée". Lovely colour, topaz, orange gold, slight powdery sediment; perfect honeyed bouquet; medium sweetness and weight, some fat but still fresh tasting. Dry finish.
*Last tasted Nov 1979*****
Ch Suduiraut Old gold; one with tainted old cork, the second cleaner but, though attractive, drying out. Should have been better.
*In San Francisco, May 1980. At best***
Ch La Tour Blanche Very bright warm orange amber; very sweet powdery bouquet that tired rapidly in the glass; very sweet, fairly full, rich but with very high, tangy acidity.
*Sept 1988**
Ch Voigny Preignac. Startlingly bright yellow shot with gold; gentle waxy and honeyed Sémillon nose; medium-sweet, lightish, fragrant, charming, refreshing acidity.
*Nov 1983*****

1938**

Picking began Sept 26. Not a notable Sauternes vintage. Rarely seen. However, **Ch Lafaurie-Peyraguey** and **Ch de Rayne-Vigneau** both pretty good when tasted in the 1970s.

1939***

Picking began Sept 20. Drying out, variable now.
Ch d'Yquem Four slightly variable notes on bottles with various levels. At its best, in 1983, surprisingly good, fairly deep amber gold; very rich crème brûlée nose demonstrating bottle age and *pourriture noble*; fat, rich, good length, life and aftertaste. More recently, upper-shoulder: a rather strange medicinal, caramelly nose; fairly sweet and fullish, with an assertive singed-raisins taste. A bit too acidic and short.
Last tasted Feb 1988 to *****

1940*

Picking began Sept 25. Mediocre.
Ch d'Yquem Good level; good colour, medium orange amber; curious, high-toned, caramel-and-honey nose; medium-sweet, slightly singed rich flavour, quite attractive.
*At Bud Moon's tasting Feb 1988***
Ch Climens Drying out.
1976.

1941

Picking began Sept 30. Poor vintage.
Ch de Mayne Haut Barsac. Belgian bottled. Pale for age. Drying out but soft and pleasant. In excellent condition.
*Nov 1980**

1942****

Picking began Sept 30. A fine rich vintage.
Ch d'Yquem Two very good notes. Fairly deep; warm orange, green rim; low-keyed, gentle, fragrant, developed and held well; medium-sweet, full-bodied, more power than nose indicated, good dry acidic finish.
*Last tasted at Schloss Johannisberg, Nov 1984*****
Ch Climens Pleasing.
*1971****
Ch Coutet Three good notes. Bright, lively gold, lime rim; lovely rich bouquet; sweet, rich, lovely, excellent crisp acidity.
*Last tasted June 1988*****
Ch Lafaurie-Peyraguey Glorious rich gold; rich, hefty, honey and barley-sugar nose; fairly sweet, full-bodied, very rich, excellent acidity.
*Oct 1987*****

1943****

Picking began Sept 15. The best wartime vintage. Powerful wines, now drying out a little.
Ch d'Yquem Three consistently good notes. Warm orange amber; classic bouquet, very forthcoming, fairly powerful, noticeable acidity and alcohol; medium-sweet, drying out though warm rich and positive, its highish volatile acidity merely adding a high-toned fragrance. Aftertaste like the crust of crème caramel.
*Last tasted Nov 1984******
Ch Guiraud Distinct depth of colour; very little bouquet, minty, varnishy; drying out, lean and leathery.
*Jan 1983**

1944***

Picking began Sept 24. Quite good. Variable now.
Ch d'Yquem Two good notes. Medium-deep, bright, orange amber with vivid apple-green rim; remarkably attractive, fresh, crème brûlée, lanolin and honeyed bouquet; medium sweetness and body, fairly assertive flavour, good acidity.
*Last tasted Feb 1988*****
Clos Haut-Peyraguey "1er cru Sauternes". Good level. Beautiful colour; lovely classic nose; sweet, excellent flavour, balance and condition.
*Jan 1981*****

1945*****

Picking began Sept 10. The miraculous first post-war vintage. Highest quality, refined, concentrated. Keeping well.
Ch d'Yquem A very great wine which I have been privileged to taste on many occasions. Six very consistent notes since 1983: pure gold, highlight of amber, orange tints; perfect bouquet that blossoms in the glass, floral, peachlike, apple crumble! Still fairly sweet, intense, concentrated, great power and attack, great length,

orange blossom aftertaste. Magnificent.
*Last tasted Sept 1990***** Will continue well into the 21st century.*
Ch Filhot Warm, lively amber; caramelised barley-sugar, but lacking zest; drying—but still fleshy, with high extract, very good acidity.
*At Belle and Bernard Rhodes', April 1986*****
Ch Lafaurie-Peyraguey Fabulous colour, deep orange amber, lemon rim; fragrant, high-toned, slightly citrus tang; sweet, rich, powerful but not heavy—a deft touch. Marvellous acidity.
*Last tasted May 1984******
Ch La Tour Blanche Exquisite, concentrated.
*1978******

1946

Picking began Sept 30. After rain and rot, the vintage saved by extremely hot weather. However, of little interest.
Ch d'Yquem Level between mid- and high shoulder. Cloudy. Colour a grubby amber. First whiff pricked, oxidised yet with richness beneath. After an hour: chocolate and coffee fudge. Still sweet. Taste of singed liquorice. A poor bottle and, at best, unlikely to be more than interesting.
Feb 1988.

1947*****

Picking began Sept 15. A very great rich, ripe vintage. Glorious. Watch out for acidity.
Ch d'Yquem Tasted 13 times since 1954. Very consistent notes. Glorious colour: warm orange amber, light powdery sediment (worth decanting for the beauty of its colour alone); bouquet sheer perfection; orange pekoe, peach and orange blossom, soft, harmonious; very sweet still, medium-full body, soft, plump, fleshy, masking volatile acidity (result of fermentation in very hot conditions).
*Last tasted Sept 1987***** At peak.*
Ch Climens One of the best-ever vintages of Climens, on a par with '29. 10 excellent notes, five since 1980. Colour medium-deep, glowing old gold; perfect bouquet, always sweet, rich, classic crème brûlée, mint leaves, apricots. On the palate it varies from fairly sweet to very sweet, soft, creamy, barley-sugar flavour, great length, superb aftertaste.
*Last tasted Jan 1988***** Plenty of life left.*
Ch Coutet Several notes. Most attractive. Recently, London-bottled by Lebègue's, with unbranded cork. Fairly deep orange amber; deliciously caramelised nose; fairly sweet and full, rich, fat, soft, with dry, slightly acidic finish.
*July 1990. At best*****
Ch Gilette Waxy yellow; grassy, mustard and cress, peach kernels nose; very sweet, full-bodied, oily, assertive. Disappointing.
*Sept 1990***
Dom de Jaussans Cérons. Palish; honeyed; drying out, short, acid-edged, but still worth looking out for minor wines of great vintages.
Dec 1980.
Ch de Mayne Barsac. Orange amber; excellent nose, mandarins, orange blossom; sweet, fullish, lovely fresh honeyed taste. Excellent acidity.
*Sept 1987*****
Ch La Tour Blanche A glowing yellow gold; rich, vanilla, barley-sugar bouquet; sweet, fairly full-bodied, glorious flavour, silky texture, fleshy, good acidity.
*Sept 1990*****

1948**

Picking began Sept 22. Quite a good vintage but on the lean side.
Ch d'Yquem Several notes. Perfect in the early 1960s. Most recently: a lovely warm gold; honeyed bouquet; fairly sweet, soft, fleshy, tolerable sustaining acidity. Lacking the length and aftertaste of a great vintage.
*Last tasted Oct 1987*** Drink soon.*
Ch Climens Fairly deep rose apricot colour; smooth, harmonious, sweet but touch of varnishy old age; still fairly sweet, lean, acidity catching up.
*Tasted in half-bottles in 1981 and Feb 1986** Drink up.*

1949*****

Picking began Sept 27 and continued through the driest Oct on record.
Ch d'Yquem 10 notes, all showing consistent quality and correct development. Most recent: lovely amber colour, faint orange tinge and lime rim; perfect bouquet, fragrant, blossomed in the glass: apricot, orange, honey; medium-sweet, lacking the fat of '47 and concentration of '45 but supple, lively, slightly singed character, dry finish.
*Last tasted Feb 1988******
Ch Climens Consistently good.
*Last tasted 1977******
Ch Coutet Several notes, all good. Most recently, a half-bottle: wonderfully rich amber gold; perfect, harmonious, honeyed bouquet; medium sweetness and weight, excellent flavour and acidity.
*Last tasted July 1983******
Ch de Fargues Very heavy powdery sediment; powerful, toasted barley-sugar nose; fairly sweet, full-bodied, assertive. Hot, bitter finish.
*Sept 1986**
Ch de Rayne-Vigneau Lovely colour; perfect nose and flavour.
*Feb 1987******
Ch Rieussec Medium-gold; pears, kerosene, toffee; medium-sweet, high-toned, dry finish. Disappointing. Poor bottle?
Sept 1989.

1950**

Picking began Sept 17. Damp weather compensated for by Indian summer. Some good wines.
Ch d'Yquem The Comte de Lur-Saluces and I disagree about this Yquem. I simply do not like the almond kernel smell, though I confess it does wear off in the glass after an hour or so. It has a good colour, deepish pure glowing amber. At the remarkable tasting at Schloss Johannisberg in 1984 M Lur-Saluces described it as a great classic, but I found it to be drying out a little, though rich, its inner fragrance offset by a bitter touch. More recently, sweet, fuller, positive, barley-sugar flavour and good finish.
*Nine notes. Last tasted Feb 1988** to **** depending on condition and personal taste.*
Ch Coutet A dozen notes. At birth, very high alcohol and sugar. At a dinner party in 1981 David Peppercorn produced one, bottled in Margate by his family firm, Osborne & Co. Drying out a little, otherwise very good, with vanilla cream flavour and excellent acidity. Two years later, château bottled: a lovely warm orange gold; perfect rich honeyed, crème brûlée bouquet; still pretty sweet, a pleasant crispness balancing richness and fat.
*Last tasted Jan 1983*****

Ch Gilette *Crème de Tête*. Held for a minimum of 20 years in tanks or vats – no wood used! Idiosyncratic but excellent. Fairly deep-coloured; peach and mint bouquet; fairly sweet, rich, fat.
*June 1984**** Years of life left.*

1951

Picking began Oct 4. Poor year. Yquem not made. No '51 Sauternes tasted.

1952***

Picking commenced Sept 17 except at Yquem whose crop was destroyed by hail and no wine made. Once substantial wines, now drying out but worth looking out for.
Ch Climens Pale and unimpressive when young. Tasted a dozen times since, probably at its best in the mid-1970s. The most recent, possibly English bottled, with tartaric acid crystals, unknit nose, taste bright, appealing Sauvignon Blanc and rich waxy Sémillon, sweetish, soft yet crisp.
*March 1982*** Not much future.*
Ch de Rolland Barsac, *cru bourgeois*. No vintage on label. Cork branded "Sauternes 1952". Colour of bright buttercup and vaseline; ripe nose; fairly sweet, rich, excellent flavour and waxy, honeyed aftertaste. A nice surprise.
*July 1988*****

1953****

A lovely Sauternes vintage. Beautiful Aug, wet Sept, picking beginning Sept 28 in perfect weather. Now fully mature, the best still lovely.
Ch d'Yquem One of my favourite Yquems. Stylish rather than a block-buster, though it started life full and rich. Noticeably *not* deep in colour though lovely, orange-tinged; soft, gentle, harmonious bouquet, crème not brûlée. Fairly sweet, medium weight, lovely crisp flavour. A charmer.
*Last tasted Feb 1988**** Despite its comparative delicacy, will last into the next century.*
Ch Doisy-Daëne Lovely colour, rich yellow gold; perfect nose, peaches and cream and melted barley-sugar; lightish style and weight, drying out a little. Delightful.
*Oct 1986**** Perhaps lacking further staying power.*
Ch Gilette A late-bottled *Crème de Tête* and, because of its storage in stainless steel tank, still youthful and holding well when tasted in 1983. Another, noted as "Doux" pale for its age, with a fabulous though unusual bouquet, very fruity, with a raspberry-like piquancy; medium-sweet, medium-light, charming, peachy endtaste.
*April 1987*****

1954

Poor late vintage, a wash-out in Sauternes. How Yquem came to be made I do not know. None other tasted.
Ch d'Yquem Apart from a noticeably deep colour, two contrasting notes, unknit and acidic in 1971 and more recently, very rich on nose and palate, lovely flavour, good length and acidity.
*Last tasted June 1983. At best****

1955*****

A well-nigh perfect Sauternes vintage. Weather conditions all conspired favourably to produce quality and quantity. Picking from Sept 21 through to fine dry Oct. The best still good though slipping: years of life left.
Ch d'Yquem 12 notes. Impressive in cask, wonderfully even development throughout the 1970s into the 1980s. Summarising recent notes: an astonishing orange rosehip amber with pale lemon rim; intense and heady fragrant floral bouquet. Still very sweet and full-bodied, with classic barley-sugar flavour and balance, good length, acidity creeping into prominence, lovely aftertaste.
*Last tasted Feb 1988***** Magnificent wine. Despite, or perhaps because of, the acidity, a long and appealing life.*
Ch Climens Deepish amber gold; fragrant, forthcoming, spicy. Perfect harmony after 20 minutes. Spearmint in cream caramel after an hour in the glass; sweet, fullish, fat. Slightly peppery end.
*Last tasted May 1988*****
Ch Gilette *Crème de Tête*. 25 years in cement vat. First tasted after five years in bottle: marvellous rich gold; very fragrant, creamy, crisp bouquet; fairly sweet, medium body, rich, touch of caramel and honeyed aftertaste. Now a polished, waxy yellow; nose of vanilla and spearmint, but almost no evolution in the glass; powerful, rather hard finish. Touch of volatile acidity. Liked it less.
*Last tasted June 1990*****
Ch Rabaud-Sigalas Deepish amber; rich, fully-developed nose, lanolin and honey, minty; good flavour but lacking fat and drying out a little.
*Last tasted at the Kreegers' in New Orleans, May 1981****

1956

A poor vintage everywhere. By dint of careful late picking, Yquem managed to produce some wine. Have tasted no other Sauternes. A curiosity.
Ch d'Yquem Four notes. First tasted in cask, pale, fruity. Now deepening in colour to orange amber; distinct *Botrytis* nose, not bad but faded; sweetish, flavoury but a bit raw and short.
Last tasted Feb 1988 just.*

1957***

An up-and-downer of a vintage, in growing conditions and end results. Warm spring, extremely cold summer, late harvest in great heat. Acidic tendencies. Past best.
Ch d'Yquem Never Yquem at its best. Now a deepish amber; oily, whiff of mercaptan which cleared, sweet, rich, vanilla; very sweet, fullish, strong toffee-like flavour, highish acidity, short.
*Last tasted Feb 1988**
Pre-1980 notes:
Suduiraut, **Rieussec** and **Rabaud-Sigalas** good; **Coutet** and **Doisy-Daëne** refreshing, acidity probably catching up; **Lafaurie-Peyraguey** thin.

1958**

Good summer, late harvest from Oct 7. A perfectly pleasant vintage but not destined for longevity.
Ch d'Yquem Sweet and ripe from the start. Still very sweet, a positive, assertive flavour, better than the nose which initially I found a bit oily and cheesy but which opened up creamily.
*Last tasted Feb 1988***
Ch Suduiraut Six notes. At its best in the early 1970s. Showing age on colour and nose but still fairly sweet, with a soft, quite rich flavour, but pasty end acidity.
*Last tasted June 1983***
Pre-1980 notes:
Climens and **Coutet** attractive; **Doisy-Védrines** quite nice.

1959★★★★★

A very great Sauternes vintage. Long hot summer, some rain mid-Sept but cleared for relatively early harvest from Sept 21. The best should still be excellent and will keep well into the next century.

Ch d'YQUEM *Superb. Very high sugar content and extract. Sweet and immensely rich from first tasting in 1964 to the most recent. The last six notes very consistent. Fairly deep amber gold, very bright; beautiful bouquet variously described as heavenly crème brûlée, vanilla, duck-egg custard!, creamy, honeyed, whiff of Cox's orange pippins and charred oak, with enormous depth and more to yield. Always sweet, full-bodied, powerful, masculine (as opposed to the more feminine '53), touch of caramel and black treacle, luscious yet could do with even more time in bottle.* Last tasted Feb 1988★★★★★(★) *Yes: 5 star+*

Ch RIEUSSEC *Five notes. Most recently from two half-bottles, both shipped by Sichel and bottled by Saccone & Speed, for whom I happened to have worked from 1953 to 1955. The first half at a Bordeaux Club dinner in 1984 with foie gras, excellent level, quite deep colour; perfect bouquet, flavour and balance; still sweet, full-bodied, "25 years more life". The other, a lovely warm amber colour; sweet, rich, full, excellent acidity.* Last tasted Sept 1985★★★★

Ch SIGALAS-RAUBAUD *Lovely amber colour; perfect bouquet: crème brûlée, orange blossom, vanilla; sweet, flavour to match nose, lovely acidity.* May 1986★★★★

Ch SUDUIRAUT *Eight consistently good notes. Distinct yellow colour in 1978, now deepened with bottle-age to a medium-deep amber gold, with slight sediment; gloriously rich, ripe, honeyed, harmonious nose. Very sweet, full, fragrant. Perfection.* Last three notes in 1980, 1982 and June 1988★★★★★

PRE-1980 NOTES:

Climens magnificent; Coutet tinglingly beautiful; Guiraud nine variable notes; Lafaurie-Peyraguey Beerenauslese-like.

1960★

Not much past, present or future. Interesting only. The fault of a cold and wet summer.

Ch d'YQUEM *Orange amber; quite good classic nose and taste. Fragrant, spicy; medium sweetness and body. Citrus.* Last tasted Feb 1988★★

Ch COUTET *Crumbly cork. Colour rather deep and too orange; crème brûlée, yet not quite right; medium-sweet, lightish, soft, leathery, butterscotch finish.* From an American private cellar, Oct 1982.

1961★★★

It is a common mistake to think that '61 was as great a vintage in Sauternes as it was for the red Bordeaux. The crop was small and the conditions not ideal. Good but overrated.

Ch d'YQUEM *Several notes. Colour now a deepish orange-tinged amber gold; soft, caramel fudge nose; fairly sweet, quite powerful, drying out at the finish. Not a great Yquem.* Last tasted Feb 1988★★★

Ch CLIMENS *Eight consistently good notes since 1967. Now a rich yellow gold; attractive, ripe, barley-sugar and cream bottle-age and* Botrytis *bouquet; sweet, fairly hefty, rich, perfect acidity.* Last tasted June 1990. *At peak*★★★★

Ch COUTET *Eight consistent notes since 1964. Rich, creamy, well-knit, lanolin bouquet; sweet, rich, lovely, good acidity.* Last tasted Aug 1980★★★

Ch DOISY-VEDRINES *Two notes. Both bottled by Averys. Pleasant enough wine. Palish yellow; blancmange, peaches and cream; sweet, lightish. Perfect condition and state of development in 1986.* Last tasted Nov 1989★★★

Ch LAFAURIE-PEYRAGUEY *Deepish gold; a crisp, honeyed nose but not much evidence of* pourriture*; sweet, fullish, rich, ripe, waxy, honeyed flavour masking a touch of bitterness.* Last tasted April 1983★★★

Ch La TOUR BLANCHE *Three fairly recent notes. Lovely colour; soft, sweet, honeyed bouquet; medium sweetness and body, rich, touch of caramel, dry finish.* Last tasted May 1987★★★

1962★★★★

Much more favourable conditions in 1962 than in 1961. Hot summer, late picking. Not heavyweight like 1959, but supple, elegant, more tautly refreshing. A Sauternes to keep and drink.

Ch d'YQUEM *I have been fortunate to have had this wine on 15 occasions, eight since 1980. Consistently good. Now a deepish amber; marvellous fruit variously noted as mandarin, ripe peaches, honey and orange blossom; not overpoweringly sweet, a nice weight, intense, elegant, good acidity.* Last tasted June 1988★★★★ Drink now to 1995.

Ch CLIMENS *Many notes, consistently good from 1964 to date. Now buttercup gold; perfect, harmonious, creamy bouquet; sweet, fullish, apricots, wonderful acidity and aftertaste.* Last tasted July 1988★★★★ Will last well beyond 2000.

Ch COUTET *Also consistently good notes. Lovely colour, nose and flavour. Less sweet, crisper than Climens, much more of the Barsac-style. Dry finish. Excellent aftertaste. One bottle woody.* Last tasted Sept 1990★★★

Ch GUIRAUD *Slightly variable notes. Ripe, sweet, touch of oiliness(?) yet lovely flavour.* Not tasted *since June 1982*★★★

Ch RIEUSSEC *Pale for age and a light Barsac-like style, fragrant but lacking middle. Not tasted since Feb 1982*★★

Ch SIGALAS-RABAUD *Glorious yellow gold; equally glorious waxy, harmonious, nose and taste. Fairly sweet, very rich, barley-sugar flavour. Last tasted April 1990*★★★★

Ch SUDUIRAUT *Lovely bright yellow gold; excellent bouquet and flavour. Sweet, rich, some fat but not too hefty. Good acidity. Five notes though not tasted since 1982*★★★★ *Years of life ahead.*

1963

Weather conditions dreary from start (poor flowering) to finish.

Ch d'YQUEM *By dint of picky picking, some wine was made though it should never have been marketed. In 1975 it was too deep and too brown; rich yet tinny and cheesy; acidic and short. No recent notes and not worth seeking.*

1964

A promising summer was ruined by torrential rain. Mostly washed out in Sauternes. Ch d'Yquem not made.

Ch CLIMENS *Several notes. Good colour; unknit nose, superficially rich and waxy, but green and a bit raw; some sweetness, richness and body. Light dry finish. At a Bordeaux Club dinner at Culham Court, May 1984.*

Ch GUIRAUD *Gold-tinged, curiously attractive nose; sweetish, crisp, with a touch of bitterness. Good for a mediocre year. Not tasted since Feb 1982.*

1965

The third poor Sauternes vintage in a row. Heavy rains. Rot-inducing humidity. The châteaux proprietors must have been in despair. Even if they had been able to make good wines, the sweet-wine market was at a low ebb.

Ch d'YQUEM *Lemon gold; oily nose — I didn't bother to taste it. The second bottle faded, dried out. Feb 1988.*

Ch SUDUIRAUT *Thanks to highly selective picking and an experienced winemaker, not bad, with sweetness and character. 1978.*

1966★★★

A good but not wholly satisfactory Sauternes vintage. Lacking the fat and flesh of a great year, the wines are lean, sinewy, with higher than usual acidity that should enable them to keep well.

Ch d'YQUEM *First tasted in cask, six notes since 1986. Warm, orange-tinged gold; consistently good notes relating to the bouquet, deep, rich, butterscotch, and to its sweetness. An assertive wine. Full, rich yet with a lean, long, fragrant but slightly acidic finish. Last tasted Sept 1989*★★★★ *Should keep well.*

Ch BASTOR-LAMONTAGNE *Many notes, all half-bottles. Nose of lanolin and peach kernels. Fairly sweet. Satisfactory. Last tasted Jan 1987*★★

Ch CLIMENS *Four notes. Rather pale and skinny in 1970. More recently, bright yellow; extra dimensions yet a touch of hardness. Sweet, rich, flavoury. Touch of bitterness on finish. Last tasted at the château, June 1982*★★★

Ch GUIRAUD *Good colour, nose and flavour. Harmonious, waxy,* pourriture. *Sweet. Well-balanced. June 1982*★★★

Ch LAFAURIE-PEYRAGUEY *Pale for its age, green-tinged; pleasant bouquet, waxy Sémillon, honeyed bottle-age; medium sweetness and body, some flesh. Last tasted May 1983*★★★

Ch SUDUIRAUT *Amber gold; harmonious, peach-nosed, barley-sugar bouquet and flavour. Sweet, lovely flavour, balance, acidity. Very good old-fashioned winemaking around this period. Last tasted July 1985*★★★★

1967★★★★★

A great Sauternes vintage. Late flowering, hot dry summer, rain in Sept cleared for picking in warm sunshine from Sept 28.

Ch d'YQUEM *I am abashed to admit that I have consumed this wine on over 40 occasions since 1973, nearly half since 1980. With the exception of a slightly woody bottle and one slightly maderised, due, I suspect, to poor keeping, it is a great wine, as its owner, Alexandre de Lur-Saluces, is not too modest to admit. I have noted slight differences in colour, ranging from a palish pure yellow gold to a rich burnished old gold; sometimes it appears to be very sweet, at other times medium-sweet with a dryish finish. Doubtless the latter depends on the context, the place, the company, above all the food it happens to accompany. But it is an outstanding Yquem. I have more than once, out of curiosity, timed the way the nose blossoms in the glass: very positive, buttery. Ten minutes later, lovely fruit, pineapple; after 35 minutes, sweet, ambrosial Turkish delight; 70 minutes later glorious; after 90 minutes perfection; after four hours starting to turn into a tea-like decline. On the palate, assertive yet beguiling, with zestful acidity. In weight more like '53 than '59. Last tasted Nov 1990*★★★★★ *Years of life ahead.*

Ch COUTET *15 notes, somewhat variable. A disappointing number of insubstantial half-bottles, but at best lovely, honeyed, fairly sweet. Not great. Not tasted since June 1983*★★ *to* ★★★

Ch de FARGUES *Another, very old, Lur-Saluces family property. First tasted with pleasurable surprise prior to the Asher Story sale in 1974.*

More recently: gold; quite powerful nose and palate; drying out a little, highish acidity but most attractive. Last tasted Dec 1985★★★

Ch GILETTE Crème de Tête. *Buttercup yellow; minty; medium-sweet, very assertive flavour, some fat, hard end.* Oct 1990★★(★)?

Ch GUIRAUD *Several notes. Fairly deep orange-tinged amber; lovely ripe bouquet, honeyed bottle-age and* Botrytis, *harmonious, with hint of fresh mint; sweet, fullish, soft, rich, caramelly, good acidity. A reassuringly good, if not great, Guiraud.* Last tasted Aug 1990★★★★

Ch LIOT *Barsac. Pale and wan.* Last tasted April 1984★

Ch RIEUSSEC *A fine classic Sauternes, sweet, rich, long.* Last tasted at the château, April 1984★★★★

Ch SIGALAS-RABAUD *Good colour; pineapple and passion fruit; medium sweetness and weight, excellent flavour, balance and finish.* Several notes but not tasted since Sept 1981★★★

Ch SUDUIRAUT *15 consistently good notes since 1974, half since 1980. Lovely bright warm gold; "celestial" used twice, barley-sugar and marmalade. Pretty sweet, fullish, rich excellent* pourriture, *fragrant aftertaste. Vying with Yquem in this vintage.* Last tasted May 1991★★★★(★)

Ch La TOUR BLANCHE *London-bottled by Dolamore's. Pure yellow gold; light, waxy bouquet — with a whiff that reminded me of oyster shells!; lightish weight. Needs drinking.* Tasted July 1986★★

1968

Terrible vintage entirely due to poor weather; no sun, cold wet summer, unripe grapes.

Ch d'YQUEM *Tasted, still in cask, in 1973. Though it was never marketed, a bottle managed to find its way into Bud Moon's Yquem tasting in Chicago. It had a mahogany colour and needed decanting; harsh, medicinal, caramelised nose; dry but strangely rich. A singed, brackish taste.* Last tasted Feb 1988.

1969★ to ★★★

Another far from perfect year. Sauternes saved by an Indian summer. The wines can be flavoury and attractive but lack harmony and balance. Acidity on the high side but tolerable as it is masked by residual sugar.

Ch d'YQUEM *First tasted in cask in 1973. Marked acidity noted on this and subsequent occasions. Medium-pale; lanolin with a twist of lemon; sweetish, crisp, high but tolerable acidity.* Last noted Feb 1988★★

Ch CERONS, GRAND ENCLOS DU *Pale, bright; fresh, piquant; medium-sweet, flavoury, '69 acidity.* June 1982★★

Ch CLIMENS *First tasted in 1973. Several consistent notes since. As with Yquem, a waxy, lanolin nose, sweetish, very flavoury but lacking flesh, with pasty, slightly tinny, piquant finish.* Last tasted Jan 1984★★

Ch FILHOT *Excellent appearance; good nose; sweet barley-sugar flavour, good finish.* June 1986★★★

Ch GUIRAUD *Four slightly variable notes in early to mid-1980s. Amber gold, green-tinged, like shot silk; pretty good balance of waxy Sémillon, acidic Sauvignon Blanc and* pourriture; *sweet, glorious flavour, length, dry finish.* Last tasted May 1984.

Ch LAFAURIE-PEYRAGUEY *Now golden amber; hefty honeyed nose, almond paste; sweetness temporarily destroyed by* mousseline *of almonds but revived.* Last tasted March 1986★★

Ch RIEUSSEC *Yellow gold, pale for Rieussec; gloriously rich, cheesy bouquet; big, flavoury, a bit overdone.* Last tasted Nov 1986★★★

Ch SIGALAS-RABAUD *Yellow; fragrant, spicy, mouth-watering nose; medium sweetness and weight, Sémillon (75%) giving it a waxy flavour, the balance of Sauvignon Blanc a clean acidic finish.* Last tasted March 1985★★

Ch SUDUIRAUT *Amber gold; harmonious, classic Sauternes nose; medium-sweet — drying out a little. An old fashioned style, toffee and old apples.* Last tasted June 1988★★★

1970★★★

Just as the '61 Sauternes bask in the reflected glory of the reds, so do the '70s. Good growing conditions, but the long hot autumn lacked the humidity to produce *pourriture noble*. Ripe, sweet wines but lacking that extra dash and finesse.

Ch d'YQUEM *10 notes. From the cask in April 1973, pale and lemon-tinged, slightly bitter finish. Deepening in colour as it ages; nose becoming more harmonious, vanilla, lacking* Botrytis. *Now a medium yellow gold; fairly hefty, apricot, vanilla nose gaining honeyed bottle-age. Consistently sweet, fairly powerful, barley-sugar flavour, reasonable length. Good but uninspired.* Last tasted Jan 1990★★★(★)

Ch BASTOR-LAMONTAGNE *Fairly sweet, straightforward, always good value.* Jan 1981★★

Ch CLIMENS *Palish; clean, sweet nose; medium-sweet on palate, lacking fat but pleasant. If Climens cannot produce an outstanding wine, no one can. Confirms the vintage.* Four notes, but not tasted since 1982★★(★)?

Ch COUTET *Six consistent notes. A very pleasant wine. Palish, bright yellow; slightly scented, slightly singed, cress-like bouquet; sweet, medium weight and style, lively, well-balanced. Nice now.* Last tasted Feb 1986★★★

Ch de RAYNE-VIGNEAU *Three slightly variable notes. On the pale side for its age; lively, waxy, white currant nose, kerosene and almond kernels; fairly sweet, not a heavyweight, at best pleasant enough but not up to its old classic standards.* Last tasted July 1984★

Ch RIEUSSEC *Surprisingly pale; sweet, spearmint nose; medium sweetness and body, nice rich*

*flavour, good acidity. Last tasted June 1988****
Ch ROUMIEU-LACOSTE *Yellow; waxy, grassy; sweet, fat, creamy, powerful. March 1983***
Ch SUDUIRAUT *Six notes: not great but good. Sweetness but not* Botrytis. *Bouquet relatively low-keyed but fragrant, peaches and barley-sugar; fairly sweet, trace of kernels, four-square. Last tasted Nov 1990***(*)*

1971★★★(★)

A very good vintage with further development possibilities. More supple and subtle than the '70s. Growing conditions fairly normal with, clearly, more *pourriture noble* when picking began early Oct.

Ch d'YQUEM *Distinctive yellow gold; beautiful bouquet, classic, the initial pineapple and honey now floral, peachy, harmonious; very sweet, fullish body, very positive flavour, rich, good length and aftertaste. The best Yquem between 1967 and 1975. Lovely now but will keep and develop. Last tasted Feb 1988***(*) Drink now 'til death do us part.*

Ch CLIMENS *Seven notes, all in the 1980s. Perfection. Climens at its best. Now a glorious buttery gold; lovely classic* Botrytis *bouquet gaining extra dimensions with bottle-age. Caramel cream. Sweet, not at all hefty, rich yet elegant, soft, smooth, excellent life-enhancing acidity. Last tasted Feb 1988****(*) Drink now and until well into the next century.*
Ch COUTET *Seven good notes. Palish, pure gold; minty honeyed bouquet; fairly sweet, medium weight, very stylish, good acidity. Last tasted Sept 1986***(*) Drink now to 2000.*
Ch COUTET *'Cuvée Madame'. The ultimate* cuvée, *made only in great years. Pure gold; glorious, sweet ripe peaches, gushing out of the glass; sweet, blissful, great style, length and aftertaste. In magnum April 1985****(*) Drink now and indefinitely.*
Ch LIOT *Palish; good nose; sweet, nice flavour and balance. Liot is usually attractive, always good value. July 1981****
Ch RABAUD-SIGALAS *Palish, hint of green; low-keyed but harmonious, medium-sweet. Nutty, kernelly smell and taste. May 1982** Drink up.*
Ch RIEUSSEC *Very bright yellow gold; most attractive bouquet and flavour; rich, honeyed; sweet, not heavy, stylish, well-balanced. Three notes but not tasted since Sept 1984*****
Ch SUDUIRAUT *Palish; attractive; medium-sweet for Suduiraut, soft, pleasing but not as good as expected. Not tasted since March 1980**(*)?*

1972★

Climatically an erratic year with unsuitable growing conditions. A poor, graceless vintage. Many declassified. But not all that bad. Not for keeping.

Ch CLIMENS *Six notes. Initially pale, now palish yellow gold; somewhat pungent at first, perhaps too much sulphur, otherwise quite decent nose and even better flavour. Slightly pasty, acidic finish. Last tasted Oct 1989**
Ch SUDUIRAUT *Also six notes, mainly at pre-sale tastings. Palish, bright yellow; light but surprisingly attractive nose despite the odd "Gripfix" note; medium sweetness and weight, lean but positive, barley-sugar flavour. Not at all bad. Last tasted June 1988***

1973★★

A lightish, moderate — indeed modest — vintage though not poor. Drinking rather well now, but not destined for the next century.

Ch d'YQUEM *Three notes. Lovely colour: amber with gold highlights; attractive bouquet, orange blossom, still youthful, vanilla, — opened up in the glass; medium sweetness and body, surprisingly rich and flavoury, elegant, with a deft touch. Crisp acidic finish. Last tasted Feb 1988*** Drink now to 2000.*

Ch CAILLOU *Pale; light, lean style but sweet and flavoury. Sept 1982***
Ch CLIMENS *Seven notes. Waxy yellow; fragrant, creamy bouquet; fairly sweet, lighter and leaner than a classic Climens vintage, pasty acidity but attractive. Last tasted April 1991*** just. Drink now to 1995.*
Ch COUTET *Pleasing and positive yellow; equally pleasing ripe Sémillon nose; sweet, more power than expected. '73 acidity. April 1981** Drink soon.*
Ch DOISY-DUBROCA *Unknit nose, waxy Sémillon and peach-kernelly acidic Sauvignon Blanc. Sweetish, lightish. Flavoury though modest. Aug 1982***
Ch FILHOT *Two notes. Pale gold, very light sediment; grassy Sauvignon, piquant acidity; fairly sweet but on the light side. Some fruit, and acidity. Not tasted since Nov 1983***
Ch NAIRAC *Two notes. Quite nice bouquet and flavour but no finesse. Not tasted since May 1982***
Ch de RAYNE-VIGNEAU *Three somewhat variable notes. Buttery gold; hard-nosed though ripe Sémillon; sweet, lightish, pleasant enough. Dry finish. All tasted in 1981***

1974

A cold, damp and dismal vintage. The worst of the decade — until 1977 arrived. But the leading first-growth Barsac managed to make a palatable wine.

Ch CLIMENS *Pale, rim a bit watery; honey-sweet nose masking green acidity and hardness. Fairly sweet, quite mouthfilling, with herbaceous honeycomb flavour. Good for a '74. Tasted four times in 1987***
Ch COUTET *Bright, lemon-tinged; rich, grassy, straw-like nose; medium-sweet, clumsy, dry finish. Three notes, but not tasted since Aug 1982**

1975★★★★★

An important year. My second opinion better than early impressions, partly because of the development of the wines in bottle. But it seems apparent that only the top châteaux, making wine in a traditional way, have maximised the innate quality of the vintage.

Ch d'YQUEM *In the early 1980s rich, impressive but almost raw immaturity. Eight notes later: lovely, star-bright but still rather pale; attractive creamy bouquet, harmonious, fragrant, honey and barley-sugar opening up in the glass: orange and peach blossom; very sweet, rich, full-bodied yet with beautifully counterbalancing acidity. Soft, fleshy, peach-like flavour. Great class, great future. Last tasted Sept 1990★★★★(★) Lovely now but should develop even more marvellously over the next 50 years.*

Ch d'ARCHE *Deep for age; medium-sweet. Nice. Nothing special. July 1982★★*

Ch CLIMENS *Six good notes. Still relatively pale gold; fabulous harmonious bouquet, honey, apricots; sweet, full, fat yet refreshing acidity, crisp fruit. Delicious. Last tasted Oct 1988★★★★(★) Lovely now until well into the next century.*

Ch COUTET *First tasted in 1978. Rich but grassy nose, tangy, unready. Still palish; lanolin, honey and cress; fairly sweet, medium weight and style, pleasant, nice finish. Not tasted since a memorable lunch in the company of H M the Queen Mother in Christie's boardroom, Feb 1982★★★(★)*

Ch DOISY-DAENE *Pale; grassy, some fruit and* Botrytis*; sweet, light style but rich and very attractive. Last tasted April 1986★★(★) Now to 2000.*

Ch DOISY-VEDRINES *Quite different in style from Daëne, deeper, heavier. Noticeable* Botrytis*. Medium-sweet; positive, stylish. Bitter aftertaste. Last tasted Sept 1982★★★(★) Drink now and just into the 21st century.*

Ch de FARGUES *Pale gold; pineapple, high-toned; medium sweetness and weight, lovely positive flavour, rather spiky acidity. Should be more rounded by now. Oct 1983★★(★)? Now until 2000.*

Ch FILHOT *Pale and rather unimpressive in 1978. Four years later, still too pale, green-tinged; fresh but light fruity grassy style. Medium-sweet. Cannot see this developing into a really good classic Sauternes. Not tasted since Sept 1982★(★) Now to 1995.*

Ch GUIRAUD *Curious, piquant, in 1978. Yellow; fragrant but tom-cat reminiscent Sauvignon nose; medium sweetness and weight, some fat, grassy style, though attractive. Might have matured and broadened out by now. Not noted since* Decanter *tasting, Sept 1982★★(★)? Now to 1995.*

Ch GUITERONDE *Two notes in early 1980s. Then unknit, sulphury nose; sweet, fairly fat and rich, almost oily. Needed time to settle down. Last tasted March 1983★(★)? Try now.*

Ch LAFAURIE-PEYRAGUEY *Palish; cress; sweet, powerful, waxy. May 1991★★★(★)*

Ch LIOT *Five notes: pleasant grassy Sémillon nose. Now rich though gently honeyed, crusty, lanolin; fairly sweet, vanilla, peaches, barley-sugar. Trying hard to be classic and, in 1975, almost succeeding. Last tasted Sept 1989★★★ Nice now to 2000.*

Ch RABAUD-PROMIS *Deepish yellow; very sweet nose and taste. Mint, raisins, syrup of figs. Attractive but headache making. May 1987★★★(★)*

Ch de RAYNE-VIGNEAU *Three notes: pleasant but undeveloped in 1978. Bouquet emerging quite well. Sweet, medium weight, plausible style. Should develop satisfactorily. Not tasted since Sept 1982★★(★)*

Ch RIEUSSEC *Seven notes, starting in 1978. Distinctly deep old gold, orange-tinged; curiously appealing fragrance, spicy apricot; sweet, full-flavoured, concentrated. Very Beerenauslese-like. Idiosyncratic. Very good in its way. Last tasted May 1991★★★(★) Drink now to 2000+*

Ch SIGALAS-RABAUD *Pale, immature, in 1978. Four years later, still green-tinged, raw-nosed though sweet and pleasant on the palate. Last at the* Decanter *tasting, Sept 1982★★★*

Ch SUAU *A Barsac, rarely seen in England. One can see why. Tasted three times in the early 1980s. Palish; grassy; fairly sweet, cherry-like flavour. Could do with more ripeness, more* pourriture *and, perhaps, more new oak? Last tasted April 1983★(★)?*

Ch SUDUIRAUT *Five notes. Impressive in cask, April 1978: deep-coloured, rich. Recently: gloriously fragrant nose, peach, orange blossom,* pourriture*, honey; sweet, full, classic flavour, good length. Should develop further. Last tasted June 1988★★★★(★)? 1995 to mid-21st century.*

Ch La TOUR BLANCHE *Seven notes. First tasted in cask Sept 1976. A bit stalky and unimpressive in the early 1980s. More recently: distinctly pale yellow; a bit raw, though some* pourriture *and honey. Fairly sweet, medium weight, attractive, firm, slightly hard. I have mixed feelings but would like to try it again in five years. Last tasted April 1987★★(★)?*

LESSER GROWTHS OF BARSAC AND SAUTERNES

Noted at the Decanter tasting of '75s in Sept 1982:

Clos HAUT-PEYRAGUEY *Deep, rich ★★(★)*
Les JUSTICES *Straightforward ★(★)*
Ch de MALLE *Too pale; sulphury; sweet, rich ★★(★)*
Ch NAIRAC *Like a sweet Graves ★*
Ch ROMER-DU-HAYOT *Flavoury, needs time ★★(★)*

1976★★★★

A more immediately impressive vintage. Perfect picking conditions, over a period of three weeks at Yquem. Incredibly beautiful in cask. Luscious. Like a precocious child, Shirley Temple, perhaps, who will settle down to normality. Glib, specious. Time will tell.

Ch d'YQUEM *Five notes, first tasted with Alexandre de Lur-Saluces in 1983. One corky bottle in 1986. More recently: medium-deep yellow gold; bouquet blossomed in glass: first citrus and melon, rich, spicy, peaches, apricots, honey; very sweet, powerful and intense, typically highish volatile* *acidity (a level that, for example, the Quebec Liquor Board's quality controllers might find unacceptable), wonderful length, dry zestful finish.* Last tasted Sept 1988****(*). Drink now, if you must. Will continue to develop.

Ch BASTOR-LAMONTAGNE *I bought a useful case of half-bottles and made many notes in the early to mid-1980s. Pleasant enough.* Last tasted Feb 1984**

Ch CLIMENS *Another stunning wine, even sweeter than the '75. Yellow gold with tears or legs like gothic arches; glorious, rich, honeyed nose; fairly full body, alcohol and extract. Marvellously rich yet crisp.* Last tasted Oct 1989****(*)

Ch COUTET *Slightly disappointing. Gentle, unknit, grassy nose, and a touch of peach kernels, which I never like; medium sweetness and body though light style. Fairly high acidity and hard finish.* Last tasted Jan 1990**

Ch de FARGUES *Lur-Saluces puts this wine into old Yquem casks. Golden colour; powerful, high-toned nose; sweetness and body masking high acidity. Excellent flavour.* April 1985***(*)

Ch FILHOT *Very appealing in cask (May 1977), but less impressive, in the early 1980s: palish; fragrant but grassy nose, lacking depth; medium sweetness and weight, a bit of plumpness. Straightforward.* Last tasted May 1983**(*)?

Ch GUIRAUD *Deepish amber gold; apricots; sweet, full, rich. A somewhat beefy, caramelly style.* Tasted only once, Nov 1984**

Ch NAIRAC *I admire the efforts made at this* 2ème cru *Barsac but find the '76 sweetish, alcoholic yet lean and a bit hard, with a swingeing finish.* Sept 1989*

Ch RIEUSSEC *First tasted, from an impressive half-bottle, in 1982. Eight notes later: fabulous colour, a recognisably Rieussec deepish orange gold; glorious bouquet of ripe peaches and cream, honey and a touch of toffee; fairly sweet and full. Rich, soft yet firm. Lovely flavour, good acidity.* Last tasted June 1988****(*)

Ch SUDUIRAUT *Immensely attractive and impressive in cask (April 1978). Most recently, at a Suduiraut tasting in London, Mme Frouin gave me her opinion that it was peaking and that her '75 would be showing best. She was right. Nevertheless, the '76 is a lovely wine: a glowing amber gold; creamy, minty, chocolaty, rich yet refreshing bouquet; fairly sweet, with a beautiful crisp barley-sugar flavour and dry finish.* Last tasted June 1988****

OTHERS NOTED IN THE EARLY 1980s:

*Ch La Brie A Sauternes-type wine from Monbazillac. Grassy, caramelly-rich, a bit coarse. Ch Doisy-Daëne *** Ch Doisy-Védrines *** Ch Liot ** Ch Menota Very deep, rich *** Ch Padouen *** Ch Romer-du-Hayot *** Ch Sigalas-Rabaud ***(*) Ch Trillon Paint-stripper.*

1977

Poor weather. Even the very late picking of a small crop could not produce anything much. Amazing that they can be drinkable at all.

Ch d'YQUEM *Surprisingly positive colour; broad, waxy, touch of greenness with unripe and slightly varnishy underlay; sweet, more body than expected, rich but raw, flavoury, but still hard. Different.* Tasted at the château, Sept 1983*

Ch CLIMENS *Palish, slightly green; nose seemed a bit stewed at first, but a certain harmony apparent; sweet, not at all bad, acidity reasonable. Noted before a Climens promotional wine auction, and later the same year.* Last tasted May 1987*

1978**

A dismal growing season saved by a protracted Indian summer which ripened the grapes but, as in 1970, did not allow *pourriture* to form. Slightly overrated at first — I now assess it as just above mediocre. Perhaps, like the Indian summer, extended bottle-age might transform the best. Anyway, not enough tasted to form a firm opinion.

Ch d'YQUEM *When first tasted at the château in 1983 it was the palest of the vertical range, but positive, with lemon-like acidity. Five years later it had developed a buttercup colour; a curious, sweet, almost soapy nose; medium sweetness and weight, rather hot, still rather raw, lacking length.* Last tasted Feb 1988**

Ch BROUSTET *Pale; scented; sweet, adequate.* May 1991*

Ch CLIMENS *Pale, green-tinged; initially fragrant and floral, then simmered down; sweet, fullish, attractive easy flavour. A bit short.* At the Climens tastings, Jan and May 1987**(*)

Ch COUTET *Palish; low-keyed, warm crusty smell, lanolin and honeycomb; sweet, clean, nice fruitiness, barley-sugar taste, crisp acidity. Needs more time, but encouraging.* Tasted only once, Oct 1984 **(*)?

Ch La RAME *Ste-Croix-du-Mont. Pale; medium-sweet, lightish, fresh, nice acidity. Included merely to demonstrate that a relatively minor wine can go well with foie gras.* At Dr Louis Skinner's in Florida, Jan 1987**

Ch SUDUIRAUT *Four notes from mid-1980s. Most recent: palish straw yellow, still green-tinged; sulphur dioxide wore off but, though attractive, the 80% Sémillon and 20% Sauvignon Blanc not yet married. Nevertheless, rich, honeyed, asparagus, piquant, curranty, vanilla and nectarines — quite a cocktail on the nose; fairly sweet, lanolin and honey, but though flavoury, with a dash of peach kernels which are not to my taste. Lacking length.* Last tasted June 1984**(*) Not for the 21st century.

MINOR WINES TASTED IN THE EARLY 1980s

Ch COULLAC *Ste-Croix du Mont. Sweet, short.*

Ch GUITERONDE *Grassy, sweet, light, kernelly* **

Ch de la JAUBERTIE *A fragrant well-made Monbazillac* ***

Ch LOUPIAC-GAUDIET *Sweet, honeyed, pleasing* ***

Ch PADOUEN *Odd nose, over-oaked and over sulphured. Sweetness and acidity. Might have settled down by now* *(*)?

Ch de VAYRES *Good in its class* ***

1979***

Another late harvest, but with *pourriture noble*. As different in character from 1978 as the '79 to '78 Médocs. A good enough vintage but no more, though bottle-age will help.

*Ch d'*YQUEM *More charm, fat and assertiveness than the '78. Nose low-keyed when first poured, but grew in the glass. Sweet, fullish; fair length. A caramelly shortbread-like flavour and endtaste. Still a bit hard.* Last tasted Jan 1990**(*)

Ch CLIMENS *Rich yellow gold; waxy Sémillon, grassy, herbaceous; sweet, fairly powerful, peach kernel flavour and finish noted consistently. Rather clumsy for Climens.* Last tasted Nov 1989***

Ch COUTET *Highly polished appearance; honeycomb wax (80% Sémillon), fragrant, fruity — apricots, pineapple — mouthwatering (the 20% Sauvignon including a dash of Muscadelle); sweet, very attractive, reasonably long on the palate.* Last tasted May 1988***(*)

Ch COUSTET *(Note the 's'. A minor Barsac). Vanilla; sweetish, lightish, pleasant.* Jan 1986**

Ch de FARGUES *Yellow; the smell reminded me of duck-egg custard; sweet, fullish, rich, positive. With pâté de foie gras at lunch after the tasting at Yquem.* Sept 1983***

Ch FILHOT *(65% Sémillon, 33% Sauvignon Blanc, 2% Muscadelle). Palish yellow; honey, wax, crisply acidic and Muscadelle grapiness noticeable; fairly sweet, fleshy, fruity, lovely tingling acidity.* Last tasted March 1989***(*)

Ch GUIRAUD *Fairly intense, and of an old-fashioned style, almost chocolaty, when first noted in 1983. Five notes later: now medium-deep amber gold; good, rich, slightly caramelly nose and taste. Sweet and pleasant enough. Lemon vanilla flavour, good aftertaste.* Last tasted Jan 1991***

Ch LAFAURIE-PEYRAGUEY *Plump* pourriture *nose; sweet, nice flavour and flesh. Good length. After several years of well-made but rather light wines, the '79 a bit more my style.* June 1987***(*)

Ch LARRIVAT *Ste-Croix-du-Mont. Pale; oily, minty; fairly sweet, very pleasant flavour and weight. Good acidity.* Jan 1990***

Ch de MALLE *Pale, bright; sweet but 'Gripfix' glue paste nose; sweet, flavoury, curiously interesting.* Last tasted July 1986*(*)

Ch RAYMOND-LAFON *Lightly honeyed; sweet, nicely plump, good length, violet/peach kernel aftertaste.* Last tasted April 1987**

Ch de RAYNE-VIGNEAU *Palish yellow; grassy, honeyed, rich nose; fairly sweet, crisp, peach kernels again (I am told this is correct, so a matter of taste I suppose). It always makes me think of unsuitable fining agents.* July 1985*

Ch RIEUSSEC *Three consistent, perhaps overcritical, notes in the mid-1980s. Bright gold; rich, assertive but unknit; fairly sweet, fullish, fat, lacking finesse, length and finish.* Last tasted Sept 1984*(**)

Ch SUDUIRAUT *Rather pale, Lafaurie-like; the bouquet seems to be uncertain and struggling; fairly sweet and full, rich, rather obvious, still a bit hard. Dry finish. Give it time.* Last tasted June 1988*(**)?

THREE MINOR WINES

Tasted in the early 1980s:

Ch LOUPIAC-GAUDIET *Yellow gold; fairly sweet, fruity, very attractive and outstanding value* ***

Ch PADOUEN *Sweet, honeyed* **

Ch ST-AMAND *Sweet and quite stylish* **(*)

1980**

Terrible spring and early summer resulting in poor, prolonged flowering. July cold and wet, Aug hot, Sept cold and wet again. Sauternes saved by a sunny and dry 'back season' in late Oct, early Nov.

A light, not too serious Sauternes vintage, but some quite nice wines made. They will improve in bottle, but not for long keeping.

*Ch d'*YQUEM *Bright yellow; minty, quince peaches, barley-sugar, vanilla and a touch of caramel — and taste to match. Fairly sweet, and richer than expected.* Last tasted April 1991**

Ch CLIMENS *Green gold, deeper than the '82 and '83; a forthcoming, almost opulent nose of some depth. My notes range from medium-sweet to very sweet, which must reflect the context. More forthcoming and richer than one might expect of an '80. Fair length, crisp acidity.* Last tasted Nov 1988**(*)

Ch de FARGUES *Surprisingly attractive nose and taste. Sweet. Light.* Feb 1990**

Ch FILHOT *Pale; grassy, herbaceous nose, crisp, honeyed; straightforward, sweet enough (Filhot is never cloying), quite attractive flavour, waxy, crisp. But I did not anticipate a great future.* Tasted only once, Oct 1984**

Ch GUIRAUD *Yellow; mint; sweetish, lightish, touch of caramel, short, and a touch too much end acidity.* Dec 1989*

Ch PADOUEN *A lot of experimentation and effort being made at this 10 ha vineyard property. Picking commenced Oct 5, small crop, quite a lot of rot. Bunches bench-sorted and destalked, the 'green' grapes becoming Bordeaux blanc. Nevers and Limousin oak tried. Tasting note: palish; grassy; medium-sweet, fairly light, nice flavour, short. Not a very encouraging vintage but it will be interesting to see how this, and more important years at Padouen, will develop.* Oct 1982*(*)

Ch de RAYNE-VIGNEAU *How the mighty have fallen. Even allowing for the vintage, very pale; sulphury, 'blown'; sweetish, on the light side, no finish. Little to it.* April 1985.

Ch RIEUSSEC Crème de Tête. *Rather hard, dusty, whiff of acetone nose; medium sweetness, rich, quite nice flavour but a bit of a kick at the rear. Slightly raw acidity. See below. Sept 1984*★★?

Ch RIEUSSEC *Second wine. Lower-keyed, more waxy than the* Crème de Tête. *Paradoxically, sweeter and richer, with nice acidity. Much preferred. Both tasted at the château with Eric de Rothschild and Professor Peynaud. The Domaines Rothschild had taken a major interest in Rieussec, Sept 1984.*

Ch SUDUIRAUT *Piquant Sauvignon and waxy Sémillon only just coming together on the nose; sweet, pleasant flavour and better balance than expected. Tasted only once, March 1984*★(★★)?

1981★★

A hot summer resulted in high sugar levels. 'Noble rot' well developed, and good late harvest. Rather like the reds, a little on the lean side and by no means great. Very satisfactory for the mid-term, say 1995 to 2010.

Ch d'YQUEM *Very bright, green-tinged gold; extraordinary nose: lemon, lanolin, herbaceous, scented, spicy; sweet, medium-full body, spicy flavour, good length, fairly high end acidity. Needs time to settle down and develop. Last tasted June 1988*★(★★★)? *Think about drinking in five to eight years.*

Ch CLIMENS *Five notes. Consistent reference to lovely texture. Palish; forthcoming grassy nose, yet after 30 minutes in the glass, complete, rich; medium-sweet, nice touch of plumpness; good fruit and acidity. Attractive. Last tasted April 1991*★★(★★)

Ch COUTET *Very attractive nose; lovely flavour. Even better than Climens. July 1989*★★★(★)

Ch FILHOT *Palish; sweetish, light, quite nice. May 1989*★★

Ch GUIRAUD *Grassy nose and taste. Fairly sweet, and medium full-bodied. I found it soft in 1983 yet a bit hard and bitter-ended four years later. Must try it again. Last tasted July 1987*★★?

Ch LAFAURIE-PEYRAGUEY *Three notes. Still rather pale and green-tinged; forthcoming, creamy yet crisply acidic barley-sugar and pineapple nose; sweet, some flesh and fat, grassy, refreshing acidity. Last tasted July 1990*★★(★)

Ch de MALLE *Lovely waxy lemon gold; honeyed but kernelly and sulphury; sweet, rich, fat, spoiled a little for me by its peach kernels endtaste. July 1990*★★

Ch de RAYNE-VIGNEAU *Pale; nose reminds me of watercress. Pleasant enough. Oct 1989*★(★★)?

Ch RIEUSSEC *Six recent notes. Pure gold; crisp, mustard and cress, celery-like nose; sweet, fullish, rich, slightly kernelly, honeyed* pourriture, *waxy Sémillon, crisp Sauvignon. Last tasted May 1991*★★★(★)

Ch ROMER-DU-HAYOT *Two recent notes. Traces of carbon dioxide, palish warm gold; honey and cress; medium sweetness, rather light, curious upturned flavour, hot, slightly bitter acidic finish. Last tasted July 1990*★

1982★★★

June and July pleasantly warm, Aug to mid-Sept very hot resulting in grapes with a very high sugar content. The weather then changed, enabling *Botrytis* to form. However, hopes of a great Sauternes were dashed by torrential rain which washed the *Botrytis* away. Sweet but sodden grapes were picked in appalling weather. Some growers picked ripe grapes before the rain, some hung on until much later. Some substantial wines made, but all lack the touch of 'noble rot'.

Ch d'YQUEM *Because of the ripeness and high sugar content, Yquem started picking Sept 16, but after the 24th the weather was terrible and later grapes not used. The wine was three and a half years in new oak. A rich and enticing golden colour; honeyed but not a very clear-cut nose, vanilla and peaches; sweet, fairly full-bodied, considerable fat and weight, good length, highish acidity. Needs time. Last tasted Sept 1988*★★(★★)

Ch CLIMENS *Lovely colour, pure yellow; a bit on the hefty side though nice supporting honey and fruit. Developed a liquorice-like fragrance. Sweet, fullish, good solid four-square character, yet rich, good flesh and length. A touch of caramel and hard edge. Needs time but will never catch up with the '83. Last tasted May 1987*★★(★★) *Say 1995–2000+*

Ch GUIRAUD *Seemed attractive when tasted in cask. Sept 1983.*

Ch LAFAURIE-PEYRAGUEY *A pleasant half-bottle consumed not long after bottling. Sugary sweet, fat, but clumsier than the '83. Dry finish. Dec 1985*★★(★)

Ch LAMOTHE *Pale; unknit; sweet, quite powerful, good length. July 1986*★★(★)

Ch RAYMOND-LAFON *Sweet, full, very alcoholic. July 1986*★(★★)

Ch RIEUSSEC *Waxy nose; fairly sweet, hefty, rich, soft, gentle, with taste of caramel and peach kernels. Last tasted May 1991*★★★

Ch ST-AMAND *Palish; barley-sugar nose; sweet, fairly powerful, pleasant. June 1986*★★(★).

Ch SUDUIRAUT *Roasted grapes, picked exceptionally early (Sept 16). Alcoholic content 14%. Sweet, hefty, flavour of mint leaves and cinnamon, good length and acidity. June 1988*★★(★)

Ch SUDUIRAUT *'Cuvée Madame'. Grapes picked towards the end of this early harvest, on Sept 26. Richer, more harmonious nose than the standard* cuvées*; sweet, rich and powerful. Very good flavour and lengths. June 1988*★★(★★★)

1983★★★★★

Perfect weather conditions, with an Indian summer lasting until mid-Nov enabling some châteaux, such as Suduiraut, to comb their vineyards up to six times to select well advanced *Botrytis*-endowed grapes.

No question about it, a marvellous Sauternes vintage: the best between 1975 and

1988. Full of flavour, fruit, finesse. Rich, vibrant, long-lasting.

Ch d'YQUEM *The youngest vintage at Bud Moon's remarkable vertical tasting of Yquem in Feb 1988: very bright buttercup yellow; lanolin and vanilla, rich, fragrant, honeyed* Botrytis *character; sweet but not intensely sweet, medium weight, crisp orange blossom flavour. More recently: glorious peachy bouquet; excellent length, perfection. Last tasted at a luncheon hosted by Tony Terlato of Paterno Imports, Chicago, Feb 1990***** Years of life ahead.*

Ch CLIMENS *Six notes since 1984. Still rather pale; sweet, creamy nose, lovely, fruity, slightly spicy (new oak), with positive and powerful underpinning. Developed beautifully in the glass. Sweet but not overpoweringly so. A nice weight and feel despite its alcoholic content. Last tasted May 1991***(*)*

Ch DOISY-VEDRINES *Palish yellow gold; light, sulphury, unknit as yet; moderately sweet, nice flavour, rather hot acid finish. Oct 1984*(**)*

Ch FILHOT *Yellow gold; sweet, with the blackcurrant smell of Sauvignon and gentle honeyed waxiness of Sémillon; on the palate, sweet, fullish, nice flesh, excellent crisp flavour and length. A really good Filhot (I nearly added, at last). March 1987***(*)*

Ch GUIRAUD *Pale; grassy, slightly common and artificial, burnt matchstick-like sulphur; sweet, fullish, assertive, good length. Better on palate. Needs time to settle down. Last tasted Oct 1987*(**)?*

Clos HAUT-PEYRAGUEY *Fairly rich, soft, sweet, grassy (mustard and cress) flavour. May 1987***

Ch Les JUSTICES *Sweetish. Nice acidity. June 1987**(*)*

Clos LABERE *The second wine of Rieussec. Very good colour, nose and flavour. Just lacking the length and finish of the* grand vin. *Tasted June 1987***

Ch LAFAURIE-PEYRAGUEY *Nose like toasted marshmallows; fairly sweet and full, nice crisp style and length. Tasted only once, Dec 1985*(***)*

Ch de MALLE *Fat, waxy, unknit; medium-sweet, unusual, pasty, powdery flavour. Touch of bitterness. Last tasted April 1991**

Ch NAIRAC *Palish; fragrant, peach kernels; sweetish, light for an '83, crisp, almond finish. April 1991***

Ch RABAUD-PROMIS *Two recent notes. Attractive. Fairly deep yellow gold; agreeable barley-sugar nose; fairly sweet, rich, good acidity. Last tasted Sept 1989****

Ch de RAYNE-VIGNEAU *Four notes. Fragrant; fairly sweet, quite powerful, lovely flavour, good length and aftertaste. Last tasted June 1987**(**) Needs time.*

Ch RIEUSSEC *Tasted four times in the autumn of 1984: two* cuvées *at the château, quite different. One had a rather ordinary nose, stuffed with sulphur and spicy new oak; very sweet, positive, attractive. The 'special' was deeper coloured, more orange; hard, alcoholic, not quite as sweet, lively, powerful, with taste of boiled sweets. Then, during lunch at Lafite, delightful despite its youthfulness. In 1990, a glorious duck-egg custard nose; fleshy, still hard about the midriff, with a touch of tangerine on the finish. Most recently, orange; showing age, almost Tokay-like; hefty, barley-sugar. Last tasted June 1991***(*)*

Ch ROMER-DU-HAYOT *A waxy-sheened yellow gold; equally smooth waxy texture. Attractive bouquet though a touch of peach kernels and kerosene; sweet, crisp acidity. Oct 1989**(*)*

Ch SUDUIRAUT *Picking began relatively early, Sept 26, due to its high natural sugar content (306 gr/litre). Palish gold; crisp, honeyed, nutty bouquet; sweet, assertive, trace of almond paste in flavour, good length, dry finish. Needs time. Last tasted Sept 1988**(**) 1995–2025*

1984★★

This was the year that Merlot failed; but clearly not Sémillon and Sauvignon Blanc. Until I had assembled a few notes, I hadn't realised that the '84 Sauternes are better than I had expected. Not classic, not for long keeping, but for pleasant mid-term drinking.

Ch d'YQUEM* *Rich, slightly minty, honeyed and quite harmonious nose; sweet, fullish, good fat and, to my surprise, a lovely and lengthy flavour. At the château, June 1989**(*) 1994–2000+*

Les CYPRES DE CLIMENS *Palish; waxy; sweet, firm, quite a bite. May 1987**(*) 1994–2000.*

Ch de FARGUES *Palish, lovely; very light, waxy, honeyed nose; sweet, medium body, very attractive, very good acidity. June 1989**(*) 1994–2000*

Ch LAFAURIE-PEYRAGUEY *Palish yellow gold, watery rim; sweet, rich, some honeyed* Botrytis, *butterscotch, herbaceous; sweet, fullish, some fat but a slightly woody taste and youthful acidity. From a sample half-bottle, Dec 1985. Hard to judge. Probably **(*) like the others.*

Ch SUDUIRAUT *Palish; crisp, 'green', minty; fairly sweet and full-bodied, dry mint-leaf finish. June 1988**(*)*

Ch La TOUR BLANCHE *Rather tinny, hollow nose; touch of bitterness which will probably wear off. Not particularly impressive. Try again. Oct 1986.*

1985★★★

Paradoxically, the weather was too good; certainly too dry for Sauternes, the lack of humidity preventing the formation of *Botrytis* until Oct.

Ch d'YQUEM *Already harmonious, creamy, peachlike; sweet, medium-full, very good flavour, good acidity and dry finish. June 1989**(**)*

Ch BROUSTET *Pale, slightly green tinge; fairly neutral nose; moderately sweet, moderately full, soft, with interesting mint chocolate flavour. April 1987***

* *From 1984, to prevent forgery and fraud, labels watermarked with specks which can only be seen under ultra-violet light.*

Ch FRANCOYE *Loupiac. I had never come across this wine before, but its being bottled by or for Anthony Barton, and shipped by The Wine Society, was reassurance enough. Very pale; light, slightly minty nose; sweet, lightish, with a very appealing slightly scented flavour and fragrant vanilla finish. At an IW & FS dinner at Vinton's, Coral Gables, Jan 1990****

Ch GUIRAUD *Palish; lanolin and mint; very sweet, minty, fruity flavour, crisp, acidity. Tasted twice, April 1987*(**)*

Ch de RAYNE-VIGNEAU *Medium-pale; light and quite attractive minty 'tom-cats' (Sauvignon) aroma; very sweet. April 1987*(**)*

Ch RIEUSSEC *Walnuts and barley-sugar, some depth; fairly sweet, rich, nice texture and acidity, with peach kernelly flavour and aftertaste. Jan 1989**(*)*

Ch SUDUIRAUT *Pale; medium sweetness and body. June 1988.*

1986★★★★

Unlike 1985, conditions were ideal in the autumn of 1986, with later autumn sunshine and morning mists to form 'noble rot'.

The majority of recent notes were made at a blind tasting organised by *Wine* magazine in Oct 1990. A very satisfactory vintage. Needs time.

Ch BROUSTET *Buttercup yellow; sweet, honeyed fruit, still somewhat unknit; sweet, fullish, assertive, somewhat piquant. Good for its class. Oct 1990***

Ch CLIMENS *Bottle variation, one not quite right, the second with heavy honeyed nose; sweet, assertive, boiled sweets, still a bit hard but with good aftertaste. Oct 1990**(**)*

Ch COUTET *Grassy, cress-like nose though hefty with honey underlay; very sweet for Coutet, fairly full-bodied, some fat, crisp, lacking the length expected and rather a hard acidic finish. Oct 1990*(**) Probably improve with bottle-age.*

Ch DOISY-DAENE *Three recent notes. Pale, greenish tinge, watery rim; honey and fruit, some depth but unknit; medium-sweet, lighter weight and style, gentle fruit and cress flavour, a touch of acidity. Tailed off. Last tasted June 1991***

Ch DOISY-VEDRINES *Two recent notes: good, fairly 'hot', alcoholic nose, sublimated honey, some depth; sweet, nice weight, good crisp minty flavour, acidity and length. Nice wine. Last tasted Oct 1990***(*)*

Ch Le DRAGON *Three notes: good yellow colour; forthcoming, minty nose; sweet, attractive mint leaf and honeycomb flavour. Last tasted Sept 1989**(*)*

Ch FILHOT *Very grassy, herbaceous nose and taste. I thought it was Lafaurie. But good depth, honeyed* Botrytis, *decent finish. A bit hard. Will benefit from more bottle-age. Oct 1990**(*)*

Ch GUIRAUD *Fairly consistent notes. Soft yellow colour; lovely floral fragrance, crisp, honeyed, delicate, touch of Muscatelle; flavour to match. Sweet, delicately poised, dry finish. Last tasted Oct 1990***(*)*

Ch LAFAURIE-PEYRAGUEY *Classic, harmonious, waxy bouquet of some depth which will evolve further, given time; very sweet, full of body and flavour, fat and rich — a great improvement on the light grassy style of some earlier vintages. Barley-sugar taste, length and aftertaste. My highest rating in the blind tasting of 24 '86 Sauternes and Barsacs held by* Wine *magazine. Oct 1990****(*)*

Ch de MALLE *An attractive cask sample in April 1987: lovely flavour, good length and acidity. Two recent notes: crisp, minty, tea-like nose. Fairly sweet, classic, waxy, honeyed flavour but a bit raw. Not too keen on its finish. I gather this was the handiwork of a new winemaker. Will be interesting to see how this copes with bottle-age and whether future vintages will show an improvement. Last tasted Oct 1990*(*)*

Ch NAIRAC *Not very impressed in May 1988: honey and sulphur on nose; rather artificial, boiled sweets taste. Two recent notes confirm my reservations. An unusual, appley, slightly woody nose, not like Barsac at all; one bottle distinctly woody, the other fresher. Flavour not bad. Last tasted Oct 1990*?*

Ch de RAYNE-VIGNEAU *Even a cask sample was lovely to drink. In May 1988 I noted a classic sweet Sémillon/Sauvignon nose, herbaceous; very sweet, a hefty, rather obvious wine. At the recent blind tasting, I thought the nose strange, a kerosene oiliness though it had an attractive barley-sugar flavour. Alas, inconclusive. I must retaste. Last noted Oct 1990. Probably****

Ch RIEUSSEC *Although very sweet, rich and full-bodied, I detected an oiliness on the nose and touch of peach kernel stalkiness on the palate. Must re-taste. A half-bottle sample, Oct 1990.*

Ch SUDUIRAUT *Two admiring notes in the summer of 1988: palish and slightly lean style for Suduiraut; very fragrant, floral, tea and mint; sweet, crisp, honeyed. Most recently: taking on colour; very distinctive soft peach and apricot bouquet, with flavour to match. Fleshy yet delicate. Good length. Dry finish. Last tasted Oct 1990***(*)*

OTHERS TASTED ONLY ONCE, IN OCT 1990

*Ch d'*ARCHE *Very positive, honeyed, minty nose, needs bottle-age; sweet, nice weight, soft, reasonably long. Dry finish ****

Ch CAILLOU *Pale yellow; herbaceous, unknit; sweet, soft, quite pleasant ***

Ch DOISY-DUBROCA *Very distinctive nose, rich, honeyed; sweet, a rich, assertive mouthful, good length, butterscotch aftertaste. Good for its class and deserves to be better known ****

Clos HAUT-PEYRAGUEY *Light herbaceous style; sweet, soft, a bit short and flat **

Ch LAMOTHE-GUIGNARD *Very Germanic nose, more like a Rhine Riesling; sweet, light, soft, quite nice. Rather hard acidic finish *(*)*

Ch RABAUD-PROMIS *Soft, pleasant, harmonious, clover honey fragrance; fairly sweet, lovely delicacy of flavour, light style, good finish. Very agreeable ***(*)*

Ch ROMER-DU-HAYOT *Lovely, sweet, broad, glowing bouquet of some depth; sweet, medium-full, very flavoury, good length and finish* ★★★★

Ch SUAU *Palish yellow; low-keyed, waxy, honeyed, butterscotch nose; sweet, soft, pleasant flavour, reasonable length, good acidity. Finished a bit hard* ★★★

Ch La TOUR BLANCHE *I thought I detected mercaptan amidst its sweet, honey and pineapple nose; very sweet, fairly full and fat. Needs more time in bottle* ★★(★)?

1987

Unfavourable weather conditions. Not a Sauternes vintage.

SAUTERNES, BARON PHILIPPE Pale; peachy, pleasant; fairly sweet, lightish, good flavour, balance and acidity. New to me, and surprising. Dec 1989★★

1988★★★★★

A hot dry summer and early autumn ensured fully ripe grapes with an exceptionally high sugar content. Humid conditions in early Oct encouraged the formation of 'noble rot' and a balmy Indian summer enabled growers to harvest perfect grapes to make great classic Sauternes. A fairly wide range tasted in April 1989. It was a bit too early for some of the wines, but confirmed as an outstanding vintage.

Ch BROUSTET *A very sweet though bitter cask sample in April 1989. One year later: still fairly pale and green-tinged; gentle, honeyed nose; powerful, hard and peppery. Needs time.* Last tasted April 1990★★★ 1993–2000

Ch CLIMENS *Impressively deep, highly polished, yellow gold; a heavyweight: hefty, buttery nose, honeyed, distinct peachy fragrance; very sweet, full-bodied, rich, barley-sugar flavour, great intensity, length and aftertaste.* April 1989★★★★★

Ch DOISY-DUBROCA *Showing well in cask, April 1989. Palish, bright; fragrant, minty; very sweet, fullish, fat for this class of Barsac, crisp, firm, honeyed, dryish though flowery finish. Good fruit, length and potential.* Last tasted April 1990★★★★

Ch GUIRAUD *Although a cask sample in April 1989 was not bright, its nose was glorious, and immense sweetness and body showed great potential. A year later, confirmation: honey,* Botrytis, *pineapple, power. A wine to buy and to keep.* Last tasted April 1990★★★★ Possibly five star 1994–2010

Ch LAFAURIE-PEYRAGUEY *Fragrant, honeyed but unknit; very sweet, crisp full flavour, some fat and a sweet finish.* April 1989★★★★ 1994–2010

Ch de MALLE *Still slightly cloudy; very good though lacking a little length.* Unready for tasting in spring 1989.

Ch NAIRAC *Unready cask sample. Most recently, pale gold; little nose; medium-sweet, fairly light body and style. Good crisp acidity. A pleasant enough middle-term wine.* Last tasted April 1990(★★) 1992–97

Ch de RAYNE-VIGNEAU *Immensely impressive cask sample: deepish yellow gold; lovely honeyed* pourriture, *peach-like; also very sweet, full, rich, glorious flavour, pineapple and honey, high extract, fat, acidity. Confirmed 12 months later. Powerful. Spicy.* Last tasted April 1990(★★★★★) 1995–2020

Ch SUDUIRAUT *Three notes. Slightly cloudy and bitter cask sample but clearly a massively impressive wine. A year later: distinct golden tinge; forthcoming, excellent, honey and mint nose, exuding power in all directions. Sweet, loads of grip. Needs plenty of bottle-age. Confirmed recently.* Last tasted June 1991(★★★★★) 1995–2020

1989★★★★★

Another exceptional year. The summer heat-wave concentrated the sugars and Sept's early morning mists provided perfect conditions for *Botrytis*. Those who picked early, not wishing to risk a change in the weather, were able to make good, rich wines. Those who waited made wines of exceptional richness, richer even than the excellent '88s. Most are still hard, needing bottle-age.

The following notes were made at three recent tastings: one a selection from Justerini & Brooks who provided a basic analysis of each wine (alcoholic content, acidity, residual sugar), another with the Union des Grands Crus in Bordeaux, and the third organised by the Hungerford Wine Company, in March, April and June 1991 respectively.

*Ch d'*ARCHE *Medium yellow; hard, cress-like; medium-sweet, lightish weight and style, good acidity.* At Hungerford Wine tasting, June 1991(★★★) 1993–98. Drink now!

Ch BASTOR-LAMONTAGNE *Palish, slight green tinge; ripe, creamy, clover honey; sweet, fullish, very fruity, apricots, youthful pineapple.* Last tasted June 1991(★★★★) 1984–2000

Ch BROUSTET *Pale; low-keyed, grassy; fairly sweet, fullish, distinctive, fragrant. A bit short.* Last tasted June 1991(★★★) 1994–99

Ch CLIMENS *Three notes: up to its usual high standard. Paler than expected but lovely, shimmering; luscious, honeyed, bacon fat, harmonious; very sweet, full body, extract, flavour (alcohol 14.1%, acidity 5.10, residual sugar 112). Taste of apricots, ripe peach, butterscotch, assertive, great length, lovely texture and aftertaste.* Last tasted June 1991(★★★★★) 1995–2010

Ch COUTET *Yellow green; forthcoming, melon, grapefruit, honey; very sweet, fullish, lovely flavour and flesh, peachy, good length, aftertaste (13.5%, 4.60, 102).* March 1991(★★★★★) 1995–2010

Ch DOISY-DAENE *Palish; crisp fruit and* Botrytis; *very sweet, fullish, flavoury, barley-sugar.* June 1991(★★★★) 1994 to beyond 2000.

Ch DOISY-VEDRINES *Flowery, lanolin, peaches, honey; very sweet, full, luscious, excellent balance fruit and acidity. Fragrant.* Last tasted June 1991(★★★★★) 1994–2010

Ch FILHOT *Palish; cress, slight peach kernels; medium sweet, lean, crisp.* June 1991(**) 1992–98

Ch GUIRAUD *High-toned,* fraise du bois, *floral, clover honey; sweet, fairly full-bodied, good length and acidity.* Last tasted June 1991(***) 1994–2000

Ch LAFAURIE-PEYRAGUEY *Half-bottle sample from J & B. One of the deepest: yellow gold; fragrant, herbaceous, slightly smoky, depth; very sweet, full, powerful, hefty, four-square, toast oak endtaste (15.5%, 3.90, 106).* Last tasted April 1991(****)? 1996–2010+

Ch LAMOTHE-GUIGNARD *Scented; sweet, fullish.* June 1991(***) 1993–98

Ch LIOT *Rich, grassy Sauvignon Blanc; medium-sweet, better flavour than nose. Some coarseness.* June 1991(**) 1993–98

Ch de MALLE *Three notes. Palish; minty, unusual scent, ripe melon, fresh mint leaf, fulsome* Botrytis*; fairly sweet, full, rich waxy. Hot finish.* Last tasted June 1991(***) 1994–2000

Ch NAIRAC *Very scented, hyacinth, melon; sweet, extraordinary, unclassic, attractive but tails off.* Last tasted June 1991(***)? 1993–98

Ch RABAUD-PROMIS *Palish; lightly honeyed, vanilla; sweet, lightish, crisp fruit, lacking depth and conviction (13.8%, 4.00, 110).* March 1991(**) 1993–98

Ch de RAYNE-VIGNEAU *Slight haze; closed, peachy, then like milk chocolate; fairly sweet, fullish, delicacy of flavour, good length.* April 1991(***) 1994–2000+

Ch RIEUSSEC *Yellow; sweet, herbaceous, touch of 'greenness'; sweet, fullish, rich, good length and acidity (14.5%, 4.10, 101).* Last tasted June 1991(****) 1994–2010

Ch SIGALAS-RABAUD *Very fragrant, honeyed* Botrytis*; fairly sweet, crisp.* June 1991(***) 1994–2000+

Ch SUDUIRAUT *Waxy yellow; lovely, honeyed, peach, classic; very sweet, full-bodied and fat yet elegant, good length, finish.* Last tasted June 1991(*****) 1995–2010+

1990★★★★★

Not since 1928/9 has there been another twin Sauternes vintage like this and the '89. A hot dry summer concentrated the sugar, then Aug rain induced *Botrytis*. Overall the highest sugar content since 1929. My notes made at two tastings, the first organised by the Union des Grands Crus at Ch de Malle in April, the second by the Hungerford Wine Company in June 1991.

Ch d'YQUEM *Alas, the Comte de Lur-Saluces no longer permits tasting in cask.*

Ch d'ARCHE *Rich, bright; harmonious, waxy Sémillon; sweet, fullish, rich, crisp.* June 1991(****) 1995–2005

Ch BASTOR LAMONTAGNE *Palish; lovely, flowery, harmonious,* Botrytis*; very sweet, full, intense, rich.* June 1991(****) 1995–2010

Ch BROUSTET *Medium yellow; lovely, honeyed, rich, scented; very sweet, lightish style, crisp, delicious.* Last tasted June 1991(****) 1994–2010

Ch CLIMENS *Alas, not considered ready for tasting.*

Ch COUTET *Not tasted but good reports.*

Ch DOISY-DAENE *Richly coloured; low-keyed, a bit soapy; sweet, powerful, good length, aftertaste. Impressive but lacks finesse.* June 1991**** 1995–2010

Ch DOISY-VEDRINES *Palish; fragrant, crisp, grassy, Sauvignon Blanc uppermost; medium sweetness and weight, flavour, good acidity.* Last tasted June 1991(****) 1994–2000+

Ch FILHOT *Palish, green-tinged; grassy, Sauvignon; medium sweet, fullish, lean, flavoury, good length and aftertaste.* June 1991(***) 1994–2000

Ch GUIRAUD *Unready, hard though rich in the spring of 1991. Medium yellow; now very rich, slightly chocolaty, depth; very sweet, powerful wine.* Last tasted June 1991(****) 1995–2010

Ch LAFAURIE-PEYRAGUEY *Deep yellow gold, marvellous sheen; high-toned, floral, fragrant; intensely sweet, full, heady, assertive, impressive. Totally different from the light grassy style of yesteryear.* April 1991(*****) 1996–2010

Ch LAMOTHE-GUIGNARD *Richly coloured; light, toasted Sémillon; very sweet, powerful.* June 1991(****) 1994 to beyond 2000.

Ch LIOT *Palish, cress; medium sweet.* June 1991(**) 1992–97

Ch de MALLE *Fairly deep green gold; lusciously rich, honeyed, apricot; very sweet, fat, fleshy, assertive, flavoury. Surely the best ever?* Last tasted June 1991(****) 1993–2010

Ch NAIRAC *Pineapple, honey, boiled sweets; fairly sweet, crisp, flavoury.* Last tasted June 1991(***) 1994–2000

Ch de RAYNE-VIGNEAU *In April 1991 subdued, smell like skin of rice pudding; full, alcoholic, herbaceous, lacking charm. More recently hard, almost woody nose, taste of gravy.* Last tasted June 1991 ??

Ch RIEUSSEC *Pale for a change; rich, ripe; sweet, crisp, flavoury.* June 1991(****) 1994–2000+

Ch SIGALAS-RABAUD *Palish, green-tinged; curious, boiled sweets; very sweet, rich, powerful.* June 1991(***) 1994–2000

Ch SUDUIRAUT *Buttery gold; dumb at first, then mint leaf, honeyed, scented, lilies; fairly sweet, full-bodied, positive, needs time.* Last tasted June 1991(*****) 1996–2010+

Ch La TOUR BLANCHE *Palish; grassy, hard; very sweet, full, assertive, good acidity.* June 1991(****) 1995–2010

RED
BURGUNDY

Hospices de Beaune

Burgundy is a minefield: challenging, infuriating, unpredictable, often disappointing, most often misunderstood. If claret at its best appeals to the head, burgundy appeals to the heart. It must, I believe, be approached with an open mind, neither using Bordeaux as a touchstone, nor in comparison with Pinot Noirs from elsewhere. The Pinot Noir is one of, if not the most difficult and fickle of all the 'noble' grape varieties. Moreover, in Burgundy the soil and climate differ from that in Bordeaux, California or Oregon. It is still a tight community, where, despite technological advances, traditions are handed down from one generation to the next. The vineyard plots are small, sometimes just strips of vines, each strip under different ownership. One man's vines might be older, with different subsoil and better drainage; he will tend his vines in his own way, pick and ferment in his own time. He might make and market his own wine, or sell his grapes or newly made wine to a merchant. The permutations are endless. All of which militate against a complete knowledge of burgundy, even if one has lived there for generations. Recommending wines without prior tasting is hazardous, for there can be no definitive guide to the wines of Burgundy.

On tasting burgundy

Perhaps the most misunderstood feature of red burgundy is its colour or, more specifically, its not infrequent lack of colour. On occasion, as with some '82s, the heading "*red* burgundy" seems inappropriate. Given that all red wine derives its pigmentation from the skin of black grapes, the relative paleness of burgundy must therefore be attributed, first and foremost, to the grape. The Pinot Noir variety, particularly some modern clones, has a relatively thin skin. Moreover, it is susceptible to grey rot, which affects the pigment. Speedy fermentation can also reduce the time of colour extraction, though the deep-coloured wines of the past were due less to prolonged fermentation than to blending with more robust and colourful wines from the Rhône and elsewhere. Uncontestably, the high yields of some recent vintages have had a diluting effect. For those used to claret and New World Cabernet Sauvignons, a pale colour and watery rim looks unconvincing and off-putting. Misleading too, for the wine itself can, in fact, be remarkably high in alcohol and extract. To sum up, do not expect the appearance of red burgundy to be deep, or very red. Also, a practical tip: make due allowance for the size and shape of glass. *Any* red wine will look relatively pale and very translucent in a traditional broad-bowled burgundy glass.

Next, the nose. The smell is frequently difficult to grasp, and will not necessarily evolve in the glass. Though the Pinot Noir aroma is often more obvious than that of Cabernet Sauvignon, it might only reach its apotheosis – vivid, intensely fragrant, earthy yet sublime – in say, La Tâche, just as the *cassis*-like Cabernet will be most dramatic in a first-growth claret like Mouton-Rothschild. Do not anticipate a pronounced Pinot Noir aroma: the smell of burgundy is sometimes neither fruity nor flowery; more frequently it is earthy, beetroot-like, more vegetal, even bush-like, reminiscent of bramble, hawthorn.

In my experience, red burgundy's major feature is taste, in particular the peculiar ability of the flavour to expand in the mouth, filling every part of the palate, and, after swallowing, releasing a fragrant aftertaste. It is sweeter than claret, due partly to the nature of the Pinot Noir grape, partly to chaptalisation, but significantly to its high alcoholic content (ethyl alcohol is sweet). At its best, burgundy is sublime. The quest is endless and rewarding. The purpose of the following notes is to assess the state of evolution of a given vintage by describing the principal features and condition of individual wines. This is an anthology not, definitely not, a gazetteer.

EARLY 19TH CENTURY

The following note serves to make two important points: that burgundy will keep, and that the best chance of it remaining in good condition is if it has never been moved from the original bin in a cool dark cellar. The other important proviso is that it should have been of top quality to begin with.

Richebourg Contemporary hand-blown burgundy bottle with striated neck and lozenge or cushion-shaped string lip. Remains of original bin-soiled 'bottle ticket', "Richebourg" just discernible, no vintage date. Original bin label: "3 DOZEN RICHEBOURG", again vintage not stated. One of several old wines and liqueurs occupying a number of bins in the extensive cellars beneath Badminton House, packed up by my wife and myself and sold at Christie's, in Dec 1989. 12 of the least ullaged bottles, which had been purchased by Hardy Rodenstock, were opened for the final dinner of one of his annual rare-wine weekends. Half were, as catalogued, ullaged and in poor condition, the rest remarkably drinkable. I opened the first bottle. Level about 2½in below the cork, very good for its age. When I cut round the old wax capsule, the wizened cork came out with it. To everyone's surprise the wine looked impressively deep in the decanter and had a good colour in the glass. The initial whiff reminded me of Amarone, the Italian liqueur, then calf's-foot jelly, finally a rich, ripe, raisiny Pinot Noir and walnuts scent which lingered in the glass until late into the evening. On the palate it had a distinct sweetness and substantial body, good flavour and grip, and virtually no decay. Though its vintage not identifiable, somewhere between 1806 and, at the latest, 1825. Certainly the oldest burgundy I have ever tasted.
*At Arlberg, Sept 1990****

c 1860

Bourgogne Old mould-blown deep punted bottle with wax seals embossed "Bourgogne". Cork blackened with age, sides and end like charcoal. Still a good, deep, mahogany-tinged red brown; rich nose, rather medicinal, reminding me of lint and bandages; high acidity but flavoury. Clean finish.
Oct 1985.

1861***

Romanée-St-Vivant *BOUCHARD PERE ET FILS* The first of a series of vintages of the 1860s from the cellars of the Ch de Beaune. All kept cool and dark and periodically recorked. An occasional bottle sold at the various Heublein rare-wine auctions I conducted in the US between 1969 and 1982, and almost all purchased by

Lloyd Flatt and cellared in New Orleans. High level. Flaky sediment. Colour of wine palish tawny but with a healthy glow; completely sound, slightly meaty nose; distinct sweetness on palate, light, delicate yet not faded. Elegant, Pinot Noir flavour and lovely aftertaste. Not as big or rounded as the 1865s but a wonderful wine.
*At lunch in New Orleans. Host Lloyd Flatt, May 1981******

1864****

Beaune, Clos de la Mousse *BOUCHARD PERE ET FILS* Tasted on three occasions, first at Heublein's pre-auction tasting, May 1974. Next, also pre-sale, at Bouchard's 250th anniversary tasting in 1981. A bottle, purchased by Lloyd Flatt, served at a dinner six years later. Of the three tasted, the earliest had a touch of tartness, though still attractive, the other two were remarkably sound: both had quite a deep colour for their age; a lovely old Pinot bouquet; both were drying out somewhat, and lacking flesh, but otherwise faultless.
*Last noted Oct 1987*****

1865*****

A magnificent vintage. Deep, firm, flavoury wines.
Beaune, Première Cuvée, Grizot *BOUCHARD PERE ET FILS* Tasted on four occasions, the first three, 1977, 1978 and 1981 at Heublein pre-sale tastings. All good. Lovely, expansive, soft autumnal red; lively yet delicate, slightly smoky bouquet; rich, retaining good fruit, intensely flavoured, finish still dry and tannic, good length and aftertaste.
*Last noted dining with Lloyd Flatt in New Orleans, Oct 1987******
La Romanée *BOUCHARD PERE* Good colour; sweet, fragrant bouquet; smooth, soft yet perfect tannin and acidity. Years of life remaining. A glorious drink.
*At Heublein pre-sale tasting, May 1981******
Volnay, Santenots *BOUCHARD PERE* Two notes, both at Heublein tastings. Very good smoky Pinot nose; good, light Volnay character.
*Last tasted May 1981*****
Clos Vougeot *BOUCHARD PERE* Three notes, all at Heublein pre-sale tastings. Made prior to the Clos being split into small parcels. Last recorked in 1960. Beautiful colour, still deep; sweet nose, no signs of decay, perfection; touch of ripe sweetness on palate, assertive yet languorous flavour; full of character, and all the component parts — fruit, extract, alcohol, tannins and acidity — for a long life.
*Last tasted May 1981******

1898***

Bonnes Mares *FAIVELEY* Three bottles tasted in the early 1980s. All had good levels, a good, remarkably deep colour, fully mature of course; sweet, sound bouquet, no faults; touch of sweetness, full-bodied, high alcoholic content and extract, meaty, singed, rounded flavour, dry finish.
*Last tasted Aug 1981*****

1904****

The first really outstanding vintage after 1887. Hot dry summer, adequate rain at the end of Aug to swell the berries. Ripe grapes harvested early, from Sep 15.
Chambertin *JULES REGNIER* Excellent level, lively though very mature colour, very little red remaining; nose aged but attractive; fading but flavoury.
*At Christie's, pre-sale, Chicago, June 1984****
Grand-Musigny *FAIVELEY* Bought at auction and served at a couple of dinner parties. Good (2in) levels but poor corks. Fairly pale, very mature; on each occasion rather dusty and showing its age at first, but the nose cleared, a touch of vanilla, overripe, not much Pinot in evidence but fascinating. Far better on the palate. Distinctly sweet, light elegant style, yet rich, fragrant, delicate. Surprisingly well balanced.
*Last noted July 1981****
Richebourg Capsule embossed *J CALVERELL*. Level 2½in below the firm, unbranded cork. Magnificent colour, rosy-hued, rich rim; nose a bit varnishy at first but developed a rich, singed old Pinot fragrance; sweet, fairly full-bodied, excellent beetroot-like Pinot Noir flavour. Silky perfection.
Tasted with the buyer, Douglas Logan-Kuhs, at Christie's, May 1986.

1906*****

Great vintage. Perfect growing season, the hot summer increasing the sugar content but reducing the yield by concentrating the grape juice. Early harvest.
Romanée-St-Vivant *DUFOULEUR* An amazingly good half-bottle. Excellent level, 1in below a sound, well-stained cork. A rosehip tawny hue with pale yellow rim; lovely, fragrant old beetroot-like Pinot bouquet that opened up in the glass, sweet, glorious, mulberry-like fruit; sweet, beautiful smoky flavour, good length and intensity, excellent finish. Opened on the spur of the moment and poured, undecanted.
*At dinner, with our weekend guests, Belle and Bernard Rhodes, both great connoisseurs, April 1990*****

1911*****

A great classic burgundy vintage. Weather conditions similar to 1906.
Chambertin, Clos de Bèze *GUICHARD PROTHEROT ET FILS* Despite its very considerable ullage, surprisingly good. Fairly pale; mushroomy old nose; firm, good body and length. Complete.
*Oct 1981***
Corton, Clos du Roy (*sic*) Level 2¼in below a firm unbranded cork. Pale orange-tinged amber; sweet and gentle bouquet, faded but lovely; amazingly powerful wine, laden with sweetness and alcohol.
*A sample bottle from Lady Birley's cellar in Sussex, Nov 1980****
Vougeot, 1er cru "Grand vin; 1er cuvée", grower and shipper unknown. Plain lead capsule, very good level. Fairly pale amber orange; maderised, nutty nose, almonds, banana skin. Dry, with flavour like an old amontillado. Surprisingly good acidity.
May 1986.
Clos de Vougeot *LUPE-CHOLET* Fully-embossed Lupé-Cholet capsule, body label and vintage neck label. Crumbly cork. Good level for age. Autumnal colour, mahogany centre, amber rim; fine smoky old Pinot nose — beetroot and cold tea — that remained fragrant for three hours. Dry. Fullish. Fine rich old flavour. Good class. Sound.
*From a cellar near Biarritz, tasted Nov 1987*****

1914***

Seldom seen wartime vintage.
Clos de Tart *BOUCHARD PERE* Recorked by Bouchard. Medium-deep, still very richly coloured, with an amber brown rim; an old farmyard smell, then soft leather; very sweet, good old smoky Pinot flavour and aftertaste. Good grip but acidity nibbling at the edges. A rare and solitary bottle found by Patrice Noyelle of Mommessin.
*Tasted at Clos de Tart, Oct 1990***

1915*****

It is easy to remember the great burgundy vintages: '06, '11, '15 and '19, then a veritable spate in the 1920s. The weather in 1915 was good throughout the growing season, resulting in a large crop of superb early-harvested grapes.

Aloxe-Corton Bottled in Holland. Curious dumpy bottles. It had not survived Dutch cellaring.
Nov 1980.

Corton Grower unknown. Short wartime cork. Had also failed to survive, despite its deep intense appearance. Malty and acidic.
May 1986.

Musigny Shipper unknown but from a good English cellar. Level high, and good, long, unbranded cork. Palish, little red but very healthy glow. At first fairly light, delicate and faded on both nose and palate, but got its 'second breath' and developed richly in the glass. Crisp, clean and refreshing on the palate. Dry, lightly acidic finish.
*From Lady Birley's cellar at pre-sale tasting, Oct 1980***

1916***

Climatic conditions similar to Bordeaux. Good quality. Faded and fatigued now.

Gevrey-Chambertin Unknown source, almost certainly bottled in Burgundy. Palish, very mature appearance; sweet, rich old roasted Pinot nose and flavour. Showing age but not at all bad.
*Pre-sale tasting, Christie's, Amsterdam, Oct 1980****

Nuits-St-Georges French bottled. Good level, fairly pale; rich, rather sickly sweet bouquet but quite good flavour.
*From the same Dutch cellar, Oct 1980***

1919*****

Great vintage. Perfect growing season though a little more rain during the hot dry summer would have fleshed out the grapes. Below average production of magnificently ripe wines. Over two dozen notes, though only four since 1980.

Beaune, Clos des Avaux *DOM DU CH DE BEAUNE* Lovely, expansive, mature appearance; initially the nose reminded me of cold seawater but whilst remaining 'cool' it developed a lovely fresh fragrance; slightly sweet, beautiful flavour and acidity. Perfection.
*At Lloyd Flatt's, New Orleans, Oct 1987******

Chambolle-Musigny *BAROLET* Though an old note, worth mentioning that this was one of the most beautiful of all the Barolet burgundies.
*Last tasted in 1970******

Hospices de Beaune (*sic*) *CALVET* From Mme Teysonneau's 'young wine' cellar in Bordeaux. Her uncle had been a Calvet, and the cellar was full of Calvet burgundy, vintages '19 to '29, in pristine condition. A perfect bottle in 1979. The following year a good deep colour; showing age on the nose, rich, gamey, with a singed Pinot character; rich and velvety on the palate. Good quality. Firm, dry, slightly acidic finish.
*Last tasted at lunch with Peter Palumbo, Feb 1980*****

Nuits-St-Georges *FAIVELEY* Deep-stained, unbranded cork with wizened and crystalline end. Medium colour, fully mature of course; slightly old mushroomy nose that evolved richly in the glass; medium sweetness and weight. As so often, high in alcohol yet lightish in style. Elegant, smooth, good dry finish.
*Dining at Houston House, near Edinburgh, May 1982*****

Richebourg *CALVET* Level 2½in, normal for this age of burgundy. Rich, hefty 'tears'; the sweet decay of a well-hung pheasant. Nice old flavour. Clean finish. Another wine from the Teysonneau cellar.
*March 1980****

1920****

A good start to the best-ever burgundy decade. Too little sun in July and Aug slowed development in an otherwise good growing season. Late Sept harvest in perfect conditions. Small production.

Chambertin, Héritiers Latour Medium-pale but with bright and beautiful colour; a whiff of the 'fishy' Pinot I associate with Chambertin, slightly smoky, waxy bouquet of great style and quality; medium dry, very crisp, flavoury, with a lean sinewy character. Perfection.
*Bought at Christie's sale of Fernand Woltner's Paris cellar, Oct 1980, and served at dinner, June 1981******

Charmes-Chambertin Cork branded with an unreadable restaurant name. Breaking burgundian traditions I decanted this and served it four hours later. Lovely warm colour, a sweet, soft bouquet that seemed to become even more fragrant after an hour in the glass. A delicious wine.
*At home, Oct 1980******

1921***

Exceptionally hot summer. Early harvest.

Corton The same provenance as the Charmes-Chambertin '20. Good hard cork branded "Restaurant Foy ...." (?) Excellent level, deep, warm orange-tawny colour; nose rather mushroomy; better on palate, sweet, rich though lacking length.
*Nov 1980***

Clos de la Roche *BAROLET* There were three huge bins of this wine alone, some 2,000 bottles, so considerable bottle variation can be expected. Moreover, after Christie's inaugural sale for the new owners, de Villamont, the latter recorked an unspecified quantity. All bear "Collection du Dr Barolet" labels. I first tasted the '21 Clos de la Roche with Harry Waugh at our initial inspection in the autumn of 1969. Next, at the pre-sale tasting, and several times subsequently, some being very good, some oxidised. Two notes in the mid-1980s exemplify the differences: the first, recorked by de Villamont, was pale, with a slightly pink tinge; very fragrant bouquet with whiff of raspberry; dry, fairly lightweight, pleasant enough (April 1985). The second, with its original cork, had a broad, expansive burgundy appearance, fully mature, with long rich 'legs'; first impression was a chocolaty style, high alcohol, herbaceous, hawthorn character, that aged noticeably in the glass, eventually a Graves-like tobacco smell, pungent, tangy. On the palate a touch of sweetness, fairly full-bodied, with singed old taste. Drying out but powerful.
*Last tasted at a Wine & Food Society dinner given by Professor Nils Sternby in Malmö, Feb 1986. At best****

1923****

Cold wet spring, dry June and July, excessively hot and dry Aug, merciful rain in Sept. Small crop, high quality.

Beaune *BAROLET* Harry Waugh and I considered that this Beaune, admittedly the equivalent of a simple 'village' wine, was not good enough for the Christie's sale in 1969, though I have tasted it since, presumably shipped by de Villamont. It had a healthy, ruddy, glow; a sound but slightly stalky nose; distinctly sweet. Quite nice for its age and class.
*Last tasted Jan 1981***

Hospices de Beaune, Santenay-Volnay (Cuvée Gauvin) (*sic*) Judging by the very original Berry Bros & Rudd label, it must have been imported during the restricted period just after WWII. Fairly pale but very lively colour; nose low-keyed and a trace of fungi at first; striving to be sweet but drying out. After a bit of airing it turned into a charmer.
*A half-bottle produced towards the end of a remarkable great wine dinner given by Mutsuo Okabayashi at the Imperial Hotel, Tokyo, June 1989****
Musigny *CALVET* Three notes, all bottles from Mme Teysonneau's cellar, and all good. Lovely colour; showing age on the nose, gamey; all better on the palate: sweetish, crisp, some Musigny femininity and elegance, nice consistency.
*Last tasted Jan 1981****
Romanée, La Tâche *BERRY BROS* Original, crumbly cork. Good 2in level for age. Palish but with a good ruddy glow; touch of vanilla and sweet old oak, fragrant but with a fringe of decay; sweet, nice weight, high extract, very positive flavour, clean but slightly raw dry finish.
*Aug 1984*****
Other '23s tasted in 1980:
Nuits-St-Georges Unknown French bottling from a Dutch cellar: deep colour; meaty almost malty nose; sweet, rich, mulberry jam flavour**
Unknown Cork branded "Chauvenet" and vintage. Deep, rich appearance; sweet, smoky nose; very rich, chunky flavour.
*From Lady Birley's cellar****

1924***

Despite insufficient summer sun and poor weather at harvest time, some pleasing wines made. Several tasted but none during the 1980s.

1925*

Its reputation as a small and relatively poor vintage of rather hard, astringent wines not borne out by the four I have tasted, though only one tasted since 1980.
Chambertin, Héritiers Latour Excellent level. Palish, soft brown mature edge; dusty and a bit cheesy at first, then rich, fragrant singed Pinot nose of great depth; good weight, crisp, sound. Surprisingly nice wine.
*Drunk at dinner alongside the 1898 and 1904 burgundies referred to earlier, July 1981****

1926****

Cold weather during flowering and a long summer drought severely reduced the size of the crop but some excellent wines made. Variable, some acidic, some good, tasted in the 1960s and 1970s, few recently.
Corton *J DROUHIN* Despite crumbly cork, very good level; once very deep and rich; old, singed bouquet and flavour. Distinct Corton style and weight. Good for its age.
*From a New York cellar, at Christie's in Chicago, June 1984***

1927

Cold wet summer, poor harvest conditions. The worst vintage of the decade.
Gevrey-Chambertin *FAIVELEY* Several bottles bought and consumed in the early 1980s. Consistently good colour, deep, lively – its best feature. Nose ranged from creaking but sound enough to acetic; flavour from pleasant and flavoury to tart.
*Last tasted Oct 1981. At best**

1928****

Hot summer but not without hazards, hail in particular. Good, firm-structured wines made. If well cellared, still good. (Overall, the best Barolet vintage, though none tasted since the 1970s.)
Beaune *MARCILLY* Bottled April/May 1929 and imported by Shaw & Co, New York. An odd half-bottle with 2¼in ullage. Deep, rich, with faint red glow; clearly oxidised, with meaty, stably, old sherry nose; dry, fairly full-bodied, chewy and, surprisingly, clean and drinkable.
*Tasted at Sunday's post-Chicago auction get-together at Schaefers, Skokie, March 1985***
Bonnes Mares *EDOUARD BELORGEY* Fairly deep; sweet, rich, *faisanté* nose; flavour to match. Venerable.
*At dinner following Arthur Hallé's remarkable first growth tasting in Memphis, Tennessee, April 1987****
Romanée-St-Vivant *CALVET* Two bottles, one with 3in ullage, quite good colour and nose, flavoury but dried out, and one mid-shoulder (a rather vague term in respect of burgundy bottles) hopelessly oxidised.
*Last tasted Jan 1981. At best**

1929*****

Rare combination of abundance and high quality. Excellent weather conditions, hot summer with rain at the end of Sept to swell the grapes. Although '29 burgundies had a soft, elegant reputation, I have found some fairly mammoth, long-lasting wines.
Beaune, Clos de Roy (*sic*) *BOUCHARD PERE* Fabulous depth; still cherry-tinged ruby; massive nose, laden with alcohol and blackberry-like fruit; sweet, very full-bodied (14°), powerful, intense, very tannic. Slightly bitter finish.
*At dinner after Flatt's big Ausone tasting, Oct 1987******
Bourgogne, Vieilles Vignes *BOUCHARD AINE* Two bottles. Fully mature though still some red; the first 'over the top', smelling of wet wood; touch of sweetness, flavour better than nose, chocolaty, held together by its flesh. The other leaner but more fragrant.
*At the Fondation Cartier, May 1988***
Corton *CALVET* Good though palish colour; old, sweet, singed nose that developed beautifully over two hours; very sweet on palate, nice weight, full, punchy flavour. Very rich mouthful.
*The youngest of three Calvet burgundies served at a family dinner at home, Jan 1981*****
Corton *PASQUIER-DESVIGNES* Good level. Aged appearance and nose, yet ripe and appealing in its way. Acidity at the edges.
*Dinner at Brooks's, July 1984***
Gevrey-Chambertin *BAROLET* Lovely garnet; in marvellous condition, gentle bouquet, walnuts, held well; very sweet, full-bodied, beautifully balanced.
*Served at a magnificent Christie's/Schaefers dinner, Chicago, Oct 1983******
Volnay, Champans (Provenance unknown) Fabulous colour; glorious bouquet, celestial beetroot; taste of singed heather, excellent length, still tannic.
*Dinner at Becky Wasserman's, Bouilland, Sept 1988******
Clos Vougeot *BAROLET* High volatile acidity but fruity, lively and flavoury.
*Dec 1984***

1930–32

Three disastrous vintages. Even Dr Barolet could do little with the '30 or '31. '32 never tasted.

1933****

A small but very good vintage. Upstaged by the '34s, mainly, I suspect, because 1934 was better than 1933 in Bordeaux, and this always has an influence. Several very good, tasted pre-1980, only one tired example since.

Mazis-Chambertin *LEROY* Deep, brown and murky; singed, chocolaty nose; gripping tenaciously but really too fatigued, dry and acidic.
The oldest wine in a remarkable tasting of Mazis, Gevrey-Chambertin and Cazetiers vintages presented by Mme Bize-Leroy at Dom d'Auvernay, Sept 1984.

1934****

Almost too perfect growing conditions. An over-abundance of ripe and deservedly popular wines. Heat during the vintage caused problems and some were, and still are, overblown and over-acidic. The best are glorious.

Many '34s tasted, from the early 1950s, and several dozen since 1966. The following noted during the 1980s.

La Tâche Recorked. Not much red left; a whiff of kerosene at first, but after 30 minutes opened up extraordinarily, really spicy; sweet, huge, mouthfilling, almost chewy wine with typical La Tâche fragrance.
*Tasted with Fritz Hatton in the extensive cellar of a country house in New York State, March 1985****

Chambolle-Musigny *A & R BARRIERES FRERES* Short original cork, good level. Pale but lively; fungi and walnuts nose but much better on the palate: fairly sweet, lovely flavour, good acidity.
*April 1985****

Chambolle-Musigny *LABAUME AINE* Slip labelled "A Fougères & Co Beaune and imported by Zaphiro, Fantizzi & Trucco, Chicago". Clearly post-prohibition, but only just. Surprisingly deep for its age, sweet, soft and attractive. Good old ZFT!
*Appropriately at Christie's pre-sale tasting, Chicago, April 1987****

Grands-Echézeaux *BAROLET* Very attractive colour; warm, singed, stewed Pinot nose, somewhat medicinal – it cracked up a bit; fairly sweet, lovely flavour, nice dry finish.
*Dinner at the Rhodes' after the Napa Valley Wine Auction, June 1986****

Clos des Lambrays Magnificent: very rich, ripe, opulent bouquet and flavour. Lovely texture, length and finish.
*July 1981******

Musigny Sweet, coffee and chocolate nose, low-keyed, some decay; chewy, flavoury, nice clean fresh flavour. Very dry finish.
*The oldest wine at Tawfig Khoury's de Vogüé tasting in San Diego, Oct 1984*****

Volnay, Caillerets, Ancienne Cuvée Carnot *BOUCHARD PERE* Fairly deep, rich; good smoky Pinot bouquet; medium sweetness and body, rich, toffee-coffee flavour.
*At the Flatt collection pre-sale tasting, Sept 1990*****

Volnay, Pousse d'Or *SAVIN ET FILS* Pale but good.
*June 1983****

1935****

A very good vintage but little shipped to the UK, as the merchants had stocked up with the popular '34s.

Grands-Echézeaux A most original label depicting an Italianate château, "du Domaine de la Romanée-Conti" in small lettering under the name of the wine and "George Thienpont à Etichove" written large beneath. Good long firm cork. Deep, lively colour; sound, attractive, citrus-touched bouquet; sweetish, fairly full-bodied, rich, very sound but rather unsubtle, with very hot spirity finish.
*Dinner at Arnaud's, New Orleans, April 1986*****

1936*

Cool damp summer. Small crop. None tasted.

1937*****

A great vintage, at its best rarely equalled. Well-nigh perfect growing conditions, warm from May until Sept when a spell of rain refreshed and swelled the fully ripe grapes. Picking began around Sept 27 in excellent weather. Very many tasted over the years. The top wines, well kept, can still be wonderful. Some of my more recent notes follow.

Romanée-Conti Magnificent. Four good notes, most recently, in magnum, medium-deep, lovely warm, broad, autumnal colour with fine gradation to mature, mahogany-hued rim; ripe, rich, classic 'beetroot' Pinot, gentle, fragrant, sustained bouquet; very sweet, fairly full-bodied, fleshy, lovely flavour. Seemed to grow richer in the glass. Perfect tannin and acidity.
*Last tasted in Sept 1988***** Hardy Rodenstock tacked a magnum of Romanée-Conti and DRC Richebourg (see below) to the end of a range of over 60 '37 red Bordeaux, including all the first growths (in magnums). It was a revelation. The '37 clarets were completely thrown out of orbit by the marvellous burgundies.*

La Tâche Wonderfully deep, almost syrupy-rich appearance; magnificent bouquet that unravelled fragrantly in the glass. Rich, intense, fairly high acidity yet creamy textured. Fabulous aftertaste.
*Last tasted April 1980******

Gevrey-Chambertin *LEROY* Attractive colour; lovely sweet ripe old bouquet and flavour. Lovely, elegant.
*At Lalou Bize's tasting, Sept 1984*****

Gevrey-Chambertin *L TRAMIER* Soft red; mild, ripe; quite good rich flavour with marked but tolerable acidity.
*Sept 1988****

Clos des Lambrays Two good notes, first in 1981. More recently: medium-pale though still with a healthy red tinge; rich, ripe though subdued old Pinot Noir nose and taste. Well-stacked, crisp, aromatic.
*Last tasted Sept 1988*****

Mazis-Chambertin *LEROY* Lovely colour, autumnal, mahogany; touch of decay on the nose but, as is so often the case with top-class burgundy, much sounder on the palate. A lovely flavour, soft, dry finish.
*March 1980*****

Musigny *DE VOGUE* Not domaine-bottled. Deep, lively; sweet, singed, very medicinal nose – like some disinfectant; full-bodied, high-toned, power-packed, a bit too severe.
*At Khoury's de Vogüé tasting, San Diego, Oct 1984***

Nuits-St-Georges, 1er cru *THOMAS BASSOT* Lovely rich red glow; an unmistakable smoky Pinot Noir bouquet; sweet, full-bodied, very good flavour and length.
*Sept 1988*****

Pommard, 1er cru (Rugiens) *CAMILLE GIROUD* Topped up and recorked. Healthy appearance; scented Pinot, touch of vanilla; soft, pleasing.
*Dec 1980****

Richebourg *DRC* Magnum. Magnificent depth of colour, rich, luscious legs; fine bouquet that evolved richly in the glass; very sweet, full-bodied, great depth of flavour, firm, more grip than Romanée-Conti itself. A

great wine.
*At the Rodenstock dinner, Sept 1988******
Clos de la Roche *MOREY* (No note of which.) High fill, fabulous colour, lovely smoky Gouges-style bouquet; very flavoury.
*Pre-sale, June 1984*****
Romanée-St-Vivant *SAVIN* Very pale; perfumed Pinot; sweet but light and delicious.
*Pre-sale tasting, Chicago, June 1983****
Volnay, Hospices, Cuvée Blondeau *C GIROUD* Magnificent bouquet, excellent flavour, soft, fragrant, dry finish.
*Dec 1980*****

1938**

Variable weather conditions, frost and hail in the spring, heavy hailstorms in the summer. Vines slow to mature. Picking started Oct 4 but those who delayed benefited from the autumn sun. Bottled during the war.
La Tâche Clearly picked late. A warm, expansive autumnal maturity; an extraordinarily chocolaty nose; distinctly sweet on the palate, exquisite, incandescent, lingering flavour.
*At La Pyramide, Vienne, thanks to James Halliday at a neighbouring table, Sept 1984******
Clos des Lambrays Palish, fully mature but lively-looking. Too lively: positively crackling with volatile acidity.
July 1981.

1939**

Moderate quantity, modest quality. None tasted recently.

1940**

Good growing season spoiled by mildew though the Dom de la Romanée-Conti managed to make quite good wine. None tasted recently.

1941**?

Poor reputation, yet judging by the only two tasted, one fairly recently, can be very good. Despite the reappearance of mildew, the vines were healthy, though a cold, damp autumn inhibited ripening.
Chambolle-Musigny *J DROUHIN* Magnum. Sweet, soft, spicy, very fragrant. Most attractive and holding well.
*At dinner with Parry de Winton, Drouhin's London agent, Feb 1983*****

1942***

Undoubtedly a good, very early vintage. The start of picking coincided with hailstorms in the Côte de Beaune. These freak storms can do untold damage, from mere bruising to stripping the vines bare. La Tâche and Richebourg DRC both good in the 1970s.
Ruchottes-Chambertin *THOMAS BASSOT* Brown, alas oxidised.
May 1981.
Clos Vougeot, Tête *THOMAS BASSOT* First tasted at a Heublein pre-sale tasting in 1981, and recently. Consistent notes: palish, very mature but healthy colour; attractive bouquet reminiscent of smouldering leaves; dry, flavoury, soft yet a touch of acidity.
*Last tasted Sept 1990****

1943****

Very good vintage. Well-nigh perfect spring, summer and autumn though the crop was reduced by frosts in May and hail in July. Perfectly ripe grapes. Well-cellared wines still drinking beautifully.
La Tâche Two notes, first in 1977. Medium colour, attractive; rich, ripe, scented, almost a Pinot 'beetroot' caricature; very fragrant, piquant flavour, very dry rather acidic finish. An exciting drink.
*Last tasted May 1983****
Chambolle-Musigny, 1er cru *THOMAS BASSOT* Noted at two pre-sale tastings, Heublein's in May 1971, and Christie's in Chicago. The stock, originally from Maxim's in Paris, was bought by Lloyd Flatt and the remaining bottles formed part of his collection, sold recently. The wine had kept well, palish but healthy; fragrant, spicy old Pinot; dry, fading a little but in good condition.
*Last noted Sept 1990****
Clos St-Denis *THOMAS BASSOT* High-toned, spicy, fragrant. Noted at two Heublein tastings.
*Last tasted May 1981****

1944*

Another fine growing season spoiled by heavy rains throughout the harvest. Light, rather washed-out wines. Only one tasted, a watery **Romanée-Conti** in 1959.

1945*****

Unquestionably a great vintage. As in Bordeaux, nature did the pruning and old-fashioned winemaking did the rest. Spring frost, followed by remarkably early and speedy flowering and a hot summer with low rainfall resulting in a small crop of highly concentrated ripe grapes. The best, and best kept, still magnificent.
La Tâche Tasted, memorably, twice. First in 1961. More recently, the last and unquestionably the greatest of 26 vintages of La Tâche laid on at the Domaine for John Arlott, Christopher Fielden and myself. The concentration resulting from the small crop could be seen, smelled and tasted: amazing depth of colour, still red; and extraordinary mulberry-rich fragrance, great depth and, after 45 minutes in the glass, exuding incredible power; sweet, the sweetness of ripe grapes and high, well-integrated, alcohol. Full-bodied yet not heavy. Rich texture. Bursting with flavour. Still with perfect balance of tannin and acidity. Great length and inimitable La Tâche aftertaste.
*Last noted May 1983******* *Yes, six stars!*
Chambolle-Musigny *FAIVELEY* Fairly deep, intense, still red; an extraordinary bouquet, rather medicinal and ripe, a very fragrant, harmonious powerhouse of scents; fairly sweet, silky, stylish, excellent length.
*At Dr Norman Burrows' burrow beneath Devonshire Place, Aug 1985******
Charmes-Chambertin *CAMILLE GIROUD* Decanted and recorked in Giroud's cellars. Fine colour; sweet, slightly fishy, medicinal Chambertin Pinot nose; high-toned, flavoury, lacking flesh and with a slightly metallic finish.
*Dec 1980***
Gevrey-Chambertin *LEROY* Medium-deep; fine rich colour; very sweet, singed, almost chocolaty nose; very elegant and complete though lacking the length expected. A lovely wine.
*At the Bize-Leroy tasting, Sept 1984*****
Clos des Lambrays Three fairly ecstatic notes. First in 1981, next in 1983: fabulous appearance, great richness and depth, virtually opaque, still red-tinged and lively; massive nose, singed Pinot, walnuts, the pepperiness of

high alcoholic content, reminiscent of Pétrus '47; incredibly sweet, sweeter than the port (1887 Sandeman), huge, soft, rounded, perfect condition. Most recently: deep, rich, powerful.
*Last noted at a pre-sale tasting in Oct 1987******

Mazis-Chambertin *ROUSSEAU* First noted at a 'paired' luncheon at Le Taillevent. My guest, Georges Prade. The first pair were '77 Leflaive, Pucelles and Chevalier-Montrachet, the second, Rousseau's Mazis of two vintages: '45 and '37. The '45 was very good. Despite a broken cork and 2½ in level, it had a seemingly boundless colour; a rich peppery bouquet and flavour with a touch of acidity. More recently, a high-toned, ripe, flowery-nosed bottle with Faiveley's Chambolle, noted above. Soft, though getting a bit edgy.
*Last noted at Dr Burrows' luncheon, Aug 1985*****

Musigny *DE VOGUE* Magnum: deep, lively—the unmistakable '45 depth of colour. Nose low-keyed at first, slowing evolving in the glass, with a passing scent of baked apples pricked with cloves, still not fully developed after 90 minutes in the glass; a firm, still youthful, spicy flavour with dry, tannin and acid finish. Years of life in hand.
*Noted at Khoury's de Vogüé tasting, Oct 1984******

Musigny, Vieilles Vignes *DE VOGUE* Magnificent, exquisite, silky magnum in 1958 and bottle in 1961. Most recently a sadly recorked bottle with whiff of old rubber and '45 tannin, but a shadow of its former self.
*Last tasted in March 1985. At best******

Nuits-St-Georges, Clos des Forêts *JULES BELIN* Very good original cork. Medium, very mature appearance; waxy, singed, smoky coal-tar bouquet and flavour. Powerful. Dry.
*Feb 1989****

Vosne-Romanée *NOELLAT* Palish, tawny, little red; low-keyed but sound; dry, fading and a bit screwed up.
*April 1984**

Vosne-Romanée, Beaumonts *NOELLAT* Ruddy-tinged tawny; gentle, fragrant, toasted bouquet; dry, lightish, thinning but flavoury and clean.
*April 1984****

Vougeot Bottled in Burgundy. Avery selection label. Deep but mature brown tinge; magnificent nose, opulent, forthcoming, boiled beetroot; a ripe, singed, hot-vintage Pinot taste, high alcoholic content, sweet but with rather a ragged finish. Needed drinking.
*Jan 1981****

Other notes:

Charmes-Chambertin *ROUSSEAU* 3in ullage, deepish but little red, amber-rimmed. Oxidised. A disappointing bottle from the Darroze cellar.
March 1981.

Mâcon Rouge *PATRIARCHE* Bottled in Copenhagen. Deep, heavy sediment; sweet, rich, remarkably good, if you do not object to a touch of brown treacle.
*July 1989***

1946*

Uncannily similar to the red Bordeaux vintage, totally overlooked but not bad. A tolerably good growing season, sunny, abundant crop until hail struck in Aug, followed by a cold rainy period. Last half of Sept warm, prior to a decent enough harvest.

Chambertin *THOMAS BASSOT* Though too brown, surprisingly good with a deep, rich, true 'fishy' Chambertin Pinot nose.
*At a Heublein pre-sale tasting, May 1981***

1947****

A wonderfully rich vintage, following an excellent growing season: warm summer, fully ripe crop picked early from Sept 16. Despite the problems encountered when the grapes are picked and fermented in heat, the '47 burgundies seem, in retrospect, more stable than their peers in Bordeaux.

I was fortunate to have started my wine trade career in the early 1950s when these '47s were shipped, mainly *en barrique*. The quality of wine and of British merchants' bottling reassuringly high, allowing for some commercial 'stretching' at either end.

La Tâche Medium-pale; fragrant, singed, slightly malty bouquet; very sweet. A wine of great power and length.
*Oct 1987*****

Beaune, Marconnets *BOUCHARD PERE* Medium-deep; lovely, ripe, slightly smoky old Pinot nose; very sweet, full, rich and holding well.
*In Memphis, April 1987*****

Chassagne-Montrachet *BOUCHARD PERE* Rich colour, bouquet and flavour. Very sweet. Touch of toffee.
*At the Flatt collection pre-sale tasting, Sept 1990*****

Corton *C GIROUD* Deep; very sweet, soft, full, rounded.
*Dec 1980*****

Clos des Lambrays Very deep, intensely rich; curious, high-toned, stalky, slightly malty; soft, ripe, citrus-like fruit flavour and acidity.
*July 1981***

Mazis-Chambertin Bottled by Avery in Bristol. Warm, opulent, singed, vegetal, showing age; fairly full-bodied, walnut flavour, 'hot', alcoholic, good acidity.
*Dining with Len Evans in the Hunter Valley, March 1985****

Musigny *DE VOGUE* Several notes. Served blind at Layton's towards the end of lunch when I was expecting port. I thought the colour and nose not quite right, but the taste brought me back in the right direction. Because of its heavy sediment it had been decanted. Colour perfect. Very distinctive, smoky bouquet, with a whiff of charming decrepitude that reminded me of Lafite '12. Marvellous flavour. Rich. Still very tannic. This was in 1982. Two years later: a low-level, oxidised bottle and a gloriously rich, ripe bottle at Khoury's de Vogüé tasting. Fragile bouquet, arsenic and old lace. Fabulous warmth and length.
*Last tasted Oct 1984. At best******

Some other '47s tasted in the 1980s:

Beaujolais Bottled by Williams Standring, from Lady Birley's cellar: lovely colour; smoky old Gamay beginning to resemble a mature Pinot Noir; soft, lightish, flavoury.
*Nov 1980****

Beaune, Clos des Mouches *J DROUHIN* Alas, oxidised.
March 1981.

Chambertin *CAMUS* Maxim's selection. One bottle corky, the other lovely.
*Heublein, May 1980. At best****

Corton *J DROUHIN* Variable. At best dry, fullish, good.
*April 1988****

Grands-Echézeaux *MORIN* Variable, at best fairly deep; lovely, toasted bouquet; soft, ripe, good aftertaste.
*May 1981****

Pommard, Grands Epenots *LOUIS POIRIER, SELECTION RAYMOND BAUDOUIN* Deep, a bit too brown; rich but malty nose and flavour. Lacking elegance and cracking up.
July 1983.

1948**

Fairly good, somewhat idiosyncratic wines, as in Bordeaux, and just as unpopular with the trade, which wisely focused on the flanking '47s and '49s. Variable weather conditions, the late spring and early summer too cold and wet though good from mid-Aug to the early Oct harvest. Few tasted recently. Variable: from tired to very good.

La Tâche Impressive but immature aged 10, perfection when last tasted.
*May 1980*****

Richebourg *DRC* First tasted when it was 10 years old. Massive and magnificent. Alas, on the only other occasion it was the colour of burnt amber, clearly oxidised. It *should* still be good.
Last tasted March 1981. Variable.

Clos Vougeot *L GROS* Medium, coppery-tinged. Good ripe bouquet, sweet and refreshing in 1980. At the next Heublein tasting its nose resembled Ovaltine. Fatigued but drinkable.
*Last noted May 1981***

1949*****

One of the most beautiful and one of my favourite of all burgundy vintages. The vital flowering took place in worryingly unsettled rainy conditions but thereafter the climate behaved admirably, warm and dry to ripen and concentrate, sufficient rain to swell the grapes prior to picking from Sept 27. Elegant, well-balanced wines, the best the epitome of burgundy. The '49s filled both private British cellars and the merchants' coffers.

Bonnes Mares *DE VOGUE* Magnum: rich red colour with orange-pink tinge; showing some age and drying out, fruit faded, rather acidic finish. Disappointing.
*At Khoury's de Vogüé tasting, Oct 1984***

Chambertin *LEROY* Lovely colour; nose showing some age, brambly fruit, smoky Pinot. After 10 minutes or so attained a fluttery fragrance and perfume, then expired. Surprisingly powerful on the palate, a touch of sharpness, yet scented aftertaste.
*Cercle de Vingt, May 1988****

Chambolle-Musigny, Les Charmes *DOUDET-NAUDIN* Good colour; bouquet of pickled walnuts and wet straw; sweet, nice weight, delicious flavour, good length. The *cognoscenti* tend to turn up their noses at Doudet-Naudin's wines, but though generally lacking finesse I have always found them dependable, and rarely have I come across even old vintages that are over-the-hill.
*July 1988****

Charmes-Chambertin Bottled by Prunier's, Paris. A wax-capsuled half-bottle, fairly big wine, still with a touch of hardness. A month later, at a pre-sale tasting, very mature-looking; a nose that reminded Oz Clarke of radishes; flavour better. Attractive.
*Last noted Dec 1982***

Corton *L JADOT* Very deep colour; meaty, almost volcanic earthy nose, sound as a bell; very sweet, full-bodied, high extract and alcohol, and fairly high acidity. Impressive.
*Lunching with Pierre-Henry and André Gagey at the elegant Hostellerie de Levernois, Oct 1990*****

Gevrey-Chambertin, Les Cazetiers *LEROY* Very deep but showing age; sweet chocolaty bouquet, with whiff of volatile acidity; markedly sweet, rich, warm, elegant, with considerable length. Touch of bitterness on the finish, otherwise great.
*At the Bize-Leroy tasting, Sept 1984*****

Mazis-Chambertin *LEROY* Opaque centre, very mature brown rim; deep, singed hot vintage bouquet; also very sweet, a massive wine, tannic, great length but showing its age.
*Also at Lalou Bize-Leroy's, Sept 1984*****

Musigny *DE VOGUE* In 1972, it embodied everything I expected of a great vintage and great domaine. Perfect then. A magnificent future. This was amply confirmed 12 years later: still a rich red; a hot, alcoholic, medicinal nose that evolved and held well; sweet, fairly full-bodied, luscious, fragrant Pinot fruit, the most persistent flavour and lingering aftertaste of all.
*For me, the star of Tawfig Khoury's de Vogüé tasting, Oct 1984******
Now to 2000.

Nuits-St-Georges *CHARLES NOELLAT* Palish but healthy; fragrant, smoky Pinot; slightly sweet, lighter style, charming, fragrant and flavoury.
*April 1984*****

Richebourg *LEROY* Remarkably deep, red brown; quite understandably, not a trace of varietal aroma, just a lovely old bouquet. Positive flavour, soft yet with dry finish. Though well past its best and creaking, a lovely drink.
*April 1985****

Volnay, Santenots *CAMILLE GIROUD* Good colour though showing considerable maturity, amber-edged; slightly singed, chocolaty, deliciously ripe *gibier* bouquet; sweet, still vigorous, lovely wine. Dry finish.
*Brought by Becky Wasserman for the closing burgundy dinner of the Hollywood (Florida) Wine Society's wine weekend, Jan 1990*****

Clos Vougeot *NOELLAT* A healthy rosy glow; vanilla, singed; sweet, nice weight, lovely flavour, firm, still tannic, good finish.
*April 1984*****

1950*

Burgundy seems susceptible to summer hailstorms. Not only do they do considerable damage, but grapes, even if not struck from the vines, can give the wine a peculiar mousy taste. 1950 suffered hailstorms in July, Aug and Sept, the last two months being wet. An abundant crop of rather feeble grapes picked during the last half of Sept. The English trade, used to picking and choosing, chose not to pick the '50s for sale, so few tasted.

Volnay, Hospices, Cuvée Jehan de Massol From the Quancard family cellars almost literally unearthed by Russell Hone, shipped to London and sold, part of the quite remarkable "Quancard Collection", in the 1970s. Two ullaged bottles tasted later, the first a not unreasonable 2in below the cork had a pale but attractive *pelure d'oignon* colour; a light, slightly vanilla-scented Pinot bouquet; light, good length and acidity. The other, at 3in, was paler and more tawny; slightly oxidised, dried out but perfectly drinkable. Had the vintage been more robust, there would have been little or no problem.
*May 1989. At best****

Vougeot, Clos du Prieuré *PIERRE PONNELLE* Two notes. Medium, mature; gentle, rich, slightly vanilla nose that evolved in the glass and held its fragrance over a long period; medium dryness and weight, soft, rather short but lovely flavour, and in good condition.
*Last tasted Oct 1984****

Older note:

La Tâche The only DRC '50 tasted. Brown and tired in 1963 and unlikely to have survived. Yet . . . see 1951.

1951

A dismal summer and late vintage, ostracised by the British trade. Yet of the six or so tasted, some surprises.

La Tâche Medium-pale, lively, rosy—a better colour than '82 Clos de Tart; nose rather hard, beetroot-like, sound; dry, light yet positive flavour. Crisp, fresh. Sound. Quite a surprise.
Oct 1985★★

Grands-Echézeaux *POULET PERE* Quite a good colour, noticeable legs; lovely clean-cut Pinot Noir aroma which held well; sweet, rich, soft and lovely, with excellent acidity. I was informed by Bernard Rhodes that this was made from declassified grapes from the newly planted Romanée-Conti vines.
At a remarkable dinner at the Rhodes' in the Napa Valley, June 1986★★★

Clos des Lambrays Fairly pale; remarkably attractive, toasted, chocolaty Pinot. For a change, nose better than palate. Despite lacking length and highish acidity, not at all bad.
July 1981★★

1952★★★★

A top-class vintage. Sturdy, often massive, and one of the most dependable of all burgundy vintages. Its toughness and concentration due to drought in June and a very hot, though showery, July and Aug. Sept lacked warmth; picking started Oct 7.

Romanée-Conti Several notes. A great wine. Evolving in the 1960s and perfection in the early 1970s. A decade later, in magnum, a lovely medium-deep colour, maturing perfectly; an indescribably magnificent bouquet of great complexity and overwhelming fragrance: an intriguing *mélange* of raspberries and celestial beetroot that churned out of the glass for an hour or so, and would doubtless have continued overnight; sweet ripe entry, huge yet not heavy, velvety yet firm. Opulent. A touch of bitterness in its tannic finish.
Last tasted at a magnificent wine dinner given by Richel and Tawfig Khoury. Despite being flanked by two highly scented ladies, the wines won. In San Diego, Oct 1982★★★★★ *Now to 2000.*

Musigny *DE VOGUE* Glorious colour. No signs of age; restrained despite lively fragrance; distinctly unfeminine: a massive wine, soft, lovely, yet very dry, very tannic.
At Khoury's de Vogüé tasting, Oct 1984★★★(★★) *Now to 2000.*

Nuits-St-Georges, Clos des Porrets *HENRI GOUGES* Incredibly deep; a bouquet of truffles and freshly peeled mushrooms; full-bodied, rich, firm, still loaded with tannin.
Tasted at the Domaine, Sept 1981★★★(★★) *Now to 2000.*

Richebourg *LEBEGUE-BICHOT* Jeroboam. Broad expansive appearance—like the host; rich, overripe bouquet; sweet, fullish, very complete, excellent balance.
Cunningly wedged between Mouton '57 and Lafite '53 at Marvin Overton's mammoth 50th birthday dinner, Fort Worth, Feb 1985★★★★

Other '52s tasted recently:

Not a great vintage for Dr Barolet's burgundies. I noticed a tailing off in quality after the 1940s and the following, all with de Villamont labels, rather disappointing:

Aloxe-Corton Dry, flavoury but lean.
Tasted Sept 1990.

Beaune Cheesy nose, sour cream taste.
Tasted Sept 1990.

Chambolle-Musigny Agreeable a decade earlier.
Tasted April 1980.

1953★★★★

Lovely ripe, supple wines, some like shooting stars, others beguiling, deceptive, as only great burgundies can be, charged with longevity. Quality is determined during the later months of ripening: well borne out in 1953. After a pleasantly mild, encouraging spring, June and July were cold and wet. Happily, Aug and Sept were warm and dry, a relatively 'no problem' harvest beginning on Sept 29. Popular wines, mostly consumed by now. Some fading but the best still superb.

La Tâche An object lesson. Relatively pale and anything but sturdy when young. By 1966, fully mature-looking; incredibly fragrant; dry, delicately flavoured, good length but seemingly at its peak. Yet, 17 years later, still ploughing along, elegantly, beautifully, a lovely colour, glowing, mature; archetypal La Tâche fragrance, perfectly harmonious; slightly sweet, light style yet mouthfilling flavour, with gentle, life-sustaining tannin and acidity.
Last tasted at the Domaine, May 1983★★★★★ *Should still be perfection and will doubtless see us into the 21st century.*

Beaune, Clos des Mouches *J DROUHIN* Fairly pale but healthy glow; good rich nose; flavoury.
Pre-sale tasting, Dec 1980★★★

Chambertin *REMOISSENET* Lovely colour; fragrant, brambly nose; very sweet, full, rich, chocolaty, yet some elegance.
Dinner at the Averys', May 1987★★★

Chambertin, Héritiers Latour Sweet, soft, lovely flavour and endtaste.
At pre-sale tasting, June 1984★★★★

Mazis-Chambertin *LEROY* Rather pale but attractive; sweet vanilla chocolate nose. How it is that burgundy can be light in style yet powerful and alcoholic is one of life's mysteries. Good wine.
At the Bize-Leroy tasting, Sept 1984★★★★

Musigny *DE VOGUE* Two bottles both from an American cellar, the first level a bit lower than expected, palish tawny, thin but flavoury, elegant despite its acidity, the second low-shoulder, malty and maderised.
One—or rather two—of the disappointments at Khoury's de Vogüé tasting, Oct 1984.

Musigny, Vieilles Vignes *DE VOGUE* Coincidentally, also from an American cellar. Long but dry cork that broke as it was pulled out. Malty nose; sweet, meaty—not bad but not right. Stored in conditions too hot or too dry, or both.
Feb 1989.

Romanée-St-Vivant, Les Quatre Journaux *L LATOUR* Two notes. Medium depth but hardly any red left; ripe, mature, beetroot-like fragrance; very sweet, full, rich, almost port-like, with excellent aftertaste. Last noted, holding its own after magnums of Margaux, Lafite, Latour, Mouton, La Mission, Haut-Brion, Ausone, Cheval-Blanc and Pétrus, but nearly destroyed by Brie de Meaux.
At a mind-boggling '53 First Growth Magnum Dinner organised by the Marin County Chapter of the International Wine & Food Society at the Four Seasons Clift, San Francisco, June 1985★★★★

Some other '53s tasted in the 1980s:

Gevrey-Chambertin *LEROY* Rubbery nose and whiff of volatile acidity, dry and thinning.
Sept 1984.

Vosne-Romanée, Beaumont Of unknown origin. So sweet and powerful that it could scarcely be contained in a half-bottle.
Aug 1988★★★★

Clos Vougeot *L LATOUR* Palish, fully mature; touch of old boots, old age, tannins; flavoury enough.
June 1984★★

Two great wines last tasted in the 1970s:
Romanée-Conti Perfection in 1975.
Grands-Echézeaux *DRC* Simply ravishing in 1979.

1954***

An undeservedly by-passed vintage, presumably because the trade and its customers had stocked up with the '52s and '53s, and the quality of the '55 vintage was known before the '54s had been bottled. By no means perfect climatically for, despite a pleasant spring and successful flowering, the summer was wet. The vintage was saved by autumn sun and warmth, an abundant crop being picked from Oct 7. Rarely seen but worth a gamble.

La Tâche The Dom de La Romanée-Conti declassified all but the Romanée-Conti and La Tâche, the latter tasted twice. Deeper than the '56 and even the '75, ruddy, touch of orange at the rim; an extraordinary scent, amazing depth, piquant raspberry-like fruit; distinctly sweet, fuller, richer, more complete and greater length than expected.
*Last tasted at the Domaine, May 1983****

1955***

Described in Harvey's autumn 1957 wine list as "a most irregular vintage", yet by 1959, the 'Laying Down' list was devoted to the '55 vintage. The weather conditions were good save for a cold June which delayed flowering. The harvest took place early Oct in the best conditions for 20 years.

Of my several hundred notes of burgundy of this vintage, most were made prior to 1966. They *were* variable, but the good wines that have survived are marvellous now and woefully undervalued. The likelihood of finding bottles of precisely the same wines as those noted below is remote. However, they do give an idea of the differing styles and maturity.

Bonnes Mares *DE VOGUE* Very richly coloured and much deeper than expected though with pronounced orange-tinged mature rim; marvellous harmony, vinosity and fragrance; sweet, fullish, with fabulous flavour and aftertaste.
*At Khoury's de Vogüé tasting, Oct 1984***** Now to 1996, or beyond.*

Chambertin, Clos de Bèze *LEROY* Medium; spicy, harmonious nose that seemed to enrich itself and unfold in the glass; sweet, really too sweet, but rounded and hard to criticise.
*Feb 1989**** Now to 1995.*

Chambolle-Musigny *L LATOUR* I am not sure when the criticisms of Latour pasteurising reds began but this wine is beyond reproach: elegant, stylish, lovely texture and length.
*Following the '66 and alongside Corton-Grancey at a Gidleigh Park wine weekend dinner, Jan 1984**** Now to 1996.*

Charmes-Chambertin *CAMUS/HASENKLEVER* Surprisingly deep — but not so surprising after tasting it. A good old-fashioned souped-up wine.
At pre-sale tasting, June 1984 Drink up.*

Ch Corton-Grancey *LATOUR* Chambolle being feminine and Corton muscular masculine, it is to be expected that it should be much deeper than the former, with a '59-like thickness. Heavy sediment too. Deep, singed hefty Corton nose, and weight. Sweet, full, meaty, excellent acidity. Fine wine, in its prime but perfectly constituted for a longer life.
*At Gidleigh Park, in the snows of Jan 1984**** Now to 2000.*

Gevrey-Chambertin, Cazetiers *LEROY* Opaque, plummy, heavy sediment; wide open, brambly, with a sort of meat extract smell that reminded me of Haut-Brion '29; surprisingly dry, massive. Thought it must be a '59. Knock-out drops.
*At the Leroy tasting, Sept 1984***

Mazis-Chambertin *LEROY* First noted at the Leroy tasting. Quite different to the Cazetiers: medium-pale, mature; sweet, chocolaty, burnt bracken nose; medium, neither dry nor sweet, and similar weight. Dry, burnt flavour. Three months later, at home, I liked it better, finding it smooth yet firm, and well-balanced.
*Last tasted Dec 1984*** Drink now.*

Nuits-St-Georges, La Richemone (The grower or shipper not on menu.) Deeper than expected; very fragrant smoky Pinot; medium sweetness and weight. Quite noticeable acidity.
*At the 99th meeting of the Saintsbury Club at Vintners Hall, Oct 1981*** Drink up.*

La Romanée, Tastevinage *CAVES DE LA BUSSEROLLE* Mature; fragrant, singed Pinot; sweetish, soft, very flavoury.
*Feb 1986****

Volnay, Santenots *LEROY* Lovely colour; sweet, slightly singed earthy Corton-like nose, touch of sweetness, nice weight, Pinot flavour, meatiness, tannin and acidity. Worthy if not inspired.
*Sept 1985*** Drink soon.*

Some other '55s tasted in the 1980s:
Chambertin *AVERY* Ruddy, rosehip colour; sweet, chocolaty, vanilla and caramel nose; medium sweetness and body, meaty, with noticeable life-preserving acidity. A good drink but not a great Chambertin.
*May 1989*** Now to 2000.*

Latricières-Chambertin (Unknown origin.) Deep, scented, and stressing the sweetness and weight of the vintage.
*May 1984****

Pommard, Méthode Ancienne *BELTOUR ET FILS* By which I assume they meant 'stewed', for this is how it smelled. Mediocre.
March 1980.

1956

A disastrous vintage, the worst of recent times, entirely resulting from inclement weather. The poor spring set vegetation back a month; cold and incessant rain throughout July and Aug, with attendant pests and diseases. Sept sun too late to save the very late harvest. Small crop. Thin, deficient wines.

La Tâche Ironic that I have not a single note of any '55 DRCs yet three of La Tâche '56. First tasted at the Domaine in 1981. Bottle variation. Both fairly pale, one more orange-tinged; the latter richer and more harmonious yet some decay — the grapes not the bottle — and more complete though both were short. Two years later at the La Tâche vertical: a bit too brown and thick-looking; subdued nose, smell of grape rot again; lean, taste reminiscent of dry leaves, with edgy acidity. It should never have been bottled under the DRC label.
Last noted at the Domaine, May 1983.

Gevrey-Chambertin, Cazetiers *LEROY* The palest of the tasting, pink-tinged; overmaturity and rot on nose and palate.
At the Bize-Leroy tasting, Sept 1984.

1957***

Attractive wines spurred on, and sustained, by fairly high acidity. The acidity, though noticeable, more part and parcel of the structure of the wine and better balanced than in the '57 red Bordeaux. The first half of the growing season good, with a crescendo of heat late June, early July. Thereafter, variable, too grey, cool and rainy. A fairly big Oct vintage with an imbalance of sugar and acidity. Some good wines made. Many '57s tasted in the 1960s, fewer recently. Some nice surprises.

La Tâche The extraordinary thing about many of the DRC wines is that when first shown to the trade they often appear to be disarmingly and misleadingly pale and light – delightful and fragrant perhaps, but giving few clues as to their future. La Tâche, at three years of age, was light in style, very ripe, fragrant, sweet and immediately drinkable. Quarter of a century later, in jeroboam, still fairly pale, fully mature-looking; a lovely, ripe beetroot Pinot fragrance, almost too exotic; it had dried out a bit but had a wonderfully open, fully developed, entrancing flavour, with '57 piquant acidity.

*Last noted at Marvin Overton's birthday dinner, Feb 1985*****

Gevrey-Chambertin *LEROY* Touch of hardness on nose and palate. Dry. Lean. Short.

*At the Bize-Leroy tasting, Sept 1984**

Musigny *ROUMIER* Palish, mature; deliciously sweet, rich Pinot bouquet; dry, fairly light, very flavoury.

*May 1980****

Musigny, Vieilles-Vignes *DE VOGUE* Beautiful colour but a strange stewed nose, a bit stale and twisted, in April 1984. I thought it might be a poor bottle, poor storage. Six months later, mean, low-keyed cheese-rind nose; fairly dry, rather light, some power though fading, and fraying at the edges.

Last noted at Khoury's de Vogüé tasting, Oct 1984.

Clos de Tart First tasted in 1962: lovely, high-toned zestful acidity, fragrant aftertaste. Nearly 30 years later: palish, rather weak rim; low-keyed; ripe entry, good flavour, reasonable length, dry finish.

*Last tasted March 1990****

Some other '57s tasted in the 1980s:

Chambertin, Clos de Bèze *GRIVELET* Rather medicinal, dry, curious but fragrant**

Cuvée Brunet Very flavoury, with citrus-like acidity***

Volnay, Cuvée Général Muteau *HOSPICES DE BEAUNE* Sweet and delicious.

1958**

At the time, considered by the British trade to be a poor vintage. In fact it was not bad; it just had the ill luck to be sandwiched between the over-bought '57 and "vintage of the century", the '59. The weather was fair enough, variable June but good flowering, July warm, then heavy rain. Sept mainly fine though rain towards the end deferred picking, fortunately, until the warm and sunny early Oct. Strangely, only one '58 tasted.

La Tâche Very attractive warm, well-graduated ruddy colour. Not deep but deeper than the '53. Equally attractive nose, very sweet, slightly caramelly; palate reflecting appearance and bouquet. I felt it had been substantially but well chaptalised, masking a touch of acidity on its clean dry finish.

*At the La Tâche vertical, May 1983***

1959*****

A giant of a vintage and, for me, the end of an era. Perfect blossoming, giving promise of an early and abundant harvest. Dry in July and Aug, concentrating the crop, but enough rain to swell the grapes in time for picking in warm weather from Sept 14. A record crop of high-quality wine and a huge crop of notes to match, most being made in the 1960s. Wonderful wines and, if good to begin with and kept well, affording continuing pleasure. Perhaps, with '52 running a close second, the most dependable of the older vintages.

La Tâche First consumed, in jeroboam, in May 1980. Marvellous, though I thought it lacked the raciness of the '62, more four-square. Next, at the tasting at the Domaine in 1983: impressively deep, huge for La Tâche and with "30 years life" ahead. Two years later, in magnum: impressively deep, rich, with lovely gradations of colour; very fragrant, spicy, peppery nose; very sweet, full of alcohol, extract, flavour. Vast yet velvety. A great wine.

*Last tasted, Feb 1985***** Drink now to well beyond 2000.*

Beaune, Hospices, Avaux Lebègue bottling: still peppery but excellent in 1964, good again in 1972. Next, Avery's label: a bit too brown; nose fully developed, fragrant, but with a Rhône-like stalkiness; fairly sweet, massive, combining high alcohol and (unusual for a '59) high acidity.

*Last tasted April 1984. At best****

Beaune, Hospices, Bétault, *DOUDET-NAUDIN* Deep, lively; low-keyed coffee and chocolate nose and flavour. Massive yet well balanced.

*April 1984** Will doubtless survive the century.*

Beaune, Hospices, Nicolas Rolin *F PROTHEAU* Rich colour, nose and taste. Singed Pinot, nice fruit, sweet, soft, very attractive.

*March 1990**** Now to beyond 2000.*

Beaune, Hospices, Rousseau-Deslandes *BERRY BROS* Magnum: fairly deep, lively but mature; rich meaty nose; dry, full-bodied, powerful but swingeingly austere. "Good for 20 years".

*Oct 1988***(*) 1995 to well beyond 2000.*

Beaune, Grèves *P PONNELLE* Sweet, '59 richness on nose and palate. Chunky, nicely made, some complexity but blunt.

*Nov 1980****

Bonnes Mares *AVERY* Browner, more mature-looking than de Vogüé's. Marvellously fragrant bouquet, spicy, developing a lovely wholemeal, ginger biscuit scent. Taste to match. Fairly full-bodied. Touch of bitterness on finish.

*A single bottle put into the de Vogüé tasting, Oct 1984**** Drink soon.*

Bonnes Mares *DE VOGUE* Pinker than Avery's but, alas, not "in the pink"; a woody, cardboardy, over-the-hill bottle. Dry. Tart.

In San Diego, Oct 1984.

Chambolle-Musigny *BAROLET, DE VILLAMONT* Good colour; rich, smoky nose and flavour. A good though uninspiring drink.

*Sept 1990****

Corton *DOUDET-NAUDIN* The combination of Corton, '59 and Doudet-Naudin predictable: deep colour; toasted marshmallow nose, rich, vanilla and oak, brandy and chocolate; fairly sweet, full-bodied, solidly impressive. I felt it could almost be cut like cake.

*Dining chez Joan and Sid Cross in Vancouver, Oct 1983*** Will last forever.*

Corton, Bressandes *LEROY* Sweet, rich, vanilla bouquet, touch of malt; high strength, chewy, rich mouthful.

*Sept 1985*** Now to 2000.*

Gevrey-Chambertin *LEROY* Deep, mature-looking; hard and dumb; drier than expected but full-bodied, with lots of inherent life.

*At the Bize-Leroy tasting, Sept 1984**(*) Now to beyond 2000.*

Mazis-Chambertin *LEROY* Deep, impressive, brown-rimmed; sweet, slightly singed bouquet; full, firm, loads of grip.

*At Sept 1984 tasting**(**) 1995 to beyond 2000.*

Mazis-Chambertin *MARQUIS DE VILLERANGES* Fairly deep, lovely colour; dry, still tannic, full-flavoured.
*Chez the Sampsons, Aug 1989**(**) Plenty of life ahead, though not much joy if it's one's only bottle!*
Musigny, Tastevinė *FAIVELEY* Deep, lively, earthy, rich, very good.
*Oct 1987*****
Musigny, Vieilles Vignes *DE VOGUE* Remarkable colour, fabulous depth and intensity; glorious, warm, luscious bouquet that was still churning out of the glass an hour later; fairly sweet, full-bodied for Musigny but with lavender-and-old-lace flavour and aftertaste. Good balance and length. A great classic.
*One of the top de Vogüé wines at Tawfig Khoury's tasting in San Diego, Oct 1984***** Now to beyond 2000.*
Nuits-St-Georges A very good, rich, beautifully balanced Avery bottling.
*Aug 1986*****
Nuits-St-Georges, Ch Gris *LUPE-CHOLET* Another example of the way in which top quality burgundy can appear to be palely loitering when young, yet with the substance and stamina for a long life. In 1970, though lovely, I thought it light, piquant-nosed and almost fading away. Yet, nearly 15 years later, a fine '59 depth of colour; rich, ripe fishy Pinot scent; full-flavoured yet a touch of leanness, the piquancy noted earlier translating itself into a refreshing, squeeze-of-lemon dry finish.
*Last tasted Dec 1984**** Now to 1999.*
Pommard, Epenots *L LATOUR* Singed, rich, mature, hot-vintage smell; distinctly sweet, richly flavoured, well-balanced despite its high alcoholic content. Served, wrongly and as so frequently, with cheese. The latter has the effect of sweetening an already sweet wine, and, in my opinion, destroying rather than enhancing the flavour.
*At a Gidleigh Park wine weekend, Jan 1983*** Now to 2000.*
Richebourg *LEROY* Rich, fully mature, orange-tinged; nose at first vegetal and showing age but, after 20 minutes, opening up beautifully. Powerful, very assertive, very tannic. Impressive but lacking flesh, charm and length.
*May 1988**(*) Will keep and, hopefully, soften.*
Richebourg *VIENOT* Deep, mature; good, full-bodied, soft, richly flavoured.
*At pre-sale tasting, May 1980*** Now to 2000.*
Romanée-St-Vivant *VIENOT* Medium-pale, fully mature; sweet, very fragrant, touch of vanilla; lovely, warm, rich, stylish wine.
*Jan 1984**** Now to 2000.*
Volnay *BOUCHARD PERE* At 13 years of age the wine was light, pretty, fragrant and "not for further keeping". 14 years later, a half-bottle: still fairly pale, very mature yet with a positively sweet and chocolaty nose and taste.
*Last noted at a pre-sale tasting, Chicago, April 1986***
Volnay *LEROY* A vintage like '59 can produce atypical wines, unfeminine Chambolles, hefty Volnays, as was this. Deep, big. Good but lacking finesse.
*Sept 1988*** Drink now.*
Volnay, Caillerets *BOUCHARD PERE* Magnum: deep, lively; lovely, crisp, refreshing citrus bouquet; distinctly sweet, medium-full body, despite its substance a true Volnay elegance and very fragrant aftertaste.
*Oct 1987**** Lovely now.*
Volnay, Champans *MONTHELIE-DOUHAIRET* Topped up and recorked by the grower in 1983. Showing no age on the nose but dried out and a bit tart.
At Becky Wasserman's, Sept 1988.
Clos Vougeot *CLAIR-DAU* A gloriously glowing colour though not as deep as expected; singed, Corton-like nose, plus bottle-age. Beautifully balanced, appealingly sweet yet with good crisp acidity, finishing dry. A lovely wine.
*Jan 1981***** Should still be perfection.*
Some other outstanding '59s last tasted in the 1970s:
Echézeaux *DRC* Surely one of the best ever. Lovely and disarmingly ripe in 1964 and in 1977. Should still be a marvellous mouthful.
Grands-Echézeaux *DRC* Also richly impressive in 1964 and several notes since, last, alas, in 1979. Outstanding.
Romanée-Conti First noted at the opening Lebègue tasting in 1964: amazingly rich and concentrated. Still totally unready in 1979. Must see how it is progressing in 1999!

1960

The decade opened with another 'pariah' vintage. No-one bought it, for the usual combination of reasons – it was a poor year and the '59s had been bought heavily. Then came the promise of '61.

There was a fairly good start to the growing year with satisfactory flowering. July was too cold, Aug and Sept wet with attendant rot, inducing some growers to pick prematurely. A large crop of uneven, weary, unripe and acidic wines. Only one tasted prior to 1980.

Beaune, Vignes Franches Shipped by Jadot and bottled by Grants of St James's. Tasted twice within a month: fairly pale, mature appearance; stewed, vanilla nose; open-knit, soft, somewhat medicinal and tart.
*Last tasted, April 1980**

1961***

Came on the market with high hopes, and to some extent fortunate to benefit from the rub-off of the justifiably high reputation of the '61 red Bordeaux. But although I originally gave the vintage four stars, and quite a few wines live up to this, having surveyed my notes, I think it warrants downgrading.

The growing season started off most encouragingly. A warm spring with, by May, vegetation well in advance of normal. However, the crucial flowering in June was extended due to variable weather conditions, mostly cooler than average until hotter yet variable in Aug. Happily, Sept was fine and warm, the harvest commencing on the 25th in good conditions. A small crop and a prematurely exaggerated reputation resulting in high demand which enabled growers to get 50% more than for their '59s. Time has put the '59s and '61s into perspective.

La Tâche I described this as "a bit scrawny and green" at the Lebègue tasting in 1964. Eight years later, rich, but acidity noticeable. At 22 years of age, the wine appeared to be fully mature, medium – neither deep nor pale; rich, fruity but with somewhat muffled nose, strange, high-toned, like wet fern; dry, medium weight, soft, spongy with a raw, spiky finish. Not a patch on the '62, and certainly not worth the price paid at auction.
Last noted at the La Tâche vertical, May 1983 Drink up.*
Beaune, Grèves, Vigne de l'Enfant Jésus *BOUCHARD PERE ET FILS* Two notes, both magnums. Fine, rich colour, fully mature; lovely soft ripe Pinot nose that blossomed in the glass, most opulent; distinct touch of sweetness, soft, with attractive singed, charred flavour, finishing with a touch of hard acidity. I thought it as perfect as it would ever be.
*Last tasted Sept 1982*****
Bonnes Mares *DE VOGUE* Velvety, elegant and fully mature at 10 years of age. 18 years later, more than

surviving: medium, mature; sweet harmonious bouquet of considerable depth; meaty, well-shaped, complete.
Sept 1989★★★★
Chambertin *JABOULET-VERCHERRE* Labelled "Estate bottled". First noted in 1982. A pleasant, scented, flavoury wine. A couple of years later, at a pre-sale tasting, fairly pale, very mature-looking; the same light but fragrant Pinot nose; firm, attractive, good acidity.
Last tasted April 1984★★★
Chambertin *PIERRE PONNELLE* Bottled in Belgium by Gondrand. A good meaty Pinot nose and flavour. From a good private cellar south of Brussels.
July 1984★★★
Le Chambertin *ARMAND ROUX* (A *sous nom* of Bichot, one of many.) Indistinct, cardboardy nose; very sweet, rich, chunky. Dry finish. A good enough mouthful but a not good enough Chambertin.
Rather letting the side down at an expensive dinner in Chicago, Oct 1983★★
Chambertin, Clos de Bèze *J DROUHIN RECOLTE DU DOMAINE* First tasted in 1971, "gorgeously velvety", a lovely powerhouse in 1973. At 19 years of age, still a magnificently deep colour; incredibly rich, ripe but somehow unready nose; an enormous wine of high quality.
Le Gavroche after Drouhin's tasting of '78s, June 1980. Then★★★(★★) *Now doubtless approaching its peak.*
Chambolle-Musigny *PASQUIER-DESVIGNES* Palish, rosehip; very sweet, vegetal Pinot flavour.
March 1991★★
Charmes-Chambertin *DOUDET-NAUDIN* A characteristically chocolaty style, but elegant.
At a Saintsbury Club dinner, Oct 1983★★
Le Corton *BOUCHARD PERE* Deep; rich, jammy; huge but wholesome, massively masculine, nicely put together.
At another Saintsbury Club dinner, in Oct 1981★★★★ *Doubtless many years of life left.*
Corton *VIENOT* First tasted in 1972: stewed Pinot, flavoury "though not top drawer". Aged 20, still deep; overladen with alcohol and sweet, blackcurrant-like fruit; another hefty wine. Rich. Dry finish.
Aug 1981★★★ *Probably approaching its peak.*
Gevrey-Chambertin *LEROY* Medium-pale; firm; sweet, almost sickly sweet but 100% Gevrey 'fishy' Pinot nose. Drying out, slightly stalky, hard and tannic.
At the Bize-Leroy tasting, Sept 1984★★
Grands-Echézeaux Bottled by the Wine Society (IECWS). The first, with high level, had a lovely colour; equally lovely smoky old Pinot nose; slightly sweet, very good flavour and length but noticeable acidity. The second bottle had a roughly mid-shoulder level, looked more mature, nose less well defined and a bit raw.
Chez the Sampsons, Feb 1990. At best★★★
Latricières-Chambertin *DOUDET-NAUDIN* Ruddy; chocolaty; somewhat austere.
March 1991★
Musigny *LEROY* Low-keyed coffee-chocolate nose that evolved well in the glass. Dry, firm, high alcoholic content, a bit austere.
March 1982★★★ *Probably reaching peak now.*
Musigny, Tastevinė *FAIVELEY* Paler and pinker than expected; good, ripe, rather jammy character; sweet, stylish, charming and easy.
April 1983★★★ *Drink up.*
Musigny, Vieilles Vignes *DE VOGUE* Bottle variation: the first deep, very rich, very lively red; fragrant, harmonious, developing a spicy perfume in the glass (reminiscent of freesias); overall dry, firm, a touch too austere. The second even harder and slightly woody.
At Khoury's de Vogüé tasting, Oct 1984★★?
Clos de la Roche *PIERRE PONNELLE* A really lovely wine: luminous, beautiful gradation of colour; good crisp fruity nose blossoming gloriously after an hour in the glass; very sweet, fairly full-bodied, good full fruity flavour and length.
At the closing dinner of the Hollywood Wine Society's weekend, Jan 1990★★★★
Volnay, Caillerets *JABOULET-VERCHERRE* Palish but attractive; charred Pinot, blancmange vanilla nose; surprisingly full flavoured and tannic. In a good state of preservation.
At Schaefer's, Skokie, June 1984★★★ *Drink soon.*
Clos Vougeot *NOELLAT* Palish, bright, autumnal; beautiful bouquet; medium full-bodied, a warm, lively flavour and fragrant aftertaste. Elegant.
Jan 1984★★★★ *Drink soon.*
Some other '61s tasted in the 1980s:
Beaune, Marconnets *ARMY & NAVY STORES* (Bottler) Good old stalwart ★★★
Bonnes Mares *GONDRAND* (Belgian bottled.) Piquant, flavoury★
Chassagne-Montrachet *GONDRAND* Chewy★
Latricières-Chambertin *FAIVELEY* Palish, rich, attractive★★★
Vosne-Romanée, Suchots *CHAUVENET* Overmature and a trifle acidic★
Clos Vougeot *GONDRAND* Touched with oxidation, and acidic. Rather good.
Other DRCs tasted:
Echézeaux Piquant, showing not at all well in the early 1970s.
Grands-Echézeaux Tasted in 1964, 1967 and 1972. Less impressive than Richebourg, stringy, raw, green, not a patch on the '62.
Richebourg This was best, impressive in 1964, misleadingly pale in 1967 then generating richness, with noticeable style and quality in 1972. Probably excellent now.

1962★★★★

Superior to '61. At best five star.

Weather cool in April and May but favourable for flowering in June. Quite good July. Fine and warm in Aug, continuing with intervals of welcome rain, through to a rather late harvest of sound, fully ripe grapes, from Oct 8. To merchants' dismay prices held firm. Looking back, of course, they appear to have been excellent value and, not having the "1961" tag, have tended to be underrated. Well worth looking out for.
Romanée-Conti Whatever reservations I had – still have – about the '61 DRC wines, 'the Domaine' performed marvellously in 1962. They were first presented to the trade in London in Oct 1964. Romanée-Cônti was difficult to taste: dry, raw, tannic, closed; virtually undrinkable. Still rather hard and nowhere near fully developed even after 15 years. Last tasted, in jeroboam (a double-magnum size in Burgundy), almost exactly a quarter of a century after the grapes had been picked. Now medium-deep, richly coloured, looking mature. When first poured, the nose was low-keyed, rather twiggy. It took 20 minutes in the glass to open up. After 30 minutes it was rich and toasty. Medium-dry, full-bodied, a powerful, assertive wine with hints of liquorice, holly, walnuts. Great length. Mouthfilling.
Last noted at a dinner devoted to great wines of the '62 vintage given by Hardy Rodenstock, Sept 1987★★★(★★) *Best beyond 2000.*

La Tâche Also totally immature and by no means obvious at the Lebègue tasting in 1964 but, by 1972, had developed well. Seemed deeper and sweeter, opulence and velvet noted the following year. It filled the entire room with perfume when served at a post-midnight supper at the end of Marvin Overton's great Latour tasting in 1976. Two subsequent notes, in 1983 and, more recently: a very fine deep though mature appearance; nose hard, restrained, slow to emerge but opened up magnificently, indescribably opulent, vegetal. But on the palate, positively explosive, a touch of ripe sweetness, fairly full-bodied, concentrated, beautiful texture, mouthfilling fragrance, with the proverbial peacock's tail of multi-faceted flavours.
*Last noted at the Bresciani Collection pre-sale tasting, Chicago, Oct 1987*****(*) Now to well beyond 2000.*
Richebourg *DRC* I am always fascinated by the contrast of style between La Tâche and the DRC Richebourg. It makes a nonsense of the arguments of the 'grape and winemaker' protagonists and dramatises the importance of what the French call *terroir*: for the essential difference here is in soil, sub-soil, drainage and exposure, not grape, not winemaker, for the latter they have in common. Moreover, it demonstrates how misleading these wines are when tasted young, and how difficult for the inexperienced taster to assess. This wine was thought by me, and others, to be "curiously dry, light and thin" at the opening tasting in 1964 yet, three years later "rich and developing well". Not tasted again for 20 years: jeroboam alongside the Romanée-Conti, deeper and redder than the latter, more immediately fragrant, then a bit prune-like in its fruit. Seemed drier at first, though it managed to become sweeter and to soften in the glass. A good mouthful.
*Last tasted at Arlberg, Sept 1987****(*) Now to beyond 2000.*
Grands-Echézeaux *DRC* Alongside the Romanée-Conti, in 1964, it presented a totally different face, nice, easier to comprehend, appearing more advanced and confirmed at another Lebègue tasting three years later. By 1972, deep, rich-looking; sweet, perfectly balanced. In 1972 with the Khourys: a rich, complex "fishy Pinot" nose noted again. Fabulous flavour, soft, saffron, cloves, perfection. More recently, still holding its own. A lovely sweet wine with plenty of grip.
*Last tasted Sept 1986***** Now to beyond 2000.*
Musigny, Vieilles Vignes *DE VOGUE* Also listed here out of order, mainly because of its quality, partly because of the Khoury connection. A magnum, still deep, still red; a fully-developed, instantly fragrant bouquet, slightly singed and chocolate, but a very pure strain of Pinot, lovely after over two hours in the glass; touch of sweetness, a warm, scented, chewy, meaty wine. Very fine flavour and length. Still tannic.
*At Khoury's de Vogüé tasting, Oct 1984***** Now to 2000.*
Chambertin, Clos de Bèze *CLAIR-DAU* A lovely half-bottle "selected by Colony Wines & Spirits, New York", brought from Newfoundland to Christie's by Dr Angus Neary who had bought it from the Chicago Wine Company. A very good long, branded cork had helped preserved this peripatetic Pinot. It had a pretty colour, rather tawny-hued; very sweet, almost sickly sweet, slightly jammy, smoky, boiled beetroot nose; equally sweet on palate but rather light in style with a raspberry-like fruit flavour and good length.
*May 1989*****
Gevrey-Chambertin, Cazetiers *LEROY* Medium, cherry, ruby-tinted yet maturing nicely (red seems the predominant hue in the generality of '62s.) Bouquet sweet, ripe, good 'communal' fishy Pinot character. Equally ripe on the palate, lovely rich texture, length, dry finish.
*At the Bize-Leroy vertical of Gevrey and Mazis-Chambertin, Sept 1984*** Now to 2000.*
Mazis-Chambertin Not very deep but bright, yet with a very sweet chocolaty nose, lovely flavour, fully mature.
*At the same tasting, Sept 1984**** Drink soon.*
Nuits-St-Georges *PIERRE PONNELLE* Palish, mature; pleasant enough, scented Pinot nose; dry, agreeable. Probably fairly representative of the middling '62s.
*April 1987** Drink soon.*
Volnay, Hospices, Cuvée Général Muteau Bottled by Berry Bros. First noted in 1972 as rich, scented and stylish but "not a lightweight" Volnay. After 10 years, it had deteriorated, a situation I would not immediately put down to storage, as it had one home only after bottling, the cellars at Vintners Hall. Even allowing for candle-light, it appeared almost opaque, even in a large glass; a rich, chocolaty nose, Virol and molasses; a big chunky mouthful, devoid of elegance and charm.
*At a Saintsbury Club dinner, Oct 1982**

1963*

A promising start and a late, but some thought, promising finish. Something wrong in between. Too cold in July and too wet in Aug. The grapes did not really start to ripen until the second half of Sept, a very late harvest rambling on through Oct, ending in sunshine, early Nov. An over-abundant crop of rather thin acidic wines, given a miss by the British trade. Only one tasted recently.
La Tâche First noted at the Romanée-Conti tasting at Quaglino's in 1974. Browner and deeper than the '65, quite nice nose, balance and texture. Next, in May 1983, and again the following autumn. Good colour for its vintage and age; soft, chocolaty, chaptalised nose, slightly scented; touch of vanilla, 'green' unripe fruit beneath it all; fairly dry, lightish, lean but quite nice fruit and an interesting flavour. For a 20-year-old 'off' vintage, not at all bad.
*Last tasted Oct 1983***

1964****

A good, big vintage, approaching the weight and substance of '59 but, though completely different in style, its quality more on a par with '62.

Perfect flowering, extremely hot and dry summer though some rain in Aug. Excellent ripening weather in Sept, warm, sunny, with occasional rain showers. Crop size reduced by the summer drought conditions but fine ripe grapes picked in good conditions from Sept 18.

A deservedly popular vintage with merchants and their customers. I have more notes on the '64s than any other burgundy vintage, mainly made in the late 1960s to mid-1970s. More recent notes follow. The best are rich, rounded wines, still drinking beautifully.
La Tâche Once again, a good example of an alarmingly pale youthful DRC taking on colour and character with bottle-age. At the Lebègue presentation in 1967, it was singularly feeble in colour and on nose, yet sweet and beautifully flavoured. Then at the Romanée-Conti tasting at Christie's in 1972, bottle variation: one dull and raw, the other full of flavour with quite a bite. In 1982 a pair of slightly variable magnums: both had a lively plummy colour; the bouquet, disappointing at first, developed well; slightly sweet, rather loose-knit, good flavour and finish, one seeming to pack a bit more punch. The following year, at the Domaine, the colour was a

medium-deep, firm, pleasant red; the nose very forthcoming, elegant, fragrant, strawberry-like. Fairly full-bodied, a different character to the '62, spice, crisp, firm, with dry finish.
*Last tasted May 1983. A difficult wine to pin down, but on balance**** Probably best to drink soon.*
Aloxe-Corton, Vieilles Vignes *MICHEL COUVREUR SELECTION* In fact a Thévenot wine made from 20-year-old vines, first tasted in Bouze-les-Beaune in 1972. Still a very agreeable wine, lively, pink-tinged; nice weight, good grip.
*Last tasted Sept 1990*** Now to 2000.*
Chapelle-Chambertin *LEROY* Medium-deep, lively; smoky bouquet; lovely flavour, still tannic.
*At Dom d'Auvernay, Sept 1988*** Now to 2000.*
Corton, Renardes *LEROY* Similar smoky Pinot nose; full-bodied, touch of overripeness.
*Oct 1984** Drink up.*
Gevrey-Chambertin, Combottes *PIERRE PONNELLE* Still deep, with a touch of crimson; lovely, slightly singed bouquet; sweet, soft, most attractive.
*Shown by Becky Wasserman at an extensive tasting of wines from the Gevrey-Chambertin commune at the Hollywood Wine Society, Feb 1989*****
Grands-Echézeaux *LEROY* Good rich nose; firm, chewy.
*Oct 1984****
Mazis-Chambertin *LEROY* Magnificent.
*Oct 1984******
Musigny A magnum from Pierre Ponnelle's private stock. Fine deep colour; lovely, sweet, smoky hot-vintage Pinot, like toasted marshmallows; sweet, fullish, soft, velvety.
*Dining at the home of Juan Morales in Mexico City, March 1982**** Seemed at its peak then, but probably still delicious.*
Musigny *AVERY* Magnum: a lovely rich, ruddy colour pressing the sides of the glass; soft, expansive, harmonious bouquet of lovely Pinot warmth; fairly dry, with a powerful, mouthfilling flavour, still quite hard and tannic. Showing no signs of age, after 20 years.
*Slipped into Khoury's de Vogüé tasting, Oct 1984**** Doubtless still a good mouthful.*
Musigny, Vieilles Vignes *DE VOGUE* Medium-pale, slightly hazy; rich bouquet, figs, prunes; medium sweetness and weight, rounded, some elegance but rather disappointing.
*With the multi-professional peripatetic Ray Healy, July 1988***
Nuits-St-Georges, Clos des Porrets St-Georges *HENRI GOUGES* Fabulous depth of colour; an extraordinary bouquet, neither varietal, fruity or earthy—I just thought of a holly bush; fairly sweet, tremendously flavoury, 'hot' alcohol and acidity.
*At a Castle Hotel, Taunton, burgundy dinner, Nov 1983**** Will still be good.*
Romanée-St-Vivant *L LATOUR* Fairly deep. Lively colour and nose though showing some age. Sweet, full, rich, powerful.
*Lunch at Parrot's, Latour's London agents, Aug 1989*****
Volnay, Caillerets *POUSSE D'OR* Lovely, palish, luminous; fragrant, touch of liquorice; medium sweetness and weight, a veritable fishy-Pinot flavour, perfect to drink.
*Sept 1988*****
Some other '64s tasted in the 1980s:
Chambertin, Clos de Bèze *DAMOY* Anaemically pale and faded.
Charmes-Chambertin *PATRIARCHE* Pleasant, very mature, sweet soft wine.
Nuits-St-Georges *JAFFELIN* Sweaty.
Clos Vougeot *JAFFELIN* Similar to the Nuits-St-Georges but more acidic.
Vosne-Romanée *JAFFELIN* Lovely.
Pommard, Epenots *LEROY* Dry, austere.
Two ROPITEAU wines:
Pommard, Chanlains Sweet, singed.
Volnay, Clos des Chênes Several palish, fully mature-looking, ripe, lightish and pleasant-enough bottles. They say that variety is the spice of life. It certainly prevents one ever from generalising about burgundy.

1965

A washout, literally and metaphorically. No fault of the growers and winemakers: appalling conditions with temperature and hours of sunshine the lowest recorded since 1910. On Sept 8 the most appalling storm in living memory. Overnight, the vineyards waterlogged, those on any sort of slope had their soil washed away. Because of the earlier poor weather the harvest was already a month delayed. It started on Oct 12 in fitful and too late sunshine. Unwanted, largely unseen, mercifully forgotten.
La Tâche Although not unattractive it cannot do the Domaine much good to promote their wine in this sort of vintage. First tasted in 1972: already fairly pale, yet its nose was quite appealing, if piquant. Sweet too, though raw and short. It was served, as a light, quite refreshing, luncheon wine after a DRC tasting. It then appeared at another DRC tasting at Quaglino's in 1974: a minty, grassy nose; fairly raw and acidic. Next tasted at the Domaine: strangely, it seemed to have taken on a bit of colour, quite attractive though a fraction too brown. It had a strange, delicate fragrance, leafy, tinged with rot. On the palate fairly light, crisp, flavoury, with a short dry finish.
*Last noted May 1983**

1966****

'62, '64 and '66: three easy to remember vintages but, generalising, three different styles of burgundy, the '66s having more in common with the '62s, leaner and more elegant than the '64s. At its best, superb, five-star. Generally reliable and, if good wine to begin with, still marvellous to drink.

The growing season not spectacular until the end of Aug, the vital ripening month Sept was sunny with a fortuitous amount of rain. Picking started at the end of the month in perfect conditions.
Romanée-Conti Without doubt Romanée-Conti has extra dimensions. At Lebègue's opening tasting in Oct 1967, the earliest DRC presentation I can recall, it was richer, bigger than the rest of the 'team'. In 1977, some loss of colour and looking more mature, yet rich, ripe and clearly packing a punch. The last two notes at Christie's pre-sale tastings in Chicago: in Oct 1984, displaying a beautifully soft, classic, 'beetroot' Pinot nose; and, exactly three years later, still medium-pale and fully mature-looking, yet mouthfilling, with great length.
*Last tasted Oct 1987***** A well-structured wine with many more years of life.*
La Tâche Often more dramatic, more immediately appealing than other DRC wines when young, it was certainly aromatic and exciting the autumn after it was made. Outstandingly attractive at the Christie's/DRC tasting in 1972. By the mid-1970s, deep, almost over-opulent to drink and, at a DRC tasting in 1977, I noted a deeper richer colour than the other '66s. Firm. Great vivacity. In May 1983 it was showing well in the La

Tâche vertical at the Domaine. Still deeply coloured; crisp, very forthcoming, fragrant bouquet; dry, fairly full-bodied with a perfectly balanced, rich, root-like vegetal flavour. And later that autumn, showing some maturity at the rim; an amazingly rich, ripe, 'beetroot' scent which soared out of the glass and continued for some time; an unbelievable rich, flowery flavour, its inimitable 'peacock's tail' flooding the palate and rebounding in the aftertaste. A brilliant wine.
*Last tasted Oct 1983***** Perfect now, and doubtless still perfection beyond 2000.*
Chambertin *ARMAND ROUSSEAU* Rousseau and his Chambertin at their best. Good colour, glorious bouquet; a wine of great power and character.
*Oct 1987****(*)*
Chambolle-Musigny *L LATOUR* Fairly deep; sweet, rather sweaty and jammy. Not much development of bouquet. Sweet, rich, chunky. But lacking the style and elegance I would expect of Chambolle and '66.
*Jan 1984***
Chambolle-Musigny *LEROY* Attractive ruby colour; first impression, fruit and walnuts. Developed fragrantly and held well. Distinctly sweet entry, crisp, fruity, flavoury, lovely acidity.
*Jan 1984*****
Chapelle-Chambertin *P PONNELLE* Rich, red brown, lovely sheen; gentle fragrance, touch of tar and coffee bean; excellent balance.
*Feb 1989****
Corton, Clos de la Vigne au Saint *L LATOUR* Aged 12 a lovely soft, 'welter-weight' Corton. "Will keep" noted. 11 years later some colour loss, though lovely, with slight orange tinge; ripe Pinot bouquet; touch of sweetness, softness, very agreeable weight. Nice consistency.
*Last tasted Aug 1989**** Perfect now but will keep.*
Corton, Bressandes *REMOISSENET* Rich, meaty and expensive at Avery in 1974. Still surprisingly deep and intensely coloured six years later. A singed, scented chocolate cake nose; sweet from start to finish. An impressive heavyweight Corton.
*Last tasted Aug 1982**** Now to 2000.*
Ch Corton-Grancey *L LATOUR* A deep, hefty-looking wine. Touch of iron on the nose and palate. Sweet, full, rich Pinot flavour.
*March 1982**** Will keep.*
Gevrey-Chambertin, Cazetiers *LEROY* Virtually opaque though maturing at the rim; rich, chocolaty, brambly nose; most curious texture, tannic. Lacking '66 elegance.
*At the Bize-Leroy tasting, Sept 1984***
Mazis-Chambertin *LEROY* Fullish, cherry-hued; nice ripe, brambly Pinot nose; full of alcohol, fruit and tannin. Very dry finish.
*Sept 1984**(*)*
Musigny, Vieilles Vignes *DE VOGUE* Gloriously rich colour, red-hued depth; heavenly bouquet, very forthcoming yet perfectly harmonious, and, descending in vintage order from the '79, I thought it the first really classic nose of the de Vogüé range. Fine flavour, balance and length. A touch of '66 leanness but displaying real class.
*At Khoury's de Vogüé tasting, Oct 1984***** Perfect now and will continue well past its 30th birthday.*
Nuits-St-Georges, Les St-Georges *J DROUHIN* Fine deep colour; rather singed and chocolaty; sweet, full, chewy, rounded. Good, but more of a Corton in style and '59 in weight, not a patch on Henri Gouges' tasted a decade early.
*March 1985****
Richebourg *DRC* Noted simply as "rich" in 1967. Very attractive colour though not deep in 1972; rich, assertive flavour and aftertaste. 12 years later, bouquet fully aroused, rich, 'boiled beetroots'. Dry, full but lean, with a fabulously fragrant and positive flavour.
*Last tasted Sept 1984***** Now to beyond 2000.*
Romanée-St-Vivant, Marey Monge First tasted in 1973: lovely. Deep, fabulously fragrant and flavoury in 1975. Nine years later, ripe, rich, soft. High-toned. Great style and class.
*Last tasted June 1984***** Now to beyond 1996.*
Clos de Vougeot *CHARLES NOELLAT* Fairly deep, expansive appearance; excellent ripe, 'beetroot' Pinot nose; sweet ripe entry, distinctly dry finish. Well constituted. Good flavour and grip.
*Dec 1984***(*) Now to 2000.*
Some other '66s tasted in the 1980s:
Aloxe-Corton, Boutières Bottled by Berry Bros and from its curiously meaty character almost certainly a Doudet-Naudin wine. Sweet, flavoury, idiosyncratic, holding well.
*July 1987** Will keep without great improvement.*
Beaune, Hospices, Nicolas Rolin Bottled by Avery. Fairly deep, positive, very fragrant and flavoury, powerful yet stylish.
*Oct 1980***(*)*
Echézeaux *GOUROUX* Rather pale; smoky, low-keyed but rich, mature. Dry, medium-light, yet with a rather 'hot' alcoholic finish.
*Oct 1981**(*)*
Musigny More Berry Bros bottlings. Rather good nose; slightly sweet, a touch of elegance.
*Tasted in 1983 and 1988****
Richebourg *MOREAU-FONTAINE* Bottled by Hatch Mansfield, very mature, orange-tinged, dry, good, firm.
*October 1985****
Vosne-Romanée, Beaumonts *NOELLAT* Cloudy, mercaptan nose.
Feb 1984.

1967**

An uneven vintage. For a change, the fault more of the grower and winemaker than the weather. The latter provided opportunities that seemingly few growers took advantage of. Widespread frost at a crucial period in early May, the net result of which was a concentration of fewer grapes: nature's pruning. The summer was warm and sunny, so many did not bother with the normal vine prophylactics. This proved to be a false economy as 10 days of rain fell during Sept. Happily, fine weather returned in good time for an early Oct harvest. Some grapes gave high must readings, some were diseased. But worst of all was the general feeling of carelessness, of short cuts, quick fermentation aimed at easy wine for quick sale and consumption. It heralded a period of shortsightedness which harmed the reputation of burgundy.
La Tâche Just two notes: pale, pink-tinged; an immediacy of fragrance; dry, light, flavoury, piquant at five years of age, not much change at 16, the pink now slightly orange, nose sweet, soft but superficial. Lean, clean, firm, wiry.
*Last tasted at the Domaine, May 1983** Neither much change nor much future predicted.*
Chambertin *LEROY* Palish, fully mature, autumnal brown; very rich, very meaty; soft entry, austere finish. Good flavour but lacking length and finesse.
*April 1985***

Mazis-Chambertin *LEROY* Medium-deep, rich, starting to show maturity; good, open, mature, ripe Pinot bouquet of some elegance; firm, crisp, good flavour, length and aftertaste. A high quality '67.
*At the Bize-Leroy tasting, Sept 1984****

Vosne-Romanée *JEAN GRIVOT* My first visit to Grivot's cellars in Vosne awakened my palate to another facet of a true Pinot flavour. The wine had a lovely colour; a well-mannered, calm fragrance, and Pinot 'beetroot', aroma, yet with a lovely underlying ripeness of grape character for a '67. The wine was very sweet, very flavoury, velvety in texture, with good tannin and acid grip.
*In the cellars, Sept 1984*****

Vosne-Romanée, Tastevinė *CLERGET* First tasted in 1972: fragrant, light, rather lean, delicious. The proprietors assured me that it had "a good 10 years of life ahead", and they were right. Though palish and looking very mature, it had a slightly vanilla-scented bouquet that developed well, a touch of sweetness, also a slight touch of bitterness on the finish but showing well. I did not think it had yet another 10 years but I dare say it will have survived.
*Last tasted Aug 1983*** Drink soon.*

One or two other '67s tasted in the 1980s:

Beaune, Clos des Ursules *JADOT* Delicious.
*April 1989****

Ch Corton-Grancey Looking, smelling and tasting fully mature in 1980, slightly sweet, soft, little tannin, just enough acidity**

Latricières-Chambertin *FAIVELEY* Deep, singed, chocolaty and slightly oxidised.
Feb 1986.

Romanée-St-Vivant *DRC* Beautiful colour but, alas, corked!

1968

A poor vintage which, this time, could fairly be blamed on inclement weather. The growing season started well: good spring, absence of hail and frost, June perhaps too hot but July and Aug poor, sunless and wet. Sept not as bad, the harvest being brought in from the 30th under reasonable conditions, but the damage was done, the grapes had not ripened. A rare thing: the Hospices de Beaune auction was cancelled. As 1968 in Bordeaux was equally disastrous, and as one influences the other, the trade gave the '68 burgundies a miss. Not counting skinny, tinny beaujolais I have tasted only three wines, one of them twice, in the mid-1980s.

Vosne-Romanée, Beaumonts *P PONNELLE* Pale, with orange tawny hue; spicy, medicinal, singed Pinot nose and flavour. A touch of chaptalised sweetness, lacking body but quite flavoury. Touch of bitterness.
*Twice in Feb 1983**

1969★★★★

I suspect that many of those who live and work in the remarkably rural villages in Burgundy have little idea of the broader context in which their wines are judged. Worse still, how the British, trade and consumer alike, have their conception of a burgundy vintage influenced by the vintage in Bordeaux. This certainly applies to the '69 vintage. In Bordeaux, the reds are meagre and acidic; in Burgundy – at their best – very fine indeed. There is some tendency to leanness and acidity, though the latter adds to the wine's zest and flavour.

As the climate was more or less common to all, whether along the Côtes de Nuits or Beaune, the differences are of *terroir* and of winemaking.

The flowering was late but some catching up was done during a fine, warm July and Aug. The cold wet Sept was responsible for some less-than-ripe grapes and others high in acidity though sound. Many '69s tasted. A cross-section of the better notes follow.

ROMANEE-CONTI *Not for the first time, a misleadingly pale colour. How can a red wine that looks so lacking in pigment pack such a punch? Make no mistake about it, this wine is magnificent: an inimitably glorious bouquet; great power and length. No words of mine can do justice to it.* Sept 1986★★★★★ Now to well beyond 2000.

La TACHE *Six notes. At its presentation by Lebègue in 1972, its appearance belied its fullness and richness. Showing well in 1974, yet the colour, though deeper than the '70, already had a mature brown tinge. A bottle was returned by a puzzled American client in 1977, and I could see why. Next tasted at the La Tâche line-up at the Domaine in 1983: firm, flavoury, touch of leanness but nicely balanced. Later that autumn, not helped by* fond d'artichaut, *I thought it lacked the flair and intensity of the '62 or even the '66. Most recently, noted its fabulous, almost exaggerated Pinot fruit; medium dryness and weight, firm, flavoury, attenuated. An exciting wine.* Last tasted Sept 1990★★★★★

BEAUNE, HOSPICES, CLOS DES AVAUX *Whoever bottled this did a good job. Lovely colour, spicy bouquet, very sweet. Almost over-endowed with alcohol but a lovely rich, classic flavour.* At one of Dr Norman Burrows' little luncheons, July 1986★★★★

CHAMBERTIN LEROY *Medium-deep, intense, chestnut hue; I found it a bit smelly at first (bottle-stink?), then rich and earthy. Daphne noted it as flowery and beautiful, and she is a reliable taster. Certainly a sweet, rich, close-to-the-earth wine. All the component parts in balance. Delicious.* Feb 1989★★★★ Now to beyond 2000.

CHAMBERTIN TRAPET *Good colour; rich, authentic 'beetroot' Pinot nose; lovely rich spicy flavour.* Feb 1989★★★★ Now to beyond 2000.

CHARMES-CHAMBERTIN CHANSON *First noted, rather condescendingly, as "a good commercial wine". In fact it was very fragrant, dry, appealing. Confirmed a year later.* Last tasted April 1981★★★ Will doubtless still be drinking pleasantly.

ECHEZEAUX DRC *In 1982, detected the ripe Pinot identity which, unflatteringly, I always note as "boiled beetroot". Crisp, leaner than La Tâche, marvellous acidity. The following year, looking fully mature, with copybook Pinot aroma, distinctly sweet and fragrant with good length. Next – noting also various labels: Lebègue neck label (the London agents),* "Interdiction d'Exporter aux USA" *presumably to protect the exclusivity of the Domaine's American agents, and, even more fascinating, the back label, printed in black and grey, indicating* "Très Grandes Années" *(in the case of* "Très Bonnes Années", *the colours are black and maroon). By the mid-1980s, a touch of orange at the rim, rich, fragrant bouquet, rather taut character and despite "a taste of rusty water" rather attractive, with good length and acidity.* Last tasted March 1983. At best★★★★★ Drink soon.

GEVREY-CHAMBERTIN LEROY *Palish, colour a bit feeble; fishy Pinot fragrance; a bit loose-knit though quite elegant. I thought it was the '67.* At the Bize-Leroy tasting, Sept 1984★★

GEVREY-CHAMBERTIN, CAZETIERS LEROY *Better colour, cherry-tinged, spicy, stylish, elegant, good length and acidity.* Sept 1984★★★

GEVREY-CHAMBERTIN, CLOS ST-JACQUES CLAIR-DAU *Several notes in the mid-1980s. Fairly deep; good nose, very positive fruit reminding me sometimes of bramble, of raspberry and – not surprisingly – Pinot. Attractive.* Last tasted Sept 1985★★★ Will be nice now.

GEVREY-CHAMBERTIN, CLOS ST-JACQUES FERNAND PERNOT *Incredibly deep, complex, fragrant, with zest and bite noted in 1977. In 1984, in magnum, impressive, with very pronounced nose. Most recently, still fairly deep; low-keyed at first, slightly peppery, but fragrant, evolving beautifully in the glass; distinctly sweet, soft despite its complement of tannins and acidity. Delicious.* Last noted dining with the Peppercorns, Jan 1990★★★★ Now to 2000.

MUSIGNY, VIEILLES VIGNES DE VOGUE *Reputed to be M le Comte's favourite wine. However, at Khoury's tasting in 1984 it showed its age: a warm orange-tinged garnet; distinctive, cheesy, spicy, cloves and Pinot; elegant, considerable length but a touch of tartness. Three years later, I noticed depth of colour, elegance, lovely texture and length. Most recently, again that very mature orange tinge, honeyed bouquet but showing its age.* Last tasted Sept 1989. An open verdict.

RICHEBOURG DRC *A slow starter. Powerful but holding back in 1977. In 1986, medium-pale, very mature appearance, and both nose and flavour fully developed. A glorious, positively exotic bouquet and tremendous fragrance on the palate. Confirmed by another bottle a few months later.* Last tasted Sept 1986★★★★ Now to 1996, possibly beyond.

Clos de la ROCHE DUJAC *Fairly deep; rich, dramatic Pinot nose; dry, medium full-bodied, firm, crisp with an aftertaste reminding me of figs. A good* *example of this relatively new domaine's clear-cut, classic Pinot noirs. Dining with Jacques Seysses, Sept 1981**** Drink soon.*

ROMANEE-ST-VIVANT *Bottled (by Remoissenet?) for Avery. Bright, lively; pleasantly scented Pinot; good flavour, firm. March 1982****

Clos VOUGEOT *FELIX CLERGET Deep; sweet, vanilla chocolate nose; nice weight and flavour. Feb 1986****

Clos VOUGEOT *JEAN GRIVOT A relatively substantial individual proprietor, with over 1 ha of the famous Clos. Several bottles opened for a dinner and, because of the rather difficult cloudy sediment, double decanted. Nose lacking intensity but good; drying out a bit but still powerful and with good length. Grivot's hallmark is lack of drama but great penetration. Not the peacock's tail of the best DRC but a solidly convincing mouthful of flavour. Feb 1989*** Take care with the sediment, but will keep.*

Clos VOUGEOT *HENRI LAMARCHE The owner of Plot No 1 and two other narrow strips of vines at the top, in the middle and at the bottom of the Clos, also totalling roughly 1 ha. Was pale and understandably mature-looking aged 15 with a light but fragrant 'beetroot' Pinot scent; dry, flavoury, with just a touch of bitterness on the finish. Pre-sale tasting, Feb 1984****

Clos VOUGEOT *MUGNERET Two members of the family owned small parcels in the Clos. I think this was Jean. A different ballgame from Grivot and Lamarche. A beautiful colour; a Spanish-root earthiness and fragrance on bouquet and palate. Distinctly sweet, assertive, excellent length and dry finish. Dec 1987**** Now to 2000.*

1970★★★

I was inclined to downgrade the '70 vintage to two stars, for my notes make depressing reading. The weather was good, the crop large, the prices high. '1970' sounded just right for an overheated market. What went wrong? Overcropping? Quicker fermentation?

First the growing conditions: a poor spring but fine for the flowering in June, with the promise of a big crop. Sunny July and, save for a cold spell, warm in Aug. Sept was hot and continued from the start of picking at the end of the month into Oct. At the Hospices de Beaune sale, an accurate market barometer, prices broke all records.

From the start the wines lacked the firmness and style of the '66s or '69s. More open-knit and rounded, like the '64s but not as good. Most were pale, and appeared to reach full maturity within five years. Few were really top notch in the 1980s and, with some honourable exceptions, hardly worth pursuing. Drink up.

La TACHE *Appeared very pale when shown to the trade in 1974, but flavoury, with a tingle of youthful acidity. Next, tasted at the Domaine in 1983, its characteristic fragrance noted, yet an underlying hardness and seemed drier. Seven years later, in magnum, good bouquet, bigger than its colour indicated, growing in richness and complexity, with an assertive flavour and good length. Most recently, lovely colour; soft, scented, harmonious bouquet; still tannic. Perhaps lacking a little zest. Last tasted Jan 1991***(*) Will continue to expand.*

BONNES MARES *DE VOGUE Attractive, quite a bit to it, though I thought lacking some of its customary style and elegance in the mid- to late 1970s. Palish, soft and completely mature when last noted. April 1980*** Drink up.*

CHAMBOLLE-MUSIGNY, AMOUREUSES *DE VOGUE I presume Tawfig Khoury could not get hold of a '70 Bonnes Mares or Musigny for his de Vogüé tasting. The domaine's Amoureuses turned out to be a disappointing substitute, with a rather exaggerated aroma which my wife described as fish glue and paraffin. Gentle but short. Oct 1984***

CHAPELLE-CHAMBERTIN *BOUCHARD PERE Several notes over 10 years. Rather pale, now orange-tinged. A nose variously described as cheesy yoghurt, scented and a bit like damp cardboard. Dry, little flavour, not bad, just not good enough. Last tasted Jan 1990**

CORTON, CLOS DU ROI *PIERRE PONNELLE Pleasant, ripe, singed Pinot nose and flavour. Dry. Fair enough quality. May 1986***

CORTON, MARECHAUDES *MERODE Four notes. Although fairly pale and very mature-looking by 1979, it was fragrant and had quite a bite. But it soon seemed to fade, losing all trace of red after its 15th birthday, the last bottle having an oily, overripe nose and yeasty finish. Last tasted May 1986.*

CORTON, POUGETS *L JADOT At seven years of age, rich, powerful. 12 years later, paler with bite, a sweet bouquet and delicious flavour. Last tasted April 1989****

GEVREY-CHAMBERTIN *L LATOUR Following the same pattern, fully mature and open-knit in 1977, little nose, dry, lacking interest when last tasted. April 1988***

GEVREY-CHAMBERTIN *LEROY So pale I thought it must have been the '77. Very misleading, because the nose had a scented, oaky character that developed beautifully. Dry, open-knit like most '70s, yet firm and with good length. Sept 1984****

GEVREY-CHAMBERTIN, LA COMBE AUX MOINES *FAIVELEY Orange-tinged; nose almost sickly sweet; sweet on the palate too, yet with some tannin. Quite good flavour and body. Sept 1988*** Drinking well now.*

GRANDS-ECHEZEAUX *DRC Fairly deep; spicy Pinot nose; impressive on palate, giving the appearances of a big-vintage wine. Dining chez Angel del Valle in San Juan, Jan 1990***(*) Drink now to 2000.*

MOREY ST-DENIS *L LATOUR Noted in 1977 as good, firm and with more to come. Several recent notes. Now soft but with sufficient tannin and acidity to hold it together. Not thrilling but attractive and drinking nicely. Last tasted Aug 1990***

MUSIGNY, VIEILLES VIGNES *Another substitute at the de Vogüé tasting, this bottle with an Avery label. Lovely colour, pink-cheeked; sweet, chocolaty, scented bouquet; appeared to be drying out, but lovely flavour. Still a bit hard for a '70.* Oct 1984***(*) Probably more to come.

VOUGEOT, CLOS PERRIERE *BERTAGNA Pleasant, palish, rosy-hued; low-keyed, dry, lightweight. Quite nice.* Nov 1986**

SOME OTHER '70s TASTED IN THE 1980s:

BEAUNE, CLOS DE LA FEGUINE *CALVET Rich, ripe, flavoury***

BEAUNE, HOSPICES, ROLIN *AVERY Sweet, soft and lovely*****

BEAUNE, MARCONNETS *CHANSON Pretty; fragrant; flavoury**

CHAMBERTIN, CLOS DE BEZE *M DUROCHE The only time I have tasted wine from this ⅓ ha holding in this great vineyard. Alas I thought it smelled of stewed cardboard. Better on palate: some sweetness, chewy, quite nice flavour.* 1982**

CHAMBOLLE-MUSIGNY *JADOT Almost carrot-coloured, with a stewed Pinot nose yet dry, quite crisp and a perfectly pleasant drink***

CHARMES-CHAMBERTIN *CHANSON Stewed and screwed.*

CHASSAGNE-MONTRACHET *ALBERIC MATHIEU A pale orange brown colour, nose like wet cardboard, was very dry, and dull.*

CORTON *CHANSON Very pale tawny, stewed, scented nose, better taste.*

CORTON, BRESSANDES *AVERY Soft, the flavour swelling in the mouth, good length****

NUITS-ST-GEORGES, LES PORRETS *THOMAS FRERES Weak-rimmed, a nose like freshly picked mushrooms, quite powerful***

POMMARD, EPENOTS *DE COURCEL Overblown nose, dry and raw.*

*1971******

A magnificent vintage: rich, structurally sound, long-lasting wines. Almost from the start, certain Burgundian voices mildly protested that they were rather too big, somewhat untypical. They have been proved at least partially right. It *is* untypical.

The weather was settled and generally favourable from the spring to well past the harvest save for one or two blips: some failures at the time of flowering and hail mid-Aug followed by a poor week, happily corrected by warm sun in Sept. A small crop of ripe, concentrated grapes picked early, from Sept 15. After the depressing '70s, the heartening '71s. Still worth looking out for. Like most mature burgundy, undervalued and now underpriced.

As I have a full set of notes on the magnificent DRCs, these are listed first, in order of status (and price).

ROMANEE-CONTI *At the Domaine's and Lebègue's main trade tasting in 1974 the wine appeared already to be remarkably well developed. Misleading of course. Three years later it was filling out and at 12 years of age had actually deepened in colour. Certainly the richest and sweetest of the '71 DRCs on the nose, after only minutes in the glass, opulent, holding well for well over 1½ hours — and doubtless would have continued to exude fragrance had the glasses not been removed. On the palate distinctly sweet, full, richly flavoured. A vast, complete wine, packed with fruit, with great length and flowery aftertaste.* Last noted at the Domaine, May 1983***** Should be magnificent now, and will keep.

La TACHE *Eight notes, three from jeroboams. Pink-tinged, high-toned in 1974, dry and holding back in 1977 but opening up, assertively, fragrant in its 10th year. Its inimitable bouquet, 'ambrosial beetroot', fully in evidence at a grand Christie's/Chicago Wine Company dinner in 1982. Served in magnums. Marvellous flavour and richness but still tannic. I gave it another 20 years. 12 months later, at the domaine, tasted 'vertically' against a wide range of other vintages and 'horizontally' alongside the other '71 DRCs, it seemed comparatively restrained. Most recently, in jeroboam again, medium-deep; wonderfully fragrant; seemed sweeter but still with quite a tannic bite.* The last, served at a Rodenstock Wine Weekend dinner, Sept 1989****(*) 1995–2010

RICHEBOURG *DRC Richebourg is to La Tâche as Latour is to Ch Margaux. Usually more four-square, substantial, long living. In 1974, I noted a roasted character, in 1977, earthy, rounded. At the Domaine in May 1983, it had quite definitely deepened in colour, the darkest and most intense of the '71 DRC range. A broad, expansive, slightly vegetal nose, yet with a Chambertin-like 'fishy' Pinot aroma. Marvellous fruit. Held well. Full-bodied, rich, firm, with dry finish. Most recently, in magnum, rich, mature appearance; glorious bouquet; with the incoming sweetness of alcohol and ripe grapes, flavour of violets, great length.* Last tasted Sept 1990****(*) Now to well beyond 2000.

GRANDS-ECHEZEAUX *DRC In 1974, just under half the price of Romanée-Conti, and looking disarmingly advanced, open-knit. Three years later it was marking time, immature even; then, by 1980, surging ahead: lovely flavour and texture. Seemed perfect. At the horizontal tasting in May 1983 I noted a fairly good depth of colour though browning a little at the rim; fine, firm, crisp, fragrant bouquet. Stylish, elegant. Still tannic. Most recently, the same notes apply. Heavenly bouquet. The epitome of refinement yet still more to come.* Last tasted Feb 1988****(*) Now to beyond 2000.

ROMANEE-ST-VIVANT *DRC The old Général Marey Monge Domaine now managed, and the wines made, by the Domaine de La Romanée-Conti. Although always released at a hefty price, (the '71 the same as Richebourg): it does not hold its own on the open market and, for that reason, is better value than its peers. Delightful in 1974, with deep fragrance and great elegance in May 1983. Most recently, very mature-looking; a glorious bouquet; touch of sweetness, firm, assertive* *even, good fruit. Despite appearances to the contrary, still a certain amount of tannin and acidity ensuring a good life ahead. A very stylish wine.* Last tasted Sept 1989****(*) Now to beyond 2000.

ECHEZEAUX *DRC From the price and value point of view, the converse to St-Vivant. More correctly and proportionally lower priced by the Domaine, it not infrequently fetches at auction almost as much as the vastly superior Grands-Echézeaux. Pleasant enough but not very impressive in 1974, it was fully mature in its 12th year. Still bright and appealing, it had an orange tawny rim, an open, vinous nose, showing a bit of age. Dry, fairly mouthfilling, finishing firmly.* Last tasted May 1983*** Drink up.

SOME OTHER GOOD '71s:

BEAUNE, GREVES, VIGNE DE L'ENFANT JESUS *BOUCHARD PERE A lovely wine. Mulberry-rich fruit in 1977. A decade later: a good colour; ripe nose; excellent mouthfilling flavour. Most recently, still showing well.* Last tasted Sept 1990**** Now to 2000.

BEAUNE, HOSPICES, NICOLAS ROLIN *Bottled in Beaune for Hedges & Butler: richly coloured; a most exciting bouquet; marvellous flavour, elegance, length.* Not tasted since Nov 1980, but should still be*****

BEAUNE, VIGNES FRANCHES *L LATOUR Gentle and soft yet with a life-preserving backbone in 1977. Now pale, tawny-hued; sweet, fragrant bouquet; very flavoury.* Last tasted April 1989*** Drink soon.

BONNES MARES *L JADOT Toasted; rich, soft yet tannic. Very fragrant aftertaste.* March 1985***** Now to 2000.

BONNES MARES *DE VOGUE Deep, very rich, mahogany-tinged; nose low-keyed at first but developed well; a substantial wine. More beef and liquorice than elegance but impressive.* At Khoury's de Vogüé tasting, Oct 1984***(*) Now to 2000.

BONNES MARES, VIEILLES VIGNES *CLAIR-DAU Magnificent: lovely, broad, open, mature appearance; nose both earthy and flowery, vegetal and violets, gloriously scented after two hours; fairly sweet, fullish, soft yet assertive, rich yet dry finish.* At the Peppercorns', Jan 1990****(*) Now to 2000.

CHAMBERTIN, CLOS DE BEZE *J DROUHIN Rich, ruby; warm-singed, hot vintage scent that held well; medium-sweet, full-bodied, glorious flavour that unravelled and surged. Excellent length. Perfect.* Nov 1985***** Now to beyond 2000.

CHAMBOLLE-MUSIGNY, AMOUREUSES *DE VOGUE Fine colour; glorious Pinot aroma, yet with almost a Corton-like meaty richness; dry, full-bodied, certainly not a 'feminine' Chambolle, with scented finish.* At Khoury's tasting, Oct 1984**** Now to 2000.

CHARMES-CHAMBERTIN *A ROUSSEAU Palish, fully mature-looking; ripe, opulent, bouquet; sweet, nice weight, very good flavour and aftertaste.* July 1982**** Doubtless still very good.

Le CORTON *BOUCHARD PERE First tasted in 1973. Full, flavoury, still tannic in 1976. Most recently: a good rich, singed Corton character, with touch of caramel; lovely warm rounded flavour and good length. Yet on the verge of thinning and with a lean touch of end acidity.* Last tasted July 1984*** My original projection to 1995 probably still stands, though best to drink now.

CORTON, HOSPICES, CHARLOTTE DUMAY and DR PESTE *BOUCHARD PERE (both bottles) Both palish, very mature-looking but very rich and fragrant.* Both last tasted Sept 1990**** Drink soon.

ECHEZEAUX *J DROUHIN Lively, firm, nice weight, good length, fragrance and elegance.* Nov 1985**** Now to 2000.

GEVREY-CHAMBERTIN *L TRAPET Magnum: fragrant, scented, bouquet that opened up attractively; distinctly sweet, rich, chunky, good dry finish and aftertaste.* Nov 1983**** Now to 1995.

MUSIGNY, VIEILLES VIGNES *DE VOGUE Restrained, elegant, ripe Pinot nose; a warm, gorgeous wine with length and fullness.* At Khoury's tasting, Oct 1984***(*) Now to 2000.

RICHEBOURG *Bottled in Burgundy for Avery. Beautiful colour; perfect weight and balance. Elegant.* March 1985**** Now to 2000.

RICHEBOURG *J DROUHIN Fine classic bouquet and flavour.* Sept 1985**** Now to 2000.

Clos de TART *Stored upside down: even allowing several days to settle, its heavy sediment had adhered to the cork and the wine remained obstinately hazy; slightly meaty 'boiled beetroot' Pinot character, with almost port-like richness though rather hard and a trifle raw on the palate.* At the Castle Hotel, Taunton, Nov 1984**

Clos VOUGEOT *HUDELOT Glorious colour; deep, rich, mature, toasted Pinot nose; sweet, full-bodied, powerful charred flavour. Despite its weight and assertiveness, overall harmonious.* Produced by Becky Wasserman for the Hollywood Wine Society's burgundy evening, Jan 1990**** Now to 2000.

SOME OTHER '71s TASTED MAINLY IN THE EARLY TO MID-1980s:

BEAUNE, GREVES *AVERY Youthful for a 14-year-old, prune-like nose, unspectacular***

BEAUNE, HOSPICES, AVAUX *Rather overmature. Acidity too noticeable**

CHAMBERTIN, CLOS DE BEZE *DR MARION Outstanding******

CHAMBOLLE-MUSIGNY, 1ER CRU, TASTEVINAGE *FAIVELEY Very attractive****

CHAPELLE-CHAMBERTIN *THORIN Short cork; dried out.*

CORTON, CLOS DE CORTON *FAIVELEY Consistently good, deep, impressive, rich, perfectly balanced.*

ECHEZEAUX *AMANCE Flavoury****

ECHEZEAUX *JABOULET-VERCHERRE Bright red, flavoury but over-high volatile acidity.*

GEVREY-CHAMBERTIN *DOUDET-NAUDIN A good rich mouthful, solidly drinkable, in magnum**.*

GEVREY-CHAMBERTIN, CAZETIERS *LEROY Richly coloured but overdeveloped, slightly bitter.*

GEVREY-CHAMBERTIN, LAVAUX *AVERY French-bottled, (doubtless by Remoissenet). Lively and lovely, good fruit and grip****

LATRICIERES *REMY Palish, fully mature, chestnut*

*colour, gentle 'beetroot' and liquorice nose, medium sweet, good length, tannic**(*)*

NUITS-ST-GEORGES, CLOS DE LA MARECHALE *FAIVELEY Very fragrant but almost too sweet and rich — it gave me a port-like hangover. Very good though*****

NUITS-ST-GEORGES, LES ST-GEORGES *REMOISSENET Very disappointing at 10 years of age, with hard, spirity undertow.*

Clos ST-JACQUES *ROUSSEAU Beautifully flowery bouquet and flavour. Firm*****

VOLNAY, CLOS DES CHENES *LOUIS LESANGLIER Weak rim; light, medicinal nose yet sweet, chunky flavour***

VOSNE-ROMANEE *JADOT Earthy, surprisingly tough. A long laster***(*)*

VOSNE-ROMANEE, SUCHOTS *LOUIS LESANGLIER Similar though not as sweet. Quite good acidity***

Clos de VOUGEOT *RAYMOND-ROBLOT Advanced, high-toned, rich****

1972★★

Most Burgundians insist that this was a good vintage. In the late 1970s, I was inclined to agree; certainly compared with the distinctly poor, ungracious '72 red Bordeaux. But the early appeal, marred by occasional bitterness, has worn off. The weather was unpropitious. Despite the advantage of early budding, the summer was unusually cool and dry with a hot Sept.

La TACHE *Five notes. First tasted in the cellars at the Domaine, Sept 1975 and a month later in London. Rich and powerful. In 1980, nose even more forthcoming than the '71, lovely richness and texture. Good fruit and depth in the mid-1980s. Most recently, medium weight, mature colour; dramatically sweet, inimitable La Tâche Pinot scent. Last noted Sept 1989***(*) Good and more to come: now to beyond 2000.*

BONNES MARES *DE VOGUE Expansive, maturing but a bit weak at the rim; singed, rich, almost Corton-like, in fact it reminded me of Eyrie Vineyard's Pinot Noir from Oregon; a big, warm, slightly 'cheese' flavour, some softness and sweetness, and not a trace of '72 bitterness. At Khoury's de Vogüé tasting, Oct 1984*** Now to 1995.*

Ch CORTON-GRANCEY *L LATOUR Good, rich but slightly austere in 1975 but, more recently, a completely oxidised bottle. Last tasted May 1986. At best this should still be*** Drinkable now.*

GEVREY-CHAMBERTIN *LABOURE-ROI Palish, very mature; soft, fleshy, attractive. Sept 1988****

GEVREY-CHAMBERTIN, CAZETIERS *LEROY Good colour; rich bouquet, chocolaty, distinctive Chambertin Pinot aroma; dry, good weight, flavour and balance. At the Bize-Leroy tasting, Sept 1984***

GRANDS-ECHEZEAUX *ENGEL Very mature appearance; quite good nose and flavour, lean, uplifting. March 1985***

MAZIS-CHAMBERTIN *LEROY Pink and pretty; good Pinot aroma, sweet, singed, vanilla; dry, lovely flavour, nice acidity, good finish. Surprisingly stylish. At the Bize-Leroy tasting, Sept 1984****

MUSIGNY, VIEILLES VIGNES *DE VOGUE Two notes in the mid-1980s, showing well, rich bouquet and flavour, lacking length but with a good dry finish at the Khoury tasting. Most recently: good colour; attractive, scented, pronounced Pinot aroma. Dry, fullish, crisp, fruity. Good grip, acidity and aftertaste. Last noted Jan 1990*** Now to 1996.*

NUITS-ST-GEORGES, BOUDOTS *J GRIVOT Richly robed; sweet nose, figs and black treacle to which, on the palate, I added "beetroot". Very tannic. Correct though idiosyncratic. In the cellars, Sept 1984. In its way*** Probably at its best now.*

La ROMANEE *DOM DE LA ROMANEE (Not to be confused with DRC.) Bouquet developed nicely, a bit jammy; overall dry, good length and acidity. Nice wine. Dec 1987*** Drink soon.*

ROMANEE-ST-VIVANT *MAREY MONGE (DRC) Four notes, two in 1975, fairly pale but with a powerful backbone, good length. Colour rich and elegant in 1980. Most recently, medium, fully mature appearance, and beautifully evolved Pinot nose. Last tasted Septmber 1989*****

SOME OTHER '72s TASTED RECENTLY:

CORTON, RENARDES *GEISWEILER Very pale, poor nose but drinkable.*

ECHEZEAUX *MONGEARD-MUGNERET Orange-tinged; musty, mushrooms and beetroot — not very good.*

ECHEZEAUX, TASTEVINAGE *GEISWEILER Oxidised.*

MAZIS-CHAMBERTIN *FAIVELEY Bouquet reminding me of hazelnuts; sweet, flavoury, hint of violets, at peak.*

VOSNE-ROMANEE *JADOT Fragrant, flavoury, fairly acidic.*

SOME OTHER '72s SHOWING WELL IN THE EARLY 1980s:

Auxey-Duresses LEROY; Bonnes Mares L JADOT; Charmes-Chambertin J DROUHIN; Corton, Hospices, Charlotte Dumay LESANGLIER; Echézeaux J DROUHIN; Gevrey-Chambertin DROUHIN-LAROZE; Richebourg DRC; Clos St-Denis DUJAC.

NOT SHOWING WELL OR DISTINCTLY POOR IN THE EARLY 1980s:

Beaune, Marconnets BICHOT; Corton BICHOT; Clos de Tart.

1973★

Remarkably similar to Bordeaux: overproduction, seemingly idle and short-sighted winemaking; and both disheartening weather and market. I have marked the vintage rating down on the basis of recent and earlier notes.

The growing season started well: good flowering and dry, the driest summer since 1945, until mid-July. Thereafter heavy rain.

Sept inclement, a protracted rainy vintage from Sept 22 until Oct 18. An overabundance of watery grapes, lacking both ripeness and acidity. A dismal period in almost every respect.

La TACHE *Unimpressive, with youthful bitterness in 1977, yet after only three more years in bottle, a remarkable blossoming. But it all seemed rather premature, a distinct browning noted. At 10 years of age, rather lean, very dry. Better flavour than nose; its adolescent bloom seemed faded. Last noted at the Domaine in May 1983. Then** but it will be interesting to see how this has fared.*

BEAUNE, VIGNES FRANCHES *L LATOUR Two notes in 1975, one in 1977: pale, quick-maturing, pleasant enough. Most recently, still pale, lean, flavoury but lacking. Last tasted April 1989***

BEAUNE, THEURONS *JADOT Lively, sweet, surprisingly assertive. April 1989****

SOME '73s SHOWING WELL IN THE EARLY TO MID-1980s:

Chambertin, Clos de Bèze DR MARION; *Corton, Bressandes* TOLLOT-BEAUT; *Romanée-St-Vivant* DRC.

QUITE ATTRACTIVE BUT NO FUTURE:

Beaune, Hospices, Brunet BOUCHARD AINE; *Chambertin* TRAPET; *Chambertin, Clos de Bèze* L JADOT; *Volnay, Santenots, Hospices, Gauvin* THORIN.

POOR WHEN LAST NOTED WITHIN EARLY TO MID-1980s:

Corton, Renardes LEBEGUE; *Clos des Lambrays* BICHOT; *Musigny* CLAIR-DAU.

OTHER DRC '73s NOT TASTED SINCE THE 1970s:

ROMANEE-CONTI *Trying hard, its 'peacock's tail' with a few feathers missing.*

RICHEBOURG *Pale and pink, relatively modest in scale for Richebourg.*

GRANDS-ECHEZEAUX *Weak and watery.*

*1974**

A dismal vintage and a historic pattern of poor weather, poor wine, economic gloom. Difficult flowering, sunny and warm in July and Aug but the crucial period for ripening marred by rain, the grapes harvested in cold, wet, gusty weather. Quick-maturing wines for early sale and consumption. Prices down. One or two quite nice wines. Few shipped.

La TACHE *Three consistent notes in the early 1980s. A strange yet fragrant nose, somewhat stewed, lacking in fruit; touch of chaptalised sweetness counterbalancing its raw acidic finish. Flavoury but pasty-textured. Last tasted at the Domaine, May 1983* Will be interesting to see how this has developed, if at all.*

Clos de TART *An odd bottle opened out of curiosity by Patrice Noyelle of Mommessin after tasting a range of young vintages. Medium-deep with brown-tinged rim; earthy, vegetal nose that changed rapidly as the air got to it: Irish stew and malted milk! On the palate surprisingly sweet, assertive, fullish, malty and acidic. At the domaine, Oct 1990.*

OF MY RELATIVELY FEW NOTES ON THE '74s, THE FOLLOWING WERE MADE IN THE EARLY 1980s:

BEAUNE, CENT VIGNES *JESSIAUME Orange tawny; strange toasted nose; quite nice, singed flavour**

BEAUNE, GREVES *LEBEGUE Dull, woody.*

CHAMBERTIN, CLOS DE BEZE *ROPITEAU Scented Pinot, soft, elegant, well balanced****

ECHEZEAUX *DRC Lacking fruit and charm, but clean**

GEVREY-CHAMBERTIN *LEROY Nicely developed, vanilla nose; light style, flavoury but with raw acidity**

GRANDS-ECHEZEAUX *DRC Good Pinot aroma and very flavoury, but raw and acidic**?*

POMMARD *MARC GARAUDET Cardboardy nose, austere, stringy on palate.*

POMMARD, CLOS DE LA PLATIERE *MERODE Very attractive: a fabulously ripe Pinot nose and flavour*** Doubtless blown by now.*

RICHEBOURG *DRC Fragrant nose, nice vinosity****

Clos de la ROCHE *ROPITEAU Quite good fruit, refreshing acidity***

ROMANEE-ST-VIVANT *DRC Brown-tinged and raw at the opening tasting, and at 10 years of age a nose like old beetroots in a garden mulch heap, flavoury, but like soil clinging to roots. My host just emptied a magnum into 10 large glasses, hazy sediment and all.*

Clos de VOUGEOT *DOM DU CH DE LA TOUR Lovely colour; sweet, high-toned nose of soggy grapes with a whiff of varnish. Genuine but little and short.*

1975

Not a happy time in Burgundy: 1972, 1973, 1974 and, to cap it all, a dismal 1975. The year started off well, with marvellous spring and early summer. July and Aug mixed: heat, some hail. The rot set in, literally, at the end of Aug which was wet and humid. This carried through to early Sept, thereafter cool and dry. Small crop of rotten, unripe grapes from Sept 25. No market anyway: sales had slumped. One of the worst vintages of the post-war period, certainly since 1968. Not wines to seek out.

The controversial DRC wines are listed first. As usual, they picked the surviving grapes late and highly selectively. The *gérants* informed me that anti-rot sprays were first used at the Domaine in 1974.

ROMANEE-CONTI *Noted only once, at the Domaine's London tasting. Rather pale, prematurely orange-tinged; the 'toasted coconut' nose I found quite attractive and the wine, as always, packed a surprising punch. But its reputation languishes.* Noted March 1980 ?

La TACHE *Lacking firmness and grip at the opening tasting. The following autumn (1981) the nose was recognisably La Tâche but reminded me of damp ferns, rather 'blown' Pinot, and liquorice. Not bad but short. Aged eight, palish, bright; low-keyed, vegetal, stewed Pinot nose, the La Tâche fragrance struggling to surface; sweet, light, very flavoury but short.* Last tasted at the Domaine, May 1983*

RICHEBOURG DRC *Open-nosed; some richness. With the Richebourg signature but lacking body, firmness and frankly, quality. Despite its known recuperative ability, I doubted it would do much.* March 1980*

GRANDS-ECHEZEAUX DRC *Some depth of colour, like a '76; subdued nose, some fruit lurking; open-knit. Edgy acidity.* I predicted a short burst of development but have not tasted it since March 1980(**)?

ROMANEE-ST-VIVANT DRC *Sweet, open and also 'edgy' (acidic) in 1980; but in 1982, its rich colour slightly marred by cloudiness due to careless handling. Surprisingly sweet, richly developed and harmonious 'boiled beetroot' Pinot nose though a touch of maltiness; slightly sweet, higher alcohol than expected — heavily chaptalised I presume. Flavoury and stylish. Dry, slightly bitter finish.* Last noted Aug 1982**

ECHEZEAUX *The tail end of the DRC range, loose-knit, hollow but fragrant.* March 1980 ?

VOUGEOT 1ER CRU BERTAGNA *Stewed, gassy, short and sharp in 1982. Then, aged 11, fully mature, orange-tinged; an old, chocolaty nose and taste. Dry. Meaty.* Last tasted April 1986.

MY REMAINING NOTES MADE BETWEEN NOV 1981 AND JULY 1982:

BEAUNE, HOSPICES, BRUNET J PRIEUR *Unimpressive appearance; stewed, grassy nose and flavour, yet sweet and quite rich***

BEAUNE, CLOS DU ROI LEBEGUE *Passable.*

CHAMBERTIN, CLOS DE BEZE DOM MARION *Pale, orange-tinged; strange, uneven bouquet that improved on acquaintance; sweet, light, flavoury but acidic**

GEVREY-CHAMBERTIN, LAVAUX ST-JACQUES LEBEGUE *Sickly.*

VOSNE-ROMANEE LEBEGUE *Fruitless and grassy.*

VOSNE-ROMANEE, BEAUMONTS BERTAGNA *Curiously scented, piquant, raw and bitter.*

VOUGEOT, CLOS DE LA PERRIERE BERTAGNA *Medicinal; dry, light, piquant, flavoury but raw.*

CORTON LEBEGUE *'Blown' and bitter.*

1976***(*)?

An important vintage, seized upon by merchants after a string of poor years in terms of both quality and trade. I confess I *thought* I liked it until I put my notes into perspective. The wines had almost everything in abundance: colour, fruit, alcohol, extract. But there was, still is, one drawback: too much tannin. The wines were and still are very hard, and the worry has always been whether the harsh tannins will ease with time (after all, this is what happened to the '28 red Bordeaux) or whether the hardness will outlive the fruit.

A hot, dry growing season. Heat-wave and drought conditions which, in England, ceased abruptly on Aug 31 but which continued on the continent. The resultant grapes had thick, sunburnt skins, high sugar content and lacked lovely moist flesh. Deep colouring matter and bitter tannins were extracted from the skins during fermentation.

Certainly the English — merchant, restaurateur and consumer alike — found many of these wines strangely, unfamiliarly and unpleasantly hard, and quite a few were put back on to the market. I suspect, however, that those who cellared the best will have pleasant surprises around the turn of the century.

ROMANEE-CONTI *Already intensely, penetratingly rich, at the private preview at the Ritz in London in March 1979. The deepest of the DRC range in 1982, stern, impressive, heady, good length. Next noted at Christie's Chicago pre-sale tasting in Oct 1987: powerful, lean, flavoury. Most recently: heavenly fragrance, 'ethereal beetroot' — the inimitable, almost theatrical, DRC Pinot scent. On the palate sweet, mouthfilling flavour, still hard.* Last tasted Sept 1990**(***) Anticipate full blossoming after 1996.

La TACHE *Six notes starting with the London agents' tasting in March 1980. Deceptively light in style and elegant yet loads of fruit and quite an end-bite. The following autumn, noted that it was not as deeply coloured as the '78, yet no signs of maturing. Hard. Tannin and acidity dominant. Colour relative as it appeared impressively deep early in 1982, with its extraordinary aroma clawing its way out of the glass. Powerful. Left the mouth dry and perfumed. Next noted at the La Tâche vertical tasting at the Domaine in May 1983 and, becoming more ethereal, its peacock's tail opening up in the spring of 1985. More recently, no longer deeply coloured; an immediately forthcoming bouquet; marvellously flavoury but lean.* Last tasted Oct 1987***(*) Possibly***** if it sheds its hard edge.

BEAUNE, GREVES LEROY *Medium, mature; quite good fragrant Pinot nose; dry, firm, good finish. Sound, not startling. Just worth giving more bottle-age?* Feb 1986**(*)?

BEAUNE, VIGNES FRANCHES L LATOUR *Palish and pretty in Nov 1979, sporting a flowery, vanilla nose, good flavour, texture and fair length. In 1983 noted as still purple-tinged and immature; nose and flavour with jammy fruitiness but a hard edge. Most recently, still jammy but showing bottle-age. Tannin very noticeable. Will it shed its tannin and soften, or dry out?* Last tasted April 1989**(*)?

BONNES MARES *DE VOGUE Noted only once, at Khoury's big tasting in San Diego. Fairly intense ruby; rich brambly Pinot; dry, full-bodied, laden with hard tannins and tartaric acid. Good length but severe. "Needs time" — and only time will tell.* Oct 1984(***)??

BROUILLY *CH DE LA CHAIZE Beaujolais is really meant to be quaffed whilst still fresh and youthful. But in hot years like 1947, 1959, 1964 and 1976, and if made in a rather old-fashioned way, they develop and keep well — a far cry from the light, tinny* macération carbonique *wines that occasionally disgrace our tables. A magnum consumed aged nine: good colour, still quite youthful; excellent 'jammy Gamay' fruitiness on nose and palate. Perfection, in its way.* May 1985***

CORTON, HOSPICES, CHARLOTTE DUMAY *Put in magnum by André Gagey after 2½ years in barrel to soften. Still tannic though with a soft, harmonious vanilla nose and richness on palate. A very good mouthful — one of the few burgundies that can cope with cheese.* Jan 1990***(*)

CORTON, RENARDES *DELARCHE Sweet, fragrant nose and flavour. Dry finish. Nice wine.* Feb 1989***

DEZIZE-LES-MARANGES *B BACHELET A charmingly named Côte de Beaune new to me but, being a Robert Haas selection, bound to be more than just interesting. Scented, raspberry bush nose; light style, a minor wine, I suppose the equivalent of a decent* bourgeois *claret. Attractive.* Feb 1986**

ECHEZEAUX *DRC At the Ritz in March 1979, immature, tannic. It sprouted the following spring: very forthcoming nose, prunes and rhubarb; immediate impact on the palate but, I felt, lacking substance. Two years later, its purple hue about to mature; a lively, fragrant bouquet and flavoury.* Last noted at an Oxford University Wine Circle Subscription tasting, at New College, Jan 1982***

ECHEZEAUX *MOILLARD It is worth remembering that the Echézeaux* climat *covers some 80 acres, of which only 11½ are owned by DRC. Style depends on the ownership, the age and tending of vines, the precise time of picking, the degree of selectivity, the winemaking, its maturation in new or old barrels, the time of bottling. In short, endless permutations. Moillard's richly coloured, very flavoury, with lots of '76 tannin.* April 1988**(*)

ECHEZEAUX *MONGEARD-MUGNERET Another good Bob Haas selection noted in 1987. Most recently: medium-deep, suave but sweaty (tannins). An interesting future.* Last tasted Sept 1989***(*)?

GEVREY-CHAMBERTIN, CLOS VAROILLES *DOM DE VAROILLES Vatted quickly to prevent tannin eclipsing the fruit. Medium-deep but very mature-looking in its ninth year. Lovely, sweet, toasted Pinot. Others noted cocoa, prunes and tar. Dry, fairly alcoholic, very rich yet raw, with a slightly stalky, woody character.* Feb 1985**(*)?

GRANDS-ECHEZEAUX *DRC Deep, rich, more substantial and positive than the Echézeaux at the DRC tasting in 1980. Two years later its depth and intensity of colour very apparent; a glorious nose, ripe Pinot aroma, marvellous core of fruit. Positive entry, good middle flavour, backbone of tannin and acidity. Rather unyielding.* Last noted Jan 1982. Then***(**) Not tasted since, but should be a strikingly impressive wine.

MAZIS-CHAMBERTIN *JABOULET-VERCHERRE Several notes in the mid-1980s. Very red, warning one of the volatile acidity on the nose. A common, stalky edge to it and though lightweight in style for a '76, raw.* Last tasted Oct 1986.

MOREY ST-DENIS *DUJAC Restless in his quest for quality, constantly experimenting — the Bob Mondavi of the Côtes! — Jacques Seysses opened two bottles, both of wines from the same* cuvée *but one having spent a year* en barrique, *the other two. The latter had a finer, richer colour; the first a rich, cheesy nose with piquant fruit support, the later-bottled wine being more fragrant. It also reminded me of tripe! The early-bottled wine had a short, pleasant flavour and dry finish, the two-year bottling more opulence and richness of texture.* Tasted at the domaine, Sept 1981** and***(*) respectively. I would put my money on the latter being better now.

MUSIGNY *J DROUHIN Lovely deep colour; low-keyed but rich, elegant bouquet; fabulous, assertive, good length, dry finish.* Oct 1990***(*) Now to 2000.

MUSIGNY, VIEILLES VIGNES *DE VOGUE Expansive-looking, but with orange-brown mature rim; bouquet fragrant and delicate yet at the same time a bit hard; dry, good body, length and finish. Stylish but tannic.* At the Khoury de Vogüé tasting, Oct 1984. Then*(**) I would hope to add a star now.

POMMARD, CHANIERE *THEVENIN Fairly pale and very tawny-hued; light, chocolaty nose; dryish, nice weight, '76 tannin — but a pleasant drink.* Dec 1987**

RICHEBOURG *DRC Distinctly not deep in colour, and the most mature-looking of the '76 DRCs when presented to the trade in March 1980. But a good, expansive flavour. A certain thickness of colour, and richness noted in 1982. The nose, originally rather dumb, had evolved gloriously, sweet, beautiful by any standards; sweet on palate too. A marvellous mouthful, well endowed with alcohol, tannin and acidity.* Alas not tasted since Jan 1982. Then**(**) Should be magnificent.

Clos de La ROCHE *PONSOT Medium-deep; somewhat unknit, varnishy, dusty; tannic and not very appealing. Admittedly I tasted this quickly as time was short, but I can see why some of these '76s are not popular. People are disinclined to wait until bottle-age has had its softening effect. I can understand the risk.* At Christie's, pre-sale, Chicago, Sept 1989*(*)?

ROMANEE-ST-VIVANT *DRC Distinctly dry and assertive in March 1980. I suggested a drinking span from 1984–98. By the new year of 1982, developing nicely, sweet entry noted, good middle palate, distinctly silky texture. Elegant but with a somewhat abrupt, astringent finish. 18 months later, a lovely colour; rich, beautiful, fragrant, vegetal Pinot nose and flavour. Nice weight. Tannic finish.* Last tasted July 1983***(*) I see no reason to change my original prognostication and hope that before the turn of the century the hard tannins will have ameliorated, leaving opulent, velvety fruit.

SANTENAY, GRAVIERES, CH DE LA CHARRIERE *DOM GIRARDIN Thick skins in evidence here, fairly deep though maturing; rather stewed, vegetal nose, touch of iron; nice chunky wine, good fruit. Tannin and acidity under control. Slight taste of liquorice. From the most southerly commune of the Côte de Beaune, usually dependable and good value. Feb 1985****

Clos de TART *I have often found this a rather perverse wine. Two notes made in 1980 of the '76 prompted me to regard its name, Tart, singularly appropriate as the wine had the red tinge and high-toned citrus nose denoting high volatile acidity. Flavoury but tinny. The same noted in 1983 and, in 1985, in magnums, the wine had a plummy colour and jammy style. Soft, yet raw, touched with tannin, iron and slightly oxidised. Yet, most recently, a good deep lively colour, some of its liveliness provided by the ever present volatile acidity which, at its most tolerable, has the effect of elevating the bouquet and bringing out the flavour. I confess, I enjoyed it. A lovely crisp wine but very tannic. Last tasted Oct 1990. At best***

VOLNAY, CHAMPANS *D'ANGERVILLE An elegant wine: sweet, good fruit; dry on palate, very pleasant at just three years of age. Aged 10: I thought I detected a deeper colour, certainly more assertive, powerful even, for a feminine Volnay, on nose and palate. Quite a high alcoholic content, and tannic. Last noted Sept 1986***(*) *I wonder, will this aristocrat retire gracefully?*

VOSNE-ROMANEE, SUCHOTS *GERARD MUGNERET Deep, with slightly bitty sediment; fabulous bouquet, spicy, blackberry and hazel, opulent ripe Pinot; mouthfilling flavour, length but with swingeingly tannic finish. Will it dry out, or will its rich fruit outlast the tannin? I fear not, but time — as always — will tell. June 1988****

VOUGEOT, CLOS BERTAGNA *One of several Bertagna '76s tasted in the early to mid-1980s. Frankly, not thrilling. Nose a bit neutral. Meaty, decent length but hard. Last tasted April 1986**(*)

A SELECTION OF OTHER '76s NOTED IN THE EARLY TO MID-1980s, PRECISE DATES OMITTED AS LITTLE CHANGE OVER THIS SHORT PERIOD:

ALOXE-CORTON *LABAUME Stewed, hard, acidic.*

ALOXE-CORTON *LATOUR Chunky, tannic, short**

BEAUNE, EPENOTS *DE GRAMONT Lively, some fruit but hard**(*)

BEAUNE, CLOS DES MOUCHES *DROUHIN Normally one of my favourite Drouhin reds, meaty, somewhat stalky, high tannin and acidity**?

CHAMBOLLE-MUSIGNY *CLERGET Good colour; good ripe vegetal Pinot character, some sweetness, good flavour but bitter finish*(**)

CHAMBOLLE-MUSIGNY, AMOUREUSES *DROUHIN Lovely, nicely evolved, fragrant but with noticeable acidity (pH 3.20) and tannin***(*)

CHAMBOLLE-MUSIGNY, COMBE D'ORVAUX *JEAN GRIVOT A marvellous colour; sweet, warm nose and flavour, fairly full-bodied, very fruity but seemed to lack length, with a dry, onion-skin finish***(*)?

CHASSAGNE-MONTRACHET *COLOMB-MARECHALE Rough, hard and spirity nose; woody and tart on palate.*

CORTON *BONNEAU DU MARTRAY Attractive, ruby; fruit and vanilla; sweet, nice weight, very flavoury and attractive****

CORTON, BRESSANDES *CHANDON DE BRIAILLES Deep, rich* robe; *very rich scented Pinot; dry, full-bodied, good flavour but hard***(**)

CORTON, CLOS DES CORTONS *FAIVELEY Impressively deep but woody-nosed; rich but tainted.*

Ch CORTON-GRANCEY *L LATOUR Deep, richly coloured; lovely fruit; dry, fullish, firm, great depth of flavour and character. Good texture but laden with tannin and acidity***(**)

GEVREY-CHAMBERTIN *L LATOUR Nicely made but lacking character***

GEVREY-CHAMBERTIN *ARMAND ROUSSEAU Pink-rimmed, soft, pleasing; potentially good nose; well constructed, good fruit, dry but not as tannic as expected***(*)

NUITS-ST-GEORGES *H GOUGES Surprisingly cheesy, Bordeaux-like nose. Dry. Distinctive***(*)

NUITS-ST-GEORGES, CLOS ST-MARC *VIENOT Lively appearance — its best feature. Nose like cardboard. Dry. Not bad**

1977

A poor vintage. Some drinkable wines *were* made, also disastrous ones. The following notes were made at the opening Dom de la Romanée-Conti (DRC) tasting at Vintners Hall in July 1980.

Spring climate ideal. No frosts. The vines flowered in perfect weather, no *coulure*, so a substantial crop anticipated. However, the weather deteriorated: July and Aug were exceptionally wet, making numerous anti-rot sprayings necessary (13 by DRC in 1977 compared with seven in 1976). By the end of Aug the *gérants* began to worry about the maturity and health of the crop. The weather improved with a dry Sept and little rain in Oct. The Domaine waited until Oct 20 to pick "fully mature grapes, without disease or rot". The vintage lasted for 10 days and all the grapes were taken to the press in small boxes to prevent them from being crushed by their own weight. The fermentation was slow: three weeks. The high acidity disappeared after the malolactic fermentation in Dec.

ROMANEE-CONTI *Tasted only once. A somewhat overblown nose and taste, rather hollow, with a curious dry, flat finish. Carbon dioxide evident but would, possibly, settle down. July 1980 ??*

La TACHE *First impression, in July 1980: stewed nose; dry, hard but with good aftertaste; 14 months later, at the Domaine, a fluffy, light, pine-like smell that developed surprisingly in the glass. Softer and more forward than the '78, lightish, raw and incomplete. At the La Tâche vertical it had a similar colour to the '75, slightly redder; similar nose too. Soft, earthy, vegetal flavour. No length. Last tasted May 1983**

THE OTHER DOMAINE DE LA ROMANEE-CONTI '77s TASTED AT VINTNERS HALL IN JULY 1980:

RICHEBOURG *Dumb at first but some richness, depth and potential; surprisingly rich and powerful, with a good aftertaste*★★

ROMANEE-ST-VIVANT, GENERAL MAREY-MONGE *Pale; open-knit, slightly stalky, hint of violets; dry, elegant, flavoury but short, tailed off*★

GRANDS-ECHEZEAUX *Pleasantly sweet, stylish nose; dry, medium-full body, good flavour, hard, with reasonable follow through*★★

ECHEZEAUX *Light, jammy fruit; lightweight too yet curiously punchy. Very dry finish.*

Well, one cannot accuse the domaine of not trying. A heartbreaking and expensive business in a year like 1977. Yet, who knows, some might surprise us, like La Tâche '51 and '54.

For Armand Rousseau, one of the principal owners, growers and winemakers in the commune of Gevrey-Chambertin, 1977 was a disaster. A leading London shipper misguidedly imported a large quantity, at substantial prices. But despite offering them below cost over a lengthy period, there were few buyers.

ROUSSEAU WINES TASTED, SOME SEVERAL TIMES, IN 1982/85:

CHAMBERTIN *Slightly cloudy; quite good Pinot nose and palate. Fluffy, spicy, clove-like flavour and aftertaste. A bit yeasty on the finish.*

CHAMBERTIN, CLOS ST-JACQUES *Weak-rimmed; peppery Pinot; flavoury but raw and bitter.*

CHARMES-CHAMBERTIN *Cloudy; smell of piled up beets, pigstys and abandoned oyster shells. Stalky and tart.*

GEVREY-CHAMBERTIN *A rather beautiful but over-developed Pinot aroma. Piquant and in poor condition.*

GEVREY-CHAMBERTIN, CLOS ST-JACQUES *Four notes between 1983 and 1988: variable, some bright, some cloudy and brown; two scented, two overblown, with high volatile acidity.*

GEVREY-CHAMBERTIN, LAVAUX ST-JACQUES *Seven notes, all terrible: cloudy, yeasty, pricked.*

MAZY-CHAMBERTIN *Palish, cloudy, quite good but suffering from a secondary fermentation in bottle.*

Clos de la ROCHE *Feeble colour, orange-tinged, lingering carbon dioxide, one cloudy. Fragrant though unknit aroma; lean, piquant, over-the-top.*

RUCHOTTES-CHAMBERTIN *Cloudy; stewed Pinot; flavoury, classy but at least one acetic bottle.*

A pitiful roll-call of great names in appalling condition. And a bitter, expensive business for grower, shipper and merchant alike. Did any grower make good wine in 1977? No, but some were not bad:

CORTON, CLOS DE LA VIGNE AU SAINT *Made by Marcel Amance from a portion owned by the Bouchard family*★★

GEVREY-CHAMBERTIN, CAZETIERS *LEROY*★★

GRANDS-ECHEZEAUX, TASTEVINE *BARRAULT-LUCOTTE*★★

GRANDS-ECHEZEAUX, TASTEVINE *MONGEARD-MUGNERET*

MOREY ST-DENIS, CLOS BUSSIERE *G ROUMIER*★★

NUITS-ST-GEORGES, BOUDOTS *J GRIVOT*★

RICHEBOURG *J GROS*★★

VOLNAY, CAILLERET *CLERGET*★

VOLANY, CHAMPANS *D'ANGERVILLE*★

VOLNAY, CLOS DE VERSEUIL *CLERGET*★★

VOSNE-ROMANEE, LES BEAUX-MONTS *BERTAGNA*★

VOUGEOT, 1ER CRU *BERTAGNA*★★

VOUGEOT, CLOS DE LA PERRIERE *BERTAGNA*★★

1978★★★★★

A very good vintage, the best between 1971 and 1985. An unpromising start, the spring and the first half of the summer being cold, retarding initial growth, flowering and development. From Aug 20 the weather changed and, as in Bordeaux, a sustained period of sunshine saved the harvest, ripening the grapes in time for a late harvest, around Oct 11.

Despite the imbalance of the climate, the wines are well balanced. Better, in my opinion, than Bordeaux; and the top wines should develop further and last well.

ROMANEE-CONTI *First tasted at the Domaine in May 1983, two bottles, one at cellar temperature. Fairly deep; harmonious but restrained, with a curious dusty character but underlying foundation of fruit. A massively constructed wine. Rich. Firm. Deceptively advanced for its age. Length and excellent acidity. The cooler bottle seemed to have more vanillin on the nose, drier and spicy. Two years later: deep by burgundian standards. Makes La Tâche look fully mature. A great bouquet, slightly earthy, vegetal, rich, tangy, packed with fruit. Magnificent but unready. Complete. Fragrant but needing at least 10 years more bottle-age.* Last noted April 1985. Then★★★(★★) 1995–2020

La TACHE *Aged three a lively purple* robe*; nose already opulent; masses of fruit, rich yet elegant. Excellent potential. Two bottles in May 1983, nose fragrant, scented but still a bit hard; shapely, slender, flowery but firm. Good tannin and acidity. A lovely wine.* Last tasted May 1983. Then★★(★★★) Now, doubtless★★★★(★) 1992 to beyond 2000.

A MISCELLANY OF RECENT NOTES:

BEAUNE, CENT VIGNES *CH DE MEURSAULT* *Lively-looking; very spicy new-oak nose; dry, fleshy but lean and still tannic.* Dec 1989★★(★)

BEAUNE, CENT VIGNES *PROSPER MAUFAUX* *Fully mature, sweetish but rather acidic*★★

CHAMBOLLE-MUSIGNY, CHARMES *REMOISSENET Surprisingly deep, rich, intense, with mature rim; rather jammy sweetness, glorious fruit, harmonious; chewy, meaty, powerful. Rather old-fashioned and just a little too plausible, but an attractive drink.* At a burgundy dinner at the Grand Bay Hotel, Coconut Grove, Jan 1990★★★ Now to 2000.

CHARMES-CHAMBERTIN *CAMUS Also fairly deep, intense, mature; good fruit, flowery, walnuts; sweet, beetroot-like flavour, well-knit, good length, delicious. Feb 1989*** Now to 1996.*

Ch CORTON-GRANCEY *L LATOUR'S 'GRAND PREMIER CRU' At the opening trade tasting in 1981: lovely smoky nose; powerful, excellent balance — and future, borne out by recent tasting. Despite loss of colour, palish but pink-tinged, a warm distinctive Pinot nose, totally different from the '79; fullish, firm, still with dry tannic finish. Last tasted Oct 1990***(*) Now to beyond 2000.*

ECHEZEAUX *MONGEARD-MUGNERET Immensely fragrant, intensely flavoury — or vice versa, with marked yet excellent crisp and refreshing acidity. Sept 1989*****

GEVREY-CHAMBERTIN, 1ER CRU *BOURREE Deep, intense; low-keyed but vinous and lovely bouquet; dry, full, rich, still tannic. An impressive wine from an old-fashioned winemaker. Feb 1989*** Now to 2000.*

NUITS-ST-GEORGES, VAUCRAINS *BOUCHARD PERE Palish, mature, soft and sweet. July 1988***

POMMARD, LA CHANIERE *R THEVENIN Palish, pink; odd, oaky, port-like nose; dry and raw in 1982. Now fully mature; mediocre bouquet; flavoury but tart. Last tasted May 1988.*

POMMARD, VIGNOTS *RENE MONNIER Fragrant; good flavour, length and aftertaste in 1986. More recently, a rather indeterminate colour; very sweet, rich bouquet and flavour. A lovely mouthful. Last tasted May 1989*** Drink soon.*

RICHEBOURG *J DROUHIN Deep, rich, red-brown centre with gradation to mature amber rim; first impression vanilla, but with great depth, rich Pinot nose expanding in the glass; typical ripe burgundy sweetness, powerful, mouthfilling flavour, good length, great to drink though still tannic. At a tasting conducted for Wine Japan before an eager, over-full house, Tokyo, May 1990****(*) Now to 2010.*

ROMANEE-ST-VIVANT, QUATRE JOURNAUX *L LATOUR An impressive sample taken from the cask in Oct 1980: a wine of great depth, with a lovely ripe-grape mulberry-like aroma. Very rich. Great future. More recently, still deep, sweet and developing nicely. Last tasted Oct 1987**** Now to beyond 2000.*

Clos de TART *MOMMESSIN (sole owner). Medium depth of colour, opulent, in 1987. Most recently: rich, surprisingly well-developed appearance, brown-rimmed; lovely, forthcoming nose of ripe Pinot and grilled sausages, evolving exotically in the glass; sweet, fullish, rich ripe fruit, great length, adequate tannin. An attractive, buxom, nubile, highly scented Tart. Last noted Oct 1990**** Now to 2000.*

VOLNAY, CAILLERETS *POUSSE D'OR Medium-pale, mature, shapely, good legs; complete, harmonious bouquet; glorious flavour, very fragrant though with a touch of leanness, tannin and rather high acidity. Jan 1990***(*) Now to 1996.*

VOLNAY, CLOS DES CHENES *LAFARGE Very much a family domaine. Fairly deep-looking wine; nose of fruit and hawthorn that blossomed in the glass; medium full-bodied, very tannic — not a light feminine Volnay, but this is due to the vintage. Great class. Tasted at the domaine with Becky Wasserman, Sept 1989**(**) 1992–2000*

VOSNE-ROMANEE *LABOURE-ROI Somewhat stewed and smelly though better flavour, and tannic. Sept 1988***

VOSNE-ROMANEE *ALBERT PONNELLE Very mature-looking, chocolaty and chewy. Jan 1990***

VOSNE-ROMANEE, BEAUMONTS *JEAN GRIVOT This was lovely in cask though closed. Grivot, father and son, informed me that it had been excellent in bottle for the past two years, and that they thought their '85 would develop similarly. Certainly a good colour; at first sniff like the '82, warm fruit, with nutty (cobnuts) underlay; a rich, mouthfilling wine of great length and silky, nutty tannins. Last tasted in the cellar, Sept 1989***(*) Now to beyond 2000.*

VOSNE-ROMANEE, BEAUX MONTS *DANIEL RION An example of quirky Burgundy spelling (another example: Epenots, Epenottes, Epeneaux). Same* 1er cru *vineyard, different section, different proprietor. A good rooty Pinot nose but, for me, spoiled by a sort of tannate of iron bitterness. Feb 1988*(**)? Hard to know whether to drink up or wait for 10 years.*

Clos VOUGEOT *NOELLAT Good colour, rich nose, excellent firm flavour. Showing potential in July 1984, now*****

A SELECTION FROM THE MANY '78s TASTED IN THE MID-1980s:

BEAUNE, CLOS DU ROI *TOLLOT-BEAUT Surprisingly deep; fragrant; fruity but bitter tannins *(**) Probably softened by now.*

CHASSAGNE-MONTRACHET *LEROY Beautiful colour; good Pinot quality; very tannic*(**)*

CHASSAGNE-MONTRACHET, CLOS DE LA BOUDRIOTTE *BACHELET-RAMONET Not much red; somewhat undistinctive; soft, fragrant but not for long keeping***

CORTON, PERRIERES *DUBRENIL-FONTAINE Luscious, harmonious Pinot nose and gently rich flavour disguising high alcohol and sustaining tannins***(*)*

ECHEZEAUX *DRC Ruby, cherry red; rich, plummy; earth and fruit aroma, broad and of immediate appeal; dry, fullish, firm, slightly bitter tannins but fragrant and lingering**(*)?*

GRANDS-ECHEZEAUX *DRC Fairly deep and plummy; fragrant, refined, lovely fruit; fabulously sweet entry and mid-palate. Mouthfilling flavour, firm, great length and future**(***)*

GRANDS-ECHEZEAUX *H LAMARCHE Orange-tinged; ripe nose and taste*** Drink up.*

LATRICIERES-CHAMBERTIN *TRAPET Palish; high-toned, fragrant, mature *** Drink up.*

MAZIS-CHAMBERTIN *LEROY Very deep, still plummy purple after six years; fresh, stylish, attractive, vanilla nose; fabulous flavour, lots of fruit, tannin and acidity **(**) Should be excellent now.*

MOREY ST-DENIS *DUJAC Deep though mature; fabulously rich scent, chocolate, vanilla; fairly sweet, fullish, tannic iron endtaste****

MUSIGNY, VIEILLES VIGNES *DE VOGUE Lacking the big guns of '59 and '49 but elegant, well put together and showing well at Khoury's de Vogüé tasting* ***(*) *Probably at peak now.*

NUITS-ST-GEORGES, PORRETS ST-GEORGES *H GOUGES Attractive colour; citrus, walnuts; cherry-like fruit, taste reminiscent of heather. Nice wine. Ready****

RICHEBOURG *DRC Medium-deep, plummy, intense; a broad-based nose, excellent foundation of rich, prune-like fruit; mouthfilling, all the component parts on a massive scale*(****)

ROMANEE-ST-VIVANT *DRC Fairly deep and plummy; fragrant, refined, lovely fruit; fabulously sweet entry and mid-palate. Mouthfilling flavour, firm, great length and future***(***)

Clos VOUGEOT *NOELLAT Good colour; firm nose; excellent flavour****(*)

OF THE MANY '78s TASTED ONLY IN THE EARLY 1980s, THE FOLLOWING HAD VERY GOOD POTENTIAL:

Beaune, Clos des Mouches J DROUHIN; Beaune, Vignes Franches L LATOUR; Bonnes Mares J DROUHIN; Chambertin HERITIERS LATOUR; Chambolle-Musigny, Amoureuses J DROUHIN; Chassagne-Montrachet, Boudriottes DELAGRANGE-BACHELET; Corton, Bressandes CHANDON DE BRIAILLES; Grands-Echézeaux J DROUHIN; Griottes-Chambertin J DROUHIN; Morey St-Denis, Mont Luisant MOILLARD; Musigny J DROUHIN; Pernand-Vergelesses, Iles de Vergelesses CHANDON DE BRIAILLES; Vosne-Romanée, Beaumonts J DROUHIN.

*1979****

A good, useful, abundant vintage. Another late starter, cold spring delaying vegetation; budding and frosts coinciding in early May; moderate summer with hailstorms, a major one in June cutting through part of the Côte de Nuits. Late Sept harvest of healthy grapes.

The usual variations, but on the whole reasonable quality, less well balanced, certainly less tannic than the '78s. Many, if not most, drinking well now; the best will keep.

La TACHE *I am sorry and surprised to note that I have only tasted one DRC red, La Tâche. In Sept 1981, after just three months in bottle it had a dramatic immediacy of fragrance despite the imminence of early, and quite normal, bottle-sickness. Showing well at the extensive vertical: bright, touch of cherry red; spicy, fruity, blackberries and cloves; medium-sweet, fullish, very flavoury and attractive. Good future. Last tasted May 1983. Now probably****(*) *Plenty of life ahead.*

MISCELLANEOUS '79s TASTED SINCE THE MID-1980s:

BEAUNE, GREVES *AVERY Rich, mature; lovely, fragrant nose and flavour, good fruit, weight and texture. Dec 1990***** *Drink now to 1995.*

BEAUNE, CLOS DES MOUCHES *J DROUHIN First tasted in Sept 1981: though immature-looking, not deeply coloured; muffled beetroot-Pinot nose; light, easy style. I thought it lacked length. Nine years later, little red left; well-developed bouquet; sweet, seemed fuller-bodied, rich, fruity and ready for drinking. Last tasted Oct 1990**** *Drink soon.*

BEAUNE, CLOS DES URSULES *L JADOT Good ripe Pinot nose; nice weight, a bit lean, attractive. April 1991****

CHAMBERTIN, CLOS DE BEZE *DAMOY Very mature-looking, and carbon dioxide playing at the rim; low-keyed, singed nose and stewed Pinot flavour. Very disappointing wine from the biggest proprietor owner of both Chambertin and Clos de Bèze. Nov 1987**

CHAMBOLLE-MUSIGNY *REMOISSENET Very mature appearance; showing age on nose, mint and milk. So-so. Dec 1990** *Drink up.*

CHAMBOLLE-MUSIGNY *G ROUMIER Palish, mature; very scented Pinot. Quite attractive. Feb 1989*** *Drink soon.*

CHAMBOLLE-MUSIGNY, CHARMES *L JADOT Fairly deep, fine mature colour; hefty, rich, meaty nose, good fruit. Flavour to match. Still tannic. March 1989**** *Now to 1995.*

CHASSAGNE-MONTRACHET *GAGNARD DELAGRANGE Quite nice fruit; dry, nice quality, some tannin, slightly acidic. Sept 1990***(*) *1992–96*

Ch CORTON-GRANCEY *Many notes. Firm, slightly stalky nose, dry, raw but flavoury in Oct 1980. Not too impressed at the Louis Latour tasting the following autumn, or in 1983. It had opened up at the dinner of the Wine & Food Society Convention in Boston in 1987, though the 'assortment of New England farmstead cheeses' sweetened it up. Most recently, showing well at a vertical of Corton-Grancey, medium-pale, fully mature; gloriously ripe, fully evolved Pinot scent; sweet, medium weight, soft, spicy, rich fruit. A slight touch of bitterness on the finish. Last tasted Oct 1990***** *At its peak; drink soon.*

FIXIN, CLOS D'ENTRE DEUX VELLES *MOILLARD The suburbs of Dijon are rapidly encroaching on the parish of Fixin at the top end of the Côte de Nuits. It would be a shame if some* supermarché *was built on this quaintly named* clos. *An attractive fruity flavour. The real thing, and some style. June 1986****

MAZIS-CHAMBERTIN *FRANCOIS FAIVELEY Lovely colour; delicate, a bit withdrawn, slightly stalky; dry, rather flat, dried out, lacking length yet tannic. Feb 1989**

MAZIS-CHAMBERTIN, HOSPICES, CUVEE MADELEINE-COLLIGNON *JABOULET-VERCHERRE (bottler) Warm, rich, mature; whiff of kerosene, tar, chocolaty Pinot; flavoury, slightly bitter finish but fragrant aftertaste. Certainly interesting. Jan 1990***?

Ch de POMMARD *JEAN-LOUIS LEPLANCHE New to me, and delightful. Calm, broad, agreeable colour; earthy Pinot nose opened up gloriously but started to fade in the glass 25 minutes later; very sweet, spicy, mouthfilling, expansive peacock's tail. Good length and aftertaste. At the Svensk Vin Festival, Malmö, Feb 1986***** *Should still be lovely.*

Clos de la ROCHE *DUJAC In 1981, fairly full and rich,*

with spicy endtaste. By 1985, a certain muskiness, dried prunes on nose and slightly bitter finish. Most recently, a bottle from my own cellar: not very bright despite standing upright for 24 hours, orange-tinged; fabulously rich, meaty Pinot scent, full-flavoured but marred slightly by a bitter tannic iron finish. Seemed fuller and longer in a classic Riedel burgundy glass. But overall not too enamoured by Jacques Seysses' '79s. Last tasted Nov 1990**

Clos de la ROCHE *PONSOT Very deep; low-keyed nose; marvellously rich in 1985. Next: though still closed, sweet, fullish, lovely texture, combining opulence and elegance.* Last tasted Nov 1987****

SAVIGNY-LES-BEAUNE *DOM DU CH DE BEAUNE Fairly pale but with very lively and attractive nose and flavour, pleasant weight and good length.* Jan 1987***

Clos de TART *Similar depth to the '78 but slightly more red; low-keyed, vegetal nose that opened up fragrantly and fruitily; distinctly sweet, pleasant, harmonious, agreeable.* At the domaine, Oct 1990*** Now to 1996.

VOLNAY, 1ER CRU *HUBERT DE MONTILLE A lawyer with a formidable reputation for his winemaking. I regret that few have come my way, but here was a stylish, copybook Volnay, palish but at 6½ years of age, still youthful-looking. A pleasant Pinot aroma. Dryish, nicely made.* Served at lunch at the Waterside Inn, the day that Albert and Michel Roux and I received the French 'Personnalité de l'Année' award, April 1986***

SOME OTHER '79s SHOWING PROMISE IN THE EARLY 1980s:

Aloxe-Corton TOLLOT-BEAUT; Beaune, Cent Vignes CH DE MEURSAULT; Beaune, Hospices, Nicolas Rolin EMILE CHANDESAIS (bottler); Beaune, Vignes Franches FRANÇOIS GERMAIN; Chambertin A ROUSSEAU; Chapelle-Chambertin DROUHIN-LAROZE; Charmes-Chambertin DUJAC; Charmes-Chambertin HENRI RICHARD; Chorey-Lès-Beaune J DROUHIN; Corton, Bressandes TOLLOT-BEAUT; Morey St-Denis, Mont-Luisants MOILLARD; Nuits-St-Georges, Ch Gris LUPE-CHOLET; Pommard, Epenots L LATOUR; Clos de la Roche CHANSON; Volnay, Clos des Chênes CH DE MEURSAULT; Vosne-Romanée, Suchots L LATOUR; Clos Vougeot HUDELOT NOELLAT.

SOME DISAPPOINTING '79s:

Beaune, Vignes Franches L LATOUR; Bonnes Mares DE VOGUE; Chassagne-Montrachet AUDIFFRED; Morey St-Denis DUJAC.

1980★★ to ★★★

Quality uneven, but much better than its rather mediocre reputation. Some good wines made.

An unfavourable spring: tardy foliation, extended, uneven flowering, poor pollination. June cold and rainy but Aug and Sept temperatures above average. Some rain just before picking.

The market was in recession, the Hospices de Beaune auction registering a 17% average price drop, the second in a row.

The vintage was variously likened to '62, '70 and '74 but I think Rousseau was nearer to the mark. When tasting in cask at the domaine M Charles Rousseau told me that he thought his '80s were like his '72s, and I can see the resemblance: good flavour, but a touch of bitterness on the finish.

This was the opening vintage of two 'verticals' of the decade, of Beaune, Clos des Mouches at J Drouhin's and Musigny at de Vogüé's, which helped put the quality, style and condition of the 1980s into perspective.

La TACHE *First tasted in cask Sept 1981: bright, naturally immature-looking, but with a sweet, chocolaty — chaptalised — nose, fair body, quite good length. Next, at the La Tâche vertical, a palish pink, a* macération *sort of fruitiness, deceptively light style and acidity which was almost Beaujolais-like. But young DRCs are notoriously deceptive so — optimistically — it could be a deliciously fragrant mouthful by now.* Alas not tasted since May 1983 ??

SELECTED '80s TASTED SINCE 1985:

BEAUNE, CLOS DES MOUCHES *J DROUHIN Alcohol 12.4%, total acidity 3.6. Medium-deep, mature; a fully evolved fragrant 'boiled beetroot' Pinot nose which, after 10 minutes in the glass, I thought a bit overblown, but an hour later had opened out beautifully. On the palate, medium body, firm, slightly hard, good acidity, dry finish.* Last tasted in Drouhin's tasting room, Oct 1990*** Now to 1995.

BONNES MARES *VAROILLES Medium; rich, uneven, scent of boiled sweets; sweet, quite rich and chewy. Some tannin. Flavoury.* At pre-sale tasting April 1988** Now to 1995.

CHAMBERTIN, CLOS DE BEZE *JACQUES PRIEUR Lovely ruby colour; nutty, bramble bush, Grivot-style nose that developed, sweeter, more jammy, and fragrantly in the glass; dry, medium weight, crisp acidity, slightly bitter finish. Flavour and construction destroyed by Stilton and some other blue cheeses.* At a Wine & Food Society Gala Dinner at the Hilton Hotel, San Juan, March 1986***

GEVREY-CHAMBERTIN, CAZETIERS *PHILIPPE LECLERC Surprisingly deep and intense; sweet, fragrant, spicy, walnuts, slightly chocolaty nose, excellent depth; crisp fruit, very flavoury, piquant acidity, some tannin, dry finish.* Feb 1989*** Drink soon.

GEVREY-CHAMBERTIN, CAZETIERS *G SERAFIN Medium-deep, open, maturing; lovely fragrance and depth; sweet, soft, pronounced Pinot flavour, nice grip.* Feb 1989*** Now to 1996.

MOREY ST-DENIS, CLOS DES ORMES *FAIVELEY Rich, rather jammy Pinot.* March 1988**

MUSIGNY *DE VOGUE Good colour; very sweet, strawberry blancmange scent, soft, slightly meaty* *nose that, after 50 minutes, developed a lovely ginger biscuity bouquet with dash of paprika; nice weight and fruit. Soft underbelly yet quite good tannin and acidity. Attractive but not spectacular on the palate, and with a light, dry, slightly bitter finish. At the domaine, Oct 1989***just. Drink now to 1995.*

NUITS-ST-GEORGES, PRULIERS *H GOUGES* *First tasted in cask, Sept 1981. Medium-pale, prettily coloured; a pleasant, easy, delicately fragrant bouquet with a touch of underlying hardness; light style, attractive but a bit hollow, nice acidity, dry, with slightly bitter finish. Last tasted May 1986** Drink soon.*

ROMANEE-ST-VIVANT *C NOELLAT Medium, mature, rather weak, watery rim; ripe, stewed Pinot — old socks style! But the fruit came out. Unknit. Meaty, hefty with very dry hard finish. July 1988**

Clos VOUGEOT, CH DE LA TOUR *MORIN* *Medium-deep; fragrant, fig-like; very agreeable. Jan 1986****

SELECTED '80s TASTED IN THE FIRST HALF OF THE DECADE:

ALOXE-CORTON *TOLLOT-BEAUT Very attractive, scented Pinot nose and flavour. Delicious aftertaste****

BEAUNE, CLOS DU ROI *TOLLOT-BEAUT Surprisingly deep and still purple-tinged; fragrant varietal aroma; medium weight, quite good fruit, slightly bitter endtaste***

BEAUNE, GREVES *A MOREY Attractive, arboreal nose; chaptalised sweetness masking unripe grape acidity. Flavoury. Plausible***

BEAUNE, GREVES, VIGNE DE L'ENFANT JESUS *BOUCHARD PERE Deep; little nose; neutral flavour, high acidity**

CHAMBERTIN *CALVET Unspectacular, but attractive nose and taste, fairly full-bodied, quite well balanced***

CHAMBERTIN, CLOS DE BEZE *CHANSON Flavoury but nothing special***

CHASSAGNE-MONTRACHET *ALBERT MOREY Fresh, light fruits, Beaujolais-like scent and taste. Attractive***

PERNAND-VERGELESSES, ILE DE VERGELESSES *DUBREUIL-FONTAINE Very pronounced earthy Pinot aroma; very flavoury but a bit raw. Good aftertaste***

POMMARD *F CHAUVENET Strange scent of boiled blackcurrant sweets; an extraordinary flavour, attractive in its way, with refreshing acidity*?*

VOLNAY, CAILLERETS *POUSSE D'OR Cherry red; open, fragrant, slightly vegetal; sweetish, surprisingly high alcohol, grip and acidity. Attractive but unbalanced***

VOLNAY, CHAMPANS *D'ANGERVILLE Palish, pink; neutral nose; smooth, lightish, dry finish. Disappointing, and not for keeping**

VOSNE-ROMANEE, CROS-PARANTOUX *HENRI JAYER The one and only time I have tasted wine from this* climat. *Jayer has a high reputation and this particular '80 won a gold medal in Mâcon in 1982. A fairly deep, mulberry purple; fragrant, fruit — a sweet, raspberry-like Pinot; enters medium-dry, departs very dry. In between, good flavour, reasonable length, nice acidity****

TASTED IN CASK, SEPT 1981, AT THE DOMAINE DE LA ROMANEE-CONTI:

ECHEZEAUX *Plummy; dumb; distinctly sweet, light, fruity and spicy — needing a second winter in barrel.*

ROMANEE-ST-VIVANT *Palish, youthful mauve; fatter, fruitier on nose and palate. Good balance. Spicy aftertaste.*

TASTED IN CASK, SEPT 1981, AT DOM ARMAND ROUSSEAU:

Clos de BEZE *Broad-shouldered, packed with fruit, good length and aftertaste, dry.*

CHAMBERTIN *Impressively full, rich, concentrated.*

CHARMES-CHAMBERTIN *Fine deep colour; crisp fruit, excellent flavour, reasonable length, tannin and acidity.*

GEVREY-CHAMBERTIN *Bright, good colour; good young fruit; quite a powerful flavour and bite despite being racked the previous week. The* 1er cru, *from his vineyard on the slopes above the village was impressive, dry, full flavoured, elegant. M Charles Rousseau informed me that though most people in Burgundy thought '80s were light, he considered 1980 a* vin de garde *vintage. He also explained that he habitually bottled lighter wines in May (the second year after the vintage) and heavier wine in Sept.*

GEVREY-CHAMBERTIN, CLOS ST JACQUES *Of this 6-ha vineyard, Rousseau owns 2½ ha. Bright, good colour "that will deepen after racking — the effect of oxidation". Dry, rather hard.*

Clos de la ROCHE *Racked once in Feb, once in Sept, to be fined with eggs and finally racked and bottled in 1982. Beautiful colour; sweet, fragrant, fruity. Dry from start to finish. More feminine style and weight than the various Chambertins.*

Clos de RUCHOTTES MONOPOLE *Before racking, sweet, rich, marvellous flavour.*

TASTED IN CASK, SEPT 1981, WITH JACQUES SEYSSES AT DOM DUJAC:

GEVREY-CHAMBERTIN, COMBOTTES *Total 3ha, 1.15ha owned by Seysses: bright; rich Pinot aroma, opening up spicily in the glass; very good fruit, uplifting dry finish, crisp acidity.*

MOREY-ST-DENIS *Underwent its malolactic fermentation in Jan and had its last egg fining in Aug 1981. Palish, very bright; good straight-forward fruit nose and flavour. Moderate length, some charm, very dry finish.*

Clos de la ROCHE *Very fragrant; rich entry, dry finish, good fruit, length and tannin.*

AT DOM HENRI GOUGES IN NUITS-ST-GEORGES:

Clos des PORRETS *Bright; youthful, pear-like nose that became beautifully scented; sweet, nice weight, crisp, very fruity, excellent acidity.*

Les VAUCRAINS *Star-bright, highly polished; oaky, appley, closed up but with good depth apparent; firm, straightforward. Good tannins and acidity.*

1981★★

Moderate, mainly unimpressive, indifferently structured wines with relatively low alcohol. A warm spring induced early budding. Leaves well-developed when severe frosts hit the vineyards, though *grand* and *premier cru* sites relatively unscathed. Flowering good but July cold and wet with several waves of hail from Aug 10–31; Aug was otherwise brilliant, the good weather continuing to mid-Sept. From then on, rain, which continued spasmodically throughout the harvest, from Sept 24 to around Oct 5. Quantity small, Quality mediocre. Despite the continuing recession, a marked increase in prices due to the small crop and inflationary pressures affecting the cost of production. Relatively few tasted, particularly recently. Avoid or be highly selective. Drink soon.

BEAUNE, CLOS DES MOUCHES *J DROUHIN Alcohol 12%, total acidity 3.6. Medium, fully mature, rather weak, watery rim; sweet but curiously muffled, stably nose. Malty after an hour in the glass. Dry, medium-light, not bad flavour but short, with hard, slightly acidic finish. At Drouhin's, Oct 1990*★ *Drink now.*

CHAMBOLLE-MUSIGNY *CORON Rather pale, indeterminate, just starting to show maturity; fruit on nose and palate. A reasonably attractive drink. At pre-sale tasting, July 1986*★

CHARMES-CHAMBERTIN *BERNARD BACHELET Medium-deep, pleasant ruby; rich, rustic, earthy, stably nose, curiously meaty; rather sweet, fullish body, soft, very agreeable to drink, despite its 'whole fruit* maceration' *character and touch of bitterness on the finish. March 1986*★★

CHASSAGNE-MONTRACHET, CLOS DE LA BOUDRIOTTE *BACHELET-RAMONET Pale; sweet, stewed Pinot aroma and taste. Fuller-bodied than appearance suggested. Fragrant. Jan 1987*★★

COTE DE BEAUNE VILLAGES *CLAVELIER A curiously scented nose; dry, lightish, flavoury but tart. A minor wine admittedly. March 1986*★ *Of no interest.*

GEVREY-CHAMBERTIN *A ROUSSEAU Medium-pale, ruddy, maturing; rather nice, fragrant, strawberry-like fruit. Medium dryness and weight. Attractive though acidity a trifle high. April 1987*★★

MOREY ST-DENIS *L JADOT Rather sweaty vegetal nose; quite nice, nutty flavoured, dry finish. June 1990*★★ *Now to 1995.*

MUSIGNY *DE VOGUE Medium, maturing; immediately forthcoming, fully evolved but spiky nose, high-toned, raspberry-like fruitiness that became surprisingly fragrant in the glass; touch of sweetness, medium weight, soft yet lean, flavoury, rather short, some tannin. At the domaine, Oct 1990*★★ *Drink up.*

TASTED PRIOR TO 1986:

ALOXE-CORTON *TOLLOT-BEAUT Very fragrant; outstanding, lovely, oaky flavour*★★★

BEAUNE, CLOS DES FEVES *CHANSON Stewed fruit; quite good flavour, flesh and quality*★★

BEAUNE, MARCONNETS *CHANSON Paler, weak-rimmed though with an attractive scent, lightish in weight and style, pleasant flavour*★★

Ch CORTON-GRANCEY *L LATOUR Palish, immature, rather feeble appearance; fragrant, jammy Pinot with slightly acidic strawberry undertow; dry, a bit raw — perhaps too soon after bottling*★

POMMARD, CLOS DES EPENOTS *CH DE MEURSAULT Nose combining strawberries and straw, 'green', unripe; very dry, screwed up.*

SAVIGNY-LES-BEAUNE *L LATOUR Palish, quick-maturing, weak; light but sweet brambly fruit aroma; light, very flavoury, refreshing acidity, slightly bitter finish*★★

THE FULL DRC RANGE, LAST NOTED AT PERCY FOX'S LONDON TASTING, NOV 1985:

ROMANEE-CONTI *Low-keyed, vegetal nose; soft, flavoury, tannin and noticeable acidity(*★★*)*

La TACHE *The youngest vintage in the vertical of La Tâche tasted at the Domaine in May 1983: fresh, light style. At the Percy Fox tasting, slightly deeper than the '82, more fully developed; a very forthcoming earthy fruitiness; medium-dry, soft, loose-knit, maturing quickly*★★

RICHEBOURG *Weak-rimmed; nose low-keyed though it developed in the glass; attractive but not its usual broad-shouldered self. Just misses being hollow. Some tannin, notable acidity*★

ROMANEE-ST-VIVANT *Fairly pale; sweet, earthy, one-dimensional nose; medium dry, open, loose-knit.*

GRANDS-ECHEZEAUX *Medium-pale, fairly advanced; low-keyed; medium-full body, very flavoury, hot finish*★★

ECHEZEAUX *Spicy — cloves and cinnamon — quite well-developed nose and flavour. Some softness, slightly bitter finish(*★*)*

1982★★ to ★★★

Not remotely as impressive as Bordeaux. In retrospect, variable, neither wholly good nor wholly poor but, by and large, of little credit to Burgundy. Too many, as notes will indicate, lacking colour — even allowing for the nature of the Pinot grape as described in the introduction on tasting burgundy. With their selectivity and policy of late picking, the Domaine de La Romanée-Conti does appear to have made wines above average.

A marvellous spring ensured early flowering before the first week in June. Good summer, showers in Aug, marvellous ripening weather, harvest completed by the first week of Oct. A bountiful crop.

Many will have been drunk by now, most of the remaining wines should be drunk soon, just a few will repay keeping.

BEAUNE *MICHEL GAUNOUX Palish watery rim; low-keyed, soft, 'warm', slightly singed and chocolaty; fairly sweet and — not unusually — fuller-bodied than its depth of colour indicated, quite nice flavour and fruit, dry but not tannic finish. Dec*

*1988*** Drink soon.*

BEAUNE, CLOS DES MOUCHES *J DROUHIN Two recent notes. The first accompanying, adequately,* pigeonneau en salmis, *the second, nine months later, under more clinical and critical conditions: medium-pale, fully mature, weak-rimmed; a ripe, intriguing, fully developed Pinot nose, settled quickly, softly, harmoniously, holding well in the glass for an hour when it seemed to have taken on a strawberry-like scent; medium sweetness and weight (12.8% alcohol), soft, ready for drinking, some tannin and moderate acidity (3.5).* Oct 1990** *perhaps ungenerously. Drinking pleasantly now.*

BEAUNE, CLOS DES URSULES *L JADOT Palish, cherry red in 1984, dry, complete, good spicy flavour. Three years later, developing well: very good Pinot nose; classic, stylish.* Last tasted Jan 1987*** *Probably at best now.*

BEAUNE, HOSPICES, CLOS DES AVAUX *Bottler unknown. Medium, completely mature appearance; very sweet, slightly raisiny, vanilla nose; nice weight, attractive though faintly artificial sort of flavour.* Dec 1990** *Drink soon.*

BEAUNE, MARCONNETS *REMOISSENET Fully mature, open appearance; superficially attractive but a bit overblown, with citrus-tinged fruitiness; quite good.* Dec 1990** *Drink soon.*

BEAUNE, TEURONS *(*sic*) BOUCHARD PERE Two virtually identical notes: quite good nose, pleasant enough.* Last tasted Oct 1988** *Drink soon.*

BONNES MARES *L JADOT Palish; vegetal; not very special despite combination of names and price.* July 1990**

CHAMBERTIN, CLOS DE BEZE *A ROUSSEAU Sweet, rich Pinot nose and glorious, oaky, spicy flavour and aftertaste.* June 1987. Then***(*) *but now doubtless fully mature and needing drinking.*

CHAPELLE-CHAMBERTIN *TRAPET It strikes me, after looking at so many '82s, that they should not be under the heading* red burgundy *at all. Of two bottles recently brought in for me to taste, both being pale, one had a faint red tinge, the other none at all. One was sweet, soft, with a stewed Pinot nose, the other more chocolaty. One sweet, soft, short, the other had a bit more of a bite. Neither out of condition, just depressing.* Feb 1991.

CORTON, BRESSANDES *BOUZEREAU Scented Pinot; very pleasant weight, flavour and finish.* March 1989*** *Nice now.*

CORTON, CLOS DE LA VIGNE AU SAINT *AMANCE Quite good Pinot nose and flavour, crisper than expected.* June 1991***

Ch CORTON-GRANCEY *L LATOUR Palish, open; light, slightly meaty, stewed Pinot nose; sweet, soft, medium weight, touch of bitterness.* Oct 1990**(*) 1992–96

GEVREY-CHAMBERTIN *CHAUVENET Aged three a cherry-cheeked youth; aroma neither fruity nor vegetal, more like a bramble bush; with a good firm flavour, complete, needing time. More recently, palish, still pink-tinged; a sweet, light, raspberry nose; medium sweetness and weight, straightforward, perhaps lacking length.* March 1989** *Drink soon.*

GEVREY-CHAMBERTIN *A ROUSSEAU Fairly pale, fully mature, almost* pelure d'oignon*; little nose, just a slightly dusty old Pinot; a faint touch of fruit, stewed flavour, dry finish. The sort of wine that makes one despair of burgundy.* Jan 1991*

MAZY-CHAMBERTIN *FAIVELEY Harmonious nose though showing its age; pleasant enough sweetness, weight and flavour. Dry finish.* June 1990***

MUSIGNY *DE VOGUE Medium, maturing; strange, meaty, smelly nose with whiff of banana and* anis. *Remained low-keyed and meaty in the glass. Medium dryness and body, cheesy flavour, lacking the elegance and finesse one expects from a top-class Musigny. Dry finish.* At the domaine, Oct 1990* *Drink up.*

NUITS-ST-GEORGES *L JADOT Vegetal, sweaty— like most of the tasters; very sweet, rich, broad-based, slightly acidic.* At a crammed, hot, Jadot tasting at the Savoy Hotel, June 1990** *Ready for drinking.*

NUITS-ST-GEORGES *DANIEL RION Pale, more like a 30-year-old tawny port; very ripe Pinot nose and flavour; with dry oaky endtaste.* April 1989*** *Now to 1995.*

NUITS-ST-GEORGES, VAUCRAINS *H GOUGES Medium, still with a touch of ruby; distinctive 'fishy' Pinot, bramble-bush fruitiness; high alcoholic content, warm, full-flavoured, dry finish.* June 1988*** *Now to 1996.*

POMMARD, RUGIENS *MOILLARD Medium-deep, good, lively appearance; sweet, rich, slightly singed meaty nose that opened, fudge-like; very sweet on the palate, hefty, alcoholic, chewy,* négociant *wine with touch of iron on the finish.* Feb 1988*** *Now to 1995.*

ROMANEE-ST-VIVANT *DRC In the autumn of 1985 it was a palish, immature purple; very fragrant fruit and root aromas with spicy depth. Very assertive flavour, good length, tannin and acidity. New Year 1990: still fairly deep, sweet and full. Recently, losing some colour, mature; an attractive rather earthy St-Vivant, and very drinkable.* Last tasted Jan 1991***(*) *Now to 1996.*

SAVIGNY-LES-BEAUNE *CHANDON DE BRIAILLES Delicious. Though not very deep and already appearing to be—using Bordeaux criteria— fully mature the spring after the vintage, it had a very forthcoming nose and delicious, rather earthy flavour. Six years later, flowery bouquet, very flavoury. Such are the mysteries—and occasional delights—of burgundy.* Last tasted April 1989*** *Drink now.*

SAVIGNY-LES-BEAUNE, LES GUETTES *SIMON BIZE An up-and-coming grower with an excellent reputation. Tasted only once: medium-pale, browning distinctly; nose soft, low-keyed, earthy, singed. After 30 minutes in the glass, a marvellous scent had developed. Medium dry, medium-full body—certainly more alcohol and power than its appearance denoted. Very good flavour. Peppery finish.* Jan 1987. *Needed time then, probably at its peak now. A cautious*** Drink soon.*

Clos de TART *In Oct 1985, palish, pink-tinged, weak-rimmed and unimpressive; gentle nose, some fruit, fairly fragrant, with mouthwatering piquancy; distinctly sweet, with burgundy's contradictory lightness of style and weight of alcohol. Firm enough. Some charm. More recently: a well-developed, open-rimmed appearance with misleadingly light, soft, rather undemonstrative nose totally unpreparing one for a wine fullish on the palate with surprising weight and bite, and a raw, rather astringent finish.* Last tasted at the domaine, Oct 1990** Drink now or hope for the best?

VOLNAY *H DE MONTILLE Interesting to see what this gifted winemaker could do with his '82. Familiar '82 paleness of colour, maturing though not browning and with lovely highlights; a nutty, stemmy, hawthorn-bush nose, rather hard but with a honeyed quality beneath. Once again, its appearance belies a skilful balance of fairly high alcohol with delicacy of flavour. Marked tannin and acidity.* Refreshing but needed more bottle-age in April 1987. At least*** Now to 1996.

VOLNAY, CAILLERETS, CLOS DES 60 OUVREES, MONOPOLE *WHOLLY-OWNED CLOS OF LA POUSSE D'OR Palish, youthful, weak-rimmed; very sweet, attractive, slightly caramelly nose; the familiar combination of alcoholic body yet light style. Pleasant flavour.* April 1987*** Drink soon.

VOSNE-ROMANEE, BEAUMONTS *J GRIVOT Some intensity of colour; a rich, warm, harmonious* cassis *and cobnuts nose and taste. Sweet, fairly full-bodied. Attractive. Tannin and good acidity.* At the domaine, Sept 1988***(*) Now to 1998.

Clos VOUGEOT *CH DE LA TOUR Three notes. Consistently stewed, jammy nose; flavoury but short.* Last tasted June 1986*

SOME OTHER '82s TASTED SINCE 1986:

BONNES MARES *ARLAUT Unknown to me. Nose not good, flavour not bad.*

CORTON, POUGETS *L JADOT Deep appearance, hefty, dull.*

MOREY ST-DENIS *ROPITEAU Fairly pale; stewed Pinot; flavoury but a bit hollow***

NUITS-ST-GEORGES *ROBERT DU BOIS Another grower unknown to me. Palish, pink; stuffed and stewed; dry, light style, flavoury enough**

Clos VOUGEOT *ROUMIER Medium, pink-tinged, watery rim; sweet, vanilla nose; dry, lean, strawberry-like fruit***

SOME '82s SHOWING QUITE WELL IN THE MID-1980s

BEAUNE, BOUCHEROTTES *L JADOT Still hard***

BEAUNE, GREVES *LAFARGE Good fruit, rounded*** Probably at best now.

CHAMBOLLE-MUSIGNY, 1ER CRU *J DROUHIN Fragrant and charming***

CORTON, HOSPICES, CUVEE DR PESTE *Bought by Avery at the Hospices auction in 1982 and bottled by Jaffelin. Sweet. High alcoholic content. Hard but fragrant****

GEVREY-CHAMBERTIN *R THEVENIN Good fruit, flavour, length and aftertaste****

GEVREY-CHAMBERTIN *TRAPET Palish, pink and bright; nose like mustard and cress; very flavoury***

MOREY ST-DENIS *JEAN-CLAUDE BOISSET Fairly deep and immature; light, scented nose; quite attractive***

NUITS-ST-GEORGES *JACQUELINE JAYER Made by Etienne Grivot: lovely fruit and spice, sweet, fullish, very good flavour***

NUITS-ST-GEORGES, BOUDOTS *JEAN GRIVOT Made from 60-year-old vines. Dry, powerful, oaky, fruity, spicy****

POMMARD, CLOS DES EPENOTS *JAFFELIN Sweet, pleasant nose and flavour. Good aftertaste***

SAVIGNY-LES-BEAUNE *TOLLOT-BEAUT Good fruity, crisp, and, despite its browning rim, still rather hard**

VOLNAY, 1ER CRU *and* CLOS DES CHENES *LAFARGE Both good, the* 1er cru *having greater length, the Chênes with more concentration of fruit, very complete. Both needing bottle-age****

VOLNAY, CHAMPANS *LAFON From 60-year-old vines, very fruity, distinctly raspberry-like, deceptively light style but penetrating****

Clos VOUGEOT *JEAN GRIVOT In 100% new oak until the malolactic fermentation, then 50% new oak. Good colour; sensational impact on the palate, powerful, concentrated fruit, tannic, expansive aftertaste****

THE DRC RANGE, MAINLY AT PERCY FOX'S TASTING IN LONDON, NOV 1985:

ROMANEE-CONTI *Though a positive, immature colour, appeared to be weaker-rimmed than the '81, but with an extraordinarily rich, scented nose of great depth; a powerful wine, with length, tannin, acidity and penetrating aftertaste. Certainly impressive, amongst the very best of the '82s and infinitely superior to the DRC '81s*(****) 1992–2000?

La TACHE *Medium-pale, lively, immature; spicy Pinot aroma, great depth; dry, lean, firm, lively and already with a lovely aftertaste. A year later: very fragrant, harmonious bouquet; seemed to have sweetened a little – probably the context. Root-like, earthy, Pinot flavour, good acidity.* Last noted Dec 1986*** – at least.

RICHEBOURG *Rich, lively, immature; sweet, spicy, biscuity nose; sturdy, aromatic****

ROMANEE-ST-VIVANT *See page 221.*

GRANDS-ECHEZEAUX *Youthful; low-keyed, crisp, immature fruit; powerful, spicy flavour, excellent length. A year later, lovely red/ruby colour; harmonious Pinot nose; some sweetness, pleasant weight, good fruit and fragrant aftertaste.* Last tasted Dec 1986***

ECHEZEAUX *A positive, luminous, youthful appearance; vegetal, beetroot (Pinot) character, fruity, fragrance; assertive flavour, quite substantial tannin and acidity***

1983** to ****

An important but controversial vintage. A cool, wet, dismal spring; localised hailstorms in May, with Chambolle-Musigny and Vosne-Romanée badly affected, losing 30% of their potential crop, but in general the subsequent flowering was successful. June and July exceptionally hot and dry, advancing development, thickening skins, concentrating flesh. However, dull wet weather from the end of Aug to mid-Sept brought on rot. Harvesting took place in mixed conditions; those who picked late and selectively gathered the best grapes.

I well remember the shock of the first tasting when Robert Drouhin brought over a range the spring after the vintage: unusually deep, purple and laden with hard tannins. Indeed colour and tannin have been fairly consistently noted since then, although there is a fairly dramatic colour loss after relatively few years in bottle. Also, very normal with burgundy, a tendency to look mature — soft, rosy, orange-tinged, tawny-edged — after what seems, by Bordeaux standards, a shockingly short time. Until one takes a mouthful. Two problems, rot and hard tannins, affected an otherwise excellent vintage. Wine can be permanently tainted by rotten grapes. However, wine that manages to shake off its tannin straitjacket should, long-term, turn out well. The best will be fragrant and flavoury through the latter half of the 1990s and well into the 21st century.

DOMAINE DE LA ROMANEE-CONTI

Because of the high tannin content the DRC wines were bottled late, between March and May 1986. They were shipped to the US and on retailers' shelves within months, equally speedily tasted and roundly condemned by a leading wine journal. As a result of the subsequent controversy I was invited by the US importer to taste a range of '83 DRC wines and, on my return, the London agents laid on another tasting, this time attended by Oz Clarke and Clive Coates. The notes that follow were made at these tastings, in Nov and Dec 1986, and I have added notes on subsequent tastings of Romanée-Conti, St-Vivant, Grands-Echézeaux and Echézeaux.

ROMANEE-CONTI *On Nov 2 1986: the deepest of the range, the most purple at heart and rim; deep, rich, classic 'beetroot' Pinot nose, after 30 minutes developing an opulent blackberry aroma; massive, concentrated and tannic, yet at the same time soft, rich and chewy. A month later, in London: fine rich intensity of appearance noted; nose massive yet subdued, rich, latent power. As before, medium sweetness, full-bodied, vast, velvety and packed with fruit, its extract masking tannin and acidity. Great potential. Most recently: decanted in my office at 12.30pm as lunch was in the boardroom and I did not want to disturb the sediment. Medium-deep, warm, ruddy, not much red. Upon decanting, subdued though rich Pinot aroma; very dry, massive, with crisp 'beetroot' flavour. Served at 1.20pm. A huge tannic wine, tough but with very fragrant aftertaste. Three hours after decanting an amazingly rich bouquet, slightly singed, great depth. Tough. Clearly needs hours of decanting time, but really totally unready. Last tasted, in magnum, March 1991**(***) Beyond 2000.*

La TACHE *At both tastings: medium-deep, rich, warm, translucent; immediately forthcoming bouquet, yet hard-edged. Rich, spicy, opening up yet further, gloriously, in the glass; crisp, fragrant, lean yet with penetrating flavour expanding in the mouth. Still hard, tannic, needing bottle-age. Last tasted Dec 1986(****) 1996 to beyond 2000.*

RICHEBOURG *At the tasting in San Fancisco it appeared to be more forward; a sweet, chocolaty nose, somewhat overblown; medium sweetness, fairly full-bodied, with a broad, spicy flavour and cinnamon aftertaste. At the London tasting, two bottles, one appearing to be deeper and browner (DRC wines are bottled from individual casks which can vary); a similar singed chocolaty nose, with rich fruit foundation, yet low-keyed and unyielding for up to an hour in the glass. A big wine. Very dry, massively tannic. Last tasted Dec 1986(***)?*

GRANDS-ECHEZEAUX *At both the earlier tastings, slightly deeper and more intense than the Echézeaux. Classic, rich, 'boiled beetroot' Pinot aroma. Good weight, firm, greater length and intensity than the Echézeaux, good flavour, spicy tannic finish. Just over three years later: good colour, showing maturity at the rim; very good bouquet; sweet, well developed, lovely vinosity, nicely balanced, rich and attractive. Last tasted Feb 1990**** Now to 2000.*

ROMANEE-ST-VIVANT *First noted in Dec 1986: a lovely, limpid medium colour, rich but the rim already showing considerable development; delicate, herbaceous, higher-toned and fragrant; elegant but firm and totally unready, with high tannin and acidity. I reversed my old metaphor, describing this as "velvet glove in iron fist". Most recently: notable colour loss, now medium-pale, very mature-looking; very good bouquet; now sweeter and softer, nice weight, very attractive flavour and aftertaste. Touch of bitterness on the finish. Last tasted Feb 1990***(*) Now to 2000.*

ECHEZEAUX *At the Nov 1986 tasting: medium, slightly pink-tinged, the weakest rim; open-knit, vegetal aroma; fairly full-flavoured, tasting of cold tea with singed leaves aftertaste. The second glass appeared more chocolaty, volatile and acidic. A month later, my notes more or less matched: forthcoming, slightly 'stewed' Pinot; with quite a biting edge. Tannic. More recently, bottle variation. Both medium-pale, mature-looking; both fragrant, but one with more vanilla; both flavoury but qualified — a sort of woodiness, perhaps a touch of rot. Distinctly below standard. Last tasted Feb 1990**

BEAUNE, CLOS DES MOUCHES *J DROUHIN First tasted at Drouhin's preview presentation in April 1984: medium-deep, purple-tinged; low-keyed, crusty nose, with lovely fruit poised to make a break for cover; dry, medium-full body, lovely though raw, immature oaky/Pinot flavour and aftertaste. Most recently: now medium-pale, fully mature red brown; when first poured, a light, open, strawberry and liquorice scent, then, after 20 minutes, harmonious, very pleasant and, after an hour, calm, good, vegetal nose; sweet, fairly full-bodied, assertive, good fruit, flavour, marked tannin and good acidity. One of the best of the decade.* Last noted at Drouhin's, Oct 1990***(*) Now to beyond 2000.

BEAUNE, TOUSSAINTS *RENE MONNIER Medium-deep; 'boiled beetroot' Pinot aroma; good body, extract and fruit. Rather hard tannic finish.* March 1990***(*) Now to 2000.

BEAUNE, CLOS DES URSULES *L JADOT Deep though fully mature appearance; initially showing a lot of age, soft, singed, with sweaty tannins but in minutes it opened up, fragrant, fruit, fresh walnuts. Full of fruit, extract, velvety tannins. Good wine.* With André Gagey at Jadot's, Oct 1990***(*) Now to beyond 2000.

CHAMBERTIN, CLOS DE BEZE *DAMOY Medium-pale, maturing; sweet, rather smelly old beetroot — tannin and overripe Pinot; sweet, fullish body, dry leathery tannic finish.* Feb 1990**(*) Hard to judge whether the fruit will outlive the tannin.

CHAMBERTIN, CLOS DE BEZE *L JADOT Medium-deep, mature; low-keyed yet rich, sweaty tannins like old socks — improved greatly with air; dry, fairly full-bodied, with the very distinctive Chambertin 'fishy' Pinot flavour, tannin and acidity. I felt it was, somehow, a bit hollow.* Oct 1990**(*)?

CHASSAGNE-MONTRACHET, MORGEOTS *LABOURE-ROI Medium-deep, still ruby; not much nose; sweet, soft, singed flavour, fairly light style yet amply alcoholic. No excess of '83 hard tannins.* At Wilton's, Sept 1989*** Now to 1995.

Ch CORTON-GRANCEY *Cask sample, first noted at a Louis Latour tasting in Oct 1985: good depth of colour; nose dumb, hawthorn rather than fruit or earthy character; a big, chewy wine. Four years later: considerable colour change, now medium-pale, mature, rosehip hue; fully developed, rich, singed Pinot bouquet; very sweet, fullish body, good rich flavour, touch of liquorice. Noticeably tannic.* Last tasted Nov 1989**(*)

GEVREY-CHAMBERTIN *FAIVELEY Good colour but already mature-looking by March 1986: very positive nose and flavour, quite good fruit. Exactly three years later: medium-pale, lively, but its mature rim now tinged with orange; not a bad nose, trace of old socks, Pinot, tannin; medium sweetness and fairly full-bodied. Rich enough and quite good fruit but a tinny tannic finish.* Last tasted March 1989** I do not see this improving.

GEVREY-CHAMBERTIN, CAZETIERS *L LATOUR A cask sample: hawthorn, brambly character but fragrant and with some depth. Dry, good length in Oct 1985. Four years later: further bottle-age, colour loss, now palish warm tawny. Noted as "sweet", with good flavour, marked tannin and good acidity.* Last tasted Nov 1989**(*) The tannin will conserve, but will it improve?

GEVREY-CHAMBERTIN, CAZETIERS *PHILIPPE LECLERC Fairly deep, more crimson than Magnien's and just beginning to show maturity; sweet, medicinal, almost Pauillac-like oyster-shell nose; sweet, soft, fleshy, fruity, delicious. Dry finish.* Feb 1989***(*) Now to 1998.

GEVREY-CHAMBERTIN, CAZETIERS *H MAGNIEN Noted for austerity and long fermentation. Medium-pale, lovely brick red colour, maturing; gentle, flower-like, walnuts and dried raisins nose, with a certain earthiness; powerful, good length, swingeingly tannic.* Feb 1989**(**) An interesting future.

GEVREY-CHAMBERTIN, ESTOURNELLES ST JACQUES *CLAIR-DAU Medium-pale, mature; smell like a burnt doormat; sweet, chewy, quite flavoury, with bitter tannic finish.* Jan 1990*

NUITS-ST-GEORGES, CLOS ST MARC *DOM DU CLOS ST MARC, BOUCHARD PERE Medium, very orange-tinged; sweet, completely ready; rich, good long flavour, very tannic.* Oct 1988***(*) Now to 1996.

POMMARD *THOMAS BASSOT Medium-pale, rosy-hued; rather hard, stewed Pinot nose and palate. Slightly malty, very dry tannic finish.* Jan 1990. Not very appealing.

POMMARD, EPENOTS *L LATOUR A medium-pale, already mature-looking cask sample; dumb hard nose; huge, powerful, excellent length, very tannic. Four years later a gentle rosy glow; ripe bouquet; sweet, less mammoth, nice flavour, soft despite its tannin and acidity.* Last tasted Nov 1989**(*) Now to 1996.

ROMANEE-ST-VIVANT, QUATRE JOURNAUX *L LATOUR Dry, elegant cask sample, good vinosity, length, aftertaste and future. Four autumns later: lovely, glowing, but very mature-looking; fragrant; sweet, fairly full-bodied, lovely flavour, elegance noted again, and good length.* Last tasted Nov 1989***(*) Now to 1998.

Clos de TART *Medium-deep, lively colour; fragrant, cherry-like aroma, assertive, then a strange smell that reminded me of kerosene or lead-free petrol — the effect of hail I was told. Full body and flavour but very astringent, with an aggressive stalky tannic finish.* At the domaine, Oct 1990*(*)

VOSNE-ROMANEE *JEAN GRIVOT Rather pale; bramble-bush Pinot that developed pleasantly in the glass; medium dry, fairly full-bodied, flavour of sweet beetroot, good length, tannic but not aggressively so.* At Le Gavroche, Feb 1990***(*) Now to 1996.

VOSNE-ROMANEE, ORVEAUX *MONGEARD-MUGNERET Medium-deep but already a fully mature appearance; good, vegetal Pinot aroma becoming smoother and richer as the air got to it. Flavour to match. Despite its appearance, a fairly high alcoholic content and needing bottle-age.* Feb 1988***(*) Now to 1998.

SOME OTHER '83s TASTED SINCE 1987:

ALOXE-CORTON, FOURNIERES *GUYON Rather neutral and cardboardy at first but developed peachy overtones***

BEAUNE, TEURONS *DOM DE CH DE BEAUNE Palish, slightly brown-tinged; open, somewhat stewed Pinot nose; medium in every way, with leathery tannins***

CHAMBOLLE-MUSIGNY *EDUARD DELAUNAY Earthy Pinot aroma and taste. Quite good in its way, with a fragrant aftertaste***

NUITS-ST-GEORGES, LES ST-GEORGES *ROBERT DUBOIS Palish but ruddy; flowery, rather artificial and hard; fairly sweet, assertive, flavoury but with swingeing tannin and acidity**(*)

POMMARD, JAROLLIERES *DOM DE LA POUSSE D'OR Medium-pale, bright, ruby-tinged; fragrant, spicy, slightly nutty and touch of liquorice; dry, crisp, hard, touch of bitterness, unready(***)*

VOLNAY, FREMIETS, CLOS DE LA ROUGEOTTE *DOM DU CH DE BEAUNE Orange-tinged; warm, open bouquet, but dry, lean and very tannic. Unlikely to throw off its tannin(**)*

SOME '83s TASTED IN THEIR EARLY YEARS:

ABBAYE DE MORGEOT, CLOS DE LA CHAPELLE *DUC DE MAGENTA Deep, bright, full, rich, a touch of oak, attractive****

ALOXE-CORTON, CHAILLOTS and BEAUNE, VIGNES FRANCHES *L LATOUR Impressive cask samples.*

CHAMBERTIN, CUVEE HERITIERS LATOUR *More like port than burgundy.*

CHAMBOLLE-MUSIGNY, LES HAUTS-DOIX *SERGE-GROFFIER Good colour but smell of cabbages: rot or hail? Dry, chunky.*

CHASSAGNE-MONTRACHET *J DROUHIN Palish, little nose, disarmingly light yet packing a punch**(*)*

CHOREY-LES-BEAUNE *TOLLOT-BEAUT Ruby; raspberry and vanilla on nose, tough and tannic on palate. But very flavoury*(**)*

GEVREY-CHAMBERTIN *FAIVELEY Attractive despite tannic bitterness*(**)*

GEVREY-CHAMBERTIN *VIENOT Raw and horrid.*

GEVREY-CHAMBERTIN, CLOS DE LA JUSTICE *PIERRE BOURREE A beautiful colour; honeyed, ripe, opulent bouquet; sweet, smooth, fragrant and elegant. Tannin present but not omnipresent***(*)*

GRIOTTE-CHAMBERTIN *J DROUHIN Overwhelmingly tannic, raw, woody even, but not tasted since its cask sample.*

Clos des LAMBRAYS *Lovely, expansive appearance; sweet, meaty, alcoholic nose; beguilingly sweet and soft, yet powerful**(*)*

MOREY ST-DENIS *J C BOISSET Some fragrance but rather lean and tart.*

MUSIGNY *DE VOGUE Being racked with an old-fashioned stirrup pump; lovely colour, deeper than the Bonnes Mares; low-keyed yet richer; lovely flavour, oaky, tannic. Due to hail, it had to be vinified quickly so would not have the power of some '83s.*

VOLNAY, CHAMPANS *LAFON Extraordinary wine, dazzlingly fruity. A cherry ruby colour in cask with immensely fragrant nose, leaving a scent of strawberry jam in the glass; firm, lively****

VOLNAY, SANTENOTS *LAFON A fabulously intense ruby; deep, warm, nutty nose; good fruit, tannic finish. In cask(***)*

VOLNAY, SANTENOTS *L LATOUR Also good. Assertive. Good flavour, length, tannin and acidity(***)*

VOSNE-ROMANEE, BEAUMONTS *Already tinged with orange, fleshy yet powerful. Cask sample. Oct 1985.*

VOSNE-ROMANEE, BEAUMONTS *GRIVOT Still in new oak casks: medium-pale ruby, sweet but a bit gassy – awaiting another racking. Very lively, the flavour tinged with the spicy cloves of new oak. Excellent aftertaste. Interesting future(****)*

VOSNE-ROMANEE, SUCHOTS *Rather pale in cask, though M Grivot told me it would gain colour; sweet but raw, powerful, very tannic(***)*

1984★

Much in common with Bordeaux: uneven growing conditions resulting in wines lacking in grace. In the case of burgundy, lacking breeding and class, and over-acidic. A poor spring was followed by late flowering and *millerandage*. Fine, hot July, stormy Aug, decidedly wet Sept, one of the worst on record. Late, disheartening harvesting conditions. Few tasted recently, and no regrets. Not a vintage to pursue.

La TACHE *Medium-pale, mature, orange-rimmed; fully developed, rich, slightly chocolaty nose; fairly sweet, medium weight, quite a good deal of grip, singed, fruity flavour. Loads of tannin. Lacking the flair and dazzling fruit and elegance of La Tâche at its best but a fairly impressive mouthful. Better than expected. At the Percy Fox DRC tasting, Feb 1990** 1992–98*

BEAUNE, CLOS DES MOUCHES *J DROUHIN Alcohol 12.3%, total acidity 3.8. Medium-pale, mature, weak, watery rim; light, open, floral, minty nose that developed quite nicely; dry, raw fruit and acidic. After the '81, the least satisfactory Clos des Mouches of the decade. Tasted at Drouhin's, Oct 1990**

Le CORTON *LOUIS MAX Medium-deep, rich, mature; very sweet, hefty, vanilla-scented; good fruit and length, but attenuated and too acidic. Dec 1990**

GEVREY-CHAMBERTIN *TRAPET Palish with pink highlights; unknit; strange, piquant beetroot flavour. March 1990.*

MUSIGNY *DE VOGUE Medium-pale, open-knit, the most developed of the decade; sweet, vegetal, somewhat high-toned and medicinal nose, underlying greenness noted, yet, after 30 minutes, very scented and surprisingly nice; medium weight, not bad, earthy, slightly liquorice flavour. At the domaine, Oct 1990***

ROMANEE-ST-VIVANT *DRC Medium-pale with an orange brown edge; singed, chocolaty, chaptalised Pinot nose; medium sweetness and body, flavoury, chunky, agreeable. Feb 1990** Best to drink soon.*

VOSNE-ROMANEE *GERARD MUGNERET Rosehip tawny; mild beetroot nose; dry, some grip but unimpressive. April 1990**

Clos VOUGEOT *ROPITEAU Two recent notes: medium-pale with soft red tinge; unknit, hard to define – a dash of raspberry, vanilla. Lean, lacking fruit, swingeingly dry tannic-acid finish. Last tasted July 1989.*

Clos VOUGEOT, *CH DE LA TOUR Quite attractive colour and stewed-fruit nose; slightly sweet, not bad for an '84. Dec 1990***

SOME '84s TASTED FROM 1985 TO 1988:

ALOXE-CORTON, LES CHAILLOTS *L LATOUR Very pale, watery cask sample; unimpressive nose; dry, piquant, flavoury, acceptable acidity**

BEAUNE 1ER CRU *J DROUHIN Prematurely orange; unforthcoming; loose-knit, short.*

CHAMBOLLE-MUSIGNY, 1ER CRU *J DROUHIN Open, relaxed, watery about the edges; light but fragrant; overall dry, surprisingly attractive fruit, shape and elegance*★★

CHASSAGNE-MONTRACHET *MOMMESSIN Cherry-scented; very flavoury but piquant and slightly bitter*★

CHOREY-LES-BEAUNE *DOM DE TERREGELESSES Singed, blown, even without a whiff of oxidation, mediocre.*

GEVREY-CHAMBERTIN *J DROUHIN Premature; sweet, slightly malty nose; dry, mild but rather raw.*

GRANDS-ECHEZEAUX *The best of the Drouhin '84s*★★

GRIOTTE-CHAMBERTIN *J DROUHIN Good colour; youthful but fragrant nose; hard and tannic but coping adequately with an elaborate truffle-garnished Alsatian dish*★★

NUITS-ST-GEORGES *REINE-PEDAUQUE Rosy-hued, hard, not unattractive but tart.*

NUITS-ST-GEORGES *J DROUHIN Faint trace of violet, weak-rimmed; smell of sweaty feet; dry, lean.*

VOLNAY, SANTENOTS *L LATOUR Palish, immature; curious, spicy, stalky nose; fairly dry, oaky, flavoury, hard, with acidic edge.*

1985★★★★★

Undoubtedly one of the most attractive vintages of the decade. After four variable years, an uncomplicated, beautifully balanced year – wines of charm, style, class and, despite their accessibility, wines that will keep. Unprecedentedly low temperature in Jan (−25°C [−13°F]) was recorded in the lower-lying vineyards of the Côte de Nuits. Both young and old vines were damaged. A further cold snap in Feb, followed by heavy snow. Flowering was delayed, avoiding late frosts, but in damp conditions. June and July unremarkable, but from the first week in Aug, drought conditions. Barely ½in of rain fell during Aug and Sept. Burgundy suffers from frequent hailstorms; one on Aug 14 destroyed 25% of the crop in certain communes, notably Aloxe-Corton. From Sept 1 constant sunshine during the day and mild nights, transforming the somewhat backward grapes into a ripe, healthy crop. No rot. One of the most satisfactory vintages in most growers' memories.

On the whole about the best-balanced burgundy of recent years, certainly since 1978. Those capable of making top-class wine did so, and, judging from copious notes, there are fewer aberrations than in most vintages. Well worth acquiring, drinking, keeping.

La TACHE *Deep, rich and fairly intense, showing some maturity; at its best inimitable, and difficult to put into words, the first whiff – strange as it might seem – being of iodine, fish scales or oyster shells, crisp, opening up, after 15 minutes displaying beautiful blackberry-like fruit; touch of sweetness, ripe grapes and alcohol, long assertive flavour leading to firm, dry finish. Quite unready. Tasted at the Domaine, Oct 1990*★(★★★★) *1995–2020*

BEAUNE, BRESSANDES *ALBERT MOROT Lovely colour, luscious legs; almost a caricature of Pinot Noir, fragrant; rich, a touch of iron in its dry finish. At the Hollywood Wine Society burgundy session, Jan 1990*★(★★★) *1992–2010*

BEAUNE, CLOS DES MOUCHES *J DROUHIN Alcohol 13.2%, total acidity 3.7. Immature purple tinge, some denseness; nose unready but flesh, fruit and fragrance much in evidence in March 1986. Five years after the vintage: medium, fairly rich colour, maturing nicely; first impression, stewed Pinot, opening up richly and, after an hour, beautifully 'shaped' scent; fullish body, rich, rounded, lovely flavour, good acidity. Last tasted at Drouhin's, Oct 1990*★★★★(★) *Now to beyond 2000.*

BEAUNE, CLOS DES URSULES *L JADOT Good colour; sweet, soft and rich with raspberry-like fragrance; nice weight, balance, flavour. Last tasted Oct 1990*★★★★ *Now to 1996.*

BONNES MARES *GEORGES ROUMIER Medium, garnet; low-keyed, meaty, a bit stewed; sweet, powerful, delicious flavour but slightly bitter tannins requiring more bottle-ageing. May 1990*★★★(★) *1992–98*

CHAMBERTIN *HERITIERS DE LATOUR Fairly deep; very sweet, lovely, touch of raspberry; fullish, silky, velvety, voluptuous. Perfect balance. Lovely now. May 1991*★★★★★ *Now to 1998.*

CHAMBERTIN *A ROUSSEAU Very rich, intense, starting to mature; bouquet of tremendous power and depth, welling out of the glass, increasingly aromatic; sweet, mouthfilling, lovely aftertaste. After some less than notable wines Rousseau on top of form. Worth flying to Tokyo just for this. At Wine Japan burgundy tasting lecture, May 1990*★★★★★ *Now to beyond 2000.*

CHAMBOLLE-MUSIGNY, 1ER CRU *J DROUHIN In the spring of 1986 very deep, purple; immature but good fruit; sweet, soft, oaky. Four years after the vintage: good colour, nose and taste. Correct, flavoury, copybook. Touch of hardness, a plea for further bottle-age. At the award-winning Plume restaurant, Hong Kong, Oct 1989*★★★★(★) *Now to 2000.*

Le CORTON *DOM DU CH DE BEAUNE Palish, almost rosehip; low-keyed; sweet, rich, chunky, powerfully tannic. Feb 1991*★★(★★)

CORTON, RENARDES *REINE PEDAUQUE A delicious gold medal-winning drink, but not my idea of a rich, meaty Corton. Medium, pink-tinged; scented fruit, raspberries, an attractive confection; interesting, a strong Pinot flavour, bitter tannins on finish. At Wine Japan, May 1990*★★(★) *Now to 1996.*

Ch CORTON-GRANCEY *Fairly deep, still youthful; rather restrained, immature, slight blackberry-like aroma; excellent nutty – walnuts – flavour, good length, aftertaste, tannin and acidity. The finest of an interesting range at a Louis Latour tasting, Oct 1990*★★★(★★) *1993 to beyond 2000.*

GEVREY-CHAMBERTIN, CLOS-ST-JACQUES *L JADOT A nose and taste of great depth and length. Glorious flesh and fruit. June 1991*★★★(★) *1992–2000*

ECHEZEAUX *J DROUHIN The most completely evolved of the seven top '85s at the Wine Japan burgundy seminar, maturing, its edge tinged with* *orange; a toasted, roasted, demerara sugar nose of broad rich character which, after 25 minutes in the glass, smelled like singed hair; sweet, citrus-like acidity, slight touch of tannic bitterness, otherwise a good rich drink. In Tokyo, May 1990****(*) 1992–98?*

GRANDS-ECHEZEAUX *DRC Deep, lively, still youthful; good fruit, but unready despite its delicacy; a confident, attractive entry, good length, great style, silky tannins and acidity. With lunch at the Domaine, Oct 1990****(*) 1993 to beyond 2000.*

MUSIGNY *J-F MUGNIER First tasted at the Ch de Chambolle-Musigny in Sept 1988: good depth of colour; warm, rich nose; sweet, alcoholic, fairly concentrated with spicy new oak. Next, at the Wine Japan tasting: medium, a rather pretty red on the verge of maturity; delicate, low-keyed but very fragrant. Good, cherry-like fruit. After an hour became sweeter and seemingly deeper, less superficial; touch of sweetness on the palate, with a deceptively light, Musigny femininity. Yet — a not abnormal female trait — quite strong and assertive. Flavoury, good endtaste, the highest acidity of the group. Last tasted in Tokyo, May 1990***(*) 1992–98*

MUSIGNY *DE VOGUE Medium-deep, fairly intense, still rather immature; a welcomingly sweet, ripe Pinot aroma. Returning after 15 minutes, I noticed its richness and high extract, then after 30 minutes, a lovely, soft, blackberry-like scent and touch of cinnamon — new oak; gloriously rich, full of fruit,* crème de cassis, *firm tannins and acidity. Fine wine. Excellent future. At the domaine, Oct 1990***(**) 1992–2010*

NUITS-ST-GEORGES, PORRETS ST-GEORGES *H GOUGES Palish, mature; an immediacy of scent; very sweet and flavoury. Aug 1991**** Now to 1998.*

NUITS-ST-GEORGES, PRULIERS *H GOUGES Two recent notes: pretty colour; very forthcoming, smoky, vegetal; firm crisp fruit and more tannic than expected. Last tasted Aug 1991***(*) 1992–2000*

NUITS-ST-GEORGES, LES ST-GEORGES *H GOUGES Richly-coloured; vegetal fragrance; very sweet and fruity. Marvellous aftertaste. Aug 1991***(*) Now to 2000.*

POMMARD, HOSPICES, CUVEE BILLARDET *BOISSET Deep, rich; equally rich, hefty, vanilla and fruit nose; full body and flavour, fruit-laden and very tannic. Dec 1990**(**) 1995–2015*

Clos de La ROCHE *DUJAC Medium, maturing; cherry-like Pinot aroma leaping out of the glass, mouthwatering. After 40 minutes a simply beautiful scent, with touch of mint leaf; immediate flavour on palate, sweet ripe fruit, deceptively light style, delicate fragrance, acidity and bitter tannins. Vibrant. Delicious. May 1990****(*) Now to 2000.*

Clos de TART *Medium deep, still youthful; a lovely, open fruitiness that, after 10 minutes in the glass, evolved gloriously; sweet, medium full-bodied, lovely fruit, perfect balance. At the domaine with Patrice Noyelle of Mommessin's, Oct 1990****(*) Now to beyond 2000.*

VOSNE-ROMANEE, SUCHOTS *J DROUHIN A deep, very pretty colour with long shapely legs; tremendous impact, glorious Pinot aroma, sweet, almost jammy in its richness; sweet, lovely flesh and fruit, beautiful texture yet distinctly tannic. At Becky Wasserman's seminar in Hollywood, Florida, Jan 1990****(*) 1992–2000*

Clos VOUGEOT *J DROUHIN Alcohol 13.2%, total acidity 3.40. Medium-deep, purple-tinged but slightly weak at the rim; with the spiciness of new oak and zest of youth yet some sweetness and softness on the palate. This was in the spring after the vintage. Four years later, the weak rim noted again, yet the nose and palate anything but weak. Nose restrained but powerful, opening up, sweet, rich, with fishy Pinot aroma; an impressive, well-structured wine, its prickly finish indicating the need for more bottle-age. Last tasted May 1990***(**) 1993 to beyond 2000.*

BRIEFER NOTES ON SOME OTHER '85s TASTED RECENTLY:

BEAUNE, TEURONS *CHANSON Rich, soft, spicy. Oct 1990****

BEAUNE, CENT VIGNES *RENE MONNIER Good Pinot flavour. Feb 1990****

BEAUNE, CHOUACHEAUX *L JADOT Good flavour and balance. Jan 1990***(*)*

BONNES MARES *JADOT Vanilla chocolate nose; marvellously rich and chewy. June 1990*****

CHASSAGNE-MONTRACHET *GABRIEL JOUARD Soft cherry; vinous, harmonious; quite a powerful bite. Last tasted May 1989**(**)*

CHASSAGNE-MONTRACHET *MARC COLIN Palish, pink; sweet, light style, fruity. Dec 1990****

GEVREY-CHAMBERTIN, CAZETIERS *L JADOT Fragrant, good fruit, balance. Dec 1990****

MOREY ST-DENIS *DUJAC Fragrant, almost overscented; lean, lively, fruity, very flavoury, touch of end bitterness. Last tasted July 1989****

NUITS-ST-GEORGES, DAMODES *RODET Soft red; harmonious; smooth, rich, with dry tannic finish. Oct 1989**(*)*

SANTENAY, CLOS DE TAVENNES *REMOISSENET Palish but alcoholic, easy drinking yet with notable tannin and acidity. Nov 1989****

VOSNE-ROMANEE, BEAUMONTS *AVERY Nice weight, fruit and flavour. Dec 1990***(*)*

SOME OTHER '85s TASTED PRIOR TO 1989 AND SHOWING PROMISE:

BEAUNE, LES SCEAUX *BOUCHARD AINE Made from 15-year-old vines and matured in 50% new oak (*chêne d'Alsace*); one bottle slightly oxidised but another crisp, spicy, delicious. At best****

BEAUNE, TEURONS *BOUCHARD PERE Toasted coconut nose, lovely flavour, length and aftertaste***(*)*

BEAUNE, TOUSSAINTS *RENE MONNIER High-toned, very oaky, lean but attractive(***)*

CHAMBERTIN, CLOS DE BEZE *BOUCHARD AINE (DOM MARION) 75% new Limousin oak; cherry red; nutty; powerful*(***)*

CHAMBERTIN, CLOS DE BEZE *DAMOY Fruity and nutty; great length(*****)*

CHAMBOLLE-MUSIGNY, 1ER CRU *J-F MUGNIER A blend of grapes from the Fué and Plantes vineyards: sweet, lovely texture and component parts(****)*

CHOREY-LES-BEAUNE *TOLLOT-BEAUT Scented, crisp, lean, attractive. Dependable and good value**(*)*

GEVREY-CHAMBERTIN *J DROUHIN, L LATOUR, ALAIN BURGUET, L JADOT, ROSSIGNOL All good to very good.*

GRANDS-ECHEZEAUX *J DROUHIN Spicy(****)*

MOREY ST-DENIS *J DROUHIN Crisp. Glorious(*****)*

MUSIGNY *J DROUHIN**(**)*

MUSIGNY *J-F MUGNIER Deep, fleshy, oaky, voluptuous*(****)*

NUITS-ST-GEORGES, ARGILLIERES *CHARTRON & TREBUCHET Aroma of prunes and raspberries; lovely new oak, cinnamon, lean, flavoury**(**)*

NUITS, CLOS ST MARC *BOUCHARD PERE Crisp, fruity, good length, tannic*(***)*

POMMARD, CLOS DES EPENAUX *COMTE ARMAND Lovely flavour, style, texture, grip(****)*

VOLNAY, CAILLERETS, ANCIENNE CUVEE CARNOT *DOM DU CH DE BEAUNE Lovely toasty nose; sweet, very attractive**(**)*

VOLNAY, CLOS DE LA BOUSSE D'OR *DOM DE LA POUSSE D'OR Lean, oaky, attractive(***)*

VOSNE-ROMANEE, BEAUMONTS *J GRIVOT Given a long fermentation to increase tannin content, bottled early Sept 1987: warm, fruity, cobnut nose that sweetened in the glass; good, rich, nutty flavour, tannin very apparent(****)*

1986★★★★

Despite a somewhat hair-raising growing season, some extremely good wines made; reputed to be more successful among the top growths of the Côte de Nuits. Rather tough, less charm, more tannic than the '85s. A drab cold showery spring continued into early June. Late but well-nigh perfect flowering. Rain and thunderstorms at the end of Aug and in the middle of Sept encouraged the spread of grey rot. Although some growers started to pick in rain on Sept 24, shortly after there was a miraculous change of temperature due to an anti-cyclone, enabling *grand cru* proprietors to pick late in ideal conditions. A large crop. Better in the Côte de Nuits.

Reading back through my notes, I notice relatively consistent style and quality. Perhaps I have been exposed mainly to the better growths. It would appear, unless they lose fruit and dry out, that the best '86s will be well worth cellaring.

La TACHE *Two recent notes: medium-deep, now beginning to show some maturity; very good, rich, fairly concentrated, vegetal fragrance; touch of ripe sweetness, full body and flavour, lovely, packed with fruit, touch of bitter tannin on finish, with acidity and inimitable aftertaste. Long life. Last tasted Jan 1991*(****) 1995–2010*

BEAUNE, CLOS DES MOUCHES *Alcohol 12.6%, total acidity 4.00. Medium depth, rosy glow, slightly pink immature tinge; forthcoming, open, sweet Pinot character, touch of jamminess and liquorice, held crisply and fragrantly in the glass; very distinctive, assertive even, with high tannin content. Showing well at the Clos des Mouches vertical at Drouhin's, Oct 1990(****) 1995–2010 or beyond.*

BEAUNE, TEURONS *DOM DU CH DE BEAUNE Medium pale, with a youthful tinge in Oct 1988. Two years later: not much red; nose a bit smelly. Most recently rosy-hued; stewed; noticeably sweet and attractive on all these occasions, with more power and bite than expected. Last tasted Feb 1991***(*) 1992–98? Hard to predict.*

BEAUNE, CLOS DES URSULES *L JADOT Medium depth, seems about to mature but informed by the oenologist that it will gain colour – such is the peculiarity of Pinot Noir; soft, scented nose, powdery, raspberry blancmange, with plenty of crisp fruit beneath; fairly dry, nice weight, fruit, lightish style, and supporting tannin and acidity. Oct 1990*(***) 1992–2000*

BONNES MARES *L JADOT Surprisingly pale, appearing to show age both in appearance and on its sweet, singed nose. Yet tannic and unready. June 1990. A baffling sort of wine(***)? 1993–?*

Le CORTON *DOM DE CH DE BEAUNE Deep; crisp, neat and nutty on nose and palate in Oct 1988, very tannic, "years of life". After two years, a noticeable change in colour – less deep, more evolved; rather powdery vanilla nose that opened up richly in the glass; fairly full-bodied, good mid-palate, very agreeable. Last tasted Dec 1990*(**) Possibly**** 1992–2000*

Le CORTON *LIONEL BRUCK Medium, fully evolved colour; unknit, citronella, attractive in its way, touch of wood; dry, fullish, fruity, crisp. Dec 1990*(**) 1993–98*

CORTON, CLOS DES CORTONS *FAIVELEY Palish, pink-tinged; nutty nose that improved upon acquaintance; nice weight and flavour though I felt something was slightly lacking. Dec 1990*(**) 1992–98*

GEVREY-CHAMBERTIN, CAZETIERS *J DROUHIN Rather weak-rimmed; dusty, stewed, vanilla nose and taste. Lacking conviction. Dec 1990** Now to 1995.*

GEVREY-CHAMBERTIN, CLOS ST-JACQUES *L JADOT Ruby; very sweet, fudge-like, fragrant; good crisp flavour and finish. June 1991**(**) 1992–2000*

GEVREY-CHAMBERTIN, VIEILLES VIGNES *ALAIN BURQUET Palish, pink-tinged; sweet, strawberry-like nose, gentle, held well. Straightforward, attractive. Feb 1989**(*) Now to 1998.*

GRANDS-ECHEZEAUX *DRC Lively, distinctly sweet, rich and tannic in Feb 1990. Fairly deep yet a distinctly brown rim developing; harmonious, rich, soft, singed nose; fairly full-bodied, earthy Pinot flavour, still very tannic. Last tasted Jan 1991(****) 1994–2010*

MAZIS-CHAMBERTIN *FAIVELEY Palish red pink, transparent, rather watery; glorious, spicy nose which developed fabulously; lean yet powerful, loads of oak. Feb 1989*(***) 1992–2000?*

MUSIGNY *DE VOGUE Medium-pale, developing; fragrant, spicy, still a bit hard, very scented – like an Oregon Pinot Noir! – evolving crisp, blackberry-like nose; dry, medium-full body, lean, rather peppery, spicy, good aftertaste.* At the domaine, Oct 1990*(***) 1992 to beyond 2000.

NUITS-ST-GEORGES, DAMODES *CHANTAL LESCURE Deep; fruity, nutty, vanilla; good texture, fruit, tannic. Needs time.* Dec 1990*(**) 1992–98

NUITS-ST-GEORGES, CLOS DE LA MARECHALE *FAIVELEY Good nose; fairly sweet, chunky; full of fruit, good length.* Dec 1990**(**) 1992–98

NUITS-ST-GEORGES, PORRETS ST-GEORGES *H GOUGES Fragrant, good depth; dry, full, firm.* Aug 1991***(*) 1993–2000

NUITS-ST-GEORGES, PRULIERS *H GOUGES Fragrant but unknit; dry, fullish, hard, slightly bitter finish.* Aug 1991(***) 1993–2000?

NUITS-ST-GEORGES, LES ST-GEORGES *H GOUGES Fairly deep; a hefty, fruity wine with loads of grip.* Aug 1991(****) 1995 to beyond 2000.

RICHEBOURG *DRC Misleadingly pale; interesting nose, walnuts and deep Pinot Noir fruitiness; very powerful, loaded with tannin. Eleven months later, soft, autumnal red-brown appearance; lovely gentle open nose; silky leathery tannins.* Last tasted Jan 1990*(***) 1993 to beyond 2000.

ROMANEE-ST-VIVANT *DRC Totally different style to the Richebourg, a 'warm', coffee and chocolate nose, truffles; assertive, great length, tannic. At the second tasting, even browner-tinged than the Grands-Echézeaux. Soft, very earthy Pinot nose and taste. Despite this, very tannic and rather ungracious, raw even. Needs bottle-age.* Last tasted Jan 1990(****) 1996 to well beyond 2000.

Clos de TART *Two recent notes: still immature appearance; tight-knit, smoky, brambly, blackberry-like fruit; medium full-bodied, firm, good flavour, tannic. Needs time.* Last tasted at the domaine, Oct 1990(****) 1994–2000

VOLNAY, HOSPICES, CUVEE BLONDEAU *AVERY Very sweet nose and palate, very fragrant, full-flavoured, rich, very good acidity — perhaps a touch too tart.* Dec 1990*(**) 1992–96

Clos VOUGEOT *CHANTAL-LESCURE Very deep, fairly intense; amazing fruit; sweet; full body and flavour. Tannic.* Dec 1990**(**) 1992–2000

A SELECTION OF OTHER '86s:

COTE DE BEAUNE VILLAGES *Despite being from the Dom A Chopin and imported by R Mendelsohn, a most unmusical, unknit wine.* Jan 1990.

MONTHELIE, LES DURESSES *ROGER VERGE Skinny and acidic.* Nov 1989(*)

NUITS-ST-GEORGES, PORRETS *BOUCHARD PERE Stewed, hefty, very tannic with citrus-like acidity.* Dec 1990(**)

SANTENAY, CLOS TAVENNES *DOM DE LA POUSSE D'OR Opaque, intense; malty nose; full body and full of fruit, but strange flavour, too tannic.* Nov 1990(**)

SAVIGNY-LES-BEAUNE, MARCONNETS *SIMON BIZE Crisp, red, lively; equally lively and crisp nose; dry, lean, flavoury, refreshing. A touch of woodiness.* Oct 1990**(*)

SOME '86s TASTED IN AUTUMN 1988 AND SHOWING PROMISE:

BEAUNE, GREVES *LAFARGE Sweet, full, rich, oaky, spicy*(****)

BEAUNE, GREVES, VIGNES DE L'ENFANT JESUS *BOUCHARD PERE Sweet, lovely, good fruit; dry, full-flavoured*(****)

BEAUNE, MONTREMENOTS *ANDRE MUSSY Sweet; slightly malty nose and taste, powerful*(***)

CHAMBOLLE-MUSIGNY *GEORGE ROUMIER Hefty, mouthfilling*(***)

CHAMBOLLE-MUSIGNY, AMOUREUSES *J-F MUGNIER Most original malty, fruity nose; fairly powerful, youthful Bordeaux-like tannin*(***)

CHAMBOLLE-MUSIGNY, FUES *J-F MUGNIER Beautifully scented; lovely, oaky, tannic*(***)

CHARMES-CHAMBERTIN *OLIVIER LEFLAIVE Very attractively fragrant; lovely flavour, good but over-oaked*(****)

LE MUSIGNY *J-F MUGNIER Three notes: a strangely Italianate aromatic wine, hefty, tannic. Shortly after, a pair; the first 10 days on skins, deep, extraordinarily rich; the second from another cuvée, from old vines, slightly paler, very fragrant, rich texture, spicy, aromatic.* At best(****)

NUITS, CLOS ST MARC *BOUCHARD PERE Scented; good blackcurrant-like flavour, leathery tannins*(****)

POMMARD, CHANLINS *MONTHELIE-DOUHAIRET Walnuts and fruit; dry, lean, tannic*(***)

VOLNAY *MONTHELIE-DOUHAIRET A lovely ruby; cherry and plum-like aromas; full-bodied (13.3% alcohol), chewy*(***)

VOLNAY, CLOS AU CH DES DUCS *LAFARGE Lovely walnut nose and flavour, stylish*(****)

VOLNAY, FREMIETS *BOUCHARD PERE Good long flavour but very tannic*(***)

VOSNE-ROMANEE, AUX RAIGNOTS *DOM DU CH DE VOSNE-ROMANEE Nutty, lean, very tannic*(***)

1987***

Not at all bad. A useful vintage for early to mid-term drinking. Growing conditions: budding took place relatively early but heavy rains in May and June and exceptionally cold weather at the time of flowering caused damage, resulting in poor fruit set and *millerandage* and, hence, small crop. After a summer of changeable weather, exceptionally warm weather in early Sept enabled the small crop to ripen reasonably well. The harvest was late, starting around Oct 5 and took place in brilliant sunshine. Absence of rot ensured that the small crop was healthy, whilst good ratio of skin to flesh produced wines with a considerable depth of colour.

As I have recent notes of the wines of the Dom de la Romanée-Conti, I have listed these first. Bearing in mind that they traditionally pick late and highly selectively, and the grapes benefited from the brilliant Indian summer, there is some justification for optimism regarding quality.

ROMANEE-CONTI *Just one note at the earlier of the two Percy Fox DRC tastings: as so often, a misleadingly pale colour giving one the impression that it is soft, mild and a quick developer. Low-keyed and genuinely complex, with depth of rich fruit; powerful, assertive on the palate, considerable length, tannin and acidity.* Feb 1990(****) *It will surely develop well, but over what period I hesitate to prognosticate.*

La TACHE *In Feb 1990: low-keyed, refined, fragrant; sweet, lean, long and flavoury at the first tasting. Now quite richly coloured though not deep, more assertive and tannic than expected, with the inimitable expansion of flavour in the mouth, and aftertaste.* Last noted Jan 1991(****)

RICHEBOURG DRC *I am always fascinated by the contrast in style between La Tâche and Richebourg. Initially paler than expected; nutty, undeveloped nose. The second bottle seemed more fragrant, yet hard. Both were full-bodied and dry, though the extract masked the severity of the tannins. A year later, more of a rose pink sheen than the '86; a soft, singed, earthy nose had developed; it also seemed to be sweeter on the palate, flavoury, with greater length and more fragrant aftertaste than I had anticipated.* Last tasted Jan 1991(****) 1996 to well beyond 2000.

ROMANEE-ST-VIVANT DRC *This is, of course, from the old Dom Général Marey-Monge. Rather indeterminate appearance in Feb 1990; low-keyed, vegetal nose. Whether or not it was my imagination, I thought the second bottle was more meaty, coffee-scented; distinctly sweet, nice weight, with all the St-Vivant elegance, lots of grip and good aftertaste. More recently, an expansive, mature appearance; very soft, rather chocolaty nose; sweet and soft on the palate, very flavoury and with a good follow through. My style of wine.* Last tasted Jan 1991(****) 1993 to beyond 2000.

GRANDS-ECHEZEAUX DRC *Low-keyed, rather sweaty tannic nose; considerably more power and thrust than the Echézeaux. Beetroot Pinot flavour. Bitter tannins. At the following year's tasting: palish, open, luminous; soft, slightly chocolaty stewed Pinot nose; medium sweetness and body, soft fruit, adequate tannin and acidity but seemed likely to be a quick developer.* Last tasted Jan 1991*(***) 1992–98

ECHEZEAUX DRC *Scented Pinot aroma, the second bottle even more scented; lightish style, delicious flavour though dry tannic finish. A year later, a palish plummy colour, sporting a more mature, browner tinge; a nice soft fruit scent, like crushed strawberries; fairly lean, dry and tannic.* Last tasted Jan 1991(***) 1993–2005, at a guess.

OTHER SELECTED '87s TASTED RECENTLY:

BEAUNE, BOUCHEROTTES L JADOT *Open, attractive, but unknit; sweet, nice weight, touch of bitterness.* June 1991** Drink soon.

BEAUNE, GREVES, VIGNE DE L'ENFANT JESUS BOUCHARD PERE *Rather weak-rimmed; unknit, rich, singed, vanilla nose; quite flavoury but light and a bit unconvincing. More acidity than tannin.* Dec 1990*(*) Now to 1995.

BEAUNE, CLOS DES MOUCHES J DROUHIN *Alcohol 13.1%, acidity 3.8 — better than the '86. Pink-cheeked; crisp, very attractive, high-toned, spicy nose which opened up nicely in the glass. Quite pleasant sweetness, weight and flavour. More acidity than tannin. Robert Drouhin told me he preferred his '87 reds to the '86s, even in the Nuits.* In Drouhin's tasting room, Oct 1990*(**) Now to 1996.

CHAMBERTIN, CLOS DE BEZE L JADOT *Fairly deep-coloured; sweet, fully evolved, rather jammy; dry, fairly full-bodied, aggressive — fruit and much tannin resulting from a 26-day* macération. At Jadot's, Oct 1990(***) 1993–98

CHAMBOLLE-MUSIGNY J-F MUGNIER *Pleasant colour; slightly jammy nose and taste though nicely balanced and flavoury.* Jan 1990**(*) Now to 1996.

CHAMBOLLE-MUSIGNY, SENTIERS ROBERT GROFFIER *Low-keyed Pinot nose; giving far more on the palate: delicious, spicy, good length, slightly bitter finish.* April 1990*(**) Now to 1995.

CHASSAGNE-MONTRACHET 1ER CRU FONTAINE-GAGNARD *Plummy; very rich, jammy fruit, unusual and distinctive smell — like roast beef; full of fruit, powerful, very tannic.* Last tasted Oct 1990(***) 1993–98

CORTON, BRESSANDES CHANDON DE BRIAILLES *Very pronounced, classic, Pinot aroma; powerful, tannic.* Dec 1990(****) 1992–2000

CORTON, CLOS DES CORTONS FAIVELEY *Deep; full of fruit and alcohol, slightly scented and dusty at first but evolved richly; sweet, full, chunky, good tannin and acidity.* Dec 1990*(***) 1992–2000

GEVREY-CHAMBERTIN, CAZETIERS FAIVELEY *Pink-tinged; curiously attractive, strawberry-like scent; flavoury, lean, dry finish. Needs time.* Dec 1990(***) 1992–98

GEVREY-CHAMBERTIN, CLOS ST-JACQUES L JADOT *Open, chocolaty; soft, chewy, quite good fruit, acidity.* June 1991** Drink soon.

MOREY ST-DENIS, CLOS DES ORMES J DROUHIN *Stewed, earthy; very flavoury, nice fruit, good acidity.* Dec 1990*(**) Now to 1998.

MUSIGNY DE VOGUE *Looks like an early developer; wide open, Oregon-like Pinot nose — only better! After 20 minutes seemed uneven, with touch of caramel, but settled down. Returning to it an hour after it had been poured, a pleasant gingery bouquet; rather lean, watery and short. But a dry, easy style. Not a vin de garde.* At the domaine, Oct 1990** Now to 1995.

Clos de la ROCHE DUJAC *Fully evolved colour; sweet yet firm, nicely developed, harmonious nose; sweet, good body, very nice rich flavour, touch of tannic bitterness on the finish, but good aftertaste.* At the domaine, Oct 1990(***) 1992–96

SAVIGNY-LES-BEAUNE, SERPENTIERES ECARD *Several notes: a soft, mellow, rose-hip colour; warm, earthy nose, touch of vanilla, developing well in the glass; ginger, cinnamon, chocolate; good flavour and length, a bit green and hard at the finish.* Last tasted June 1991*(*) Now to 1994.

VOSNE-ROMANEE DANIEL RION *Run now by the young Patrice Rion. Ruby; good Pinot aroma; dry, powerful, loads of fruit. A good mouthful* *though still hard. Jan 1990**(**) Now to 1998.*

Clos VOUGEOT *J DROUHIN Very fragrant varietal aroma; good but hard. Dec 1990(***) 1992–2010*

SOME OTHER '87s:

AUXEY-DURESSES, LES ECUSSEAUX *HENRI & GILLES BUISSON Deep, velvety; sweet, assertive, fairly good length, touch of bitterness. Oct 1990*(*)*

BEAUNE, HOSPICES, CUVEE CYROT CHAUDRON Elevé, *but not very well, by NOEMI VERNAUX. Flavoury but volatile. Sept 1990.*

BEAUNE, CLOS DES URSULES *L JADOT The feeling of unripe grapes, lean but flavoury. Oct 1990(**)*

BONNES MARES *L JADOT Good. June 1990(***)*

ECHEZEAUX *LOUIS MAX Stalky, woody. Dec 1990.*

GEVREY-CHAMBERTIN *ALAIN BURQUET From 60- to 80-year-old vines, bottled Dec 1988: pale scarlet; crisp, intense, berry-like fragrance and flavour. Very spicy, very dry — harsh tannins. Feb 1989(***)*

Clos des LAMBRAYS *Smelly, abandoned cabbages; dried out, bitter. Dec 1990.*

SAVIGNY-LES-BEAUNE *CHANDON DE BRIAILLES Orange red; mellow, gentle, vinous rather than varietal; soft yet with an upturned tannic finish. Jan 1990(**)*

SHOWING WELL IN CASK, SEPT 1988:

Chambolle-Musigny, Amoureuses J-F MUGNIER; Chambolle-Musigny, Fués J-F MUGNIER; Corton BOUCHARD PERE; Musigny J-F MUGNIER; Nuits-St-Georges, Boudots J GRIVOT; Nuits-St-Georges, Roncières J GRIVOT; Pommard, Bertins CHANTAL LESCURE; Richbourg J GRIVOT; Vosne-Romanée, Beaumonts J GRIVOT; Vosne-Romanée, Les Rouges JACQUELINE JAYER, MADE BY GRIVOT; Clos Vougeot J GRIVOT.

1988★★★★★

An excellent vintage; sturdy, well-formed wines with staying power. Not as flatteringly easy to taste in their youth as the '85s but clearly impressive, the best magnificent. Alas some not good enough.

A prolonged wet spring followed a mild winter. The weather continued cool and damp, though the flowering and fruit set were satisfactory. What made the vintage was a long sunny summer, three months of hot and dry weather continuing through to Oct, fortunately interspersed with showers. A good crop of healthy ripe grapes was harvested before the late autumn rains set in. Hot sun and dry conditions produced a high sugar content and concentration of flesh, resulting in high alcohol and extract. All in all, the recipe for deep, rich, well-structured, long-lasting wines.

My most useful notes, establishing the style and quality of the wines, were made at Berkmann's tasting in London in July 1990, and at a Bin Club tasting in Wickwar, March 1991; also at the single domaine vertical tastings, notably at Joseph Drouhin's and Comte George de Vogüé's, in Oct 1990. I shall, however, start with the range tasted at the Dom de La Romanée-Conti in Oct 1990, subsequently at the Percy Fox/DRC tasting in London, Jan 1991 and a further three in March.

ROMANEE-CONTI *At the Domaine: very deep, opulently coloured; immensely rich nose, full of fruit, then a coffee-like scent, its aroma all-pervasive for well over an hour. Medium-sweet, full-bodied with rich, rounded flavour, full of fruit, high extract masking high tannins. In London much the same, its violet colour and brambly fruit altogether different from La Tâche. A powerhouse of a wine with a great future. Most recently, incredibly sweet and mouthfilling. Last noted at the Bin Club tasting, March 1991(*****) 1996–2030*

La TACHE *In Oct 1990, deep, fairly intense; vivid blackberry-like fruit, firm, hard; rich, full-flavoured, elegant, with great length and silky tannins. In January, a lovely bright cherry red with plummy purple rim; crisp, hawthorn, fragrant; powerful, concentrated, spicy, very tannic. Most recently, great intensity and length. Last at Bin Club tasting, March 1991(*****) 1998–2030*

RICHEBOURG *DRC Deep, fairly intense; expansive blackberry-like, good vinosity; full, chunky fruit, very tannic. In Jan and March: less deep than St-Vivant; rich Pinot aroma; dry, powerful, good length, silky textured tannins, and fragrant aftertaste. As usual, more four-square, less dramatic than La Tâche. Great future. Last tasted March 1991(*****) 1996–2025*

ROMANEE-ST-VIVANT *DRC Sweet, gentle, spicy nose, lovely fruit, tremendous vinosity, harmonious, developed well in the glass; medium-sweet, rich, rounded, leaner style than Grands-Echézeaux, with notable tannin and acidity. At the next two tastings: ruddy, cherry tinctured, immature; the usual DRC rich Pinot aroma, penetrating, great depth; powerful yet elegant, excellent fruit, good length, firm, spicy. Last tasted Jan 1991(*****) 1996–2025*

GRANDS-ECHEZEAUX *DRC Fairly deep, purple rim; crisp, firm fruit, at first slightly stalky, pepper and spice, but settled down in the glass confidently, elegantly; medium dry, assertive, powerful, fine fruit, great length, silky tannins, and acidity. Seemed closed and hard in Jan though spicy; also seemed drier, though packed with fruit. Two months later: wonderful fragrance; grip, length, marvellous style, aftertaste. Last at the Bin Club tasting March 1991(****) 1996–2020*

ECHEZEAUX *DRC Medium-deep, plummy coloured and a bit cloudy at the Domaine; powerful, beetroot-like Pinot aroma, very forthcoming, becoming sweet and strawberry-like; dry, full-bodied, crisp, with lively, berry-like flavour, tannic. In London: pink-tinged; crisp; good length, very tannic. Firm and hard. Needs time. Last tasted Jan 1991(****) 1996–2016*

OTHER '88s:

ALOXE-CORTON *TOLLOT-BEAUT Medium-pale; fruity; delicious flavour, good acidity, slightly bitter finish. Normally good and good value, the '88 lacking length and quality for the price.* Last tasted Nov 1990(**) 1994–2000

BEAUNE, MONTREVENOTS *JEAN-MARC BOILLOT Very good colour; deep, rich, scented; powerful, well put together, highish tannin and acidity.* July 1990(****) 1994–2000

BEAUNE, CLOS DES MOUCHES *J DROUHIN Alcohol 13.3%, total acidity 3.8. Fairly deep; immature; very sweet, almost sickly sweet, strawberry-like nose, sweaty with tannin; dry, firm, fruity, good length and potential. Very tannic.* Oct 1990(****) 1994–2000

BEAUNE, CLOS DES URSULES *Bottled in June 1990 and tasted in London the same month: fruity, fragrant; very good flavour and grip. Nearly three months later: immature, minty but powerful nose; dry, full-bodied, firm, oaky, good length and aftertaste. Tannic.* Last tasted in Beaune, Oct 1990(****) 1994 to beyond 2000.

BEAUNE, VIGNES FRANCHES *L LATOUR Good fruit, new oak; fairly sweet, fullish, fleshy.* Oct 1990(****) 1992–2000

BONNES MARES *DE VOGUE Fascinating nose, combining meat, fruit and violets; good crisp fruit and acidity, with soft tannins. Attractive.* Sept 1990(*****) 1993–2000

CHAMBERTIN *LOUIS TRAPET Two notes: deep, immature; dry, powerful, austere, very tannic.* Last tasted March 1991(***)

CHAMBERTIN, CLOS DE BEZE *BOUCHARD PERE Fragrant; assertive, powerful, tannic.* March 1991(****) 1995–2020

CHAMBERTIN, CLOS DE BEZE *L JADOT Bottled June 1990. Deep; strong scent of oysters and iodine (from the anthocyanins, pure vegetal aroma, very characteristic of Chambertin Pinot); dry, powerful, lots of fruit, great length, the tannin a bit metallic.* At Jadot's, Oct 1990(*****) 1996–2020?

CHAMBERTIN, VIEILLES VIGNES *TRAPET Similar, more laden with fruit, long, with fragrant aftertaste.* Tasted July 1990. The latter(*****) 1994–2000

CHAMBOLLE-MUSIGNY *ALAIN HUDELOT-NOELLAT Sweet, light, a* soupçon *of tannin. Some charm but lacking serious quality.* July 1990(***) 1992–95

CHAMBOLLE-MUSIGNY *DE VOGUE Not very deep; low-keyed, creamy nose; marked tannin and acidity.* Sept 1990(***) 1994–98

CHAMBOLLE-MUSIGNY, LES BANDES *J DROUHIN Crisp, raspberry-like fruit, good grip.* May 1991(***) 1993–98

CHAMBOLLE-MUSIGNY, HAUTS DOITS *J DROUHIN Crisp fruit; powerful, tannin and acidity.* May 1991(***) 1994–2000

CHAMBOLLE-MUSIGNY, CLOS DU VILLAGE *A GUYON Fragrant Pinot aroma; excellent flavour, gentle yet powerful.* March 1991**(**) 1992–2000

Le CORTON *DOM DE CH DE BEAUNE Fairly deep purple but weak-rimmed; harmonious; touch of sweetness, full body, firm, good length, tannic.* Last tasted March 1991(****) 1995–2010

CORTON, BRESSANDES *TOLLOT-BEAUT Pale for Corton and 1988; low-keyed Italianate nose—neither fruity, nor earthy, nor flowery: hawthorn bush; slightly sweet, rich, chewy, adequate tannin.* July 1990(***) 1993–2000

CORTON, CLOS DU ROI *CHANDON DE BRIAILLES Highly scented nose; sweet, chewy, rich Corton flavour and body, extract, tannin and acidity. Very good wine.* Last tasted March 1991(*****) 1996–2015

Ch CORTON-GRANCEY *First tasted at Latour tasting Oct 1990: expected a much deeper colour; nice upturned light fruitiness; sweet, medium body, soft, pleasant but lacking substance. More recently, evolved, scented, agreeable.* Last tasted March 1991*** But drink soon.

GEVREY-CHAMBERTIN *ROLAND DAGENEAU Easy, attractive*(**)

GEVREY-CHAMBERTIN *PHILIPPE ROSSIGNOL Good fruit, flavour, body, very tannic.* July 1990(****)

GEVREY-CHAMBERTIN *LOUIS TRAPET Palish; nice, scented; good flavour and bite.* Last tasted March 1991**(*) For drinking 1993–98

GEVREY-CHAMBERTIN, CLOS DU FONTENY *BRUNO CLAIR Deep; plausibly oaky nose and taste.* March 1991*(**) 1993–98

GEVREY-CHAMBERTIN, LE FONTENY *RENE JACQUESSON Rich, nutty, fruit and oak.* March 1991*(**) 1993–98

GEVREY-CHAMBERTIN, CLOS ST-JACQUES *L JADOT Firm, nutty, fragrant; surprisingly soft and fleshy. Silky tannins.* June 1991**(**) 1993–98

Clos des LAMBRAYS *F & L SAIER Sweetish, lovely wine, shapely, with class.* March 1991(****) 1993–2000

LATRICIERES-CHAMBERTIN *L TRAPET Showing well at Berkmann's: rich, very forthcoming nose; sweet, full-flavoured, soft yet tannic. Less impressed at the Bin Club tasting.* Last noted March 1991(****)? 1993–2000

MUSIGNY *JACQUES PRIEUR Good depth, weight, flavour, balance.* March 1991(****) 1993–2000

Le MUSIGNY *DE VOGUE Bottled May 1990. Strength 13–13.5% alcohol. Medium-deep, youthful cherry red; surprisingly sweet, slightly tobacco-like nose, hard underlay but developed well; after 15 minutes, singed, clover honey, and, returning to it after half an hour, wonderfully evolved; on the palate ripe fruit, full-flavoured, full-bodied yet not heavy, concentrated fruit, very tannic, good aftertaste.* At the domaine, Oct 1990(*****) 1995–2015

NUITS-ST-GEORGES *ALAIN MICHELOT Two notes: crisp fruit, fabulous flavour, loads of oak and tannin, in July 1990. Next; very sweet, spicy, very tannic, good aftertaste.* Last noted Oct 1990(****) 1994–2000+

NUITS-ST-GEORGES, CAILLES *A MICHELOT Crisp fruit; very sweet yet very tannic. Impressive.* July 1990(****) 1996–2000+

NUITS-ST-GEORGES, CHAIGNOTS *A MICHELOT Fairly deep, youthful; very rich, very fragrant; a marvellous, rich, tannic wine.* July 1990(*****) 1996–2000+

NUITS-ST-GEORGES, MURGERS *HUDELOT-NOELLAT Stewed, jammy nose; fairly sweet, soft, quite attractive.* In July and Oct 1990(***) 1992–96

NUITS-ST-GEORGES, PORRETS ST-GEORGES *H GOUGES Two notes: deep, youthful, violet-tinged; crisp, fascinating fruit; firm, full-bodied, tough and tannic.* Last tasted Aug 1991(****) 1996 to beyond 2000.

NUITS-ST-GEORGES, PRULIERS *H GOUGES Ruby; good fruit; dry, full, firm, crisp, long.* Last tasted Aug 1991(****) 1995–2005

NUITS-ST-GEORGES, LES ST-GEORGES *H GOUGES Two notes: deep; very original, intriguing, "violets" noted twice; dry, lovely crisp fruit, still austere and lean.* Last tasted Aug 1991(****) 1996–2010

NUITS-ST-GEORGES, VAUCRAINS *H GOUGES Lovely crisp youthful fruit.* Aug 1991(****) 1994–2000

PERNAND, ILE DE VERGELESSES *CHANDON DE BRIAILLES Good colour, nose and taste. Slightly sweet. Some grip. Decent finish.* Cask sample July 1990(***) 1992–96

Ch de POMMARD *LA PLANCHE Fragrant, delicious, tannic.* March 1991(***) 1993–98

POMMARD, EPENOTS *CH DE MEURSAULT Youthful; rich, flavoury, quite powerful.* March 1991(****) 1994–2000

POMMARD, SAUSSILLES *JEAN-MARC BOILLOT Good colour; lovely fruit and oakiness; sweet, rich, tannic.* July 1990(****) 1993–98

Clos de La ROCHE *DUJAC Beautiful aroma, lovely fruit, much more to give; assertive, scented, very tannic.* Oct 1990(****) 1994–2000

Clos de TART *Medium, immature; lightly scented pinot aroma; lean, flavoury, piquant at Mommessin's London tasting in March 1990. Later that autumn: tight-knit cherry, touch of oil and cloves; slightly sweet, fairly full-bodied, good fruit and grip. Complete. A tart with a heart, and a future.* At the domaine, Oct 1990(***) Possibly**** 1993–98

VOLNAY, 1ER CRU *LAFARGE Good colour; nutty, hard, closed nose; some sweetness, flesh, and powerful for Volnay. Will turn out well.* July 1990(***) 1993–98

VOLNAY, CLOS DES CHENES *CH DE MEURSAULT Very good flavour, intensity and follow-through.* March 1991(****) 1993–2000

VOLNAY, HOSPICES, JEHAN DE MASSOL *BOUCHARD PERE Deep fruit, power and length.* March 1991(****) 1993–2000

VOSNE-ROMANEE, BEAUX MONTS BAS *BERTAGNA Very fragrant but unknit; crisp, oaky, Pinot flavour. Tannic.* March 1991(****) 1994 to beyond 2000.

Clos VOUGEOT *HUDELOT-NOELLAT Not very deep; good fruit, weight, flavour and length. Sweet. Oaky aftertaste.* July 1990(***) 1992–98

BRIEFER NOTES ON SOME OTHER '88s:

ALOXE-CORTON, CHAILLOTS *L LATOUR Good fruit, body, oak, tannin.* Oct 1990(***)

CORTON, CH DE BLIGNY *ROPITEAU Dry, sturdy, tannic.* Dec 1990(***)

CORTON *L LATOUR Paler than expected though sweet, full, fleshy and tannic.* Oct 1990(***)

NUITS, PRULIERS *ROPITEAU Musty, cardboardy nose, but good straightforward weight and flavour.* Dec 1990(**)

SANTENAY, CLOS DE LA CONFRERIE *VINCENT GIRARDIN Good colour; very sweet, rich, forthcoming nose and flavour. Good value for early drinking.* July 1990(**)

VOLNAY, CLOS DES CHENES *R CAILLOT Very deep; smelly; strange, very tannic.* Nov 1990.

Clos VOUGEOT *BOISSET Artificial but attractive nose; dry, lacking conviction.* Dec 1990(**)

SOME '88s SHOWING MODERATELY WELL AT THE BIN CLUB TASTING, MARCH 1991:

Aloxe-Corton, Fournières A GUYON; Beaune, Bressandes CHANSON; Beaune, Grèves, Vignes de l'Enfant Jésus BOUCHARD PERE; Chambertin JACQUES PRIEUR; Chambolle-Musigny, Hauts Doix J DROUHIN; Corton, Bressandes CHANDON DE BRIAILLES; Corton, Renardes PARENT; Nuits-St-Georges, Procès ARNOUX; Pommard, Bertin LESURE; Pommard, Chanlains PARENT; Pommard, Epenots PARENT; Pommard, Rugiens PARENT; Clos de la Roche BOUCHARD PERE; Volnay, Caillerets CH DE BEAUNE, BOUCHARD PERE; Volnay, Frémiets PARENT; Volnay, Verseuil Y CLERGET; Vosne-Romanée, Malconsorts CLOS FRANTIN (BICHOT); Vosne-Romanée, Réas JEAN GROS; Vosne-Romanée, Reignots CH DE VOSNE-ROMANEE.

RELATIVELY LIGHT, EASY, PASSABLE AT THE BIN CLUB TASTING, MARCH 1991:

Beaune, Clos du Roi CHANSON; Beaune, Ste-Desirée, Clos de l'Hermitage VIRELY-ROUGEOT; Gevrey-Chambertin, Lavaux St-Jacques BICHOT; Nuits-St-Georges, Clos de l'Arlot DOM D'ARLOT; Volnay, Champans DELAGRANGE.

BELOW STANDARD FOR ITS NAME, BIN CLUB, MARCH 1991:

Bonnes Mares L BRUCK; Chambertin, Clos de Bèze L BRUCK; Echézeaux RENE ENGEL.

1989★★★★

Another very good year, my first impression being of wines less sturdy, less tannic than the excellent '88s, but with balance and charm, certainly quicker to develop. A highly recommended vintage for early to mid-term drinking. And, for immediate drinking, delicious Beaujolais.

Following a mild winter, early vegetation encouraged by a mild spring. Summer was exceptionally hot and sunny which resulted in an early harvest of ripe, healthy grapes. Ripe fleshy wines with naturally high alcoholic content and lower acidity than the '88s, also softer tannins.

At recent trade tastings I was particularly interested in taking the opportunity to compare the '88s and '89s, noting them in pairs. As with the earlier vintages of the decade, I found that vertical tastings of vineyards put the year into perspective. However, as last time, I shall open with the range from the Dom de La Romanée-Conti, tasted with Lalou Bize-Leroy and Aubert de Vilaine and his father in the fall of 1990. They were tasted in ascending order, Echézeaux to Romanée-Conti and not in 'status' order as noted below.

ROMANEE-CONTI *Deep, velvety purple; very good 'thick' rich nose; appears to be dry but full of body, fruit, extract. Clearly great potential. In the cellars, Oct 1990(*****)*

La TACHE *Good colour; sweet, slightly cheesy, distinctly tannic nose; lean, crisp fruit, very dry tannic finish. From the cask, Oct 1990(****)?*

RICHEBOURG *DRC Deep, rich appearance; equally rich nose, soft, meaty, touch of chocolate and vanilla; medium-sweet, full of alcohol, fruit, extract. Dry tannic finish. Ex-cask, Oct 1990. At least(****)*

ROMANEE-ST-VIVANT *DRC Fairly deep; nose already sweet and soft; perfect sweetness and weight. I confess I have a great liking for the Marey-Monge style. Despite its youthfulness, already elegant. Ex-cask Oct 1990(*****) Say 1995 to 2010.*

GRANDS-ECHEZEAUX *DRC Medium depth; hard, spicy, young Pinot aroma; sweet, chewy, lots of fruit. Ex-cask, Oct 1990(****)*

ECHEZEAUX *DRC Rich, luminous; good, scented, youthful blackberry-like aroma; distinctly sweet, very rich, very tannic. On occasion, the DRC Echézeaux lags far behind their Grands-Echézeaux, but not, as far as my palate could detect, in '89. Ex-cask Oct 1990(****) 1995 to beyond 2000.*

SELECTED '89s:

BEAUNE, CLOS DES MOUCHES *J DROUHIN Cask sample first noted at the Drouhin tasting in Sept 1990 when it seemed rather pale and pink but had a glorious, youthful, fruity nose and flavour. Sweet. Fullish. Oaky. A month later, in the vertical line up of wines of the 1980s, it appeared deeper with a light youthful purple tinge. "Gorgeous" nose this time: a really lovely young aroma with palate to match. Good fruit. It will be a charmer. Sample drawn from the cask. Noted in Drouhin's tasting room, Oct 1990(****) Probably 1994–2000.*

BEAUNE, CLOS DES URSULES *L JADOT Deep; singed, very oaky nose; dry, nice weight, fragrant, with the clove-like spiciness of new oak. Charm already apparent. A sample drawn from the cask, recently racked. To be bottled in the spring of 1991. Tasted in Beaune with André Gagey, Oct 1990(****) 1994–2000*

BONNES MARES *DE VOGUE Described as the 'great uncle' of the Comte Georges de Vogüé's family of wines. 40% to 50% new oak used, depending on the vintage, the strong Nevers oak for Bonnes Mares, Allier for Musigny. A good colour; smell of ripe grapes, cherry-like, spicy, dry, full-bodied, very fruity — cherry-like on entry, blueberry on the finish. Generously laden with tannins and acidity. Should turn out magnificently. Tasted from the cask, Oct 1990(*****) At a guess, 1996–2015.*

CHAMBERTIN, CLOS DE BEZE *L JADOT Very deep; very rich, with a ripe, raspberry aroma and vanillin of new oak; slightly sweet on the palate, medium-full body, nice fruit, '89 charm, and fragrant aftertaste. Ex-cask, at Jadot's, Oct 1990(*****) 1995–2015.*

CHAMBERTIN *CUVEE HERITIERS LATOUR Brilliant cherry red; good but subdued nose, quite a lot of oak; ripe entry, full-bodied yet soft and fruity. The bitterness of the tannins will wear off. At Louis Latour's tasting in London, Oct 1990(*****) 1995–2015*

CHAMBOLLE-MUSIGNY, AMOUREUSES *DE VOGUE A vintage that suits the name of the vineyard. Medium-deep, cherry red; lively, lovely fruit, walnuts; nice weight, firm, lean but supple, well balanced. A wine with poise. In the cellars, Oct 1990(****) 1994–2000*

CHAMBOLLE-MUSIGNY, BAUDES *J DROUHIN Palish, lovely, Sept 1990. Gentle, cherry-like fruit. A pretty wine. Last tasted May 1991**(*) Now to 1998.*

CHAMBOLLE-MUSIGNY, HAUTS-DOIX *J DROUHIN Between Amoureuses and Charmes. Two notes: deepish cherry red; rich brambly fruit on nose and palate. Good length and tannins. Last noted March 1991(****) 1993–2000*

Le CORTON *DOM DE CH DE BEAUNE Fairly deep purple; ripe mulberry-like fruit, and oak. Fairly full-bodied, chewy, soft. Adequate tannins, a touch of bitterness on the finish. Cask sample, Oct 1990(****) 1995–2000*

Ch CORTON-GRANCEY *Medium-deep, youthful purple tinge; rich, fragrant, nutty, blackberry; sweet, fullish, rich, delicious flavour and good aftertaste. Cask sample at the Louis Latour tasting in London, Oct 1990(*****) 1994–2000*

GEVREY-CHAMBERTIN, CHAMPEAUX *J DROUHIN Cherry-like in colour, nose and taste. Good aftertaste. May 1991(***) 1993–98*

GEVREY-CHAMBERTIN, COMBOTTES *J DROUHIN More floral, sweeter, long, lean. May 1991(***) 1993–98*

GEVREY-CHAMBERTIN, CLOS ST-JACQUES *L JADOT Soft fruit yet with silky tannins. June 1991(***) 1993–98*

Le MUSIGNY *DE VOGUE The youngest vintage in the instructive line up of Musigny vintages of the 1980s. A lovely colour; beautiful fruit, soft, fragrant, gentle spices; dry, nice weight, lean, supple, elegant. Drawn from the cask, Oct 1990(*****) 1994 to beyond 2000.*

NUITS-ST-GEORGES, CLOS DES CORVEES *L JADOT Low-keyed but fragrant and nutty on nose and palate. Medium-light, good length. June 1990(***)*

Clos de La ROCHE *DUJAC Medium-deep, lovely luminosity; sweet, soft, ripe, blackberry-like Pinot aroma; sweet on the palate, full of fruit and spice. Good length, flavoury, with charm. Slight bitter tannins which will wear off. I think Jacques Seysses' wines are probably best drunk when in the full vigour of youth. From the cask, Oct 1990(****) Say 1993–98.*

Clos de TART *100% new oak (Allier). Lovely ruby; good fruit, cherry-like, oak, developing fragrantly in the glass; fairly dry, medium-full body, very crisp fruity flavour. Good acidity. Stylish.* Tasted at the domaine, Oct 1990(****) 1993–98

VOSNE-ROMANEE, AUX RAIGNOTS *DOM DU CH DE VOSNE-ROMANEE Glorious depth of fruit, fragrant; sweet, very assertive yet unaggressive, with the clove-like spiciness of new oak which will, in time, simmer down.* At the Bouchard Père tasting, Oct 1990(****) 1993–98

Clos VOUGEOT *L JADOT Both bottles hard, oaky, almost woody on nose and palate. Full-bodied. Spicy.* June 1991(***)? 1995–?

BRIEFER NOTES MADE AT TWO TRADE TASTINGS IN OCT 1990:

BOUCHARD PERE ET FILS:

BEAUNE, TEURONS *Good fruit, sweet, fragrant; very soft, oaky, dry finish*(***)

NUITS-ST-GEORGES, ARGILLIERES *Fragrant, new oak — walnuts; assertive yet 'warm' and soft. Sweet, with leathery tannins*(****)

POMMARD, 1ER CRU *Medium-deep, fairly intense; very good oaky fragrances; assertive, firm, good fruit and tannins*(****)

SAVIGNY-LES-BEAUNE LAVIERES *Light, soft, fruity, easy, for early drinking*(***)

VOLNAY, CAILLERETS, ANCIENNE CUVEE CARNOT *Rich, good fruit*(****)

VOLNAY, FREMIETS, CLOS DE LA ROUGEOTTE *Good fruit, crisp, good acidity*(***)

VOSNE-ROMANEE *Intense purple; sweet, rich, perhaps too hefty?*(**)

J DROUHIN:

BEAUNE, CHAMPIMONTS *Good fruit, tannic*(***)

BEAUNE, EPENOTTES *Lovely, meaty, rich*(****)

BEAUNE, GREVES *Fragrant, spicy, tannic*(***)

CHAMBOLLE, FEUSSELOTTES *Low-keyed, oaky, dry, tannic*(***)

CHAMBOLLE, SENTIERS *Deep, sweet, very flavoury, a little too oaky and spicy*(**?)

CHAMBOLLE-MUSIGNY, AMOUREUSES *Deep, good fruit, full, rich*(****)

LASTLY, SOME EXCELLENT INDIVIDUAL DOMAINE BEAUJOLAIS AT MOMMESSIN'S TASTING IN MARCH 1990:

CHENAS *DOM DE CHANTEGRIVE Surprisingly deep; lovely fresh rich Gamay fruity aroma; lightish, fragrant. For early drinking****

FLEURIE *DOM DE LA PRESLE Good tannic grip. Needs bottle-age*(***) Probably at best 1992–95.

JULIENAS *DOM DE CONSEILLERE Very fragrant, firm, stylish. Nice now. Will keep****(*)

JULIENAS *DOM DU VIEUX CERISIER Crisp fruity aroma; soft, lovely. Drink soon*(***)

MORGON *DOM DE LATHEVALLE Very deep; lively; fullish, excellent fruit and balance. Will develop further****(*)

MOULIN-A-VENT *DOM DE CHAMP DE COUR Fairly deep; good firm fruit; rich, glorious now and will improve further with bottle-age****(*)

1990★★★★

A very good vintage, probably somewhere between the '88s and '89s, hopefully with the colour, tannin and firmness of the former and amiable fruit of the latter, and the quality of both.

Above average temperatures in winter and spring, 24°C (75°F) being registered in south Burgundy, encouraging early vegetation. April, May and June were less propitious, cooler and wetter than usual, with sporadic storms and hail. Extended flowering, followed by hot, very sunny dry weather through July to early Sept. Some welcome rain prior to the early harvest beginning Sept 17 in the Côte de Beaune and two days later in the Nuits. Late pickers benefited from glorious sunshine towards the end of the month. All in all, a good crop of ripe, healthy grapes. The wines appear, in general, to have higher extract and more tannin than the '89s. The outlook is encouraging. While at Drouhin's, on the outskirts of Beaune, and after tasting the Clos de Mouches *rouge* and *blanc* of the decade of the '80s, I had a sneak preview of their '90s. I look forward to tasting a fuller range — and to drinking them towards the end of the century.

BEAUNE, CLOS DES MOUCHES *J DROUHIN Fresh from the cask, very scented. Because of the natural tannins the grapes had been destalked and, Robert Drouhin informed me, there would be no need to use new oak.* At Drouhin's, Oct 1990.

BEAUNE, EPENOTS *J DROUHIN Very deep purple. Dry, powerful, spicy.*

CORTON, POUGETS *L JADOT Fairly deep; lovely fruit; very sweet, rich, full, very oaky. Delicious.* At the Savoy tasting, June 1991(****) 1995–2005

MOREY ST-DENIS *J DROUHIN Made from grapes bought in: opaque, bramble-like fruit, dry, lean, tannic — yet elegant, even in its kindergarten stage.* Oct 1990.

WHITE BURGUNDY

One of the great classic dry white wines of the world. The finest, grown mainly in the Côte de Beaune, are named after the village (commune or parish) and vineyard. Though these are made exclusively from the Chardonnay grape variety, this never appears on the label. As with red burgundy, the name of the grower, domaine and merchant is all important.*

One or two top-class white burgundies are made in the Côte de Nuits, and pleasing wines made in what I loosely call 'south Burgundy', mainly the Mâconnais. Only the better, more notable wines of the latter district are included.

When to drink and how to taste white burgundy

As with most of the world's dry white wine, white burgundy is made to be drunk whilst still young and fresh. However, unlike most dry whites, the finest will not only keep but positively benefit from a certain amount of bottle-age. Optimum cellaring time depends on the growth and on the vintage. I hope that the following vintage notes will give a reasonably clear indication of condition or potential. Colour is relatively unimportant. Young wines tend to be pale yellow with a greenish tinge. In certain 'big' vintages some of the top wines, particularly Meursault and Le Montrachet, can have a more pronounced buttery yellow hue. As they age, they deepen in colour and take on a golden hue. All should be star-bright.

* *A useful guide to merchants and growers can be found in* Serena Sutcliffe's Pocket Guide to the Wines of Burgundy *(Mitchell Beazley/Simon & Schuster).*

The nose is quite often hard to get to grips with. Do not expect the somewhat exaggerated waxy, buttery, flagrant as well as fragrant smell of an Australian Chardonnay; rather, a low-keyed, slightly bread-like, sometimes toasty smell which, at its best, opens up in the glass. Most white burgundy is served too cold. Do not serve top quality wines chilled. The very best smell and taste best near to room temperature (see Le Montrachet DRC 1969, page 241).

The palate is usually more explicit than the nose. At first sip, 'on entry' it will range from very dry to medium dry, never sweet. It can be surprisingly high in alcohol. Its taste can be nutty, oaky, toasty and, with bottle-age, honeyed. Acidity should be refreshing but not tart. Quality can be measured by length of flavour, and in the way it expands in the mouth and lingers.

1864*****

Le Montrachet *BOUCHARD PERE ET FILS* The Bouchard family are unusual, if not unique, in holding stocks of old wines which are stored deep in the cellars, beneath one of the bastions of the mediaeval town walls of Beaune. They have been regularly recorked. Over a period of 10–15 years, small quantities, odd bottles at a time, were offered for sale at the annual Heublein auctions of Fine and Rare Wines. In addition to conducting the first 13 of these sales, I also provided a commentary on those opened at the special pre-sale tastings. Many of the bottles were bought at auction by Lloyd Flatt who has opened them from time to time at his various tastings and dinners.

First tasted at a Heublein pre-sale tasting in May 1981, and another bottle six years later. Both notes virtually identical: lovely bright warm straw-gold with hint of orange; no faults, still fruit, the bouquet develop-

ing in the glass, toasted; dry, hefty – probably maximum alcoholic content, about 14% – but beautiful. Full flavoured, sweet honeyed bottle-age, good acidity.
*Last noted pre-dinner following Flatt's Ausone tasting in New Orleans, Oct 1987******

1865*****

Meursault *BOUCHARD PERE* Warm straw colour with slight flaky sediment – orange-gold crystals like a copper *casse*; bouquet unknit, a mixture of old damp straw and a *vin jaune d'Arbois*, varnishy old age, yet with tremendous power and depth; dry, peach-flavoured, verging on pungent, with fairly high acidity.
*At Lloyd Flatt's, Oct 1987***

Meursault, Charmes *BOUCHARD PERE* Remarkably bright buttery gold; smoky, buttery, Chardonnay nose; dry yet appearing to have residual sugar – probably alcohol and old ripe grapes – clean as a whistle. Delicious, slightly smoky flavour.
*At Heublein's pre-sale tasting, May 1981******

1888

Chablis *BOUCHARD PERE* Yellow gold, touch of ochre, bright; nose slightly varnishy; dry, firm, remarkably sound for district and age. Straightforward flavour and acidity.
*At Heublein's pre-sale, May 1981***

1906****

Le Montrachet From the cellar unearthed by Russell Hone and sold as "The Quancard Collection" by Christie's in 1978. First tasted prior to cataloguing. Three years later: good cork, good level; yellow-straw; excellent, rich, deep, nutty, smoky bouquet and flavour. Remarkably good.
*At a picnic supper in a box at the Albert Hall, watching wrestling with Peter (now Lord) Palumbo, Feb 1981******

1919****

1921*****

1923****

Wines of these three very good vintages not tasted since 1980.

1928*****

An excellent, firm, long-lasting white burgundy vintage.

Meursault *CUVEE RESERVEE AU RESTAURANT LES FEVRIERS* From the cellar of the Baroness Guillaume at La Bretèche, sold at Christie's in the mid-1970s. First tasted in Paris, at lunch with Peter Palumbo, then in New Orleans. Variable 'old apples and tokay', 'nutty, fumed-oak' and in wonderful drinking condition. On the last occasion: old gold, but bright; fragrant but resinous nose and taste. Dry, clean despite having a slightly maderised old sherry character.
*Last tasted May 1981. At best*****

1929****

Beaune, 1er cru, Montée Rouge *LEON VIOLAND* Bright yellow, touch of straw; very good toasted, crusty old bouquet; medium dry, medium full-bodied, broad beefy style, good length.
*At Hardy Rodenstock's fifth Raritätion Weinprobe at the Fuente, Mülheim, Oct 1984****

1933***

Though a good vintage, still showing well in the 1950s, recent bottles disappointing.

Chassagne-Montrachet *CHANSON* Colour of old amber; meaty, 'oxo'dised nose; rather sour.
March 1985.

1934****

A dependable vintage. The best, and best kept, can still be very attractive.

Mâcon Viré, Clos du Chapitre *JACQUES DEPAGNEUX* Original cork, slight ullage, decanted. Very bright, medium-deep old gold; not much nose but what little it had held well; fairly dry, rather old-straw, sherry-like flavour, touch of honey, good acidity.
*Ordered out of curiosity and drunk with limited pleasure at La Pyramide, Vienne, Sept 1984**

Meursault *BAROLET* Showing well at the original pre-sale tasting in 1969 and still good in 1981: bright old gold colour; sound nose; medium body, excellent, slightly nutty, flavour and acidity.
*Dining with Lloyd Flatt, May 1981****

Meursault, Charmes *BAROLET* Nearly a dozen notes from the first tasting with Harry Waugh in the courtyard above the Barolet cellars, Oct 1969. Slight variations, but all drinking reasonably well. Most recently, very good level, a powdery sediment, needing decanting, yellow-straw gold; the smell of old apples in a loft; fairly dry, well past its best but acidity holding it together.
Last noted at Jancis Robinson's Wine *programme tasting, Dec 1982. At best****

Meursault, Perrières *LEROY* The colour, smell and taste of old straw but very good acidity.
*At Gil Nickel's, San Francisco, Sept 1984**

1935***

Good vintage, not generally imported by British merchants and rarely seen.

Le Montrachet *RESERVE PRIVEE COMTES LAFON MEURSAULT* Very good appearance for its age: medium-deep, rich gold, noticeable legs; waxy nose, more like Chenin Blanc than Chardonnay, but in very good condition, distinct vanilla scent after the wine had recovered from its initial chill; medium dry, full-bodied – high alcohol, fat, with very assertive, rich, oaky flavour. A trace of hardness yet slightly lacking in acidity.
At The Great Vintage Wine Book *dinner to launch the German edition, Zurich, Oct 1983*****

1937****

A very good vintage but not seen much as the war intervened. Though many excellent red burgundies survived and were shipped in the early post-war years, most of the whites had been consumed by the French and, doubtless, by the occupying Germans. In any case, at that time, most merchants were seeking younger and fresher vintages.

Puligny-Montrachet, Combettes *LEFLAIVE* Imported by Bellows & Co, New York. Amber orange, really too tawny-tinged. Nose low-keyed but interesting. After 15 minutes, it reminded me of Cointreau, then of old pears and, surprisingly, 30 minutes after opening, it had a very good scent; bone dry, full-bodied, clean, good length and very good acidity.
*At a Rodenstock Wine Weekend dinner, Arlberg, Sept 1990*****

1938*

Corton-Charlemagne *L LATOUR* Very deep gold, but bright; lovely old charred, smoky, bouquet; dry, high

alcohol, very nutty flavour, good length and acidity.
*With James Halliday at La Pyramide, Sept 1984****

1941**

A good vintage, but one which seemingly only the resourceful Dr Barolet managed to retain stocks of.
Meursault *BAROLET* Several notes. A reasonably reliable wine. Surprisingly pale for its age; full, fragrant, oak chip, slightly vanilla nose; overall very dry, tasted of lanolin, its lemon-like acidity keeping it alive.
*Last tasted Sept 1987***

1943***

The best white burgundy vintage between 1937 and 1945. A quantity of Barolet's Chablis and Chablis, *Grand Cru* found its way on to the market, starting with the landmark auction at Christie's in 1969. Many notes, reasonably good though blunt, short.
Montagny *'QUANCARD COLLECTION'* Several notes, slightly variable. Two recently tasted blind, one the colour of old gold; harmonious orange blossom and vanilla nose though slightly appley; very dry, firm, short. The other paler and brighter; somewhat more malty but held well, creamy after 90 minutes in the glass; very good acidity.
*Really remarkably good for its age and district. Last tasted Feb 1986***

1945****

Small, very good vintage. Surprisingly few shipped to England.
Meursault, Hospices, Cuvée Jehan Humblot From Claridge's, Paris, and imported by the IECWS. A quantity sold at Christie's in the late 1970s. Tasted prior to the sale, and eight notes since. Slightly variable, colour ranging from a lovely yellow gold to deeper amber gold. Needed decanting. Bouquet lovely, rich, lanolin, nutty, the poorest being like old straw. Overall dry but rich, plump, firm, spicy, with fragrant aftertaste. Mainly excellent.
*Last tasted March 1982. At best*****
Meursault, Perrières *LEROY* Pale for age. Dry. Firm.
*Oct 1984****

1947****

Rich, rounded, good wines. Less firm than the '45s. Early maturing and mainly drunk young. All the '47s noted recently have all been served with meals, not just at tastings.
Bâtard-Montrachet, Cuvée Exceptionnelle *AVERY* Yellow gold; first whiff, delicately honeyed bottle-age, then deep, vinous, nutty, toasted coconut. Developed well, oaky, very rich. Slightly sweet, rich, oaky, four-square, meaty though rather austere.
*At John Avery's, May 1984*****
Chassagne-Montrachet *BAROLET* Medium-pale; lightly fragrant, very clean; dry, very strong flavour, firm, high strength, good acidity.
*At Lloyd Flatt's, May 1981****
Corton-Charlemagne *LEON VOILLAND* Recorked. An amazing colour, but pale; low-keyed, toasty, showing no age on the nose. Really too good to be true. Refreshed? Dry, lean, nutty, with good acidity though it tasted rather tinny with fish.
*Oct 1985*****
Mâcon Viré, Clos du Chapitre, Moelleux *JACQUES DEPAGNEUX* Interesting to note that this was a marvellous vintage in Beaujolais and Mâconnais. This wine will have been made from extremely ripe grapes, possibly slightly botrytised. Pure golden colour; soft, waxy nose; medium-sweet, very pleasant flavour, showing bottle-age but held together with very good acidity.
*With James Halliday at La Pyramide, Vienne, Sept 1984****
Meursault *DOM DAMBREME* Good old-gold colour; meaty, slightly varnishy, honeyed bottle-age; medium dryness and weight, rounded, flavoury, excellent acidity.
*Dinner with Mutsuo Okabayashi, Tokyo, June 1989****
Meursault, 1er cru *'QUANCARD COLLECTION'* Cork branded "Ets Vanier, Beaujeu, Bourgogne". Fabulous colour, buttercup yellow; creamy nose that opened up as it gained room temperature: vanilla custard with touch of pineapple; medium-sweet, full and fat with rich vanilla flavour and pasty acidity. With Bugler Crab and frogs legs.
*At Brennans, New Orleans, April 1980****
Meursault, Charmes *LEROY* Two bottles, slight variation, one yellow gold, the other with an orange tinge. The latter harmonious, creamy, sound. Very assertive burnt heather, mint and spice, excellent acidity. One with slightly unclean finish.
*At Stephen Kaplan's, Chicago, Sept 1990***
Pouilly-Fuissé Bottled in London by Williams Standring. A lovely rich buttery gold; low-keyed, smoky, vanilla bouquet; some nuttiness, overall dry and firm for its age, class and vintage. Clean. Well bottled, well stored.
*From Lady Birley's cellar, Sussex, Nov 1980***

1948**

Only one '48 white burgundy ever tasted. Few if any imported, and not listed by my old firm Saccone & Speed in the early 1950s.
Chevalier-Montrachet *BOUCHARD PERE* Very good colour; slightly peach kernelly nose; medium dry, very rich, powerful, meaty, vanilla flavour.
*At the Flatt Collection pre-sale tasting, Chicago, Sept 1990****

1949****

Very good vintage. Imported and only too rapidly sold and consumed. Only one tasted recently.
Corton-Charlemagne, Ancien Dom de Ch Grancey Bottled in London by Dolamore. Warm gold; bouquet of scented, toasted, coconut; medium dry, full-bodied, marvellous flavour, excellent acidity.
*At Jack Plumb's Bordeaux Club dinner, Christ's College, Cambridge, Nov 1989******

1950***

Good vintage. Imported, sold and consumed in the mid-1950s. Can still be excellent. None tasted recently.

1952****

Very good, firm wines. The few that remain can be excellent: Laguiche's Le Montrachet, perfection in 1969. Only one recent note.
Corton-Charlemagne *JEAN-MARIE GARNIER* Palish yellow, slight green tinge, remarkable for its age; clean, nutty nose, still a bit hard; dry, firm, both steely and nutty. Very good acidity. Perhaps lacking length.
*Dining at Crockford's, Jan 1987****

1953****

Most attractive, more amenable, but softer, less firmly structured than the '52s. Many tasted, consumed and noted in the mid- to late 1950s, some in the 1960s. Only one tasted recently.
Meursault, Genevrières French bottled for Avery.

Two bottles, one corked, tasted in Brussels, March 1986. Curiously, the more ullaged bottle was better, having a buttery colour and nose. Soft and drinkable. Three months later, quite coincidentally another bottle served at dinner by Belle and Barney Rhodes: medium yellow, touch of green; creamy, mildly smoky Chardonnay nose that held well; medium dry, slightly malty, kernelly flavour that tailed off.
*Last noted at Bella Oaks, Napa, June 1986. At best***

1954*

Not bad. Few shipped. Two tasted, neither recently.

1955****

The middle of a reasonably happy decade for white burgundy. Good wines. Nicely balanced. A deservedly popular vintage and, at the time, reasonably priced. Much shipped and many tasted from the spring of 1956 to the mid-1960s, thereafter infrequently. Some, extremely good, in the 1970s and 1980s. Only one tasted recently.

Bâtard-Montrachet *L POIRIER* Avery selection, bottled in Burgundy. Very yellow, touch of green; rich and very vivacious, lanolin and lemon, touch of vanilla; medium dry entry, very rich almost oily, but balanced by a lovely crisp, dry, acid finish. Good length.
*May 1984****

1956

Poor, thin, acidic wines. Few tasted, none since 1962.

1957***

The naturally high acidity of the vintage suiting the character of young fresh white burgundy. Severe frosts in May decimated Chablis. Otherwise firm flavoury wines mainly sold and consumed within five years of the vintage. None tasted since 1977.

1958*

Minor. Few shipped. Only one recent note.

Meursault, Genevrières, Cuvée Baudot Bottled by Leroy. Yellow; scented, herbaceous, slightly oily nose; dry, nice weight, oaky flavour, good acidity.
*At the Rhodes', Napa, June 1986****

1959***

A good but atypical vintage. Summer too hot, grapes too ripe, with high sugar content producing correspondingly high degrees of alcohol, high extract and the associated problems of low acidity, though doubtless early picking of the Chardonnay helped a little. Plump wines lacking zest, mainly consumed by the mid-1960s. Those tending to be on the substantial side, like Le Montrachet and Corton-Charlemagne, can still, if kept well, be excellent. Many tasted though few recently.

Le Montrachet *BOUCHARD PERE* Two bottles: the first medium-deep yellow gold; rich, expansive, honeyed bouquet, then sweet, fudge-like; slightly sweet on palate, a big, full, fat wine – powerful, 14% alcohol, very impressive despite slightly woody flavour. The second bottle with a touch more lemon on the nose, firmer on palate.
*At the Castle Hotel, Taunton, Wine Weekend, Nov 1985*****

Chablis, Les Clos *LONG-DEPAQUIT* Pale for its age; smoky, toasted, rather untypical hot-year Chablis bouquet; dry, sufficient acidity but showing its age. Not the sort of wine that improves in bottle.
*June 1984**

Meursault *PAUL DARGENT* Bright, buttercup yellow; waxy nose reminding me more of an old Sémillon or even Chenin Blanc; very dry, over the hill but drinkable. Neither the class nor quality to benefit from bottle-age.
*Feb 1981**

Meursault, Hospices, Jehan Humblot Variable: two bottles in the mid-1980s, one amoroso-coloured, oxidised, beery, the other yellow gold, powerful, meaty. More recently, four bottles opened, two old amber with singed, maderised nose, the other two a good colour, with creamy, sound, honeyed bottle-age nose; very dry, firm, a bit austere.
*Last tasted March 1988. At best***

Pernand-Vergelesses, blanc *P PONNELLE* The colour of old fino sherry; very good, waxy, vinous nose; dry, crisp for age and vintage.
*Aug 1983****

Puligny-Montrachet, Les Pucelles *P PONNELLE* Three notes in the mid-1980s: consistently attractive, bright pale yellow gold; smoky, oaky nose; nice weight, good crisp, charred flavour, dry finish.
*Last tasted Sept 1985****

1960

Poor thin wines, though better at the time than the reds. Few seen now. None tasted recently.

1961****

Attractive wines, most showing at their best in the mid-1960s. The top wines at the height of their maturation curve by the early 1970s. The best can still be excellent. Variable though, as some of my more recent notes demonstrate.

Bâtard-Montrachet *HENRI CLERC* Medium-pale yellow gold; lovely, a rich toasted coconut bouquet; medium dry, medium full-bodied, soft yet nutty. Slightly lacking acidity yet a glorious wine.
*With the Rhodes' at 47 Park Street, Oct 1987*****

Beaune, Clos des Mouches *J DROUHIN* Two bottles: the first quite yellow; a bit oily and overblown; dryish, rather fat and dull. The second yellower but brighter, drier and better.
At lunch after the Drouhin tasting of '78s, June 1980.

Chassagne-Montrachet, Le Château *MOILLARD* Smell like dough; fairly nondescript.
Jan 1984.

Chassagne-Montrachet, La Maltroye Good colour for age, tinged with lemon; sweet, mealy, charred bouquet; medium dry, soft and rich, with a slight twist of lemon-like acidity. Lovely. In excellent condition.
*Pre-sale, Oct 1982*****

Corton-Charlemagne *BERRY BROS & RUDD* Long, unbranded cork. Palish gold; smoky Chardonnay nose, nutty, old straw after 15 minutes, and then rich old apples. Bone dry. Medium body. Steely but rather neutral flavour. Sound but lacking character.
*At Rodenstock's Wine Weekend opening dinner, Sept 1990****

Corton-Charlemagne *L LATOUR* Fine, still youthful in 1970. 12 years later: smooth, waxy, harmonious, creamy vanilla bouquet with twist of lemon acidity; rich, fleshy yet firm. Good acidity. Oaky aftertaste.
*One of several magnificent wines, dining with the Khourys in San Diego. Last tasted Oct 1982******

Meursault, Chevalières *JEAN MONNIER, DOLAMORE LABEL* Curious colour, tinges of green and brown; very little nose, slightly maderised. Dry, dull, appley flavour.
At an Aquitaine Society Dinner, March 1982.

Meursault, Perrières *BOUCHARD AINE* Deep straw

gold; showing age, nose like old apple cores; better on palate: good rich flavour. Excellent acidity holding it together.
*April 1983***

1962*****

As marvellous a vintage for white as for red burgundy. Combining body and acidity, the wines were consumed with alacrity and pleasure in the mid- to late-1960s, the remaining top wines superb through the 1970s. To my surprise, I have only noted one since 1980 though I have no hesitation in recommending readers to look out for the best and best kept.

Corton-Charlemagne *L LATOUR* For many of us, Louis Latour makes a 'copybook' Corton-Charlemagne. His '62 is a pinnacle vintage, certainly the best at a vertical tasting in 1970. A decade later, still superb: a lovely buttery yellow; equally buttery nose – almost the old Californian style of Chardonnay richness – that developed marvellously in the glass (New World noses tend to be more static), sweet, toasty; touch of sweetness on the palate, certainly rich, with a beautiful, nutty, smoky flavour. By no means an enormous wine, if anything lean.
*Last noted at the 97th Meeting (dinner) of the Saintsbury Club at Vintners Hall, Oct 1980***** Should still be good.*

1963**

Much better for whites than reds, but not popular with the trade or consumer for two reasons, both obvious: the general reputation of '63s in France, and because it followed two good vintages, with promising weather for the next vintage during the first year of the sales campaign. Several surprisingly drinkable '63s in the 1970s but only one noted in the 1980s.

Meursault, Hospices, Cuvée Jehan Humblot *RAOUL CLERGET* Yellow; oily Chardonnay; dry, some flesh, even plumpness, not bad flavour but with raw end acidity.
*May 1984**

1964***

A vintage not dissimilar to 1959, with the same problem: the summer was too hot, grapes high in sugar, low in acidity. Untypical white burgundies, lacking suppleness, finesse and zest. Popular however. Nevertheless, lacking acidity they lacked stamina and are risky now. Contrary to my normal advice, serve these '64s well chilled.

Le Montrachet *LAGUICHE* Alas not good: dull yellow, partially oxidised in 1968, dull and flabby in 1972 and, admittedly 26 years after the grapes were harvested, a surprisingly pale yellow, though not bright; nose sweet but maderised, like sweaty old pears crossed with Tokay Szamorodni. Dry, fullish body, taste of old fino sherry.
Last tasted Sept 1990.

Bâtard-Montrachet *CAMILLE GIROUD* Old man Giroud had the reputation for hoarding his wines. This, the colour of Tutankhamen gold; a subdued, honeyed bouquet that grew and grew and grew in the glass; medium dry, fairly full-bodied, lovely texture, good length, a bit oily. Unusual. Interesting.
*Presented by Becky Wassermann at Dr Maliner's Wine Weekend, Jan 1990****

Bâtard-Montrachet *P PONNELLE* Bright, gold-tinted yellow; caramelised nose; not bad.
*At pre-sale tasting, Aug 1983**

Corton-Charlemagne *CHAUVENET* Good colour; smoky Chardonnay nose and flavour, oaky aftertaste. Dry. Holding well.
*Nov 1983****

Corton-Charlemagne *L LATOUR* In 1970: massive, lacking finesse. 12 years later, though pale for its age, fading; an odd mushroom stalk nose, though it shook this off, relapsing by the end of dinner. Flabby and lacking.
*Last tasted Oct 1982**

Corton-Charlemagne *H SICHEL* Mature, holding well. Smoky. Medium dry, medium full-bodied, lacking length and acidity but very drinkable.
*July 1984***

Puligny-Montrachet, Combettes *DE MOUCHERON* Deep colour; old straw, dry, maderised yet drinkable.
March 1982.

Savigny-Lès-Beaune, Redescul *DOUDET-NAUDIN* Orange-tinged straw, slight sediment, not bright; surprisingly good toasted marshmallow nose; dry, fair body, slightly nutty flavour, lacking length. Best feature its nose.
*Oct 1983***

1965

Climate as unfavourable for white as for red burgundy. Thin, skinny, weak, acidic wines. Only one ever tasted, 15 years ago.

1966****

The '66, like the '85, is one of my favourite vintages – almost everywhere. There is a happy common denominator that I can sum up as reliability, balance, often understated but correct, lissom, firm, long lasting.

Of the very many notes on 1966 white burgundies, the average rating has been high – in fact higher than for almost any other vintage, particularly throughout the 1970s when most were at their peak. Alas, not many tasted recently, but the wines of the top estates should still be reliably beautiful.

Le Montrachet *DRC* One of the most spectacularly lovely white burgundies ever tasted. First at a Bordeaux Club dinner hosted by Michael Behrens in 1976. Magnificent power, fragrance and future. Then, four years later, elegant, excellent – in Houston with Herbert Allen of Screwpull fame. His excellent, air-conditioned cellar was next to the workshops where he designed and made the prototypes of his original screwpull and the subsequent variations on the corkscrew theme. Next drunk at lunch with Lalou Bize, Aubert de Vilaine and his father after a marvellous La Tâche vertical. A beautiful, limpid, yellow gold; rich, slightly vanilla nose that opened up, honeyed, nutty; fairly dry, medium-full body, substantial but by no means heavy. Rich. Intense. What was extraordinary was the way the flavour expanded, unravelling, becoming sweeter until it seemed almost a dessert wine. This '66 was the first made at the Domaine in combination with grapes from the old de Moucheron patch of Montrachet vines. Certainly one of the best Montrachets that DRC has ever made.
*Last tasted – sipped, savoured, devoured – May 1983****** (yes, six stars!)*

Le Montrachet *LAGUICHE* The family of the Marquis de Laguiche sells its must (grape juice) to J Drouhin's who vinify and bottle the wine. Alas, the '66 not as magnificent as expected: good but not great in 1971, delicate, delicious though unassertive in 1975. Five years later, though a good colour, overall slightly disappointing.
*Last tasted July 1980. At best*****

Montrachet *LEROY* Pale gold; very good creamy, nutty,

toasted bouquet; dry, positive and powerful. Good acidity.

*In Wiesbaden, Oct 1985******

Meursault, Charmes, Hospices, Grivault Bright amber gold — too deep for just bottle-age; over-maturity confirmed on the nose, showing age, but rich, vanilla; firm enough, flavoury.

*At lunch with the International Wine and Food Society of Chicago, April 1982***

Meursault, Perrières *POUPON* Pale gold; light, honeyed, not very impressive. No development. Dry, straight but austere.

*At a Saintsbury Club dinner, April 1982***

1967****

A very good white burgundy vintage at the opposite end of the spectrum to '59 and '64. In short, leaner and distinctly more acidic. Never as popular or fashionable as the '66s, the '67s were at their best, judging from the many notes warranting three and four stars, in the early to mid-1970s. Few tasted recently but I still think they are worth looking out for; the occasional surprise will make up for the occasional disappointment.

Montrachet *BOUCHARD PERE* Not too deep but positive yellow; pleasant, light, waxy nose; more assertive on the palate. Nice weight, flavour and good acidity.

*Lunch with the Bouchard 'groupie', Lloyd Flatt, in between his mammoth Mouton sessions, April 1986****

Chassagne-Montrachet, Ch de La Maltroye Extremely good. Many notes, all highly complimentary, between 1970 and 1975 when I thought it probably at its best. Nevertheless, nine years later, no let-up: the bouquet exuding waves of honeycomb waxiness, fruit, rich toast, marvellous vinosity; dry, good mid-palate and endtaste, slightly pasty acidity. Determined not to give up the ghost.

*Last tasted Feb 1989. At best******

Meursault, Clos de La Barre *R CAVIN* As fresh aged 17 as it was at seven. Yellow; low-keyed, slightly spicy, fruit emerging, honey and pineapple; dry, clean-cut, touch of lemon-like acidity. Very agreeable drink.

*Last tasted July 1984****

Meursault, Hospices, Goureau Bottled in Burgundy for Avery. Palish yellow, good for age; fresh mint; dry, its flavour opening up in the mouth leading to a lean, attenuated lemon-acid finish.

*July 1988****

Ch Pouilly At nearly 20 years old, a Pouilly-Fuissé showing its paces: very good, fairly pale appearance; nose neutral at first but eventually like faint lemon and stewed pears; dry, fairly light, firm, delicious. Which just goes to show that a well-made wine will keep even from a district not noted — or needed — for its longevity.

*Nov 1986****

1968

Climatic conditions responsible for a poor, unripe harvest, equalling 1965 as the worst years of the decade. Few imported, few tasted, only two since 1980.

Chevalier-Montrachet *BOUCHARD PERE* Old gold — too deep; not bad, certainly not oxidised; dry, lean, surprisingly drinkable though rather acidic.

*At Lloyd Flatt's, April 1986**

Meursault, Hospices, Jehan Humblot Bright yellow, touch of acidic green; pleasant, slightly vanilla nose; dryish, light weight and style, flavoury.

*Feb 1983***

1969****

A very good white burgundy vintage. Firm, well constituted wines with vibrant conserving acidity, ending the decade on a high note. A mass of almost uniformly good notes throughout the 1970s, the more robust wines taking a full 10 years to evolve completely. Clearly, from my own notes, a highly satisfactory year for the big guns: Montrachet, Bâtard and Corton-Charlemagne, the finest still magnificent and well worth looking out for.

Le Montrachet *DRC* Good colour, not too deep; when first poured — chilled — crisp, refreshing, but as it lost its chill the bouquet opened up. I kept some in my glass and after an hour it had become completely transformed, sweet, forthcoming, smoky oak chip, finally a calm caramel; on the palate dry, firm, full yet delicate. Excellent acidity. This was the occasion that categorically demonstrated the error of serving top quality white burgundy too cold. My host, Michael Behrens, and fellow members had finished theirs before the bouquet and flavour had fully evolved. I handed my glass round and they all realised what they had missed.

*At Culham Court, April 1981***** Now to 2000.*

Le Montrachet, Dom Renée Pierrot *FLEUROT-LAROSE* Buttery amber; rich, rather agèd oaky Chardonnay nose that held well; good shape, touch of sweetness, good weight, toasty flavour, twist of acidity.

*July 1981*****

Beaune, Clos des Mouches *J DROUHIN* Excellent colour; lovely, fragrant, smoky, fruity — pineapple. Dry, nice weight, firm, well balanced, excellent vinosity, just a touch of bitterness — space for expansion.

*March 1981**** Should still be good.*

Bâtard-Montrachet *DELAGRANGE-BACHELET* Slight bottle variation. The first deep, old straw; glorious toasted marshmallow nose and flavour. Dry. Medium-full body. The second slightly paler, leaner, more austere. Good acidity.

*Dec 1985. At best*****

Bâtard-Montrachet *LEFLAIVE* Fabulous yellow gold; excellent oaky Chardonnay nose with an underlay of fresh, slightly pineapple-like fruit; dry, full, firm, excellent acidity and a long life ahead.

*At Peter Palumbo's Farnworth House (Mies Van der Rohe's 'glass house') on, practically in, the Fox River, Illinois, June 1984***** Now to 2000.*

Bâtard-Montrachet *ANDRE RAMONET* Lovely, soft, toasted bouquet, a bit soapy, and deteriorated in the glass; dry, powerful, toasty, austere, rapier-like.

*Oct 1985**** But on the edge.*

Bâtard-Montrachet *RAMONET-PRUDHON* Pale for its age; smoky, oaky, honey and lemon; dry, full of alcohol, extract, flavour. Toasted. Marvellous acidity.

*June 1985***** Now to 2000.*

Chablis, Les Clos *A PIC* Good colour though showing some age; distinct smell and taste of almond kernels. Dry. Austere. Even a *grand cru* Chablis of a good firm vintage is better drunk within, say, three to five years.

*Jan 1981**

Corton-Charlemagne *L JADOT* Incredible appearance: very bright, highly polished, lemon-curd colour with hint of green; initially, lemon and wax nose, then, after 30 minutes, lovely, soft, vaseline-like with touch of powdery barley-sugar and after an hour in the glass, mint, vanilla and orange blossom; 'warm', buttery, a wine of great power, opening up in the mouth, overall dry, with excellent acidity. A spectacular wine.

*At Christ's College, Cambridge, host Jack Plumb, June 1987***** Now to 2000.*

Corton-Charlemagne *L LATOUR* Bottle variation. Both surprisingly pale, the first more yellow-green; lovely, well-developed nutty oaky nose with squeeze of lemon; medium dry, marvellously evolved open flavour, with lean, lively acidity. The second slightly deeper coloured; fresh, acidic, walnut nose; drier, seemed lighter in weight and style, thinner and sharper.
*Both at a Gidleigh Park Wine Weekend, Jan 1984 At best*****

Meursault, Charmes *LEROY* First tasted in 1977, the opening wine at a tutorial in Sydney, good "quite a bite – will keep". In 1988: its original pale yellow now deeper and with a slight orange tinge; sweet, with honeyed bottle-age, a bit overblown; dryish, fullish, broad shouldered, attractive, good finish, but peak reached.
*Last noted at Lalou Bize's annual tasting, Sept 1988****

Meursault, Charmes, Hospices, Grivault *LEROY* Bitty sediment; sweet, blancmange nose – rather like vanilla ice cream; medium-dry, fullish, assertive, curious flavour.
*At the Leroy tasting, Sept 1988***

Meursault, Goutte d'Or *LEROY* Good colour; smell of hen droppings. Terrible.
Sept 1988.

Meursault, Clos de Mazeray *JACQUES PRIEUR* Very bright yellow; attractive honey and pineapple bouquet; dry, pleasant, slightly soft finish.
*Nov 1983****

Meursault, Les Narvaux *LEROY* Strange but fragrant, floral, honeyed nose; full-bodied, assertive, odd taste, boiled sweets.
*Sept 1988. At best***

Meursault, Perrières *LEROY* An extraordinary smell of charred sticks and fish skin; very dry, lean.
*Sept 1988. At best***

1970★★★

On the whole good wines but soft and lacking acidity. Without that staying power, few able to survive into the 1980s. Most were consumed, quite rightly, within the first five years. Only the very best worth pursuing. Serve chilled to crisp them up.

Le MONTRACHET *DRC Three notes, first in 1977. A year later, superb, with blossoming 'snuffed candle' bouquet and glorious flavour, then, four years later, still quite pale though with a slight sediment; an incredible, open-knit, waxy, honeyed bouquet, meaty, vanilla, opulent — yet disappointing on the palate, biscuity, touch of peach kernels, loose end acidity and on verge of oxidation. Last tasted, and commented on, at John Hart's Fine Wine dinner in Chicago, Nov 1982. At best★★★★*

Le MONTRACHET *LAGUICHE Palish, bright; vanilla pods, some fruit, underwhelming — no development; dry, fullish body, soft, lacking zest. Disappointing. Magnum at Jack Plumb's 80th birthday dinner, June 1991★★*

BATARD-MONTRACHET *Grapes grown by Bernard Clerget,* élevé *by Remoissenet, bottled after 15 months in oak. Pronounced yellow; wax, oak and honeyed bottle-age nose; medium dry, fairly full-bodied, harmonious yet unexciting in May 1985. Presumably the same wine, with Avery label, nose and flavour like toasted coconut and duck-egg custard. Quite good acidity and aftertaste. Last tasted July 1988★★★* Now to *1995.*

CHABLIS, BOUGROTS *A PIC Pale, dry, straightforward at five years of age, tiring at 12, rather kernelly flavour, austere. Last tasted Aug 1982★★ Drink up.*

CHABLIS, LES CLOS *MARCEL SERVIN Pale, but showing age on nose and palate: dry, dull, flabby. A poor start to an otherwise magnificent wine dinner at Boodle's, July 1984.*

CHASSAGNE-MONTRACHET, CAILLERETS *ALBERT MOREY Bright, still perky and green-tinged, but stewed and disappointing on nose and palate. Nov 1980.*

CHASSAGNE-MONTRACHET, CH DE LA MALTROYE *Consistently a favourite of mine but always needing bottle-age. Good but unready when first tasted in 1972, fully evolved nine years later: a lovely, oaky, smoky, slightly tarry nose; beautiful flavour and balance. Softening but firm enough. Interestingly, served at room temperature. June 1981. Then★★★ but doubtless past best now.*

CORTON-CHARLEMAGNE *MIGNON Pale and very scented in 1975. 10 years later taking on colour, distinctly yellow; first whiff very exotic, strange, vaseline, but settled down to vanilla and oak; dry, firm, good acidity. Last tasted Aug 1985★★★ Probably still good.*

MEURSAULT, LES NARVAUX *LEROY Very yellow; curious, highly spiced, touch of peach kernels on nose and palate, but good, honeyed bottle-age flavour and firm acidity. Sept 1984★★*

MEURSAULT, PERRIERES *LEROY Waxy, buttery nose; medium dry, broad, open, slightly woody and lacking acidity. June 1984. Then★★*

PERNAND-VERGELESSES *L LATOUR Palish, slight orange tinge; singed, mature bouquet; slightly sweet, flavoury. June 1987★★*

PULIGNY-MONTRACHET, *DOM COMTESSE DE MONTIVAULT, PIAT Buttery yellow, oak and caramel on nose; very pronounced almond kernel flavour, highish acidity. Feb 1985. Poor.*

1971★★★★

Rightly highly regarded at the time. Certainly fine, firm, well-constituted wines vying with '69 as the best vintage until the '78s came along. The top growths of dependable quality, the Chablis — many tasted but few recently — and the Meursaults being particularly successful; but so were the Montrachets. Because of their structure, in particular their firmness and acidity, the best are still drinking well.

Le MONTRACHET *DOM DU CH DE PULIGNY-MONTRACHET Straw yellow; vanilla, developing a good, fragrant, Chardonnay nose; ripe, rich, mouthfilling yet delicate and fragrant. Nov 1980★★★★*

BATARD-MONTRACHET *P A ANDRE Bright, yellow-gold; initially unknit, lemon, vegetal but, after 15 minutes, it opened up well, throwing off its mushroomy bottle-stink, rich, attractive; fullish, very crisp, oaky flavour. Drying out on the finish. Sept 1990★★ Only just holding up.*

BATARD-MONTRACHET *DELAGRANGE-BACHELET Deep, buttery; astonishing, lemon curd, blancmange; fairly sweet and full, high extract, concentration. Oct 1988★★★★★*

CHABLIS, LES CLOS TESTAT *LAROCHE Pale for its age, good body. Only* grand cru *Chablis of a firm vintage like '71 seem able to survive, though bottle-age confers little benefit. Dec 1984★★*

CORTON-CHARLEMANGE (*sic*) *AVERY John Avery was somewhat embarrassed when I showed him this label, evidence of a misspelled youth! The wine — in a half-bottle — was not suffering from mange though its first whiff hinted at oxidation. Rather hard and stalky. If the label was a postage stamp, I suppose it would be a rare and expensive 'error'. I have kept it, just in case. Tasted June 1984★*

CORTON-CHARLEMAGNE *DOM DE LA JUVINIERE Lovely yellow colour; nose slightly honeyed, touch of kerosene and ceps, developing a more chocolaty and stewed-apple scent; dry, firm, steely, short. Sept 1990★★*

CORTON-CHARLEMAGNE *L LATOUR Fabulous in 1976 and 1978. Then two notes in the early 1980s. A calm harmonious nose that reminded me of damp felt. It developed well in the glass, slightly smoky, very fragrant, touch of lemon; medium dry, though rich, with a smoky almost salty taste. Despite its weight, some delicacy. Good finish, lovely aftertaste. Last noted Nov 1982★★★★ Doubtless still very good.*

MEURSAULT, CHARMES, HOSPICES, PHILIPPE LE BON *P A ANDRE Slight bottle variation. The first palish yellow; buttery, nutty nose and taste, almost Corton-like. The other orange gold, rich, meaty, toffee-like nose; showing age, old apples, maderised. Both tasted in Sept 1990. At best****

MEURSAULT, CHEVALIERES *RENEE MONNIER Straw yellow, with distinctive ripe Meursault butteriness; copybook; fine, beautifully developed smoky oaky bouquet; ripe sweetness, nice weight and balance, lovely flavour, touch of fat. March 1982**** Doubtless still excellent.*

MEURSAULT, LES TESSONS, CLOS DE MON PLAISIR *GUY ROULOT Very ripe Meursault yellow; lovely, fragrant, oaky bouquet, powerful and penetrating. Medium dry, excellent oaky flavour and finish — if anything too much oak, giving it a touch of spicy rawness. Good length. On the whole very appealing even aged 13. Oct 1984*****

SOME OTHER '71s TASTED IN THE 1980s:

CHASSAGNE-MONTRACHET *LAGUICHE Too deep, like a rich Sauternes; fine oaky smoky nose and flavour, overlaid by caramel. Maderised, acidic. Poor storage. In New York, Feb 1986.*

CHEVALIER-MONTRACHET *BOUCHARD PERE Good colour; fragrant though kernelly nose; firm, good flavour and acidity. Sept 1990***

MEURSAULT, CHARMES *AMPEAU A good yellow colour; oaky, vanilla and lemon nose; very flavoury, old-fashioned style, very slightly tinny finish. March 1984****

1972★★

Uneven, depending on the success of chaptalisation and level of acidity. Useful wines at the time though lacking grace. Several tasted in the early to mid-1980s. Of little interest now.

BIENVENUE BATARD-MONTRACHET *HENRI CLERC One of the better '72s. At 11 years of age, a rich appearance, pale gold, with good 'legs'; bouquet of toasted barley, old straw, apples stored in a loft; a touch of sweetness, smoky Chardonnay, excellent length and rich finish. At a Castle Hotel, Taunton, burgundy dinner, Nov 1983****

PULIGNY-MONTRACHET, COMBETTES *ROBERT AMPEAU Pale for its age; sweet, rich, sound bouquet; medium dry, medium weight, soft, acidity somewhat lacking but pleasant. Nov 1988***

1973★★★★

A most attractive though uneven vintage. However, the delicacy and fragrance that made the best so appealing militates against long keeping. Some had too much acidity. The 'big guns', like Montrachet and Corton-Charlemagne, have the best chance of surviving.

Le MONTRACHET *LAGUICHE/DROUHIN Very good colour; honeyed, very biscuity nose; medium dry, nice weight, soft yet with a dry, nutty finish. Sept 1989*****

Le MONTRACHET *THENARD Raw and unready in 1974, mouthfillingly glorious in 1979. Three years later, a pure yellow gold that would look magical in a decanter; smoky nose, developing richly, spicily in the glass; medium dry, nice weight — neither too light and certainly not too hefty, classic, elegant, lovely aftertaste. Last tasted May 1982*****

Le MONTRACHET *REMOISSENET Medium yellow; oaky bouquet and flavour; rather sturdy for a '73, rich, good acidity. July 1987*****

BOURGOGNE BLANC *BARON THENARD Said to be a declassified Montrachet, presumably owing to the crop in 1973 being well in excess of permitted yield. Pale yellow; scented nose, touch of vanilla; dry, lightish style, soft, good delicate oaky wholemeal flavour. Acidity slightly lacking. Supplied by Avery for a Castle Hotel, Taunton, burgundy dinner, Nov 1982****

BIENVENUE, BATARD-MONTRACHET *ROLAND THEVENIN Six notes. I tried out this purchase at an annual dinner in 1979. It was searingly dry and steely. Half the members thought it was finished, the other half that it would soften and improve. A year later it was still acidic, and aged 10 had taken on a buttery yellow colour, toasted coconut nose but was still searingly acidic, the wine lacking balance. Last tasted July 1983* Alas, I doubt if the acidity will ever ameliorate.*

BATARD-MONTRACHET *ROLAND THEVENIN A more successful 'selection' by Thevenin. A positive yellow; attractive buttery, oaky, bottle-age bouquet; rich, flavoury, good acidity. April 1988****

CHEVALIER-MONTRACHET *REMOISSENET Light, vanilla, crusty, blancmange nose; speciously charming. Jan 1983****

CHEVALIER-MONTRACHET, DEMOISELLES *L LATOUR Unbelievably beautiful at the opening tasting in 1975. In 1980 taking on colour; light but with high-toned fragrant nose; dry, lightish, delicate yet with wonderful flavour and nutty aftertaste. Aged 10, showing well: marvellous vinosity, fruit, developing beautifully in the glass. Mouthfilling smoky oaky flavour and fabulous aftertaste. Last tasted Jan 1983***** Should still be superb.*

CRIOTS-BATARD-MONTRACHET *DELAGRANGE-BACHELET Superb. First tasted at a Benedicts dinner in 1979. Two years later: pale, star-bright; fine quality nose, slightly smoky, developing a fabulous toasted bouquet; lightish in style, certainly not a big wine but elegant, with a deft touch. Lovely wine. Last tasted Jan 1981***** Should still be excellent.*

CORTON-CHARLEMAGNE *L LATOUR Six notes. It fairly dominated Latour's trade tasting in 1975, a pronounced yellow and richly developing nose noted in the later 1970s. Superb in magnum, crusty bread nose, fabulously mouthfilling, in 1983, and, the following year, though not deep, very yellow, still with a faint green tinge; bouquet opening and softening, classic, buttery; nice weight, excellent crisp, charred oak flavour, good acidity.* Last tasted Jan 1984**** Should still be very good.

MEURSAULT, GENEVRIERES, HOSPICES, CUVEE BAUDOT *Nose of lemon and linoleum; lovely singed Chardonnay flavour.* July 1982***

THE FOLLOWING WERE NOTED AT THE BIZE-LEROY MEURSAULT TASTING, SEPT 1988:

CHARMES *Palish yellow; lovely bouquet, oaky, slightly 'fishy', walnuts; firm, smoky Chardonnay flavour, dry finish****

Les NARVAUX, *RESERVE PERSONNELLE* *Yellow gold; waxy, meaty bouquet; fairly full-bodied, good acidity, a bit hard****(*)?

PERRIERES *Curious nose, distinct walnuts, ie nutty, bitter; dry, fullish, hint of lemon, good but austere, perhaps, lacking length***(*)

PORUSOTS, RESERVE PERSONNELLE *Waxy, harmonious bouquet; lovely oaky flavour and excellent acidity*****

PORUZOT, HOSPICES, JEHAN HUMBLOT *Warm, oaky nose but austere, flat yet acidic, and too hard**(**)

1974*

Not a good vintage but some interesting, rather bizarre wines made. A combination of poor weather, recession and lack of quality kept it off the market. Of little interest now.

Le MONTRACHET *BOUCHARD PERE Paler than expected, slight tinge of lemon; very forthcoming, meaty but with whiff of almond kernels. It deteriorated after some time in the glass, becoming 'brown' and blown; slight sweetness, rich, soft, better on palate than nose.* March 1982* Will be well over the top now.

Le MONTRACHET *COMTE LAFON Paradoxically, the Lafon family told me they loved all their '74s. The secret: to convert sugar into alcohol takes six months, then two years in cask! Quite good colour; an amazing nose: aniseed, liquorice — like the scent of a box hedge — which, apparently, never occurs in a ripe vintage; medium dry, leading to a warm, crumbly, dry, fennel-flavoured finish.* At the domaine, Sept 1984. In its idiosyncratic way****

BIENVENUES-BATARD-MONTRACHET *LEFLAIVE Very bright, buttercup gold; waxy, honeyed bottle-age nose that opened up richly in the glass, like blancmange; a touch of sweetness and good weight, rich, meaty, malty, lanolin taste with touch of peach kernels.* At a Marin County Wine & Food Society dinner, San Francisco, June 1986**

CORTON-CHARLEMAGNE *BONNEAU DE MARTRAY First noted at a 'Krug Awards for Excellence' luncheon at the Banqueting House, Whitehall — the wine was not a recipient. The following year: an old straw yellow colour; quite good, fragrant, nutty nose; soft, quite flavoury, but lacking acidity. Quite a character: "hussy of a wine".* Last noted Jan 1981**

MUSIGNY BLANC *DE VOGUE The colour of apple juice tinged with gold; an amazing nose, spicy pineapple, with a herbaceous, buttery underlay; dry, fullish, with flavour of pear, apple and varnish. Good backbone of acidity.* At lunch with Mats Hanszon, Stockholm, March 1984***

1975

Although less disastrous for white than for red burgundy, a dreary vintage. Few shipped and relatively few tasted. Only six notes in the 1980s.

CHABLIS *J B REYNIER Bright yellow; almond kernels; full-flavoured but* passé. Served at a City Livery Company luncheon, Jan 1988. An insult to the guests.

CHABLIS, GRENOUILLES *LOUIS MICHEL Low-keyed, quite good flavour but with very marked acidity in 1983. Most recently, too oaky on the nose but still quite flavoury. Reasonable length.* At a Saintsbury Club dinner in April 1990. We all felt that we were putting it out of its misery.

1976****

A useful, timely vintage though not up to the reds in quality. Overrated at the time, yet the very same hardness that afflicts the reds might, for those that survive, turn out to be their saving grace.

Many tasted, mainly in the late 1970s. Surprisingly variable in style and quality. Some short. Some too hard. Some nutty, some steely. Fewer tasted in the 1980s, the following notes being a cross-section. The top growers' wines of this vintage could still be drinking well into the 1990s.

Le MONTRACHET *DRC First tasted in 1979. Fragrant but still hard. By 1983, the colour had deepened from lemon yellow to yellow gold; low-keyed, slightly vanilla, nutty and fragrant, developing a sweet, oatmeal bouquet; a big wine, holding back. Two years later, from a reluctant double-magnum: needed coaxing out of the glass. Very dry, firm. I felt it could do with another 10 years. Most recently another double-magnum; much more amenable, a delicate smoky oaky fragrance though still hard; fairly high alcoholic content yet lean, with lemon-like acidity.* Last noted at the Eigensatz tasting in Wiesbaden, June 1987**(**) 1992–2000

BATARD-MONTRACHET *JEAN BACHELET Good nutty charred nose and taste.* Feb 1987****

BATARD-MONTRACHET *RAMONET-PRUDHON Magnum. Classic, developing a lovely floral bouquet; dry, appearing misleadingly light, its delicate yet firm smoky oaky flavour expanding in the mouth. Perfect acidity.* Nov 1983****(*) Should still be excellent.

CHASSAGNE-MONTRACHET, LA ROMANEE *JEAN BACHELET Lovely, rich, charred nose and flavour. Fairly dry, still hard.* Pre-sale, Chicago, Feb 1987***(*) Now to 1996.

CHEVALIER-MONTRACHET, *GEORGE DELEGER* *Distinctly yellow; buttery nose; medium dry, powerful, impressive.* Sept 1989**** Now to 1995.

CHEVALIER-MONTRACHET *L LATOUR Nose dumb at first, then a trace of melon and wax; powerful, good texture.* Aug 1989***(*) 1992–2000

CORTON-CHARLEMAGNE *L LATOUR Six notes from the autumn following the vintage. An appealing youth. Slow to develop though always attractive; nutty and fragrant by 1980, great penetration of flavour in 1986 and completely out of its shell the following year: still surprisingly pale, slight lemon tinge; also, lemon the first scent one notices, then a harmonious richness and honeyed bottle-age. Though never notably dry, it seems to have become sweeter and fuller on the palate, with a gloriously mouthfilling oaky flavour and aftertaste.* Last noted Sept 1987****(*) Now to 2000.

CORTON-CHARLEMAGNE *BONNEAU DE MARTRAY Colourful and flavoury but lacking flesh and length in 1979, and a disappointing magnum four years later: minty, fennel, noisette nose; lacking body, flavour of 'Gripfix' and almond kernels. A notable grower but not my idea of a copybook Corton-Charlemagne.* Last tasted Nov 1983*

MEURSAULT *L LATOUR Five notes. Pleasant and positive between 1977 and 1980. Crisp, still hard in 1982, austere and no signs of development in 1983. Having taken on colour — very yellow — and acquired bottle-age on the nose, still not giving much: dry, short, dull, lacking.* Last tasted Sept 1989** Drink up.

POUILLY-FUISSE, CUVEE HORS CLASSE *J-A. FERRET An extraordinary wine: pronounced yellow gold; strong, honeyed, bramble-like scent; medium-sweet, fairly full-bodied, rich, almost unctuous. Presumably made from* Botrytis-*affected grapes.* Sept 1984**** in its way.

PULIGNY-MONTRACHET, FOLATIERES *DOM DE CH DE PULIGNY-MONTRACHET Pale; classic toasty oaky scented bouquet; medium dry, medium-full body, good, soft, toasty character, very good acidity, oaky aftertaste.* July 1987**** Drink now to 1995.

PULIGNY-MONTRACHET, PUCELLES *LEFLAIVE Lovely flavour and great potential in 1978. More recently, pale, greenish tinged, star-bright; still fresh, with lightly charred oak bouquet; dry, steely, lovely acidity.* Last tasted, Oct 1983. Then***(*) Probably still firm and lovely.

THE FOLLOWING WERE ALL NOTED AT THE BIZE-LEROY MEURSAULT TASTING, SEPT 1988:

CHARMES *Palish yellow; curious, oyster-shell nose; very dry, lean, too austere but good length**(**)

GENEVRIERES *Touch of orange; low-keyed, liquorice; dry, rather dull, slightly bitter finish***

GENEVRIERES, HOSPICES, PHILIPPE LE BON *Dry, powerful, still hard***(*)

Les NARVAUX *Yellow gold; lovely oaky smoky bouquet; very dry, lean, crisp, delicious flavour and aftertaste****(*)

PERRIERES, *RESERVE PERSONNELLE* *Oxidised: the colour of old gold; smell and taste of half-eaten and abandoned apples; rather grubby aftertaste.*

SOME OTHER '76s TASTED IN THE EARLY 1980s:

Le MONTRACHET *LAGUICHE/DROUHIN Pale; disappointing bouquet, more milky than oaky, no development; good but not good enough. Perhaps needed more time.* July 1981**(*)?

Le MONTRACHET *BARON THENARD Shipped by Remoissenet. Touch of lemon on colour, on nose and on palate. Good fruit, delicious flavour, good length.* July 1981****

BIENVENUES-BATARD-MONTRACHET *ANDRE RAMONET A very striking yellow; good quality nose and smoky flavour but still hard.* Sept 1981**(**)

PULIGNY-MONTRACHET, COMBETTES *ETIENNE SAUZET Fabulous bouquet, excellent flavour, outstanding.* June 1981****

PULIGNY-MONTRACHET, FOLATIERES *BOUCHARD PERE Quite good.* Jan 1981**

PULIGNY-MONTRACHET, FOLATIERES *L LATOUR* *Showing great potential in 1978, and a marvellous constitution, oaky, high-strength when last tasted.* May 1982**(**) Probably at peak now.

Clos BLANC DE VOUGEOT *(believed to be) MERAT*, Very hard and austere. March 1983*(**)?

*1977**

Poor but could have been worse. Mainly ill-constituted, meagre and acidic. Overpriced at the time. Avoid.

Le MONTRACHET *DRC Bottled April 1979. First tasted July 1980. Straw-tinged; light, slightly malty, vanillin nose and flavour. Quite good flavour. Hard to assess but clearly needed bottle-age. Aged 10: a medium yellow; rather unknit, two-part nose, vanilla and pineapple; on the palate flowery but acidic.* Last noted at pre-sale tasting in Chicago. Oct 1987** Drink up.

Le MONTRACHET *JEAN MILAN A name unfamiliar to me. Bright; light, hard, malty nose; dry, good length and finish.* Pre-sale, Chicago, Sept 1985**

MEURSAULT, PERRIERES *GUY ROULLOT* *Yellow; rich, creamy, very attractive Chardonnay nose; dry, marvellously nutty, toasty fragrance. Refreshing tartness.* Oct 1985**

MUSIGNY, BLANC *DE VOGUE Pale yellow; nose of lemon and vanilla; lightish yet firm and flavoury. Oaky. Overall dry, with '77 acidity. A whisper of style and elegance.* March 1982**

SOME OTHER '77s TASTED IN THE EARLY 1980s:

BATARD-MONTRACHET *LEFLAIVE Distinctly yellow; nutty, oaky, smoky nose; flavoury, dry, hard. Good for the vintage***

CHABLIS, VALMUR *MAURICE FEVRE Smell of wet*

dogs. Dry. Barely tolerable.

CHEVALIER-MONTRACHET *LEFLAIVE Nutty and attractive though no great future***

MEURSAULT, GOUTTE D'OR *JAVILLIER Bright yellow; fat waxy nose; lightish, soft, mild yet acidic**

PULIGNY-MONTRACHET, PUCELLES *LEFLAIVE Very pleasant but lacking finish***

1978★★★★

An important vintage. Very firm, well-constituted wines, with good alcoholic content, extract, fruit and acidity: crisp dry acidic Chablis, marvellously steely Pulignys, expansive Meursaults, substantial, hefty, Corton-Charlemagne. Delightful minor wines. Variations on the theme abound. Not all are top class, some too lean and hard. Undoubtedly the best vintage after 1971, and one of the sturdiest. The finest only just reaching their plateau of perfection.

Le MONTRACHET *DRC One of the highlights of the DRC/Leroy tasting conducted for Emerald Wines in Melbourne: yellow gold; a marvellous nose-filling smoky oaky richness, honeyed, buttery, toasted; full of alcohol, extract, flavour, rich yet with marvellous cleansing acidity. Fabulous aftertaste. Almost too big a wine to drink at supper afterwards. Last tasted April 1985****(*) Drink now to 2000.*

Le MONTRACHET *LAGUICHE Alcohol 13.2% by volume, extract 29.00, total acidity 4.40, volatile acidity 0.52. First noted at a Drouhin special tasting of '78s in June 1980. Pale, dry, nutty and intense. Not tasted since, but it should be magnificent now******

Le MONTRACHET *L LATOUR First tasted in 1985: bread-like nose — both dough and crust; dry, huge, excellent acidity, years of life ahead. More recently: pale for its age; toasted, touch of lemon, bouquet developing gloriously in the glass; powerful, mouthfilling, marvellous flavour, pineapple-like acidity. Last tasted Aug 1989***(**) Now to 2000.*

Le MONTRACHET *BARON THENARD Palish but positive colour; buttery nose; fairly sweet, full, very rich, good aftertaste. Sept 1989****(*) Now to 2000.*

CUVEE DE BARON *Bottled in Burgundy for Avery. Said to be Thénard's declassified Montrachet. Two good notes in the mid-1980s. An attractive yellow; a very fragrant oaky, smoky, bouquet, vanilla and lemon tang; medium dry, fairly full-bodied, stylish, elegant, smoky flavour, excellent acidity. Last tasted March 1986. Then***(*) Drink now to 1998.*

BATARD-MONTRACHET *BACHELET-RAMONET Toasted bouquet, great vinosity; dry, powerful. Sept 1985****(*) Now to 1998.*

BATARD-MONTRACHET *J. DROUHIN Alcohol 13.1%, dry extract 24, total acidity 4.40, volatile acidity 0.49. Wonderfully nutty, crisp and intense at the opening tasting in London in June 1980. Not tasted since. Doubtless***** and lovely now.*

BATARD-MONTRACHET *LEFLAIVE Strength in excess of 13.5%. Four notes: bright, appealing, mouthwatering just to look at, its flavour expanding in the mouth like La Tâche 'peacock's tail'. Still hard, in Jan 1982. In 1987, in magnum, a lovely yellow gold; oaky nose that after 40 minutes had the sweet scent of coconut squares; nutty, smoky flavour, powerful, great length. The following year, a gusher: rich, buttery nose, lovely smooth oaky flavour. Most recently, pure gold; very forthcoming bouquet, rich, meaty, vaseline and clover honey. Seemed incredibly sweet, nutty, ripe. Great length. Last noted at lunch with Vincent Leflaive and his daughter, who now manages the domaine, Oct 1990***** Now to beyond 2000.*

BEAUNE, CLOS DES MOUCHES *J DROUHIN Two notes in the early 1980s. Pale; smoky, toasty, spicy nose; dry, medium-light weight and style for a '78, crisp, attractive. Perhaps lacking length. Last tasted Feb 1983****

CHABLIS:

Many notes, different crus, *different growers and considerable variation in style and quality, though the firmness and acidity would seem to be appropriate for Chablis. Most should have been drunk whilst young, crisp, fresh and acidic, and most were. Of those tasted and at their best in the early to mid-1980s, I would single out Blanchots JACQUES LAMBLIN, Fourchaume JACQUES LAMBLIN and Vaulorent DOM DE LA MALADIERE.*

FOURCHAUME *FEVRE Of those tasted more recently, these are the most mouthfillingly superb. July 1987.*

CHASSAGNE-MONTRACHET:

La BOUDRIOTTE *GAGNARD A vintage seemingly tailor-made for Chassagne. This one perfection.*

LAGUICHE Superb, "what white burgundy is all about", I noted in 1981.

CHEVALIER-MONTRACHET *L LATOUR Palish yellow, glint of gold; lovely, slightly oaky nose; perfect weight, excellent, long oaky Chardonnay flavour. A wine of great style. Dining at David d'Ambrumenil's, Nov 1989**** Now to 1998.*

CORTON-CHARLEMAGNE *BONNEAU DE MARTRAY Pale yellow gold; fragrant, scented; crisp, fruity, time in hand in the mid-1980s. Still pale; waxy, honeyed bouquet, gentle vinosity, depth and persistence; dry, nutty, assertive, good length, fairly high acidity. Last tasted July 1990**** Now to 1995.*

CORTON-CHARLEMAGNE *L LATOUR Attractive yellow; extraordinarily rich, almost oily nose, vanillin; very full-flavoured. March 1987**** Now to 1998.*

OTHER CORTON-CHARLEMAGNES TASTED IN THE MID-1980s:

*BICHOT Fragrant and flavoury****

*JADOT Lovely*****

GARNIER (A sous nom *of Reine Pédauque.) Sulphur on the nose but good, classic, smoky, oaky, bouquet;*

*good length, lean, slightly acidic***

MOILLARD Marvellously flavoury.

HOSPICES, CUVEE FRANCOIS DE SALINS, *F PROTHEAU A lovely golden colour; fabulous smoky Chardonnay nose; magnificent body, flavour and acidity.* Last tasted May 1985****(*)

MEURSAULTS, MAINLY TASTED IN THE EARLY 1980s, AND VARIABLE:

*CAMILLE GIROUD Piquant, spicy, highish acidity***

*JADOT Attractive****

*L LATOUR Little better than a Mâcon blanc when first noted in 1980 but growing in interest year by year***

*MATROT 'Blown' and kernelly, but his Blagny better***

CROMIN *BERNARD MOREY Creamy, nice quality, good, slightly high acidity***

GENEVRIERES *L LATOUR Fine quality, rich, good aftertaste*****

*L LATOUR Hazelnut nose; lemon-tinged, positive and exciting****

MUSIGNY BLANC *DE VOGUE Jeroboam: medium-pale yellow gold; honeyed bouquet marred slightly by smell of sour straw and touch of maltiness, and, after a time in glass, like Château-Chalon or an old raya sherry. Dry, fullish, but with edgy acidity. Clearly in less than good condition.* At a Rodenstock dinner, Sept 1987.

PULIGNY-MONTRACHET *Many and varied. LEFLAIVE'S dry, firm, good, steely**** *REMOISSENET'S* Reserve numerotée *buttery and over-oaked*** *THEVENIN'S rather oily and disappointing, neither steely nor nutty.*

PULIGNY-MONTRACHET, CLAVOILLON *LEFLAIVE Outstanding: crisp, steely, smoky, with good length, balance and aftertaste when first noted in 1981. Still a fairly pale green gold; lovely fragrant bouquet; bone dry, very refined.* Last tasted Feb 1989****

PULIGNY-MONTRACHET, COMBETTES *ETIENNE SAUZET Curious nose, highish acidity, disappointing in 1982. Nose fully developed but leaner and more acidic than expected, with a curious, slightly artificial flavour when last tasted.* June 1988**

PULIGNY-MONTRACHET, FOLATIERES *R THEVENIN Eight notes since 1982. Its youthful pale green now distinctly yellow; vanillin and lemon nose now rich and waxy; less firm but good length. Showing its age.* Last tasted April 1991*** Drink now.

PULIGNY-MONTRACHET, PUCELLES *LEFLAIVE An attractive waxy yellow; calm smooth nose and flavour; deceptively mild, with good length and very good acidity.* Nov 1990**** Now to 1996.

OTHER PULIGNY-MONTRACHETS:

CLOS DE LA GARENNE *THEVENIN Yellow, hefty, good future when last tasted in* March 1984***(*)

CLOS DE LA MOUCHERE *HENRI BOILLOT Good flavour, balance and length. Steely.* March 1984***(*)

COMBOTTES *CH DES HERBEUX Gassy, poor, short.* April 1985.

SOME OTHER '78s:

AUXEY-DURESSES *DUC DE MAGENTA Pure lemon colour; waxy, honeyed bottle-age; dry, good flavour, short but pleasing.* March 1985***

BATARD-MONTRACHET *REMOISSENET Rich but delicate and fragrant; substantial, flavour swells in the mouth, good length, acidity and smoky aftertaste.* Nov 1982*(***)

Clos du CHATEAU *CH DE MEURSAULT An unclassified walled vineyard in front of the château. Good nose, lightish, soft, very attractive.* July 1983.

MEURSAULT, CHEVALIERES *LEROY Buttery, honey and vanilla; dry, mouthfilling, remarkably fresh, firm — stood up to Le Montrachet.* Tasted April 1985***

PERNAND-VERGELESSES *GUYON Very good indeed.* Aug 1982***

*1979*****

1978 and 1979 are beautiful but not identical twins. The '79s had an instant more obvious and easy charm and were assumed for this reason to be less good than the harder, firmer '78s. I think the '79s are the best for drinking now, and will continue beautifully well into the 1990s, but the top '78s will finally overtake them. We shall see.

Le MONTRACHET *DRC Pale yellow gold; marvellously rich, toasted, buttery, developing a creamy bouquet; medium dry, full-flavoured, nutty, great length and aftertaste. Instantly lovely, yet with the fruit and balance needed for a long life.* Oct 1983***** Now to 2000.

Le MONTRACHET *LAGUICHE 13.4%, total acid 4.25, volatile acidity 0.30. Sample bottle not showing well at Drouhin's introductory tasting in June 1980, appley, maderised. Two autumns after the vintage, low-keyed, delicate but rich; dry, good length and aftertaste.* Something lacking, but not tasted since Sept 1981. Need to retaste.

MONTRACHET *L LATOUR Palish; toasted; firm, dry, fairly full-bodied but not heavy. Toasted oak-chip flavour, very good acidity, lovely aftertaste.* April 1983. Then****(*) Doubtless lovely now to say 1999.

ALOXE-CORTON, PINOT GRIS *SENARD A most unusual and baffling wine (tasted blind): buttery yellow; rather exotic nose with touch of pineapple; dry, medium weight, four-square but flavoury. Dry, abrupt finish.* Professor Nils Sternby's mystery wine, tasted in Miami, Feb 1981***

BATARD-MONTRACHET *BACHELET-RAMONET Two recent notes: medium-pale yellow; glorious, smoky oak chips, hint of lime, toasted coconut and marshmallow; touch of sweetness, full-bodied, very rich, assertive, loads of fruit. Magnificently mouthfilling flavour and fragrant aftertaste.* Last tasted Sept 1990***** Superb now to 2000.

BEAUNE, CLOS DES MOUCHES *J DROUHIN Five notes. Attractive, fruity, fairly high acidity in Sept 1981. Developing well, a good aftertaste in 1983, pleasantly evolved by 1986, taking on a bit* *of colour, nose softening, buttery, waxy in 1988. Most recently: a bit of bottle-stink blew away leaving oak, fruit, vanilla; ripe sweet touch on entry, a very positive, quite assertive flavour, with a dry, slightly hard, acidic finish. Last noted in Drouhin's tasting room Oct 1990, the oldest vintage of a vertical range of Clos des Mouches. I enjoyed it from the start: difficult to know how much more it will develop. Possibly taking a second breath at the moment***(*) Now to 1998?*

BIENVENUES-BATARD-MONTRACHET *LEFLAIVE Lovely colour; very good, smoky, nutty bouquet and flavour. Very dry, vanilla-tinged finish. Feb 1989**** Now to 2000.*

BIENVENUE-BATARD-MONTRACHET *ANDRE RAMONET Gorgeous lemon-tinged yellow;* pain grillé *nose that opened up, vanilla. After one hour harmonious, creamy — then faded. Fullish but firm, hefty yet delicate. Oaky. Good length. Still a bit hard. Sept 1988***(*) Now to 2000.*

CORTON-CHARLEMAGNE *L LATOUR Showing well at the first Latour tasting in London, Oct 1980, with an amazingly nutty aftertaste. Seven years later, at the New York Wine Experience Gala Dinner in New York: a flat yellow-gold colour; maderised nose; out of condition if not actually undrinkable. I thought it was just the bottle on our table but I visited others and all were 'off'. My first reaction was that the wines had been badly stored, but they had been specially flown over. Last tasted Nov 1987 ?*

CORTON-CHARLEMAGNE *LEON VIOLLAND Pale; creamy, vanilla Chardonnay; dry, disarmingly lean and long with twist of lemon. Oct 1985****

MEURSAULT, CLOS DE LA BARRE *LAFON An interesting demonstration of the benefits of late bottling. One, bottled in April 1982: palish lemon yellow; warm, bread-like nose, sweet, slightly caramelly, developed well, a sort of piquant white-currant fruitiness; medium dryness and body, fresh style. Another, bottled in May 1981: deeper colour, more orange; a warm, honeyed bouquet that lay heavily in the glass and, contrary to my expectations, did not develop; yet on the palate, paradoxically, more not less oaky, and with greater power. Tasted at the domaine, Sept 1984*** It will of course be interesting to see whether bottle-age reverses these situations.*

MEURSAULT, CHARMES, HOSPICES, CUVEE ALBERT GRIVAULT *AMANCE Five recent notes, in bottles and magnums. Bright, healthy, lemon yellow; marvellous development of bouquet, initially smoky oaky vanilla with twist of lemon acidity, then a dough-like Chardonnay, and, almost an hour after pouring, a fabulous, warm, biscuity scent, finally crusty bread! On the palate still very youthful, gentlemanly, low-keyed, overall dry, stylish. Last tasted May 1989**** Now to 1999.*

MEURSAULT *CH DE MEURSAULT, DE MOUCHERON Heavenly, perfection in 1984. Then lovely crisp smoky oaky bouquet with slight citrus edge; dry, refined, good classic flavour, acidity and aftertaste. Feb 1986***** Now to 1996.*

THE FOLLOWING WERE ALL NOTED AT THE BIZE-LEROY MEURSAULT TASTING, SEPT 1988:

CHARMES, RESERVE PERSONNELLE *Pure gold; soft, smoky bouquet; surprisingly dry, austere but full-flavoured and very good acidity****

GENEVRIERES *Palish; lovely, flowery, fresh as a sea breeze; dry, very oaky vanilla taste, long lean and still youthful, with trace of almonds****

GENEVRIERES, HOSPICES, PHILIPPE LE BON *Yellow gold; very meaty, agreeable, fulsome; dryish, fairly full-bodied, good acidity****

LES NARVAUX *Yellow; very pronounced bouquet, fruity, violets; dry, full-bodied, stern, a bit blunt**(*)*

PERRIERES, RESERVE PERSONNELLE *Warm yellow gold; sweet, buttery, Pinot-like, vanilla; dry, fullish, austere**(**)*

PULIGNY-MONTRACHET, COMBETTES *LEFLAIVE Very pale, green-tinged; lean, twist of lemon; misleadingly light, the flavour expanding in the mouth, clean, lovely. Oct 1985**** Now to 1996.*

PULIGNY-MONTRACHET, COMBETTES *SAUZET Four notes, first in June 1981, deep, complex but a bit clumsy. Some months later fragrant but still lacking some element. Disappointing in 1982. Three years later, taking on colour; dough-like nose; some softness, vanilla and oak. Last tasted Oct 1985***

PULIGNY-MONTRACHET, PUCELLES *LEFLAIVE Three notes. An out-Chardonnaying Chardonnay, honeyed with glorious flavour, steely firmness and crisp acidity in the spring of 1985. Now a distinctive shade of yellow, having lost its youthful green tinge; waxy, honeyed, buttery vanilla, slightly smoky, spicy, developing fabulously in the glass; dry, fullish, firm, crisp, length, acidity and nutty aftertaste. Last tasted March 1990**** Lovely now, will keep.*

SOME OTHER '79s TASTED ONLY IN THE EARLY 1980s:

BATARD-MONTRACHET *BLAIN-GAGNARD Soft, rich, lovely*****

BATARD-MONTRACHET *L LATOUR Lovely, toasty; full-flavoured*****

BATARD-MONTRACHET *E SAUZET Broad style, needed crisping up but otherwise creamy, oaky, its bouquet after time in glass was like the skin of rice pudding. Good aftertaste. Several notes****

CHASSAGNE-MONTRACHET *LAGUICHE Great length but austere. ?*

CHASSAGNE-MONTRACHET *MALTROYE Dry, straightforward. As always, needing bottle-age**(*)*

CHASSAGNE-MONTRACHET, BOUDRIOTTE *GAGNARD-DELAGRANGE Four notes, fragrant, flavoury but not as good as his '78s.*

CHASSAGNE-MONTRACHET, RUCHOTTES *BACHELET-RAMONET Chablis-like, piercing acidity***

CHEVALIER-MONTRACHET *LEFLAIVE Delicate, subtle bouquet and flavour, good length***(*)*

NUITS-ST-GEORGES, CLOS DE L'ARLOT *BELIN*

*Buttery colour; good waxy nose; firm but fleshy, lemon vanilla acidity****

CHABLIS

Enormous variations in style and quality. As most should be consumed young, there is little point in a roll-call of notes. The few I have liked best include: Les Clos R DAUVISSAT and J MOREAU, Mont de Mileu SIMONET FEBRE, Montée de Tonnerre J FORGEOT, Les Preuses J FORGEOT, Vaudésir J DROUHIN

1980★★

Not brilliant, not bad, although acidity uppermost. Chablis, as so frequently, is the odd man out weather-wise. The district suffered a particularly cold and wet June and July, the flowering lasting five weeks instead of two. Aug and Sept, though not bad, lacking the warmer temperature of the Côte de Nuits, roughly 100 miles to the south. Few 1980s now seen and few tasted recently. All should be drunk soon.

Le MONTRACHET *LAGUICHE Alcoholic content 12.9% by volume, total acidity 4.1. Medium-pale yellow, slightly watery rim; fragrant, mint leaf and vanilla, continued fragrantly, becoming sweeter, with touch of oak, after an hour in the glass soft, very sweet, vanilla; medium dry, medium-full body, pleasant positive flavour, good length and acidity. At Drouhin's, Oct 1990**** *Drink now to 1995.*

Le MONTRACHET *DOM JACQUES PRIEUR Nose quite rich, fragrant, but peach kernelly; distinct sweetness, quite good flavour but short. Sept 1989*** *Drink soon.*

BEAUNE, CLOS DES MOUCHES *Alcohol 12.6%, acidity 4.3. Medium-pale; first impression, sweet, oaky vanilla, spicy, acidic, interesting though slightly green, later a smoky oaky character coming through, finally, at the end of the tasting, 80 minutes later, fragrance and acidity; on the palate, dry, medium weight, crisp, flavoury with rather pasty acidity on the finish. At Drouhin's, Oct 1990*** *Drink soon. Improvement unlikely.*

CHASSAGNE-MONTRACHET *A MOREY Two fairly recent notes. Pale; slightly sweet, vanillin nose; medium dry, chaptalised, giving it a sort of thickness and weight, oaky in 1987. Exactly two years later, similar description. A fairly decent mouthful. Last tasted Jan 1989*** *Needs drinking.*

MEURSAULT *GUY ROULLOT Yellow; buttery vanilla nose; quite nice. March 1988***

1981★

Mediocre. Frosts in the Yonne reduced the Chablis crop by roughly 30%.

Le MONTRACHET *LAGUICHE Strength 12.4%, the lowest of the decade, total acidity 4.3, the highest. Palish appearance, weak watery rim; nose woody and unclean, the final sniff 'green'; dry, lean, weak and woody. Might have been the bottle but clearly a poor wine. At Drouhin's, Oct 1988. Avoid. If you have any, drink up.*

BATARD-MONTRACHET *LEFLAIVE Magnum: pale; light oaky nose that developed quite well. Flavour to match. Slightly scented. Lemon-edged acidity. Feb 1989** *Drink up.*

BEAUNE, CLOS DES MOUCHES *Alcohol 12.7%, acidity 4.3. Palish, slightly green-tinged; initial impression of a 'hot', 'blown' nose with touch of caramel and vanilla, 30 minutes later not bad, finally a trace of almond kernels; sweet, chaptalised, on palate, fair body, soft, pleasant enough but no future. At Drouhin's, Oct 1988** *Drink up.*

CORTON-CHARLEMAGNE *J DROUHIN Fairly bright, positive yellow; indifferent nose; dry, fairly full and rich, slightly oily and kernelly with nutty acidic finish. Feb 1987** *Drink up.*

MEURSAULT, GENEVRIERES *L LATOUR Palish; no nose, slightly fishy; oaky verging on woody, fairly assertive, good acidity. It improved as it lost its chill and warmed in the glass. Jan 1987** *Drink up.*

MEURSAULT, 1ER CRU *J M GARNIER Bright lemon yellow; quite rich, strong vanilla scent and flavour. Dry, clean, peach kernels on finish. July 1988** *Drink up.*

MUSIGNY BLANC *DE VOGUE Jeroboam. Good, bright, yellow gold; first impression, pineapple and blancmange, vanilla and a faintly sickly smell that cleared becoming baked bread-like; fairly dry, crisp, flavoury, moderate length and aftertaste. Not brilliant but a good '81. At Rodenstock's Wine Weekend dinner, Sept 1987*** *Drink up.*

PULIGNY-MONTRACHET *LEFLAIVE Fairly pale; light, smoky nose and richer smoky flavour. Dry. Lacking length. Aug 1990*** *Drink up.*

SOME OTHER '81s NOTED IN THE EARLY TO MID-1980s:

CHABLIS, BLANCHOTS *LAMBLIN Creamy Chardonnay nose, quite nice but short. Nov 1983**

CHABLIS, FOURCHAUME *LAMBLIN Pineapple and oyster shells, steely, clean. Nov 1983**

CHABLIS, FOURCHAUME *A PIC Similar nose to Lamblin's but a bit woody. I didn't like it. Sept 1986.*

CHABLIS, VALMUR *LONG-DEPAQUIT Green-tinged; dusty, Sauvignon Blanc-like taste and acidity, not bad. 1984***

CHASSAGNE-MONTRACHET *J DROUHIN Surprisingly pleasant, low-keyed and gentlemanly. April 1985****

CHASSAGNE-MONTRACHET *L LATOUR Crisp, good. Oct 1984****

CHASSAGNE-MONTRACHET, CAILLERETS *DELAGRANGE-BACHELET Interesting but not up to his usual standard, packing quite a punch, with fairly high acidity. April 1985***

CORTON-CHARLEMAGNE *L LATOUR Lighter style than usual but with a lovely oaky nose and flavour. Feb 1985****

MEURSAULT, CHARMES *L LATOUR Distinctly yellow; soft, gentle, harmonious bouquet and flavour, with twist of lemon acidity. Oct 1984****

MEURSAULT, CLOS DE LA BARRE *LAFON Bottled Feb 1984, lemon gold; lovely flavour and aftertaste. Oct 1984****

MEURSAULT, PERRIERES *JACQUES PRIEUR Vanilla and lemon; lean, very flavoury, acidic. Feb 1986***

PULIGNY-MONTRACHET *E SAUZET Quite nicely balanced. July 1984***

PULIGNY-MONTRACHET, FOLATIERES *L LATOUR Austere, oaky, good acidity, well made but lacking character. Nov 1984***

1982 ★★ *to* ★★★★

Mixed feelings about this vintage. When they are good they are very, very good; when they are not, they are awful. Basically an attractive vintage. Ripe, flavoury wines. But, lacking a firm backbone of acidity, the majority I suspect being at their best between 1985 and 1988. Louis Latour, in *Decanter* magazine, described his '82s as "a smashing success" and in the same issue another burgundian reported that this vintage was "even more marvellous in Chablis". Regarding the latter, I cannot have been exposed to a wide or good enough range, for "neutral", "clean", "short", "lacking acidity" appear — not a single laudatory description. And a Chablis Montmain served at an annual dinner in Jan 1991 was oily, flabby and tired out. My advice: drink up.

Le MONTRACHET *BOUCHARD PERE A plump-looking yellow gold; fat, buttery, waxy nose, touch of sulphur dioxide at first, but fragrant; medium dry, full-bodied — a hefty 14% or thereabouts. Impressive but lacking zest. Good not great. March 1988**** Drink soon.*

*Le MONTRACHET COMTES LAFON First tasted the second autumn after the vintage: 'warm', crusty nose and flavour, quality of fruit, crisp enough; lovely but lacking ultimate length. More recently, a palish yellow straw gold; glorious bouquet, fully developed, very creamy, almost custardy, the oak coming through, but after 30 minutes sweet, soft, fragrant; medium dry, full, fat, rounded, buttery, oaky flavour, slightly bitter finish. Impressive. Last tasted at the Domaine, Sept 1989**** Now to 2000*

Le MONTRACHET *DRC Surprisingly pale, lemon-tinged pure gold; extraordinary nose, bread — like dough, brown toast, brown sugar and old oak; medium dry, full-bodied, a big nutty spicy wine. At an early DRC trade tasting, Nov 1985**** Should be a fairly voluptuous mouthful. Now to 1998.*

Le MONTRACHET *JACQUES PRIEUR Fairly pale lime yellow; forthcoming, fragrant, sulphur noted, mealy, and after 20 minutes the scent of Italian vanilla ice-cream; between sweet and dry, soft, yet packing quite a punch, lacking acidity yet a certain austerity. At a Rodenstock Wine Weekend dinner, Sept 1990*** 1992–2000*

Le MONTRACHET *LAGUICHE Alcohol 13.5%, acidity 3.8. Fairly pale; slightly oily, high-toned, waxy fruit, pineapple, opening up attractively and, going back to the glass after nearly two hours, still beautifully developed; slightly sweet on the palate; fairly full-bodied but not as hefty as the alcoholic content indicated, intriguing flavour, good length and acidity. At Drouhin's, Oct 1990**** Drink now to 1998.*

BATARD-MONTRACHET *E SAUZET Palish; buttery, waxy bouquet; medium dry, fullish body, richly flavoured, slightly bitter finish. Lunch at Christie's, Oct 1990**** Now to 1998.*

BEAUNE, CLOS DE MOUCHES *J DROUHIN Alcohol 13.3%, acidity 3.9. Palish; sweet, rich, very forthcoming nose, butter, vanilla, and after minutes an extraordinary confection in the glass; fairly full-bodied, positive, yet with a dry, hard finish, trace of peach kernels — a question mark. Despite the exotically rich nose I did not rate it highly. At Drouhin's, Oct 1990**?*

BIENVENUE-BATARD-MONTRACHET *ANDRE RAMONET Pale and delicate appearance; fabulous bouquet, pineapple, after an hour fully opened up, fragrant and harmonious; medium dry, medium-full body, soft yet crisp enough, acidity adequate and quite a good aftertaste, yet seemed to tail off. Sept 1986****? Drink soon?*

CHASSAGNE-MONTRACHET *J DROUHIN Nose a bit muffled at first but opened up nicely; full, dry, soft — it grew on me. Feb 1986****

CHASSAGNE-MONTRACHET *L JADOT Excellent. June 1987*****

CHASSAGNE-MONTRACHET, EMBAZEES *PRIEUR-BONNET Palish; cool, restrained; medium dry, slightly woody, fair acidity. Lacking character. Jan 1989***

CHASSAGNE-MONTRACHET, MORGEOT, TASTEVINE *CH DE MALTROYE Good colour; rich, nutty, slightly kernelly nose and flavour. April 1987*** 1992–98*

CHEVALIER-MONTRACHET *LEFLAIVE Low-keyed, sulphury nose, slow to emerge. Muffled. More positive on the palate but lightish and soft. Not tasted since Sept 1986. Then *** Will it have developed or faded?*

CORTON-CHARLEMAGNE, HOSPICES, CUVEE FRANCOIS DE SALINS *JABOULET-VERCHERRE Fairly deep, yellow, green-tinged; rich, waxy, buttery Chardonnay, with distinct whiff and taste of almond kernels. Moderate length and finish. Jan 1990** Drink up.*

MEURSAULT, BLAGNY *L JADOT Pale; not showing its age. A bit austere. Minor yet overpriced. June 1990** Drink soon.*

MEURSAULT, GENEVRIERES *BOUCHARD PERE Two recent notes. Waxy, yellow, tinged with green; nutty, oaky, vanilla nose; medium-sweet, fullish, rich, oaky — rather like an old-fashioned California Chardonnay — very attractive flavour and aftertaste. Last tasted Sept 1990**** Now to 1996.*

PULIGNY-MONTRACHET, FOLATIERES *L JADOT Palish; good enough nose; a bit lean though with quite a pleasant oaky flavour and reasonable length. March 1988** Now to 1995.*

PULIGNY-MONTRACHET, PERRIERES

A PONNELLE Bright vaseline yellow; variable: waxy, honeyed bottle-age, touch of wood. Unexciting. Last tasted May 1991* Drink up or avoid.

SOME OTHER '82s TASTED IN THE MID-1980s:

AUXEY-DURESSES *LEROY Very attractive when first tasted early in 1985: lovely fruit, flavoury, good length, yet despite an appealing lemon and pineapple nose, really rather ordinary. Still, an inexpensive, pleasing enough wine, clearly best drunk young.* Last tasted Dec 1987**

BATARD-MONTRACHET *L LATOUR A lovely nutty, oaky nose and excellent flavour.* Oct 1983(****) *Alas not tasted since. Doubtless still very good.*

CORTON-CHARLEMAGNE *CHANSON Good flavour, nice acidity.* May 1984***

CORTON-CHARLEMAGNE *J DROUHIN Pale; very fragrant, with a broad, nutty, oaky nose and flavour; lively, with good length and needing more time when last tasted.* Feb 1986**(**)

CORTON-CHARLEMAGNE *L LATOUR Also a cask sample, was very good****

MACON CLISSE *JEAN THEVENET Oaky; most attractive, soft and a delicious drink.* 1985*** *The sort of wine to be drunk at three to five years of age.*

MACON LUGNY, GEVIEVRES *L LATOUR Excellent for its class, also at its peak.* 1985***

OF THE VERY MANY MEURSAULTS TASTED BETWEEN 1983 AND 1986 THE FOLLOWING ALL GOOD:

Clos de la BARRE *LAFON Lemon-tinged Chardonnay, attractive. All Lafon's wines are bottled by hand, unfiltered, two casks a day****

BLAGNY, SOUS LE DOS D'ANE *HENRI CLERC A good yellow tinge; fresh, mouthwatering, vanilla and spice; classic taste — in May 1985, probably at its best between then and 1988.*

CHARMES *LAFON Glorious nose; mouthfilling flavour, lovely cleansing acidity (they leave their wines on the lees, the latter nourishing and cleansing the wine)****

CHARMES *PIERRE MOREY Positive flavour, charred-oak finish, good length****

Clos du CHATEAU *CH DE MEURSAULT An amazing scent; lean but supple****

*CH DE MEURSAULT Made from Perrières and Charmes. Pure Chardonnay; excellent flavour and aftertaste*****

*LAFARGE Bottled in Nov 1983, tasted a year later: soft, supple with nice fruit, but an early developer****

PERRIERES *LAFON Rich, pineapple and oak; fairly dry, soft, rounded****

TASTEVINE *DENIS BOUSSEY A grower new to me: good flavour, spicy and perfect acidity in the spring of 1986****

PULIGNY-MONTRACHET TASTED AND DRUNK IN THE MID-1980s:

CHALUMEAUX *MATROT Soft but mouthfilling.*
CHAMP-CANET *ETIENNE SAUZET Rich and flavoury.*
FOLATIERES *J DROUHIN Soft, rich, very agreeable.*
PUCELLES *J DROUHIN Leaner and lighter in style than the Folatières, with smoky oaky flavour.*
JABOULET VERCHERRE Very poor, cardboardy.

1983★★★★

A vintage of character and quality, the best wines combining high alcoholic content with ripe fruit and good acidity. For me, infinitely more exciting than the '82s.

As always, with white as with red burgundy, big variations in style and quality as the following cross section of notes will — at least partially — demonstrate.

The minor wines, like St-Aubin, Montagny and St-Véran, were richly attractive when young and most have been, or should have been, drunk by now, hence the omission of tasting notes. The best growths of the Côte de Beaune are still magnificent and will keep.

MONTRACHET *LAGUICHE Remarkably high alcoholic content, 14.1% by volume, one degree higher than the big '78, total acidity 3.7, on a par with '86 and '87 but, curiously, fractionally less than the '82. Colour a pretty distinctive yellow; when first poured a deep, rich nose, spicy with a touch of caramel — a heavyweight. After 10 minutes, it opened out fully, positively buttery and, after nearly two hours in the glass, fragrant and spicy; distinctly sweet on the palate, full-bodied and rich. A lovely wine. Beautiful aftertaste. Ready.* At Drouhin's, Oct 1990***** Now to 2000.

BATARD-MONTRACHET *LEFLAIVE Palish yellow gold; a lively, youthful, lemon-vanilla 'lid' covering innate richness; fairly full-bodied, assertive, long life ahead.* With other superlative white burgundies at a Rodenstock wine luncheon at the restaurant Die Ente vom Lehel, Wiesbaden, Oct 1985. Then**(***) Should be superb now to 1998.

BEAUNE, CLOS DES MOUCHES *J DROUHIN The highest degree of alcohol of the decade: 13.7% alcohol, 3.8 acidity. First tasted, a cask sample at Drouhin's opening tasting of '83s in London, April 1984: very pale; low-keyed, crusty nose, with whiff of youthful acetone; dry, oaky flavour that opened out and left a lovely aftertaste. More recently: deeper, now a distinct yellow; nose rather oily, pasty vanilla, at first, but took only 10 minutes to spread its wings, honey, depth; medium dry, its very pleasant flavour and balance masking a high alcoholic content. Quite a bit of fat and a lot of oak on the finish.* Last tasted at Drouhin's, Beaune, Oct 1990**** Now to 2000.

BIENVENUE-BATARD-MONTRACHET *H CLERC Palish, greenish tinge; low-keyed but buttery, supported by good depth of fruit; very good, positive flavour, soft, vanilla, Chardonnay yet with crisp acidity.* At Christie's/Len Evans' tasting in Sydney, April 1985. Then**(**) Should be perfect now.

BIENVENUES*(sic)*-BATARD-MONTRACHET *LEFLAIVE Medium-pale, still green-tinged; gentle, slightly scented; very high strength, about 14%, and certainly more powerful than the eye and nose led one to expect. Rich, beautiful shape in the mouth, sweet, mouthfilling.* At Le Montrachet restaurant in Puligny with Vincent Leflaive and his daughter, Oct 1990****(*) Now to 2000.

CHABLIS, MONT DE MILIEU *A PIC Readers by*

*now will gather that either I am exposed to few Chablis or do not like them. Neither statement is entirely true. I find some too almond kernelly and, latterly, some too Chardonnay-like, others resembling Sauvignon Blanc. I found this wine aged five and a half, flowery, grassy on the nose; dry, with nice crisp fruit, positive and delicious. April 1989*** Drink now.*

CHASSAGNE-MONTRACHET *J DROUHIN Lovely flavour, deft oak. May 1991****

CHASSAGNE-MONTRACHET, BAUDINES *BERNARD MOREY A rarely tasted* ler cru. *Positive yellow; vanilla, touch of malt; distinctly dry, fullish body, firm, rather hard finish. Nov 1990**(*) Possibly needs more bottle-age.*

CHASSAGNE-MONTRACHET, MORGEOT *L JADOT Pineapple husk nose; rather fat, coarse style. Jan 1988***

CHEVALIER-MONTRACHET *LEFLAIVE Medium-pale yellow with waxy gold sheen; harmony and vinosity, refined, with deft touch of oak; medium dry, fullish with a lovely, long, lemony flavour. Great wine. Long life ahead. Dinner at Dom de Chevalier Graves, June 1987***** Now to 2000.*

CORTON-CHARLEMAGNE *L JADOT Very positive yellow; slightly peppery, waxy, minty nose that opened up, like glorious custard! Fairly sweet, very full-bodied, rich, with lovely fruit and vinosity. At Jadot's, Oct 1990***** Now to 2000.*

CORTON-CHARLEMAGNE *L LATOUR A distinctive, luminous grape green; lovely bouquet, toasted coconut and lemon meringue; full, rich, nutty but with very dry finish. Sept 1989****(*) Now to 2000.*

MACON-VILLAGES, CLESSE, CUVEE SPECIALE, BOTRYTIS *THEVENOT-WICART Something of a novelty. Fermented Oct 6 to Nov 17. Six notes. An attractive lemon gold; sweet, clover honey, very distinct* Botrytis *nose, but also a touch of 'green fruit'; medium-sweet, rich, with counterbalancing acidity. Delightful. Last tasted June 1991*** Drink now.*

MEURSAULT, CHARMES, HOSPICES, BAHEZRES DE LANLAY *Of the many '83 Meursaults, this is definitely one of the best. Alas, I did not note the bottler's name. A beautifully pronounced ripe Meursault yellow; glorious nose and flavour, soft vanilla and oak with rich aftertaste. Feb 1990**** Now to 1998.*

MEURSAULT, CHEVALIERES *JEAN-PAUL GAUFFROY Bright buttercup yellow, shot with gold highlights; soft, waxy, toasted coconut and honeycomb. Sweetened in the glass. Like a macaroon. Hefty yet firm and crisp. Good length. Last tasted April 1987***(*) Now to 1998.*

MEURSAULT, CLOS DE BOUCHE CHERES *Excellent colour; rich; lovely wine. Some fat. In a different context I would have taken it for a top Australian Chardonnay. With Armand and Louis Cottin of Labouré Roi in Nuits-St-Georges (Philippe Cottin of Mouton is their brother), Sept 1988**** Drink now.*

MUSIGNY, BLANC *DE VOGUE Very good straw gold colour; at four years of age still youthful, with fresh pineapple scent, but opening up powerfully; medium; certainly not dry, fairly full-bodied, 'warm', chewy, good length and acidity. Sept 1987. Then **(**) Probably at peak now but will keep.*

PULIGNY-MONTRACHET *L JADOT An extraordinary wine. Alcohol an astonishing 14.6%, acidity also high: 4.6. Distinct yellow hue; very rich bouquet — reminded me of Laville-Haut-Brion of a big vintage like '71 or '89. Knockout drops! The sweetness of very ripe grapes and high alcohol, hefty, plump for Puligny — definitely not the steely sort. With André Gagey, Oct 1990***** if you like this style of wine. I do. Drink now to 2000.*

PULIGNY-MONTRACHET, CLAVOILLON *LEFLAIVE Very pale; lovely, toasted but still youthful; distinct '83 sweetness, but not a heavyweight. Lovely flavour and oaky aftertaste. Puligny should be served reasonably chilled. This wasn't. Dec 1986. Then***(*) Probably at peak now.*

PULIGNY-MONTRACHET, FOLATIERES *H CLERC Buttery yellow; oak but an almost Sancerre-like fruit and acidity; medium dry, mouthfilling flavour, good length, crisp. April 1985*****

PULIGNY-MONTRACHET, MOUCHERES *HENRI BOILLOT Slightly stewed nose, oaky flavour, mediocre. March 1988 **

PULIGNY-MONTRACHET, PERRIERES *E SAUZET Very pale, lemon-tinged; scented, oaky bouquet that opened up beautifully in the glass; medium dry, lean, rapier-like, excellent acidity. Oct 1990**** Now to 1998.*

PULIGNY-MONTRACHET, REFERTS *L JADOT Warm rich fragrance; firm, crisp, flavoury, good oak and acidity. July 1987****

SOME OTHER '83s, TASTED MAINLY IN THE MID- TO LATE 1980s:

CHABLIS, CLOS DES HOSPICES *J MOREAU Just one of several Chablis', mostly indifferent to poor, even when young, and flat by the late 1980s. Too old, lacking zest. Feb 1988.*

CHASSAGNE-MONTRACHET *ROPITEAU Slightly oxidised, dry, poor. Sept 1985.*

CHEVALIER-MONTRACHET *L JADOT Oaky and agreeable. Dec 1989****

CORTON-CHARLEMAGNE *BONNEAU DU MARTRAY Bright yellow; fruity, honeyed, opened up nicely. Jan 1987*****

CORTON-CHARLEMAGNE *CHANSON Palish; sulphur and lemon, grassy, piquant; fresh but kernelly flavour. April 1988***

SOME OTHER MEURSAULTS:

FRANCOIS JOBARD Soft, bread-like, neither fruity nor oaky; better flavour than nose, lovely mouthful with quite a powerful, austere finish. 1986(***)*

*BERTRAND DE MONCENY Palish; attractive; rather light style, dry. 1987****

Ch de BLAGNY *L LATOUR Lemon-tinged; crusty, meaty; flavoury but short. 1987.*

CHARMES *DOM CHARLES JOBARD Bottled by Robert Chenevoy, a* négociant *in Meursault: smelly nose, horrid taste. July 1989.*

Les GRANDS CHARRONS *PHILIPPE BOUZEREAU Buttery gold; gloriously rich charred, lanolin bouquet; a powerful wine with high acidity. 1988**(**)*

TILLETS *JAVILLIER A fairly pronounced yellow; intriguing, complex, slightly malty nose; powerful, assertive, good fruit and acidity.* Last tasted in 1986. Then**(**)

1984*

Arguably better for white than red, the unripe grapes if skilfully chaptalised turning into passable if, on occasion, nakedly acidic wines. What is noticeable, going through my notes to make the following cross-section, is the relative success of *négociants'* wines. The big boys probably did a more skilful job than some of the small growers. Also noted were the pleasant enough white burgundies from lesser districts, drunk with varying degrees of satisfaction mainly in 1986 and 1987.

Only the best worth bothering with now. I still have one or two major growers' '84s. They are very drinkable but undistinguished and will not improve with further bottle-age.

Le MONTRACHET *LAGUICHE Alcohol 13.2%, total acidity 4.2, made from healthy but not very ripe grapes, hence the high acidity. Medium-pale; first sniff, boiled sweets, but some sweetness, vanilla and oak. A certain artificiality persisted though it was quite nice after nearly two hours' exposure; dry, medium weight; positive though rather hard, acidic and somewhat raw on the palate, with a curious, scented aftertaste.* At Drouhin's, Oct 1990** Not bad. No great future.

Le MONTRACHET DOM RAMONET *Palish, lemon-tinged gold; crisp, acidic, lemon and oak on the nose, slightly minty, a bit hollow and tinny though not unattractive; dry, soft, a fairly gentle, subtle flavour despite steeliness and acidity.* Towards the beginning of a typical 40-wine dinner tasting at the Rodenstock Wine Weekend at Arlberg, 1988. A hard life!**

BATARD-MONTRACHET *LEFLAIVE Palish, lemon-tinged; served far too cold but the bouquet emerged as it lost its chill in the glass — lovely, vanilla; dry, a bit austere, quite good length. A touch of bitterness.* At a French banquet at the Hilton Hotel, Singapore, Oct 1984*** Fair enough. Drink soon.

BEAUNE, CLOS DES MOUCHES *Alcohol 13.6%, total acidity 3.9, pH 3.34, tartaric acid 0.9, volatile acidity 0.44. A sweet, youthful, pineapple nose; dry, firm, very flavoury. But this was a cask sample. It was the only vintage of the decade not available for tasting in Oct 1990.* At the Drouhin tasting in London, March 1986.

CHABLIS *Oddly enough, I have more even, consistent notes on '84 Chablis than of several other far better vintages. Most were tasted in 1986 and 1987 and "acidic" and "short" recur, whether straight AC,* Ier cru *or* grand cru. All should have been drunk by now.

CHASSAGNE-MONTRACHET *L LATOUR Stewed, lemon, vanilla, mediocre.* March 1991*

CHASSAGNE-MONTRACHET, MORGEOT *GAGNARD-DELAGRANGE Buttercup yellow; lemon and vanilla, quite rich extract, but still rather hard.* Oct 1989** I do not see this improving.

CORTON-CHARLEMAGNE *BOUCHARD PERE A slightly dull straw yellow; ripe, waxy though heavy-handed nose; a rich, oaky, mouthfilling wine with acceptable acidity.* June 1989***

MEURSAULT, CHARMES *L JADOT Quite good nutty, oaky flavour.* Last tasted April 1989**

MEURSAULT, CHARMES *PIERRE MOREY Many notes from 1986. Initially a fairly pale yellow but becoming more stridently yellow; nose lemon-tinged, minty when young, a softer, sweeter, smoky, oaky bouquet developing; distinctly dry, medium weight, a touch of lemon and pineapple when young, then soft fruit, touch of leanness and austerity. Lacking the length bestowed by a better vintage.* Last tasted Aug 1990** Will not improve.

PULIGNY-MONTRACHET *LEFLAIVE Palish; served too cold, nose dumb, some vanilla, gradually opened up; dry, assertive, good length, honeyed endtaste. As usual, Leflaive making the best of a less than good vintage.* At the Chao Zhou Garden, Hong Kong, Oct 1989*** Now to 1994.

PULIGNY-MONTRACHET, FOLATIERES *Deep gold; distinctly fat yet reasonably harmonious, scented vanilla nose. The must had been heated and the wine heavily chaptalised, its rawness due more to immature grapes than overhigh acidity.* With André Gagey, Oct 1990* Drink up.

SOME OTHER '84s TASTED FROM 1987–89:

Corton-Charlemagne CHANSON Corton blanc CHANDON DE BRIAILLES** Meursault J DROUHIN** Meursault L JADOT*** Meursault L LATOUR** Meursault Blagny L LATOUR*** Meursault Chevalières PRIEUR-BRUNET* Meursault Clos Cromin MICHELOT** Puligny-Montrachet L LATOUR** Puligny-Montrachet CHANSON* Puligny-Montrachet, Folatières J DROUHIN***

1985***

A good year. Northerly Chablis suffered cold winter and frost, but the undamaged grapes turned out well. On the Côte de Beaune, flowering was late resulting in a late harvest of healthy grapes.

Le MONTRACHET *CHARTRON & TREBUCHET The distinguishing feature of this partnership's range of white burgundies is — to me — leanness, steeliness, a certain austerity, though the combination of Le Montrachet and 1985 does not exactly bear this out: pale yellow, waxy sheen; nose minty at first, developing a lovely smoky vanilla bouquet, spicy; dry, fairly full-bodied, very oaky flavour, good length, still a bit austere.* July 1990***(*) Needs to prove itself. Drink say 1992–98.

Le MONTRACHET *LAGUICHE Alcohol 13.3%, total acidity 3.4. First noted at the opening Drouhin tasting in London in March 1986. It was very pale; nose unknit, youthful fruit, acetone, pineapple; very oaky flavour and aftertaste. Next tasted at the complete line-up of Montrachets of the 1980 decade, the first bottle being* *embarrassingly poor: woody, lacking fruit. Another was put on the bench, happily better, fragrant nose and lovely flavour. Finally, as if to clinch matters, Robert Drouhin produced yet another bottle for lunch after the tasting. It was superb: a lovely bright positive yellow; delicate, oaky fragrance that lingered in the glass; a distinct touch of sweetness, perfect weight, rich, buttery flavour and pleasing finish. Last noted chez Drouhin, Oct 1990***** Now to 1998.*

Le MONTRACHET *THENARD A jeroboam two autumns after the vintage: still pale; a light, lean, smoky lemon nose that blossomed in the glass, lovely youthful fruit, finally nutty but crisp. Long, very spicy, fairly powerful yet elegant. Sept 1987. Then***(**) Doubtless excellent now to 1998.*

BEAUNE, CLOS DES MOUCHES *J DROUHIN Alcohol 13.3%, total acidity 3.7. First noted at Drouhin's opening tasting in March 1986 and three times since. A mild, pleasant young nose, good fruit, pineapple; dry, very flavoury, oaky, notable length and aftertaste. In 1987, noted the way the flavour swelled in the mouth. Most recently, in rather clinical conditions: medium-pale; initially crisp fruit, oak and twist of lemon on the nose, after 15 minutes developing a lovely, broad, peach-like scent, finally a soft discreet vanilla; the sweetness of good, sound, fruity, ripe grapes noticeable, fairly full-bodied, soft on the palate yet with quite a powerful finish. Needs time. Last tasted Oct 1990***(*) 1992–98*

CHABLIS, 1ER CRU *A PIC Very pale; indifferent nose; dry, light, slightly peach kernelly flavour. A very ordinary wine in a flashy designer bottle. At a Cantonese dinner, Hong Kong, Oct 1989**

CHABLIS, MONT DE MILIEU *A PIC Now owned by Ladoucette of Ch du Nozet. Good colour; very good, rather waxy nose; dry, good body, vinosity, shape, though a trace of the peach kernels that I so dislike. Presumably, because of the very ripe grapes, lacking the expected acidity. Oct 1990***

CHASSAGNE-MONTRACHET:

CHAMPS-GAINS *JEAN-MARC MOREY Good nose and flavour, fairly rich; oaky, touch of bitterness, needs time. March 1989**(*)*

*LOUIS JADOT Palish yellow green; curious nose, somehow artificial; oaky, improved in glass; positive flavour. Jan 1989***

*LEFLAIVE Palish, highly polished, dry, good, complete. July 1989***

MORGEOT *OLIVIER LEFLAIVE Fabulous colour; minty, grassy nose, developing smoke and oak; positive and attractive flavour but sharpness on finish probably due to acidifying. June 1987****

La ROMANEE *PAUL PILLOT Yellow straw, waxy sheen; waxy nose, buttery like a honeyed Australian Chardonnay; rich, fullish, very oaky. Attractive in its way. Nov 1990****

CHEVALIER-MONTRACHET *DOM CHARTRON A highly polished green-tinged yellow; a warm rich open bouquet, touch of grassiness, honeyed; fairly dry, rich yet rather lean, nutty flavour, good acidity. Last tasted Oct 1990***(*) 1992–98*

CHEVALIER-MONTRACHET *L LATOUR Two good notes in the autumn of 1987: pale; an excellent toasty nose; very good oaky flavour, elegant and, I thought, a good future. But when last tasted the nose was decidedly coy, admittedly served too cold, a common fault, eventually developing a sweet, malty character; fairly dry, good flavour but somehow lacking zest. Last noted Sept 1989** Now to 1995.*

CORTON-CHARLEMAGNE *L JADOT Magnums: distinct yellow hue; lovely nose, nutty; fairly dry, fullish body, very attractive mouthfilling flavour, good length. Jan 1989***(*) Now to 1998.*

A CROSS-SECTION OF THE MANY MEURSAULTS TASTED IN 1989 AND 1990:

*LABOURE-ROI Two notes, dry, fragrant, unspectacular***

BLAGNY, LA GENNELOTTE *MARASLAVAC-TREMAU Curious, bread-like nose, lacking character and definition; dry, austere*(*)*

CASSE-TETES *R THEVENIN Dry, raw, flat.*

CHARMES *OLIVIER LEFLAIVE Rather pale; lovely, crisp nose and taste; dry, delicious*****

CHARMES *R MONNIER Not quite right, some oak, fair acidity***

GENEVRIERES *LEROY Long, lean, pineapple nose; very flowery, attractive considerable length, nutty finish***(*)*

Les NARVAUX *LEROY Spicy; dry, full, very austere, assertive, needs time*(***)*

Les ORMEAU *BOYER-MARTENOT Dry, clean, vanilla aftertaste****

MUSIGNY BLANC *DE VOGUE Jeroboam. Very pale, lime-tinged yellow; lightly scented crisp nose that opened up, with traces of cumin (aniseed) and vanilla. It blossomed beautifully after 20 minutes in the glass and after an hour displayed a lovely, open, waxy bouquet; fairly dry, nice weight, subtle flavour, crisp, delicately balanced. Who else would serve it in jeroboams but Hardy Rodenstock? At the Arlberg Hospiz, Sept 1990***(*) Now to 1998.*

A SELECTION OF THOSE PULIGNY-MONTRACHETS TASTED IN 1989 AND 1990:

*CHANSON Raw, unknit; lean, lightish, short**

*L JADOT Good, positive, oaky, crisp.****

*R MONNIER A bit lacking**

*PROSPER MAUFOUX Quite good***

FOLATIERES *J DROUHIN Nutty, very fragrant; distinctly dry, nice weight, steely**(*)*

FOLATIERES L JADOT Jadot own one-third of a hectare of Les Folatières' east-facing vineyard, soil light and stony with calcareous subsoil. The grapes were picked early Oct, the juice remaining one day on its lees, fermented in 20% new oak then 14 months in small barriques, *fined with skimmed milk. The result, when first tasted in 1988: a pale but pure yellow gold; rich oaky, smoky, buttery Chardonnay nose; dry, powerful, firm, needing bottle-age. In 1989 fragrant, oaky bouquet evolving in the glass, positive, attractive, still a bit raw. Last tasted June 1989**(**) Say 1992–98? Hard to predict.*

REFERTS *L JADOT Good****

REUCHAUX *ROGER VERGE Dry, lean, clean, acidic.*
TRUFFIERE *L LATOUR Glorious nose, delicious, rounded and mouthfilling*****

Clos Blanc de VOUGEOT *L'HERITIER-GUYOT The colour of a ripe Australian Chardonnay; most unusual nose, very distinctive, waxy, touch of vanilla; medium dry, a distinct heavyweight in body and style. Good length and acidity. Tasted only once, in April 1987. Then**(**) Should be drinking well now to say 1998.*

SOME OTHER '85s SHOWING PROMISE, WHEN TASTED IN 1987 AND 1988:

CHASSAGNE-MONTRACHET *OLIVIER LEFLAIVE*
MEURSAULT, 1ER CRU, RES PERSONNELLE *LEROY* and PERRIERES *JADOT*
PULIGNY-MONTRACHET, COMBETTES and FOLATIERES *REMOISSENET*
PULIGNY, FOLATIERES and PUCELLE *CHARTRON & TREBUCHET*

*1986*****

Good, firm, well-structured, crisp, acidic wines. A complete contrast to the soft, ripe, supple '85s. Archetypal Pulignys.

It will be interesting to follow this two-horse race: the '85s have fruit but perhaps lack backbone, the '86s have backbone but are a bit lean. The former might sag with bottle-age, the latter might outlive its fruit and savour. It is this that makes vintage predicting so difficult and the passage of time so fascinating.

The notes that follow are selective examples of wines tasted in 1990, then a string of briefer notes in commune order, demonstrating the variety of styles — and quality — produced by the different growers and merchant *éléveurs*.

A word about Chablis. Chablis is different, or, to re-emphasise a bias, Chablis is too often indifferent. It is a risky, frost-prone area which, over the years, has had more than its fair share of disasters. The '86s were, judging by the large numbers of notes, on the whole quite good, despite the late — early October — harvest. However, I do note the increasing use of oak. For me, Chablis should be dry, clean as a whistle, crossing the palate rapier-like, with a crisp acidic finish. Increasing the oak increases the flavour: buttery, oaky Chablis might well be speciously attractive, but is it classic Chablis?

MONTRACHET *LAGUICHE Alcohol 13.3%, total acidity 3.7. Good colour; low-keyed, vanilla, oaky, very slightly woody nose — like a heavily laden Boeing 747 trying to get into the air — even after an hour, bouquet not very forthcoming, touch of spearmint, muted, hard, needing bottle-age. Medium dry, medium-full body, straightforward, good length, teeth-gripping acidity. Unready. At Drouhin's, Oct 1990*(***)? 1995 to beyond 2000.*

AUXEY-DURESSES *BERNARD BATTAULT Palish; lemony; slightly sweet, medium-light weight and style, vanilla and oak. Feb 1990*** Drink soon.*

BATARD-MONTRACHET *PIERRE MOREY This M Morey used to farm the Lafon estate and is now winemaker for Olivier Leflaive. Palish, slightly green tinge; nutty, oaky, vanilla, youthful pineapple — a lovely Chardonnay ensemble; dry, medium weight, crisp, firm, fragrant. Very much a (Vincent) Leflaive steeliness and style. Good length. Jan 1990***(*) Now to 2000.*

BEAUNE, CLOS DES MOUCHES *J DROUHIN Alcohol 13.5%, acidity 3.9. First tasted in Jan 1988. Hugh Johnson, Colin Anderson and I placed it first in a range of 26* grand cru *and* 1er cru *white burgundies. Deep, oaky, delicious. The following Dec the British Airways Wine Committee flew to Barbados by Concorde to taste again. Though a lovely bright buttery colour, I thought it was a bit* too *oaky on the palate, though attractive. Most recently, in more down-to-earth surroundings: a heavy, assertive, hard and spicy nose, exuding power, mint and 'ivy', still immature; a mouthfiller, with length and fragrant aftertaste. Of the entire range of Mouches* blancs *from 1979 to 1989 I rated '86 highest. Last noted in Drouhin's tasting room, Oct 1990(*****) 1993 to beyond 2000.*

CHABLIS, MONT DE MILIEU *A PIC Good colour; rich, good fruit, vinosity. Touch of almond kernels on nose and palate. Bone dry, crisp, very fragrant, with floral aftertaste. Oct 1990****

CHABLIS, LES PREUSES *DOM DE LA MALADIERE First tasted in Jan 1988, pale; youthful 'green' lemony nose; lean, oaky aftertaste. Next tasted on Concorde, its nose very Sauvignon Blanc-like, a positive flavour, but cruising at 40,000 feet it appeared to deepen slightly in the glass, nose scented, the flavour even more explosively oaky, and more acidic. Two months later, the oak and vanilla taste overcame all else, even spicy sausages! Speciously attractive. Last noted Jan 1989*** for presumptuousness. Drink up.*

A large number of Chablis tasted, mainly in 1988; too many to record, and frankly mostly forgettable, despite the reputation of the vintage:

CHASSAGNE-MONTRACHET, MORGEOT *OLIVIER LEFLAIVE Lemon yellow; very rich nose, lemon curd, acidic pineapple and peach kernels; too dry, good body, positive meaty minty flavour. Nice wine. In the cellars, Oct 1990***(*) Now to 1998.*

CHASSAGNE-MONTRACHET, MORGEOT *JEAN-NOEL GAGNARD Pale; dry, fairly full-bodied, nutty flavour, good length. Dec 1990***(*) Now to 1998.*

CHASSAGNE-MONTRACHET, MORGEOT CLOS CHAPELLE *DUC DE MAGENTA Crisp, scented; firm, still hard. Good acidity. Jadot tasting, June 1991**(**) 1992–2000*

CORTON-CHARLEMAGNE *OLIVIER LEFLAIVE Initially deep, rich, vanilla, kernelly and, after several minutes, explosive, nose-filling — rather liberal use of new oak, and after an hour* *fabulously full rich bouquet; medium dry, full-bodied, powerful yet very fragrant, with refreshing lime-like acidity. A jeroboam at a Rodenstock dinner, Sept 1990***(**) Now to 2000.*

MEURSAULT *J-P GAUFFROY Palish; heavier, dough-like, slightly malty nose with some fruit; medium dry, open, chewy, quite nice. The only '86 at an extensive tasting at Layton's. And sold out, I noticed. April 1990*** Drink soon.*

MEURSAULT *FRANÇOIS JOBARD Well-honed pale yellow; at first a touch of honey and butteriness, it sweetened in the glass, like toasted marshmallows; very positive though not assertive, medium full-bodied, stylish, overall dry, good acidity and oaky finish. I would like to think of this as a typical '86 Meursault, but there are swings either way. Jan 1990*** Now to 1996.*

MEURSAULT, CHARMES *H BOUZEREAU GREURE Very yellow; rich, vanilla, blancmange; fairly full-bodied, waxy oaky flavour, firm, dry, acidic finish. Feb 1990*** Drink soon.*

MEURSAULT, CLOS DU CROMIN *P JAVILLIER Good colour; fresh, touch vanilla; firm, delicious, discreet oak, good length. Feb 1991*****

PERNAND-VERGELESSES *LALEURE-PIOT Lovely colour, yellow gold; rich, spicy nose; medium dry, powerful, assertive, long, good acidity. Feb 1990****

PULIGNY-MONTRACHET *ETIENNE SAUZET Palish nose, neither positive nor interesting; dry, with little character and not much style. Frankly boring after a New Zealand Chardonnay (the '87 Kumeu River). At the bi-annual dinner of the Institute of Masters of Wine, March 1990** Drink soon.*

PULIGNY-MONTRACHET, FOLATIERES *BOUCHARD PERE Youthful, pineappley in 1988. Now full, rich, long, nutty. Last tasted Feb 1991****

PULIGNY-MONTRACHET, FOLATIERES *L JADOT Softer and sweeter than expected. June 1991**** Delicious now.*

PULIGNY-MONTRACHET, PERRIERES *LEFLAIVE Palish, bright; lemon-tinged; not too dry or too full, excellent texture and flavour. Copybook. With Lloyd Flatt at Mosimann's, June 1990**** Now to 1996.*

SOME OTHER '86s TASTED IN 1988 AND 1989:

AUXEY-DURESSES *OLIVIER LEFLAIVE Nicely rounded****

CHABLIS:

*DOM STE CLAIRE Very pale; Sancerre-like; flowery****

1ER CRU *DROUHIN Dry, oaky****

1ER CRU CH DE MALIGNY *DURUP A vineyard replanted in the early 1970s; pale yellow; sulphury and green at first but developed a pleasing honeyed bouquet; dry, fragrant, a 100% malolactic fermentation making it less aggressive****

BEAUROY *LAMBLIN Grassy; mediocre***

Les BUTTEAUX *Good fruit, very pleasant flavour, not too dry, slightly acidic****

Les CLOS *MOREAU Raw and stalky.*

La FORET *VOCORET A surprising waxy yellow; again, almost Sauvignon Blanc-like fruit and acidity, hint of laurel; dry; broad, kernelly flavour, attenuated acidic finish****

FOURCHAUME *HENRI DUPAS Fragrant; pleasant, good acidity****

MONTMAIN *MOREAU Despite sulphur, acetone, stewed nose, a pleasant enough flavour with youthful acidity**

VAUDESIR *J DROUHIN Pleasant enough****

VAUDESIR *MOREAU Grassy with Sauvignon Blanc-like aroma; dry, clean, straightforward****

VAUDEVAY *LAROCHE Mouthfilling, good length and acidity****

CHASSAGNE-MONTRACHET:

*PHILIPPE BOUZEREAU Floral nose; very dry, lean, austere and acidic***

*J DROUHIN Curious style, good in its way, nose developed well****

BOUDRIOTTE *GAGNARD-DELAGRANGE Dry, rounded, classic*****

MALTROIE *FONTAINE-GAGNARD Full, good length, fragrant oaky finish and aftertaste*****

Clos ST-MARC *A RODET Waxy, gooseberry-tinged nose that sweetened in the glass; quite pleasant flavour, finish rather weak***

VIEILLES VIGNES *BERNARD MOREY Pale; distinctive; good length, very pleasant scented flavour; nice quality****

VIGNE BLANCHE *CH DE LA MALTROYE Of Dom A Cournat. Very fragrant, crisp fruit; dry, lean****

LES CHAMPS-GAIN *JEAN GERMAIN Very smelly, grubby, awful. ROPITEAU Not bad, lacking charm** CHARTRON & TREBUCHET Very dry, typically firm and steely*** LAROCHE Crisp***

MORGEOT *BOUCHARD PERE Very attractive, youthful, sweet, oaky nose that developed gloriously, peach-like; full-bodied yet soft, rich with oaky aftertaste**** GAGNARD-DELAGRANGE Dry, fullish but lean. Good acidity*** LABOURE-ROI Fairly deep straw yellow; rich fragrant, spicy nose and flavour*** DOM LAROCHE Rather bread-like and slightly chocolaty on the nose, dry, straightforward, nice acidity****

CHEVALIER-MONTRACHET *BOUCHARD PERE Minty; 'warm', nutty; good length**** DOM CHARTRON Rich honeyed nose; dry, lean, powerful yet elegant, excellent length and acidity*****

CORTON-CHARLEMAGNE *CHARTRON & TREBUCHET Dry, lean with vanilla, oaky cinnamon flavour, good length and acidity, but the oak rather too specious, lacking fat and fruit for long-term*** L A MONTOY Yellow gold; odd, soft nose, not liked**

MEURSAULTS

*Of the very many tasted, those that stood out were: VIRELY-ROUGEOT**** THEVENOT-MACHAL**** BOYER-MARTENOT**** J P GAUFFROY**** CHARTRON & TREBUCHET Good but not oaky*** LABOURE-ROI****

CHARMES *DOM ROUGEOT Lovely. B VIRELY****

CHEVALIERES *GAUFFROY*** CHARLES JOBARD** R MONNIER Speciously spicy and oaky***

GENEVRIERES *BOUCHARD PERE Three notes, rather*

*raw fruit, assertive, unenthusiastic***
PERRIERES *BOYER-MARTENOT***** *J DROUHIN****
PORUSOTS *DOM GAUFFROY*****

PULIGNY-MONTRACHET:

*CHARTRON & TREBUCHET Walnut nose, long oaky flavour****
*ANTONIN RODET Very flavoury, attractive, fragrant aftertaste****
CHARMES *THEVENOT-MACHAL Honeyed; lovely*****
FOLATIERES *DROUHIN Elegant, lean, steely, rapier-like acidity***** *L JADOT**** *A RODET**** *DOM CHARTRON Hard***
Clos de la MOUCHERE *BOILLOT Hard, acidic**
Clos de la PUCELLE *DOM CHARTRON Hard, acidic**
Ch de PULIGNY-MONTRACHET *Oaky, spicy****
Les REFERTS *BOUCHARD PERE Soft, slightly chocolaty*** *A complete contrast to CHARTRON & TREBUCHET Very dry, oaky, spicy, acidic***(*)
REUCHAUX *LOUIS MAX Uninteresting** *ROLAND THEVENIN Austere***
TRUFFIERE *L LATOUR Yellow gold, opened up nicely***
Clos du VIEUX CHATEAU *LABOURE-ROI Assertive, oaky****

1987★★★

Quite attractive, useful vintage. Already well developed.

Le MONTRACHET *LAGUICHE Alcohol 13.4%, acidity 3.7 — surprisingly similar to the '86. Medium yellow, lightly tinged with gold; ginger, pineapple, good vinosity, quickly opening up, a lovely subtle, tea-like scent; medium dry, mouthfilling, rounded, quite good end acidity, perhaps lacking length. At Drouhin's, Oct 1990**** *Drink soon, say 1992–97.*

BEAUNE, CLOS DES MOUCHES *J DROUHIN Alcohol 13.6%, total acidity 4.1. First tasted in Aug 1989: palish yellow; light fruit and oak; served too cold it appeared to be distinctly dry and firm, but as it warmed up so the flavour evolved. Most recently, in Drouhin's tasting room, it appeared to have taken on more yellow, but perhaps this was just in the context of the other vintages; nose initially all vanilla and spice, very good fruit emerging; medium dry, medium full-bodied, nicely balanced, rounded, delicious. Last tasted Oct 1990**** *Now to 1997.*
CHABLIS, GRAND CRU *DOM MALADIERE Fresh, appealing, touch of spice and pineapple; firm, assertive, oaky flavour, good length, lean, lively and refreshing. Almost too rich and oaky, but very attractive. From May 1989 to Oct 1990****
CHABLIS, 1ER CRU, MONT DE MILIEU *A PIC Harvested mid-Oct in the rain, soft, kernelly. Oct 1990**

OTHER CHABLIS TASTED 1988–89:

BEAUROY *LAMBLIN Clean, a bit short***
BLANCHOTS *LAROCHE Sauvignon Blanc sort of rawness on the nose, but softness on palate***
BOUGROS *COLOMBIERES High-toned, a bit appley, good length****
CHABLIS *JEAN DURUP Very pale; delicious, dry, full of fruit****
CHABLIS *ROLAND THEVENIN Stewed, nondescript nose; very dry, ordinary flavour, acidic**
CHABLIS GRAND CRU *LOUIS LATOUR Stewed, soapy and expensive.*
Les CLOS *LAROCHE Bright, touch of pale gold; vanilla and lemon, nose that developed beautifully; very dry, trace of honey and wax, good acidity masked by fruit****
Les CLOS *MOREAU Raw nose, not bad flavour***
FOURCHAUME *DOM DU COLOMBIER Rich, acidic***
FOURCHAUME *HENRI DUPAS Quite attractive, tailed off a bit***
Les PREUSES *HENRI DUPAS Grassy, hollow nose; dry, long but mean and very acidic.*
VAILLONS *LAROCHE Very dry, little to it**
VALMUR *MOREAU Very fragrant, forthcoming, acidic nose, but on the palate light and little to it***
VAU DE VAY *(sic) MOREAU Peachy, scented; positive flavour, minty, slightly 'green' and with kernelly endtaste. Lacking length**
VAUDEVAY *LAROCHE Positive, fresh, oaky***

CHASSAGNE-MONTRACHET *FONTAINE-GAGNARD, DOM RICHARD Toasted, fruity nose; very powerful, assertive, lacking elegance, needs time. April 1990***(*)
CHASSAGNE-MONTRACHET *OLIVIER LEFLAIVE Fragrant, spicy but a bit hollow and yeasty when first tasted in Sept 1988, but with pleasant oaky flavour when last tasted. May 1990****
CHASSAGNE-MONTRACHET *CHARLES MONCAUT Minty, fruity; straightforward. June 1989***
CHASSAGNE-MONTRACHET, BOUDRIOTTE *GAGNARD DELAGRANGE Minty, refined oak and fruit; dry, good flavour and length, elegant, fragrant aftertaste. Oct 1990****
CHASSAGNE-MONTRACHET, MORGEOT *OLIVIER LEFLAIVE Very positive flavour, slightly 'hot' acidic finish, quite nice. Oct 1990***
CHASSAGNE-MONTRACHET, MORGEOT, CLOS CHAPELLE *DUC DE MAGENTA Fully evolved; broad, open, acidic. June 1991***
CHASSAGNE-MONTRACHET CHAMPS-GAIN *ROPITEAU Assertive yet neutral flavour, very dry and not very clean finish. June 1989*
CHEVALIER-MONTRACHET *CHARTRON & TREBUCHET High-toned, fruit-salad nose; powerful, assertive, masculine, mouthfilling, hot acid finish. Sept 1989***(*)
CHEVALIER-MONTRACHET, FOLATIERES *J DROUHIN Yellow gold; lovely nose, soft, waxy, fruit and oak; dry, medium-full body, some steeliness, classic flavour. Consistently good. Last tasted July 1990*****
MEURSAULT *BOYER-MARTENOT Several consistently good notes: lovely, star-bright, rich but pale gold; flowery, attractive, touch of honeycomb, developing well in the glass; dry, medium full-bodied, teeth-gripping acidity, good length. Last tasted Nov 1990****
MEURSAULT, BLAGNY, 1ER CRU *Pale smoky*

*nose that opened up gloriously; dry, very flavoury but still hard. June 1990**(*)*

MEURSAULT, PORUSOTS *J-P GAUFFROY Yellow; flowery, spicy — rather strangely individual mint-leaf nose, flavour and aftertaste. Full and rich. Last tasted Oct 1990****

MEURSAULT, PERRIERIES *Y-B MARTENOT Very attractive, mouthfilling, spicy oak. March 1990****

PULIGNY-MONTRACHET *CHANSON 'Green', fragrant; pleasant, a bit lean and short. Jan 1989***

PULIGNY-MONTRACHET *L JADOT Long on its lees, resulting in gloriously rich, rather powdery scent; medium dry, very agreeable, slightly appley flavour, fair length. Oct 1990****

PULIGNY-MONTRACHET *CHARLES MONCAUT Scented, grapey; dry, firm, steely — finish a bit yeasty. June 1989***

OTHER MEURSAULTS TASTED IN 1988–89:

CASSES-TETES *LABOURE-ROI Aroma of apples and tom-cats; strange flavour. Jan 1989.*

CHARMES *CHARTRON & TREBUCHET Four* barriques *from the same grower, Tronçais oak, good colour; low-keyed, slightly honeyed nutty nose; dry, warm, nutty, oaky flavour. Sept 1989**(**)*

CHEVALIERES *LABOURE-ROI Beautiful, gentle, fragrant, oaky bouquet; fairly dry, full-bodied, rich, elegant, firm oaky flavour. June 1989*****

GENEVRIERES *BOUCHARD PERE Rich, scented, youthful pineapple nose; good acidity, still unknit, needing further maturation. Oct 1988*(**)*

PORUSOTS *RENE MANUEL Yellow; dry, clean, nice texture, teeth-gripping acidity. Sept 1988**(*)*

*R MONNIER Stewed nose but quite good oaky flavour. June 1989***

*ROPITEAU Attractive vanilla, oak, fruit nose; lovely flavour, enough fruit to balance the excellent oaky flavour. June 1989****

1988***

Basically very nice wines, ripe and fresh, with good balance of fruit and acidity. But yields were high, sometimes excessive, due to unusually big bunches and berries. This inevitably resulted in lack of concentration.

I have tasted a wide range at several trade tastings in London, some in Burgundy. For me the most illustrative was at a Bin Club tasting in Gloucestershire in March 1991 of 30 *1er* and *grand cru* Côte de Beaune.

Le MONTRACHET *DRC Palish yellow; rich, rounded, dough-like nose, with fruit, touch of youthful pineapple and vanilla underlay; distinctly sweet, fairly full-bodied, flesh, good fruit and acidity. Already an attractive mouthful but will develop. At the Domaine, Oct 1990***(*) 1992–98*

Le MONTRACHET *LAGUICHE Palish, slightly green tinge; intense oak, fruit and vanilla, expansively lovely after 10 minutes in the glass, and sitting in the glass perfectly after an hour; dry, medium weight, light style, very fragrant, good length, lovely aftertaste. March 1991***(*) Now to 1998.*

BATARD-MONTRACHET:

BOUCHARD PERE Light, rather indifferent nose; dry, very oaky but unconvincing. March 1990(*)?*

LIONEL BRUCK Very pale; malty, almond kernel nose and flavour. Expensive and poor. March 1991.

*L LATOUR Lovely, warm, crusty, rich, fragrant bouquet; dry, fragrant and fruity flavour and nutty aftertaste. March 1991**(**)*

LEFLAIVE Palish, touch of carbon dioxide; low-keyed; sweet, quite a big wine on the palate, rich but adolescent. Oct 1990(**)?*

BEAUNE, CLOS DES MOUCHES *Alcohol 13.6%, total acidity 4.0. Pale; immature pineapple aroma, good fruit though, relatively low-keyed, some oak; medium dry, soft, pleasant acidity. Needs time but not overly impressive. At Drouhin's, Oct 1990(***)? Say 1992–97.*

CHABLIS TASTED BETWEEN DEC 1989 AND OCT 1990:

*LABOURE-ROI Oaky, fragrant; nice if somewhat artificial flavour, curious dry finish, but inexpensive***

1ER CRU *J DROUHIN Frankly horrible.*

1ER CRU *LABOURE-ROI Sweet, slightly honeyed, crusty bread, cinnamon nose; dry, clean, scented flavour, crisp, acidic****

COTE DE LECHET *DOM A JANNET Pale, fruity, crusty; dry, rather dull — cardboard and acid.*

MONT DE MILIEU *A PIC Grapes picked early Oct. No wood used. Very pale; rather appley fruit and youthful pineapple; very dry, very acidic, strong almond kernel taste.*

VAILLONS *LAROCHE Vanilla, touch of acetone; dry, neutral, hard*(*)*

VAUDEVAY *LAROCHE High-toned, rather artificial; dryish, somewhat neutral, acidity adequate**(*)*

CHASSAGNE-MONTRACHET, BOUDRIOTTE *GAGNARD-DELAGRANGE Pale, slightly green tinge; low-keyed youthful Chardonnay, vanilla, aniseed developing fragrantly in the glass; fairly dry, fullish body, lovely classic flavour and length. Firm, still a bit hard, good acidity. Last tasted June 1991**(**)*

OTHER CHASSAGNE-MONTRACHETS TASTED 1990:

*CHARTRON & TREBUCHET Dry, assertive — even aggressive, hard. Needs time****

*OLIVIER LEFLAIVE Pale, lime-tinged; very scented, oaky, spicy, vanilla; medium dry, full-bodied, very positive, lovely flavour, crisp dry finish**(**)*

La MALTROYE *RICHARD FONTAINE-GAGNARD Very bright yellow-green; open, scented, fruit and oak; medium dry, full-bodied, lovely rich oaky flavour, good length and finish**(**)*

MORGEOT *L LATOUR Light, slightly nutty vanilla; dry, fullish, firm, good acidity**(*)*

CHEVALIER-MONTRACHET *BOUCHARD PERE Good nose, slightly minty, depth; medium dry, mouthfilling, nice richness, balance, oak, length. Oct 1990***(*) Now to 1998.*

CORTON-CHARLEMAGNE *BOUCHARD PERE Rich, kernelly nose; dry, full-bodied, firm, good acidity. Rather austere. March 1991**(**)*

CORTON-CHARLEMAGNE *L BRUCK Stewed nose; almond kernel taste. March 1991.*

CORTON-CHARLEMAGNE *LABOURE-ROI Clean, quite good nose; dry, oaky, slightly woody. March 1991*(**)*

CORTON-CHARLEMAGNE *L LATOUR Pale; lovely, nutty, scented, vanilla, new oak nose; dry, fullish, soft yet spicy with good acidity. Last tasted March 1991***(**)*

MEURSAULT:

*BOYER-MARTENOT Palish, star-bright; dancingly fragrant, crisp, spicy cloves and fruit; medium dry, medium-full body, very flavoury, nutty, oaky, and bit austere. Last tasted March 1991***(*)*

*J DROUHIN Pale; youthful, fragrant pears, pineapple; lovely fruit and acidity. Sept 1990**(*)*

*CH DE MEURSAULT Open, bread-like scent; dry, mild, youthful pineapple, fragrant. March 1991**(*)*

BLAGNY *CH DE BLAGNY (L LATOUR) Very pale; fragrant, unknit; dry, slightly appley flavour, light, oaky, vanilla. March 1991*(**)*

CHARMES *BOUCHARD PERE Very pale; broad, fruity, cress and mint; medium dry, very flavoury and fragrant. March 1991***(*)*

CHARMES *L LATOUR Very pale; fragrant, scented but as yet unknit; pleasant youthfulness, quite powerful, time will tell. March 1991*(**)?*

CHEVALIERES *Y CLERGET Four notes. Dumb but clean and correct in Jan 1990. On palate, dry, assertive, good acidity. Last tasted June 1991**(*)*

Clos des CORVEES, DE CITEAUX *BOUCHARD PERE Pale; little nose; dryish, fullish, assertive, slightly bitter finish. Oct 1990*(**)?*

GENEVRIERES *BALLOT-MILLOT Pale; crusty bread and peach kernels; very dry, austere. March 1991(**)*

GENEVRIERES *BOUCHARD PERE Slightly variable notes; more forthcoming in Oct 1990 but a bit closed in Feb and March 1991, restrained nose, trace of walnuts; fairly dry, oaky, one bottle verging on woody, four-square. Last tasted March 1991*(**)?*

GENEVRIERES *L LATOUR Pale; light; dryish, good flavour and length. March 1991****

GENEVRIERES *MICHELOT-BUISSON Very pale; old socks; mediocre. March 1991.*

GENEVRIERES, HOSPICES, CUVÉE BAUDOT *F PROTHEAU Superb; fragrant, lovely. March 1991***(**)*

GOUTTE D'OR *L MAX Attractive, nutty; excellent flavour, weight, balance. March 1991***(*)*

PERRIERES *BOYER-MARTENOT Fragrant, immature, slight acetone; medium dry, full-bodied, lovely rich flavour, good length, teeth-gripping acidity. Oct 1990*(***)*

PERRIERES *J DROUHIN Disappointing: stewed nose; dry, slightly woody, lacking length. March 1991?*

PORUZOT *RENE MANUEL Good vinosity, fragrant, oaky, depth; nutty, very fragrant flavour and aftertaste. March 1991**(**)*

PORUZOTS *(sic) J P GAUFFROY Nice depth of fruit and oak, lightly honeyed; aggressively dry, assertive flavour, good length, acidity, hard. Needs time. Oct 1990*(**)*

PULIGNY-MONTRACHET:

L JADOT Bottled March 1990. Pleasant, open, vanilla; dry, fullish, rather hard, steely, aggressive. Oct 1990(**)*

LEFLAIVE Picked Sept 27: pale; spearmint, grapey, pineapple; fullish, soft yet firm, touch of peach stones. Oct 1990(**)*

COMBETTES *JACQUES PRIEUR Nice fruit; a bit lacking. March 1991***

Clos de la GARENNE *J DROUHIN Pale; lovely, fragrant nose; dry, crisp, lean, oaky, delicious. March 1991***(*)*

FOLATIERES *BOUCHARD PERE Low-keyed; dry, firm, steely. Oct 1990*(*)*

FOLATIERES *L LATOUR Palish, honeyed fruit, good depth, hint of walnuts; dry, steely, fragrant. March 1991**(*)*

FOLATIERES *THEVENOT-MACHAL Good colour; low-keyed, hint of vanilla, unyielding; dry, full, assertive yet lacks follow through, austere. Oct 1990*(**)*

PUCELLES *BOUCHARD PERE Pale; indifferent nose; rather ordinary. March 1991***

PUCELLES *LEFLAIVE Very pale, fragrant, spearmint; slightly sweet, medium body, good flavour, very fruity, nice acidity. Oct 1990***(*)*

Clos du VIEUX CHATEAU *MAROSLAVAC Better flavour than nose; full-bodied, good acidity. March 1991*(**)*

1989*****

An immediately attractive vintage following good growing conditions and an early harvest of healthy, ripe grapes. The flowering, though early, was long, taking one month (one week in 1988). Aug very dry, with enough rain at the end of the month to swell the grapes just sufficiently. Early Sept warm. Small, concentrated berries, picked from the 15th. The only thing to look out for is the level of acidity. Undoubtedly agreeable wines, the lesser growths, the Mâconnais and Chablis for early drinking, the middle- to good-class wines best whilst still full of beguiling fruit, between say four to six years after the vintage. Don't worry too much about the softness and ripeness, the big guns have the fruit, extract and alcohol for a fairly long life.

A limited number tasted, mainly from cask samples shown to the trade in London in the early autumn, and from the cask in Burgundy mid-Oct 1990. But sufficient to give me at least an idea of the style and quality. Clearly wines of charm and elegance.

Le MONTRACHET *DRC The scale of production, and the price, can be readily understood when one visits the cellar: 10 small* barriques *of nectar. 12 months after vintaging: colour a distinctive lime yellow; no holding back: equally distinctive waxy, spicy,* *vanilla and oak that opened up fabulously with a scent of fresh ground coffee; touch of sweetness, fairly full-bodied, lovely fragrance and acidity. Clearly going to be a beauty.* Tasted from the cask, Oct 1990(*****) Say 1995–2010.

Le MONTRACHET *LAGUICHE Good colour; lovely, fragrant nose, vanilla, oak and fruit, medium-sweet, medium-full body, lovely flavour, length and aftertaste.* Cask sample in Drouhin's tasting room, Oct 1990(*****) 1995–2010

Le MONTRACHET *BOUCHARD PERE Lovely, fragrant, oaky nose; medium-sweet, fairly full-bodied, rich, soft, lively, warming with oaky finish.* Last tasted from the cask, Oct 1990(*****) 1995–2005

BATARD-MONTRACHET *L LATOUR Sweet, nutty, oaky and spicy nose of great depth; dry, full-bodied, powerful, great length.* Cask sample, Oct 1990(*****) 1995–2010

BATARD-MONTRACHET *DOM LEFLAIVE Medium-pale; low-keyed fruit and oak; medium dry, full-bodied, rich, dry finish, fragrant aftertaste. Racked July 9.* Tasted from the cask, Oct 1990(*****) 1995–2010

BATARD-MONTRACHET *OLIVIER LEFLAIVE Just six* barriques. *Rich entry, mouthfilling flavour of pineapple and vanilla, firm, dry finish, good grip.* Tasted from the cask, Oct 1990(*****) 1995–2005?

BEAUNE, CLOS DES MOUCHES *J DROUHIN Cask sample tasted in London mid-Sept 1990: rather muffled nose, slightly sweet, with lovely fruit and oak, forthcoming and lively. A month later, in Beaune, it appeared still to be 'working', with a light, youthful pineapple and vanilla nose, slightly appley. Medium weight and lightish in style, soft mid-palate, oaky.* Last tasted from the cask, Oct 1990. Will doubtless turn out well. Say 1993–98.

CHABLIS, VAU LIGNEAU HAMELIN *THIERRY Unknit, slightly artificial nose, but quite attractive fruit.* May 1991*

CHABLIS, VIEILLES VIGNES *LA CHABLISIENNE Agreeable fruit, dry, straightforward. Perhaps a little too soft. A certain '88 type of austerity suits Chablis better.* Tasted Aug 1990*** Judging by the nature of the vintage, one might expect agreeable fruity wines for drinking early, say now to 1993.

CHASSAGNE-MONTRACHET *CHARTRON & TREBUCHET Soft, youthful aroma, good fruit, deft touch of oak; soft mid-palate but acidic finish.* Oct 1990(***) 1993–96

CHASSAGNE-MONTRACHET, MORGEOT *OLIVIER LEFLAIVE Pale, lime-tinted; very scented aroma of apples, pears and peaches; a ripe wine, scented, fullish, with charm.* From the cask, Oct 1990(****) 1993–96

CHASSAGNE-MONTRACHET, MORGEOT, CLOS CHAPELLE *MAGENTA Pale; lovely, lots of oak.* June 1991*(****)

CHEVALIER-MONTRACHET *BOUCHARD PERE Very attractive, spicy, oaky cask sample.* Oct 1990(***)

CHEVALIER-MONTRACHET *LEFLAIVE Slightly minty nose; sweet, fullish, spicy. Due to be fined early Dec and bottled in Feb.* Tasted from the cask, Oct 1990(****) 1993–98

CORTON-CHARLEMAGNE *L LATOUR Slightly more colour than the '88; broad, open, softer nose than the '88, good fruit and vinosity; medium dry, fairly full-bodied, nice fruit, soft, beguiling, with warm oaky aftertaste.* Cask sample in London, Oct 1990(****) 1993–2000

MEURSAULT, CLOS DES CORVEES DE CITEAUX *BOUCHARD PERE Pale; soft, almost peach-like, touch of youthful acetone; medium dryness and weight, soft, easy yet with refreshing acidic finish.* Cask sample tasted, Oct 1990(****) 1993–96

PULIGNY-MONTRACHET, CLOS DU CAILLERET *DOM CHARTRON Very forthcoming, young, appley nose with fragrant fruit and oak; pleasant sweetness and body, soft, rich — almost the antithesis of the lean steely Chartron & Trebuchet Pulignys. A heavier, oakier style. Good aftertaste.* Oct 1989(****) 1993–98

PULIGNY-MONTRACHET, CLAVOILLONS *LEFLAIVE Yellow; full, buttery, ripe pineapple and mandarin nose; sweet, lovely peachy flavour, marked acidity.* From the cask, Oct 1990(*****) 1993–96

PULIGNY-MONTRACHET, PUCELLES *LEFLAIVE Yellow; surprisingly harmonious for its youthfulness, slightly spicy, oaky; sweet, medium weight, rich, subtle flavour, vanilla, pasty end acidity. It was in oak until the end of the malolactic fermentation, April (1990). Then in steel vats.* Tasted from the vat, Oct 1990(****) 1993–98

OTHER PULIGNY-MONTRACHETS, ALL TASTED OCT 1990:

FOLATIERES *BOUCHARD PERE Pale; youthful, fresh, pineapple aroma; slightly sweet, soft, oaky. Still a bit yeasty and unfinished — or might have been the cask sample.*

FOLATIERES *DOM CHARTRON Palish; rich, open, fulsome, rich, oaky, honeyed nose; dry, full-bodied, rather stern, masculine and powerful. Cask sample.*

FOLATIERES *L JADOT Pale; lovely youthful pineapple and Chardonnay aroma, touch of acetone, still on its lees; medium dry, fullish, good length, nutty, rather hard acid finish.*

FOLATIERES *L LATOUR Pale, bright; open, youthful vanilla and fruit nose, some depth; dryish, lean, elegant, nice fruit, attenuated end acidity.*

FOLATIERES *OLIVIER LEFLAIVE Lightly cloudy; medium sweetness and body, rich, even fat, oaky pineapple flavour and good length. Tasted from the cask.*

1990(★★★★)

Possibly — and in the opinion of some respected domaines — a five-star vintage. Growing conditions not dissimilar to those of 1989, mild spring, advanced vegetation, long, uneven flowering, a dry summer followed by rain early Sept. Surprisingly big crop, high in sugar, low in acidity. Net result a fair abundance of soft fruity wines for relatively early consumption. As always, time will tell.

Le MONTRACHET *LAGUICHE Minty, grapey; fairly sweet, powerful. Interesting potential. In Drouhin's cellars, Oct 1990.*

BEAUNE, CLOS DES MOUCHES *DROUHIN Pineapple; sweet, crisp, loads of fruit. In the cellars, Oct 1990.*

CHASSAGNE-MONTRACHET, MORGEOT, CLOS CHAPELLE *MAGENTA Very pale; youthful, pineappley, attractive; medium dry, soft yet full body and flavour, good length and potential. At Jadot tasting, June 1991.*

RHONE

The Rhône can reasonably claim to be the oldest major wine district in France: in Roman times a sort of trunk road to the north. The reds were renowned for their quality and have always had a strong local and Parisian following, though they have been shamelessly abused over the past two centuries, the best red Hermitage being used to add strength and balance to even first-growth claret. Until 1971, when the *Appellation Contrôlée* laws started to take hold, Rhône reds were blended with red burgundy for stylistic and commercial reasons.

Although British wine merchants always listed Rhône wines, they rarely featured individual growers of renown, tending to concentrate on reasonably priced district wines bought from the producers. The real pioneer in England was a dentist, Robin Yapp, who in the late 1960s spotted a gap in the then modestly priced Rhône market for individual growers' wines, in particular Auguste Clape, Robert Jasmin, Gérard Chave, to name just three now illustrious names. There is, however, little doubt that standards have improved since the mid-1950s and, to cap it all, the Rhône has been blessed with three recent wonderful vintages, 1988, 1989 and 1990.

RED

The division of the Rhône into two regions, northern and southern, is not merely a geographical convenience. The styles of wine are different. In the north, the steep 'roasted slopes' of Côte Rôtie, as difficult and expensive to work as Wehlener Sonnenuhr in the Middle Mosel, produce wine that combines explosive power and finesse. Hermitage is elegant, the most Bordeaux-like in weight and style. To the south, a totally different scene, the wide valley and flatter vineyards of Châteauneuf-du-Pape. There, the 'soil' consists of enormous pebbles which act like night storage heaters absorbing the sun's rays during the day and emitting its retained heat at night. No wonder that the wines are full of colour, rich and alcoholic.

The wines of different regions need a different approach. Expect the Rhône reds of the best years to be opaque when young and a deep ruby when maturing, particularly those from the extremities, Côte Rôtie and Châteauneuf. The bouquet of Côte Rôtie and Hermitage tends to be far more distinctive than that of Châteauneuf, partly because only one variety, Syrah, is used. Guigal's Côte Rôtie is packed with fruit, Jaboulet's Hermitage is more suave. But in Châteauneuf up to 13 varieties are used, which, with the heat and the alcohol, tend to 'muddy' the aroma. In my opinion the nose of southern Rhône wines is relatively unimportant, it is the palate that counts: the sweetness of ripe grapes and high alcoholic content, roundness and fleshiness. These are better drunk within say three to six years, whereas further north the finer red Hermitage wines have more finesse and improve with bottle-age. My notes aim to give an idea of the quality of the vintage and the current state of play. Remember, the Rhône is a hot valley and the *vignerons* are blessed with more ripe vintages than most, hence the number of high star ratings.

1825

Lanerthe (*sic*, now Ch de La Nerte) This and the next wine were from an old French cellar near Lyon, unearthed by Sandy McNally who organised and catalogued, effulgently, the annual Heublein wine auctions. According to Livingstone-Learmonth and Master, La Nerte was the first Châteauneuf-du-Pape to be bottled as opposed to being sold and drawn from the cask (this was in 1785). First tasted over a century and a half later in San Francisco. One bottle tart, the other remarkably sound: dry, full, spicy. Two years later: old tawny, healthy but little red; very rich, meaty, slightly oxidised nose; a vestige of sweetness, still some fruit and plenty of body. Edgy acidity, dry finish.
Last tasted at the Heublein pre-sale tasting, New Orleans, May 1981.

1832

Ermitage (*sic*) Same provenance as Lanerthe, above, and all tasted and noted at Heublein pre-sale tastings, the first in May 1977. Five bottles opened in May 1979, levels and condition variable. Another pair two years later: the first bottle had high neck level. Despite the cork dropping in it decanted well, a fabulous colour. Nose sour, though fruit lurking. Better on palate. The second bottle: very good colour for age, old tawny with rosy hue; pretty good nose, a bit varnishy but with fruit; touch of sweetness, clean.
*Both May 1981**

c 1870

Hermitage From a cellar of old wine in Northampton. Contemporary burgundy-shaped bottle, original wax seal. Unlabelled. Very good level despite shrunken cork. Tawny, faintly amber green rim; interesting nose, like Victorian milk punch, spicy, scented, high-toned; slightly resinous, lavender oil taste.
*At a pre-phylloxera wine tasting for the Wine & Food Society at Christie's, April 1986***

1871

Hermitage Surprisingly deep, plummy; singed, chocolaty, deteriorated in the glass; very sweet but with a hard old woody finish.
*Sept 1990**

1929*****

Into the realms of reality. An excellent vintage.
Hermitage *CHAVE* Lovely soft red with mature amber orange edge; sweet old nose, walnuts; touch of sweetness leading to very dry acidic finish. Flavour reminiscent of gnarled old oak, past best but sound.
*At a remarkable tasting of Chave vintages presented by Robin Yapp, the Rhône and Loire wine specialist, at the Garrick Club, March 1984****

1933****

Very good in the northern Rhône.

1934****

Very good in the southern Rhône.

1937****

At their magnificent best, such as Chapoutier's 'Grand Hermitage', in the mid-1950s.
Châteauneuf-du-Pape *ST MARC ET SANDERS, BARSAC* Deep colour; high-toned, citrus, walnuts, spicy, friar's balsam; fairly full-bodied, in very good shape. Seemed to get sweeter.
*Dining at Saling Hall with Hugh Johnson, Aug 1986****

1942***

Hermitage *CHAVE* Lively and lovely; fading a little and a touch of decay; lean, leathery texture, short but sweet. Light dry acid end.
*At the Chave tasting, March 1984****

1943****

Very good in northern Rhône. None tasted since 1973.

1944***

Good in southern Rhône.

1945*****

As elsewhere in Europe, outstanding, particularly in Hermitage. Jaboulet's La Chapelle magnificent in 1973.
Châteauneuf-du-Pape, Tête de Cuvée, Grande Réserve *J VIDAL FLEURY* Richly coloured; sweet, slightly sickly nose; sweet on palate, medium weight, 'warm', singed flavour.
*From a private cellar in Holland, April 1984****
Gigondas *PIERRE AMADIEU* Bottled in Belgium. Strange amber orange colour; sweet, smoky; singed old nose; old but flavoury.
*April 1984**

1947****

Hot vintage. Rich, alcoholic, voluptuous wines. But a period of depression still, particularly in the northern Rhône. Côte Rôtie prices so low they were uneconomical to make.
Châteauneuf-du-Pape *ARMAND ESTABLET, PROPRIETAIRE ET NEGOCIANT A CHATEAUNEUF* Imported by Kjaer & Sommerfeldt, a leading Copenhagen wine merchant. Fine, orange amber rim; sweet, meaty, hefty, ungracious. Probably souped up for the Danish market.
*From the Aalholm Castle cellars, July 1989***
Hermitage, Rochefine *JABOULET-VERCHERRE* Still a lovely ruby red; sweet, touch of raspberry, not showing its age on nose or palate. Mild, perfect weight, charm, condition.
*Chez Alistair Sampson, Aug 1989****

1949*****

Excellent vintage throughout the region.
Hermitage, La Chapelle *P JABOULET AINE* Medium-deep; ripe, rich, mature nose, like a fine burgundy; pleasant sweetness and weight, with warm toasted flavour, perfect balance and condition.
*May 1985******

1952*****

Also excellent.
Hermitage *CHAVE* Palish, very mature; rich, smelling like old fertiliser, tannin still lurking; fairly sweet, soft, rich, lovely.
*March 1984*****

1953****

Exceptionally successful in the northern Rhône. Most of the Rhônes tasted around this vintage were bottled by Harvey's, an exception being a "curious and interesting" Ch Fortia in 1960.
Hermitage, La Chapelle *P JABOULET AINE* Bottled Sept 1954. Immensely impressive, rich and youthful

when first tasted in 1960. More recently, deep, intense, mature rim; corky, woody nose that deteriorated in the glass, fishy. Alas, horrid. A bad bottle, I hope.
Last tasted at Burg Windeck, May 1983.

1955****

Very good vintage, fully mature in the northern and southern Rhône.
Châteauneuf-du-Pape *DOM DE BEAURENARD* A 70-acre vineyard north of Châteauneuf. Extremely fine deep colour; beautiful spicy nose; very rich, impressive, smooth, perhaps lacking length and finish.
*March 1980****

1956

Odd and unimpressive in the early 1960s.

1957****

Very good year. Seemed at best after 10 to 12 years. No recent notes.

1959*****

Excellent vintage, particularly in the northerly vineyards. Masses, mainly Chapoutier's, tasted in the early 1960s. The Hermitage La Chapelle first noted in 1960 was like Mouton '45 in concentration and power.

1960*

A mediocre vintage. Dull even in the early 1960s. Of little interest now.
Côte Rôtie, Les Jumelles *P JABOULET AINE* The 'twins' referred to are the Côtes Brune and Blonde, adjacent hillside vineyards. Fine, rich in 1973. More recently, a lively ruby; some fruit and fragrance but a bit cardboardy; drying out, a bit thin, just a touch of sourness, and short.
At Thornbury Castle, Sept 1982.

1961*****

A superb vintage throughout the Rhône, the Hermitage reputed to be the best of the century, with the '29, Châteauneuf the best after 1945 and only rivalled by the '78.
Côte Rôtie *J VIDAL FLEURY* Established in 1781, the oldest *maison du vin* in the northern Côtes du Rhône. Even after 20 years, opaque; little nose at first but evolved raspberry-like fruit then a tobacco-like scent; dry, massive, unready.
At a Wine and Food Society Miami branch dinner, Feb 1981. Then(***) 1990–2000*
Côtie (*sic*) Rôtie *P JABOULET AINE* London bottled (hence misspelling). Intensely deep, blackcurrant-tinged; very fragrant, like a top-class Pauillac — surely not 'hermitaged' in reverse? Dry, massive, magnificent. Another quarter century of life.
At Hugh Johnson's, Jan 1981(****) 1990 to beyond 2000.*
Hermitage, La Chapelle *P JABOULET AINE* First tasted in 1967: "a lovely strapping mouthful". Still opaque in 1983, sweet, laden with fruit. At nearly 30 years of age, still very deep; mulberry and prunes nose, its rich fleshiness reminding me of the '61 Pétrus or Trotanoy; very sweet on palate, full-bodied, soft, velvety, tarry taste. Magnificent.
*Last tasted at 'Le Montrachet' in New York, Oct 1990***** Now to beyond 2000.*

1962****

A very good year though the quality of the wines was overshadowed by the great '61s.
Hermitage *VIDAL FLEURY* Curious fig-like nose that improved in the glass; fullish, some elegance.
*Feb 1981*** Probably passing its best now.*

1964****

Tannins long-lasting in Hermitage, La Chapelle particularly fine; very good but limited production in Châteauneuf. Many tasted in the late 1960s and early 1970s when most were at their peak.

1966****

Very good year. Peaking around now.
Châteauneuf-de-Gadagne *DOM DE LA CHAPELLE* An old Côtes du Rhône property just to the east of Avignon. Medium-red, very mature; the bouquet of an old burgundy; medium dryness and weight, lovely flavour and texture.
*July 1981*****
Châteauneuf-du-Pape, Les Cèdres, 'La grappe des Papes' *P JABOULET AINE* Deep, rich; a sweetish hefty wine, velvety but powerful. Slightly bitter aftertaste.
*Christmas dinner, Dec 1984****
Côte Rôtie, Les Jumelles *P JABOULET AINE* Fairly deep, fine colour; very rich, high-toned, fascinating — strawberry jam and the smell of the *chai*; seemed to grow sweeter in the glass, excellent flavour and balance.
*March 1980. Then****

1967****

Very good throughout the Rhône, particularly good in Châteauneuf, the latter now thought to be on a par with 1978.
Châteauneuf-du-Pape, Ch Fortia Fairly deep, rich, mature rim; ripe, showing a bit of age; sweet on palate, good flavour but very dry, hard and with acidic finish.
*Aug 1982***
Côte Rôtie, Brune et Blonde *GUIGAL* Good colour; not very distinctive; flavoury. Unimpressed.
*Pre-sale tasting, Chicago, Oct 1983***
Côte Rôtie, Les Jumelles *P JABOULET AINE* Several notes in the early 1980s. Still fairly deep, violet-rimmed; very forthcoming nose; lovely texture, elegant.
*Probably at best when last tasted Dec 1984**** Now doubtless in decline.*
Hermitage *P JABOULET AINE* Fine, deep; mulberry-like richness of fruit on nose and palate. Fairly full, soft.
*Not tasted since Nov 1979. Then****

1968

Poor vintage. None tasted.

1969*** *to* ****

Good to very good in Châteauneuf, better in Hermitage, a small but outstanding crop in Côte Rôtie.
Châteauneuf-du-Pape, Ch de Rayas Massive and magnificent in 1978. Two years later: a stunningly beautiful colour; rich spicy nose; sweet, full-bodied, lovely flavour and finish.
*Not tasted since March 1980. Then**** Should still be lovely.*
Hermitage *CHAVE* Medium-deep, richly coloured; deep, crisp, fragrant nose, rich tannin and fruit foundation; fantastic flavour, lean, spicy, very long dry tannic finish.
*March 1984. Then***(**) Now to beyond 2000.*
Hermitage *GUIGAL* Deep; immensely rich, alcoholic nose; dry, huge, tannic.
*Sept 1986***(**) 1992 to beyond 2000.*

Hermitage *CAVE CO-OP DE VINS FINS* Medium-pale; showing age on nose but soft, long and lovely on palate.
*Sept 1986*** Drink now.*

1970*** *to* *********

Excellent in the south, very good in the north. Only one tasted recently.

Hermitage, La Chapelle *P JABOULET AINE* First noted in Nov 1972: enormous, tough. Most recently in magnums: deep, lovely; fragrant, glorious fruit emerging; dryish, medium full-bodied, very good flavour, texture and balance. Elegant.
*Last tasted at the Wine & Food Society's French Banquet at the Hilton, Singapore, Oct 1989*****

1971**** *to* *********

Very good to excellent. All probably at peak now.

Châteauneuf-du-Pape, Clos des Papes *PAUL AVRIL* Medium, mature, chocolaty; rich, soft yet tannic.
*March 1985***(*)*

Châteauneuf-du-Pape, Ch de Rayas Very deep; creamy, honeyed fruit; fairly sweet, a marvellous wine, silky, great vinosity, good future when last tasted.
*Oct 1981. Then***(**) Probably perfect now.*

Côte Rôtie, Les Jumelles *P JABOULET AINE* Amazingly rich spicy wine.
*March 1984****(*)*

Côte Rôtie, Tête de Cuvée *J VIDAL-FLEURY* Fine, deep; rich; dry, firm, fragrant.
*Pre-sale, April 1986****

Hermitage *CHAVE* Gold medal, Concours Agricole Paris. Good colour; marvellous ripe fragrance; slightly sweet, full-bodied and earthy yet a light touch, very rich, good length, fragrant aftertaste.
*Jan 1984****(*)*

Hermitage, La Chapelle *P JABOULET AINE* First noted in Feb 1975. Rich, and expensive at £32 per dozen! At 10 years of age: deep; magnificent bouquet; fine flavour, balance and finish. Elegant but still not fully ready when last tasted.
*Dec 1981. Then****(*) Doubtless perfection now.*

1972* *to* ********

Good in Châteauneuf, the best excellent in Cornas and Hermitage (La Chapelle, deep, sweet in 1974); mediocre in Côte Rôtie. Drink now.

Châteauneuf-du-Pape, Dom de Beaucastel Opaque; peppery, alcoholic and unready at seven years of age.
Not tasted since Dec 1979. Then(***) Doubtless ready now.

Cornas *P JABOULET AINE* A good young wine. At eight years: marvellous depth of colour though showing maturity; bouquet blossomed in the glass with scented, Bordeaux-like fruit; good length, tannin, acidity, fragrance. A splendid wine.
*Last tasted April 1980***(*) Doubtless excellent now.*

Hermitage *CHAVE* Very deep; nose like mustard and cress in 1984, spicy, very flavoury. Most recently, now palish, soft, warm red; extraordinary fruit; sweeter, medium weight, soft original flavour, refreshing acidity.
*Last tasted Dec 1990**** Now to 1996.*

1973* *to* *******

Very large crops throughout the region. Variable quality.

Châteauneuf-du-Pape, Dom de la Petite Bastide Deep, rich; very alcoholic, scented, unusual — like prunes in vodka; extraordinary flavour, rich, strong tasting, tannic. A slightly bitter, medicinal finish.
*March 1986**

1974* *to* *******

Moderate in the south, abundant and mediocre in the north.

Hermitage *CHAVE* Low-keyed, nothing special; dry, chewy, short.
*At Chave vertical, March 1984***

Hermitage, Monier de la Sizeranne *CHAPOUTIER* Malty, jammy, stalky, dry.
*April 1989**

1975* *to* ******

Mediocre to poor throughout the region, Cornas about the best. None tasted recently.

1976** *to* ********

Variable in Châteauneuf mainly due to rain at vintage time; very good in Cornas, Hermitage and Côte Rôtie.

Cornas *CLAPE* Fine, deep; marvellous nose, peppery, good fruit, unusual; dry, full of alcohol and fruit, excellent balance, length, acidity. Very flavoury.
*Sept 1981***(*).*

Cornas *P JABOULET AINE* Purple; nose more obvious than Clape's, fully developed; some sweetness, chunky, good mid-palate but lacking Clape's length and aftertaste.
*Sept 1981. Then**(*)*

Côte Rôtie *DELAPINE* Rich, warm; toffee-like; soft.
*Ready when tasted in March 1980***

Hermitage *CHAVE* Deep, lively colour; marvellous bouquet, spicy, almost La Tâche-like intensity and fragrance; some sweetness, pleasant weight, concentrated but not intrusively so, marvellous fruit, flavour, length, aftertaste.
*In bottle and magnum, March 1984*****

Hermitage *DELAPINE* Palish; stewed fruit nose and flavour.
*March 1981**

1977* *to* ******

Light, mediocre, from southern to northern Rhône.

Châteauneuf-du-Pape, La Bernadine *CHAPOUTIER* Very sweet yet drying out on finish.
*Ready in April 1980***

Châteauneuf-du-Pape, Dom de Nalys Pale; waxy, kernelly; rather woody.
*Dec 1986**

Hermitage *CHAVE* Woody.
March 1984.

Hermitage *GAMBERT* Lovely nose but lean and tart.
*April 1989**

Hermitage *P JABOULET AINE* Deep; medicinal, rich yet dry, tannic.
*April 1989***

Vacqueyras, Dom des Lambourtins Stewed fruit, 'blown' nose; sweetish, light, flavoury but slightly bitter.
Nov 1985.

1978*****

Outstanding. The best vintage since 1911.

Châteauneuf-du-Pape, Dom de Beaurenard *PAUL COULON* Medium-deep, attractive colour; nose and palate sweet and full of fruit. Full-bodied. Delicious.
*Feb 1988**** Now to 1998.*

Cornas *P JABOULET AINE* Deep purple; difficult nose to pin down; fullish, a marvellous style but raw and rasping at five years old.
July 1983. Then(***) Say 1993 to beyond 2000.*

Côte Rôtie, Brune et Blonde *EMILE CHAMPET* Very deep, huge and tannic in the mid-1980s. More recently, less deep, lovely colour; an extraordinary nose, fruit, fruit bushes, a citrus-like whiff; ripe entry, very dry tannic finish, earthy, vegetal flavour. Powerful.
*Last tasted Oct 1988****(*) 1992 to beyond 2000.*

Côte Rôtie, Brune et Blonde *GUIGAL* At five years old, the heat of the Côtes positively simmering on the nose, the richness and weight of heftily ripe grapes. Unready. Five years later, still very deep; rich, meaty, singed nose; distinct touch of sweetness, full-bodied, a gloriously expansive flavour, good length and superb aftertaste.
*Last noted Nov 1988***(**) Now to beyond 2000.*

Côte Rôtie, La Mouline *GUIGAL* Opaque, making the Brune et Blonde look feeble! Close-knit, harmonious, rich almost malty nose; medium-sweet, full-bodied, complex and concentrated, loads of tannin and acidity. Glorious.
*Nov 1988***(**) 1992 to well beyond 2000.*

Côte Rôtie, La Landonne *GUIGAL* Having unified the Landonne Vineyard, Guigal launched his new Côte Brune in 1978. The first vintage immensely impressive: opaque; different from Mouline on nose and palate: rich, very tannic. Enormous weight, power, extract, alcoholic content. Massive. Crisp. At 10 years of age quite unready.
Nov 1988(*****) 1998–2020

Crozes-Hermitage *JABOULET-ISNARD* Opaque at three years old. A big, fluffy wine. By the mid-1980s a lovely velvety ruby colour; high-toned bouquet; fullish, nice fruit, touch of acidity.
*Last tasted Jan 1984*** Probably at peak now.*

Crozes-Hermitage *VIDAL-FLEURY* Medium-deep; crisp, berry-like fruit; walnut flavour, good tannin and acidity. Years of life left.
*Feb 1989***(*) Now to 2000.*

Hermitage *CHAVE* Deep, fine, rich, mature; low-keyed at first then rich, biscuity, very fragrant, fabulous; fairly dry, fullish, perfect fruit, richness, balance.
*At the Chave vertical, March 1984. Then***(**) Drink now to beyond 2000.*

Hermitage, La Chapelle *P JABOULET AINE* So massive that it was given an extra year in cask. Tasted only aged three years old: opaque, purple; youthfully peppery; packed with fruit. Tannic.
July 1981. Then(*****) Drink, say, 1992–2010.

St-Joseph, La Grande Pompée *P JABOULET AINE* St-Joseph, an appellation created in 1956, is across the river from Tain. The first vintage tasted was the '61, noted in 1963. The reds made mainly from Syrah grapes as in Hermitage. Medium-deep; low-keyed though scented; dry, lean, supple, attractive.
*Last tasted Feb 1988*** Drink now to 1996.*

1979** *to* ****

Moderately good. Lighter style. Some lacking acidity.

Châteauneuf-du-Pape, Dom de Monpertuis Ruby; walnuts; unusual flavour, very dry.
July 1984.

Châteauneuf-du-Pape, Dom Tour St-Michel Sweaty, stalky; too sweet.
*May 1986**

Châteauneuf-du-Pape, Réserve des Papes *SALAVERT* Deep; raw, stalky, like red ink.
*Jan 1982(**?) Doubtless softened by now.*

Cornas *DELAS* Ruby; stylish; dry, firm, excellent flavour.
*March 1984**(*)*

Côte Rôtie, Brune et Blonde *GUIGAL* Many notes. At nine, still deep, plummy, just starting to mature; massive, harmonious, fig-like fruit; sweet entry, dry tannic finish. Fleshy, almost exotic yet crisp. Good texture. Marvellous wine.
*Last tasted Nov 1988***(*) Now to beyond 2000.*

Côte Rôtie, Brune et Blonde *VIDAL FLEURY* Fine, deep; magnificent nose; deep, rich, long dry finish.
*April 1986****

Côte Rôtie, Les Jumelles *P JABOULET AINE* Very good, fruity and forward.
*May 1983****

Côte Rôtie, Cuvée Beaufort *CHAPOUTIER* Rather dull.
*June 1983**?*

Crozes-Hermitage *VIDAL-FLEURY* Lively, ruby; very sweet nose; fullish, assertive, chocolaty.
*Feb 1989*** Drink now.*

Hermitage *CHAVE* Deep ruby; sweaty-saddle nose; extraordinary, rich yet refined. Lively.
*Last tasted Sept 1984**(**)*

Hermitage *GUIGAL* Impressively deep, black cherry; hefty fruit, plummy, fig-like – like a ruby port; ripe, alcoholic, concentrated mid-palate, raw tannic finish.
*Nov 1985**(**)*

Hermitage *GRIPPAT* Dry, fullish, fresh, clean.
Not tasted since April 1982(***)

1980** *to* ***

The harvest the largest ever recorded. Generally fairly good.

Châteauneuf-du-Pape, Dom de Mont Redon Medium, still immature; neutral nose; dry, nothing special.
March 1985(*)*

Cornas *P JABOULET AINE* Fine, deep; lovely young fruity aroma; fairly dry, fullish, very flavoury, touch of iron and lemon.
*Dec 1986**(*) Drink now to 1995.*

Côte Rôtie *CHAMPET* Strange, unknit, medicinal; delicious flavour, interesting character.
*April 1989****

Côte Rôtie *CHAPOUTIER* Malty, stewed, slightly oxidised.
April 1989.

Côte Rôtie *DELAPIN* Very dry, very fruity.
March 1984(**)*

Côte Rôtie *GUIGAL* Very deep yet mature; low-keyed, chocolaty, showing age; slightly sweet, positive, flavoury, moderate length.
*Nov 1988** Drink soon.*

Hermitage *CHAVE* Plummy; sweet, ripe, earthy but dry and a bit tart on palate.
*Not tasted since March 1984(**?)*

Hermitage *GUIGAL* Very deep; full-bodied, lusty, very tannic – needs food, and more bottle-age.
Oct 1987(**)*

Hermitage, La Chapelle *P JABOULET AINE* Deep; medicinal; developed pleasingly; dry, medium weight, touch of bitterness.
*Dec 1984**(*)*

1981**

Moderate. Summer drought in the south, rain during harvesting in the north. Some better than others, depending on the skill of the winemaker.

Châteauneuf-du-Pape, Ch de Beaucastel Two recent notes. Surprisingly deep, opaque centre, intense; fruit and a metallic character; fairly full-bodied, rich, mouth-filling, bitter tannins.

*Last tasted Oct 1989**(*) 1992–98*

Châteauneuf-du-Pape, Dom du Père Caboche Cherry red; lovely sweet, raspberry-like fruit; very flavoury, good texture, refreshing acidity, slightly bitter finish.
*Aug 1987**(*) Now to 1996.*

Cornas *P JABOULET AINE* Deep; sweet nose, dry palate. Scented flavour.
Not tasted since July 1983(*)*

Côte Rôtie, Brune et Blonde *CHAMPY* A rather sweaty, medicinal nose and flavour.
*June 1986**(*) Perhaps more bottle-age needed.*

Côte Rôtie, Brune et Blonde *GUIGAL* Still relatively deep and youthful, but with a slightly woody flavour.
Nov 1988.

Côte Rôtie, La Mouline *GUIGAL* Far more mature-looking, with a lovely, fully evolved, singed nose, rich like syrup of figs; sweet, full, rich, chewy. Delicious.
*Nov 1988*****

Hermitage *CHAVE* Forward; sweet, rich fruit; amazing bite and flavour, piquant and delicious.
Not tasted since March 1984. Then(****)

Hermitage, La Chapelle *JABOULET* Impressively deep, beautiful colour; harmonious, well assembled, stylish nose and palate. Dry finish though not very tannic.
*Feb 1986**(**)*

1982****

Excessive summer heat, even for the Rhône, and lack of rain. Hot weather continued through the harvesting period making fermentation difficult to control except in the more modern cellars. Some wines spoiled. Despite this, a large crop.

Châteauneuf-du-Pape, Dom du Vieux Télégraphe Despite its quaint name, very modern and efficient cellars. M Brunier's '82 has a deep, self-satisfied look; nose noted "par for the course" (Christie's wine course) but after an hour exciting, a surprisingly lovely scent emerging from its alcoholic base; delicious, soft and sweet, with an upturned touch of bitterness on the finish like some top Italian wines.
*April 1985**(**) Now to 2000.*

Côte Rôtie, Brune et Blonde *GUIGAL* Deep; very rich, fragrant, meaty; fairly sweet, excellent fruit, full, chewy. Noted as "perfect" in 1986.
*Last tasted Nov 1986***(**) Now to beyond 2000.*

Côte Rôtie, Les Jumelles *P JABOULET AINE* Not as deep as expected; deliciously sweet nose, strawberry jam-like fruit; drier, lighter and leaner than Guigal's.
*Last noted at pre-sale tasting, Nov 1987**(*) Now to 1997.*

Crozes-Hermitage, Dom du Thalabert *P JABOULET AINE* Crozes is rarely up to Hermitage quality, but the price is commensurate. Firm, tannic.
Last tasted Dec 1984(***)*

Crozes-Hermitage *MOILLARD* Immature, dry, raw.
March 1985(**)

Gigondas, Dom St Gayan One does not normally take Gigondas tremendously seriously. At best, fruity, quaffable, not for keeping. But Roger Meffre makes superb wine. At five years: ruby red; rich, baked fruit; rich mid-palate, lovely flavour, length, citrus-dry finish.
*Sept 1987***(*) Now to 1995.*

Hermitage *CHAVE* Good potential.
March 1984(***)?

Hermitage *GUIGAL* Fairly deep; beautifully made, harmonious, good vinosity; a bit of everything on the palate.
*Last tasted April 1987**(**)*

Hermitage, La Chapelle *P JABOULET AINE* Impressively deep; very rich, fruity, evolved beautifully in the glass; fullish, fleshy, meaty, mouthfilling. Unready.
*Last tasted April 1987**(**)*

Hermitage, Cuvée Marquis de la Tourette *DELAS* Deep, intense; beautiful, fig-like richness of fruit, radiating heat; rich, full-bodied, flavour swells in the mouth but still bitter tannins. Several consistent recent notes.
*Last tasted Jan 1989***(*) 1992–2000*

1983*****

Poor flowering of the Grenache reduced yield but a magnificent summer, one of the hottest and driest on record.

Châteauneuf-du-Pape, La Bernadine *CHAPOUTIER* Full-bodied, very tannic, but needs more bottle-age.
Feb 1990(***)*

Châteauneuf-du-Pape, Chante Cigale *CHRISTIAN FAVIER* Surprisingly, not deep, maturing; Italianate at first but developed scents of cigars, singed sultanas; rich, 'warm', tangy.
*Aug 1987****

Châteauneuf-du-Pape, Château Rayas Several notes. Deep lively colour, long legs; very fragrant, harmonious; sweetish strawberry-like fruit, lovely flavour swelling in the mouth, touch of tar on the finish. Vibrant.
*Last tasted April 1991*****

Châteauneuf-du-Pape, Dom du Vieux Télégraphe Rich, very fruity, delicious.
Jan 1985. Then(***) Doubtless lovely now.*

Côte Rôtie, Côte Brune *E CHAMPY* Plummy; very medicinal; very sweet, ripe, curious.
*June 1986**?*

Côte Rôtie, Brune et Blonde *GUIGAL* Very deep, still youthful; low-keyed, dumb but deep, fragrant, figgy; full-bodied, powerful yet silky, packed, fleshy, good length. Glorious.
*Last tasted Nov 1988***(**) Now to beyond 2000.*

Hermitage *CHAVE* Tasted only in its youth. Intensely purple; already a lovely fragrance, spicy, the La Tâche of the Rhône; rich, lively, tannic.
March 1984(*****) Should be superb now to beyond 2000.

Hermitage *GUIGAL* Still violet-rimmed; nose like a holly bush, still hard; yet fairly sweet on the palate, the sweetness of ripe fruit and high alcoholic content, good character, flavour, texture and shape. Crisp fruit. Attenuated finish.
Jan 1988(****) 1992 to beyond 2000.*

Hermitage, La Chapelle *P JABOULET AINE* Intense, impressive; a hot singed alcoholic nose, yet suave; lovely fruit, flavour of figs, prunes, chocolate, crisp, tannic. Excellent. Needs time.
*Nov 1987**(***)*

Hermitage, Monier de la Sizeranne *CHAPOUTIER* Medium-deep, thick appearance; unusual, as yet unknit, fig-like fruit; sweet, chewy, flavoury, very tannic.
*Last tasted April 1989**(**)? 1992–2000*

Hermitage, Marquis de La Tourette *DELAS* Opaque; massively hot alcoholic nose; sweet, full-bodied, flavour of blackberries, needs bottle-age.
*May 1988**(**) 1993–2000*

1984**

Moderate vintage. Three weeks of rain in Sept dampened the spirits as well as the harvest. Nevertheless some agreeable wines made, though not for the long haul.

Châteauneuf-du-Pape, Les Cèdres *P JABOULET AINE* Medium colour, dryness, and weight. Chewy.

Feb 1987(*) Drink soon.*
Châteauneuf-du-Pape, Dom de Marcoux Deep; firm fruit, huge, meaty, tannic.
May 1987(**) Now to 1997.*
Côte Rôtie, Brune et Blonde *GUIGAL* Deep, plummy; fairly sweet, full, fruity, touch of silk, spicy.
Last tasted Nov 1988(**)*
Côte Rôtie, Les Jumelles *P JABOULET AINE* Good colour; jammy fruit; very tannic.
Feb 1987(**) Both 1993 to 2000.*
Hermitage *GUIGAL* Deep; positive, powerful, good fruit, grip.
Jan 1988(**)*
Hermitage, La Chapelle *P JABOULET AINE* Vinous; medium-full, reasonable length, tannic.
Last tasted Jan 1989(**) Both 1993 to 2000.*
Muscat de Beaumes de Venise, Dom de Coyeux Although out of place here being a *vin doux naturel* dessert wine, mentioned because M Yves Nativelle, the proprietor of this domaine, is one of the few local *vignerons* to concentrate on muscat, most having substantially greater plantings for Côte du Rhône Villages wines. Moreover, few Beaumes de Venise sport a vintage, the vast proportion being churned out, agreeably enough, by the enormous co-operative. The '84 surprisingly pale; delicate muscat grapiness; medium-sweet, clean, light, with a deft touch. Very flavoury. Without the straw colour and clumsiness of the more ordinary muscats.
*Sept 1986. Then*** and should have been drunk by now.*
Tavel Rosé *J VIDAL-FLEURY* Tavel, once regarded as the only rosé a serious wine drinker would consider, tends to be rather dull. This one pink; little nose, a light somewhat nondescript fruitiness; fairly dry, a touch of bitterness on the finish.
*Feb 1989**

1985*****

An outstanding vintage. Freezing in Jan and Feb, cool into March and April. Some late flowering. A glorious summer, no rain in the south until after the vintage, though a little in Aug in the middle Rhône was enough to swell the grapes.
Châteauneuf-du-Pape, Beaucastel Virtually opaque, intense; opulent, earthy; very strange, heftily ripe, immense alcohol, extract, fruit, silky tannins.
Nov 1988(*****) 1995–2015
Châteauneuf-du-Pape, La Bernadine *CHAPOUTIER* Medium-deep; scented; sweet, pleasant enough.
*Sept 1990**(*)*
Châteauneuf-du-Pape, Le Bosquet des Papes A small vineyard, M Borion sharing bottling and storage facilities with nine other growers under the banner 'Prestige et Tradition', surprisingly well developed; meaty; sweet, fullish, chunky, rounded.
*Nov 1988**(**) Now to 2000.*
Châteauneuf-du-Pape, Les Cèdres *P JABOULET AINE* Fragrant; crisp, tannic, good future.
Feb 1987(****) 1993 to beyond 2000.
Cornas *A CLAPE* The best and best-known grower in this small *appellation*. His '85 a glorious cherry red when young; a wonderful, high-toned, sweet, raspberry-like scent; slightly sweet, soft, ripe fruit yet crisp and firm, good tannins and lovely aftertaste.
Aug 1987. Then(*****) 1992–2000
Cornas *P JABOULET AINE* Deep; glorious fruit; very agreeable.
Feb 1987(****) Now to 2000.
Cornas, La Geynale *ROBERT MICHEL* A scion of one of the two oldest families in the district. Initially virtually opaque, now a medium-deep, still youthful, cherry red; low-keyed, sweet; fleshy fruit, no hard edges; fairly full-bodied, lovely flavour and texture. Dry tannic finish. A beautiful wine.
*Last tasted Jan 1990***(**) 1993 to beyond 2000.*
Côte Rôtie *EMILE CHAMPET* Deep with purple rim; glorious fruit but a touch of something like raspberry vinegar, then mirabelle; fullish, soft, warm, crisp fruit, loads of tannin and acidity.
*July 1987. Then(*****) Say 1995 to 2010, maybe***** in due course.*
Côte Rôtie *ROBERT JASMIN* Ruby, purple-rimmed; lower keyed than Champet's, more vegetal, crisp, violets; softer, broader, good extract, loads of alcohol, flavour expanding, almost exploding, in the mouth. Lovely at two years old. Should be terrific in due course.
July 1987(*****) 1995–2010
Côte Rôtie, Brune et Blonde *GUIGAL* Very deep but developing; glorious bouquet, fleshy, fig-like fruit, spicy, great depth; major impact, mouthfilling, substantial yet refreshing. Excellent flavour. Needs more bottle-age.
*Last tasted Nov 1989***(**) 1993–2010*
Côte Rôtie, Chantillonne *VIDAL-FLEURY* A single vineyard wine from the Côte Blonde: very forthcoming, opening up even further, with Mouton-Rothschild-like opulence and spice; lovely fruit, medium full-bodied, lean, long, fragrant.
*Nov 1988***(**) 1993–2010*
Côte Rôtie, Les Jumelles *P JABOULET AINE* Very deep; full, very good fruit and expensive.
At Loeb's introductory tasting, Feb 1987(*****) 1995–2010
Côtes du Rhône, Ch de Fonsalette Owned by the Reynauds of Ch Rayas. Despite the dip in their reputation I found this attractive: a brilliant ruby and black cherry colour; a bit stalky on the nose but very sweet, full of fruit, crisp.
*Nov 1988*** Now to 1995.*
Crozes Hermitage, Dom Thalabert *P JABOULET AINE* An 86-acre vineyard producing on average 9,000 cases. Deep cherry; distinctive style, rich; prune-like fruit; lovely flavour, texture, length, enough tannin, refreshing acidity, very fragrant. Surely one of the best Crozes for years?
Nov 1988(***) 1992–2000*
Hermitage *CHAVE* Still ruby; 'warm', medicinal, at first rather Bordeaux-like, then, after an hour, sweet, slightly caramelly; dry, singed, crisp berry-like fruit, long, dry finish.
*Dec 1989***(*) 1993–2015*
Hermitage, La Chapelle *P JABOULET AINE* Macerated for three weeks. No new wood used: 12 to 18 months in two to three-year-old burgundy *barriques*, spicy, tannic, great length and future in 1987. More recently, a fine deep colour; low-keyed, meaty nose, later a touch of liquorice; full, warm, fleshy, lovely rich flavour.
*Last tasted Nov 1988***(**) 1993–2010*
Hermitage, Monier de la Sizeranne *CHAPOUTIER* Medium, maturing; deep, sweaty nose; sweet, rich, fruity.
*Sept 1990***(*) 1991–2000*

1986** *to* ****

Difficult summer conditions. Hot, no rain until Aug 24, then dull through to mid-Sept, a week of rain from Sept 20 delaying the harvest. Picking began on Oct 1 in the north, on Oct 6 in the south.
Châteauneuf-du-Pape, Dom de Mont Redon Indis-

tinct nose, slightly stalky, youthful, tannic.
July 1987(**)

Châteauneuf-du-Pape, Dom du Vieux Télégraphe Deep, cherry red; very fragrant, spicy; rather sweet, full-bodied, crisp, fruity, good length, very tannic.
Nov 1988(***) 1994–2000

Cornas *VERSET* Just six acres out of a total AC of 240. 100% Syrah. Deep, immature; amazing nose, crisp, violets, reminded me of Normandy cider; dry, crisp, very flavoury.
Nov 1988(***)

Cornas *P JABOULET AINE* Rather stewed fruit; dry, chewy, soft tannins.
Feb 1991(*)*

Côte Rôtie *CHAPOUTIER* Low-keyed fruit; dry, comparatively light.
Sept 1990(*)*

Côte Rôtie, Les Jumelles *P JABOULET AINE* Soft mature colour; fig-like fruit; dry, brambly flavour, assertive, tannic.
Feb 1991(**) 1995–2000*

Côte Rôtie, La Mouline *GUIGAL* Medium-deep, richly coloured; slightly stalky nose, straw, walnuts; medium sweetness and body, crisp, lovely brambly fruit, distinctly tannic.
*At the French Wine Farmers' tasting, Oct 1990**(**)*

Côte Rôtie, La Landonne *GUIGAL* Deep, immature; hefty, rich, smell of roast beef; very rich, mouthfilling, loaded with fruit, alcohol, tannin.
*Oct 1990 *(***)*

Côte Rôtie, La Turque *GUIGAL* Formerly a Vidal-Fleury vineyard on the Côte Brune, opaque, intense; enormously rich, harmonious, developed soft vanilla and strawberry scents; full-bodied, lovely oaky flavour, tannic. A massive mouthful.
*At the French Wine Farmers' tasting, Oct 1990**(***) 1996–2030*

Crozes-Hermitage, Thalabert *P JABOULET AINE* Deep, intense, dark ruby; a hot, powerful yet smooth nose, rich, port-like; substantial wine, suave yet very tannic. A good mouthful.
Last tasted Nov 1990(**) 1993–2000*

1987* *to* ***

Most dismal weather of the decade. Northern Rhône: wet spring, good flowering, frequent showers in early to mid-summer but persistent rain in Aug. Harvest late: mid-Oct. Worse in the south: satisfactory flowering followed by rain, tempest, rain again and a mass invasion of caterpillars. A week of rot-inducing fog and more rain.

Châteauneuf-du-Pape The worst affected. Jaboulet's Cèdres not made. None tasted.

Cornas *P JABOULET AINE* Stewed prunes and malt extract, poor cork, May 1990. Most recently: medium colour, brambly fruit, tannic. Price increased 50% in nine months.
Last tasted Feb 1991(*) For early drinking.*

Côte Rôtie *GUIGAL* Deep; rich, very sweaty tannic nose; medium full-bodied, soft yet spicy oak, tannins, well made and reasonably priced.
Oct 1990(***) 1992–96

Hermitage *GUIGAL* Immature; gloriously sweet, rich, rather toffee-like; fairly dry, fullish body, rich, soft. Good tannins and fruit.
Oct 1990(***) 1992–96

Hermitage, La Chapelle *P JABOULET AINE* Touch of stalkiness; swingeingly tannic, an '*osso buco*' wine when first tasted in Jan 1990. Rich but a bit malty by May. Most recently: less deep, softer colour; nose stewed; strange flavour.
Last tasted, hastily, Feb 1991(*)? Say 1992 to 1995.*

1988****

An excellent vintage. Big wines, particularly in northern Rhône, which have high extract and a good future. Côte Rôtie vineyards were badly hit by two hailstorms during flowering, reducing and concentrating the crop. In southern Rhône problems created by humidity were countered by timely spraying. Showers swelled the grapes in Aug. Early picking avoided the problems caused later by heavy rains.

Châteauneuf-du-Pape *GUIGAL* Attractive, surprisingly forward appearance; crisp fruit; sweet, medium-full, soft, chewy, touch of iron.
Oct 1990(***)

Châteauneuf-du-Pape, Dom de Beaurenard Deep, immature; curiously attractive; dry, fullish yet lean, good fruit, length and acidity.
May 1990(****)

Châteauneuf-du-Pape, Clos de Brusquières Maturing; speciously attractive, boiled sweets; elegant, nice texture and flesh, touch of bitterness. An early developer.
May 1990(**)*

Châteauneuf-du-Pape, Petite Cuvée *CHAPOUTIER* Somewhat artificial, scented, sugary nose; sweet, medium-light for Châteauneuf, easy, another early developer.
May 1990(**)

Châteauneuf-du-Pape, Dom de Mont Redon Very good deep colour; Médoc-like oyster-shell nose, some depth; sweetish approach but somewhat astringent finish, fullish, spicy.
May 1990(****)

Châteauneuf-du-Pape, Ch de Vaudieu Adjacent to Ch Rayas. Fairly deep, immature; nose both burgundian and Italianate, beetroot and bramble bush; good fruit, fullish body, very tannic.
May 1990(***) 1995–2010

Crozes-Hermitage, La Petite Ruche *CHAPOUTIER* Sweet, sweaty, jammy; rather tinny fruit, bitter tannin and rather acidic.
May 1990(**)?

Gigondas, Ch Raspail *GABRIEL MEFFRE* Meffre also owns Ch de Vaudieu (above). Good colour and fruit but a bit woody and very tannic. The sort of wine to drink when young and lusty (take that either way).
*May 1990***

Hermitage, Monier de la Sizeranne *CHAPOUTIER* Lean, a bit hollow though quite good fruit on nose and palate. Medium dryness and fullness, lean, good tannin and acidity.
May 1990(***)

1989****

A drought year. Young vines and vineyards with low water reserves had a difficult time but deeper-rooted older vines on heavier soil did better, the best being excellent, particularly in Côte Rôtie. Châteauneuf also successful, producing rich and complete reds. Picking in the south was two weeks sooner than usual, some early-ripening varieties being picked at the end of Aug.

Châteauneuf-du-Pape, La Bernadine *CHAPOUTIER* Fairly deep, immature of course in colour and on nose; good fruit; very sweet, chewy, oaky with excellent aftertaste. After some relatively disappointing Chapoutier wines, a step in the right direction.
Sept 1990(****)

Châteauneuf-du-Pape, Les Cèdres *P JABOULET AINE* Similar appearance; very sweet nose, full of fruit; tannic. Will be lovely.
Feb 1991(****) Say 1995 to 2005.
Cornas *P JABOULET AINE* Good fruit; elegant, nice texture, good flavoury.
Feb 1991(****) 1994–2000
Côtes du Rhône-Villages, Vinsobres A sleepy Provençal village with a most evocative name, and an unusually attractive '89 made by the elder of the two cooperatives, the *Vinsobraise*, and marketed by the Cellier des Dauphins. Full of fruit; sweet, lovely texture, highly quaffable.
*May 1990*** Drink now to 1993.*
Côte Rôtie *CHAPOUTIER* Cask sample: deep; sweet, very spicy, 'hot' and tannic.
Sept 1990(****)
Côte Rôtie, Les Jumelles *P JABOULET AINE* Very deep; very good fruit, body, flavour and length.
Feb 1991(****) 1996–2005
Crozes-Hermitage, Dom de Thalabert *P JABOULET AINE* Opaque cask sample in May 1990, extraordinary aroma, rather Gamay-like whole-fruit fragrance; fulsome and flavoury. Most recently, spicy; soft, agreeable though a touch of stalkiness. Nice weight.
Last tasted Feb 1991(***) 1993–98
Hermitage *CHAPOUTIER* Very deep; immature spicy nose and flavour; dry, lean, fullish.
Sept 1990(****)
Hermitage, La Chapelle Distinctive nose and flavour, rich, tannic.
Feb 1991(****) 1996–2010

1990*****

Mild weather and spring, early flowering leading to an early harvest. In between, a hot and dry summer. The result a good healthy crop of rather small, concentrated grapes. Careful winemakers will have made top-class wines. The best should certainly turn out to warrant five stars.

WHITE

As Robin Yapp was the first to elaborate in his marvellous annual lists, the Rhône and Loire are totally complementary. One tends to think only of red Rhône; indeed the production of whites is relatively small. They are quite different from the light acidic Loire wines. In weight, and to a certain extent in style, the white Rhône, Hermitage in particular, is most like good white Graves. The best white Hermitage wines can be magnificent, and will keep. They are distinctive yet hard to describe; the words "nutty" and "lemon-tinged" recur. Their life span is not unlike dry white Bordeaux: most should be drunk young, between two and four years after the vintage, but the finest, in common with, say, Haut-Brion, need bottle-age.

1929*****

A great vintage for white as well as red.
Hermitage blanc *CHAVE* At 55 years of age a lovely yellow amber gold; bouquet like toasted coconut; medium dry, soft, gentle nutty flavour, good length. In remarkable condition.
*At Yapp's Chave tasting at the Garrick Club, March 1984*****

1952*****

Hermitage blanc *CHAVE* Straw colour; fabulous, mature, smoky, honey and leather bouquet; dry, medium-full body, marvellous flavour, length and fine acidity.
*March 1984******

1957****

Châteauneuf-du-Pape, Ch Rayas '1er Grand Cru Réserve' "A notable year" for Rayas (Masters and Learmonth). Pale gold; creamy nose that developed well with air and after losing its chill; very dry, fullish, flavour of old straw, nutty finish.
*Oct 1981****

1962***

Hermitage, Chevalier de Sterimberg *P JABOULET AINE* Jaboulet's white, named after Gaspard de Sterimberg, a 13th-century knight who returned wounded from a crusade and en route came across the Hermitage hill. Delighted with the peaceful view, he built a retreat, the famous Chapelle. The '62 still remarkably fresh: scented, spicy cinnamon, pineapple and lemon – I always associate lemon with white Hermitage; bone dry, very firm, austere even (like the hermit), excellent acidity.
*May 1981*****

1967*****

Hermitage blanc *CHAVE* Delicate fruity nose, honeyed; medium dry, sound but more than 'nutty', with the almond kernel flavour I dislike.
*March 1984**

1969***

Hermitage, Sterimberg *P JABOULET AINE* Two magnums, one dull, unclean, the other bright, pale yellow; nose hard to describe, not varietal, no bottle-age, a whiff of lemon; dry, four-square, good acidity.
*At a Gidleigh Park Wine Weekend, Nov 1980. At best** Doubtless tiring now.*

1970***

Hermitage, Chante Alouette *CHAPOUTIER* Very bright, good colour; low-keyed, waxy nose, touch of lemon; dry, medium weight, soft yet firm enough. Unexciting.
*Oct 1982** Not to be kept.*

1971*****

Château-Grillet, Cuvée Renaissance A tiny $7\frac{1}{2}$ acre vineyard owned, since 1820, by the Neyret-Gachet family. I cannot resist recording that in 1829 James Christie, King George IV's Lord Steward, ordered two cases of 72 bottles for delivery to St James's Palace. Demand has always exceeded supply, with consequent high prices not always reflected in the quality. Many notes of older vintages but few recently. The style and quality seems to veer violently, but in 1971, excellent: good colour; soft, peachy, fragrant bouquet; medium

dryness and body though light style. Good mid-palate, excellent acidity.
*Feb 1982*****

Châteauneuf-du-Pape, Ch de Rayas blanc Good colour, palish lemon yellow; nose vinous not varietal; dry, perfect weight, smoky oaky, a dash of lemon. Absolutely delicious.
*Nov 1980**** Probably still good.*

Hermitage blanc *CHAVE* Straw yellow; strange, individual scent, bread-like, very good fruit, depth; medium dry, great length, excellent acidity.
*March 1984*****

1972***

Although reputed to be a good white Rhône vintage they have escaped me. Vernay's Condrieu lacking 'oomph' even when young (1974). More recently:

Hermitage blanc *CHAPOUTIER* Pale; poor, flat, sulphury; dry and dreary.
Oct 1983.

Hermitage blanc *CHAVE* Colour of old straw. *Passé.*
March 1984.

1973***

Château-Grillet Lemon yellow; sweet, vanilla, touch of caramel; flavour of vanilla and walnuts. Marvellous aftertaste.
*Feb 1988*****

1976***

Good ripe vintage, the whites rich but lacking acidity.

Condrieu, Ch de Rozay Owned by M Paul Multier but vinified at this time by M Georges Vernet. Even without bottle-age a pleasant yellow gold; scent of the Viognier grape, baked apples and cloves. Medium dry, meaty. The richness of old vines and a good vintage – yet said to be best between two and four years after the vintage.
*Nov 1979*****

Hermitage blanc *CHAVE* Interesting, multi-faceted, good length and adequate acidity.
*March 1984**** Probably at peak.*

Hermitage blanc, Chante Alouette *CHAPOUTIER* Distinct yellow, good flavour and balance in 1981, showing honeyed bottle-age on the nose and good texture in 1985, thereafter somewhat dull, nutty.
*Last tasted Oct 1987. At best*** Now over the hill.*

1977*

The opposite to 1976. Over acidic.

Hermitage blanc *CHAVE* Extraordinarily rich nose; medium dry, flavoury, marked but agreeable acidity.
*At peak in March 1984***

1978*****

An excellent vintage. No relevant tasting notes but the best should still be on top form.

1979***

Good vintage, mainly consumed in the mid-1980s.

Château-Grillet Bright yellow; bouquet expanded in the glass, sweet, oak, vanilla; medium dry, a good long warm flavour, slightly biscuity finish. Very good acidity.
*May 1988****

Hermitage blanc *CHAPOUTIER* Bright palish yellow; fruit, lemon, almond kernels on nose and palate, touch of sweetness, coarse texture.
*March 1983***

Hermitage blanc, Sterimberg *P JABOULET AINE* Attractive yellow; positive, rather oily and kernelly flavour.
*March 1990***

1980**

Moderate. For quick drinking.

Château-Grillet The Neyret-Gachets' biggest-ever vintage: 116 hectolitres. Rather pale, green-tinged; nice clean nose; dry, firm, reasonably body, balance, length.
*July 1983****

Condrieu, Ch de Rozay Distinctive straw yellow; strange nose, damp straw and watercress; dry, fullish, firm.
*Last tasted Aug 1983***

Hermitage blanc *CHAVE* Fragrant, appley, pineapple nose; good shape, dry finish.
*March 1984***

1981***

Châteauneuf-du-Pape, Dom de Nalys blanc Reputed to be the best white in Châteauneuf, made from a cluster of grapes headed by Grenache Blanc and Clairette, and best drunk within three years. Low-keyed, whiff of sulphur, waxy, touch of honey; surprisingly dry – white Châteauneuf can be distinctly sweet – rather neutral flavour but good finish.
*Nov 1984****

Hermitage blanc *CHAVE* Low-keyed but harmonious, sweet nose; rather disappointing, ordinary flavour, so-so finish.
*March 1984**

Hermitage, Vin de Paille *CHAPOUTIER* Although rarely seen, straw wine is still occasionally made by Chapoutier, the oldest and largest family *Maison du Vin* in Tain. The alcoholic content is quite high, 15.2% in '81, with 35g residual sugar. Colour buttercup yellow; very unusual nose, reminded me of my grandmother's family dye-works, touch of chlorine, nutty; medium-sweet, fairly full-bodied, rich, powerful, good length.
*May 1988. In its idiosyncratic way**** but something of an acquired taste.*

1982****

Condrieu *GEORGES VERNAY* Lemon-tinged; squeeze of lemon, fresh walnuts; dry, fragrant, good flavour and length. Opened up and improved in the glass.
*Dec 1984. Then***(*)*

Hermitage blanc *CHAVE* Vanilla, marshmallow and fudge; slightly sweet, medium weight, soft yet with grip and adequate acidity.
*March 1984****

Hermitage blanc *VIDAL-FLEURY* Pale, raw and almond kernelly when first tasted. Most recently: straw gold, showing age; dry, spicy, touch of liquorice. Intriguing.
*Last tasted at a Miami Wine & Food Society dinner, Feb 1989****

Hermitage, 'Velours' *CHAPOUTIER* 'Vin de Marsanne Passerillé sur Pied' – the last year the grapes dried on vines instead of on straw. Buttercup yellow, strange Tokay Aszú-like bouquet and flavour: waxy, honeyed, medicinal, medium-sweet, soft, grapey, good length and aftertaste. Rare. Unusual.
*May 1991*****

1983***

Condrieu *J PINCHON* Yellow; youthful fragrant, walnuts; lovely flavour, soft, just enough acidity.
*Jan 1985****

Condrieu *GEORGE VERNAY* Bright buttery yellow; creamy, touch of walnuts, developed well; slightly sweet, solid, smooth, perfect weight and balance, gentle finish.
*Last tasted Dec 1985*****

Crozes Hermitage, Mule Blanche *P JABOULET AINE* Pale; fulsome; dryish, nice style but with the peach or almond kernel flavour I dislike.
*April 1986. In its way****

Hermitage blanc *CHAVE* First tasted the spring after the vintage: pale straw; touch of youthful pineapple, a powdery, appley scent; slightly sweet, soft, very pleasant chewy flavour, light acidity. Two years later surprisingly flat and dull.
*Last tasted April 1986. At its youthful best****

Hermitage blanc, Sterimberg *P JABOULET AINE* Deepish waxy yellow; strong peach kernelly nose and taste, good smooth texture, full-bodied.
*Feb 1991****

1984*

Condrieu, Ch du Rozay Lemon yellow; dry, unusual flavour, mild, delightful, perhaps lacking acidity.
*Feb 1989***

1985****

Châteauneuf-du-Pape blanc, Ch de Beaucastel Surprisingly pale; light, nutty nose; dry, assertive with lots of grip, and nutty, slightly peach kernelly flavour.
*Jan 1990****

Condrieu *A CUILLERON* Waxy yellow; very unusual, minty, lemon curd; dry, quite powerful, flavour reminiscent of juniper.
*June 1988**(*)*

Condrieu, Viognier *G VERNAY* As Viognier is the only permitted grape in this small AC commune it is unnecessary to put it on the label. Distinctly disappointing. Medium-pale yellow, very slight green tinge; nose of wax and lemon, touch of kerosene, oak and meatiness; medium dry, fairly hefty, rich, taste of walnuts and pronounced almond kernels. Had I kept it too long? Or is it just not to my taste? After two sips I tipped it away.
April 1991 ?

Hermitage blanc *CHAVE* Very pale; charred lemon; medium dry, fullish, flavour hard to pin down, oaky, good acidity, length, finish.
*Jan 1990****

Hermitage blanc, Sterimberg *P JABOULET AINE*
Sulphur on nose; dry, firm in Feb 1987. Variable bottles recently: pale; one raw with strong almond taste, the other still kernelly but softer, better balanced.
Last tasted May 1991 ?

1986***

Châteauneuf-du-Pape blanc *DE LAUZE* The only time I have come across the Comte de Lauze's wine. Pale lemon; immature, slightly pineappley nose; dry, medium-full body, an interesting and unusual uplift of flavour, hot, youthfully acidic finish.
Nov 1987. Then(***) Probably delicious now.

Hermitage, Sterimberg *P JABOULET AINE* Virtually colourless; immature, pineappley, fragrant; dry, firm — really like almost any other young dry white wine. Good finish.
Feb 1987 Then(***) Probably showing well now.

1988****

Good vintage, firm wines. Possibility of long life.

Hermitage blanc *GUIGAL* Medium-pale yellow; lovely, intriguing, spicy nose; dry, medium-full body, firm, good flavour, needs time.
Nov 1990(***) Say 1992–96.*

Hermitage blanc, Sterimberg *P JABOULET AINE* Medium yellow; still a youthful appley nose; dry, nutty, oaky.
*Feb 1991**(**)*

1989*****

Glorious vintage. Marvellous richness and fruit. Probably best though between four and eight years of age.

Condrieu *GUIGAL* Pale; lovely, rich, nutty, oaky nose — marvellous after a range of austere Chablis; medium dry, medium full-bodied, lovely flavour, warm spicy finish. Sold out before I had a chance to order!
*Nov 1990**(**) Possibly ***** Say 1993–97.*

Hermitage blanc, Sterimberg *P JABOULET AINE* Pale; touch of recognisable Hermitage lemon; extraordinary, powdery, scented flavour. Attractive.
*Feb 1991**(**) 1992–96*

1990****

Yet another very good vintage throughout the Rhône.

Condrieu *GUIGAL* Palish yellow; youthful, floral; fairly dry, ostensibly mild, misleadingly powerful. Good acidity. Needs bottle-age.
*May 1991**(**) 1992–98*

LOIRE

Château de Chenonceau

Essentially Loire wines are made to be drunk young and fresh. The bone-dry Muscadet and Sancerre, perfect shellfish wines, are the staple of restaurants everywhere, and one vintage tends to succeed the other. The same applies to the attractive medium dry to dry Anjou rosés. Apart from the firm, dependable, sometimes austere Savennières, my interest, and the main subject of this necessarily brief section, lies in the few top-class *demi-sec* and *doux* wines from the mid-Loire: Vouvray, Coteaux du Layon and Quarts de Chaume. Certain vintages are supreme, need bottle-age and last well.

Being a rather northerly vineyard area and, towards the west, subject to a maritime climate, the weather pattern can be very changeable — a total contrast to the continental clime of Alsace and the southern warmth of the Rhône. Vintages are easy for the English to predict. If there is a heat-wave in southern England it will be a good vintage in the Loire! If a cold wet summer in England, the wines in the Loire are likely to be thin and even more acidic than usual.

The following notes deal almost exclusively with the top-class sweeter wines, save for comments on very recent vintages. Prior to 1988, most of the more commercial dry whites are either passé or unavailable or both.

How to taste and when to drink:

The *demi-sec* and dessert wines have much in common with their German counterparts and are best drunk alone as delicious summer wines, not with food. The exception is slightly sweet Vouvray, which used traditionally to be drunk — and is delicious — with Dover sole.

*Pre-***1928**

One or two long-established growers in the mid-Loire have wines going back to the 19th century in their cellars. The vintages tally with those known to be outstanding for white wines in northern Europe, particularly in districts on a similar or more northerly latitude: the Côte d'Or, Champagne, Alsace, the Rhine and across to Hungary. Doubtless the 1811 would have been the greatest though I have not come across any of that age in the Loire, also the 1865, 1874, 1900, and scorchingly hot years like 1893 and 1921.

I have several notes on '21s made in the early to mid-1970s. Marc Brédif's Vouvray Liquoreux: amber gold, consistently delicious; and Alfred Arrault's Saché (AC Azay-le-Rideau), a *demi-sec*, almost as good. In short, the best, from cool cellars, can be a revelation.

1928*****

The best vintage between 1921 and 1937.

Anjou, Rablay *Bottled by Prunier's, Paris* In 1982 Mme Prunier informed me that they had large stocks of old wine surplus to their requirements. I visited the restaurant Prunier Traktir and found that the cellars extended from near L'Etoile a long way down their side of the street. Amongst other wines, mainly old Sauternes, I found binned roughly 100 dozen bottles of '28 Anjou and the same number of half-bottles. M Barnagaud-Prunier asked if I was free to lunch so, in view of the enormous quantity of Anjou, I asked if I could try a half. He brought a bottle. It was delicious. I drank the lot.

The story of the wine is the story of changing fashion and economies. Being a famed fish restaurant, white wines featured heavily. Old M Prunier was knowledgeable and visited the Loire annually on buying trips. The 1928 vintage had an unusually high reputation and on his visit in the spring of 1929 he purchased a quantity which was delivered in cask and bottled in his own cellars. This coincided with the slump. Then came the war. The cellars were bricked up. After the war, semi-sweet wines were out of fashion. Muscadet and Sancerre were preferred, as they still are. Moreover, the French do not like to drink old wine. This was the problem.

The solution was to brazen it out and put it all into one sale at Christie's. Thanks to tasting notes and sound samples it all sold. I bought some for Christie's and some for myself. Consequently I have nearly 36 notes from 1982 to the present day. One or two half-bottles were a bit tired. But none less than glorious: a beautiful burnished gold (it looks fabulous in a decanter); heavenly, waxy, lanolin-like Chenin Blanc nose with honeyed bottle-age; medium, neither sweet nor dry (perfect with any fish dish), medium weight, a glorious flavour and perfect acidity. Just a little short. Dry finish.

*Last tasted at a boardroom luncheon, May 1991**** A revelation, as always.*

Moulin Touchais Undoubtedly the most renowned sweet Loire white. An Anjou Chenin Blanc, made — hoarded — by the Touchais family. The wines sprang into prominence in the late 1970s, and my first exposure was at a tasting of seven vintages, including this, organised by Dr John Jenkins. A beautiful yellow, like satin, shot with gold; touch of age on the nose but rich, complete — the smell of a thoroughbred stables! Medium-sweet, rich, marvellous acidity holding it together and giving it a fine dry finish. Austere but good.

*At an Imperial College Senior Common Room tasting, Jan 1981*****

1933***

Bonnezeaux, Ch de Fesles Rich, glowing, green-tinged amber; medium — drying out but good flavour and more power than the Touchais. Dry finish.

*June 1982****

Moulin Touchais Several notes in the early 1980s. One bottle woody, raw, acidic. A lighter style, pale for its age; at best a very good classic mature Chenin Blanc nose; medium-sweet.

*Last tasted June 1982****

1934****

Vouvray, Clos Baudoin An estate owned since 1918 by the family of Prince Poniatowski. Remarkably pale for its age; soft, slightly peachy, waxy, harmonious bouquet with a squeeze-of-lemon acidity. Dry, lightish style and weight, flavour like oil of walnuts.

*At dinner with Janet and Freddie Price, Aug 1983*****

1937*****

One of the most successful white wine vintages of the century. Arrault's Saché, tasted twice in 1977, excellent.

Moulin Touchais Two notes. The colour and smell of Tate and Lyle's Golden Syrup. Lovely, honeyed: *pourriture* and bottle-age; medium-sweet (one bottle drying out a bit), rich, complex, refreshing. Excellent '37 acidity.

*Last tasted Feb 1982*****

1945****

Very good vintage. Fine firm wines. The best still good.

Ch de Breuil Bottle variation, one tawny, maderised, the other yellow amber gold; scent of crème brûlée; fairly sweet, rich, excellent flavour, good length and acidity.

*Oct 1982*****

Coteaux du Layon *MAURICE BOUGRIER* Amber gold; waxy, vanilla, slightly appley Tokay-like nose; medium-sweet, excellent acidity.

*Dec 1972****

Moulin Touchais Wonderful colour, pure gold; nose low-keyed at first but blossomed in the glass; sweet, assertive mid-palate. Drying end acidity. Faultless.

*Jan 1981******

1947*****

The most successful, the most luscious post-war vintage and the best virtually guaranteed still to be excellent.

Bonnezeaux, Ch de Fesles Marvellous colour, a rich, glowing, green-edged amber; excellent bouquet, soft, sweet; sweet on palate, full body, full flavour, touch of wood, excellent acidity.

*June 1982*****

Bonnezeaux, Ch des Gauliers *FOURLINE-BOIVIN* As always with old white wines, I decanted it. A marvellously deep amber with, in the glass, an apple green rim;

whiff of 'vaseline', oily richness and a dash of mandarin, then meaty, like fried bacon, finally, sweet, barley-sugar bottle-age and *Botrytis* bouquet; medium-sweet (drying out), lovely concentration of flavour, tangy acidity.
*May 1991*****

Moulin Touchais Deep buttercup yellow; *Beerenauslese*-like nose; fairly sweet, lovely flavour, crisp finish.
*Feb 1982*****

Vouvray *BREDIF* Bought by the family in 1893 — a good year to start. In 1965 Marc Brédif handed over to his son-in-law who subsequently sold out to the ubiquitous de Ladoucette. Two notes: golden; classic waxy honeyed Chenin nose; medium-sweet, a bit more four-square than the Foreau but all the component parts there.
*Last tasted June 1982*****

Vouvray Doux *FOREAU* Several notes. First in 1979. Now medium-deep orange gold; low-keyed but piquant nose, touches of peach and honey; medium-sweet, crisp, lightish style, gentle, lovely flavour, at best perfectly balanced, one with a little pasty acidity.
*Last tasted June 1986*****

1949*****

Though not as luscious as the '47s, perfect fruit, structure, with firmer and better acidity.

Coteaux du Layon, Chaume, Ch Guimonière Chaume is the most superior of the seven designated Coteaux districts, with restricted *rendement*, as in Sauternes. A marvellous amber gold; slightly scented, classic *Botrytis* and bottle-age, five-star bouquet; medium sweetness and weight, slightly chewy, exciting flavour, excellent acidity.
*June 1982*****

Moulin Touchais Several notes in the early 1980s. On one, a touch of pineapple and slightly sickly nose though perfect weight and flavour. Medium-pale, green-tinged; classic; fairly sweet, assertive flavour, low-keyed but can be very good.
*Last tasted June 1982. At best*****

1953***

Good vintage though none tasted recently.

Vouvray, Clos Paradis *Demi-sec*. Showing well.
1972

1955**

Good but not a hot enough summer to produce the luscious wines.

Coteaux du Layon, Chaume, Ch Guimonière Clean, crisp, very good bouquet; well-nigh perfect flavour, rather hard acidic dry finish.
*June 1982*****

Moulin Touchais Only tasted once, possibly a less-than-good bottle. Singed, slightly oloroso-like nose; medium-sweet, some fat cut by lively acidity.
*Jan 1981***

Vouvray *BREDIF* Medium-deep yellow; waxy, slightly oily nose; dry, crisp, rather austere.
*June 1983****

1959*****

A marvellous vintage. Best since 1947 and unequalled in weight and concentration.

Coteaux du Layon, Chaume, Ch Guimonière Perfect bouquet and taste but surprisingly austere, leaner than expected. Good grip but needing even more bottle-age.
*June 1982***(*)*

Moulin Touchais The youngest and in many ways the most impressive vintage at the Imperial College tasting in 1981. Another five notes, the earlier ones remarking that it was not as deep-coloured as expected though more recently amber gold; extraordinary nose, rich, minty, candle wax, 'varnishy', 'furniture polish', 'celluloid' noted; sweet, powerful yet not heavy, assertive, good length, flavour of vanilla, butterscotch, excellent aftertaste.
*Last tasted Oct 1987. Idiosyncratic but warranting***** Years more life ahead.*

Vouvray *BREDIF* Fairly deep yellow; plump, waxy Chenin nose and flavour. Medium-sweet, some vanilla, crunchy, flavoury.
*June 1982*****

Vouvray *FOREAU* A flat yellow; very good honeyed nose, the aroma reminding me of a soft ripe Sémillon. Medium dry, very good flavour. 10–15 years more life.
*Oct 1982*****

Vouvray, Clos Naudin, moelleux *FOREAU* Very pale for its age and style; calm, waxy nose, like a snuffed candle; slightly sweet, gentle, rich: perfect balance.
*Nov 1983*****

1961** *to* ***

Not remotely as good as 1959 for the sweet, though the dry wines — now too old — were crisp and refreshing.

Moulin Touchais Very yellow; rather peach-kernelly nose and taste. Medium-sweet.
*Feb 1982***

1962****

Good fruit, balance and acidity.

Moulin Touchais Impressively buttery colour; hefty, buttery nose; medium-sweet, fairly full-bodied, surprisingly crisp acidity.
*Feb 1982*****

1964*****

A hot summer and the best vintage of the decade for the semi- and sweet Loire wines. The dry whites however lacked acidity, some being flabby. Many tasted, mainly prior to 1980.

Bonnezeaux, Ch de Fesles First tasted in 1972, labelled "*1er grand cru*" and "médaille d'Or, Concours du Comité Interprofessionel des Vins d'Anjou et de Saumur 1965": a whiff of aniseed, pineapple husks; lovely flavour. A decade later: more delicate than the '47, fragrant; sweet, fairly full-bodied, flavoury, fat but with good refreshing end acidity.
*Last tasted June 1982*****

Bonnezeaux, Ch des Gauliers Several notes in the 1970s. I bought some in 1973 and noted it again more than once the following year. An attractive yellow, bright and lively; low-keyed waxy Chenin Blanc nose; medium-sweet, seeming to sweeten in the mouth, refined, well-balanced, not great but very satisfactory.
*Last tasted Nov 1980**** Doubtless still good.*

Coteaux du Layon, Ch Guimonière Classic honeyed *Botrytis* nose; medium sweetness and body, some '64 fat, dry finish. Beautifully made.
*June 1982*****

Moulin Touchais Several notes in the early to mid-1980s. Fine bright golden colour; an extraordinary nose, high-toned, linoleum, but amazingly fragrant and refreshing; fairly sweet, plump yet shapely, slightly varnishy flavour, very good acidity and finish.
*Last noted Nov 1984**** Strangely attractive.*

1966***

Well-balanced wines, the dry were excellent, the sweet less successful.

Bonnezeaux, Ch de Fesles Gentle waxy nose; fairly dry, rather dull.
*June 1982***

1969***

Good vintage. The sweeter wines holding well.

Bonnezeaux, Ch de Fesles Fairly pale; well-knit, honeyed nose; medium-sweet, some fat, well-balanced.
*June 1982****

Coteaux du Layon, Ch Guimonière Pale; fragrant; rather raw, slightly bitter finish.
*June 1982**

Moulin Touchais Open, oily; sweet, rich, meaty, good acidity.
*June 1982****

Vouvray demi-sec *BREDIF* Yellow; calm waxy harmonious nose; much drier than expected, well made, attractive, good acidity.
*Nov 1980*** Probably dried out by now.*

1970**

Noted more for abundance than class. Pleasant enough wines. Ripe grapes but not a dessert wine year.

Vouvray sec *BREDIF* Very good nose. Really dry.
*Jan 1983****

Vouvray demi-sec *FOREAU* Very *demi* – like a German *halbtrocken*, fairly dry, soft, rather neutral flavour.
*May 1980***

1971***

Stylish, elegant, well-balanced. Still good. Acidic.

Quarts de Chaume *DOM BAUMARD* Surprisingly pale and youthful for its age; lovely waxy vanilla nose (once again the Chenin reminding me of Sémillon) and flavour. Medium-sweet, good acidity. Perfect condition.
*An unusual marie-jeanne brought by Hugo Dunn-Meynell to a Wine & Food Society dinner, Aug 1989*****

Vouvray *BREDIF* Lovely, pale, medium dry, lean and crisp. Marvellous for an 11-year-old. In this sort of vintage, keeps better than good dry white Rhône.
*June 1982****

Vouvray, Pétillant, demi-sec *FOREAU* Though somewhat out of place here, included to demonstrate how good these sparkling Vouvrays can be and how well they keep. At 15 years a lovely gold with lethargic sparkle; medium-sweet, pure Chenin flavour, good acidity. Delightful.
*Nov 1986****

1973**

Pleasant, somewhat overlooked. Better for dry whites. Brédif's Vouvray very good in 1978.

Quarts de Chaume *DOM BAUMARD* Very dependable grower. Very pale; fragrant bouquet, good depth; medium-sweet, slightly malty finish.
*April 1989***

1975***

Surprisingly good. The richer wines will continue to please.

Moulin Touchais The familiar rich, slightly goaty, oily, extraordinary nose; sweet, full, very rich. A powerful, almost pungent wine, good length and aftertaste.
*June 1982*** If I were more generous, four stars. Doubtless still going strong.*

Quarts de Chaume *DOM BAUMARD* Pale; creamy, touch of raspberry, good depth; medium-sweet, lightish weight, crisp, excellent acidity.
*Aug 1985****

1976****

A very good vintage. The year of exceptional heat and drought in England, broken by rain, incessant from Aug 31. Continental Europe more fortunate. The sun and warmth continued. Result: marvellously ripe grapes. Rather to my surprise I have tasted very few recently.

Jasnières *JEAN-BAPTISTE PINON* Jasnières is an *hameau*, a hamlet, giving its name to a rather rarified wine made from Chenin Blanc with very limited yield grown within the larger Coteaux du Loir (*sic*, a confusingly named tributary of the Loire). First noted in 1980, very dry, rather Savennières-like. A bottle was then given to me by the Marquis de Goulaine, a prominent Muscadet grower, to demonstrate Jasnières' keeping qualities. The '76 certainly made the '83 I tasted alongside appear raw and immature. The colour had deepened to waxy yellow gold, the nose acquired nutty honeyed bottle-age; it seemed less dry, a lovely flavour, perfectly balanced.
*Last noted July 1987*****

Saumur Champigny *DOM FILLIATREAU* A relatively old note, included to make the point that, in my opinion, Loire reds are tolerable only in really good vintages like '59, '64, '76 and doubtless '89. In a poor vintage they are thin, raw and acidic. The major reds, Chinon, Bourgueil, St Nicolas-de-Bourgueil are all made from the Cabernet Franc. Usually a good colour, purple-tinged when youthful as this was, with a slightly jammy raspberry fruitiness; fairly dry, medium-light, pleasant fruit and not over-acidic.
*Nov 1980****

Vouvray, Aigle Blanc, demi-sec *PONIATOWSKI* Buttery yellow; faint whiff of geraniums suggesting sorbic acid, and strange taste. Medium-sweet. A bit disappointing.
Oct 1989.

1978*** *to* ****

Particularly good for Sancerre and Pouilly and the dry whites of the mid-Loire. Roblin's rapier-like Sancerre and two Savennières, Mme Joly's Coulée de Serrant and Baron Brincard's La Roche aux Moines, particularly notable in the early 1980s.

1979***

An attractive vintage destined for early drinking. Virtually all showing well in 1981 to 1983: several Muscadets, Pouilly Blanc Fumé, including du Nozet, bone dry Sancerres and agreeable medium-sweet wines with tingling acidity from Bonnezeaux and Coteaux du Layon.

1980**

The best early spring and the worst summer of the period. Six weeks of uninterrupted rain delayed and extended the flowering, though the early autumn was warm and sunny. Late harvest during second week in Oct and snow reported in Vouvray, Quarts de Chaume and Bonnezeaux. Despite all this some surprisingly pleasant wines, including attractive medium-sweet Quarts de Chaume, Ch de Bellerive and Dom des Baumard, both very pale, grassy, light, and Ch de Fesles from Bonnezeaux, with more colour and body, all noted between 1983 and 1986. Just one recent:

Vouvray (presumably demi-sec) *BREDIF* Palish

waxy yellow; pleasant Chenin Blanc nose and flavour. Touch of sweetness, on the light side, good acidity. Still fresh and bright.
*Oct 1989****

1981**

Generally small harvest of modest wines, mostly consumed within a year or so of the vintage. Strangely, I noted a lack of acidity in two Savennières, Clos de la Coulée de Serrant and Ch de Chamboureau, and a Sancerre, Les Roman, yet Vouvrays had good acidity, in particular Poniatowski's Aigle Blanc and Clos de la Meslèrie.

1982***

Well-nigh perfect weather during the growing season: warm spring, hot summer, sufficient rain though some violent storms during the vintage. Generally large and satisfactory harvest. Some Pouilly-Fumé wines plumper than usual, Michel Redde's in particular had almost a creamy nose, not the usual tart Sauvignon Blanc aroma, very agreeable on palate. Drinking well between 1984 and 1986 when my notes were made. They were not wines to keep.

1983**

Ideal flowering then hot. Warm and very humid in July and Aug with frequent storms and some hail. Constant spraying. Heavy rain and variable temperatures from mid-Sept. Dry wines for early drinking; keynote crisp acidity. Not for keeping. No sweeter wines noted.

1984*

Very dry acidic wines of no distinction. Refreshing enough when young, some blowsy, some too thin and tart. Mostly, and rightly, consumed. Not to be sought after.

Pouilly-Fumé, Les Moulins à Vent Attractive, in a light fruity way.
1988

Saumur Champigny *DOM FILLIATREAU* Combining a delicious raspberry nose with a touch of rot. Went well with garlic sausages.
1987

1985****

Generally good conditions. The mid-Loire, Anjou and Vouvray benefited from a rare, sustained run of hot and dry weather from the third week of Aug until early Nov. The reds and the sweet whites particularly notable.

Azay-le-Rideau, Touraine Sec *G PAVY* Practically colourless; youthful, herbaceous; very dry, lean, rather rasping.
*Aug 1987**

'Bouquet' *ALBERT BESCOMBES* A new AC, Anjou-Villages, first noted at a trade tasting in Jan 1988. A low yield, 90% Cabernet Franc, 10% Cabernet Sauvignon: immature purple, refreshing but not over-acidic. Still youthful; glorious fruit gushing out of the glass; dry, lightish, distinctive berry-like flavour, oak discernible, tannic, good acidity. An exciting wine.
*Last tasted Sept 1990**(*)*

Bourgueil, Dom des Ouches *PAUL GAMBIER 'Cuvée Assemblage'* — a medium red; strange nose and taste, not fruity, rather stalky. Another cuvée, the winner of a *Medaille d'Or, Mâcon, en barrique*, had the characteristic piquant raspberry-like aroma, was not too dry, fairly light and surprisingly soft and easy. Yet another 'brew' that had won a gold medal in Paris had a similar nose but more grip and bite on the palate. When to drink? Summer luncheons, picnics, after-theatre suppers — with something spicy.
At a Thorman Hunt tasting, April 1987. From to**(*). Drink when reasonably young and fresh, the best, say, now to 1993.*

Coteaux du Layon, Chaume *CH DE LA ROULERIE* Palish waxy yellow; scented, honeyed Chenin nose and taste. Medium-sweet, good acidity.
*June 1991*****

Sancerre, Clos des Romains *VACHERON* Here the reds are made from the Pinot Noir. The 1985 seemed a conducive vintage. A plummy ruby colour; sweet, distinctly Pinot aroma, softer, less raw than the Cabernet Franc; a distinct touch of sweetness, very pleasant flavour — much softer than its counterpart from Bourgueil.
*July 1987****

1986****

Ideal for the dry whites. Many notes of light dry, crisply acidic wines mainly from Sancerre, Pouilly-Fumé, the latter reputed to be the best of the decade.

Vins d'Orleans, Auvernat Blanc *ROGER MONTIGNY* A VDQS new to me from the enterprising merchant of Mère, Robin Yapp. *Auvernat* is the local synonym for Chardonnay. Distinctive: pale lime yellow; amazingly full, scented nose erupting out of the glass, honeysuckle, pineapple; medium dry, youthful scented flavour, light style and weight, Loire acidity, dry finish.
*Sept 1987****

1987*

Muscadet perhaps the most successful due to earlier flowering and earlier harvesting than further up the valley. Nevertheless, variable from producer to producer. Likewise Pouilly-Fumé. My advice: choose carefully, drink quickly. There was plenty of sun from mid-July to early Sept but the month ended in rain. Early pickers here and in Touraine did best. The red grapes of Chinon, Bourgueil and Saumur were rain-gorged, resulting in a large production of acid-deficient wine.

Muscadet Ch de la Galissonière Very ordinary, dry, dull, stalky.
July 1989.

Muscadet Ch des Montys *MARQUIS DE GOULAINE* Much more fruity, crisp, good length, Sancerre-like acidity.
Sept 1988.

Muscadet, Cuvée du Millenaire *MARQUIS DE GOULAINE* Sulphury, very dry, very acidic.
Sept 1988.

Pouilly-Fumé *DOM PABIOT* Pale, distinct green tinge; aroma of raw blackcurrants, mint, mouthwatering acidity; dry, light yet full of flavour. Flowery mid-palate, lingering acidity.
*Nov 1989****

Pouilly-Fumé Les Champs des Plantes *B PLANCHET* Very pale; hollow, grassy; dry, austere, unattractive.
March 1989.

Sancerre Several growers, also variable, too pale, "acetone" noted, also gooseberry-like acidic fruit, mostly lean and on the tart side. At best refreshing. Drink up.

Savennières *MME JOLY* The most agreeable '87.
*Tasted Oct 1989***

1988****

A very satisfactory vintage for the dry whites, reds and

sweet whites following a good growing season, warm summer, harvest two weeks earlier than usual. Drinking well now. The *demi-sec* and *moelleux* will keep.

Baron de 'L' Ladoucette's top wine. Very pale, almost colourless; grassy nose; dry, fragrant, tangy, high acidity.
*At a Chinese banquet in Hong Kong, Oct 1989****

Quarts de Chaume *DOM DES BAUMARD* Pale; fragrant; medium-sweet, light style, almost spritz. Hopeless with pudding.
*April 1991****

Sancerre, Dom de Montigny *HENRI NATTER* Tinged with lime, a shade to make the mouth water; gooseberry-like fruit-acid – a touch of tom-cats; dry, light, refreshing. Which is what Sancerre is all about.
*Jan 1990****

Savennières, Clos des Papillons *DOM BAUMARD* Dry pleasant weight, very good firm flavour and acidity. Archetypal.
*At Restaurant Markwitz, Bristol, April 1991****

Vouvray Demi-sec, Le Peu de la Moriette *JEAN-CLAUD PICHOT* Rather more Chenin Blanc aroma, lightly honeyed nose, but though lean and clean, more *sec* than *demi*.
*April 1990** to*** For early drinking.*

Vouvray Moelleux, Le Peu de la Moriette *JEAN-CLAUD PICHOT* Grassy, minty nose; also drier than expected but very attractive flavour and nicely balanced.
*April 1990** to*** For early drinking.*

Vouvray Sec, Coteaux de la Biche *CHRISTOPHE PICHOT* Pale; dry, grassy, flavoury.
*April 1990** to*** For early drinking.*

1989*****

This, surely, is *the* vintage for the semi-sweet and sweet whites. Rather like Sauternes, a felicitous twin of the '88, different style, the '89s being softer, more luscious. The sun-enriched grapes produced, as in 1959 and 1964, untypical dry whites: plumper, riper, less acidic than in a more normal Loire year, particularly at the two extremities, Muscadet, and the twins Sancerre and Pouilly. Many tasted. It is quintessentially a Chenin Blanc vintage, the quality and richness of the best on a par with the legendary '47s. They also have something in common with German dessert wines though higher in alcoholic content. Some analyses stated where known.

Bonnezeaux, La Montagne *DOM DE PETIT VAL* Pale, green-tinged; light, grassy grapey aroma, acidic, some depth; medium-sweet (residual sugar 73g/l), misleadingly light style despite remarkably high alcoholic content (14.2%), crisp fruit, refreshing acidity (4.9). Fragrant.
*May 1991***(*) 1992–2000*

Coteaux du Layon, Beaulieu, Clos des Ortinières *DOM D'AMBINOS* Lemon yellow; floral, waxy, honey, cloves, sulphur (which blows away); medium-sweet, soft, lovely, excellent acidity.
*May 1991**** Now to beyond 2000.*

Montlouis, Moelleux *CAVE CO-OP DE MONTLOUIS* Montlouis tend to be drunk on the spot, or in Paris. Certainly a district overshadowed by its neighbour, Vouvray. This wine was a gold medal winner and I can see why: medium-sweet, a light charmer with crisp, refreshing acidity.
*May 1990****

Quarts de Chaume, Ch de Bellerive Medium-pale waxy yellow; rich, scented, distinctive, minty, touch of stalk; medium-sweet (residual sugar 82g/l), fullish body (14% alcohol), positive waxy Chenin flavour, rich, slight trace of peach kernels, good acidity (4.9), still rather hard. Needs time.
*May 1991**(**) 1993 to beyond 2000.*

Sancerre *PIERRE DEZAT* Many tasted. This, another Paris gold medal winner, was very pale; hard acid nose; dry, lean; achieving crisp fragrant acidity despite the riper than usual grapes.
*April 1990****

Sancerre, Chavignol *VINCENT DELAPORTE* Several notes: very pale, distinct greenish tinge; fresh, with the raw currants and tom-cats scent of Sauvignon Blanc, herbaceous, squeeze of lemon; very dry, lightish, good length, flavoury, adequate acidity.
*Last tasted Feb 1991*** Drink now.*

Vouvray, Clos du Bourg, Moelleux *HUET* Medium-deep yellow; lowish keyed, buttermint nose; medium-sweet (residual sugar 64g/l), good body (13.65% alcohol), very positive and firm flavour, length, excellent acidity (5.70) and aftertaste. Needs time.
*April 1991***(**) 1993–2000+*

Vouvray, Cuvée Constance, Moelleux *HUET* Mind blowing! Rabelais described Vouvray as "like taffeta". I can see what he meant. Made from selected grapes affected by 'noble rot' from Huet's three domaines, Le Haut Lieu, Le Mont and Le Clos du Bourg. The yield was only 5 hectolitres per ha. There were 390g/l of natural sugar in the grape juice, a long fermentation in barrel just managing to achieve 10.9% alcohol and leaving 162g/l of residual sugar. The result a deliciously sweet wine with marvellous counterbalancing acidity (6.05). Colour already a medium-deep yellow gold; soft, rich, waxy, honeyed *Botrytis* nose, touch of 'vaseline'; full, delicious peachy honeyed flavour, good length, perfect acidity. All the components for at least 50 years.
*May 1991****(**)! Lovely now but best 1994 to 2020, but will go on.*

Vouvray, demi-sec, Le Marigny, 2me trie *J-C PICHOT* Good positive Chenin Blanc aroma; medium dry, certainly more *demi* than his '88.
*April 1990**(*)*

Vouvray, Le Haut-Lieu, 1er trie *SA HUET* Lovely waxy yellow green; harmonious, honeyed *Botrytis* nose; medium-sweet (residual sugar 100g/l), agreeable weight (12.9% alcohol), lively, honeyed flavour and excellent acidity (5.70). Still a bit hard.
*May 1991***(*) 1992–2000*

Vouvray Moelleux, Vieilles Vignes, 2me trie *C PICHOT* Yellow green; light, grapey, slightly honeyed nose and flavour. Medium-sweet. Stylish.
*April 1990***(*)*

Vouvray, Vieilles Vignes, Moelleux, 3me trie *C PICHOT* Young, rather appley nose and taste. Medium-sweet.
*April 1990**(**)*

1990(*****)

Yet another *annus mirabilis*. Timely too for the erstwhile Cinderellas of the wine world, Vouvray and Coteaux du Layon. These are easy to drink but sometimes difficult to place (do not waste the sweeter ones on puddings. Cheese perhaps. Best by themselves). All – dry, medium dry, sweet and red – should give pleasure.

Sancerre, Chavignol *VINCENT DELAPORTE* Very pale, green-tinged; mouthwatering, gooseberry-like aroma; bone dry, fragrant fruitiness, high acidity – the sort of wine to drink young and fresh.
*Last tasted June 1991****

ALSACE

Of all the world's wine districts Alsace is hard to match, let alone beat, for dependability and good value. This is no place to restate its chequered history, one minute being German, the next French. Suffice it to say that, after World War I, determined producers systematically planted better quality vines and the resultant quality is plain to see.

The wines are named after the grape variety, the 'noble' Riesling and Gewurztraminer*, both capable of producing copybook styles of wine, the Tokay, which is now known as Tokay Pinot Gris to avoid confusion with the Hungarian wine, and the idiosyncratic Muscat. Secondary grapes such as Sylvaner now appear less frequently and these less distinctive wines scarcely feature in the notes that follow. Individual vineyard names are beginning to feature more and more, such as Sporen and the *grands crus* vineyards, Kitterlé, Rangen and Brand. However, most important of all is the name of the producer. If the Hugel family appear to dominate my notes it is because they have long been in the forefront as pioneers between the wars and indefatigable exporters since. First Jean then his son Johnny, through regular visits to England managed to make 'Hugel' and 'Alsace' synonymous. Some of the greatest Alsace wines I have ever tasted have been Hugel's, several noted at their 350th anniversary celebrations in Riquewihr, June 1989. But there are many other excellent producers.

* *In Alsace the umlaut ü is omitted*

1865*****

A great vintage in northern Europe and one that proves, if proof be needed, that if wine is good to begin with, and stored cool and undisturbed, it will keep.

Tokay d'Alsace *HUGEL* One of the very few remaining bottles in the family cellars, opened by Jean and André Hugel in Riquewihr after the remarkable rare-wine tasting at Burg Windeck. A deep warm amber tawny and, as it was an impromptu gesture, the wine being brought from the cellar at short notice, not quite bright; sweet honeyed grapey bouquet, no signs of decay, oxidation or over-acidity on nose or palate. Sweet – the Hugels thought it would have been over 200° Oeschle – rich, still vestiges of fat, perfect flavour and acidity. Remarkable.
*May 1983*******

1900*****

Riesling:

HUGEL Medium-pale amber brown, with a fairly heavy, bitty sediment; good old Riesling nose, lovely, scented not oxidised; fairly dry, but losing its punch and acidity.
At the dinner at L'Auberge de l'Ill to celebrate Hugel's 350th anniversary, June 1989.

Sélection Grains Nobles* *HUGEL* Decanted but still cloudy, amber; very rich, old stably nose, intense, magnificent in its way; dry, high acidity, rich but not appealing.
*Sept 1985*****

1921*****

Great vintage. Not tasted.

1928****

Riesling *ALBERT SCHOER* Vineyard believed to be **Kaefferkopf**. Excellent colour, deep yellow gold; gentle though very fragrant, trace of Muscat; medium dry, lovely calm, even flavour not unlike an old Chenin Blanc. Rich. Good acidity keeping it sprightly.
*At lunch with Mme Teysonneau in Bordeaux. It was the youngest white wine in her cellar! April 1979*******

1934****

One of the best inter-war vintages. Several tasted, three recently.

Riesling Mittelbergheim Stein *E BOECKEL* 2½in ullage. Lovely colour, honey, amber; toasted nose; dry but rich, quality, length.
*Pre-sale, March 1985*****

Traminer Réserve Exceptionnelle *HUGEL* If labelled today, would be "*Gewurztraminer, Sélection Grains Nobles*", or *SGN*. Made from *Botrytis*-infected grapes from the Spoerren vineyard. The potential alcohol at time of picking was 18.6%, a reading of 190° Oeschle and 55g/l residual sugar. Two consistent notes, the first in the mid-1980s. Lovely old gold; extraordinary bouquet, sweet, peach-like, old barley-sugar and butterscotch – like an old Yquem; fairly sweet, sugar content clearly high but drying out a bit, still rich and powerful, soft, marvellous acidity. Complete.
*Last noted at Hugel's 350th anniversary tasting, June 1989********

* *Sélection Grains Nobles* are known as, and in the notes that follow are shortened to, SGN.

1937*****

As in every other European wine district, an excellent year for white wines. However, acidity beyond the merely life-preserving.

Tokay d'Alsace, Grande Réserve *CAMILLE PREISS* Assertive but showing its age, more like its famous Hungarian namesake; very dry, high acidity. Alas, revolting!
Sept 1988.

1943***

The best of the wartime vintages, but difficulties due to German occupation.

Gewurztraminer, *CAVES JACOBERT* Despite its good level, rather drab old straw colour; old, appley nose; dry, tired.
At pre-sale tasting, Chicago, Feb 1986.

1945*****

Great year, as in all districts, white as well as red.

Gewurztraminer, SGN Colour rosehip tawny; very good, raisiny, green-tea bouquet, rather like Tokay essence; medium-sweet, which means drying out, full-bodied, flavour of dried raisins, excellent acidity.
*At Hugel's 350th, June 1989*******

1947****

1948***

1949****

1950***

1952****

Noted as "outstanding". Destined to be drunk young, and were. And I have no recent notes.

1953***

An attractive vintage. Ripe wines, tending to lack acidity. Masses of notes in the mid- to late 1950s. "Flabby" recurring frequently. The best can still be marvellous.

Riesling, Vendange Tardive *HUGEL* With late-harvest wines the problem is to manage to retain enough acidity to counterbalance the naturally high sugar content. In this instance it failed. The bouquet, though honeyed, was somewhat maderised.
May 1980.

Tokay, Vendange Tardive *HUGEL* Rich gold colour; smoky, honeyed bouquet that opened up, like warm toast; originally 150° Oeschle, now medium dry, four-square, solid yet stylish, just enough acidity to give the finish an uplift.
*A magnum at Peter Ziegler's rare wine lunch at Burg Windeck, May 1983*******

1955***

Good vintage. Mostly tasted, and drunk, in the late 1950s.

Riesling, Réserve Exceptionnelle *HUGEL* Mellow and lovely.
Early 1970s.

1957***

A naturally acidic vintage.

Riesling:

Réserve Exceptionnelle *HUGEL* A lovely fresh grapey aroma and flavour when first listed by Harvey's in the

summer of 1959. *Botrytis* noted, and its good acidity, when last tasted.
1961

Réserve Spéciale *SCHLUMBERGER* Dry, charming, drinking well.
1968

1958*

Mediocre vintage. Lacking acidity. None tasted recently.

1959*****

A great vintage. Because of the hot summer and extremely ripe grapes some of the lesser wines tended to lack acidity and 'zing' but great dessert wines were made.

Alsace wines were commonly shipped in cask. I have notes on '59s covering all grapes and qualities ranging from Zwicker up to a Gewurztraminer Réserve Exceptionnelle bottled by Harvey's (Harvey's name on the label not the producer's). The best can still be magnificent.

Gewurztraminer, SGN *HUGEL* Lovely rich gold; very sweet, harmonious, an almost powdery, custardy scent; unquestionably sweet on the palate, full-bodied, powerful even, firm, lovely, soft, spicy grape flavour. Dryish finish.
*At Hugel's 350th, June 1989*****

Riesling:

Sélection Exceptionnelle *DOPFF & IRION* Although an old note, memorable for me, and for perhaps one or two older readers of Kathleen Bourke's *Wine* magazine, the opening wine of the first of a series entitled "Dining with a Master of Wine". Our guests were the Duke of St Albans and Nubar Gulbenkian. We drank bottle no 4277 (out of a total of 4683 produced): a pale lemon straw; refreshing, lightly fruity; dry but not too dry, fairly assertive flavour.
*April 1966. Then****

Réserve Exceptionnelle *HUGEL* Distinctly dry and drinking perfectly.
*Oct 1967*****

Sélection Spéciale, Cuvée 27 *SCHLUMBERGER* Of *feine Spätlese* quality.
*July 1968****

Traminer:

Réserve Exceptionnelle Auslese *HUGEL* Slightly cloudy as it had been brought to Burg Windeck the morning of the tasting. It needed decanting but insufficient time had elapsed. The old straw smell and taste eventually opened up: rich old muscatelle, mouthfilling fruit.
*May 1983*****

Of the many tasted in the late 1960s and early 1970s:
Cuvée 37 *SCHLUMBERGER* Rich, ripe, powerful***
Cuvée Exceptionnelle *BEYER* Top class****

1960*

An abundance of light rather acidic wines, listed by Harvey's and first noted in 1961. Refreshing enough in the early 1960s. Not substantial enough to keep.

1961*****

Very good vintage. Less overripe, better acidity than 1959. Still worth looking out for, though most at their peak in the late 1960s and early 1970s.

Gewurztraminer, SGN *HUGEL* Surprisingly pale, still green-tinged; strange cheesy nose, spicy (*Gewurz*), showing no age; medium, neither sweet nor dry (35g/l residual sugar), medium-full body, pure spicy 'lychee' flavour, perfectly balanced, overall effect dry. A long life ahead.
*At Hugel's 350th, June 1989*****

Riesling *Although I detest 'rationalisation', Hugel's quality descriptions can be rather confusing.*

Réserve Exceptionnelle Beerenauslese (Would this now be SGN?) *HUGEL* A rich grapey nose; fairly sweet, fullish fat and rich.
Sept 1973.

Vendange Tardive, Personnelle Sélection *HUGEL* A refined wine of great depth.
May 1968.

Gewurztraminer:

Cuvée Exceptionnelle *BEYER* Delicately honeyed; beautiful richness and depth.
March 1973.

Traminer Sélection *SCHLUMBERGER* Mentioned mainly because of the old varietal name still used. Soft and lovely.
Late 1960s.

1962**

Rather hard but fairly light wines with crisp refreshing acidity.

Noted mainly in the mid- to late 1960s. The best tasted:

Gewurztraminer Spätlese *HUGEL* (note the Germanic late-picked suffix).

Riesling Réserve Spéciale *SCHLUMBERGER* A charmer.

1963*

Noted, at Deinhard's wide-ranging tasting of Trimbach wines in March 1965, as "a good year". In fact the wines were light and acidic. Refreshing. For quick drinking. None tasted recently.

Pinot Gris Riquewihr Sélection *DOPFF & IRION* Smelled and tasted of seaweed.
July 1973.

1964****

Hot year. Very ripe grapes. Better for the richer wines, Gewurztraminer in particular.

Many tastings between 1965 and 1973. Particularly notable:

Gewurztraminer, Vendange Tardive, Réserve Exceptionnelle Auslese, Sélection Personnelle Jean Hugel, bottle no 14 (What a lot to fit on that small yellow label.) Combining great richness and delicacy.
*April 1966. Then*****

Traminer *HUGEL* Very like its counterpart in the Pfalz, fragrant but earthy.

Riesling, Cuvée Exceptionnelle *BEYER* Attractive.
March 1973.

1965

Dreadful weather. Poor vintage, one of the worst ever.

1966***

A very satisfactory vintage: wines with good structure and acidity. The lesser wines consumed by the late 1960s, the better quality wines excellent in the early to mid-1970s.

Riesling:

Réserve Exceptionnelle *HUGEL* Drunk at lunch at the British Embassy in Paris with Christopher Soames.
June 1972.

Reserve Exceptionnelle Auslese Personnelle Sélection *HUGEL* Noted as the best Riesling ever tasted, at the André Simon Memorial tasting luncheon lecture I

gave at Christie's in 1971, confirmed when retasted in 1973.
Oct 1973.

Gewurztraminer, Réserve Exceptionnelle Vendange Tardive Personnelle Sélection *HUGEL* Rich, ripe, fabulous.
Oct 1974.

1967****

A very good vintage with some excellent late-picked wines. But, as in Germany, best in the early 1970s. Several attractively scented Gewurztraminer noted, and a particularly lovely **Tokay Réserve Exceptionnelle Spéciale Sélection** *JEAN HUGEL* in Oct 1974.

Gewurztraminer:

Réserve Exceptionnelle Vendange Tardive Personnelle Sélection *JEAN HUGEL* Smelling of old apples and honey, very rich, very fine.
Sept 1973.

SGN *HUGEL* Tasted 16 years after the above: a warm gold colour; showing considerable bottle-age on the nose, straw-like, akin to a Tokay Aszú, soft, peachy; now medium-sweet – drying out, full-bodied, a bit hard. Long past best but interesting.
*Last noted at Hugel's 350th, June 1989***

1968

Nearly as bad as 1965.

1969**

Average, though some attractive wines noted between 1971 and 1976, the Rieslings being dry and steely, the Gewurztraminers with more acidity than usual.

Muscat d'Alsace Carelessly the producer not noted, but interesting to drink a 17-year-old Muscat: positive yellow, considerably deepened with age; good ripe, mature, grapey bouquet; on the dry side but not bone dry or austere like some Alsace Muscats. Nice quality. Holding well. Attractive.
*June 1986****

1970**

Late flowering, some *coulure*, summer fine, harvest from mid-Oct yielding an abundant crop of ripe grapes. Wines very commercial but lacking zest. The majority recorded in 1972 and 1973 when they were best for drinking, "dull", "short" noted. Tired by now.

Gewurztraminer:

DOPFF Soft and spicy.
1974

Eichberg Récolte Tardive *DOPFF* Very good, very spicy, stylish.
1973

'Own Harvest' *DOPFF* Palish yellow; rather disappointing on the nose and rather dull and four-square on palate. A heavyweight clod-hopper.
*Last tasted March 1980**

1971*****

Very small harvest due to *coulure* and a very dry summer, the hot ripening autumn enabled wines of the highest quality to be made. Many notes, all grape varieties, several producers, mainly between 1973 and 1978, not one less than admiring amongst the best.

Gewurztraminer:

Cuvée Anne *SCHLUMBERGER* The finest of all the wines produced only in great years when they can rate their *grand cru* grapes 100%: very yellow; ripe, honeyed bouquet; fairly sweet, spicy, rich yet delicate. Superb.
July 1978. Doubtless still excellent.

Réserve Exceptionnelle *KUENTZ-BAS* Lovely, soft, scented, ripe, several notes.
Last tasted April 1982.

Clos St-Landelin, Grande Réserve Lovely.
At Hellmers annual tasting, Sept 1975.

Cuvée des Seigneurs de Ribeaupierre *TRIMBACH* Exhibiting typical delicacy.
Sept 1974.

The following all Hugel wines. Every grade of quality excellent:

Réserve Exceptionnelle Vendange Tardive Medium dry, delicate, spicy.
Last tasted in 1978.

SGN Pale for its age; a strange, high-toned cheesy, minty nose with a touch of kerosene, like a Riesling, but which opened out beautifully in the glass; fairly sweet, fat, strange earthy style, fully developed.
*Last tasted June 1989****

Sélection Premier Soft and delicious.
1973

Spätlese Surprisingly dry but excellent.
Noted several times in 1976 and 1977.

Muscat:

Grand Cru *PREISS-ZIMMER* Typical of this superb vintage for piquant wines with very grapey aromas and abruptly dry palate. Best drunk by the mid-1970s.

Réserve Exceptionnelle Vendange Tardive *HUGEL* Lovely when last tasted.
1978

Riesling *A perfect Riesling vintage, many tasted, none less than good in the mid-1970s:*

Réserve Cuvée Fredric Emile Trimbach *TRIMBACH* Dry, firm and delicate.

Cuvée Particulière *LEON BEYER* Surprisingly pale for its age (sulphur?); curiously scented, displaying neither Riesling character nor bottle-age; dry, nice weight, delicate, held in trim by its excellent acidity.
*Sept 1989***

Clos Ste-Hune *TRIMBACH* Yellowing with bottle-age yet still fresh with a light style despite ripeness and fullish body.
Last tasted, Jan 1983.

Réserve Exceptionnelle Vendange Tardive *HUGEL* Achieving a rare refinement.

Tokay *(now known as Tokay Pinot Gris) Also very good in 1971.*

Réserve Exceptionnelle Vendange Tardive *HUGEL* Excellent in 1973/4 but not tasted since though doubtless will have survived.

1972

Large crop. Poor acidic wines resulting from a combination of heavy rains, cold, drying winds from mid-Aug through the whole of the potential ripening period. Several notes in the mid-1970s: 'hard', 'green' Sylvaner; highly acidic Riesling; un-spicy and insubstantial Gewurztraminer, Muscat smelling of 'cold cats', austere.

1973***

Record crop thanks to good flowering and satisfactory summer. Undoubtedly overproduction, as in Bordeaux, but some nice wines made. My notes mainly made between 1974 and 1978. Amongst the Gewurztraminers Trimbach's Seigneurs de Ribeaupierre stood out, with an aroma like Turkish Delight, though short on palate; some attractive Muscats, Trimbach's again being very fragrant. Rieslings dry but tending to lack length.

Riesling, Vendange Tardive *HUGEL* The only '73 tasted in the 1980s. On both occasions: pale; a piquant, minty, almost Sauvignon Blanc-like aroma; dry, nice weight, firm and crisp. Good though not thrilling.
*Last tasted Jan 1983****

1974*

Small crop. Poor wines. After a cold start, a pleasant summer but the anticipated quality did not materialise owing to continuous rain during the last month of the potential ripening period. Only three '74s ever tasted: two short, dry, dumb and hard Rieslings in 1976 and 1977 and, in 1978, a passable fruity Tokay Kuentz-Bas that tailed off. Avoid.

1975***

Good summer. Late Oct harvest. Agreeable wines though some, particularly the Muscats, lacking acidity when tasted in the late 1970s, by which time most should have been drunk. No notes since a pleasantly scented Gewurztraminer (Hugel) in July 1980.

1976*****

A great year. Good flowering mid-June, sunny summer, early Oct harvest. Ideal conditions for late-picked wines of high quality, still superb. Many tasted, of which I report only the top wines.

Gewurztraminer, Vendange Tardive, Sélection Grains Nobles par Jean Hugel, Fût 20 Hugel's greatest cask: 137° Oeschle, a *Beerenauslese*, alcohol 13.7%, residual sugar 53g/l. Several notes: lively golden sheen; glorious bouquet, honey and barley-sugar from 100% *Botrytis*-affected grapes – ambrosial syrup of figs! Not as sweet as expected, full of flavour and richness, soft, ripe, peachy flavour, fragrant.
*Last tasted Jan 1990***** Now to 2000+*

Muscat, Réserve Personnelle *HUGEL* Surprisingly pale, very bright; developed grapey, spearmint aroma; dry, flowery and flavoury but a bit flat.
Last tasted April 1985. Drink up.

Riesling:

Clos Ste-Hune *TRIMBACH* Palish; lightly scented; dry, soft, fragrant, very agreeable.
*Lunch at Ch Lynch-Bages, May 1986****

SGN *HUGEL* One of Hugel's greatest Rieslings. Grapes, brought in late at 142° Oeschle, fermenting from Oct 20 to mid-July 1977. Residual sugar 51g/l. Six notes from 1982: pronounced buttercup yellow; initially a surprisingly delicate, grapey aroma, ripe, fragrant, with the honeyed richness of *Botrytis* and gaining additional dimensions with bottle-age; medium-sweet, pleasant weight, a lovely uplift of flavour, marvellous acidity.
*Last tasted June 1989***** Now to beyond 2000.*

Vendange Tardive *HUGEL* Grown in the *grand cru* Schoenenberg vineyard. Yellow gold; harmonious, rich, touch of oiliness; medium dry, soft, fruit and lemon.
*Last tasted Jan 1990****

Tokay Pinot Gris, SGN *HUGEL* Hugel's first SGN since 1865. Bouquet of spicy peach skins, rose cachou, crystallised violets; very sweet, medium body, marvellously gentle, rich, soft, rounded.
*Last tasted June 1989***** Now to 2000.*

1977*

Fair-sized production, mediocre quality. Some attractive enough Gewurztraminers, notably Boekel's, Hugel's and Trimbach's and the latter's dry, light Riesling, tasted in 1979. Only one since: a characterless Gewurztraminer of René Schmitt in 1980. Forget the '77s.

1978**

Delayed and unsatisfactory flowering, very late and small harvest. Nevertheless some quite good wines made. Of Gewurztraminers tasted 1980–82, Dopff au Moulin very scented and flavoury, the best was Trimbach's fragrant Cuvée des Seigneurs de Ribeaupierre.

Tokay Pinot Gris, Clos St Urban *ZIND-HUMBRECHT* A producer whose reputation has soared. Certainly justified by what must be one of the best of all the Alsace '78s: 105° Oeschle, 14.3% alcohol. Buttery gold; bouquet of milk and honey supported by good fruit; fairly dry though rich and fairly hefty.
*Sept 1986*****

Riesling, Clos Ste-Hune *TRIMBACH* Green-tinged; delicate, piquant fruit; fairly dry, light, crisp.
*Feb 1984***

1979**

Large crop of good commercial wines. Best in the early 1980s.

Gewurztraminer:

Réserve Personnelle *HEYT* Gentle, scented, light style.
*May 1984****

Cuvée Seigneurs de Ribeaupierre *TRIMBACH* Yellow; lovely, spicy lychee and soft grapes; a bit short.
*Oct 1984****

Riesling:

Réserve Personnelle *HUGEL* Delicate, light, dry.
May 1983.

Clos Ste-Hune *TRIMBACH* Lemon yellow; attractive, subtle, lanolin, grapey; pleasant weight and flavour.
*An ideal light lunch wine, with Ab Simon at The Four Seasons, June 1985****

1980*

Small crop. Muscat and Gewurztraminer severely reduced by poor flowering. Cold wet summer. Late, chilly harvest. My only notes are of Hugel's Gewurztraminer, fragrant, acidic for this grape, dry and fairly austere, last tasted in Nov 1982.

1981****

Very good year, quality and quantity. Good flowering, sunny summer, early harvest for Alsace but conditions continuing to enable excellent late harvest wines to be made. Many tasted. The reds about as good as they come.

Gewurztraminer:

HUGEL Muscat-like, spicy; better acidity than usual.
*July 1984***

LEON BEYER Highly scented; light, flavoury.
*March 1983****

Récolte Tardive *DOPFF AU MOULIN* Spicy, grapey, lychees; dryish, delicate, fragrant.
*Nov 1984****

Réserve *HEIM* Grapey, spicy; dry mouthfilling flavour.
*Nov 1984****

Réserve Personnelle *KUENTZ-BAS* Palish lemon; very scented; dryish, good acidity.
*May 1984*****

SGN *HUGEL* High potential alcohol: 19%, 75g/l residual sugar. Palish; soft, classic, gentle cachou; medium-sweet, spicy. Finishes hard.
*June 1989***(*) Now to 1998.*

Pinot Blanc, Les Lutins *JOS MEYER* An early-ripening variety grown in the sandy plain. Bottled July 1982. Good colour; neutral when young, developed well in bottle and at five years old good vinosity; dry, lightish, clean, nice fruit, fragrant but a bit hollow.
*Sept 1986***

Pinot Noir:

HUGEL Three months in oak: light, rather Beaujolais-like appearance; fruity, jammy—more Gamay than Pinot; slightly sweet, lightish, fruity.
*May 1983***

KUENTZ-BAS Palish, strawberry-like; dry, fullish, strange cardboardy flavour and bitter finish.
*Sept 1986**

Riesling:

Cuvée Emile *TRIMBACH* Green, grapey, acidic; dry, light, delicate, refreshing.
*Nov 1984***

Rangen (vineyard) *ZIND-HUMBRECHT* Low-keyed, gingery; flat, kernelly.
June 1990.

Schoenberg *DOPFF AU MOULIN* Very good nose; dry, light style, crisp, fruity.
Jan 1990.

Sélection Personnelle *HUGEL* Very flowery, almost Muscat; dryish, light, nice acidity.
*Feb 1983****

Cuvée Tradition *HUGEL* Dry, firm.
*Oct 1983****

Tokay d'Alsace:

Réserve Millésime *ROLLY GASSMANN* Grassy; toasty flavour, lovely.
*Nov 1984****

Réserve Particulière *PREISS-ZIMMER* Kernelly, sulphury, no character, expensive.
*July 1983**

Cuvée Tradition *HUGEL* Neutral but very pleasant.
*May 1983***

Tokay Pinot Gris, Vendange Tardive *HUGEL* Small production (100 cases). Lovely colour; beautiful nose, harmonious, cress; medium dry, glorious grape and melon flavour, fragrant aftertaste.
*Last tasted Jan 1990***** *Now to 2000.*

1982**

Huge crop, biggest since 1944. Local saying: in large harvests grapes sprout from the stakes—in 1982 surely from the wires! Good early flowering, hot summer, marvellous ripening period. But unexciting wines, mainly tasted in the mid-1980s. Passé now.

Gewurztraminer:

HUGEL Soft, spicy, boring.
*May 1985***

GUSTAV LORENTZ Yellow; spicy; firm and crisp***

ZIEGLER Soft, gentle, powdery; fragrant**

ZIND-HUMBRECHT Gold-tinged; floral, violet cachous; rich, 13%, a bit stolid***

Cuvée des Evêques *HUGEL* Yellow gold; scented, grapey; exotic yet lacking.
*May 1985****

Réserve Personnelle *HUGEL* Yellow gold; spicy cachous; dry, soft, blunt.
*Sept 1985***

Sporen *HUGEL* Delicate; gentle spice, fruit.
*April 1985****

Pinot Noir, Brandberg *R JOGGERST* Rosé; stewed fruit; highish alcohol, clean, pleasant.
*July 1984***

Riesling:

Brand *ZIND-HUMBRECHT* Dry, austere, good; short.
*Last tasted Aug 1985***

TRIMBACH Neutral, austere, flavourless.
*Feb 1985**

Vendange Tardive *HUGEL* Medium dry, good acidity.
*May 1983***

1983*****

The warmest winter, wettest spring and driest summer on record. Grapes ripened under ideal conditions, harvest from early Oct to mid-Nov. Well-balanced, exciting wines, the top, late-picked Gewurztraminers and Tokay Pinot Gris still excellent and will keep.

Gewurztraminer:

Altenberg *GUSTAV LORENTZ* Deep yellow; soft, like sea water; fairly sweet, ripe, lovely.
*May 1990*****

Cuvée des Comtes d'Eguisheim *BEYER* Buttercup yellow; powdery scent; massive, great potential.
*Sept 1986**(****)

Hengst Spicy, rose cachou; surprisingly dry, austere.
*June 1990****(*)

Kessler *SCHLUMBERGER* Palish; good nose; pleasant, easy.
*Oct 1987****

Cuvée Particulière *RENEE SCHMITT* Yellow gold; powdery scent, harmonious; dryish, grapey, good quality and flavour, needing time.
*Jan 1986***(**)

Rangen Gentle, harmonious, grapey nose; rich, powerful, lovely.
*June 1990*****(*)

Réserve *PREISS-ZIMMER* Dryish, solidly made.
*Oct 1986***(*)

Réserve Personnelle 'Jubilee' *HUGEL* Six notes. Grassy, spicy; dry, rather hefty style, good length.
*Last tasted Jan 1990****

Ribeaupierre *TRIMBACH* Distinctive yellow; copybook ripe Gewurztraminer, spicy, rose cachou, mildly exotic; touch of residual sugar, its spicy grapey flavour swelled mid-palate, hefty, overall dry, firm finish.
*Oct 1987****(**)

SGN *HUGEL* Glorious colour, pale gold; beautiful bouquet and flavour; medium-sweet, great length.
*June 1989******

Vendange Tardive *BLANCK DOM COMTES DU LUPFEN* Gloriously rich, scented; medium-sweet, hefty, opulent.
*Sept 1988*****(*)

Vendange Tardive *M KREIDENWEISS* Pale; lychee; well made but austere, needing time.
*Sept 1986***(**)

Vendange Tardive Guebersschwir *ZIND-HUMBRECHT* Nose reticent; very dry, assertive, length, excellent aftertaste.
*June 1990****(*)

Vendange Tardive, Réserve Personnelle *HUGEL* Peachy, aromatic, high alcohol (14.5%), hard dry finish.
*Last tasted Jan 1990****(*)

Muscat:

HUGEL Dramatic grapey tom-cats aroma, delicious if plausible.
*Oct 1986****

Réserve *TRIMBACH* Pale; very flowery, piquant, bone dry, flavour expanded in the mouth.
*Oct 1986****(*)

Tokay Pinot Gris:
Crystal *DOPFF & IRION* Uneven, needing time.
*1986***
Crystal *GISSELBRECHT* Dry, nice quality, needing time.
*1986**(*)*
Jubilee *HUGEL* Dry, powerful, good acidity.
*June 1989**(*)*
Réserve *BEYER* Yellow; still youthful, pineapple, flowery; dry, powerful but neutral flavour.
*Last tasted June 1989**(*)*
Réserve Personnelle *HUGEL* Difficult to define but a very individual flavour, fairly dry, good aftertaste.
*Jan 1990***(*)*
Réserve Personnelle *KUENTZ-BAS* Fragrant, creamy, lightly scented; full-flavoured, grapey, lively.
*Last tasted June 1991*****
SGN 192° Oeschle, 220g/l residual sugar. Deepish yellow; soft, slightly smoky, harmonious, like Williamine pears and apples in a loft; fabulously sweet and rich, fat, fleshy, concentrated, perfect acidity. Great, TBA quality.
*June 1989***** Now to beyond 2000.*
Riesling *Of the several noted in 1986:*
Cuvée des Ecaillers *BEYER* Bone dry, crisp, lean.
*June 1986**(**)*
Cuvée Fred Emile *TRIMBACH* 90° Oeschle. Light style despite components, fragrant, needing time.
*Sept 1986**(***)*
Jubilee *HUGEL* Dry, firm, good acidity. Needed time.
*Sept 1985**(*)*
Princes Abbés *SCHLUMBERGER* Austere but good.
*Sept 1986**(**)*
Cuvée Ste Catherine *MME THEO FALLER* 92° Oeschle, high for a late-ripening variety, green-tinged; very good flavour, length, acidity, aftertaste.
*1986***(*)*
Tradition *HUGEL* Firm, hard, good acidity.
*Sept 1985**(*)*
Vendange Tardive *HUGEL* Only 1% of Hugel's production even in a good vintage. Held for six years before release. Highly polished yellow-gold; harmonious, honeyed, crisp, grapey; fairly dry despite fractional residual sugar, full-bodied, spicy, rounded, acidity masked by richness.
*Jan 1990***(**)*

1984*

Late spring, protracted flowering, sunless summer, rot but sunny and dry Oct saved disaster.
Riesling:
Brand *ZIND-HUMBRECHT* Some colour; vinosity as well as some bottle-age; dry, still fresh, good length and acidity. Demonstrating what a good grower can do in a mediocre vintage.
*June 1990****
Rangen *ZIND-HUMBRECHT* Palish; slightly earthy, bottle-age nose; medium dry, open grapey flavour.
*June 1990***
Riesling de Wolxhein, Altenberg *JUSTIN-REGIN* Very dry, acidic, more like Sauvignon Blanc.
*May 1986**
Tokay Pinot Gris, Réserve *TRIMBACH* Walnuts, cardboard and sulphur — but it opened up; lightish, bland.
*June 1986**

1985****

After a bad start, cold spring, some frost damage, difficult flowering, from end of June to end of harvest warm and sunny. A large crop, the best, particularly the late-picked, still marvellous and with time in hand.
Gewurztraminer:
ZIND-HUMBRECHT Showing well when young, very scented crystallised violets nose; fairly dry, good fruit still a bit hard when last tasted.
*Jan 1988**(*)*
des Evêques *HUGEL* Perfumed, powdery; dry, austere.
Feb 1988(**)*
Gueberschwihr, Vendange Tardive *ZIND-HUMBRECHT* Curious nose, very pronounced lychee and rose cachou fragrance and taste; drier than expected, full-bodied.
*June 1990***(*)*
Clos St Landelin SGN *MURE* A 1.6ha terraced vineyard, chalk, facing south, in an area renowned for its lack of rain. A blockbuster: yellow gold, hint of orange; rich, earthy, scented Gewurztraminer; medium-sweet, 15.8% alcohol, almost too powerful to drink. Impressive.
*Sept 1988***(**)*
SGN *HUGEL* Deep, rich, peachy; sweet, glorious flavour, length.
*Feb 1991******
Cuvée Tradition *HUGEL* Slight spritz; heavy, pungent opulence; dry, gently scented, refreshing.
*March 1987**(**)*
Vendange Tardive *HUGEL* Surprisingly pale; low-keyed; peach kernelly.
*Feb 1991***
Others showing well when tasted 1986–88:
Hatschbourg *MARC KREIDENWEISS* Grand Cru. Flowery***
Grand Cru *J LORENTZ* Gentle, scented, powdery, roses, lychees; fairly dry, highish alcohol, delicious flavour****
Grand Cru *PREISS-ZIMMER* Pale; fragrant; lightish***
Grand Cru *R SCHMITT* Flowery, grapey, touch of raspberry; dry, spicy***
Muscat:
Rangen *ZIND-HUMBRECHT* Lovely scent, vanilla; medium dry, full, assertive, spicy, grapey — splendid combination of *grand cru* vineyard and winemaker.
*June 1990****(*)*
Réserve *PREISS-ZIMMER* Pale; light but fragrant (Muscat is a difficult grape. The aroma is in the skin and is, more pronounced in a poor year); dry 85° Oeschle, and light (11.5%). Fragrant. Lean.
*Sept 1986****
Rothenberg, Vendange Tardive *ZIND-HUMBRECHT* Deeper colour; ripe, fat, almost goaty nose, grapey; medium-sweet, rich, spicy, lovely wine.
*June 1990****(*)*
Pinot Noir, Réserve Personnelle *HUGEL* Palish, mulberry; very sweet, strawberry-scented; slightly sweet entry, good dry acidic finish, flavoury. If you must drink red Alsace, it should be a wine like this.
*Last tasted June 1990*** Drink now.*
Riesling:
Cuvée Ecaillers *BEYER* Dry, touch of peach kernels, unimpressed.
*April 1991***
Cuvée Fréderick Emile *TRIMBACH* Delicate, gra-

pey; fairly dry, lightish, deft touch of fruit, lovely acidity.
*Oct 1989*****

Furstentum, Vieilles Vignes, Late-picked *DOM COMTES DE LUPFEN, M. BLANCK* Very pale; deliciously fragrant; bone dry, crisp, lean.
*Sept 1988****(*)

Clos Hanserer *ZIND-HUMBRECHT* Goaty; medium dry, rather drab.
June 1990.

Rangen Grand Cru *ZIND-HUMBRECHT* Pale; ripe, cheesy, sweet, pineapple nose; yet dry, full-bodied, austere.
*June 1990****(*)

Reserve *DOM L ALBRECHT* Very good flavour, balance, acidity.
*March 1990*****

Sporen *HUGEL* Pale, rich, fairly deep, flavoury.
*Jan 1990****

Vendange Tardive *HUGEL* Very Mosel-like, crisp, grapey; light style, delicate flavour, good acidity. One of the best Hugel Rieslings.
*Feb 1991***** *Now to 1995.*

Tokay, Moenchberg, Vendange Tardive *KREIDENWEISS* Pale; herbaceous, crisp; medium-sweet, soft, gentle style, yet very good acidity. Excellent with *foie gras* but needed bottle-age.
*June 1987****(**)

Tokay Pinot Gris, Jubilee, Réserve Personnelle *HUGEL* Very pale; subtly scented; dry, soft, slightly peachy.
*Last tasted July 1990****

Vendange Tardive *HUGEL* Scent of cress; medium, fairly hefty, good length and aftertaste.
*Feb 1991****(*)

1986 *At best*****

Tricky growing conditions: harsh winter, frost damage, vegetation retarded, poor late spring but ideal weather from mid-June, perfect flowering, three weeks of cold and damp from mid-Aug encouraged rot, then a return to ideal conditions, picking beginning Oct 9. Mist and sun encouraged *Botrytis*. Most drinking well now but the best will continue to improve.

Gewurztraminer:

ZIND-HUMBRECHT Many notes. An attractive, pure yellow gold at two years; very flowery, scented, copybook powdery rose cachou and lychees; fairly dry, nice weight, lovely flavour.
*Last tasted May 1989****(*)

M SCHOECH Pale gold; opulent, assertive; dry, alcoholic, flowery, hard dry finish but leaves mouth fragrant.
*May 1988****

Clos des Capucins, Cuv Théo *DOM WEINBACH* Very pale; flowery, scented; dry, fullish, firm, rather austere.
*Sept 1989***(*)

Goldert, Vendange Tardive Crisp, spicy, grapey; very sweet, full-bodied, very good, assertive flavour but a bit short.
*June 1990*****

Hengst, Vendange Tardive Rich yet gentle; sweet, full, rounded, lovely aftertaste.
*June 1990*****(*)

Herrenweg, Vendange Tardive Sweet, rich, earthy, rustic.
*June 1990*****

'Jubilee', Réserve Personnelle Pale; lychee and cachou; dry, spicy, good flavour and length.
*Last tasted Jan 1991****(*)

Kitterlé Grand Cru *SCHLUMBERGER* Pale; sublime, harmonious; medium dry powerful, glorious scented flavour, good length, years of life.
*Feb 1991*****(*) *Now to beyond 2000.*

Médaille d'Or *CAVE CO-OP RIBEAUVILLE* Beautiful bouquet; dry, scented, hard finish in lieu of acidity but deserves medal.
*Nov 1989****

'Tradition' *HUGEL* Many notes. Originally fairly pale, now a highly polished yellow gold; powdery rose cachou scent; fairly dry, a surprising 13.2% alcohol, good fruit, velvety yet with hard finish.
*Last tasted June 1991****

Pinot Blanc *HUGEL* Light, fragrant; bone dry, some body, positive, slightly caramelly endtaste.
*Oct 1989***

Riesling:

Cuvée des Evêques *HUGEL* Dry, light, straightforward.
*Nov 1990***

Clos Hauserer *ZIND-HUMBRECHT* Nutty, sulphur; very dry, crisp, slightly short and acidic.
*June 1990***

Kitterlé Grand Cru *SCHLUMBERGER* Palish; very fragrant, piquant grapiness; dry, lean, firm, excellent acidity.
*Feb 1991****(*)

Rangen Grand Cru *ZIND-HUMBRECHT* Little nose; dry, fruity, attractive.
*June 1990****

Schlossberg *DOM COMTES DE LUPFEN, M BLANCK* Bone dry, austere but very good.
*Sept 1988***(**)

Tokay Pinot Gris: *These are very satisfactory workhorses, like a diffident piano accompanist. Difficult to describe. Of all Alsace wines, probably best with food.*

Jubilee *HUGEL* Grassy, cress-like; fairly dry, soft, good length, interesting aftertaste.
*Feb 1991****

Réserve Personnelle *HUGEL* Palish yellow, waxy sheen; lovely nose, peachy; medium dryness and body, a bit four-square but pleasant.
*May 1991****

1987* *to* ***

A difficult vintage. Record flowering (Hugel reported five days, all varieties) followed by cold. Then hot July, Aug cold and wet; heat-wave in Sept through to early Oct. Picking from mid-Oct in variable weather, though Hugel picked very late in glorious weather, but interrupted on Nov 9 and their best vineyard being left until later. Not many tasted. Variable. Drink up.

Gewurztraminer:

HUGEL Scented; dry, light, flavoury.
*Last tasted in Oct 1989**

Hengst Grand Cru *ZIND-HUMBRECHT* Powerful, scented; dry, fullish, fine, needs time.
*June 1990***(*)

Rangen Grand Cru *ZIND-HUMBRECHT* Pale gold; soft, honeyed, grapey; medium sweetness and body, rich, lovely flavour and aftertaste.
*June 1990****

Réserve *G LORENTZ* Scented; dry, hollow, slightly woody.
*Oct 1989**

Réserve *ROLLY-GASSMANN* Grapey, rose cachou, lychees; medium dryness and body, dryish, spicy finish.
*Jan 1990***

Vieilles Vignes *DIETRICH* Yellow green; very forthcoming, lychees; dry, fairly full and assertive, spicy, lacking length but fragrant aftertaste.
*March 1989****

Riesling:

HUGEL Bone dry. Austere.
Oct 1989(*)*

Clos Hauserer *ZIND-HUMBRECHT* Fresh, youthful, pineapple; crisp, dry, good flavour, hard, steely.
*June 1990***

Tokay Pinot Gris:

Cuvée Particulière *KUEHN* Nose, as so often with Pinot Gris, hard to pin down, but good; positive flavour, grip, body, nice length.
*July 1989**(*)*

'Jubilee' *HUGEL* Remarkably good, due to the addition of some late-picked grapes.
*Feb 1991****

1988*** *to* *****

A wonderful summer: a fine crop of ripe grapes, then heavy rain just before the early Oct harvest which began in hot humid conditions. The weather cooled, some frosts but hot Nov with *Botrytis* enabling quantities of top-quality late-harvest wines to be made by the top estates. Avoid the inexpensive early-picked, go for the best – for future drinking.

Gewurztraminer:

CLAUDE DIETRICH Several notes: very pronounced scent; fairly dry, austere yet with powdery fragrance.
*Last tasted April 1990**(*)*

HUGEL Pale, youthful, green-tinged; lightly scented, rose cachou and lychee; fairly dry, good finish.
*Jan 1990***

Cuvée Anne *SCHLUMBERGER* Made only from '100%' grapes, the last being in 1976 (Schlumberger rated their best in 1983 at 97%, 1985 98%). Picked Nov 16: just one 60l cask. Yellow gold; heavenly honeyed *Botrytis* nose; fairly sweet, full-bodied, lovely flavour, soft. Perfection.
*May 1991***** Now to well into the 21st century.*

Goldert Grand Cru *ZIND-HUMBRECHT* Similar but lower-keyed nose; sweeter, soft, lovely.
*June 1990***(*)*

'Jubilee' *HUGEL* Refreshing; medium dryness, soft yet powerful, good length.
*Feb 1991***(*)*

Rodelsberg *DIETRICH* Pale; very peachy, vanilla and lychee scent; distinctly dry, nice weight, firm. Surprisingly good with roast beef.
*Last tasted March 1991**(*)*

SGN Rather Germanic: honeyed Traminer; sweet, assertive, fabulous flavour, acidity, finish, aftertaste.
*Feb 1991***** Now to beyond 2000.*

Cuvée Tradition *HUGEL* Pure lychee and scented cachou; soft, fragrant.
*Feb 1991****

Cuvée Tradition *KUENTZ-BAS* Scented, delicate; fragrant.
*June 1991*****

Clos Windshuh *ZIND-HUMBRECHT* Soft, scented; medium dry, full-bodied, rich, fragrant, yet hard. Needs time.
*June 1990**(**)*

Pinot Blanc:

DIETRICH Very attractive, pineapple, *poire Williamine*; dry, lightish, soft mid-palate.
*Aug 1989***

Cuvée Amours *HUGEL* Very pale; fresh, minty, mouthwatering, with whiff of sulphur like a burnt match; very dry, light, slight spritz, refreshing acidity. Quaffable.
*Jan 1990***

Riesling:

HUGEL Grown on light soil: pale; subtly grapey; bone dry, lightish, very good acidity, decent length.
*Last tasted Nov 1990***

'Jubilee' Formerly **Réserve Exceptionnelle Personnelle** *HUGEL* Grown on clay and limestone soils: pale, star-bright; low-keyed but whiff of 'kerosene' Riesling, touch of honey, grapiness, good depth; very dry – completely fermented out – assertive, 'limestone' flavour, rather austere, firm acidity. Will take bottle-ageing.
*Last tasted Feb 1991***(*)*

SGN 17.4% potential alcohol, 19 g/l residual sugar: hefty polished medium pale yellow; lovely, fresh, minty nose, touch of vaseline; fairly sweet, lovely crisp, firm flavour, a touch of fat, spice.
*June 1989***** Now to beyond 2000.*

'Tradition' *HUGEL* Pleasant light grapiness; dry, crisp acidity**

Vendange Tardive *HUGEL* Glorious, peachy nose; medium dry, lovely, soft, like the flesh of a ripe grape, fragrant aftertaste.
*Feb 1991****(*) Now to 2000.*

Tokay Pinot Gris:

DIETRICH Very forthcoming, youthful, grapey scent; fairly dry, surprisingly soft – indeed a touch of fat though finishing hard. Fragrant.
*April 1990**(*)*

HUGEL Youthful acidity and rather neutral 15 months after the vintage. Nose hard to define but a light grapey flavour, firm, fragrant aftertaste.
*Last noted Feb 1991**(*)*

Clos Jepsal *ZIND-HUMBRECHT* Crisp fruit, scented; medium, fairly full-bodied, lovely rich mid-palate, hard finish. Needs time.
*June 1990**(**)*

'Jubilee' *HUGEL* Minty; fairly dry, spicy, soft, good length and aftertaste.
*Feb 1991***(*)*

Vendange Tardive *HUGEL* An aroma like mown grass, mint and clover honey; drier than expected, fullish body, fabulous flavour and fragrance.
*Feb 1991******

Vin de Paille du Jubilee *HUGEL* 200 half-bottles made. Pale gold; glorious scent, nose and taste, a *mélange* of Muscat, Gewurztraminer and Riesling; slightly sweet, delicate, lovely.
*Served at the end of Hugel's 350th anniversary dinner at L'Auberge de L'Ill, June 1989****(*) Will keep for decades.*

1989*****

Combination of abundance and high quality. Even the more modest quality wines are attractive, the *grand cru* vineyards and late harvest wines being exceptional and with a long future. All this followed a hot, dry summer, some rain in early Sept to swell the berries and an unusually early harvest, from Sept 27. Fairly wide range. Selection follows.

Gewurztraminer:

Cuvée Anne Made but not yet tasted. I ordered some on the strength of the '88 which, alas, had sold out.

TRIMBACH Cachou-scented; good flavour, acidity, aftertaste.
*June 1991****

Brand Grand Cru *DOPFF AU MOULIN* Rich, earthy, lychee; good flavour.
*June 1991***(*)*

Cuvée Christine *SCHLUMBERGER* Heavenly nose, soft, spicy; medium dry, high quality, good future.
*May 1991****(*)*

Muscat *SCHLUMBERGER* Réserve quality. Sauvignon Blanc-like piquant grapiness; dry yet rich, scented.
*May 1991**(**)*

Pinot Blanc, Réserve (Médaille d'Or, Colmar) *PIERRE SPARR* Positive, vinous; dry, clean, good fruit.
*Feb 1991*** For early drinking.*

Riesling:

Brand Grand Cru *ZIND-HUMBRECHT* A notable year: Olivier Humbrecht was the first French national to pass the Master of Wine examination. The wine: very fresh, young, grapey; pineapple aroma; dry, good fruit, steely, firm crisp acidity.
June 1990(****)

Buhl *DIETRICH* Very pale, almost colourless; bone dry, light.
March 1991(**)*

Princes Abbés *SCHLUMBERGER* Scented, attractive; dry, firm.
*June 1991***(*)*

Saering Grand Cru *SCHLUMBERGER* Very scented, youthful, gooseberry-like; fairly dry, firm, powerful dry finish. Needs time.
May 1991(****) 1993–2000

Schloss *DIETRICH* Pale, green-tinged; equally dry, austere, good length.
*March 1991**(**)*

Tokay Pinot Gris:

Kitterlé Grand Cru *SCHLUMBERGER* Bottled early, Jan 1991. Palish, lovely colour, polished; fragrant, the 'pineapple' of youth; surprisingly sweet (medium dry, ripe grapes) and high alcohol (13.7%), lovely spicy flavour, length, fragrant aftertaste.
Last tasted May 1991(****) 1993–2000*

1990*****

Yet another marvellous vintage following almost unique growing conditions: mild winter with no snow or frost, early budding though Muscat, Tokay Pinot Gris and Gewurztraminer affected by *coulure* and *millerandage* due to one cold week during flowering, reducing the crop by roughly 25% compared with 1989. Otherwise a fine summer and excellent harvest of healthy, rot-free grapes. The only problem: very high sugar content and low acidity demanding a high level of careful winemaking. Relatively few yet tasted. The following are a selection.

Gewurztraminer:

de Riquewihr *DOPFF AU MOULIN* Nose combination of peeled grapes, lychees and rose cachou; medium dry, fairly full-bodied, flavoury, hard finish.
June 1991(***)*

Cuvée St Leon *WOLFBERGER* Pale; grapey; medium-sweet, hollow, short.
*June 1991***

Pinot Blanc:

HUGEL Very pale; peach fruit; light, easy.
*June 1991***

Les Cuveliers *WOLFBERGER* Dryish, lightish, pleasant enough, 'hot' finish.
June 1991(**)

Médaille d'Or *DIVINAL* Muffled, pineapple; dry, light, fair acidity.
June 1991(**)

Riesling:

CAVES RIBEAUVILLE Green, grapey; dry, hard, acidic.
June 1991(***)

Cuvée des Seigneurs *WOLFBERGER* Rich, goaty, dry, artificial, horrid.
June 1991.

Médaille d'Or *DIVINAL* Fragrant, scented, lovely; fairly dry, delicate, elegant, good acidity.
June 1991(***)*

Tokay Pinot Gris:

Caves Rabelais Pfaffenheim Damp cardboard; medium dry, fullish, soft centre, hard finish.
July 1991(***)?

Other FRENCH WINES

France abounds with wine districts, some historic such as Jurançon, of ancient lineage like Cahors, the Muscat and *vins doux naturel* of the fringes of the Mediterranean, the idiosyncratic *vins jaunes* of the Jura, notes on all of which are dotted through my volumes of tasting books. Most of the minor French districts produce wines for local consumption, for drinking young. Vintages merely come and go. I shall therefore confine myself to brief descriptions of some lesser classics and a closer look at significant new developments, specifically in Languedoc, and Hérault.

Château-Chalon

The odd man out. Not a château, a village name. The wine, made from Savagnin grapes (Traminer), spends six years in cask, mould (*flor* in Spain) growing on the surface, producing an inimitable *vin jaune*. Several notes, several vintages. Just one included to indicate style.

1961 *HENRI MAIRE* (This firm dominates wine production in the Jura): pale yellow, like a fino sherry; very malty, pungent but fragrant; exceedingly dry, curious oxidised sherry and deep straw flavour, highish, pasty end acidity.
Feb 1985 to**** A matter of taste.*

Ch d'Arlay *LAGUICHE* Another *vin jaune* from the Jura.

1978 Bottled 1985: fine colour; distinctly sherry-like 'flor' nose; dry, extraordinary length of flavour, tangy like manzanilla, twist of lemon acidity.
*Aug 1986****

1983 Waxy straw yellow and smell to match, touch of walnuts; dry, some fat, sherry-like taste.
*June 1988***

Of the many other French wines tasted I particularly recommend **Fitou, Bandol** and **Faugères**: the reds from these districts are best drunk when young, but will keep; **Ch Vignelaure** a pioneer in Provence: intense lusty reds reminding me of Taltarni in Western Australia. The rosé of **Dom Ott** deserves its reputation. Serve at room temperature (chilled, lacks flavour). Also from Provence another attractive red, **Ch Sainte Roseline**: redcurrants, orange blossom, mouthwatering acidity; lightish, distinctive, unusual, lovely. Of the Jurançon's I prefer the sweet, the **Dom Cauhapé Moelleux**, the '85 having a bouquet like kiwi fruit; rather Vouvray-like in weight and style though fatter, less acidic. The *sec* is flowery, rather Alsace-like, full-flavoured; good acidity. Of recent vintages of **Cahors** I liked the '86 of **Dom Les Hauts de Chambert**: deep; lovely crisp fruit. Will keep.

Mas de Daumas Gassac *AIME GUIBERT*

A striking new *Vin de Pays d'Hérault* which demonstrates what can be done with good grapes, on sympathetic soil and subsoil, and with intelligent winemaking in an area better known for high production of indifferent quality wine. Also interesting to follow its development, young vines, early vintages, maturing vines young vintages, the proprietor M Guibert being guided by top Bordeaux agronomists and enologists.

1978 The first vintage to be put on the market. Now losing initial depth of colour though still youthful; medicinal, low-keyed, not much development; fairly dry, nice weight, good fruit, attractive, still tannic.
*Last tasted May 1990*** Further development unlikely.*

1979 Deep, plummy; tannin and fruit; medium dryness and body, lean, austere yet some softness, leathery textured tannins.
*Last tasted July 1990** Unlikely to improve.*

1980 First tasted in 1987: opaque; packed with fruit and tannin, the latter producing a smell of wet leather and

sweaty armpits. Raw. Two notes later: still plummy purple; rich, rustic, high-toned; the sweetness of ripe fruit, lots of grip, tannic iron finish.
*Last tasted May 1990**(*)*
1981 The first vintage sent to me to taste, in 1984. Intensely purple; spiciness of new oak; taut and very tannic. Professor Peynaud the advisor: certainly very young Bordeaux-like. Youthful cherry red in 1987, Cabernet fruit discernible, gooseberry, radishes! Lean but shapely. Medium-full body (12.5% alcohol). Now plummy; fragrant, the nose developing in the glass; still very tannic.
*Last noted July 1990***(*)*
1982 80% Cabernet Sauvignon, the rest Cabernet Franc, Merlot, Malbec, Pinot Noir, Syrah and Tannat. Seven notes. First at a pre-sale tasting in July 1986 and, coincidentally, a month later guessed at Hugh Johnson's purely on the strength of its extraordinary intense purple colour. Light, crisp fruit; packed, tannic, inky, impressive. Most recently, still deep, rich, velvety though maturing at the rim; thick, rich fruit, and sweaty tannin that decanting and air in the glass failed to budge; sweetish, ripe, fairly full-bodied, high extract, rich yet austere.
*Last tasted Oct 1990***(*)?*
1983 Similar *cépages* to the '82 but no Tannat. Rich, mature; very fragrant, vigour and sap in 1987 though cheesy tannins noted later. But unlike earlier vintages it evolved in the glass, cedar, citrus; rich, fullish (13%), extremely high dry extract, elegant, lovely flavour, cinnamon, dry tannic finish. Daumas Gassac getting into its stride, due not just to the vintage but to maturer vines.
*Last tasted May 1990***(**)*
1984 Two notes. First in 1987. Less intensity; touch of stalkiness, celery. More recently light, 'stewed'. Fairly dry, chewy, its rawness softening but short.
*Last tasted May 1990***
1985 Five notes, from a cask sample drawn Jan, and tasted May 1987: opaque; packed with fruit, sweet, raw blackcurrant, then figgy, port-like. Full (13.3%) yet surprisingly lean. Most recently, still deep purple; fruit and sweaty tannins; fairly sweet, very rich, full, soft, fleshy, good fruit, extract, tannin and acidity. Becoming seriously good.
*Last tasted April 1991****(*) 1993–2000*
1986 Less Cabernet Sauvignon (75%). Very deep, fine; fragrant, spicy, fruit and oak; sweetish entry, dry tannic finish, crisp fruit.
*May 1990**(**)*
1987 Plummy purple; muffled; sweet, soft, pleasant enough.
*May 1990** Drink soon.*
1988 Two notes: opaque; packed with fruit, oak, spice; medium dry, full-bodied, rich, tannic yet fleshy. Very good potential.
Last tasted June 1991(****) 1993–2000+*
1989 A bit rough-textured in May 1990. Most recently: gloriously deep cherry red; aroma of peaches, blackberries; fullish, soft, fleshy, a lovely drink without food.
*Last tasted June 1991***(**) Now or wait.*
Mas de Daumas Gassac, Blanc
1988 Touch of gold; vanilla, walnuts, lovely; medium dryness and body, slight bitterness, fair length, attractive flavour.
*Last tasted May 1990**(*)*
1989 (Chardonnay up to 40%, 25% Viognier) Three notes: raw pineapple husks, attractive young fruit; rich, mouthfilling, Chardonnay apparent, oaky spicy finish.
Last tasted July 1990(***)*
1990 Very attractive, youthful, pineapple and vanilla nose and taste, almost too rich, immature yet soft, very oaky aftertaste.
April 1991(****)?
Mas de Daumas Gassac, Blanc de Raisins Blanc
1986 (Viognier 80%, Chardonnay 10%, Muscat 10%, two months in wood) Pale waxy yellow; youthful, pineapple; dryish, very good fruit and spicy flavour, length and acidity.
June 1987(**)*
1987 (Chardonnay increased to 30%, Viognier reduced to 60%) Pale, steely, fragrant in 1988. Most recently: straw yellow; meaty, minty, waxy, unusual nose; fairly dry, good mid-palate but tails off.
*Last tasted Nov 1990***
Mas de Daumas Gassac, Rosé Frisant Made mainly from Cabernet Sauvignon, 1/3 Syrah, skin contact enough to leave the wine pale pink.
1985 Slightly fizzy; clean but indeterminate; dry, light, acidic.
*Nov 1986**
1986 Cork pops but no *mousse*; strawberry-like; dry, slightly salty finish. Very refreshing summer drink.
*May 1987***
1989 Very pale pink; light, tinny fruit, quite attractive but short.
*May 1990**
1990 Pale pink, slightly *pétillant*; fragrant; dry, austere.
*May 1991** Drink whilst still young and refreshing.*

Prieuré de St Jean de Bebian *A ROUX*

Another marvellous new wine from the south, this time Coteaux du Languedoc. Unlike Daumas Gassac not remotely a Bordeaux 'clone', rather following the 13 *cépages* of Châteauneuf, principally Grenache (30%), Mourvèdre (18%), Syrah (18%).
1985 The first vintage, tasted in Dec 1986: lovely blackberry colour; *nouveau*, almost Gamay-like fruit; full-flavoured, spicy, attractive fruit. Two notes later: medium-deep, rich ruby; very crisp, fruity; seemed very sweet, fullish, rich fruit. Delightful, easy.
*Last tasted July 1989*****
1988 In July 1989 advised by M Roux to decant and leave an hour to release excess carbon dioxide: intense purple, spritz; lovely fruit, as if macerated; spicy, tannic. Already fragrant, chunky, a good fruity mouthful.
Last tasted Feb 1990(***)
1989 Two notes: vivid purple; very minty, spicy, good fruit; distinctly sweet entry, very dry tannic finish, sandwiching lovely fleshy fruit.
Last tasted April 1990(***)*
1990 'Brut' Deep, rich; intriguing fruit, touch of tangerine, oaky; soft, fleshy yet spicy tannins. Attractive.
Jan 1990(****)

ITALY

One of the oldest, biggest and most varied of all wine countries, Italy is, in some ways, one of the last to come in out of the cold; the most recent decade has witnessed a transformation. When I came into the wine business, Italian wines were scarcely more widely represented than Spanish: the odd *fiasco* of Chianti, perhaps a Soave. Italian restaurants were more or less confined to London's Soho, the range of wine extending to Orvieto and Verdicchio in funny shaped bottles, and mainly of indifferent to poor quality. The best stayed at home, served in the better restaurants of Florence or Milan. Commercially, the Italian wines were notoriously unreliable. I remember on our first visit to Italy, in the mid-1950s, while idly watching a bottling line in one of the biggest and best-known firms in Asti, my wife noticed that different vintage labels were being affixed to bottles of the same wine. It hardly inspired confidence.

Tuscany and Piedmont were then, as now, the principal classic regions. Each had, and still has, producers of high quality. Nevertheless, the reds tended to be strange to British taste, with their extended cask-ageing and severe tannic finish. As for Italian whites, many were drab, oxidised. The emergence of the oenologists cleaned up the act—perhaps too much, in fact, for at a tasting for wine writers at Vintners Hall in 1979, a range of top reds and whites were presented by some distinguished producers. But the whites all seemed to taste the same, whether from Sicily or the Veneto. Pale, clean, dry, uniform. Clearly modern winemaking had triumphed at the expense of regional and varietal characteristics.

Happily, the pendulum has swung back to what seems like a healthy middle position, and a combination of enlightened owners and competent winemakers is transforming the scene. These are not just newcomers, but also old families like Antinori and Frescobaldi, and the larger than life characters like Gaja. And the principal changes, all for the better, are taking place in the classic areas already mentioned.

For a quarter of a century, Italian wines have not been my business, so the following notes are a smattering of those made over the past 10 years. They are far from being comprehensive; they merely report one or two unexpected joys, and hint at a newly rekindled interest. I love Italy, I like Italians; I look forward to spending more time there, with them and their wines.

1930

Carmignano Riserva *CAPEZZANA, BONACOSSI* Rebottled at the estate, 1960. Pale rosy tawny; faint at first, with that 'hawthorn bush' nose, neither fruity nor earthy, that I associate with so many Italian reds. Then a bit of old fustian, sweet, sage-scented; a lovely gentle character, slightly smoky flavour, reminding me of an old recorked Lafite. Later it seemed sweet; faded but sound and delicious.
*Dining with Ted Hale, Oct 1983*****

1947**** *to* *****

Chianti Rufina *SELVAPIANA* Deep, rich; lovely old nose, reminding me of milk and old stables; rich, intense, uplifting flavour. Long. Still tannic.
*May 1982*****

Vin Santo *BROLIO RICASOLI* Frankly I have never been much of a fan of this strangely made white wine but the old ones can be delicious. Colour old gold, tawny-tinged;

sweet, rich, chocolaty nose, harmonious, singed oloroso, later like warm mellow straw; medium-sweet, smooth. An oddity but very good in its way.
*At the opening 'probe' at Rodenstock's 5th annual tasting in Mülheim, Oct 1984*****

1952****

Pia Barolo *MARCHESI DI BAROLO* Beautiful colour. Spoiled by high volatile acidity.
Oct 1984.

1954***

Spanna *VALLANA* With the '54 Bordeaux and Burgundy vintage at the back of my mind I did not have high expectations. I was pleasantly surprised. A deep plummy colour; high-toned 'brambly' nose, holding well after 30 years. Fleshy, fruity, chewy. More iron than tannic. Remarkably good drink.
*With Elin and John Walker at Spark's Steakhouse in New York, Oct 1984*****

1955*** *to* **** *(Tuscany)*

Spanna *VALLANA* A very deep rich appearance; curious singed nose; full-bodied, rich, soft, slightly malty, very heady. Interesting but not really enjoyable.
*Oct 1984***

1957*** *to* **** *(Tuscany)*

Chianti *POGGIO* Earthy red; rich, curious nose. Very dry.
*July 1982***

1958*** *to* *****

Great year in Barolo, less good in Chianti.
Chianti *POGGIO* Palish; rich but stalky; dry, hard.
July 1982(*)*

1959** *to* *** *(Tuscany)*

Chianti *POGGIO* Fairly pale, very mature-looking; nice, Pinot-like nose; pleasant weight, positive flavour, very dry finish.
*July 1982****

1960**

Chianti Classico *FOSSI* A different ballgame. An early DOC. Autumnal red; rich, singed, fragrant, mature bouquet; attractive flavour, like a mature Graves, and warm tiles. Pleasant weight, excellent acidity.
*At home, a present from David Peppercorn, perfect, May 1983*****

1961** *to* ***** *(Piedmont)*

Barbaresco *GAJA* One of the most glorious Italian wines I have ever drunk. Fine mature red; soft, warm nose, singed fruit lurking beneath, holding beautifully in the glass; medium — the sweetness of ripe grapes, medium full-bodied, soft, with a flavour that opened up into a crescendo. Lovely texture. Gentle tannins.
*Provided by the very generous proprietor, Pat Cetta. At Spark's, Oct 1984******

1962** *to* ***** *(Tuscany)*

Chianti Rufina *CASTELLO DI NIPOZZANO, FRESCOBALDI* The only '62 tasted since 1980. Tasting it at 1.30 pm and finding it slightly oxidised, I discovered that due to excess zeal, the wines had been decanted by the staff of the Savoy Hotel at 7.00 am. Bad luck on the Frescobaldis and their clients. It should have been delicious.
Sept 1983.

1964*****

A notable vintage, successful throughout Italy.
Barolo Riserva:

GIACOMO BORGOGNO Attractive, intense ruby; slightly vanilla nose, its high volatile acidity masked by tremendous richness.
*Oct 1983***

CONTERNO Rich in colour, on nose and palate. Sweet, nutty and slightly peppery bouquet, fullish, malty flavour, good tannin and acidity.
*Oct 1983*****

Barolo Riserva Partic *CANTINA ROSSA* Smell of old boots, showing its age; very dry, high acidity, coarse.
Aug 1982.

1967**** *to* ***** *(Tuscany)*

Barolo Riserva *BORGOGNO* Fine deep ruby; curious, high volatile acidity; good flavour but tart.
*Oct 1983**
Brunello di Montalcino Riserva *COL D'ORCIA* Sweet, chocolaty nose; combining richness on palate with typically dry, rather bitter, tannic finish.
*July 1986***(*)*
Chianti Classico Riserva:

VILLA ANTINORI Magnums: very deep colour; very Bordeaux-like nose, weight and style. Again, very tannic.
*Sept 1986***(*)*

BROLIO RICASOLI Palish and very mature-looking; strange meaty style; on the light side but with lovely firm texture and the usual upturned tannic finish.
*March 1982***(*)*

1968** *to* ****

Variable — after all, Italy is a country of contrasting geography and climate. Outstanding in Tuscany.
Brunello di Montalcino *COL D'ORCIA* A very good vintage for Brunello. Rich but bitter.
*July 1982***(*)*
Rubesco Torgiano *LUNGAROTTI* First noted in 1976: claret-like, very attractive. The nose with immediately familiar 'sea breeze', Médoc-like; very pleasant weight, and if I can mix my Bordeaux metaphors, a Pomerol-like texture. Good iron/tannic finish.
*Last tasted Jan 1981***(*)*

1969** *to* ***

Vin Santo *POGGIO ROMITA* Only '69 tasted since 1980. Made from Malvasia and Trebbiano grapes laid out on racks, like raisins, under the roof, then five years in small oak. Orange amber; curious nose and waxy taste; medium-sweet, high acidity. Very much an acquired taste not, alas, acquired by me.
*July 1981**

1970***

Barolo Riserva *FRANCO FIORINA* A beautiful, rich, briar-like, singed character; ripe yet too tough, also with fairly high volatile acidity. Not softened by food. I wondered whether it would ever come round and am told that it *did*, but needed three days to breathe!
*Aug 1982**?*
Barolo Riserva Speciale *GIACOMO CONTERNO* Fine deep rich colour, old oak, mature — but no sediment; a ripe, really old smell, like a '24 Bordeaux, plus whiff of volatile acidity; positive, assertive flavour swelling in the mouth but acidic. Just short of magnificent.
*Jan 1987*****

Chianti Rufina *CASTELLO DI NIPOZZANO, FRESCOBALDI* I first visited Florence in the late 1950s and, with my architectural studies still fresh in my mind, I gawped when I saw a Brunelleschi church in the gardens of the Frescobaldi palazzo in the centre of Florence. The wine was good, with a rich, port-like nose, good length and finish.
*Last tasted Sept 1983*****

Rubesco Torgiano *LUNGAROTTI* Deep ruby; a rich, powerful nose and taste. Attractive despite a strong rustic, pigsty whiff.
*Jan 1984****

1971*****

An excellent vintage in Piedmont and Tuscany.

Barbaresco *GAJA* A few days after drinking Gaja's '61, I returned to Spark's with Sam and Michael Aaron as my guests. The '71 had a good reputation but was considerably less expensive. A lovely wine, with well-nigh perfect weight and balance. Touch of iron on the finish. Had I not previously drunk the '61 I would have rated it higher.
*Oct 1984**** Doubtless still lovely.*

Barbaresco *PRUNOTTO* A beautiful colour; odd nose, high acidity; dry, with firm, rather hard, backbone. Good in its way and doubtless needing more time.
*Nov 1981. Then***(*)*

Barbaresco Riserva Ovello *CANTINA SOCIALE* Smell and taste reminiscent of hen droppings and seaweed, but soft, fleshy and rich.
*Oct 1986****

Barolo Riserva *PRUNOTTO* 'Selezione 1981 dei Vini dell'Albese' First tasted in 1981: still deep; nose still rather dumb, laden with alcohol, totally different from any French classic red, unvinous, unfruity, walnut-like; massive, severe, laden with tannin, power, grip, marvellous length and finish. Marvellous in 1985, "needs 20 years" noted. And most recently: a lovely colour, soft red, warm, rich; beautifully bricky nose, high-toned fruit and after a time in glass sweetening, a mixture of Verdelho, madeira and fudge, wonderfully fragrant. Its hardness mollified. Now seemingly sweet, fleshy, soft fruit and soft tannins, good acidity.
*Last tasted Feb 1991****(*)*

Barolo Riserva Speciale *CONTERNO* Deep; huge, impressive but not very fruity.
*Feb 1987*****

Rubesco Torgiano *LUNGAROTTI* A lovely ruby colour; warm, appealing bouquet and flavour; ripe, pleasant weight, elegant, excellent fruit and acidity. One of those rare (for me) reds that is beautiful to drink both by itself and with food.
*Oct 1987******

Tignanello *ANTINORI* Despite their ancient lineage the Antinoris have always been aware of the rest of the world's wines and have not hesitated to experiment. This is their most successful *vino da tavola*. First tasted June 1977 with Piero Antinori: firm, fine. Three notes: sweet, meaty, jammy nose; ripe, elegant, dry tannic iron finish.
*Last tasted Aug 1982***(*) Doubtless fully mature now.*

1973***

Only one tasted since 1980. Reputation better in Tuscany than Piedmont.

Chianti Classico Riserva *VILLA ANTINORI* Excellent flavour and balance. Perfect at nine years of age but time in hand.
*May 1982****

1974*** to ****

A good year in Tuscany, very good in Piedmont.

Barbaresco *GAJA* A bit stalky and showing age after eight years. Full body and flavour, with swingeingly dry finish.
*Sept 1982***(*) Probably at peak now.*

Brunello di Montalcino *BARBI* Slightly singed, 'hot' nose, rich, touch of honey; ripe sweetness, fullish but not heavy, soft, velvety, very good indeed.
*Feb 1983***(*)*

Cabernet Sauvignon di Miralduolo *LUNGAROTTI* Very deep, opaque centre; distinctive but stern, hard Cabernet aroma more California than Bordeaux, good fruit lurking beneath; slightly sweet, full-bodied, excellent flavour, with a refreshing tingle at its edge, avoiding the customary Italianate tannic bitterness.
*Oct 1982**(*)*

1975* to *****

A mediocre vintage in Piedmont, excellent in Tuscany.

Brunello di Montalcino:

CASTELGIOCONDO, FRESCOBALDI Very scented, spicy; leathery satin texture, elegant.
*March 1982***(*)*

ISABELLA DE MEDICI Rather brown; also scented, sweet yet stalky nose and taste. Laden with leathery tannins.
*Sept 1982**(*)*

RIGUARDO Seemed maderised, richness masking high acidity.
Aug 1983.

CASTELLO POGGIO ALLE MURA Rather pale; nose of walnuts and prunes; pleasant weight, good flavour, very tannic.
*June 1984**(*)*

TENUTA CAPARZO Lovely colour, mature; very pleasant fruit, after an hour, coffee-like; well made, attractive but still with severely tannic finish.
*June 1988**(**)*

Carmignano *CAPEZZANA, BONACOSSI* A Tuscan wine, a Chianti that went its own way to pursue an individual varietal mix and style. Already very mature-looking at under six years of age, a sweetish, well mannered, very drinkable wine.
*July 1981*** Probably tiring now.*

Montepulciano d'Abruzzo *VALENTINI* Opaque, still immature; sweet, alcoholic, figs and blackberry nose; a very odd wine, full-bodied, meaty, chewy, with a strong taste of coffee.
*Jan 1987**(*)?*

Vin Santo *AVIGNONESI* All the way from Montepulciano to the Napa Valley. One of Hugh Johnsons' 'fast balls' tasted blind at the Trefethens' annual picnic. A flat yellow straw, orange-tinged; maderised nose; fairly sweet, finish rather grubby, short but flavoury. I had no idea what it was, thought it very peculiar but not unappealing. Then the penny dropped.
*In the Napa, Oct 1982*** in its way.*

1976**

Torricino *PIO* Ruby; fragrant, appealing; flavoury, with a light dry uplift of slightly spritz acidity and pleasant aftertaste.
Feb 1982.

Venegazzu *GASPARINI LOREDAN* Known as the dean of Veneto reds and made from grapes only too familiar to Bordeaux lovers: Cabernet Sauvignon and Franc, Merlot

and Malbec. Deep, now mature; unsurprisingly a very mature claret-like nose; dry, medium body, curious un-French upturned flavour and showing its age.
*Jan 1988*** Needs drinking.*

1977** *to* ****

A very good vintage in Tuscany. Only one tasted since the early 1980s.

Chianti Rufina Riserva *SELVAPIANA* A very attractive soft mature red; bouquet conjuring up the smell of a stack of wood being seasoned, and a vague whiff of bushes in blossom; medium dry, pleasant weight and flavour.
*July 1983****

1978****(*)

The best all-round Italian vintage of the 1970s. Originally tough and tannic. Starting to come round. Many notes.

Barbera d'Alba *ALDO CONTERNO* Very deep purple; stalky Rhône-like nose; raw, swingeingly tannic. Impressive, needed 10 years.
At VIDE tasting, May 1980(****)

Barbaresco *SORI TILDIN, GAJA* Still a youthful ruby when first noted in 1982, with a sweet, strangely attractive smell like rice pudding, vanilla, that opened up in the glass, fennel and walnuts. Piercing flavour, lean but fruity – coped marvellously with Lancashire hotpot and Piccalilli! More recently, richly coloured and now maturing; bottle-age on nose but still tannic, vinous; curious crisp middle fruit, lean, with very dry tannic finish. Not an easy wine but impressive.
*Last tasted Jan 1987***(*)?*

Barolo *CERETTO* Lovely colour and bouquet; dry, fine, tannic.
*April 1986****

Barolo Riserva *VIGNA SAN GIUSEPPE, CAVALLOTTO* Medium, cherry-tinged yet maturing; singed, deep, rich, coffee-like bouquet; touch of sweetness, a rich, meaty wine – one could almost chew it, powerful, complete, lovely by itself.
*Jan 1987*****

Brunello di Montalcino:

BARBI Deep, mature, fairly sweet, flavoury, tannic.
*Feb 1988*****

CASTELGIOCONDO, FRESCOBALDI From Brunello grapes, a clone of Sangiovese grown on yet another Frescobaldi estate. Minimum four years in Slav oak. Palish, already mature-looking, good flavour and length but with bitter walnut finish.
*Feb 1983****

Carmignano Riserva *VILLA DI CAPEZZANA, BONACOSSI* Nose curiously lacking in fruit, more like thorns, bushy; yet on the palate soft, rounded, very pleasant.
*Oct 1983**(*)?*

Chianti Rufina Riserva:

CASTELLO DI NIPOZZANO, FRESCOBALDI One of the finest estates in the Chianti Rufina zone, only the best vintages being bottled under the estate label. Indigenous grapes plus Cabernet Sauvignon. Alas, opened too long (a situation already referred to; see 1962).
*At the Savoy Hotel, Sept 1988. Potential*****

MONTESODI, FRESCOBALDI From small crop of local grapes, plus Cabernet Sauvignon, grown in the hills of the Nipozzano estate. 18 months in small oak. Deeper colour; walnuts; touch of sweetness, good middle palate, length and aftertaste. An appealing style.
*Feb 1983****

Sassicaia *TENUTA SAN GUIDO, MARCHESI INCISA DELLA ROCCHETTA* A very fashionable Italian red made from Cabernet grapes planted, most unusually, on the coast due west of the centre of the Chianti Classico district. First noted at 10 years of age; opaque, black cherry; lovely classic nose and flavour – that is to say, perfect harmony of bouquet and on palate. I placed it first, the group placed it third, in a rather mischievous blind tasting of 10 reds including Pétrus '77, Vega Sicilia '60 (which the group placed second), and others, at Rodenstock's wine weekend in 1988. More recently less deep yet still richly coloured; a curious high-toned Brie crust nose; medium-sweet, nice weight and grip though needing drinking.
*The oldest vintage at the Sassicaia tasting at Brooks's, March 1990****

Solaia *ANTINORI* A single vineyard next to Tignanello on the Antinori estate in the Chianti Classico region, 75% Cabernet Sauvignon, 25% Cabernet Franc, 18–24 months in small French oak. Small production. The '78 never released ('79 the first to be marketed). Initially opaque. Still a good deep rich colour; gorgeously rich nose with unmistakeable Bordeaux character, like an '82; medium dry, medium full-bodied, spicy (oak) rich, chewy, citrus-like acidity, still tannic.
*Last tasted March 1988***(*)*

Tignanello *ANTINORI* A Chianti made without the traditional inclusion of Malvasia and Trebbiano white grapes, and with the addition of Cabernet Sauvignon aged in French *barriques*. Sweet nose, dry palate, excellent flavour.
*Feb 1988*****

Recioto Amarone della Valpolicella *BERTANI* I have never developed the taste for Recioto or Amarone, sweet or dry. Deep mature red; curious warm stalky, twiggy, bush-like plus honey bouquet that developed interestingly; slightly sweet, full-bodied (15% alcohol), a strange powerful wine, very dry finish. Good with fresh figs.
*Sept 1988*** in its way.*

1979****

A good vintage, the 'new classics' and *vino da tavola* reds getting into their stride: Ghiaie della Furba, Torre Ercolana, Rubesco, above all Sassicaia and Tignanello. But the older DOC and DOCG classics also good.

Barbaresco:

ASILI, CERETTO Scented attractive nose; dry, nice quality.
*July 1983****

GAJA An extraordinary scent, citrus, figs, high-toned but also great depth; medium-sweet, full, very rich, very fruity, still a bit coarse and tannic. Accompanying fallow deer, juniper and balsamic vinegar.
*At a mammoth red wine tasting banquet in Frankfurt, Sept 1988***(*)*

Barolo *GIACOMO CONTERNO* Very deep, plummy; hard, dry, alcoholic, tannic. An old style, uncompromising wine needing many years of bottle-age.
Feb 1985(****) 1995 to beyond 2000.*

Chianti Classico Riserva *VILLA ANTINORI* Just to show that Antinori's Chianti Classico is also good: medium, cherry-tinged; very fragrant nose, delicate fruit, dry, lightish, perfect weight and balance.
*March 1984**** Probably passing its peak now.*

Dolcetto d'Alba *PRUNOTTO* Opaque; dry, full, lots of grip, demanding bottle-age.
March 1982(****)

Ghiaie Della Furba *CAPEZZANA, BONACOSSI* A *vino da tavola* blend of Cabernet and Merlot. Immensely impressive when young. Excellent flavour and balance.
Alas not tasted since July 1981(****)

Rubesco *LUNGAROTTI* Still fairly deep; bramble-like nose; an extremely pleasant drink and underpriced.
*Dinner at the Breakers, Palm Beach, Jan 1991****
Sassicaia *ROCCHETTA* Outstandingly the best of all the Sassicaia vintages from 1987 back to 1978: medium-deep, very rich, mature – like a good '59 claret; sweet, glorious, harmonious bouquet, with marvellous flesh and fruit; very sweet for a red table wine, medium full-bodied, rich, fleshy, rounded, perfection yet with well-tempered tannin and acidity to keep it another decade.
*March 1990***** Now to 2000.*
Tignanello *ANTINORI* Beautiful gradation of colour; medium-sweet, most agreeable Bordeaux weight and style yet different. Good texture, refreshing acidity, dry tannic finish.
*Last tasted April 1984***(*) Probably at peak now.*

1980*

A late harvest. One of the least satisfactory vintages of the period. Drink up.
Chianti *NOZZOLE* Good body, balance and flavour for vintage and price.
*Feb 1986***
Chianti Classico Riserva *BADIA A COLTIBUONO* Palish; pleasant enough, short.
*Jan 1987***
Sassicaia *ROCCHETTA* Several notes. Showing quite well in the mid-1980s but unknit, herbaceous nose with touch of tea and green stalkiness; comparatively lean and short at the Sassicaia vertical.
*March 1990***

1981***

A relatively light but attractive vintage. Several quite appealing Chiantis in particular, though acidity noted fairly consistently.
Chianti Classico:
CASTELLO DI VOLPAIA My first introduction to Volpaia by Christopher Tatham. A delightful wine, fragrant, easy, agreeable.
*March 1986****
Riserva *BADIA A COLTIBUONO* Full fragrant bouquet; very good flavour and length. Tannin and marked acidity.
*Oct 1987****
Riserva Prima *VIGNA CASTELLO DI VICCHIO-MAGGIO* Slightly sweet, elegant, good length.
*Nov 1987****
Chianti Rufina Riserva *MONTESODI, FRESCOBALDI* Still youthful; pleasing sweetness, lightish, very attractive fruit, good acidity.
*March 1987*****
Sassicaia *ROCCHETTA* Richly coloured, good extract; curious, rich, sweet, slightly cheesy nose; distinctly sweet on the palate. Quite a chunky wine. Very tannic.
*March 1990**(*)*
Tignanello *ANTINORI* Three magnums, one corked. The other two fairly deep, intense; sweet, strawberry-like nose; sleek texture, fragrant fruit but, somehow, not quite right.
*Sept 1988**?*
Torcolato *MACULAN* 'Passito Naturale, Vino Liquoroso' A semi-dessert wine new to me and much preferred to Vin Santo. Palish yellow gold; nose faintly Beerenauslese-like, with whiff of vanilla; fairly sweet, very distinctive, assertive flavour and excellent acidity.
*Dining with the Rhodes, Oct 1986****

1982*** *to* *****

Only one less than good note and most (reds) drinking well now. Particularly fine in Piedmont.
Barbaresco *SORI TILDIN, GAJA* Idiosyncratic (for those inured to Bordeaux!): rich, strange, fruity, figgy, slightly resiny, tarry nose; intense, great length, hot, almost burning alcohol on finish. Immensely impressive and needing much bottle-age.
*June 1987**(***) 1995 to well beyond 2000.*
Barolo:
CAVALLOTTO Very sweet and sweaty tannic nose though lots of fruit; high extract, rich but far too raw and tannic – perhaps with wild boar, in 15 years time!
Aug 1987(****) Beyond 2000.
FONTANAFREDDA A huge deep fruity long-term wine.
Jan 1988(****)
MONPRIVATO, GIUSEPPE MASCARELLO Quite different style: full-bodied but soft, fleshy and delicious.
*June 1987**** Now to 1997?*
Granbussia *ALDO CONTERNO* A wine which used to spend an astonishing four to seven years in oak vats. As this was tasted six years after the vintage I would hazard a guess at four to five years in wood. A fairly deep luminous, lively and lovely appearance with rich legs like Romanesque arches; crisp, fresh, fruit: figs, grapefruit; ripe entry traversing an immensely fruity path to a dry, very tannic finish. Impressive to say the least.
Sept 1988(*****) Drink 1995–2010 or beyond.
Brunello di Montalcino *BANFI* Somehow the concept of creating a classic wine on a vast scale, bulldozing acres of rolling hills, strikes an odd chord to the purist. However, install 'state of the art' equipment and put in charge an oenologist of the calibre of Ezio Rivella, and results can be achieved. My first taste certainly endorsed the good chunky richness of the '82. So did the most recent.
*Sept 1989*** Drink now to, say, 1996.*
San Giorgio *LUNGAROTTI* Another *vino da tavola* from this distinguished winemaker. Lovely colour; strangely attractive nose, rich fruit, honeycomb; distinct touch of sweetness, nice weight, interesting upturned flavour, crisp, refreshing, with silky leathery tannins.
*Last tasted April 1991***(*) Now to 1996.*
Sassicaia *ROCCHETTA* Deep rich plummy colour; very sweet, tannic nose of great depth; sweet on palate, plenty of fruit, extract, silky tannins.
*Last tasted at the Sassicaia vertical, March 1990***(**) 1992 to beyond 2000.*
Vintage Tunina Bianco *SILVIO JERMANN* An interesting white wine, a blend of Chardonnay and other grapes from the Collio area. Pale; very fresh, minty nose; fairly dry, lightish, very clean and pleasant, with good acidity. A good example of the 'new wave' of whites. Not tasted recently, but worth trying younger vintages.
*Oct 1984****

1983***

The vintage that rekindled my interest in Italian wines. The Chiantis in particular, well-balanced, with deftness and charm.
Bardolino Classico *MASI* Very attractive light ruby; a curious bushlike stalky nose that could only be Italian; agreeably sweet on the palate, refreshingly light in weight and style, with a soft, easy, strange but appealing flavour. Touch of end bitterness. A good food wine.
*Jan 1986****

Brunello di Montalcino:

BARBI Lovely but astringent.

April 1990(***)

CASTELGIOCONDO, FRESCOBALDI Marvellous names again. Not very deep-coloured; nose of fruit, briar and sweaty tannins; sweet, fullish, crisp, fruity, attractive.

*Dec 1989**(*)*

POGGIO ANTICO Scented, attractive.

*May 1990****

Riserva *COL D'ORCIA* Good fruit, tannic.

April 1990(***)

Cepparello *ISOLE E OLENA* A Vino da Tavola di Toscana, 100% Sangiovese, with a name like a character in a Mozart opera. And a light-comedy colour: pretty, cherry red; lively nose, crisp, fruity; lean, crisp and flavoury but more tannin than anticipated. It needed air, and food.

*July 1987**(*)*

Chianti Classico:

ISOLE E OLENA A soft, easy, delightful wine and marvellous value.

*Sept 1987****

Riserva *CASTELLO DI VOLPAIA* Prettily coloured but quite assertive. Good wine.

*Sept 1988****

Riserva *SELVANELLA* Excellent fruit, rounded.

*Jan 1988****

Sassicaia *ROCCHETTA* Two recent notes. Dry, lean, tannic, Cabernet taste in 1989. Not showing well at the vertical tasting, smelly nose, raw, slightly oxidised.

Last noted March 1990 ?

Valpolicella Classico *PALAZZO DELLA TORRE, ALLEGRINI* Soave and Valpolicella, good, inexpensive, white and red merchants' wines in the mid-1950s and 1960s, are nowadays more associated with cheap and cheerful Italian restaurants. A well-made Valpolicella can be delightful. Best drunk reasonably young. This one had a bittersweet nose and taste, very flavoury, good fruit, refreshing acidity.

*Aug 1988****

Recioto della Valpolicella Amarone *SEREGO ALIGHIERI* Beautiful name, beautiful label, very good in its way. But who drinks it and when? Bouquet fragrant, nutty, trace of almond kernels and walnuts; medium-sweet.

*April 1990****

Ca' del Bosco *MAURIZIO ZANELLA* A very smart new, expensive, designer label white *vino da tavola*. Very unusual, attractive fruit, crisp, nice weight (not heavy: 12.2% alcohol) and style, great length and a powerful finish. Clearly to be taken seriously and, judging by its very long cork, to be kept.

*Jan 1987**(**) Say 1992–98.*

1984**

Wedged between the charming '83s and the splendid '85s, a vintage understandably by-passed, though the northern (Piedmont) and southern (Sicily) extremities not bad.

Duca Enrico *CORVO-SALAPARUTA* I mention this as it was the first vintage I tasted of a Sicilian *vino da tavola* of a distinctly higher, and most welcome, quality. Deep, impressive, still youthful-looking; sweet, hot, spicy nose; sweet on the palate, medium-full body, very flavoury, spicy tannins.

*Dec 1989**(*)*

1985*****

Here, I felt, was a turning point. All the improvements, the well-meaning and earnest experiments with indigenous and French grape varieties, the fresh look at winemaking, came to a head in a lovely vintage. One became conscious of owners and winemakers working in tandem — almost like California.

Superb in Piedmont, 1985 was even more successful in Tuscany, and it was a special offer of 1985 Tuscan wines, well described and presented by a London company, Wine Cellars, specialising in Italian wines, that caught my imagination. I ordered a wide range, tasted and drank. As before, however, I found — still find — that there is no predictable correlation between price and drinkability.

Barbaresco:

GAJA A wine of great depth. Mouthfilling. Long dry finish.

*Sept 1988**(***)*

DI GRESY Two vineyards on the Martinenga estate: the first, Camp Gros, jammy nose; extraordinarily sweet, full-bodied (13–14%), peppery, a touch of volatile acidity on its finish. Made from heavily pruned subvarieties of Nebbiolo, up to three years in oak and clearly needing long cellaring.

June 1989(***) Say 1995–2010.*

And from the Gaiun vineyard, different, a softer red; sweet, bramble-like nose; medium-sweet, full-bodied and powerful, high tannins and acidity.

Last tasted June 1990(**)*

Barolo:

PIO CESARE Fragrant, sweet, fruity, fully endowed.

*Last tasted April 1990***(*)*

MONPRIVATO, GIUSEPPE MASCARELLO Nose like the crust of Brie; sweetish, high in alcohol (14%) yet not heavy in style, flavour opening up, with a peppery, swingeingly tannic finish.

April 1990(***) 1995 to well beyond 2000.*

Brunello di Montepulciano:

BANFI Deep; rich; good fruit; touch of bitterness.

*April 1990**(*)*

CASTELGIOCONDO, FRESCOBALDI Deep; lovely rich fruit; full, very attractive.

*Last tasted June 1990***(*)*

IL POGGIO Full, soft, fleshy, loads of grip and fruit, a hefty, soporific wine.

*Last tasted May 1990***(*)*

TALENTI Lovely ruby; rather medicinal, iron nose; sweetish but with swingeingly dry finish.

*April 1990**(**)*

Chianti Classico:

CASTELLO DI CACCHIANO One of the oldest properties in Chianti. Medium pale, mature appearance; very sweet, strawberry-like fruit; lightish style but assertive and tannic.

*Dec 1989**(*)*

CASTELLO DI VOLPAIA Firm. Well made. Soft, sweet — seemed much better the next day.

*Last tasted Feb 1990****

ISOLE E OLENA Fairly deep, pleasant enough.

Last tasted Nov 1987(**)*

Poggio *SAN FELICE* Pretty colour; arboreal; lightish style, pleasing fruit, an uplift of refreshing acidity.

*Last tasted May 1990****

Riserva *FELSINA BERARDENGA* (Owner Giuseppe Mazzocolin, winemaker Franco Bernabei.) Medium-deep, richly coloured, starting to mature; fragrant but

hard, dusty; very sweet, full-bodied (13% alcohol), better flavour than nose, its swingeingly high tannins masked by sweetness and extract.
*Feb 1990**(**)*

Riserva di Fizzano *ROCCA DELLE MACIE* Very lean, dry, tannic, bitter.
April 1990(*)

Riserva Millennio *CASTELLO DI CACCHIANO* Sweet, very rich, fruity, slightly jammy and brambly nose; sweetish, pleasant weight, good fruit and grip. Nice now, will keep. The top wine at a *Decanter* magazine tasting of 30 *riservas*.
*Feb 1990***(*)*

Ser Lapo *FONTERUTOLI* Light, youthful, slight spritz giving the flavour a pleasant uplift, piquant fruit. Refreshing.
*Jan 1990****

Chianti Rufina:

Banda Blu *GRATI* Mild, too plausibly soft and easy.
*Aug 1987***

MONTESODI, FRESCOBALDI A scent of fragrant figs and sticks; rich, chewy but lean and oaky.
*Last tasted April 1990**(*)*

SELVAPIANA Rich ruby; sweet rich and chewy but with dry tannic 'rusty nails' finish. Good value.
*Last tasted Sept 1990**(*)*

Riserva *VILLA DI VETRICE, GIAN FRANCO GRATI* A top estate. But I found the '85 had a hard, dusty, concrete-like nose; a lightish piquant wine with an odd flavour.
Dec 1989(**)?

Dolcetto d'Alba *MASCARELLO* Immensely impressive. Opaque; ripe sweetness, full of fruit but packing a punch.
Jan 1987(***) 1994–2000*

Montepulciano d'Abruzzo *BIANCHI* Very deep; fragrant, elegant, good fruit. Incredibly good value.
*Jan 1987**(*)*

Vino Nobile di Montepulciano:

POLIZIANO Black cherry; low-keyed at first but opened up fragrantly; delicious.
*Sept 1988*****

TENUTA TREROSE Rich colour, nose, taste, almost too sweet for a non-dessert wine, soft yet with an attractive touch of tangerine-like acidity.
*May 1990****

VINO DA TAVOLA:

Cepparello *ISOLE E OLENA* Soft ruby colour; harmonious; lightish agreeable style.
*Jan 1990****

Duca Enrico *CORVO-DUCA DI SALAPARUTA* This relatively new Sicilian table wine showing very well in 1985: very fragrant, raspberry scented and very oaky nose; good, crisp, blackberry-like fruit, spicy, very drinkable. Several notes.
*Last tasted June 1990****

Fontalloro *FELSINA BERARDENGA* Made from Sangiovese grapes, under Wine Cellars' heading of 'Super Tuscans'. Lovely soft red; spicy, sage-like nose; fairly sweet, fullish, rich blackberry-like fruit, silky tannins. Excellent with *osso buco*.
*Dec 1989**(**)*

Franciacorta Rosso *MARTINONI* An unbelievably inexpensive red from Piedmont. Delicious!
*Aug 1987****

Ghiaie della Furba *CAPEZZANA, BONACOSSI* 40% Merlot, 30% Cabernet Sauvignon, 30% Cabernet Franc. Many notes. Deep, very rich-looking wine confirmed by the palate. Fairly sweet, delicious, chewy, fruity, a lovely mouthful.
*Last tasted March 1991*****

Tignanello *ANTINORI* Deep, intense; good fruit; tannic.
*Sept 1990***(*)*

Ca'del Bosco *MAURIZIO ZANELLA* A new white, from Chardonnay grapes picked in Oct, vinified in small oak. A positive yellow gold; very fragrant, delicate, oaky spicy nose; fairly dry, delicious flavour, a deft touch, good texture and acidity.
*Last tasted May 1987****

1986****

A very satisfactory vintage, a good follow up to the '85, though producing wines of a different, initially less obviously approachable style. In Piedmont, Barolo and Barbaresco are surprisingly forward and will make good mid-term drinking; in Tuscany the Chiantis and top *vini da tavola*, initially lacking charm, now show some elegance. Very noticeable was the increase in prices, the leading estates displaying new found confidence and, presumably, reacting to a welcome increase in demand.

Balifico *CASTELLO DI VOLPAIA* Another new Tuscan blend. Two-thirds Sangiovese, one-third Cabernet Sauvignon, one year in wood, one-third new oak. Sweet, fruity, soft, touch of pepper on the nose; sweet, charming, tannic finish.
*Sept 1988**(*)*

Bricco dell' Uccellone *GIACOMO BOLOGNA* I know that if my old friend Count Riccardo Riccardi brings over some bottles, they must be superb. This was new to me, a *vino da tavola* made from Barbera grapes and though not DOCG, reputed to be the best of all Barberas. *Bricco* in Piedmontese means top of a hill, *uccellone* a big bird – or words to this effect. Fine colour, still immature; marvellous nose, very fruity, sweet, touch of strawberries, singed brown paper, whiff of aniseed and Spanish root; medium, certainly not dry, excellent weight and balance, fruity, fleshy, with the cinnamon spiciness of new oak.
*Last tasted July 1989***(**) 1992 to beyond 2000.*

Cepparello *ISOLE E OLENA* Soft cherry red; good nose, opening up in the glass; good fruit, firm.
*Last tasted Oct 1990**(*)*

Chianti Classico:

Ser Lapo *FONTERUTOLI* Delightful wine. Good fruit, length, fragrant aftertaste.
*Oct 1990****

Riserva Ducale *RUFFINO* Also fragrant; good taut fruit, length, tannin and acidity.
*April 1990**(*)*

Chianti Rufina, Riserva *VILLA DI VETRICE* Rather unknit and stalky; lightish, easy style, short but a pleasant drink.
*Nov 1990***

Fontalloro *FELSINA BERARDENGA* A now well-established *vino da tavola*. Deep, rich, velvety, youthful; rich fruit on nose; very assertive, fullish, good crisp fruit and length. Touch of tannic bitterness.
*Oct 1990**(**) 1993–2000*

Sammarco *CASTELLO DEI RAMPOLLA* A very ambitious *vino da tavola* from the Chianti region: 75% Cabernet Sauvignon, 25% Sangiovese. Deep fleshy appearance; sweet, very rich, lovely fruit on nose and palate, sweet, full-bodied, high extract, fleshy, velvety texture. Bitter tannin on finish. Good, high-priced.
*Dec 1990***(*) 1992–2000*

Sassicaia *ROCCHETTA* Cherry red; sweet, lovely fruit,

crisp berry-like; distinctly sweet, medium-full body, good fruit, extract, tannin and acidity. Showing well at the Sassicaia vertical but lacking the glory and richness of the '85.
*March 1990***(*)*
Piodilei, Chardonnay delle Langhe *PIO CESARE* From the several attractive dry whites, I have singled out this very appealing, scented Chardonnay. Touch of ripe sweetness, medium-full body, lovely soft, oaky flavour and aftertaste.
*April 1990****

1987** *to* ***

Some nice wines. Fruity, attractive, for early drinking. More whites tasted than reds. Some of the newer whites are interesting:
Bianco di Valguarnera *CORVO-SALAPARUTA* The white *riserva* equivalent of this firm's red Duca Enrico. Medium-pale yellow; very scented, peachy, buttery, very attractive nose, with whiff of vanilla; very good shape in the mouth – that is to say a gentle entry, swelling mid-palate and closing well. Pleasant weight, nice flavour, good length.
*Last tasted April 1990****
Borro della Sala *ANTINORI* Nice fruit. Coped admirably with a lunch at the Tandoor restaurant of the Holiday Inn, Singapore.
*Oct 1989***
Chardonnay *DI GRESY* Bottled Aug 1988. Five-year vines. Palish; youthful, slightly oaky, pineapple aroma; austere yet very flavoury, good length, very dry, acidic finish, fragrant aftertaste.
*Last noted June, 1990****
Gaia & Rey Chardonnay *GAJA* Named after Angelo Gaja's formidable grandmother, and his daughter, born in 1979, the year the vines had been planted. Bottled unfiltered. Very pale, slightly green tinge; peach-like aroma and just the right touch of oak; fairly dry, fragrant, lovely wine.
Tasted with Gaja 20 days after bottling at the International Wine Festival, Frankfurt, Sept 1988(**)*
Piodilei, Chardonnay delle Langhe *PIO CESARE* Lovely rich buttery nose with deft oakiness; medium-full body (13% alcohol), a sliver of fat, crisp, hard dry finish. What must it be like in a perfect vintage?
*April 1990****
Tocai Friulano, Colli Orientali del Friuli *LIVIO FELLUGA* Finally, a white to send me scurrying towards the borders of Yugoslavia to drink the wine – and admire the scenery: a very unusual scent, spicy, original; medium dry, light, delicate, very fresh, lovely peach-like flavour.
*Sept 1988****
Dolcetto d'Alba *DI GRESY* Deep cherry red; low-keyed, still hard but with good depth; not exactly a soft, easy, early drinker. Quite powerful. Needs cellaring.
At the red wine dinner tasting at the International Wine Festival, Frankfurt, Sept 1988(**)*
Sassicaia *ROCCHETTA* Medium-deep; sweet, quite good fruit; pleasant weight and style, a quick developer.
*The youngest vintage in the Sassicaia vertical, March 1990***

1988*****

A fine classic vintage. I see a similarity between the '88 and '85 vintages in Tuscany and in Burgundy, the earlier vintage having tremendous style and charm, beautifully balanced, the latest more firmly structured and, in the long run, probably better. We shall see.

First tasted in the spring of 1990, the reds unready, needing bottle-age, the dry whites showing well.
Bricco dell' Uccellone *BRAIDA* Giacomo Bologna, the brilliant winemaker of this Piedmontese *vino da tavola* died in 1991. Deep, youthful, lovely black cherry; glorious fruit, raspberry-like; distinctly sweet, full-bodied, lovely crisp fruit flavour, spicy, tannic, acid finish.
June 1991(****)*
Rosso di Montalcino *TENUTA IL POGGIONE* Glorious fruit, touch of tar; crisp, very tannic.
April 1990(****)
San Giocondo, Novello di Toscana *ANTINORI* No-one can accuse Antinori of not keeping up with times. Ahead of time in this instance: an Italian *novello* vintaged Sept 26 for consumption from Nov 7, and tasted at home alongside new Beaujolais 12 days later. Slightly sweet, blancmange and raspberry nose, quite nice soft fruit flavour. *Frizzante*, a distinct prickle.
*Nov 1988***
Gavi *PIO CESARE* Pale, green-tinged; very appealing fresh, youthful pineapple and mint aromas; fairly dry, lightish, excellent flavour and acidity. A highly acceptable style. Several notes.
*Last tasted April 1991****
Le Moie *FAZI-BATTAGLIA* Very pale; dry, lightish, refreshing, reasonable length. A world of difference between this newish *vino da tavola* and the boring, flat old Soaves.
*One of many whites tasted April 1990****
Vintage Tunina *SILVIO JERMANN* Blend of Sauvignon Blanc, Chardonnay, Picolit and other local varieties. Touch of spice, caraway; dry, fresh, good but not surprisingly indeterminate fruit, excellent acidity.
*At the Port Hole, Bowness, May 1991****

1989* *to* ****

Not as successful a summer as in France. Mixed results: Piedmont producing attractive whites and some very good reds, arguably amongst the best of the decade, but Tuscany suffering from poor weather, wines reported to be light, early developers.
Barbera d'Asti, Ai Suma *BRAIDA* Fairly deep purple; lovely fruit, sweet, good oak; fairly sweet, hefty (14.5% alcohol) yet deft, glorious fruit, oak. A lusty mouthful now. Will develop.
*June 1990***(*)*

1990****

David Gleave and Nicolas Belfrage, both Masters of Wine, and directors of Wine Cellars in London, report that the vintage in Piedmont was excellent, making 1989 and 1990 remarkable 'twins'. Tuscany also reported to be outstanding.

SPAIN

So accustomed are we to the great 'New World' developments that we tend to forget the changes – for once, all for the better – in the old world, and none more old-worldly than Spain.

In my early days in the wine trade, in the early and mid-1950s, if a wine merchant listed Spanish wine at all, apart from sherry, it would invariably be the cheapest and, I am afraid, often the nastiest. It was easy to recognise Spanish whites in blind tastings, they smelled of vomit. Rioja was to change the image. It established a beachhead and – I do not think it was a deliberate marketing ploy – played down its Spanish background. Torres then came along and almost single-handedly consolidated the quality image.

Rioja

Until recently life was simple – there was Rioja. Now it is complicated. The reds vary in style from Bordeaux-like to a *macération carbonique* cross between Côtes du Rhône and Beaujolais, the whites from modern and bland to old-style, verging on maderised. 'Vintages' exist and, of course, vary. But though there are old vintages around drinking well, the oldest tasted recently being a 1925 *reserva* of the Marquès de Riscal, most are best consumed whilst young and fruity.

Of the producers, I have always liked the style of the old-established Riscal and Murrieta, probably because they are more claret-like, but there are some very interesting new wineries, amongst the most intelligent being a new 'boutique' operation called Remelluri. Some of the mature CVNE reds are attractive, their lovely velvety 1973 *Gran Reserva* for example. I do not much care for the white Riojas, particularly the older vintages.

Penedès

I first visited this part of Spain in 1959. It was then another world. The best hotels charged £1 a day and for two pence a glass you drank the local wine and asked no questions. The Torres family put Penedès on the map. Of their various styles of red, their moderately priced, easy going *Coronas* suit me best. The other now prominent firm is Jean León. But I was recently startled at the price of his Cabernet Sauvignon and decided to stick to Bordeaux.

Vega Sicilia

There is little point in dwelling on Spanish vintages in general as the trade and consumer tend to live from hand to mouth. I shall concentrate therefore on Spain's one really great classic red wine, Vega Sicilia, and begin by deflecting, if not refuting, the charges that it is wildly overrated, over-priced and badly made, seething with volatile acidity. It *is* expensive. It is anachronistic. It happens to be great. Unlike the only other recently fashionable contender from the Duero (a river that flows into Portugal, becoming the Douro) Vega Sicilia uses only grapes from its own vineyard.

Vega Sicilia is a 1,000 ha estate with 150 ha under vines; Bordeaux and local varieties are grown on chalky soil. What is peculiar is the winemaking, in particular the length of wood ageing. The top wine, *Vinho Fino 'Unico'* (Unique), spends eight months in wooden vats followed by approximately 10 years in *barriques*, 25% French, 75% American oak, the wines being racked every six months and barrels topped up "every Friday"! Unsurprisingly, the wine has a distinctive character and tremendous intensity. The less expensive *Valbuena* spends three years in new oak. Sometimes referred to as the Lafite of Spain, 'Unico' has the ability to evolve fragrantly in the glass. Australian tasters, renowned for their competence but who tend to look for faults and aberrations, doubtless hate the wine. I admire Vega Sicilia for its individuality: an exciting flamenco dancer in the world of classical ballet.

I have tasted Vega Sicilia spasmodically over the years, but most recently at two verticals in parallel, as it were, first at the winery in Oct 1989, then at Christie's pre-sale tasting in Sept 1990 at which even hardened critics succumbed, particularly after comparing the freshly poured wine with one that had been in the glass for an hour or so. A summary follows of vintages noted twice, in 1989 and 1990 unless otherwise stated.

VEGA SICILIA VINHO FINO 'UNICO'

1941 Made in the depths of the post-civil war depression. Unusually high volatile acidity. I always notice its sediment annealed to the bottle; colour, a warm, soft rosehip; fragrance and elegance battling with acidity. An attenuated dry finish**

1942 Totally different, richer colour; nose of scented walnuts and singed honey, its bouquet developing beautifully in the glass; a charming old *señor****

1948 A bottle from John Arlott's cellar opened to taste in 1980. Rich, orange-tinged red. Nine years later it reminded me of Cheval Blanc '48 though more tangy, its high extract masking high acidity***

1953 First tasted in 1979: amazingly powerful, impressive. At two recent tastings, an extraordinary bouquet, at first singed, chocolaty, touch of mint, opening up richly and, after 90 minutes in the glass very scented, roses, blackcurrants. Fig-like fruit on palate****

1957 Nose malty, sherry-like when first poured, next a Pinot-like fruit, then evolving, like a fine claret. Fairly sweet, full, soft, flavoury. Still tannic***(*)

1960 Lovely colour; earthy Graves-like nose; very sweet for a red wine, lively, idiosyncratic****

1962 Medium dryness and weight, good flavour and texture***

1964 Four notes over the last decade, in 1980, 1984 and at the two recent vertical tastings. "Fragrant" repeated. A lovely sweet rich nose; tannic and unready when first noted. Now sweet, soft and lovely but more to come***(*)

1965 A difficult vintage, selection important and the wine kept longer in old casks. Anthocyanins still evident, its colour redder than the '66. Singed, spicy, shapely bouquet; good rich fruit but overall dry***

1966 First tasted: a bottle from Lamont and Shaw, the UK agents, in 1980, and thrice recently. Vying with '64 as everyone's favourite wine at the pre-sale tasting. Good colour, touch of orange maturity, rich 'legs'; an excellent bouquet, distinctly Lafite-like in its refinement and the way it opened up in the glass: lovely fruit, violets, and still surging out of the glass after an hour; fairly sweet, perfect weight, great depth, stylish, with 'Unico' acidity — but lovely*****

1967 Extraordinarily sweet, chewy, attractive but lacking length**

1969 Made from a typical blend of Cabernet Sauvignon, Merlot, Malbec, Albillo and Tinta Fino (Tempranillo), equally typical — and extraordinary — nose: sweet, chewy (tannins), singed, vanilla (oak), toffee and hot horses! On palate sweetish, elegant but still tannic**(**)?

1973 Short vegetative cycle, late blossoming, an interesting change of climate: hot days, very cold nights. A good harvest. Three consistent notes, in 1988, 1989 and 1990. An unquestionably lovely wine, lighter than many of the older vintages, elegant, good texture, delicious now****

If you can afford it: try some. For the less affluent, Spain provides many excellent, good value reds. Happily they are easy to find.

PORTUGAL

The Palace Hotel, Bussaco

For the English, for the French – still the biggest importers – and latterly for the Americans, Portugal means port wine. Yet historically, the table and dessert wines grown in the middle of Portugal and around Lisbon were immensely popular. Calcavella, Colares and Bucelas, for example, appeared regularly in Christie's catalogues from the second half of the 18th century, reflecting the contents of the squirearchy's cellars. These have faded, sometimes into complete obscurity, their popular place being taken by the light, acidic *vinho verdes* from the north and the reliable, also inexpensive, Dãos from the south of the Douro. All in all, Portuguese reds deserve better recognition. Most are well made and all are very reasonably priced. Old vintages can be excellent, even back to the 1940s; the 1960s and 1970s, seemingly ageless and virtually given away in even the top restaurants in Lisbon.

The old established but newly delineated area,

Bairrada, is worth noting. The Caves of São João make excellent wine, and to the south J M da Fonseca (not to be confused with the brand of port of the same name) are also more than dependable, their lively Periquita and the softer, red Graves-like Pasmados being two excellent brands. Beware of the *vinho maduro*, mature whites, as they tend to be straw-coloured and tired by modern standards.

The outstanding dry white is João Pires from Palmella, bottled by the ubiquitous J M da Fonseca. The first vintage I tasted was the '83 in 1985. The 1989 is delicious: minty, with touch of Muscadelle grapiness. *The* classic red is Barca Velha made from Douro grapes by Ferreira. At 20 years of age the '66 was lovely: a beautifully deep colour; scented, briar-like bouquet; perfect richness, weight, balance. A taste of heather. Other good vintages are '78; '82, soft and round; '83; '85, opaque, lovely but unready in 1988; '86, like a young claret; and '87 showing well in cask in March 1988.

As with Spain and Vega Sicilia, I shall concentrate on what will be, for most readers, a completely unknown wine, another idiosyncratic 'classic': Bussaco or Buçaco. I first came across this in the cellars of Gorhambury. A collection of vintages had been built up by John Grimston. It was John's son, the third Earl of Verulam, whom I persuaded to sell a few bottles at auction — and promptly bought some myself, notably the '45s. On the strength of the label alone I determined to find Bussaco. I first stayed there in 1979.* I have returned to it since. It appeals to my romantic nature: a palace hotel built at the turn of the century in the ornate 'Manuelesque' style, as a royal hunting lodge, in a magnificent forest on a hill in the middle of Portugal. They have always made a red and a white wine from their own vineyards, but it is never sold except to those who stay and eat there.

Quite coincidentally, the oldest wine listed was of my own birthyear, 1927, famous for port but infamous otherwise.

BUSSACO TINTO

1927 Decanted, with 'beeswing' fliers, rather like old port. Palish, attractive, lively, fully mature; distinct smell of green olives, a bit decayed; touch of sweetness, lightish, overall gentle and delicate. Highish end acidity. Delicious but decadent.
*Nov 1979****

* *On my first visit, I asked Sr Almeida, the manager, who also makes the wine and guards the cellar beneath the hotel, how long he had been at Bussaco. "Too long," he said wearily: "since 1934!" He was still there in 1985, and one of my happy memories was a Saturday afternoon spent in the cellars with Sr Almeida, who cooked local sausages in Aguardiente distilled from his own wine, sipping a young* Bussaco tinto. *I can't wait to go back.*

1940 Slightly ullaged, faintly spicy, soft yet acidic.
*Nov 1979**

1945 Reserva Especial First tasted at the Palace Hotel do Bussaco in Nov 1979: beautiful colour, perfect maturity; nose a bit dusty at first, showing age, then meaty; fairly dry, full-bodied — clearly a hot year as in the rest of Europe, peppery yet soft, rich, well balanced. The following year from the cellars at Gorhambury: good nose, touch of sweetness, lovely flavour, by no means trounced by the Pichon Lalande '20 that followed.
*Last tasted at home July 1980*****

1950 Ullaged and oxidised.
Nov 1979.

1951 *Reserva* A palish but beautiful colour; slightly lactic nose; soft, light, spicy cinnamon flavour but its acidity more apparent as the evening wore on.
Nov 1979.

1953 Beautiful colour, not unlike a top class '53 claret: ruby centre, fairly intense though mature; cedary nose that developed well; lovely weight, shape and texture. Full of charm.
*At dinner on our second visit in May 1985******

1959 Also a marvellous colour, ruby centre, mature rim; extraordinary nose: at first like mushrooms cooked in butter, hazelnut, then a classic 'chewy', Bordeaux-like scent; well-nigh perfect on the palate: medium dry, medium-full body, very original high-toned, refined, slightly varnishy flavour, lovely texture, perfect tannin and acidity.
*May 1985******

1960 Almost as good, a whiff of straw on nose but lovely, soft, heavenly fruit, less tannic, more acidic.
*May 1985*****

1963 Still a bit youthful and peppery on the nose; a very positive swooping, sweeping flavour, sweet, chewy, unready. Needing 10–20 years' bottle-age.
*May 1985**(***)*

As with most Portuguese white wines, the older vintages are more interesting than enjoyable. Out of curiosity, I drank with meals the following:

BUSSACO BRANCO

1934 Amber; old straw, stably nose; dry, rich but acidic.
*Nov 1974**

1944 Unfiltered, I was told: a deep yellow gold like a '37 Climens, bright, warm and appealing; intriguing bouquet, gentle, waxy, resinous: a touch of Tokay, of Ch Chalon, a whiff of fennel; smoky, nutty flavour. In excellent condition.
*Nov 1979****

1956 Straw yellow; sherry-like nose and flavour, but otherwise not showing its age. Nice in its way.
*May 1985***

1958 Orange-tinged straw; resiny, lacking fruit.
*Nov 1979**

1966 Jan Read, an Iberia authority also at Bussaco, thought the slightly resinous nose was from Bical (an indigenous grape); medium dry, good body, flavour and acidity.
*May 1985****

1977 Fresh, light style.
*May 1985***

GERMANY

If Burgundy is a minefield, Germany is a labyrinth, but one worth exploring. At their best German wines are sublime; even at the inferior, more commercial end, they are rarely undrinkable —bland perhaps, or a little too sweet, but innocuously so.

The Rhine, being one of the major thoroughfares of Europe, has a long commercial history. Rhenish wines were shipped to London in substantial quantities in the Middle Ages. It was a safer trade route than that from the Mediterranean and across the Bay of Biscay where, from Bordeaux for example, it was prudent to ship only twice a year, in convoy. Old Rhine wines were fashionable and expensive in the 18th and early 19th centuries, with high prices being paid at Christie's for venerable vintages. "Old Hock", (and never, to my knowledge, just "Hock"), was engraved on silver decanter labels of the period. The wine must have tasted like sherry from the south of France (see 1727 Rüdesheimer below). Hock was also extremely popular in Victorian times, with a famous vineyard in Hochheimer being named Königen Victoria Berg after the Queen's visit. The top German wine estates sensibly anglicised their labels at this time.

World War I sounded the death knell for all things German. Recovery was slow and further set back by World War II. However, it is little known that, at the end of the last war, the English were instrumental in saving German vineyards from the depradations of our own allies.

Alas, German officialdom, commercialism and 'rationalisation' have, in the wake of the disastrous

1971 Wine Laws, inflicted damage which, though not irreparable, is infinitely disheartening for both quality producers and discerning consumers. The simplification of names has in practice made it difficult for the non-expert to understand the difference between an ordinary district wine and that from a top-growth vineyard of a major estate. And the flood of cheap imports, though reasonably palatable, has debased the reputation of German wines.

How to taste German wines

Just as one should not approach red burgundy in the same way as claret, so one must not have, say, white burgundy in mind when tasting and drinking good Rhine or Mosel wine. Quite simply, leaving aside the differences of grape, soil and climate, the aim of the German winemaker is not the same as that of his French counterpart. For a start, alcohol does not play a principal role, nor is dryness the be-all and end-all. What the German winemaker seeks to achieve is a balance of fruit and acidity. The end product is not essentially a 'food wine', but an agreeable drink. One drinks white burgundy with food, one opens a bottle of Moselwein to sip, to quaff, with friends, and, judging by those who live in or travel to the Rhine or Moselle, at any time of the day from breakfast time to late evening. The alcoholic content is low, sometimes around 8%, compared to a 14% Montrachet, and therefore less dangerously heady.

An effort to switch from agreeable, light fruity wines to food wines has been made, not altogether successfully. Remove the slightly sweet fruitiness and one is more than occasionally left with little else. These Trocken (more or less fully fermented out, dry wines) do not interest me greatly and hardly feature in the notes that follow. The similar sounding Trockenbeerenauselen do. The latter are the rare, small production, late-picked grapes with *Edelfäule*, the same *Botrytis cinerea*, or 'noble rot', responsible for the great Sauternes. These great, and very expensive Trockenbeerenauslesen (vulgarly but economically referred to as TBAs) should be sipped, rolled around the tongue then swallowed, luxuriating in the aftertaste, perhaps with a ripe nectarine, *never* at meals with a sweet dish—they are not pudding wines. Puddings sabotage fine sweet wines.

The quality rungs are clearly indicated on all German wine labels. Never mind the minor Qba wines, start with the Qmp, the Prädikat wines: Kabinett, then Spätlese, next Auslese. The first two are generally dryish, but Auslesen, confusingly, can be medium dry or medium-sweet. Next come the *Beerenauslesen*, always sweet, usually with a lovely bouquet, and finally the *Trockenbeerenauslesen*. They are all gloriously easy to enjoy.

I happen to like fine German wines and I drink them regularly, mainly at weekends in the country. The following notes have been made on every conceivable sort of occasion, many, particularly of the younger vintages, at trade tastings, some at pre-sale tastings. But, most memorably and surely unrepeatably, at a tasting entitled *Homage a Château d'Yquem und Schloss Johannisberg 1984* hosted by the Fürst von Metternich and the Comte de Lur-Saluces. The wines were presented mainly in pairs, from 1967 back to the 1892 vintage of Yquem and the 1846 Johannisberg.

1727

Rüdesheimer Apostelwein Although not the oldest tasted (1653 Rüdesheimer in 1977), I have sipped this on six occasions, twice since the early 1980s. From time to time odd half-bottles come on to the market, five or more at Christie's over the past 15 years. All come from the famous Ratskeller (Town Hall cellar) in Bremen. Tiny amounts are drawn from the huge original mother cask which, from time to time, is topped up with younger Rüdesheim wine of a good vintage. The large volume of older wine is thus kept refreshed. My second visit to these medieval cellars was in 1981. Direct from the cask the wine had a straw amber colour, the smell of old apples and a nutty, appley taste. Dry. Good length. High acidity. More recently from a half-bottle "Reserve du Bremer Ratskeller", paler than I had previously noted, Sercial-like; bouquet also reminded me of an old madeira, then more like a *raya* sherry. After two hours in the glass, like rich old stables; an hour after that an amazing pungency lingered in the empty glass. On the palate medium dry, lightish weight, a soft, gentler, slightly toasted old straw flavour, tolerable acidity, and clean finish.

*Last noted at the Great Vintage Wine Dinner in Zurich to mark the publication of the German edition, Oct 1983** for pleasure***** for interest.*

1748*****

Reputed to be the most renowned vintage of the 18th century.

Schloss Johannisberger Cabinets Wein *FURST METTERNICH* Original 'flute' bottle with the oldest label in the cellars of the Schloss. Original short, blackened cork. Decanted. Very bright and warm old amber, a rosy glow, almost as though it had been a faded old red wine; smell of wet hazelnuts and walnuts; intolerably high acidity and not drinkable.

From the cellars of the Schloss, presented at Hardy Rodenstock's annual tasting, in Wiesbaden, Oct 1985.

1846****

Schloss Johannisberger Blaulacke (Blue label) The oldest vintage at the Schloss Johannisberg/Yquem tasting. Fürst von Metternich told us that, from the castle's records, the grapes were brought in from Oct 12. Medium amber gold; light but sound when first poured, touch of linoleum and faded fruit but fragrant, cracking up after 10 minutes, resembling charcoal and sultanas; dry, positive flavour, like a refined old amontillado, good length and remarkable for its age.

*At Schloss Johannisberg, Nov 1984. As a drink*** for its age******

1862***

A very big crop. Shipped in quantity to England.

Schloss Johannisberg Goldblaulack (Auslese) Lovely colour, warm amber; very rich, slightly smoky, minty sultanas bouquet, after minutes developing a rich old-straw nose, like a 5-putt Tokay Aszu, cracking up 15 minutes after it was poured, charred, akin to an old fire in a grate, then pungent, stably. Medium-sweet, very assertive flavour, high acidity, fragrant, exciting.

*At the Schloss, Nov 1984*****

1868***

Schloss Johannisberg *MANSKOPF & SOHNE, FRANKFURT* Pre-1880, believed to be 1868. Very deep brown colour; full, rich, honeyed and harmonious nose with

touch of black pepper; still fairly sweet, excellent flavour, long dry finish and lovely aftertaste.
*Oct 1984****

1893*****

After 1811 and 1865, the best vintage of the century.
Schloss Johannisberger Goldlack Very ripe grapes, very high sugar content: 130° Oeschle. Still surprisingly pale for its age, though deeper than the 1921; initially a scent of cold tea and slightly powdery Muscat. After 30 minutes a spicy, complex bouquet, honey, tea, sultanas; medium dry at first sip but fading to a very dry finish; too lean, too austere despite its fleeting fragrance.
*At the Schloss, Nov 1984***

Marcobrunner Cabinet Riesling feinste Auslese Glorious, warm, bright, rosehip colour; bouquet of sultanas and apricots; dry, full rather meaty flavour and high, pasty acidity.
*One of three bottles from an English private cellar, bought by Hardy Rodenstock and tasted at Ch d'Yquem, Sept 1986***

1897*

Stein Auslese *BURGERSPITAL ZUM HEILIGEN GEIST* Fairly deep, amber, like strong tea, cloudy and deathly; off and oxidised yet with spicy old pears fragrance. Nosed only, not tasted.
Bought at Christie's, noted at Yquem, Sept 1986.

1904***

Geisenheimer Mäuerchen Riesling Beerenauslese *FRIEDRICH VON LADER* Very short, half-inch cork. Very deep brown, like black treacle; an amazing scent, gentle yet powerful, surprisingly fresh, muscadelle; sweet, very rich, singed grapey.
*At the Fuente restaurant in Mülheim, Oct 1984****

1911*****

Magnificent vintage, the best between 1900 and 1921.
Steinberger Cabinet Beerenauslese *H SICHEL SOHNE* The colour of orange pekoe tea, not quite bright; very powerful, but 'blown', mercaptan; medium-sweet, rich, high-toned, slightly pungent but with a fragrant uplift at the finish.
*In Mülheim, Oct 1984**

1920***

Forster Ungeheuer Riesling Auslese *VON BUHL* Fairly deep orange, like dried apricot; bouquet of sultanas, with a combination of honeyed *Botrytis* and bottle-age; medium-sweet, fairly full-bodied, lovely old barley-sugar flavour, rich, good extract, length and aftertaste.
*Bought at Christie's, served at dinner at home, Oct 1988*****

Schloss Johannisberg Goldlack (Auslese) 57% Riesling, 43% Sylvaner, the ripest at 115° Oeschle. In oak until bottled, 1930. Warm, lively amber gold; lovely, gentle, honeyed, grapey nose—no signs of old age, holding well in the glass for an hour; medium-sweet, very assertive flavour and acidity. Dashing and fragrant, some charm but a bit austere after the nose.
*At the Schloss, Nov 1984*****

1921*****

Still the greatest vintage of the century. Small crop of extremely ripe, healthy grapes picked early after a scorching summer. Rich wines.
Schloss Johannisberger Cabinet 105° Oeschle. Colour of pure burnished gold; lovely, lightly grapey nose, remarkably fresh for its age, but after 30 minutes tiring, slightly strange, touch of resin; dry, fairly assertive, 'kerosene' (Rieslings quite often have a slightly oily, petroly smell and taste). Good acidity.
*At the Schloss Nov 1984****

Johannisberger Weiher Auslese *WEINGUT KOMMERZIENRAT KRAYER ERBEN* Broken cap, poor cork, 5 inch ullage. Drab amber, oxidised.
Aug 1989.

Liebfraumilch feinste Auslese *B M & J STRAUSS* (London) Amber shot with gold, weak rim; amazing scent, of lilies, of raisins, slightly Tokay-like and varnishy; medium-sweet, with very good, rich, singed grape flavour which tailed off, reflecting its appearance.
*Bought at auction, served in Mülheim Oct 1984***

Niersteiner Auflangen Riesling Auslese *FRANZ KARL SCHMITT* Good cork, 2 inch level. Marvellously rich colour, nose and taste. Brilliant pure gold, touch of orange; sweet, honeyed, barley-sugar nose, then spearmint; medium-sweet, fairly full-bodied yet gentle, soft, good length, perfect acidity.
*From the Aalholm Castle cellars, Denmark, noted prior to cataloguing, Aug 1989******

1929****

A lean decade in Germany, the 1929 the next best after 1921. For obvious reasons these ripe and appealing wines were virtually all consumed in the 1930s. Few seen and only two tasted recently.
Liebfraumilch Superior *H & J BROOKS* Old gold; caramel beneath old walnut; sweetish, soft, easy, tired but drinkable.
*May 1991**

Nierstein (*sic*) **Riesling** *H SICHEL SOHNE* Very good level and general appearance. Lovely golden colour; rich, slightly smoky bouquet; very dry, very good flavour for its relatively lowly status. Remarkably sound and interesting.
*From an American cellar at Christie's pre-sale tasting in Chicago, June 1983****

1933***

An abundant vintage. Pleasant wines. Several tasted, warranting three and four stars, only one recently.
Rauenthaler Baiken TBA *STAATSWEINGUT, ELTVILLE* Palish yet rich and warm gold; low-keyed, touch of mushrooms; drying out, now medium-sweet, flavour of singed sultanas, good acidity.
*At Peter Ziegler's Club Meeting at Burg Windeck, May 1983***

1934****

Very satisfactory vintage. Several previous good notes up to five star in quality and condition. Only two recently.
Schloss Johannisberg Dunkelblaulack (Deep blue capsule.) The picking started Oct 3, the earliest for their Auslesen for 30 years. A lovely gold colour, pale for its age; delicate, smoky, but a bit smelly—cracking up. Pure lanolin after an hour. Medium dry, lightish, an odd oily taste with twist of lime and touch of bitterness. Short.
*At the Schloss, Nov 1984**

Piesporter Goldtröpfchen Auslese *BOTTLED IN LONDON BY BERRY BROS* Pale gold, excellent colour for its age; almost Sémillon-like buttery waxy nose; medium dry, excellent flavour and acidity, dry finish.
*Pre-sale tasting, Chicago, June 1983****

1937*****

A top-class vintage in Germany, as for white wines

elsewhere in Europe. Magnificent wines, full of fruit, concentration, acidity. The best still excellent if well stored. Unquestionably my favourite German vintage.

Erbacher Marcobrunn Riesling TBA *SCHLOSS RHEINHARTHAUSEN* Lovely warm orange gold; perfect fragrance: peach blossom, apricots, touch of vanilla, then raisiny; still fairly sweet, nice weight, lovely flavour, drying out a little.

*At Rodenstock's Festival des Jahrgangs 1937, Arlberg, Sept 1988*****

Schloss Johannisberger Auslese Bottled after two years in oak. Still relatively pale, a perfectly polished gold, with watery rim; an old Riesling bouquet whose oak and smoke reminded me of a venerable Chardonnay, with touch of caramel and lanolin; sweeter than expected, with very lively, fresh, fruity flavour and good length, but just lacking the persistence and aftertaste of a truly great wine.

*At the Schloss, Nov 1984*****

Rauenthaler Baiken TBA *STAATSWEINGUT* A warm deep, almost tawny colour; perfect crème brulée bouquet, very Sauternes-like; sweet, mouthfilling flavour, fresh, raisiny style, perfect condition and acidity, magnificent.

*At Peter Ziegler's, Burg Windeck, May 1983******

Wachenheimer Goldbachel-Gerümpel allerfeinste Goldbeeren-TBA *J L WOLF-ERBEN* Very deep but beautiful tawny with amber green rim; glorious concentrated essence of honey and raisins; fairly sweet, very rich, very conentrated and with intense extract and flavour. Touch of prune. Fabulous length.

*At Rodenstock's annual tasting, at Ch d'Yquem, Sept 1986*******

Wachenheimer Mandelgarten Natur *WINZERVEREIN DURKHEIM* Imported by Kjaer and Sommerfeldt, Copenhagen. Extremely high level. Good, unbranded cork. Medium-deep amber gold; rich honeyed bouquet, apricots and lanolin, no faults; medium-dry, yet rich, soft, honeyed bottle-age flavour. Good dry finish. Typical of the pure, well-made *naturrein* wines of the good vintages of the 1930s.

*From the Aalholm Castle cellars, Aug 1989*****

1943**

As in France, the best of the wartime vintages.

Schloss Johannisberg Beerenauslese, Fass Nr 92 Very good colour, a lively gold; a lovely gentle bouquet that opened up beautifully, exuding an almost Gewürztraminer spiciness that held well and, even after two hours, had a heavenly rose cachou and lychee-like scent; medium-sweet, good but rather one-track, holding well but lacking fat — indeed thinning out and a bit lean, tasting of Gewürz and ferns.

*At the Schloss/Yquem tasting, Nov 1984*****

Schloss Johannisberg Goldlack Beerenauslese 900 litres produced. Re-corked 1973. Lovely rich gold; delicate floral bouquet, scented ripe Riesling. Medium-sweet, rich yet a delicate touch — alcohol only 5.5%. Easy to drink, good acidity but touch of earthiness, even rot.

*Lunch at the Eigensatz's, Wiesbaden, June 1987*****

Steinberger Kabinett Naturrein *STAATSWEINGUT* Very bright yellow gold; harmonious, mellow, sound, reminding me a little of a Chenin Blanc with a twist of fruit. Dry, fairly solid healthy core, mild fruit, good texture but lacking length and zest.

*Brought by Hugh Johnson to lunch, with Maynard Amerine, at our home near Bath, May 1984****

Steinberger TBA Half-bottle. Pure bright yellow gold; curious, light, delicate bouquet; completely dried out but refreshing and sound.

*One of six old vintage TBAs produced by Ziegler at his magnificent tasting at Burg Windeck, in Baden, May 1983****

Wehlener Sonnenuhr feinste Auslese *J J PRUM* Pure gold touched with orange; spicy, honeyed, calm; fairly dry, good but unusual flavour, perfectly mature but a bit short — blunt, like '43 clarets.

*At Burg Windeck, May 1983*****

1945*****

A great but pitifully small vintage thanks to a hot, dry summer and to lack of labour to tend the vineyards. Few shipped, few seen. I have tasted only seven over the past half-century, only one since 1980.

Schloss Johannisberg Auslese, Fass Nr 62 Slightly dull amber yellow, weakish rim; nose muffled at first, dough-like, lacking fruit support, then powdery, rich yet a touch of decay. After an hour reminded me of white chocolate, after two hours appley, Tokay-like, finally after three hours light, honeyed and holding on well. Surprisingly sweet on the palate, an old smoky flavour, crisp dry acid finish.

*At the Schloss, Nov 1984****

1947****

A very hot year with half the normal rainfall. Very rich, soft wines of high quality.

Schloss Johannisberg TBA, Fass Nr 163 155° Oeschle. Very bright amber gold; deep, honeyed bouquet with touch of spice, developing fragrantly, low-keyed perfection after an hour then a lemon eau-de-cologne-like scent. Held beautifully on the palate, drying out, now medium-sweet but with excellent flavour and balance, a deft touch and high, lip-licking acidity. Finally a wonderful caramelly aftertaste.

*At the Schloss, Nov 1984******

Schloss Vollrads TBA Deep amber with apple green rim; very powerful bouquet of great depth, singed raisins and honey; sweet, full-flavoured, high extract yet delicate. Glorious length and aftertaste.

*With Graf Matuschka and other members of the Vintners Pride group of estates, at Vollrads, Sept 1988******

1949*****

A beautiful vintage. Perfectly balanced wines. By 1949 the vineyards had recovered, and so had the trade. A very popular vintage, many of my notes starting in 1954. Most of the notes made in the mid-1950s to early 1960s are no longer relevant, though 10 of the best, noted between 1961 and 1973, were reported in the first edition. It is rather strange that the only '49s tasted since 1980 have all been from the Mosel.

Leiweiner Laurentiuslay feine Auslese (Grower not known) Very bright yellow gold; ripe, grapey, lanolin bouquet; slightly sweet, lovely flavour and acidity.

*Pre-sale tasting, Feb 1984****

Trierer Kreuzberg Naturrein, Fass Nr 41 *LANDES WEINBAURANSTATT* Colour of apple juice; scent of baked apples and sultanas; dry but rich. Flavour a bit dull. Good acidity.

*Pre-sale, Feb 1984***

Wehlener Zeltinger-Sonnuhr (*sic*) **TBA** *J J PRUM* Yellow gold; scent of ambrosial lemon curd, slightly pungent, touch of lime and vanilla; very sweet, immensely rich, fat, with delicious flavour of lemon and honey.

*At Burg Windeck, May 1983******

1950**

Harvey's, in their autumn 1954 retail price list, equated

the 1950 with the 1947, by stating that both "proved to be excellent vintages". Despite this rash statement, the quantity they listed was comparatively modest, and most disappeared without trace in the mid-1950s. Yet, at the time, an estate-bottled Schloss Johannisberger Spätlese was more expensive than any '50 first-growth claret, and an Auslese from Deidesheim over twice the price. Few tasted since the late 1950s and only one since the early 1980s.

Wehlener Nonenberg Natur *S A PRUM* Yellow gold, green tinge; clean, nice fruit, honeyed bottle-age, some depth; distinctly dry, lean, austere, a bit tart. The oldest vintage brought out by Raimond Prüm Jr to demonstrate the range produced from their 12.5ha of holdings dotted around the middle Mosel.
*In Wehlen, Sept 1988**

1951

Poor thin wines. Few if any shipped. None listed by Harvey's in the mid- to late 1950s.

Graacher Humberg Natur *S A PRUM* Graacher Humberg (now part of Himmelreich.) Buttery gold; slightly earthy, heavy honeyed bottle age; medium dry, lightish, tasting older than nose. "Natur" implies unsugared. How they managed to make this without chaptalisation I do not know, but it had evidently — by its taste — been sustained by sulphur. Not bad though.
*At Prüm's, Sept 1988***

1952***

A good vintage. Harvey's, in 1954, listed no fewer than 18, over half of them bottled in Bristol. Many tasted, mostly sold and consumed in the mid- to late 1950s. Few recently.

Graacher Abtsberg Natur *S A PRUM* An unfair example as the cork was poor, the wine slightly cloudy, a nose like cream cheese, then cow feed. Dry. Unclean.
Sept 1988.

Hattenheimer Stabel Spätlese *SCHLOSS RHEINHARTHAUSENER* Good level. Pure gold; musty at first, then honeycomb, after 1½ hours lovely, creamy; rather stern '52 Rheingau character, good body, waxy, clean dry finish.
*March 1991****

1953*****

Wines of enormous charm and appeal, deservedly popular when put on the market. In those days vintages tended to be first listed retail in the spring of the second year after the vintage. I tasted masses at the time and many since. One word of warning, the quality of corks used by the Germans in the mid-1950s was variable, often poor; on the other hand, the wines were mainly expected to be drunk young, not cellared for 10 or 20 years. Having said that, the best are still lovely to drink now.

Assmannshauser Hüllenberg Spätburgunder Rotwein Kabinett *STAATSWEINGUT, ELTVILLE* Made from the Pinot Noir in the principal red wine district of the Rhine just north of Bingen. Tawny, no red left; very pronounced, exciting bouquet, soft yet piquant, *framboise*-like fruit on nose and endtaste. Flavour like old cognac. Curious hard dry finish.
*At Ziegler's spectacular wine luncheon, Burg Windeck, May 1983***

Berncasteler Doktor und Graben hochfeine Auslese *THANISCH* Pale for age; remarkable fresh peach nose, some sulphur dioxide; medium-sweet, soft and ripe yet with a hard, earthy, Graves-like finish.
*At Burg Windeck, May 1983****

Burg Windecker Spätburgunder Spätlese *WEINBAUSCHULE, WEINSBERG* Pale and pretty; totally different, light, crumbly fruit, preferred to the Assmannshauser; dry, good though thin, nice acidity.
*The local red at Burg Windeck, May 1983***

Eitelsbacher Karthauserhofberg Burgberg feinste Auslese Fresh, peachy bouquet; medium dry, light weight yet full flavour. Rather short, blunt-ended.
*At Burg Windeck, May 1983****

Eitelsbacher Marienholz kabinett *BISCH KONVIKT* Lovely bright yellow; equally lovely honeyed bottle-age bouquet, peach and pineapple; dry, good flavour but lacking length.
*With Simon Smallwood, in Bath, May 1984****

Graacher Domprobst feine Auslese *MEYER-HORNE* Orange gold; nose like peaches and cream; medium dry, lightish, lovely.
*At Christie's pre-sale, Chicago, Feb 1984*****

Hochheimer Steinern Kreuz Naturrein *DOMDECHANT WERNER* Many notes made between 1978 and 1982. Corks variable, some hard. Most levels good. All a palish yellow gold; noses variable, from old apples to spicy and peachy; dry, lightish, some livelier than others, but attractive.
*Last tasted Aug 1982*** *to****

Kanzemer Berg feine Auslese *VON OTHEGRAVEN* Nose hard and sulphury; dryish, delicate, managing to be both flat and acidic.
*May 1983**

Maximin Grünhäuser Herrenberg Beerenauslese *VON SCHUBERT* Yellow gold; touch of vanilla, heavenly ripe peaches; medium-sweet, full, even assertive flavour. Powerful, years of life though drying out.
*At Burg Windeck, May 1983*****

Rauenthaler Pfaffenberg TBA *STAATSWEINGUTER, ELTVILLE* Marvellously rich, expansive, pale orange-tawny; creamy bouquet, perfection; sweet, rich, fat, fabulous length, balance and flavour. One of three TBAs from Rauenthal at Peter Ziegler's Club Meeting. On a par with the '37 Baiken though lacking the latter's intensity.
*At Burg Windeck, May 1983******

Wehlener Sonnenuhr Beerenauslese *J J PRUM* Brought by Manfred Prüm to Peter Ziegler's tasting. Yellow; fabulous bouquet, like ambrosial lemon curd; flavour to match. Fairly sweet, fleshy, buttery texture. Lovely.
*At Burg Windeck, May 1983******

Wehlen-Zeltinger Sonnenuhr feinste Auslese *J J PRUM* Yellow; soft, ripe, honeyed bouquet that opened up beautifully; medium-sweet, light style, charming, delicate attenuated acidity, attractive flavour.
*At Burg Windeck, May 1983*****

1954

Disastrous weather. Only one ever tasted, in the New Year of 1955. It hadn't aged well!

1955**

A moderately good vintage that made a modest appearance in retail wine lists around the autumn of 1957, the high water mark for German wines at Harvey's. All sold for quick consumption and none tasted since the late 1950s.

1956

Even worse than 1954. Frost damage, miserably cold wet summer — my first visit to Germany in June: cold and rain every day—damp-induced rot, vineyards largely abandoned. None tasted.

1957**

Moderate quality. Heavy frost damage early May, midsummer warm and sunny, almost continuous rain throughout Aug and Sept. Some were bought in 1959 to succeed the '55s and mainly consumed by the early 1960s. Most of my notes made between 1958 and 1967.

Graacher Domprobst Natur *S A PRUM* Yellow gold; mint leaf and honeyed bottle-age, unknit but interesting; dryish, clean, attractive but slightly lacking in acidity and with a touch of bitterness.
*At Prüm's in Wehlen, Sept 1988***

1958**

Mediocre but abundant. After a shaky start, a fine Aug and Sept augured well. Rain during an exceptionally prolonged harvest filled the grapes but diluted the quality. Had the trade followed the more recent practice of buying—even listing—wines the spring after the vintage, more would have been imported. Happily, the quality of the 1959 vintage was ascertained before major purchases had been made. Few '58s tasted.

Graacher Himmelreich Natur *S A PRUM* Yellow gold; soft, creamy, milky, lactic, settling down to a cool fragrance; fairly dry, still reasonably fresh and attractive. Flavour reminded me of vaseline and vanilla. Firm dry finish.
*At Prüm's, Sept 1988****

1959*****

At last, to end a mixed and mainly disappointing decade, a magnificent vintage, though the excessively hot summer created unusual, unprecedented, winemaking conditions. However, from sun-enriched grape juice with an extraordinarily high sugar content, glorious wines were made, resulting in a record number of Beeren and Trockenbeerenauslesen in the Mosel-Saar-Ruwer districts.

My favourite vintage after the 1937, though I have many more notes of the '59s. The top wines are still beautiful and will continue to be so for many years to come.

Affenthaler Spätburgunder Rotwein Auslese *WINZER EISENTHAL* A selected late-picked Pinot Noir from Baden. Palish, a nice ruddy glow; sweet, singed, bouquet reminding me of blancmange and Turkish delight; sweet on palate, meaty, charred flavour, smoky Pinot aftertaste.
*At Burg Windeck, May 1983*****

Brauneberger Juffer feinste Spätlese *LICHTWEILER PRUM* Fat, rich vintage, bottle-age nose; medium-sweet, fullish, plump, very attractive, slightly lacking acidity.
*Sept 1981******

Brüssele Lemberger Auslese *GRAF ADELMAN* Attractive colour, weak rim; very sweet, almost overpowering nose, like strawberry jam, sweaty; dry, fullish, firm. Flavour more neutral. Made from the Lemberg grape in Würzburg.
*Another curiosity, at Peter Ziegler's tasting lunch at Burg Windeck, May 1983*** in its way.*

Erbacher Marcobrunn Riesling Auslese Cabinet *SCHLOSS RHEINHARTHAUSEN* Lovely orange gold; sweet, ripe bouquet with honeyed bottle-age and *Botrytis*; sweet, full body and glorious flavour, ripe, rich, perfectly balanced.
*At Rodenstock's 9th annual tasting, at Arlberg, Sept 1988*******

Erbacher Marcobrunn Spätlese Cabinet, Fass No 59/24 *EBERHARD RITTER UND EDLER VON OETINGER* Very high level. Excellent cork branded Kjaer & Sommerfeldt. Palish, still green—unusual for a 30-year-old Rhine wine of a vintage like 1959; nose still very fresh and youthful, mint leaf; dry, medium-light, mild, touch of peach kernels.
*From the Aalholm Castle, Denmark, Aug 1989****

Rauenthaler Baiken TBA *STAATSWEINGUTER* An astonishing 248° Oeschle, 13° total acidity. Warm rich gold; massive, intense bouquet, the smell of singed raisins; sweet, full-bodied, high extract, concentrated, raisiny, counterbalancing acidity. Magnificent.
*The best of an outstanding range of wines produced by Peter Ziegler at Burg Windeck, May 1983********

Dom Scharzhofberger *HOHE DOMKIRCHE* With golden sheen and prickly acidity I thought it was cracking up in 1972. 13 years later, from a good English cellar, a lovely bright yellow; honeyed bottle-age and mint; dry, nice weight, firm, very good acidity for a '59.
*Aug 1985******

Schloss Staufenberger Schlossberg Spätburgunder Spätlese, Fass Nr 2 *MARKGRAF VON BADEN* Palish, soft mature red; curious nose, no fruit at first, then raspberry-like, charming, developing further in the glass; distinctly sweet, rather 'hot' and alcoholic yet light in style, and with very good acidity. The second bottle more positive and powerful.
*At Burg Windeck, May 1983*****

Steinberger Auslese *STAATSWEINGUTER* In old, tall, slender, amber bottle. Yellow; ripe bottle-age nose, rich, smoky, excellent; medium-sweet, fullish, rich, deep, smoky, good acidity, dry finish. Great classic.
*Sept 1987*******

Steinberger TBA *STAATSWEINGUTER* Rich amber with pronounced apple green rim; fabulously rich, raisiny, like Tokay essence; very sweet, mouthfilling, glorious barley-sugar flavour, great length, excellent acidity.
*Two notes, last at Michael's Restaurant, Santa Monica, Sept 1989*******

Wehlener Sonnenuhr feinste Auslese *JJ PRUM* A remarkably pale yellow colour for a '59, still retaining a youthful green tinge; quiet, lightly herbaceous, grapey; medium-sweet, fleshy, soft, perfect flavour, just enough acidity.
*At a dinner organised by Jim Craig of the Hollywood Wine Society, Feb 1985******

Wehlener Sonnenuhr feinste Auslese *S A PRUM* A hearteningly similar feinste Auslese by another Prüm. Fairly pale yellow; note at first mild but rich, peachy, then an eruption of fragrance; medium-sweet, plump but not fat, good length and acidity. If this was in Burgundy, I would have expected that the wines, made from the same grape variety in adjacent parts of the same vineyard would have been very different.
*Tasted in Wehlen, Sept 1988******

Zeltinger Sonnuhr (*sic*) **Beerenauslese** *JJ PRUM* Colour of old straw; vanilla; medium-sweet, attractive though slightly 'off' flavour.
*July 1988****

1960*

A return to poor weather. An abundance of mediocre quality wine, not unlike 1958. None tasted recently.

1961* *to* **

Not remotely tarred with the Bordeaux brush. Another

poor summer in Germany sandwiched between an encouraging spring and an extraordinarily hot Sept which saved the day. Wide variations of quality, from fairly ordinary to Spätlese quality; no great sweet wines. None tasted recently.

1962* *to* ***

A moderate vintage, best known for its *Eiswein*. Another difficult growing year; late, cold spring, uneven blossoming, extremes, dry but not hot, grapes unripe, and, after giving up hope a sudden change in early Oct, picking continuing well into Nov, the last grapes being picked early Dec in below-freezing temperatures.

Baudenberg Sylvaner Auslese Eiswein *WIRTH* Deeper colour and bouquet than the Wollsteiner, below: meatier, fuller and richer.
*Sept 1987*****

Forster Mülweg Riesling Auslese *BURKLIN-WOLF* The Mülweg vineyard no longer exists. Good colour for age; slightly oily nose; distinctly dry, peach stones flavour, raw.
At the estate, Sept 1980.

Wehlener Sonnenuhr Riesling feine Auslese *S A PRUM* Picked in Nov and first noted as a feinste Auslese that should, I was told, have been an *Eiswein*: low-keyed, mild, plump, by no means sweet. Coincidentally, six years later, at the estate, a half-bottle: palish lime gold; lovely, warm, harmonious, grapey, lightly honeyed — touch of kerosene; medium-sweet, lovely flavour, soft yet firm, perfect, understated acidity.
*Last tasted in Wehlen, Sept 1988****

Wollsteiner Affchen Sämling Auslese Eiswein *WEINGUT WIRTH* A prize-winning wine: straw gold; ripe, rich nectarine fragrance, touch of 'petrol', very sweet though light in style and a bit of a let-down on the palate, straw-flavoured.
*Sept 1987****

1963* *to* ***

Amazing how any decent drinkable wines can be made after such a growing season: the Rhine frozen, cold spring, late flowering, sunny July then rain through to an abrupt Indian summer at the end of Oct. Yet I have a surprising number of good notes, though few recently.

Schloss Vollrads Pale for its age; still youthful and grapey, a lovely fragrant Riesling; dry, lightish, mild, easy, still fresh but drying up.
*Sept 1988***

Ungsteiner Michelsberg Scheurebe Auslese *KARL FUHRMANN* Good yellow colour; very opulent scented grapey Scheu aroma, like grapefruit with sugar; medium-sweet, very flavoury, intense.
*Jan 1981****

Wachenheimer Rechbachel Riesling Cabinet *BURKLIN-WOLF* Very bright Tokay-like yellow amber; very fragrant, remarkably fresh, slightly grapey, spicy, like a sea breeze; dry, lightish, firm, fresh but kernelly.
*At Burg Windeck, May 1983***

1964****

A rich, ripe vintage following an almost too good summer, the hottest and sunniest year ever, hours of sunshine exceeding 1959, though the resultant wines not so massively structured. The same problems though; tricky winemaking, ripe grapes, high sugar content and low acidity.

Undoubtedly most successful in the northerly Mosel-Saar-Ruwer districts where the naturally high acidity of the Riesling grown on steep slate slopes counterbalances the unusually ripe sweetness. Popular, attractive, the best vintage between 1959 and 1971, many still lovely.

Alsheimer Rheinblick Beerenauslese *THEO LAUTH* Almond kernelly nose and flavour. Medium-sweet. Not good enough.
Oct 1988.

Bernkasteler Doktor Auslese *DEINHARD* Palish straw; ripe, sweet underlay; ripe, fruit, surprisingly firm acidity for a '64.
*Aug 1981****

Erbacher Hohenrain Riesling Spätlese Cabinet *SCHLOSS RHEINHARTSHAUSEN* Waxy yellow; rich, honeyed, soft, grapey; medium dry, quite pleasant flavour but lacking zest.
*Sept 1988***

Niersteiner Hipping u Oelberg TBA *H SEIP* An alarmingly deep amber gold; muscadelle fragrance; very sweet yet starting to dry out, deliciously fat, adequate counterbalancing acidity.
*Dec 1987*****

Niersteiner Hipping u Rehbach TBA *RHEINHOLD SENFTER* Medium-deep, bright yellow; honeyed, rather raisiny; medium-sweet, more of a feinste Auslese — very disappointing.
*Oct 1980***

Oppenheimer Schützenhütte Riesling Spätlese Nikolauswein Naturwein *GUNTRUM* Loose cork. Waxy yellow; hard yet honeyed; dry, old straw flavour, good length. Slightly disappointing condition.
*Oct 1988***

Dom Scharzhofberger Riesling Fass Nr 7 *HOHE-DOMKIRCHE* Good, rich, yellow; buttery, fragrant, harmonious; dry, lovely flavour, excellent acidity.
*July 1983*****

Wehlener Sonnenuhr feine Auslese *S A PRUM* Very pronounced lime-tinged gold; lovely honeyed bottle-age and *Botrytis*, peachy, developing heather and honeycomb; medium-sweet, lovely mild grapey and slightly smoky flavour, with very good clean dry finish.
*Sept 1983*****

Wehlener Sonnenuhr Spätlese *JJPRUM* Still remarkably pale and green-tinged; very gentle fruit; dry, lightish, mild, a bit faded but well-balanced.
*A sunny Sunday lunch in the country, guests Herbert (Screwpull) Allen and Ted Hale, June 1983****

1965

Back to bad times. Vying with 1956 as one of the worst vintages this century. Growth uneven and retarded, cold wet summer. Harvest delayed until Nov then largely abandoned. Some quite drinkable wines tasted between 1966 and 1974, none since.

1966***

Good but totally different in style to the '64: paler, firmer, more steely, good sustaining acidity. A relatively small crop, harvested late due to cold and rain at the end of an otherwise well-balanced growing season. Few sweet dessert wines made save for some very late-picked grapes made into *Eiswein*.

Notes made in the late 1960s and early 1970s remarkable for the evenness of quality: wines with considerable style. Few tasted recently, the following being a contrasting cross-section.

Bermatinger Leopoldsberg Riesling x Sylvaner Naturrein *MARKGRAF VON BADEN* Positive yellow; lovely, waxy, grapey aroma, honeyed bottle-age, slightly

smoky; medium dry, rather dull and flat. A curiosity. Baden wines can be very good and good value, but this did not have the natural zest to be more than faintly interesting after 22 years, though perfectly drinkable.
*July 1988***

Erdener Prälat Riesling feinste Auslese *DR LOOSEN* 90–94° Oeschle, from 100% ungrafted Riesling planted in red sandstone soil. Wines matured in 1000-litre *Fuder*. Palish yellow; fairly hefty, slightly malty nose; dry, medium-full weight and flavour. Bracken-like endtaste.
*The oldest vintage of a wide range of Loosen's wines introduced by Stuart Piggot, Sept 1988***

Hattenheimer Hinterhaus Riesling Beerenauslese *WINZERVEREIN HATTENHEIMER* (the Hattenheim Co-operative winery) Very good colour for its age, lemon-tinged; good clean attractive fruit; sweet, fresh, unspectacular, sound.
*March 1980****

Rüdesheimer Bischofsberg Riesling Cabinet *VON RITTER* Good pale colour; nose of grapefruit and pineapple; medium dry, delicate and delicious.
*Pre-sale, Oct 1984****

Würzburger Neuberg Silvaner *WEINGUT BURGERSPITAL* Buttercup yellow; peachy, rose cachou-scented; dry, lightish, touch of peach kernelly bitterness and rather losing its grip.
*Aug 1986***

1967* *to* *****

Fairly ordinary in the lower quality range but some excellent, late-picked, *Edelfäule* (*Botrytis*)-affected, sweet wines due to the switchback climatic conditions: very variable spring, retarded growth, lovely summer but high hopes dashed by heavy rains in Sept which washed out many vineyards. Those great estates that hung on for the late autumn sunshine made superb TBAs.

Not much note was taken of the '67s by the English trade which, apart from specialists in German wine, seems psychologically affected by what happens in French districts, and 1967 was not particularly notable in Bordeaux. I tasted many '67 German wines prior to and during a tour in 1969, most notably at a fine wine auction in Wiesbaden that spring which really opened my eyes to the quality of the top wines of this vintage. Forget the lesser wines but look out for the big guns: much underrated. The following tasted since the early 1980s.

Casteller Hohnart Silvaner Natur *FURST CASTELL* Palish; broad milk-and-honey nose; dry, powerful, strange, unfamiliar but attractive Franconian wine.
*Tasted with other wines of the Pride of Germany group at Schloss Vollrads, Sept 1988****

Deidesheimer Leinhölle Riesling TBA *VON BUHL* First tasted in 1973, then a medium-pale lemon gold with a rich yet delicate and grapey Palatinate nose; very sweet, rich. Several notes since then: now a rich amber gold; bouquet now richer, heavier, toffee-like, with singed raisin fruitiness, great depth; still very sweet, full, fat, with high volatile acidity and caramelly aftertaste.
*Last tasted Sept 1988****** *Magnificent but needs drinking.*

Forster Kirchenstück Riesling TBA *BURKLIN-WOLF* Strange that I should have tasted von Buhl's twice in the mid-1970s and Bürklin-Wolf's twice in the early 1980s. The latter two were deeper in colour and more raisiny on the nose: a very deep warm amber with a touch of orange and green amber rim, not unlike a '21 or '29 Yquem; fabulously rich bouquet and flavour. Sweet, concentrated, fat, caramelly flavour, lovely acidity and aftertaste.
*Last tasted Jan 1981****** *Should still be excellent.*

Forster Pechstein Riesling Auslese *BURKLIN-WOLF* Lovely amber gold; beautiful bouquet: overripe grapes, *Botrytis* and honeyed bottle-age; medium-sweet rich, lovely flavour, length, acidity and endtaste.
*Oct 1982*****

Johannisberger Erntebringer Riesling Cabinet *DEINHARD* Fairly deep yellow gold; showing some age and acidity but with deep, rich, grapey support; dry, good mid-palate, honeyed. Very dry, slightly too acidic finish.
*April 1982***

Oppenheimer Sackträger Riesling u Silvaner Beerenauslese *JACOB GERHART* Bright yellow, touch of orange; rich, slightly grapey nose; sweet, fullish, rich; fat, almost a TBA.
*June 1984*****

Rauenthal Herberg Auslese Cabinet *VON SIMMERN* Beautiful palish yellow gold; lovely ripe honeyed bouquet, with Rauenthaler richness; fairly sweet, fat but not heavy, exquisitely balanced: perfect fruit and acidity.
*At pre-sale tasting, March 1980****** *Should still be lovely.*

Schloss Johannisberger Riesling TBA This was paired with Ch d'Yquem '67 at the opening of the never to be forgotten Johannisberg/Yquem marathon at the Schloss, Nov 1984. Both wines were superb. Each distinctive in its own way. I knew, the moment I had tasted from the two glasses in front of me, that it was not going to be a competition, more a comparison of styles. The following autumn, quite coincidentally paired again with the Yquem. As both the notes of the TBA were similar, I combine them: medium-deep, lively amber gold with hint of orange; glorious bouquet, refined, orange blossom and a rich, crisp, sultana grapiness developing in the glass, intense spiciness, cinnamon, tea; sweet and rich yet delicate, fabulous acidity, touch of caramel, fragrant finish.
*Last noted at Rodenstock's annual rare wine tasting, at the Nassauer Hof, Wiesbaden, Oct 1985******

Wehlener Sonnenuhr feinste Auslese *S A PRUM* My host told me that, despite 50–60% rot in his vineyards, the late-picked grapes were excellent. I noticed a lot of tartaric acid crystals at the bottom of the bottle, perfectly harmless of course. Medium yellow; low-keyed at first, with an underlay of wax and 'greenness' that reminded me of Sauvignon Blanc; medium-sweet, lively gooseberry-like flavour and acidity.
At Prüm's, Sept 1988.

1968

A poor year in virtually every European wine district, due entirely to weather conditions (cold, wet, rot — black rot not 'noble' rot) that makes life an unrewarding misery for the grower. Largely thin, raw wines of low quality and short life. One or two drinkable wines in the early 1970s, none tasted since.

1969 *at best* ***

Reasonably good, firm, acidic wines. A good growing season spoiled by lack of rain, then, at the crucial ripening period, three weeks of thick fog obscured the sun. The Palatinate and Rheinhessen districts suffered most, particularly with their early ripening varieties, but estates in the Rheingau and Mosel, with their classic later-ripening Rieslings, took advantage of the late Oct and early Nov sun.

After the '71s came along, the '69s were largely forgotten. Many tasted when young, several showing well in the mid- to late 1970s. The best can still be very agreeable to drink.

Bernkasteler Doktor *DEINHARD* Gentle, mealy, bottle-age bouquet, with trace of almond kernels on nose and endtaste. Dry, lightish, crisp acidity, short.
At a comparative tasting of von Buhl and Deinhard estate wines for Decanter *magazine, prior to a promotional sale at Christie's, Aug 1981***

Erbacher Rheinhell Riesling Cabinet *SCHLOSS RHEINHARTHAUSEN* Palish, slightly green-tinged; crisp 'green' grapey aroma, whiff of kerosene, reflected on the palate. Dry, flat, waxy, kernelly.
*Sept 1988**

Erdener Prälat Riesling hochfeine Auslese *DR LOOSEN* Natural sugar content of grapes 100–105° Oeschle, close to Beerenauslese, hence the *hochfeine* suffix. Nowadays 83–110 entitles the grower to the Auslese category. It is the abolition of these fine distinctions, and the changing of vineyard boundaries and names by the German Wine Laws of 1971, that have done so much to blur and damage the image and perception of German wines by handicapping the great estates in order to give others, and the ignorant public, an equal opportunity! Back to the wine: an attractive yellow colour; honeyed bottle-age and ripe grapes; medium-sweet, fairly full-bodied for a Moselwein, even fat, but with very good acidity. Touch of bracken on the endtaste.
*At the Loosen tasting, Sept 1988****

Graacher Himmelreich Riesling hochfeine Auslese Natur *VON SCHORLEMER* Yellow; good sweet nose; medium-sweet, lovely fruit, pleasing acidity.
*July 1983*****

Wachenheimer Mandelgarten Scheurebe Beerenauslese *BURKLIN-WOLF* Gold; heavenly, honeyed, high-toned, with whiff of Scheu's grapey 'tom-cats'; sweet, rich, its fatness cut with high (12°) acidity.
*Sept 1980*****

Wehlener Abtei hochfeine Auslese Naturrein *KLOSTERHOFGUT, WEHLEN* Bright lemon gold; deep, rich, slightly oily; medium-sweet, fairly rich, some fat, touch of almond kernels, possibly old sulphur, but a clean finish with good acidity. Should make a pleasant summer drink.
*March 1987***

Wehlener Abtei Riesling hochfeine Auslese Naturrein *MICHEL SCHNEIDER, AT ZELL* Interesting to compare notes. I first tasted this a month after the Klosterhofgut's, and again two years later. Palish but brilliant buttercup yellow, perhaps a bit more gold with the extra bottle-age; waxy, honeyed *Botrytis* and bottle-age with a touch of peach kernels — reminded me of certain vintages of Ch Climens; fairly sweet, rich, some fat, good acidity.
*Last tasted Oct 1989****

1970**

Definitely not comparable with the best French districts. Rather plodding wines due to late blossoming, dry summer and moderate autumn. Early pickers made passable wine for quick consumption. Some growers took advantage of the late autumn sunshine; one or two picked even as late as Jan 6 1971! Some have survived but few are of interest.

Deidesheimer Hofstück Riesling Spätlese *VON BUHL* Very yellow; buttery, slightly maderised; medium dry, rich, good acidity. A silver prize-winning wine in its youth. No prizes after a decade.
*At the estate, Sept 1980***

Erbacher Rheinhell Riesling Beerenauslese Strohwein *SCHLOSS RHEINHARTHAUSENER* To make this, the individually picked, very ripe grapes were spread out on corrugated asbestos roof panels! Of the 280 bottles made, I have consumed just two with, I must confess, *slightly* different descriptions — either me or bottle variation. The first (May 1982) a deepish straw gold; waxy bottle-age and *Botrytis* nose; fairly sweet, excellent flavour, consistency (texture), balance and aftertaste. Developed well in the glass. Slightly pasty end acidity. 18 months later a pure yellow gold; very fragrant forthcoming nose that appeared to sweeten, muscat-like, in the glass; some sweetness and weight though light style. The original acidity appears to have settled in. Fragrant. Perfect.
*Last tasted Oct 1983. At best******

Forster Pechstein Riesling Auslese *BURKLIN-WOLF* The sulphur content kept low because the grapes were in cask 3½ hours after picking. An incredible yellow; glorious, broad, buttery, slightly peachy, honeyed and raisiny bouquet; medium dryness and body. Lovely flavour.
*At the winery, Sept 1980****

Forster Ungeheuer Riesling Spätlese *VON BUHL* Colour of old gold; sweet, honeyed, meaty — an archetypal fat Pfalz wine; medium dry, quite rich but a bit ploddingly four-square.
*Aug 1981***

Geisenheimer Kirchgrube Riesling feinste Auslese *SCHUMANN VON HORADAM* Pale for its age; lovely honeyed bouquet and flavour.
*At a Christie's tasting in Chicago, June 1985****

Hattenheimer Nussbrunnen Riesling Spätlese *BALTHAZAR RESS* Rather oily Riesling nose; dry, firm, not very interesting.
*Oct 1981**

Schloss Böckelheimer Kupfergrube Riesling Kabinett *DEINHARD* Very yellow, tinged with gold; buttery, harmonious, dry, four-square, with enough acidity for its survival.
*Aug 1986***

Trierer Thiergarten Unterm Kreuz Auslese, Weihnachts Eiswein-Edelwein *FRITZ VON NELL* A remarkable wine made from grapes picked on Dec 24 and 25. Palish; bottle-age and *Eiswein* honey; fairly sweet, good acidity. I feel somewhat ashamed that my pre-sale tasting note is shorter than the name of the wine.
At Christie's, July 1983.

Wachenheimer Luginsland Riesling Kabinett *BURKLIN-WOLF* A couple of notes, on separate occasions. Both poor. 'Blown' and tart.
Last tasted Oct 1981.

1971★★★★★

A magnificent vintage. More on a par with the '49 and '53, rather than the heavyweight '59 and the sweet ripe '64. Early flowering and well formed; a fine summer, with sunshine and warmth from early July through to the autumn, the lack of rain concentrating the flesh. Perfectly healthy, fully mature grapes picked in ideal conditions. Arguably the most perfect in the Mosel and its tributaries, the best Saar and Ruwer for decades, the early morning mists providing moist nourishment and burning off to continue the ripening. Overall the quality was high, almost too high for the bigger commercial houses.

My recommendation: drink up the Spätlesen and lower qualities, but look out for Auslesen from the better estates, even from *Winzerverein* (cooperatives). All are woefully undervalued at auction even though they have been off merchants' lists for years. The Beeren and Trockenbeerenauslesen are still magnificent but scarcer and more pricey, though not compared to the price of Yquem. Of the dozens tasted since the early 1980s I have made a selection to illustrate development, quality, and condition.

AVELSBACHER ALTENBERG KABINETT *HOHE DOMKIRCHE In a less good year, a wine, of Kabinett quality from the Ruwer valley Trier, would be hard and acidic. In 1971, grapey, rich, even a touch of oiliness; fairly dry, flavoury, very pleasing a decade after the vintage.* Oct 1981★★★ *Probably thinned and dried out by now.*

AYLER KUPP SPATLESE *PAUL AY A step up in the German wine quality scale and from the neighbouring Saar valley which also discharges into the upper Mosel. Glorious buttercup yellow; lovely honeyed rich vintage nose; medium-sweet, lightish style and weight, grapey, mild — just enough acidity, a far cry from the sharp tartness of a lesser vintage. Needed drinking.* Feb 1986★★★

AYLER HERRENBERGER AUSLESE *BISCH KONVIKT Same district, neighbouring vineyard, and another step up the quality ladder. Several notes, firmer and more acidic than the Spätlese. Aged 10 still fairly pale; delicate, yet with ripe peachy bouquet; medium dry — drier than Ay's Spätlese: Auslesen are rich but not necessarily sweet. Lovely flavour. Crisp dry finish.* Oct 1981★★★★ *Should still be good.*

BERNCASTELER BADSTUBE AUSLESE *DR PAULY-BERGWEILER Lovely lemon gold; spicy bouquet; medium — neither sweet nor dry, lovely flavour and acidity.* June 1985★★★★ *Will still be good.*

BERNCASTELER DOKTOR SPATLESE *DR THANISCH Very pale, with slightly green tinge; very fragrant; medium dry, lightish, very attractive.* Feb 1986★★★

BERNKASTELER BADSTUBE BEERENAUSLESE *KARL DILLINGER Same vineyard, different grower and the fourth rung of the Prädikat ladder. But a disappointing half-bottle: pale; rich but with a hard stalky edge; medium-sweet, short dry finish.* Oct 1982★★

BERNKASTELER BRATENHOFCHEN RIESLING AUSLESE *DEINHARD A vintage like 1971 gives a wine of this quality extra dimensions. Complete, ripe, slightly vanilla nose; medium dry, great length.* Aug 1981★★★★

BERNKASTELER DOKTOR AUSLESE *DEINHARD Palish, bright; good gentle fruit; medium-sweet, lovely fruit, balance and acidity.* Oct 1981★★★★

BERNKASTELER DOKTOR SPATLESE *DEINHARD (The second of the three owners of the famous Doktor vineyard. The third is Lauerberg.) Well-developed flowery nose, good depth of fruit; medium dry, good flavour, distinctly dry finish.* Aug 1981★★★

ELTVILLER SONNENBERG RIESLING AUSLESE *SCHLOSS ELTZ Three notes on a classic Rheingau. Buttery yellow in the summer of 1980, with honeyed nose, very good fruit, perfect balance. By 1989 the colour of a Beerenauslese, deep warm gold; rich, honeyed* Botrytis *bouquet; medium-sweet, lovely and lively, very fragrant aftertaste. Prior to the 1971 Wine Laws this would surely have been a feinste Auslese. Most recently, a shade of orange noted; glorious bouquet of peaches and peach skins; heavenly wine, ill-matched with crème brûlée.* April 1990★★★★

ELTVILLER TAUBENBERG SPATLESE *SCHLOSS ELTZ Yellow gold; grapey, honeyed, soft, flowery bouquet and taste. Harmonious but fractionally lacking acidity.* March 1981★★★

ERBACHER MICHELSBERG RIESLING BEERENAUSLESE *WINZER ERBACH Touch of orange; soft, apricots bouquet; medium-sweet, soft, slightly caramelly. A cooperative wine, nice but on the verge of drying out and certainly needing drinking.* July 1988★★★

ERBACHER SIEGELSBERG RIESLING SPATLESE TROCKEN *SCHLOSS RHEINHARTHAUSEN Still in the heart of Rheingau but slipped in first slightly out of alphabetical order to describe one of the earlier, fully fermented-out Trocken wines: very pale lemon gold even after 17 years; delicate, grapey, slightly powdery nose; bone dry, lean. Why anyone should want to, in effect, leach out all the ripe flesh and fruit of a richly rare vintage like 1971 I do not know, though it went quite well with calf's liver.* Sept 1988★★

ERBACHER SCHLOSSBERG RULANDER TBA *SCHLOSS RHEINHARTHAUSEN Alcohol 10%, 147g/l of sugar, 8.9 acidity. One of the few and probably the last* Rülander TBA. *Clearly this estate was in the throes of great experimentation, what with the Trocken, above, and now a TBA from the Pinot Gris. Two notes, the first, memorably, at a dinner given by Christopher York at Boodle's in 1983, fellow guest Prinz Nicholaus von Preussen of the Schloss (the TBA had been preceded by several glorious clarets). Virtually identical notes the following year. Fairly deep, distinctly orange tawny with light lemon green rim; bouquet out of this world: high-toned, honeyed, sultanas; very sweet, very rich, fairly concentrated, fabulous flavour and caramelly aftertaste.* July 1984★★★★★

ERDENER PRALAT RIESLING AUSLESE *DR LOOSEN Back to the middle Mosel. Lovely, classic, slightly*

* *The spelling of Bernkastel varies, as labelled.*

'kerosene' Riesling grapiness, well-developed; medium-sweet, fine flavour, slightly hard finish. Sept 1988**** Now to 1996.

GEISENHEIMER KLAUSERWEG RIESLING TBA *DEINHARD Two notes, a year apart: lovely bright yellow gold; beautiful, rich yet gentle, honeyed, spicy nose — one could smell the fleshily ripe grapes; sweet, fullish, rich, fat yet with perfect counterbalancing acidity.* Last tasted March 1984***** Will still be lovely.

GEISENHEIMER SCHLOSSGARTEN RIESLING BEERENAUSLESE *SCHONBORN Positive yellow; fabulous, honeyed* Botrytis *nose; fairly sweet, very attractive but more of a feinste Auslese than a Beerenauslese (not as rich as another tasted five years later from the Mäuerchen vineyard, with deeper colour and barley-sugar flavour).* Noted March 1980***

GRAACHER HIMMELREICH RIESLING TBA *VON SCHORLEMER Palish for a TBA; crisp, concentrated grapey nose; very sweet, rich, excellent acidity. Balanced enough for another 20 years.* After lunch in Kies with Karl Meyer, Sept 1980***** Will still be good.

HATTENHEIMER WISSELBRUNN TBA *SCHLOSS RHEINHARTHAUSEN Alcohol 11%. Noted at the first of Christopher York's wine dinners in April 1982: an extraordinary colour, warm, orange red, clearly due to extraction of pigment from the shrivelled, sunbaked grape skins during fermentation. Very bright, very exciting, with a light tartrate deposit; ambrosial bouquet, touch of muscadelle grapiness; sweet, lightish in style though with '71 fat, marvellous acidity. And a half-bottle six months later. Identical. Years of life ahead.* Last noted Oct 1982****(*)

HOCHHEIMER KONIGEN VICTORIA BERG AUSLESE *PABTSMANN 100° Oeschle. From the top end of the Rheingau, virtually out of that district, not all that far from Frankfurt. At 10 years, bouquet low-keyed but rich; medium dry — much drier, overall, than expected. Good length.* July 1981***

HOCHHEIMER KONIGEN VICTORIA BERG BEERENAUSLESE *Grapes brought in at 148° Oeschle, 2° short of TBA level: deeper colour; a bouquet from a different world, rich, grapey, honeyed, penetrating; fairly sweet, medium-full body, fairly powerful, still a touch of hardness. Many years of life.* Tasted July 1981****(*) Will be approaching peak now.

NIERSTEINER KLOSTERGARTEN SILVANER U HUXELREBE TBA *WINZER NIERSTEIN 235° Oeschle, acidity 12.5°, 250 bottles produced by the local Rheinhessen cooperative. First tasted at H Sichel's tasting in 1975. Further consistent notes from the early and mid-1980s: incredibly deep old amber, like a Verdelho madeira; bouquet indistinguishable from an old Sauternes,* crème brûlée, *gently caramelised; very sweet, rich, fat and fleshy, taste of singed raisins, matching acidity.* Last tasted April 1984*****

OESTRICHER LENCHEN RIESLING AUSLESE *JOS SPREITZER Very yellow; lovely honeyed Rheingau Riesling nose; medium-sweet, good flavour, quality, balance.* March 1981***

OESTRICHER LENCHEN BEERENAUSLESE *JOS SPREITZER Same vineyard, same grower as previous entry. Golden colour with hint of orange; a lovely calm, harmonious, honeyed combination of* Botrytis *and bottle-age; fairly but not very sweet, medium body, very good flavour and acidity, the latter a bit hard, with a lemon peel twist, leaving the wine with a dry finish.* Jan 1983**** Doubtless drinking well now.

OESTRICHER LENCHEN BEERENAUSLESE EISWEIN *DEINHARD Yellow gold; glorious bouquet; sweet, rich, beautiful flavour and acidity.* Dec 1981*****

OESTRICHER LENCHEN RIESLING TBA *DEINHARD Five notes made at various dinners. Bright yellow gold deepening to a glorious old gold; bouquet full of fruit, peaches, apricots, sugar and spice. Sheer nectar; one of the sweetest wines I can recall, rich, concentrated, fat but not cloying, saved from unctuousness by its marvellous acidity. Years of life.* Last noted Aug 1985***** Probably peaking now but with another 10 to 15 years' life.

RAUENTHALER BAIKEN RIESLING SPATLESE *STAATSWEINGUT Aged ten: yellow, slightly* spritzig*; rich, almost meaty, at first, developing honey and fruit — touch of pineapple; medium dry, light style, the trace of carbon dioxide giving the finish a refreshing uplift.* With Willi Reitz at his country house near Bingen, Sept 1981***

RAUENTHALER BAIKEN AUSLESE *STAATSWEINGUT Warm gold; rich, hefty, old honey bouquet; sweet, custard-like flavour, quite high acidity.* At a dinner in Miami after Bob Paul's mammoth tasting of 1982 Pomerols, Feb 1989***

RAUENTHALER BERG AUSLESE *SCHLOSS ELTZ Orange tinge; attractive, 'kerosene'; medium sweetness and body, good flavour, lovely.* April 1991*** Drink up.

RAUENTHALER STEINMACKER RIESLING KABINETT *HANS GALLO (Unfamiliar name, from Hochheim.) Deep; delicate honey and pineapple nose; dryish, lightish, nice but bland and needing more acidity. Surviving 10 years but not the sort of wine to keep.* Sept 1981**

RUDESHEIMER BERG ROTTLAND RIESLING SPATLESE *SCHLOSS GROENESTEYN Already a distinct yellow gold; fine honeyed nose; medium dry, crisp, light but uplifting flavour.* July 1980***

RUDESHEIMER BERG ROTTLAND RIESLING SPATLESE *DEINHARD Very good limpid appearance, on the pale side for its age; lightly honeyed nose; medium — slightly sweeter than Groenesteyn's, soft, easy, very pleasant.* Oct 1985***

SCHARZHOFBERGER SPATLESE *Rather like a nobleman dropping his Christian name when signing a letter, Egon Müller, the sole owner, does not prefix his estate name with that of the village, Wiltingen. A rare and perfect vintage: ripe, grapey nose; slightly sweet, plump for a Saar wine, very attractive.* A simple little wine served at lunch at Dr Lou Skinner's tasting of '61 clarets, Feb 1981****

SCHLOSS JOHANNISBERGER RIESLING BEERENAUSLESE *Yellow gold, rather like '67 Yquem; gloriously honeyed bottle-age and* Botrytis, *touch of sultanas; sweet, pleasantly light in style, crisp, lovely acidity. Like an exquisite ballet dancer.* Served just before two classic vintage Yquems at Rodenstock's tasting dinner at the restaurant Die

*Ente vom Lehel in Wiesbaden, Oct 1985***** Will be perfect now, and for many years to come.*

SCHLOSS VOLLRADS RIESLING BEERENAUSLESE *The other aristocratic Rheingau tasted, coincidentally, a month later. 133° Oeschle. Glorious amber gold; almost identical bouquet to the Schloss Johannisberger, lovely; slightly less sweet but similar weight and style, glorious flavour, firm, very good acidity and aftertaste. Bought at Christie's and consumed by the family, March 1985***** Now to beyond 2000.*

TRITTENHEIMER ALTAERCHEN SPATLESE *BISCHOF PRIESTERSEMINAR Buttery yellow; smelled like custard pie, ripe, good fruit; medium dry, delicious, dry acid finish. I also added "perfectly ripe now", applying equally to my wife: at her 49th birthday at Brooks's. July 1980*** Bit thin and tired now.*

WALLHAUSENER FELSENECK RIESLING AUSLESE *SCHLOSS WALLHAUSEN Grown on steep slopes of blue slate soil on a tributary of the Nahe. Very pale for its age; most distinctive nose, in between the Rhine and Mosel geographically and stylistically; medium-sweet, fairly light, very fresh for a 17-year-old, touch of woodiness on the finish. With Michael, Prinz zu Salm-Salm at the Schloss, Sept 1988****

WILTINGER BRAUNE KUPP AUSLESE *LE GALLAIS Palish; good fruit, slightly oily Riesling; fairly sweet, soft yet excellent acidity. June 1984****

WILTINGER HASENSPRUNG RIESLING TBA *DEINHARD Warm old gold; fabulous bouquet, honeyed, creamy but crisp and fruity; sweet though not too sweet, marvellous wine with lovely flavour and length. March 1983***** Will still be excellent.*

ZELTINGER SCHLOSSBERG RIESLING SPATLESE *EHSES-BERRES One of the top growers. Showing age in colour, on nose and taste, slightly "brown"-tinged and tired. July 1989* Should have been drunk prior to 1980.*

1972★

Unimportant and not notable though it did supply the trade with a quantity of lesser wines after the quality, and expense, of the '71s. Only a couple of dozen tasted, mainly in the mid-1970s. None recently. Avoid.

1973★★

Abundant — in fact the biggest crop on record — and some charming light wines made for early consumption. Late spring; almost tropical summer heat made up for the late flowering, and rain in late Sept for the near drought conditions. Despite this, disappointing wines, diluted through overproduction (as in Bordeaux) and lacking acidity.

AVELSBACHER ALTENBERG KABINETT *HOHE DOMKIRCHE This Saar wine was served as an aperitif, for which, I suppose, its acidity qualified it. Not bad in its way but really too old. Saintsbury Club, April 1987**

BERNKASTELER DOKTOR RIESLING BEERENAUSLESE EISWEIN *DEINHARD Several notes from 1981. A lovely warm, glowing yellow gold deepening to old gold; extraordinary bouquet: lanolin, lemon, roses, spice; sweet, a taste like golden syrup, lively and lovely with good fruit and tingling acidity. Bought at a charity sale and last noted at an after-theatre supper in March 1984*****

FORSTER JESUITENGARTEN RIESLING SPATLESE *VON BUHL Two notes. Fairly pale, bright; the smell of lavender wax furniture polish; medium dry, lightish, pleasant enough, short. April 1981***

HOCHHEIMER KONIGIN VICTORIA BERG SPATLESE *PABSTMANN 88° Oeschle. Broad, open, honeyed, slightly oily bouquet; dryish, not bad, short. July 1981**

SCHLOSS JOHANNISBERG *GELBLACK Fresh and agreeable for a '73. June 1981****

OCKFENER BOCKSTEIN SPATLESE *Alas the grower not noted, but another example of an old white, this time from the Ruwer, being served as an aperitif. A very pleasant, light and easy drink. At the 106th Meeting of the Saintsbury Club, April 1985***

WALLHAUSER MUHLENBERG GRAUER BURGUNDER EISWEIN *SALM-DALBERG'SCHES The Pinot Gris grapes picked early Dec. Michael zu Salm's first vintage at the 800-year-old family estate. Palish buttery yellow; delightful peach and melon bouquet; sweet, lovely flavour and acidity. Perfect. At the Schloss, Sept 1988*****

WALLHAUSER MUHLENBERG RULANDER EISWEIN TBA *SALM-DALBERG Very positive yellow; distinctly minty, fragrant bouquet; sweet, rich but not fat, with a pleasantly light delicate touch and delicious apricot flavour and lovely acidity. Half-bottle: a perfect after-theatre dessert wine. Oct 1988******

1974

Weather conditions the opposite to 1973: a dismal summer with one of the wettest autumns in memory. A few lacklustre wines tasted in the 1970s. None tasted since.

1975★★★★

A good vintage but, as soon as the very attractive '76s appeared on the market, buyers seemed to lose interest. But the firm, slightly more acidic '75s have overtaken the softer, more plausible '76s.

Late spring but warm, speedy flowering. Extremely hot, late summer, heavy rain early Sept followed by ripening sunshine. Some very good wines made though variations of style and quality due to conflicting wine-making approaches: the old-fashioned and the sweeteners.

Looking back at my notes it also seems to be a period when experimentation — mainly, it seems, in the Rheinpfalz — with strange grape varieties and crossings was coming to a head: Ehrenfelser (Riesling x Sylvaner), Kanzler u Perle, Optima, Rülander, which I always like, the older-established Müller-Thurgau (Riesling x Sylvaner) and, of course, the Silvaner or Sylvaner which is really at its best in Franconia. All of which appear in my notes of '75s. Conspicuous by its absence is the Traminer or Gewürztraminer, a scented, exotic grape I used to associate with the rustic, sometimes goaty, Palatinate wines.

Good '75s are incredibly undervalued and those of genuine Auslese quality are still lovely. First a small selection mainly tasted recently:

AYLER KUPP RIESLING SPATLESE *HUESGEN Yet another inappropriate mature Saar wine, attractive but too sweet to be served at dinner. Oct 1988***

BERNKASTELER DOKTOR RIESLING SPATLESE *DEINHARD Several recent notes. Palish, bright yellow gold; lovely, clover honey, peach and bottle-age; fairly dry, with an attractive soft grapey flavour, still fresh with lively acidity. Last tasted July 1989****

BERNKASTELER JOHANNISBRUNNCHEN MULLER-THURGAU BEERENAUSLESE *S A PRUM Palish lemon gold; lovely, fragrant peachy ripe bouquet with incredible depth of fruit, more flowery than a straight Riesling; fairly sweet, rather light and lean for a Beerenauslese, elegant, flowery with a slightly kernelly finish and raisiny aftertaste. At the estate, Sept 1988****

BRAUNEBERGER JUFFER-SONNENUHR RIESLING BEERENAUSLESE *FRITZ HAAG Again, not very sweet and a rather light style, but lovely, fresh, and perfectly balanced. Nov 1982*****

DEIDESHEIMER LETTEN OPTIMA AUSLESE *WINZER FORST A gold medal winner made from the rather exotic Optima grape by the cooperative at Forst. After five years a very deep old-apple gold; overripe honeyed scent; fairly sweet, rich, ripe — very Palatinate. Really a feinste Auslese, almost Beerenauslese. At supper, Oct 1980*****

EITELSBACHER KARTHAUSERHOFBERG SPATLESE *RAUTENSTRAUCH Probably the smallest, the prettiest of all classic wine labels. Dry, fresh, attractive. April 1983**** *and will still be good.*

ERDENER PRALAT RIESLING AUSLESE *DR LOOSEN Winner of two major prizes and one could see why: an extraordinary scent, creamy, vanilla, blancmange and fruit, showing no age; overall distinctly dry, lovely mid-palate fruit, touch of fat but good acidity, length and aftertaste. In June and Sept 1988***** *Now to 1998.*

FORSTER FREUNDSTUCK RIESLING SPATLESE *VON BUHL Palish yellow; classic, sweet, honeyed, 'kerosene' Riesling nose; medium dry, very pleasant but rather low-keyed, slightly lacking acidity, fragrant aftertaste. Sept 1988**** *Drink soon.*

WACHENHEIMER KONIGSWINGERT RIESLING BEERENAUSLESE *Made by the Wachenheimer cooperative, selected by H SICHEL. Deepish, orange-tinged; lovely honeyed bouquet; sweet, fairly full-bodied, rich, good acidity. A classic style Pfalz Beerenauslese. May 1987*****

WILTINGER SANDBERG RIESLING AUSLESE *VON SCHORLEMER Pale lemon yellow, peachy, nicely developed by the spring of 1980. By 1986 the bouquet had developed gloriously, fragrant, touch of 'tom-cats' fruit, like a Sauvignon Blanc; medium in sweetness and body. Lovely flavour and acidity. Last tasted April 1986**** *Drink soon.*

SOME OTHER 1975s TASTED IN THE EARLY TO MID-1980s:

AYLER KUPP RIESLING AUSLESE *LEONARD KREUSCH Pleasant fruit and flavour, light style***

CANZEMER ALTENBERG RIESLING AUSLESE *BISCH PRIESTERSEMINAR Two notes: amazingly rich despite its sulphur; soft, rich yet more delicate than the '76. Very pleasant light fruit**** *Probably still good.*

FORSTER SCHNEPFENFLUG AN DER WEINSTRASSE RULANDER AUSLESE *WINZER FORST A massively impressive cooperative-made Palatinate wine worthy of its gold medal for its name alone! Several notes: a deep orange-tinged amber gold; a rich, heavily honeyed nose with Rülander grassiness and grapiness, very Beerenauslese-like; medium-sweet, hefty, assertive flavour***** *A wine for Wagnerian Rhine maidens.*

GRAACHER HIMMELREICH RIESLING AUSLESE *DEINHARD Two notes: soft, fat,* Botrytis *nose; medium dry, good, rich, ripe penetrating flavour that seemed to stop half-way. But firm and refreshing****

HOCHHEIMER VICTORIA BERG AUSLESE *106° Oeschle, more colour; rich, grassy, honeyed, old-fashioned style; medium to dry finish, some fat, exciting flavour, much superior and will last****(*)

HOCHHEIMER KONIGIN VICTORIA BERG SPATLESE *PABSTMANN 87° Oeschle, no* Botrytis. *Somehow hollow, stuffed full of sulphur; assertive, some richness but a bit short***

KALLSTADTER KOBNERT SILVANER KABINETT *EDUARD SCHUSTER An interesting, bronze medal-winning wine made from the Silvaner grape grown on limestone soil. Very distinctive yellow; almost Traminer spiciness, with strawberry and honey-rich depth of fruit; lightish, clean fresh, firm and dry****

KANZELER HITZLAY RIESLING *VON BEULWITZ Very attractive, light style, pleasing acidity. Oct 1984**** *but better then than now.*

NIERSTEINER KLOSTERGARTEN TBA *H F SCHMITT Straw colour; sweet, sultana-like nose and taste, yet (despite its fat) a light style and nice acidity. Oct 1984*****

RUPPERTSBERGER LINSENBUSCH EHRENFELSER SPATLESE *VON BUHL Palish; light, fragrant, unusually scented bouquet; medium dry, easy, attractive, perfect — at its best. Aug 1981****

SERRIGER VOGELSANG SPATLESE *VER HOSPITIEN Dry, little to it**

SERRIGER VOGELSANG AUSLESE *Dry and short**

1976****

A gloriously ripe vintage. Soft, fleshy, extremely attractive wines, the only handicap being a certain lack of acidity. The sort of year that brings out the best in the Mosel and, in particular, its normally acidic tributaries, the Saar and Ruwer.

A vintage with more than its fair share of lovely Auslesen and fabulous Beeren and Trockenbeerenauslesen wines. These, on the whole, still lovely, some at their peak, some with time in hand. Most Kabinett and Spätlesen should really have been drunk. 1976 was a year of great heat and drought in northern Europe though the weather broke at the end of Aug, bringing much-needed rain. However, in southern Germany, with its milder continental climate, the weather pleasantly warm from mid-Sept to early Oct, dampness returning to encourage the formation of *Edelfäule* ('noble rot').

Although in terms of depth of quality 1976 ranks slightly below the firmer, perhaps greater all-round 1971, I cannot think of any German wine vintage whose wines have given me more pleasure. Hence the effort to report on and to try to describe quite a wide range.

BURGHORNBERGER WALLMAUER TRAMINER AUSLESE *FREIHERR VON GEMMINGEN-HORNBERG Some very individual and attractive wines are made in Würtemburg though few are shipped to England. Wallmauer is a very steep, terraced, south-facing vineyard, the* Traminer *grapes being picked on Nov 4th. At twelve years of age a very positive yellow colour; scented* Gewürz *nose, a bit earthy, slightly malty; medium dryness and weight, soft, open flavour and texture. Hard rather than acidic finish — a* Traminer *trait. Sept 1988*** Now to 1995.*

DEIDESHEIMER KIESELBERG RIESLING BEERENAUSLESE *WINZ NIEDERKERK Lovely amber gold; sweet, honeyed* Botrytis *and bottle-age bouquet; fairly sweet, rich yet with a lean touch, peach-like flavour and good acidity. Jan 1988**** Perfect now.*

ERDENER PRALAT RIESLING AUSLESE *DR LOOSEN Sweaty, bitter almond nose; medium, neither sweet nor dry, with a hot acid end. A disappointing wine at an otherwise excellent Loosen tasting. Sept 1988.*

ERDENER TREPPCHEN RIESLING BEERENAUSLESE *DR PAULY-BERGWEILER, C H BERRES ERBEN Several recent notes: palish yellow; rich, minty, oily Riesling nose; fairly sweet, perhaps drying out a little, gentle, flavoury but lacking acidity. Last tasted Oct 1990*** Needs drinking.*

FORSTER JESUITENGARTEN RIESLING AUSLESE *BASSERMANN-JORDAN Lovely old-gold colour; at first an oily, petroly Riesling nose but very perfumed, combining a citrus-like piquancy and honey. After an hour in the glass, a beautiful calm, ripe fruit smell with a whiff of raspberry; medium-sweet, rich, flavoury, with a touch of lemon and Cayenne pepper end. June 1988****

GRAACHER DOMPROBST AUSLESE *CLEMENS, FREIHERR VON SCHORLEMER Fat, grapey,* Botrytis *nose; sweet, good flavour, length and aftertaste. April 1986****

HATTENHEIMER NUSSBRUNNEN RIESLING AUSLESE *VON SIMMERN Several notes: perfection aged 10. Still lovely: a glorious buttercup yellow; soft, rich, peachy bouquet with hint of barley-sugar; medium-sweet, ripe, fleshy, good length and acidity. To be drunk by itself, not with food and emphatically not a pudding wine. Last tasted June 1988**** Now to 1996.*

HATTENHEIMER WISSELBRUNNEN RIESLING TBA *SCHLOSS RHEINHARTHAUSEN Straw gold; whiff of kerosene; very sweet, raisiny, but lacking penetration. Sept 1990*** Drink soon.*

IPHOFER JULIUS ECHTERBERG SPATLESE *JULIUSPITAL A typically firm steely Franconian wine, clearly successful in '76: palish lemon yellow; fragrant, peachy, buttery, honeyed ripeness; medium dry, very fragrant, great length, excellent aftertaste. Aug 1986*****

SCHLOSS JOHANNISBERGER RIESLING ROSALACK (AUSLESE) *Two notes: buttercup yellow; deliciously rich, petroly, honey and pineapple nose; medium-sweet, attractive, good acidity. Last tasted April 1986*** Should still be good.*

LORCHER BODENTAL-STEINBERG RIESLING AUSLESE *VON KANITZ The only outstanding estate in the most northerly Rhine wine district, down-river from Assmannshausen. Fairly deep orange gold from ripe* Botrytis*-infected grapes; petroly, rich, honey, peaches and apricots nose; fairly sweet, perfect* Edelfäule *flavour, lovely but a bit flat at the end. Lacking acidity. Sept 1988*** Drink up.*

MAXIMIN GRUENHAUSER ABTSBERG AUSLESE *VON SCHUBERT Medium-sweet, rich fruit but with gentle, light style. A perfect combination: the Ruwer, a ripe vintage and a great estate. Last tasted July 1987**** Drink soon.*

MAXIMIN GRUENHAUSER HERRENBERG RIESLING AUSLESE *VON SCHUBERT Glorious at 10 years of age, plump for an upper tributary of the Mosel. A lovely , positive yellow gold; rich, ripe, honeyed bouquet; medium, beautiful fruit and consistency of texture, well-clad, adequate acidity. Last tasted May 1988**** Drink soon.*

MEDDERSHEIMER RHEINGRAFENBERG KERNER TBA *An exotic wine from the Nahe made at the cooperative in Meddersheim. A lovely buttercup yellow; heavenly, very forthcoming bouquet, fragrant, honey and acidity; sweet, nice weight, lovely lanolin-like flavour, crisp, fresh as a daisy. Last tasted Sept 1989*****

MORZHEIMER PFAFFENBERG GEWURZTRAMINER BEERENAUSLESE EISWEIN *Little known and even more exotic, from another cooperative, this one in the Rheinpfalz. A beautiful orange amber with gold highlights; soft, wide open, laidback peachy apple strudel nose; fairly sweet, powerful flavour, even at 10 years of age, needing more time. At Rodenstock's rare wine tasting, Sept 1986*****

NEUMAGENER ROSENGARTCHEN RIESLING BEERENAUSLESE *JOSEF SCHMITT Back to the middle Mosel. Six notes over five years. Now a yellow gold with heavy — quite harmless — tartrate deposit; pleasant peachy nose and taste. More of a feine Auslese in sweetness and quality. Despite good acidity, at its peak. June 1989*** Drink soon.*

NIERSTEINER HOLLE SPATLESE *GUNTRUM In a*

curious dumpy bottle. Peachy, soft, touch of oiliness, violet cachous; trace of almonds, easy, ripe. Just enough acidity. This sort of wine needs drinking early. Sept 1988**

NIERSTEINER FINDLING SCHEUREBE BEERENAUSLESE *GUNTRUM The Rheinhessen region was very partial to the various new crossings to the extent that by the 1970s the classic Riesling only accounted for about 5% of the total. A very grapey grape, I always think of Scheurebe (named after its originator, Georg Scheu) as a plausible performer, a peroxide blonde of a wine, but at its best joyfully exotic. Two very recent notes: waxy yellow gold; delicious bouquet: fresh peeled grapes, peaches and honey; very sweet, almost Wagnerian in its voluptuous stridency. Just enough acidity.* Last tasted Aug 1990**** Drink up.

NIERSTEINER FINDLING HUXELREBE BEERENAUSLESE *Made by the Rheinfront cooperative at Nierstein. 10.7% alcohol, acidity 8.2. Coincidentally another exotic crossing from the same vineyard. Also developed by Georg Scheu, the Huxel, legal since 1968, is only used to make top Prädikat wines, Auslese to TBA. Fairly deep orange gold; fabulous, rounded, peachy ripe nose with touch of malt, creamy, honey and apricots; very sweet, mouthfilling grapey flavour, a bit obvious. Excellent acidity.* Sept 1988***** Now to 1996 or beyond.

NIERSTEINER OELBERG GEWURZTRAMINER U SILVANER BEERENAUSLESE *GEORG ALBRECHT SCHNEIDER Sweet soft fragrant bouquet and flavour. Ripe, fat.* April 1987**** Drink soon.

NIERSTEINER OELBERG RIESLING AUSLESE TROCKEN *GUNTRUM Palish; rich, flowery nose; dry — Trocken, not TBA — full flavour, a bit earthy.* Sept 1988** Holding well.

OESTRICHER DOOSBERG RIESLING BEERENAUSLESE *WEGELER-DEINHARD Golden; honeyed* Botrytis *bouquet, crisp acidity; sweet, perfect weight, flavour and acidity. I disapprove of wasting lovely sweet wines on puddings but this went beautifully with elderflower fritters.* At the Deinhard Heritage Selection lunch at the Hilton, London, July 1988****

OPPENHEIMER HERRENGARTEN RULANDER TBA *RUHLING-GILLOT I cannot recall drinking a TBA made from this grape before. The colour of old gold; rich, raisiny smell and taste; very sweet, soft, lacking length and acidity but attractive.* July 1987*** Drink up.

OPPENHEIMER SACKTRAGER GEWURZTRAMINER TBA *GUNTRUM Buttery yellow; the richness of the TBA overpowering the* Gewürz *character; sweet, rich but less fat than expected. Good length. Lovely.* Sept 1988***** Now to 1996, or beyond.

PIESPORTER GOLDTROPFCHEN AUSLESE *WELLER-WEIT Lovely lemon yellow, pale for its age; fragrant, mint leaf nose; medium-sweet, attractive. Too sweet for fish or chicken, not dry enough as an apertif, not sweet enough for dessert. Quite simply, an agreeable drink by itself.* At a Christie's pre-sale tasting, July 1988** Drink up.

SCHLOSS VOLLRADS AUSLESE *Soft, gentle, fragrant bouquet and flavour. Medium-sweet. Subtle grapey flavour and aftertaste.* March 1986*** Drink up.

SCHLOSS VOLLRADS BEERENAUSLESE *Several notes over the past five years. Now a fairly deep amber gold with lime green rim; lovely bouquet, mint leaf, peachy, touch of raisins, barley-sugar stick; fairly sweet, perfect weight, slightly caramelised mid-palate, soft, hints of lapsang souchong tea, Seville oranges, marmalade! Marvellous wine.* Last tasted Oct 1990***** Now to 1996.

SCHLOSS VOLLRADS TBA *Fairly deep, orange-tinged; very powerful nose, a bit hard and with the maltiness of Bavarian beer; sweet, full, very rich, meaty, toffee and chocolate, very assertive but also very fragrant with an extraordinary mint leaf aftertaste.* Sept 1990***(**) 1996 to well beyond 2000.

WACHENHEIMER LUGINSLAND RIESLING BEERENAUSLESE *WINZERGENOSSENSCHAFT WACHTENBURG-LUGINSLAND Just to demonstrate again that cooperatives as well as great estates can make beautiful wines, and can win gold medals. A couple of notes. Gloriously ripe at 10 years of age. More recently: lovely rich gold; sweet, vanilla, orange blossom bouquet; sweet, low alcohol, rich, glorious fruit and acidity.* Last tasted March 1988***** Now to 1996.

WEHLENER SONNENUHR RIESLING AUSLESE *S A PRUM The harvest began on Oct 4 and the sugar content was so high it was classed as Auslese from the start. Buttery gold; rich, ripe, slight touch of kerosene, deep, fragrant with almost gooseberry-like fruit; fairly sweet, really of feinste Auslese quality, very good acidity. A bit hard on the finish. Could do with more time.* In Wehlen, Sept 1988*** Now to 1996.

WINKELER HASENSPRUNG RIESLING AUSLESE *DEINHARD When I bought this in the early 1980s it needed more bottle-age. By the mid-1980s a bright yellow with tartrate deposit; fabulously ripe bouquet; flavour of peaches and cream, just enough acidity.* Last tasted July 1988****

WINKELER HASENSPRUNG RIESLING TBA *DEINHARD A marvellous golden colour, very sweet, concentrated and in 1984 needing more time. Most recently, a fairly deep, warm orange gold; very rich, tangy, almost Tokay Aszú-like nose; sweet, hefty, assertive, raisiny, great length, fragrant aftertaste. Finishes a little hard. Needs more bottle-age.* Sept 1990****(*) 1994 to beyond 2000.

ZELTINGER SONNENUHR RIESLING TBA *EHSES-BERRES Very similar colour to the Winkeler; glorious, ripe, peachy nose, almond oily richness; sweet, surprisingly delicate, refined, very good acidity.* Sept 1990***** Now to 2000.

OF THE 200 OR SO OTHER NOTES OF THOSE TASTED LAST IN THE EARLY TO MID-1980s, THE FOLLOWING WERE WELL ABOVE AVERAGE:

BERNKASTELER BADSTUBE AUSLESE *J J PRUM Ripe, lovely*****

BERNKASTELER GRABEN RIESLING AUSLESE *DEINHARD Fine, firm.* Aug 1981***

DEIDESHEIMER HERRGOTTSACKER RIESLING AUSLESE *VON BUHL GROSSER PREIS DMG — a top medal winner. Two notes. Perfection******

DEIDESHEIMER HERRGOTTSACKER BEERENAUSLESE EISWEIN *Harvested Dec 9. Very strange, a bit acetic.*

DEIDESHEIMER HOFSTUCK AUSLESE *Flowery, honeyed and perfectly balanced******

DURKHEIMER HOCHMESS RIESLING SPATLESE *A cooperative wine. Clean, grapey****

EITELSBACHER KARTHAUSERHOFBERGER BURGBERG SPATLESE *Lovely, complex****

ESSINGER RULANDER TBA EISWEIN *WINFRIED FREY 174° Oeschle, sugar 225g/l, acidity 9.1: deep orange amber stained by shrivelled brown skins; honeyed, scented; very sweet from start to finish yet with a deft touch******

FORSTER FREUNDSTUCK RIESLING AUSLESE *VON BUHL Another big prize winner; lovely*****

FORSTER KIRCHENSTUCK RIESLING AUSLESE *VON BUHL Winner of the DLG Grosser Preis in 1979: deep buttery yellow; ripe fruit and honey. Delicious******

GEISENHEIMER MAUERCHEN RIESLING BEERENAUSLESE *BASTING-GIMBEL Glorious, sweet, full, rich — touch of end bitterness. May 1986*****

GRAACHER HIMMELREICH TBA *S A PRUM Golden; blissful bouquet, soft, exquisite flavour*****(*)

HATTENHEIMER WISSELBRUNNEN BEERENAUSLESE *MOLITOR Rich. Perfect balance*****

HOCHHEIMER KONIGEN VICTORIA BERG RIESLING BEERENAUSLESE *PABSTMANN 130° Oeschle. Buttercup yellow; honeyed, peach, apricot, piquant, spicy; medium-sweet, lovely crisp flavour, dry finish, fragrant aftertaste. Several notes*****(*)

HOCHHEIMER KONIGEN VICTORIA BERG TBA *164° Oeschle. Only 144 bottles produced: yellow gold; beautiful bouquet; sweet, fabulous flavour that expanded in the mouth, great length******

JOHANNISBERGER HOLLE RIESLING AUSLESE TROCKEN *VON MUMM Made from ripe grapes fully fermented out. Lovely, peachy nose; dry, good firm and long flavour****

KESTENER PAULINSHOFBERG RIESLING BEERENAUSLESE *JOS SELBACH Several notes: palish for its style and age; high-toned, peachy with a scent also reminding me of ripening tomatoes in a greenhouse; medium-sweet, lovely flavour, lemon-tinged acidity****(*)

KIEDRICHER GRAFENBERG RIESLING SPATLESE *DR WEIL Rich, ripe, honeyed, raisiny, harmonious nose and taste. Lovely shape in the mouth. Dryish, lightish, gentle. More like an Auslese****

KIEDRICHER SANDGRUBE AUSLESE *SCHLOSS GROENSTEYN Ripe and excellent*****

KONIGSCHAFFAUSER STEINGRUBE SPATBURGUNDER WEISSHERBST TBA *An extraordinary rosé wine made from the Pinot Noir by a cooperative in Baden and winner of two top medals. Several notes: a rich, warm, ruddy tawny colour; fabulous nose, grapey, honeyed, hint of grass and straw; very sweet, immensely rich, marvellously Wagnerian, lovely acidity******

MULHEIMER HELENENKLOSTER RIESLING AUSLESE *MAX FERD RICHTER Lovely, ripe, floral; touch of lanolin, nice acidity****

MULHEIMER SONNENLAY AUSLESE *MAX FERD RICHTER More delicate and grapey; two notes****

NIERSTEINER AUFLANGEN SCHEUREBE TBA *STAATSWEINGUT Pure yellow gold; overwhelming yet crisply honeyed bouquet; very sweet, fat, luscious, great length and acidic uplift. Several notes******

RANDERSACKERER PFULBEN SILVANER BEERENAUSLESE *JULIUSPITAL Winner of the DLG Grosser Preis, 1977, and a Würzburg gold medal. Several half-bottles: golden; rich, raisiny, spicy nose; medium-sweet, Sauternes-like flavour, fat but a consistently hard, short, dry finish****

RUDESHEIMER BERG ROSENECK RIESLING AUSLESE *NAEGLER Fairly deep yellow gold; almost Beerenauslese honeycomb-wax richness, harmonious, like pineapple in syrup, scented, spicy; medium-sweet, plump yet gentle and fragrant. Perfection*****

RUPPERTSBERGER LINSENBUSCH MULLER-THURGAU SPATLESE *BURKLIN-WOLF Lovely peachy nose and flavour but a bit dull and flat on the finish. Too ripe a year for the Müller-Thurgau***

RUPPERTSBERGER LINSENBUSCH SCHEUREBE BEERENAUSLESE *VON BUHL Sweet, soft, plump and lovely*****

SCHARZHOFBERGER KABINETT *RUDOLF MULLER Nicely balanced****

SCHARZHOFBERGER KABINETT *VER HOSPITIEN Surprisingly dry, austere and variable** to***

SCHARZHOFBERGER AUSLESE *VON HOVEL Medium dry, excellent*****

SCHARZHOFBERGER RIESLING AUSLESE *VER HOSPITIEN Pale gold; gentle, honeyed plus pure lime; medium dry, ripe, very flavoury — would have been feinste Auslese prior to the 1971 Wine Laws*****

SERRIGER VOGELSANG RIESLING TBA *STATE DOMAINE, TRIER Concentrated, syrupy, lovely richness and racy acidity. Aug 1982******

The wide range of 1976s from Meyerhof, Franz Duhr, Schloss Lieser and von Schorlemer tasted in Bernkastel and prior to the auction in 1980 were vastly superior to the 1975s, mainly because they ranged from Auslese to Beerenauslese in quality. I see no point in reporting further of the 120 or so not already referred to above.

1977*

Modest quality wines for early consumption. Late flowering and poor summer followed by marvellous warmth early Oct. Then, in Nov, conditions right to enable some *Eiswein* to be made. Average production, very few quality wines. Quite a lot of '77s tasted in 1980/1 including far too many raw and acidic Mosel wines, but some quite passable from the more southerly Rheinpfalz. All should have been consumed long before now.

FORSTER ELSTER RIESLING SPATLESE *VON BUHL Winner in 1978 of an* Ehrenpreis *("special" prize), higher than a gold medal. First tasted in*

Deidesheim in 1980: good colour, good flavour. In 1982, lunching at home, distinct yellow hue; fairly hefty, grapey nose; medium, neither sweet nor dry, nice flavour, reasonable acidity and finish. Most recently, a rich, positive, attractive but not altogether harmonious fruit salad bouquet, with bottle-age — more mango than honey. A very fruity complex flavour, lively acidity. Michael Hiller, the American who was running the estate at that time, described it as a "wine with a beard"! Last tasted at von Buhl's, Sept 1988★★★

1978★★

Moderate quality. A poor spring, late flowering, wet summer but lovely, balmy sunshine Sept through Oct. Late harvest. Small crop of useful, commercial wines. A reasonably representative range of districts and estates tasted between 1980 and 1983, very few recently. The overall impression: pleasant enough, most mild and gentle, lacking distinction and length. Drink up.

BERNKASTELER BADSTUBE RIESLING *DEINHARD* *Although this is an old note I include it because it was a declassified Doktor with sugar-free extract of 29g. It had a typically fragrant, somewhat raw Riesling aroma but untypical, slightly cardboardy flavour due to frost on Oct 10 which destroyed the leaves. The grapes continued to develop for some three weeks, the vines extracting minerals from the soil, the grapes increasing in extract but not sugar, and the acidity reducing.* Tasted at the Deinhard estate in Bernkastel, Sept 1982★

DURKHEIMER SPIELBERG SCHEUREBE BEERENAUSLESE EISWEIN *KLOSTER LIMBURG Yellow; very grapey Scheu aroma plus honey; sweet, rich, soft, fruity, lovely acidity.* May 1981★★★★ And might have survived.

FORSTER MARIENGARTEN SCHEUREBE BEERENAUSLESE NICHOLAUS EISWEIN *BURKLIN-WOLF Picked Dec 6, 140° Oeschle, 12° acidity and a gold medal winner. High-toned yet delicate spicy nose; very sweet, some fat, an amazing flavour and uplift of acidity.* At the estate, Sept 1980★★★★

HOCHHEIMER KIRCHENSTUCK SPATLESE *ASCHROTT Two notes: grapey, sour cream nose, a bit raw but curiously attractive; medium sweetness, lightish, soft, easy, a bit lactic. Needed drinking.* Last tasted Nov 1986★★

JOHANNISBERGER SCHWARZENSTEIN RIESLING AUSLESE EISWEIN *G H MUMM Very bright yellow; singularly creamy, earthy, acetone nose, like powdered blackberry-flavoured boiled sweets, lacking fruit support; medium-sweet, lean, quite good length, light, acidic finish. Really rather raw.* After-theatre supper, May 1984★

OPPENHEIMER SCHUTZENHUTTE RIESLING KABINETT *GUNTRUM Pleasant enough grapey nose and taste; a bit flat. Needed drinking.* Sept 1988★★

SCHLOSS VOLLRADS GRUNSILBER TROCKEN *Pale; rather Sylvaner-like, pleasant enough; dry, light straightforward.* Sept 1988★★

WALLHAUSER JOHANNISBERG TROCKEN *SALM-DALBERG Very pale; flowery Nahe fruit salad nose; dry, lightish, rather flat.* Sept 1988★★

WINKELER HASENSPRUNG RIESLING AUSLESE EISWEIN *BASTING-GIMBEL Palish, still slightly green-tinged; sweet, fat, peachy; fairly sweet, attractive, a touch of rot(?) but nice crisp acidity.* May 1986★★★

1979★★★

Pleasant, on the whole light and easy wines. Very severe frosts in Jan damaged dormant vines. Inclement spring, late flowering, poor summer but lovely, sunny ripening autumn which saved the late harvest. District variations, Rheingau and Pfalz bigger and better, Rheinhessen small but good, Mosel small, quite good.

Not as much *Edelfäule (Botrytis)* as in 1983 and, Guntrum told me, problems with an assault by red spiders.

A broad spectrum of notes in the early 1980s. Looking back I rather liked the wines, certainly far more agreeable than adverse comments. Lacking the excitement, grandeur, finesse of a good classic vintage, but pleasant to drink. A selection of some unusual, more recent, notes follow. Now cheap and still worth picking up.

BRAUNEBERGER JUFFER RIESLING KABINETT *WILLI HAAS Pale; rich, aromatic bouquet and flavour. Fairly dry.* June 1990★★

ERDENER PRALAT RIESLING AUSLESE *DR LOOSEN High-toned, rather petroly Riesling, violet scent, depth of fruit; medium dry, good positive fruit, no signs of age, with nice acidity.* Sept 1988★★★

GRAACHER HIMMELREICH RIESLING KABINETT *DEINHARD First tasted in 1981: very pale; rich, attractive fruit and some depth; fairly dry, almost Saar-like acidity. One could taste the slate soil. The winemaker said he would not drink this before 1983. However, pleasant enough in 1982. By the mid-1980s still pale; nose very fresh; dry, good refreshing acidity.* Last noted May 1985★★

GRAACHER HIMMELREICH RIESLING KABINETT *JJ PRUM Still very pale; very dry, almond kernels flavour. However much I admire 'JJ', distinctly unexciting and not to my taste.* With Manfred Prum, June 1990★

HATTENHEIMER PFAFFENBERG RIESLING SPATLESE *SCHLOSS SCHONBORN The vineyard faces south, overlooking the Rhine at its widest point. No chemicals used in the vineyard, late and selective picking, individual oak barrels. The result a lovely, palish yellow colour; a rich, honeyed, bottle-age and ripe grape nose; medium-sweet, soft, grapey, attractive, with fragrant aftertaste. Completely evolved.* Sept 1988★★★

KREUZNACHER BREITENWEG RIESLING KABINETT TROCKEN *FINKENAUER Although roughly parallel and to the south of the Mosel, the latter's steep slopes of slate become, in the Nahe, sandstone* *slopes, hence the different style. I am not a great Trocken fan but this is one of the best I have tasted: subdued, immature (then), nose with hint of Nahe "fruit salad" and mint. After the appealing scent a shock: bone dry, austere. At Lay & Wheeler's, Oct 1982*** but likely to be tired now.*

MEERSBURGER SONNENUFER RULANDER TBA *STAATSWEINGUT MEERSBURG An extraordinary wine, made from vines grown at a fairly high (500m) elevation overlooking Germany's largest lake, the Bodensee. Amazingly deep, almost ruddy, with an intense apple green rim, reminding me of an Australian 'Liqueur' muscat; glorious bouquet: intensely rich amalgam of apricots, barley-sugar, vanilla, the skin of muscadelle grapes and syrup of figs; sweet, of course, as if the must had been concentrated, unctuousness tempered by good acidity, taste of black treacle. Not for those who seek length, finesse, delicacy. A luscious mouthful. July 1988*****

NIERSTEINER AUFLANGEN SILVANER BEERENAUSLESE EISWEIN *GUNTRUM Picked Dec 31 yet not much* Botrytis. *148° Oeschle, 1,800 bottles produced. A marvellous deep gold; beautiful honey-sweet, pure raisin nose; fairly, not very, sweet, fullish, some plumpness yet still hard. Good acidity. After lunch at 'Hajo' Guntrum's, Sept 1988**** Now to 1999.*

NIERSTEINER BERGKIRCHE RIESLING SPATLESE *GUNTRUM Tasted in the vineyard on the hill by the church (which had one of those pretty south German onion-shaped domes). Good colour, positive yellow; light, gentle, honeyed bottle-age bouquet; dryish, touch of fat—clay soil, slightly petroly Riesling flavour, soft. With Guntrum and his vineyard manager, Sept 1988*** Needs drinking.*

SCHLOSS VOLLRADS BLAUSILBER HALBTROCKEN KABINETT *Palish and green-tinged; crisp, green, with Sauvignon Blanc-like acidity; very dry, light, lean and almost tart. By my reckoning very, not halb, trocken. At Vollrads, Sept 1988***

WOLLSTEINER ZIFFCHEN OPTIMA RULANDER BEERENAUSLESE *P MULLER An exotic combination of grapes, the full-bodied juicy Rülander (Pinot Gris) and the newer, grapey, Optima. Two notes in 1987: bright yellow gold; very attractive scented, peachy flavour; a fairly sweet, plump, muscadelle-flavoured wine with excellent acidity. Most recently, as above but a slightly deeper waxy gold; intriguingly novel bouquet, spearmint, perhaps lacking length but with tingling acidity. Last tasted Aug 1990****

1980

A strange and difficult vintage for the vinegrower. After a cold wet winter, spring arrived tentatively, but lovely warm weather arrived in May and continued until early June. Then, just as there were hopes for a bumper crop, the weather changed and from mid-June it was cold and wet, resulting in the latest flowering in memory, finishing end July, with, on average, only half setting. Moreover, bunches and grapes were of very variable size which made vinification difficult despite the good ripening autumn weather. The harvest was late and meagre, the smallest since 1962.

Very few tasted, only one of even *Spätlese* quality, but quite flavoury with refreshing acidity. Passé now.

HOCHHEIMER KONIGEN VICTORIA BERG* RIESLING KABINETT *PABSTMANN Only Qba and Kabinett qualities produced in 1980 but the wines had enormously high sugar-free dry extract partly or mainly due to the 30% of normal crop. Pale; immature, amyl acetate and sulphur dioxide; fairly dry, lean, light refreshing acidity. At a Victoria Berg tasting in London, July 1981.*

1981**

Variable, mainly modest to moderate quality. Somewhat below-average crop. Warm weather induced advance vegetation in April but premature shoots were damaged by frosts at the end of the month. May to mid-June unusually moist but warm weather induced early flowering of part of the remaining crop, the rest delayed in less than ideal conditions. However, those that flowered early, ripened early. When I visited the Königin Victoria Berg vineyard on Sept 2, Mr Hupfeld told me that he had never known such advanced, well-formed and tightly bunched grapes in his life—they were at least a month ahead of normal as his flowering took place earlier than in the Rheingau proper. He expected an average harvest. Alas the weather turned cool and wet at the end of the month. Probably at best in the Rheinpfalz.

A fairly wide range tasted mainly in 1983 and 1984, few of higher than *Spätlese* quality, and quite variable. A few tasted recently, and noted below: a Deinhard estates selection tasted to demonstrate the variety of district styles and qualities.

In short, not bad. Some will be pleasant enough now but not meriting a detour.

FORSTER PECHSTEIN GEWURZTRAMINER AUSLESE TROCKEN *VON BUHL A hefty, opulent, earth-scented Gewürztraminer nose; very dry, quite full-bodied, hefty, austere. Sept 1988****

* *Prior to a visit by Queen Victoria and the Prince Consort in 1850, the five-acre vineyard was known as Hochheimer Dechantenruhe. The tradition of Royal gifts, which started in 1857, resumed in 1945 when the Auslese was given as a christening present for Princess Anne (HRH the Princess Royal). When HRH Queen Elizabeth II visited Wiesbaden in 1965 she was presented with wine, and the '75 vintage was drunk at the Jubilee Banquet at the Guildhall in 1977. More recently, the '76 Beerenauslese was presented to HRH the Prince of Wales and Lady Diana Spencer as a wedding present.*

FORSTER UNGEHEUER SCHEUREBE SPATLESE TROCKEN *VON BUHL Palish, yellow; honeyed bottle-age and acidity, delicate, ripe yet "green" and unexaggerated Scheurebe aroma; dry, highish alcohol, with fine fragrant flavour and aftertaste.* Sept 1988***

HALLGARTENER SCHONELL GREEN/GOLD CAPSULE, QBA *GRAF MATUSCHKA-GREIFFENCLAU (Formerly the old Loewenstein estate.) Dryish, on the light side, soft, easy.* As good as it would ever be, Nov 1985**

HATTENHEIMER NUSSBRUNEN RIESLING QBA *One would be forgiven for not noticing the name of village and vineyard as Schloss Rheinharthausener dominates the label. Very bright yellow; the smell of an old-fashioned waxy, commercial Sauternes, with almond kernels equally reminiscent of white Bordeaux; distinctly dry, steely, crisp to the point of tartness.* Sept 1988*

OPPENHEIMER SCHUTZENHUTTE RIESLING KABINETT *GUNTRUM A silver prize winner: lively, highly polished yellow green; attractive, crisp; dryish entry, dry somewhat acidic finish, but fresh for its age with a pleasant delicate touch.* Sept 1988***

RUPPERTSBERGER LINSENBUSCH SCHEUREBE SPATLESE *DEINHARD First noted at Deinhard's trade tasting of '81s: aroma rather like the "lychee" of Gewürztraminer; a broad fragrant flavour. Now more yellow; lovely grapey nose, hint of passion fruit; medium — a bit too sweet for food, plump yet crisp and with adequate acidity. A flavoury drink.* Last tasted Jan 1989***

SCHLOSS VOLLRADS GREEN CAPSULE QBA *The lowest quality rung of the Vollrads ladder. Presented by Erwein Gräf Matuschka-Greiffenclau — the 29th descendant of the first* Gräf *or Earl — who explained that even this quality was best three years after the vintage. Pale, very bright; nose still youthful but developed peachy, soft scent in the glass; fairly dry, light, pleasant enough acidity but short.* At a Castle Hotel, Taunton, Wine Weekend, Nov 1985**

WEHLENER SONNENUHR RIESLING SPATLESE *JJ PRUM If not as old as the Greiffenclau's, Manfred is, at least, a 10th-generation Prüm. Broad, sweet, fruity nose of pleasing depth; medium-sweet, lightish, flavoury, fruity, very good acidity.* Sept 1988***

OF THE WIDE RANGE OF DEINHARD ESTATE WINES TASTED IN 1983/4, THE BEST:

BERNKASTELER DOKTOR RIESLING SPATLESE *The scent of blown grass; some richness and breadth of flavour, with pleasant grapey aftertaste****

BERNKASTELER GRABEN RIESLING BEERENAUSLESE EISWEIN *Scented, rich bouquet; sweet, plump, fruity, lovely*****

FORSTER UNGEHEUER RULANDER AUSLESE *Fragrant, grassy, just enough fruit support; medium, soft, fleshy****

OESTRICHER LENCHEN RIESLING AUSLESE EISWEIN *A gold prize winner with a rather prickly honeyed nose; sweet, soft, loose-ended acidity and with touch of bitterness***

1982*

Yet another mediocre vintage. This time a bumper harvest in quantity if not in quality thanks to heavy rain — to the extent that some growers had storage problems. The wines as unpredictable as the weather, the latter ranging from deepest winter frosts, through sunshine and drought to the rain already mentioned at vintage time. The biggest ever crop recorded in Germany, half as much again as 1973. A wide range tasted when they came on to the market in the summer and autumn of 1983. Few meant to be stayers and even fewer tasted since 1984.

BERNKASTELER DOCTOR (*sic*) RIESLING SPATLESE TROCKEN *DEINHARD Pale, limpid; spicy — but nose and taste spoiled for me by almond kernels. Ugh! 'Exclusive' to the excellent Die Ente vom Lehel restaurant. They were welcome to it.* In Wiesbaden, Oct 1985.

SCHLOSS BOCKELHEIMER FELSENBERG RIESLING SPATLESE *H CRUSIUS Another quite agreeable wine, but Nahe fruit nose and flavour were better after only one year than after two, when I thought it lean and needing drinking.* Last tasted July 1984.

SCHLOSS BOCKELHEIMER KONIGFELS RIESLING *ANHEUSER & FEHRS Grapey and grapefruity in the winter of 1984; in the spring of 1985 was too light to survive and needed drinking that summer. My initial two stars fizzled out to one.* Last tasted July 1985*

CASTELLER KUGELSPIEL RIESLANER SPATLESE *FURST CASTELL Another grape crossing. From Franconia. Yellow; an extraordinarily flowery aroma plus scent of banana; dry, curiously pungent, with strange apricot skin flavour and aftertaste.* Sept 1988*?

INGELHEIMER SPATBURGUNDER *J NEUS A district in the Rheinhessen specialising in soft reds from the Pinot Noir. This one had a jammy, slightly caramelly nose; medium dry, quite attractive but with a rusty nails finish like some South Australian reds.* May 1987**

KASELER KEHRNAGEL RIESLING SPATLESE *B SIMON Mild, grapey, medium dry, light, rather acidic.* Last tasted Nov 1987**

MAXIMIN GRUNHAUSER HERRENBERG SPATLESE *Not unlike the* Kaseler, *fractionally sweeter. Fresh but as good as it would ever be.* In July 1985**

WEHLENER SONNENUHR KABINETT *JJ PRUM A dryish, light, easy, pleasant enough drink at a jet-lagged early supper.* At the University Club, Chicago, Feb 1988**

THE BEST (***) '82s NOTED AT EARLY TRADE TASTINGS:

BERNKASTELER GRABEN RIESLING SPATLESE *DEINHARD Nose of cress and grape skins; firm, good flavour and aftertaste****

GRAACHER HIMMELREICH RIESLING SPATLESE *FRIEDRICH WILHELM GYMNASIUM Rich yet delicate, dry, firm, very pleasant****

OESTRICHER LENCHEN RIESLING SPATLESE *DEINHARD Nose of egg and cress; good flavour and light****

WEHLENER SONNENUHR AUSLESE *DEINHARD Earthy, sweaty but attractive****

*1983****

At last, a real vintage, the best since 1976. When I say 'real' I mean respectable, natural, unforced, thanks to better growing conditions.

A relatively mild winter with no frost damage was followed by a cool wet spring, with rains in April and May. Good flowering conditions during the latter half of June were followed by a long dry spell in July and Aug. A judicious combination of rain and sun in Sept swelled and ripened the berries. Good vintage. However, little or no *Botrytis*.

Though highly rated at the time, the overall reputation of 1983 has eased back a little. It was, however, unreservedly successful in the Saar and Ruwer, also in the Nahe. As always, the best growers make the best wine. A wide range and large number tasted, of which the following are a recent cross-section, including some of the most bizarre. A most invigorating vintage, still well worth looking for and drinking.

AVELSBACHER HAMMERSTEIN RIESLING AUSLESE *STAATSWEINGUT Lightly grapey, assertive, still hard, needing more time. Sept 1990***(*)

AVELSBACHER HAMMERSTEIN RIESLING AUSLESE *PETER JOSS HAUTH Lovely, delicate fruit and acidity, Sept 1988*****

BERNCASTLER (*sic*) DOCTOR (*sic*) RIESLING AUSLESE *LAUERBERG (Labelled for Japanese market?) Still pale, lime green-tinged; positive rich ripe grapey nose, with honey, melon; medium-sweet yet a nice light style, agreeable grapey flavour, just a slight touch of bitterness. At a tasting conducted for Shibata, the Japanese publisher of* Wine Tasting, *in Tokyo, Nov 1989****

BERNKASTELER BRATENHOEFCHEN RIESLING AUSLESE *DEINHARD Lovely peachy nose and pleasant acidity when first shown to the trade in July 1983. By 1986 it was lacking some finesse and, at five years of age, had taken on more colour; nice fruit but a bit oily. Needed to be served well chilled to crisp it up. Last tasted May 1988***

BRUSSELE KLEINBOTTWARER LEMBERGER KABINETT TROCKEN *GRAF ADELMANN A vineyard in Würtemberg dating back to Roman times: Lemberger a red grape (*blau Frankreich*). Medium-deep, youthful cherry red; rather green fruit, blackberry-like, plus whiff of fresh banana; slightly sweet, medium-full body, curious earthiness and tinny tannins. Lacking length but at least with more guts and interest than most of the Rhine reds. At the 2nd Europäisches Wein-Festival in Frankfurt, Sept 1988***

CASTELLER FEUERBACH DOMINA KABINETT *FURST CASTELL 95° Oeschle. Not chaptalised. Another curious red wine, this time from Franconia, the grape being a Portugueser crossed with Spätburgunder. A surprisingly deep red, slightly spritz; crisp, Gamay-like fruit; dry, medium-light, correct balance of tannin and acidity. Attractive. Like a young Chinon without the rasping acidity. Two notes. Last tasted Sept 1988****

EITELSBACHER MARIENHOLZ RIESLING SPATLESE *BISCH KONVIKT Several very consistent notes: most recently, yellow green but still slightly spritz; soft, grassy, grapey nose, a 'green' undertow; medium dry, grapey, peach kernels, very dry gooseberry-like acidic finish. Last tasted July 1989****

FORSTER PECHSTEIN GEWURZTRAMINER AUSLESE *VON BUHL Pale; delicate, harmonious, powdery rose cachou-scented* Gewürz *bouquet and taste. Medium-sweet — but not sweet enough for plum dumplings with strawberries and cream — a delicate touch, perfumed. At lunch in Deidesheim, Sept 1988****

GAILINGER RITTERHALDE SPATBURGUNDER ROTWEIN SPATLESE TROCKEN *STAATSWEINGUT MEERSBURG A 1984 silver award-winning Baden Bodensee red wine. A complete contrast to the Casteller: a palish, mature, rosehip colour; fragrant, raspberry-scented; fairly dry, lightish, flavoury, not unlike some lighter '83 burgundies. Touch of spritz. Nov 1986***

GAU-HEPPENHEIMER PFARRGARTEN EISWEIN *CHRISTMANN-ROLL Tartaric acid crystals on the cork. Distinct yellow hue, hint of green; scented and a bit sulphury; sweet, pleasant though somewhat artificial flavour. April 1988***

GEISENHEIMER KLAUSERWEG RIESLING EISWEIN *FORSCHUNGSANSTALT, GEISENHEIM Palish yellow gold; deep, minty, bread-like nose; very sweet, rich, fairly concentrated with counterbalancing acidity. Several notes. Last tasted Oct 1987****

GRAACHER HIMMELREICH RIESLING AUSLESE HALBTROCKEN *S A PRUM Neutral; correctly 'half-dry', soft, flavoury. Sept 1988*** *Drink up.*

HALLGARTENER HENDELBERG RIESLING SPATLESE HALBTROCKEN *FURST LOWENSTEIN Grapes now vinified at Schloss Vollrads. Fragrant, but it smells dry and acidic and, as usual, Matuschka Greiffenclau's idea of 'half-dry' is not mine. This is dry. But flavoury. Sept 1988***

HOCHHEIMER DOMDECHANEY RIESLING SPATLESE *WERNER'SCHEN A silver prize DLG in 1986 for Dr Franz Werner Michel, the 7th generation of the Werner family: pale; low-keyed; fairly dry, lean, crisp, very flavoury, good acidity. Sept 1988***(*)

HOCHHEIMER DOMDECHANEY RIESLING, SPATLESE *SCHLOSS SCHONBORN More fruit and slightly sweeter, soft, ripe. June 1987****

HOCHHEIMER HOLLE RIESLING SPATLESE *WERNER Lovely gentle, fruity crisp acidity. Feb 1988****

HOCHHEIMER KIRCHENSTUCK RIESLING SPATLESE HALBTROCKEN *WERNER This vineyard is next to Domdechaney, a heavy soil said to produce fresh and elegant wines even in dry years. Werner does not overproduce. The wines are fermented and aged 1½ years in old oak barrels. Peachy nose but a bit dull.* Sept 1988**

HOCHHEIMER KONIGIN VICTORIA BERG RIESLING SPATLESE *PABSTMANN First tasted in July 1984. It was fragrant, rather unusual and unsettled but soft, gentle and agreeable on palate. Several years after the vintage it has taken on colour, an attractive, bright, yellow gold; deep, warm, earthy, grassy bouquet and flavour. Seems sweeter.* Last tasted Oct 1990** Drink soon.

HOHENTWEILER OLGABERG RULANDER AUSLESE *STAATSWEIN MEERSBURG A gold medal Baden wine with surprisingly deep amber gold colour; very rich, grapey, delicious bouquet; medium-sweet — went well with parma ham and melon, rich yet nicely balanced, perfect acidity.* June 1988****

HOHENTWEILER OLGABERG TRAMINER AUSLESE *Yellow and mellow; bouquet of peaches and apricots; medium-sweet, glorious flavour, fleshy, grapey, good acidity.* July 1989****

HOHENTWEILER OLGABERG WEISSBURGUNDER SPATLESE *Straw yellow. Rich, soft, fleshy, a bit too heftily sweet.* Aug 1987**

KASELER DOMINIFANERSBERG RIESLING AUSLESE *VON NELL Yellow green; attractive low-keyed grapiness; medium, kept fresh by its rather sharp Ruwer, gooseberry-like acidity.* Sept 1989***

KASELER DOMINIFANERSBERG RIESLING AUSLESE HALBTROCKEN *A lovely soft yellow colour; soft, waxy fruit; medium dry, light dry acidic finish, touch of bitterness.* Sept 1989*

KASELER DOMINIFANERSBERG RIESLING AUSLESE TROCKEN *Dry, lightish, crisp, very dry acidic finish and slightly harsh, rubbery endtaste.* May 1989*

KASELER DOMINIFANERSBERG RIESLING SPATLESE TROCKEN *Pale; nutty; bone dry but fragrant.* Sept 1988**

MAXIMIN GRUENHAUSER ABTSBERG KABINETT *VON SCHUBERT A perfect light refreshing luncheon wine on a hot day at the zoo restaurant in Jo'burg (South Africa, not Rhine).* Dec 1987***

MAXIMIN GRUENHAUSER ABTSBERG RIESLING AUSLESE *Several notes: glorious, peachy, pineapple nose and taste, yet great delicacy, refreshing, fragrant aftertaste.* Last noted April 1987***(*) Will still be delicious.

RAUENTHALER BAIKEN RIESLING SPATLESE *VON SIMMERN Bright, appealing, pure yellow with gold highlights; gentle grapiness, low-keyed, touch of honey, good depth; medium dry, lovely firm fruit, crisp, hard, steely finish. My sort of Hock. Time in hand.* Oct 1987***(*) Should be perfect now.

SCHARZHOFBERGER *VON VOLXEM Light and dry, perfect with oysters Rockefeller.* At Antoine's in New Orleans, April 1986***

SCHARZHOFBERGER SPATLESE *HOHE DOMKIRCHE Medium-sweet, with a delightful light grapiness and beautiful balance of fruit and acidity.* May 1980***

SCHLOSS BOECKELHEIMER FELSENBERG *DEINHARD More attractive, with a lightly honeyed nose and distinctive Nahe pineapple and grapefruit taste. Acidity adequate.* Dec 1988**

SCHLOSS BOECKELHEIMER FELSENBERG RIESLING SPATLESE *H CRUSIUS Sulphur dioxide obscuring fruit in July 1984; still a bit disappointing, better on palate in 1986. Most recently: fairly dry, on the light side, so-so.* Last tasted July 1989*

SIEBELDINGER 'IM SONNENSCHEIN' SPATBURGUNDER WEISSHERBST AUSLESE *IKONOMIERAT REBHOLZ A dependable grower, according to Schoonmaker. Makes an attractive, dry white wine from ripe red grapes. Not exactly white: a palish, warm orange amber gold; lovely, harmonious, honeyed grapey nose; surprisingly dry, firm, good length and aftertaste. Excellent acidity. Went well with figs.* Sept 1988****

WINKELER HASENSPRUNG RIESLING SPATLESE *DEINHARD Two very consistent notes, the first at the opening tasting in July 1984: very scented, violets; dry, flavour less exciting than nose. In 1988 a deeper yellow but otherwise similar. So-so.* Last tasted Dec 1988**

WINKELER HASENSPRUNG RIESLING SPATLESE *WILM WASUM Distinctly sweeter but rather oily and peach kernelly. Just misses.* March 1987*

WINKELER HONIGBERG RIESLING SPATLESE *Noted over a three-year period. Yellow-tinged; grapey, mild yet fat; medium dry, a bit four-square, slightly kernelly but reasonably rich. Needs drinking.* May 1990**

To reel off all the wines tasted 1984–86 would be superfluous and space-consuming. They ranged from Qba to Auslese but mainly Spätlesen and Auslesen, of which I would generalise by saying that the latter were the most attractive, whether Mosel or Rheinpfalz.

1984

Poor, acidic wines; one of, if not the worst of the decade. Unseasonable weather throughout northern Europe. In Germany, late budding, late flowering, poor summer, delayed harvest (mid-Oct) in reasonably warm dry conditions. I have only tasted four and have no burning desire to taste more.

ASSMANNSHAUSER FRANKENTHAL SPATBURGUNDER TROCKEN *R KONIG Palish, auburn-tinged; delicate, fruity, recognisably Pinot, a bit green and malty; unknit, curious cheesy flavour, taste of rotten grapes.* April 1989.

RUPPERTSBERGER REITERPFAD RIESLING SPATLESE *VON BUHL Admitted to be an 'off' year. A curiously scented nose and taste. I thought there was some Scheurebe but was informed that 1983 was the last vintage they used this grape. High acidity.* At the winery, Sept 1988*

SCHARZHOFBERGER EISWEIN *EGON MULLER Orange amber, apple green rim; astonishing, apricots, honey; intensely sweet, waxy fruit, very high acidity.* With Hugh Johnson, June 1991****

WEHLENER SONNENUHR RIESLING KABINETT *J J PRUM Light, easy to drink, fruity, acidic.* After-sale supper at the Cape Cod Room, Drake Hotel, Chicago Feb 1990*

1985★★★

An attractive vintage. To quote Ian Jamieson in *Decanter*, "the vineyards suffered trial by frost, hail and drought finishing with some of the best harvesting weather for 20 years". The long hot summer extended into autumn, producing ideal ripening conditions – sunny days, cool nights, hazy mornings. A few welcome showers to succour the grapes. At best wines of charm rather than substance. The worst that can be said of some is that they are a little dull, lacking, short. Most are, or were, very agreeable. Districtwise, a reasonably wide spread of notes, mainly in the Kabinett, Spätlese and Auslese quality range, with rather too many Trocken wines for my liking. A selection of my more recent notes follow.

BERNKASTELER DOCTOR RIESLING SPATLESE *DEINHARD Slightly kerosene Riesling aroma, became chocolaty after exposure; medium-sweet, soft, slightly peach kernelly flavour, plus violets.* Oct 1990★★

SCHLOSS BOECKELHEIMER FELSENBERG RIESLING SPATLESE *CRUSIUS Very pale; austere yet scented, a face-powdery fragrance; dryish, very agreeable fruit; good length.* Aug 1988★★★

BRAUNEBERGER JUFFER-SONNENUHR RIESLING SPATLESE *WILLI HAAG Six recent notes. Steely grey green, star-bright; subdued kerosene grapey aroma but, as one gently sniffed, a touch of clover honey; medium-sweet, light (alcohol 7.8%) yet with hidden backbone. Elegant wine, fresh and fruity. A delicious drink.* At Christie's Wine Course. Last tasted June 1991★★★

CASTELLER BAUSCH MARIENSTEINER EISWEIN *FURST CASTELL Really an '86 as the Mariensteiner Main Riesling grapes (a crossing of Sylvaner and Rieslaner, which in turn is Riesling Sylvaner) were picked on Dec 31, 1985 and Jan 1, 1986, the first* Eiswein *made in Franconia. Sylvaner is the principal grape variety used in Franconia. It has thick stalks and skins and is very disease-resistant. First tasted with Michael Prinz zu Salm-Salm, the son-in-law of Fürst Castell, who has been in charge of winemaking since 1983. Then, a half-bottle a few months later. Bright, buttercup yellow; very powerful honey and spicy nose, with youthful, greengage-like fruit; very sweet, very rich with high tangy acidity, clean and crisp.* Last tasted Nov 1988★★★★

DHRONER HOFBURG RIESLING SPATLESE *BISCH PRIESTERSEMINAR Pale and polished; powerful but rustic farmyard smell, slight grape and honey; overall dry, clumsy, unimpressive, astringent finish.* Feb 1988★

ERDENER PRALAT RIESLING AUSLESE *DR LOOSEN Mild, gentle, grapey nose and taste. Dryish. Rather disappointing.* Sept 1988★★

FORSTER MUSENHANG RIESLING KABINETT TROCKEN *VON BUHL Not much colour; scented, almonds; dry, assertive, fragrant but raw and tart.* Sept 1988★

INGELHEIMER SCHLOSS WESTERHAUS RIESLING EISWEIN *VON OPEL Picked Dec 31 and Jan 1 (1986). Alcohol 6.1%. Pure yellow gold; glorious, zestful, grape, peach, mango and honey; very sweet, delicious crisp fruity flavour, perfect acidity. The best 'ice-wine' I can recall.* Sept 1988★★★★★

SCHLOSS JOHANNISBERG GRUNLACK RIESLING SPATLESE TROCKEN *Dry, firm, light fruit, nicely made.* March 1989★★★ Drink soon.

JOSEPHSHOFER RIESLING AUSLESE *VON KESSELSTATT exclusive vineyard in Graach. 8.5% alcohol. Silberner Preis DLG 1988, Silberne Kammerpreismunze 1987. Rich, hefty, goaty nose; medium dry, richness balanced by very good acidity. Vanilla aftertaste. Will keep.* Nov 1990★★★(★) Now to 1995.

JOSEPHSHOFER SPATLESE *VON KESSELSTATT Pale; medium dry, light, gently quaffable.* May 1991★★

MAXIMIN GRUNHAUSER HERRENBERG RIESLING KABINETT *VON SCHUBERT Several notes. Fairly pale, slight spritz; peach skin, strawberry, mouthwatering acidity; overall dry, light, a bit too much of a carbon dioxide prickle, but an enchanting flavour and rapier-like acidity. Moderate length.* Last tasted May 1985★★★ just.

OPPENHEIMER HERRENBERG SILVANER EISWEIN *GUNTRUM Palish yellow; gooseberry and honey; sweet, a touch of fat yet pleasantly delicate, good acidity. A bit short.* Dec 1988★★★

SCHARZHOFBERGER RIESLING SPATLESE *EGON MULLER Medium dry, light, fresh, delicate, peach-like flavour. Served with skate but much better alone.* Sept 1988★★★

SERRIGER SCHLOSS SAARSTEINER RIESLING KABINETT *Green-tinged yellow; mildly fruity; light, pleasant. Rather high sulphur dioxide.* Last tasted Jan 1989★★

TRAISER BASTEI RIESLING AUSLESE TROCKEN *CRUSIUS Acidity 8.5°. Bastei is a 1ha suntrap, reputed to be the warmest vineyard site in Germany. Palish yellow; delicate, warm, grapey nose, great charm; dry, light, crisp, a bit earthy and a hard edge. Needed further bottle-age.* Sept 1988★★(★) Now to 1995.

UERZIGER WURZGARTEN RIESLING AUSLESE *MONCHHOFF Kerosene Riesling aroma plus a touch of bottle-age; attractive, firm, still hard. Short but good finish.* June 1990★★(★★) Now to 1995.

VERRENBERGER VERRENBERG LEMBERGER SPATLESE TROCKEN *FURST ZU HOHENLOHE-OEHRINGEN The village and vineyard in Württemberg bear the same name. Impressively deep, intense, cherry/ruby colour with immature purple rim; hot, deep fruit, sweaty tannins, vanilla and an explosive depth; dry, raw, tannic – a strange, rather mouldy taste. Drink with German sausages or wild boar.* Red wine dinner-tasting in Frankfurt, Sept 1988★? Hard to place. Needs bottle-age.

VERRENBERGER VERRENBERG RIESLING SPATLESE TROCKEN *HOHENLOHE-OEHRINGEN Very pale; a similar earthiness to the Lemberger, Camembert rind; very dry. Also a similar curious mouldy taste. Prinz Kraft zu Hohenlohe-Oehringen, the son of the Duke, thought it might be the soil. I wondered about the casks.* At the European Festival tasting, Frankfurt, Sept 1988?

WEHLENER SONNENUHR RIESLING SPATLESE *DEINHARD First tasted in Aug 1986: very pale, quite good fruit, still too youthful. Six notes since, taking on some colour; "grapiness" occurs over and over again, as if freshly peeled, sweet, delicate; medium dry, lightish, flits across the palate. A charmer.* Last tasted Nov 1988***

WILTINGER BRAUNE KUPP KABINETT *EGON MULLER Lovely, ripe, slightly oily Riesling; fairly dry, light, not much flavour.* Nov 1990** Drink up.

WINKELER HASENSPRUNG RIESLING KABINETT *DEINHARD Pleasant grapey flavour and good dry acidic finish. A very pleasant summer drink.* June 1990***

1986★ to ★★★

A vintage of blasted hopes. Superb flowering in June, very hot Aug, indifferent Sept, rain encouraging rot, and very changeable weather in Oct—severe storms tore grapes from their vines. Pickers had to salvage what they could find. Variable, mainly light, thin, fairly acidic wines, though acidity in Germany is a crucial structural element. The Rheinpfalz was reputed to be the most successful region though the wines have evaded me.

I certainly did not home in on this vintage and have only a few dozen notes, mainly made in 1988, hardly any since.

ERDENER TREPPCHEN RIESLING SPATLESE *MONCHHOF Medium, slightly oily, chaptalised taste and character.* June 1990*

JOSEPHSHOFER RIESLING SPATLESE *VON KESSELSTATT 8% alcohol. Acidic nose: gooseberry, pineapple; some sweetness and fruit to mark the acidity, but a tinglingly tart finish. Refreshing!* Nov 1990*

KANZEMER SONNENBERG RIESLING KABINETT TROCKEN *CARL GRAFF Slightly scented, fragrant; distinctly dry, lightly grapey. A successful Trocken wine. (In the old days, Saar wine of an acidic vintage would be sent to the manufacturers of Sekt, but the growers can't afford to sell it cheaply and the Sekt makers can import less expensive wine.)* Oct 1989**

OBEREMMELER HUTTE RIESLING KABINETT *VON HOVEL Pale; grassy; bone dry, hard, acidic. (The foregoing remarks apply.)* June 1990*

PIESPORTER GOLDTROPFCHEN RIESLING KABINETT *VON KESSELSTATT Hard to get drunk on this: alcohol 7.5% by volume, just over half the strength of a good white burgundy (and a fifth of the price!) Light grapey, peach-like nose; fairly dry, light, firm, good acidity. Short.* Nov 1990**

SICHEL'S TBA *A novel marketing ploy. District and vineyard name(s) expunged. This is H Sichel's TBA, and very good too: fairly deep orange-tinged gold; rich, ripe peach and apricots nose; very sweet, fat, rich, lovely flavour, grapey, minty, excellent acidity. Although I do not approve of the emasculation I approved of the wine.* June 1989***(*) Now to 2000.

OF THOSE TASTED IN 1988, THE FOLLOWING WERE ABOVE AVERAGE:

SCHLOSS BOECKELHEIMER KUPFERGRUBE RIESLING HALBTROCKEN *STAATSWEIN The 'copper mine' vineyard boasts a Mediterranean microclimate. The grapes were picked Oct 23, untreated, matured in oak, strength 11%. An extraordinary scent, like ladies' face powder, almost Gewürz; medium dry, chaptalised but complete, with an attractive flavour****

HALLBURGER SCHLOSSBERG SILVANER QBA *DR GRAF KARL VON SCHONBORN (Schloss Hallburg in Franconia.) The purest Silvaner aroma, fragrant; bone dry, clean, crisp***

HATTENHEIMER PFAFFENBERG RIESLING SPATLESE *VON SCHONBORN Estate in the Rheingau. A gold medal-winning wine. Lovely 'green' fruit aroma; fairly dry, lightish, mild and gentle****

KESTENER PAULINSBERG RIESLING KABINETT *PETER JOS HAUTH Dry, clean, attractive***

RAUENTHALER BAIKEN RIESLING KABINETT TROCKEN *STAATSWEINGUT Grapes picked Oct 26–28. In stainless steel. Bottled April 27, 1987. The Baiken vineyard: its soil the most expensive in Germany, after Berncastel's Doctor. Palish yellow; fresh, almost Sauvignon Blanc tom-cats fruity acidity; dry, positive, classic flavour but austere***(*)*

SPATBURGUNDER *LINGENFELDER (technically* GROSSKARLBACHER BURGWEG*) A Pinot Noir from the Rheinpfalz, 8–10 days on the skins, then the malolactic fermentation followed by 12 months in small oak (not new) casks. A pretty colour; fruity, Gamay-like aroma; fairly dry, firm, good length, hard dry finish. Needs bottle-age*(*)*

WEHLENER SONNENUHR KABINETT *S A PRUM Palish yellow; soft, harmonious, fruity nose; dryish, fairly light, good fruit and acidity***

1987

Yet another rather uninspiring vintage. Running through my notes makes me more and more depressed. I *like* German wines but pity the poor winemakers. Good leaf break and flowering but summer cool and wet. However from mid-Sept the weather improved and continued relatively dry through to early Oct. Mainly light, dryish acidic wines of modest distinction. Few wines of Spätlese, fewer of Auslese quality made but, in fairness, some useful steely, attractive Kabinett wines, the best of which will keep. Most of my notes were made in 1988, relatively few since.

EITELSBACHER KARTHAUSERHOFBERG RIESLING KABINETT *7.4% alcohol. Palish yellow; trying hard, its chaptalised grape aroma sitting on green, gooseberry-like fruit acidity. Quite clearly even a great estate like this cannot do much in a year like 1987. The wine perfectly drinkable.* Oct 1990*

HATTENHEIMER PFAFFENBERG RIESLING KABINETT *VON SCHONBORN Pleasant, light, green grapey aroma and taste. Fairly dry, some Rheingau steeliness, good acidity.* Oct 1989**

KESTENER PAULINSHOFBERG RIESLING EISWEIN *Good colour; mildly grapey nose; fairly sweet, some intensity, nice weight, delicious flavour, good length. A surprise half-bottle pulled out of his briefcase by Hugh Johnson en route to Tokyo, June 1989****

WALDRACHER ROMERLAY RIESLING *PETER SCHERF* *First tasted in 1988: very pale; soft, creamy, grapey aroma; crisp, attractive. The following autumn, returning from Los Angeles, noted a fragrant aftertaste. Most recently, also served on BA flight, taking on a bit of colour. Light and fruity. Excellent with mulligatawny!* May 1990**

WEHLENER SONNENUHR RIESLING SPATLESE *JJ PRUM Bone dry. Austere.* June 1990.

WESTHOFENER BERGKLOSTER SILVANER HALBTROCKEN *WINZER WESTHOFEN* *Virtually colourless; minty, slightly spicy; mildly fruity, short when first noted in 1988. Passable in 1989. More recently, surprisingly dry for halbtrocken, moderate quality.* Last tasted June 1990*

A CROSS-SECTION OF '87s TASTED IN 1988:

BERNKASTELER LAY RIESLING KABINETT *ZACH BERGWEILER PRUM (Ernst Loosen's mother's estate, now combined with Dr Loosen's under the umbrella, Weingut St-Johannishof.) All Loosen's wines matured in 1000-litre* Fuder. *Pleasant fresh fruitiness, flowery even; touch of earthiness, very dry, acidic finish***

DEIDESHEIMER LEINHOLLE RIESLING SPATLESE *VON BUHL Dry, lightish, agreeable but more of Kabinett quality. Acidic finish***

ERDENER PRALAT RIESLING KABINETT HALBTROCKEN *DR LOOSEN Prälat is the best part of Treppchen (Little Steps) vineyard, beneath the rocks, facing south: very pale; very scented; a surprisingly warm rich wine, with broad dry finish****

ERDENER PRALAT RIESLING SPATLESE *LOOSEN* *Harvested before the rains; mild, grapey, blackcurrant aroma; medium dry, lightish, nice flavour, very good mouth-drying end acidity****

ERDENER TREPPCHEN RIESLING KABINETT *LOOSEN* *Red soil, sandstone: the wine had hardly any colour; youthful, grapey, touch of vanilla; dry, light, lean, lively but short***

GRAACHER HIMMELREICH RIESLING KABINETT *LOOSEN Deep soil, of clay loam and grey slate: very attractive fruit, grapey, touch of lychee, acidic; delicate, crisp, very dry finish****

GRAACHER NONNENSTUCK RIESLING KABINETT HALBTROCKEN *Very pale and wan, dry, just enough fruit, acidic**

ROXHEIMER BERG RIESLING HALBTROCKEN *DALBERG Immature, acetone; dry, light, lean, grapey, good acidity***

WALLHAUSER JOHANNISBERG RIESLING *DALBERG* *Also immature; dryish, light, grapey, fresh and easy, dry finish***

WEHLENER SONNENUHR RIESLING KABINETT *LOOSEN Shallow soil, half a metre thick, Devonian slate, good drainage: crisp, delicate yet hard pineapple aroma; very slight residual sugar, crisp high, 70% tartaric acidity***

1988****

Overall a very good vintage that missed being great due to the vagaries of the weather at a critical mid-harvest period. Certainly the best since 1983, in some respects, and in some districts on a par in style and quality with 1975.

It is foolish to generalise about 'the vintage' in Germany as the climate on the more balmy slopes of the Palatinate to the south (although due north of Alsace) differs from that of the more northerly and serpentine Mosel, whose every bend has its own microclimate, and its tributaries, the Saar and Ruwer. Not to mention immense differences in soil types, soil depth and drainage.

The run up to the vintage was excellent: successful flowering in June, pleasant July then warm, sunny, dry weather in Aug and Sept, *Edelfäule* being prevalent towards the end of that month. What was lacking was rain. Welcome rain arrived early Oct, followed by an unwelcome 10–14 days in the middle of the vintage. Those who picked early were successful. Those who courageously waited to the end of the month made superb Auslesen. Frost on Nov 7 in the Nahe, for example, hit some mid-harvest. But frost can be turned to advantage. Some superb *Eisweins* were made.

I confess I have not tasted as wide a range as I would have liked. But, by and large, what I have tasted, and bought, or drunk, I have liked. In common with many, I love wines from the Mosel-Saar-Ruwer. But I think we are all very foolish not to re-explore the other classic districts. Some lovely wines are being made.

BERNKASTELER BADSTUBE KABINETT *JJ PRUM* *Very pale; youthful, grassy, touch of lanolin, harmonious; light grapey flavour, hard, very dry, slightly metallic acidic finish. Crisp. Refreshing.* March 1991**

BERNKASTELER BADSTUBE RIESLING SPATLESE *DR THANISCH Very pale; mild, very grapey aroma; fairly dry, nice weight, a good positive flavour, soft yet very acidic.* Last tasted Oct 1990**(*)

BRAUNEBERGER JUFFER AUSLESE *WILLI HAAG* *Peachy nose; medium-sweet, rich, good length.* June 1990***

BRAUNEBERGER JUFFER RIESLING KABINETT *WILLI HAAG Pale, slightly spritzig; very mild grapey nose; medium dry entry leading to very dry acidic finish with spritz uplift. Fragrant but lacking length.* March 1991**

BRAUNEBERGER JUFFER-SONNENUHR SPATLESE *WILLI HAAG Very pale; touch of kerosene Riesling, nice fruit, pleasant acidity; medium dry, light (7.8% alcohol), fruity, very pleasant end acidity, enchanting.* Jan 1990****

EITELSBACHER KARTHAUSERHOFBERG RIESLING KABINETT *RAUTENSTRAUCH Green-tinged; light, youthful fruit — pineapple, peach, fragrant though sulphury; very dry, fairly light (9% alcohol), delicate fruit and acidity. Oct 1990***

EITELSBACHER KARTHAUSERHOFBERG RIESLING SPATLESE *Very dry, delicate, firm, good length and acidity. June 1990****

ERDENER PRALAT RIESLING AUSLESE *DR F WEINS-PRUM Earthy, sweaty bouquet; medium-sweet, rich, ripe, fragrant aftertaste. June 1990****

FORSTER UNGEHEUER RIESLING SPATLESE *DEINHARD Rich, sweet, warm, lightly honeyed and spicy; medium — neither sweet nor dry, medium full-bodied, excellent flavour, violets, good acidity and aftertaste. Replanted in the rearrangement of vineyard sites that followed the 1971 Wine Laws, this wine reflects the heavy soil, rich in minerals, of the Rheinpfalz, such a contrast to the light, steely, acidic Mosel wines. Oct 1990**** Now to 1998.*

GRAACHER HIMMELREICH RIESLING KABINETT *LAUERBERG Palish; oily Riesling grapiness; medium, medium-light, flavoury. Adequate. Must be served well chilled. Oct 1990***

GRAACHER HIMMELREICH RIESLING SPATLESE *DEINHARD Pale; delicate, spicy, acidic, gooseberry-like; dry, light weight and style, fragrant, good acidity. Oct 1990****

HOCHHEIMER KONIGIN VICTORIA BERG RIESLING KABINETT *PABSTMANN Palish yellow; grapey, vanilla, whiff of sulphur dioxide; dry, rather austere, steely. Oct 1990***

HOCHHEIMER KONIGIN VICTORIA BERG RIESLING SPATLESE *Ripe grapes but curious nose (sulphur?); medium dryness and weight, touch of fat, very positive rather earthy Hochheim flavour, very good aftertaste. Oct 1990****

MAXIMIN GRUENHAUSER ABTSBERG KABINETT *VON SCHUBERT Just about my most favourite wine label in the world. A pretty wine too. Fairly pale, star-bright; lovely fragrant fruit, touch of melon, pineapple; fairly dry, very light, dry finish. Slight but charming. March 1991****

MAXIMIN GRUENHAUSER ABTSBERG SPATLESE *Sweet, plumper, peachy nose; touch of sweetness, a heavier grapier style, rather hard acidic finish. Needs more time, Sept 1990***(*)?*

NIERSTEINER AUFLANGEN SILVANER SPATLESE-TROCKEN *GUNTRUM Pale; intensely grapey nose, raw youthful acidity; after the nasal fanfare abruptly dry on the palate, rather hollow, steely, with firm finish. Sept 1989*(*)*

NIERSTEINER OELBERG RIESLING KABINETT TROCKEN *GUNTRUM Fresh, young, grapey, peachy nose; dry, light, rather austere. A "Guntrum Classic" in a handsome old-style tall flute bottle. Feb 1990***

OBEREMMELER HUTTE RIESLING SPATLESE *VON HOVEL Some depth of fruit; dry, lean, austere, good length. Needs time. June 1990**(*)*

OBEREMMELER HUTTE RIESLING AUSLESE *Lovely bright yellow gold; honeyed, waxy, melon nose, still hard; medium, rich fruit though still light, refreshingly tart. Needs time. March 1991**(**)*

OBEREMMELER HUTTE RIESLING EISWEIN *Rich, honeyed bouquet; intensely sweet, delicious balance of fruit and acidity. Almost a TBA. June 1990***(**)*

OPPENHEIMER SACKTAGER RIESLING KABINETT TROCKEN *GUNTRUM Youthful, peachy aroma, lemon-like acidity; dry, light, grapey flavour, fragrant but short. May 1990***

OPPENHEIMER SACKTAGER GEWURZTRAMINER AUSLESE TROCKEN *GUNTRUM Palish; scented lychee, medium, certainly not dry, ripe, with a goaty, earthy fragrance. An odd style but good in its way. April 1990****

OPPENHEIMER SACKTAGER SILVANER AUSLESE *GUNTRUM Waxy yellow; hefty Silvaner fruitiness; medium, rich, quite powerful, fruity, dry finish. It palled a bit. I prefer a wine that becomes more interesting with every sip. July 1990***

RAUENTHALER BAIKEN RIESLING SPATLESE *STAATSWEINGUT An appealing appearance, tinged with green; classic Riesling aroma, whiff of peach and ripe grape honey; touch of sweetness, grape skin taste, dry finish. Poised, balanced. Nov 1989***(*) 1992–98*

SCHARZHOFBERGER RIESLING EISWEIN *EGON MULLER Amber; amazing honeyed sweetness; intensely sweet, very rich, plump for a Saar wine, good length, fabulous acidity. June 1990******

WEHLENER SONNENUHR RIESLING KABINETT *DEINHARD Pale; lovely positive grape aroma, peach and a trace of vanilla; fairly dry, crisp, delicate, very good acidity. Reasonable length for Kabinett quality. Oct 1990****

WEHLENER SONNENUHR RIESLING SPATLESE *PAUL BERGWEILER PRUM Alas, terrible — whether the wine or the bottle I know not. Oct 1990.*

WEHLENER SONNENUHR RIESLING AUSLESE *MARIENHOF Intriguing bouquet of walnuts and violets; medium sweetness and weight, still hard. June 1990**(**)*

WEHLENER SONNENUHR RIESLING AUSLESE GOLDKAPSEL *J J PRUM J J makes several qualities of Auslese, the bottles with the long gold capsules being his best. Deliciously grapey; medium-sweet, good length. Lovely wine. June 1990*****

WINKELER HASENSPRUNG RIESLING KABINETT *DEINHARD Palish, green-tinged; good ripe spicy grapiness with reasonable depth for Kabinett quality; fairly dry, nice weight, good crisp positive flavour and aftertaste. Still a bit hard. Oct 1990***(*)*

1989★★★★★

Bordeaux has its twin vintages, so do the German wine districts: 1975 and 1976, for example, and now 1988 and 1989. In fact, the comparison of '89 with '88 rings a bell, reminding me of the same vintage relationships in Bordeaux and in Burgundy: '88s are firm, '89s have grace and charm. 1989 combined both quality and quantity. Above all it is a classic Riesling vintage. It is arguably the best of the decade, and has the soft ripeness of the 1976 and approaches, sometimes matches – for there are variations – the quality of 1971. Add to this the biggest crop since 1983 and one can sum up the 1989 as 'success'.

An exceptionally mild winter, growth started early, satisfactory setting in April, though cool wet weather slowed the growth. Excellent flowering early June followed by a sunny, relatively dry summer. In Baden, to the south, the Müller-Thurgau started to be picked on Sept 11, in the Saar some estates picked from the 22nd (the earliest in living memory), the Ruwer a few days later, the Middle Mosel and most of the other classic districts in early Oct in fine weather. Towards the end of that month, warm southerly winds caused the *Botrytis*-affected grapes to shrivel, concentrating the juice and enabling firm Auslesen, Beeren, and Trockenbeerenauslesen wines to be made. Not since 1976 have there been so many wines of that quality. Hard frosts at the end of Nov also enabled *Eiswein* to be made.

Although the great TBAs, made in such small quantities, will always be expensive, even in a year like 1989, the lower rungs of the quality are woefully (for the producer) and remarkably (for the consumer) underpriced. My recommendation: taste, buy, and drink.

BERNKASTELER BADSTUBE RIESLING KABINETT *WWE DR THANISCH Austere. Needs time. June 1990**(**)? 1992–98*

BERNKASTELER DOKTOR RIESLING SPATLESE *THANISCH Very pale – little colour; good, positive nose and palate, very good acidity, dry finish. June 1990**(*)*

BERNKASTELER DOKTOR RIESLING AUSLESE *THANISCH Youthful fragrance; medium dry, good fruit, fine, attractive. June 1990***(*)*

BERNKASTELER DOKTOR RIESLING AUSLESE *THANISCH A different* Fuder. *Incredibly richer: ripe, honeyed nose; sweet, great length. Prior to 1971 this could, would, have been marketed as feinste Auslese but, thanks to the idiotically restrictive Wine Laws, it can only be sold as Auslese, so this cask will be kept for special friends and customers! At the Grosser Ring tasting in London, June 1990****(*)*

BRAUNEBERGER JUFFER RIESLING KABINETT *WILLI HAAG Virtually no colour; light, fragrant, spicy nose and taste. Dry. Light. A bit short. June 1990**(*)*

BRAUNEBERGER JUFFER-SONNENUHR RIESLING KABINETT *FRITZ HAAG Dry, mild, fragrant. June 1990**(*)*

BRAUNEBERGER JUFFER-SONNENUHR RIESLING SPATLESE *FRITZ HAAG Very pale; grapey nose; fairly dry, firm, good, still hard. June 1990**(**)*

BRAUNEBERGER JUFFER-SONNENUHR RIESLING AUSLESE GOLDKAPSEL *FRITZ HAAG Ripe, kerosene Riesling aroma; fairly sweet, almost oily rich, delicious, round rather than long. June 1990***(*)*

CASTELLER FEUERBACH DOMINA QBA TROCKEN ROTWEIN *FURST CASTELL A surprisingly deep, youthfully purple wine from Franconia; sweet, jammy aroma, some depth, leaving fragrance in the glass; dry, fullish, fruity but steely, well-endowed with tannin and acidity. Keeping qualities? I cannot say but it seems to have all the component parts. April 1990(***) 1994–2000?*

CASTELLER KUGELSPIEL MULLER-THURGAU QBA TROCKEN *FURST CASTELL Youthful, lightly grapey, touch of honeycomb; dry, steely, austere, short. April 1990(**)*

CASTELLER KUGELSPIEL KERNER SPATLESE *CASTELL Flowery, some honeyed ripeness; dry, surprisingly assertive, long dry finish. April 1990*(**)*

CASTELLER KUGELSPIEL RIESLANER AUSLESE *CASTELL More colour; delicate, honeyed nose; medium sweetness and body, lovely flavour, length and aftertaste. At the 'Pride of Germany' tasting in London, April 1990***(*)*

DALBERGER RITTERHOLLE MULLER-THURGAU KABINETT TROCKEN *SALM-DALBERG Youthful, peachy, grapefruit and a whiff of sulphur dioxide which will wear off; dry, austere, short but fragrant aftertaste. Inexpensive. April 1990*(*)*

DALBERGER RITTERHOLLE SCHEUREBE KABINETT HALBTROCKEN *SALM-DALBERG Faint, crisp, lacking a pronounced Scheu grapiness on nose, but a pleasant light grapey flavour. Dry, not half-dry. Good acidity. April 1990*(**)*

DALBERGER SCHLOSSBERG RIESLING SPATLESE *SALM-DALBERG Immature, peachy, hint of the characteristic Nahe fruit salad nose; medium dry, flavoury, acidic. Needs time. April 1990**(*)*

EITELSBACHER KARTHAUSERHOFBERG RIESLING KABINETT *RAUTENSTRAUCH Lovely, delicate bouquet; very dry, fragrant, delicious upturned end of acidity. June 1990***(*) 1992–98*

EITELSBACHER KARTHAUSERHOFBERG RIESLING AUSLESE *Virtually colourless but will doubtless deepen with bottle-age; youthful, grapey, almost Sauvignon Blanc, like tom-cats; medium dry, surprisingly mild, easy and attractive but, I thought, lacking length. June 1990**(*)*

ERDENER PRALAT RIESLING SPATLESE *VER HOSPITIEN Very pale; youthful, peachy, medium dry, light, very good acidity. Delicious. June 1990***(*) 1992–98*

ERDENER TREPPCHEN RIESLING KABINETT *MONCHHOF Young, crisp, grapey aroma and flavour. Fairly dry. Light. No great length but an easy charmer. June 1990**(*) Drink soon.*

NIERSTEINER FINDLING SILVANER AUSLESE *GUNTRUM Yellow gold; soft, scented, peachy; medium-sweet, good rich mid-palate, hard dry finish. March 1991*(**)*

NIERSTEINER OELBERG RIESLING KABINETT TROCKEN *GUNTRUM Very attactive peachy nose and flavour; medium dry, not trocken, attractive fruit, youthful acidity. April 1990*(**)*

NIERSTEINER PATERBURG MULLER-THURGAU KABINETT HALBTROCKEN *GUNTRUM Powdery scented, vanilla; medium dry, well-balanced though still hard. April 1990**(*)*

OBEREMMELER HUTTE RIESLING KABINETT *VON*

HOVEL Light, youthful, grapey, acidic, still a bit sulphury; dry, lean, acidic, hard. Needs bottle-age. June 1990★(★)?

OBEREMMELER HUTTE RIESLING EISWEIN *Surprisingly low-keyed nose but considerable depth; incredibly sweet, peachy flavoured. Glorious. Needs time. June 1990★★★(★) 1992–2000*

OCKFENER BOCKSTEIN RIESLING KABINETT *DR FISCHER Very pale; rich, rustic, almost goaty; bone dry. Interesting to see how this will develop. June 1990★(★★)?*

OCKFENER BOCKSTEIN RIESLING SPATLESE *FISCHER Grapey, nutty nose; assertive yet mild. Needs time to show its paces. June 1990★★(★) at least.*

OPPENHEIMER HERRENBERG SCHEUREBE SPATLESE *GUNTRUM Fairly rich, peachy; medium-sweet, deliciously grapey flavour, very good acidity for a Scheurebe and fragrant aftertaste. April 1990★★★★ Will doubtless expand further, say to 1998.*

OPPENHEIMER SACKTRAGER SILVANER AUSLESE *GUNTRUM Another example of a wine that would have been a feinste Auslese, had this been permitted: distinctly yellow hue; gloriously rich, honeyed, fabulous flavour, length, toffee-like aftertaste. April 1990★★(★★)*

OPPENHEIMER SACKTRAGER RIESLING TBA *GUNTRUM Yellow gold; most extraordinary nose, spicy, honeyed; great sweetness balanced by high acidity, marvellous concentration, length and aftertaste. And precisely 10 times the price of the* Auslese*! April 1990★★★(★★) 1992 to beyond 2010.*

SCHARZHOFBERGER RIESLING KABINETT *EGON MULLER Virtually colourless; broad, peachy, grassy nose and flavour. Dry. June 1990★★(★) 1992+*

SCHARZHOFBERGER RIESLING SPATLESE *EGON MULLER Pale; peachy, considerable depth; dry, good flavour and length. June 1990★★★(★) 1992+*

SCHARZHOFBERGER RIESLING AUSLESE *EGON MULLER Distinct yellow tinge; equally distinctive spicy nose; very rich, honeyed* Botrytis*. June 1990★★★(★) 1992–2000*

SCHARZHOFBERGER RIESLING SPATLESE *VON HOVEL Light, tight, grapey nose. Medium dry, fresh as a daisy, good length. June 1990★★(★)*

SCHARZHOFBERGER RIESLING AUSLESE *VER HOSPITIEN Sulphury nose; fairly sweet, rich, good length and acidity. June 1990★(★★★) 1993 to beyond 2000.*

SOMMERLOCHER RATSGRUND SPATBURGUNDER SPATLESE TROCKEN ROSE *SALM-DALBERG I am surprised there are not more German rosés. This one from the Nahe: very pale pink; quite attractively scented, touch of raspberry, boiled sweets; fairly dry, not particularly light, or distinctive, but pleasant. April 1990★★ Drink whilst young.*

UERZIGER WURZGARTEN RIESLING KABINETT *F WEINS-PRUM No colour at all; youthful, hard, grapey aroma; dry, austere, firm but decent length. Needs time. June 1990★(★★)*

UERZIGER WURZGARTEN RIESLING SPATLESE *MONCHHOF Medium dry, in fact quite rich, lozenge-shaped: what it lacks in length it makes up for in girth. June 1990★★(★★)?*

WAWERNER HERRENBERGER RIESLING EISWEIN *DR FISCHER Spicy, grapey aroma; incredibly sweet yet with a deft touch, power and acidity. June 1990★★★(★★) 1993 to beyond 2000.*

WEHLENER SONNENUHR RIESLING KABINETT *MARIENHOF Somewhat muffled grapey nose; unimpressed. June 1990(★★)*

WEHLENER SONNENUHR RIESLING SPATLESE *MARIENHOF Cool grapey aroma; fairly dry, straightforward, a bit short. June 1990★(★★)?*

WEHLENER SONNENUHR RIESLING SPATLESE *DR F WEINS-PRUM Light, grapey also, I thought, short though pleasant. June 1990★(★★)?*

WEHLENER SONNENUHR RIESLING AUSLESE *DR LOOSEN Almost colourless; lovely grapey, peachy nose and taste medium-sweet, excellent acidity, length, aftertaste. My style of Mosel. From John Boys, June 1991★★★★*

WEHLENER SONNENUHR RIESLING AUSLESE *S A PRUM Medium-pale; very distinctive, very fragrant, slightly peachy nose; medium dry, crisp, good flavour and length, dry finish. Needs time. April 1990★★(★★) 1993–2000*

WILTINGER BRAUNE KUPP RIESLING SPATLESE *EGON MULLER Broad, powerful, peachy nose and flavour. Good acidity. Good future. June 1990★★(★★)*

WILTINGER HOLLE RIESLING SPATLESE *VER HOSPITIEN, TRIER (The Hölle vineyard wholly owned.) Very pale; fresh, light, grapey, touch of youthful pineapple; medium dry, light weight and style, still a bit hard. June 1990★★(★) 1992–99*

WILTINGER HOLLE RIESLING AUSLESE *Pale; surprisingly earthy; medium-sweet, fuller-bodied, very pleasant grapey flavour, nice length. June 1990★★★(★) Drink from 1992–99.*

1990★★★★?

The third good vintage in a row, but totally different to 1989 in several respects. First of all a much smaller crop, below the 10-year average, but firmer, many of the major estates having the highest sugar/acid levels but little *Botrytis*.

Another mild winter and early growth. Flowering early in the Mosel, followed by a hot dry summer, later in Rheinhessen, and some heavy rain. Rather like 1976 in England, the hot summer abruptly ended with serious rain at the end of Aug, followed by a cool wet Sept, and rot. The surviving crop benefitted from sun and warmth in late Sept and Oct. Another classic Riesling vintage. Unhappily, I have not been able to follow up the many good reports.

WALLHAUSER MUHLENBERG GRAUER BURGUNDER EISWEIN *SALM-DALBERG Very unusual nose: roses, stewed apples; very sweet, richly textured. Needs bottle-age. June 1991★★(★★) 1994–2000*

CHAMPAGNE

There are a surprising number of types of champagne: the rich man's *de luxe marques*, of which Dom Pérignon is the supreme example; 'straight' vintage blends of the major houses; the well-known and big-selling non-vintage champagnes of the *grandes marques*; the lesser-known smaller houses; the *sous marques*; the BOBs (buyer's own brands) which might or might not be supplied by the big firms in the business; and the small artisanal champagne producers, some quite fashionable, some virtually farm producers with a small but loyal following of private customers.

However, this book is about vintages — what makes a good vintage, which vintages were great, which wines are still drinkable and, of the more recent vintages, which will keep and improve.

I readily concede that most champagne is bought either on name or on price, or both; a high proportion is scarcely tasted and much is wasted, by motor racing champions for example. Critical faculties are rarely brought to bear on festive occasions, and even prior to a serious wine-orientated dinner, it is, I find, difficult to concentrate enough on the sparkling pre-prandial to make a valid note. I try, but the skimpy nature of some of my notes bears witness to the difficulty. I also realise that not everyone, not even every Englishman, has a passion for old champagne. So, if you are not that way inclined, turn straight to the young and currently fashionable vintages.

The condition of old champagne

A cool, dark cellar, preferably in which the champagne has been lying since original delivery, is

Remuage

crucial to condition. Also, in common with other wines, the state of the cork has a direct bearing on that which it protects. Champagne corks are, of course, designed not only to prevent air getting in but also to stop the carbon dioxide, held under great pressure, from prematurely blowing out. It is aided by being wired to the top of the neck. However, there is a tendency for champagne corks to harden and shrink with age, in which case the wire becomes vital to hold the cork fast.

The most common misunderstanding in champagne context is that of 'ullage'. With age there is a tendency for the carbon dioxide to come out of solution. What originally consisted of tiny bubbles becomes, in effect, a smaller reservoir of carbon dioxide. The size of this reservoir, best seen by tipping the bottle upside down, gives a clear indication of the liveliness, but not necessarily of the intrinsic life and drinkability, of the wine. Occasionally so much carbon dioxide is in the neck that the level of the wine can be seen below the foil. At this, as at other stages, the cork is crucial. If it has failed, carbon dioxide will have escaped and been replaced by air, in which case the wine will be oxidised, its colour a drab straw brown, the wine flat, with a grubby, beery endtaste. If, however, the cork has maintained its grip, the champagne will be more like an old white burgundy, with just a prickle of life and—with luck—an exquisitely honeyed nose and great character on the palate.

1815–1900

I must stress that champagne, of *all* wines, has enjoyed an unvarying high reputation: always fashionable, always rather expensive. Champagne was served in the best houses in England throughout the 18th century. The top-quality wines were in great demand and commanded remarkably high prices. 'Champagne' was first sold by James Christie in 1768, just two years after he founded his auction house, and this and subsequent catalogues faithfully record the types of champagne most in demand and the prices paid. During the last quarter of that century, the best champagne sold for double the price of top claret, and by the early 1800s the prices were double those of good port.

Around the middle of the 19th century sales took off, tracking a boom period, with, alas, the inevitable result. In the Jan 1872 issue of Ridley's wine trade journal, Veuve Clicquot's agent reported that "the consumption of champagne in all parts of the globe increases regularly, while the area of production remains necessarily limited. This want of proportion, which is one cause of the exaggerated demands of our growers, threatens to assume a permanent character . . . hence the increase of prices".

Champagne was most fashionable during the third quarter of the 19th century and in the period preceding World War I. The high peak, an era of extravagance and luxury, was personified by the Prince of Wales, later King Edward VII, and his set, by *fin de siècle* Paris society, and even far beyond European shores. South America now seems an unlikely part of the world for vast consumption of champagne, but some of those countries were very rich; Chile, for example, was the world's biggest importer and consumer of champagne in the early years of this century. Price apart, what is interesting to me is the fluctuation in fashion, not of champagne the drink, but of champagne houses. The most expensive, the most fashionable champagne of all time was Perrier-Jouët. Delbeck and Ayala were then the familiar top names, not Krug and Bollinger. The only two constants appear to be Moët, which first appeared by name in a Christie's catalogue in 1835—it was of the famous 'Waterloo' vintage, 1815—and Clicquot.

The ratings for the years 1815–1910 are summarised below:

1815****	**1868******	**1892*******
1822**	**1874*******	**1893******
1825***	**1875–9** *all terrible*	**1894**
1837**	**1880*****	**1895****
1842***	**1881****	**1898*****
1846*****	**1882**	**1899*******
1857*****	**1884*****	**1900******
1858***	**1887****	**1904*******
1864**	**1889*****	**1906******
1865*****		

1911*****

A great vintage, the best since the renowned and most highly priced 1874. Early flowering, hot dry summer, early vintage, picking from Sept 9. Small but perfect harvest. Average yield 1,600 kilos per ha.

Pol Roger Disgorged *c* 1955. Level below foil (see note on 'condition' above). Straw gold, good colour for age, no bubbles, just a slight prickle; nose sound, no 'old straw' or oxidation; medium dry, still fairly full-bodied, with excellent flavour, length and acidity. Smell and flavour always difficult to put into words, but I will try: a soft, nutty—walnut, hazelnut—scent and taste, rather like a creamy old Chardonnay.
*At a Pol Roger tasting, March 1989*****

1914****

A difficult growing season not made any easier by the German army's occupation. Nevertheless, very good wines made following the harvest which commenced on Sept 21. Average yield 2,640 kilos per ha.

Pol Roger Disgorged 1944. Old straw gold, with just the faintest signs of life. Nose withdrawn but sound though it developed in the glass the rich, damp, arboreal nose that champagne gains after considerable bottle-age. Distinctly sweet on the palate. Rich. Flavour of old oak. Good length and acidity. Perhaps I should add, perfectly drinkable and most enjoyable—if one likes the peculiar character of old champagne.
*March 1989****

1921*****

Probably the greatest white wine vintage in Europe this century, including champagne. A long, very hot summer. Small crop harvested from Sept 19. Average yield 1,800 kilos per ha.

Pol Roger 80% Pinot Noir, 20% Chardonnay. Two bottles, disgorged *c* June 1979, opened by Hugh Johnson before dinner at Saling Hall in Jan 1981 to demonstrate the inaccuracy of my note in the first edition of *The Great Vintage Wine Book*! Well, no bottles are the same. As it happens, the first Hugh opened more or less matched my earlier description. It was certainly rather pale for its age

and a bit short on the palate, with an old, slightly charred, bouquet. The second bottle was a deeper amber gold and less lively, had more of an old damp straw character on the nose but was much fuller, more flavoury and complete on the palate. Noted more recently at a Pol Roger tasting, a bottle disgorged Sept 1988: medium-pale straw gold, apparently little life; rather meaty, old straw nose; medium dryness and body, good flavour and surprising liveliness, a refreshing prickle.
*Last tasted March 1989*** to*****

1923****

Good quality. Small crop.
Heidsieck, Dry Monopole I opened the most ullaged of seven bottles. Its level was low-shoulder, well below foil, and with a poor cork. Risky. In appearance, drab old gold, with just a prickle of life; a rich though maderised nose, like old apples. Just a bit too far gone to invigorate by opening and adding a young non-vintage, a trick that sometimes works!
March 1980.

1928*****

Excellent vintage following a fine summer. Fine, firm wines capable of long life. Many '28s tasted. If previously well kept they can still be magnificent.
Veuve Clicquot, Rosé Palish, orange rose, with a slight uplift of bubbles; a distinct whiff of old age yet notably sweet, soft, clean and sound. The whole character of the wine impressed itself the more one sipped. It was ripe and delicious.
*Before dinner at Peter Palumbo's, May 1987****
Pol Roger Two bottles at the Pol Roger vertical tasting held at L'Escargot restaurant in London's Soho. The first a lovely gold colour though showing no life; slightly appley, mushroomy nose; distinct touch of sweetness on the palate, with soft, honeyed, bottle-age flavour. Not the slightest sparkle of carbon dioxide but a delicious drink. The second: slightly paler colour, fresher on nose, drier, crisper and more acidic with a touch of spritz.
*March 1987** to****
Roederer Around 1954/55, I organised a young merchants' tasting group, all contemporaries. Roederer was the first really old champagne, certainly the first '28, I had ever tasted. It was a revelation. It still can be. For example, a magnum opened in 1981, still rich, with excellent acidity. More recently a '28 Roederer Brut, its colour like a good '66, still bright, with encouraging signs of life; an excellent, deep, creamy bouquet; rich yet dry. Fabulous.
*Last tasted Feb 1984*** to*****

1929****

Totally different in character to '28. An abundant vintage of soft, charming wines.
Avize Producer unknown. Probably a straight *blanc natur*. Certainly a still wine now. The colour of an old cut apple, with nose to match. Some vinosity. Rather like a Tokay Szamorodni. Dry. Alas, spoiled by its beery finish.
March 1984.
Bollinger Magnum: pale for age, though age showing on the nose. Despite this, a richly attractive bouquet; dryish, medium weight, soft, mature. Rich.
*Consumed in a box at the Albert Hall—watching wrestling! Feb 1981****

1934****

A fine, abundant vintage to meet the end-of-slump demand.
Bollinger A superb creamy-nosed freshly disgorged bottle in 1976 and, more recently, in magnums and doubtless also recently disgorged: a medium-deep yellow colour; dry, full-bodied, with lovely smoky flavour.
*Last tasted at a Bollinger lunch at Vintners Hall, March 1988*****
Pol Roger Two bottles: the first, amber, a bit drab, maderised though not totally undrinkable. The second bottle, its level just above the bottom of the foil, had a lovely colour, bright, shot with gold, and showing reasonable life. It had a smoky old Chardonnay bouquet, of walnuts; medium dryness and weight, a good mature taste and nice spritz-like uplift.
*March 1984. At best****

1937*****

In common with 1921, a superlative vintage for all European white wines, including champagne. Firm, well-constituted wines with life-sustaining acidity.
Veuve Clicquot, Brut First tasted in 1978, both bottles disgorged in 1976. Variable. More recently the 'Bicentenaire 1772–1972', disgorged in 1986: palish, warm straw colour. Not much life. Rich, old straw nose, sweet, a touch of toffee, very like a mature Tokay Aszú. On the palate, dry, fullish, firm, with a good long rich old flavour and excellent acidity.
*Last tasted at David Allan's 50th birthday dinner, March 1987. At best*****
Pommery & Greno From a stock in almost pristine condition removed from the Dublin cellars of a former Pommery agent. Original cork, the top of which broke off. But level good and a lively pop. Palish gold, good *mousse* and steady stream of bubbles. Deep, creamy, bottle-age bouquet; a touch of sweetness, nice weight, firm, positive, clean, and with very good acidity.
*At Christie's pre-sale tasting, Dec 1987*****

1941**

Despite early wartime problems, quite good quality wines produced.
Pommery & Greno An orange gold wartime foil, good level. A tired cork was pulled out effortlessly. It had managed to contain the wine but not retain the fizz. An attractive though flat gold colour; sweet, rich, honeyed old nose; a touch of sweetness, clean, good acidity. Presumably shipped to Pommery's Irish agent immediately after the war.
*At pre-sale tasting, Dec 1987***
Roederer, Brut Colour of old straw. No *mousse*. Alive but not kicking. Lovely bottle-age bouquet; fairly dry, rich, clean. Excellent acidity.
*Oct 1987****

1942***

A good vintage.
Pommery & Greno A half-bottle from the same Irish stock as the '37 and '41. Cork broke. No pop. Bitty, but with a good colour for its age and a light grip of carbon dioxide. Good old bouquet. Correct. Fairly dry, very positive flavour. Clean, with good length and acidity.
*At pre-sale tasting, Dec 1987****

1943****

A very good vintage, nicely timed to replenish depleted wartime stocks, and mainly consumed too young.

Veuve Clicquot An excellent bottle in 1975. A flat, dull, jeroboam in 1977 which should have been drunk when it was shipped, to celebrate the Coronation in 1953. Next, alongside the Lanson, a deep amber with copper tinge; old straw nose; dryish, rich, deep. Showing its age but characterful. Very good acidity buoying it up.
*Last tasted May 1985****

Lanson With wax seal over foil. Good yellow colour though not as bright as the Clicquot above. Lovely creamy bouquet. Medium dryness and weight. Beautiful texture and flavour though a bit short.
*Prior to dinner, with '43 Clicquot, at 'Barney' Wilson's, a delightful wine-loving lawyer, May 1985*****

Pommery & Greno Two bottles from the Dublin consignment. Both with good levels. The first with good colour but lacking *mousse*; a lovely, creamy, wet cardboard and caramel nose; touch of sweetness, lightish, spoiled by a grubby finish. The second had a better colour and nose; slightly sweeter, soft, but also a bit unclean on the finish.
*At pre-sale tasting, Dec 1987**

1945*****

A small crop of excellent, firm, initially hard, long-lasting wines.

Pol Roger Magnum: fairly pale still, despite its age, and with nice life; sound nose; very dry, good firm body and acidity.
*An excellent interval wine between bouts at the Albert Hall, Feb 1981*****

Pommery & Greno Several bottles. Understandably good, full, fruity and deliciously smooth in 1955, still most attractive in 1968, but a bottle 'on the turn' a year later. More recently, an extremely good bottle from the stock originally shipped to Dublin and never moved until transported to Christie's. Sample bottle removed from a previously unopened and wire-banded case: good cork, excellent level, a good pop followed by a steady stream of fine bubbles. Pale for its age. Lovely creamy bouquet. No faults. Dry, firm, good acidity.
*Last noted at the pre-sale tasting Dec 1987*****

1947****

Despite its soft fruitiness, still a wonderful drink if well cellared. Lovely rich wines, the product of a very good summer, with record sunshine levels in Aug. Picking started early, from Sept 5, under excellent harvesting conditions. Quantity below average because of lack of rain, but uniformly regarded as being of excellent quality.

Veuve Clicquot First tasted 1955: substantial. Needing more bottle-age. By 1959, reaching maturity but continuing to improve, changing character the while. By 1981, a magnum had acquired a rich golden colour whilst retaining plenty of life. Though rich and impressive, the acidity seemed a bit high. Most recently, still a good colour but very little *mousse*; deep, nutty — walnuts — bouquet; a rounded, warm, nutty flavour reminding me a little of the taste of a good old cognac.
*Last tasted Sept 1989*****

Pol Roger Bottled 1948, disgorged May 1981: a beautifully refined wine. Palish colour, fine bubbles; 'fishy' Pinot and creamy Chardonnay combining to produce a lovely harmonious bouquet. Dry yet full-flavoured, with excellent length and finish in June 1981. A month later, a deeper-coloured, more meaty, richer bottle. Most recently, at the Pol Roger tasting in Soho, a bottle disgorged towards the end of Sept 1988: palish gold colour, very fine *mousse*; fragrant oyster shell and walnuts bouquet; dry, fairly high alcohol, firm, a bit austere.
*Last tasted March 1989******

Roederer Colour of rather drab old straw. Slightly cloudy. Though somewhat oxidised, the nose still meaty and creamy. Rich. A hefty old-vintage wine, its excellent acidity just tipping it over the edge and failing to subdue its slightly grubby aftertaste.
April 1986.

1949****

A very good year, excellent in its heyday. Climatically, a slow start, with prolonged flowering period followed by an exceptionally warm and dry summer.

In my early days in the wine trade, this was one of the most popular vintages, and I have many notes from the mid-1950s though only a few have been tasted since 1980.

Veuve Clicquot Slight bottle variation, the first a lovely tarnished gold with faint but fine *mousse*; nose like freshly peeled mushrooms; dry, very assertive flavour, very good acidity, a bit appley. The second paler, with creamier bouquet though showing some age. Dry, firm, excellent flavour. Fresher and better balanced.
*Both tasted Jan 1984. At best, now****

Charles Heidsieck Straw-coloured with gold highlights, the few bubbles being very fine. Creamy, slightly honeyed bouquet and flavour; slightly sweet, full-bodied and rich. Excellent acidity.
*From a good English cellar, March 1990****

Pommery & Greno Perfect level. Pale for its age, with a fine stream of bubbles. Nose light but sound. Dry, firm, with slight almond kernel taste. In remarkable condition. From the pristine Dublin stock already referred to.
*At a pre-sale tasting, Dec 1987****

Salon Le Mesnil Surprisingly pale; smell of old mushrooms; soft, ancient flavour. Flagging but drinkable.
*Oct 1981**

1952*****

Very good, firm, long-lasting wines, a result of favourable growing conditions. Still worth looking out for, with the usual provenance provisos.

Bollinger Several notes since it was first 'landed' in 1957. It has, with age, completely changed its character. By 1985: fairly deep, distinctly orange in colour; lovely, calm, rich, harmonious bouquet; fullish, soft, rich, chewy. Delicious. Most recently, sheer perfection.
*Last consumed, with infinite pleasure, before dinner with Camilla and Alistair Sampson, Jan 1991******

Krug Many notes since 1957, nine since 1980, in bottles, halves and magnums. At its magnificent best from the mid-1960s to mid-1970s, but though now showing age, still a remarkably good drink. The best was a magnum "Private Cuvée, Extra Sec for Great Britain" consumed in 1983: pale for its age, nose of cream, toast and refined straw, with a whiff of lemon; rich yet austere, with lovely crisp dry acidic finish. Bottles are now, of course, variable. Of the last two tasted, one was maderised, with a drab amber colour and taste of old straw, the other two, one in 1987, one most recently: a lovely rich gold colour with lively *mousse* and a continuous stream of fine bubbles; creamy, meaty yet refined bouquet; medium dry, fairly full-bodied, firm, rich, good length and with powerful finish.
*Last tasted Nov 1987. At best******

Mailly, Rosé A curiosity. The wine had lain undisturbed since the mid-1950s in the cool dry cellar at Aalholm Castle in Denmark. The two bottles tasted were

part of a mixed lot which included some great classics: Krug '28, Roederer '28, Dry Monopole '29 and Goulet '37. But clearly the Mailly was originally bought for fun, as all rosé champagne should be, not for posterity. The corks were unusually short and only just retaining their grip. The colour palish amber, neither gold nor pink. The carbon dioxide had been more or less dissipated. Little nose but not a bad flavour despite levels 5 in and 6 in below the lower lip.
Tasted Nov 1989. Moral: drink, don't keep, pink champagne.
Pol Roger A consistently good wine that reached its zenith in the mid-1960s but which has kept well. Aged 31, fairly pale still, with a very fine steady flow of bubbles. A cool, low-keyed, mild, creamy bouquet plus hint of walnuts. Distinctly dry, firm and crisp. Excellent length and condition. Not sure where I acquired this.
*An excellent aperitif, Feb 1983******

1953****

A very good vintage. Not as firm and sturdy as the '52s but, as in Bordeaux, supple, elegant wines.

A good growing season with perfect balance of sunshine and showers, and an unusually early harvest, from Sept 14. A deservedly popular champagne in the 1960–70 period, and ageing gracefully.
Veuve Clicquot An interesting trajectory: soft but refreshing at six years of age, fully developed at 14, holding well for another 10. An odd half-bottle, with excellent level and appearance and a good firm cork, tasted at the ripe age of 31: a lovely yellow gold; good, old straw, nutty, Chardonnay bouquet and flavour. Nice acidity. Clicquot is a survivor.
*Last tasted April 1984*****
Charles Heidsieck Several notes from 1960, the adjective 'meaty' cropping up frequently. Certainly still most enjoyable in the late 1970s and early 1980s. Levels usually excellent. Amber gold colour with lively and steady *mousse*; good nose, creamy, smoky old Chardonnay; slightly sweet, fresh, quite rich, nice balance, good acidity, dry finish. Occasional bottle variation.
*Last tasted Oct 1981. At best, then*** Probably faded now.*
Krug The father of Rémi and Henri Krug considered this his best vintage between '45 and '55. Certainly a lovely rounded wine at four years of age, and sheer perfection 10 years later. Bottles stored in English cellars keep well though the sparkle tends to ease back after five minutes or so in the glass. The most recent two notes are both from magnums of the Private Reserve disgorged at the normal time but stored in Krug's own cellars. Both were outstanding: good pale gold colour for age, little *mousse*, just a prickle – but this is how English lovers of old champagne like it. Bouquet combining rich cream with smoky Chardonnay; fairly dry, good body, rich, with a nutty, toasted taste, perfect length and finish.
*Last tasted Oct 1983***** Should still be good.*
Pommery & Greno Good firm cork. Pale for age. Smoky bouquet. Very dry, medium weight, good flavour, nice bite.
*July 1981****

1955****

High quality. Firm, drier and more acidic than the '53s. Early spring cold and wet, excellent later. Latter half of June hot, leading to good flowering early July. Equable summer. Large crop picked end of Sept, early Oct. Many notes, mainly, and understandably, made in the early to mid-1960s. But they held well through the 1970s and, if stored in cold cellars, can continue to please.
Bollinger, RD This was the pioneer vintage of the now well-established series of 'recently disgorged' wines, establishing a rich, to me sometimes perverse, style. My first note, of a bottle disgorged in 1968, was made in 1969. The best, perhaps influenced by the context in which it was drunk, had a good yellow colour and was still lively. Sweet, creamy nose; plump and rich, very fine, and overall very dry.
*Last noted at supper in Tawfig Khoury's summer house, San Diego, Oct 1982*****
De Castellane A brand not much seen in England. Only one note. Some life but slightly cloudy; an old straw nose. Despite this, a sweetish, very pleasant ripe flavour.
*June 1987****
Veuve Clicquot Although, at a Clicquot tasting, we were informed that '55 was "an outstanding and exceptional harvest", my notes do not fully bear this out. Of those tasted since 1980: a magnum disgorged in Feb 1980 and presented in London the following month was almost too pale, had a rather ordinary nose and was a bit tinny. However I noted a well-nigh perfect bottle in 1984. Most recently: still very lively; a fishy Pinot nose; crisp, good length and acidity. 'Fishy' sounds rather unappealing, but the Pinot Noir often has this character, for example in Chambertin. Others will describe it differently. But it is in stark contrast to the smoky, creamy, sometimes buttery nose produced by the Chardonnay grape.
*Last tasted Sept 1989. At best*****
Dom Pérignon Not being a bloated plutocrat, I do not keep the great Dom in my cellar, and certainly could not afford the '55 when it was first released. Unfortunately my most recent note is of a magnum which, despite its good level, was clearly let down by its 'easy' cork. It had no life and was a dull, maderised, straw brown colour. Sherry-like nose. Powerful, but its finish yeasty.
Jan 1986. But better-kept bottles should still be good.
Charles Heidsieck Several notes in the 1960s and 1970s. The most recent in 1981. Three bottles, variable. One, surviving a fairly loose cork, had a pale straw colour and nose to match. Clean. Meaty yet very dry. Another, with a tighter cork, was more lively but had a similar taste. And the third, a month later, sporting a good firm hard cork and resounding pop, had good *mousse*, a fragrant bouquet, light style and nice texture. Flavoury but short.
*Last tasted July 1981. Now, at best***
Krug I think it is worth repeating what Rémi Krug told me about the make-up of their '55 because it indicates the essential difference between good champagne and even the very best sparkling wine. Any firm with a supply of grapes and sophisticated methods of production can make a decent sparkling wine. But even the most perfect Chardonnay grapes, converted by an induced and efficiently controlled secondary fermentation will produce only a one-track taste. Moreover, hardly any sparkling wine, however good, remotely approaches the finesse and length of champagne. The answer lies in the blending. For their '55 vintage, Krug made a final blend of 23 different wines, of varying styles and from different vineyards. Overall *cépages* mix, Pinot Noir 59%, Chardonnay 26%, Pinot Meunier 15%. I first noted the result of the final blend in their tasting room in Reims in Oct 1957 though it was not shipped to the UK until 1962. I have had several mainly excellent bottles, and magnums, since. Only one criticism: the corks have not always been perfect.
*Not tasted since March 1980. Then******

Laurent-Perrier Good old straw nose with hint of apricot. Medium dry, good body and flavour. Showing well.
*June 1986****
Pommery & Greno Very good wine, first noted 1962. Most recently a bottle from the pristine stock shipped from Dublin. Excellent level. Healthy pop. Pale, lively appearance. Slightly singed, 'charcoal' bouquet; dry, clean, with good acidity but a slightly odd peach kernel taste.
*Last noted, pre-sale, Dec 1987. Now***

1959****

A mighty vintage in Champagne as elsewhere in France. Long hot summer, excellent, early harvest.

An extremely popular vintage with the UK, for not only was it good but extremely timely as stocks of the '52, '53 and '55 vintages were depleted.

Mostly, and rightly, consumed by now; the best, such as Dom Pérignon, and the best kept, worth looking for.

Bollinger Perfection in the mid-1960s and still excellent 20 years later. Touch of orange gold in 1985; a massive nose, rich, open, like caramel cream; a wine of great depth. Most recently, a magnum, remarkably pale for its age and weighty vintage: yellow straw, lively; creamy nose; drier than previously noted, fairly full-bodied, with lovely old smoky charred flavour, good length and acidity.
*Last tasted July 1988*****
Veuve Clicquot The most recent, disgorged in 1980: a good pale colour for its age but a bit lifeless; bouquet of refined old straw; excellent flavour, considerable length, lovely uplift and acidity.
*March 1983****
Charles Heidsieck Notes range from the mid-1960s and through the 1970s. The most recent bottle resurrected in its 21st year: a very lively head of *mousse*, palish straw colour, large bubbles. Very good, deep, rich, typically meaty Chas Heidsieck nose. A good big flavoury wine. Nevertheless, I helped it on its way by refreshing it with some non-vintage Laurent-Perrier. Very effectively too: it seemed to uplift bouquet and taste.
*Last noted prior to an office luncheon, Dec 1980***
Lanson Originally considered a bit flabby, a magnum rose to the occasion at a very grand luncheon given by Woodrow (now Lord) Wyatt to celebrate his umpteenth birthday. The wine was a good colour for its age and showing reasonable life; a deep smoky nose (his Lordship smokes endless cigars); a fine, deep, rich, classic wine.
*Last tasted July 1980*****
Moët & Chandon Good wine. Last tasted in jeroboam: palish straw, good, bright, lively enough; nose, though not youthful, still not showing much sign of age; a distinct touch of sweetness, nice weight, firm, crisp, with very good acidity.
*Last tasted Feb 1986*****
Paillard Good colour and life for its age; touch of old straw on the nose which then opened up, finally taking on a slightly malty character. Dry, firm, Montagne de Reims-style, good body, length and acidity.
*Sept 1983****
Pol Roger Harvest started early, Sept 10. Production 7000 kilos per ha. High alcoholic content, the best since 1893. A good wine from the start. Last tasted from a bottle, disgorged Sept 1988: a surprisingly pale yellow gold. Fine *mousse* when first poured but settled down indolently. Fresh, crisp, oyster shell nose, fairly dry, full-bodied, excellent flavour and acidity. Nutty dry finish.
*Last noted March 1989*****
Pommery, Rosé Excellent level, good cork. Resounding pop turned out to be a 'flash in the pan' as the initial lively *mousse* soon deflated. Its colour was that of a pale dead rose, and it was not star-bright. Yet it was clean on both nose and palate, with a fullish, singed flavour. Despite its favourable provenance (the Dublin stock), my old stricture applies: do not keep rosés.
*Noted at the pre-sale tasting, Dec 1987***
Salon Le Mesnil Tasted only once, at a Salon presentation given at the Travellers' Club by the late Colin Fenton, the UK agent. It was totally unlike my conception of Salon, which is elegant and rapier-like. It was fairly deep in colour, relatively hefty and, I thought, lacking length.
*Tasted Oct 1981***

1961****

I gave this only three stars in 1980. Less obvious, more refined than the '59s, I now rate the finest '61s more highly.

The growing conditions were completely different from 1959. A good mild start to the season though storms in April and cold in May. Happily the flowering took place in June in warm, sunny weather. July variable, then fine and warm, some refreshing rain and a brilliant harvest.

By the time it was put on the market, the vintage already had the rub-off benefit of the reputation of the '61 red Bordeaux. But it was deservedly popular in its own right, and its style a refreshing contrast to the almost Wagnerian '59s.

At its best in the 1970s. Still, in its mature years, a lovely drink, though bottle variation is to be expected.

Bollinger Several notes since the first tasting at Mentzendorff's, Bollinger's long-established London agent, in 1966. Distinctly lighter and leaner than the '59. At 10 years of age it was fully developed and much superior to the '62. A fine mature wine by 1975, and just one note 10 years later: singed, oaky bouquet; a bit loose-knit, soft yet with crisp dry finish.
*Last tasted in Aug 1985****
Bollinger, RD Noted simply as "dull" in 1982. In 1984, at John Avery's, it had the colour of apple juice, though quite a steady spread of bubbles; and it smelled of old apples. A mixed reception on the palate: fairly meaty flavour, some length, dry finish. Most recently, in magnum, straw-coloured, austere and acidic. This was probably the time I started to wonder about these RDs. Basically a style I find an odd man out. A freshly disgorged wine should, I think, be drunk – rather like LBV port – soon after being put on the market.
*Last tasted March 1990***
De Bonneville A champagne unfamiliar to me but drunk with pleasure, despite it showing its age, at a seafood dinner in Fort Lauderdale. Rich, nutty. Little if any sparkle, but very attractive – if one likes old champagne.
*May 1981****
Dom Pérignon First tasted in 1971. Refined. Classic. Exactly 10 years later, a limited number of Royal Wedding magnums were presented by Moët & Chandon (UK) Ltd to friends and special customers. It was labelled "Specially shipped to honour the marriage of His Royal Highness the Prince of Wales and Lady Diana Spencer, 29 July 1981. Champagne Cuvée Dom Pérignon Vintage 1961. Disgorged 1981". Very good they were too. My own magnum, and one brought as a

present, were consumed, with dutiful loyal toasts, that July. It was a palish, dry, firm, almost taut wine. In 1984, a very fine bottle with a difficult-to-extract cork. It had a creamy, oaky, fruity bouquet that developed a characteristic old champagne straw-like smell. Rich. Mouthfilling. Perfect flavour and length. The next bottle was served alongside the Krug '61 mentioned below. It was superb. Pale for its age. Lively; a most beautiful bouquet, creamy, harmonious with hints of 'fishy' Pinot Noir and smoky Chardonnay. After a little time in the glass, it became even more creamy, with a hint of barley-sugar. Slightly sweet for Dom, with perfect weight, flavour and length. I rated it as high as my previous best-ever champagne, Krug '28, tasted in 1957. Having acquired this at auction I kept my eyes open for more, but a bottle, and later a magnum, for which I paid high prices, though good, just missed the previous peak. Each had a more mature yellow gold colour though both had very fine bubbles. Old straw accompanied the creamy bouquet. However, both were rich, with a good dry acid finish. But it was like trying to rekindle an old love. Best to move on.

*Last tasted Oct 1988. At best*******

Krug 12 notes and, surprisingly, not as great as it should have been. A slow developer, it was approaching its best in the early to mid-1970s. It certainly has character. However, for me, the best was, undoubtedly, a magnum consumed in 1982. It had a lovely yellow gold colour but its initial sparkle soon simmered down. An equally lovely bouquet, meaty, smoky, almost charred. Dry, fairly full-bodied, a fine deep flavour. Rich yet austere. Then a couple of ageing, creaking, old straw halves, a nutty-flavoured bottle and, a few months later, another bottle I served alongside the '61 Dom Pérignon. It had a deeper colour than the Dom but was lively enough, with a very meaty, rich bouquet which reminded me of the smell of a timber yard. Distinctly sweet, full, rich, tangy with very good acidity. But it seemed lumbering and ponderous alongside its rival.

*Last tasted Dec 1986. At best*****

Pommery & Greno Initial notes made in 1967 and 1969, then a hiatus. When the remarkable cache of Pommery came to light in Dublin, amongst the wide range of vintages was a quantity of the '61, some of which I bought for special luncheons at Christie's. I have 12 notes, from Feb 1988. Despite bottle variations, a splendid wine. Pale for its age, with a green-gold sheen and good *mousse*. At its best a gentle, fragrant, creamy bouquet; touch of sweetness at the tip of the tongue, but overall dry. Lovely flavour. Soft yet with crisp acidity. Some must have been brought by one of Christie's German clients for the last bottle was served before the La Mission tasting in Wiesbaden. After noting it, I poured it into my glass of the '52 to invigorate the older wine.

*Last tasted June 1990. At best*****

Pommery & Greno Avize Pale for its age. Not a vestige of sparkle so presumably a straight Chardonnay from that district. Touch of vanilla and slightly maderised. Medium dry, fairly light in weight and style. Smoky flavour. Nice acidity.

*With the Rhodes at Bella Oaks, Napa, June 1983***

Roederer Consistently one of my favourite brands. They made a well-nigh perfect '61. It came top in the first blind tasting of '61s in 1967 and, despite some bottle variation, I enjoyed many in the mid-1970s. At 21 years of age, in magnum, some depth of colour showing, though with reasonable life for its age. An extremely good bouquet. Overall dry. A wine of great style and character. Touch of end acidity.

*Before lunch at the Stevens' (David is now Executive Director of the Institute of Masters of Wine), May 1982. At best***** Should still be good.*

Taittinger Extra dry: straw gold, little life. Life ebbing too on nose and palate, its old, rich, honeyed, straw flavour fighting a losing battle with acidity and oxidation.

June 1987.

Taittinger, Comtes de Champagne Amber-coloured. Scarcely a flicker of life. Nose maderised. Kept too long, the only clue to its original quality being its length. Flat, a bit tart.

Nov 1989.

1962****

Another very good vintage, vying with the '61. Perhaps drier and more austere but, like the '52, firm and long-lasting. The result of a cold spring, dry June, mild July and a lack of summer sun made up for by a fine, hot, ripening Sept. Worth looking out for.

Bollinger A refined, rather steely wine in its youth. Most recently: deeper in colour and leaner than the '64; 'fishy' Pinot Noir nose; good acidity.

*Last tasted Aug 1985*** Should still be good.*

Veuve Clicquot I do not seem to have tasted this when young. At a recent Clicquot tasting, I noted that the grapes had been picked from Oct 4 "in beautiful autumn weather". Described as a wine of "elegance and finesse". And so it was, still. A nutty, crusty bread-like bouquet; a lot of flavour and character, with good acidity.

*Sept 1989*****

Henriot A magnum presented to me by M Henriot. A gloriously bright pale yellow gold with gentle spread of fine bubbles. Nose not particularly notable. Fairly dry, nice weight, good flavour, stylish, a bit short.

*April 1990****

Lanson A characteristically extravagant methuselah to greet guests at the opening dinner of Hardy Rodenstock's marathon tasting weekend: very pale; little nose, touch of straw; pretty well bone dry, with good length and acidity.

*Sept 1987****

Dom Pérignon Several notes, "bone dry" and "very dry" appearing and reappearing, from 1971. A fine, firm, highly refined champagne. Then not tasted for 10 years but still pale, with a fine *mousse*. To oversimplify: a 'dry' Chardonnay character on the nose. On the palate, very dry, medium weight, refined, excellent flavour and considerable length – what the French call *persistence*.

In magnum, at the Marie Antionette *in New Orleans. My host, the ever munificent Lloyd Flatt. Last tasted May 1981******

1964*****

A very good vintage but entirely different in character to the '61 and '62, as rich as the '59 but not as fat. Rich, fruity, marvellous wines made following a warm spring, early flowering, hot dry summer yet enough rain in Aug to swell the grapes, and a wellnigh perfect early harvest.

Ayala, Brut Quite a number of notes in the early to mid-1980s. All in magnums. Part of a substantial stock sold by Ayala, presumably because there is no market for old champagne in France. It showed consistently well at Christie's pre-sale tastings. Pale for age and vintage, very lively; meaty nose; dry, fullish, firm, with good flavour and acidity.

*Last noted May 1985*** Will still be good.*

Bollinger Many notes, mainly in the 1970s. Showing the meaty style that I associate with Bollinger. Most recently: a pleasant straw gold, its lively initial froth subsiding to a

gentle spray of fine small bubbles; a hefty, rich, meaty nose and flavour, open-knit, dry finish.
*Last tasted Aug 1985*****
Bollinger, RD First tasted at the Christmas meeting of David Allan's '45 club at Gravetye Manor in 1979. Good, nutty, rich. More recently: medium dry, good length.
*Last tasted Aug 1985****
Bollinger, Tradition Magnums, on their lees until disgorged in July 1978. Colour distinctly golden, fine bubbles; fairly rich meaty bouquet; rich entry, dry finish. Flavoury. Oaky. Touch of acidity. Needed drinking.
*Nov 1980****
Renée Brisset, Brut Bright. Straw colour and good old straw nose. Dry, meaty, squeaky clean, good acidity.
*Aug 1989****
Charles Heidsieck An easy cork. Good colour, still frothy, with large languid bubbles; glorious old oak-chip bouquet; medium dryness and body, lovely meaty '64 flavour and character. Very attractive.
*Oct 1980*** Probably still good.*
Krug Many notes, mainly in 1970s. A rather unfortunately corked magnum in 1980 though the other was perfect. A rich wine of great character. And seven very good notes since. In the mid-1980s still relatively pale for its age, with neatly spaced small bubbles. An exceptionally good bouquet, rich, meaty, evolving beautifully in the glass. Great length consistently noted. At a Bordeaux Club dinner, at Christ's College, Cambridge, in 1986, promptly after foil was removed, the wire broke, the cork shooting out with remarkable vivacity, just missing our host, Jack (Sir John) Plumb and his precious porcelain. In 1990: its colour now deepening to a distinct straw gold though with a very good old bouquet. Dry, good length.
*Last tasted June 1991. Now*****
Pol Roger Many notes, in bottles, halves and magnums, the latter reaching my theoretical plateau of perfection at 12 years of age. A lovely wine. Latterly a palish straw gold; smoky, and with a sweet, slightly caramelised smell reminiscent of the brown edge of a rice pudding. Good old flavour. Well clad.
*Last noted June 1986. At best*****
Pommery & Greno Strangely, only one note. Very good level, cork and life. Smoky bouquet. Dry, a bit austere. Good finish.
*Oct 1980****
Roederer, Cristal Brut Fine wine. Perfection in the mid-1970s. Lively; a bouquet of many dimensions, Chardonnay, fruit, piquancy, bottle-age; rich and appealing. Long dry finish.
*Last tasted May 1981***** Probably still good.*
Salon Le Mesnil A beautiful wine. First tasted, in magnum, at a dinner given by the Rhodes in 1987: pale for its age; fairly dry, firm, fine – very refined for a '64. Perfect. And a year later, also in magnum from the Rhodes' cellar, colour pure gold, with very fine *mousse*. Dry, good body, firm, great persistence of flavour.
*Last noted at a Bordeaux Club dinner at Christie's, Nov 1988******

1966****

It is interesting how similar in character the classic '66s are. Not just champagne but claret, burgundy, even vintage port. A coincidence repeated, incidentally, in 1985, though the style differs. The '66 champagnes were firm, sometimes steely, lean, long, and long-lasting. A contrast to the meaty, ripe-fruit '64s. If I were to use one word to describe the best, it would be "finesse".

Very hot June, early blossoming. Wet and rather sunless Aug. Fine weather prior to harvesting.

Paul Barron In the early 1980s some of the smaller producers and secondary *marques* started to put in an appearance. This, from that most evocative of all wine village names: Bouzy. Meaty, smoky nose. Soft old flavour. Needed drinking.
*Sept 1982***
Bollinger This was the first '66 I tasted. Unlike bordeaux and burgundy, vintage champagne is 'released', to use a Californian term, ie put on the market when the producer thinks the time is ripe, in the case of champagne several years after the vintage in question. The '66s were launched in 1971. This wine was good, and developed well throughout the 1970s. Only one recent note: colour medium-straw, with a steady but well-spaced stream of fine bubbles; rather 'cool', hard nose; dry, still frothy, firm.
*Last tasted Aug 1985**** Clearly plenty of life in hand.*
Veuve Clicquot Some good, firm, elegant bottles in the mid- to late 1970s but only two less-than-perfect half-bottles since. Showing age but drinkable.
*Last tasted June 1985. At best still probably*****
Deutz & Gelderman, Brut Many notes. Agreeable in the mid-1970s, and a good bottle in 1985: pale for its age; slightly sharp, Chardonnay, bread-like nose; dry, good acidity. And an odd half-bottle with very light *mousse* but fine bubbles, always a sign of quality; warm, crusty, harmonious bouquet and flavour. Dry. Touch of old sherry on the endtaste.
*Last tasted July 1988. At best****
Dom Pérignon, Rosé 'DPR', the most fashionable champagne in Palm Beach! Very good too. One of the relatively few rosés I like, and that will keep. Two fairly recent notes. An extraordinary colour, a rosy orange, not – I must admit – unlike Mateus rosé. Very rich, assertive nose redolent of its Pinot Noir base; a touch of sweetness for the Palm Beach palate, nice weight, soft, mellow. A very easy drink to enjoy.
*Last noted at 'the Flatt collection' pre-sale tasting in Chicago, Sept 1990*****
Alfred Gratien, Crémant Brut Only the vestiges of a sparkle, scarcely creaming. Showing age on the nose too. Better on the palate, but lacked zest. Moral: drink *crémant* young.
*In Stockholm, March 1987**
Charles Heidsieck 60% Pinot Noir and showing it. Flavoury. Drinking well through the 1970s. A magnum *à point* in the early 1980s but a disappointing freshly disgorged bottle at a recent Charles Heidsieck tasting: straw gold; Tokay-like flavour and finish.
*Last tasted March 1990. At best****
Lanson, Red Label Good wine. Approaching cruising altitude at 10 years of age. Magnum: good, pale, still youthful lemon yellow; rather hard, herbal nose; dry, firm, good flavour and length.
*Last tasted Sept 1986**** Plenty of life yet.*
Laurent-Perrier Not really up to top vintage quality though agreeable. Slightly sweet, very flavoury but lacking length.
*Last tasted Jan 1981***
Roederer, Cristal Brut Top wine in a tasting of champagnes in 1972 and, 10 years later, though showing some age, the epitome of elegance: palish, refined, delicate *mousse*; nose a bit hard at first, slightly nutty, opening up beautifully; dry, medium body, the flavour swelling in the mouth in parallel with the evolution of the bouquet. Wonderful length and finish.
*Last tasted in Oct 1982***** Will still be excellent.*

1967

Growing conditions not bad, but the harvest spoiled by heavy rain which not only prevented ripening but caused widespread rot. Only one tasted recently.

Roederer Showing age, straw gold, yet lively; light, damp straw; medium dryness and body, good flavour, excellent acidity.
*Jan 1991****

1969***

I have the feeling that the champagne shippers had two motives for marketing the '69 vintage: the first to catch up after two non-vintage years, the second to supply a hyper-inflated wine market which, by the time it was released in 1974, had in fact deflated severely.

Poor spring, late flowering followed by a cold and wet period that lasted until mid-July. A hot summer, with some cool spells in Aug. Grapes ripened in time for a late, Oct, vintage. A moderately good vintage. Flavoury but acidic.

Bollinger Not the meaty style of Bollinger. Clean cut and dry. First noted shortly after its release in 1974 and several times later that decade. All needed bottle-age. Then, fairly appropriately, served in magnums at the launch, at Christie's, of the first edition of *The Great Vintage Wine Book*, on Oct 27 1980. By then a very attractive yellow gold, with good nose and flavour. Approaching its peak of perfection. Some variable half-bottles, a touch of austerity lingering in the mid-1980s, though, conversely, it seemed to be getting sweeter. Most recently an attractive half-bottle, soft, yet with an extended citrus-acidic finish.
*Last tasted March 1988. At best****

Bollinger, Rosé Tasted only once. Still a fairly pale pink. Dry, nice weight and style. A good rosé, and holding well.
*Aug 1986****

Bollinger, Tradition Specially disgorged in Jan 1980 and opened five months later. Very good, crisp, dry.
*Last tasted April 1981*****

Bollinger, Vieilles Vignes Made from ungrafted 'pre-phylloxera' vines grown in a five-acre vineyard. Scarce and expensive. A different style of wine. Rich, high-toned nose, considerable length, touch of wood, piquant acidity.
*Aug 1985*****

Veuve Clicquot, Brut Showing well in the mid- and late 1970s. Just one more recent note: palish straw yellow; slightly meaty nose; medium dry, good long flavour and nice acidity.
*Last tasted Feb 1987**** Should still be on top form.*

Dom Pérignon Medium-pale, steady flow of fine bubbles; surprisingly scented bouquet; medium dryness and weight. Rich. Good length. Excellent acidity.
*Nov 1989***** Should continue to improve.*

Charles Heidsieck The annual Champagne Academy dinner, only one of which I have missed since 1958, is usually an opportunity for the *grande marque* houses to show their newest release. The '69 was first released in May 1974. I noticed its unusually ripe yellow colour. Nice wine. Several notes, but none recent. I considered it crisp and perfectly developed when last tasted.
*Nov 1981****

Alfred Gratien A champagne I associate with the Wine Society and its former chairman, Edmund Penning-Rowsell. In fact, he served it before his recent '45 vintage first growth Bordeaux dinner. It had a good colour for a 21-year-old, not vigorous but with a steady flow of small bubbles; a pleasant mature bouquet, but showing more age on the palate. Medium dryness and body. Agreeable, though slightly tart finish.
*June 1990****

Krug Showing well, as indeed it should, at 10 years of age. In 1981, prior to another Penning-Rowsell first growth claret dinner, lively, with a fragrant, but rather low-keyed and, for Krug, delicate bouquet; smoky flavour but with slightly acidic finish. At 20 years of age, presented in a handsome 'Krug Collection' box with vintage information: "cold winter, cold rainy spring, summer dry and fine, similar Sept". It is worth mentioning that the time of flowering more or less dictates the date of the vintage. Krug reported that the flowering took place between June 16 and July 7, and the picking – a small crop – from Oct 1–13. And the wine: medium-pale straw yellow with very fine *mousse*. A lovely rich meaty bouquet, redolent of walnuts, and with great depth. Excellent length. Surprisingly low alcohol content, about 10%.
*Last tasted Oct 1989**** Will keep.*

Perrier-Jouët, Belle Epoque I first saw this clever and attractive *art nouveau* flower bottle in the cellars of a noted Danish connoisseur, Holger Ewald, in Hobro in 1978.* We did more than admire the bottle. It was consumed with relish. More recently, still fairly pale; a good, clean, distinctly 'fishy', Pinot Noir tang; dry, firm, good flavour but a bit lean and with pronounced acidity.
*Last tasted Aug 1986*** Drink up.*

Pol Roger Strangely, only one note. Magnum. Flavoury, good length.
*Sept 1986****

Roederer *Last tasted at the David Rutherford's, Feb 1991*****

Salon Le Mesnil First noted at its 're-launch' in London in 1978. I have several notes either side of 1980, all good. One, disgorged just before shipment and with no dosage, had a pronounced scent of walnuts and a lively, frothy style. Shortly after, a very noteworthy magnum with an excellent bouquet. This time definitely with some dosage as it had a touch of sweetness, more body, was rich and very flavoury.
*Last tasted Oct 1981**** Could still be excellent.*

* *The first vintage put into the now well-known flower bottle was the '64, launched in 1969 but, initially, exclusive to Maxim's and Fauchon in Paris. It was generally released the following year. There is no doubt that this brilliant marketing concept – the design was based on an original* art nouveau *bottle – gave the very old-established firm, Perrier-Jouët, a new lease of life.*

1970★★★★

A substantial vintage, though not as hefty as I first thought it would be. Nevertheless, 'broader' and less acidic than the '69s. Cold spring, late blossoming, heavy rain in June, then good growing conditions through to the vintage. Good wines, the best keeping well.

BOLLINGER *First tasted 1977 and somewhat austere until well into the 1980s. Gaining colour, and with a speedily settling* mousse*; nose creamy and rich yet still with a hard core; quite powerful, great persistence. Dry finish. Last tasted Aug 1985★★★(★) Will still be developing.*

BOLLINGER, TRADITION, RD* *Several notes, the first made in 1979 so, presumably, the wine had been disgorged either the same year or in 1978. Next tasted in 1980: lively, creamy, touch of vanilla, rich flavour swelling in the mouth. More '70s were disgorged in 1980 and one of these I drank the following year: bouquet of cream and walnuts. Dry. Good length. Very stylish. My most recent notes from magnums disgorged in 1978, the straw colour endorsing its age in 1989 but still drinking well: nutty; dry, firm, excellent flavour, acidity. Last tasted June 1991. At best★★★★*

BOLLINGER, VIEILLES VIGNES FRANCAISES *First tasted 1979. In 1981 a couple of notes: fairly pale. Very frothy when first poured but quickly settled to a gentle, idle, even flow of small bubbles. A sweet, mealy nose; sweeter and richer than the RDs, soft yet mouthfilling. Most recently: straw-coloured; soft, lovely, perfect now. Last tasted June 1991★★★★*

DEUTZ, BRUT *Thanks to the energetic salesmanship of fellow MW Kit Stevens, Deutz was, and presumably still is, all over Australia, which is where I tasted both the '66 and '70. I suspect that the latter might have been recently disgorged as it had a pale, rather lemony colour, and was dry, light, clean but short. Before a 'museum tasting' at Yalumba, April 1985★★ Nowhere near as good as the Cuvée William Deutz.*

ALFRED GRATIEN, CREMANT *Pale and lively for a 14-year-old* crémant. *Fresh crisp Chardonnay nose and flavour. Lightish. Oct 1984★★★*

CHARLES HEIDSIECK, BRUT *56% Pinot Noir. I liked this when it first came onto the market. Most recently, a magnum, disgorged Sept 6 1989: good fine* mousse*; gloriously 'fishy' Pinot, crusty nose of marvellous depth. Slightly sweet at first sip, full-bodied, excellent flavour, length and aftertaste. Nutty dry finish. Last tasted March 1990★★★★ Drinking well now.*

KRUG *Surprisingly, only one brief note. Pale for its age; some weight, great class. Aug 1983★★★★ Will last.*

1971★★★★★

I have upgraded this vintage. At its best, quoting one of my notes below, "the epitome of elegance". More shapely than the '70s, less acidic than the '69s, firmer than the '73s. In short, champagne with finesse. A rough start to the growing season: storms in May, June hot and humid, flowering uneven. More storms in Aug but Sept hot and dry.

Probably at its peak from 1979 through to the mid-1980s. The finest and firmest are still beautiful to drink.

DEUTZ, CUVEE WILLIAM DEUTZ *Pale, lively; nice smoky Pinot nose; dry, good length, considerable finesse though not mind-blowing. Last tasted May 1980★★★★*

DOM PERIGNON *Still pale, with slightly green tinge; twist of lemon and straw nose (though I doubt whether Moët, or the reader, will be satisfied with such a trite note); distinct sweetness, excellent flavour and considerable length. Refined. Certainly warranting its reputation. Sept 1990★★★★★*

CHARLES HEIDSIECK, BLANC DE BLANCS *Pale, with noticeably large bubbles; clean fresh nose; dry, lightish style, nutty endtaste. April 1980★★★ Will be tired by now. Most* blanc de blancs *champagne should be drunk young.*

HEIDSIECK, DIAMANT BLEU *These Heidsiecks are very confusing. The Diamant Bleu is the* de luxe *version of Heidsieck Dry Monopole and has no connection with Chas Heidsieck. Despite its horrible skittle-shaped bottle, a good wine. Palish, uneven but fairly fine bubbles; probably quite a bit of Chardonnay, judging from the nose; fairly dry, lightish, good middle flavour but a bit austere even at 10 years of age. Jan 1981. Then★★(★★) Now fully mature and probably still drinking well..*

KRUG *Like most of the '71s first noted in 1978, impressive. Reaching the top of the plateau at the age of 11: palish, lively; very fine bouquet, good fruit, perfectly evolved; fairly dry, medium weight, beautifully balanced, lovely flavour, acidity and length. Last tasted Sept 1982★★★★★ Krug at about its best. Should be well worth looking out for even now.*

MOET & CHANDON *Shipped in 1977 to celebrate the Silver Jubilee of HM the Queen. Strictly speaking, it should have been drunk around the time of the Jubilee for, 11 years later, it had deepened somewhat in colour and lost its pristine sparkle. Showing age on the nose too. Slightly sweet, fully mature, good acidity. Nice drink but flagging a little. June 1988★★*

MUMM, CORDON ROUGE *Not very exciting when first tasted in 1977, though I thought it might well benefit from bottle-age. Then, at what I would consider its peak period, I had only a half-bottle. The wine was an attractive yellow gold; had a 'warm' nose, rather like wet flannel; meaty middle, with dry, slightly acidic finish. Last tasted Feb 1984★★ I do not think this worth pursuing in bottles or even in magnums.*

ROEDERER, CREMANT *This was privately imported by the late Jack Rutherford, then head of Roederer's London agents. Pale for its age, lemon-tinged and lively; lovely bouquet, nutty, with touch of honeyed bottle-age. Usually the* crémant *style is light and dry. This wasn't. Lovely flavour and finish. Only a top-quality wine will keep as*

* *The name 'Tradition' has been dropped; now just 'RD' with the date of disgorgement on the back label.*

well as this. Jan 1990★★★★

ROEDERER, CRISTAL BRUT *Noted in 1979 as "the ultimate in refinement". Two and then three years later, a good colour; rich yet refreshing, smoky Chardonnay, touch of piquant fruit with flavour to match. Great length, firm, refreshing acidity, dry finish. Last tasted Oct 1982*★★★★★ *Should still be magnificent.*

SALON LE MESNIL *Enthusiastically noted at its presentation in 1978. Showing off its elegant self at the 91st meeting of the Bordeaux Club hosted by Harry Waugh in 1981. Creamy perfection in bottle and magnum in the mid-1980s but a disappointing bottle recently: colour of old straw, flat, with matching nose and taste. Last noted Aug 1990. At best*★★★★★ *Possibly risky now.*

TAITTINGER, COMTES DE CHAMPAGNE, BLANC DE BLANCS *Three notes, all in the early 1980s. Palish, lively; nose a bit austere, some creaminess. Light style, a rather obvious but long enough flavour. Attractive but plausible. On the last occasion tasted I preferred the '73. Last noted July 1983*★★

1973★★★

The second biggest vintage of the century. Certainly prolific and, possibly because of the over-high production, somewhat lacking in grip. The quality derived from the hot dry summer, the quantity due to heavy rain in Sept. Most '73s are tired now but, if well kept, the best can still be delicious.

BOLLINGER, BRUT *I suppose that 'meaty' and 'fishy' are not particularly appealing adjectives, but the old classic Bollinger style was often referred to as meaty, that is to say rich, almost chewy, in contrast to the lighter, leaner styles of champagne. And 'fishy', or oyster shells, is a more literal description of the scent emanating from the Pinot Noir. For me, the '73 had these odorous characteristics. On the palate, fairly dry. Firm. Last tasted Aug 1985*★★★

BOLLINGER, TRADITION, RD *I must confess that for a long time I thought that there was basically only one RD per vintage, which is why I frequently referred in my notes merely to "'73 RD" though, looking at them again now that they are in order, I notice "'73 RD 1981" tasted in 1984, "'73 RD 1983" tasted three years later. All rather confusing.*

I now think of RD in floral terms, as an "RD perennial". I am of course joking! Of my seven notes on the '73 RDs, all were admiring though, in addition to the Bollinger 'meat', I have remarked on its leanness and austerity. Last tasted Aug 1986. At best★★★★ *Should all be drunk by now.*

BOLLINGER, VIEILLES VIGNES FRANCAISES, BLANC DE NOIRS *The latter part of this label description informs us that the ungrafted vines are all of the Pinot Noir variety. From the start (first tasted in 1981) a much deeper colour than the Brut or '73 RD, and with a broader, richer nose and taste than even the latter. Fairly assertive, with a light, lemon-like, tingling acidity. Similar in 1984. Most recently, a many-layered herbaceous bouquet and the most persistent flavour of the entire Bollinger portfolio. Last tasted Aug 1985*★★★★

VEUVE CLICQUOT, GOLD LABEL BRUT *A 'straight' Clicquot vintage, and very good too, showing well at its opening presentation in 1978 and subsequently. Not a big wine, medium light, refined. In general, I have noted an overall dryness, perhaps a trifle too acidic. Fine colour, crisp bouquet, good length. Last tasted Jan 1984. Then*★★★★ *Probably at best shortly thereafter.*

VEUVE CLICQUOT, LA GRANDE DAME *This is Clicquot's* de luxe *brand, and the 'Grande Dame' pictured on the label is, of course, the formidable widow herself. The wine has the anticipated Clicquot character on the nose, perhaps more Chardonnay and possibly more refined, very dry and steely. Alas, just one rather old note. Nov 1980. Then*★★★(★) *Probably still very good.*

DEUTZ, BLANC DE BLANCS *Gentle* mousse*; sweet, creamy nose; dryish, light in style and weight. Elegant. A copybook* blanc de blancs*, perfect at around six or seven years of age. Aug 1980. Then*★★★★ *Worth looking out for more recent vintages.*

DOM PERIGNON *Magnums: lovely colour and bouquet. Surprisingly sweet and rich, with beautiful flavour and notable length. At 13 years of age, a perfect drink. Nov 1986*★★★★★

DOM RUINART, BLANC DE BLANCS *The relatively new* de luxe *brand of the oldest champagne house, now part of the Moët-Hennessy-Vuitton empire. Perhaps, as a* blanc de blancs*, designed to compete with Taittinger's Comtes de Champagne. Certainly not in the same* de luxe *league as the flagship, Dom Pérignon. First enjoyed in 1981. A couple of years later, similar notes: very pale, slight tinge of lemon, lively with very fine bubbles; creamy nose; dry, lightish, fresh and flavoury. Perfect at 8–10 years of age but not intended to age longer. Last tasted Jan 1983. Then*★★★★

GEORGE GOULET, CUVEE DE CENTENAIRE *Many notes in the mid- to late 1980s as a quantity had been bought by my colleague Duncan McEuen for Christie's boardroom. Initially pale, by 1978 it had deepened to a pure gold, losing its liveliness en route. When first noted, I described the bouquet as "cream and smoke", a Danish friend adding "black bread and walnuts". Latterly, more meaty, more mature on the nose. Rich, soft yet with good acidity. I enjoyed it. Last tasted July 1989*★★★

GOSSET, GRANDE MILLESIME *Several recent notes: developed pale yellow gold, lively, fine* mousse*. Very good nose, fruit, walnuts. Medium dry, lightish body and style, soft yet holding well. Nice quality. Demonstrates that it is not just the more high-profile brands that satisfy the discerning palate. Last tasted March 1989*★★★★

CHARLES HEIDSIECK, LA ROYALE, BRUT *The now firmly established 'Champagne Charlie' was in fact conceived in 1973. His parents were 'Royal Charles' and 'La Royale'. Both these names appeared on the Charles Heidsieck* de luxe *blends, presumably for different markets. Both, I think, have been completely superseded by the Edwardian* roué. *My first note in Jan 1985, on the '73 'La Royale' reads as though it was scribbled on the sole of an actress's slipper: very golden, lively froth, generous bubbles; creamy, smoky nose; fresh, with lightly acidic finish but tailed off a bit. Six months later I tasted 'La Royale' and 'Royal Charles' in tandem. They were different. The latter a very bright, pleasant yellow colour, with crisp vanilla nose and flavour. Distinctly dry. 'La Royale' had a warm straw gold colour and was livelier; a meatier, more crusty, bread-like nose; softer and more mature. A similar note a year later.* Last tasted April 1986★★★

KRUG *The flowering, Krug reported, took place from June 14–19, picking from Sept 28 to Oct 15. First tasted in May 1980: marvellous, deep, nutty flavour that reminded me of a good Corton-Charlemagne. Good notes subsequently. Then, in 1989, stocks were released of the straight vintage, not freshly disgorged, packed in individual wooden cartons branded 'Krug Collection'. Colour still pale, with very fine* mousse, *small bubbles; nicely developed, very fragrant bouquet; medium dry, fairly full-bodied for a '73, rich, lovely flavour, good length and acidity, with nutty finish.* Last tasted Oct 1989★★★★★ *Worth looking out for.*

PERRIER-JOUET, FLEUR DE CHAMPAGNE *First tasted at a Champagne Academy dinner in 1978. A charmer. Most recently, exactly 10 years later: still pale, smoky bouquet, fairly dry, very attractive.* Last tasted Feb 1988★★★★

POL ROGER, CHARDONNAY *This must have been one of their earliest straight vintage Chardonnays, certainly the first I tasted. My earliest impression was of a fresh nose but no great character. Fairly dry, lightish, charming and easy. Well-nigh perfect, in its way, at 11 years of age.* Not tasted since Dec 1984★★★

POL ROGER, EXTRA DRY *Literally dozens of notes, starting with the first of the batch I bought in 1983. My last bottle finished only recently. Initially pale, lively, lighter in body and style than the '76, of which I also bought several cases; the '73 seemed thinner or more acidic. But by the mid-1980s I thought it had mellowed beautifully. It appeared to have sweetened a little, certainly opened up, soft and rich. A charming easy-to-drink champagne, sheer perfection. Latterly the colour has deepened to a straw yellow, the bubbles arising more slowly, albeit steadily and, by the late 1980s, the bouquet had become fully evolved, gushing out of the glass and touched with malt, lanolin, straw and honey. Slight bottle variation, one or two bottles more tired than others but acidity, its nervous system, keeping it going. In 1989, Pol Roger brought over to a tasting some '73s disgorged the previous year. It was quite different. Still a palish green gold. Dry. Frothy and fresh. Frankly, late disgorging is akin to a face-lift. I prefer a well-cellared, untampered original wine and cork.* The last bottle of my own stock consumed with infinite regret at its passing, in July 1990. At its best★★★★

SALON LE MESNIL *Presented, in a new-style bottle, in 1981. It was fairly pale in colour with a green tinge. A light, rather indolent* mousse. *Somewhat raw and appley on the nose. Dry. In 1988, showing its age, with an old straw nose and taste.* Last noted June 1988★★

MAXIM'S SALON LE MESNIL, BLANC DE BLANCS *Maxim's in Paris had one or two exclusivities (see also Perrier-Jouët's flower bottle, page 339) including Salon which was very much associated with this* fin de siècle *restaurant. I thought Maxim's '73 Salon creamy, dry, fairly light, elegant and very stylish.* Feb 1983★★★

TAITTINGER, COMTES DE CHAMPAGNE, BLANC DE BLANCS *Perfection either side of the mid-1980s. Pale for its age, lively; a rich creamy bouquet with added touch of spice; slightly sweet — distinctly* not *dry, nice weight, soft, quite delicious. Although past its peak, a lovely, easy, unaggressive and very appealing champagne.* Last tasted Feb 1986★★★★★

SOME OTHER '73s TASTED IN THE 1980s:

LANSON, RED LABEL *Firm, crisp, good length.*

LAURENT-PERRIER *Good, smoky Chardonnay nose, good fruit and acidity.*

MUMM, RENE LALOU *Lacking fizz. Disappointing.*

PERRIER-JOUET, FLEUR DE CHAMPAGNE *Pale, smoky, dryish, good.*

JOSEPH PERRIER, RESERVE ROYALE *Bottle variation, some like old straw and austere, others creamy, with a pleasant charred flavour.*

1974★

The sort of vintage that can damage the reputation of champagne. Wedged neatly between 1973 and 1975, it might well have been more prudent to have kept it to replenish non-vintage stocks. A roller coaster of climatic conditions. Poor weather just after the start of flowering, then excessively hot and dry. Welcome rain in Aug and very unwelcome rain at vintage time. Give '74 a miss.

DE CASTELLANE, CUVEE COMMODORE *Quite good.* Sept 1982★★

ROEDERER, CRISTAL BRUT *First tasted in Cognac in 1982 after checking a large stock of venerable vintages and old blends. It was welcome enough after some dusty work, but no more. In 1984 fairly pale, lively, pleasant. Most recently: still pale for age, fine bubbles; sweaty but harmonious old straw bouquet; assertive, good acidity. Not up to Cordier standard.* Last noted at Cristal Brut tasting, March 1991★★

ST-MARCEAUX *Noted with lack of enthusiasm at a Vintners' dinner and, alas shortly after, at the 104th meeting of the Saintsbury Club in the same hall. Unimpressive. Unmemorable.* April 1984★

1975★★★

Good vintage. Stylish wines tending to be a bit acidic, like the '69s but with a more satisfactory character, more harmonious. A cool damp start to the growing season, with snow in March. Yet by the end of April, hot and sunny. Summer temperature higher than average but lack of sun and a wet second half of Sept delayed picking until Oct.

Not many '75s seen around but those with body as well as sustaining acidity should still be delicious to drink.

BOLLINGER, BRUT *My first introduction to the '75 vintage was a rather unimpressive half-bottle in 1981. It tailed off. In 1982, a palish, lively bottle with a good, smoky, charred nose; flavoury, elegant but a bit austere. Gaining colour after 10 years, the bouquet gathering itself together, rich, creamy. A lovely wine. Good fruit. Flowery. An even more characterful magnum in 1986, the Pinot Noir character noted, also its good length and acidity. More recently a pale, frothy magnum, nose by now perfection. Dry. Very good flavour. Last tasted July 1987**** Worth seeking out.*

BOLLINGER, RD *Several notes starting in 1984 but no disgorging dates noted. A different character to the Brut: a positive yellow gold colour from the start, with a very fine* mousse. *Nose of considerable depth, rich, fragrant, complete—redolent of walnuts. A rich, classic, meaty Bollinger style. Good length. A rogue jeroboam in Sept 1986: pale, creamy, dry, lightish style, a bit lean and rather neutral. Not up to RD standard. The following autumn, one bottle corked, the other very good. Last tasted at the Ritz Carlton, Montreal, Oct 1987*****

VEUVE CLICQUOT *Five notes, all magnums. In 1982 and 1983, I thought it scented, flowery, slightly artificial on nose and palate. Very flavoury, a bit acidic. Similar expressions, "scented", "acidic", noted quite independently in 1987 and, most recently, at a very civilised bubbly and oyster breakfast at Scott's, noting that "despite poor weather earlier in the year, one of Clicquot's more memorable vintages. Acidity 8.5 gr/l". Alas, despite being a Clicquot admirer, I find the '75 memorable for the wrong reasons. Last tasted Sept 1989***

DOM PERIGNON *Tasted, in magnum, in its youth: a light, refreshing, lemon-tinged nose; dry, nutty, austere, long, with slightly acidic finish. Oct 1983. Then**(**) Probably at peak now.*

KRUG *Good, creamy, rich, nose; surprisingly high acidity. A birthday drink with John Arlott, July 1987***(*)*

LANSON, RED LABEL *Launched in spring 1984 in a hideously contorted skittle-shaped bottle. Despite the silly marketing pretentiousness, a good firm wine. Later notes from magnums. Most recently: pale for its age, refined* mousse*; twist of lemon in the bouquet resolving itself into a lively refreshing wine. Dry. Firm. Time in hand. Last noted March 1990***(*)*

MOET & CHANDON *I have often admired the standard vintage Moët, though wedged between the immensely popular—and reliable— Moët non-vintage and the ritzy Dom Pérignon, it seems to be overlooked. I commend it for quality and value. Nice wine. Consumed without much note-taking at a grand Hennessy "Paradis" Cognac dinner at the Mansion House, Jan 1981. Then**** Probably still very good.*

LAURENT-PERRIER, GRAND SIECLE *Pale, elegant, creamy, firm, long, very appealing. Feb 1985*****

PERRIER-JOUET, BRUT *Excellent, smoky bouquet and flavour. Very attractive. May 1985*****

POL ROGER *The Pol '75 must have come on the market fairly early as I noted it in May 1980. A very refined wine. Good body and clean lines noted a couple of months later and, the following year, surprising bottle variation, one fairly lifeless and flabby, the other zestful. It seemed to grow with age, mouthfilling perfection with a slightly smoky aftertaste. Last tasted in Oct 1986. Then**** but firm enough to last.*

POL ROGER, CHARDONNAY *The second vintage of Pol Roger's Chardonnay. Pale, youthful, dry, fairly light in weight and style. Excellent acidity. As good as it would ever be in Dec 1984****

POL ROGER, CUVEE SIR WINSTON CHURCHILL *Known to have been Churchill's favourite champagne, it seemed wholly appropriate that Pol's* de luxe *brand should be named after him. First noted Dec 1984: palish, surprisingly little* mousse, *and what there was dissipated quickly. However, a very attractive nose, scented, walnuts and a 'fishy' Pinot aroma. Medium dryness and weight, rich, flavoury, good length and finish. Very good indeed. More recently, still fairly pale, with lovely bouquet and fresh flavour. Softer than the '76 Pol Roger. Last tasted May 1987***** Should still be on top form.*

ROEDERER, CRISTAL BRUT *The opening wine at a magnificent dinner of the Houston chapter of the Wine & Food Society in Oct 1983 hosted by Lenoir Josey. In magnums: gentle, creamy bouquet, less 'toasted' than the '76. Rich, frothy yet very elegant, with measurable length and acidity. A similar note two years later, save that the acidity was more noticeable. Last tasted June 1985*****

TAITTINGER, COMTES DE CHAMPAGNE, BLANC DE BLANCS *Provided for our 30th wedding anniversary supper in 1984 at the luxurious Bel-Air hotel in Hollywood by an old friend, George Reese, sadly now departed. Delicious. Two years later, in magnum, a palish yellow, with, as before, rather light* mousse; *dry, light style, firm, hard even. Needed more time in bottle. Preferred the '73. Last tasted Feb 1986. Then**(**) Probably reaching its peak now.*

SOME OTHER '75s TASTED IN THE 1980s:

DE CASTELLANE, BRUT *Fairly dry, elegant, firm, good balance and finish.*

DE CASTELLANE, ROSE *A somewhat artificial pink touched with orange. Rather stalky, meaty, nose. Fairly dry. Quite good length.*

DEUTZ, CUVEE WILLIAM DEUTZ *Positive yellow green colour, short with gold, refined* mousse*; nose a bit hard but "refined" noted again. Dry, low-keyed, genuinely subtle, elegant.*

DOM RUINART, BLANC DE BLANCS *Good colour, excellent nose, decent length but lacking the style and delicacy of Taittinger.*

GOSSET *Very unusual style and muscadelle grapiness — but memorable because served at Ch Pavie in the company of Douglas Fairbanks Jr.*

J JASSALLE, BLANC DE BLANCS *One of the several small producers to be introduced to the English market in the mid-1980s. Initial lively froth quickly subsided. Lemon-like acidic nose. Very dry, pleasant enough, good length. A bit one track.*

LAURENT-PERRIER *Pale, lively; a touch of woodiness diverting its cream and fruit. A bit acidic.*

MUMM *Little nose. Dry. Fairly light. Flavour expanded in the mouth but seemed to deflate rather quickly. Not a deeply satisfying wine.*

PERRIER-JOUET, FLEUR DE CHAMPAGNE *In jeroboams: palish, lively, fresh, youthful nose of no great depth; dry, lightish, frothy and lacking length. Why anyone bothers with jeroboams I do not know. At least,* I do *know, but the best maximum size for champagne is the magnum.*

PERRIER-JOUET, ROSE *Very lively pink and blushing, like Tavel rosé, in a silver cup. The luxurious chalice did nothing for the nose but the wine had surprisingly good flavour, fruit and finish. One of the best pink champagnes I have tasted.*

JOSEPH PERRIER, BRUT *Shipped to celebrate the Queen's Silver Wedding anniversary. Magnums, with magnum-size bubbles, but with a very good, meaty nose, flavour and length.*

ROEDERER *A recent note: good colour; ripe, very mature nose; distinctly sweet, medium body, very rich, delicious. Worth seeking.*

1976★★★★

One of my favourite champagne vintages. Firm, well-structured wines. For those with long memories, this was the year of the heat-wave and drought, when the blissful English summer developed an alarming water shortage; when a Minister of Sport became the Minister of Moisture. The weather in the south of England is not dissimilar to that in Champagne which, after all, is the most northerly of all the great French vineyard areas. In England, the heat and drought ended abruptly on Aug 31 and thereafter it rained incessantly until the following spring. Happily the rains came a little later in Champagne, fleshing out the early ripening grapes.

I never recommend hanging on to rosé or *blanc de blancs*, but this is the sort of vintage in which the best can still survive. As for the top 'straight' vintage and *de luxe* champagnes, the '76s are superb now and, if you like mature champagne, will keep and improve further.

BOLLINGER *Several notes from the London launch with Christian Bizot at Mentzendorff's, June 1982. Very impressive. Marvellously rich in the meaty Bollinger style. Really powerful, with an almost anaesthetising effect on the palate. At least three mentions of "needs more time" in 1983 and 1984, particularly in magnum. I would judge it at its best at 10–12 years old for, more recently, I thought it showing age and slightly disappointing on the nose, rather hollow on the palate and a touch acidic on the finish.* Aug 1990. At best★★★★

BOLLINGER, RD *The first, matured on its lees, disgorged in March 1987 and drunk six months later. Very dry, straw-like flavour. The following year, in magnum, the same old straw nose but good length.* Last tasted March 1988★★★

BOLLINGER, ROSE *Positive colour, orange-tinged pink; nose rather hard and woody; overall dry, firm, rather beefy for a rosé, touch of bitterness on the finish. Not a wine to convert me to pink champagne.* Feb 1985★★

VEUVE CLICQUOT *The '76 'Gold Label' was launched in July 1982 by Clicquot with panache at the Henley Royal Regatta, in sweltering heat, the mirror image of the summer of the vintage itself. Despite this, not overly impressed by the earlier magnums though it has developed well with bottle-age. Nutty and firm in the mid-1980s, I thought it at its very pleasant peak when last tasted: a good colour, superfine bubbles, attractive bouquet; rich, flavoury.* Last noted, Oct 1989★★★★ Now to 1996.

CLICQUOT, ROSE *Unreal-looking orange rose; slightly peach kernelly nose; dry, curious flavour, slightly bitter finish. Not very nice.* July 1982★

DEUTZ, BLANC DE BLANCS *Palish, very little* mousse, *almost* crémant*; very clean, fresh, lightly scented nose; light style and weight, elegant, fresh, lovely.* April 1982★★★★ Will be well past its best now.

DEUTZ, BRUT *Perhaps an obvious '76, but how or why I also correctly placed this as Deutz in a blind tasting in April 1982 I do not know. It was rather pale, with a youthful green tinge; creamy nose of nice quality; dry, on the light side, very straightforward. 'Cream' still apparent but developing meatier bottle-age on the nose and palate.* Last tasted July 1988★★★ Now to 1994.

DOM PERIGNON *Champagne is the wine of celebration. Appropriately, magnums of '76 Dom greeted guests at a great reception and dinner held at Ch Margaux in Sept 1984 to celebrate 50 years of the wine trade between Bordeaux and the US. The champagne was dry, firm and impressively long. Tasted only a couple of times since, noting its yellow gold colour developing, its excellent fresh Chardonnay and walnuts bouquet; a certain quality of femininity and inimitable finesse and length.* Last tasted April 1985★★★★★ Will still be excellent.

DOM RUINART, BLANC DE BLANCS *Very positive green-tinged yellow with an indolent stream of not very small bubbles. More positive flavour than indefinable nose. Fair length. Two notes and considered at its peak soon after its release.* Last tasted Dec 1984★★★

DOM RUINART, ROSE *Pink when young, later more of an orange rose. Fresh nose and taste. Good fruit. As rosés go, good.* Last tasted Dec 1987★★★

CHARLES HEIDSIECK, ROSE *Rather artificial colour, moderately lively; pleasant nose; soft, gentle, nice quality but lacking length. Should have been consumed soon after its launch.* Nov 1982★★★

HEIDSIECK MONOPOLE, DIAMANT BLEU *The*

apéritif d'honneur *at the Champagne Academy dinner in May 1983. A very nicely put together wine. Palish, very fine, minute bubbles; very positive elegant nose, with style and depth, redolent of walnuts. Dry yet rich. Good length.* Last tasted Dec 1984**** Should still be good, though changing in character and liveliness with bottle-age.

HEIDSIECK MONOPOLE, ROSE *Pale pink; somewhat overblown nose but some fruit. Light, dry, firm, short.* Early 1980s*

HENRIOT'S RESERVE BARON PHILIPPE DE ROTHSCHILD *Identical phrase "creamy and crusty" applied to nose and palate at two separate tastings a decade after the vintage. Already showing age, fairly yellow. Soft, toasty flavour.* Last tasted April 1986*** Will be past its best now.

KRUG *First presented at the Champagne Academy dinner in May 1982. Deeper and more yellow in colour than the preceding '76 Pol Roger (see below); impressive nose though still hard and a little stalky. Clearly a big wine, rich mid-palate "better in five years". Next served at the* Dîner Classique *in Oct 1983 at the Dolder Grand in Zurich to mark the publication of the German edition of* The Great Vintage Wine Book. *A lovely creamy classic bouquet which held its perfume in the glass for two hours. A wine combining substance and elegance. Perfect in 1986 and, most recently, still displaying a lively youthful tinge; delicious bouquet, with elements deriving from the Pinot Noir, and a smoky character; fairly full-bodied, firm, considerable length, crisp finish. Despite its body, seemed leaner alongside a rather disappointing bottle of '61 Dom Pérignon.* Last tasted with Lloyd Flatt at our house near Bath, June 1988****(*) Now to beyond 2000.

LANSON, RED LABEL *Well over two dozen notes since the spring of 1985. Then on the pale side, with fine* mousse*; fresh, youthful and fruity on nose and palate. Overall dry. Good acidity and length. Apart from one rather tart bottle, an immensely satisfying champagne. Now gaining colour, more yellow; nose still fresh, minty; fleshy yet with firm, mouthfilling flavour. Touch of oakiness. Excellent structure.* Last tasted May 1990**** Now to 1996.

MOET & CHANDON *First noted before dinner at a wine weekend at The Castle Hotel, Taunton, Nov 1982. A pale, lemon-tinged and moderately lively wine poured out of jeroboams. Little nose. Dry, less full-bodied than expected of a '76 but perhaps this was just reflex reaction after the Californian Domaine Chandon. Certainly delicate in comparison. But its flavour swelled in the mouth, ending with a refreshing lemon-tinged end acidity. Next, in magnums, at a Wine & Food Society dinner at* Max au Triangle *in Hollywood. In 1985 the wine had evolved well. Creamy. Excellent flavour, balance and finish. Most recently showing its age but still a very good drink: lovely golden colour, still lively; crisp, nutty bouquet; equally crisp and firm, with good body and excellent flavour.* Last tasted at David Searle's in Hong Kong, June 1989**** Drink now to 1996.

MOET & CHANDON, ROSE *Already a fairly deep orange-tinged straw gold — not much pink to be seen. A curious — to say the least — nose that reminded me of New York State hybrids; clumsy style, slightly bitter finish. It was awful.* May 1982.

PERRIER-JOUET *As all three types were tasted within two years of their launch I shall lump them together in one paragraph. The 'standard' Perrier-Jouët had, when young, a very good fruity nose, both the Pinot Noir and Chardonnay elements discernible. The* 'Fleur de Champagne rosé' *had a faded rose colour, almost* pelure d'oignon *— fashionable in the late 18th century; more of a Pinot Noir aroma; nutty and fruity on the palate. A* good *rosé for a change. And lastly an attractive* 'Belle Epoque' *rather unfortunately upstaged by the '76 Dom Pérignon at the Ch Margaux reception already referred to.* Last tasted Sept 1984. All***

PIPER HEIDSIECK, RARE *Pale, very little life; an unusually scented, rather artificial, Asti-Spumante-reminiscent nose; dry, fairly light, ordinary and short.* Dec 1984*

POL ROGER *I well recall the launch of the '76, overlooking Kensington Gardens, on a sunny spring day in March 1982. It had a good colour, a fine and interminable* mousse, *lovely nose and flavour. Dry but not too dry, noticeably impressive mid-palate, excellent finish. "Will be perfect in five years" I noted at the time and, shortly after, bought several cases. Which is why I have literally dozens of notes. I drank it with great pleasure. Recently deepening slightly in colour, a yellow straw, but still lively; a gloriously rich, wholesome bouquet; fairly — but not too — dry, well constituted, with loads of character and good length. One of my favourite champagnes.* Last tasted Nov 1990**** Now to 1996.

RENARD-BARNIER, BRUT *Imported privately from a producer who refuses to sell to the trade. It was good: creamy-nosed, dry and firm. A* blanc de blancs *style.* With George Rainbird, at Whichford, Aug 1984***

ROEDERER, CRISTAL BRUT *Alas, tasted only once. But, memorably, when young. It was on the occasion of my first visit to the home of Herbert Allan, the inventor of the Screwpull corkscrew. Superb. A very attractive pale gold with steady flow of bubbles. An intriguing nose: fresh straw, smoky, slightly toasted; dry, positive, in fact quite assertive, fairly full-bodied, steely yet elegant, with good length and acidity.* Still a bit hard and youthful in Oct 1983. Now doubtless***** I must look out for some, both on its own account and to remember the gentle giant who died in 1990.

ST-MARCEAUX *Rather flat, dull and drab.* April 1988.

SALON LE MESNIL *A fairly distinctive yellow colour, rich, creamy, mealy, meaty nose, touch of sweetness, good length. A very stylish wine, interesting, needing more time to settle down.* Before lunch at Christie's, Nov 1983. Then***(*) Will now just be passing its peak.

TAITTINGER, COMTES DE CHAMPAGNE, BLANC DE BLANCS *My second highest mark at a blind tasting in 1984 of 18* de luxe *champagnes, vintages ranging from '75 to '79. Next noted at 10 years of age: a lovely lemon gold, refined; nose still a bit hard; lightish* blanc de blancs *style. Last tasted June 1986***** Firm but not recommended for long keeping.*

1977

The rains in the previous autumn continued through to the spring. An altogether damp and dismal growing season with an improvement, though too late, in Sept.

ROEDERER, CRISTAL BRUT *A blend of Pinot Noir picked Oct 9 and Chardonnay, Oct 13. Palish yellow gold; creamy, crusty, developed well; medium dryness, weight, soft yet good acidity, slightly malty finish. Surprisingly good for a '77. March 1991***

1978★★

A strange vintage. Weather pattern not dissimilar to 1977. Poor flowering, retarded growth. A poor summer but sun, though lacking great heat, throughout Sept which, as in Bordeaux, saved the day. The musts were sweet but acidity high. It seems strange to me that *de luxe* brands were produced in 1978 but, as we shall see, they were not at all bad. It was clearly a marketing ploy, I suspect, mainly for the US as comparatively little was shipped to the UK.

VEUVE CLICQUOT *I have never cared for sailing, even on azure seas and under a cloudless blue sky. The '78 Clicquot was not on top form either. With Robin Blackburne in Bermuda, Sept 1985**

DOM PERIGNON *Several notes. Good clean fun in 1985, fresh and fishy nosed in 1987. Most recently: pale yellow green; a lovely gentle toasted, creamy nose; dry but not too dry, rich yet not overstated. Good length. Last tasted Sept 1989****

DOM PERIGNON, ROSE *Tasted only once. A quite positive, fairly deep pink, its bubbles struggling a bit. Nutty, rich bouquet of some depth. Rather sweet, fairly full-bodied, a surprisingly lovely (for a '78, and for a rosé) mouthfilling flavour and excellent acidity. Dinner with David Allan, Sept 1990*****

DOM RUINART *Surprisingly dry, austere and rather acidic. Served at Ch Loudenne, June 1988**

MOET & CHANDON, BRUT IMPERIAL *Quite nice when it came on to the market in 1982. In 1984, showing extremely well even though it did not, strictly speaking, qualify to be represented at the blind tasting of* de luxe *champagnes previously referred to. It was at this tasting I realised how good yet how under-appreciated the straight vintage Moët can be, floating commercially between the non-vintage and Dom Pérignon. It had quite a deep straw yellow colour but refined* mousse, *tiny bubbles. A rich, fragrant, Pinot-dominated nose of great depth. Soft, rounded, excellent flavour, good length and acidity. My next experience was at a tasting not of wine but of five types of oyster, caviar and so forth. Mouthfilling. Very flavoury but not very* brut. *March 1986. By then*** Probably past its best now.*

MOET & CHANDON, DRY IMPERIAL, ROSE *The sort of title that would have appealed to the Czars, except they would have preferred a* sweet *pink champagne.* This *was definitely dry. Palish, with a distinctly orange tinge and lacking vitality. Nose rather tinny, though some fruit on the palate. Jan 1985**

PERRIER-JOUET, BELLE EPOQUE. *Showing extremely well at the blind tasting of* de luxe *champagnes in 1984, rich and full flavoured. The* BRUT *pale, very dry and acidic. Last tasted March 1986*** and* respectively.*

ROEDERER, BLANC DE BLANCS *A curiosity, produced for the French market and not normally shipped to the UK. Some colour, a curious nose and strange flavour. Frothy yet aged. I am a long-time admirer of Roederer, but the French can keep this sort of* blanc de blancs. *May 1985.*

ROEDERER, CRISTAL BRUT *Just two notes in the mid-1980s, the first, probably stored too warm, was very disappointing, slightly caramelly, dull. On another occasion palish, with a fine* mousse*; a lovely creamy nose; slightly sweet, good length, very attractive. Last tasted April 1985. At best****

1979★★★★

A major vintage. Stylish wines, notable for their refreshing acidity. Severe winter, cold spring, heavy May frosts. Growth retarded but good flowering anticipating a large crop which would be picked late, as indeed was the case. Summer heat and sun adequate.

Champagne is a naturally acidic wine. If bubbles provide the uplift, it is the acidity that gives champagne its inimitable zing and zest. Acidity is also a life preserver – up to a point. The best '79s are drinking well and will keep.

BOLLINGER, BRUT *Distinctly not the meaty style of 'Bolly' but dry and stylish. Good length. Several notes. Last tasted Aug 1988****

BOLLINGER, GRANDE ANNEE *A positive yellow colour; very fresh but straw-like nose and taste. I found it rather disappointing. March 1986. Re-taste.*

BOLLINGER, RD *Seven notes over the past two years and surprising variations in both bottles and magnums. Mainly an unusually deep straw gold in colour. On at least two occasions caramelly and with a strange oily, malty nose. In a line-up of top vintage champagnes it was distinctly the odd man out. Sometimes noted as too hefty, sometimes a bit on the lean side. Clearly I must record more carefully dates of disgorgement, otherwise I cannot assess the wine in any – I hate the word – 'definitive' way. Last tasted March 1990.*

CHARBAUT, CERTIFICATE *Additionally described as 'Blanc de Blancs Brut' and presented in a clear glass bottle. A new brand to me, and the first vintage I tasted, soon after it came on to the market in 1986. A pale lemon gold, lively, small bubbles; a tangy, dough-like nose; distinctly dry, with clean, light* blanc de blancs *style, good acidity and length.* Last tasted April 1987★★★★ Probably at best now.

VEUVE CLICQUOT *Several recent notes. Good colour, golden, lively; excellent nose now beginning to show bottle-age, fresh yet rich, creamy; medium dry, nice weight, good flavour, style, balance.* Sept 1990★★★(★) Now to 1996 or beyond.

VEUVE CLICQUOT, LA GRANDE DAME *First noted at the* de luxe *champagne tasting in Dec 1984. Then frothy; rich walnut-like nose with overtone of powdery rose cachou scent; intriguingly rich taste of walnuts and mushroom soup! Fairly high acidity. Distinct richness and sweetness noted on a later occasion.* Last tasted Nov 1986. Then★★★★ Possibly now★★★★★ in its idiosyncratic way.

DOM RUINART, BLANC DE BLANCS *Very scented, rather artificial nose; very frothy, youthful, with lemon-like acidity.* Nov 1986★★

DOM RUINART, ROSE *Rich orange rosé colour, its initial froth fairly soon subsiding; rich nose, like beef extract; dry, assertive flavour but short and slightly bitter.* The oldest vintage at a tasting of rosé champagnes in Tokyo, Nov 1989★

CHARLES HEIDSIECK *Good colour, very fine* mousse*; deep, rich, nutty Pinot nose; good, firm, positive flavour, with crisp acidity. Still climbing to cruising height.* March 1990★★★(★) Now to 1996.

CHARLES HEIDSIECK, CUVEE CHAMPAGNE CHARLIE *Showing quite well at the blind tasting of* de luxe *champagnes in 1984. Good fruit. The following year, in magnums: enticingly fresh and fruity nose; dry, firm, good length.* Last tasted May 1986. Then★★★(★) Doubtless excellent now and will develop further.

KRUG *Two recent notes. Palish yellow, lively; soft, rich, meaty bouquet; very rich, very distinctive, slightly scented flavour, with great vinosity and good length.* Last tasted before lunch at Ch Pétrus with Colin Parnell and host, Christian Mouiex, Nov 1990★★★★(★) Now to 2000.

KRUG, LE MESNIL *Le Mesnil is in the heart of the Côtes des Blancs, so this must be a straight vintage Chardonnay. Palish, lemon-tinged; strange somewhat scented nose and flavour. I thought it fresh and attractive but lacked length.* At the Peppercorns', Dec 1984. Then★★★ Should have been drunk by now.

LANSON, NOBLE CUVEE *Lovely colour, good length and bite.* April 1986★★★★(★) Now to 1998.

LANSON, RED LABEL *Lively; classy bouquet; dry, firm, excellent now, will keep.* June 1990★★★(★) Now to 1995.

MUMM, RENE LALOU *Several notes in the mid-1980s. Pale. Preferred when young, fresh and frothy. Not quite up to* de luxe *standard.* Last tasted Sept 1986★★

PIPER HEIDSIECK, BRUT SAUVAGE *One is tempted to observe that its title adequately describes its taste, for although I rather liked its scented peach-like nose I found it very dry and austere, with a short, hard acidic finish.* Two notes, the last in Nov 1986★

PIPER HEIDSIECK, RARE *Apple green colour; equally 'green', stalky, corky nose and taste. Might just have been one particular bottle, but it was one of the worst champagnes in a major vintage line-up, tasted blind.* Sept 1988.

POL ROGER *First tasted in May 1985. First rate. In 1986 noted as dry, lovely, crisp and oaky. However, most recently I found it rather disappointing. Possibly the bottle, or me, not on top form.* Last tasted Oct 1989. At best★★★(★) Should be approaching its peak now.

POL ROGER, CUVEE BLANCS DE CHARDONNAY *Subtitled* "Cuvée Prestige". *First noted in April 1984: palish, slightly green-tinged; very fragrant, creamy nose; fairly dry, and light, with lovely flavour. Several similar notes over the next two years when it was probably at its best: crisp, stylish, elegant.* Last tasted March 1986★★★★

POL ROGER, CUVEE SIR WINSTON CHURCHILL *Several notes. It is always a pleasure to meet the Pol Roger family on their stand at VinExpo, and it was in June 1985 that they introduced me to their new '79* de luxe cuvée. *It really was delicious, with excellent length and acidity, but needing—for my taste—another five years of bottle-age. An opinion confirmed by magnums the following year. It was still rather austere. Back at VinExpo in 1987, I was startled by an appley malic acid sort of nose and thought it altogether too tart. Most recently, also in magnums, at a Chinese banquet in Hong Kong. It was very good.* Oct 1989★★★★ Should still be improving.

POL ROGER, ROYAL WEDDING CUVEE *I thought I detected a whiff of aniseed nestling in the cream. Slightly sweeter than usual. Soft. Nice weight. Good length. A couple of good notes.* Last tasted Jan 1987★★★★

ROEDERER, CRISTAL BRUT *First tasted in 1984, surprisingly yellow; frothy, flavoury. Three recent notes: golden fine steady stream of bubbles; lovely, sweet, soft, crusty nose; excellent long toasty taste. Perfect acidity.* Last tasted April 1991★★★★

TAITTINGER, COMTES DE CHAMPAGNE, BLANC DE BLANCS *Had I sipped this at some reception, making a casual note, I would have ignored it. However, notes made at major comparative tastings at which wines of similar class are tasted blind is, for me, more significant and telling. This is a preamble to the rather poor showing of the '79 'Comtes': hollow, grassy nose; slightly sweet, with artificial, flavour.* Nov 1986. In theory a re-taste would be fair, though it is now rather old for a blanc de blancs.

TAITTINGER, LA FRANCAISE *Much better: yellow-tinged, bright and appealing; good nose, nice style, ageing well; touch of sweetness, good body, excellent flavour. Mellow.* April 1990★★★★ Now to 1998.

BRIEF NOTES ON SOME OTHER '79s:

BINET, BLANC DE BLANCS *Very good, clean, dry.* Nov 1985★★★

DEUTZ, BLANC DE BLANCS *Creamy, dough-like nose. Dry, austere, lean, rather acidic.* Jan 1986★★

ANDRE DRAPIER, CARTE D'OR, BRUT *Dry, nice weight, fresh tasting, prominent acidity.* Jan 1985★★★

GOSSET, GRAND MILLESIME *Dry enough, nice weight, very pleasant.* Oct 1989★★★

A GRATIEN *Magnums struggling against the odds: asparagus and hollandaise sauce. Good. Firm. Better on its own. July 1987****

ABEL LEPITRE, BLANC DE BLANCS, CREMANT, BRUT *Indefinable, and unappealing nose; better flavour. Dry. Light. March 1985**

ABEL LEPITRE, PRINCE DE BOURBON PARME, BRUT *A startling buttercup yellow, with gold sheen, but lively, fine* mousse*; fresh rather acidic nose, combining creaminess and meatiness. Curious flavour. Rather raw and acidic and lacking the length expected of a* de luxe *brand. Dec 1985***

G H MUMM *Very nice wine. March 1987****

MUMM, CREMANT DE CRAMANT *A half-sparkling Chardonnay from Cramant in the Côte des Blancs: attractive, slightly raisiny nose; very refreshing, lightweight but perfectly balanced. Best drunk when young and fresh. Nov 1986*****

PERRIER-JOUET, BRUT *Sept 1989****

PERRIER-JOUET, BELLE EPOQUE, ROSE *Orange pink, pleasant nose and flavour. In magnums. May 1985****

POMMERY LOUISE *The new Pommery & Greno* de luxe *blend. Pale, dry, lighter than anticipated. May 1985*****

THEOPHILE ROEDERER, JAMIN, BRUT *Yellow straw colour; creamy, dough-like nose; in the mouth both frothy and chewy, with light dry acidic finish. Pleasantly refreshing. Feb 1985****

1980★

Frankly, this vintage should never have been 'declared'. Mainly lacking body and with a surfeit of acidity yet, on occasion, refreshing in a sherbet-powder sort of way.

By May 1980, everything in the vineyards was perfect and promising: no frosts, healthy vines. From June 15, when flowering should have started, until July 21, the weather was disastrous – cold and wet, and its effect was calamitous as far as potential quantity was concerned. Thereafter, the summer was pleasant enough but the harvest was small and one of the latest on record.

VEUVE CLICQUOT, TEXAN ANNIVERSARY CUVEE *Whatever next! However, doubtless the enterprising widow would have approved. Pale; dry. Very pleasant smoky flavour. Good acidity. Before dinner, in San Francisco, with my son and Clicquot's representative, M Stephan Lambert. Feb 1989*** Assez bien.

DOM PERIGNON *Three notes. First tasted around the time of its release: very acidic unripe-lemon scent; flavoury, good length but with tooth-tingling acidity. The acidity now seems less raw, and it has more creaminess on the nose and nuttiness on palate. Oct 1989*** But the price/quality ratio inequitable.*

LANSON, RED LABEL *Tasted only once, shortly after its release. Fresh, clean, positive, creamy nose, still youthful, with a touch of oak and nuttiness. A young frothy actress's-slipper type of bubbly, rather short, with teeth-gripping acidity. June 1986***

LECHERE, GRAND CRU, BLANC DE BLANCS BRUT *I had never before come across this imposingly labelled champagne but it is worth noting for one simple reason: the best '80 I have tasted. Pale, dry, light, crisp, refined. Jan 1990*****

MOET & CHANDON *Just one note convinced me that it was short-sighted of Moët to put on the market as 'vintage' a non-vintage quality wine. Pale, with large, clumsy bubbles. Dry, loose-knit. Lacking style and conviction. July 1985**

POMMERY & GRENO *In magnums. Fairly pale, greenish tinged; strange yeasty nose with a grapey, acidic aroma, more like a Sauvignon Blanc. Dry, light, immature, acidic, unimpressive. May 1986.*

POMMERY, LOUISE POMMERY, ROSE *Two recent notes. Rosehip colour; meaty nose; medium dry, some fruit, fair finish. Last tasted Sept 1990.*

SALON LE MESNIL, BLANC DE BLANCS *Pale, dry, refined, refreshing. March 1987****

1981★★★

A small crop, most of it kept for the non-vintage blends. A limited amount of high-quality wine made and marketed.

The weather – always the great dictator – mild during the early months of 1981, promoting heavy and premature growth. The vines were literally nipped in the bud by a single night's frost at the end of April. Scattered hailstorms in May did further indiscriminate damage. To make matters worse, a cold spell at the beginning of July induced irregular flowering. Happily, Aug was hot and sunny, though Sept was wet. The best of the limited number of '81s have considerable finesse. "Refined" is a word that crops up several times in my notes. The '81s are firm and will keep.

HENRIOT, CUVEE BACCARAT *Good colour; interesting but unknit nose, meaty, malty, crusty, finally with a smell like apples stored in a loft. On the palate a rich mix, but hard to know how it will develop. Oct 1989***

KRUG *At the launch of the vintage in May 1988 it was explained that May frosts and poor flowering conditions had particularly affected the Pinot Noir and the Meunier, hence the high percentage of Chardonnay (50%), in their '81 blend. I noted a very positive colour, lime-tinged, and a strangely old, straw-like nose, reminding me of a '55. Medium dry, a lighter style than usual because of the preponderance of Chardonnay, but a very distinctive and attractive flavour, and good length. Developing well in bottle, a few months later I noted walnut-like fragrance, nutty, meaty character and great length. A fine wine with good life ahead. Jan 1990***(*) 1991 to beyond 2000.*

KRUG, CLOS DE MESNIL *A unique Clos, or walled vineyard, of 4.61 acres in the middle of the village, Mesnil-sur-Oger. 100% Chardonnay. Production in 1981, 12,793 bottles. Pale, lime-tinged, very lively; forthcoming and intriguing scent of oyster shells and lime; dry, fairly light but steely and rather austere. Fresh. Acidic. Needs more bottle-age.* Oct 1989**(**) 1991–96

MOET & CHANDON, DRY IMPERIAL, ROSE *First noted May 1987. A pleasant enough colour though rather pale. Sweet-nosed. A bit four-square but, for one lacking enthusiasm for rosés, better than expected. More recently, in magnums, pale pink, dry, austere, raw, unappealing.* Last tasted June 1989*

PANNIER BRUT *Pale, dry, firm.* June 1987***

POMMERY, LOUISE POMMERY, CUVEE SPECIALE *Several not wholly consistent notes, depending, I think, on context. For example, on the second occasion it was impeded by* crème d'avocat froid. *But, at its best, a good pale yellow gold colour; crisp, crusty nose with delicate fruitiness; medium dry, nice weight, good length, excellent acidity.* Last tasted Sept 1990***(*) The extra potential star is dependent on bottle-age smoothing away its slight 'greenness'.

ROEDERER, CRISTAL BRUT *First noted in Oct 1987. Very lively, with a heavy white froth like the 'head' of a glass of Guinness; a classic creamy, crusty, very slightly malty nose; lovely refreshing flavour, good length and crisp acidity. Most recently, in magnums: a fairly pale soft waxy yellow colour, its* mousse *a bit more subdued. Nutty bouquet. Good length. Refined.* Last noted March 1991**** Now to 2000.

TAITTINGER, COMTES DE CHAMPAGNE, BLANC DE BLANCS *Noted fairly recently, in magnums and in bottle. Firm yet lively. Fine quality. Dry. Refined.* Last tasted Sept 1989**** Now to 1998.

1982★★★★

An important and substantial vintage in all respects. For a change, well-nigh perfect climatic conditions, the vines sitting out a cold winter with snow and frosts. The spring entered coolly but became mild and sunny. June perfect for flowering, with light rain at the end of the month. July warm and dry, Aug sunny and dry. Grapes fully ripe in Sept, some rain mid-month helping to swell the berries and produce the biggest crop on record, three times the size of the '81. Although it would have benefited from a dose of '81 acidity, the wines are well structured, and the best are still improving in bottle.

BOLLINGER, GRAND ANNEE *First noted Nov 1986. Some depth of colour; a sweet, broad, meaty old-style Bollinger nose with just a whiff of sultanas; medium dry, fairly full-bodied, rich, chewy. More recently: fairly pale, lively; good rich creamy nose; dry, medium-full body. Showing well. Latterly I have found it somewhat acidic on nose and palate, but a wine of refinement.* Last tasted Nov 1990**(**) 1992–98

BOLLINGER, GRAND ANNEE, ROSE, BRUT *A deeply tinted rosé. Distinct touch of sweetness on palate. Rather heavy and clumsy and lacking finesse.* Sept 1988.

BOLLINGER, RD *Palish yellow; straw nose and taste.* May 1991**

CHARBAUT *Rather green and immature when first tasted in 1988, flavoury, very scented, and with very dry finish. Most recently: pale, unimpressive nose; a touch of my least favourite taste, peach kernels, and a rather limp end. Might have been the context.* Last tasted in New York, Oct 1990. At best**(*)

VEUVE CLICQUOT *A large number of notes starting in Sept 1988; drunk as an aperitif, as a reviver, with cooked cheese dishes, at a British Airways tasting — wherever and whenever, showing well. I was told that 160kg of fruit was pressed to produce 100l of juice. A good colour from the start, when it had a slightly green youthful tinge, now beginning to settle down. Lovely nose, fairly assertive, crusty, scented, considerable depth. A distinctly dry wine, firm, with good weight and length. Will benefit from a good deal more bottle-age.* Last tasted Sept 1990***(**) 1992 to beyond 2000.

DOM PERIGNON *Three recent notes. Very lively, small bubbles; crisp steely; distinctly dry, fairly full-bodied, rather austere.* Last tasted May 1991**(***) At least 1995 to 2005.

CHARLES HEIDSIECK *A tasting in Nov 1982 of some of the newly made wines destined for Brut Réserve or, possibly, for the vintage* cuvée. *The malolactic fermentation had not taken place, hence the raw acidity and sourness of some of the samples. A Grand Blanc Chardonnay from Avize, classified 100%, which would make up approximately 20% of the Brut Réserve; Petit Blanc, an 85% classified Chardonnay from Sézanne; a Grand Noir Pinot Noir from Bouzy, rated 100%, which would make up roughly 30% of the non-vintage blend. The others were a Petit Noir, from a Vallée de la Marne Pinot Meunier. Attractive when young, Meunier wines are fast-maturing and do not keep as long, so only 10% in the final blend; another Pinot Noir, from the Montagne de Reims, classified 94% and which might make up 20% of the final blend; lastly, Taille Noir, the end of the first pressing of a Pinot Noir mix from the Vallée de la Marne and the Grand Noir: its natural rosé colour fades in the final blend, giving the wine a gold tinge. The smell of these new wines varied, some sweet, fruity and fragrant, some like pear drops, amyl acetate. The blender has a vital and difficult job. I am glad that mine is merely to enjoy the fruits of his labours.*

My first taste of the '82 vintage cuvée *was in Sept 1988: a pleasing colour, yellow gold; creamy, fragrant nose; surprisingly sweet, almost too sweet, but attractive. Quite a complex, powerful wine.* Last tasted March 1990**(**) 1992–98

CHARLES HEIDSIECK, CUVEE CHAMPAGNE CHARLIE *Several notes. A more substantial wine than the standard vintage blend. Still a bit raw and appley on the nose though meaty on the palate, yet the 'Cuvee Charlie', same price, and tasted at the same time (in Oct 1989) had a nutty, classic nose of some depth, was soft, flavoury and very attractive. Two recent notes. Very distinctive yellow colour, dry, still full of youthful zest and with excellent flavour and length. A jolly good drink now, though I would give it more time.* Last tasted on British Airways en route back from Chicago, Sept 1990***(*) 1992–2000

CHARLES HEIDSIECK, ROSE *Made with 10% Pinot Noir. Two notes. Curious autumn orange tints, fairly pale, almost* pelure d'oignon. *Firm, positive flavour, tolerable acidity, lacking length but quite a good rosé.* Last tasted March 1990** Drink soon.

KRUG *Preferred in magnum to bottle, the latter having a strange scented bouquet. In magnum: a lovely toasty bouquet; good rich flavour, long dry finish. Good future.* Last tasted Sept 1990***(**) 1992 to beyond 2000.

LANSON *The 'Special Anniversary Cuvée' tasted in Nov 1986 was stylish but acidic, needing bottle-ageing. The 'Brut', tasted in 1989, had notable depth of colour, distinctly yellow. In fact, I found it peculiar in other ways, rather neutral on the nose, hard, a whiff of lemon and wet cardboard. An oddly scented, somewhat artificial flavour but good length.* Oct 1989** ?

LANSON, BRUT, ROSE *Two notes. Pale pink, firm, very good.* Last tasted Feb 1989*** Drink up.

MUMM, CUVEE RENE LALOU *Four notes, one — memorably — on Concorde, climbing out of Shannon en route for Barbados. Happy anticipation prevailed over the less-than-ideal British Airways glasses. Palish yellow, tinged with straw, lively; good nose; most definitely dry — if not brutally dry, certainly bone dry. Good flavour and length. Still a bit austere. Would benefit from further bottle-ageing.* Last tasted Jan 1989***(*) 1992–98

PERRIER-JOUET, BELLE EPOQUE, FLEUR DE CHAMPAGNE *Tasted only once, after its release. Then lime-tinged and lively. Sweet, creamy nose; nice wine. Fairly high marks. Should be at peak now.* Nov 1986. Probably**** Now to 1998.

PIPER HEIDSIECK *'Brut Millésime' too sweet, rather light and short, the 'Brut Sauvage' crisper, fruitier, not as dry as anticipated and with a more expansive flavour. Rather hard at the time.* Both tasted Sept 1988* and**(*) respectively.

POL ROGER, BLANC DE CHARDONNAY *First tasted in Dec 1987. Nose of cream and walnuts, rich, nice fruit but somewhat unknit. Lovely flavour, good length. Many notes since. Now taking on colour and less vigorous: a lovely yellow gold, languid. I frequently noted a particular scent, most recently pinning it down as lilac. Dry, of course, but fairly full-bodied for a straight Chardonnay, with lovely penetrating smoky flavour, and twist of lemon acidity on the finish. A very successful and stylish wine.* Last tasted Jan 1990**** Now to 1996.

POL ROGER, CUVEE DE RESERVE *Only one note since I first sipped it on the Pol Roger stand at VinExpo in June 1987. Fine colour; straightforward classic bouquet and flavour. Medium dry, fairly full-bodied, rich.* Last tasted Oct 1989***(*) 1992 to beyond 2000.

POL ROGER, CUVEE SIR WINSTON CHURCHILL *Six recent notes. Fairly pale lemon yellow with steady stream of ultra-fine bubbles; very forthcoming, fragrant bouquet, still with youthful zest and a touch of hardness; like the straight vintage, medium dry, medium full-bodied, rounded, its flavour expanding in the mouth. Top class.* Last tasted May 1990****(*) 1992 to beyond 2000.

POL ROGER, ROSE *The colour of Mateus Rosé or an orange pink Tavel. Light, fresh, fruity aroma with whiff of gooseberries. Fairly dry, medium-light, rather neutral flavour, fair length, quite nice only.* June 1989** Drink up.

POMMERY, LOUISE POMMERY, ROSE *Two recent notes. Pink and lively; very attractive, positive, crusty bread bouquet; fairly dry, medium-light, pleasant fruity flavour, moderate length.* During Rodenstock's wine weekend at the Arlberg Hospiz in Austria, Sept 1990*** Now to 1994.

ROEDERER, BRUT *In magnums and halves. Crisp and creamy, firm, dry, excellent flavour and length.* Last tasted May 1988***(*) Now to 2000.

ROEDERER, CRISTAL BRUT *In magnum and bottles. Bright lively and appealing; creamy, touch of mint; fairly dry, lightish style though firm, with lemony, appley taste.* Last noted March 1991****

TAITTINGER, BRUT *Good colour, lively. Fresh and attractive, and with very appealing flavour when first tasted in the autumn of 1987. The following year, good, but by no stretch of the imagination* brut. *In fact, a touch too sweet.* Last noted Sept 1988*** Probably on top form now.

TAITTINGER, COMTES DE CHAMPAGNE, BLANC DE BLANCS *Extremely good, judging from three recent notes. Pale straw yellow, lively; very fragrant bouquet and flavour. Crisp. Stylish. With tingling acidity.* Last tasted at Ascot on our 36th wedding anniversary, June 1990**** Now to 1998.

TAITTINGER, COMTES DE CHAMPAGNE, ROSE *Outstandingly the best of a small but high-class selection of rosés tasted with a number of exquisitely varied dishes in one of Tokyo's top restaurants. Pale salmon pink colour, very refined* mousse; *firm, scented bouquet of some depth; fairly dry, lightish but firm, good flavour and fragrant aftertaste.* With Mme Arisaka of Vinothèque Magazine, Nov 1989**** Now to 1996.

OTHER NOTES:

BRICOUT *Dry, crisp, good fruit, length and aftertaste.* Sept 1986***(*)

CHARBAUT *Two poor notes. Pale; green, lean, unimpressive nose; slightly scented, peach kernelly flavour, dry, acidic finish on the first occasion, rather flat on the second.* Oct 1990.

DEUTZ, BLANC DE BLANCS *Fairly pale, lively; creamy nose; dry, on the light side, firm, acidic. Probably at peak now.* In magnums Oct 1987***

DOM RUINART, BLANC DE BLANCS *Unexciting.* June 1989*

ALFRED GRATIEN, BRUT *Yellow-green, fine* mousse; *very good fragrant bouquet though still a bit hard; high-toned assertive flavour, good length but rather acidic finish. Needs more bottle-age.* Oct 1989**(*)

HEIDSIECK, DRY MONOPOLE, BRUT *Not particularly impressive. Bottle-age might have improved it. May 1987***

HEIDSIECK, DIAMANT BLEU *A very disappointing bottle in a blind tasting: hard, yeasty nose; dry, strange flavour, tinny.* Oct 1989.

MOET & CHANDON *Extremely good flavour, body, length.* Nov 1989***(*)

MUMM *Rather pale but lively. Dry. Clean. Nothing special.* Jan 1988***

JOSEPH PERRIER, CUVEE ROYALE *Nutty; slightly sweet, very positive, long, rich yet lean, with an extraordinary core and attenuated finish.* Sept 1988***

LAURENT-PERRIER *Agreeable.* Jan 1990***

LAURENT-PERRIER, CUVEE ALEXANDRE, ROSE *Palish orange rosé; very little nose, dry, neutral, short.* Oct 1989*

PERRIER-JOUET, ROSE *Pale pink and harmless.* Jan 1988**

PHILIPPONNAT, CLOS DE GRAND, BRUT *Very pale; curiously and highly scented nose and taste. Dry, rather light, lean, tailed off. Completely upstaged by stone crab terrine.* Jan 1990*

POMMERY, BRUT ROYAL *Creamy, toasted nose; slightly sweet, chewy, easy, pleasant but minus length and finesse.* May 1987**

POMMERY, LOUISE POMMERY, CUVEE SPECIALE *Very flowery bouquet and flavour. Touch of sweetness.* Sept 1985***

RUINART 'R' *Appley, indifferent.* Feb 1989*

1983***

Another major vintage and the biggest crop ever recorded in Champagne: the equivalent of approximately 300 million bottles. The early claims of 'exceptional' quality hardly justified, though the wines are of pleasant style and weight, flavoury and nicely balanced – on the whole.

A cold wet spring following a dismal winter. Flowering started around June 25, and from July 3 for later varieties, and took place in excellent conditions. Aug also warm and sunny, with adequate rainfall. The beginning of Sept damp and rather cool but the second half sunny, picking beginning on the 25th on the Côte des Blancs and from Oct 3 elsewhere.

BOLLINGER, GRANDE ANNEE *Pale; creamy; very good. My style of Bollinger.* March 1990***(*) *Now to 1998.*

VEUVE CLICQUOT *A blend of 20* crus *made up of 62% Pinot Noir, 33% Chardonnay and 5% Meunier grapes. Lively; warm, crusty, bread-like nose; medium dryness and weight, fresh, youthful, perhaps lacking the length of a great vintage.* Sept 1989*** *Now to 1998.*

VEUVE CLICQUOT, ROSE, BRUT Pelure d'oignon, *large bubbles; fairly sweet, dough-like nose that became more assertive as the chill wore off; dry, a bit pushy, fairly acidic.* Nov 1989**(*) *1991 to 1995.*

DOM PERIGNON *Lovely colour, lively, small bubbles; an oaky, smoky, soft, fruity bouquet; quite unlike the '82, much sweeter, medium weight, soft, gentle fruit, long smoky finish.* Prior to a Bordeaux Club dinner at Gonville and Caius, Cambridge, Nov 1990**** *Now to 1998.*

CHARLES HEIDSIECK, BLANCS DES MILLENAIRES *Good colour, fine* mousse*; crusty, lemon-tinged; dry, firm, excellent balance and length.* Feb 1991****

CHARLES HEIDSIECK, BRUT *First tasted with the winemaker, Daniel Thibault, at Mosimann's, spring 1990. We were informed that the Pinot Noir was slightly* botrytised. *The result was certainly attractive. Delicious. Fragrant.* Last tasted May 1990***(*) *Now to 2000.*

CHARLES HEIDSIECK, CHAMPAGNE CHARLIE *Pale. Fairly dry. Lighter weight and style than usual. Very good flavour.* Feb 1990***(*) *1993–2000*

CHARLES HEIDSIECK, ROSE *Three recent notes. Pale orange pink. Quite a bit of character on the nose. Distinctly dry.* Last tasted May 1990*** *Now to 1993.*

POL ROGER *Very pale; smoky, walnuts; dry, light, crisp, short, acidic; weight and style not unlike the '73. Good length and acidity. Decidedly elegant. A comparatively early developer and will probably remain a delicious middle-term wine.* Last tasted Nov 1990. *Just warranting***** *Now to 1998.*

ROEDERER, CRISTAL BRUT *Lemon gold, excellent flow of bubbles; fresh, attractive, rich; nutty fragrance; dry, firm, acidic, pleasing.* Last tasted March 1991***(*)

TAITTINGER *Classic nose. Medium dry, agreeable weight, positive character, firm, good balance and length. Showing well in a comparative tasting.* Oct 1989***(*) *1991–2000*

BRIEF NOTES ON SOME OTHER '83s:

DE CASTELLANE *Very good nose; dry, attractive flavour but lacking length.* Sept 1988***

JACQUART, BRUT *Good colour, nose, flavour and length. Dry.* Feb 1990***

LANSON, BRUT *Fairly full, rich nose and flavour. Assertive. Not the Lanson style familiar to me. Perhaps a matter of taste – and I must taste it again.* Sept 1988***?

ABEL LEPITRE *A brand rarely seen on the English market. It was served at the Marina Club, Aberdeen, on Hong Kong Island after a tour of 'Fragrant Harbour'. The champagne was more fragrant than the harbour, though not as colourful. Dry, light style, scented, twist of lemon acidity.* Nov 1989***

MAILLY, GRAND CRU, BRUT RESERVE *Fairly deep yellow gold; not too sure about the nose. Two conflicting notes, neither wholly complimentary. Distinctly dry, austere, scented flavour, marked acidity.* Oct 1989**

MOET & CHANDON, BRUT IMPERIAL *Attractive nose, rather* blanc de blancs *style; youthful, frothy, with fairly high acidity, but attractive.* Sept 1988***

BRUNO PAILLARD, BLANC DE BLANCS, BRUT *Fairly pale, green tinged; immature, rather artificial nose; very dry, bitter flavour, good length, noticeable acidity.* Sept 1988**

POMMERY, BRUT *Pale, lively.* June 1988***

TAILLEVENT, BLANC DE BLANCS *Fairly pale green gold; intriguing nose of bread and limes; dry, scented flavour, acidic but attractive. May 1990****

1985*****

An extremely good vintage, very stylish wines. In my opinion, likely to be the best balanced and most elegant of the 1980s. A year of dramatic weather patterns. Temperature in mid-Jan was down to −25°C, the lowest recorded for 150 years. Another very cold spell in Feb (−15°C). During both periods, the vineyards were blanketed with snow which gave some protection, though 62,000 acres of vines had to be uprooted. Night temperatures dropped to −5°C towards the end of April, causing more damage. However flowering and fruit set took place in good conditions and sunny weather continued through July. Grapes started to ripen from mid-Aug and high temperatures were recorded during Sept, the harvest starting on the 30th. Despite relatively high prices, well worth tasting, selecting and buying. Several notes, the most salutary made at a blind tasting arranged by *Decanter* magazine.

BOLLINGER *Three notes. At* Decanter *a slightly oxidised, unclean bottle. Two subsequently showing well: lovely colour; rich, crusty, slightly scented; dryish, rich, meaty, good length, style. Last tasted May 1991***(*)*

VEUVE CLICQUOT, LA GRANDE DAME *Three top notes. Showing well at a comparative blind tasting in Oct 1989 of* de luxe *champagne brands of recent vintages. Clean, classic, fragrant; youthful frothiness, dry, good acidity. Most recently: lovely warm pale gold colour; distinctive, fragrant, smoky — like a burnt match; medium dry, reasonably full-bodied, lovely fruit, rounded, good acidity. Top-class wine with good life ahead. Last tasted Dec 1990***(**) Excellent now, even better between, say, 1995–2005.*

CHARLES HEIDSIECK, BRUT *Good positive colour; light, nutty (walnuts); fairly dry, medium-full, lovely uplifting flavour, good acidity, hard, needs time. Last tasted May 1991**(**)*

MOET & CHANDON, BRUT IMPERIAL *Strange style, buttery; dry, hard, lacking length, a bit stalky. April 1989*(*)? Re-taste.*

MUMM, CORDON ROUGE, BRUT *Palish, yellow green, lively, small bubbles; pleasant open style, crisp, fresh, lightly fragrant and creamy bouquet; dry, lightish in weight and style, still young and frothy, retaining an immature hardness, good acidity and touch of sweetness on the finish. Tasted blind Oct 1985**(**) 1992–2000*

MUMM, RENE LALOU *Pale yellow green; quite nice but unknit, immature, appley nose; dry, assertive, lean, acidic. Preferred the 'Cordon Rouge' but doubtless the* de luxe *Lalou needs bottle-age to evolve. Tasted blind Oct 1989*(**)? 1994–2005*

MUMM DE MUMM *More presumptuous than prestigious. To give benefit of doubt, not served cold enough. May 1991****

PERRIER-JOUET, BELLE EPOQUE *Perfect appearance; light, dry, hard, steely, fragrant but austere. Needs time. April 1991**(***)*

PERRIER-JOUET, BELLE EPOQUE, BRUT ROSE *Pale rosehip colour with steady stream of fine bubbles; nose still hard but sweetened up, becoming strawberry-like in the glass; dry, medium weight, crisp, clean, with good acidity. Tasted in Tokyo, Nov 1989**(**) 1991–95*

PERRIER-JOUET, RESERVE CUVEE, BRUT *Straw gold; rich, meaty; interesting character, good flavour, balance. Last tasted April 1991****

POL ROGER *Brilliant appearance, fine* mousse*; lovely creamy nose; dry, light yet firm style, very rich fruit. Attractive now but with good mid-term life. Last tasted April 1991***(*) Now to 2000.*

POL ROGER, BLANC DE CHARDONNAY *Fine* mousse*; distinctive, crusty; dry, rather hard and acidic. Stylish though. April 1991**(**)?*

POL ROGER, GRANDE RESERVE, BRUT *Fresh, fruity; not* brut*, light style, charming. June 1991*****

ROEDERER, BLANC DE BLANCS *Extremely pale,* mousse *like a* crémant*; light lemon and honey; fragrant, but a bit hollow and stalky. Feb 1991*(*)*

ROEDERER, BRUT *66% Pinot Noir, 34% Chardonnay from 100% rated vineyards in the Côte des Blancs. Pale. Creamy, slightly scented nose, still a bit immature and hard; medium dry, very good body, flavour and length. Excellent acidity. A very satisfying wine with a good future. Last tasted Feb 1991***(**) 1992 to well beyond 2000.*

ROEDERER, CRISTAL BRUT *55% Pinot Noir, 45% Chardonnay. Pale; lovely fruit though suppressed, unyielding; medium dry, light style, youthful froth yet soft and beguiling, creamy, slightly scented aftertaste. Last noted March 1991***(**)*

OTHER '85s TASTED BLIND AT *DECANTER*, APRIL 1991:

AVERY *Though* brut*, touch of sweetness, crisp acidity***

BEAUMONT, BLANC DE NOIRS, BRUT *Low-keyed, dry, firm, lean**(*)*

BILLECART-SALMON, BRUT *Attractive, classic nose, richly flavoured, good length*****

BINET, BLANC DE BLANCS *Distinctive, very scented, stylish nose and taste. Dry, lean, steely***(*)*

CHARBAUT, CUVEE DE RESERVE, BRUT *Crusty, meaty style; medium dryness and body**(*)*

MARGUERITE, CRISTAL, BRUT *Very odd, slightly corky; dry.*

DEUTZ, BLANC DE BLANCS, BRUT *Lightly scented, aniseed whiff; dry, good, clean, crisp****

GOSSET, BRUT *'Warm', walnuts; dry, fullish, hard, slightly kernelly finish***

JACQUESSON, PERFECTION *Pale; sweet, smoky, lot of character, very dry, lean, steely, hard, lacking length?**(*)*

LANG-BIEMONT, BLANC DE BLANCS *Yellow green; flowery, attractive, oaky/smoky; positive, good length, very dry acidic finish**(**)*

BRUNO PAILLARD, BRUT *Almost orange-tinged; forthcoming, rich, almost too meaty; dry, hefty* *weight and style, good mid-palate and length**(*)*

JOSEPH PERRIER, CUVEE ROYAL, BRUT *Pale; like a cold fish slab, walnuts; medium dry, frothy, positive but rather common, dry acidic end***

RUINART, BRUT *Penetrating, classy; dryish, steely, good mid-palate, still youthfully hard. April 1991**(**)*

DE SAINT GALL, CRU PREMIER, BRUT *Quickly dispersing bubbles; attractive though unknit, smoky; lightish, attractive, smoky charred flavour**(**)?*

ALAIN THIENOT, BRUT *Scented, violets; dry lean, attractive, still hard**(*)*

ALAIN THIENOT, ROSE *Palish, orange tinge; rather common; dry, boring, short**

DE VENOGE *Fine gold; slightly scented, fishy Pinot, walnuts; dry, good nutty flavour and length****

1986

Another hard winter. Late budding, but warm May advancing vegetation. After another cool period, sunshine and heat, with flowering towards the end of June in perfect conditions. Nevertheless, the cold had caused some *millerandage* and the warmth, *coulure*. High temperatures during the summer months followed by rain prior to picking on Sept 28 and finished the beginning of Nov.

Whether 1986 will be shipped as a vintage will depend on the quality of the top wines and, most importantly, on the economic climate. It is unlikely that any pronouncements will be made before the end of 1991.

1987

Budding took place in April, speedily and in excellent conditions, but this was followed by an unusually wet spring. The weather improved for flowering though rain returned in the second half of July. Three weeks of magnificent weather in Aug was followed by a cold, wet period that ran on into Sept. From the 8th to the 22nd, a hot, and humid Indian summer, some growers starting to pick on the 28th, others waiting until Oct 10. Although it rained during harvest, the grapes were healthy. A useful crop for replenishing non-vintage stocks but unlikely to be shipped as 'vintage'.

1988

As elsewhere in France, a high-quality vintage year though quantity more than 10% lower than 1987. In the context of the current overheated world demand, this was a serious shortfall. Satisfactory growing season, the vintage starting early, on Sept 19.

The '88s will not be put on the market until 1993, and then only if demand, quality and quantity meet on equal terms.

1989

Undoubtedly a vintage year. Mild weather, early sunny spring advancing the vegetation. Unfortunately severe frosts towards the end of April affected some 20% of the Champagne vineyards, reducing the potential harvest. May was sunny but there was a cold spell in the middle of the flowering. The summer, as in England, was exceptionally hot and sunny, leavened with light rain, resulting in an unusually early harvest, commencing Sept 4 on the Côte des Blancs (the Chardonnay), and a week later for the Pinot Noir. Equally unusual was a second harvest between Oct 10 and the beginning of Nov, the result of the interrupted flowering earlier in the year. Both crops were fully mature and of high quality. The net result of the double harvest was a large production, equivalent to 274 million bottles, though not considered sufficient for the champagne houses to replenish stocks, which should be equal to three years' shipments.

1990

Another exceptional year. A bumper crop of nearly 330 million kilos of grapes, making the equivalent of 288 million bottles, though not as abundant as 1982 (295 million) or 1983 (302 million bottles).

Once again, widespread frost damage in April, affecting 45% of the region in differing degrees, and unseasonable weather during the flowering period which caused *coulure* and, later, *millerandange*. Despite this, it was noted by mid-July that not only were there a remarkably large number of bunches but that the grapes were notably big. The summer was hot and dry. Rain in Sept was followed by cooling winds, both of which encouraged healthy maturation.

Because of the extended and interrupted flowering period, from as early as late May to as late as early July, the harvest was equally extended, beginning on Sept 11 on the Côte des Blancs and on the 24th for the Pinot Noirs.

1990 was also noted for the failure of the *négociants* and growers to renew long-term agreements, resulting in the upheavals of a free market – a situation resembling the end of the boom period reported in the British trade press just 119 years ago. *Plus ça change.*

1991

Recession causing a huge drop in sales, which might sober up growers' demands and steady the market. The weather will probably have the last word.

VINTAGE *PORT*

Vintage port has always been at the top end of the port market, a market that has had its ups and downs. Starting as a rough and ready red table wine in the late 17th century, the sweet fortified wine we know today was created by enterprising English merchants who developed the trade during the 18th century to an extent that scarcely seems credible now. The taste for port continued through the 19th century and reached new peaks in the 1920s. There followed three desultory decades: slump, wartime conditions, post-war restrictions and a disheartening lack of interest meant that, when I first visited Oporto in the autumn of 1953, it seemed that the once thriving port trade was on its last legs. Happily it is now thriving again.

Although referred to as 'the Englishman's wine', a nourishing cockle-warming beverage created by the English for the English, other equally cold and draughty northern European countries also imported the wine, Scandinavia in particular. Now the United States, a market-in-waiting, has started to take off—and the vanguard is vintage port. It must also be said that, although once almost the preserve of English shippers, a very large portion of modern port production is, quite fairly, in Portuguese hands. However, the pacemakers in style, certainly in the field of vintage port, are the very British Symington family who own the Dow, Graham, Warre, Quarles Harris, Smith Woodhouse and Gould Campbell brands, the Robertsons and, despite the un-English name, Guimaraens, with Taylor and Fonseca, plus multi-national-owned Cockburn, Croft, Martinez and Sandeman. Excellent wines are made by Portuguese firms, the best known for vintage port being Noval and Ferreira.

It is not the purpose of this chapter to cover all types of port but to put the wines and the vintages into perspective. I must remind readers that most of the port made and shipped is 'wood' port, port matured in wood rather than in bottle, and shipped for immediate consumption. Young 'ruby' port, older 'tawny' port: both types are sold under brand names. Also, rather confusingly, 'crusted' and 'late-bottled vintage' (LBV) port, the latter a pseudonym for what is, in effect, a fairly youthful ruby. A step in the right direction has, in my opinion, been the introduction of 'time-span' tawnies: 10, 20, even 30 years old. I love the inimitable pale-coloured, nutty-nosed old tawny. Having said this, the greatest heights are scaled by true vintage port: the *crème de la crème* of the lodge *lotes* following a particularly good vintage, bottled after two years and cellared until maturity. Notes of such wines and vintages follow.

c 1700

Unknown Contemporary bottle with almost stone-like, pitted sides, tall neck and wide-flanged string lip. Tawny, cloudy; strange un-vinous nose, touch of marzipan. All flavour lost. Deathly. *Oct 1985*

Unknown Onion-shaped bottle of the period. Very good level. Surprisingly deep, opaque centre, prune-like colour, amber rim; faded, sound and very definitely port; still fairly sweet and with body, excellent old port flavour and high, madeira-like, acidity. *Sept 1987****

c 1720

Unknown In contemporary hand-blown bottle. Deep-coloured, intense, brown with apple green rim; bouquet faint, slightly raisiny, touch of cinnamon; still sweet, quite full-bodied, spicy edge to flavour. *June 1987****

1734*****

A great 18th-century vintage.

1755***

Abundant but slump conditions.

1771–1774

All shipped as vintage years.

1775*****

Highest quality, good quantity reported.

1779, 1788, 1790

All offered in London as single vintages.

1791–1796

The trade in port reached its peak, with 45,000 pipes shipped to England in 1792.

1797*****

According to George Sandeman, writing in 1809, "the best port vintage ever known".

1804–1809

Fairly good vintages, in particular 1804 and 1806.

1811****

In common with virtually every European wine district, superb weather conditions produced magnificent wines.

1815****

Referred to by the British as the 'Waterloo' vintage.
Ferreira Aged in cask for about 50 years, bottled and recorked every 40 years. (These old wines take two years to recover their bouquets after recorking.) A pale but healthy amber with lemon tinge; woody and acidic at first but settled down after decanting, rich, waxy, still with fruit, slightly estery, like old lace; medium-sweet, medium-light, a wonderful spicy yet soft long flavour, madeira-like acidity, dry finish. *Four consistent notes, all from Ferreira's cellars, last tasted July 1991*****

1816–1819

Terrible vintages.

1820***

After many poor ones, this good vintage eagerly bought.
Ferreira Lovely bright pale amber; rich; high-toned, a bit varnishy; medium sweetness and body, soft, agreeable. *At a pre-sale tasting, April 1981****

1834*****

One of the most renowned of the mid-19th century.
Ferreira Last recorked 1980. Reputedly made from a single grape variety. Palish, a bit cloudy; high-toned; still sweet. *Tasted in a BBC recording studio for the* Today *programme, April 1981***
'C & S' (F Chamisso Filho & Silva) Velho Particular Amber tawny with rim that looked like olive oil; high-toned, madeira-like, singed, lemony; sweet, mouthfilling, and despite a taste like liquid linoleum, varnish, linseed oil and metheglin, marvellous acidity. Very good – in its way. *April 1986****
Roriz, Qta do Kopke's Roriz, the giant of the vintage but somewhat withered after a century and a half. This was one of 13 three-part moulded bottles removed from a country house in North Wales. Recorked in Jan 1878. Pale, pure amber; faded, rather medicinal and sound at first but after 30 minutes cloves and acetone; completely dried out, lean. *Bought at a Christie's sale and tasted Dec 1983**

1840***

Ferreira Warm amber; rich, peppery, spicy (cloves); a rich wine with very good end acidity. *Pre-sale, April 1981****

1847*****

Unequivocally the greatest vintage of the period, with around 30,000 pipes being shipped to England (but compare 1792).
Ferreira Records show that this was Ferreira's sweetest wine of the century. A medium-deep, rich yellow amber; rich, fat and fruity bouquet and flavour. Still very sweet, and perfectly balanced. *Last tasted July 1990***** for age.*
Shipper unknown Labelled "'Rare old Port' Vintage 1847, guaranteed over 65 years in wood. Bottled in Oporto 1913 for Marten & Co, New York". Short cork. Lovely old tawny colour with green rim; sweet, powdery, pungent and slightly resinous nose; medium sweetness and body. Rich but a touch of mercaptan on nose and palate that grew more noticeable but otherwise excellent flavour. *With Jack Strauch in New York, April 1983****
Shipper unknown Thought to be 1847 or 1851. In magnum. Good, lively, rosehip colour; high-toned, slightly varnishy, ethereal liquorice bouquet that settled down perfectly harmoniously; medium sweetness and body but powerful flavour, tremendous attack. *Bought at Christie's in 1983 and opened at a Rodenstock tasting, Sept 1987*****

1851****

Prince Albert's Great Exhibition lent its name to this excellent vintage.
Ferreira Amber, slightly cloudy; a bit decayed; fairly sweet and powerful. Marked though good acidity. *Pre-sale April 1981****
Stibbart Tasted twice, one with Freddie Cockburn who could not believe it wasn't a recent post-war vintage despite clearly embossed wax seal and bin label – and evidence that it had never been moved from the Gladstone cellar in Scotland until sold at Christie's in 1972. And next, when I recognised it, lunching at Christopher's in 1975. On both occasions, an amazingly deep colour; sound, fruity; sweet, rich, assertive flavour. Still the most magnificent old port I have ever drunk. *Old notes, but worth repeating.*
Shipper unknown Pale tawny, just a glimmer of red; old, high-toned, medium-sweet, faded, high acidity verging on acetic. *Oct 1981.*

1853****

Hankey Bannister One of three half-bottles from the cellars of Kingston Lyle Park. Clearly rebottled, and with this Sackville Street wine merchant's embossed capsule. Level top-shoulder. Warm amber colour with pale apple green rim; sweet, soft, vanilla, spicy and waxy old bouquet with a high-toned powdery scent that mellowed in the glass; fairly sweet, with a marvellously long spicy flavour masking fairly high acidity. Its flavour reminded me of a lovely old cognac. *Opened rather casually, not expecting much, at Chippenham Lodge for Walter Eigensatz, May 1988******

1854***

Another good 'comet' vintage.
Ferreira Slightly cloudy; rather low-keyed; some sweetness, good 'grip'. *Pre-sale April 1981****

1858***

Ferreira The first bottle brown, with maderised nose. Unclean and acidic. The second, a month later; bright amber mahogany with green rim; sound, gentle, sweet, 'warm', excellent. *Pre-sale April 1981. At best*****

1863*****

A great vintage.
Ferreira Tasted twice, once at the great pre-sale tasting in 1981, nose a bit mushroomy, sweet, high acidity. More recently: palish amber; muscadelle and lime bouquet. A lovely old wine, medium-sweet (1.4 Beaumé), with lime-like acidity, holding well. *Last tasted March 1988*****
Johnstone & Sadler's Probably bottled by them in 1866. From a Norfolk cellar, tasted twice. Bottle variation. The first, in 1977, drying out, ethereal, clean. The second with original wax seal embossed "PORT, Johnstone & Sadler". Ullaged almost to low-shoulder. Spongy cork. Pale yet still with a ruddy glow; faded, old and varnishy; a vestige of sweetness, light and faded, yet with gentle old flavour, good acidity. It held well and charmed my guests. *Last tasted Sept 1982****
Shipper unknown Rewaxed. Hard cork. Fairly deep for age, slightly hazy; clean, lovely, rounded, surprisingly un-pungent bouquet reminding me of Spanish root and liquorice; still sweet, alcoholic, nice fruit though faded. Clean. Beautiful. Outstanding for its age. *April 1986*****

1864, 1865 *and* 1867

The first two vintages not very good, but some good wines made in 1867. None tasted.

1868****

A great pre-phylloxera vintage. Generally declared, with the exception of Croft. Sandeman, "the biggest ever" and "very dry", considered the finest.
Martinez An old note. The only '68 tasted. Faded, drying out, yet retaining power. Acidic. *From Sherborne Castle, Sept 1976****

1869***

"Total absence of quality" reported by Ridley's trade journal. Shipped only by Croft.

1870*****

Made under most favourable circumstances though "ravages of phylloxera noted – one quinta, whose production averaged 50 pipes in the mid-1840s, was reduced to 2 pipes in 1870" (*Ridley's Wine Trade Monthly*). 19 port houses declared and shipped this vintage, the greatest between 1863 and 1878.
Warre Labelled "Warre's/1870 Vintage Port matured, and bottled in 1918". Recorked in Oporto at some later date. Yellow-tinged tawny; sweet, quite good despite acetone-edged aged bouquet; fairly sweet, very rich and spicy, but with a medicinal flavour, a cross between cough mixture and *Punt è Mes*. *March 1985***
Agrello (José Carlos Agrello) Palish tawny amber; aged, meaty, liquorice bouquet; fairly sweet, very rich, citrus-like and raisiny flavour, ethereal, good quality and length. *Jan 1985****

1871

Spring cold and wet, oidium in the vineyards, Aug intensely hot, heavy rains during the harvest. Not declared.
Delaforce's Royal Palace Port by special warrant to His Majesty the King of Portugal. Bin label "PORT 1871": I include this because of its provenance. It was either an old white port or more likely a cask-aged 'vintage tawny'. Tasted twice: good levels; palish warm amber, apple green rim; high-toned, raisiny; medium sweetness and weight, good rich middle palate, lovely warming endtaste. Volatile acidity on the high side. From the Aalholm Castle cellar, Denmark. *April 1989***

1872***

16 shippers. Not tasted but of good repute.

1873***

Also shipped by 16 port houses. Only one tasted, Meyer's, drying out though still a good drink. *1972*

1874*

After all the activity in 1870, 1872 and 1873, only three port houses shipped this vintage. None tasted.

1875****

18 shippers. Light, fine, elegant wines – as in Bordeaux – but small production. Only one tasted, bottled by Bell, Rannie of Perth for the Gladstone family. Showing its age (in 1972) but still some sweetness, gentle, faded but refined.

1877***

Ferreira An appealing amber colour; good spicy bouquet and flavour, still sweet. Lovely aftertaste. *Pre-sale, April 1981*****

1878*****

20 port houses declared and shipped. None tasted recently but older notes still relevant.
Cockburn Recorked in 1920. Lovely, sound, spicy, holding well. *In 1972*****
Dow According to George Saintsbury in his *Notes on a Cellarbook*, "one of the best ports of the century". Still powerful and punchy. *In 1967****
Harvey's Sealed "Port, 1878, Rich", still sweet, powerful and lovely. *In 1978*****

1880**

Not a generally declared vintage. Only six shippers.
Vinho Velho do Porto, Frasqueira Particular Bottled in 1980 from a cask in the cellars of the Duke of Palmella. Tasted twice: palish amber tawny; sweet, touch of muscadelle, high-toned, pungent; palate sweet, soft and gentle, with lovely singed flavour and madeira-like acidity. Fragrant finish. *Last tasted pre-sale, March 1986*****

1881***

Optimistically declared by 20 port shippers but never lived up to expectations.
Martinho (Qta de São) Amber, clouded (not decanted); meaty, liquorice bouquet; fairly sweet, fabulous racy flavour, excellent length, acidity and aftertaste. *June 1985****

1882–1883

Substandard vintages. Not declared.

1884*****

21 shippers got this right, but I am not sure that Charles Walter Berry did when he described it (in 1935) as "the last of the classic vintages".
Cockburn Certainly excellent. *Tasted in 1972.*
Shipper unknown Excellent. *Tasted in 1967.*

1885*

Moderate. Only five shippers declared.

1886

Not declared.

1887***

Popular and good vintage. 20 port houses shipped it to celebrate Queen Victoria's Golden Jubilee.
Sandeman Four bottles from Tim and David Sandeman's cellars decanted 6.30pm after standing for 6½ hours. Crumbly corks. Rich amber tawny in decanters, more buff-coloured in glasses. Acetone and liquorice bouquet; drying out, faded, nutty flavour, good length. Seemed better at midnight. *At* The Great Vintage Wine Book *dinner in Zurich, Oct 1983****
Schofield Shipper unknown but bottled by Schofield Bros, Manchester, who, like many good wine merchants, went out of business in the 1950s. Wax capsule impressed "1887 PORT". Three-part moulded bottle. Level into neck. Fine mature colour; fine old spirity nose, spicy, nutmeg; losing sugar, weight and fruit but very clean. Excellent. *From a Christie's sale, Sept 1985*****
'Starling' In original heavy-based mould-blown bottle. Cork, much of it blackened, branded "Starling" (the name of the General Steam Navigation Company's ship – all were named after birds). In May 1981: pale tawny, hint of red; remnants of fruit; still retaining some sweetness, body and power. Held well. A second bottle, recorked *c* 1934 by Oliver & Laver, was in excellent condition despite a slightly varnishy bouquet. Well balanced. Must have been a big wine. *March 1982*****

1888–1889

Not declared.

1890***

Tough tannic wines. 20 shippers.
Cockburn Variable, one attractive, one 'pricked'. *Early 1970s.*
Dow Bottled by Schofield: fragrant and refined. *Tasted in 1979*

1891–1892*

1891 not declared, 1892: 10 shippers. Not tasted.

1893***

Number of shippers unknown.
Dow Palish, tawny, yellow rim; low-keyed but sound; drying out, gentle, faded, but otherwise in excellent condition. *Sept 1983*****

1894**

Moderately good. 13 shippers.
Sandeman Holding remarkably well, tasted twice. *1966*

1895

Not declared, which does not mean that only poor wines were made but that, as always, commercial factors played a part. In any case, at the time the major shippers would be considering a declaration, they were aware of the higher quality and great potential of the 1896s.

1896****

A good, well-received vintage, declared by 24 shippers.
Cockburn Tasted several times. Consistently good for age. Pale but rich tawny – a better colour than the 1900; sweet, chocolaty, liquorice-like bouquet; still some sweetness and considerable body. A rich and distinctly powerful wine. *Last tasted Feb 1990*****
Cockburn (believed to be) Capsules embossed 1896. One bottle opened for further identification but the cork too crumbly. Excellent level, into neck. Medium, very rich tawny, amber rim; showing a lot of age on the nose, meaty, rich, chocolaty; medium-sweet, full-bodied for its age and with powerful flavour. Dry, slightly acidic finish. Bin label information probably correct. *Feb 1990*****
Croft Branded cork. Pale autumnal tawny, no red; very sweet nose, lovely character, showing age but sound and still fragrant after eight hours; medium-sweet, good middle-flavour and an excellent 'warm' dry finish. *A half-bottle, Oct 1984*****
Eira Velha, Qta One of the oldest quintas in the Douro, a vineyard since 1588 and owned since 1809 by the Newman family, traders in wool and wine established in Oporto in 1735. Confusingly, they traded as Hunt, Roope and their vintage port brand was Tuke Holdsworth. Two magnums from the Newman family cellars in Devon, and probably the same stock as the magnums of Tuke '96 tasted in 1952 and 1968. At 84 years of age, both had a palish but healthy appearance. The first had a sweet, old, spirity nose, a whiff of mushroom; plummy, peppery but some decay. The second had a soft sweet bouquet with a touch of hardness and spirit lurking beneath. Drying out, lighter than the other magnum, faded but sound. *Both tasted Oct 1980***
Sandeman Alas, on two occasions unclean and over-the-hill, once in 1967, later, with a hazy unhealthy appearance; muffled, malty nose; first sip not bad but a grubby, yeasty finish. *Last tasted March 1982.*
Skinner & Rook's Shipper unknown, bottled by this old established Leicester wine merchant. Low-shoulder. Pale, no red; sweet nose and taste, a bit varnishy, with attenuated spicy finish. Good for age and level. *From the Forman-Hardy family cellar near Nottingham, June 1984**
Taylor Lead capsule embossed "Skinner & Rook" (the bottler). Pale, rosehip orange; light, peppery at first, opened up rich, scented, after an hour, glorious; still surprisingly sweet, lean yet good fruit and texture, elegant, excellent acidity. *From Bernard Rhodes' cellar, April 1991******

1897****

Coming hard on the heels of the heavily marketed '96, the '97, though very good, had to take a back seat. Only seven port houses shipped the Royal Diamond Jubilee vintage.
Sandeman Following the prolific 1896 vintage, there was a shortage of brandy to make the '97. Sandeman, in desperation, used Scotch whisky. A tregnum (three-bottle bottle) from Tim Sandeman's cellar was magnificent in 1976. More recently from a rather odd-looking bottle with "Sandeman" embossed on a raised tablet: still a touch of ruby; sound, meaty but madeira-like nose; medium-sweet, full-bodied, rich, fruity with a powerful tangy tawny finish. *Last tasted Sept 1987*****

1898–1899

The first not declared, the second by only one shipper. In any case, the market was saturated and palates sated.

1900*****

The first of four classic vintages declared, rather neatly, at four-year intervals. 22 shippers.

Cockburn Sweet, vinous bouquet that held well. Drying out, elegant, very nice texture, complete and sound. *March 1982*****

Ferreira Very much a plummier Portuguese-style vintage compared with the British shippers'. *April 1981****

Niepoort A *colheita*, matured in wood, put into demijohns in 1955 and finally bottled in 1972. The colour of a good old 'vintage tawny': deep amber with greenish rim and rich legs; high-toned madeira-like bouquet and acidity; sweet, showing age yet fleshy. The oldest of several excellent though sometimes idiosyncratic Niepoort vintages. *March 1988****

Noval, Qta do In cask for approximately 40 years. Stencilled bottles. Recorked fairly recently. Palish amber; high-toned, varnishy, fragrant, spicy; still sweet though lightish weight, with very good raisiny flavour, excellent depth and aftertaste. High strength and high acidity. *At a Noval tasting at the Portuguese Embassy, Nov 1989****

1901–1902

Not shipped as vintage wines.

1903

Not generally declared.

Gonzalez Byass Bottled in Oporto, 1906. Fairly pale orange-tinged tawny; spirity, no fruit; medium-sweet, lightish, slightly unclean finish. *From the shipper's cellar, Nov 1980.*

1904****

25 shippers. Though reckoned at the time to be a lighter vintage than 1900, the wines have kept very well.

Cockburn Due to the shortage of local brandy, Cockburn used brandy from the Azores for their '04. Tasted twice, old but firm in 1972. More recently, bottled by the Army & Navy Cooperative Society: palish but with a healthy glow; smoky, high-toned, slightly varnishy, brandy laid bare; medium-sweet, elegant, clean, dry finish. *Last tasted March 1982*****

Martinez "Martinez Gassiot & Co Ltd/Oporto/Finest 1904". Recorked. Very pale, no red but healthy appearance; old, rather sherry-like, touch of liquorice; fairly sweet, good rich old flavour but no fruit left. *March 1985****

Sandeman Tasted several times, bottled by different merchants. Harvey's and Avery's both very good. Most recently: fully branded cork; pale but very lively; delicate bouquet that blossomed in the glass; sweeter than expected, lean, with a dry spirity/acidic finish, but very good for age. *Last tasted March 1982*****

Smith Woodhouse Rather unusually, a glass button on the shoulder embossed with the name of the bottler "RW Taylor (& Co) Barton/1904". Cork branded "Smith Woodhouse". Pale but healthy; sweet, rich, spicy, fragrant; medium sweetness and body, some fat, fruit, good long finish. Still a powerful wine. *Oct 1984*****

Taylor Excellent level, original cork disintegrated. Palish, very little red; sweet and dusty, restrained though ethereal; sweet, lightish though with a powerful, spirity dry finish. Sound. Fragrant. *Taylor's tercentenary tasting at Christie's, April 1991*****

1905–1907

Not declared though some eventually bottled.

Sandeman (1906) Unknown time in cask, bottled in their lodge. Pale tawny; light, spirity; still surprisingly sweet though loss of body and fruit. Nice gentle flavour, fair length, slightly singed aftertaste. *May 1983***

1908*****

Great vintage. 26 shippers.

Cálem Chanceleiros Probably cask-aged. Palish pure amber, apple green rim; high, madeira-like acidity; still sweet. Good old flavour. Sound. *With Dr Cálem, March 1988****

Cockburn Arguably the greatest-ever Cockburn. Tasted several times. At a pre-sale tasting in 1984, one bottled by Skinner & Rook, level just below top-shoulder: palish, orange-tinged, appealing; fragrant, sultana-like, a whiff like turpentine giving away its age; still fairly sweet, assertive, powerful. Most recently, from an old three-part moulded bottle, top of lead capsule embossed "Cockburn's 1908 Port", fully branded cork, level top-shoulder. Palish ruddy-hued old tawny; good fruit, touch of mint and liquorice, fully opened out after 40 minutes, sweet, slightly raisiny, glorious, and still excellent the next day. Medium-sweet, full-bodied, very rich, good texture. A very assertive heavyweight, ethereal, cognac-like, fabulous flavour. Great wine. *Last tasted Nov 1990******

Croft Four consistently good notes, the first and last, coincidentally, from the same stock. Most recently, opened to celebrate Dr John Potter's 70th birthday. The port had decanted bright (through a matron's silk stocking!) and still had a lovely colour; a touch of age, old liquorice, on the nose; still sweet and fleshy though fading, with a good, dry, somewhat peppery finish. *Last tasted at Wadham College, Oxford, March 1990*****

Dow Originally purchased as an unknown '08. Wax seal crisply and delicately impressed "Hill Thompson, PORT 1908, Edinburgh". Having knocked off and broken the neck to retain the cork in one piece I found it clearly branded "DOW'S Vintage 1908 bottled 1910". The level had been good, well into the neck but the colour was pale, rosy-hued. The nose when first poured smelled of old cork, a bit mushroomy. It remained restrained, low-keyed. Medium sweetness and weight, elegant, very flavoury, good length but with a distinctly dry finish. Another, identical, a year later. *Last tasted April 1991****

Ferreira Lovely warm tawny; still sweet, rich, delicious bouquet and flavour. *Last tasted March 1989*****

Gould Campbell Palish; harmonious, faded but sound; sweeter than expected. Very flavoury. Delightful. *March 1982*****

Graham Very good in 1967. Still an excellent warm ruddy colour; glorious bouquet, spicy, fine brandy; drying out a little, not fleshy but great length, excellent finish. *Last tasted 1985******

Offley First tasted March 1984: cork drawn for identification in a substantial private cellar. Bottled by Skinner & Rook, fully branded, and the wine sound. Another opened at the pre-sale tasting three months later. The third, believed from the same cellar. Consistent notes: pale amber tawny; light; sound, liquorice bouquet and flavour. Medium-sweet, fading but firm. Good acidity. From a different cellar: plain wax capsule but cork branded "Offley Boa Vista 1908", level into neck. Palish old tawny, amber green rim; a sweet, gentle, dusty bouquet that opened up nicely; still sweet on the palate, powerful flavour, lean yet some flesh, taste of liquorice, dry finish. Overtones of old age, and acidity catching up. *Last tasted Nov 1990. At best*****

Taylor Low neck. Cork completely disintegrated on removal. Palish amber, green rim; rich, peppery old fruit, then meaty, chocolaty; medium sweetness and body, like an old Verdelho, 'hot' finish. *April 1991****

Shipper unknown Recorked by Skinner & Rook in the 1930s. Very good level. Palish, lively, ruddy glow; low-keyed, waxy, sound; medium sweetness and body but lacking length, probably due to recorking. *In the Forman-Hardy cellar, March 1984.*

1910***

Good but not declared.

Gonzalez Byass Bottled 1913. Palish, a blush of red; nice, slight, raisiny bouquet; sweet, lightish, delicious. *Pre-sale, Nov 1980****

1911***

Good vintage but only one loyal (King George V Coronation) shipper. Other port houses concentrated on shipping the '12.

Sandeman Tasted several times in the 1960s, prior to discovery of a remarkable bin-full at Hopetoun House, sold by Christie's in 1967. Lovely wine. *Nov 1964*****

1912*****

The last great classic vintage of the period. 25 shippers. The best are still excellent.

Cockburn Tasted many times. The last two notes in the mid-1980s, both bottles with fully branded corks, both with excellent levels. Fairly pale but with an attractive rosy hue; fragrant, forthcoming, one with light crisp fruit on the nose, the other a bit high-toned, varnishy and with peppery alcohol. But both fabulous on the palate, still sweet, firm, with the power and backbone I usually associate with Taylor's, plus cinnamon spiciness and great length. *Last at a pre-sale tasting, June 1984******

Ferreira Four notes, all bottles from Ferreira's remarkable old-wine cellar, the biggest and best stock of old vintages in Oporto*. Though pale and fully mature, more plummy-coloured and pinker than the usual amber tawny I associate with ageing in cask; also more plummy, prune-like fruit on the nose. On the palate sweet, with good fruit, power, length and aftertaste. *March 1988******

Taylor Tasted 11 times over the last 20-odd years, all but one extremely good. Two in 1987 with lead capsules embossed "PORT 1912" and corks fully branded. However, one with a very worm-eaten cork and ullage upper mid-shoulder. It was acetic on nose, still refined but with a yeasty endtaste. The other, from the same cellar, had a perfect cork and level, a lovely warm rose-tinted tawny colour with amber rim; spirity, dusty and muffled when the cork drawn but 15 minutes after decanting rich and spicy – and held its richness all day. Still fairly sweet, lean, powerful but refined, great length, lovely acidity. Perfect. Most recently, recorked. Very sweet, lovely, slightly raisiny flavour, good length, opening up beautifully. *June 1987******

1913–1916

The first three years affected respectively by drought, mildew and intense heat. Good in 1916, but, doubtless due to wartime and economic factors, not declared.

1917***

A relatively light, supple and attractive vintage declared by 15 shippers.

Capucho, Fonseca and Frias Lds's 'Celebration Porto Velho' An agreeable oddity from a Portuguese private cellar. Bright amber; raisiny nose; sweet, some fat and flesh, good flavour and preservation. *Nov 1980****

Delaforce Tasted on two occasions, both in Oporto. Both good. Both deeper in colour than expected of a '17; very sound and appealing bouquet, with a plum/prune richness; both drying out but still fleshy. Excellent firm fruit, flavour and balance. *Last tasted, Nov 1979*****

Ferreira Pale; sweet and delicate on nose and palate. A curious aftertaste. *At pre-sale tasting, April 1981***

Quarles Harris Pale, very little red left; medium-sweet, lightish weight. Faded and showing age on nose and palate but sound. *At David Rutherford's, March 1981****

Taylor The first, in 1989, believed to be Taylor: old tawny; very old nose; drying out and faded. Next, capsule and cork branded 1917. Surprisingly deep, warm, ruddy; singed, meaty, chocolaty; sweet, fullish, good long rich flavour. *Last noted at Taylor tasting, April 1991****

1918–1919

1918 – scorching summer, small quantity. Vintage not declared. The following year abundant but few shipped as 'vintage'. Offley reputed to be good.

1920****

23 shippers. Small production but high quality. Sturdy, and if well kept can still be very good.

Croft First tasted in 1952, seven notes, variable condition. Of the three bottles tasted since 1980, one had too much volatile acidity. The other two: palish old tawny; lovely soft harmonious bouquet; still sweet and powerful, fleshy, perfect flavour and condition. *Nov 1986*****

Graham Four consistently good notes. Lead capsule embossed "Graham 1920": good colour, some depth and a beautiful red tinge; lively Spanish-root bouquet; fairly sweet but losing weight, a bit spirity but delicate and flavoury. *Nov 1980; should still be good if well cellared*****

Taylor Several notes. The last, bottled by Skinner & Rook: palish warm amber; showing age at first, fragrant, liquorice, opening up beautifully, harmonious, a whiff like Havana cigars; medium sweetness and weight, smooth, refined. *Taylor tasting at Christie's, April 1991*****

1921

Unlike France and Germany where intense heat scorched the vines, in Portugal the grapes failed to ripen fully. This is not to say that port wine was not made. Indeed Rebello Valente at 40 years old was delicate and delicious.

1922***

Another small crop though of nice quality. Lightish in style like the 1917. 18 shippers.

Avery bottling, shipper not stated. Medium tawny; rather spirity nose; medium sweetness and weight, very dry finish. Showing its age. *A magnum, July 1981****

Martinez One of the problems of old vintage port is identification. The owner thought this was '19 or '22. It had a plain wax seal. The cork confirmed "Martinez" but the vintage was not visible. Level good. Pale, little red left. Showing a lot of age on nose and palate. Spirity, rather acidic but some sweetness and good fruit. We opted for '22. *At Christie's, Oct 1990***

* *The word Oporto used, though all the port lodges are actually on the south side of that large, rather drab city, on the left bank of the Douro at Vila Nova de Gaia.*

Porto Velho Unknown Portuguese house. Tawny brown; nose sour at first but developed rich stably bouquet. Not very attractive. *Vila Nova de Gaia, Nov 1980.*

1923**

A bigger crop than 1922 and good quality wine made. Despite this—probably for commercial reasons—not declared. However Offley, who had started to ship their single-quinta wine in good but undeclared vintages, a practice more recently adopted by Taylor with Vargellas, and Graham with Malvedos, put their Boa Vista on the market. It was light, somewhat ethereal, though very pleasant when tasted, more than once, in the late 1970s.

1924****

Below-average production. Good quality. 18 shippers. The port market recapturing a new high. By and large the wines are keeping well.

Graham Six notes. All but one good. Very attractive lively colour; marvellously rich ripe bouquet; still sweet, very much the Graham style, warm, soft, delicious. *Last tasted March 1983******

Taylor 13 notes, starting in 1953, but only four since 1980. Consistently good, though high-toned and perhaps lacking length. Unusually sweet for Taylor and for its age. An immediacy about the bouquet, at best rich, mellow, ethereal, scented; very positive flavour, the characteristic Taylor backbone, dry finish. *June 1991*****

1925*

A year of pests and diseases. Poor summer saved by good late harvest conditions. Not declared.

Offley Boa Vista Bottled by the Army & Navy Cooperative Society (later known as the Army & Navy Stores, whose wine department was legendary). Pale but attractive, a tawny hue; nose light, still fruity but a bit 'dusty'; still sweet, sound, very pleasant flavour, with a dry, lightly spirity, finish. *Last tasted, pre-sale, Nov 1979****

1926*

Almost the opposite, weather-wise, to 1925. Too hot, too dry, small yield. Not declared.

1927*****

A great classic, the best between 1912 and 1935. Declared, at the top of the market, by a record 30 shippers.

Cockburn A great classic. Tasted (and drunk) many times since 1959 and never disappointing. Of the four tasted in the mid- to late 1980s, the best bottled by Arnold Perret & Co of Gloucester, and consumed at my 60th birthday lunch in May 1987. A filmy crust, decanted clear and bright. Medium depth, lively ruddy ruby hue; perfect bouquet, low-keyed and spirity at first but after 20 minutes opened up, spicy, nutty; medium-sweet (as always, since its extreme youth), but fullish body, firm, lean, lissom, gloriously rich and spicy, silky tannin and acidity, marvellous length. *Last tasted Dec 1989******

Croft Many notes. Two recently: a rather unconvincing colour, and cloudy; sweet, creamy, high-toned; still sweet and fairly powerful, lean, alcoholic and a bit hard. Dry acidic finish. Classic but thinning. *Last tasted Dec 1989****

Dow First tasted in 1955: soft, full, attractive. More recently: fully mature colour, palish rosy-tinged tawny; light, spicy, high-toned madeira-like bouquet; still fairly sweet, medium weight, faded though remnants of power, good length, acidity. *Last tasted Dec 1989****

Fonseca Also first tasted in 1955. Many good notes except for a poor bottle in 1971. The best, bottled by Grantham's of Sherborne, removed from a good private cellar in Dorset and tasted pre-sale in 1988. Most recent: fine colour, still fairly deep; extremely good rich classic liquorice 'Pontefract cakes' nose; still sweet, fullish, marvellous flavour, touch of eucalyptus, lots of bite and length. A great '27. *Last tasted Jan 1990******

Graham Three notes in the mid-1950s: very sweet, rich, chocolaty but brandy showing. A lovely chocolaty-nosed, beautifully balanced bottle in Oporto in 1967 and, in 1971, showing full maturity with good rich bouquet and flavour though drying out a little. An odd, hopefully unrepresentative bottle at a major tasting of '27s in 1989. Strange clear glass bottle. Rosehip tawny; slightly scented, malty and acidic nose; sweetish, lean, trace of aniseed. Most recently, slight bottle variation: sweet, chocolaty, waxy, spirity; lovely texture and flavour. *Last noted at Graham tasting, May 1991. At best*****

Martinez Several notes from the mid-1960s, some variable. At best excellent. Still fairly deep in colour; high-toned with brandy showing at first but mellowed in glass; medium-sweet, elegant, spicy. *Oct 1981*****

Niepoort Rolf Niepoort, like me, was born in 1927 and his father kept a cask and bottled off 360 bottles in 1941, all of which were recorked in 1978. Several of these very recognisable dumpy bottles have been presented to me, and drunk, over the past five years. Five consistent notes: a fairly deep, rich, mahogany colour; well developed, very attractive, slightly raisiny, chocolaty, spicy old wax and liquorice nose; considerable sweetness balanced by crisp, slightly citrus components, touch of tar, high alcohol. A startling contrast to the English shippers' classic ports but extremely good in its way. *Dec 1989*****

Noval, Qta do Seven notes. One bottle spoiled by a poor cork. Still fairly deep, richly coloured; massively impressive, penetrating bouquet, slightly medicinal but fragrant, rich, spicy vanilla, black treacle; medium-sweet—drying out slightly, though fairly full-bodied. Intense, almost Taylor-like backbone and tannin. Firm fruit. Good length. Dry finish. *Last tasted Jan 1991*****

Rebello Valente It had "REBELLO VALENTE PORT" embossed on the original lead capsule. The owner thought it was a '35 but the cork revealed all: it was clearly branded "1927". The level was top-shoulder; colour a pale, warm amber, no red left; nose faint but sound; still very sweet on palate. Lightish, lean but flavoury. Acidity catching up. *Sept 1990***

Rosa, Qta de la Oporto-bottled. A pretty colour; forthcoming, ethereal nose showing age; medium-sweet, soft, strange flavour, dry finish. *Tasted Dec 1989***

Sandeman Six notes, the best from a 'cock' or 'tregnum' (three-bottle bottle) from the Sandeman family cellars. Most recent: palish but lovely colour with hint of cherry red and mature yellow rim; nutty-nosed, opened up in the glass; fairly sweet, now lightish, long, lean, spirity but elegant. Dry finish. *Last tasted Dec 1989*****

Taylor First tasted in 1954 and on 19 occasions since. Slight variations which would seem to depend partly on the bottler but mainly upon cellaring. One of the best was bottled by Justerini & Brooks, tasted in 1973. Another, from Earl Bathhurst's cellars at Cirencester Park, a marvel in a half-bottle, beautiful when first opened, rich, spicy, developing a strawberry-like nose five hours later. A bottle in 1989: fairly deep, lively ruby, lovely graduation of colour; very attractive classic 'British' liquorice bouquet; drying out, full-bodied, hot, high alcohol, fig-like fruit, good length, dry finish. Most recently rich, incredible depth and power; very sweet, mouthfilling,

rounded, still tannic. *Last tasted April 1991******
Warre Several notes, all good. Now palish but like all the top '27s, lively-looking with ruby tinge; gentle, fragrant, classic bouquet of great depth; very sweet, full-bodied. High alcohol, extract, tannin and acidity. Impressive. *Last tasted Dec 1989****** *Will continue to improve.*

1928**

A good vintage but, at the time a declaration might have been considered, the economic slump was biting and the market for vintage port, then solely British, was sated with the abundantly shipped 1927.
Lagrima do Douro José Francisco Frias da Fonseca. Very much the Portuguese style, matured in cask: deep, firm amber gold with touch of orange and rich green rim; fabulous sweet honeyed nose; drying out and fading somewhat but still some fat, with a clean though short finish. *Nov 1980****

1929**

Small quantity, good quality but not declared for similar reasons to the 1928. Boa Vista shipped: flavoury in 1967.

1930

Unsettled weather. Intense heat damaged the grapes. Not declared. Only one tasted, from a quarter cask of Vargellas, in 1977.

1931*****

A splendid – nay great – vintage but, for reasons stated earlier, slump conditions and cellars still stocked with '27s made the British port houses, who at that time dominated the trade, decide not to declare. Though good wine was made, but the towering reputation of this vintage rests on Noval, a wine I have long since thought of and described as the Everest of vintage ports.
Foz, Qta do Warm amber brown; sweet, lovely, harmonious bouquet, touch of brown treacle; fairly sweet, full, excellent flavour, weight and condition. *March 1988******
Noval, Qta do I have been privileged to note this on no fewer than 16 occasions and at fairly regular intervals since 1972. A variety of bottlings, all good, some unstated on cork or capsule but including Justerini & Brooks, H & G Simonds of Reading and, perhaps the most superlatively typical, by Fearen, Block, Bridges, Routh, consumed in 1985. Also one, at a Wine and Food Society luncheon in Chicago in 1982, "shipped by Avery's and imported from Bristol, where it had been bottled in 1933 by Louis Glunz, Lincolnwood, Ill.". Both still very deep, opaque at the centre; huge, sweet, spirity bouquet that reminded me of caramelised raisins and then, as it opened up in the glass, of prunes and cloves. Still sweet but not overpoweringly so, full-bodied, an assertive prune-like flavour, hot, peppery, mouthfilling, still plump, with marvellous acidity. *Last tasted Dec 1989****** *Years of life left.*
Noval Nacional Some of the above Novals might have been made from the 10% of the vineyard traditionally planted, ungrafted, with the local fruiting varieties. Usually however, "Nacional" appears somewhere on bin label, wax seal and/or cork. This particular bottle came from a Nacional wooden case, had a black wax seal and its cork branded "Noval 1931 bottled 1933". I noted its amazing high-toned bouquet which reminded me of eau de cologne, Armagnac and a sort of ultra-refined liquorice. Although only medium-sweet, incredibly full-bodied, a rich, bitter-sweet wine, spicy, of great length. *At dinner at Tawfig Khoury's, San Diego, Oct 1982******
Martinez Surprisingly pale, very mature-looking yet fine, rich colour; ethereal, waxy, wisp of fruit; sweet, lightish and delicate, complete and sound though fading. Good acidity. Really very good but needed drinking. *Jan 1981******
Niepoort Several notes: one clearly labelled "bottled 1938 decanted (ie rebottled) 1979" with a lovely, sweet, soft, fragrant bouquet; sweet on the palate. A charmer. Another, rather paler in colour with delicate grapey nose and fabulous sultana-like flavour. Yet another, very deep-coloured; a nose like syrup of figs, very sweet, full, rich and rounded. But all good to drink. *Dec 1989*****

1932

Poor year, not declared.
Gonzalez Byass Oporto-bottled. Rather dull amber tawny; not bad but no fruit; faded but sound. Dry finish. *Nov 1980**

1933***

Early flowering, heat-wave, early harvest. Not declared, for market reasons and because of the promise of the 1934s then, even more so, the 1935s.
Niepoort Oporto-bottled 1936. Pale but warm old tawny; very good bouquet, sweet, nutty, raisiny; still pleasantly sweet though thinning and fading. Excellent flavour and length. *July 1988*****

1934****

Once one of my favourite vintages. Fairly scarce as only 12 shippers declared. Worth looking out for.
Ferreira Considerable colour loss; scent like the liqueur, Kahlua; medium sweetness and body yet more assertive than its appearance indicated. *March 1981****
Fonseca Several consistently good notes starting in 1953. In 1983: still deep-coloured; lively peppery nose; fairly sweet, fullish body, powerful, hot, rich, a little unyielding. *Last tasted July 1983*****(*)
Foz, Qta do Slightly weak rim; showing some age; sweet, pleasing weight, fully mature. *March 1988****
Martinez Several notes, deeply coloured in 1957. Palish, fully mature appearance 30 years later; bouquet of singed caramel; still fairly sweet, ageing gracefully, elegant, with very good length. *Last tasted June 1987*****
Noval, Qta do Several notes. Lively colour, touch of pink; drying out a little, lean, firm, flavoury. Excellent length, lovely aftertaste. *Last tasted Aug 1984*****
Taylor Tasted only twice. Rich, beautiful in 1966, and, strangely, one late-bottled in 1977: pale old tawny from extended cask-age; attractive old tawny cobnuts bouquet; fairly sweet, lovely flavour, dry finish. An old 'vintage tawny' of high quality. *Chez Morales-Doria, Mexico City, April 1980*****
Shipper F.S. unknown Thought to be Fonseca, possibly Warre. Soft waxy nose harbouring brandy, developed richly; sweet, soft, silky, Spanish-root flavour, long lingering aftertaste. *Oct 1987******

1935*****

A classic year. Similar harvest conditions to 1934 but smaller crop. Market slowly recovering. 15 shippers. The best still superb, with many years of life ahead.
Cockburn Notes starting in 1953, four since 1980. Flavoury but spirity, never my favourite '35. Now fully mature appearance, bouquet and palate. Sweet, gentle bouquet; medium-sweet, lightish and lean. Brandy and acidity a bit obtrusive. Good length. *Nov 1990****
CSC Campbell W & T Restell's (City auctioneers and wholesalers) brand: pink-tinged tawny; gentle, vanilla,

still fairly sweet. *Produced 'out of a hat' by Bill Skitt, who once worked for Restell's, on his 65th birthday, Aug 1984****

Foz, Qta do Similar colour to the '31; lovely fruit, harmonious, perfection; fairly sweet and full-bodied, good texture and length. *Tasted twice in March 1988*****

Graham Several notes since 1955. Glorious. Good rich mature colour; marvellous bouquet, liquorice and prunes, some spirit now showing; fairly sweet, brandy sheathed in fleshy fruit, fragrant, perfect acidity, length. *Marvin Overton's 50th birthday dinner, Fort Worth, Feb 1985******

Niepoort *Colheita* (matured in cask) Orange amber; very rich, nutty, estery, almost madeira-like acidity; better flavour than nose, rich, ethereal, refined, long dry finish. *Last tasted Oct 1986****

Sandeman Several notes. Now palish, very tawny; pleasant liquorice-like bouquet; still sweet, fullish, classic soft waxy flavour. *Last tasted May 1987*****

Smith Woodhouse Bottled by Laing of Sunderland. Rather tired-looking; sweet gentle mature bouquet and flavour. Lightish, dry, peppery, slightly acidic finish. *Pre-sale tasting June 1980***

Taylor Outstandingly the best 1935 and one of the greatest ports of this century. Tasted (and drunk) on 22 occasions since 1953. My notes describe its appearance as ranging from medium to very deep, but this might well result from variations of light in dining rooms as well as different bottlings. The bouquet and taste more consistently marvellous: full, rich, spicy, touch of vanilla and liquorice, overall harmony, depth and power; still sweet, fairly full-bodied, almost chewy, with the inimitable Taylor backbone, great length and ethereal aftertaste. Perfection. The most recent, a pair, Oporto-bottled and recorked in 1986. One was horrid: codliver oil and malt, the other superb. *April 1991. At best***** Years of life yet.*

1936**

Good wines but not of vintage quality and, in any case, too soon to declare after the 1934s and 1935s.

1937**

Sound, nice quality; not declared by British shippers.

Gonzalez Byass Bottled in 1940. Pale tawny; quite nice, some fruit; medium sweetness and weight, some flesh and softness. *Pre-sale tasting Nov 1980***

Flagman's 'Porto' *Colheita*, bottled 1986. Warm amber; rich yet lean, tangy, Verdelho-like. *Pre-sale, Chicago, Sept 1988**

Hooper Bottled 1972. Rosehip colour; high-toned; medium-sweet, hot grapey flavour. Nice quality. *Chicago, Sept 1988***

Noval, Qta do Matured in wood. Warm amber gold; nutty nose and flavour; medium-weight, on the lean side, very dry finish. *Sept 1988**

Silva, AJ da Bottled *c* 1980. Probably the same as Noval (da Silva was the trading company). Similar style. A bit more raisiny. *April 1987**

Taylor Not, strictly speaking, Taylor's vintage but a fascinating tasting of straight '37s from different grape varieties and quintas. Slight variations in depth of colour, some (Tinta Francisca) marvellously rich, sweet, long but lean, others like Rori with more acetone on the nose yet meatier on palate, and a fabulous wine of small production but high quality made from three grape varieties at Cão. *Tasted at Taylor's, Nov 1979.*

1938**

Quite good wines made but, owing to wartime restrictions, not declared or shipped. None tasted recently.

1939

Poor quantity and quality. Not declared.

Gonzalez Byass Bottled 1942. Very attractive. Rich, fruity nose and taste, well balanced, dry finish. *One of a wide range of vintages from Gonzalez Byass lodge, pre-sale, Sept 1980****

1940**

Small crop. Quite good wines. Not shipped.

Niepoort Bottled 1945. Old tawny; malty, meaty, singed raisins; very sweet, fullish, good nutty flavour, high biting volatile acidity. *Jan 1989**

Niepoort Put into demijohns in 1945, bottled in 1970. Strangely, little nose; medium-sweet with good firm fruit and acidity. *March 1988****

Taylor wax seal "4xx Taylor", relabelled, cork fully branded. Recorked 1986. Medium, rich, rosy-hued; rich, warm, stably; very sweet, fairly full, good rich flavour, excellent length and condition. *April 1991****

1941*

Moderate quality. Not shipped.

Noval Bottled 1944 and tasted 10 years later, rich and luscious. Probably faded now.

1942***

A good wartime year. Though declared and bottled in Oporto by 10 shippers, very little actually shipped but just worth keeping an eye open for.

Graham Noted as stylish but lacking usual plumpness in 1955 and 1971. Most recently: palish, rosy-hued tawny; low-keyed, old tawny nose; medium sweetness and body, sound, rich, stylish. From the colour and nose probably bottled in 1945. *Last tasted April 1990****

Niepoort Two very similar notes. First tasted in 1985. Deep colour; sweet, forthcoming, vinous nose; very sweet, fairly full-bodied, soft, fleshy, slightly toasted flavour. *Last tasted April 1990****

Noval, Qta do Bottled in 1945. Palish, very mature appearance; nose harmonious but a bit dusty; medium sweetness and weight, nice fruit, stylish – in fact remarkably similar to the Graham but with higher acidity. *Last tasted April 1990****

Rebello Valente Fully branded cork (which broke – not uncommon). Labelled Robertson Bros & Co – Rebello was their vintage *marque*. Lovely in 1960, and still delicious 20 years later: sweet, waxy, high-toned; still sweet, lightish, fruit and acidity. *Fully mature and nowhere to go when last tasted, April 1980****

Taylor Fairly pale tawny; rich, roasted, toasted nose; sweet, fairly full-bodied yet lightish in style. Good length. Still harbouring tannin and noticeable acidity. More recently, corked by Taylor in 1986: amber; dusty then ethereal; elegant but drying. *Last tasted April 1991***

1943**

Not bad but not up to vintage standard. Not declared.

Dow Fairly deep, mature; waxy, liquorice nose; sweet, lightish, soft, with a very pleasant chocolaty flavour. Short though finished well. Good for a 40-year-old 'non'-vintage. *March 1983****

Eira Velha, Qta I have always had a soft spot for this lovely old quinta perched on the spur of a hill above Pinhão and looking across to Noval. Had 1943 been declared it would have been shipped by Hunt, Roope as their Tuke Holdsworth vintage. Pale tawny; beautiful bouquet that expanded in the glass, fragrant, nutty;

medium-sweet, lightish, elegant, nice texture, harmonious, lovely finish. *Feb 1986*****

1944****

Excellent quality but the majority of the shippers concentrated on the 1945. In any case, good wine was needed to boost stocks to meet British post-war demand. None tasted recently.

1945*****

The first end-of-war vintage was of superb quality, although, as in other European wine districts, the quantity was small. The growing season was perfect, although great heat at harvest time created some vinification problems, resulting in over-high volatile acidity. All were Oporto-bottled. 22 shippers, Cockburn the only major abstention.

Tautly constructed concentrated wines still – if well cellared – superb, as demonstrated at the horizontal tasting of 1945s I conducted for the Hollywood (Florida) Wine Society in Feb 1989.

Butler Nephew The least good '45 at tasting mentioned above. Pale, very little red left; *garrafeira* (wood-aged) smell, linoleum-like, faded; dried out. Too much time in cask. *Feb 1989. Drink up.*

Croft 15 fairly consistent notes. Good colour, lively, rosy-hued; delicate low-keyed but fragrant bouquet, great depth; fairly sweet still, medium-weight, lean but firm, interesting leathery silky tannic texture, good quality, crisp dry finish. *Sept 1990**** Drink now to 2000.*

Dow Noted many times since 1959. Only five pipes shipped for bottling in England. One by British Transport Hotels, tasted in 1989 showed considerable colour loss, a palish tawny hue; sweet, surprisingly fruity nose, lean, liquorice, yet after an hour or so became more and more fragrant. Surprisingly sweet for Dow, relatively light for the vintage, marvellous acidity, lean, dry finish. Most recently, bottled October 1947 by Rigby & Evens with pre-war corks, fully branded: palish, no red left; meaty, lean, touch of acetone on the nose and palate. Dry finish *Last tasted with Jim Hood, March 1991. At best*****

Eira Velha, Qta Very fragrant, fruity, some brandy pushing through; medium-sweet, very flavoury, highish acidity. *Oct 1980** Drink up.*

Ferreira Unready in 1966, lovely in the mid-1970s, perfect in the early 1980s. Most recently: palish, fully mature, not much red left and a slightly weak tawny rim; crisp, peppery bouquet with a lot of bare brandy; more fruit and life on the palate than its colour suggested. A singed, sooty taste of scorched grapes, with end acidity and touch of bitterness. A powerful and interesting wine with some of the sweetness of Graham and backbone of Taylor. Good dry finish. *Last tasted Feb 1989*** Drink now.*

Fonseca A rather faded look, though healthy. Again, as with the Dow, the colour a bit misleading as the nose richer and more positive than anticipated. A touch of singed caramel and a whiff of volatile acidity, the result of picking in great heat, developing in the glass a curious, explosive fragrance: hot, high-toned, fruit fading exposing spirit. Rather disappointing. *Feb 1989** Drink up.*

Graham Outstandingly the loveliest '45. Tasted many times over the last 20 years. Seven consistently good notes since 1980. Deep-coloured, fairly intense, lively, attractive, long 'legs'; immediately forthcoming fragrance, spice, sweetness and fruit masking high alcoholic content; the sweetest of the 11 '45s tasted in Florida. An extremely powerful wine yet with wonderful balance and harmony. *May 1991***** Drink now to 2020.*

Niepoort Bottled March 1948. Four fairly recent notes: still fairly deep, rich and intense; rich, idiosyncratic, prune-like nose, more like meat than fruit; sweet, full, chunky, velvety, good length and life ahead. *Last tasted Nov 1988**** Drink now to 2020.*

Noval, Qta do Tasted several times since 1956 and "charm" noted fairly consistently. At the Hollywood tasting, bottled by Churtons, Liverpool: palish but still with a youthful tinge; fragrant, rich, perfectly harmonious bouquet; sweet, perfect weight, lovely fruit, good dry finish. A wine of feminine graciousness. Most recent, labelled "da Silva", with short cork; rather unimpressive colour; unknit and spicy, orange blossom and candlewax bouquet; sweet, fullish, lean, intense, citrus-like acidity. *Last noted at the Noval tasting Nov 1989. At best***** Drink now to 1995.*

Rebello Valente Overpowering in the late 1950s, lovely in mid-1960s. Most recently: an attractive, lively rosy-hued appearance of some intensity; shy at first, lively, refreshing nose, spare but fruity; lean, flavoury, touch of liquorice, noticeable acidity. A crisp, lissom charmer. *Last tasted Feb 1989**** Drink now to 2000.*

Sandeman Several notes, including two good London bottlings. In the early 1970s chunky, needing another 10 years. And after nearly 20 years, mature-looking, rose-hip-hued, nice gradation of colour; suave, silky, harmonious bouquet; drying out on palate, now on the light side, gentle, touch of vanilla, crisp, lacking length. *Last tasted Sept 1989*** Drink now to 1995.*

Taylor A big strapping wine, totally unready in the mid-1960s, with magnificent depth and concentration in the late 1970s. Recent notes fairly consistent: still a fine deep lively plummy colour; a well-spread, beautifully sublime bouquet with touch of liquorice, slightly malty; fairly sweet, loaded with fruit and alcohol, firm, intense, nutty, great length. *Last tasted April 1991****(*) 1995–2030.*

Warre Variable notes, including one framboise-scented, one woody. Showing marvellously well at the '45 tasting in Florida: beautiful colour, lively, lovely gradation; very forthcoming, indeed fairly forceful nose, brandy evident; a powerful wine with cockle-warming alcohol, crisp, lovely texture and elegance – for me the hallmarks of Warre. Good length. Splendid life ahead, if well kept. *Last tasted Feb 1989***** Drink now to 2000.*

1946*

Uneven quality, not declared and none tasted recently.

1947****

A very good vintage though only declared by 11 shippers. Certainly very attractive and popular in the wine-starved 1950s, which is why little remains, and so few tasted recently. Good weather conditions: wet spring, long hot summer, a little rain before picking which began towards the end of Sept in excellent conditions.

Cockburn Up until this time, Cockburn were very sparing with the number of vintages they declared: '27, '35 – not the '45 – and then the '47. Several notes. Slightly variable, depending on bottler rather than condition. Sometimes a rather odd, medicinal bouquet and flavour with rather high, prickly acidity. Most recently: fully labelled and wax seal impressed with shipper and vintage. Crumbly cork. Good warm tawny colour, fairly heavy 'crust' or sediment. Soft barley-sugar nose which developed lovely powdery vanilla fragrance. Fairly sweet, nice weight, flesh, flavour and balance. Dry, liquorice finish. Attractive. *Oct 1990*****

Delaforce Only three notes. A palish, orange-tinged

tawny; ethereal, fragrant but unknit; sweet, medium weight, a positive but rather estery flavour and highish acidity. *Last noted at a Delaforce tasting, April 1989*** Drink up.*

Sandeman Surprisingly deep, rich appearance; pronounced liquorice and vanilla bouquet; very sweet, pleasant weight and balance. Beautifully developed. *Sept 1990*****

Taylor's Special Qta (bottled 1949) Although Taylor did not declare the '47 vintage, a limited quantity shipped. Several notes, most recently with wax seal impressed "1947 SP Quinta Taylor, Dolamore Ltd London W1", presumably bottled by the latter. Good warm tawny colour with flush of red; rich, fragrant bouquet, a bit spirity, seemed very sweet, full-bodied, assertive Taylor flavour and backbone, so presumably from Vargellas. Hot dry finish. *Last tasted Oct 1990*****

Tuke Holdsworth Several notes. Now rather pale, rosy-hued, weak-rimmed; faded yet opens up, soft and sweet. Lightish though fairly assertive flavour, with attenuated spirity and slightly acidic finish. More like a '34. *Last tasted May 1991*** Drink up.*

Warre Several notes since 1958, none recent. The last, bottled by Berry Bros, fully mature but lively appearance; a gently waxy, harmonious bouquet; fairly sweet, lightish; perfect balance. *Jan 1982**** Drink up.*

1948****

A very good vintage but declared by only nine shippers which, in retrospect, was an unfortunate error of judgement as it turned out to be so successful. It was seven years before another vintage of real quality was declared.

The top three '48s were Fonseca, Graham and Taylor. The first, a deep, spicy wine not tasted since 1979.

Graham First tasted 10 years after the vintage, then immensely deep, magnificent. 17 consistently good notes since then. A recent Christopher's bottling still fairly deep; fragrant, spicy, a bit spirity; medium sweetness and body, a bit lean and tannic for Graham, good firm though abrupt finish. Most recently, deeper, richer fruit; sweet, warm and strong with almost Taylor-like backbone. *Last tasted Sept 1990**** Drink now to 2000.*

Taylor Tasted 19 times since 1958, invariably magnificent. Still fairly deep and intense; beautiful bouquet, lovely fruit, scented, citrus, vanilla; sweet, full-bodied, powerful yet perfect flavour and balance with glorious blackberry-like ripeness. Most recently lovely, shapely, ethereal. *Last tasted April 1991******

1949

Not declared. Freak weather conditions. Drought from the previous autumn until June, followed by a heat-wave, unprecedented, even in Portugal. None tasted.

1950**

Cockburn 15 notes since 1959 and always found to be lean and spirity. Pale, fully mature, watery-rimmed; fragrant but reminiscent of an old Sercial madeira; medium-sweet, flavoury, dry finish. The most recent bottle rather undistinguished. *Sept 1990. At best** Drink up.*

Dow Several notes, once full and rich, now palish and very mature-looking. The last bottle a bit mushroomy; drying out, fading, a bit too acidic. *Sept 1983** Drink up.*

Graham's Malvedos Bottled 1952. Palish, orange-tinged; rich, sweaty, raisiny; medium sweetness and weight, chewy, sandy texture, dry acidic finish. *May 1991**

Noval Lovely wine. Most recently, bottled by James Hawker, Plymouth. Level upper mid-shoulder. Warm, chocolaty tawny colour; bouquet to match. Very sweet, nice weight, soft, agreeable. *Last tasted Nov 1988****

Ferreira Pale, red-tinged. Delicious, slightly scented fruitiness. *April 1981*** Drink now.*

Sandeman Tasted more than any other '50. Fragrant, sweet but a bit spirity and acidic. *July 1986*** Drink up.*

Sandeman A curiosity: a pipe (110 gallons) shipped to Wales in 1952 and not bottled until 1985 after the owner's death. It had evaporated to 50 gallons and was bottled unfiltered. Though it had lost bulk it had gained strength. A lovely colour; rich, tangy, singed toffee, high-strength bouquet; sweet, full, very rich. Almost burning alcohol and acidity yet fat, smooth and velvety. *Tasted on two occasions, with David Sandeman, shortly after bottling, then, five months later, in Aug 1985*****

1951*

Not bad, but not of vintage quality. None declared.

Graham's Malvedos Palish, weak-rimmed; fragrant but unknit, powdery, estery; medium sweetness and body, spirity, pungent, high acidity. *Magnum at a Graham's tasting, July 1986**

1952

Damp and dismal year. Not declared.

Graham's Malvedos Deeper and more intense than the '51; complicated, unharmonious but interesting nose: boiled sweets, caramel, rich, earthy, fulsome; sweet, full, soft, with rather hot spirit and acidity. *Graham's tasting, July 1986***

Niepoort Late bottled (1984). Pale tawny; sharp, estery volatile nose but sweet and nutty; drying out, light, some softness. *Aug 1985***

1953**

Too dry, excessive heat in Aug. Better than the two preceding years but not up to vintage standard.

Eira Velha, Qta Very pale, tailing off; rich, roasted, forthcoming bouquet; medium-sweet, soft, very pleasant flavour, peppery finish. *Oct 1988****

Graham's Malvedos Fine crisp colour, deeper than the '52; taut, hard at first but bouquet unravelled pleasingly; sweet, fullish, soft, fleshy, nice fruit and finish. *At Graham's tasting, July 1986****

1954***

Excellent harvest but small yield. Coming after so many poor to middling vintages, some thought was given to declaring the '54, but the quantity available was insufficient (which would merely irritate potential buyers). Also by that time, the quality and quantity of the '55 was known – so no declaration. Rarely seen.

Foz, Qta do Tasted twice, full, fruity in 1977, still deepish, ruddy-coloured; rather spirity nose; fairly sweet and full-bodied, characterful. *Last tasted March 1988****

Graham's Malvedos Rich and ruddy; gentle, fragrant, powdery-scented bouquet but something lacking; sweet, fullish, very good fruit, tannin and acidity. *At Graham's tasting, July 1986*****

1955*****

At last, a vintage of quality and quantity to meet an equally ripe and responding market. The best since 1948, the most widely declared – 26 shippers – since 1927. Yet strange weather conditions with some excessive heat. Some still think that '54 was better. They are surely mistaken. Unquestionably my favourite vintage for drinking now.

Cockburn I have been able to follow the progress of this port from cask, pungent and purple, to maturity. At random: bottled by Hunter and Oliver, still deep and plummy in 1980; by the IECWS (The Wine Society), tasted in the early 1980s: good flavour and balance, and, more recently, by unknown bottlers: each medium-deep, with a warm glowing tawny rim; brandy showing on the nose; still fairly sweet, assertive, with good fruit, fair length but a bit hot and sharp. Latterly, lead capsule embossed and cork branded "Cockburn's 1955 Vintage" but bottler unknown: excellent level, lovely colour, beautiful gradation; soft, fragrant yet a touch of pepper and liquorice; sweet, medium full-bodied, lovely flavour, texture. Extended dry finish. *Last tasted Nov 1990. At best*****

Croft 11 notes. Slightly variable bottlings. Medium, mature; firm yet fruity; fairly sweet, medium-weight, excellent flavour and balance. Dry, slightly spirity finish. *Last tasted Feb 1986. At best**** Lovely now to 2000+*

Delaforce Deep and dense in 1961. Now a warm mature appearance; low-keyed but harmonious fragrance; very sweet, lovely flavour, smooth flowery style. *Last tasted April 1989**** Perfect now to 2000.*

Dow 10 good notes from the mid-1960s. Very mature, though still a touch of brick red; fabulously rich, fully-developed bouquet; still fairly sweet and fullish body, soft, good texture and length, dry finish. My favourite Dow vintage. *Sept 1990***** Now to 2010+*

Ferreira Several notes. Still fairly deep, classic; sweet, fairly full-bodied, rich, fruity, lovely. *Last tasted Jan 1985**** Now to 2000+*

Fonseca Almost as deep and full as when first tasted in 1958. Lively-looking and rich; perfect, complete, harmonious bouquet with touch of tobacco and Spanish root; sweet, powerful — almost Taylor-like backbone — but shapely and fleshy. *July 1988***** Perfect now to 2020+*

Gould Campbell Lovely colour, bouquet and flavour. Still fairly deep; forthcoming bouquet, waxy, liquorice; sweet, full, soft, fleshy, good length, hot finish. *Last tasted Dec 1988*****

Graham Over 20 notes since 1958, 14 since 1980. Recently, bottled by Harvey's: medium, mature but rosy-cheeked; glorious bouquet, smooth, rich, erupting out of its depths a fabulous fragrance. Sweet, refined, silky, yet still tannic, fleshy yet firm. One of my favourite ports. *May 1991***** Perfect now to 2020+*

Noval, Qta do 11 notes, good but not great. Palish, light-rimmed; low-keyed and delicate though with some depth, toasted liquorice; sweet, lean, spiky spicy flavour, good length, dry finish. *Last noted, Oporto-bottled, at Noval tasting Nov 1989*** Now to 2000.*

Noval Nacional Less intense than anticipated; very rich, liquorice nose; sweet, fullish, marvellous flavour and character. Spirity finish. *Nov 1989*****

Taylor Despite well over two dozen notes, not a wine I have yet come to grips with. An opaque blockbuster when young, astringent and unready up until the early 1980s. Still fairly deep-coloured; a vast, deep, high-toned, spicy nose; fairly sweet, full-bodied, packed with fruit, extract, tannin and acidity. Taylor backbone and '55 vintage flesh which, I trust, will outlive its spirit and tannin. *Last tasted April 1991****(*) 1995–2020*

Tuke Holdsworth Two recent bottles, with fully embossed wax seals and long branded corks, Gough Bros slip labels: medium, mature yet rich and lively-looking; bouquet of wax and liquorice; fairly sweet — one was drying out a little — medium-weight, good fruit but lean, with high alcohol and acid levels. Good drink though. *Last tasted April 1990*** Drink up.*

Warre For some strange reason, all four notes relatively recent, indeed three made in 1990. The first with a fully branded cork but with an all-too-rare spelling mistake on the Newcastle Breweries label "WARNE 1955"! Medium colour; fragrant bouquet, touch of vanilla; drying out a little but elegant, lovely, great length. A more recent, unknown bottling, very sweet, silky. Lastly, one with a noticeably long, 2 in, branded cork; a bit sour at first until it opened out. Assertive. Good texture. A bit peppery and acidic. *Oct 1990. At best******

Other 1955s:

Berry Bros' Own Selection Sweet, soft, rich, peppery. *March 1989****

1956

The worst weather conditions of the period. Snow followed by cold, wet spring, summer and autumn. A washout.

1957

Irregular weather. Wine not up to vintage standard.

Cálem Bottled 1990. Medium tawny; fairly high volatile acidity; sweet, fullish, rich, raisiny flavour. Very good in its way. *Dec 1990****

Graham's Malvedos Very peppery, spirity, clumsy nose; sweet, fullish, soft, short. *July 1986**

Sandeman Peppery; very flavoury, charming, nice fruit, dry finish. *Last tasted May 1991** Ready.*

1958***

A pleasant enough vintage made in an unusually wet year, declared by 12 shippers. A light stop-gap vintage, nice now but needs drinking.

Delaforce Nine notes. At best in mid-1970s but still pleasant, rosy-hued; slightly medicinal bouquet; medium-sweet, soft. *Last tasted March 1986** Drink up.*

Graham's Malvedos Palish; a bit unyielding; quite attractive, short peppery finish. *Last tasted April 1988***

Martinez Nine notes. Bigger than the other '58s from the start. Still a fine colour; good fruity bouquet; fairly sweet and full, spicy, excellent flavour. *Last tasted Jan 1983*** Good now to 2000.*

Noval, Qta do Over 12 agreeable notes. Most recently, bottled by Berry Bros: very sweet, good spicy flavour, but short. *Last tasted Nov 1989** Drink up.*

Noval Nacional Two slightly variable bottles. Both very deep for '58s; one citrus-scented, one with quite an alcoholic kick. Each had wonderfully intense grapiness. *Both tasted May 1980**(*)*

Tuke FS Holdsworth Two recent notes, both Oporto-bottled by Hunt, Roope: palish, fully mature; singed, substantial bouquet; sweet, nice weight, rich, good fruit, plumper than expected. A very agreeable '58. *Last tasted Jan 1991*** Now to 1998.*

Warre The most often seen. 18 notes, all demonstrating that this has always been a sweet, lightish, soft and very agreeable wine. *Last tasted June 1988*** Drink now.*

Other '58s:

Sandeman Sweet, soft, lean and a bit edgy. *March 1986***

Taylor's Vargellas Lots of fruit, dry finish. *Jan 1985****

1959

The odd man out in Europe: the 1959 port harvest disappointing. Not declared. None tasted.

1960★★★

An enthusiastically declared, and received, vintage. 24 shippers. The weather dictated the style of wine. A very hot summer. Picking, which began in some areas as early as Sept 12, and in a heat-wave, ended in rain. The heat accounts for some noticeable acidity and, for those who picked late, a little weakness. Nevertheless agreeable, flavoury wines. More or less fully developed.

COCKBURN *Over 20 notes since 1966. Started losing its deep colour in the early 1980s. Now palish, fully mature and fully developed bouquet. Still fairly sweet, lean but elegant, dry, slightly acidic finish. Last tasted Oct 1986★★★ Now to 2000.*

CROFT *Many notes. For long a rather deep-coloured, ruby wine. Now maturing. A stylish, attractive wine, sweet but lean, nice weight, firm dry finish. Last tasted Nov 1988★★★ Now to 2000+*

DOW *24 notes. Now completely mature-looking with touch of orange at rim; attractive but high-toned nose; fairly sweet, lean, flavoury, dry finish. Rather high volatile acidity. Sept 1987★★★ Drink up.*

FONSECA *Tasted only seven times over the past 20 years. Rain at the end of harvesting, so a lighter wine than usual. Nevertheless very flavoury and attractive if a bit lean and lacking structure and length. Last tasted Nov 1987★★★ Drink now to 1995.*

GRAHAM *Lovely to drink from the start. Lively, attractive, sweet but lacking a little concentration. A rare aberration: a bottle with a dry and wormy cork resulting in loss of colour and sharp acidity. The most recent, both Oporto-bottled: mature-looking; fragrant bouquet, violet, citrus; medium sweetness and body, rather lean for Graham but good length and acidity. Last tasted May 1991★★★★ Drink now to 2000.*

MARTINEZ *Many notes. Slightly variable bottlings but at best a good wine, lovely vinosity, fairly sweet, full-bodied, hard, rather Taylor-like backbone, distinctive style. Oct 1986★★★(★) Now to 2000.*

NOVAL, QTA DO *"Charm" appears in several of the 11 notes. Now palish, mature; tangy, attractive nose; still fairly sweet, medium weight, rather idiosyncratic spicy violets flavour. 1960 acidity noticeable. Last tasted Nov 1989★★★ Drink now to 1995.*

SANDEMAN *Tasted many times. With the high tone and leanness I associate with the '60s. Still sweet, nice weight, attractive, flavoury. Last tasted Dec 1989★★★ Now to 2000.*

TAYLOR *Many notes, slight variation due mainly to different bottlers. Three bottles from the same London livery company's cellars tasted in the mid-1980s were variations on a theme. What I believe was Oporto-bottled looked the most mature; hefty, sweet, chocolaty on the nose; medium-sweet, fairly full-bodied. The Army & Navy Stores bottling was deeper and plummier; a low-keyed but alcoholic nose; sweeter, fuller, with a better and longer flavour. The third, bottler unknown, less sweet, lean and uncompromising on the palate, good texture and endtaste. More recently Oporto-bottled: still sweet, fleshy but 'hot' peppery and alcoholic. It will be interesting to see how this turns out. Last tasted April 1991★★(★★) 1995–2010*

TUKE HOLDSWORTH *Three notes, two recent, both Oporto-bottled by Hunt, Roope, both fully mature, rosy-hued, the first (in July 1989) had a rich raisiny nose, the second a scented almost ethereal bouquet. Both were medium-sweet, medium-light, with good length and dry, slightly acidic finish. Last tasted Jan 1991★★★ Now to 1996.*

WARRE *Also many notes, different bottlings. Variable: one Oporto-bottled corked, another very flavoury. On average medium maturing appearance; a fairly sweet, classic and elegant wine, sometimes with twist of 1960 acidity. The most recent bottle had a lovely, slightly singed, almost muscadelle aroma; very sweet, lovely flavour, texture and length. Last tasted Sept 1990★★★(★) Now to 2010.*

OTHER '60s:

BURMESTER *Bottled in Oporto, March 1962; fragrant, touch of liquorice on the nose, attractive, fresh and fruity. Last tasted Oct 1983★★★*

CALEM *Amber-coloured, ethereal, raisiny; surprisingly fat and sweet. March 1980★★★*

DELAFORCE *Bottled by Harvey's, ruddy-tinted; two-part nose, hard yet very forthcoming; sweet, lean, light style, touch of acid on the finish. April 1989★★*

FERREIRA *Good colour; lovely fruit, high-toned, fragrant; sweet, fullish, crisp, flavoury, hot peppery, end acidity. March 1981★★*

SERRAS *Single-quinta port, quite nice, sweet, soft, fruity. Oct 1986★★*

1961★★★

Good wines made but vintage not declared. Too soon after the '60 and, by the time the decisions were made, the high quality of the '63 was known. In a way a pity, as the '61 vintage was so brilliant elsewhere, in Bordeaux particularly, that there would have been a sales rub-off. However, this was the year not only when single-quinta wines began to show their paces but LBVs (late-bottled vintage ports) put in a major appearance.

DOW *Bottled 1965. Very spirity; plummy fruit, a bit raw. Last tasted June 1984 and not destined for the 1990s.*

GRAHAM'S MALVEDOS *Bottled 1963. In 1971 I advised "drink up". This was a premature observation for in the mid-1980s it still had a fine, deep, fairly intense look about it; an excellent sweet, fragrant, fruit and liquorice nose; very sweet, full-bodied, soft, fleshy, good length. Last tasted July 1986★★★ Drink now.*

1962★★

Quite a good growing season but, between the much-shipped '60 and upstaged by '63, not declared. Some nice wines, still pleasant to drink. One great classic.

GRAHAM'S MALVEDOS *Four notes. Now palish, very mature; light, spirity, sweet, rich, lovely texture, twist of lemon.* Last tasted May 1991★★

FONSECA GUIMARAENS RESERVE *Palish, weak rim; estery, black treacle; very sweet, chewy, raisiny, pasty texture, slightly acidic.* Last tasted March 1991★★

HARVEY'S *An interesting blend of Cockburn and Martinez shipped and bottled in Bristol. (Cork branded "Harvey's 1962"). Rather weak-rimmed; clove-like, singed raisin nose; sweet, spicy, soft yet spirity.* Last tasted twice in 1991★★★

NOVAL NACIONAL *This is a great wine, made from grapes grown in the 10% of the vineyards at the quinta planted with the ungrafted local fruiting varieties. Three notes: black strap in 1969, hardly any change in 1979 and, in 1989, still deep, thick and intense yet with a mature rim; an unusual bouquet, peppery, old spice, dusty, alcoholic and with a distinct tea-like scent — a sign of quality. Sweet, full-bodied, powerful, concentrated, chocolaty, touch of black treacle, excellent acidity to bear it into the next century.* Last tasted Nov 1989★★★★(★) 1995–2050

OFFLEY BOA VISTA *Following a long-established pattern, wine from the Quinta Boa Vista marketed in a good but undeclared vintage. Five notes: elegant, flavoury, nice weight.* Last tasted Oct 1985★★★ Drink now.

OTHER '62s:

FERREIRA RESERVE *Despite poor corks, fragrant bouquet and flavour, lightish with nice uplift in the middle and excellent aftertaste.* In Oporto, Nov 1985★★★

NIEPOORT *Bottled 1985. A typically idiosyncratic but good Niepoort* colheita*: orange tawny; high-toned, raisiny nose; sweet, good length, slightly acidic, caramelly finish.* Oct 1990★★★

ROYAL OPORTO *Sweet, plummy, pleasant.* Sept 1987★★

WARRE *Bottled 1966. Palish, rosy-hued, hot spirity nose and taste.* Aug 1987★

WARRE'S GRANDE RESERVE *Bottled 1984. Very pale tawny; lovely, nutty, spirity bouquet; sweet, soft, rich, smell and taste of sultanas,* April 1985★★

1963★★★★★

An extremely good vintage. 25 shippers. Very straightforward growing and harvesting conditions towards end of Sept. A large quantity of vintage port made, probably the biggest volume since '27. Some very beautiful wines. The top: Dow, Warre, Fonseca, Graham and Taylor. Most are now fully mature.

COCKBURN *Opaque, liquorice and raw brandy in 1965. 20 years later, lively-looking with ruby glow; interesting bouquet, tea, chocolate, liquorice, citrus. Never very sweet or hefty, lean, sinewy, dry finish.* Last tasted Nov 1986★★★★ Now to 2000.

CROFT *Many notes since 1965, nine since the early 1980s. All good though slight bottle variations. Now medium, mature; nose a bit hard. Some distinctly sweet, some drying out a little — but this might have been the context in which they were drunk. Firm, lively, lacking some flesh but nice texture. Two almost identical recent notes: liquorice bouquet, very sweet, rich, soft, excellent length, peppery finish. Good, not great.* Last tasted Dec 1990★★★(★) Now to 2000.

DELAFORCE *Five notes, much liked. Fragrant, sweet, elegant. Nice in its youth, perfect in the mid-1980s. Liquorice and tangerine flavour, good length. Becoming a bit lean and drying out, otherwise holding well.* Last tasted April 1990★★★★ Now to 2000.

DOW *From 1965, a plethora of notes, 20 since the early 1980s. On the whole very good though one, with a wormy cork, was distinctly 'pricked'. Warm reddish brown with long sticky legs; beautiful nose: a great tunnel of smell, honeyed, harmonious, fragrant — but time in hand; sweet entry, long dry finish, shapely, spicy. Drinking well.* Last tasted March 1991★★★★★ Now to 2020.

FONSECA *From start to finish a consistently beautiful wine. One of the top '63s, and one of the best-ever Fonsecas. Still fairly deep; great classic bouquet and flavour. Perfect weight, texture. Great finesse.* Last tasted March 1988★★★★★ Now to 2020.

GRAHAM *32 idyllic notes since 1968, no matter where or by whom bottled. Amongst the most recent a superb Corney & Barrow bottling, even with the bottling date on the cork, and an excellent Oporto-bottled wine: medium-deep, slightly plummy, maturing nicely; sweet, rich, compact, slightly chocolaty bouquet; very sweet compared to the '60 and '66, fairly full-bodied, chunky fruit, rich yet lissom, great power and penetration. Still with great potential for further development.* Last tasted May 1991★★★★★ 1995–2025+

NIEPOORT *Three notes since the mid-1980s. The first, though clearly a two-year bottling, had a rose tawny hue, the most recent fairly deep and intense. But both were sweet, with a full fruity flavour and good length.* Last tasted Aug 1990★★★

NIEPOORT *Bottled 1987. One of the many permutations of this small production but high quality family firm. A* colheita*, what I call a 'vintage tawny', with characteristic pale amber colour, high-toned walnut bouquet, very sweet, crisp on palate.* Aug 1990★★

NOVAL, QTA DO *First tasted 1965. Even then soft and sweet. Many notes but only a few since the early 1980s. Good but not great. With the exception of a rather sharp Cockburn & Campbell bottling, fragrant, elegant, lean, and lightish in style, spicy and with slightly hot, spirity dry finish. Now relatively pale in colour, fully mature; sweet bouquet, vanilla and liquorice; still sweet, lightish, easy.* Dec 1990★★★ Now to 2000.

NOVAL NACIONAL *As different as night and day: a deep, intense-looking wine just striving to mature; immense, expansive, fig-like nose of great depth; medium-sweet but very full-bodied. An enormous, concentrated spicy wine with great length.* At Noval tasting, Nov 1989★★★★(★) 1995–2050

OFFLEY BOA VISTA *Several very consistent notes. Medium, lively, mature; spicy, fragrant; fairly sweet, medium-weight, good length. A scent and flavour of singed raisins and liquorice. Crisp. Very flavoury.* Last tasted Jan 1990★★★★ Now to 2000.

SANDEMAN *Six slightly variable notes since the early 1980s. Fairly good colour; rather peppery and spirity (touch of caramel and figs my wife noted); not very sweet or full. I said "lean"; my host said "elegant". Good acidity. Last tasted Sept 1989***(*) Now to 2000+*

TAYLOR *Over two dozen notes since 1968, mostly since 1980. Originally a block-buster, no matter whether English- or Oporto-bottled. Though deep, suddenly showing maturity from the mid-1980s. The most recent, Oporto-bottled, was palish, retaining very little red. Peppery spirit, toffee and tobacco on the nose heralds a powerful, lively wine with not only the Taylor backbone but quite a kick. Still a fairly sweet mouthful. Last tasted April 1990**** Now to 2015.*

WARRE *For me, one of the best and most elegant of all the '63s. 11 notes since the early 1980s. Has lost quite a lot of colour: a lovely warm, ruddy tawny; crisp, fruity, rounded, forthcoming bouquet; sweet, pleasant weight, lovely and lively flavour, silky texture. Last tasted Feb 1990***** Now to 2010.*

OTHER '63s:

AVERY'S *Figgy, liquorice nose and taste. Nice wine. April 1988****

BERRY BROS SELECTION (reputed to be from Taylor) *Sweet, soft, lovely. Last tasted March 1990*****

BURMESTER *Very deep, rich, smell of sugared raisins; very sweet light style, flavoury. Feb 1991***

CALEM *Deep; rich, plummy; very sweet, soft, fleshy. March 1988*****

HUNT'S *(Hunt, Roope) Pale for a '63; mature; sweet, lightish, soft yet spicy. July 1985****

MACKENZIE *Palish, mature, unconvincing; sound though slightly high-toned, vanilla, fragrant; sweet, lightish, lean, flavoury. Noticeably 'hot' spirity and acidic finish. June 1990***

MARTINEZ *Several consistent notes. Palish, unimpressive; low-keyed; sweet, hollow, short. Disappointing. Last tasted Oct 1986***

ROSA, QTA DE LA *Just down-river from Pinhão and only recently marketing their wine as a single-quinta wine. Touch of ruby with tawny rim; soft sweet nose, touch of liquorice; a very sweet, powerful wine with loads of grip, tannin and acidity. Nov 1988***(*)*

ROYAL OPORTO *Very sweet, prune-like, fruity. June 1987***

SMITH WOODHOUSE *Just one recent note: medium, mature, slightly weak rim; attractive, high-toned, well-developed, citrus tinge; sweet entry, dry finish, crisp, still a bit hard. Dec 1990****

*1964**

As in France, a hot summer and very hot mid-Sept. Not easy, and not declared.

GRAHAM'S MALVEDOS *Bottled in Oporto, 1966. Six notes. Deep colour in the early 1980s, now a very mature orange-tinged appearance; very fragrant; medium-sweet, nice weight, flavour and style. Refreshing finish. May 1991*** Drink up.*

OTHER '64s:

GUIMARAENS RESERVE *Bottled 1966. First tasted shortly after bottling and still, in the mid-1980s, thick and plummy and very sweet. High-toned. Last tasted Feb 1984****

*1965**

Some nice, ripe wines but, sandwiched between the '63s and '66s, not declared.

GRAHAM'S MALVEDOS *Four notes: lovely long flavour save one sharp and woody bottle. Last tasted July 1986. At best*** Drink up.*

TAYLOR'S VARGELLAS *Powerful Taylor backbone noticeable in the mid-1980s. A recent magnum deep ruby, sweet, crisp and fruity, and a bottle showing more maturity, softer, flatter. Both tasted in April 1988. At best****

OTHER '65s:

BORGES & IRMAO *20 years in cask: amber, high volatile acidity, madeira-like. May 1985.*

CALEM *Bottled 1990: rosehip tawny; bouquet of oranges and cobnuts; sweet, soft, raisiny, attenuated. Dec 1990****

*1966******

A marvellous vintage declared by 20 shippers. Cockburn and Martinez decided not to declare. Firm yet flexible wines with a perfect weight. Sinewy, not unlike the best '66 red Bordeaux, and long-lasting. Some will probably outlast the '63s, some might even turn out greater in the end. All this due to a hot year which ripened but did not singe the grapes, and some rain at vintage time which reduced concentration. Slightly underestimated and undervalued. Upgraded during the last decade.

BERRY BROS SELECTION *A superbly balanced wine blended and bottled in Berry Bros' style and, of course, only available from No 3, St James's Street. Still deep, relatively youthful for its age; harmonious, waxy bouquet; fairly sweet, nice weight, elegant, well balanced. In short, delicious. (I have since learned that this was shipped via Percy Fox & Co, then the agents for Warre.) Several notes, last tasted Feb 1989***** Now to 2010.*

CALEM *Deep, still ruby; lovely wine, long dry finish. March 1988*****

CROFT *Plummy; fruity; harmonious; good depth, nice weight, with a Graham-like sweetness. Not tasted since 1983. At least**** Drink now.*

DELAFORCE *Still surprisingly deep and immature; deep, firm, citrus touch; sweet, full, chunky for Delaforce, good length, alcohol and acidity. Last tasted April 1989***(*) 1993–2010*

DOW *Several notes, several bottlings, all good. Some colour loss over the last 10 years, but rich and attractive; nicely developed, very fragrant;*

medium sweetness and weight, lean, elegant, very appealing. Last tasted June 1988****(*) Now to 2010.

FERREIRA *Beautiful bouquet; sweet, fullish, firm, stylish, elegant.* March 1988**** Now to 2010.

FONSECA *Still fairly deep; fig-like fruit. Fragrance lingered in the glass five hours: spicy, ripe mulberries. Very sweet, very rich. Magnificent.* Last tasted Feb 1990***** Now to 2020+

GOULD CAMPBELL *Surprisingly deep, virtually opaque in the early 1980s, well-knit, plump and peppery. Now medium, mature; very scented, slightly citrus-tinged bouquet; very sweet, rich, lovely texture. Still an impressively powerful wine.* Last tasted Dec 1990***(*) 1993–2010

GRAHAM *23 notes since 1968. All but one woody bottle, excellent. Still quite deep though less red than the '63; fragrant, citrus, China-tea and liquorice-like bouquet; fairly sweet and full. Nice plump flesh though leaner than the '63. Rich, spicy, lovely flavour and texture, perfect balance.* Last tasted May 1991***** Now to 2020.

NIEPOORT *Bottled 1969. Deep, hot, highish acidity — needed plenty of time in decanter. Sweet. Good shape, weight, finish.* Last tasted May 1988***

NOVAL, QTA DO *Many notes since 1968. Still deep and rich-looking; figgy, Spanish root; very sweet and full-bodied for Noval, assertive even. Intense.* Last tasted June 1989***(*) 1995–2010?

SANDEMAN *Six notes, four since the mid-1980s: sweet nose, vanilla, liquorice; lighter style, lean, elegant, nice balance, hot, dry, slightly acidic finish, delicious.* Last tasted Feb 1991**** Now to 2000.

SMITH WOODHOUSE *Medium, mature though ruddier than the Gould Campbell; rich fruit; very sweet, nice texture. Very good wine.* Dec 1990**** Now to 2000.

TAYLOR *12 notes. Deep, rich, maturing; sweet, full-bodied, shapely, firm, good length, still tannic.* Last tasted April 1991***(*) 1994–2020

WARRE *The most frequently noted seem to have been Oporto-bottled and consistently attractive and elegant. A wine with suppleness and a bit of a swagger. Maturing nicely, fairly sweet, lean, stylish.* Last tasted April 1991****(*) Now to 2010.

1967★★

The weather conditions were conducive to the making of good wine although the yield was small. I wonder if Cockburn and Martinez were wise to buck the '66 trend and only declare the '67. It did not make a lot of marketing sense. Sandeman (who still regard this as one of the most underrated vintages) and Noval joined them, making four major declarations. Graham and Taylor treated it as a second-class vintage.

COCKBURN *Tasted 18 times, though not very recently, and consistently unimpressed. Its initial depth of colour and richness sagged throughout the 1980s. Since 1985 palish and mature-looking; rather hard, pasty, spirity nose; drying out, medium weight, lean though some flesh and nice texture. Dry finish.* Last tasted June 1987** Drink now though it might well linger on.

CROFT'S QTA DA ROEDA *Five notes through the 1980s. Still deep; lean, spirity nose, some acidity showing. Sweet, fullish, surprisingly powerful, slightly raw but flavoury.* Last tasted Oct 1988***

MARTINEZ *Bottled in Oporto and, I think, otherwise only by Harvey's in Bristol. The latter was very good in 1980. Altogether a better colour, sweetness and weight than Cockburn. A curious, fragrant, spicy, pine-fresh bouquet; complex yet balanced. Opened up nicely.* Oct 1987***(*)

NIEPOORT *A* garrafeira *'vintage tawny', put into demijohns in 1971 for bottling as required. All very complicated, but it works. Lovely garnet colour; walnuts and fruit; sweet, full, opulent fig-like fragrance. Very good in its way.* Oct 1985***

NOVAL, QTA DO *Lively ruby; evolved, rich, tangy nose with a whiff of grape skins; medium-sweet, lean, spicy, slightly short with a dry finish.* Jan 1991*** Drink soon.

NOVAL NACIONAL *Very deep, intense; a hefty but slightly unknit nose; fairly sweet, powerful yet lean liquorice flavour and dry tannic finish.* At Noval tasting, Nov 1989**(*) 1994–2010

SANDEMAN *Initially deep, now maturing but rich; rather hard nose; very sweet, fullish, fleshy, attractive.* Last tasted Oct 1988*** Now to 1995.

TAYLOR'S VARGELLAS *Several notes. Still fairly deep; a fairly sweet, very positive and attractive wine. Remains a bit hard.* Last tasted in July 1989***(*) Now to 1995+

TAYLOR *Notes on an unusual tasting of three wines, made from different grapes, five years in cask in the Douro, five years in Gaia. Each had lost considerable colour, pale tawny, rather Verdelho-like appearance and nose. The best, sweet, fat and lovely was made from a mixture of grapes including the Nacional, Tinta Francisca, Bastardo, Sousão and Flor de Douro.* Nov 1979.

1968★★

Exceptionally hot summer, then an unsettled period improving in time for picking. Some nice wines made but not declared. A year of LBVs and single-quinta wines.

CROFT *Late-bottled, palish, pink-tinged; raisiny; pleasant light easy style in mid-1980s.* Not for keeping**

GRAHAM'S MALVEDOS *Initially assertively hard, lacking Graham charm. A recent bottle seemed to be nutty and drying out but two others delicious, with fragrant, spicy nose like an old* garrafeira; *sweet, fullish, yet lean, expanding and expansive flavour.* Last tasted May 1991*** Drink now.

GUIMARAENS RESERVE *Deep, immature, full-bodied and tannic for the mid-1980s. Probably softened by now.* May 1985** Drink up.

1969

Hot summer flanked by cold and rain. Grapes unripe, wines acidic. Not declared.

TAYLOR'S VARGELLAS *Taylor's prime-site quinta, well up the Douro, managed to produce good enough grapes to make a deep, sweet and powerful wine tasted several times in the early to mid-1980s.*

WARRE LBV *Around the same time proved adequate: fairly deep, nice weight, refreshing. Last tasted March 1986. Drink up.*

1970★★★★(★)

Ideal growing and harvesting conditions. A serious vintage, still somewhat underrated. 23 shippers. It was also a turning point. After 1970 there were to be no more shipments in pipe for bottling by the British trade. A unilateral decision was taken to make bottling at source, ie in the shippers' own lodges, mandatory.

I had not given the vintage much thought until Justerini & Brooks laid on a tasting of major shippers' '70s and '75s. For me it was a revelation. A much sturdier vintage than I had expected, confirmed by subsequent tastings. Classic. A good future.

CALEM'S QTA DO FOZ *Very impressive. Opaque; prune-like fruit; very sweet and full in the early 1980s. Still very deep though maturity showing at the rim. Extraordinary fruit, reminded me of figs. Full-bodied and fleshy. Last tasted Aug 1990★★★(★) Now to beyond 2000.*

COCKBURN *Correctly opaque at the time of bottling. At 10 years of age still fairly deep though maturing; a hard, rather unyielding, cardboardy nose; medium-sweet, medium full-bodied. Its initial fieriness simmering down, but still hard. A good long lean tannic finish. Nine notes since 1980. Rather unexciting. Sept 1990★★(★) 1995–2010*

CROFT *An impressive youth. Sweet, with good flavour, texture and length in the early to mid-1980s. Two recent notes: now medium-deep, a bit weak at the edges; high-toned citrus-like nose and flavour, with whiff of volatile acidity. Sweet, medium-weight, lean yet fleshy, good length. Last tasted Dec 1990★★(★) Now to 2000.*

DELAFORCE *Several notes, the most interesting at a Delaforce tasting in 1989, comparing a bottle and a magnum. The wine from the bottle had a very distinctive citrus (hint of mandarin) flavour whereas the magnum's look was distinctly deeper, plummier, less mature; a rather hard cheesy bouquet that developed richly. Both were fairly sweet, but the magnum packed greater power and length. Most recently: forthcoming, rich, high-toned bouquet; sweet, full-bodied, plenty of grip. Good dry finish. Aug 1990★★(★★) 1995–2010*

DOW *17 well-spread and pretty consistent notes. Still fairly deep and youthfully plum-coloured; excellent nose, fragrant, forthcoming, an almost Cabernet Sauvignon-like fruit, plus liquorice. Sweet, full-bodied, nice texture, fleshy — as Dow goes. A rich exciting drink with considerable future. Last tasted Sept 1990★★★★(★) 1995–2020*

FONSECA *Virtually black when young and still very deep, with the plumminess of maturity-in-waiting; restrained though fruity nose; initially very sweet, now merely sweet, full-bodied, rich, ripe, fleshy, fruit and grip. Ten notes through the 1980s, two recent. Excellent. Last tasted April 1991★★★(★★) Drink now (if you must) to well into the 21st century.*

GOULD CAMPBELL *First tasted in 1973, deep, fine, rich. Three good notes in the mid-1980s, two bottled by Clode & Baker, slow to mature but good balance and length. Two recent notes, the last, possibly both, Oporto-bottled: now medium-deep but, interestingly, with more of a youthful purple tinge than the '75. Very sweet, fruity nose, slightly high-toned, tea-like; also sweet and fairly full on the palate, yet lean. Very flavoury. Dry finish. Good wine. Good future. Last tasted Dec 1990★★★(★) Now to well beyond 2000.*

GRAHAM *The Graham family's last vintage. Originally opaque, still deep, plummy and fairly intense, showing rich extract, fragrant, high-toned yet harmonious bouquet though still a bit hard; very sweet, full-bodied, lots of fruit, grip, length, tannin and acidity. Chocolate and spice. Will be glorious. Over 16 notes since 1982, all consistently good. Last tasted May 1991★★★(★★) 1995–2050*

MARTINEZ *Seven notes since 1977. Retaining most of its original depth of colour though bottlings have varied. For example, Gilbey Vintner in 1988 was medium-deep and looking mature. More recently, bottler unknown (probably Harvey's), was opaque. "Spirity" in relation to the nose recurs over the past 11 years. Unusual style, vinous, fragrant. One bottle ruined by being served with unripe Cox's orange pippins and digestive biscuits. Last noted Feb 1991★★(★) 1995–2015*

NIEPOORT *'Straight' vintage, two-year bottling and in curiously attractive, stencilled, dumpy bottles. Two notes, first at a very extensive Niepoort tasting in 1985. Still deep, richly coloured; rather restrained nose, "classic" noted then and more recently. Very sweet, fairly full-bodied, firm, fleshy, still a bit peppery. Last tasted Aug 1990★★★(★) Now to well beyond 2000.*

NOVAL, QTA DO *Many notes, nine since 1981. Not a big '70, a charmer. Not deep, and soft enough to drink even at the time of bottling in 1972. Now medium, maturing; fairly sweet, middle-weight, a bit lean but soft and smooth, stylish and appealing. Last noted no fewer than 10 times in different types of glass. More of a glass tasting than a port tasting, but Georg Riedel made a good point: the shape and size of glass* does *make a difference, to the perception of depth of colour, nose and taste. Ironically, Christiano van Zeller had to agree that his own 'Noval' glass was not ideal. Even more ironically, the exercise made it difficult to sum up the wine: there were too many variations on the theme. Last tasted March 1991★★(★) to ★★(★★) depending on the glass! Now to 2010.*

NOVAL NACIONAL *Not as deep as the '67 Nacional but rich, displaying high extract; bouquet hard, with fig-like fruit and considerable depth; fairly sweet, full-bodied. Impressive. At Noval tasting, Nov 1989★★★(★★) 1995 to well into the 21st century.*

OFFLEY BOA VISTA *Many notes. Originally very*

deep, its colour started to change to plummy after 10 years and to show maturity around the mid-1980s. Now fully mature-looking, a medium-pale tawny. It has also softened, the bouquet fully evolved by the late 1980s. Still sweet but the originally lean, attenuated acidity noticeable throughout. Firm. Flavoury. Last tasted Aug 1990*** Now to 2000. Drink soon.

REBELLO VALENTE *Never very deep, now fully mature. Hard, spirity nose after five years in bottle. Most recently, rather smelly, on the verge of oxidation though it was very good on the palate, still very sweet, fairly full-bodied, soft, velvety yet powerful. Far better to taste than to look at and to smell.* Last noted Aug 1990. At best*** Now to 1998.

SANDEMAN *11 notes, revealing bottling variations. One, bottled by Paten of Peterborough with a short cork, looked fully mature in 1986 and was chunky with rather a sandy texture. Other bottlings tasted more recently: medium-deep but still a little immature-looking; sweet, harmonious bouquet with pleasing fruit masking a hard core and considerable depth. Sweet, fullish, good flavour, firm, with lots of tannin and acidity. Attractive wine.* Last tasted Aug 1990. At best**(**) 1995–2015

SMITH WOODHOUSE *Six notes. After five years in bottle deep, hard-nosed, and 10 years later little change. However, since 1987 some colour loss, now looking mature. Bouquet has opened up; mint, liquorice, fruit. Still fairly sweet, nice weight, flavoury, but tannin and acidity giving the wine a dry finish.* Last tasted Dec 1990**(*) Now to 2000.

TAYLOR *First tasted in 1972, many notes, 13 since the early 1980s. Originally opaque, virtually black-purple, it remained plum-coloured for nearly 20 years and — with the exception of an unusually precocious Russell and McIver bottling in 1983 — is still a vigorous ruby. Recent notes, probably different bottlings, slightly variable, particularly on the nose: whiff of mercaptan, rawness and volatility, at best harmonious though subdued. Certainly sweet, full-bodied, rich, good fruit, lovely mid-palate, still powerful, high alcoholic content, good length, tannin and acidity. Impressive.* Last tasted April 1991**(**) Possibly***** but not until well into the 21st century.

WARRE *A mass of notes. 19 since the early 1980s, all complimentary. Pristine purple now easing a little, starting to mature; lovely fruit, fragrance and vinosity. My notes range from medium-sweet to very sweet but, as so often, this depends on the context in which the wine is tasted and drunk. Let's settle for sweet, full-bodied, rich, almost too rich, yet not overpowering, with the perfect weight and balance I expect from Warre at its best.* Last tasted March 1991***(**) Now to 2020.

OTHER '70s:

BARROS *Medium, plummy; sweet, soft, well-developed, fragrant nose; very sweet on palate, excellent fruit, lively, touch of citrus-like acidity, good length and aftertaste.* Aug 1990**** Now to 2000.

BERRY BROS SELECTION *(believed to be Warre) Medium depth of colour and sweetness, fullish body. Very good.* Dec 1990****

BORGES & IRMAO *Plummy; very sweet, fullish, lively, full of fruit, nice texture.* Nov 1985***

BURMESTER *Bottled 1973. Quite good in 1981: broad, singed nose; medium-sweet, dry finish. More recently, a pair, one rich but woody, the other, maturing, with raisiny nose.* Aug 1990. At best**

BUTLER NEPHEW *Raisiny, sweet, reasonable fruit and flesh.* Two notes in the early 1980s**

DALVA *Fully mature appearance; over-high volatile acidity; medium-sweet, tart.* 1990

FEIST *Deepish, maturing; rich, peppery, classic nose and flavour. Very sweet, soft.* Aug 1990****

HUTCHESON *Masses of notes throughout the 1980s and into the 1990s. Its initial deep ruby now medium and plummy; undemonstrative nose; sweet, fleshy, quite attractive and good value.* Aug 1990**(*)

KROHN *Plummy in 1979, now tawny; original hardness ameliorated, singed, minty, raisiny bouquet; very sweet — like many Portuguese house ports, lean, flavoury.* 1990***

KOPKE'S QTA S LUIZ *Fully mature; chocolate and liquorice; very sweet, fullish, lovely flavour, texture, softness and finish.* 1990***(*)

OSBORNE *Bouquet of* raya *sherry and sultanas; sweet, fullish, endtaste of dried raisins.* Aug 1990*

ROSA, QTA DE LA *Not very deep; nose still hard and undeveloped; medium-sweet, fairly full-bodied, piquant, flavoury.* Nov 1988*(**)

ROYAL OPORTO *Originally noted as having a rather insubstantial appearance, nose and taste. Two recent notes: now a medium-deep but fully mature tawny with amber rim; very sweet, rather high-toned, raisiny bouquet and flavour. One bottle I thought lean and acidic.* Sept 1990**

SANTOS JUNIOR *Medium, plummy, maturing; rich fruit, slightly acidic; sweet, good body yet lean. Attractive.* Aug 1990***

SOUZA *Medium-deep, maturing nicely; powerful, fruit, vinosity; very sweet, very rich, soft, fruity. Somewhat hot and acidic finish. Nice wine though.* Aug 1990***

1971★

Useful wines made for standard blends. Not declared.

1972★

Heat and drought sandwiched between heavy rains. Though some passable wines made, not generally declared.

DOW *The odd man out. Having made a nice wine it was belatedly declared. Only two notes. Deep, brown-coloured; prune-like nose; fairly sweet, nicely put together, reasonable length.* Oct 1983** Drink up.

DOW RESERVE *Bottled 1985. The appearance of a very old, rose-tinted tawny; sweet nose, figs and malt; drying out, lean, flavoury. A bit of an oddity.* Tasted Feb 1986**

EIRA VELHA, QTA *Lovely colour, sweet, peppery, very flavoury.* 1980**(*)

REBELLO VALENTE *Fairly sweet, nice weight, soft,*

*elegant, rather lean, good acidity. Two notes in 1985****

ROSA, QTA DE LA *Medium-pale, maturing nicely in appearance but still rather hand and spirity on the nose. Enters sweet, departs dry. Pleasant flavour in the middle but lean and lacking length. Nov 1988***

1973

Weather pattern not unlike 1972. Not declared.

1974★

Vintage marred by heavy rain. Abundant crop, but mostly of mediocre quality.

WARRE *Late bottled. Very deep, straightforward, pleasant. July 1987***

EIRA VELHA, QTA *Sweet, positive, quite nice. 1980***

FEIST *(Barros Almeida) Sweet, flavoury, charming. Oct 1986***

ROZES *Sweet, full-flavoured, raisiny. 1982***

1975★★

Mild winter, warm spring, hot and dry summer. Rain in early and late Sept. Picking early Oct. A rare example of a port vintage that has not lived up to the original cheerily optimistic expectations. I suspect that the 17 major shippers declaring the wine, despite the proximity of the excellent '77s, turned a blind eye to the heavy early autumn rain. Something of a damp squib. The first mandatory bottling at source of a widely declared vintage did not get off to a good start. Unless, the '75s have a 'second breath', an 'Indian summer' or a 'swan song', I do not foresee a great future.

COCKBURN *Opaque at the time of bottling but considerable colour loss by the mid-1980s. Strange, stalky, wet straw nose; sweet, fruity, spirity. Last tasted Oct 1986*(*) Drink soon.*

CROFT *Only two notes, both in the early 1980s. Plum-coloured; nice fruit; well clad and good length. Must retaste. Last tasted Nov 1983**(*)*

DELAFORCE *Palish, ruddy-tinged, attractive; chocolaty, malty nose; sweet, lightish, muscadelle flavour, lean. Last noted at Delaforce tasting, April 1989** Drink now.*

DOW *Tasted when bottled, and with over 15 notes straddling the 1980s. Deeply impressive when young, consistently good notes but seemed at its best at 10 years of age. Though some colour loss, still youthful-looking and luminous; fragrant, hazelnuts and liquorice bouquet; fairly sweet, nice weight, soft yet crisp, lean, spicy, good length, attractive. Last tasted Feb 1991**(**) 1995–2010*

FERREIRA *Opaque, raw, powerful in 1977. 11 years later medium-deep, still some red; very sweet, medium weight, quite flavoury. Fernando d'Almeida, the venerable blender, thought it not very good, rather like the 1917, but will, paradoxically, be best when it is very old. Last tasted March 1988***(*)*

FONSECA *Initially huge, opaque, very sweet, now a medium-deep ruby; moderate sweetness and body, lively, good flavour but not Fonseca at its best. Last tasted Sept 1989*** Drink now to 1995.*

GOULD CAMPBELL *Purple and pleasing in 1977, maturing nicely in the mid-1980s. Now pale, rather weak; nutty — walnuts; medium-sweet, fuller than it looks, rather original flavour. Last tasted Dec 1990** Drink soon.*

GRAHAM *Also impressively purple when young, but 15 notes since 1983 indicate that it was probably at its best at 10 to 12 years of age. Now showing considerable maturity, slightly weak-rimmed; brown sugar and figgy nose, not completely knit; still fairly sweet, lacking a little flesh but nice, flavoury with refreshingly dry finish. Last noted June 1991*** Drink soon.*

NOVAL, QTA DO *Youthful purple now paler and pleasantly mature; bouquet as evolved as it is ever likely to be; fairly sweet, flavour of walnuts, lightly clad. Last tasted Nov 1989** Drink soon.*

NOVAL NACIONAL *Two notes. Fairly deep and rich colour, nose and flavour. Strange sweet fig-like nose; powerful, concentrated, tannic, unready. Last noted at Noval tasting, Nov 1989*(***) 1995, into the 21st century.*

SMITH WOODHOUSE *Now pleasing but plummy; grapey, whiff of tangerine; sweet, surprisingly powerful yet soft and easy. Dry finish. Last tasted Dec 1990*** Now to 1998.*

REBELLO VALENTE *Never very deep and full, now rather weak and watery with touch of malt and iron on the nose. Sweetish, fairly light. Dry finish. Last tasted Nov 1988* Drink up.*

TAYLOR *The best '75 by far. Immensely impressive in 1977 and despite losing its concentration, richness and sweetness in the early 1980s, still relatively deep, youthfully plummy; hard, prune-like fruit; very sweet, quite powerful, stern, lean yet fleshy for a '75, dry tannic finish. Showing well when last tasted, April 1991**(**)? Not fully developed and hard to predict its future. Taylor's vintage port always seems to be about 10 years behind that of most other shippers so perhaps it will start to soften from about 1995.*

WARRE *More notes than any other, 15 since 1980. One can trace its change in appearance from opaque in 1977, plummy in 1980, less deep but still fairly plummy in 1983, a touch of red in 1987 and in 1988 medium, mature, with a weak tawny rim. In parallel, the nose has changed from a youthfully stalky, spirity character, developing fragrance in the mid-1980s, and, latterly, a refreshing citrus, lean, fruity character. On the palate it has ranged from sweet, full and rich, through an elegant attractive 10-year-old stage to a touch of leanness, losing weight, still elegant but lacking the length of a really good vintage. Sept 1990*** Now to 2000.*

OTHER '75s:

BUTLER NEPHEW *Unimpressive in the early 1980s.*

EIRA VELHA, QTA *At five years of age pale, mercaptan*

nose, high acidity. Admittedly only tasted once.

FOZ, QTA DO *Quite nice light luncheon port. Tasted March 1988***

GONZALEZ BYASS *Ruby, sweet, fat, not bad in 1980***

GOULD CAMPBELL *Purple and pleasing in 1977, maturing nicely in the mid-1980s, and with a rather original flavour***

MARTINEZ *Impressive in 1977, in 1986 evolving nicely, a lovely colour, a bit hard, lean and peppery. Retaste*****?*

OFFLEY *Full, fat and rich in 1977, attractive and just ready at 10 years of age, medium-sweet, lightish and refreshing in 1987***

POCAS JUNIOR *Weak rim; singed, raisiny nose and taste, very sweet, quite nice in the early 1980s, not tasted since***

ROZES *High-toned, spirity, very sweet, full-flavoured and nice quality, fruity, cherry-like in early 1980s***

1976*

Drought from winter to end Aug. Heavy rain end Sept. Not declared but some nice wines made, the best appearing as single-quinta wines or LBVs. For drinking not keeping.

GRAHAM'S MALVEDOS *Several notes from the mid-1980s. Lively colour and character. Sweet, good flavour, nice texture. Refreshing, citrus-like elements, touch of tannic bitterness. Last tasted Feb 1990*** *Drink soon.*

NOVAL *Late bottled, probably in 1980/1. Deepish ruby, drinkable but unmemorable. Tasted in 1982. Off the market now. Perhaps as well.*

SMITH WOODHOUSE *bottled 1980. A lean, attractive LBV. June 1988***

WARRE *Bottled 1980. Quite assertive flavour. Crisp. Good length. June 1988****

1977*****

Wet winter, cold spring and cool summer which delayed development. The weather changed for the better at the beginning of Sept and was followed by the hottest autumn since 1963. Declared by 20 shippers, notable exceptions being Martinez, Noval and Cockburn. The latter have admitted that this was an error of judgement. But this was a period of rather odd policy decisions. Whether this was due to the directors of Cockburn and Martinez on the spot or by their overlords in England I have not ascertained. The major port shippers and their London agents held a tasting at Christie's shortly after the '77s were bottled, in Nov 1979, at which the majority of my first notes on the vintage were made.

CROFT *At the tasting of '77s at Christie's: dense black, prune-like, tangy, high acidity. Eight years later still fairly deep and relatively immature; nose restrained; sweet, full-bodied, elegant, good length, peppery alcohol, tannin and acidity. Most recently, starting to mature; bouquet opening up; rich, rather chocolaty flavour. Good future. Last tasted April 1990***(**) *1995–2050.*

DELAFORCE *Deceptively easy style in 1979. Several notes 10 years later. Still youthful; figs, liquorice and malt; sweet, full-flavoured, lots of tannin and acidity. Last tasted Sept 1989**(***) *1995–2015*

DOW *In 1979 crisp, ruby purple; spirity, beef-tea nose; sweet, full yet fleshy. Loads of all the right component parts. 16 well-spaced notes later illustrating the beginning of colour loss in mid-1980s, though still ruby, intense, translucent. The nose endlessly fascinating with sweet, fig-like fruit, a squeeze of tangerine, cognac-like spirit, tight-knit but developing fragrance. Apart from one corky, woody bottle recently, consistently exciting flavour, now medium-sweet, fairly full-bodied, rich, intense, almost explosively assertive, with the grip of a good vintage and long lean dry finish. Last tasted Nov 1990**(****) *1995–2050*

FERREIRA *In Nov 1979, deep plummy purple; sweet but raw. Two half-bottle samples in 1980 were full of fruit, impressive. Most recently, medium-deep; nose light but pleasing with tea-like fragrance; sweet, nice weight, lightish style yet with noticeable tannin and acidity. Attractive. Last tasted July 1990****(*) *Now to 2010.*

FONSECA *Very impressive at the opening tasting: deep purple; hard, spirity nose; powerful, well-balanced. Most recently, a perfect colour, still fairly deep, plummy; classic, still hard, black cherry fruit nose; very sweet, fairly full-bodied, rich, lovely texture. Great future. Last tasted April 1990****(**) *1994–2020, or beyond.*

GOULD CAMPBELL *Enormously impressive at two tastings in Nov 1979 and certainly one of my favourite '77s: very deep, red-black centre, purple rim. Despite appearance, a sweet, easy, attractive wine on nose and palate. Not tasted again until 1990, at a line-up of Smith Woodhouse and Gould Campbell vintages in the Symington tasting room at Vila Nova de Gaia. Still notably deep, purple, intense; sweet, low-keyed nose with a strange scent that reminded me of bacon rind (I noted a "meaty" taste in 1979). Very sweet, with a totally different character from the Smith Woodhouse. Lean. Dry finish. A good future — certainly of* grande marque *status. Last tasted Dec 1990**(****) *1995 to well beyond 2020.*

GRAHAM *14 notes since 1979 when it was a black red colour; big, fruity, green leaf, almost appley-nosed; very sweet, full, rich but angular. Very gradual colour loss but still fairly deep, plummy and only just starting to mature; extraordinary mélange of fragrances, pure liquorice, figs, strawberry, with citrus crispness; sweet, full-bodied, fleshy, soft, lovely fruit, balance and backbone. Flavour like liquorice 'Pontefract cakes' — as previously made in Yorkshire. Great future. Last tasted May 1991***(***) *1995–2050*

NIEPOORT *Two notes, first in 1985: deep cherry red, rich; good nose, walnuts; sweet, full, unusual but lovely flavour and acidity. "Unusual" noted again, very fragrant, considerable extract and depth. Good if somewhat idiosyncratic. Last tasted April 1990***(**) *Now to 2010.*

OFFLEY BOA VISTA *A surprisingly short cork for a vintage needing bottle-ageing. Deep, plummy; curious, malty, wet blankets and figs nose; sweet, fullish, lean, hot, spicy.* Last tasted Dec 1988*(**) 1995–2010, corks permitting.

QUARLES HARRIS *Extremely good. Appeared to develop quickly but this was misleading as it is still very deep; rich, full of fruit; a sweet, massive, well-stacked wine with high alcohol, good length.* Last tasted Oct 1988**(***) 1995–2020

SANDEMAN *At the opening Christie's tasting: opaque russet purple; a bit lean and spirity, but with good potential. Five years later, delicious but unready. Now medium-deep, still youthful-looking though starting to mature; nose rich yet still hard, liquorice, depth; very sweet, fairly full-bodied, evolving nicely, alcoholic peppery finish.* Last tasted Nov 1989**(**) 1995–2010

SMITH WOODHOUSE *Bottled 1980 though a sample shown at the tasting in 1979: black, ruby-rimmed; slightly singed, prune and blackberry-like nose; very fat, voluptuous. A lively, fruity, pronounced flavour in 1983. Two recent notes: very deep, still immature-looking; rich, figgy, slightly malty nose and taste to match. Sweet, full-bodied, hot alcoholic character, still well endowed with tannin and acidity. The '77 certainly not a second-rank Symington brand.* Last tasted Dec 1990(****) 1995 to well beyond 2015.

TAYLOR *Black; harmonious but closed up; concentrated but reined-in at the opening Christie's tasting in 1979. Deep and fairly intense after a decade; equally deep and rich nose, singed raisins and liquorice; sweet, full-bodied, powerful, packed with all the requisite components, vigorous, great length. Classic.* April 1991(*****) 2000–2050

WARRE *Very deep, hard, tea-leaf taste in 1979. 17 notes showing a slow but gradual development. Though slightly less deep, still youthful, with soft cherry centre; fragrant, tea noted again, scented, mouthwatering acidity; sweet, fullish, a stunning wine, lissom, citrus, spicy, lovely texture, good length and finish.* Nov 1990***(**) 1995–2040

OTHER '77s:

CALEM *Sweet, loaded with fruit. Impressive.* Oct 1986(****)

DIEZ *Lovely gradation of colour; nose unforthcoming but some potential; sweet, full-bodied — notably high alcoholic content, rich, good length.* April 1990*(***)

FEUERHEERD *Pale and unimpressive.* July 1987.

FOZ, QTA DO *Very sweet, full of fruit, lovely.* March 1988**(**)

ROYAL OPORTO *Deepish purple; sweet, raisiny, harmonious; prune-like flavour.* Feb 1986*(**)

1978

Not an easy year. Cold wet winter, spring and early summer followed by drought from late June until early Oct. Great heat in Sept. Net result, a small crop of beefy wines. Noval, which did not declare the '77, did, for good reasons, ship the '78. But the year is notable for an increasing plethora of other single-quinta wines.

CROFT'S QTA DA ROEDA *A fine property, Croft's equivalent to Graham's Malvedos and Taylor's Vargellas. Palish, youthful, a bit feeble; slightly spirity, sweet, fair quality and length.* April 1988**

DELAFORCE'S QTA DA CORTE *The first vintage that Delaforce have marketed a single-quinta wine. Tasted twice. Palish, pink tinge; 'warm' raisiny figgy nose; fairly sweet, easy, dry, slightly bitter finish.* Last tasted April 1988**

DOW'S QTA DO BOMFIM *A few minutes walk from the delightful station at Pinhão is Dow's winemaking centre in the Douro. Bomfim '78 has a good colour, meaty nose, and is sweet, fairly full-bodied, with a fig and blackberry-like flavour. Rich yet with dry finish.* June 1988**(*)

FERREIRA *Two notes, the first, 10 years after the vintage: surprisingly deep-coloured; great power; sweet, massive, full of fruit, tannin and acidity. Still very impressive; fleshy, lovely.* Last tasted July 1990**(***) 1995–2020

GRAHAM'S MALVEDOS *Four notes. A delicious wine. Good colour; very attractive nose, slightly raisiny, touch of liquorice; fairly sweet, medium weight, soft, fleshy.* Last tasted May 1991***(*) Drink soon.

HARVEY'S EIRA VELHA *Bottled Jan 1981. A rather misleading name as this famous old quinta still belongs to the Newman family. But the wine is matured and bottled by Cockburn and now exclusively marketed by Harvey's of Bristol. When first tasted before bottling, exactly two years after the vintage, it was quite impressive, with a pleasing richness and balance. In the mid-1980s deep crisp ruby; bouquet holding back; medium sweetness and weight, a bit leaner than expected. I found the style strange. Must taste again.* Last tasted Oct 1986**?

KOPKE *Another famous old name, but one relatively little known in England. I found their '78 very sweet but short.* Oct 1986**

NOVAL, QTA DO *Mature; rather hard nose, whiff of tangerine; sweet, nice weight and style. Feminine and flavoury.* At Noval tasting, Nov 1989**(*) Can be drunk now but will keep.

NOVAL NACIONAL *Plum-coloured; rich, broad, very figgy nose of great depth; very sweet, full-bodied, rich, fat, concentrated.* Nov 1989*(***) Great future.

ROSA, QTA DE LA *Surprisingly pale; immature nose, reminding me of an apple core; medium-sweet, fairly powerful, crisp fruit, still tannic. I assume colour was lost in cask at the quinta.* Nov 1988(**)

ROYAL OPORTO *Prolific producer, one of the biggest port houses. Somewhat looked down upon by the British (both here and there) but a big seller, on price, in America. Four notes in the mid-1980s. Fully mature-looking; the sweetness and richness (almost) of syrup of figs, soft and agreeable.* Last tasted June 1987**

TAYLOR'S VARGELLAS *I had an unusual opportunity to taste from the casks separate grape varieties grown in different parts of this renowned estate. 'TN' (Touriga Nacional) was incredibly deep in colour, a crisply defined purple, sweet and firm. 'Roris', or Tinta Roriz, was also deep but less crisp. Nose and palate softer, more open-knit. 'Mistura' (mixture of varieties) the most forthcoming on the nose, sweet, with lovely fat and fruit. Clearly promising components.* At Taylor's, Nov 1979(★★★)

WARRE'S QTA DA CAVADINHA *An old vineyard but the wine not previously marketed as single-quinta wine. The grapes are late maturing here. After eight years in bottle I found the nose a bit spirity and like wet cardboard. Very sweet, fullish, crisp, lean and attractive. Quite a lot of tannin still and citrus-like refreshing acidity.* June 1988★★(★)

1979★★

Another summer of drought until heavy rain shortly before harvesting at the end of Sept. Abundant, above average quality but not declared. Some useful LBV's marketed. These should really be drunk fairly soon.

DOW'S LBV *Appears to have been bottled over a period of three years: in 1983, and tasted soon after bottling, lusty but raw; bottled in 1984, pleasantly fruity in 1985; and bottled in 1985, a mélange on the nose, very sweet and soft with a distinctly grapey flavour, but short.* Tasted in 1986 and 1987.

GRAHAM'S MALVEDOS *Very nice sweet, fullish, crisp, fruity flavour. Refreshingly acidic finish.* Last tasted May 1991★★

1980★★★

A good vintage, approachable now as the tannin levels are below '83s'. A useful vintage to drink whilst waiting for the '85s and '77s to mature. A particularly dry summer, picking started towards the end of Sept in fine dry weather. Cockburn, Martinez and Noval did not declare the vintage, whereas the Symington family group did, and regard it as a very underrated vintage. Most of my recent notes on the '80, '82, '83 and '85 vintages were made at a tasting for wine writers and the trade organised by Tim Stanley-Clark at Christie's in June 1990.

BARROS *A very Portuguese port as opposed to the British style, deep, intense; sweet full plummy chocolaty wine with a fragrant aftertaste.* Oct 1986★★★ Now to 2000.

CALEM *Medium, maturing nicely; very sweet, chocolaty, vanilla bouquet and flavour. Rich, figgy, soft, good length. Showing well.* June 1990★★★ Now to 2000.

CROFT *Did not declare but produced LBV. Opaque, prune-like, sweet, citrus cladding, hot acidic finish.* Last tasted Jan 1988★. Drink soon.

DOW *First noted at a tasting held by Michael Symington at Christopher's to launch the Dow 1980 vintage. Preceding the final blend were six* lodge lotes, *wines made from different grape varieties and grown in different districts, all of course of the 1980 vintage. For example 'BFQTA', a wine from two low-lying vineyards on the north bank of the Douro at Pinhão and made at Dow's Quinta do Bomfim: a tough bitter wine, unbalanced on its own but a vital part of the final blend. 'URT', a single-quinta wine from the upper Rio Torto. A high proportion of old vines: opaque, to me very classic. A similar tasting of individual '80s and the final vintage '80 was presented by Michael Symington the following Sept. After one year in bottle the final blend was still hard and figgy on the nose, sweet, hot and spirity on the palate. Two years more in bottle and developing nicely, softer, revealing more flesh. Most recently still impressively deep and intense; rather stalky on the nose, touch of liquorice; very sweet, fullish, flavoury. Plenty of alcohol, tannin and acidity. Needs time.* Last tasted June 1990(★★★) 1995–2020?

FERREIRA *Deepish but maturing quickly; curious high-toned but harmonious nose; sweet, fullish, agreeable, nice acidity.* March 1988★★(★)

FONSECA *Not very deep but after six years in bottle still with a youthful tinge; low-keyed, fig-like, rich though still hard; sweet, medium weight, straightforward, hot dry finish. After another two years, considerable maturity apparent; sweet, chocolaty; spirity, peppery nose, scented, attractive. Very sweet alongside other '80s, fuller than it looked, on the lean side. Dry finish.* Last tasted June 1990★(★★) Now to 2010.

FOZ, QTA DO *Soft rich meaty nose; very sweet, full, fruity.* Oct 1986★★(★)

GOULD CAMPBELL *Two recent notes. Showing pretty well at the big tasting in June and six months later. Virtually opaque, still a plummy immature purple; rich, figgy, harmonious nose; sweet, full of flavour and body, very rich, good fruit, fat for an '80, good length.* Last tasted Dec 1990★★(★★) 1992 to well beyond 2000.

GRAHAM *Seven notes from the mid-1980s. Still impressively deep and intense yet showing some development; rather hard, spicy, curious, muted, slightly raisiny nose; sweet, fairly full-bodied, youthful, fig-like flavour. Lean, peppery, spicy, tannic.* Last tasted May 1991★(★★★)? 1995–2010

HUTCHESON *(owned by Barros Almeida) Deep, crisp, plummy; very sweet, spirity; sweet, rich, firm. Hard end.* Oct 1986★★(★) 1994–2000

NIEPOORT *Four notes in the mid-1980s: singed walnuts and raisins; very sweet, rich, soft. Nice wine. Two recently: still deep and youthful; almost sickly sweet on the nose, ripe figs; medium full-bodied, very attractive fruit. Dry finish.* Last tasted Oct 1990★★★(★) Now to 2000.

OFFLEY *Deepish, still slightly plummy — neither immature nor mature; lean, sharp fruit on the nose. Later a trace of woodiness. Sweet, fairly full-bodied, rather stalky and spirity.* June 1990★ Drink up.

QUARLES HARRIS *Medium, plummy; sweet, slightly chocolaty, figgy nose and taste. Fragrant. Rich. Good tannin and acidity.* June 1990★★★ Now to 2000.

REBELLO VALENTE *Medium, maturing; sweet,*

*classic, vanilla nose of some depth; sweet, medium weight, lean but shapely, lovely flavour, good length. June 1990*** Now to 2000.*

ROYAL OPORTO *After only four years in bottle, maturing quite quickly. Nose of warm nuts and raisins; sweet, fleshy. Two poor bottles at the recent comparative tasting: pale, weak rimmed; high volatile acidity; sweet, thin and sharp. Not recommended. Last tasted June 1990.*

SANDEMAN *Impressive depth, weight and fruit before and just after bottling. Still deep, intense and immature-looking after six years in bottle; low-keyed though with some depth; fairly sweet, fairly full-bodied, flavoury, moderate length, tannin and refreshing acidity. Most recently, beginning to show some maturity; straightforward, rather spirity nose; nice weight, lean, flavoury. Last tasted May 1991**(*) Now to 2000.*

SMITH WOODHOUSE *My highest rating of the 14 '80s tasted blind at Christie's in June 1990. Equally impressive at the line-up arranged by James Symington: notably deep, plummy; very forthcoming fruit on the nose, richness, almost malty; very sweet, full-bodied, lovely flavour, intensity and length. Dec 1990**(**) 1992–2000+*

TAYLOR *Opaque, purple; highly alcoholic but dumb; sweet, full-bodied, with bitter tannic finish in Dec 1982. Now medium-deep, plum-coloured; low-keyed, harmonious, rich yet ethereal bouquet; fairly sweet, opening up pleasantly, good flavour, reasonable length and finish. Leaner than the '83. Last tasted May 1991*(**) 1995–2010*

WARRE *Just one recent note: medium-deep, rich, plummy; sweet, quite fragrant nose though still with unsettled peppery spirit; very sweet, fairly full-bodied, despite its 'heat', very attractive. Agreeable and ready soon. June 1990*(**) Now to 2000.*

1981

Not declared. Noted for some reasonably successful LBV ports. The rest of course used for standard blends.

DOW'S *Late bottled in 1986. Palish; unknit; very sweet, pleasant, easy, short. Dry acidic finish. April 1987* Drink up.*

GRAHAM'S LBV *Some depth, lively. Last tasted April 1988***

NIEPOORT *Bottled 1986. Medium-deep, maturing; good fruit, reminded me of mincemeat (sweet mince pies!). Very sweet. Good fruit. Nice body and balance. Dry finish. Oct 1990****

TAYLOR'S LBV *Very deep, very sweet, full-bodied, fruity and vigorous. Extremely good when last tasted, Nov 1987****

1982★★★ *at best* ★★★★

12 shippers. Some — Cockburn, Graham, Warre for example — conspicuous by their absence. They plumped for '83. Very dry winter, some spring rain but summer exceptionally hot and arid. One of the earliest harvests in living memory, early to mid-Sept. Frankly, mixed results, some warranting four stars. But this ambiguity over quality and style is leading to confusion. Consequently they are at present distinctly underpriced.

CALEM'S QTA DO FOZ *See* **Foz**

CHURCHILL GRAHAM *The marriage of a scion of the Graham family to a Churchill justified the name of a new port brand — the first to start up for many years. However, there were strong objections to the use of 'Graham', on grounds of possible confusion. I was not overly impressed by Churchill's new range of ports though the '82 when tasted in 1984 had a pretty impressive depth of colour; a youthful, stalky, syrup of figs nose; hard, lean, spirity, but reasonable length and potential. Showing badly at the big tasting at Christie's, high volatile acidity and woodiness. June 1990. Try again?*

CROFT *First tasted in 1985: broad, malty sultanas nose; sweet, full, nice flesh and fruit. Good length. Two recent notes: palish, rosy-hued, rather advanced for its age. Bouquet also very forthcoming, raisiny, attractive in its way. Very sweet, almost chocolaty, full of flavour, stylish, silky tannins and lively acidity. More in it than meets the eye. Last tasted June 1990*** Now to 2000.*

DELAFORCE *Their first declaration since 1977. Limited quantity. Two recent notes: medium-deep, attractive, quick-maturing; sweet, raisiny, slightly malty nose; sweet on the palate, fullish but lean, with crisp fruity flavour, tannin and highish acidity. Last tasted June 1990**(*) Now to 2000.*

DOW *Just one note, three years after bottling: then still opaque, intense; sweet, full, rich, slightly short and with an edge of acidity. April 1987(**?)*

FERREIRA *Deep, still immature; hefty nose, stewed prunes; very sweet, full-bodied, packed with fruit. March 1988*(**) 1992–2010*

FOZ, QTA DO *In 1986, after two years in bottle: deep, crisp, intense; youthful, fruity, spirity. Most recently, still impressively deep, plummy; good fruit; very sweet, medium full-bodied, lovely flavour. Delicious wine. Last tasted June 1990**(**) 1994–2010*

GRAHAM'S MALVEDOS *Deep, rich, plummy; curiously evolved and open aroma of thick fruit, figs, raisins; very sweet, smooth, fleshily endowed and full of fruit, tannin and acidity. May 1991**(**) 1993–2000*

GRAHAM'S LBV *Alas, date of bottling not noted. I found it rather lean and too dry. But, like RD champagnes, drink when put on the market. Not for keeping. Tasted June 1990**

GUIMARAEN'S QTA DO CRUZEIRO *Deep; warm crusty nose; pleasing. May 1985. Then(***) Now to 2000.*

MARTINEZ *Under the same ownership, yet always playing second fiddle to the heavily promoted Cockburn. Usually excellent — as with this '82. Showing well at the big blind tasting in June and, more recently, at Cockburn's. Fairly deep, plummy, trying to make a start at maturing; very good, rich, intense, rather high-toned, figgy, raisiny nose; a big sweet wine, with a very attractive, slightly raisiny flavour, touch of leanness, otherwise excellent balance.* Last tasted Dec 1990**(**) *Almost a five star future.* 1995–2015

NIEPOORT *The standard two-year bottling. Five notes since the mid-1980s. Though an intense mulberry colour a year after bottling it seemed destined for early maturity. An unusual style, tasting of singed stalky raisins, gingery, meaty. Attractive in its way. It went very well with strawberries in its fifth year but I thought it a bit hard and dull in the recent line-up of 10 '82s.* Last tasted June 1990** Possibly**(*) 1992–98

NOVAL, QTA DO *The first vintage declared by the new generation of the van Zeller family. Four admiring notes from the mid-1980s. Initially opaque, still fairly deep and very impressive, intense, youthful after five years in bottle; a lot to it: deep plummy fruit with a tannin smell like soft shoe leather, figs and walnuts. Sweet, full-bodied, rich, high extract, excellent length, tannin and acidity. Most recently, as described but beginning to show some maturity. Intense. Good potential. A top '82.* Last tasted June 1990*(***) 1992–2020

NOVAL NACIONAL *Bottled Feb 1985. Surprisingly, slightly paler than the 'standard' Noval, but with a rich, spicy nose of great depth; sweet, full, rich, dry finish.* At Noval tasting, Nov 1989(****) 2000–30

OFFLEY *Very deep, intense; low-keyed, still rather hard and spirity; sweet, full-bodied, assertive. Lovely flavour but unready.* June 1990*(**) 1992–2000

OFFLEY BOA VISTA LBV *Malty and — to me — unattractive.* May 1989.

RAMOS-PINTO *Two recent notes: deep, immature; sweet but hard, with touch of mint and figs; sweet, crisp assertive fruit, powerful, lean yet shapely. Unready.* Last tasted Oct 1990(***) 1995–2005

'RIO TINTO' *An unnamed single-quinta wine from the Rio Tinto, a tributary of the Douro, imported by Eldridge Pope and included to demonstrate an interesting new marketing concept. Good colour, lovely fruit, good value.* July 1990*** Drink soon.

ROYAL OPORTO *My lowest rating in the blind tasting of '82s. Both bottles poor, one smelly, sulphide, the other oxidised. Both unclean.* June 1990.

SANDEMAN *Four notes. Opaque, huge, hard and peppery around the time of bottling. Still a youthful rich ruby after four years in bottle; strange nose, still hard, figs and brambles; distinctly sweet, fullish, a refreshing citrus touch, good length. Most recently, less deep, now plummy; straightforward, low-keyed, Spanish-root nose.* Last tasted June 1990*(**) 1992–2000+

TAYLOR'S LBV *Medium-sweet, lean but fruity and flavoury with characteristic Taylor bitter finish.* May 1987** Drink up.

TAYLOR'S VARGELLAS *Fairly well-developed even under three years of age. Sweet, soft, pleasing.* May 1985. Probably at best now.

1983****

A very attractive vintage. Superficially similar vintage to '82 but overshadowed by the excellent '85s. Roughly 10 major shippers plus minor and LBV's. Good mid-term drinking. A cold, wet May caused *desavinho (coulure)*. Sept was fine and sunny with average temperatures over 30°C almost throughout the month. The hot and dusty grapes "freshened up", to quote Michael Symington, by a few isolated rain storms during the last few days of Sept which merely interrupted the long hot autumn. A good, but exceptionally late harvest in Oct, with high sugar readings.

Quite a few notes but first put in perspective at a blind tasting of nine of the major '83s in Oporto in May 1985 and at the more extensive blind tasting at Christie's in June 1990 which included a dozen '83s.

Like the '82, currently undervalued and will remain so until the confused market has shaken down.

CALEM *Fairly deep, pleasant colour, maturing nicely; nose rather hard at first but developed and sweetened in the glass; very sweet, full-bodied, crisp citrus-edged flavour, lean. Good. Family-owned, traditional, rather British in style, very good.* June 1990*(***) 1993 to beyond 2000.

COCKBURN *Cockburn's first declaration since 1975, "production small but of first-rate quality" (Peter Cobb). Three notes made in summer 1985 confirmed its blackness of colour and exceptional sweetness and concentration, character, length and tannin — all harbingers of long life. The following Nov (1986) still intense with a hard immature spirity nose. Sweet, full-bodied, peppery (alcohol) and dry tannic finish. Two more recent notes: still impressively deep and youthful-looking; sweet, scented, attractively piquant nose, still peppery. On both occasions noted as medium-sweet and medium full-bodied. A leanish, long and tangy wine. Very flavoury.* Dec 1990(****) 1998–2020

CROFT *Did not declare but produced an LBV. Three recent notes: still deep, plummy, fairly sweet, a bit lean and raw but quite flavoury. Easing up now and pleasant to drink.* May 1990** Drink up.

DOW *In May 1985 Michael Symington produced another of his fascinating but arduous tastings of the individual lodge* lotes *which made up their 1983 vintage blend. They ranged in appearance from deep purple to opaque with intense violet rim. Aromas varied between the dumb but spirity and broad soft tones with liquorice, figs, sultanas, a baked character and herbaceous scents. On the palate the sweetness cut, and counterbalanced by, tannins and acidity. Some were lean, some fleshy, most had good length. Seven notes since. In 1987, still opaque but more complete and evolved on the nose. Sweet for Dow. Most recently still fairly deep, lively, youthful; very rich, harmonious bouquet reminding me of stewed prunes; sweet, hot, assertive, almost maltily rich, good fruit and length. Dry, tannic, acid finish.* March 1991(****)

FONSECA *Seven notes. Predictably opaque in 1985; a lot of vinosity and flesh; sweet, full, fruity. Now deep and plummy; a hefty, rich bouquet and flavour of prunes and figs. Seems very sweet, fairly powerful, still rather hard yet elegant. Lovely* *wine. Last tasted June 1990(****) 2000–20*

GOULD CAMPBELL *First noted in the Symington's tasting room in May 1985. It was as opaque as the Warre and fatter than Fonseca and Graham. Certainly rich and impressive. A couple of months later, noted a meaty almost malty richness on the nose, coupled with brandy. Also showing well at the blind tasting at Christie's: good grip, firm. Most recently, still impressively deep, immature; considerable depth of fruit; fairly sweet, flavoury, like a pretty child with an upturned nose. Dry finish. Last tasted Dec 1990(****) 1995–2015*

GRAHAM *Nine notes. Black velvet in 1985 and 1986, fine wine, great length. More recently still impressively deep, a fine crisp appearance with youthful edge; rather muted nose, figgy, fruity, peppery, not unlike the '80. Sweet, full-bodied, rich, chewy, lean yet with a good flesh, tannin and acidity. Up to Graham's high standard. Last tasted May 1991(****) 1993–2015*

NIEPOORT *Deep purple in 1985 with curious malty, coffee-bean nose; soft yet highish acidity, good length. Showing well at the recent blind tasting of '83s: still fairly immature; good, peppery, fruity nose; very sweet, full of fruit, extract and flavour. Good length. An attractive wine. Last tasted June 1990*(***) 1992–2015*

RAMOS-PINTO *Two recent notes. Deep, plummy, starting to mature; nice nose, good fruit, slightly raisiny, figs, touch of stalkiness but inherently soft and harmonious. Distinctly sweet in the Portuguese style, medium full-bodied, assertively fruity, hard still yet fleshy. Dry finish. Needs time. Oct 1990*(**) Possibly**** in due course. Say 1993–2015.*

REBELLO VALENTE *Just one note: medium, showing considerable maturity; a fully evolved, broad, figgy nose and flavour. Whiff that reminded me of a* raya *sherry. Very sweet. Quite nice in its way. Unenthusiastic. June 1990** Drink soon.*

ROYAL OPORTO *As with the '80 and '82, by far my lowest mark at the blind tasting at Christie's. Medium-deep, still rather immature; high volatile acidity on nose and palate. Sweetness and fruit but . . . not recommended. June 1990.*

SMITH WOODHOUSE *Four notes. Showing well at the initial blind tasting in May 1985, rich, fat, attractive. Sweet, agreeable shortly after. Though impressively deep, intense and still youthful looking at Christie's I found a stalkiness on nose and palate. Most recently, a much better note: very fruity on the nose; sweet, rich, lovely flavour. Last tasted Dec 1990. On balance*(***) 1993–2015*

TAYLOR *Six notes. Opaque; high-toned, spirity; good rich crisp flavour in 1985. By June 1990 colour less deep, developing quicker than expected and rather weak at the rim. Rich, peppery, liquorice nose; medium full-bodied, straightforward. Most recently, soft, very sweet, fleshy. May 1991(****)*

WARRE *Seven notes. The usual classic appearance in 1985: opaque centre and violet rim. Very deep plummy purple by autumn 1986. Still fairly deep, still with a fairly immature plummy hue; a powerful yet restrained, almost chewable, peelable nose of intriguing character; sweet without being cloying, nice weight, lovely flavour and texture, a bit lean but with characteristic Warre elegance and firm dry tannic finish. June 1990(****) 2000–20*

OTHER '83s:

CALEM *LBV Very good. March 1988****

FERREIRA'S QTA DO SEIXO *Fabulously intense appearance; very powerful nose; sweet, fairly full, lovely citrus-edged fruit. March 1988**(**)*

FOZ, QTA DO *Fine big classic wine. Oct 1986*(***)*

HUTCHESON *Malty, peppery, figgy. May 1989*(*)*

QUARLES HARRIS *Warm, soft, flavoury. 1985*(**)*

NOVAL *LBV Good, rich, flavoury. Oct 1989****

1984

Not declared.

FONSECA GUIMARAENS *Bottled 1989. Deep, immature. Horrid nose. Taste of prunes and figs. Not liked. Preferred the cheese and celery. At the Wine Trades' Benevolent Banquet, May 1989.*

QUARLES HARRIS *Probably LBV. Thick. Ruby. Quite nice. July 1990***

TAYLOR'S VARGELLAS *Tasted in cask. Typically massive and tough Taylor character. Will probably develop and keep well.*

1985★★★★★

An outstandingly attractive, vibrant vintage. The best since 1977 and one of the top post-war vintages. 26 shippers. Very cold and long wet winter, damp spring, hot summer and excellent conditions for the harvest which began around Sept 30.

20 '85s tasted blind at a June 1990 tasting at Christie's arranged by Tim Stanley-Clark with the cooperation of shippers and their agents. At that and at tastings before and since, the quality and great style of the vintage patently apparent.

CALEM *Three notes in the summer and autumn of 1987. Good wine. At the Christie's tasting: still quite deep though about to turn into its maturity curve; rich, fruity nose with the lively acidity noted on quite a lot of the '85s. Very sweet, full, glorious flavour. Rich, extract masking the acidity. Last tasted June 1990(****) 1995–2010*

CHURCHILL *Intense and fragrant in July 1987. More recently, opaque, youthful appearance; high-toned, good fruit on nose and palate. Fairly sweet, full-bodied. Their best vintage to date. June 1990(***) Possibly a future **** Time will tell. 1995–2010*

COCKBURN *Opaque, intense; very distinctive — fish skin and iron — nose; fairly loaded, overall dry in July 1987. Two recent notes, a distinct whiff of volatile acidity noted at the blind tasting in June and in Cockburn's tasting room six months later. Still impressively deep and youthful; good fruit and a more evolved nose and palate than the '83. Very flavoury but a rather sharp attenuated finish. Last tasted Dec 1990(***) 1995–2005*

CROFT *Just two years old: deep thick rich appearance; sweet, soft, malty nose; full, fat, nice texture.*

Most recently, though fairly deep and of course still immature, it gave me the impression of a wine likely to develop fairly quickly. Extremely good rich nose and fine flavour. An attractive, well-balanced wine. Last tasted June 1990(****) 1995–2010.

DELAFORCE *Four notes. Very deep plummy purple; beetroot and tobacco, tannic nose; very sweet, plump, fleshy and smooth in July and Aug 1987. In spring 1989, still youthful-looking; rich malt and fruit nose; fairly full-bodied, some flesh, fruit, balance, tannin for longevity and acidity. At the blind tasting at Christie's: lovely colour, showing some development; the same rich, meaty nose; very sweet, rich — one of the best vintages of Delaforce I can recall.* Last tasted June 1990(****) 1995–2015

DOW *Two notes in the spring and summer of 1987: vigorous, lots of grip. Two in Feb 1989: still very deep and purple; nose holding back but spicy fig-like fruit lurking beneath the brandy and sweaty tannins. Very sweet, intense and powerful. Fleshy yet still raw. Very tannic. A slow starter, long keeper. At the Christie's tasting: deep, plummy; nose and palate much as described though I upgraded the former when returning to it (still blind) several hours later. With some of the leanness and acidity — its vibrant nervous system — I associate with Dow's style. Very flavoury.* Last tasted June 1990(*****) 2000, just, to past 2030.

FONSECA *Deep, intense; malty; powerful, great potential in July 1987. High marks at June 1990 tasting, particularly on the palate, the nose being a bit restrained despite its rich, figgy fruit. Full-bodied. Powerful. Still opaque; soft, sweet, fleshy. Well endowed with fruit, alcohol and tannin for longevity. My style of wine. Magnificent.* Last noted May 1991(*****) 1998–2030

GOULD CAMPBELL *Loaded with tannin, July 1987. Very high marks at the June 1990 tasting: deep, rich, velvety; good nose that seemed to expand richly in the glass over three hours; sweet, full-bodied, lots of fruit, life-preserving tannin and good acidity. Most recently, confirmation. A lovely deep rich wine.* Last tasted Dec 1990(****) Possibly***** future. 1998–2025

GRAHAM *Nine notes. Distinctive style. Very floral, malty richness, rich and fat in April and July 1987. Gloriously velvety purple colour; deep, equally velvety, harmonious nose that developed a honeycomb sweetness in the glass. A wonderfully complete wine in Feb and March 1989. A year later, at a Graham vertical tasting, superb. Bouquet evolving well and very appealing; lovely flavour, texture, length and acidity. High-toned. Perfect weight, flesh, fragrant aftertaste. Beautiful to drink now — though a pity, as it has so much more to offer. A lovely wine.* Last tasted May 1991**(***) 1995–2025

MARTINEZ *When first tasted (July 1987) I noted it as having a very curious nose and distinctive flavour, with a dry, rather acidic finish. Three years later, the citrus twist of acidity still noticeable but otherwise rated quite highly. Deep, rich, plummy colour; richness of fruit that so often calls to mind ripe figs; sweet, fullish body, hot fruity flavour.* Last tasted June 1990*(**), possibly*(***) 1995–2010

NOVAL, QTA DO *Picking began on Sept 27 in excellent conditions. First tasted in July 1987. Exciting flavour. Lovely fruit. Two autumns later: powerful, figgy nose; very sweet, full-bodied, a fine shapely wine, good length. Showing well at Christie's tasting: attractive colour, starting to mature; deep, rich nose; touch of elegant leanness, long dry fruity-acid finish. Very attractive.* Last tasted June 1990*(***) 1992–2015

NOVAL NACIONAL *Medium-deep, rich, starting to mature; rich, harmonious, slightly subdued nose with whiff of walnuts; very sweet, immense, powerful, packed with fruit and vigour.* At the Noval tasting, Nov 1989(*****) 1995–2030

NIEPOORT *Tasted in April, May and Aug 1987 from sample half-bottles on which were notes made at the time of fermentation. A natural 12.9° alcohol, 27.00 dry extract, total acidity 3.5, volatile acidity 0.52, and 6.2 iron. Not surprisingly, opaque; rich, good fruit but with immature stalkiness and brandy; sweet, concentrated, spicy and fleshy. Then, showing well at the blind tasting at Christie's: still opaque-centred with immature purple rim; high alcoholic content noted on the nose, plus figs, liquorice. Sweet, nice weight, good balance and fruit.* June 1990(****) 1995–2015

OFFLEY *Good note July 1987 and exceptionally good, earning equal top marks tasted blind at Christie's. Still opaque, intense, immature; classic nose, with the rich, figgy, almost maltiness of very ripe grapes; very sweet, full-bodied, loaded with fruit, extract, tannin, acidity. Good length. Hot finish.* June 1990(*****) if it keeps up the pace. 1996–2020

QUARLES HARRIS *Just one note. Medium-deep, starting to mature; very forthcoming, lean, raisiny nose which after some hours in the glass reminded me of a late-harvest Zinfandel. Fairly sweet, medium-full body. Good, straightforward flavour. Long, lean, dry finish.* June 1990(****) 1995–2015

RAMOS-PINTO *Two recent notes. Deep, attractive, a clean-cut youthfulness; dusty and hard at first but rich underlying fruit; very sweet, fairly full-bodied, lovely flavour, soft and fleshy despite its tannin and acidity. Good length.* Last tasted Oct 1990(****) 1993–2015

REBELLO VALENTE *A good opening note in July 1987. At the Christie's tasting, fairly deep, but though still purple looked to me like a quick developer; odd nose, like a wet blanket, hard, spirity, but fruit lurking. Much better on the palate: very sweet, full, with lovely spicy fruit, good length, hot finish.* Last tasted June 1990*(**) Possibly **** when it shakes down. 1995–2000+?

ROYAL OPORTO *Another questionable performance in the blind tasting at Christie's. One of the least deep and impressive '85s. Plummy but a fairly weak rim. Nose unknit. After time in glass, sweaty, coarse. Better on the palate. A very sweet, powerful wine, full of fruit.* June 1990*(*)?? Retaste.

SANDEMAN *First tasted in July 1987: sweet and spicy. A year later, at a vertical of Sandeman vintages: very rich, meaty, malty, prunes and figs, slightly singed nose; sweet, full-bodied, loaded with tannin, acidity and alcohol, vanilla and spice. I gave it my highest mark, fractionally above the '77. At the Christie's tasting, still fairly deep, poised to start maturing; lots of fruit, pepper and high-toned acidity on the nose and palate. Very flavoury.* Last tasted June 1990(★★★★) 1995–2015

SMITH WOODHOUSE *First noted in July 1987: stylish, nicely put together. Showing well at the recent blind tasting: fairly deep, youthful but at the point of departure; lovely rich nose but still with hard-edged immaturity; sweet, medium-full body, good fruit. Confirmed, plus a note relating to its good balance and texture.* Last tasted Dec 1990★(★★★) 1992–2015

TAYLOR *In July 1987 a predictably substantial wine. Tannic. Great length and aftertaste. Showing well at the recent horizontal of '85s. Tasted blind, one of the eight top-ranking wines, with just a half to one and a half points between them. Still impressively deep, intense, plummy; rich, figgy concentrated nose; fairly sweet, full-bodied, rich, good length, still hard but with that extra Taylor aftertaste. Great potential.* Last tasted May 1991(★★★★★) 1998–2030

WARRE *Four notes since April 1987. A touch of toffee on the nose (malt, meat, toffee all reflecting the almost unctuous richness of the vintage, as is a thickness of colour). Still a fine deep red purple; extraordinary nose, whiff of wet oilskin, great vinosity, prunes, figs; sweet, fairly full-bodied, fleshy, elegant, beautifully balanced. Excellent tannin and acidity. An archetypal Warre. I put this top of the '85s.* Feb 1989(★★★★★) 1995–2030.

OTHER '85s:

FERREIRA *Deep, crisp; plummy, sweet, full, figgy.* March 1988(★★★)

FOZ, QTA DO *(Cálem's) Opaque, huge, opulent, very sweet, full but lean.* March 1988(★★★★)

HOOPER'S *Indistinct nose; sweet, full, fat, smooth but lacking length.* July 1987★(★)

HUTCHESON *Plummy colour and nose; very sweet, fig-like flavour.* Sept 1989★(★)

KOPKE *Medium colour; hard, lean, spirity; not very sweet, lean, crisp, nice length.* July 1987★(★)

MESSIAS *Thick, plummy; sweet, smooth texture, a rather odd, slightly stalky flavour.* July 1987★(★)

POCAS *Opaque, sweet, full and figgy.* Sept 1987★(★)

DA SILVA *Very sweet, impressive.* July 1987★(★★)

1986

Not a very propitious growing year. After 3½ months of virtually unbroken drought, the wind suddenly turned to the south and, during the second week of Sept, the Douro — indeed all Portugal — was inundated with rain, 2in being recorded at Pinhão over the weekend of Sept 13–14! Picking in the upper Douro continued from Sept 24 under good, crisp autumn conditions. Not declared.

DOW *Cask samples tasted in the spring after the vintage to compare two of the leading classic grape varieties. Touriga Nacional, considered the best: extremely deep and intense; vast aroma of prunes and figs; fairly sweet, very full-bodied, very rich, severe. Touriga Francesa, which makes useful blending wine: totally opaque; softer, more feminine, citrus nose and flavour; slightly less sweet, and lighter-bodied, leaner, very flavoury. The more I taste young ports, the more I admire the incredible stamina and experience of the 'noses', the master blenders, who must be the lynch-pins of all the great port houses.*

FOZ, QTA DO *An intensely purple wine from a sample pipe. A sweet, gutsy yet lean wine. Impressive.* March 1988.

NIEPOORT LBV *Bottled 1990. Deep, youthful; syrup of figs; very sweet, soft, fleshy, long, hot, slightly acidic end.* Oct 1990★★(★)

SANDEMAN *Bottled 1990. Plummy; figgy, horrible; sweet, not liked.* Feb 1991.

1987

Another uneven year. The early development of the vines hampered by the previous winter's low rainfall. Then a long bout of hot weather, reaching a near record 38°C (just over 100°F) in Oporto, early Aug. Intermittent violent storms in July and Aug. Heavily laden vines consisted of rather small, dried-up grapes, picked in excessive heat (reaching 40°C in Pinhão) in mid-Sept, followed by rain. Nevertheless, some yields were above average and sugar readings of the early-picked grapes were high, and there were considerable variations from district to district. So far, declared only by Martinez.

FOZ, QTA DO *Interesting samples from vineyards on the hot barren slopes of the excellent Cima Corgo district and the lower Baixa Corgo, both opaque, the former with a hot, youthful, straw-like nose; full and lean, loaded with tannin and acidity, the latter more open-knit on nose and palate, slightly sweeter, less full-bodied.* Tasted in April 1988.

GRAHAM'S MALVEDOS *Opaque, intense; very rich young fruit; sweet, raisiny yet lean.* May 1991★★(★)

MARTINEZ *Opaque, intense; rather hard, oaky nose with fig-like fruit and rather high acidity; medium-sweet, medium-full body, lean, dry finish.* Dec 1990(★★★)

NIEPOORT *Rolf Niepoort suggested that I might try drinking young port with steak au poivre. I tried it in Feb 1990 with his '87, a thick-set, intense wine with an immature appearance; surprisingly fragrant only a few months after bottling; sweet, full-bodied, loads of fruit, tannin and acidity which coped admirably with the pepper steak. In fact it seemed to hot-up even the pepper. Most recently: as described, a good mouthful of a wine with an equally promising future.* Last tasted Oct 1990(★★★) 1995 to well beyond 2000.

TUA, QTA DA *Cockburn's first single-quinta vintage port. Gordon Guimaraens informed me that the grapes were 100% from their quinta at Tua, just across that tributary of the Douro from Malvedos. An impressive, mouthfilling wine: opaque, intense; very good fruit; sweet, fairly full-bodied. A good start.* At Cockburn's, Dec 1990(★★★)

*1988**

After the abundance of recent years, relatively sparse budding followed by three exceptionally damp and stormy months, causing mildew and *desavinho* (*coulure*). Also hail damage. Early Sept, an intense heat-wave caused some scorching, but also accelerated maturation, and harvest began towards end Sept. The smallest crop in memory. Financial disaster for farmers, serious shortage for shippers.

1989

Excessively dry winter, sporadic spring rain. Summer began early and was long and hot, though heavy rain in June. Harvest began some three weeks early and was completed in ideal conditions by early Oct. Though quality high, production below average.

Shippers need stock for standard blends so the 1988 shortfall means they are unlikely to cream off the best to declare a vintage.

* *I am indebted to Michael Symington, Bill Warre and* Decanter *for recent weather and vintage reports.*

1990

Propitious conditions: successful budding and flowering; a big potential crop. However, searing heat late July into Aug 'burnt' the ripening grapes and dried up young vines. Heavy rain again mid- and end-month swelled grapes. A large healthy crop, final yields surprisingly high. Problems caused mid-harvest by an unforeseen brandy shortage, then, paradoxically, official permits issued for quantities in excess of the original authorisation.

Whether 1990 will be declared a vintage year will depend on 1992 market conditions.

GRAHAM *Tasting of wine made from grapes vinified separately. Tinta Barroca grown at Malvedos: opaque, purple; raw stalky nose; sweet, lean, swingeingly tannic. Tinta Roriz, also from Malvedos, softer yet with quite a kick. Touriga Nacional, even more intense, figgy fruit; less sweet, full-bodied, firm, classic. Tinta Francesa: incredible aroma, violets; fabulous flavour and length.* Tasted May 1991.

MADEIRA *and* TOKAY

Madeira was an immensely popular wine throughout the 18th century and up to the mid-19th. It was the most versatile of all wines: perfect for mid-morning, mid-afternoon with cake, before, during and after meals. It was also the only wine that could survive both icy cellars and hot climates. For this reason it was shipped to and consumed in large quantities in the Americas, the plantations in the West Indies, trading posts in the East Indies and British regimental messes in India and elsewhere.

Between 1850 and 1875 the Madeira vineyards suffered two blows, the deadly mildew oidium then the aphid phylloxera. Though decimated, some vines survived and, against all odds, a few fine wines were made. The American Civil War put an end to extensive shipments to the Southern States and, except for British regimental messes, the popularity of madeira declined as production diminished.

A note about the order

The wines have been arranged chronologically, whether 'true' or straight vintage or solera. This is because it is sometimes impossible to know whether a wine is vintage or solera when only the year appears on the label, also because it is not easy to know whether old vintage wine had been judiciously refreshed in cask. Solera madeiras are often more vigorous and more beautiful to drink than an unblended vintage wine which can dry out and take on a woody taste from the cask. However, vintage madeiras usually command a higher price at auction, though not necessarily justifiably.

Tastings

I have tasted madeiras in a variety of contexts. Many individually, with friends and from my own modest collection; at madeira tastings for *Decanter* magazine and other groups, one organised by a small Belgian company specialising in fine madeiras and, most memorably, Dr Robert Maliner's collection forming the opening session of a Wine Weekend organised by the Hollywood Wine Society in Florida: 11 wines of the rarest and 'shyest' of all madeira grapes, Terrantez and Bastardo. When we drew the corks the room filled with an almost intoxicating perfume.

On several visits to Madeira I have also taken the opportunity to taste on the spot (not at the quintas, but in the tasting rooms in Funchal, the island's capital) wines of the Madeira Wine Association (MWA), whose brands include Blandy, Cossart Gordon, Leacock, Rutherford & Miles; also the still-independent Henriques & Henriques, and the family-owned Barbeito.

How to taste madeira

Island-bottled corks are often miserably short but seem to do the job. The colour of the wine usually ranges from the pale yellow of Sercial, the amber yellow of Verdelho, through to the amber gold of Bual and amber brown of Malmsey. Quality shines like a beacon and one of the clues, apart from richness of sheen, is a distinctive apple green or yellow gold edge or rim. One peculiarity of madeira is that, unlike most other wine, age and maturity cannot be judged by its depth or hue.

The expressions 'high-toned', 'ethereal' and 'tangy' crop up endlessly. I make no apology. They result from the high acidity, fixed and volatile, that is an essential part of the make-up of top-class madeira, an acidity that sometimes reaches levels that would be quite intolerable in any other wine but which, being masked by rich extract and 'dried fruit', and supported by high alcohol, lifts the bouquet and flavour to heights unmatched. On the palate they range from the swingeingly dry old Sercials (something of an acquired taste but, at their best, ultra-refined), dryish Verdelhos, richer Buals and sweet Malmseys. All in all, marvellous variations on the theme of amber tanginess.

1746

Verdelho, solera *JUSTINO HENRIQUES* In the decanter the wine had a ruddy colour, in the glass pure amber; singed old bouquet that evolved in the glass, richly, like old stables, touch of malt; still some sweetness but thinning, burnt toffee taste and typically high acidity. My wife guessed the century, I got the grape! *Served by Dr Louis Skinner at the end of a Commanderie de Bordeaux dinner in Miami, Jan 1990*****

1792****

A high-quality vintage famed for its association with Napoleon's last exile.

'Madeira, Blandy, 1792–1840' One of the rarest and most historic of all wines. On Aug 7 1815 HMS *Northumberland*, with Napoleon on board, put in at Funchal, en route to St Helena, to purchase fresh fruit and wine. The British Consul-General, Henry Veitch, persuaded Napoleon to take with him a pipe of the excellent 1792. The ex-Emperor had a stomach complaint and did not touch the wine. After his death in 1820 it was returned, unbroached, to Madeira, acquired by Charles Blandy and, after further maturation, bottled in 1840 by his son. One or two of these bottles, with the original 'bottle ticket' or label, have survived. The wine still has a rich, beautiful colour and, despite an acetone-like whiff and being now dried out on the palate, the flavour is good. *Tasted in the MWA 'wine library', Dec 1983.*

Malmsey, solera *BLANDY* Blandy's clearly had additional stocks of the 1792 which they used as the basis of perhaps their most famous solera. Its final yield, in 1957, was 1,228 bottles, of which I have had the privilege to drink and taste from two: lovely brown-tinged amber colour; rich, meaty, tangy bouquet; still fairly sweet and full-bodied, rich, intense yet soft on the palate with seemingly endless persistence of flavour. *Dec 1983******

1795****

Generally very good.

Terrantez Several notes. One bottle, labelled "South Side Madeira Association Ltd Funchal", turned out to be rather a curiosity: a bit too deep in colour, a peculiar nose, a cross between lightly malty calf's-foot jelly and a rather drab *raya* sherry; fairly sweet, rich, quite a nice old drink. On six other occasions I have tasted an excellent solera originally from the cellars of the Vasconcellas family, one, I noted, bottled in 1980. They had similar characteristics: medium-pale amber with lovely gradation to a soft lime-gold rim; a fabulous bouquet that expanded in the glass, high-toned, ethereal, spicy; fairly sweet, incredible intensity yet refined, high alcohol, very high acidity, great length. *Last tasted at the Hollywood Wine Society's Great Wine Seminar, the oldest of nine Terrantez, Jan 1990. At best******

1802

Terrantez *ACCIAIOLY* Labelled "Special Reserve 1802 Produced, bottled and guaranteed by Oscar Acciaioly". I had never heard of this firm before I was approached by one of the two surviving sons to sell through Christie's a wide range from the family cellars in Funchal. All were of outstandingly high quality. The Acciaiolis are (or were, as they no longer live there) one of the oldest families on the island, being descended from Simon Acciaioli (*sic*), originally from Florence, who settled there in 1525. As the English and colonial trade was virtually the monopoly of the British family firms, Acciaioli concentrated on Scandinavia, "by appointment to HM King Gustav VI Adolf" (of Sweden) appearing on some of the labels. I have two fairly recent notes, one prior to cataloguing. Both medium-deep amber with a very pronounced apple green rim; refined, ethereal, high-toned, a scent like crystallised violets; sweet, full-bodied as all Terrantez should be, and coping well with its high acidity. A wine of great power and persistence of flavour. *Last noted at the Hollywood Wine Society's Terrantez tasting, Jan 1990******

1808*****

An excellent vintage. Malmsey "best ever known" (Cossart).*

Malmsey, solera, *COSSART GORDON* Three notes. Very rich, deep tawny brown; gloriously harmonious nose encompassing caramel, coffee, meatiness, yet with inimitable 'ethereal' old madeira fragrance; very sweet, its characteristically high acidity counterbalanced by its richness and power. A lovely warming wine. *Oct 1984******

Sercial *LOMELINO* Labelled "Sercial de 1808 Do Velho Conde do Carvalhal, Re-engarrafado an 1914 Recorked 1962. Tarquinio T da C Lomelino". Great names, great vintage. Alas it had not survived rebottling and recorking. It smelled of Evostick glue applied to linoleum. I did not taste it. *Dec 1983.*

1811***

Unknown origin Large bottle, good level. Warm amber, slightly cloudy; nose soft, more like old sherry; sweet, rich, lacking the pungency of old madeira but a recognisably 'singed' aftertaste. *Sept 1987***

1815***

Known as the 'Waterloo' vintage; the Bual particularly successful. Several tasted but none recently.

Bual, solera *COSSART GORDON* Light in style, very elegant. *1980*****

1821*****

An excellent vintage. Several notes but none recent.

Bual, solera *COSSART GORDON* Variable but at its best rich, elegant, tangy. *1979****

Bual, solera *RUTHERFORD & MILES* Good though rather sharp. *1965***

Bual, solera *BLANDY* Tasted twice, magnificent, fragrant, ethereal, exquisite. *1976******

1827*****

Boal, Qta de Serrado In oak casks for 108 years, then

* *Madeira, the Island Vineyard by Noël Cossart (Christie's Wine Publications, 1984).*

put into demijohns and finally bottled in 1988. Part of a considerable stock from the estate of one of the Henriques family. Tasted five times. A fabulous wine: a rich glowing amber with pronounced apple-green rim; sweet, slightly caramelly with scent of vanilla and spirit resembling a fine old cognac; still fairly sweet, full-bodied – high alcohol, extract, sustaining power, intensity, incredible length and tingling acidity. *Last noted at a pre-sale tasting at Christie's, June 1990******

Verdelho 'V.L.' Though not identifiably an 1827, a magnificent wine, roughly a century old, bottled in 1927. Bouquet like a venerable cognac. Fragrant, delicate, lovely texture. *In the MWA tasting room, Dec 1983******

1830****

Malmsey Another Henriques family wine, 105 years in oak casks, then in demijohns and bottled in 1988 just before shipment to London. Short unbranded corks. Like the 1823, a very large quantity entered for sale over a period of two years. Seven notes: a deep, rich, oloroso-like colour; hefty, concentrated bouquet, lime blossom, slightly chocolaty; very sweet, full, rich, luscious and long. *Last tasted June 1990*****

1832

Terrantez, 'Special Reserve Medium-sweet' *ACCIAIOLY* Short, rather loose, deeply stained cork. High level. Rich amber; tangy nose; distinctly original varietal flavour, medium sweetness and body, austere, good length but hot dry acidic finish. *April 1989****

1834****

"Generally very good, especially Bual" (Cossart).

Terrantez *BARBEITO* A magnificent wine, seventh in the Terrantez line-up: richly coloured yet not deep; beautiful, harmonious, low-keyed bouquet; very sweet, marvellous mid-palate, very powerful, its high acidity leaving the mouth clean and dry. *Florida, Jan 1990******

1835****

Sercial, solera *BLANDY* Three notes. Amber, sweet, pungent; dry, light style, marvellous acidity, lovely long lingering flavour and aftertaste. *Last tasted Oct 1984******

1836****

"Generally very good, especially Sercial" (Cossart).

Malmsey, 'Special Reserve Sweet' *ACCIAIOLY* Deeply stained but clearly branded cork. Deeper than the 1802 Terrantez but less definitive rim; rich, smooth, harmonious bouquet of considerable depth; very sweet, fairly full-bodied, smooth rich texture, fabulous flavour and excellent finish. *April 1989******

1837****

In the middle of a high-water period in Madeira, one of eight vintages rated by Cossart as "very good" in all districts and for all grapes.

Boal *BARBEITO* Warm amber brown; soft, powdery, touch of cognac; fairly sweet, very rich, excellent flavour and acidity. *April 1991*****

Bual, Special, 'Medium-sweet' *ACCIAIOLY* Short cork faintly branded "Oscar Acciaioly". Amber gold, green rim; glorious, high-toned, refined bouquet; medium-sweet, as labelled, medium weight, exquisite flavour and great length. Excellent acidity and a finish like crystallised violets. *A favourite amongst half-dozen old Acciaioly madeiras tasted prior to cataloguing, April 1989******

Terrantez, *BARBEITO* Deep amber, apple-green rim; very fragrant bouquet, like an old Bas Armagnac, touch of vanilla; medium-sweet, lovely tangy flavour, attenuated, squeeze-of-lemon acidity. *With Doña Maria Manuela de Freitas and her son Riccardo after visiting their Christopher Columbus museum and library in Funchal, Dec 1990*****

1838****

Bual From the Companario district. Very warm, red orange tinge with strong amber-green rim; extraordinary, rich, herbal, somewhat medicinal bouquet; very rich, concentrated, like syrup of figs. *MWA, Dec 1983***

1839****

Another very good vintage.

Verdelho, 'Special Reserve, Dry' *ACCIAIOLY* First tasted in 1986. Rich warm amber-green rim; refined, slightly 'singed', toffee and cognac bouquet; medium-sweet entry, long dry finish framing lovely mid-palate flavour and flesh. Refined. Great length and fragrance. *Last noted April 1989******

1840****

"Generally very good, especially Sercial and Verdelho" (Cossart).

'The Rebel' *NEWTON, GORDON, COSSART & CO* Bottled by William H Fearing, 24 Old Broad Street. In old moulded bottle with wax seal and original bottle ticket. Cossarts were trading under this name between 1828 and 1835 and must have shipped the wine towards the end of that period for bottling by this City of London wine merchants, Fearing. It was quite a common practice to name the wine after the vessel in which it was shipped, in this instance the *Rebel*. The wine had survived. The level was above top-shoulder, the colour good, the nose and flavour very high-toned and varnishy. *June 1984***

1845***

"Generally very fine, especially Bual" (Cossart).

Bual, 'Centenary Solera' *COSSART GORDON* Rather confusingly stated that the 'mother' was the 1844 but the solera was started in Cossart's centenary year, 1845. Some, bottled in 1975, tasted several times, rather malty tangy acidic nose, medium-sweet, attractive. *Oct 1985****

Boal *BLANDY* Apart from the different grape spelling (both are correct), also labelled "Centenary Solera". In oak 85 years, shipped and bottled either just before or after the war (presumably in demijohns in between) and rebottled in 1988. Strength 21%, sweetness 4° Baumé. Low-keyed, rich, relatively soft and gentle. *At a tasting conducted for MADAS in Bruges, May 1990****

1846

A great vintage. Noted for its Terrantez, Bual and Verdelho.

Terrantez, vintage *H M BORGES* Bottled 1900. Several notes since 1973. Magnificent. Rich, slightly orange-tinged amber; fabulous bouquet, rich, intense, refined, squeeze of lime; amazingly powerful wine, great intensity, wonderful length and acidity. Will clear anyone's catarrh! This is what great madeira is all about. *Last noted at the Terrantez tasting conducted for Robert Malliner's Wine Weekend in Florida, Jan 1990******

Terrantez *H M BORGES* Bottled in 1950. This later bottling had a much deeper 'Jacobean oak' colour; its first whiff like a Tinta Negra Mole; sweeter, very rich and concentrated. Lots of grip. *Last tasted in Dec 1983****

Verdelho, Val de Pariso, Avery label Almost certainly 1846, provenance Dr Grabham, then Sir Stephen Gaselee (both noted collectors), bought by Ronald Avery and sold to Harry John Johnson. Pale amber; ethereal, cognac and violets fragrance; intense, assertive yet delicate. Long dry finish. *Dec 1982******

1850****

"Generally very good, especially Verdelho" (Cossart).

Verdelho *PERRIERA D'OLIVEIRA* In oak 130 years. Bottled in 1980. Strength 21%, 6° Baumé. One adjective covers appearance, nose and palate: intense. Fabulous, fairly deep colour for an old Verdelho, very rich, powerful, peppery acidic bouquet and flavour. *At the MADAS tasting in Bruges, May 1990*****

THE EARLY TO MID-1850s

1851 was the last all-round successful vintage before oidium struck. In 1852, wine production on the island down from an average of 50 million hectolitres to 8m, to 3m in 1853 and only 600 hectolitres in 1854, resulting in an economic crisis, unemployment and a 'wine famine', though a few high vineyards produced some good Sercial. By 1855 only 15 British shippers remained out of the 70 trading in 1850. However, they profited from the occasion by buying old stocks.

Leacock Out of place but included to demonstrate that the benefit of long sea voyages, so much in vogue in the 18th century, lingered well into the 19th. Original wax seal embossed "MADEIRA", tag label and bin label "Leacock, shipped for the W Indies, Sept 13 (18)52, bottled at Antony House Aug 6 (18)55". Also continuing the 18th-century tradition, in a bottle with a glass button or seal bearing the Carew family crest. Lively amber; sound, old, tangy nose. Drying out and fairly light but with good flavour, acidity and finish. *At lunch with Sir John Carew Pole after checking the Antony House cellars, in Cornwall, Jan 1981****

1856***

Minute production, yet some fine wine made.

Boal *BLANDY* In oak 65 years, bottled in 1921. 19% alcohol, 3.1° Baumé. Palish amber; a fabulous, ethereal, lime, vanilla, cognac-like bouquet; initial sweetness overtaken by sharp dry finish. Very high volatile acidity but marvellous in its way. *At the Bruges tasting, May 1990****

1860****

Small production. Some very good wines made, especially from the Sercial grapes.

Bual *BLANDY* Two consistent notes 16 years apart. Lovely warm amber; rich, highly aromatic bouquet and taste. Initial sweetness, very dry finish. *July 1987*****

Sercial, solera *COSSART GORDON* Three notes since the mid-1980s, the last rebottled in 1988. In oak 65 years, imported and bottled by Cossart's London agents, Evans Marshall. High alcohol (21%), low sugar (1.4°). Consistent notes: fairly pale amber; glorious, scented, refined, gentle but high-toned mouthwatering bouquet. Assertive, touch of sweetness overtaken by long, sharp, rapier-like, dry acidic finish. Lean but elegant. Good texture. Not the easiest of wines but excellent in its way. *Last tasted May 1990*****

1862*****

Though by no means all the vineyards back in production, some excellent wines made, the Terrantez generally considered the best ever.

Malvazia 'Velho' Stencilled bottle. Short cork, so doubtless island-bottled. Fabulous; high-toned fragrance; sweet, plump, velvety. Waxy honeycomb texture and sweetness. Perfect flavour. *Jan 1983******

Sercial *PERREIRA D'OLIVEIRA* In oak 120 years, bottled 1982. 21.2%, 3.4° Baumé. Green-edged amber; rich, tangy, acidic nose; fairly sweet for Sercial. Fabulous, ethereal quality. Great length. *In Bruges, May 1990******

Terrantez *H M BORGES* Four magnificent bottles in the mid-1980s. Borges, famous for their stocks of vintage wines, were not founded until 1877. They acquired this particular wine from T T de Camara Lomelino 'successors to Mr Robert Leal', the founder of Lomelino, whose grandson was the maternal grandfather of Noël Cossart. Such is island life. What does one of the greatest madeiras look, smell and taste like? Impossible really to put into words: a medium warm amber colour with highlights of gold — beautiful in the sunlight or by candlelight — and lemon-green rim; an overwhelming bouquet, pungent, caramel and honey, high-toned scent of crystallised violets. All this repeated on the palate. Still fairly sweet, very rich, sharing power and delicacy, intensity and fragrance. Boundless length, beautiful acidity. Not a wine to spit out. Even if you did, it would leave an indelible impression. *Last enjoyed at one of Dr Norman Burrows' intimate luncheon parties in Devonshire Place, July 1986******* *(six stars!)*

1863****

Another small but very fine vintage, the Malmsey being particularly good.

Boal, Velho *BLANDY* Sweet, delicate, high-toned; high alcohol and acidity. Rich, warming. *May 1984*****

Malmsey, Finest old, solera *BERRY BROS* Until I compared notes I thought this must be the same as Blandy's, below, but it seemed paler and more ethereal on the nose. *Jan 1990******

Malmsey, solera *BLANDY* Eight notes. The last had been in oak 68 years and rebottled in 1988. Strength 21%, high sugar content: 5.8° Baumé. Fairly deep amber gold; soft, rich, meaty, chocolaty nose; very sweet, fairly powerful, lovely tang, length, acidity, aftertaste. *Last tasted May 1990******

Sercial *COSSART GORDON* Glorious amber gold; mint and chocolate, long, refined wet straw bouquet and flavour. Singed, tangy, attenuated, rapier-like acidic finish. An uncommon taste, worth acquiring. *Dec 1985*****

1864***

A vintage not dissimilar to 1863, small but good, "especially for Bual and Malmsey" (Cossart).

Gran Cama de Lobos Tasted six times, noted (as presumably labelled) with either the name of this famous district (the 'Pauillac' of Madeira) or "Verdelho Blandy's", or both. With the exception of one smelly mercaptan bottle, all lovely, with exciting tangy, smoky, slightly tarry, refined spirit bouquet; medium-sweet, fabulous flavour, great length, cockle-warming yet exquisite. *Last tasted March 1990*****

Madeira *BERRY BROS* Bottled, unusually early, in 1869 and recorked in 1933. Fairly pale amber; a rather varnishy gnarled old character; still fairly sweet but difficult to tell whether old sherry or madeira save for the latter's typically high acidity. *March 1982***

1865***

Another small but good vintage. The trade still at a low ebb.

Malmsey, solera *RUTHERFORD & MILES* Interesting

to compare MWA island bottling with Harvey's 1963 Bristol bottling. The latter pale, the MWA browner; both with light nose; the MWA sweeter, rather like syrup of figs, possibly reduced and concentrated in hotter storage conditions. *Harvey's tasted in 1967, the MWA Dec 1983. Both, in their way****

1866 and 1867***

Small crops, good quality.
Terrantez A blend of both vintages bottled in 1900, re-corked by the MWA in 1962. Beautiful, lively bright. Slight, bitty sediment; incredibly rich, tangy, high-toned; palate also rich yet with sizzling, long, dry, rather varnishy finish. *Dec 1983**** for nose,** for palate.*

1868***

Good vintage, Bual particularly excellent.
Cama de Lobos Bottled in 1883. Lovely, refined, ethereal nose. Low-keyed on palate. *Dec 1983**** for nose ** for palate.*

1869***

Small. Good in all districts. Bual again showing best.
Malmsey Identified by bin label. Gentle, sound on nose and palate. Still very sweet, with some fat, good flavour and length. Lacking the usual pungent acidity. A half-bottle, probably binned in the late 19th century. *Opened and tasted in the cellars at Badminton House, Sept 1989****

1870****

Although at the time growers and merchants were unaware of it, this was the last of a series of good but small post-oidium vintages and the last top-class pre-phylloxera year.
Bual, solera *LOMELINO* Meaty, rich but not outstanding. *Nov 1980***
San Martinho Bottled 1893, recorked 1962. Two notes: fairly pale; thin, spiky nose smelling of bandages and TCP. Dry, lightish, lean, with rapier-like acidity. Doubtless an old Sercial. *Last tasted Aug 1985***
San Martinho 'Challenger' So named because it returned to the island on HMS *Challenger*. And I can see why. A high acetone nose. *Dec 1983.*
Sercial, solera *LOMELINO* Also meaty and not dry enough but a fragrant finish. *Nov 1980***
Terrantez *ADEGAS DO TORREO* Pale; caramelly, sickly, lacking tanginess; sweet, raisiny, high acidity, bitter finish. *Jan 1990.*

1872***

Another turning point: the year that the phylloxera arrived to destroy the vines planted after the devastation of oidium. Once again the growers and the trade were badly hit. The actual vintage in 1872 was reported as "good", but none tasted.

1874**

Very small production but good wines made from vines grown in vineyards not fully infested by the phylloxera.
Boal *SHIPPER UNKNOWN* Pungent, smoky. Sweet, meaty, fabulous flavour. *March 1980*****

1875****

Tiny crop but some outstanding wines made in sheltered vineyards.
Bastardo *COSSART GORDON* Made from grapes grown at the Qta do Satão in Cama de Lobos. An exquisite wine: green-rimmed pure amber; extraordinary bouquet, complete, harmonious, refined spirit, that evolved marvellously in the glass. Fairly sweet, rich yet lean. Great length. *One of the top wines at the magnificent tasting of old Terrantez and Bastardo in Hollywood, Florida. Jan 1990******
Sercial *D'OLIVEIRA* In oak 107 years, bottled 1982. 22% alcohol, 3.3° Baumé. Rich, tangy, deep and sweet for Sercial. Marvellous length and acidity. *At the Bruges tasting, May 1990*****

1877***

Terrantez *H M BORGES SUCRS* Bottle stencilled "T 1877". Very short island-bottled cork. Palish amber; low-keyed nose though soft, sweet and ethereal; medium-sweet though with a swingeingly dry, twist of lime finish. Impressive and refreshing. *Jan 1990****
Verdelho, 'Mistura', Torre Bella Difficult to pin down its precise date but the oldest wine in the remarkable stock inherited by Captain Fairlie who had married into the Blandy family. All the wines had come from the famous Casa Torre Bella estate in Camara, or Cama, de Lobos. *Mistura* means mixture: in this instance a blend of vintages all of the Verdelho grape. Chocolaty nose, good length. *Tasted prior to cataloguing, Nov 1988****

1878**

Bual, solera Bottled by the Wine Society (IECWS). A good enough wine, fairly sweet. *At the 92nd dinner of the Miami Chapter of the Wine & Food Society, Feb 1981***

1879****

Verdelho, Torre Made from grapes grown in the Torre vineyard of the Casa Torre Bella in Camara de Lobos, stored in the family *frasqueira* and recorked in 1987 just before shipment to the UK. On arrival at Felixstowe the entire consignment was, in error, put aboard a ship destined for San Francisco via the Panama Canal. It was eventually returned, unscathed, and was penultimately delivered to the Fairlie family castle in Scotland, later to Christie's. (See also 1877 and 1905). Two notes, one made from a sample bottle brought prior to shipment for me to taste and the next at a pre-sale tasting. A fabulous colour, amber with lime-green rim, the hallmark of maturity and quality; beautiful bouquet, rose cachou, ethereal like a Grande Champagne cognac, and high volatile acidity. Fairly sweet, touch of caramel, high alcohol and acidity. Clean as a whistle. *Nov 1988******

1880***

A vintage with a high reputation but, from my notes, seems to suffer from higher than usual acidity. Cossart Gordon & Co were by far the biggest shippers, exporting 1,073 pipes in 1880, nearly a third of the island's total.
Malmsey *BLANDY* Stencilled bottle. The smell of wet straw in a thoroughbred stable. Fairly sweet, tangy, a bit too sharp. *Oct 1985***
Malmsey, solera *JUSTINO HENRIQUES* Only 700 bottles produced. Not bright; meat extract nose; sweet, soft and cuddly but lacking class, particularly as 1880 Malmsey was reputed to be the best since 1808. *In Savannah, April 1980**
Sercial *VEIGA FRANCA* Short cork. Old amber; rich, highly volatile nose but very acidic, with unclean finish. *Feb 1981.*
Terrantez *D'OLIVEIRA* "Over 100 years matured in oak cask". Not very bright; volcanic nose; medium entry, very dry finish, 'hot', with swingeing acidity, fixed and volatile. *Jan 1990***

Verdelho, solera *BLANDY* Nine notes over 10 years. Mostly English bottled, probably mainly bottled in the late 1950s, a decade after shipment. Variable. Two distinctly malty, oxidised, one rubbery, mercaptan, another quite good. At best intensely fragrant, ethereal on nose and palate, expanding in the mouth like La Tâche '62 but richness barely shielding the very high acidity. *Last tasted May 1990. At best****

1883****

After 10 years of futile petitioning, the Portuguese government in Lisbon appointed an inspector and initiated an anti-phylloxera campaign. Meanwhile, struggling growers managed to produce a small crop of high-quality wine.

Vinho Velho, Chrozinha Old amber brown, intense green rim; lovely, high-toned bouquet; very sweet and rich, so presumably Malmsey, very high acidity, great length. *Dec 1986*****

1884–1889

The lowest period for the growers and the trade. Very small production, though Cossart reports some fine Sercial made in 1884 and Malmsey in 1885. None tasted.

1890**

Small. Adequate quality.

Malmsey, solera *BARBEITO* The excellent family firm of Barbeito was not founded until World War II but, being wealthy, they were able to buy considerable stocks of old wine, both from other merchants but mainly, I suspect, from growers who, then as now, tend to hoard casks of madeira. Amber with olive-green rim; lovely nose; sweet, soft, fleshy, good length and acidity. *May 1985****

Verdelho *D'OLIVEIRA* In cask 96 years. Bottled in 1986. 20% alcohol, 5.3° Baumé. Alcohol predominant, nose muted, vanilla. Medium dry, rather pasty flavour and bitter finish. *In Bruges, May 1990**

1891***

Cama de Lobos Bottled 1897, recorked 1953, rebottled 1960. Three notes. Although grown and made in Cama de Lobos, the wine had been stored in a hot barn in Santana on the north side of the island. First noted in the MWA tasting room in 1983: the medium-pale amber of pure Verdelho, confirmed by the nose of 'dry almonds', refined, fragrant; also typically 'medium', neither dry nor sweet, medium weight too, soft, mellow but with dry madeira 'acetone' finish. Most recently, a similar note, nose amazingly pungent – it filled my office with its fragrance; rich, tangy, good length. *The last noted given to me at Christmas in Madeira by Richard Blandy and opened for the Wine Department to taste in the wine's centenary year, Jan 1991*****

1892***

Yet another small crop. As always, some interesting wine made.

Sercial A simple, rather anonymous stencilled bottle. Exquisite flavour and length. Dry. Ravishing acidity. *July 1980*****

1893****

The first major vintage since the phylloxera had struck in 1872.

Malmsey Another anonymous stencilled bottle. Rich, glowing amber; intensely fragrant; very sweet, full, great length, superfine brandy and acidity. *At a Yalumba 'museum' tasting in the Barossa Valley, April 1985******

1895***

Malmsey *D'OLIVEIRA* In oak 92 years. Bottled 1987. 20.6% alcohol, 5.6° Baumé. Fairly deep, rich; tangy acidity; very sweet, fullish yet refined. Very attenuated dry acidic finish. *In Bruges, May 1990*****

1898****

Overall the most successful vintage since the phylloxera arrived on the island.

Boal, solera *HENRIQUES & HENRIQUES* Two notes in the early 1980s. Rich amber; rich but refined bouquet; sweet, very striking flavour, burnt, pungent, ethereal. Naturally high acidity. *Last tasted Dec 1983*****

Cama de Lobos Bottled 1921. Gentle yet high-toned with very dry finish. Probably Verdelho. *Dec 1983***

Verdelho, solera *HENRIQUES & HENRIQUES* Drab tawny; very high volatile acidity; nutty flavour, grubby finish. *May 1988.*

1899****

A difficult period ending on an encouraging note.

Terrantez *BLANDY* Stencilled "AO-SM". Glorious wine. Fabulous bouquet, slightly chocolaty, touch of toffee as if given a dollop of Malmsey. Ethereal, oyster shell. Very sweet, high alcohol, teeth-gripping acidity. *At Robert Maliner's Great Wine Seminar in Florida, Jan 1990*****

1900*****

A great vintage, signalling the full recovery of the vineyards though not a resurrection of trade.

Boal, Velho Reserva *MIGUEL JARDIM* First bottled in 1906, shipped by Henriques & Henriques (there is still a Jardim in the business). Sweet, rich, tangy, high acidity. *Feb 1989*****

Malmsey *JUSTINO HENRIQUES* Deepish amber; ethereal bouquet; sweet, fat, rich, long, acidic. *Feb 1990*****

Malvazia Rather pale straw amber; strange mustard-and-cress nose; fairly sweet, clean, straightforward on palate. *Dec 1983***

Moscatel *D'OLIVEIRA* First tasted shortly after shipment in bottle in 1980. Very sweet, balancing very high acidity. Next, stated to be in oak 87 years and bottled in 1987. Strength 20.6%. A very high 6.8° Baumé, the highest in the group. Singed, tangy bouquet. Very sweet, with a tremendous uplift of flavour and excellent acidity leaving the palate marvellously clean and dry after such a rich mouthful. *Last noted at the Bruges tasting, May 1990*****

Moscatel *POWER DRURY* In oak 60 years, bottled 1985. 19.6%, 5.4° Baumé. Soft, singed, soapy nose; sweet, great length, high acidity. Strange that I should have to talk about two madeiras made from the Moscatel grape, both from the same vintage – the oldest Moscatel I have tasted. Also strange that the anticipated grapey nose and taste did not materialise. *In Bruges, May 1990*****

1901

An undistinguished year.

Cama de Lobos *MWA* The appearance and smell of cold wet straw. Dry, screwed up. Yeasty. *Dec 1983.*

1905***

Small but good.

Sercial *MWA* Pale amber; twist of lemon and violets; fragrant, flavoury, very dry. *Dec 1983****

Verdelho, Nogueira From the Nogueira vineyard of the Torre Bella estate in Camara de Lobos. Part of the

Captain Fairlie stock (see also the 1877 and 1879). Surprisingly sweet, rich, chocolaty. Excellent acidity. *Pre-sale Nov 1988****

Verdelho, Torre As above but from the Torre vineyard. Totally different. More of a Sercial-like piquancy. Dry. Flavour of damp cardboard, yet, somehow, exquisite. *Nov 1988*****

1906**

Another small crop. "Malmsey especially good" (Cossart).

Malvasia *LEACOCK* There are several types of Malvasia or Malvazia grape. The oldest, *Malvasia babosa* was brought to Madeira by Simon Acciaioli (*sic*) (see 1802) and is thought to be the French *malvoisie*. They tend to be pressed and made together to make rich Malmsey, of which this is a good example. Amber brown; pungent; intense. Marvellous smell and taste. *Nov 1980******

1907***

Boal, vintage *BLANDY* Two recent notes. Very deep, glowing mahogany colour, intense; beautiful bouquet, herbaceous, spicy; sweet, richly flavoured: coffee, chocolate, brandy. A warm mouthfilling wine, powerful yet refined. *Last tasted Feb 1989******

Malvazia, reserva *D'OLIVEIRA* Very deep in colour; hefty, incredibly sweet, full, rich, chocolaty. Lacking refinement. *Last tasted May 1990****

1910*****

A great vintage and successful for all types of wine.

Bual *COSSART* Nose like mustard-and-cress though rich and tangy; sweet, rich, chewy, with high end acidity. Lovely wine. *Dec 1990*****

Sercial *BELIEVED COSSART* Very assertive. Fine. *March 1980*****

Sercial *MWA* Fragrant, flowery; lovely long, dry, clean, acidic finish. *Dec 1983****

1911****

Bual *BLANDY* Glorious colour and bouquet; sweet, rich, yet with an almost Sercial-like leanness. *From the cellar of the late Mills B Lane of Savannah, June 1990*****

1912***

Malmsey *COSSART* Very rich amber; marvellous nose, singed, crystallised violets which carried on to the palate and through to the aftertaste. Lovely, rich, characterful wine. *Nov 1983*****

1913***

Verdelho *MWA* Amber gold; refined bouquet like old cognac; equally refined taste, long, rapier-like acidity. One bottle oxidised. *Both tasted Dec 1983. At best****

1914***

Small crop. Noted for its Bual.

Bual *MWA* Medium-sweet, firm, rich, stylish. *Dec 1983****

1915***

Generally good for all types of wine.

Bual *COSSART* Fabulous, high-toned, lemon and tom-cats; medium sweetness and weight though a light elegant style. Crisp. Flavoury. *Two notes, July 1981*****

Bual *RUTHERFORD & MILES* In cask until 1978 and first tasted in 1983. Lovely wine. High acidity. More recently, meaty nose, sweeter than Cossart's, refined, acidic finish. *Last tasted Sept 1989****

1916***

An excellent year for Malmsey. The best, the richest wines, had been destined for the Imperial Russian Court but the market disappeared overnight. A diverted and diverting bottle of Cossart's vintage Malmsey sweet, soft, rich and tangy in 1979.

1917

Balthazar The name of a ship not size of bottle. Bottled 1930, recorked 1962. High acetone type of nose. Fairly sweet, crisp, clean. *Dec 1983***

1920****

Bual *BLANDY* In cask 30 years. Strength 19.5%, 2.9° Baumé. Amber; crème brûlée, vanilla and mint; medium-sweet, delicate, fragrant. *May 1990*****

Boal *BLANDY* Amber brown; toasted, tangy; sweet, full, soft, very rich. Lovely finish. Clearly another cask. *Dec 1990*****

Malmsey *COSSART* A famous wine made from the last *Malvasia Candida* variety from Faja dos Padres and considered by Noël Cossart to be as good as the 1880. Tasted six times: lively colour, rich amber, gold highlights, apple-green rim; highly scented, violets, strawberry, fine cognac; sweet but not too sweet, offsetting its piquant acidity, meaty, singed, fleshy yet ethereal. *Last tasted Sept 1987******

Malvazia *MWA* Crystallised fruit; very sweet, lovely. *Dec 1983*****

1926****

Very good vintage.

Malmsey (vintage) *COSSART* Magnificent. Made like port, restraining fermentation and retaining sugar, nothing added, no *estufa*. In cask 40 years, in demijohns 10 years, bottled in 1976. *1976*****

1927***

Bastardo *LEACOCK* Trust Leacock's to have made a wine with a grape of that name in my birth year! A rare, shy-bearing and difficult black grape. Amber; touch of honey, a refined bouquet like the finest cognac, evolving marvellously after 20 minutes in the glass but after a further hour slightly chocolaty. Sweet, rich, thick, excellent tangy flavour. Dry acidic finish. *At the Maliner Madeira tasting, Jan 1990*****

1931*

Verdelho *BLANDY* Bottled in 1979. From John Blandy's private cellars. Two notes. Yellow amber; rich, malty, touch of acetone; sweet for Verdelho, tangy, extended acidic finish. *Last tasted June 1990***

1932**

Verdelho *BLANDY* Rarefied, violet-scented; medium-sweet, with flesh and fat to support an extended dry finish — like a cantilever construction. *June 1989****

1933***

Bual *BLANDY* Bottled in 1979. Lime and linoleum, mint and chocolate; very sweet, soft, better on palate than nose. Good length. Fragrant aftertaste. Trace of old wood. *Last tasted June 1990. At best*****

1934****

All grape varieties and districts excellent.

Bual *COSSART GORDON* Two notes: rich, meaty, sweet,

soft. *Last tasted Dec 1983****

Bual *LEACOCK* Beautiful, rarefied bouquet, twist of lime; sweet, full-flavoured, tangy, good length, excellent acidity. *Dec 1990******

Malvazia *HENRIQUES & HENRIQUES* Deep; rich, high-toned; very sweet, fat, warm, 'singed' flavour. *Dec 1983*****

Verdelho *HENRIQUES & HENRIQUES* 21.4% alcohol, 2.5° Baumé. Harmonious, medium dryness and weight. Elegant. Tangy. Good length. *Dec 1983****

1936*****

Generally very fine. Cossart Sercial "the finest this century" (Cossart).

Cama de Lobos *BLANDY* Unlabelled but cork fully branded. Lovely amber gold, fine apple-green rim; beautiful, refined, ethereal bouquet; medium sweetness and weight, lovely flavour, fleshy, very high acidity, dry finish. *March 1986******

1939****

Calheta (*sic*) Bottled 1979. From John Blandy's cellar. Not to be confused with *colheita* (aged in wood), Calheta is a village on the south coast, beyond Magdelena. Rich amber, green rim; glorious bouquet, very sweet, high-toned, with citrus-like acidity; medium dry yet very rich and full flavoured. Good length, acidity and aftertaste. *Last tasted June 1990******

1940****

Especially noted for its Sercial.

Sercial *RUTHERFORD & MILES* Colour of weak tea, a bit cloudy, with crystalline sediment. Nose of lemon-tinged butterscotch, softened to become more fruity in the glass. Medium dry, lean, rapier-like acidity crossing the palate but with a lovely warming aftertaste. Glorious. *Sept 1987*****

1941****

Good, particularly Bual and Malmsey.

Bual *BLANDY* Rich, cheesy; medium-sweet, light for Bual, fragrant, slightly chocolaty flavour, good acidity. *May 1989*****

Bual, 'CDGC' *COSSART* A straight unblended vintage Bual made by Noël Cossart to mark the birth of his son, David. Soft yet ethereal bouquet; same sweetness and weight as Blandy's. Exquisite flavour, like delicate violet cachous. *Oct 1984******

Sercial *INSTITUTO DO VINHO DA MADEIRA* Bottled 1986. 19.8%, 2.7° Baumé. Palish; pleasant nose and taste. *May 1990****

1944***

Sercial Strength 21.5%. *Vinho Surdo* added in 1948/9 to raise the sweetness to 5° Baumé. (Surdo is made by adding brandy to unfermented juice of the same quality of grape.) Fairly deep for Sercial; very tangy, exhilarating, high acetone nose; lovely flavour. Dry, acidic finish. *Still in cask when tasted at the MWA, Dec 1983****

1950**

Sercial *LEACOCK* Very rich, tangy nose and flavour. Medium dry, twist of lemon acidity. *Feb 1989****

Tinta Negra Mole, Torre Bella Bottled 1970. An interesting wine made from the ubiquitous and versatile Tinta* grape grown in the Torre vineyard, Camara de Lobos. Medium-pale amber; meaty yet with a curiously refined edge; medium dry, lean, flavour of old straw and old cognac. Rather a harsh finish. *Nov 1988***

1952***

A good vintage, Malmsey and Verdelho particularly notable.

Malmsey, 'Jubilee Selection' *LEACOCK* Very rich but distinctly acetic and not fully integrated nose; very sweet, tangy, dry, acidic but acceptable finish. *Dec 1983***

Verdelho, 'Jubilee Selection' *LEACOCK* Rather deep, amber brown; high-toned, singed, spirity, acetone nose; medium-sweet, rich, tangy. *Last tasted Dec 1983***

1954****

Boal and **Bual** Both tasted in the MWA's tasting room, the former being better: rich, toasty bouquet, fairly sweet, rich, good acidity; the latter browner, more chocolaty on nose, sweeter and meaty on palate. *Dec 1983. At best*****

Malvazia 19.3%, 5° Baumé. Distinctly brown; heavy, chocolaty nose; very sweet, rich, lovely flavour and tang. *At the MWA, Dec 1983****

Malvazia *INSTITUTO DO VINHO DA MADEIRA* In oak 32 years, bottled 1986. High strength, 21% alcohol and with unusually high sugar content, 10.1° Baumé. High-toned, a bit too sharp. Not as sweet on the palate as expected, it had a curious taste and tailed off. *At the Bruges tasting, May 1990**

Sercial, Vintage *MWA* Warm amber; rich, high, acetone nose with caramel and spirit; flavoury. A long, very dry, acidic finish. *MWA, Dec 1983***

Terrantez *BLANDY* Fairly deep amber, gold highlights, yellow edge; slightly malty, caramel nose; very rich, tangy. Sweet entry and sweet finish, despite its twist of acidity. *The opening wine at Robert Maliner's memorable Terrantez tasting in Florida, Jan 1990****

1957****

Boal *RUTHERFORD & MILES* Beautiful rich, ethereal crystallised violets bouquet; very sweet for Bual, very rich, lovely, rarefied flavour and fabulous length. Dry finish. *Dec 1990*****

1960***

Bual *BARBEITO* Tawny, amber-green rim; very rich, spiky nose and flavour. Medium-sweet. Finely pointed taste, refined, distinctly dry finish. *Last tasted Dec 1985*****

1964***

Malvazia Astonishingly powerful, 27.4% alcohol and high volatile acidity, 2.57, but enough rich flavour to be supported comfortably by the spirit and to mask the acidity. Which is what madeira is all about. *MWA, Dec 1983****

1967****

Boal 21.4%, volatile acidity 0.89. Fabulously rich, fragrant bouquet, flavour and finish. *MWA, Dec 1983*****

Verdelho 20%, extract 101.4, volatile acidity 0.73. Bright amber gold; fragrant, high-toned, medium dry, good firm mid-palate. Long dry finish. *MWA, Dec 1983*****

* *The Tinta Negra Mole is prolific and has useful chameleon-like characteristics. It is said to make wine like Sercial when grown in high altitude vineyards, like Bual at lower levels and so forth, though doubtless the amount of sweetening wine helps. The practice of naming wine made from the Tinta grape Sercial, Verdelho, Bual and Malmsey became widespread and is now, particularly since Portugal joined the EEC, regarded as a malpractice.*

1968****

Boal *PERREIRA D'OLIVEIRA* In oak 20 years, 20.4%, 2.4° Baumé. Glorious nose, rich yet delicate, touch of vanilla. Flavour to match. Sweet, excellent acidity. *At the Bruges tasting, May 1990*****

1971

Sercial *HENRIQUES & HENRIQUES* 19.4%. Straight Sercial, nil Baumé, therefore bone dry, with rather swingeing acidic finish. Fragrant. *With the late Peter Cossart at Henriques in Funchal, Dec 1983.*

1972

Sercial Fragrant, clean-cut; bone dry, rapier-like acidity. Tasted alongside the Tinta Negra version: more acetone on nose; sweetened, meatier. *At the MWA, Dec 1983.*

1973

Bual 19.2%, nil Baumé yet tasting medium dry due to its richness. Light, rather neutral nose. *MWA, Dec 1983.*
Verdelho Similar strength and nil Baumé. Low-keyed, spirity, dry almonds nose; distinctly dry. *At the MWA, Dec 1983.*

1974

Bual Unsweetened and therefore dry; fragrant, volatile, acidic. *At the MWA Dec 1983.*
Malvazia 23.1%, volatile acidity 1.9 and very noticeable on nose. Very dry, acetic. I was informed that a very tiny percentage of this went into Cossart's Malmsey and 'Old Company' Bual, presumably to pep up those blends. *At the MWA, Dec 1983.*
Verdelho A straight varietal, with high volatile acidity — far too sharp on the palate. *At the MWA, Dec 1983.*

1977

Malvazia A relatively low 17.2% Gay Lussac, extract 19.4, volatile acidity 1.20. Yellow orange. Acetic. I was told this had been picked in the rain. It had certainly acquired an acetone sort of spoilage at an early stage. *Sample tasted at the MWA, Dec 1983.*

1978

Bual 'SRD' 18.6%, volatile acidity 0.79. Amber colour and not very bright; straightforward, classic, singed, meaty nose and flavour. Medium-sweet. Lacking length. *At the MWA, Dec 1983.*
Verdelho Green amber; a cool, damp straw, cellar-reminiscent nose, spirity. Hint of raisins. Very dry. *At the MWA, Dec 1983.*

1980

Bual With *Boal Surdo* added. Curious musty, dusty, cold tea leaves in teapot smell. Fairly sweet, rich, meaty. *At the MWA, Dec 1983.*
Malmsey *Malvasia tinta* warm amber, touch of orange; rich, figgy, muscadelle-like nose and taste. Sweet. Rich. Nice acidity. *At the MWA, Dec 1983.*
Verdelho Palish, orange tinge; immature, slightly sickly sweet; dry, dough-like flavour. *At the MWA, Dec 1983.*

1981

Bual, 'very old', Special Reserve Not vintage, but part of an old solera shipped in 1981 by Cossart Gordon to celebrate the Royal Wedding. First tasted in July of that year, it had a bouquet that could aptly, and almost literally, be described as 'loyal toast': singed, meaty, ethereal. Sweet. A wine with a lovely, long warm glow. *Last tasted, March 1988*****

1982–88

Wines still maturing in cask. None tasted.

1989

Boal Yellow amber gold; distinctly immature, yet already a distinct meatiness on the nose. Medium sweetness. Nose and taste reminding me of a *raya* sherry. *Vat sample tasted at the Madeira Wine's São Francisco Lodge, Christmas 1990.*
Sercial A warm amber colour; dry, not raw but very austere on the palate, with swingeingly, penetratingly, dry acidic finish. *Christmas, 1990.*

1990

Bual From grapes grown on the windswept north coast harvested at the end of Aug. Very distinctive yellow; harmonious, slightly honeyed nose, with lemon-like acidity; medium-sweet, lovely flavour, nutty, honeyed, touch of muscadelle grapiness, good acidity. *Christmas 1990.*
Malvasia Mainly from south coast vineyards. Small production. A lovely bright yellow gold; very forthcoming, upturned, fruity nose; sweet, tangy, good length. Slightly yeasty finish. *Christmas 1990.*
Sercial Also from the south coast. Summer unusually warm. Early harvest for Sercial, towards the end of Sept. Fermented to around 11% and fortified immediately after to 17%. Pale yellow; smell of pineapple and pear skins — like *poire Williamine*, also honey and lemon. Very fragrant. Brutally dry and acidic. *Christmas 1990.*

TOKAY

The least known of all the great classic European wine districts, Tokay is a tiny region in eastern Hungary, close to the Soviet-Ukraine border. The finest dessert wines have an almost indefinite life and, even when opened, will be drinkable for months. The older, more concentrated wines can have a very heavy and obstinate sediment, so store upright.

Apart from the very old straight-sided dumpy types, all Tokay bottles are of the very distinctive traditional slender-necked half-litre bottles, in use from the early 19th century to the present day. Almost invariably, mean little corks are used, but they seem to serve their purpose. Unless otherwise stated all the wines will have been made from the traditional Furmint grape.

There are various grades of Tokay or Tokaji made: **Szamorodni** ('as it was grown') can be dry or sweet. The most distinctive wines are **Aszú**, those which have had, in effect, concentrated grape juice paste added in measures called *puttonyos* (putts), three putts being medium-sweet, four sweet, five Sauternes-like, six, now fairly rare, sweeter still. **Aszú-Eszencia** is like a fairly concentrated Beerenauslese, and the extremely rare '**Essence**' (*Esszencia, Eszencia or Essencia*) is intensely rich, TBA-like.

Mád, Tolcsva, Tarcal and Tolestan are all village names.

Throughout I have used the spelling that appears on the labels or, in the case of very old wines, in catalogue descriptions. The dry wines are odd, sometimes sherry-like. Stick to the sweet Aszú wines which, once one is used to their style, are delicious, and at best are beautiful, poignant, blissful and memorable.

c 1650

Imperial Tokay believed to be 1649. From the Royal Saxon cellar (sold at Christie's Nov 1968). Dumpy straight-sided bottle with glass seal bearing arms. Medium-deep amber, crisp yellow-green edge; not surprisingly showing age on nose, Malmsey-like, malty, then distinct *Aszú Essencia* raisiny scent, held well; medium-sweet, drying out, unclean finish. *At Rodenstock tasting, Oct 1985***

c 1790

Tokay believed to be 1794. From the cellars of Count Radziwill. Dumpy bottle, stump-necked. Deep, rich warm amber, mahogany shading to olive rim; magnificent old bouquet, sweet, supple, raisiny; sweet, full-bodied, excellent honey and raisiny flavour, good length, excellent acidity keeping it vigorous. *Sept 1987******

1811*****

Essence Bottled circa 1840. From the cellars of the 'Princely family of Bretzenheim'. Walled up in 1849, unearthed and imported by Berry Bros in 1925. Amber; ambrosial; sweet, concentrated, lingering. *Last tasted May 1973******

1825

Aszú Two bottles, one mid-shoulder, brown, acetic, the other with 2½in ullage, original short but firm cork, cloudy tawny; more like a very old sherry; high acidity. Not Aszú, as catalogued. *Heublein pre-sale tasting, May 1981.*

1834

Essence Provenance Bretzenheim, Berry Bros. Bright, medium amber, slight orange tinge; high-toned, intense, singed; drying out, delicate, excellent muscadelle flavour, perfect acidity, finish and aftertaste. More four putt than essence. *At Hans Jorissen's 'Vinum Tokayens' tasting, Leiden, Nov 1982*****

1865

Aszú, 5 putts *HERCZEG WINDISCH-GRAETZ, SAROSPATAK* Mid-shoulder. Lovely warm amber; wonderful bouquet despite slightly varnishy overtone, rich, multifaceted after time in glass; no longer sweet, but rich with somewhat beery finish. *Leiden, Nov 1982**

Aszú (putts unknown). Amber, green-tinged; excellent, harmonious, like a soft yet tangy Sauternes; medium-sweet, lightish, drying and fading, marvellous acidity. *Noted at Etienne Hugel's rare dessert wine tasting, Riquewihr, Sept 1985*****

1876

Tokayer Ausbruch *MILLUM VINUM NISI HUNGERICUM* Imported (pre-1914) by Lorenz Reich, New York. Three bottles. Short fully branded corks. Very bright amber; marvellous singed, madeira-like bouquet, slightly resiny and pungent; sweet, tremendous extract, lovely flavour — a cross between old Bual and old Yquem. High acidity. *Heublein's, pre-sale, May 1980*****

1885

Imperial Tokay From the cellar of Count Potulicki, Gex. Lovely colour, Bual-like amber, bitty sediment; good but curious nose, resinous; medium dry yet rich, rounded, soft, with acidic finish like madeira. *Dec 1969***

1889*****

Tokay Essencia *ZIMMERMAN LIPOT* Several reasonably consistent notes. Deep, fairly intense warm amber; glorious fragrance, deep, rich, chocolaty, spicy; sweet, fat, concentrated, meaty, singed sultanas, excellent balance, acidity, finish. *Last tasted in Leiden, Nov 1982******

Tokay Szamorodni *WINDISCH-GRAETZ* From a Swedish cellar, with original 1924 shipper's invoice. Slip label only. Grubby, hazy, straw colour and nose to match: pungent, maderised though still sweet, raisiny; dry, firm, like old sherry. Whiff of acidity. *Pre-sale, Christie's, Nov 1983**

c 1900

Tokayer Ausbruch 'Medical wine' *UJVEDIK, TOLCSVA, A ADAMOVITCH* Fabulous, like a great old Sercial, crystallised violets, old cognac; medium dry rich, positively fat in the mouth, yet ethereal and light style. Perfection. *At Jorissen's tasting, Leiden, Nov 1982******

1901***

Tokay Szamorodni *GROWTH OF THE TOKAJ-HEGYALIA COURT VINEYARDS BOTTLED BY THE IMPERIAL AND ROYAL COURT CELLARS, HOFBURG, VIENNA.* Palish amber; warm, spicy, honey, old apples; matching flavour, fairly dry, rich, lovely. *Pre-sale Aug 1981*****

1904****

Sweet Szamorodni *BORSAI MIKLOS, MAD* Deep rich tawny; amazingly deep, meaty almost malty; honey-sweet, rich, high extract, lovely flavour, balance, finish. *At Leiden, Nov 1982*****

1905***

Dry Szamorodni *STAATLICHE HOFKELLEREI, WIEN* Bought at Christie's in 1981. Straw-amber gold; extraordinary, very forthcoming, like fresh-picked mushrooms and a harness room; firm, excellent fragrance, singed raisins, dry acid finish. Strange style but excellent in its way. *Leiden, Nov 1982*****

1906*****

The last great vintage of the Austro-Hungarian empire.

Tokaj-Hegyaljai-Ausbruch *TERINYI HENRIK PINCZEJEBOL, TALLYA* Pre-1918, possibly '06. Bright amber; rich, toasted; still sweet, good flavour and acidity. *D Zivko's collection, Chicago, Oct 1982****

1920****

Dry Szamorodni *ZIMMERMANN LIPOT* Dusty, woody, smoky nose and taste. Very dry, austere, unclean. *Leiden, Nov 1982.*

1924*****

Aszú, 6 putts *ZIMMERMAN* Warm, intense oloroso colour; amazingly sweet, rich bouquet and flavour of great depth, ethereal cognac and Sauternes. Perfect flavour, balance, acidity. *At Leiden, Nov 1982******

1937*****

Aszú Essencia Medium, cloudy; cold, spicy, smell of squashed raisins, stalks, citrus whiff; fairly sweet, rich, crisp, high-toned, aftertaste like fish skin. *At Leiden, Nov 1982***

1943***

Aszú, 3 putts *FLEGMANN SV ES FIA, ABAUJSZANTO* Two notes. Beautiful amber; lovely, gentle, rich, grapey, honeyed; medium-sweet, delicate richness, nice, fair finish. *Last tasted Jan 1981****

1945*****

Aszú, 5 putts *CHARLES MONTROSE & CO, LONDON* Yellow amber; sweet, meaty, rich, touch of *raya* sherry and damp cardboard; sweet, soft, singed, earthy aftertaste. *July 1989***

Essencia Warm, oloroso-like, touch of orange, viscous; sweet, slightly raisiny, whiff of apples; sweet, very rich, fat, perfect flavour, length, aftertaste. *With soufflé Rothschild, the 11th and last wine at the* Great Vintage Wine Book *dinner in Zurich, Oct 1983******

1947*****

Reputed to be the best post-war vintage.

Aszú, 5 putts Rich, high-toned, acetone, meaty; sweet, sultanas and oloroso, dry finish. *At Etienne Hugel's, Sept 1985***

Esszencia *TOKAJI WINE TRUST* Medium-deep amber, apple-green rim; apples, honey, whiff of cloves; very sweet, soft, velvety, fat, ripe, luscious, good length. Glorious. *With Gábor Egressy at VinExpo, June 1991******

1956***

Aszú, 4 putts *HUNGARIAN STATE WINE TRUST* Two notes. Green-rimmed rich amber; sweet, complex, old apples, straw, calf's-foot jelly, demerara sugar; fairly sweet, rich but not heavy, refined, long dry finish. *Last tasted pre-sale, Sept 1989****

Aszú, 5 putts Two notes, both at pre-sale tastings at Christie's for the Hungarian Wine Trust, in 1985 and 1989. Similar colour to four putts; very full, rich, slightly oloroso-like bouquet; very sweet, rich, soft, fleshy, pronounced, slightly grapey, good length, finish, aftertaste. *Last noted Sept 1989*****

1957*****

Aszú, 6 putts Three notes, from 1982. Amber; rich, crisp, sultanas, treacle tart; fairly sweet, glorious. *Sept 1989*****

Aszú Esszencia Several notes starting in 1973. Warm amber, gold highlights; very rich, baked apples, raisiny, TBA-like; intensely sweet, full yet not heavy, soft, fat, glorious flavour, aftertaste. *Last noted Sept 1989******

1958***

Muskotàlyos Aszú, 4 putts From the Muscat grape. Three notes. Tawny amber, orange highlights, apple green rim; rich, grapey, Beerenauslese-like, marrow, spearmint overtone; fairly sweet, soft, grapy, like a rich, refined Verdelho, marvellous upturned finish. Lovely. *Last tasted Nov 1990*****

1959*****

Aszú, 5 putts Two notes. Very deep orange amber; ripe, honeyed, singed sultanas; sweet, full, intense, fabulous acidity. Great wine. *Both tasted Aug 1986******

Aszú, 6 putts Orange amber; sweet, *raya* sherry, Malmsey, chocolaty; very sweet, full flavour and body yet more refined than nose, fabulous acidity. *Last tasted pre-sale, Sept 1989*****

Aszú Esszencia Lovely colour; rich, harmonious, perfectly rounded, grapey, great depth; very sweet, luscious though clean-cut, fat yet with counterbalancing acidity. *Last tasted pre-sale Sept 1989******

Dry Szamorodni *MONIMPEX* Deep amber; walnuts, old apples; dry. An acquired taste. *Jan 1985**

Edes Szamorodni Two notes. Amber gold; glorious, honeyed, orange blossom, depth; medium-sweet, lovely flavour, vivacity, weight, length, dry finish. *Last tasted pre-sale, Sept 1989*****

Sweet Szamorodni *MONIMPEX* Pure amber, warm, vibrant; fabulous, rich, honeyed, baked, toffee-like, apricots; medium-sweet, rich but lean, dry finish. Nose best. *Nov 1984****

Száraz Szamorodni First tasted at Heublein's, pre-sale, 1976: oxidised. The next two prior to Christie's promotional sales, in 1985 and 1989. Palish yellow; malty, calf's-foot jelly, fino-like, pears; dry, flavour like *vin jaune* and sherry, good length, tangy. *Last noted Sept 1989***

1962****

Edes Szamorodni/Szamorodni Sweet Seven fairly consistent notes, however labelled. Warm orange amber, rich legs; very sweet, honeyed, raisins and caramel; medium-sweet, medium weight, lovely flavour, good acidity. *Last tasted Aug 1990*****

1963*****

Muskotàlyos Aszú, 5 putts Three notes. Glowing amber gold; well-knit, spicy, raisiny, Beerenauslese-like, barley-sugar, very sweet, great finesse yet intense, muscadelle and peach. Lovely. *Last tasted Sept 1990******

Muskotàlyos Aszú, 6 putts Four notes. Deepish amber; strange, sweet, Riesling sort of grapiness, singed raisins, pineapple husk; sweet, rich, yet crisp and lean, good flavour, length, acidity, aftertaste. *Last noted July 1990*****

Edes Szamorodni Honeyed, straw-like; medium-sweet, crisp, excellent. *Pre-sale Nov 1985*****

Sweet Szamorodni Rich, very raisiny, tangy; fairly sweet, straw and raisin flavour, dry acidic finish. *Dec 1989****

1964****

Aszú, 5 putts Yellow amber; soft, honeyed, harmonious, old stables; sweet, rich, well-knit, crisp. Will develop further. *At the two major pre-sale tastings, Nov 1988 and Sept 1989***(*)*

Aszú Essencia Six notes from its first launch by Berry Bros in 1972. Good then, but after a further 10 years' bottle-age, even better: ethereal fragrance; concentrated, raisiny, ambrosial. I thought it had even more to come but, judging from two more recent honeyed-old-straw notes, possibly at its best in the early 1980s. *Last tasted June 1989*****

Szaraz Szamorodni Lemon yellow; like old brown apples and maderised Graves; dry, 'strange' flavour noted on two separate occasions, excellent acidity. *Last tasted Jan 1986***

1966★★★

Aszú, 5 putts From Tolestan, one of the principal Tokay wine villages. Mid-amber; rich, meaty, 'hot', slightly raisiny; sweet, intense, good length, high acidity. *At Leiden, Nov 1982★★★(★)*

1967★★

Aszú, 5 putts Five early 1980s notes. Variable: straw yellow; raisins, old apples; sweet, good acidity. One, a different producer but also exported by Monimpex, deep amber; beautifully sweet, Beerenauslese-like nose; less sweet on palate but very rich, perfect flavour. *Last tasted Jan 1981. At best★★★★*

Aszú Essencia Bright amber; raisiny; sweet, lightish, attractive, lovely acidity. *July 1980★★★★*

1968★★★★★

Aszú Essencia Fairly deep orange tawny; rich, old honeyed apples, crème brûlée like '37 Yquem; fairly sweet, very rich, its fat cut by excellent acidity. *Oct 1983★★★★(★)*

1972★★★★★

Essence A rare taste of pure essence: medium amber, still working; immensely rich, raisiny, a pervasive tangy scent remained in the empty glass; intensely sweet, only 2% alcohol, high acidity completely masked by incredibly high grape sugars. Remarkable. *A sample brought by John Lipitch, March 1985★★★★(★★)*

1973★★★

Aszú, 5 putts Surprisingly deep orange-tinged amber; sweet, honeyed, rich, raisiny, with the characteristic old-apples-in-the-loft smell and taste. *Nov 1980★★★*

Essencia, from Mád Palish amber tawny; unexpected scent of walnut oil, salty, tangy, sweaty leathery tannin yet citrus fragrance; very sweet, very fat, curious flavour, concentrated fruit, high-end acidity. *Nov 1982★★★??*

1975★★★★

Aszú, 5 putts Deepish straw; sweet, rich, soft, muscadelle, lovely. *July 1983★★★★*

1976★★★

Aszú, 4 putts Straw colour and smell; medium-sweet. *May 1983★★★*

Aszú, 5 putts Three notes. Orange amber; pungent, singed apples and raisins; fairly sweet, slightly malty, good acidity. *Last tasted Aug 1985★★★*

1978

Szamorodni, dry Straw yellow, watery rim; very strange, sealing wax, wet straw; very dry, acidity carrying it along. Like a *vin jaune*. *Nov 1982★★*

Best more recent vintages

1979, 1981, 1982, 1983 (excellent), 1988 (excellent), 1989 and 1990.

CALIFORNIA

My first visit to California was in 1970. Though the pioneering days of André Tchelistcheff and Maynard Amerine were long past their infancy, the winemakers were still striving, and some, like the redoubtable Robert Mondavi, indefatigably experimenting. Looking back, it was another world. By 1980, there had already been a transformation; since then, a proliferation – of wineries as well as wine.

My introduction to the taste of California was through the generous guidance of the Doctors Adamson and Rhodes, and through the medium of the Heublein pre-auction tastings for 13 years from May 1969. Later came the Napa Valley wine auctions which I conducted for the first five years from 1980. These acted as a magnet.

My notes are far too numerous to catalogue, yet not remotely deep or wide enough even to attempt to be fairly critical, let alone definitive. What I have done, therefore, is to be highly selective.

RED

My original intention was to split the reds into varietal sections, the most important being, of course, Cabernet Sauvignon. But in view of the increasing practice of blending this with other related Bordeaux-type grapes, Merlot, Cabernet Franc, even, on occasions, Petit Verdot, resulting in often high-quality reds under the umbrella title of 'table wine', I finally decided to lump the red wines together under vintage headings. For brevity, I have not prefaced the earlier vintages with a summary of weather conditions, but, as demonstrated by the decade of the 1980s, these can vary enormously, with interesting consequences. The vintage star ratings are based on historic, perceived or reputed quality, using the Napa as a fulcrum. As with all old wines, bottle variation can be expected.

Lacking on-the-spot exposure to a vast range of wines, I have tackled the subject of assessing the vintages by drawing on notes made at vertical tastings, notably of Beaulieu Vineyard, Charles Krug and Robert Mondavi, and to corroborate these with random tastings. To assess the present-day 'classics', I have concentrated on major horizontal tastings of the '82 and '85 vintages, the latter being Cabernets at their most uniform best.

One of the questions I am frequently asked is "Will California wines keep?", to which I invariably reply that those – and there are many – that are well made and well constituted will certainly keep. More questionable is whether they will benefit from keeping. The following notes provide some clues.

1941****

This can fairly be regarded as the first of the 'modern' classic vintages of the Napa.

Beaulieu Vineyard,* Cabernet Sauvignon Sugar 23.5° Balling. First noted in 1972 at a Heublein pre-sale tasting: a deep, fine, rich wine in marvellous condition. Most recently: still deep and intense though fully mature

* *Beaulieu, or beautiful place, named by the wife of the founder, Georges de Latour, is variously referred to as Beaulieu Vineyard, Beaulieu Vineyards (and there are several) or, more recently by aficionados, simply and familiarly as BV. From here on I note it as Beaulieu.*

with an orange-brown rim that reminded me of syrup of figs; powerful, meaty bouquet now showing considerable age, malty, tarry, like an old brown sherry; on the palate dry, still fairly full-bodied, despite being almost half a century old, clean, tannic but with acidity catching up. *Last noted at an unforgettable open air BV tasting in the gardens at Inglenook, June 1990***

1943****

Beaulieu, Cabernet Sauvignon Fine, deep, intense and lively appearance; equally deep, rich, singed nose, then honeycomb and fruit noted, developing well over an hour in the glass: rich, fragrant, a marvellous scent; a distinct touch of sweetness, the sweetness of very ripe grapes and alcohol, fairly full-bodied, a lovely rich flavour, excellent tannins and acidity. *June 1990*****

Inglenook, Cabernet Sauvignon Old vines. Incredibly deep and intense; warm, spicy, very slightly eucalyptus bouquet, showing no signs of old age; medium dry, huge, ripe, velvety, with an alcohol-laden dry finish. A sort of Napa Latour. *June 1982******

1944****

Charles Krug, Cabernet Sauvignon Still very deep, centre almost opaque, fine mature mahogany rim; nose old and oaky at first with a strange uplift, after 15 minutes sweet, chocolate and coffee, after 30 minutes in glass glorious; drying out on the palate, medium body, holding well. The oldest wine at what could fairly be described as a historic vertical tasting of Charles Krug and Robert Mondavi vintages conducted to mark the reunion of the two brothers Peter and Robert Mondavi. *June 1985*****

1945***

Beaulieu, Cabernet Sauvignon Deep, fine, lively, very mature rim; marvellous vinosity, like an old Pétrus, but the nose collapsed, oxidising after 40 minutes, smelling like cold tea after an hour in the glass; dry, chunky, complete, still with fruit and pleasant when first poured, but rather short. *June 1990***

Sebastiani, Casa de Sonoma Opaque, mature rim; low-keyed, very sweet, malty nose; dry, full-bodied and very rich. Strange but good. Tannic. *Sept 1988****

1946*****

Charles Krug, Cabernet Sauvignon Vintage Selection Fully fermented out, fined with egg whites. Fine deep colour, still ruby; beautiful spicy, cinnamon, eucalyptus nose; perfect weight, lovely vinosity, smooth silky texture, length and excellent endtaste. In its 40th year, a perfect drink. *June 1985******

1947****

Charles Krug, Cabernet Sauvignon Fairly deep, fine, rich, mature; dusty and cedary at first, touch of meat extract, developed well in the glass; sweet, full, soft, velvety, good length, excellent acidity. *June 1985******

1950**

Charles Krug, Cabernet Sauvignon Vintage Selection Lovely colour, broad mature rim; low-keyed, elegant, touch of old varnish, some development, whiff of spice, cloves; medium weight, lean touch, teeth-gripping. Will not improve. *At Krug/Mondavi tasting, June 1985*** *Drink up.*

1951*****

Beaulieu, Cabernet Sauvignon Private Reserve A great wine, rich and lovely at 20 years old and on three occasions since. Most recently: fabulous appearance, great depth and richness; low-keyed, massive and concentrated, the bouquet clasped tight, slow to emerge, walnuts, almost smoky, a sort of sooty richness; the sweetness of ripe grapes and maximum alcoholic content, huge, fleshy, velvety, perfect acidity but a touch of overripe bitterness if left too long in the glass. A sort of amalgam of '55 Latour and '59 Cheval-Blanc. *Last noted dining with Zelma Long and the Louis Martinis at Maynard Amerine's, June 1984******

Charles Krug, Cabernet Sauvignon Very attractive colour, more intense than the '50; nose a bit woody; strange, low-keyed, mushroomy taste. *June 1985.*

Charles Krug, Cabernet Sauvignon Vintage Selection Colour a bit too brown; oaky but also more floral, herbaceous, with depth of fruit though malty, like Haut-Brion '29; great richness and concentration but oxidised. *June 1985.*

1952**

Charles Krug, Cabernet Sauvignon Lovely colour, open-knit garnet, mahogany rim; sweet, vanilla, well developed, after minutes very attractive, complete; nice weight, crisp, lively, lovely fruit, refreshing tannin and acidity. *June 1989******

Charles Krug, Cabernet Sauvignon Vintage Selection Paler, more mature-looking; meaty, more oxidation but fragrant; slightly lacking, drying out and thinning. *June 1985***

1956****

Charles Krug, Cabernet Sauvignon Vintage Selection Medium-deep, rosy glow, rich 'legs'; lively vanillin, medicinal, iron, Bordeaux-like nose, evolving quickly and gloriously, mulberry-rich fruit; sweet, medium full-bodied, fleshy, excellent fruit, balance, length and finish. *Last tasted June 1985******

1957**

Charles Krug, Cabernet Sauvignon Vintage Selection Deep, intense, mature rim; spicy bouquet, cinnamon, eucalyptus; fullish, crisp, positive flavour, good tannin and acidity. *June 1985****

1958*****

Beaulieu, Cabernet Sauvignon Private Reserve Georges de Latour Six notes since 1975. Seemed at its best around 1980. A great vintage and reputation, though Barney Rhodes told me in 1986 that André Tchelistcheff considered that it had not aged well and had no wish to taste it. In fact the bottle Barney produced that evening had a touch of mercaptan on the nose which I further described as high-toned, muffled mulberry, and a bit tart. Four years later: still impressively deep; very rich, fig-like nose, slightly dusty at first but a glorious bouquet emerged from its depths; dry, full-bodied yet with a certain leanness, and lissom for BV. Good length and marvellous life-supporting acidity. *At the BV tasting, June 1990. At its best******

Inglenook, Cabernet Sauvignon Cask F10 Tasted first in 1967: strong, piquant. Then several good notes between 1969 and 1979. More recently: very deep yet open-knit; deep, fig-like richness of fruit, closed at first, opening up over 45 minutes in the glass; a huge yet soft spicy wine with an attractive, dry finish. *At Maynard Amerine's, June 1986*****

Charles Krug, Cabernet Sauvignon Peter Mondavi

told us that press wine had been added. Powerful but curious flavour, sea salt, a bit stalky. Very dry finish. *June 1981***(*)

Charles Krug, Vintage Selection Opaque, ruby; spicy, high-toned, Ch Latour-like depth and substance, needing long decanting time; medium-sweet, full-bodied, high extract, lovely dry finish. *Last noted at the Krug/Mondavi tasting, June 1985*****(*) *Now to 2000.*

Louis Martini, Cabernet Sauvignon Special Selection Medium, mature; a gentle, slightly spicy nose that opened up beautifully, rich, ripe mulberry-like fruit; perfect weight, balance and flavour. Soft. Gentle. At peak. *Dining at the Rhodes', Napa, June 1981******

1959****

Heitz, Cabernet Sauvignon Fine deep, cherry-red, rich vintage colour; glorious minty bouquet; dry, full, fragrant, spicy, tannic. *Oct 1985*****

Inglenook, Cabernet Sauvignon Opaque, intense; spicy, tobacco-like, showing age, whiff of volatile acidity; very sweet, huge, soft, fleshy, delicious. Dry, slightly tart finish. *June 1986*****

Charles Krug, Cabernet Sauvignon First tasted in the 'Dining with the Masters of Wine' series in 1967: fine, deep, richly flavoured. Perfect in 1977. Eight years later: plummy; very Bordeaux-like, oaky, hard, rich, developed well; rich, chewy, thick, Médoc-like tannin and acidity. *June 1985****

Charles Krug, Cabernet Sauvignon Vintage Selection Slightly paler but better-defined colour; lighter, more open, higher-toned, elegant, developing fabulous fragrance; slightly sweeter, good length, texture, finish. Elegant. Perfect state of evolution. *June 1985*****

Charles Krug, Vintage Selection Lot B Deeper, ruby; dusty, rich fruit but too much oak on nose; sweet, very good fruit, mid-palate, endtaste and length. *Tasted June 1985*****(*) *Will keep.*

Louis Martini, Cabernet Sauvignon 'California Mountain' Fine, deep, mature; firm, touch of mulberry-ripe fruit; dryish, medium-full, understated but perfectly matured and complete. *At dinner with Maynard Amerine, June 1982*****

1960***

Beaulieu, Cabernet Sauvignon Private Reserve Georges de Latour First tasted with the Rhodes in 1967: fragrant, attractive. Came of age at 21: very deep, still plummy; sweet, rich, waxy, slightly spicy; also sweet on the palate, full, ripe, velvety, good extract. Five years later: medium, rich, mature; more malty, jammy on nose and flavour. Good fruit, good length. *Last tasted Oct 1986**** *Drink up.*

Heitz, Cabernet Sauvignon Deep red; cherry-like fruit on nose, touch of volatile acidity, but great after an hour in glass; nice weight, stylish, zest and zing. *With Belle and Barney Rhodes at 47 Park Street, Oct 1986*****

Charles Krug, Cabernet Sauvignon Expansive garnet, tinged with orange; fragrant, developed beautifully, then muffled, chocolaty; sweet, positive attack and mid-palate, good length, nice acidity. *June 1985**** *Drink up.*

1961***

Heitz, Pinot Noir The oldest California Pinot Noir tasted since 1980. Grapes bought in and vinified by Joe Heitz. Medium-deep; a muffled, sweaty nose with no discernible Pinot character; sweet, full-bodied, undoubtedly impressive. Like Jean Grivot's burgundies, better in the mouth, the warmth expanding the flavour. *Oct 1986***

Charles Krug, Cabernet Sauvignon Deep, plummy; low-keyed but opened up well, lovely fruit; overall dry, with slithery, silky, leathery tannic texture. *June 1985****

Charles Krug, Cabernet Sauvignon Vintage Selection Less deep, more developed; glorious, fully evolved bouquet, touch of vanillin; dry, silky tannins, better, citrus-like acidity. Time in hand. *June 1985*****

1962**

Charles Krug, Cabernet Sauvignon Medium-deep, ruby centre, maturing rim—like a '62 Médoc; spicy, lively but a touch of farmyard rusticity, cheesy, medicinal. Reminded me of Brane-Cantenac; sweet, soft, chewy, edgy acidity. *June 1985***

Charles Krug, Vintage Selection Deeper colour; woody—too much oak, but developed richly; less sweet, elegant, too oaky, very tannic. *June 1985***

1963****

Inglenook, Cabernet Sauvignon Several notes in the 1970s, all good. Opaque, intense, mature rim; fabulous, ripe Cabernet and eucalyptus bouquet, plus Lapsang Souchong! Overall dry, fairly full-bodied, rich, chewy, vigorous. *Last tasted (blind) with Hugh Johnson and Bob Thompson at the Trefethens' annual picnic, Oct 1982*****

Charles Krug, Cabernet Sauvignon Same depth of colour as the '60 but a bit weak at the edges; very forthcoming, fully evolved bouquet of fragrance and charm; nice weight, crisp yet silky, perfect balance, elegant. Will keep. *June 1985*****

1964****

Beaulieu, Cabernet Sauvignon Private Reserve Georges de Latour Sugar 23.5°. Huge, austere, unready when first tasted in 1970 but had developed agreeably by the end of that decade. Most recently: medium; nose a bit unyielding, crisp, deep; dry, Médoc-like weight and style. *Last noted at Christie's pre-sale tasting in April 1986*****

Charles Krug, Cabernet Sauvignon First tasted in 1979, very fine. In 1984, remarkably good, spicy, shapely. 12 months later, at the Krug/Mondavi tasting in the Napa: now medium-deep, but a glorious colour; lovely spice and fruit overcoming initial dusty, 'linoleum' bottle-stink; perfect weight, crisp; elegant, not unlike the '63, perhaps drier. *Last tasted June 1985*****

1965*****

Beaulieu, Cabernet Sauvignon Private Reserve Georges de Latour Lovely when only five years old, maturing nicely at 10. Perfection at the end of the 1970s and again in 1983, though paler than expected and with a fully evolved bouquet, with whiff of aniseed; firm, lively. Most recently: a crisp lively appearance, nose and taste. Gentle mulberry-like fruit, developing liquorice-like bouquet; dry, crisp, lovely texture, firm. Lots of life left. *Last noted at a Christie's dinner at Michael's, Santa Monica, Sept 1989*****

Charles Krug, Cabernet Sauvignon Gorgeously glowing colour, rich garnet, mature rim; dusty and tannic at first, the bouquet unravelled, with good fruit and perfect harmony, then warm, toasty, a hint of wholemeal and ginger, distinct mint, and after 30 minutes, heavenly; rather sweet, lightish weight and style, most elegant, adequate tannin and acidity. *June 1985******

1966****

Beaulieu, Cabernet Sauvignon Private Reserve Georges de Latour Early vintage, sugar 23°. First tasted in 1972, nicely balanced, but unready. Most recently: fairly deep, hint of ruby, mature brown rim; low-keyed but rich. Nose reminded me of port. Developed well, spicy, trace of tobacco; sweet, nice weight, soft, easy, elegant, still tannic but just lacking length of a major vintage. *Last noted at the BV tasting to celebrate the 50th anniversary of the Private Reserve wines, June 1990*****

Charles Krug, Cabernet Sauvignon Immature but attractive in 1972. Nine years later, less deep, very mature; elegant, fragrant but showing some age; very flavoury but with a dry, rasping finish. *Last tasted March 1981***

Robert Mondavi, Cabernet Sauvignon Peter Mondavi's marvellous 21-year vintage span of Charles Krug ended with the '65, after which he handed over the vertical tasting baton to brother Robert, whose range started with the '66. First, in bottle: deep, opaque at centre but mature and looking tired; oily eucalyptus nose that developed fig-like fruit but was over-the-hill in an hour; some sweetness and elegance, chewy, hot dry finish. Far better in magnum: less deep but redder and livelier; crisp fruity nose that opened up attractively but which also faded after an hour; medium sweetness and weight, soft, fleshy. *At the Krug/Mondavi tasting in the Napa, June 1985. At best****

Robert Mondavi, Zinfandel This was Bob's first Zin: opaque centre but mature rim; calm, harmonious bouquet, sweet, jammy; dryish, fullish, velvety. Remarkably good. *June 1983*****

Martin Ray, Cabernet Sauvignon Incredibly deep, plummy; very powerful but very odd, smelly, peppery nose; horribly acidic. Undrinkable. *Dropped in at the end of an extensive tasting of '66 red Bordeaux in San Diego, Nov 1986.*

1967***

Inglenook, Cabernet Sauvignon First tasted shortly after bottling: fragrant, elegant. 16 years later: lovely colour; nice vinosity, fig-like richness of fruit; dry, medium weight, Graves-like earthiness. *Last tasted Sept 1985****

Robert Mondavi, Cabernet Sauvignon (10% Cabernet Franc) Beautiful colour; pleasant, open, ripe fruit aroma, quickly developing blancmange-like vanilla scent, after 30 minutes fully evolved, after an hour glorious; medium sweetness and body, very positive, lively flavour, slightly bitter finish. One of Bob's earlier varietal blends. *June 1985****

1968*****

Beaulieu, Cabernet Sauvignon Private Reserve Georges de Latour Several notes in the 1970s, "Napa at its best". Twice in the early 1980s. Incredibly deep, a great vintage appearance, orange-tinged mature edge; nose dumb at first, well-knit, touch of eucalyptus, stewed prunes; sweet, rich, concentrated, with lovely texture and warm alcoholic glow. Marvellous wine. Years of life. *Last tasted Oct 1982******

Beaulieu, 'Special Burgundy' From vineyards 2 and 4 at Rutherford. The best barrel. First noted at a Heublein pre-sale tasting in 1980: deep, ripe, well balanced. Next, as opaque as a big vintage of Ch Latour; figgy, minty, meaty, earthy bouquet; sweet, fullish, rich, touch of iron. Complete. Delicious. *Last tasted Feb 1986****

Freemark Abbey, Cabernet Sauvignon Bosché The first vintage at Freemark made with grapes from John Bosché's vineyard. Attractive colour; broad, fruity nose; velvety, fragrant — touch of overmaturity. Cracked up a bit. *June 1981***

Harbour Winery, Zinfandel Made by Charles Myers from grapes grown by the Doctors Adamson and Rhodes, the latter supplying medical alcohol to fortify the wine. Opaque; sweet, powdery vanillin/blancmange nose; fairly sweet, fullish, fresh, fruity and craftily made. Amazing what these academics get up to. *June 1981****

Heitz, Cabernet Sauvignon First tasted in 1974. Vastly impressive. In 1979 described as a cross between Ch Pétrus and Mouton-Rothschild. More recently: still magnificently deep; fabulous, spicy — eucalyptus, though Joe Heitz hates this description; full, intense, packed with fruit and life-sustaining tannin. *Last tasted Sept 1986***** Now to beyond 2000.*

Inglenook, Cabernet Sauvignon Deep; concentrated; sweet in 1979. After six years less deep; broad, open, cheesy, tannic nose; excellent weight, balance, flavour. *Last tasted March 1985*****

Louis Martini, Cabernet Sauvignon Deep, lively; plummy, prune-like; fairly sweet and full, ripe, plausible, tannic-iron finish. *June 1982****

Louis Martini, Mountain, Cabernet Sauvignon Fine deep rich appearance, bouquet and flavour. Glorious. *Feb 1987*****

Robert Mondavi, Cabernet Sauvignon (8% Cabernet Franc) Four notes, first in 1985 at the Krug/Mondavi tasting: beautiful colour; rich, quickly developing nose; also rich yet firm on palate, with time in hand. Twice in 1986, again displaying that remarkably rapid development in the glass, its tannic finish a bit like rusty nails. *Most recently at a luncheon given by Andie Lawlor at the Chicago O'Hare Sofitel, Jan 1988*****

Souverain, Cabernet Sauvignon Deep, rich; equally rich nose, Napa volcanic earth and iron, jammy fruit; curious stalky dry raw finish. Somewhat unknit. *June 1981**?*

1969** *to* *****

Beaulieu, Cabernet Sauvignon Private Reserve Georges de Latour Still a lively ruby; figgy, then a crisp berry-like fragrance, becoming scented; medium sweetness, pleasant weight, excellent fruit, crisp — the result of cool growing conditions, finely balanced Cabernet fruit, American oak and higher tannins. Bordeaux-like in style, weight, tannin and acidity. *June 1985*****

Heitz, Martha's Vineyard Cabernet Sauvignon Bottled four years after the vintage, Sept 1973. First tasted in 1981. Similar note four years later: wonderfully rich, thick, ruby-centred, maturing; great bouquet: unmistakable spicy, cloves, pine, cinnamon, eucalyptus Cabernet, developing even further traits of old stables; full of extract and flavour, elegant despite its magnitude, fine flavour, length. Dry finish. The last bottle given me by Tim and Martha May of Martha's Vineyard (Heitz makes the wine from their grapes). *Last tasted June 1985******

Robert Mondavi, Cabernet Sauvignon (15% Cabernet Franc, 3% Merlot) Very deep, about to mature; rich, vanilla, oak opening up fragrantly, chocolaty after 30 minutes, faded after an hour. Full-bodied. Very tannic. *June 1985**(*)*

Robert Mondavi, Cabernet Sauvignon Unfined Slightly more ruby; more peppery, spicy, scent of Earl Grey tea and Cabernet Sauvignon, then faded; very flavoury, high-toned, very piquant. Neither this nor the regular blend really very successful. After the steady progression of the earlier Charles Krug vintages, Bob Mondavi's annual experiments yielded very varying results. *Noted at the Krug/Mondavi tasting, June 1985.*

Other '69s tasted only once:

Chappellet, Cabernet Sauvignon Opaque, rich; crisp, slightly medicinal, almost port-like, and spirity; dry, rather lean, crisp, eucalyptus flavour, slightly high volatile acidity. *At the Chappellets', Napa, June 1982***

Freemark Abbey, Cabernet Sauvignon Sweet, biscuity, vanillin nose with citrus piquancy and spice; medium body, crisp, fruity, lively, dry, acidic. *Oct 1982***(*) *Probably needs drinking now.*

Freemark Abbey, Petite Sirah Opaque; huge, alcoholic nose and palate, four-square, years of life. *June 1983***(**)

Charles Krug, Cabernet Sauvignon Good weight and flavour, but tannic. *June 1984***(**)

Sterling, Cabernet Sauvignon Broad, leathery, cheesy (tannic) nose; soft, nice texture and weight. *June 1983***(*)?

1970****

Beaulieu, Bosché Cabernet Sauvignon The last vintage of BV made from John Bosché's grapes. Deep, velvety; good fruit but a bit unyielding; soft, fruity, hard finish. *Dining with Maynard Amerine, June 1981***(**)

Beaulieu, Cabernet Sauvignon Private Reserve Georges de Latour First tasted in cask in 1972: deep purple, full of fruit, stalky. Towards the end of that decade, still deep but harmonious, rich, tannic. Showing very well in the early 1980s, soft, lovely consistency. Most recently at the BV Private Reserve Anniversary tasting: richly coloured but showing maturity; nose a bit hard, figgy, struggling to crawl out of its shell, a squeeze of spicy Cabernet; very sweet yet very tannic — concentrated, due to one-third normal crop, tarry, intense, silky yet leathery. Years of life. *Last noted June 1990*****(*)

Heitz, Martha's Vineyard Cabernet Sauvignon Bottled four summers after the vintage, Aug 1974. Opaque centre; extremely fruity, spicy, scented; fabulous mouth-filling flavour. Glorious. *Pre-sale, Chicago, March 1985******

Robert Mondavi, Cabernet Sauvignon (83%) Unfiltered Deep ruby; dusty and hard at first, good, mulberry-like fruit; full-bodied, fruity, chewy, excellent flavour. *Last tasted June 1985****

Robert Mondavi, Unfined (80% Cabernet Sauvignon) Even deeper yet more mature; peppery, vanilla, hint of raspberries; drier, more massive, excellent flavour, hot alcoholic finish. *June 1985****(*)

Ridge, Fulton Zinfandel Nice weight, lovely texture, elegant. *May 1980*****

Other '70 **Cabernet Sauvignons** *tasted only once:*

Chappellet Deep, ruby; well-knit, fragrant bouquet of richness and depth; full-bodied yet soft and velvety, good length and life, complete. *June 1982****

Inglenook Opaque, still immature; lovely harmonious bouquet, touch of iron; full, fleshy, very pleasant flavour, good tannin and acidity. *June 1986****(*)

Mayacamas 13% alcohol. Deep-coloured, loaded with tannin. *June 1982**(**)

Sebastiani, North Coast, Sonoma Rather pale; jammy. *Sept 1986***

1971***

Robert Mondavi, Cabernet Sauvignon (4% Cabernet Franc, 5% Merlot) Fairly deep but indeterminate appearance and nose though the latter very sweet, fruity; good weight but overburdened with tannin and acidity, very dry, rather raw. *At the Krug/Mondavi tasting, June 1985**(*)

Robert Mondavi, Reserve (60% Cabernet Sauvignon, 40% Franc) Deeper, more ruby; dusty Cabernet fruit, high alcohol, revealing Pétrus-like fruit and flesh; sweeter, softer, more chewy and better balanced. *At the Krug/Mondavi tasting in 1985, and again in Nov 1986****

Ridge, Geyserville Zinfandel Bottled Oct 1972. Medium-pale; delicate, refreshing fruit, squeeze of lemon, a 'medicinal' whiff, ripe, sweet. Slightly sweet on the palate too, soft, elegant, flavoury. *Feb 1989*****

Ridge, Montebello Cabernet Sauvignon Bottled Oct 1973. The Montebello vineyard is in the hills south of San Francisco, unusual for its height, 2,300 feet above sea level. The wines have a relatively modest alcoholic content, this '71 being 12.2% by volume. First noted at dinner at home in July 1984 when it still had a youthful appearance, with touch of spritz. The dominating impression of the nose was iron, repeated on the palate. A lean, concentrated wine. Next tasted with Paul Draper the following year on my first visit to the vineyard, a long climb to this century-old, massive timber-beamed winery. The wine's very distinctive character not only due to the vineyard's elevation but its limestone 'island' outcrop. The concept of picking when the *vine* is fully mature was new to me. The nose is medicinal, arboreal — a sort of piquant laurel. Fairly full-bodied, considerable length, complete, overall dry. *Last tasted June 1985. Then***(**) *Doubtless approaching peak, but with long life.*

1972*** *to* ****

Heitz, Martha's Vineyard Cabernet Sauvignon Total contrast to Ridge's classic two years in cask and early bottlings of Zinfandel: Heitz bottled this in June 1976. At 10 years old still opaque, intense, its youthful hue pressing the sides of the glass like a referee trying to keep two heavyweights apart; very attractive, forthcoming, minty, eucalyptus, Cabernet; full-bodied, concentrated, an almost exaggerated Bordeaux-like fruit, but much sweeter despite its tannin. Blatant, obvious, appealing, brilliant. Next, showing well at a pre-sale tasting in Chicago but given away at $320 a case. *Last noted March 1985****(*) *Probably at peak now.*

Mayacamas, Late Harvest Zinfandel 17½% alcohol. One of Napa's strange classics, often port-like and, incidentally, very good with Stilton. Medium, not as deep as expected, fully mature-looking; sweet, fragrant, fruit like plums and damsons; medium-sweet, not as hefty as its strength suggested, fresh, lovely acidity. *March 1985***** *Should be perfect now. Will keep.*

Robert Mondavi, Cabernet Sauvignon (5% Cabernet Franc, 2% Merlot) Very deep; two-part nose, lots of fruit and cheese-rind tannin; fairly sweet, full-bodied, hefty, rich, chewy, dry finish. *Krug/Mondavi tasting, June 1985***(*)

Mount Eden, Pinot Noir Released in 1975. At nine years old, a fabulous colour; incredibly rich, harmonious nose; fabulous fruit, opulent style. Not remotely a Côte de Beaune but lovely. *At dinner with the Dierkhisings, Silverado Restaurant, Calistoga, June 1981*****

Brief notes on three '72 **Cabernet Sauvignons**:

Louis Martini A charmer. *June 1982****

Mayacamas 13%; deep, thick, plummy purple; very sweet jammy fruit, spicy, attractive. Quite a contrast in the mouth, short sharp mid-palate fruit, very dry, a bit raw. *June 1983**(*)

Ridge, Montebello Deep; 'volcanic' nose; very flavoury, very stylish. *March 1985****(*)

1973★★★★

Chappellet, Cabernet Sauvignon Opaque at 11 years old; stylish, strawberry-like fruit; tannic. Later, still deep, richly coloured; very fragrant, unusual, slightly raisiny nose. *Last noted, hastily, pre-sale, Chicago, Feb 1987*★★(★)

Fetzer, Petite Sirah Still opaque and youthful; not a strongly varietal aroma, sweaty, alcoholic, reminding me of Rhône and port; rich, full, thick, peppery. Hard to place. *Oct 1983*★★(★)?

Forman's, Cabernet Sauvignon 'Grand Vin' Made by Ric Forman from a two-acre vineyard in Grass Valley, leading up to Lake Tahoe. Brilliant: still opaque, hardly aged in 13 years: amazing fruit, linseed oil, blackberry then blackcurrant oozing out! Excellent fruit on palate, nice flesh and texture, still very tannic. *With the Dierkhisings, Calistoga, June 1986*★★★(★) *Probably still evolving.*

Freemark Abbey, Cabernet Bosché (Grapes from the Bosché family vineyard.) Very deep; a bit rustic, sweet, Brane-Cantenac-like nose; nice weight, lovely texture. *June 1983*★★★ *Drink up.*

Heitz, Cabernet Sauvignon Marvellous colour; spicy and interesting in 1980. In 1983, still intense; delicate, fruity, spicy nose; fullish, lean but assertive, with severely dry finish. Recently I noticed more eucalyptus than in his Martha's Vineyard. Less dry, meaty, fruity. Maturing nicely. *Last tasted Jan 1989*★★★★

Heitz, Martha's Vineyard Cabernet Sauvignon Bottled June 1977 and first tasted in 1981. A 'big vintage' appearance; assertive, characteristic eucalyptus scent; rich, ripe, soft, full. Rich complexity noted in 1985 and, most recently, pure mint, sweet, very fragrant; lean, very tannic, lovely aftertaste. Years of life. *Feb 1989*★★(★★★)

Robert Mondavi, Cabernet Sauvignon (5% Cabernet Franc, 6% Merlot) Deep, mature; glorious, rich, spicy, fruity and tannic on nose and palate. Soft and fleshy. *June 1985*★★★★ *Lovely now.*

Robert Mondavi, Reserve Cabernet Sauvignon (12% Cabernet Franc) 23° Brix, 13.2% alcohol, 2 g/l residual sugar. Fermented for three days at 88° F, 12-day skin contact, aged 29 months in new 60-gallon Nevers oak casks. First tasted alongside the 'regular' in June 1985, opaque, more intense; a huge oaky nose, tannic, peppery; immense, packed with fruit. A bit "harsh" noted in 1986 but remarkably speedy development thereafter. Most recently, less deep, showing maturity; lovely soft spicy bouquet; seemed far less massive, refreshing, delicious. *Last noted at a tasting of Mondavi Reserve wines conducted with Michael Mondavi for Southern Wine, Miami, Feb 1988*★★★★

Joseph Phelps, Pinot Noir Fig-like nose and taste, mild, not burgundy but very agreeable. *June 1981*★★

Sterling, Merlot (100%) The first bottle oxidised, the second brighter; citrus fragrance; sweet, nice weight, fleshy, good tannins. *Both Sterlings presented by Ric Forman at a Hollywood Wine Society Seminar, Feb 1989*★★★

Sterling, Reserve Cabernet Fragrant, refreshing nose, described by the winemaker as "gauzy spice"; sweet, very fleshy and shapely, rounded rather than lengthy. *Feb 1989*★★★

Three other '73 **Cabernet Sauvignons**:

Beaulieu, Private Reserve Low-keyed, meaty, showing signs of age. *Feb 1987*★★★ *Drink up.*

Chateau Montelena From Redwood Ranch, Sonoma. Not marketed. Still virtually opaque; minty, peppery, touch of resin, liquorice, 'petrol'; dry, lean, edgy, attractive but raw. *Feb 1986*★(★)

Stag's Leap Wine Cellars Medium depth, maturing; meaty cedary nose. Attractive. *Chicago, Sept 1985*★★★

1974★★★★★

This vintage needs a preface. Long cool growing season, very hot weather during harvest. Regarded as the best year since 1968 in the Napa but the butt of endless "is it as great as all that" questions and doubts about whether it has kept well. Unhappily I was unable to attend Dr Steve Mandy's horizontal tasting of over 80 Cabernet Sauvignons in 1990. It was remarkable in that there were so many wineries and that so many wines were showing signs of fatigue. I have barely 50 notes on the wines of this vintage. The most interesting were made at a blind tasting of 11 major Cabernets at the 'California Wine Experience' on their 10th anniversary. Here is the briefest and most up-to-date summary I can muster.

Beaulieu, Cabernet Sauvignon Private Reserve Georges de Latour Deep, plummy purple, tannic, "great potential" noted in 1979 and 1981 yet at 10 years old, though richly coloured, was no longer deep, and with a red-brown mature rim; its nose rich and spicy, then after an hour soft, harmonious, understated; fairly sweet, hefty, nice texture, stylish. Three other notes in the mid-1980s repeated "soft", "sweet", "rich" and warned of a heavy sediment. Most recently, nose malty, meaty; rather medicinal Médoc flavour, great depth, good length. Dry finish. I would say this was at its best at about 12 years old. *Feb 1989*★★★★★ *Now to 1994.*

Caymus, Cabernet Sauvignon Fairly deep, indeterminate plummy colour, slow-maturing; blatantly sweet and jammy at first, over an hour later high-toned, peppery, Cabernet blackcurrant – I liked it; a delicious, fascinating wine with nice texture, length, tannin and acidity. Elegant. Beautifully made. Needed time. *Oct 1984*★★★★(★) *Probably at peak now to 1998.*

Clos du Val, Cabernet Sauvignon Two notes in 1980: impressively deep, good fruit, unready. Displaying its Bordeaux weight and style at the 10-year tasting: nose low-keyed at first, Médoc-like 'fruit bush' with Pomerol-like mulberry, fleshy fruit, the bouquet evolved beautifully in the glass, crisp, fragrant; a lovely wine, silky texture, lean for a '74, elegant. Tannic but no bitterness. Endorsed at a pre-sale tasting. *Last noted Nov 1986. Then*★★★★(★) *Should be superb now.*

Conn Creek, Cabernet Sauvignon Grapes grown by Milton and Barbara Eisele at Lyncrest, their gravelly hillside vineyard. The wine was made by John Henderson, and 'finished' at Conn Creek then bottled Feb 1977. It showed very well at the California Wine Experience tasting: the deepest of the range, like Ch Latour of a big vintage; powerful, forthcoming, sweaty tannic nose; a glorious wine, very positive fruit, crisp, good length, fragrant aftertaste. "Will keep 20 years." Voted top at Dr Mandy's tasting of '74s in Feb 1990. More recently: still very deep, almost opaque; a very pronounced 'medicinal' scent that became very Bordeaux-like in the glass; medium dry, medium weight (12.5%), fleshy, velvety, ripe flavour and aftertaste. Silky tannins. Dry finish. *Last tasted May 1991*★★★★(★) *Now to 2000.*

Freemark Abbey, Cabernet Sauvignon This was the wine that came second, after Ch Trotanoy '61, in the Cabernet Sauvignon class at the Gault-Millau 'Olympiade' in 1979. It was lovely . Five years later, rich, with a mature appearance and nose, slightly scented, fairly assertive with tannic iron finish. *Pre-sale, April 1984*★★★★

Freemark Abbey, Cabernet Sauvignon Bosché Bright cherry red; rather cool, oyster shell nose, tight-knit, lean even after an hour in the glass; a bit too raw and tannic, not perfectly balanced and frankly not showing brilliantly against the competition in Oct 1984. However, in 1986 I liked it better. More recently: lovely fruit and cinnamon on the nose. *Last tasted Sept 1986*****

Heitz, Cabernet Sauvignon First tasted at the winery in 1979: spicy; massive, magnificent. Three years on, in magnum, opaque, plummy; fragrant, eucalyptus; fine rich flavour but unready. Joe Heitz turned down Marvin Shanken's invitation to the 10-year tasting. Cost aside, I suspect that his attitude is rather like that of the first-growth château proprietors in Bordeaux: he and they do not need to compete. Most recently, a bottle given to me by the Rhodes, who informed me it was from Martha's Vineyard (they should know, they planted it, and have close connections with Heitz). The first thing I noticed was the deeply stained, sediment-covered cork – a 2in cork, short by first-growth Bordeaux standards. The wine looked so thick I thought I should have decanted it through a filter paper, but it was in fact translucent, its thickness giving a dramatic indication of its extract and other components. Deep, though with a tinge of orange maturity at the rim. Fragrant, rich, cedary, spicy and scented bouquet; mouthfilling flavour, glowingly heady (13.5% alcohol), incredibly rich, almost chewable, leathery tannic texture. The nose later reminded me of Haut-Brion, earthy, slightly tobacco-like. The eucalyptus hallmark noticeable on the palate. A fabulous mouthful but showing its age. *Easter Day, 1991***** It will keep but can it improve? Drink now.*

Inglenook, Cabernet Sauvignon Cask A 9 Distinctive, enchanting colour, rich, lively, orange-tinged maturity; rich, syrup of figs, subdued after an hour but beautiful, the most elegant and harmonious bouquet of the 11 top Cabernets shown; sweet entry, pleasant weight, spicy, fine quality. Beautiful. *Oct 1984***** Now to 2000.*

Charles Krug, Cabernet Sauvignon Lusty and still youthful nine-year-old. *June 1983***(*)*

Charles Krug, Cabernet Sauvignon Vintage Selection Lot F 1 Did not show too well at the Wine Experience 10-year tasting. Although impressive in appearance and lovely on the nose at first, it developed an overripe pig-manure, barnyard odour laced with iodine. Two notes later: very soft, velvety but with bird droppings flavour, though I next noted "lovely fruit and style". *Last tasted Nov 1986** or**** A matter of taste.*

Robert Mondavi, Cabernet Sauvignon (About 5% Cabernet Franc, 9% Merlot.) Six notes: opaque, immature in 1980; gloriously spicy nose, cinnamon new oak scent, austere, twice in 1981; mulberry-ripe but dry in 1982 and 1984. Still deep but maturing, vanilla and fruit, silky leathery tannin texture. *Last tasted June 1985***(*)*

Robert Mondavi, Cabernet Sauvignon Reserve Starting to mature in its 10th year: flowery, touch of raspberry; nice weight, '74 richness, very drinkable. In June 1985, alongside the 'regular', deeper, more intense; a beautifully evolved bouquet, sweeter, massive, packed with fruit. More recently, the unmistakable '74 thickness, its bouquet needing time to develop, drinking well. *Last tasted Jan 1988*****

Joseph Phelps, Insignia (CS 94%, Merlot 6%) Sweet, multi-layered in 1985. (One of the top three wines in Mandy's extensive tasting of '74s.) Recently very deep, velvety ruby; fragrant, rich, un-Bordeaux-like scent; very sweet on the palate, too sweet with food but delicious to drink by itself. Full-bodied (13.5%), glorious fruit and flesh. High extract, great length. I can see why it would score highly in a comparative tasting. *May 1991******

Simi, Cabernet Sauvignon Special Reserve Top marks at the 10-year tasting. Plummy purple; cool, low-keyed at first, but eventually exuded a very pronounced Cabernet aroma, like Mouton-Rothschild '59 put through a sieve, yet restrained to the point of arrogance; lovely, blackcurranty, Mouton-like flavour. A lovely wine. *Oct 1984****(*) Should be perfection now.*

Stag's Leap Wine Cellars, Cabernet Sauvignon First tasted two years after the vintage: distinctly impressive. In 1979, still opaque, with marvellous fruit, perfect balance, great future. At the 10-year tasting, richly coloured, intense, maturing; an immediately warm, vanillin nose that developed and held well in the glass. Classic. Very pronounced, somewhat idiosyncratic character, fine fruit, crosses palate well. *June 1985******

Stag's Leap Wine Cellars, Cabernet Sauvignon Cask 23 Opaque, magnificent 'robe' in 1981, rich mulberry-ripe fruit, harmony, depth; full, velvety, lovely acidity. Three years on, rich ruby; same sweet, velvety fruit; soft, beautiful flavour, rich, tannic acid for long keeping. *May 1984****(*) Doubtless approaching peak. To beyond 2000.*

Sterling, Cabernet Sauvignon First noted in 1981, a thick chunky '74 appearance; fragrant, complex; rich, though unknit and with raw acidity. Fruity nose but very tannic in 1984. Most recently, less deep, more mature, but a slightly corked bottle. *Last noted Feb 1989. At best**(*)*

Sterling, Reserve Cabernet Medium-deep, mature; citrus, strawberry-like fruit; rather sweet, full, rich, with lovely ripe fruit. *Ric Forman's tasting, Feb 1989*****

Brief notes on some other '74s:

Caparone, Cabernet Sauvignon From three-year-old vines, 25 months in 50-gallon oak barrels, unfined, unfiltered. I didn't know one could make wine from vines this age, but in Paso Robles anything goes. A rich, toasted, vegetal nose; sweet, fabulously rich, chewy, more acidity than tannin. Interesting. *July 1985**? Future uncertain.*

Chateau Montelena, Cabernet Sauvignon Well developed; herbaceous, lovely fruit; nice weight and style, fairly soft and ripe, finishing dry. *Feb 1986***(*)*

Clos du Bois, Cabernet Sauvignon (planted 1964) Deep, not mature at 12 years; low-keyed, good fruit, depth; big, fleshy; soft tannins. *June 1986**(**)*

Clos du Bois, Pinot Noir Soft, spicy, attractive but not quite right, slightly hollow, 'blown'. *Dec 1984**

Mayacamas, Mountain Cabernet Opaque; full of fruit, tannin in 1986. Most recently, still youthful-looking; sweet, fleshy, harmonious though tannic nose; an immense, swingeingly dry tannic wine. I hope it will come round. *Last tasted Feb 1989(****)?*

Raymond, Cabernet Sauvignon Rich and attractive in 1981. *For early drinking?*****

Ridge, Montebello, Cabernet Sauvignon Tremendous potential. *April 1980. Then*(****)?*

Sonoma Vineyards, Cabernet Sauvignon Prune-like nose, sagged a bit in the glass, but fragrant; good fruit, loaded with tannin. *June 1985**(**)*

1975***

Beaulieu, Cabernet Sauvignon Cold season, vines retarded, the latest harvest on record. Nevertheless two good notes in 1980, well-balanced wine. 10 years later, still a fine deep colour; soft, fragrant, fully evolved bouquet, violets; medium sweetness and body, lively, citrus-like fruit. *June 1990*** Drink soon.*

Hoffmann Mountain Ranch, Pinot Noir A lovely wine first admired in 1979. Fragrant, rich in the mid-1980s. Most recently, still very deep with noticeably rich 'legs'; deep, fine fruity nose; amazingly sweet, soft, delicious. *Last tasted May 1989**** Drink now.*

Robert Mondavi, Cabernet Sauvignon Six notes. Ruby in 1982. By 1987, less deep, more mature; a warm fleshy harmonious nose and soft, lovely flavour. A very attractive 'regular'. *Last tasted Sept 1987****

Robert Mondavi, Cabernet Sauvignon Reserve (10% Cabernet Franc, 5% Merlot) 33 months in oak (24% new). Initially lacked vinosity and charm. By 1983 noticed mouthwatering acidity, spicy, good finish. Deeper, more intense than the 'regular', more spicy too, and better length. Most recently, fruit coming out nicely; dry, lean, elegant but a bit hard. All right with food. *Last tasted Feb 1988***(*) Drink now to 1995.*

Short notes on some other '75s:

Alexander Valley, Zinfandel Bouquet like avocado and thyme; some sweetness, fresh mint. *June 1981****

Caymus, Cabernet Sauvignon Overpowering. *June 1982(***)*

Chateau Montelena, Cabernet Sauvignon (74% from Napa, 26% Sonoma) Deep, flavoury, tannic, lacking length. *Feb 1986*(*)*

Clos du Val, Cabernet Sauvignon First tasted in 1980. Very distinctive style. Tannate of iron. Deep, still immature after eight years; mulberry-rich nose and palate, excellent flavour. Still a touch of iron. *Oct 1983*(***)*

Cuvaison, Spring Mountain Reserve Cabernet Sauvignon Deep purple; crisp Cabernet fruit; very dry, high acidity. *Feb 1987*(*)*

Eisele Valley, Cabernet Sauvignon (5% Merlot) Packed with fruit; a tannic blockbuster. *March 1985(***)?*

Freemark Abbey, Cabernet Sauvignon Bosché Deep ruby; sweet, harmonious; full, ripe, soft, fruity. *Last tasted Sept 1986***(*)*

Freemark Abbey, Pinot Noir The last they made. Palish, viscous; authentic 'fishy' Pinot aroma, slightly scented; very firm, lovely acidity, very good. *June 1983****

Heitz, Martha's Vineyard Cabernet Sauvignon Bottled July 1979: opaque; spicy; massive, dry. *Pre-sale, March 1985(****)*

Mayacamas, Mountain Cabernet Sauvignon Deep and rich, port-like, tannic. *Pre-sale, Sept 1986*(**)*

Joseph Phelps, Cabernet Sauvignon (5% Merlot) Bottled Aug 1977. Fragrant, rich, very tannic. *March 1985**(*)*

Ridge, Geyserville Zinfandel Sonoma, 100-year-old vines. Beautiful ruby; deep, strawberry-like aroma; ripe grape sweetness countered by tannate of iron. Curiously attractive. *June 1985**(*)*

Ridge, Montebello Cabernet Sauvignon Bottled Nov 1977. Very fragrant, lightweight (only 11.7% alcohol), lean, refreshing, attractive. Ready. *June 1985****

Sebastiani, Proprietor's Reserve Cabernet Sauvignon 4½ years in redwood and oak. Lovely colour, fully mature-looking; sweet, caramelly, earthy; soft, attractive, silky tannins. *Jan 1990****

Joseph Swan, Zinfandel Deep ruby; crisp berry-like fruit on nose and palate. Touch of iron and distinctly tannic. *Feb 1989*(*)*

Trefethen, Cabernet Sauvignon (25% Merlot) Deep, plummy; rich, whiff of furniture polish spiciness; chunky (13.3% alcohol), flavoury, good length. *Oct 1982*(**)*

1976***

Beaulieu, Cabernet Sauvignon Private Reserve Georges de Latour Stressed vines, small crop. Incredibly deep, intense, rich; lovely fruit, crisp, low-keyed, clearly more to come, harmonious but closed; very sweet, an immense wine, packed with fruit and silky tannins. Impressive. *At the BV tasting, June 1990**(**)*

Calera, Zinfandel Essence Bottled by La Noche, Soledad. A curiosity, sold in half-bottles. Extremely fruity; sweet, extract of Zinfandel, but instead of effecting a balance, the acidity aggressive and raw. *Dining with the Adamsons at The Ahwahnee, Yosemite, June 1983.*

Heitz, Bella Oaks Cabernet Sauvignon The first Bella Oaks vintage. Bottled in 1980. An extraordinary story: Belle and Barney (Dr Bernard) Rhodes bought a property in the Napa Valley, uprooted plum trees and in 1971 planted Cabernet Sauvignon. They then sold it to Tom and Martha May who named it Martha's Vineyard. The grapes were sold to Heitz. The Rhodes bought another piece of land further up the valley, uprooted another plum orchard, built a house and planted Cabernet Sauvignon. The grapes from Bella Oaks are sold to Heitz. Between them they have created in Bella Oaks a wine to almost rival Martha's Vineyard! The '76 Bella Oaks first tasted in 1981: fragrant, young and a bit stalky, but good flavour. Impressively deep; crisp, rather raw youthful fruit, spicy but immature; rich, stylish. A good future predicted for Bella Oaks, particularly as the vines mature. *Last tasted Oct 1984*(**)? Best to drink up.*

Heitz, Martha's Vineyard Cabernet Sauvignon Four years in cask and served at dinner rather prematurely by the Mays at Martha's Vineyard. Opaque, sweet, massive – something like 14.5% alcohol. I noted that it "needs 10 years, could take 20+!" *June 1981, then**(***)*

Jordan, Cabernet Sauvignon Another first wine, and an overnight success. First tasted in New York shortly after its release and highly impressed. Next with Tom Jordan at the château-like winery in Alexander Valley. Mulberry ripe fruit; soft, velvety, complete. Softness and elegance noted in the mid-1980s and a bouquet at first like cold tea but which blossomed in the glass. *Last tasted Sept 1986. It it past its best? Say****

Louis Martini, Cabernet Sauvignon Special Selection I have always had a soft spot for the Martinis. Old-established, decent, experienced, making consistently good wines and always modestly priced. And they keep well. The '76 still impressively deep; a whiff of mushroom soup when first poured but it opened up, fleshy, blackberry-like fruit; sweet, rich, good texture, a pleasant mouthful. *Feb 1989*** Now to 1996.*

Robert Mondavi, Cabernet Sauvignon Magnificent colour; cool, crisp, attractive fruit; shapely, very dry finish. *Last tasted Sept 1986**** Excellent now.*

Robert Mondavi, Cabernet Sauvignon (100%) Reserve Although very deep, showing brown-edged maturity as early as 1982. In the New Year of 1983 I gave it fulsome praise: "Mouton character, Pétrus weight and flesh, delicious but will develop further". Alongside the 'regular' at the Krug/Mondavi tasting in 1985, it was distinctly richer, with a nose that reminded me of syrup of figs. Big. Flavoury. *Last tasted June 1985*****

Sterling, Reserve Cabernet Sauvignon Very open, forthcoming, eucalyptus and iron on nose; fairly sweet, fleshy, delicious but short and with a hot, noticeably acidic finish. *Feb 1989*** Drink up.*

Some other '76 **Cabernets** *tasted in the mid-1980s:*

Beringer Fleshy, flavoury but endtaste of rusty nails**

Chappellet Very deep, rich, fragrant***

Chateau Montelena Rich nose, liquorice and coffee beans. Hefty (13.7% alcohol) but nice texture and style. Good length. Flavoury****

Chateau St Jean Cherry red; good fruit but very tannic and with high acidity*(***)*

Clos du Val Crisp, Médoc-like***

Conn Creek Opaque; hefty; fairly sweet, fleshy, lovely fruit****

Cuvaison Opaque; singed, spicy; chewy, very fruity, attractive****

Ridge, Montebello Characteristic, idiosyncratic fragrance, weight and quality***(*)?

1977**

Drought year.

Beaulieu, Cabernet Sauvignon Private Reserve Georges de Latour Deep, intense, rich ruby, maturing; loads of fruit, whiff of pear skins, volcanic, very Napa; full, velvety, fig-like richness of fruit, silky tannins. Good finish. Impressive. *Oct 1984***(*) Probably peaking now.*

Robert Mondavi, Cabernet Sauvignon Beautifully made. *June 1985****

Robert Mondavi, Cabernet Sauvignon Reserve (3% Cabernet Franc, 5% Merlot) Deep, minty, piquant, fragrant in 1983. More spicy and flavoury than the 'regular' at the 1985 tasting. Still a beautifully intense colour; fleshy, ripe on nose and palate, good length, dry finish. *Excellent when last tasted, Oct 1987***(*) Drink now to 1997.*

Ridge, Montebello Cabernet Sauvignon An amazing scent, crystallised violets, and, as always, a distinctive 'iron' touch on nose and palate. Dry, crisp, medium weight, lean. Good finish. *Feb 1989***(*) Now to 2000.*

Sterling, Cabernet Sauvignon Very ripe grapes from the Calistoga area. Lovely soft red, maturing; smell of meat extract and malt, citrus-like fruit, violets; weedy flavour, tannate of iron. Not much liked. *Feb 1989*(*)*

Some other '77 **Cabernets** *tasted in the mid-1980s:*

Burgess, Vintage Selection Opaque; dumb but good; heavy, fruity, tannic*(**)

Clos du Val High-toned, raw, figgy, hint of volatile acidity*?

Cuvaison Opaque; old, oaky, Bordeaux-like; curious old claret flavour, cheesy, very tannic**

Firestone Visited in Oct 1984, the morning after an earthquake had bodily shifted huge steel tanks and collapsed stacks of bottles. Rich, purple; plump, ripe, full-bodied, fleshy, impressive*(**)

Firestone, Vintage Reserve Sweeter. Well structured, good length***(*)

Heitz, Bella Oaks Lovely colour, broad, minty, harmonious; lovely fruit, excellent mid-palate, good length and grip***(*)

Jordan Deep, full of fruit but initially, I thought, lacking length**(*)?

Raymond Opaque; very sweet nose and palate, full, rich, chocolaty fruit***

Silver Oak Good fruit, nose developed impressively, well made**(*)

Trefethen Opaque; very fruity, spicy; dry, lean, elegant, flavoury***

Zaca Mesa Good fruit, nice quality***

Other varietals tasted around the mid-1980s:

Inglenook, Charbono An unusual grape virtually unique to Inglenook: medicinal, rustic, ripe; dry, severe. "Robust" on the back label an understatement(*)

Carneros Creek, Pinot Noir Plummy; chocolaty; sweet, very flavoury, good aftertaste***

Mark West, Pinot Noir Palish, orange-tinged *pelure d'oignon*; fragrant; dry, crisp, attractive flavour**

Mayacamas, Pinot Noir Blackthorn bush nose; excellent flavoury, velvety but bitter tannic finish*(*)

Nichelini, Zinfandel Cherry red; pigsty and pig-iron smell and taste. Horrid.

1978****

A good vintage, a big vintage, a late vintage—Heitz picked his Cabernet Sauvignon before the Chardonnay. I probably have more notes on this year than any other and recall taking part in an early competitive horizontal ('78 California Cabernets against '78 red Bordeaux) organised by the Dutch for an article in a glossy journal. Space confines me to a cross-section of the better known wineries for which I have recent notes.

Though not opulent like '74s I like the firmness and style of the '78s. The best will surely keep well.

Beaulieu, Cabernet Sauvignon Private Reserve Georges de Latour Still opaque in the mid-1980s, like plum juice; good fruit but hard-cored, needing bottle-age. Full, rich, ripe. Recently, nose warming up, sweet, fragrant; very good weight and flavour but excessively dry tannic finish. *Feb 1989***(*) 1992 to beyond 2000.*

Diamond Creek, Red Rock Terrace I well remember the outrageous price sought, and exceeded, at the first Napa Valley Wine Auction I conducted in 1980. What I later discovered was not an inflated ego but a more modest passion dedicated to making the best 100% pure Cabernets in a valley off the top end of the Napa. Red Rock Terrace describes the terrain. At 10 years old the '78 still deeply coloured; powerful, tannic. *Feb 1988**(**)*

Diamond Creek, Volcanic Hill The other side of the stream, facing the tiny winery, has very volcanic soil. Deep, lively, still youthful; crisp, berry-like nose; surprisingly sweet, fairly full-bodied, a rich style, crisp, flavoury, with a finish that reflected its origin, volcanic ash, iron on the finish. *At dinner in Miami, after Bob Paul's mammoth tasting of '82 Pomerols, Feb 1989***(*) Now to 2000.*

Grace Family Vineyard, Cabernet Sauvignon Vinified by Caymus, I suspect that the wine was not fined or filtered for it had a thick, cloudy sediment which, even though I gave it time, made it difficult to decant. Dusty nose, fairly high volatile acidity; chunky, fruity but a bit too raw and acidic. *April 1990**

Charles Krug, Cabernet Bosché Lovely colour, highly polished ruby; beautiful, harmonious bouquet and flavour. Just the right sweetness, perfect weight, lovely texture in the mouth, good length. *Lunching with Maynard Amerine at the Bohemian Club, Oct 1983**** Now to 1998.*

Robert Mondavi, Cabernet Sauvignon There is a considerable difference in price and quality between Mondavi's 'regular' and Reserve wines, whether Cabernet, Chardonnay or Fumé Blanc, though sometimes the differences are blurred. Not in 1978. The 'regular', which I tasted from 1982 to 1985, was good, flavoury***

Robert Mondavi, Reserve Cabernet 10 more detailed notes from 1983 have, with the exception of one oxidised bottle, been adulatory. Never very deep, a pleasant maturing cherry red; fragrant, spicy fruit, opening up in the glass; rich, nice weight, crisp. Brilliant. *Last tasted Nov 1989**** Now to 1998.*

Ridge, York Creek Cabernet Sauvignon Very deep; nose of matching depth, rich, sweaty with tannins; seemed very sweet, full-bodied, rich, good length, lovely. *Feb 1988****(*) Now to well beyond 2000.*

Rutherford Hill, Cabernet Sauvignon I am more familiar with their Chardonnays, always dependable and reasonably priced. This Cabernet equally agreeable, good colour, nose, flavour, weight and balance. *Jan 1990*** Now to 1996.*

Stag's Leap Wine Cellars, Cabernet Sauvignon Lot 2 I confess I have not had this recently. It was my top wine of eight '78 Cabernets at a blind tasting conducted at the

1982 California Wine Experience. Then, a couple of years later, I noted that its rich colour reminded me of the '75 Pichon Lalande but, of course, on the palate softer, rounder, fleshier. Excellent depth of nose and taste. Full-flavoured but not heavy or overdone. *Last tasted Sept 1984. Then**(**) Possibly***** and doubtless perfection now.*

Of the many '78 **Cabernets** *tasted in the early to mid-1980s, the following stand out:*

Beringer, Knight's Valley Private Reserve****

David Bruce From the hills behind Santa Cruz, amazingly fragrant***

Chateau Montelena, Napa 'Centennial' Huge, 14.3% alcohol, massive yet fragrant***(**)*

Clos du Val Beautifully made, unsubtle***

Freemark Abbey, Cabernet Bosché (including some Merlot) One of the best I can recall****

Heitz, Martha's Vineyard*****(*)*

Jordan The sort that wins gold medals. Latour-like dimensions. Huge. Fleshy***(**)*

Louis Martini Total contrast in style to Jordan, unaggressive, lovely flavour and texture****

Phelps Elegant****

Silver Oak Bordeaux-like****

Of the several very variable '78 **Pinot Noirs** *tasted in the early to mid-1980s:*

Firestone, 'Stirrup Cup' Port-like, 17.2% alcohol, glorious nose, blackberry-like, powerful, with an incredible aftertaste***(*)*

Charles Krug Very drinkable***

Robert Mondavi Spicy, scented***

Sterling Nutty, very good**

ZD Excellent in its way****

Of the not very exciting '78 **Zinfandels**, *just one notable:*

Ridge, Late Harvest Prunes, figs on nose; fairly sweet yet still with the deft Ridge touch. Lovely. *Dec 1982***(*)*

1979***

Moderately good, with the usual winery variations, some unexpected. A useful vintage.

Beaulieu, Cabernet Sauvignon Private Reserve Georges de Latour Deep, velvety; very rich fruit; full, chunky, flavoury. *Last tasted June 1990***(*) Now to 1999.*

Beaulieu, Rutherford Cabernet Green and tannic. *June 1990***

Buena Vista, Cabernet Sauvignon Section Selection Bottled Nov 1981. Alcohol 13.2%, pH 3.45, winner of six gold medals. Admittedly an early note: opaque; huge, plum-like, alcoholic nose and flavour. Loads of fruit, very dry tannic finish. Overwhelmed the lamb, demonstrating that gold medal winners do not necessarily drink well. It leaves the 'food wine' field wide open to Bordeaux. *Oct 1983*(**) I suppose it will keep, and simmer down a bit.*

Heitz, Martha's Vineyard Cabernet Sauvignon Two notes, both unsatisfactory, in the mid-1980s. Curious, unknit; rather metallic, odd. A third, eucalyptus; dry, spicy. *Last tasted Nov 1987. At best**(*) Must retaste.*

Robert Mondavi, Cabernet Sauvignon (6% Cabernet Franc, 6% Merlot) Grapes grown on loamy soil next to Oakville. 12.9% alcohol, 6.8 total acidity, low pH 3.4, 24 months in new French oak. What I have always liked about Bob Mondavi, apart from his boundless enthusiasm, is his quest for perfection within commercial bounds, and the way he is totally open about the wine he makes, hence the 'vital statistics'. A nice wine. Its bouquet developed fabulously in the glass. Spicy, lean — reminded me of a '66 Médoc — with good length, 'persistence'. *Sept 1986**(*) Now to 1998.*

Robert Mondavi, Reserve Cabernet Compared to the 'regular', extra dimensions, glorious fragrance, more spice, greater length. Several notes. *Feb 1987***(*)*

Opus I The first vintage of the Mondavi/Rothschild joint enterprise. First noted in June 1984 at George Reece's birthday lunch at the Skandia restaurant. It and the '80 preceded a line-up of great classic Bordeaux! It was tannic. Not all that impressive. More interesting, fragrant, full-flavoured at the Krug/Mondavi tasting in 1985. More recently at a vertical of Opus 1: good fruit, sweet, nice weight. *Sept 1988*** Now to say 1994.*

Other **Cabernets** *tasted in the early to mid-1980s:*

Chateau Montelena Napa More forward, more vinosity, meatier, greater length but raw. *1986**(*)*

Chateau Montelena Sonoma Opaque, intense, Latour-like weight (13.2% alcohol). Very tannic. *1986*(**)*

Clos du Val Dependable dry Bordeaux style***(*)*

Durney Very full, fleshy***

Fisher Rich, flavoury***(**)*

Freemark Abbey 100% from John Bosché's grapes, the wine aged in American oak: spicy, Graves-like tobacco whiff and taste. With 10% Merlot, aged in French oak: deeper colour, fleshier, broader style; and with 40% Merlot in the blend: sweeter, fleshier, fatter. Very flavoury***

Jekel Attractive***

Jordan First tasted in cask, purple, high-toned, 'whole fruit' character, lacking length. Showing well aged six, a distinct Bordeaux style, tannic, with attractive bell pepper flavour, good fruit. ***(*) Possibly*****

Niebaum-Coppola Intense, austere**(*)*

Shafer From seven-year-old vines grown in the Stag's Leap district. Huge, spicy, loaded**(***)*

Simi Preferred the 'regular' to the Reserve which I found in 1983 too raw, but the former probably overtaken by now. *Say****

The two best **Merlots** *tasted in the early 1980s:*

Louis Martini Light style, lovely flavour and texture***

Stag's Leap Wine Cellars Flavoury but very tannic**(**)*

Some **Pinot Noirs** *all noted in the early 1980s:*

Acacia Excellent rich Pinot aroma, good flavour, touch of bitterness****(*)*

Chalone, Pinnacles True Pinot character, high alcohol yet elegant****(*)*

Hacienda Full (14%), flavoury, aromatic but a bit short**

Jekel Dry, elegant, flavoury, oaky aftertaste***(*)*

Kistler Chocolaty nose, good flavour but very bitter*

Robert Mondavi A pretty wine but not very Pinot and not remotely burgundian.

Zaca Mesa Huge, velvety, impressive***(*)? It will be interesting to see how this has developed.*

Of many **Zinfandels** *just two:*

Mastantuono, Dusi Vineyard Unfined, unfiltered: opaque; soft, rich, plummy. Following an excellent '75 Brunello I rather lavishly described the '79 Zinfandel as the Cheval-Blanc, then the Pétrus, of California. Might have been the occasion. *Dining with Robert Sakowitz in 1982**** I wonder what has happened to it.*

Ridge, York Creek (12% Petite Sirah) Bottled May 1981. Minty, iron nose with whiff of sweaty saddles, reminding me of a Hunter Valley Shiraz. Lovely, rich, very fruity, loads of iron, firm end acidity. *June 1987**(**)*

1980★★★★

Some growers reported the strangest spring and early summer they had ever seen. After a mild winter the growing season began early. A good but extended flowering. A long cool summer with almost daily fog blowing in from the Pacific. Sept was warmer, with a heat-wave towards the end which sent the sugars soaring. Geoffrey Roberts, the leading British importer of California wines, reported that near perfect growing conditions produced fruit with excellent sugar and acid levels, though quantity down, adding, "undoubtedly the best vintage since 1974".

In my view, a more even vintage than many, though the heat produced some rather hefty wines: power rather than elegance. But well worth seeking out.

BEAULIEU, CABERNET SAUVIGNON *Still opaque, intense, red-rimmed; a bit dumb and dusty, but lovely fruit lurking; powerful, its initial sweetness leading to a teeth-gripping dry tannic finish. At the BV tasting, June 1990*(★★)

CARNEROS CREEK, PINOT NOIR *Harsh, raw and distinctly unharmonious when first tasted in 1983, though I thought it had potential. The latter only partially realised. Nose still 'green', minty; some sweetness, rich flavour, singed Pinot finish, residual tannin and acidity. Sept 1989*★★ *Drink up.*

KALIN, PINOT NOIR CUVEE DD *Medium-deep, lively appearance; crisp, smoky, peaty Pinot nose, rather Italianate; some sweetness, high alcoholic content, very good fruit, with an upturned hard tannic finish. Preceding some excellent burgundies at the Peppercorns', Jan 1990*★★★(★)

MAYACAMAS, PINOT NOIR *Palish, very mature; rich, earthy, scented nose; medium-sweet, nice weight, 'warm', with silky tannic finish. One of the least massive, least tannic wines from this marvellous hilltop winery. Nov 1988*★★★ *Will probably last longer than its typical Pinot colour might suggest. Say now to 1996.*

OPUS I, CABERNET SAUVIGNON *(4% Merlot) Seven notes spanning five years. Preferred this to the '79 when first tasted in 1984 though still a bit hard. Opaque and still youthful at the Krug/Mondavi tasting in 1985, noted as dry, lean and sinewy like a fine '66 Médoc. More recently, in magnums, still a lively ruby; a low-keyed charmer; showing well at an Opus I vertical. At the Rodenstock wine weekend in Austria, Sept 1988*★★★ *Drinking well. Best, of course, with food. Now to 1995.*

PHELPS, INSIGNIA *(A Cabernet Sauvignon blend.) In the mid-1980s I thought it almost too sweet despite the tannins. Most recently still a fine deep ruby; good fruit, fragrant, blackcurrant; full-bodied (13.8%), lovely flavour, fine balance, lovely citrus edge of acidity. A double-magnum from Robert Charpie's cellar, at a Wine and Food Society Council dinner in London, Aug 1989*★★★(★) *Now to 1998.*

A CROSS-SECTION OF CABERNETS TASTED IN THE MID-1980s:

CAYMUS *From the Grace Family Vineyard. Intense, dense; spirity, prunes and port-like but on this last occasion a distinct whiff of volatile acidity; sweet in, dry out, massive, fleshy alcoholic, fabulous mid-palate — impressive but lacking grace*★★(★★)

CLOS DU VAL *Excellent fruit, length, finish. A nice weight — never a blockbuster*★★(★★)

CONN CREEK *Sweet, beefy, impressive*★★(★★)

CUVAISON *Not softened by its 8% Merlot*★(★★)

DRY CREEK *Full, fleshy*★★(★)

JORDAN *Lovely full, rich wine spoiled for me by its tannic acid finish which I hope will wear off*★★(★)?

ROBERT MONDAVI RESERVE *Spicy, crisp, flavoury*★★★

RIDGE, YORK CREEK *(15% Merlot) Marvellous flavour but, unlike the Montebello style, hefty (14.1% alcohol), a wine with extra dimensions but very tannic*★★(★★)

ST CLEMENT *Very good, big, tannic*★★(★★)

SIMI *(10% Merlot) Very distinctive, vegetal; sweet, rich, lovely character*★★★(★)

STAG'S LEAP WINE CELLARS *Classic*★★★(★)

A SELECTION OF PINOT NOIRS TASTED BETWEEN RELEASE AND THE MID-1980s:

ACACIA *Good. I hope its initial acidity and bitterness will have simmered down*★(★★)?

DAVID BRUCE *Pomerol-like Pinot, if such a comparison can be made; sweet, rich, meaty*★★

CALERA *Almost a caricature, Grivelet-style stewed Pinot, remarkable, very flavoury, like a '72 Côte de Nuits — from Santa Barbara County*★★★

CALERA, JENSEN *Copybook Pinot Noir beetroot nose; a bit too severe on the finish in 1983. Hopefully softened by now*★(★)

CHALONE *Outstandingly the best of a major 'horizontal', tasted in Oct 1983: almost La Tâche-like scent; copybook Pinot character, wonderful flavour, finish and fragrant aftertaste*★★★★

CLOS DU BOIS PROPRIETOR'S RESERVE *Soft, fleshy, stylish*★★★

CLOS DU VAL *Their first, from seven-year-old vines in Carneros, aged one year in new oak. Better flavour than nose*★★

EDNA VALLEY *Rich, ripe nose, like* borsch, *full-flavoured, slightly bitter end*★★(★)

FIRESTONE *Very rich, jammy; powerful, fragrant, tannic*★★(★)

HANZELL *More like a Rhône*★(★)

IRON HORSE *Pleasant light style though a touch of artificiality*★★

MONDAVI *Agreeable, silky, short*★★

PEDRONCELLI *Harmonious, herbaceous Pinot aroma; plump, well made, most agreeable*★★★

OF THE MANY ZINFANDELS, NOTES OF FOUR:

RIDGE, PASO ROBLES *(5% Petite Syrah) Two notes. Rustic, earthy, spoilt by its bitterness. I simply did not like it. Last tasted June 1986.*

SUTTER HOME, AMADOR COUNTY *A mass of scents and flavours: leather, Shiraz, strawberry, port; its fruit like raspberry jam. Attractive in its way*★★

SUTTER HOME, EL DORADO COUNTY 'DESSERT' *(100% Zinfandel) Deep purple; very sweet nose, figs, raisins, caramel; sweet — high residual sugar, full-bodied yet soft and most agreeable*★★★

WENTE *Soft red; fragrant, herbaceous; distinctly sweet, Pinot-like, lip-licking acidity. April 1991****

1981 at best★★★

Fleshy reds. Moderate quality. The result of a hot growing season with the earliest harvest in recent memory, mid-Aug. Continuing warm temperatures brought many grape varieties to full maturity at the same time, causing frenzied activity at the wineries. The weather broke late Sept (see 1981 California whites).

Quite a wide range tasted between 1983 and 1987, few recently. Drink up.

JEKEL, HOME VINEYARD PRIVATE RESERVE CABERNET SAUVIGNON *Bill Jekel pooh-poohs French* 'terroir' *theories, advocating the supremacy of the grape and winemaking. This wine was made from 500 tonnes of his own grapes grown in Monterey. In small oak three years. First noted in the spring of 1986: opaque, intense purple; spicy mulberry-like fruit; a huge wine, crisp, very tannic. After three more years in bottle still fairly deep, plummy; very good fruit and citrus-like refreshing acidity on nose and palate. Seemed to be sweetening up. Jan 1989*** Now to 1996.*

OPUS I *Two notes in 1985, one tasted blind: good fruit, flesh and spiciness, but acidic. More recently, less deep; curious nose, a bit stalky; dry and too tart. Last tasted Sept 1988* Drink up.*

SHOWING WELL IN THE MID-1980s:

Caymus, Cabernet Sauvignon; Clos du Bois, Briarcrest (100% Cabernet Sauvignon); Clos du Bois, Marlestone Vineyard (55% Cabernet Sauvignon, 40% Merlot, 5% Cabernet Franc); Clos du Val, Cabernet Sauvignon; Gundlach Bunschu, Cabernet Sauvignon; Jordan, Cabernet Sauvignon — very high marks; Kalin, Pinot Noir; Joseph Phelps, Cabernet Sauvignon — glorious; Ridge, Montebello (92% Cabernet Sauvignon, 8% Merlot); Simi, Cabernet Sauvignon Reserve — very tannic; Trefethen, Valley Floor Cabernet Sauvignon.

1982★★★★

Following the heaviest winter rains of the century a wet though generally frost-free spring. Good weather for flowering followed by a long cool summer, temperatures picking up late Aug through Sept for the main harvest. Heavy localised rains mid-Sept and a tropical storm that surged through California from Sept 23–25. High pressure, brisk winds and warm temperatures dried and ripened the remaining grapes. Large, reasonably good quality crop picked prior to heavy autumn rains. Some attractive wines. Remarkably few that I did not like even amongst the lower priced and unpretentious. Drinking soon.

A large number of notes, perhaps the most interesting, for me, and salutary, made at two horizontal blind tastings in Nov 1986. The first, at one of my annual tastings at the California Wine Experience, was of eight leading 1982 Cabernets. The next, the following day (Nov 4) was of 26 California Cabernet Sauvignons and all the top growths of Bordeaux, organised in San Francisco by *The Wine Spectator*. Unlike an earlier competitive tasting of '74s, the '82s in Bordeaux and California were well matched: both rich in fruit, extract and tannins. The best were and are luscious, and will, I believe, keep, despite worries about tannin outliving the fruit. Notes on these blind tastings and more recent notes follow.

BEAULIEU, CABERNET SAUVIGNON PRIVATE RESERVE G DE LATOUR *Picked at optimum maturity. Showing well at the Nov 1986 tasting, excellent flavour, easy to comprehend. Most recently: still very deep, its colour like intense blackcurrant juice; very sweet nose, opening up well; sweet on palate too, full-bodied, silky, leathery tannins enfolding marvellous fruit. Last noted at the BV Private Reserve tasting in the Napa, June 1990***(*) Now to 2000.*

BERINGER, KNIGHTS VALLEY CABERNET SAUVIGNON *I and a ballroom of earnest tasters placed this second out of the eight major Cabernets at the Wine Experience tasting, and it also showed well at the more extensive tasting the following day. Mouthfilling and tannic of course, the latter smelling like the armpits of a healthy, clean-living youth after exercise. Two notes since but not recently. Very good fruit and flavour. Last tasted July 1987. Now***(*) Now to 2000.*

CAYMUS, SPECIAL SELECTION CABERNET SAUVIGNON *Generally voted third of the eight '82s on Nov 2 1986 but I placed it 8th, following day I found this rather an oddball. An extremely spicy, cinnamon and eucalyptus nose, herbaceous, very scented — a bit 'artificial' I noted after an hour in the glass. A mouthful of strawberry jam-like fruit and with excessively dry finish. Noted twice in Nov 1986. Then**(*) 1992–2000*

CAYMUS, GRACE FAMILY VINEYARD CABERNET SAUVIGNON *An excellent, chunky wine. July 1988**(**)*

CHATEAU MONTELENA, CABERNET SAUVIGNON *Gloriously deep colour, vibrant, long legs; classic 'medicinal' Cabernet nose but needing time to harmonise; somewhat metallic and very ripe 'hen-droppings' taste, good length and aftertaste. I felt it would shake down, and overall rated it pretty highly. At the Nov 3 tasting, 1986. Then*(***) Will be interesting to see how it has developed.*

DIAMOND CREEK, RED ROCK VINEYARD *Holding its own alongside the '82 Lafite but of course a totally different style. Lovely deep cherry red; rich fragrant nose making an extraordinary impact; lean, dry, tannic. Nov 1986. Then**(**) Say 1992 to beyond 2000.*

DOUGLAS VINEYARDS, CABERNET SAUVIGNON *Bottled by Zaca Mesa. Very deep, rich, plummy; curious, high-toned; dry, full-*

bodied, lovely fruit, delicious by itself. June 1991***(*) Now to 2000.

DUNN VINEYARDS, HOWELL MOUNTAIN CABERNET SAUVIGNON *This was the eye-opener of the blind tasting of '82s. In the same flight as Lafite, Latour, Mouton, BV, Heitz Martha's, and sandwiched (blind) between Haut-Brion and La Mission, I thought it the best of the entire tasting. Opaque, black at the core, intense purple rim; sweaty tannin armpits smell, dumb at first, but with classic Bordeaux Cabernet aroma, opening up gloriously in the glass; huge yet elegant, with beautiful shape and texture. "Iron fist in velvet glove." When all the names were revealed I was surprised. I had never heard of Dunn!* Nov 1986. Then***(**) Dying to taste it again.

GROTH, CABERNET SAUVIGNON *Very much an 'in' wine (see 1985), I just noted this as "quite attractive" at a buffet supper at Christa and Bob Paul's the evening prior to his great tasting of '82 Pomerol and St-Emilion.* Feb 1989*** (Probably underestimated.)

HEITZ, MARTHA'S VINEYARD CABERNET SAUVIGNON *Beautiful colour; spicy, minty, lean nose; packed with minty fruit, flavour, extract and tannin.* At the Nov 3 1986 tasting***(**) 1992 to well beyond 2000.

WILLIAM HILL, CABERNET SAUVIGNON *Mr Hill advertises the favourable results of his wine tasted blind against better-known competitors, including top Bordeaux. My sixth in* The Wine Spectator *line-up of eight good Cabernets. To distil my 70 words of description: a sweet, harmonious Pomerol-like nose; nice texture, good fruit, slightly bitter tannins, elegant. A fairly quick developer.* Nov 2 1986*** Now to 1995.

INGLENOOK, RESERVE CASK CABERNET SAUVIGNON *Unanimously the top '82 of the eight on Nov 2 and showing well the following day between what turned out to be Chateau Montelena and Chateau Palmer (which, incidentally, I thought was excellent). Spicy Napa nose; an extraordinary texture and fascinating flavour.* Noted twice, Nov 1986**** Now to 1998.

JORDAN, CABERNET SAUVIGNON *(15.5% Merlot) Matured in 60% French, 40% American oak. A lively red; precocious nose: fishy, fruity, tangy; ripe fruit, lovely, crisp, flavoury. Very agreeable but perhaps lacking length.* Tasted twice, Nov 1986*** Now to 1996.

ROBERT MONDAVI, RESERVE CABERNET SAUVIGNON *(7% Merlot, 2% Cabernet Franc) 13% alcohol, total acidity 0.65, pH 3.4, 100% new oak. Barrel sample in June 1985; lively, good fruit. In 1986, at the blind tasting of eight '82 Cabernets, my fourth and group fourth. Fruity, piquant, appealing and suave yet with teeth-gripping acidity and pepperiness on the finish. Distinctly not a blockbuster. By California standards a 'lunch wine'. The following day, sited between Lynch-Bages and Beringer, it showed well: a lovely flavour, an immediacy of appeal but not for long keeping. More recently, lovely soft gentle spicy fragrance, touch of tar. Impressive but ready for drinking.* At a Reserve tasting with Michael Mondavi in Miami, Feb 1988*** Now to 1996.

OPUS I *Two notes in June 1985, one bottle woody and raw, the other: deep cherry-skin colour; rich, dusty; spicy new oak. By Nov 1986 a very fragrant, flavoury charmer. More recently, in magnum and in bottle: a bright cherry red; dry, good fruit and length.* Sept 1988*** Now to 1996.

SIMI, CABERNET SAUVIGNON *I am a great admirer of Zelma Long. Like Bob Mondavi, she is an indefatigable seeker after truth in wine. I first tasted the '82 at the winery from experimental casks: the first cask upright, high sulphur dioxide, next with low sulphur dioxide, then one from a cask rolled and racked at three-monthly intervals. The latter had the least impressive colour but marvellously rich fruit. The Reserve blend was excellent. Amongst the eight '82s the following year I rated it 4th equal with Mondavi. A silky texture, gripping tannins though a mid-, not long-term, wine.* Last tasted Nov 1986*** Now to 1996.

STERLING, DIAMOND MOUNTAIN RANCH CABERNET SAUVIGNON *Good fruit but hard. The nose opened up delightfully. Well made. Dry. Needing time. For me seventh out of the eight selected '82s at the Wine Experience tasting.* Nov 1986. Then*(**) Probably 1992–98.

VILLA MOUNT EDEN, CABERNET SAUVIGNON *(100%) Six notes. Very full, rich, chewy and tannic in 1984. Over the last three years explosively attractive fruit noted but also a fishy, tinny, medicinal touch, half-way between a ripe Ch Talbot and a South Australian 'rusty nail' red. Far from ameliorating, it was horrid with cheese.* Jan 1990**(*) in its way but not to my taste.

OF THE MANY OTHERS TASTED IN THE MID-1980s, THE FOLLOWING CABERNETS WERE SHOWING WELL:

Chateau Bouchaine, Private Reserve; Clos du Bois, Briarcrest; Cuvaison, Dry Creek (24% Merlot); Mayacamas; Ridge, Montebello; Ridge, York Creek; Shafer, Hillside Res.

SOME OF THE PINOT NOIRS:

David Bruce, lovely fruit, excellent acidity; Robert Mondavi, Reserve — too sweet and jammy; Saintsbury, Carneros — restrained.

SOME OF THE MERLOTS:

Clos du Val, soft, fruity; Duckhorn, lean, elegant; Sterling, soft, fleshy.

1983**

Moderate. An unusual growing season following the wettest winter on record. Summer more like spring. Heavy rain mid-Aug. Most of my notes made between 1985 and 1987. Relatively few since then.

CHALONE, PINOT NOIR *Good Pinot aroma and taste. Silky leathery tannins, but spoilt for me by stalkiness, though I was assured this would wear off.* Nov 1988 ?

DUCKHORN, MERLOT *Very deep; hard-nosed; raw, tannic. Pétrus without flesh.* Feb 1988(**)?

KALIN, PINOT NOIR CUVEE DD *Good broad Pinot appearance; very fragrant, distinctive Pinot beetroot nose; sweet, fairly full-bodied (13.2% alcohol), rich, very good flavour but touch of bitterness, with acidic finish.* Feb 1991**(*) 1993–98

ROBERT MONDAVI, CABERNET SAUVIGNON *(13.8% Cabernet Franc, 9.3% Merlot) Small crop after Aug rains. Alcoholic content unusually low: 12.2%, acidity 0.60, pH 3.45. Grapes 19 days on their skins after fermentation. No sulphur dioxide used. In new French oak 24 months. Very spicy, assertive, minty, eucalyptus and (new oak) cloves taste in June 1985. More recently: a most appealing harmony of strawberry-like fruit, spices and leather; crisp, refreshing, mouth-cleansing tannins and acidity. Nice weight, elegant but unready.* Feb 1988**(*) 1993–98

OPUS I *Dumb but flavoury in June 1985. More recently: light, open, bell pepper nose, attractive, well-knit; good texture, tannic, lean and dry.* Last noted Sept 1988*(**) 1993–2000

TREFETHEN, CABERNET SAUVIGNON *Two notes. Fairly deep, still youthful; quite rich, powerful, jammy fruit, nose and palate. Good tannins. Lacking length.* March 1989*(*) 1992–98

SOME OTHERS TASTED IN 1986–87:

CUVEE BELLEROSE *(80% Cabernet Sauvignon, 13% Cabernet Franc, 5% Merlot, 2% Petit Verdot and Malbec.) A very Bordeaux varietal mix planted in 1978 in a surprising range of soils on 35 acres of hilly bench and valley floor vineyard in north Sonoma. A one-man band, owner and winemaker, small by California standards yet, compared to an average Burgundy vineyard holding, substantial. Fermented in steel, up to 20 months in 60-gallon French oak. Good fleshy fruit, nice balance. Query its length***

BERINGER, CABERNET SAUVIGNON *Good, tannic**(*)

CARMANET, CABERNET SAUVIGNON *Raw, tannic*(*)

CLOS DU BOIS, MARLSTONE CABERNET SAUVIGNON *Fragrant, flavoury, easy, appealing***

CLOS DU BOIS, MERLOT *Rich, sweaty saddle nose; jammy, attractive***

CLOS DU VAL, PINOT NOIR *Extraordinary, powerful, thyme-like scent; despite its power, not heavy. High acidity****

CLOS DU VAL, ZINFANDEL *A lovely wine, with interesting gradations of colour; mouthwatering, delicate, mint-leaf fragrance; delicious fruity flavour and, despite lots of tannin and very good acidity, a charmer, ready for drinking****

CUVAISON, CABERNET SAUVIGNON *(100%) Sweet, fleshy, very tannic, good***(*)

DRY CREEK, CABERNET SAUVIGNON *Rich, jammy fruit, tannic**(*)

DUCKHORN, CABERNET SAUVIGNON *Opaque; spicy; massive, austere, very tannic*(**)

FORMAN, CABERNET SAUVIGNON *Hot, peppery, full of fruit, sweet, with well-masked tannins***

JORDAN, CABERNET SAUVIGNON *Stylish but very dry, very tannic*(**)

CHARLES KRUG, CABERNET SAUVIGNON *Heavenly fruit, very flavoury, like Lynch-Bages***(*)

MONTICELLO, CABERNET SAUVIGNON *Crisp, fruity, very good****

NEWTON, MERLOT *Unusually pretty colour; soft, fleshy, fragrant***

RIDGE, PASO ROBLES ZINFANDEL *Dry, very flavoury, great length***(**)

1984***

A moderate and, judging by my relatively few notes from 1985–1987, somewhat uninspiring vintage. The weather conditions, apart from a wet winter, were almost the opposite of 1983. A long dry period from early spring to the end of harvest. Warmth in March encouraged early bud break. No frosts. Record high temperatures in May. Grapes small though juice yields average.

DOMINUS, 'NAPA VALLEY RED TABLE WINE' *(75% Cabernet Sauvignon, 25% Merlot) A new contender in the high profile stakes, produced by the John Daniel Society, a joint venture with Christian Mouiex. At four years old, fairly deep and intense, with a black cherry centre, still immature purple at the rim; good sweet fruit, some spice, cinnamon (new oak), tannin and depth; on the palate sweet, full body, full-flavoured, rich and powerful, with lots of fruit and flesh, good length, tannin and citrus-like acidity at the end. Not a bad start.* Aug 1988**(**) I suggest 1992–98.

FREEMARK ABBEY, CABERNET SAUVIGNON *Medium-deep; good nose; nice weight, good flavour.* Sept 1988*** Now to 1994.

HEITZ, BELLA OAKS CABERNET SAUVIGNON *Bottle variation, one distinctly woody the other slightly woody though both had a good colour and were soft and fleshy.* Feb 1990. Judgement reserved.

HESS COLLECTION, CABERNET SAUVIGNON *Deep; sweet; full, impressive.* May 1991***

ROBERT MONDAVI, CABERNET SAUVIGNON *(11.3% Merlot, 5.4% Cabernet Franc) In Feb 1988: very spicy, harmonious, self-confident and nicely put-together; but with rather a gritty texture and almost spirity on the tongue despite its moderate 12.5% alcohol. More recently, stupidly served chilled. It was hard to taste, and common.* Lost noted Oct 1989. At best**(*) Now to 1996.

OPUS I *Opaque; curious nose but soft, sweet and flavoury when first tasted, a cask sample in June 1985. More recently, at a Rodenstock dinner in Austria, still fairly deep; muffled fruit, slightly peppery; good body, long but tart.* Last tasted Sept 1988. Then(***) Probably getting its second breath by now.

TREFETHEN, PINOT NOIR *Correct broad, open Pinot appearance; low-keyed root-like Pinot aroma and flavour, sweet, nice weight, quite pleasant but tinny, bitter finish.* March 1989*(*)

ZACA MESA, CABERNET SAUVIGNON *Several fairly recent notes. Deep ruby; positive but sweaty Talbot-like nose; good fruit but with tinny, rusty nails endtaste.* Sept 1988. Not to my taste.

A SMALL SELECTION OF BETTER-MADE CABERNETS TASTED IN 1987:

*Caymus**(*) Clos du Bois*** Inglenook**(*) Ridge, Montebello**(**)*

A MERLOT LAST TASTED IN 1987:

CUVAISON *(14% Cabernet Sauvignon) Unfined. Soft, fleshy, tannic, good fruit**(*)*

PINOT NOIRS LAST TASTED IN 1988:

ACACIA, IUND VINEYARD *Forthcoming, fragrant; sweet, powerful, rich, prune-like fruit, excellent flavour****

BOUCHAINE *One corked, the other nondescript on nose but good crisp flavour***

CALERA, JENSEN VINEYARD *Stewed, singed Pinot nose; dry, powerful, flavoury****

CALERA, SELLICK *Very fragrant; sweet, flavoury, appealing****

KALIN, POTTER VALLEY *Singed smelly nose; Italianate style, quite attractive***

SANFORD *Very pronounced, scented aroma; sweet, full, ripe Pinot flavour, tannic iron finish**(*)*

OF THE VERY FEW 1984 ZINFANDELS TASTED:

RIDGE, GEYSERVILLE *A most extraordinary nose: hefty, figs, prunes and tar; loads of grip and spice. Fabulous – in its way. Nov 1987*(***) 1994–2000*

1985★★★★★

A thoroughly satisfactory vintage. Many good wines. Early spring, fine summer, very dry, relatively cool save for a heat-wave in June. Two inches of rain stopped picking in Sept, continuing afterwards in short cool spells. Towards the end of the month the sun returned to complete the ripening. Faced with the impossible task of assessing the character and quality of California vintages and wineries I had decided to tackle the subject in two ways: to use some of the classic stalwarts like BV to try to evaluate different vintages, their quality, and current condition, and to select one good vintage to compare the style and quality of the major players. The extraordinarily generous Bob Paul came to the rescue. He helped me select a cross-section of 55 wines, all Cabernet Sauvignon and related varietals from well over 100 1985 Cabernet Sauvignons in his commodious air-conditioned Florida cellar. I tasted them blind in random order. Where there were two or more wines from the same winery, these were put alongside each other towards the end, which was, in retrospect, a mistake. However, to avoid 'first wine bias' I initially nosed them all first, went back to the beginning noting colour, and back again to note any development of nose, and to taste. Overall a marvellous range of lovely wines. California reds have really come of age. And I certainly recommend the '85s – the Cabernet Sauvignons at any rate. The Merlot and Pinot Noirs seem less satisfactory.

ARROWOOD, SONOMA CABERNET SAUVIGNON *Assertive but flavoury in 1988. Showing well at Bob Paul's: very rich fruit on nose and palate. Last tasted Jan 1991****

BEAULIEU, CABERNET SAUVIGNON PRIVATE RESERVE G DE LATOUR *Deep, very rich, maturing; attractive fruit, opening up well, very good, meaty; medium dryness, very flavoury, with rather piquant acidic finish. Jan 1991***(*)*

BERINGER, PRIVATE RESERVE CABERNET SAUVIGNON *Very deep, still youthful; full of fruit, brambly, oak, tannin, opening up richly and fragrantly; sweet, full-bodied, crisp. May 1991****

BERINGER, KNIGHT'S VALLEY PROPRIETOR GROWTH CABERNET SAUVIGNON *Even better: a rich, bricky rather Graves-like colour; soft, meaty, harmonious nose; very sweet, full of fruit, extract, flesh, with silky leathery tannins. Jan 1991**** 1992 to beyond 2000.*

BUENA VISTA, PRIVATE RESERVE CARNEROS CABERNET SAUVIGNON *Forthcoming, fragrant, marvellous attack, fabulous development in glass; nice weight, elegant, full of character, good length, very tannic, excellent acidity. Jan 1991***(*) 1994–2005*

CAYMUS, SPECIAL SELECTION NAPA CABERNET SAUVIGNON *Plummy; lovely, crisp, oaky spicy nose, elegant, great depth opening up sensationally in the glass; fairly sweet, 13%, full of fruit and flavour, spicy oak, fragrant aftertaste. Jan 1991**** 1992 to beyond 2000.*

DIAMOND CREEK, GRAVELLY MEADOW *Very deep but with an odd nose; dry, uplifting, high-toned but lean and hollow. Jan 1991?*

DIAMOND CREEK, RED ROCK TERRACE *First noted in Oct 1987: lovely fruit, but raw and tannic, needing bottle-age. At Bob Paul's: though deep, starting to mature; nose nearer to Gravelly Meadow but attractive in its way; nice weight (12.5%), soft and rich despite fairly marked tannin and acidity. Last tasted Jan 1991***(*) Though tasted blind I particularly wanted to compare wines made from three contrasting soil types within this one small vineyard. They were the last to be tasted and fatigue was setting in so perhaps I did not do justice to Al Brounstein, or myself.*

DIAMOND CREEK, VOLCANIC HILL NAPA CABERNET SAUVIGNON *Opaque, impressive appearance; forthcoming, fruity, citrus touch, tannic nose; despite alcohol "12½ degrees" on label, a huge wine, fleshy, full of fruit. Jan 1991**(**) 1995–2005*

DOMINUS, NAPA TABLE WINE *Neither varietal mix nor alcoholic content on label (see also 1984). Deep, plummy, heavy legs; fragrant but weedy fruit and cheesy tannins, not fully integrated. Dry, full, loads of fruit and grip. Impressive. Needs time. Jan 1991**(**)? Will be interesting to see how Mouiex's relatively new wine develops.*

DUNN VINEYARDS, HOWELL MOUNTAIN CABERNET SAUVIGNON *Opaque; very sweet nose, developing rich, stably overtones; sweeter on palate yet very raw, tannic and tart. When this was revealed as Dunn's I was most surprised, after my experience with his marvellous '82. I will follow its progress with interest.* Tasted at Bob Paul's, Jan 1981(**??)

DUNN VINEYARDS, NAPA VALLEY CABERNET SAUVIGNON *Deep, crisp, youthful; dumb, peppery, sweaty tannins; fairly full-bodied yet lean, nice flavour, refreshing acidity.* Jan 1981 **(*)

FREEMARK ABBEY, CABERNET BOSCHE *Good nose, heftily tannic but opened up well; fullish, bitingly hot alcohol (13.3%), fair tannin, considerable acidity.* Jan 1991*(**)

FREEMARK ABBEY, NAPA CABERNET SAUVIGNON *Horrible on nose, terrible on palate. The bottle or the wine?* Jan 1991.

FREEMARK ABBEY, SYCAMORE VINEYARDS NAPA CABERNET SAUVIGNON *Opaque, rich; quite good fruit, slightly raisiny; fairly sweet, full, peppery. The best of the three, but with reservations.* Jan 1991*(**)?

GRGICH HILLS, NAPA CABERNET SAUVIGNON *I have long admired Mike Grgich (particularly for his whites). A fine deep cherry red; refined brambly fruit on nose; lovely texture, flavour, length, elegance.* Jan 1991***(*) 1992–2000

GROTH, NAPA RESERVE CABERNET SAUVIGNON *This is the wine that Bob Paul said "people kill for"! It is scarce and expensive. My notes did not quite measure up to its reputation. It had a consistently sweet nose, slightly caramelly, blancmange; sweet and attractive on the palate too. A curiously easy style but I would not kill for it.* Jan 1991**** Now to 1996.

HEITZ, BELLA OAKS *The best of the three: deep and still youthful; lovely rich figgy nose; sweet, full of fruit, extract, tannin and acidity.* Jan 1991***(**) 1993 to beyond 2000.

HEITZ, MARTHA'S VINEYARD *Very deep, rich, maturing; slightly woody at first but attractive eucalyptus nose; sweetish, full (13½%), meaty, fruity.* Jan 1991***(*)

HEITZ, NAPA CABERNET SAUVIGNON *A sweet, full, rich, chewy, hefty style.* Jan 1991***

HESS COLLECTION CABERNET SAUVIGNON *Sweet, soft, excellent tannins and acidity. Lovely drink.* May 1991****

INGLENOOK, RESERVE CASK NAPA CABERNET SAUVIGNON *Unknit; dry, raw, tannic — disliked.* Jan 1991.

INGLENOOK, REUNION NAPA VALLEY TABLE WINE *Good fruit but too tannic.* Jan 1991. Needs time*(**) 1993–98

KENDAL JACKSON, 'CARDINALE' LAKE PORT, LAKE COUNTY CABERNET SAUVIGNON *Now here was a bottle worthy of its reputation. Very deep plummy purple; hard, very crisp, excellent spicy Cabernet nose opened up gloriously — rare full marks for nose; dry, fullish (13%), crisp, lean, excellent fruit length and aftertaste.* Jan 1991****(*) 1992 to beyond 2000.

MAYACAMAS, NAPA CABERNET SAUVIGNON *Deep plummy purple, rich legs; also full marks for its lovely, very soft though penetrating nose, tannic but beautifully evolved; fairly sweet, nice weight (12.5%), full yet lissom, lean, fruity, tannic.* Jan 1991***(**) 1995–2005

ROBERT MONDAVI, NAPA VALLEY CABERNET SAUVIGNON *Six good notes, flavoury, soft, refreshing.* Jan 1991*** Now to 1996.

ROBERT MONDAVI, RESERVE CABERNET SAUVIGNON *Deeper than the 'regular', still youthful-looking; good, fragrant, brambly nose; not as sweet or as soft, fuller-bodied, lovely fruit. Complete.* Jan 1991***(*) Now to 2000.

OPUS I *Modestly subtitled* NAPA VALLEY TABLE WINE *(ie no longer 100% Cabernet Sauvignon.) Three good notes, and at Bob Paul's, tasted blind. Impressively deep, youthful, with legs like gothic arches; lovely, rich, spicy, fruity nose; full of fruit and flesh but relaxingly light in alcohol (12.1%), all in balance.* Jan 1991****(*) Now to 2010.

JOSEPH PHELPS, 'INSIGNIA' AUCTION RESERVE *(50% Cabernet Sauvignon, 10% Cabernet Franc, 40% Merlot) Opaque; lovely, eucalyptus-tinged, balanced.* April 1990****

JOSEPH PHELPS, 'INSIGNIA' NAPA VALLEY RED *(60% Cabernet Sauvignon, 15% Cabernet Franc, 25% Merlot) An extraordinary scent, bell peppers, touch of spearmint, then lime blossom; lovely, very distinctive flavour, touch of 'rusty' tannin on finish.* Jan 1991***(**) 1993–2000

ROMBAUER, 'LE MEILLEUR DU CHAI' NAPA VALLEY RED WINE *Marvellous Mouton-like nose; elegant, flavoury, stylish, silky tannins but too tart.* Jan 1991***

RUTHERFORD HILL 'XVS', NAPA CABERNET SAUVIGNON *I normally associate Rutherford Hill with nicely made, reasonably priced Chardonnays. The XVS came as a surprise: impressively deep and rich; very fragrant bouquet; very good fruit and flavour with nice uplift on finish and tannins to conserve.* One of my top marks at Bob Paul's, Jan 1991****(*) 1992 to beyond 2000.

SCHAFER, HILLSIDE SELECTION CABERNET SAUVIGNON *Attractive nose that opened up, rich, beguiling; full, chewy, crisp fruit, on the lean side, very tannic.* Jan 1991***(*) 1993 to beyond 2000.

SCHAFER, STAG'S LEAP DISTRICT CABERNET SAUVIGNON *Started in 1973, replanted in 1978. First tasted from the barrel. Packed with fruit.* June 1986(***)

SILVER OAK, ALEXANDER VALLEY CABERNET SAUVIGNON *Well-developed colour; nose fragrant but hesitant, then evolving gloriously in the glass; sweet, full, chewy, full of fruit, its richness masking substantial tannins.* Jan 1991***(*) 1992 to beyond 2000.

SIMI, ALEXANDER VALLEY RESERVE CABERNET SAUVIGNON *Lovely, open, vinous bouquet; dry, full-bodied, crisp, severe tannins. Good quality. Needs time.* Jan 1991**(**) 1995–2005

STAG'S LEAP WINE CELLARS, CASK 23 *Fabulous appearance; very rich, plummy, high-toned, minty nose. Laden with fruit. Sweet, full-bodied (13.8%), rich, ripe, Médoc-medicinal flavour. Classic.* Jan 1991****(*) 1993 to beyond 2000.

STERLING, RESERVE RED TABLE WINE *Opaque; rich, hefty nose, still dumb; sweet, rich, full but lacking finesse.* Jan 1991***(*) 1992–2000

STERLING, 'THREE PALMS' *Sweet and packed with fruit but still a bit raw.* Feb 1989***

OTHER CABERNET SAUVIGNONS TASTED BLIND, JAN 1991:

BUEHLER, NAPA *Dry, lean, crisp fruit****
BURGESS, NAPA, VINTAGE SELECTION *Good brambly fruit, tannic***(*)
CARNEROS CREEK, LOS CARNEROS *Very good fruit, nice weight (12.5%), very tannic**(**)
CHATEAU MONTELENA, NAPA *Very deep, impressive, youthful; fragrant, eucalyptus-scented nose; fairly full-bodied (13.5%), very good fruit and flavour, complete, tannic****(*)
CLOS DU BOIS, MARLSTONE, ALEXANDER VALLEY *(28% Merlot, 7% Cabernet Franc) Not very deep; floral; pleasant, early developer***
CLOS DU VAL, NAPA, RESERVE *Sweet, stylish, good fruit, balance****
DONN CHAPPELET, NAPA *High-toned, sweaty, tannic, improved in glass; dry, medium full (12.8%), lean, lacking flesh, very tannic**(*)
DUCKHORN, NAPA *Rich, hefty (13.2%), good fruit, very tannic***(*)
FAR NIENTE, NAPA *Alas, slightly corky, sour: in short poor. A bad bottle?*
WILLIAM HILL, NAPA RESERVE *Dusty, weedy nose; very dry, raw though with crisp fruit***
JORDAN, ALEXANDER VALLEY *Rich though low-keyed nose, hard to get to grips with; dry, medium-full body (12.8%), crisp fruit, tannin and acidity***(*)
KALIN, SONOMA RESERVE *Advanced appearance; very attractive, forthcoming, spicy, singed Graves-like nose that opened up fully; sweet, 13%, unusual flavour, good texture. Nice in its way. Must retaste****
LYETH, ALEXANDER VALLEY *Plummy; soft, open, slightly soapy nose, quite shapely fruit and vanilla; fairly full-bodied (13.7%), fleshy, good tannin and acidity. Pleasant mid-term drinking****
LOUIS MARTINI, NORTH COAST *Sweet nose yet a background of hardness; good fruit, touch of woodiness, tannic***(*)
NEWTON *Quick maturing; nose strange at first, but I rather liked it; fairly sweet, sensible weight (12.5%), lovely texture, nice flavour, perhaps lacking follow-through****
NIEBAUM-COPPOLA, 'RUBICON', NAPA VALLEY RED WINE *Very odd, sweaty tannic bovine nose, unattractive yet not bad. Will it improve in bottle?**
RIDGE, MONTEBELLO *(7% Merlot) Its usual idiosyncratic self. A tinny, fish-skin medicinal nose. The unfolding bouquet was as if Lafite had been made from Pinot Noir. Strange, slightly metallic taste, very fragrant. I admire Ridge but sometimes it is not to my taste. Or rather, like Haut-Brion, it should not be tasted alongside its peers. It is different***(*)??
RUTHERFORD ESTATE, NAPA *Odd, vegetal, volatile, though it improved with air; dry, strange, not bad but hard, raw*(**)
ST CLEMENT, NAPA *Taut, spicy, hefty; rich, full of fruit but a bit of a clod-hopper, lacking finesse. Tannic***(*)
VICHON 'SLD', NAPA *Very deep yet advanced; rich, meaty, nose that evolved well; slightly sweet, good flavour and style, crisp fruit****(*)

PINOT NOIR: OF THE DOZEN OR SO TASTED, TOO MANY FAULTS AND FAILINGS. SOME RECENT NOTES, ALL MADE IN 1988:

BUENA VISTA, CARNEROS *Jammy***
CALERA, LOS ALAMOS *Orange-tinged; overblown though with true Pinot aroma and flavour; fragrant but screwed up.*
CARNEROS QUALITY ALLIANCE *An unharmonious alliance, lacking balance, acidic.*
CAYMUS *Sweet, soft, strawberry-like fruit****
DAVIS BYNUM, ARTISTS SERIES *Rich cabbages and hen-droppings, tinny.*
ETUDE *A bit stalky, attractive fruit***
CHARLES KRUG, LOS CARNEROS *Attractive flavour but unknit**
MIRASSOU, MONTEREY '5TH GENERATION HARVEST RESERVE' *Jean Grivot style, good fruit***
ROBERT MONDAVI *Good Pinot flavour, hot dry finish***
SCHUG, CARNEROS-NAPA *Lovely intense Pinot fruit; flavoury, good finish but something lacking***
WILD HORSE, SANTA BARBARA *Fragrant, well made, good crisp flavour and finish***(*)

1986★★ to ★★★

"Long and cool growing season, slow maturation, optimum varietal character" (to quote Beaulieu Vineyard). The coolest summer on record. "One long spring", said another. Though the vintage started early it was more protracted than usual as winemakers waited to achieve ideal must weights, the final Cabernet Sauvignon grapes being brought in during early Oct.

Relatively few, mainly unspectacular Cabernets but Merlot and Pinot Noir seemingly more attractive than in 1985. In Nov 1988 a good range of Pinot Noirs noted at a Wine Appreciation Guild Tasting in San Francisco and, that evening, a blind tasting of 12 California and Oregon Pinot Noirs at the Vintners Club. Contrary to expectations California came out best, taking the top four places.

BEAULIEU, CABERNET SAUVIGNON PRIVATE RESERVE GEORGES DE LATOUR *The youngest vintage in the Private Reserve line-up: opaque, intense purple; 'green', immature Cabernet aroma, minty, 'moth balls'; crisp young fruit, moderate length, totally unready. June 1990*(***) *1995 to beyond 2000.*
FORMAN, CABERNET SAUVIGNON *(15% Merlot, 10% Cabernet Franc and a tiny amount of Petit Verdot) Grown on deep gravel (to depth of 100ft (30.5m)). Very bright cherry red; lively, lovely scent, berry-like, spicy oak; crisp, youthful, very fragrant. Feb 1989***(**) *1992–98*

OTHER CABERNET SAUVIGNONS TASTED BRIEFLY AND ONLY ONCE:

HESS COLLECTION *Hard, very tannic. May 1991****
ROBERT MONDAVI *Deep ruby; tannin and fruit; dry. Feb 1989**(*)

SEQUOIA GROVE *Soft, attractive. June 1990**(*)*

SOME MERLOTS:

CUVAISON *The same wine in six different shapes of glass. Interesting variations, the shape of glass affecting intensity of colour, nose and flavour. On balance a lovely soft, fruity wine. Rodenstock's Wine Weekend, Sept 1990*** Now to 1996.*

DUCKHORN *Deep; lovely fruit; sweet, fleshy. Nov 1989****

GUNDLACH BUNDSCHU *Lovely fruit; medium sweetness and body, rich. Nov 1988****

SHAFER *Rather jammy. Nov 1988***

PINOT NOIRS:

ACACIA, CARNEROS *Fragrant, lean, highish acidity. June 1988*(**)*

ACACIA, ST CLARE VINEYARD *Impressively deep; lovely earthy, rich, soft nose, lots of character. A beautiful wine. Nov 1988*****

CHATEAU BOUCHAINE, CARNEROS NAPA *Palish; good Pinot aroma; sweet, soft, delicious. Last tasted June 1990****

ROBERT MONDAVI, RESERVE *Crisp, fruity nose that developed a sweetness and fruitiness almost too good to be true; crisp, fruity but not very Pinot, bitter finish. Oct 1989***

SAINTSBURY, CARNEROS *As a member of the Saintsbury Club I have mixed feelings about the Professor's name being purloined. But they make attractive wine (and brandy). Palish, luminous pink; well developed, sweet, slightly caramelly nose; though lightish, packs a punch. Good fruit. Last tasted Nov 1988****

STERLING, WINERY LAKE *Polished ruby; walnuts, caramel, alcoholic; flavoury but lean. Three notes. Feb 1989**(*)*

OTHER PINOT NOIRS TASTED ONLY ONCE, IN NOV 1988:

CALERA, JENSEN *Marvellous Pinot beetroot aroma and flavour. Sweet. Full. Rich. Slightly tinny, hot alcoholic finish**(*)*

CARNEROS CREEK, LOATH'S *True Pinot colour and aroma; good flavour, flesh, tannin**(*)*

SANFORD, SANTA BARBARA *Deep, rich; very opulent, scented Pinot aroma — a La Tâche look-alike; crisp, very flavoury, stylish*****

SINSKY, CARNEROS NAPA *Lovely flavour, texture, length and aftertaste. My top wine at the Vintners Club blind tasting*****

WILLIAMS SELYEM, RUSSIAN RIVER *Powdery, artificial, unattractive.*

ZACA MESA, SANTA BARBARA RESERVE *Vegetal Pinot aroma, then like roast beef; very flavoury, touch of tinny tannin, fragrant aftertaste***(*)*

1987**

Moderate quality. Mild winter, frost-free spring but potential yields affected by a series of heat-waves in May. Summer dry. Sept cool, then rain and excessive heat. Early harvest. The smallest crush for five years.

Alas, few tasted, mainly due to infrequent visits to California during the latter part of the decade.

BEAULIEU, CARNEROS PINOT NOIR RESERVE *Palish, soft; sweet nose; very sweet, full-bodied and alcoholic yet — true to type — a disarmingly light style. June 1990****

HESS COLLECTION, CABERNET SAUVIGNON *Deep; sweet, spicy, blackberry-like fruit. Excellent with food. May 1991**(*)*

ROBERT MONDAVI, PINOT NOIR *Deep; sweet, gentle, fragrant nose; fairly full-bodied, pleasant and positive flavour but touch of bitterness on finish consistently noted. Last tasted Sept 1990***

SAINTSBURY, 'GARNET' CARNEROS PINOT NOIR *Ruby rather than garnet; lovely fruit; fairly sweet, medium-full body, rich Pinot flavour, fragrant oaky aftertaste. Last noted Nov 1988****

SHAFER, MERLOT *(Includes some of the two Cabernets.) Lovely deep velvety red; soft, fleshy, meaty nose and flavour. Very good, but with fairly severe tannic finish. Jan 1990**(**)*

1988

A difficult year for the growers. Warm dry winter through to the spring. Cold showers then prolonged flowering. Sharp swings of temperature during the summer months with a heat-wave end Aug/early Sept. Thereafter a warm dry autumn. Another small yield. Only two reds tasted.

CARNEROS CREEK, PINOT NOIR 'FLEUR DE CARNEROS' *Dry. Beetroot flavour. Boring. May 1991**

CHARLES SHAW, GAMAY BEAUJOLAIS NOUVEAU *Up until now, the 'Gamay Beaujolais' varietal of California has born no relation to the delightful wines made in Beaujolais from the Gamay grape. The few I have tasted are a travesty. When I saw 'Nouveau' I groaned. But though too deep in colour, the wine had a very positive Gamay aroma — jammy, strawberry-like, acidic — but was mediocre on the palate and short. A brave, or rather foolhardy, attempt. Nov 1988**

1989

Third year of drought eased by spring rains. Summer cool, equable. Early harvest interrupted by heavy rains, cold, fog and rot affecting remaining grapes. Then earthquake damage. Quality dependent on selectivity. Not yet tasted.

1990

Drought continuing; yet the rain, when it came, was ill-timed, hampering flowering. Nevertheless, a good early harvest in rising temperatures. Quality generally good.

WHITE

Chardonnay is to the whites of California what Cabernet Sauvignon is to the reds – a highly successful and deservedly popular varietal, and one of the earliest to achieve recognition as a West Coast classic. The best date from the 1960s, my first exposure being to Stony Hill's. Riesling (Johannisberg Riesling) was notably unsuccessful until well into the 1970s, though the progress since has been nothing short of miraculous, winemakers coping with acidity and *Botrytis* with amazing skill. Sauvignon Blanc, sometimes labelled Fumé Blanc, was reasonably successful in the 1970s and is now ubiquitous and good. Chenin Blanc can also be good though is not widely grown or marketed. Gewurztraminer is not, on the whole, successful and is nothing like the Alsace classic.

As with the reds, I originally intended to arrange my notes under varietal headings but finally decided to list them by vintage.

Most of the whites are for early consumption, though some of the top Chardonnays will not only keep but will improve with bottle-age. Although I have a large number of notes of earlier vintages I have only recorded them here if they are recent, relevant or salutory.

1962**

Heitz, Pinot Chardonnay Made by Brad Webb at Hanzell and 'finished' (*élevé*) by Joe Heitz. Reputed to be the first commercial Chardonnay matured in (French) oak. First tasted in 1967, in March with Darryl Corti, then in May with the Rhodes. Scented. Attractive. More recently, bottle variation: the first a good, bright, medium-pale yellow; very good crisp oaky nose and flavour. Dry. Holding well. The other distinctly deep, straw-tinged; slightly oxidised 'straw' nose. Neutral. Short. *Last tasted, again with the Rhodes, June 1983. At best****

1965**

Beaulieu, Dry Sauternes Further described as "a light wine of Semillon". Very pronounced buttercup yellow, rather like an old Vouvray; low-keyed, harmonious, Semillon waxiness, touch of mercaptan; dry, medium-pale body, rather neutral flavour. Slightly peppery, sulphury end. Interesting, but no more. *At Christie's, Dec 1987**

1969**

Freemark Abbey, Chardonnay In 1977, fine and firm. But six years on: straw gold, too deep; smell of old apples; dry, not bad; clean enough but passé. *Oct 1983.*

Robert Mondavi, Fumé Blanc Buttercup yellow and lime; hard, oily nose. It reminded me of tinned asparagus. Then it softened and became more peachy – but not a glimmer of Sauvignon Blanc fruit. Curious flavour, very dry, bitter finish. Swingeingly acidic. *Dining with the Rhodes, in the Napa, June 1986. Don't hang on to this style of wine!*

1970****

Hanzell, Chardonnay Deepish yellow; sound, unexceptional; dry, very fresh for age. Excellent balance. Demonstrating that a well-made Chardonnay will keep for over 20 years, though that's about all. *Dining at Maynard Amerine's, June 1981****

1971***

Freemark Abbey, Chardonnay Warm yellow; nice quality, sound, still an agreeable drink. *June 1983****

Heitz, Chardonnay Z11 Beautiful lemon gold colour; waxy, minty, lemon-curd bouquet, slightly buttery, more like an old Semillon; dry, medium body, harmonious, trace of peach kernels. Almost like an old-fashioned Graves. *At a Christie's/Schaefer pre-auction dinner, Chicago, Feb 1986****

Mayacamas, Chardonnay Palish, with a buttery gold sheen; still fresh, slight varietal development then touch of acetone; dry, good mid-palate but short. *Oct 1981***

Stony Hill, Chardonnay The Napa Chardonnay pioneers. However, not all that impressive on the nose, neither buttery nor varietal nor oaky, but good; medium dry, extremely attractive on the palate, good flavour, fleshy yet firm. *At the Rhodes', June 1981****

1972**

Chappellet, Chenin Blanc Good rich yellow; lovely waxy, oily, cress-like nose; medium (dryness and body), excellent flavour, slightly plump yet with good acidity. The sweetness and acidity reminiscent of Loire. *June 1984****

Freemark Abbey, Chardonnay Very minty bouquet; dry, rather severe. *Dining at the winery, June 1983***

1973****

A landmark vintage.

Chateau Montelena, Chardonnay This is the wine that, in 1976, trounced the white burgundies at Steven Spurrier's blind tasting in Paris. It shocked the French! At seven years old: fairly pronounced yellow; broad, sweet buttery nose, very much my style of Chardonnay; medium dry, fairly full-bodied, fine, rich, meaty nose, very good acidity. *April 1980*****

Freemark Abbey, Chardonnay Very yellow; some fat and honeyed bottle-age; surprisingly sweet, waxy Chardonnay flavour, good acidity. *June 1983*****

Freemark Abbey, Riesling Edelwein At a period when nothing much was being made of the Riesling in the Napa, a highly successful first use of *Botrytis*-affected grapes. At nine years old: a deepish gold with warm orange tinge; rich, honeyed bouquet; medium-sweet, excellent balance of fruit and acidity. Lovely wine. *June 1982*****

1974*****

A very good vintage. Many notes but only a dozen or so in the 1980s. The following are the most recent.

Robert Mondavi, Reserve Chardonnay As usual, abundant information: picked the third week in Sept, no skin contact, the juice centrifuged to make it leaner, 16 months in French oak. Alcohol 13.6% – the average for a top white burgundy vintage. Total acidity 7.4. Residual sugar 0.2. Fairly high sulphur dioxide which accounts for its relatively pale colour. First noted at 'California Wines and the Pursuit of Excellence' at the Palais du Congrès, Strasbourg, and again two years later. Pale for its age; delicious waxy lanolin nose combining delicacy and power, lovely pineapple-like fruit noted on both occasions, and high acidity; medium dry, and despite its alcoholic content not heavy, though substantial. 'Hot' finish. *Last noted at a tasting 'moderated' with Michael Mondavi, Miami, Feb 1988*****

Robert Mondavi, Fumé Blanc At its zenith in 1984, still remarkably fresh, dry, crisp. However, a bottle two years later showing its age: more yellow; nose no longer varietal, a bit varnishy, spicy; rather bland, flat and fat, with loose acidity. *Past its best, June 1986.*

Sterling, Chardonnay Made by Ric Forman. Very bright palish lemon, with an almost sickly sweet nose and still hard in 1981. Most recently: now a deeper yellow; good vinosity, vanilla, walnuts; medium-sweet, fairly full and fat, rich toasty flavour, very good acidity. *Forman's presentation at the Hollywood Wine Society Seminar, Feb 1989****

A summary of '74 **Chardonnays** *at a tasting in June 1981:*

David Bruce Not very bright, slightly oxidised.

Chalone The palest of the group, lemon-tinged; classic Chardonnay varietal nose, subtle oak, buttery; medium, neither dry nor sweet, rich, excellent flavour, fresh as a daisy. Added acidity?****

Chappellet Delicate, dry, good balance and length***

Freemark Abbey Sweet, touch of pineapple, slightly oily nose and taste. Pineapple and lemon — reminded me of the Nahe***

Heitz Bottled Feb 1976. Very yellow; harmonious, honeyed bouquet; dry yet rich, excellent flavour and acidity****

Mount Eden Low-keyed, cool, hard; dry, uplifting flavour, lovely spicy (oaky) finish****

Stony Hill Very refreshing lemon-curd nose; high-toned, a bit varnishy, excellent aftertaste***

1975***

Not many tasted in the 1980s.

Hills Cellars, Pinot Chardonnay Another landmark, more for its background than for the wine. This was made by Mike Grgich (of Chateau Montelena fame) for Austin Hills, the start of the Grgich/Hills partnership. The wine was aged in 60-gallon Limousin oak barrels. Sugar 24.1, total acidity 1.23g/100ml, pH 3.32. Dry, lightish, good acidity. *Feb 1981***

Mayacamas, Napa Mountain Chardonnay Yellow; Chardonnay nose; dry, excellent acidity. Holding well. *Feb 1986****

Joseph Phelps, Selected Late Harvest Johannisberg Riesling One of the successful pioneers of *Botrytis*-affected, late-picked Rieslings. (Phelps also experimented with picking early whilst acidity levels were still high.) A lovely warm gold, tinged with orange; honeyed, peachy nose; sweet, nice weight, excellent flavour, an uplift of acidity. Perfection and, I thought, would keep. *June 1981******

Some other '75 **Chardonnays** *tasted 1981–82:*

Chateau Montelena Well-made, soft yet good acidity***

Freemark Abbey Fresh and delicious in 1978. By Oct 1982 had gained colour; rich waxy nose; hefty style, but surprisingly acidic*?

Spring Mountain Spicy, aromatic**

1976**

Few dry whites of interest in my recent notes but four interesting-to-great sweet wines.

Chateau Montelena, Late Harvest Johannisberg Riesling Crisp, honeyed bouquet, surprisingly not sweet, more like a medium dry Rheingau Spätlese. Fairly pure Riesling nose but more 'foreign' on palate. Firm. Upturned acid finish. *Jan 1982***

Freemark Abbey, Edelwein Sweet Johannisberg Riesling Very bright and appealing gold; wonderfully sweet, ripe, honey and wax, *Botrytis* bouquet; sweet, rich, excellent flavour and aftertaste. *April 1980******

Monterey Vineyard, Botrytis Sauvignon Blanc Amber orange; very scented, grapey, almost muscadelle nose; fairly sweet, rather like a Tokay Aszú of 4 putts. *Feb 1987***

Joseph Phelps, Late Harvest Johannisberg Riesling First tasted, a half-bottle, in 1980: intense yellow gold; very rich *Botrytis* nose; sweet, intense, like a good Beerenauslese. Recently noted, labelled "Selected Late Harvest and Botrytis". Both a fairly deep warm amber, almost rosehip; a glorious, rich, raisiny, honeyed bouquet; very sweet, fat, full-flavoured, an intriguing uplift and excellent acidity. *Last tasted Jan 1990******

Worthy of mention:

Chappellet, Napa Chardonnay Pale yellow gold; stylish, waxy, Chardonnay fruit; dry, very flavoury. Lovely wine. *June 1984*****

Inglenook, Gewurztraminer Bright, honey-coloured; slightly scented; soft, mildly grapey, not spicy. Plumper than its Alsace namesake. *April 1980***

1977*

Some flabby and fairly indifferent Chardonnays, none tasted since 1986. Most probably tired by now.

Amongst the most curious, and best:

Cuvaison, Napa Chardonnay An astonishing 15.1% of alcohol giving the wine a distinct sweet taste as well as body. Unintegrated when young but quite pleasant and flavoury at seven years of age. *Last tasted June 1984***

Robert Mondavi, Late Harvest Johannisberg Riesling Two notes. Even at under four years old a deep amber gold, like '47 Climens or an old Tokay Aszú, the juice stained by overripe grapes; very rich, very pure, honeyed *Botrytis* nose; intensely sweet, full-flavoured, soft yet good acidity, fabulous flavour and finish. Hard to tell the difference between this and TBA from a top German estate. *Tasted twice, June 1981******

St Clement, Chardonnay Showing well when young. The bouquet and flavour opened up in the glass. Rich, nutty, buttery. The old style I like. *March 1980****

Smith-Madrone, Johannisberg Riesling Although I did not see "*Botrytis*" on the label, it must have been late-picked. Good colour, not deep, still green-tinged; lovely crisp fuity nose, honeyed; medium-sweet, lovely balance of fruit and acidity. *June 1986*****

1978****

A very satisfactory vintage. I have many notes, and all the grape varieties appear to have been successful. However, as most were tasted and drunk around 1981–83, I shall confine the record to those I found particularly interesting.

David Bruce, Santa Cruz Chardonnay Dr Bruce's vineyard and winery is high up in the hills, well to the south of San Francisco and close to the epicentre of the 1989 earthquake. Deep and buttery yellow, like a young Yquem of a good vintage; magnificent nose: fragrant, vanilla, touch of grass, of oak; rich, powerful, smoky flavour, still a bit hard. *Last tasted Nov 1981. Then**(**) I wonder how it has fared?*

Firestone, Chardonnay Even further to the south, inland from Santa Barbara. Good buttery colour; very pronounced rich, waxy, fruity nose, reminding me of the weight and style of a '59 Bâtard-Montrachet. Very rich, honeyed Chardonnay with a lovely smoky aftertaste. Slightly lacking in acidity. Nowadays, a very unfashionable style. *Jan 1983. Then**** Probably well past best.*

Trefethen Also several notes, one of their best, good flavour and finish. *Last tasted April 1987****

Other '78 **Chardonnays** *showing well when tasted in the early 1980s:*

Carneros Creek Heavy but flavoury**

Chappellet Grassy, buttery***

Chateau Montelena Heavy buttery style (14.3% alcohol), good but lacked finish**

Chateau St-Jean Very yellow, waxy**

Freemark Abbey Lovely, but added acidity?***

Grgich Hills Highly polished lemon yellow; rich, oily; fascinating and attractive but a bit uneven**(*)

Lambert Bridge Buttery yellow; crusty bread Chardonnay; good flavour, lacking length***

Mark West Nice quality, good length**

Matanzas Creek Glorious ripe bouquet; gentle peachy fragrance, perfect balance****

Robert Mondavi, Reserve Several notes. Old-fashioned buttercup yellow; good nose; smoky oaky flavour. Good acidity***

St Clement Very good nose and flavour. Crisp. Good length***(*)

Stag's Leap Wine Cellars A marvellous mouthfiller. Outstanding flavour, extract, length**(**)

Stony Hill Many notes, memorably — more than once — at the Oyster Bar at Grand Central Station, New York. Flavoury, good not great***

Other grapes and styles:

Robert Mondavi, Fumé Blanc Bob was the pioneer and great promoter of this craftily named Sauvignon Blanc, and the '78 was one of his best. Dry, firm, flavoury. Always more substantial than the Loire equivalent, but, as we have seen, does not keep well. *Last tasted and probably at best, Oct 1981****

Robert Mondavi, Johannisberg Riesling First noted, in 1984, as "Special Bunch Selection". Warm, orange-tinged gold; lovely, honeyed *Botrytis* nose; sweet, full, fat, rich yet very firm with good acidity*****

Robert Mondavi, Johannisberg Riesling Late Harvest Deep orange gold; deep, raisiny, honeyed bouquet; palate also sweet, with a singed sultanas flavour and scented endtaste, still quite hard. *Tasted Jan 1988****(*) Will keep.*

Phelps, Selected Late Harvest Johannisberg Riesling Alcohol 10%, residual sugar an extraordinary 30%. First tasted in June 1981. Perfection, despite its youthfulness. Four years later: an amazing colour, glowing, orange-tinged amber; fabulously rich nose, honeyed; incredibly sweet yet not heavy or clumsy because of the crisp counterbalancing acidity. Like a great Trockenbeerenauslese. *Last tasted March 1985******

Rutherford Hill, Gewurztraminer Palish yellow; delicate, piquant, scented — not very spicy but good; medium dry, delicate grapey flavour, good dry finish. One of the most satisfactory I can recall. *June 1981****

Other Rieslings:

Monterey, Thanksgiving Harvest Very yellow; smell of kerosene, like the engine room of an old fishing boat with sea water coming through; medium-sweet, positive yet hollow. Interesting. *June 1984**

Trefethen Medium dry, plump for a Riesling but nice acidity. For quick drinking. *Oct 1982***

1979***

A surprisingly large range of Chardonnays tasted but nearly all between 1981 and 1983, just a few at five and six years of age and mostly pleasant enough, though several were what I call 'two sip' wines: after the second sip one loses interest.

Chateau St-Jean, Robert Young Vineyard Selected Late Harvest Johannisberg Riesling Warm orange amber; excellent bouquet, fruit and honey; sweet, peach and apricots flavour, zestful acidity. *April 1987**** Lovely now. Will keep.*

Stony Hill Well-made though unexciting, better I think when young. *Last tasted Feb 1987***

Short notes on some '79 **Chardonnays** *tasted in the early to mid-1980s:*

Acacia Nose far too herbaceous; dry, powerful wine***

Chalone Rich, fragrant, attractive**(*)

Chateau St-Jean Fragrant, shapely, appealing***(*)

Conn Creek Firm and flavoury***

Freemark Abbey Very good flavour, rich, good acidity***

Grgich Hills Creamy, elegant, stylish; light toasted flavour, excellent acidity****

Lambert Bridge Vanilla and pineapple**(*)

Matanzas Creek 73% Sonoma, 27% Napa. Fragrant, like fresh crusty bread; good, crisp, oaky flavour though tails off a bit***

Robert Mondavi, Reserve Buttercup yellow; buttery, touch of sweetness, soft and relatively fat***

J W Morris, Black Mountain Vineyard Very pale; lemony; dry, acidic, poor.

Mount Eden, Santa Cruz Very dry, lean, well-balanced***

Stag's Leap Wine Cellars Good colour; nose developed beautifully; excellent flavour, well-balanced****

Stonegate Good flavour, balance***

Fumé Blancs *tasted early 1980s:*

Chateau St-Jean Outstanding. Quite unlike any other Fumé Blanc: extraordinary nose, pineapple, very ripe grapes, rich, developing spicy Sauvignon Blanc fragrance; lovely flavour, rich middle palate, dry finish. Served too cold but, like a top-class white burgundy, improved as it warmed up*****

Robert Mondavi Grass-like Sauvignon Blanc; well-made***

1980★★★

Again, a wide range of Chardonnays, mostly tasted and drunk between 1982 and 1984, plus other varietals. Generally good to very good.

SOME BETTER '80 CHARDONNAYS TASTED FROM 1985:

ACACIA *Distinctly yellow; very rich herbaceous nose and flavour. A powerful wine. Sept 1985*★★★

CLOS DU BOIS, FLINTWOOD *Picked late, 100% malolactic fermentation, still working in March 1981, 12 months in wood. Rich, slightly oily vanillin nose; soft, attractive, somewhat lacking in length. June 1986*★★

MARK WEST, RUSSIAN RIVER *Soft vanillin nose; very flavoury, good length, lemon-like acidity. Last tasted Feb 1987*★★★

STONY HILL *Several notes in the mid-1980s. Now taking on colour, waxy yellow; rather waxy nose too; dry, fairly full body, touch of oak on finish. Well made and holding well. March 1989*★★★

ZD *Very pronounced yellow; nose like crusty bread; dry, fairly hefty, the flavour expanding in the mouth, good fruit and aftertaste. Last noted April 1987*★★★

SOME '80 CHARDONNAYS SHOWING WELL IN THE EARLY 1980s:

BERINGER, PRIVATE RESERVE *Picked at 24.4 Brix, aged seven months in Nevers and Limousin oak: medium dryness and weight, somewhat buttery style, flavoury, fresh mouth-cleansing acidity*★★★(★)

EDNA VALLEY *Many notes: charred, toasty, smoky nose and taste. Fairly dry, good and, I suspect, added acidity. Very flavoury*★★★

GRGICH HILLS *Attractive old-fashioned style; dry, crisp, fabulous aftertaste*★★★★

RUTHERFORD HILL *Straightforward, attractive flavour and texture*★★★

TREFETHEN *Fragrant aroma and aftertaste. Dry. Flavoury*★★(★)

OTHER VARIETALS:

BERINGER, NIGHTINGALE BOTRYTISED NAPA VALLEY SEMILLON *Named after the distinguished winemaker Myron Nightingale. A fair attempt at a Napa 'Sauternes'. Fresh grassy nose, more Sauvignon Blanc than Semillon, vanilla and lively fruit. Medium-sweet, excellent flavour, balance and acidity. June 1984*★★★

CHRISTIAN BROTHERS, FUME BLANC *Mont La Salle Centennial bottle. Holding remarkably well: good, medium-pale colour; rich, grassy, scented nose; medium dry, rich minty flavour, short hard finish. April 1991*★★★

JEKEL, LATE HARVEST JOHANNISBERG RIESLING *Outstanding, Beerenauslese-style, in 1984. More recently, rich amber, gold highlight, green rim; rich, honeyed, 'kerosene' Riesling nose; very sweet, lovely peach-like flavour, rather pasty, slightly artificial, acidic finish. Very attractive. Probably best at five to seven years of age. March 1990*★★★★

PHELPS, EARLY HARVEST RIESLING *An interesting development. Picked early to capture the acidity before it dropped so low as to require acidifying. Fairly pale; lightly grapey aroma, fairly dry, light (11% alcohol), good clean acidic finish. June 1981*★★★

STONY HILL, WHITE RIESLING *Very fragrant, flowery, slightly minty; lightish, very attractive flavour, firm dry finish. A style I like. June 1983*★★★

1981★★★★

A fascinatingly attractive vintage. My mouth waters as I read my notes. A hot summer and early harvest is not conducive to making crisp, dry wines, but the best winemakers coped admirably though some necessary acidification noted – the end acidity not fully integrated. The weather change in mid-Sept, ending with a powerful storm in late Oct, enabled some superb late-harvest wines to be made from grapes left to develop *Botrytis*.

Most of my notes were made in 1983 and 1984. Some of the more recent follow.

CHALONE, CHARDONNAY *Still pale, with distinct green tinge; very forthcoming fragrant bouquet and flavour. Dry, rather lean, oaky. April 1987*★★★

FRANCISCAN, CHARDONNAY *The first estate-bottled Chardonnay made from seven-year-old vines on their Alexander Valley Vineyard. The wine was 'finished' by Tom Farrell, formerly winemaker at Inglenook. First tasted in Oct 1982: a highly polished, flavoury wine with a lovely, buttery, oaky aftertaste. Scented vanilla the next spring. Most recently, despite an odd branded stopper cork that I was able to pull without the aid of a Screwpull, still very good: medium-pale yellow; slightly oily, rather Germanic nose, vaseline, honeyed bottle-age; medium dry, surprisingly nice flavour, good length, dry loose-acidic finish. Past best but quite good. April 1991*★★★

GRGICH HILLS, FUME BLANC *A dazzlingly exciting wine: star-bright; very pronounced floral, minty, herbaceous aroma; dry, delicious, very good acidity. With Marvin Shanken and Fritz Hatton at the Oyster Bar, Grand Central Station, Feb 1986*★★★★

KISTLER, CHARDONNAY *Fairly deep yellow; ripe waxy nose; a fairly hefty, rich wine, flavoury but showing age. Feb 1989*★★

ROBERT MONDAVI, CHARDONNAY *Most unusual nose and flavour, lychee-like; medium dry, plumpish, lacking zest. Jan 1988*★★

ROBERT MONDAVI, RESERVE CHARDONNAY *13.6% alcohol, 7.4 total acidity, skin contact 9 hours, not centrifuged, 100% new French oak. Absolutely superb when first tasted in April 1985. Rich, great power, length. A year later, a very positive yellow gold; lovely nose, ripe Chardonnay, very oaky; excellent flavour, soft, highish end acidity. Last tasted Sept 1986*★★★★

SONOMA-CUTRER, CHARDONNAY *This Russian River winery specialises in Chardonnay. A wonderful colour; creamy buttery nose; fabulous flavour, powerful, oaky. June 1984*★★★★

SONOMA-CUTRER, CUTRER VINEYARD *A pronounced yellow green colour; lovely oaky smoky Chardonnay nose and flavour with a twist of* *lemon; sweeter, lovely.* June 1984*****

SONOMA-CUTRER, LES PIERRES VINEYARD *Initially harder, more closed up; great length, great potential. Two years later a glorious yellow gold with touch of lime; sweet, rich, toasty nose; fairly dry, full-bodied (14.2% alcohol), with a deft touch of enlightening acidity.* At the winery, June 1986. Then ***(**) Interesting to see how this has developed.

TREFETHEN, CHARDONNAY *Good depth, very fragrant; flavoury, buttery.* March 1989***

SOME OTHER CHARDONNAYS SHOWING WELL IN THE EARLY TO MID-1980s:

ACACIA, WINERY LAKE *Yellow; flowery, scented, elegant*****

S ANDERSON *Pure gold; high quality****(*)

BERINGER, PRIVATE RESERVE *Rich, herbal; soft, flavour swells in the mouth, deft use of oak, fragrant*****

DELOACH, RUSSIAN RIVER *Overwhelming, scented, buttery nose; medium dry, very flavoury, excellent aftertaste***(**)

DOLAN *(Made by Fetzer's winemaker from his own small vineyard.) Heavenly, fragrant nose; nutty, elegantly oaky****

KALIN, CUVEE D *Pale; fresh, still youthful; good swell of flavour, hint of oak****

STAG'S LEAP WINE CELLARS *Beautifully made. Harmonious, elegant, lovely flavour, good texture, length and aftertaste*****

OTHER VARIETALS TASTED IN THE EARLY TO MID-1980s:

Several unexceptional Chenin Blancs and quite good Gewurztraminers, Phelps being the best.

CHALONE, PINOT BLANC *Highly polished, very burgundian, dry, marvellous acidity, austere****(*)

DELOACH, ZINFANDEL BLANC *The first of the 'blush' wines tasted. A pale, slightly orange rosé; good fresh fruity nose and flavour. Very attractive****

STONY HILL, WHITE RIESLING *Beautifully made, attractive, lightly grapey nose, medium dry, perfect balance*****

DESSERT WINES:

FELTON EMPIRE, SELECT LATE HARVEST RIESLING *Yellow gold; excellent honeyed* Botrytis *nose; sweet, rich yet lean. Flavour of honey and raisins. Excellent acidity.* June 1986****

FIRESTONE, SELECTED HARVEST JOHANNISBERG RIESLING 'THE AMBASSADORS' VINEYARD *23.5 Brix. Medium-deep orange gold; very rich, grapey nose; sweet, plump, fabulous flavour, length, acidity and aftertaste.* Tasted at the winery, Oct 1984*****

ROBERT MONDAVI, BOTRYTIS JOHANNISBERG RIESLING *From the Oakville vineyard. Sugar 34 Brix, 9% alcohol. Pleasant apple gold colour; very good* Botrytis *nose, apricot, honeyed; medium-sweet, good rich mid-palate, 'hot' dry acid finish.* June 1985***(*)

ROBERT MONDAVI, BOTRYTIS SAUVIGNON BLANC *(15% Semillon) Also from their Oakville vineyard. Sugar at harvest 34.6 Brix, residual measured at 95g/l. First tasted in Nov 1984: lovely. Needed more bottle-age. Served blind the following spring: apart from the somewhat unknit nose, it never crossed my mind that it could be anything but Sauternes. It had the '67 Yquem deftness of touch, Climens top-vintage quality. More recently: shining bright yellow gold; hefty, oily, minty, rich figs and honey nose; sweet, almost lethally assertive, full, rich, crisp honey and lemon acidity. Remarkable.* Nov 1987****(*)

QUADY, ORANGE ESSENCIA *The first commercial California bottling of the Orange Muscat, now of course well known. A striking label. Amber; first whiff reminded me of tea, but sweet, very slightly caramelly; medium-sweet, rather Tokay-like, excellent acidity. Although 15% alcohol, light in style. I found it neither very orange blossom nor very muscat, but very attractive.* Ahwahnee Lodge, Yosemite, with the Adamsons, June 1983***

1982★ to ★★★

Long cool summer slowed ripening, though end Aug and early Sept warmer. Then rain, a tropical storm. From my notes, not a good Chardonnay year, "hard", "acidic", "bitter finish", "short", "sharp" cropping up often. Better for some of the other varietals. Most of my notes made around 1984/5.

CUVAISON, CHARDONNAY *Dry, oaky, assertive but hard and short.* Last tasted Jan 1987*

ROBERT MONDAVI, RESERVE CHARDONNAY *Nutty but not very pronounced nose and flavour. Dry. Fair length.* Last tasted Jan 1990**

ST CLEMENT, CHARDONNAY *Fairly deep straw yellow showing signs of oxidation; tired nose; not bad flavour but showing age.* Nov 1988.

SIMI, CHARDONNAY *Very attractive, lemon vanilla, crushed bread nose; good flavour, length and acidity.* Last tasted April 1987***

TASTED MAINLY IN MID-1980s:

ACACIA, CHARDONNAY *More like a fat Sancerre, very dry, 'green', bitter.*

FREEMARK ABBEY, RIESLING EDELWEIN *This was to be the fourth Edelwein vintage. I tasted it as grape juice in Oct 1982: still milky, cloudy but very sweet, delicious and not at all yeasty.*

GRGICH HILLS, LATE HARVEST JOHANNISBERG RIESLING *Crisp, youthful, oily Riesling nose and taste. Raw acidity. The only Grgich wine I have not cared for.*

JORDAN, CHARDONNAY *Assertive, oaky, unknit**

MIRASSOU, LATE HARVEST RIESLING *(25%* Botrytis*) Yellow; gentle, fragrant, grassy undertone; medium-sweet, pleasant enough but short**

ROBERT MONDAVI, MOSCATO D'ORO *Palish yellow; pleasant light muscadelle aroma; medium-sweet, lightish, pleasant flavour but short***

ROBERT PECOTA, MOSCATO DI ANDREA *Very pale, green tinge; similar aroma and taste to Mondavi's. A charmer with nice uplift, hint of spritz****

PHELPS, GEWURZTRAMINER *Pale; excellent scent — I thought it was one of Trimbach's; dry, better body and acidity than some Alsace Gewurztraminers, very attractive****

SHAFER, CHARDONNAY *Delicate, very good****

SONOMA-CUTRER, LATE HARVEST CHARDONNAY *Unusual to have a* Botrytis *Chardonnay, and the first at Sonoma-Cutrer: yellow gold; low-keyed, honey; fairly sweet, fullish flavour, rich texture, excellent acidity****

SONOMA-CUTRER, LES PIERRES CHARDONNAY *Very fragrant but too assertive***

SOUVERAIN, MUSCAT CANELLI *Pronounced tom-cats grapiness; medium-sweet, light style and weight, very flavoury, fragrant aftertaste. A gold medal winner*****

1983★★ to ★★★★

Moderate vintage judging from my notes: almost all tasted and consumed 1985 to 1987. However, more sensational late-harvest wines.

GRGICH HILLS, CHARDONNAY *Positive yellow colour; vanillin nose; not so much rounded as square, but good flavour and very dry, oaky finish.* Last tasted Feb 1988***

ROBERT MONDAVI, RESERVE CHARDONNAY *96% barrel-fermented, "over 90%" in French oak for 10½ months. Alcohol 13.6%. Very positive yellow; attractive floral nose with crisp fresh fruitiness; medium dry, clean-cut, lovely Chardonnay flavour, oak, a touch of pineapple.* At peak at the Mondavi seminar in Miami, Feb 1988****

SIMI, RESERVE CHARDONNAY *A stylish, perhaps richer and more 'oily' nose than Mondavi; similar dryness and weight, oaky.* July 1990****

A SELECTION OF THE BEST '83 CHARDONNAYS TASTED PRIOR TO 1988:

S ANDERSON *Fragrant, honeyed; dry, positive flavour, noticeable acidity****

DAVID BRUCE *Dry, crisp, lovely flavour, aftertaste**(*)*

CHALONE, MONTEREY *Herbaceous; full-bodied, crisp, dry**(*)*

CUVAISON *Refreshing, flavoury, good length****

FAR NIENTE *Notes vary from slightly corky/woody, to at best "Leflaive–like", classic weight and style. More recently, in jeroboam, rich but lacking zest.* At best***?

MAYACAMAS *Good but expensive****

PHELPS *Good fruit, flavour, length****

SHAFER *Harmonious, lovely****

SONOMA-CUTRER, LES PIERRES *Fresh, medium dry, nice quality****

STONY HILL *Fragrant****

VICHON *Dry, firm, elegant****

OTHER VARIETALS TASTED IN THE MID-1980s:

CHALONE, PINOT BLANC *An interesting grape variety beginning to make an appearance around the early 1980s. Not easy to define but Chalone is extremely pleasant, soft yet with perfect acidity****

DRY CREEK, FUME BLANC *Good mouthwatering Sauvignon Blanc blackcurrant fruit and acidity****

GRGICH HILLS, FUME BLANC *Not the first vintage tasted of the Grgich Fumé Blanc but the one that awakened my interest in June 1985: a spicy, herbaceous, zestful wine, lively, uplifting, which, I am sorry to say, makes the Mondavi prototype — certainly the '83 — stodgy and dull.* At the *Casablanca, Santa Cruz***** *Youthful charm probably lost by now.*

MORE DELIGHTFUL LATE-HARVEST WINES:

BERINGER, NIGHTINGALE BOTRYTIS RIESLING *Aroma of wax, honey, pineapple husk and gooseberry, 'maiden's armpit'! Grapey flavour, silky texture.* Dec 1989****

CHATEAU ST-JEAN, GEWURZTRAMINER *The first late-harvest wine I have tasted made from this grape variety. Finely perfumed, honeyed* Botrytis, *rose cachou and lychees nose and taste. Sweet. Rich. Lovely.* Feb 1985****

CHATEAU ST-JEAN, RIESLING SPECIAL SELECTION *Magnificent. Creamy; fat, luscious.* Nov 1987*****

CLOS DU BOIS, JOHANNISBERG RIESLING *Bottled Dec 1983, and capturing the fresh fruit and acidity. Apricots, honey, sweet, a bit raw.* June 1986**

PHELPS, SPECIAL SELECTION JOHANNISBERG RIESLING *Sweet, stylish, elegant.* Nov 1987****

STAG'S LEAP WINE CELLARS, SELECT LATE HARVEST WHITE RIESLING *Sugar 31% by weight. A 'fluke' wine, very little made, from Dirk Meyer's vineyard, feinste Auslese sweetness, refined raisins, lean compared with others of the genre. Several notes.* Last tasted March 1986****

1984★ to ★★★★

A fairly hefty, hot vintage, conditions unsuitable for *Botrytis* so none of my favourite late-harvest wines. Most of my notes made in 1986 and 1987. Impossible to generalise about the Chardonnays: some lacking acidity, some very acidic. Rieslings seem soft, Sauvignon Blancs equally variable but for drinking whilst young anyway.

EDNA VALLEY, CHARDONNAY *An example of the increasing complexity of California wines. An interesting partnership, between Paragon Vineyard, the major grower in the area, and Chalone, responsible for the winemaking and marketing. Very rich, grassy nose that developed gloriously in the glass, butter and pineapple; full-bodied (13.9% alcohol) but not hefty, with very attractive oaky flavour and aftertaste, good length and acidity.* April 1987****

IRON HORSE, CHARDONNAY *Grown in West Sonoma, a cool coastal region. Grapes picked early, Sept 2, 12 hours' skin contact, 65% fermented in small French oak, the rest in French and Jugoslav vats. Aged for four months in small French* barriques. *Its extraordinary scent first noted in Feb 1987. Most recently: now a medium pale yellow; scent still lovely, waxy vinosity, underlayer of 'green' fruit; medium — not very dry, fullish, very good rich Chardonnay and oak flavour, dry finish. Has kept well.* March 1991****

RANDOM CHARDONNAYS NOTED BRIEFLY:

GRGICH HILLS *Bone dry and very acidic. June 1986**
JORDAN *Hefty style. July 1987***
KISTLER *Distinctly dry, good fruit, austere. Feb 1987***(*)
ROBERT MONDAVI, RESERVE *Many notes. Lovely smoky oaky charred flavour. Last tasted Feb 1988****
MONTICELLO, JEFFERSON RANGE CHARDONNAY *Lovely flavour. Last tasted Feb 1987***(*)
SIMI CHARDONNAY *Very dry, below standard. July 1987**

WORTH A MENTION:

GRGICH HILLS, FUME BLANC *Light, deft, the best of nine Sauvignon Blancs. Feb 1988****
QUADY, ORANGE MUSCAT ESSENCIA *Orange-tinged amber gold; very strange scent of barley-sugar and celluloid — reminding me of table tennis balls and ducks in a child's bath; fairly sweet, powerful flavour, apricots, trace of Muscat, very high end acidity. Original but not all of a piece. June 1987***

1985★★★★★

As good a vintage for whites as for reds, and for all the varietals. The best Chardonnays approaching their peak but will develop and keep well. Hard to know where to start so I will concentrate on the more interesting Chardonnay tastings.

CLOS DU BOIS, CHARDONNAY *What I presume was their 'regular' was rather neutral, dull and lacking length. Feb 1987.*
CLOS DU BOIS, FLINTWOOD *Fairly pronounced yellow colour but an odd, thin, slightly medicinal vanillin nose and taste. July 1987.*
CLOS DU BOIS, CALCAIRE *In July 1987: a more classic Chardonnay nose and flavour; later the same year, creamy, powerful yet avoiding coarseness. Most recently: yellow; good 'waxy' nose, medium dry, very attractive. Jan 1990****
NEWTON *A very interesting tasting in June 1986, at the new winery built by the Englishman who had created Sterling then sold out, of various 'natural', ie not 'acidulated' Chardonnays from different vineyards: Hudson in Carneros, picked at 23 Brix, youthful, pineapple, nice shape in the mouth; from Konsgaard in the Napa, a Stony Hill clone, more peachy, fatter and assertive; and two from Dr Bob Adamson's Rutherford Vineyard, one picked at 21 Brix, the next picked two weeks later at 23 Brix, the first with noticeably higher, raw acidity, the second softer, fuller, fleshier. The final blend, including grapes from two other growers, was a nice full peachy combination on the nose but too bland (neutral, soft) on the palate. Most recently: it has turned out well, a rich Chardonnay nose; fairly dry, fairly full-bodied, good balance and length. April 1990****
SONOMA-CUTRER *First tasted at the winery with Belle Rhodes at component-part blending stage. Some fabulously flavoury elements. June 1986.*
SONOMA-CUTRER, LES PIERRES *Tasted three times: pale, green-tinged, star-bright; very distinctive nose and taste: massive, rich, oaky, pineapple and lemon acidity. Delicious. Time in hand. Nov 1987. Then***(**)
DOMAINE WOLTNER, WOLTNER ESTATE *Having for many years known François Dewavrin and his wife Françoise, née Woltner, the previous owner of Ch La Mission-Haut-Brion, I was most interested to see their vineyard and winery built on top of the Howell Mountains. First tasted in cask in June 1986 along with the Thomas and Titus (see below): powerful young wines. Bottled Aug 1986; delicious the following spring, with very good oaky flavour and length. Next, at VinExpo in June 1987: scent of honeysuckle, dry, firm, steely. Last noted, pre-sale, Christie's, Oct 1988.*
DOMAINE WOLTNER, ST THOMAS VINEYARD *Bottled Sept 15–20 1986. In June 1987, more colour than the Woltner Estate, quite different on the nose, fragrant, delicate yet firm; distinctly oaky, greater body and length. Last noted Oct 1988.*
DOMAINE WOLTNER, TITUS *Their top vineyard wine. At VinExpo, June 1987, restrained, peachy, oak and pineapple, good length, needed time. Most recently: an attractive buttercup gold colour; gentle waxy harmonious nose; medium dry, full-bodied, assertive flavour, finishing rather raw and with lip-licking acidity. Steely. I preferred it the day after I opened it. Will be interesting to see how this relatively new and high-priced wine ages further in bottle. April 1991***(**)?

SOME OTHER '85s:

ACACIA, CHARDONNAY *More like a Sauvignon Blanc. The 'new' style? I prefer the old, the buttery. Last tasted Feb 1987***
CLOS DU BOIS, EARLY HARVEST GEWURZTRAMINER *Glorious, soft, peachy, lychee fragrance and flavour. Good acidity. June 1986*****
EDNA VALLEY, CHARDONNAY *Lovely. Feb 1987***(**)
GIRARD, CHARDONNAY *Very fragrant, very oaky. Nov 1988****
KENDALL-JACKSON, BARREL FERMENTED CHARDONNAY *Surprisingly pale; youthful nose; full-flavoured, oaky. Feb 1988****
KENWOOD, SAUVIGNON BLANC *Very pale; floral Sauvignon aroma; dry, clean, classic. Nov 1986****
ROBERT MONDAVI, BOTRYTIS SAUVIGNON BLANC *Minty; sweet, rich, powerful. Feb 1989*****
SUTTER HOME, WHITE ZINFANDEL *Pale pink; fresh, fruity; light, crisp, very flavoury. Feb 1986***

1986★★ *to* ★★★

This was the year of the 'one long spring', one of the coolest summers on record. Most unusually, amongst the earliest grapes to be picked were *Botrytis*-affected Rieslings, at Jekel's for example, in the Salinas Valley. These were marketed as 'late harvest' while the 'regular' Rieslings were still being picked the second week of Oct. The Chardonnays, many on the lean side, are satisfactory and are holding well, though I am critical of the increasing tendency to produce a steely austere style, eliminating the flesh and lovely buttery oaky character. The Germans have done the same, eliminating fruit to produce *Trocken* wines. Frankly, if I want to drink Chablis I shall buy Chablis, the real thing. The Sauvignon Blancs are particularly crisp, acidic and true to form.

CHARDONNAYS TASTED SINCE 1988:

CHATEAU BOUCHAINE *Dry, minty, acidic — not very Chardonnay but refreshing. Aug 1990***

CUVAISON *A curious scent, slightly minty and vanilla, and two-part flavour. Dry, dull. March 1991***

FORMAN *Lovely spicy wine. Feb 1989****

GRGICH HILLS *Lovely vinosity, well balanced. Last tasted May 1990****

HESS COLLECTION *Medium dry, nice flesh, deft oak. May 1991****

ROBERT MONDAVI, RESERVE *Eight months in new oak. Lovely yellow colour; nutty nose and taste, violets, custardy vanilla; dry, pale, lots of spicy oak. Delicious. Last tasted Sept 1989****(*)

RUTHERFORD HILL *As pleasant and dependable as always. Last tasted Sept 1989****

STERLING, WINERY LAKE *Most unusual colour, pure waxy pale gold; lovely soft buttery spicy wine. Feb 1989*****

OTHER CHARDONNAYS, TASTED IN 1988:

ACACIA *Very dry, with Sauvignon-like nose, taste, acidity. Not my idea of a Chardonnay but good in its way***

CLOS DU BOIS *Austere.*

CLOS DU BOIS, FLINTWOOD *Spicy, oaky, attractive****

CLOS DU BOIS, CALCAIRE *Flowery, youthful pineapple aroma; dry, crisp, flavoury, zestful, long***(*)

MATANZAS CREEK *Steely. Typical of the new breed of California Chardonnays.*

NEWTON *Too pale; no nose; dry, lean***

SANFORD *Attractive****

SONOMA-CUTRER *Austere**(*)

WOLTNER, ESTATE RESERVE *Bottled June 29–July 2 1987, very pale, positive***

WOLTNER, ST THOMAS VINEYARD *Bottled July 21/22 1987, dry, steely**(**)

WOLTNER, TITUS *Bottled Aug 12 1987, very pale; dry, powerful, lean but assertive**(**)?

SOME OTHER VARIETALS TASTED:

BANDIERA, WHITE ZINFANDEL *A winery better known for its exceptionally pretty labels. Pale pink; raw, hollow nose; dryish, light, easy. Bottled three days prior to tasting. Nov 2 1986. (Conjures up the illicit 'whiskey' motto: not a drop is sold till it's three days old!)*

INGLENOOK, LATE HARVEST GEWURZTRAMINER *Fabulously rich* Botrytis *nose; fairly sweet but not as sweet as anticipated, lovely flavour, short. June 1990****

KONOCTI, FUME BLANC *A cooperative in Mendocino specialising in Sauvignon Blanc. I can see why. Dry, lightish, crisp, fresh, delicious. Feb 1988****

LAKESPRING, SAUVIGNON BLANC *Very pale; scented, minty nose; a touch too sweet really for the style but flowery, almost a Scheurebe-like grapiness, attractive. Several notes. Last tasted Jan 1990****

SANFORD, SAUVIGNON BLANC *Curious, meaty, nutty nose; dry, very attractive, not the usual Fumé Blanc style. Feb 1988****

1987★★★

Early harvest. Summer dry. Sept cool. Wines lean rather than fat which appears to suit the *nouvelle vague* of Chardonnay. Not many tasted, so unfair to pronounce on the vintage.

AMONGST THE FEW CHARDONNAYS:

CUVAISON *Pale; dry, oaky, almost woody, austere but nice wine. Last tasted May 1990***(*)

FORMAN *Made by Ric Forman from grapes grown in the Rutherford Star vineyard bought from the redoubtable Dr Robert Adamson. Six months in oak, lightly filtered. Spicy, fragrant, crisp, oaky. Feb 1989***(*)

ROBERT MONDAVI *Rich, toasty, dry, overwhelmed by oak and with a touch of bitterness that I trust will wear off. Aug 1989*(**)?

PHELPS *Very pale; nose and taste more like a Sauvignon Blanc. Grassy. Dry. Fragrant. Sept 1990***

SOME OTHER WINES:

JEKEL, LATE HARVEST RIESLING *Golden; rich, honeyed; sweet, fat, lovely flavour, good acidity. Feb 1989*****

ROBERT PECOTA, MOSCATO DI ANDREA *Peach and spearmint nose; sweet but light, crisp, delicious grapey flavour. Feb 1989****

QUADY, ORANGE MUSCAT ESSENCIA *Delicate, scented nose like lychees and grape skins; medium-sweet, nice weight, deft though a touch of fat. Dry finish. Feb 1989*****

1988★★★

Small crop of Chardonnays of quite nice quality. Sauvignon Blanc fair. Few tasted.

OF THE CHARDONNAYS:

CHATEAU ST-JEAN *Good, positive, nutty, interesting future. Jan 1990***(*)

CUVAISON *Estery nose; good length, acidity. Very stylish. Aug 1989***(*)

DE LOACH *Very pleasant nose; medium dry, soft, oaky, nice fleshy mid-palate, highish alcohol (turned out to be 13.5%), smoky aftertaste. Jan 1990*****

EDNA VALLEY *Touch of vaseline yellow; nose as yet unknit; full-flavoured, rich, attractive — my style of wine. Aug 1989***(*)

GLEN ELLEN, PROPRIETORS' RESERVE *Astonishing production: overall sales around 3 million cases per annum, and at very reasonable prices. Mint leaf, vinosity. Medium, rather hefty and obvious but crisp and with good grip. Aug 1989***

HESS COLLECTION *Dry, firm, acidic. May 1991****

RAYMOND *Lovely colour: waxy melon yellow; oakiness verging on woody but good length. Sept 1989**(*)

SWANSON *A relatively new name but 'grafted' on to the Cassayre-Forni winery. The first vintage was the*

'87. The '88, first tasted at the winery after the Napa Valley Wine auction on a scorching day in June 1990. Most recently at Andrew Lloyd Webber's wedding reception, Feb 1991**

ONE OR TWO OTHER VARIETALS:

GRGICH HILLS, FUME BLANC *My favourite Sauvignon Blanc: lively, deliciously fruity, fairly high acidity.* Last tasted at an International Wine & Food Society Council Dinner in Palm Beach, Janaury 1991***

KENDALL-JACKSON, SAUVIGNON BLANC *Assertive, firm.* Jan 1991*(**)

KONOCTI, FUME BLANC *Very pale; grassy; a bit too sweet and a rather obvious scented flavour that palled a bit, but attractive.* Last tasted Aug 1990**

MATANZAS CREEK, SAUVIGNON BLANC *Grassy; dry, lightish, minty, good acidity.* Jan 1991***

STONY HILL, WHITE RIESLING *Dry, refreshing, always well made.* June 1990***

1989

The third year of drought. A long cool summer. Heavy rains mid-Sept interrupted the harvest. Happily many Chardonnays were brought in fully ripe, before the damage was done. A week of sun allowed more to be picked, then heavy rain again. Well-drained hillside vineyards coped best but there had to be a lot of selective picking, and sugar levels were low for California. Few as yet tasted.

FETZER, SUNDIAL VINEYARD CHARDONNAY *If you can imagine a soft, oaky, slightly grapey, rather short Sauvignon Blanc-like Chardonnay, this is it. A highly successful large family firm, dwarfing the Brown Brothers of Australia, with a top-class winemaker producing very good inexpensive wines.* April 1990**

HESS COLLECTION *Youthful vanilla, pineapple; medium dry, attractive, good acidity.* May 1991***

J LOHR, CHARDONNAY *Fragrant; strange, singed, toasted flavour. Assertive.* Last tasted Oct 1990**

LOUIS MARTINI, SAUVIGNON BLANC *Too pale; vanilla, white currants and tom-cats; medium dry, grapey flavour, acidic.* April 1990**

MONTEREY, CLASSIC CHARDONNAY *Waxy green; light, soft, grassy nose; mild, easy. An agreeable large-production Seagram wine.* March 1991**

SWANSON, SAUVIGNON BLANC *Grassy; dry, very flavoury, acidic.* June 1990**

TREFETHEN, CHARDONNAY *Very pale; very light, scented nose; fairly assertive but very dry, austere. Needs bottle-age.* Jan 1991**(*)

1990

In general, prospects for California white wines are good, certainly as far as the consumer is concerned. Were consumption increasing at the same rate as production all would be well. But the state of the economy and the insidious pressures of the anti-alcohol lobby are having an effect. Land prices have been too high, winery building too extravagant and I cannot help foreseeing difficulties. But on the plus side, top-class winemaking and healthy competition to make better and better wines will pay off long term.

AUSTRALIA

How can one summarise a continent? The distances are immense, 800 miles from the Hunter Valley in New South Wales, the cradle of Australian wines, across hot NE Victoria to the broad Barossa in South Australia, a further 1,300 miles to the relatively new wine areas south of Perth, in Western Australia. Space does not permit even a summary of the climatic variations in all the major wine districts. My brief notes reveal, to a certain extent, the effect, but not the cause.

Although viticulture is old, introduced in penal colony times, the real resurgence of interest began, slowly, in the 1950s, gathered strength in the 1960s, and came on stream in the 1970s. Few old wines remain to be tasted and drunk. A wine of the 1950s is a scarce commodity and, in my limited experience, is likely to have survived less well than its French counterpart. Reds are complicated by blending different varietals from different districts. As in California, superb Rieslings are a relatively new success; Chardonnays are triumphant.

I have been to Australia only twice but, thanks to good friends like Len Evans, have visited all the major districts except Western Australia. Equally important have been the tastings I have attended, notably the *View Australia* marathon. What follows therefore is a description of the older wines tasted since 1980 and highly selective notes on younger vintages. Bear in mind that Australia's harvest takes place in what is early spring for us.

1900

Penfolds' 'Burgundy' Two-part moulded screw-top flagon. Excellent label: "Dr Penfold, Grange". Shipped in cask, bottled in London. Top-shoulder. Fairly deep, healthy glow but no red left; excellent, rich, slightly biscuity nose and taste, no faults. Drying out, losing body but sound. Not the oldest Australian wine I have tasted, but demonstrating the sound quality of some early commercial reds. *Bought at Christie's, noted at Rodenstock's tasting, Sept 1987****

1922

Yalumba, 'Old Constantia' Two bottles, both amber brown, one malty, oxidised, the other better, sweet, soft, concentrated, figgy. *At Yalumba's museum tasting, April 1985**

1927

Yalumba, 'Adelaide Show Tawny Port' Old amber; varnishy, singed sultanas; still fairly sweet, soft yet spirity. *At Yalumba, April 1985***

1932

Yalumba, 'Sauternes' An early sweet white, fermentation arrested or sweetened with Mistella, and bottled in March 1932 soon after the vintage: warm gold; very sweet crème brûlée, caramel, touch of tangerine; medium-sweet, soft, gentle, nice acidity. Remarkable. *At Yalumba, April 1985****

1933

Quelltaler, Riesling Lovely medium gold; sour old straw; dry, smoky, fishy, yeasty. *At Yalumba, April 1985.*
Yalumba, Riesling F8 The first trial 'Carte d'Or' made by Rudi Kronberger who arrived in Australia in 1929, introducing yeast cultures and early bottling. Two bottles: one old straw colour and smell, malty. The other a better colour, caramelised but clean. Both raw, horrid on palate. *At Yalumba, April 1985.*

1943

O'Shea's Hunter Valley 'Burgundy' Deep, amber rim; rich nose, malty; very sweet, chewy, old bark and medicinal aftertaste. O'Shea's legendary reputation outlives his wine. *At Yalumba, April 1985**

1944

Seppelt's 'Great Western' Sparkling 'Burgundy' Orange, sparkle reduced to slight spritz; lovely sweet old Pinot nose and taste. Soft. Sweet. Touch of iron on aftertaste. *At Yalumba's museum tasting, April 1985****
Yalumba, 'Carte d'Or' Riesling Orange gold, copper casse sediment; more like a smoky old Semillon on nose and palate. Lacking acidity. Dry. *Yalumba, April 1985***

1945

Hardy's 'Vintage Port' Lovely deep rich colour; soft, sweet, sultanas and eucalyptus; medium-sweet, full-bodied, spicy, rich, great length. Glorious. *At Yalumba, April 1985******

1953

McWilliams' Maria Montils Shiraz A rare blend of Montils and white Shiraz. Deep, yellow; smoky, oaky, singed, honeyed, coconut; dry, touch of old straw, ie some unsurprising oxidation, good acidity. *April 1985***
Wynns' Coonawarra Estate 'Claret' Deep, rich; sweaty, chocolaty; very rich, high-toned, swingeingly dry finish. Unbalanced but interesting because the produce of that narrow strip of red earth at Coonawarra was not then fully appreciated. *At Yalumba, April 1985.*

1955

Very dry year. Bushfires.
Penfolds' Grange Hermitage A famous wine, a turning point. Max Schubert, born in South Australia, visited Bordeaux and returned determined to make a top-class wine to last 20 years. His first was made in 1951 from Hermitage (Shiraz) grapes from the Grange vineyard. The new style did not take on. Penfolds nearly gave up, but in 1962, after a 10-year avoidance of wine competitions, entered the '55 Grange for the Sydney Wine Show. It won a gold and, subsequently, 170 major awards on the Australian show circuit. Max Schubert and Grange Hermitage never looked back. 100% Shiraz. Eight months in new American oak hogsheads. Bottled in 1956. Three remarkably consistent notes, first at Yalumba in 1985. Not as deep as expected; excellent, fully evolved, rather like an old Bordeaux, but after 20 minutes overblown, very chocolaty; medium sweetness and weight, warm, toasted, rather Graves-like flavour, good length, fully developed. *Last noted at Bob Berenson's Grange tasting, New York, Oct 1990******

1956

Lindeman's 'Porphyry', Hunter Valley Said to have '49 in the blend made from late harvest raisin grapes. Waxy lemon-curd yellow; honey and touch of malt; sweet, crisp. *April 1985****
Yalumba, 'Carte d'Or' Riesling Rich ripe Riesling, kerosene and bottle-age; dry, mild, clean, short. Like a Loire Chenin Blanc. Dried-peach aftertaste. *April 1985***

1958

Saltram's Dry Red, Bin 23 Made from Shiraz, bottled Nov 1962. Marvellous colour, opaque centre, mature rim; very good, complete, vinous, old leather; not dry, sweetened and softened with age, chewy, delicious, long. *April 1985*****
Yalumba, Galway 'Vintage Claret' Deepish, fine, mature; dryish, mild, chewy, touch of end acidity. *April 1985***

1959

Lindeman's Hunter River 'Burgundy', Bin 1590 (Australian 'bin' numbers are very confusing. A higher number seems to indicate higher quality.) A classic, first tasted with Len Evans in 1977. Very rich, orange-tinged, legs; very sweet Hunter Valley sweaty-saddle nose, so presumably made from Shiraz not Pinot Noir. Sweet, rich, rustic — like a milking parlour. *Last tasted at Yalumba, April 1985*** just.*
Lindeman's Hunter River Shiraz Either 'unbinned' or number not noted. Very deep, very rich, very mature; sweetish, soft, full, ripe, fleshy. Lovely velvety tannins. *April 1985*****
Yalumba, Cabernet Sauvignon One of their first 100% Cabernets: deep, mature; curious minty cheesy nose, volatile; raw, sour, tannic. *April 1985.*

1960

Penfolds' Grange Hermitage One of my earliest notes of the famous Grange, served blind – not burgundy, not claret, no obvious 'foreign' taste. Very rich, clearly of good quality. *At John Avery's, Aug 1973****

Yalumba, Galway 'Vintage Claret', Special Reserve stock Blend of Cabernet and Shiraz later to become the 'signature' series. Neutral, with strange oxtail undertow. Better on palate: sweet, good body and finish. *April 1985**

1962****

Another turning point. Prior to this, purely on the basis of the few remaining and the few tasted, the older Australian wines in general appeared to lack the stamina of their European counterparts.

Hardy's C 407 Cabernet Sauvignon Grapes from Coonawarra and McLaren Vale, matured in French oak, bottled March 1965. Same colour as a '62 red Bordeaux. Perfect weight, length, balance. *With Len Evans en route to the Hunter Valley, March 1985******

Mildara, 'Golden Bower', Bin 10, Vintage Riesling Fabulous colour, pure rich gold; a good but extraordinarily confusing nose, reminiscent of Chenin Blanc, at the same time more Riesling in character than the Hunter Semillon from which it was made! Dry, lemony, downhill from now on. Short but good for age. *April 1985***

Penfolds' Bin 60 A Another Max Schubert success, blending Coonawarra Cabernet Sauvignon with Kalimna Shiraz. Two notes. Opaque, mature; fragrant, floral bouquet developing magnificent glow; fairly full-bodied but lean, perfect balance of oak and fruit, tannin and crisp acidity. *Last tasted April 1985******

Penfolds' Grange Hermitage My first ever taste of Grange, in 1972, thanks to Hugh Johnson. Next, memorably, tasted on the spot, at Grange in 1977. Marvellous wine. *Last tasted at Grange, March 1977******

1963****

Lindeman's Hunter River 'Burgundy' Palish, orange; sweet, sweaty; soft, touch of bitterness. *At Wine Press Club dinner, Melbourne, April 1985**

Mildara, Cabernet Shiraz, Bin 32 Fairly deep, very rich; a stately nose, singed; fullish, excellent, long, chocolaty flavour. Magnificent. *At the Crittendens', April 1985******

Penfolds' Grange Hermitage, Bin 95 Opaque; fragrant, iron; rich, full-bodied, high extract. A vast wine, its colour, nose and taste reminiscent of prunes. *At the Evans', March 1985***(*)*

Wynns' Ovens Valley 'Burgundy' Lovely ruby; hard, varnishy, spicy; fairly sweet, excellent flavour, balance, length and acidity. *At Berek Segan's, April 1985*****

1965***

Average rainfall spring and summer, warm ripening period.

Brown Bros' Cabernet Shiraz Opaque, intense; sweaty saddle, farmyard; immense yet soft and rich. Earthy. Impressive. *April 1985***(*)*

McWilliams' Mount Pleasant O H Hermitage Rich, harmonious, not a trace of 'sweaty saddle'; excellent flavour, balance. Tannic. *Oct 1981***(*)*

Seppelt's Grange Hermitage 95% Shiraz, 5% Cabernet Sauvignon grown in Magill, Kalimna, Southern Vales and the Barossa regions. 18 months in new American oak. Deep, rich, mature; lean, dusty, like dry brick, then liquorice; sweet, medium weight, raw texture, loads of tannin, acidic. *At Berenson's, New York, Oct 1990***

Tyrrell's Vat 11 Very deep; peppery, rich; dry, fullish, very flavoury. *July 1981****

1966****

Very dry season. Hardy vines produced excellent quality (South Australia).

Penfolds' Grange Hermitage 12% Cabernet Sauvignon. Opaque; huge but velvety in 1977. Now medium-deep, mature; sweet, elegant, harmonious, with class, depth; very sweet on palate, losing weight, lovely flavour, silky texture. *My equal top wine, with the '71, at the Grange tasting, New York, Oct 1990******

1967***

Normal year. Slightly below average rainfall. Warm summer. Fully mature grapes.

Chateau Tahbilk Cabernet Sauvignon A picturesque old winery in NE Victoria. Richly coloured but looked more like a mature Pinot; overripe, pigsty nose; soft, decadently attractive, touch of bitterness. *April 1985***

Penfolds' Grange Hermitage 6% Cabernet Sauvignon. 16 months new American oak. Deep, lively, black cherry; good ripe fruit, coffee, lovely; medium dryness and body, chocolaty flavour, slightly short but good grip. *At Berenson's tasting, Oct 1990****

Tyrrell's Vat 61 Shiraz Fabulous colour; peppery, vinous, good fruit; delicious. *July 1981***(*)*

1968***

Extremely dry growing season, half the average rainfall.

Chateau Tahbilk Shiraz Sweaty; soft, fleshy, iron. *Melbourne, April 1985****

Lindeman's Semillon Pronounced yellow gold; smoky oaky nose and taste, dryish, full flavoured, already showing age and, confusingly, resembling a mature Chardonnay. *April 1985****

Orlando, 'Steingarten' Riesling Tasted twice and recorded here because Australian and California Rieslings were at roughly the same state of evolution around this period. They have both made incredible strides since. Yellow, a rich fino colour; oily, waxy, showing bottle-age; dry, livelier on palate than nose though lacking acidity. *April 1985**

Penfolds' Grange Hermitage 5% Cabernet Sauvignon, 20 months in new American oak hogsheads. Medium-deep, open rim; sweet, fully mature, ginger biscuits nose, opening out marvellously, coffee, then very chocolaty; sweet, Graves-like, nice weight, texture and acidity. *At Berenson's tasting, Oct 1990**** Drink now.*

Rothbury, Semillon The earliest Rothbury vintage tasted. Very yellow; oaky, smoky, Chardonnay-like, but neither Chardonnay nor oak used. Dry. *At Doyle's, Sydney, April 1985****

1970**

Average year. Good rain, good ripening conditions.

Penfolds' Grange Hermitage 10% Cabernet Sauvignon, 18 months oak. Medium, mature; forthcoming, cheesy, then toffee-like; medium dryness and weight, rather lacking yet attractive. *At Berenson's, Oct 1990** Drink up.*

1971*****

Overall growing conditions and rainfall slightly below average in all regions. Excellent for reds.

Penfolds' Grange Hermitage, Bin 95 With '79, highest percentage of Cabernet Sauvignon: 13%. Several notes, all good, first on my original visit to Australia in 1977, dining with Len Evans: opaque; packed, peppery; huge, velvety – in retrospect a cross between Latour and Pétrus. Still very intense and tannic in 1982 and 1985. Two more recently: deep, rich, 'thick' – high extract; high alcohol pepperiness but sweet, good fruit, great depth, after an hour perfect, like a mature Latour; very sweet, full of alcohol, extract, fruit, fleshy, great length yet rounded. Great wine. *Last noted at Bob Berenson's Grange tasting, New York, Oct 1990****** *Now to 2010.*

1972

Rothbury, Semillon Several notes. These Hunter Valley Semillons, though sometimes unimpressive when young, age well and change character gaining a smoky oaky Chardonnay-like nose and taste although neither that grape nor oak used. Very yellow, well made, fairly dry. *Last tasted July 1988****

Seppelt's 'Great Western Hermitage' Lovely deep ruby; very rich, jammy; claret-like weight, curious mid-palate flavour, dry, citrus, slightly bitter finish. *April 1985***

1973***

Leeuwin, Chardonnay The price of this relatively new estate's wines stunned Australians accustomed to bargains resulting from chronic over-production and severe competition. Pale too, not the usual buttery colour; attractive, sweetened in glass, a touch artificial, vanilla; fairly dry, fullish body, good oaky Chardonnay flavour. *With shark's fin at Wine & Food Society Convention dinner in Hong Kong, Oct 1989****

Leo Buring's Reserve Bin DWC 17 Rhine Riesling Winner of six gold medals in its first year, one silver and one bronze the next. Palish yellow; very good waxy Riesling, the honey of ripe grapes and some bottle-age; fairly dry, excellent firm, oaky, Chardonnay-like flavour, dry finish. Impressive. Just lacked finesse, but clearly Rieslings on the way up. *July 1982****

Lindeman's Hunter River 'Burgundy', Bin 4810 Opaque, mature rim; rich, medicinal, earthy; fullish, velvety, well made. *A silver medal winner at* View Australia, *April 1985*****

Penfolds' Grange Hermitage Bin 95 Deep, rich, beautifully mature; sweet, chocolaty; immense, chewy, concentrated, iron on finish. *At Doug Crittenden's mammoth lunch tasting, April 1985*****(*)

1974

Climatically disastrous: very high spring and summer rainfall; hot, humid, mildew prevalent.

Penfolds' Grange Hermitage 100% Shiraz, 18 months in oak, production 30% that of the '71. Fairly deep, mature rim; cheesy nose, tea, mint, brambly, difficult to pin down; fairly dry, fleshy, Graves-like tobacco taste, fair length, chunky, tannic. *At Grange tasting, New York, Oct 1990***

1975****

Chateau Tahbilk Cabernet Sauvignon, Bin 62 Cherry red; a touch volatile though well tucked into the fruit; slightly sweet, very pleasant flavour and weight, refreshingly dry finish. *May 1982****

Penfolds' Grange Hermitage, Bin 95 Two notes first at Christie's New World wine sale tasting and, coincidentally, a month later: dark mulberry; gnarled oak, tannic, dumb, peppery; dry, massive, astringent, magnificent but undrinkable! *Last at Rodenstock's tasting, Oct 1984*(*****)

Rothbury 'Individual Paddock' From Hunter Hermitage grapes. In 1981 maturing, though hard tannate of iron. Later, gentle lightish garnet; a bit overblown, blowsy; soft, better taste than smell but spoiled by excessive tannin and acidity. *Last tasted Jan 1984. Could it have recovered?*

Stanley Leasingham, Cabernet Sauvignon, Bin 49 Very attractive, light style, spicy. *At Christie's pre-sale, Sept 1984*****

Wynns' Oven's Valley (NE Victoria) Shiraz Mature; appropriately, a smell of hot oven; sweet, rich, lovely flavour, length and aftertaste. *Sept 1984*****

1976****

Good spring rains. Warm days; cool nights leading to above average vintage. Many notes. Big, excellent reds. Few good whites tasted.

Hickinbotham's Anakie Shiraz Deep rich ruby; bell pepper; sweet, full of fruit, tannate of iron. *Dec 1989****(*)

Penfolds' Grange Hermitage 11% Cabernet Sauvignon, large production. Deep, maturing; low-keyed, vegetal, then bramble, tar, black treacle, evolving fragrantly over an hour; slightly sweet, nice weight, balance, open chocolaty flavour, strange drying finish. *At Grange tasting, New York, Oct 1990****(*)

Other reds showing well in the early to mid-1980s:

Hill-Smith, Cabernet Sauvignon Deep, plummy; good, classic; fullish, good flavour and bite***(*)

Hill-Smith, Signature Partner's blend 55% Cabernet Sauvignon 45% Shiraz. Very good flavour and texture***(*)

Lindeman's Limestone Ridge Cabernet Sauvignon Opaque; curious but attractive, high-toned; very sweet, full of fruit, perfect flesh, lovely flavour****(*)

McWilliams' (Hunter) Cabernet Merlot Tangy, powerful**(**)

Mildara, Coonawarra Cabernet Sauvignon Palish, early maturing, lovely style and flavour***

Penfolds' St Henri Cabernet Shiraz Black; rich, huge but soft, excellent flavour, tannic***(*)

Tyrrell's Pinot Noir Three notes, at first strong, singed, Pinot, leathery. Best after nine years, fine, mature; rich, fig-like; a good warming wine***

Wynns' Coonawarra Cabernet Sauvignon Deep, rich, earthy, needed time**(**)

1977***

Penfolds' Grange Hermitage 9% Cabernet Sauvignon. Fine, dark, intense cherry; berry-like fruit, iodine, evolving fragrantly; Pomerol-like silky leathery tannins, sweet yet with refreshingly acidic finish. *At Grange tasting, New York, Oct 1990*****

Tyrrell's Chardonnay After all the Semillons tasting like Chardonnay, the real thing: very bright; fabulous smoky oaky nose, flavour and aftertaste. Oak too dominant? Yet a light uplifting touch at the end. *Not tasted since Oct 1981 but a successful wine***** *Probably over now.*

Some good whites tasted in the mid-1980s:

McWilliams' Auslese Riesling Orange gold; rich, kerosene and honey; sweetish, scented***

Orlando Coming into its own with a delicately scented Gewurztraminer/Rhine Riesling***

Some interesting reds in the mid-1980s:

Mount Mary, Lillydale Cabernet Sauvignon Rich; spicy, eucalyptus; very agreeable flavour, good quality***

Mount Mary, Lillydale Pinot Noir Very burgundy-like; rooty, herbaceous; delicious fruit, a touch volatile***

Tyrrell's Vat 5 Hunter Red Very deep; hefty, Rhône-like, well made, balanced***

1978****

Below average rainfall, lower yields in all regions.
Brown Bros' Milawa Cabernet Sauvignon Deep; harmonious; a very complete, lovely wine. Brown's dependable and good value. *Sept 1988*****
Penfolds' Grange Hermitage 10% Cabernet Sauvignon. Very deep, maturing; faint at first, hard to get to grips with, then fragrant, later marvellously rich; distinctly sweet, nice weight, leathery tannins. *New York, Oct 1990*****
Some other reds showing well in the early to mid-1980s:
Blass, Grey Label 80% Cabernet Sauvignon, 20% Shiraz. Typically skilful blend, sweet; good fruit, soft***
Cape Mentelle Cabernet Sauvignon Opaque; rich, mulberry-ripe; dry, full, flavoury***(*)
Chateau Tahbilk, Shiraz Sweaty, medicinal; sweet, rich, plummy, chewy***
Hardy's Pinot Noir Strange scent; chocolaty — yet a silver medal winner***
Mount Mary, Pinot Noir Flavoury, good length***
Taltarni Cabernet Sauvignon Several notes. Impressively deep; very good but noted twice as not distinctly varietal on nose or palate. Full, chewy — needed 10 years bottle-age in 1985. Will be interesting to see how the new classics turn out*(***)?
Tyrrell's Vat 70 Cabernet Sauvignon Deep; dry, good flavour, length***
Some whites enjoyed early to mid-1980s:
Orlando, Rhine Riesling Yellow gold; rich, honeyed; medium-sweet, 'fishy', flavoury****
Petaluma, Chardonnay 11 notes, one of my favourite wines, made by Brian Crozer in the hills above Adelaide. I frequently refer to 'Petaluma style', to me typical of the bright yellow buttery, smoky Australian Chardonnays. Glorious fragrance, opulent, charred flavour. At its best up to five years****
Tyrrell's Vat 47 Chardonnay Lemon yellow; fragrant; lightish, high acidity. Attractive but preferred his '76**

1979

Good rainfall, normal growing conditions yet below average production of all varieties.
Penfolds' Grange Hermitage 13% Cabernet Sauvignon. Lovely colour, deep, rich, maturing; low-keyed, meaty, opened up sweetly; medium richness and body, soft tannins, elegant. *New York, Oct 1990*****
Some other reds tasted early to mid-1980s:
Cape Mentelle, Hermitage Deep purple; sweaty saddle, fruit; somewhat sweet, full, fleshy***(*)
Hardy's Claret Classic Bordeaux weight, balance**(*)
Lindeman's 'Rouge Homme' Cabernet Sauvignon Lovely flavour, weight, balance***(*)
Moss Wood, Cabernet Sauvignon Purple; strong rusty nails nose; rich, soft, good flavour though 'iron' character**(*)
Tyrrell's Vat 70 Cabernet Sauvignon Sweet, figgy; fragrant, spicy**(*)
Warrenmang Cabernet Sauvignon Deep; very fragrant, eucalyptus nose and flavour. Dry. Initial impact exciting but a bit one dimensional, palled**
Some whites tasted early to mid-1980s:
Brown Bros' Rhine Riesling Botrytis Orange gold; excellent, honeyed; fairly sweet, rich but firm. Good acidity****
Montrose, Chardonnay Green yellow; lovely, fragrant, estery, lemon-curd nose and taste****
Petaluma Rhine Riesling Grapes from Clare. Appetizing yellow green; delicate fruit, whiff of Riesling kerosene, hint of spice; fairly dry, lovely crisp uplifting flavour. Several notes****
Tyrrell's Vat 47 Pinot Chardonnay Fragrant but sulphury (Murray Tyrrell told me he had sacked the winemaker for over-sulphuring the casks). Very dry, oaky flavour and aftertaste. Good acidity***

1980****

Cool growing season. High reputation. Long-living reds.
Penfolds' Grange Hermitage High percentage Shiraz, only 4% Cabernet Sauvignon. Acidified but unfined. Bottled in 1982. Two recent notes. Dark cherry, intense; peppery at first, better after an hour; despite fig-like flavour, a lean, full and hard tannic finish — reminded me of a '79 Médoc. *Last tasted, New York, Oct 1990***(*)
Some other reds tasted in mid-1980s:
Leo Buring's Pinot Noir Wood-matured. Very good. Nose reminded me of a good Grivot Côte de Nuits; slightly sweet, fullish, excellent flavour, texture, length, finish***(*)
Taltarni, Cabernet Sauvignon Spicy; dry, chewy, chunky(***)
Wakefield River Estate Shiraz and Cabernet Sauvignon. Opaque; eucalyptus; soft, velvety yet tannic***(*)
Wynns' Coonawarra Cabernet Sauvignon Very sweet, smooth though rather tinny Cabernet taste*(**)?
Yalumba, Shiraz In *impériale*: nice weight, texture, touch of iron, earthiness***
Some whites tasted early to mid-1980s:
Brown Bros' Chardonnay Petaluma-style; dry, lightish, pleasant**
Brown Bros' Noble Riesling Golden yellow; oily, mint-leaf; fairly sweet, rather four-square and dull. Hard end. Lacked panache of Napa late-harvest Rieslings. Two notes. *1980***
Brown Bros' Special Limited Production Chardonnay More yellow; gentle, creamy, charred oak and vanilla; dryish, lightly toasted flavour, good crisp acidity****
Leeuwin, Chardonnay High-toned, scented, very oaky; fairly dry, light style, lovely; nutty oaky finish****
Orlando, Premium Chardonnay Glorious colour; rich, buttery, oaky style****
Tyrrell's Vat 1 Hunter Semillon Yellow; harmonious, smoky, walnuts; dry, soft, fully-developed (in 1986), perhaps lacking acidity**
Tyrrell's Vat 47 Chardonnay Nutty; mild, soft, delicious, dry finish***
Yeringberg, Chardonnay Historic vineyard, planted in 1860, uprooted 1920, replanted 1970. Vanilla, fruit; light buttery oaky flavour. Very attractive****

1981**

Drought in South Australia and the east. Hot early vintage. Yields down.
Hill-Smith Estate, Cabernet Sauvignon Sediment annealed to sides of bottle. Medium cherry red; sweet, spicy, whiff of iron; sweet on palate, pleasant to drink by itself, nice weight, crisp fruity flavour. *March 1990****
Penfolds' Grange Hermitage 11% Cabernet Sauvignon. Two notes. Immediately forthcoming nose, extraordinary flavour, very tannic in 1988. Most recently: still deep; strange, appley, Rhône-like nose; berry-like fruit,

gritty texture, tannic. Liked least of entire range at Berenson's tasting. *Last noted, Oct 1990**(*)?

Wynns' Coonawarra Cabernet Sauvignon Nicely matured; gentle, soft, harmonious nose, palate. Deserved its gold medal though lacking persistence of flavour. Ready. *June 1987****

Some other reds tasted in mid-1980s:

McWilliams' Limited Release Coonawarra Cabernet Sauvignon Deep; sweet, caramelly; good fruit, flavour, tannins and acidity***

Meadowbank, Tasmanian Cabernet Made by Hickinbotham. Orange-tinged ruby; grassy, eucalyptus; stylish, tannic*(*)

Mildara, Coonawarra Cabernet Sauvignon Very deep, intense; good fruit; sweetish, full-bodied, good length and finish***(*)

Tyrrell's Hunter Pinot Noir Several notes. Deep when young, broad mature rosy-pink hue in 1986; neutral at first, then raspberry-scented. Flavoury, rounded**

Wynns' Ovens Valley Shiraz Good fruit; soft, pleasant, easy***

Some whites tasted early to mid-1980s:

Evans Family, Coonawarra Botrytis Rhine Riesling 156° Oeschle. Sweet, soft, attractive; lacking follow-through***

Lindeman's, Padthaway Rhine Riesling, Bin 5814 Gold; scented cachous, honey, more like overripe Semillon; sweet, very rich, touch of caramel****

Petaluma, Chardonnay Several notes. Bright yellow; slight oiliness and acetone at first, unknit but exciting. Stylish, flavoury, but needed time to pull itself together**(*)

Primo Estate, Beerenauslese Made from *Botrytis*-innoculated grapes. Weak yellow gold; good *Botrytis* nose though with a raw green undertow; fairly sweet, lightish, good flavour, nice acidity**

1982*****

After the drought of 1981, winter rains restored stressed vineyards. Good growing season, warmth, good fruit. Considered one of the top vintages of the decade.

Brown Bros' Late-picked Muscat Blanc Soft buttercup yellow; assertive, spearmint, grapey, honeyed; fairly sweet but light (10% alcohol), attractive flavour. *Aug 1990****

Penfolds' Bin 707 Cabernet Sauvignon from the Barossa and Coonawarra. Winner of five trophies and 10 gold medals. Beautiful deep ruby; glorious, ripe mulberry scent; sweetish, good weight, soft, velvety, lovely fruit. *March 1988******

Penfolds' Grange Hermitage 6% Cabernet Sauvignon. As usual, 18 months in new American oak hogsheads. Two impressive notes, first in 1987. Still virtually opaque, intense; packed with well-developed fruit, sweet, marvellous vinosity, depth; initially sweet on palate, full-bodied, high extract. Tannin ameliorating. *Last noted at Berenson's Grange vertical, Oct 1990****(**)

Petaluma, Chardonnay Harmonious, oaky, perfect weight, very good flavour in 1985. Seemed more forceful when last tasted. *Feb 1989*****

Tyrrell's Vat 47 Chardonnay Many notes from 1984. Waxy, buttery yellow; sweet, soft, butterscotch nose; medium — not dry, full-flavoured, mint and butter, excellent length. *Last tasted Oct 1987*****

Wynns' Coonawarra John Riddock (limited release) Cabernet Sauvignon Opaque; rich, fruity; sweet, laden with fruit, shapely — a glorious mouthful. *Last noted March 1988*****(*)

Some other reds tasted 1985–87:

Maxwell Wines, Cabernet Shiraz Intense black; magnificent nose; sweet, huge, great length***(**)

Orlando, St Hugo Coonawarra Cabernet Sauvignon Opaque; good, jammy fruit; full, fleshy**(*)

Rosemount, Coonawarra Show Reserve Cabernet Sauvignon Plummy; mulberry; flavour like ruby port but dry, rough, tannic*(**)

Seaview, (100%) Cabernet Sauvignon Soft, wooded; sweetish, soft, velvety, nice tannins, acidity***

Taltarni, Shiraz Deep; crisp, fruit, stylish; raspberry jam flavour, very tannic and raw (in 1987)*(**)?

Wynns' Coonawarra Cabernet Hermitage Soft, too sweet, lovely flavour ruined by bitter rusty nails finish.

Some of the better **Chardonnays** *tasted mid-1980s:*

Wolf Blass Buttercup; old oak; not dry, full, soft, oaky***

McWilliams' Mount Pleasant Good expanding flavour***

Penfolds Buttery, oaky; firm***

Quelltaler, Wood-aged Yellow; classic Australian Chardonnay; assertive, good aftertaste**(*)

Saxonvale Yellow; lovely, fragrant; rich, stylish****

Late-harvest wines all tasted spring 1985:

Leo Buring's Barossa Reserve Riesling Auslese Deep gold; fabulous peachy, buttery, Sauternes-like bouquet; sweet. Outstanding*****

Petaluma, Botrytis Riesling Bottled March 1983. Two notes: Palish lemon yellow; nose like chocolate ice, honeyed, crisp fruit beneath; sweet (13.5% residual sugar), light (9.9% alcohol), fresh, crisp, lovely, Beerenauslese-like****

Rosemount, Rhine Riesling TBA Too deep, too orange; apricots; incredibly sweet, rich, luscious, touch of 'kerosene', citric?****

Yalumba, Heggies Vineyard Botrytis-affected Late-harvest Rhine Riesling Pale lemon; sweet, honeyed, squeeze of lemon; fairly sweet, rather sharp, acidic, but fragrant aftertaste***

1983**

A disastrous start, with severe drought, bush fires and flooding affecting many vineyards. Best in the Hunter Valley.

Lake's Folly, Hunter Cabernet Sauvignon Very distinctive colour, light purple rim; sweet, jammy, tannin and iron; nice weight (12% alcohol), equally distinctive fruitiness, dry acidic finish. *May 1991***

Penfolds' Grange Hermitage 6% Cabernet Sauvignon. Very deep; dusty, peppery fruit, pear core; dry, lean, a bit raw, unimpressive. *New York, Oct 1990**(*)?

Rosemount, Roxburgh Chardonnay Steel-fermented, into barrels March (1983), bottled Jan 1984. Yellow gold; rich, barley-sugar nose; slightly sweet, full (13.5% alcohol), rich, well developed, good acidity. *June 1989****

Taltarni, Shiraz Deep; despite its age, still raw. *Dec 1990*(**)?

Some good reds tasted 1985–87:

Bridgewater Mill, Cabernet Sauvignon Sweet; crisp fruit**(*)

Henschke, Cabernet Sauvignon Opaque; medicinal, figgy; full, rich, velvety***(*)

Krondorf, Cabernet Franc Glorious, tannic; very fruity**(*)

Lindeman's Rouge Homme Pinot Noir Plummy; fragrant, Grivot-like; very good flavour, balance, length****

Penfolds' Bin 707 Cabernet Sauvignon Rich, forthcoming, plummy, lovely; full-bodied, slightly strange tannins, and iron. Good fruit***(**)*

Penfolds' Dalwood Cabernet Shiraz Rhône-like; most agreeable***

Rosemount, Cabernet Sauvignon From the Hunter. Opaque; peppery, Cabernet, cloves; spicy, iron, very tannic**(**)*

Rosemount, Cabernet Sauvignon From Coonawarra. Ruby; more classic, fruity; better flavour and balance, good length, finish***(**)*

Wyndham Estate, Hunter Bin 444 Deep; sweet, jammy Cabernet Sauvignon aroma; rich, fullish, soft***

Some good whites tasted 1985–87:

Wolf Blass, Chardonnay Too deep, gold; lovely, oaky, waxy; glorious flavour, excellent finish and acidity****

Cooper's Creek, Fumé Blanc Piquant, tom-cats, gooseberry and cardboard; dry, clean***

Houghton, Frankland River Chardonnay Yellow; oaky, exciting; good flavour, length****

Matthew Lang, Fumé Blanc Very pale, green; dry, light, acidic. Remarkably Loire-like**

Leeuwin, Chardonnay Palish; pineapple; lightish style, nice fruit, some delicacy***

Lillydale, Chardonnay Palish; lovely, fragrant; perfect flavour, length****

Orlando, St Hilary Chardonnay Buttercup; hefty, buttery***

Rothbury, Cowra Chardonnay Waxy, lemon; soft, easy Petaluma style***

Rothbury, Semillon Yellow gold; estery, rich, honeyed, like Suduiraut; very sweet (270° Baumé), full-bodied (14.8% alcohol), rich, fat, slightly volatile. A Hunter TBA!

Saltram's Mamra Brook Chardonnay Sweet, rich, powerful***

S Smith's Pewsey Vale Botrytis Rhine Riesling Amber gold; mint, touch of caramel; sweet, some fat yet light style, very fragrant***

Tyrrell's Chardonnay (Presumably Vat 47) Lovely colour; fresh, fruity; some fat, delicious****

1984****

"Ideally cool during ripening period with late summer rain" sounds paradoxical to European ears until one remembers heat, drought, bush fires.... A good year, wet in the Hunter. Many tasted, the wide range of producers and styles summarised in the following notes.

Wolf Blass, Bilyara, Brown Label (Shiraz) 'Wolfie' deserves his success: a sweetish, soft, easy wine to drink, with vinosity and judicious use of oak. *Nov 1988****

Chateau Tahbilk, Shiraz Dark cherry; forthcoming, peppery, jammy; curious flavour of violets, raspberry, iron. Slightly sweet. *Nov 1988*** in its way.*

Leeuwin, Chardonnay Two recent notes: straw gold; smoky, oaky, "blancmange" noted both times, some spice; slightly sweet though balanced by good acidity, full-flavoured, waxy, almost Semillon-like. *Oct 1989****

Penfolds' Grange Hermitage 95% Shiraz, 5% Cabernet Sauvignon. Grown in Magill, Kalimna, Clare, Barossa and Southern Vales. Very deep; peppery, good fruit, depth; very sweet for a 'dry red', full-bodied, good fruit, tannins and acidity but finishes abruptly like a '43 Médoc. *At Berenson's Grange vertical, Oct 1990***(*) Now to 2010.*

Rosemount, Botrytis Semillon Unreleased, unlabelled. Apricot amber; warm, waxy, honeyed with crisp fruit support; sweet, assertive, long hard finish. Needed time. *July 1988**(**)*

Rosemount, Roxburgh Chardonnay Five notes from 1985. Deepened in colour, buttercup yellow. Its initial vanilla, curds-and-whey nose now fully developed, buttery, oaky; flavour to match, with good body and length. A bit austere. *Last tasted June 1989****

Of the '84 **Cabernet Sauvignons** *tasted 1985–87, I found the following attractive:*

Brown Bros' Koombala Minty, pleasing lightish style, spicy***

Lindeman's Limestone Ridge Coonawarra Deep, attractive, shapely, with lively acidity****

Lindeman's St George's Vineyard, Coonawarra Spicy, vanilla; dry, lean, flavoury, tannic****(*)*

Petaluma Classic, stylish***(*)*

Of the '84 **Pinot Noirs** *tasted 1985–87:*

Yarra Burn Fragrant, violets; lightish soft, oaky Pinot flavour***

Rothbury Beetroot; flavoury**

Two **Shiraz***:*

Brand's Laira, Old Vineyard Opaque; huge, sweet, rich, great length****

Penfolds' Magill Estate Lovely fruit; sweetish, elegant****

Of the 36 other **Chardonnays** *tasted 1985–87 many were disappointing. The best notes:*

Wolf Blass Toasted oak, rich****

Craigmoor Soft, lovely flavour, length, aftertaste****

Edinglassie Roxburgh Vineyard Yellow gold; glorious, butter, honey; flavour to match*****

Andrew Garrett The first vintage tasted. Dry but rich, oaky***

Hill-Smith Estate Grown high in Barossa ranges. In Nevers oak quarter casks six months. Fragrant, spicy; very dry, fresh***

Stanley Leasingham Estery; silky texture, excellent flavour, length****

Peter Lehmann Very fragrant, lean, oaky***

Lillydale Full, estery; fragrant, floral, superb*****

Lindeman's, Padthaway Pineapple, limousin oak; lovely flavour, fruit, length, acidity****

Robert & Butler Pineapple, peaches; flavour, stylish***

Rothbury Cowra, Original Paddock Full, good acidity and aftertaste***

Seppelt's Show Chardonnay Fragrant, stylish****

Tulloch Yellow, waxy, dry, oaky***

Tyrrell's Vat 47 One of my favourites. Long, dry, mouthfilling****

Of the late-picked the following are just some of the many, to show that advances had been made by the mid-1980s:

De Bortoli, Beerenauslese Riesling Very Sauternes-like nose; sweet, classic****

De Bortoli, Beerenauslese Traminer Yellow gold; peachy; sweet, full-flavoured, Gewurztraminer cachou fragrance*****

Krondorf Special Late Harvest Riesling Beautifully balanced****

Peter Lehmann, Riesling Auslese Medium-sweet; peachy nose and taste, lovely****

Petaluma, Botrytis Coonawarra Riesling Gold Cap Honeyed, Tokay-like; sweet, soft, lovely****

St Hubert, Rhine Riesling, Beerenauslese Sweet, good flavour, acidity****

Seppelt's Rhine Riesling Auslese Lovely, ripe; almost too sweet but good acidity****

1985****

Another good vintage. Unusually cool dry summer. Rain delayed vintage in the Barossa. Chardonnays picked mid-

March, Cabernet Sauvignon mid-April.
Wolf Blass, President's Selection, Cabernet Sauvignon Deep ruby; rich fruit, peppery; sweet entry, dry finish, full body and flavour. Rich. *Oct 1989****(*)*
Brown Bros' Floral and Orange Muscat A new dessert wine, fairly sweet, light, original, attractive flavour, good acidity. *Oct 1989****
'The Hardy Collection', Padthaway Rhine Riesling Beerenauslese Palish gold, distinct spritz; barley-sugar; sweet, full, rich, fat, lovely. *Oct 1989*****
Lake's Folly Chardonnay Max Lake is a latter-day pioneer. If he did not discover Coonawarra, he surely exposed it; his was one of the first successful Australian Chardonnays, and certainly the first I tasted. Lake's '85 Hunter Chardonnay is extremely good: very bright yellow; fragrant, buttery fruity nose and taste. Spicy. Good acidity and aftertaste. *Last noted Dec 1988*****
Montrose, Shiraz Lively; positive; attractive. *July 1989****
Penfolds' Grange Hermitage Almost entirely from Shiraz, only 1% Cabernet Sauvignon. Deep; a bit varnishy at first but good fruit, harmonious; dryish, nice weight, style, texture. Elegant. A relatively quick developer? *New York, Oct 1990***(*) Now to 2010.*
Penfolds' Magill Estate Shiraz Deep; crisp, spicy fruit; fleshy, walnuts, fullish, fragrant. *Dec 1988**(**)*
Petaluma, Coonawarra 70% Cabernet Sauvignon, 30% Merlot, vinified separately in new Nevers oak. Still youthful; good fruit; medium dryness and body, crisp, dry spicy oak finish. *July 1989**(**)*
Rosemount, Roxburgh Chardonnay Hard, closed, dry, full, firm but lacking fruit. Much preferred the Show Reserve Chardonnay tasted in 1986–87. *Last noted June 1989**(*)??*
Rouge Homme, Coonawarra Cabernet Sauvignon Deep; hefty, full of fruit but lacking zing and style. *Sept 1989***
Rouge Homme, Shiraz/Cabernet Sauvignon Deep, rich; gloriously ripe fruit; soft, touch of iron, very agreeable. *July 1990**(**)*
Wynns' Coonawarra Estate Cabernet Sauvignon Deep, velvety; fragrant; distinctly sweet, fullish body (13% alcohol), lean but very fruity. Good, dry, refreshing finish. *Aug 1990***(*)*
Of other '85s tasted 1986–87, outstanding:
Petaluma, Chardonnay Crisp, lean, flavoury, long***(*)
Seppelt's 'Black Label' From Padthaway, Barossa, Langhorne Creek. Lively ruby; very fragrant; fruity, stylish***(*)

1986*****

Excellent climatic conditions. Cool dry summer. One of the driest and latest-ever harvests. Long-lasting wines of power and balance.
Coldstream Hills, Chardonnay A relatively new wine from James Halliday's Yarra Ridge Vineyard. Palish yellow; waxy, scented varietal nose, held well; dry, full, a bit austere and four-square, attractive smoky, oaky flavour. *April 1991**(**)*
Penfolds' Grange Hermitage Relatively high percentage of Cabernet Sauvignon (13%). Very deep; strange, holding back, brambly fruit; very sweet, immense, packed with soft fruit, high extract masking high tannins. Pétrus-like. *New York, Oct 1990*(****) 1996–2020*
Penfolds' Shiraz Bin 28 Deep, rich; sweet; soft, rich, lovely. *July 1990***(*)*
Petaluma, Chardonnay 20% grown in home vineyard, Piccadilly Valley, 40% Clare, 40% in Coonawarra. One year in Limousin and Vosges oak. Distinctive yellow; touch of vaseline, lemon, waxy Chardonnay, charred oak, pineapple; positive entry, good mid-palate, dry finish, with lip-licking acidity. *May 1991***(*)*
Rosemount, Roxburgh Chardonnay Several notes. Powerful when young. An old-fashioned heavyweight: yellow gold; cool, fresh nose opening opulently; medium dry, fullish body, lovely combination of fruit and oak, good length, charred vanilla aftertaste. *June 1989*****
Tyrrell's Vat 47 Chardonnay Glorious expanding and expansive flavour in Oct 1987. Buttercup and gold; oaky, spicy, lanolin; assertive charred flavour, good length, dry finish. *Last tasted Nov 1989*****
Other particularly notable wines tasted in 1987–88:
Andrew Garrett's Chardonnay Buttery, oaky, opulent nose and flavour. Good length, aftertaste****
Heggie's Vineyard, Barossa Botrytis-affected Late-harvest Riesling Lemon gold; orange blossom and peach; sweet, glorious flavour, barley-sugar****
Stephen Hickinbotham's Anakie Shiraz Deep, plummy; rich, jammy; good rich fruit, good length, stylish, agreeable***(*)

1987****

The fourth and last cool, dry summer following spring rains. A late harvest, perfect grapes.
Some marvellous **Chardonnays** *noted first:*
Evans Family Vineyard Pronounced yellow; deliciously buttery, pineapple, oak; dryish, spicy cloves, touch of end bitterness. *April 1990**(*)*
Andrew Garrett First tasted Oct 1988. Masses of notes as I bought several cases. Lovely yellow; vanilla, pineapple, deft touch of oak; rich, assertive, buttery oaky flavour and aftertaste. Delicious. *Last tasted Oct 1990***(*)*
Lake's Folly Buttery; opened up; dry, lovely flavour, good acidity. *Oct 1989*****
Lindeman's Padthaway Highly polished yellow; very fresh, fruity, no oakiness; sweet, fullish, touch of fat, lovely. *Last tasted Nov 1988***(*)*
Lindeman's Victoria, Bin 65 Rather Sauvignon Blanc-like aroma; soft, flavoury, curious. *Nov 1987***
Rosemount, Giant's Creek Pale; fresh; dry, crisp, Chablis-like. *June 1989***
Rosemount, Roxburgh Buttery; good nose, touch of oak; fairly dry, full flavoured, rich, slightly hard finish. *Last tasted April 1990***(*)*
Rothbury Estate Reserve Bottling First tasted Nov 1988. Now fully developed, buttery yellow; glorious, sweet, honeyed, fat, waxy bouquet; distinct touch of sweetness, luscious, plump, rounded. *Last tasted May 1991*****
Seppelt's Oak-Matured Pale yellow; delicate oak, vanilla; dryish, lovely, good acidity, fragrant aftertaste. *Dec 1988***(*)*
Tolley's Palish; still immature; dryish, clean, attractive. *Jan 1989**(*)*
Other grape varieties:
Brown Bros' Chenin Blanc Waxy green; fairly dry, fullish, very flavoury. *Oct 1989****
Cape Mentelle, Semillon and Sauvignon Blanc The classic white Bordeaux mix. Slightly waxy, harmonious but 'cold'. Dry, fullish, Semillon uppermost, better as it warmed up. *Oct 1989***
Len Evans' Rothbury Vineyards, Semillon Chardonnay Good waxy yellow; low-keyed, soft, scented, peaches, oak; bone dry, lightish (11.5%), rather austere. *July 1990*(*)?*

Heggie's Vineyard, Adelaide Hills Cabernet Sauvignon Deep; good fruit, tannin and lively acidity. Very attractive. *May 1991****

Hill-Smith, Botrytis Semillon Palish amber; damp cardboard; sweet, rich raisiny flavour, good acidity. *July 1990****

Leeuwin, Riesling Pale, green; vanilla, grassy, acidic; very dry, light, short, one-dimensional. *Oct 1989**

Petaluma, Rhine Riesling Grown in Clare in the coolest of four cool vintages. Bottled Oct 1987. Slightly scented; fairly dry, pleasant, fresh. *Jan 1990***

Rosemount, Pinot Noir Medium, immature, soft Pinot appearance; almost Gamay-like aroma and flavour. Touch of strawberry; dry, flavoury, slightly bitter finish. *June 1989**(*)*

Taltarni, Fumé Blanc Scented; dryish, powerful, a bit too assertive. *Oct 1989*(*)*

1988***

Wet spring. Exceptionally hot summer leading to unusually early harvest, though damaging rainfall in the Hunter. Few tasted as yet.

Coldstream Hills, Chardonnay 100% Yarra Valley, hand-picked. Cold fermentation in stainless steel, finished in Vosges oak *barriques*. Prolonged lees contact. Palish yellow; lemon, pineapple, oak, lightly honeyed; full flavour, assertive yet modest 11.8% alcohol. Hard finish. Will benefit from bottle-age. *June 1991**(**)?*

Coldstream Hills, Four Vineyards Pinot Noir Medium-deep; scented, curious, depth; fairly sweet, full-bodied, rich, meaty, touch of iron and acidity. Better the following night. Needs time. *May 1989**(*)? Say 1994–99.*

Krondorf, Late-picked Muscat Extremely minty; medium-sweet, very scented but raw. *July 1990**(*)?*

Penfolds' Barrel-fermented Chardonnay Buttery yellow; blancmange; medium-dry, full body, flavour, very oaky. *Oct 1990**(*)*

Petaluma, Botrytis Riesling Pale; spearmint and honey; rather like a Gewurztraminer Beerenauslese. Very good acidity. Delicious. *Oct 1989*****

Rothbury, Semillon Palish; attractive, buttery, flavoury enough, soft, easy waxy, short. *June 1991***

1989

After five good vintages, terrible growing conditions, rain disrupting flowering, winds, summer heat-wave, downpours at harvest time. All areas affected.

Thomas Hardy, 'Bird Series' Riesling Gewurztraminer Blend Lovely, fragrant, excellent acidity giving Gewurztraminer a lift. *July 1990****

Henry Lindeman, Traminer Riesling Soft, spicy Traminer nose; firm yet soft Riesling flavour. *July 1990****

Penfolds' Bin 202 Gewurztraminer Riesling Very attractive aroma and flavour. Spicy finish. *July 1990****

Rothbury, Export Shiraz Extremely deep; marvellous fruit; lovely flavour, dry, brambly, great style, good tannin and acidity. *April 1991(****)*

Rothbury, Reserve Shiraz Opaque; nose more restrained, brambly; medium dry, full-bodied, very fleshy, attractive, violet oaky aftertaste. *April 1991(****)*

Tolley's Pedare Late-harvest Muscat Very pale, green-tinged; grassy, minty nose and taste. Medium-sweet, light, easy, short. *Jan 1991***

Wynns' Coonawarra Chardonnay Good colour; Chardonnay and oak; dryish, fairly full-bodied, good flavour, a bit severe. Needs time. *Sept 1990**(*)*

1990****

High quality, large production.

Mornington Vineyards, Chardonnay New vineyard. One of the first wines. Only 100 cases produced. Bright yellow; youthful, mouthwatering, vanilla and peardrops; dryish, nutty, oaky, lean, touch of immature coarseness, good acidity. Perhaps lacking length. *Jan 1991(***)?*

Rothbury, Barrel-fermented Chardonnay Bottled Sept (1990). Positive yellow gold; waxy, herbaceous, minty, buttery; sweet, soft, fat, mild. Enough acidity. Dry finish. *April 1991(***)*

1991****

Early harvest, small crop due to drought and heat. Particularly successful reds. Cask samples tasted in London with Len Evans, Chairman of Rothbury.

Evans Family, Pinot Noir From block of vines below the Evans' very original house 'Loggerheads', near Rothbury. Very sweet jammy fruit; medium dryness and body, soft yet very tannic. *April 1991(***)?*

Rothbury, Barrel-fermented Chardonnay On lees for 12 months. Fairly deep yellow, still cloudy; sweet, rich, honeyed, overpowering; sweet on palate, soft – its malolactic fermentation over, already an oaky flavour, fat, spicy aftertaste. *April 1991(****)*

Rothbury, Brokenback Vineyard Cabernet Sauvignon Rothbury's best vintage for red since 1965. Opaque; smooth yet two-part, blackberry, intense violets; delicious, rather piquant, original flavour. Slightly figgy fruit. Leathery tannins. *April 1991(****)*

Rothbury, Reserve Chardonnay Part barrel-fermented in new wood. No 'malo', also cloudy; leaner, more youthful pineapple; fairly powerful, nice shape, short, dry finish. *April 1991(***)?*

Rothbury, Shiraz Opaque, intense purple; restrained, minty, bramble; enormous, port-like flavour, loads of tannin and acidity, good aftertaste. *April 1991(****)*

Other WINES

NEW ZEALAND

The land of butter and sheep is now the land of wine. Unlike Australia's, its wine industry is new. Timely too, for vine growers and winemakers can draw on recent global experience without wasting too much time and money experimenting. In short, the pioneering has already been done. New Zealand only has to come to terms with its own climate – and vineyard sites.

Despite many invitations I have not yet been to New Zealand, nor, as it is not my business, have I attended the big tastings organised in recent years by the promotionally-minded official and trade bodies. For these reasons my notes are limited and arbitrary. Nevertheless it has been interesting, at any rate for me, to observe – if from afar – the progress from the early 1970s through the increasingly confident and successful 1980s. The reds, impressive but as yet relatively untried, have insufficient track record; the whites, all made to be drunk young, are immediately attractive, though Chenin Blanc, which seemed such a good starter, seems to have fallen by the wayside, overtaken by the more fashionable and dependable Sauvignon Blanc and, latterly, by Chardonnay.

It is significant that the 1991 *Decanter* magazine Vintage Guide is the first issue to report on New Zealand. New Zealand has come of age!

1970

Almost pre-historic.

Nobilo's Collector's Cabernet Sauvignon The earliest vintage tasted: deep, plummy, mature; strange, stewed, like boiled milk, yet harmonious; dry, medium weight. Showing its age. *Nov 1987.*

1975

Montana, Pinotage Another pioneer. Palish, fully mature; rich, sweet, smoky nose; medium sweetness and body, flavoury, easy, short. *Sept 1987***

1976

Cooks, Cabernet Sauvignon Picked on my birthday, 2nd May. Purple; immature colour, nose, taste. Quite good fruit. Dry, light style, flavoury. *April 1980. Then(***)*

Montana, Cabernet Sauvignon The first vintage from the Marlborough vineyard, planted 1973. Youthful, raw, lacking intensity in 1983. Piquant yet mature varietal nose; light, flavoury, jammy, short. *Last tasted Sept 1987***

1978

Faltering footsteps.

Cooks, Te-Kauwhata Pinot Gris Odd colour; curious, unattractive. *Sept 1984.*

Cooks, Matawhero Gewurztraminer Raisiny, aromatic nose and taste. Dryish, light, clean. Clearly an early step in the right direction. *Tasted 1982 and 1984****

Nobilo's 'Classic Claret' Cabernet Sauvignon Plummy; stewed; dry, rather artificial. Certainly not classic. *Nov 1982.*

Nobilo's Pinotage Already mature; broad, jammy Pinot-like nose and taste. Dry. Finish like red ink. *Nov 1982.*

1979

Cooks, Te-Keuwhata Pinot Gris Picked March 26, bottled Sept 27 (1979). An improvement: delicious, scented aroma; dry, austere, short but flavoury. *Nov 1982***

Corbans, Henderson Chenin Blanc Good colour; stewed; slightly sweet, good varietal flavour and acidity. My first taste of what proved to be a successful NZ grape. *Sept 1984****

1980

Generally average for white and red.

Cooks, Gewurztraminer Very yellow; lovely, spicy aroma and taste. Dry. Another early varietal success. (Their Traminer Riesling appley and dull.) *Sept 1984.*

1985****

Generally above average, some excellent.
Babich, Henderson Valley Chardonnay Yellow gold; high-toned, Australian Petaluma-like nose and flavour. Slightly spritz. *July 1986****
Delegat's Proprietor's Reserve Chardonnay Positive yellow; rich, waxy; dry, nicely made. *Nov 1987****
Montana, Fairhall Estate Cabernet Sauvignon Deep, plummy; sweet, vinous, slightly jammy, mint leaf, asparagus; fullish, very attractive, fruity but, somehow, odd. *May 1988***

1986*****

The pace hots up. The first — for me — top Cabernet tasted, and some excellent Chardonnays.
Babich, Hawkes Bay Sauvignon Blanc Pleasant, grassy; dryish, distinctly fleshy (unlike Loire), blackcurrant taste. *May 1988****
Cloudy Bay, Chardonnay My first exposure to a new very fashionable winery. And a good start: pleasant colour, long legs; very pronounced varietal flavour, good length and endtaste. *May 1988***(*)*
Matua Valley, Cabernet Sauvignon (plus small percentage Merlot) Opaque; crisp, very good, iron-tinged, excellent varietal aroma and flavour. Rich, full-bodied, good length, spicy. *May 1988(****) Will be interesting to see how this develops in bottle.*
Matua Valley, Yates Estate Chardonnay Youthful fragrant varietal nose and taste. Dry, lean, oaky aftertaste. *Presented by the indefatigable Margaret Harvey, now an MW, Nov 1987*(***)*
Matua Valley, Late-Harvest Muscat Fairly sweet, lightish, pleasant, cachou-scented Muscat. Good acidity. *Last tasted May 1988*** just.*
Morton Estate, Hawkes Bay Chardonnay Deep buttercup yellow; rich, vanilla; fullish, very oaky, flavoury, attractive. My sort of wine. *Sept 1988***(*)*
Nobilo's Chardonnay Palish; soft, creamy; good flavour, some oak. *May 1988****

1987*****

Some excellent reds and outstanding whites.
Some **Chardonnays**:
Collard, Rothesay Vineyard Yellow gold; pineapple and oak; massive, charred vanilla flavour, dry finish. Impressive but too assertive. *Nov 1989**(*)*
Kumeu River Yellow; very good, slightly scented, oaky; very attractive smoky oaky flavour and aftertaste. *March 1990*****
Noble Hunter, Botrytis Amber gold; honeyed, peachy; sweet, lovely flavour and acidity. *A superb sample half-bottle brought by Margaret Harvey. At dinner with Dr Norman Burrows, July 1991*****
Stoneleigh (part of Cooks) Petaluma style. Pleasant fruit, weight. *May 1988****
Several **Sauvignon Blancs**:
Corbans, Marlborough Yellow; sweet, honeyed; neither dry nor acidic enough, but a pleasant grassy flavour. *May 1990***
Delegat's Hawkes Bay Pale; good varietal aroma; rich, ripe, grassy, raw blackcurrant flavour. *May 1988****
Matua Valley, Brownlie Bay Estate Dryish, light, clean, grassy Sauvignon character. Adequate acidity. *April 1988****
Morton Estate, Hawkes Bay Very pale; bone dry. *May 1988****
Nobilo's, Hawkes Bay Hefty, flowery, oaky, dryish. *May 1989****
One **Semillon**:
Selaks Unusually scented, more like Sauvignon Blanc, good acidity, one track. *May 1988***

1988* *to* ****

North Island, including Hawkes Bay, hit by cyclone, affecting quality and quantity. Excellent reds and whites in South Island districts.
Babich, Hawkes Bay Sauvignon Blanc Fairly pronounced 'tom-cats' aroma; dry, firm, good flavour and acidity. *June 1990****
Nobilo's Gewurztraminer Yellow, too deep, too sweet. Hefty Gewürztraminer varietal aroma, a bit too plump, flavoury but lacking grace. *Sept 1988**
Redwood Valley Estates, Late-Harvest Riesling Pale; excellent peachy ripe Riesling nose and taste, fairly sweet, very good acidity. *May 1991****

1989*****

Outstanding vintage, overall best of the decade for whites and reds, all districts.
Cloudy Bay, Sauvignon Blanc First tasted Oct 1989 at the opening dinner of the Wine & Food Society Convention in Hong Kong. Very pale; almost exaggerated minty 'tom-cats' Sauvignon aroma and taste. Fairly dry, flavoury, short. Next, blind at a III Form Club tasting. Then on Christmas Day at home. *Last noted Dec 1989****
Montana, Chardonnay Palish; good nose; medium dryness and body, very good flavour, fair acidity. *Sept 1990****
Vidal, Hawkes Bay Private Bin Chardonnay Palish; mild grapey aroma, touch of vanilla; fairly dry, perfect weight, nutty Chardonnay flavour, good finish. *Last tasted June 1991***(*)*

1990** *to* ****

Moderately good vintage. Reds variable; some excellent whites.
Aotea, Hawkes Bay Sauvignon Blanc Pale; lightly scented varietal aroma; dry, light, crisp, refreshing acidity. *July 1991****
Redwood Valley Estate, Chardonnay Palish, slightly straw-tinged; young, scented Chardonnay; dry, nice weight, firm, steely yet good fruit and discreet oak. *July 1991**(**)*
Redwood Valley Estate, Rhine Riesling Palish; hard, crumbly, unknit; medium-sweet, lovely grapey flavour, long sweet finish. *July 1991****

1991****

An above average vintage, according to Bob Campbell, the first New Zealand Master of Wine. Good growing conditions, a dry summer (Jan and Feb) but autumn (March, April) very wet in Hawkes Bay and other areas. Extended ripening period resulted in good acid levels, but Sauvignon Blanc and Chardonnay wide-ranging in quality, the best first-rate.

THE CAPE

South Africa has come in from the cold. Soon we will be able to drink, with fewer inhibitions, some of the good, and excellent value, wines made in one of the most beautiful wine lands in the world.

South African wines are not 'New World'. The wine farms established in the 17th century pre-date most of the châteaux of Bordeaux. Cape wines, Constantia in particular, were both fashionable and expensive in the 18th century. Leaving history aside, post-1945 witnessed successes mainly with good, and good value, 'sherry'. Table wine improvements, as in Australia, are a relatively modern phenomenon.

South Africa can be very hot, but vintages do vary. Perversely the less good and certainly the cooler years, seem — judging mainly from verticals, of Pinotage in particular — more satisfactory.

Most of my notes were made in the Cape in 1977 and, somewhat more up-to-date and relevant, in 1987; also, most recently, at an excellent tasting laid on in London by the Cape Independent Wine Makers Guild. For recent vintage weather/quality reports I am indebted to John Platter.

c 1750

Constantia Highly prized, highly priced: one of the classic first growths of the 18th century. Two bottles, different sources, tasted in Oct 1985, one a pure amber; earthy, chocolaty nose like an old Tinta Negra Mole madeira; fairly sweet, nice weight, nutty, sherry-like flavour, excellent acidity; the other a deeper tawny, more cloudy; similar nose and taste, meatier, very rich, tangy, like an old Bual. A third, provenance the Hopetoun House cellar (sold at Christie's, May 1967): characteristic dumpy straight-sided bottle with tall, swelling neck. Excellent level. Deep amber, olive-green rim, very rich legs, slightly murky; distinctly spicy, gingery, rich, tangy; sweet, powerful, assertive, very high acidity, almost burning finish. *Last tasted at a Rodenstock rare wine tasting, Sept 1987. At best*****

1940

Ch Libertas Black cherry; glorious old nose despite whiff of mercaptan; sweet, full-bodied (over 14% alcohol), rich, fat, singed taste. Good tannin and acidity. *At Stellenbosch Farmers Winery, Dec 1987****

1945****

Stellenbosch Farmers, Cabernet Sauvignon Top vintage colour; singed, spicy bouquet that held fragrantly in the glass; dry, rich, firm, tannic. *March 1977, then***** *Doubtless still good.*

1959

Ch Libertas Fairly deep, mature; forthcoming, crisp, cherry-like acidity; fairly dry, spicy, jammy, citrus — slightly volatile. Twice the same day, one at a tasting, another at dinner. *Dec 1987***

1961

Zonnenbloem, Cabernet Very deep, rich, mature; low-keyed varnishy; dryish, fairly full-bodied, good fruit, tannic. *Dec 1987****

1963

Lanzerac, Pinotage Lovely old Cape farm, now a hotel. Deep; opened up gradually, sweet, leathery fruit; nice weight, elegant, good texture. *Dec 1987*****

Ch Libertas Open, mature; lovely, firm, fig-like fruit; light style, crisp, flavoury, short dry acidic finish. *Dec 1987****

Rustenberg, Dry Red (50% Cabernet Sauvignon, 50% Cinsault) Medium, mature; fragrant, high-toned, stylish; nice weight — like a '55 claret, gentle faded fruit, dry finish. *Dinner at Peter Devereux's, Nov 1987*****

1966

Alto Estate Opaque; deep, rich, port-like nose; dry, fullish. *Tasted with Dr Julius Laszlo at the Bergkeller, Dec 1987****

1967

Alto Estate Deep; rich, unusual, like clover honey; sweetish, full-bodied, fat, medicinal. *Dec 1987***

1969

Nederberg, Cabernet Sauvignon, Special Selection Fine, deep; fragrant; dry, crisp yet opulent flavour. *Dinner in Stellenbosch, Dec 1987*****

Nederberg, Edelkur Bottled Nov 1969. The first vintage tasted of this magnificent *Botrytis* Chenin Blanc. *March 1977*****

1970***

KWV, Pinotage First tasted March 1977: deep, plummy, dumb, rather neutral. 10 years worked wonders: harmonious, fragrant; medium-sweet, fullish, rather fig-like fruit, high extract, rich yet tannic. Certainly impressive. *Last tasted Dec 1987****(*)

Ch Libertas Translucent; vegetal; fleshy, soft fruit, a bit lacking. *Dec 1987***

1971***

A good but relatively light vintage judging by a vertical in 1977.

KWV, Pinotage Intense; muffled, root-like; sweetish, sinewy, good flavour and length. *Dec 1987****

Nederburg, Cabernet Sauvignon Mature; like fresh paint; positive, interesting. *Sept 1984***

1972** *to* ****

Hot vintage. Soft, flabby whites; good to excellent reds.

Groote Constantia, Shiraz The most famous old estate in the Cape, behind Table Mountain. Lovely colour; crisp, slightly peppery; medium dry, lighter, softer, easier than expected. Lovely though lacking length. *Dining in Stellenbosch, Dec 1987****

KWV, Pinotage Deep; four-square, stodgy, clumsy, short. *Dec 1987**

Oude Libertas, Pinotage Ruby; gentle, sweet, singed; jammy flavour, swingeingly tannic acid finish though lingering aftertaste. *Nov 1987***?

Zonnenbloem, Cabernet Delicate, oyster shells, good fruit support; lovely, slightly singed flavour, good length, tannins. *Dec 1987****

1973***

Cool vintage.
KWV, Pinotage Medium, fully mature, orange tinge; Bordeaux-like, harmonious; slightly sweet, lightish though good vinosity, nice texture, sinewy, flavoury, good length. Perfect drinking. *Dec 1987*****
Vergenoegd (a name that will not catch on), **Cabernet Sauvignon** Deep ruby; blackberry-like aroma; dry, vigorous, showing little age. *Dec 1987**(**)*
Vergenoegd, Shiraz Fairly powerful, rich, fleshy. *Dec 1987***

1974* *to* *****

Average whites but some great reds. Cabernet Sauvignon particularly successful.
KWV, Cabernet Sauvignon Sound, soft, fleshy. *Dec 1987***
KWV, Pinotage Fragrant; lean, sinewy, elegant. Drinking well. *Dec 1987****
Nederberg, Cabernet Sauvignon (Also 10% Shiraz, 25% Cinsault and Pinotage.) First tasted at the estate, March 1977: plummy; full-flavoured. More recently impressively deep; citrus touch; slightly sweet, rustic, overripe flavour, soft, beguiling. *Last tasted Dec 1987****
Overgaauw, Cabernet Sauvignon (10% Cinsault) First tasted March 1977: nose unknit; rich, ripe, taste of burnt iron. A decade later: ruby; soft, sweet, nice fruit. Medium sweetness and body, soft, fleshy, 'rusty', iodine endtaste. *Last tasted Dec 1987**** in its way.*
Zonnenbloem, Pinotage Thick, plummy; assertive, singed, hefty fruit underlay; massive, powerful (14.7% alcohol), raw tannins reminding me of Underberg bitters. Representing 'the unacceptable face' of Cape reds! *Dec 1987*(*)*

1975**

Average.
KWV, Pinotage Meat extract yet lively fruit; sweet, rich, good length. *Dec 1987****
Nederberg, Cabernet Sauvignon Consistently good winemaking. Fragrant; very attractive. *Sept 1984*****

1976****

Moderate whites, excellent reds.
KWV, Pinotage Deep but orange-tinged; sweet, warm, flavoury, good fruit and texture. *Dec 1987****
Meerlust, Cabernet Sauvignon A beautiful Cape farm estate benefiting from a maritime climate, claiming the heaviest dew in the world: 14 inches. Three notes, first at the estate in March 1977: surprisingly not very deep, high-toned; dry, still raw. Next, in 1982: good flavour and weight but very tannic. More recently, a good but not obvious (like California) Cabernet character, still hard, peppery; sagged in middle with severe iron/tobacco finish. Needs bottle-age. *Last noted dining at Miller Howe, Windemere, April 1983**(*)?*
Nederburg Edelkur Three notes. First tasted from the cask, March 1977: fabulous, pure gold colour; nose like a TBA; intensely sweet, rich. More recently: rich, viscous, orange tawny with green rim; fabulously rich, honeyed nose; sweet, verging on unctuous, lovely ripe grapey taste, lively acidity. *Last tasted April 1984******
Rustenburg (Two-thirds Cabernet Sauvignon, one-third Cinsault) Palish, weak mature rim; cheesy, fruity; slightly sweet, light weight and style, soft, amenable, mouth-drying finish. *Stellenbosch, Dec 1987****
Uitkyk, Carlonet A late 18th-century town house on a farm. Pronounced 'oatcake'. The owner, von Carlowitz, blended Cabernet and Cinsault and called the wine Carlonet. Palish, mature; slightly jammy; dry. *At New World pre-sale tasting, Christie's, Sept 1984***

1977* *to* **

Very wet at harvest time. Poor reds, passable whites.
KWV, Pinotage Orange-tinged; the first corky, the other stalky, rot? Like a wet dish cloth; light, curiously elegant but little to it. *Dec 1987.*

1978*** *to* ****

Good vintage, particularly for red wines.
Allesverloren, Cabernet Sauvignon Another 18th-century estate well north of Paarl. Attractive fruit, smoky, high quality; more like a rich burgundy. Tannic. *Feb 1988**(**)*
KWV Pinotage Sweet, jammy, like syrup of figs though leaner than expected. At this stage of the vertical tasting I reckoned that Pinotage was best made in cooler summers. *Dec 1987****
Meerendal, Pinotage Another old estate rather off the beaten track and making good wine only since the late 1940s. Opaque; rich, powerful, full of fruit. *Dec 1987***(*)*

1979** *to* ***

Cool growing year. Generally better reputation for reds.
KWV, Pinotage Confirming my opinion of the advantages of a cool year. Fragrant, appealing fruit; nice weight, elegant. *Dec 1987*****
de Wetshof, Noble Late Harvest (50% Riesling, 50% Chenin Blanc) Buttery gold; pure clover honey; sweet, firm, crisp. Touch of spritz. *July 1981***(*)*

1980** *to* ****

Very hot summer. Extremely ripe grapes. Dry whites average, lacking acidity. Reds very good.
KWV, Pinotage Deep, thick appearance; sweet, ripe figs, varnishy; full-bodied (13.7% alcohol), assertive, strange, port-like. *Dec 1987****
Nederburg, Edelkur Gunter Brozel continuing his brilliant winemaking, with naturally *Botrytis*-affected grapes. Beautiful amber, slight tartrate deposit; heavenly bouquet, rich honeyed *Botrytis*, touch of cinnamon, more scented than a German Beerenauslese; sweet, lovely flavour, high acidity balancing the natural residual sugar. *At MW Symposium dinner, Oxford, March 1982******

1981** *to* ****

Cool vintage producing good naturally acidic wines. Reds less notable. Of the several tasted, just two as illustrations:
KWV, Pinotage Using a vertical tasting of this wine as a sort of vintage barometer: far more elegant than the beefy '80, harmonious, good vinosity, lean, flavoury. *Dec 1987*****
Uitkyk, Carlsheim The white wine made on this estate, mainly from the ubiquitous Steen cultivar (variety), originally the Chenin Blanc. Pale; slightly scented; dry, lightish, pleasant flavour. Though not very distinctive, clean and does not pall. *Dinner at Miller Howe, April 1983***

1982****

Reds, particularly Cabernets, very good indeed. A wide range of commercial and single-estate wines tasted.
Blaauwklippen, Cabernet Sauvignon Two notes. Deep ruby; good fruit; fullish, fleshy, bitter metallic tannins (tamed by roast pork). *Last noted Sept 1988**(*)*

Blaauwklippen, Reserve Cabernet Franc from the same vineyard ripened at the same time and added to the Cabernet Sauvignon to make this Reserve blend: impressively deep; rich, vinous, ripe fruit; soft, ripe, sweetish approach, good texture, very fragrant, touch of spice, warm dry finish. *At Cape Independent Wine Makers' Guild tasting at Laborie, Dec 1987*****

Blaauwklippen, Zinfandel Ruby; very good fruity mouthful but a tinny tannic finish. One of several wines bought from Collinsons in London, Cape specialists. *Last tasted June 1989***

KWV, Pinotage Low-keyed, harmonious, figgy; fragrant, flavoury, good length, flesh and aftertaste. *Dec 1987****

Meerlust, Rubicon The Rubicon blend varies from vintage to vintage but is predominantly Cabernet Sauvignon. Visiting the estate I suggested, mischievously, changing the name to Petrus as this was the Christian name of one of the family's 18th-century ancestors. Biscuity, ginger, wholemeal bouquet after decanting; somewhat sweet, curious brown leaf flavour, high acidity, tannate of iron. *Last tasted April 1990. Keeping my last bottle hoping for**** 1995–2000*

1983**

Abundant crop, wines low in acidity, most of moderate quality. Many notes. Once again, a cross-section.

Blaauwklippen, Zinfandel Curious, medicinal at first but evolved fragrantly; nice weight, excellent texture, very tannic. Improved on acquaintance, and with roast duck. *Dec 1987**(**)*

Delheim, Grand Reserve (Cabernet Sauvignon plus Franc) Extremely good though almost too sweet. Full, rich, chewy. *Dec 1987***(*)*

KWV, Noble Late Harvest (Chenin Blanc) Yellow gold; excellent, like a *Botrytis* Coteaux du Layon; sweet, crisp, waxy fruit, lovely flavour and acidity. *Dec 1987*****

KWV, Pinotage Plummy, immature; citrus, cherry-like, lively fruit; for a change, dry, crisp, fresh. *Dec 1987**(*)*

Stellenryck, Blanc Fumé Not exactly a Loire lookalike, too deep, yellow gold; aroma more like a ripe flowery Riesling; but very dry with pronounced Sauvignon Blanc tom-cats flavour and good acidity. *Dec 1987***

1984** *to* ***

Great heat mid-harvest, overripe whites with low acidity, better reds. Interesting developments in the mid-1980s and more notes than any other vintage. A selection:

Delheim, Edelspatz, Noble Late Harvest, Superior — It was. Golden; honey, pineapple, spices; sweet, fullish though with a deft touch, very good acidity. Delightful. *Dinner at the Devereux's, Johannesburg, Nov 1987******

Groot Constantia, Cabernet Sauvignon Harmonious but static; sweetish, pleasant weight, smooth, good texture, pleasantly dry finish. *Dec 1987****

Neil Ellis, Cabernet Sauvignon (From bought-in grapes.) Deep; lovely crisp fruit. A new breed of 'boutique' winemakers. *Dec 1987****

Kanonkop Estate A Bordeaux-like blend: 75% Cabernet Sauvignon, 15% Franc, 10% Merlot. 18 months in Nevers oak. Deep ruby; very sweet fruit, almost jammy, iron; attractive, nice weight and acidity. Decidedly not Médoc, but successful. *Last tasted March 1988**(*)*

Meerlust, Rubicon (Merlot and Cabernet) First tasted on the estate. Most recently, a bottle given to me by Hannes Myburgh: still deep purple; its original spice now assimilated, fleshy, strawberry-like; rich, high extract, packed with fruit, crisp tannin and acidity. *Shared with the Rhodes, April 1991****(*)*

John Platter, Reserve (Cabernet) I admire the rare critic who can write a play. Still youthful of course, spicy, new oak cinnamon; dry, crisp, tannic. *With the author, Dec 1987*(**)?*

1985** *to* ***

Cool summer. Variable. Quite good whites, less good reds. Much winemaking experimentation, new blends, old European varieties. Some excellent sparkling wines.

Backsberg, Chardonnay Sydney Back's first Chardonnay harvest. Siquin Moreau's Nevers oak used. Almost a Morio-muscat scent. Dry. Austere. *Dec 1987(**)?*

Backsberg, 'John Martin' (100% Sauvignon Blanc, barrel-fermented, left on lees.) Named after a 'very difficult' estate manager! Very pale, green tinge; hefty varietal aroma; dry, austere, short. *Dec 1987*(*)*

Blaauwklippen, Pinot Noir (Their first Pinot made in 1979.) Broad open varietal colour; hazelnuts, strawberry; slightly sweet, good warm Pinot flavour, dry finish. *Dec 1987**(**)*

Delheim, Grand Reserve (Blended red) Fully mature; dry, nice weight, attractive, slightly short, ready. *Aug 1991****

1986** *to* ****

Hot vintage. Average whites. Good to excellent reds. Many notes, mostly tasted in cask at the estates or in winery tasting rooms. Great strides being made. Nine cultivars (varietals) noted, particularly good Chardonnays, previously considered too difficult.

Backsberg, Chardonnay Great improvement over Back's first (1985): delicate, youthful, pineapple; dry, lean, oaky. Very good classic flavour, length, acidity. *Dec 1987*(**)*

Blaauwklippen, Cabernet Sauvignon Deep, rich; excellent nose; medium-sweet, fullish body, fleshy; very good fruit. *Aug 1991*****

Boschendal, Chenin Blanc Palish yellow; like soft grapefruit plus oak; medium dryness and body, rich fruit, judicious oak, very well made. A bargain from Cavendish Wines in 1988. *Consumed April 1991**** For its class and price.*

Delheim, Grand Reserve (Blended red) Sweetish, fairly full-bodied, soft, fleshy yet very tannic. *Aug 1991***(*)*

Groot Constantia, Special Late-Picked Superior Furmint Interesting use of the Tokay grape. Palish yellow; low-keyed slightly spicy; fairly sweet, fullish, youthful pineappley fruit, very good acidity. *With the winemaker, Pieter de Toit, Dec 1987(***)? Longing to know how this has developed.*

Hamilton-Russell, Chardonnay First tasted in magnum at the Devereux's, Nov 1987. Youthful, elegant, smoky oaky, impressive. Five notes since. Palish; dry, firm, well made. *Last tasted April 1989****

Klein Constantia, Sauvignon Blanc Four notes, two from different tanks at the spectacular modern winery, Dec 1987. Both pale, one bone dry, acidic, the other sweeter and an astonishing 14% alcohol. Next, showing well in bottle: minty, Sauvignon, cats, clover honey; dry, tolerable weight. Most recently, tasted blind: waxy, grassy, scented; fairly dry, quite powerful, assertive but good flavour and finish. *Last noted with Nils Sternby in Grasmere, May 1991****

Meerlust, Cabernet Sauvignon (100%) Opaque, intense; curious, distinctive, oyster shell; cinnamon,

cloves, packed with fruit. Great future. *In cask Dec 1987(****) Doubtless to be blended with Merlot to make the '86 Rubicon. If so it should be top class.*
Meerlust, Merlot Very deep; high acidity; Merlot fruit and flesh, complete, tannic. *In cask Dec 1987(***)?*
Nederburg, Auction Reserve Cabernet Sauvignon Good colour, maturing; hot, jammy, alcoholic; rich, assertive, very tannic. Impressive but not my style. *May 1991**(*)*
L'Ormorins Blanc Fumé 'Vin de Nuit' (Picked at night.) Pale in cask, now a lovely glowing yellow; youthful grassy pineapple, evolved, deep fruit, oak; fairly dry, but losing freshness, soft. *Last tasted Aug 1991. Now***
Schoongezicht, Chardonnay Innoculated with Montrachet yeast. Lovely colour; vanilla; attractive, excellent acidity. Good potential. *Nov 1987*(**)*
Zevenwacht (Blended red) With eyes closed the scent of a refined old madeira — crystallised violets, fine cognac. Rather metallic on palate but curiously attractive. *Aug 1991**(*)?*
Zevenwacht, Cabernet Sauvignon Rich but tinny, metallic nose, taste. *Aug 1991(**)?*

1987* *to* ****

Variable growing season and vintage results. Better for reds. A wide range tasted mainly in cask in Dec 1987 (harvested around March). Some notably good Rieslings and late-harvest wines, few tasted.
Blaauwklippen, Cabernet Sauvignon Rich; lovely brambly fruit; sweet, full, soft, fleshy. *Aug 1991*****
Groot Constantia, Gewurztraminer The old estate coming to life with yet another classic European variety. Palish yellow; very good, powdery, rosewater scent; medium-sweet, typically broad Gewurz character, fatter than its Alsace counterpart. Equally typically dry and not acidic. *Dec 1987*(**)*
Hamilton-Russell, Pinot Noir Reputed to be the best. Certainly a very good 'beetroot' Pinot aroma; full-bodied, attractive, oaky, with somewhat bitter tannic finish. *July 1990**(**)*
Hamilton-Russell, Vin Blanc Pale; dry, well made but little character. Not a patch on his Chardonnays. *At the Port Hole, Windermere, May 1991***
Rustenberg Gold (Blended red) Sweet, soft, easy, ready. *Aug 1991****
Warwick 'Trilogy', Special Reserve Virtually opaque; crisp fruit, well-masked tannins, oak; full-bodied, ripe, rich, lovely fruit, power, finish. *Aug 1991*****

1988****

Hot year. Some very good wines.
Blaauwklippen 'Cabriolet' (Blended red) Good fruit, sweet, fullish, very attractive, ready. *Aug 1991*****
Hartenberg, Cabernet Sauvignon Reserve Openly evolved, jammy — more like the old-style Pinotage; sweetish, fleshy, curious overtones. *Aug 1991**
Kanonkop (Blended red) Plummy; scent and aftertaste of crystallised violets. Dry, tannic. *Aug 1991*****
Rust-en-Vrede, Cabernet Sauvignon Lots of fruit, good balance and finish. *Aug 1991****
Rust-en-Vrede, Shiraz Virtually opaque; powerful; crisp fruit, high alcohol and tannin. *Aug 1991**(*)*
Villiera, Auction Reserve (Blended red) Deep, firm; very good, great depth of brambly fruit; rich, excellent flavour, balance and dry finish. *Aug 1991*****
Villiera, Cabernet Sauvignon Deep, rich; good varietal aroma; dry, tart tannins. *Aug 1991*(*)?*

1989** *to* ****

Moderate whites, some very good reds.
Buitenverwachting, Cabernet Sauvignon Deep; brambly fruit; soft, fleshy, good fruit, acidity. *Aug 1991****
Buitenverwachting, Gewurztraminer Pale; very good, scented lychee nose; dry, soft, spoiled by kernelly taste. *Aug 1991**
Buitenverwachting, Reserve (Merlot) Deep, intense; very good, blackberry-like; sweetish, full fleshy flavour, excellent fruit, tannin and acidity. *Aug 1991***(*)*
Delheim, Merlot Deep, plummy; rich fruit but sweaty tannins; dry, fullish body, good flavour. Hard tannic finish. *Aug 1991**(*)*
Groot Constantia, Cabernet Sauvignon Rather woody; dry, hard. *Aug 1991.*
Lievland, Shiraz Purple; jammy; full-bodied, good fruit, balance. *Aug 1991****
Overgaauw, Chardonnay Reserve Distinctive 'bread-like' style; full, soft; fragrant aftertaste. *Aug 1991****
Overgaauw, DC (Dria Corda) **Classic** Youthful; meaty, unknit; soft, fleshy, easy wine. *Aug 1991***
Rust-en-Vrede (Blended red) Very deep, youthful; good fruit, very tannic on nose and palate, full, fleshy. *Aug 1991***(*)*
Simonsig, Chardonnay Nutty, fumed oak; fragrant, violets and peach kernels. Strange. *Aug 1991.*
Simonsig Pinotage Good brambly fruit but curious flavour: rhubarb, boiled sweets. Sweetish. *Aug 1991**
Thelema, Cabernet Sauvignon Reserve Deep, rich; dramatic varietal aroma and taste like Mouton, varnished; fleshy, soft fruit, fragrant. *Aug 1991***(*)*
Vriesenhof (Blended red) Good fruit, strangely attractive. *Aug 1991****

1990** *to* ****

A hot growing season. Moderate whites but should prove an excellent Cabernet vintage. Only a few Cape Winemakers' Guild whites tasted but a distinct softness, even soapiness noted. Much preferred the only red tasted.
Boschendal, Pavillon Blanc Great estate, but this Semillon more like a Sauvignon Blanc: exceedingly pale; raw gooseberry nose; dry, soft middle, good flavour and acidity. *Aug 1991***
Buitenverwachting, Chardonnay Also gooseberry-like — early picked for acidity? Attractive, refreshing but not the varietal flavour one expects. *Aug 1991***
Glen Carlou, Chardonnay Reserve Scented nose and endtaste but well made. High alcohol. *Aug 1991****
Glen Carlou, Pinot Noir Reserve Walnuts, oak; fullish, soft, good flesh, excellent fruit and finish. *Aug 1991**(*)*
Kanonkop Pinotage Opaque; gloriously rich, blackberries; sweetish, full-bodied, top class. *Aug 1991***(*)*
Neil Ellis, Chardonnay Youthful, pineappley; dry, firm, crisp, good finish. *Aug 1991**(*)*
Thelema, Chardonnay Faintly oaky but not very varietal. Mild, soft. *Aug 1991.*

1991(*****)

The wettest April (winter) ever recorded in the Cape. May and June also wet. Spring arrived suddenly and early (in Sept) followed by a cool, dry summer. Healthy grapes from a long ripening season. Great potential.
KWV, Cape Nouveau Blanc Pale; raw pineapple husks; dry, rather hollow, good acidity. *Tasted a month or so after the vintage, May 1991.*

APPENDIX I

Major Tastings, Tasting Groups and Hosts

III Form Club The senior UK trade tasting club, founded 1947. Regular tastings, annual dinners.
Beaulieu Vineyard 50th Anniversary of Georges de Latour Private Reserve, 12 vintages, '41–86. In the Beaulieu Vineyard Garden, Napa, June 1990.
Bob Berenson Penfolds' Grange Hermitage vintages '55–80. Le Montrachet restaurant, New York, Oct 1990.
Johann Bjürklund's 'Stockholm' Group Ch Pétrus, 28 vintages from '45–86. 47 Park Street, London, April 1990.
Bordeaux Club Six members host dinners in turn. During the period covered: Michael Behrens (died 1989), John Jenkins, Dr Neil McEndrick, Jack (Sir John) Plumb, Harry (Lord) Walston (died 1991), Harry Waugh and myself. Approximately three dinners per annum, at which we all produce, in turn, our best wines.
British Airways Wine Committee Senior member of wine tasting panel since 1982; frequent and regular tastings range from Economy Class quarter-bottles, through Club, to First Class and the Concorde cellar.
Brooks's (Club) Wine Committee Regular tastings, wine dinners for Ch Margaux (April 1988), Ch Léoville-Barton (Nov 1989), Ch Haut-Brion (March 1991).
Champagne Academy 'Old boys association' annual *grande marque* dinners dating from 1957.
Christie's Pre-Sale Tastings Frequent, regular — an average of 50 wine sales a year — tastings taking place mainly in London, and also in Geneva, Amsterdam and now, importantly, in Chicago, Tokyo and Los Angeles.
Christie's Wine Course Regular sessions in association with *L'Académie du Vin* throughout the year, since 1982, at Christie's, South Kensington.
Commanderie de Bordeaux Several dinners and tastings, the most notable: red Bordeaux of the '66 vintage, 106 châteaux tasted by district, the Médocs in classification order. In San Diego 1986.
Decanter magazine panel tastings: Ch La Tour-de-Mons, Sept 1982; St-Emilion '79–80 vintages, 52 châteaux, Sept 1983; Ch Lagrange, Sept 1988; '85 red Bordeaux, Jan 1989; '80 vintage port, Aug 1990; '85 Médoc, 54 châteaux, Dec 1990.
Bipin Desai Regular organiser of major vertical and horizontal tastings: '59 red Bordeaux, 31 châteaux, by district, Nov 1983; '45 red Bordeaux, a retrospective, 57 châteaux in flights, by district, Los Angeles, Feb 1986; Ch La Mission-Haut-Brion, 66 vintages 1878–1982, attended by the Duc and Duchesse de Mouchy, Los Angeles, Feb 1985; Ch Margaux, 61 vintages, 1771–1984, also Pavillon Rouge and Pavillon Blanc, attended by Corinne Mentzelopoulos and Paul Pontallier, at the Beverley-Wilshire, Hollywood, May 1987; Ch Figeac, 34 vintages from '05–88 attended by M Thierry Manoncourt over an extended lunch, Le Taillevant, Paris, Dec 1989.
Walter Eigensatz One of the group of keen German amateurs of wine. Lives in Wiesbaden. Lavish big-bottle tastings of 1893s, '26s, '61s in June 1987; 1899s, '29s, '59s, May 1989; and with Maurice Renaud, Cercle de Vingt, Versailles, May 1988.
Len Evans 'Mr Wine' of Australia, top taster, chairman of Rothbury, writer, TV personality, raconteur, wit — organised tastings, visits to wineries and hospitality on my two visits to Australia.
Fête du Ch Latour 86 vintages of Ch Latour, 1861–1979, presented by Kerry Payne and Denis Foley at Clift Hotel, San Francisco, June 1981.
Lloyd Flatt One of the most serious and generous of all hosts. Many dinners and three outstanding tastings: Ch Mouton-Rothschild, 75 vintages from 1867–1984, two days, April 1986; Ch Ausone, 56 vintages from 1877–1985, two days, Oct 1987; Ch Lafite, 116 vintages from 1784–1986, plus Carruades, three days, Oct 1988.
Hans-Peter Frericks Ch Pétrus, 27 vintages in magnums from '45–83, plus 1900, '08, '21, '23 and '26. Munich, 1986.
Hans-Peter Frericks and Hans-Peter Wodarz Every vintage of Latour and Mouton, from '45–86, tasted in pairs. Eight 'probes' over two days. Wiesbaden, March 1989.
Arthur Hallé Long-time collector, connoisseur and host of top-class wine dinners and tastings, of which I have been able to attend only a few, notably first growth claret of the '29, '45, '61 and '82 vintages. Memphis, April 1987.
Ch Haut-Brion Tastings and sale to celebrate the 50th anniversary of the château's purchase by the Dillon family. 25 vintages from '53–82, dry white Haut-Brion: seven from '78–83. Christie's, May 1985.
Heublein Annual pre-sale tastings each May, in different cities in the USA, dating from 1969–84. These were the major annual American wine events of the period — extensive tastings preceding spectacular wine auctions.
Hollywood Wine Society Tasting of '53 clarets, Feb 1985. I was also 'moderator' of two great wine seminars in Feb 1989 and Jan 1990, including great port of the '45 vintage, rare and outstanding Terrantez and Bastardo madeira, and other wines. Held in Hollywood (Florida) and Miami.
Homage à Château d'Yquem und Schloss Johannisberg Memorable tasting co-hosted by Comte Alexandre de Lur-Saluces and Fürst Metternich: 10 great vintages of Yquem, 1892–1967, 11 of Schloss Johannisberg 1847–1947. At Schloss Johannisberg, Nov 1984.
Hans Jorissen *see* Vinum Tokayens.
Tawfig Khoury Owner of one of the finest private cellars in the USA. Several great wine dinners, and a major de Vogüé tasting: Bonnes Mares and Musigny, 30 vintages from '34–79. San Diego, Oct 1984.
Charles Krug/Robert Mondavi Historic tasting marking the reunion of the brothers Peter and Robert Mondavi: 16 vintages of Krug '44–65, 16 vintages of Mondavi, '66–91. 'Moderated' at the Mondavi winery, Napa, June 1985.
Leroy Lalou Bize's annual tastings in, and of, Burgundy. Notably Sept 1984 and Sept 1988.
MW Tastings organised by the Institute of Masters of Wine including: '76 red Bordeaux, March 1980; VIDE Italian Wines, May 1980; '78 red Bordeaux, 46 châteaux, May 1982; '79 red Bordeaux, 37 châteaux, May 1984; '79 red Bordeaux, June 1987; Symposia, Oxford, July 1986, and in Cambridge, July 1990.
Dr Robert Maliner A major collector and power behind the Hollywood Wine Society (qv).
Bud Moon's Yquem tasting 51 vintages, 1825–1983. At the University Club, Chicago, Feb 1988.
Robert Paul Owner of a vast private cellar. Major verticals and horizontals of wine mainly from his own collection. Tasting of '78 red Bordeaux, 59 châteaux, Coral Gables, Feb 1988; '82 St-Emilions and Pomerols, 95 châteaux, Coral Gables, Feb 1989; '85 California Cabernet Sauvignons, 55 wines, Coral Gables, Jan 1991.
Edmund Penning-Rowsell The 'dean' of Bordeaux wine writers, with a magnificent cellar at his country house in Oxfordshire. First growth claret tasting dinners: eight châteaux, tasted with Jancis Robinson and respective spouses, 10 years after the vintage. Annually at Wootton. Also the first growth '61s, March 1983, and '45s, June 1990.
Port tastings Mainly organised by individual shippers. Sandeman's, June 1988; Delaforce '47–85, April 1989; Noval 1900–85 including Nacional, Nov 1989; James Suckling's '27s, 11 shippers, Dec 1989; Graham '45–85 including Malvedos, Feb 1990 and May 1991; tasting of 56 ports of the '80, '82, '83, '85 vintages at Christie's June 1990; Taylors 1896–1985, April 1991.
Hardy Rodenstock An extraordinarily generous host who spends a year organising lavish annual tastings, of which I have attended six between 1984 and 1990. A total of 1,000 wines tasted, including some of the greatest, the rarest and most beautiful. The first (Rodenstock's 5th Rräritäten-Weinprobe) at the Fuente Restaurant, Müllheim, then at Die Ente vom Lehel in Wiesbaden, at Ch d'Yquem, and latterly weekend events at the Alberg Hospiz, Austria.
Saintsbury Club Founded in 1931 by André Simon and friends in memory of Professor George Saintsbury. 50 members, literary, legal, wine. Twice yearly 'meetings' (dinners) at Vintners Hall. Attended twice

yearly since spring 1969.
Dr Louis C (Lou) Skinner Founder member of Miami Chapters of the International Wine & Food Society and Commanderie de Bordeaux. Indefatigable, extremely knowledgeable and generous host and organiser. Two major tastings: both of the '61 vintage classed growth Bordeaux, with 50 châteaux, Coral Gables, Feb 1981 and Feb 1986.
Sotheby's Tasting of '78 red Bordeaux, 93 châteaux, May 1985; '75 red Bordeaux, 77 châteaux, May 1984.
'Stockholm' Group See Bjürklund.
Union des Grands Crus de Bordeaux At Christie's, Oct 1984, March 1987, May 1988, May 1989. In Bordeaux, March 1989, April 1991. In London, April 1990, April 1991.
View Australia International tasting and tasters: 325 wines over three days. Melbourne, April 1985.
Vintners Club Weekly tastings for amateurs and professionals, of which I have attended a few major sessions: white burgundy, first growth Bordeaux, Pinot Noirs etc. San Francisco.
Vinum Tokayens A tasting of old and rare Tokay. Leiden, Nov 1981.
Wine magazine panel tastings. Two notable blind tastings: '82–83 Margaux, 50 châteaux, Aug 1990; '86 Sauternes, 34 châteaux, Oct 1990.
Wine festivals Tastings conducted, particularly overseas, including: WINE JAPAN in Tokyo, June 1989, May 1990; International Wine Festival, Frankfurt, Sept 1988; Svensk Vinfest, Malmö, March 1986; Conventions of the International Wine & Food Society, in Boston, Copenhagen, Hong Kong and Singapore, Oct 1989; Lake District, June 1991.
The Wine Spectator Conducted eight major blind tastings, from the First Annual Grand Award Seminar in New York in 1981, at the California Wine Experience in San Francisco, then alternating between New York and San Francisco. This is now the most important annual wine event in the USA. Thousands attend, and an average of 900 are seated at these blind tasting sessions. Also a major blind tasting of '82 red Bordeaux vs California Cabernet Sauvignon, 26 top growths and wineries. San Francisco, Nov 1986.
Wine Weekends at hotels Studley Priory, Nov 1980; Gidleigh Park, Nov 1980, Jan 1982, Jan 1983, Jan 1984; The Castle, Taunton, Oct 1983, Oct 1985.
Karl-Heinz Wolf One of the German group of collectors, but also in the trade. La Mission-Haut-Brion, 74 vintages from 1877–1987; Ch Laville-Haut-Brion, 37 vintages from '28–82 and Ch La Tour-Haut-Brion, 18 vintages from '43–79, plus 13 vintages of Ch Haut-Brion in Wiesbaden, June 1990.
Peter Ziegler A German schoolteacher and organiser of 'Club Meetings', only one of which I have been able to attend. It was spectacular. 36 great wines over an extended lunch. With Jean Hugel. Burg Windeck, Baden, May 1983.

The following are some other private hosts who have organised major tastings and dinners, and whose wines are reported in this volume: Mutsuo Okabayashi, Tokyo; Dr Maynard Amerine, many in Napa; Dr and Mrs Bernard L Rhodes — two great connoisseurs, many top-class tastings and dinners; the late Mills B Lane, Madeira Club, Savannah; Dr and Mrs Robert Adamson; Christopher York, four superlative wine dinners at Boodle's, 1982–84; Berek Segan, DRC tasting and dinners, Melbourne; Dr Marvin Overton; Doug Crittenden, 40 rare Australian wines over a 'light lunch' at his seaside house near Melbourne, April 1985.

And finally, I have to thank the many UK shippers and wine merchants for their trade tastings; also many château proprietors, négociants *and domaines in Burgundy; Hugels particularly in Alsace; wineries in the USA; DRC and their London agents; estates in Australia; not to mention producers who occasionally send me bottles to appraise.*

APPENDIX II

The Jefferson Bottles

Thomas Jefferson, later to be the third US President, was Envoy (Ambassador) to France from May 1784 to October 1789. He was a noted connoisseur and, visiting Bordeaux in May 1787, he ordered on the spot the 1784 vintage of Ch Margaux and other first growths, insisting that they be bottled at the château as he did not trust wine merchants. He also ordered more top growths and other wines for himself and the President, George Washington, instructing his agent in Bordeaux to have the wines etiquetté *with the name of the wine and the initials TJ and GW so that the content and ownership of bottles could be identified. For the shipment of less expensive wines destined for his own use he requested that the initial of the wine (eg F for Frontignac) should be engraved on the bottle with a diamond point.* The inference is that for expensive first growths (his letters mention the exceedingly high price for Ch Margaux 1784 and others), the slightly more costly method of wheel engraving, presumably by a local Bordeaux artisan, would be used.*

The 1784 Ch Margaux, Yquem and the 1787 Lafite and Branne-Mouton referred to in the main text are from a small cache of wines claimed to be originally in the possession of, or at least ordered by, Thomas Jefferson. Though the present owner is reticent about the provenance, there is a considerable body of evidence supporting their authenticity. The bottles themselves, three examined independently by two Christie's glass experts, are unquestionably of the period. More significantly, these experts state that the type of wheel engraving employed was not used after the end of the 18th century; and a distinguished expert in letter-design and letters from The British Library confirms the contemporary style of the engraved letters and figures.

Hardy Rodenstock, a noted German collector, was not aware of the significance of the initials TJ until the first bottle (of the 1784 vintage) was opened at Château d'Yquem. The Comte de Lur-Saluces found, from the archives, that Thomas Jefferson had ordered directly from the château wine of that vintage. The remains of the wax capsule, the cork and the wine, all believed to be original, were sent for laboratory analysis in Germany, the results being satisfactory if not conclusive.

The wines themselves are as described in my tasting notes. I have since opened and tasted 1787 Lafite prior to analysis by an independent laboratory in Munich. The cork looked to me original, the wine was old but sound — in fact, though fairly brown and faded, remarkably good. At the time of writing we are still awaiting the chemical and carbon dating analysis to pinpoint the age of the wine itself.

* *All the above facts are well documented. Jefferson kept copies of all his correspondence; archive research has been published, notably in* Jefferson And Wine *(The Vinifera Wine Growers Association, Virginia, 1989).*

Index of Wines and Vintages